THE BIG GUIDE TO LIVING AND WORKING OVERSEAS

4th Edition

JEAN-MARC HACHEY

Intercultural Systems / Systèmes interculturels (ISSI) Inc.
Toronto, Canada

www.WorkingOverseas.com

Published by

Intercultural Systems / Systèmes interculturels (ISSI) Inc.
296 Sackville Street
Toronto, Ontario   M5A 3G2
CANADA

Tel: 416-925-0479
Fax: 416-925-9650

E-mail: publisher@workingoverseas.com
Web site: www.workingoverseas.com

Jean-Marc Hachey—publisher, author, editor

The BIG Guide to Living and Working Overseas
Fourth edition: first printing October 2004

Library and Archives Canada Cataloguing in Publication

      The big guide to living and working overseas.

Triennial
4th ed.-
Continues: Canadian guide to working and living overseas.
ISSN 1713-3599
ISBN 0-9696001-3-5 (4th edition)

      1. Job hunting—Canada. 2. Canadians—Employment—Foreign countries.
3. Employment in foreign countries. 4. Economic development projects—Directories.
5. International agencies—Directories.

HF5549.5.E45H33   650.14   C2004-904881-3

Every attempt has been made to provide correct information. However, the publisher and the
author do not guarantee the accuracy of the book and do not assume responsibility for
information included or omitted from it.

Cover and Web site design by Shane Stuart

Printed in Canada by Transcontinental Inc.

DEDICATION

This book is dedicated to THE STEPHEN LEWIS FOUNDATION in recognition of its work in helping those struggling with the ravaging effects of the HIV/AIDS pandemic in Africa. There are millions who are suffering throughout the world—get involved!

the Stephen Lewis
FOUNDATION

Easing the pain of HIV/AIDS in Africa

www.stephenlewisfoundation.org

C O N T E N T S   A T   A   G L A N C E

THE BIG GUIDE TO LIVING AND WORKING OVERSEAS (Fourth Edition)

A P P E N D I X   O N   T H E   C D – R O M

THE BIG GUIDE TO LIVING AND WORKING OVERSEAS (Fourth Edition)

Appendix numbers correspond to the chapter numbers in THE BIG GUIDE.

APPENDIX: Organization Profiles (indexed in Print Edition)

APPENDIX: Guest Contributors

SEARCHABLE INDEX

Retrieve and use the Search feature (CTRL+F) to locate organizations or resources, and click through to the Web sites. ID Numbers from the book are also indexed.

INDEX & HOTLINKS to Organizations
INDEX & HOTLINKS to Resources
INDEX to ID Numbers

Instructions for the CD-ROM

- Cut the top of the CD sleeve carefully with scissors to create a durable CD storage pocket.
- Adobe Acrobat Reader (version 5.0 or higher) is needed to view the individual PDF files.
  If you do not have Acrobat Reader, you can download it for free from http://acrobat.com.
- The "Appendix on the CD-ROM" file should open automatically when you insert the CD in your CD drive.
  If it does not, you can open the "index.htm" file manually. For example, in Windows you can open your CD drive (usually drive D:) in My Computer and double-click "index.htm."
- File names are sorted by Appendix number and abbreviated title. To open manually, double-click the file name.

Table of Contents

Part One: Your International IQ

Chapter 1
The Effective Overseas Employee   15

Chapter 2
Myths & Realities   45

Chapter 3
Living Overseas   49

Chapter 4
What Expats Say About Living Abroad 77

Chapter 5
Learning a Foreign Language 91

Chapter 6
Women Living & Working Overseas 99

Chapter 7
The Canadian Identity in the International Workplace 109

Chapter 8
Re-Entry 123

Part Two: Acquiring International Experience

Chapter 9
Starting Your International Career 141

Chapter 10
Short-Term Programs Overseas 145

Chapter 11
Hosting Programs 191

Chapter 12
Cross-Cultural Travel   197

Chapter 13
Study Abroad   207

Chapter 14
Awards & Grants   223

Chapter 15
International Studies in Canada   253

Chapter 16
International Studies – The World's Top Schools   277

Chapter 17
Internships Abroad 289

Part Three: The International Job Search

Chapter 18
Your Career Path & The Ideal International Profile 321

Chapter 19
The Hiring Process 329

Chapter 20
The Job Search & Targeting Your Research 335

Chapter 21
Resources for the International Job Search   357

Chapter 22
Phone Research Techniques   383

Chapter 23
Selling Your International Skills   393

Chapter 24
International Resumes   409

Chapter 25
Covering Letters   453

Chapter 26
Interviewing for an International Job   465

Chapter 27
Jobs by Regions of the World   475

Chapter 28
Job Hunting When You Return Home   533

Part Four: The Professions

Chapter 29
Teaching Abroad   541

Chapter 30
Careers in International Development   565

Chapter 31
International Law Careers   587

Chapter 32
Engineering Careers Abroad   633

Chapter 33
Health Careers Abroad   653

Chapter 34
Spousal Employment & Freelancing Abroad   683

Part Five: International Career Directories

Chapter 35
Private Sector Firms in Canada $\qquad$ 693

Chapter 36
Private Sector Firms in the US $\qquad$ 789

Chapter 37
Canadian Government $\qquad$ 801

Chapter 38
NGOs in Canada $\qquad$ 855

Introduction

THE BIG GUIDE TO LIVING AND WORKING OVERSEAS is the authoritative guide on international careers for university students and young professionals. At a whopping 1,600 pages (including CD-ROM), THE BIG GUIDE contains expert advice on gaining experience through study and internships, succeeding and adapting to overseas living, career planning, job searching, international resumes, international interviews, specific professions abroad and 3,045 carefully researched organizations offering professional jobs and international career resources. Available on-line and in print, the Fourth Edition of THE BIG GUIDE is your ticket to success and adventure!

So you want to work overseas. You're not alone! Estimates of Canadians currently working overseas vary from 50,000 to 100,000 and some 4.1 million Americans are living abroad. Obviously, there are plenty of people who have successfully found international jobs. Now you can find them! In this book, we discuss ways to crack the international job market, to make the system work to your advantage. With careful planning and investigation, an international career is waiting for you!

Who Is This Book For?

THE BIG GUIDE is written for Canadians as well as Americans. The Guide is written for all types of international job seekers, from the entry level to the seasoned professional, from university students and recent graduates to senior consultants, entrepreneurs, teachers, academics, guidance counsellors, managers, civil servants and world travellers. It is for those making long-term career plans to work overseas and for those ready to make a career change now. This book is also for anyone interested in understanding the individual circumstances of those moving abroad: spouses, children, teenagers, women, gays and lesbians, singles and managers conducting international work anywhere in the world.

This Fourth Edition is an indispensable desk companion—a comprehensive directory of international activities in North America and an authoritative guide to working and living overseas.

Is This the Best International Career Book?

We are leaders in our field because of the expert advice we provide on the international job search. We clearly and systematically explain how finding a job overseas is different from looking for work domestically. Our flagship chapters provide you with a road map to living overseas, building international experience, the ideal international profile, the ways to sell your international skills, international resumes, international interviews and job search techniques. No other publication provides you with the same depth of advice or level of detail. Our many fans of earlier editions simply refer to our book as *"the bible on international careers."* We are proud to present you with this expanded Fourth Edition.

What's in This Book?

Everything you need to know about living and working overseas. THE BIG GUIDE is, in fact, the biggest international career publication in the world. At over three quarters of a million words and 1,622 pages (including 500 pages on the CD-ROM), the Fourth Edition has 41 percent more information than the Third Edition. The guide contains 3,045 career-building entries, 2,215 organizations and 830 resources organized under 62 subject headings.

Forty-one chapters describe business, government, NGOs, IGOs, volunteer opportunities, internships and academic programs. Carefully researched profiles include contact information and most profiles include size, areas of specialization, regions of operation and qualifications required. This book offers successful strategies and practical information to guide you through all the necessary steps of your international job search. Detailed, insightful chapters dealing with living overseas include advice on such things as moving and taxes, culture shock, cross-cultural communications and our business and managerial identity overseas.

What Is New in the Fourth Edition?

Almost everything! The Fourth Edition has 41 percent more information than the Third. Twelve exciting new or substantially rewritten "how-to" chapters are here for you. We are proud of our two flagship chapters: Selling Your International Skills (Chapter 23) and International Resumes (Chapter 24), and new writing about the career path, hiring process and job search (Chapters 18, 19, 20). There is new and innovative advice on internships (Chapter 17) as well as on health and international law careers (Chapters 32, 33). There is a massive expansion of US information including 716 profiles on US NGOs and private firms. The CD-ROM contains 27 articles from guest contributors including sample resumes as well as searchable hotlinked indexes to 3,040 contacts in the book. Enjoy!

About the Web Edition—the Choice Is Yours

You can access the entire guide on-line at *www.workingoverseas.com* by purchasing a subscription for one week, two months, or three months. The Web edition is portable, accessible and value-priced below the cost of the print edition. With a subscription, the *"My Guide"* feature remembers your written notes for each resource and organization you flag and will retain these notes for 24 months if you resubscribe within that time.

Why Encourage People to Work Overseas?

How can we learn to co-exist in the global village if we don't understand each other first? If North Americans are to make globalization work, we must become skilled in the art of crossing cultures. Professional and technical expertise alone is not enough—we must harness understanding of others in their milieu, and develop the foresight to handle cross-cultural situations effectively.

International work is fascinating, rewarding—and attainable. Good luck with your voyage!

Acknowledgements

THE BIG GUIDE TO LIVING AND WORKING OVERSEAS owes its success to the enthusiastic support it receives from many individuals and institutions. I am grateful for the encouragement and appreciate the validation of the Guide's advice over the years. To all of you—Thanks! I'm sure you'll appreciate this latest edition.

This Fourth Edition could not have been written without the assistance of the numerous organizations that responded to our initial questionnaire and provided countless suggestions for improvement. Many thanks for your participation. I appreciate the support of the sponsors whose ads appear at the end of the book.

There were 28 staff members who dedicated themselves to this edition. Production editors researched the profiles and updated the chapter introductions. They were well organized, professional and reliable. *Marie Green* was relentless and fast in compiling an exhaustive list of organizations for the Canadian NGO chapters (Chapters 10, 11, 30, 38). *Alexis Yanaky* provided a solid base for the initial research on these NGO chapters. *Lisa Alfano* precisely managed the complex profiles in the academic chapters (Chapters 13, 14, 15, 16) while effectively networking with over 500 hard-to-reach university professors and administrators. *Lydianne Ouimet* was the production editor for the French profiles; she mastered her portfolio quickly and charmed everyone. *Anne Brandner* applied her excellent writing, research and administration skills on a broad sweep of projects. These included research on internship and intergovernmental organization profiles (Chapters 17, 41), numerous writing tasks including writing important copy to launch our Web site, as well as supervisory and training activities for three production editors. *Carmen Brubacher* ably took up the challenge of finalizing the engineering chapter (Chapter 32) after some research and writing by Anne Brandner and others. *Nicole Robins* was careful, attentive and steadfast with two chapters: the hard-to-research Canadian private sector chapter (Chapter 35) as well as on the profiles for the smaller health chapter (Chapter 33). *Sean Fraser* crafted two difficult chapters: a new one on international law careers (Chapter 31) and the updated chapter on careers with the Canadian government (Chapter 37). He also wrote most of two chapters on international organizations (Chapters 40, 41) and provided insight when we designed the business model. *Jeff Ollis* researched and wrote the insightful and often witty commentary for the many resources in THE BIG GUIDE—a complex task which he documented professionally.

Special mention must go to *Alana Lewis* who was instrumental in many aspects of this project. As a production editor, she competently researched a large number of profiles of US private firms and NGOs (Chapters 36, 39). As the marketing manager, Alana successfully spearheaded the sponsorship campaign—adding a welcome new element to my business model. Alana also played a key role on the layout team, helped to vet a stream of business and administrative decisions and applied her project management skills. Many thanks, Alana. *Carina Kwan* was responsible for the professional and meticulous layout of THE BIG GUIDE and we often relied on her good judgement. *Min Wong* managed our comprehensive and complex database layout process. She was accurate and paid keen attention to the final product.

The technical team was equally important to this project. *Karen Cossar*, the Web design manager, skillfully walked us through the steps of launching a new Web site. *Shane Stuart*, a talented graphic designer, conceptualized the Web and book cover designs. We relied on *Paul Brandner* as a Web site consultant and efficient HTML coder. *Michael Macaulay* consulted on design and layout issues. *Paul Gross* is our indispensable database consultant and has worked with me on all four editions. *James Harding* found solutions to hardware installation issues.

I was glad of the help of some top-notch writers. *Susan Brown* served as in-house staff writer during the research and editing phase. She applied her writing skills to refresh numerous chapters and worked closely with me on the guide's flagship chapters. She organized and managed the inventory of new ideas—and amazingly, no idea was lost. She also competently managed the ISSI Style Guide, guest contributors, the emerging writers contest, as well as aiding copy editors. *Annik Chalifour* applied her valuable expertise in writing the health careers chapter (Chapter 32) with the collaboration of MÉDECIN SANS FRONTIÈRES. *Sheena Zain* knowledgably updated the chapter on regions of the world (Chapter 27). My sincere thanks to 27 *guest contributors* accredited in the Appendix on the CD-ROM located on the inside back cover.

Tara Tovell and *Joe Zingrone* jointly copy-edited the entire guide while working under tight deadlines. *Christiane Cadrin* provided English-to-French translation services. *Solange Beaulieu* edited the French text. *Christopher Cantlon* copy-edited last minute changes. The final version of THE BIG GUIDE was read by an assemblage of 17 professionals who donated their stipends in support of the STEPHEN LEWIS FOUNDATION. Thanks to all.

The success of this edition builds on the fine work of numerous researchers and writers from previous editions. Some of the excellent work by writers from previous editions was updated in this edition. The original writers are *Betty-Ann Smith* assisted by *Jennifer Smith*, who wrote Re-Entry (Chapter 8) and *Elizabeth Smith* who adapted that chapter for this guide. Elizabeth also wrote the first draft of Living Overseas (Chapter 3); *Dianne Lepa* wrote Women Working and Living Overseas (Chapter 6); *Denise Beaulieu* wrote The Canadian Identity in the International Workplace (Chapter 7); *Peggy Berkowitz* wrote Jobs by Regions of the World (Chapter 27) and Spousal Employment and Freelancing Abroad (Chapter 34). *Terry Cottam* also made significant and varied contributions to the First, Second and Third Editions, and I wish to remember him here.

4

Many thanks also to the numerous people who provided expert advice, quotations, copy-editing or friendship: John Aimers, Hussein Amery, Cheryl Arneson, Shubha Balasubramanyam, Denise Beaulieu, Bernard Boudreau, Andrea Boysen, Val Brandt, Richard Brooks, Moninder Bubber, Carolina Budiman, Barbara Chant, Aubrey Charette, Kathleen Dennis, Parin Dossa, Mary Douglas, Ann Duggan, Philippe Eddie, Edna Einsiedel, Larissa Fast, Pierre Francq, Kelli Fraser, Ivan Gayton, John Geiger, Lucie Goulet, Joni Guptill, Linda Haché, Heather Harding, Charlen Hofstetter, Robert Hunter, Denise Iamonaco, Isabelle Jeanson, Marina Jiménez, Beth Kaplan, Ken King, Mike Klobucar, Judy Kopelow, Jennifer Latham, Tommi Laulajainen, Geoffrey Little, David Long, Kevin Makra, Saskia Meckman, Tony Meehan, Joan and John Merriam, Danuszia Mordasiewicz, Sarah Moreault, Danielle Morin, Christine Nadori, Linda Nagy, William Nolting, Latif Nurani, Nicolas Papadopoulos, Robin Pascoe, James Pickard, Harry and Ann Qualman, Sarah Reynolds, Katiana Rivette, Ken Roberts, Mike and Marion Rudiak, Tsehayou Seyoum, Leslie Shanks, Graham Sim, Sandra Steinhause, Laura Thomas, Kirk Thompson, Jane Thorpe, Barry Tonge, Alan Travers, David Waite, Scott Walter, June Webber, Edelayne Westgate, Melissa White, Michael Wile, Tom Williams, Robert Wilson, Sophia Wong, David Zakus, Richard Zereik and staff at THE UNIVERSITY OF TORONTO PRESS.

Warm affection to my Acadian family from Bathurst, Moncton and Drayton Valley for their continuing good company, love and support. (Hi Mom!) This year, we Acadians are celebrating 400 years since arriving as the first Europeans to settle in North America. So with such a long history of cross-cultural living, it is with equal pride that I now live in the heart of Toronto, the most ethnically diverse big city in North America (and perhaps the world). Forty-four percent of its population is born on foreign soil. A third of its residents are members of visible minorities. All live comfortably side by side in my neighbourhood and throughout the city. Ethnic diversity enriches our lives across North America.

My last acknowledgement is for my supportive partner, Richard Berthelsen. Richard provided me with wise advice at crucial moments in the production of this guide and has kept the home fires burning while I laboured away for long hours at the office.

Jean-Marc Hachey

How to Use this Book

This book organizes contact information as either a *profile* of an organization, or as a *resource*. An organization is profiled if it helps you gain experience or can offer you an international job. A resource, on the other hand, is either a book, a Web site, or an organization which provides services to help you with your international job hunt.

PROFILES OF ORGANIZATIONS

There are 2,215 profiles of organizations listed in 17 separate categories. The profiles offer up-to-date contact information and details on organization size, type, objectives, activity and recruitment procedures. Profiles are located at the end of the 16 chapters with profiles in THE BIG GUIDE. There are three sets of profiles: *Part Two, Acquiring International Experience* has seven chapters with profiles; *Part Four, The Professions* has two chapters with profiles; and *Part Five: International Career Directories* has seven chapters with profiles. For a detailed list of all organizations, consult the *Index by Organization Name* at the end of this book. The CD-ROM also has a searchable index with hotlinks to these organizations.

Four chapters have their profiles on the CD-ROM and an index located within the chapter in the print edition. Chapters with profiles on the CD-ROM are: Chapter 15, International Studies in Canada; Chapter 36, Private Sector Firms in the US; Chapter 39, NGOs in the US; and Chapter 40, NGOs in Europe and the Rest of the World. CD-ROM chapters have the added benefit of being electronically searchable.

ORGANIZATIONS BY CHAPTER

Organization Address, Phone, Fax, E-mail and Web Site

Web sites are the primary source for all your information needs. Only 5 of 2,215 organizations listed in this book do not have a Web site. The easiest way to find a

Web address is to Google the organization name. Prior to sending an e-mail to someone, always contact the organization to confirm the correct e-mail, address, department, and title of the contact person. This may be done via information on the Web site, but because you want to start building a relationship with potential employers, it is often better to e-mail or phone to confirm this information before submitting a formal job application.

Size of Organization

Five of the organization types are categorized as SMALL, MID-SIZED, or LARGE, according to the size of their international budget or number of employees with international responsibilities. For example, Canadian NGOs with budgets in excess of $2,000,000 are designated as LARGE. Similar distinctions apply to private firms. The five types of organizations where size is indicated are: NGOs and private sector firms in Canada, NGOs and private sector firms in US, and the Canadian government.

Type of Organization

Every profile has an organization type written in upper-case letters, immediately following the size of the organization (if sized is listed) or organization address. The organization type identifies broad areas of activity and expertise. For example, NGOs have such types as RELIEF AND DEVELOPMENT AGENCY or MEDICAL ASSISTANCE GROUP, while private firms have such types as MANAGEMENT CONSULTING FIRM or ENGINEERING FIRM.

Job Categories

Five of the organization types have job categories: NGOs and private sector firms in Canada and the US, as well as Canadian Government. These are listed alphabetically in Title-Case and provide a useful reference guide to an organization's principal activities and skill requirements. Consult the *Job Categories Index* at the end of this book. Note that this index is to be used as a guide only. Some unique job categories have not been indexed.

Description of Organization

Profile descriptions begin with the diamond symbol ◆.

Profiles in *Part Two: Acquiring International Experience* are designed to familiarize the reader with the wide variety of international study opportunities available in Canada and abroad, as well as the short-term (generally unpaid) opportunities overseas. International study profiles list the degrees conferred, contact information, and brief descriptions of the nature and structure of programs. Profiles documenting short-term opportunities overseas detail eligibility requirements, duration, program objectives, and financial information.

Profiles in *Part Four: The Professions* and *Part Five: International Career Contacts* generally follow a standard sequence. First, an organization's principal activities and areas of expertise are outlined, followed by information on the substance and location of recent international projects. This is followed by a description of the qualifications and skills sought by prospective employers, and an indication of whether or not an organization maintains a data bank for resumes and if the organization offers internship possibilities. Where appropriate, an editorial comment is given about the organization's Web site, especially in terms of their jobs page.

RESOURCES

A resource is either a Web site 💻, a book 📖, or an organization ⚕. Organizations listed as a resource provide services to help you with your international job hunt. (If the organization provides international experience or is a source for jobs, it is listed as a profile rather than as a resource.)

There are 830 separate resources listed alphabetically in 62 subject areas located at the end of chapters. For ease of reference, many resources are listed in more than one subject area, for a total of 1,210 entries. Of the 830 resources, 382 are Web sites, 334 are books and 150 are organizations. (Some resources have two or more designations.) For a detailed list of all resources, consult the *Index by Resource Title* at the end of this book. The CD-ROM also has a searchable index with hotlinks to these resources.

Index by Resource Subject

Resource Web Sites 🖥

Web sites in the Resources sections are listed by title in **bold** with a 🖥 icon after it, followed by the Web address and a description of the site's contents. When a resource can be either purchased as a book or accessed on the Web, both the book and computer symbols are shown.

Web resources are diverse in what they offer. Many of the sites we selected post job or study opportunities and internship information. International job boards top the list of valuable services. Other sites give you the current information you will need about the regions or countries that you are targeting. The Web offers a growing number of online versions of journals and other print material. We have also suggested sites that can contribute to your international and cross-cultural knowledge as well as help you with your international job hunting.

To inform us of new interesting Web sites, please e-mail us at feedback@workingoverseas.com.

Resource Books 📖

In the Resources sections, book titles are in **bold** with a 📖 after it, followed by year or frequency of publication, author or editor (if specified), then publisher. After the symbol ➤ we list the distributor's address, followed by a brief description of the book. (If the publisher and distributor are the same, only the distributor is specified.)

Some books are easily found in large bookstores, but most are specialty publications which need to be ordered directly. Every book is conveniently available through the big Internet distributors such as Amazon.com, Amazon.ca or Chapters.ca. We have, however, only listed alternative distributors because these are often more closely affiliated to the publisher of the book. A large research library is the best place to consult expensive, frequently updated reference volumes.

Call, fax, write, e-mail, or visit the distributor's Web site to confirm current prices, availability, and distributor's address. Prepayment is usually required. Prices listed are an approximate guide only; they do not include postage, or taxes. The most convenient method to pay for books is to order with a credit card by phone, fax, e-mail or Web site. We have listed specific credit cards accepted by the distributor.

Resource Organizations ♛

In the Resources sections, names of organizations are in **bold** with a ♛ symbol after it, followed by the organization's contact address (sometimes limited to a Web address). After the ◆ symbol, a description of the services is provided.

Organizations that offer services to job seekers and do not themselves offer direct employment are listed as resources. Examples of organizations included in this category are international employment agencies, umbrella organizations for professional associations, and a host of other organizations offering information or services of interest to people wanting to work and live overseas.

LANGUAGE ICONS ❑Fr ❑Sp ❑En or FR◆

Efforts have been made to facilitate the use of the English language publication for French and Spanish speakers. A total of 567 of 3,045 records (organizations and resources) are available in French and 207 are available in Spanish.

- **Organizations with French or Spanish services:** When an organization's only language of operation is French, their profiles are written in French. (There are 112 such profiles.) For bilingual organizations that operate in both English and

French, the profile is written in English. When an English Web site is also available in French or Spanish, the following symbols appear after the Web address: ⬚*Fr* ⬚*Sp*. (There are 469 Web sites available in French and 207 in Spanish.) For profiles written in French, an English symbol ⬚*En* is inserted if an English Web site is also available.

- **Resources with French Services:** When a resource is only available in French, the description is written in French. (There are 16 such resources.) If an English Web site is also available in French, or if an English publication is also available in French, an *Fr* icon will precede the ◆ symbol. (There are 98 resources with this symbol.)

ID NUMBERS [ID:1218]

Every resource and organization profile has a unique ID number. For example: [ID:7128] is for GREENPEACE-CANADA. We expect that some of you will use this number as a quick reference when doing your job research with this book. (For example, you may note to yourself, *"Call ID:5683 page 624 re application procedures."*) The *INDEX to ID Numbers* is located on the CD-ROM and is used to locate page numbers. The CD-ROM's *Searchable Index & Hotlinks* also include ID numbers as well as organization names and resource titles. The same ID numbers are also used in the Web edition of THE BIG GUIDE at *www.WorkingOverseas.com*.

CD-ROM APPENDIX

The CD-ROM Appendix is a companion to the print edition of THE BIG GUIDE TO LIVING AND WORKING OVERSEAS. It has allowed us to greatly expand the quantity of information provided to our readers. See the *Appendix on the CD-ROM* on the inside back cover of this book for a full description of all that it contains as well as instructions for using the CD-ROM. The CD-ROM files are either HTML files or Adobe files. Each file is named starting with a prefix-number corresponding to its respective chapter in THE BIG GUIDE.

ABOUT THE WEB EDITION

You can access the entire guide on-line at *www.workingoverseas.com* by purchasing a subscription for 1 week, 2 months, or 3 months. The Web edition is portable, accessible and value-priced below the cost of the print edition. The Web edition is convenient for those who travel and want to access THE BIG GUIDE while on the road. Check it out.

UPDATES UNTIL THE YEAR 2008 ON OUR WEB SITE

This print edition will be regularly updated until December 2008 on the *Free Services* page at *www.WorkingOverseas.com*. If you find information that needs updating, please send an e-mail to update@workingoverseas.com.

Thanks and enjoy THE BIG GUIDE.

PART ONE

Your
International IQ

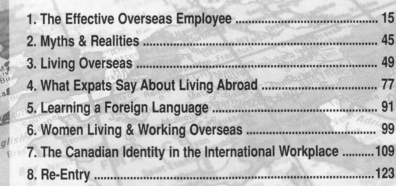

CHAPTER 1
The Effective Overseas Employee

WHY DO PEOPLE GO OVERSEAS?

It's Monday morning and you are at your desk, staring out at the bleak, cold February landscape. Imagine instead that you are gazing at palm trees and ocean surf, being fanned by tropical breezes. Many of you want to escape to warmer, friendlier climates and explore new cultures and lifestyles. While working overseas is not as simple as our February fantasy suggests, it *is* possible with the right strategy.

The reasons for working overseas are endless—from a love of new foods and the desire to travel, explore new cultures and learn new ways of living, to an interest in making new friends, improving your language skills, widening your professional experience and heightening your understanding of the world. Overseas work often requires you to take on more responsibility than you have been used to. The scope of your professional skills may be tested: you could develop a whole new perspective on your field. Certainly you'll have to develop some new skills, particularly in the area of cross-cultural communication.

For those of you with families, living overseas can be a wonderful adventure. The slower pace allows for more quality time together, and for many children, immersion in another culture can be one of the most profound experiences of their early lives. (Of course, your family must be involved in the decision to move overseas, and must understand where you are going and what to expect when you get there.)

One of the best reasons for working overseas is to gain a heightened sense of your own culture. Most returning workers find they have a greater appreciation for home. They also develop pragmatism, initiative and the confidence to take on further challenges.

Overseas work can be a truly enriching experience. While you can't escape the hardships and challenges of adjusting to a new environment, most people find that they gain immensely from the experience.

At this point in your plans for working overseas, you may be trying to determine whether you are suited to this kind of work, both in a personal and a professional sense. This chapter will help you begin your assessment.

WHAT IS YOUR INTERNATIONAL IQ?

An international employer's assessment of candidates for overseas work generally has two components:

- The *professional* component
- The *"international IQ"* component, which measures your level of international and intercultural awareness

Much of this book is concerned with helping you acquire the international knowledge and skills necessary to develop what we call your "international IQ." Building your international IQ will substantially increase your chances of finding an overseas job, even when you don't have overseas work experience.

Why is previous overseas experience so often a critical factor in getting that first international posting? Because employers want effective employees who know how to get the job done in a culture other than their own. In an overseas work situation, it is not enough to know the technical aspects of your work. You must understand the people, their country and their culture. You must see how cultural factors fit into the task at hand. Once you understand the "whats" and "whys" of a new culture, you'll have a greater chance of succeeding in that context.

It is possible to acquire this type of cultural and international knowledge without actually working overseas. Your international IQ is made up of your awareness and ability in four areas:

- Political, economic and geographic knowledge
- Knowledge about the international aspects of your field
- Cross-cultural knowledge and skills
- Personal coping and adapting skills

While many of these skills can be acquired over time, this book helps you get a jump start on qualifying for the international job market. The following sections provide more details on the above four areas.

Political, economic and geographic knowledge: If you can converse intelligently about international news and world events, you are probably sufficiently aware of world politics and economics. You also need a firm grasp of world geography and knowledge of the world's major ethnic groups and their distributions. And of course, you need detailed knowledge about the country in which you hope to work.

To increase your knowledge, you might consider the following: listening regularly to international news broadcasts; keeping a good, up-to-date world atlas close at hand; subscribing to one or two international magazines or newspapers; joining a multicultural group in your community; vacationing in offbeat places; and enrolling in courses on the politics or history of regions in which you are interested.

Knowledge about the international aspects of your field: You have a good knowledge of the international aspects of your area of expertise if you know which organizations work internationally in your field, what jobs exist, and what aspects of your work have an international application. This information is extremely important in your job search and in managing your career path. Knowing how your specialization is practiced in an international setting allows you to focus your education, your job research, your networking contacts and your discussions with peers on landing the right overseas job for you.

To start, a few phone calls to international organizations in your line of work will reap rewards. A bit of research will tell you what trade magazines you should be reading. Join an international trade association. Learn when international conferences take place. Talk to people in your field who work or have worked overseas. Find out which skills and what types of experience they think are important.

Cross-cultural knowledge and skills: You have sufficient cross-cultural knowledge and skills if you know what it takes to be effective in another culture. A good approach, once you know what country you want to work in, is to find out about that country's belief systems, modes of behaviour and attitudes.

An effective overseas employee needs a lot more than specialized technical knowledge. You should have a sound knowledge of the local culture and be able to apply it in your workplace. As well, the ability to speak the country's main language will be a great asset to you. You can generally acquire these skills at home by seeking out people from other cultures, becoming active in cross-cultural groups, and learning a second or third language.

Personal coping and adapting skills: You can improve your personal coping and adapting skills which, in turn, will help you deal with culture shock. People who enjoy living and working overseas are adaptable and tend to embrace challenges. You will face changes in culture, friends, work and climate. Therefore, having a sense of adventure, as well as humour, curiosity, and a great deal of patience, is invaluable.

To prepare yourself, you can do volunteer work or participate in organizations that put you in contact with other cultures. If you have never visited a country where the culture is radically different from your own, you should try to do so before embarking on an international career.

The remainder of this chapter details the skills and personal traits of a successful international worker.

CHARACTERISTICS FOR OVERSEAS WORKERS

This list of characteristics will help you assess your suitability for overseas work and assist you in preparing to live in a foreign environment. Self-knowledge is power in today's job market. When you understand your skills and job objectives, when you have a professional self-assessment of your cross-cultural work skills, you can be much more effective and focused in your international job search.

- **General traits:** enjoyment of change, desire for challenge, street smarts, sense of adventure, open mind, patience and curiosity
- **Adaptation and coping skills:** emotional stability and ability to deal with stress, understanding of culture shock, receptivity, flexibility, humour and self-knowledge

- **Intercultural communication skills:** tolerance, sensitivity, listening and observing skills, nonverbal communication skills and second language speaking skills

- **Overseas work effectiveness traits and skills:** independence and self-discipline, training experience, resourcefulness, versatility in work, persistence, organizational and people skills, leadership, energy, calm demeanour, project planning skills, writing skills, verbal communication skills, diligence and dedication, loyalty, diplomacy and tact, and philosophical commitment to field of work

This list divides skills and traits into blocks of information. Grouping your skills this way will help you to compile a skills inventory and then convey these qualities to prospective employers. (For more information on developing a skills inventory, see Chapter 23, Selling Your International Skills.) Each item is discussed in more detail in the following chapters.

A word of caution: this list is by no means exhaustive. The importance of each skill or trait will vary with different work environments and countries of posting. If you have no previous overseas experience, it will be difficult to measure yourself against this list, as you probably have strengths you are not yet aware of. And if you don't currently have these skills, don't forget your ability to adapt and acquire new skills.

GENERAL TRAITS

The following skills and traits can usually be found in successful overseas employees and their families.

Enjoyment of Change

Change will permeate your life in an overseas career. You should, therefore, ask yourself: do I adapt well to new situations? If you get upset when you find your toothpaste on the wrong shelf, chances are overseas life is not for you. You must adapt to new customs ("I now love drinking tea in the afternoon!") and give up old ones ("I can live without coffee!").

Change is an important part of an interesting life, and while it may be frightening for even the most daring people, you must learn to embrace and enjoy it. Make "when in Rome, do as the Romans do" your rule to live by.

Desire for Challenge

All people who move overseas encounter challenges in their work and personal life. Whether you are shopping for tomatoes, having the car repaired or struggling to meet a production deadline, every activity can seem like a challenge in an unfamiliar environment. You should ask yourself whether you enjoy tasks that require special effort or unusual solutions. Do you revel in the thought of overcoming difficulties even with mundane tasks? Do you continue to face challenges even when there is a possibility of failure or disappointment? Do you remain cheerful in the face of those challenges? If your answers are clearly yes, then you have made an informed decision about working overseas, and you should demonstrate this to prospective employers.

Street Smarts

When in a foreign country, you need to know when to remove yourself from the company of others, when to turn back and leave an unsafe situation, and when to say no to the overtures of strangers. Living and working overseas is all about interacting with new people, but there is a fine line between being open to new things and putting yourself at risk. This can be particularly hard to gauge in a new culture. Ask yourself whether you usually trust your instincts about people and new situations. Do you consistently remain aware of your surroundings in unfamiliar places? Are you cool-headed and able to react quickly when things go wrong? Do you know what steps to take to avoid being a victim of street crime? (For more information on security concerns abroad, see Chapter 3, Living Overseas and Chapter 12, Cross-Cultural Travel.)

Sense of Adventure

Moving overseas involves navigating uncharted waters. You don't know what living arrangements you will have, what friends you will make, or how far you will have to travel for gas. Every aspect of overseas life holds unknowns. Indeed, for some of you, the proportion of unknowns may seem comparable to those faced by the explorers discovering the new world!

Having a sense of adventure is important if you are to enjoy overseas life. Expatriates revel in stories about their escapades—both pleasant and unpleasant. Many overseas employers look for a sense of adventure in applicants. In discussions and interviews with potential employers, *don't* exaggerate your taste for adventure, but *do* present yourself as someone who looks forward to tackling unknowns.

Open Mind

North Americans tend to look for only one solution to a problem. Once we find it, we package it and try to franchise it across the country. Much is standardized and meticulously measured. In an overseas environment, it is important not to try to apply North American solutions to the problems you encounter. You must keep your mind open to new approaches and, equally important, be able to recognize local solutions that work and need not be changed.

The effective individual overseas is open to and interested in other people and their ideas. The CANADIAN INTERNATIONAL DEVELOPMENT AGENCY'S (CIDA) briefing material offers a good example of open-mindedness: when his boat broke down, a young man travelling down the Amazon discovered a special use for green bananas. He had heard locals talking about their sealant quality, and although he had questioned the idea at the time, his willingness to try it out got him out of a tight spot.

An open mind is a basic ingredient to success and survival in an overseas environment.

Patience

You need patience for virtually every aspect of overseas life. As a stranger to a new land, you must listen and learn. Don't jump to conclusions. Remember the old African saying that the stranger who does not suffer from alienation falls short of his role as a stranger. You should expect to feel out of place in your new surroundings. However, overcoming your impatience and learning to follow the pace of life will ease your sense of alienation. Proceed slowly, especially in your first few months abroad.

Curiosity

Your spirit of curiosity will help you uncover much about a new culture—new land, plants, animals, customs and people. No matter what the circumstance, those who enjoy living overseas are curious about their surroundings. Think of the possibilities! You are delayed in a Middle Eastern airport—what better place to study differences in traditional dress? A trip to the hospital in an African city may offer you a chance to talk with an orderly about her village. You've been waiting outside a bureaucrat's office for an hour, enough time to witness an argument between two market women across the street, and now they are making up.... Curiosity can help you appreciate, understand, and learn from virtually any situation. Don't leave home without it!

ADAPTATION AND COPING SKILLS

Culture shock is the term used to describe the difficult process of adapting to a new culture. Adaptation skills are synonymous here with coping skills, which enable you to deal with the unfamiliar aspects of your new environment and with your overall sense of alienation.

Emotional Stability and Ability to Deal with Stress

Evidence of emotional stability is critical to an employer's assessment of a candidate's suitability for overseas work. The trouble and expense of dealing long distance with emotionally overwrought individuals make employers especially wary. Fragile personalities and those who lack a realistic self-image are particularly unsuitable. This is not to say that many successful overseas employees are not somewhat eccentric!

Think about how you have coped with stressful situations in the past. If you haven't had previous overseas work experience, international employers will look for other concrete examples of your ability to cope under stress. Surviving a two-week trek through the wilderness, studying Spanish in Mexico, taking on particularly challenging social work, or enduring a long and disruptive labour strike—all of these are indicators to a recruitment officer that you can deal with the pressures of a new environment. Situations in which you were socially isolated are also good examples: travelling by yourself for two months; living in a northern community; working alone as a forest fire warden, etc.

Employers are especially wary of applicants trying to avoid problems at home. If you imagine that an overseas post will help you escape an unhappy relationship or a drug problem, for example, your chances of succeeding overseas are slight. Remember, to survive overseas your main motivation must be the experience itself, not a personal situation. Drug dependency is a particularly bad reason for working overseas. While drugs are readily available in most countries, addiction and the consequences of being caught with illegal drugs make them something to be avoided. Literature on cultural adaptation is full of warnings about applying for overseas postings for the wrong reasons.

Another aspect of emotional stability is the effect of leaving loved ones behind. For example, if you are planning to leave your family at home, or if you rely on a small circle of friends, and you have little experience being separated from these support networks, adapting to overseas life may be very difficult. Recruiters are looking for people who are flexible and adapt quickly to new situations.

Understanding of Culture Shock

Any serious overseas job hunter knows about culture shock. Recognizing the symptoms and dealing with the problem will help you adapt and cope overseas. Many an international career has been cut short by a severe case of culture shock. In recent times, however, excellent resources have been produced to help prospective overseas workers understand and prepare for it. This awareness may be crucial to your self-preservation and professional survival, and may help you assist others through their crises. (For a more detailed description of culture shock, see Chapter 3, Living Overseas.)

Receptivity

Learn to stand back, observe, and adjust your behaviour accordingly. If you don't, life overseas will be very difficult, if not impossible.

The successful international employee can observe, react sensitively, if not appropriately, to new situations and come to understand how local customs influence behaviour. People in many West African countries believe that "a stranger is like a child," and afford strangers and children a similar degree of tolerance. Indeed, until you learn appropriate social behaviour in your new environment, you *are* like a child. Tolerance for your mistakes won't last forever, however, and some Asian cultures, for example, have little tolerance for social faux pas.

Flexibility

An important skill in cultural adaptation is the ability, when necessary, to change the way you do something. You will have to abandon many of your North American "tried and true" methods, find new ones and roll with the punches. Leave your ego at home.

Why is flexibility so important overseas? First, a correct assessment of a situation on Monday may be incorrect on Thursday. Second, being rigid in a new society will hurt your chances of getting things done. You must learn to bend. The traditions and practices of the local culture are much stronger than your ability to persuade. Don't ask them to "do it my way"—rather, try to learn their approach before dismissing it. Third, flexibility will help you enjoy yourself in your new environment. Learning to play soccer where there is no ice hockey or accepting the friendship of an older couple when all your friends at home are from your age group: these are examples of the value of flexibility. Fourth, being flexible will enable you to quickly switch back to North American behaviour patterns when dealing with head office, meeting Western delegations, or returning home.

Humour

A good sense of humour is absolutely invaluable. Your ability to laugh and remain cheerful under pressure is of prime importance to recruitment officers, who know that humour can help employees adapt to even the most difficult circumstances. The ability to see the lighter side of things will make the difference between enduring and enjoying the whole adaptation process.

Self-knowledge

When you move to a new country, everything from shampoo to politics is different. The way you greet people, the way they respond, your new position as an outsider— all of these things will force you to change, to make adjustments, to adapt to your new life. When so many demands are being made on you to change, it is important to know yourself.

You need to know what aspects of your personality will help you in your overseas environment and what aspects will not. Realistically, however, you might not even appreciate certain traits until they surface in your new environment. Westerners travelling abroad for the first time are often surprised by their need for space and time alone. We may not recognize our need for solitude until we are deprived of it, which is particularly likely to happen if you are working in developing countries, where most cultures do not recognize this Western trait. Prepare yourself— you may find it difficult to cope with people continually entering your home without being invited or even knocking.

Knowing yourself will also help you distinguish your need to be flexible from your need to establish limits. While you must be willing to adapt, you must also be able to say no to social customs that you simply cannot accept. For example, you can recognize and appreciate the importance of superstition and black magic in a society without participating in rituals you find offensive or frightening. Or, if you are a female travelling by train and you are assigned to an all-male sleeping compartment, you need not accept the situation out of fear of causing trouble or offending someone. Remember, you *do* have limits. You owe it to yourself to act accordingly.

Figure out what you can live with and what you can live without. People's quirks make them unique, so if coffee in the morning is crucial or you feel like you'll die without country and western music, take care of these needs. In summary, being able to cope in a new society depends as much on understanding yourself as it does on your openness and flexibility. Indeed, your hosts will appreciate and admire your individuality. Nothing can be gained by pretending to be something you're not.

INTERCULTURAL COMMUNICATION SKILLS

Of all the skills required for overseas work, intercultural communication skills are the least understood by prospective employees. Indeed, they are very difficult to grasp and even more difficult to demonstrate that you possess.

Our links with other cultures are growing stronger and more permanent. In an increasingly interdependent world, more and more emphasis is being placed on intercultural communication skills, which allow you to transmit your knowledge to people of other cultures, and, in return, share in the wealth of information they can give you.

Don't assume cross-cultural communication is limited to language proficiency. Effective communication includes nonverbal skills, such as understanding body language and demeanour. Mastering life skills in your new environment depends on your ability to communicate across cultural barriers.

The following traits and skills are invaluable in developing good intercultural communication skills.

Tolerance

Tolerance in a foreign environment is critical to your ability to communicate. Try to get beyond your North American reaction to the new culture to understand why people behave as they do. For example, to dismiss foreign societies as inefficient because their productivity appears low by your standards is to pass judgement in haste. You may discover that a group of workers is actually more cost-effective than you thought, once you understand that labour in developing countries is cheaper and spread among more people than it is in Canada or the US, where labour and capital are more expensive.

Tolerance is crucial when you live in a society you don't fully understand. If someone is late for an appointment, assume there is a cultural reason. If someone invites you to supper and is then surprised when you show up, assume the situation has a cultural origin. Being tolerant means you can accept frustrating situations. Henceforth, prepare to go one step further: study the cultural background or traditions behind the behaviour at hand.

Sensitivity

When you exercise tolerance in a new cultural setting, you become more aware of the makeup of your host society. Be sensitive in your dealings with others. To understand a new cultural milieu, you often have to put others before yourself. Practice sensitivity toward people in your new workplace. Try to see a situation from all sides. For example, do not assume that "they are ignoring me" or "they are mocking me by being late." A better approach, especially at the beginning, is to ask "why have they reacted this way?" or "what is the reason for this behaviour?" Often there is a simple cultural explanation for behaviour that seems frustrating to an outsider.

Like your readiness to listen and observe, your sensitivity will enable you to understand the cultural puzzle around you and help you adapt to your new environment.

Listening and Observing Skills

Many books have been written about living in specific countries. While some can be helpful, your own listening and observing skills will determine how much you learn about your new environment. It takes a keen eye and a sense of curiosity to make these skills work for you. Observe people, and then ask tactful questions of your hosts and other expatriates. Just remember: listening and observing more carefully than you've ever done before are the keys to good intercultural communication skills.

Nonverbal Communication Skills

If you've never lived abroad, you may be unaware of the diversity of nonverbal communication styles throughout the world. Confronted by the strange mannerisms of other cultures, we begin to see how much in our own culture is communicated nonverbally. Body language and facial expression can be as important as what is said.

In certain Arab countries, for example, you will be considered very rude if you pass an object with your left hand, as this is the one used to handle toilet paper. Other nonverbal communication forms extend from burping after a meal to indicate satisfaction, to practically ignoring visiting friends as a sign that the friendship has gone beyond the boundaries of formality. Manner of dress is another example of nonverbal communication. In some instances, it is considered the height of rudeness for a man not to wear a tie. Awareness of these subtleties is a key to success overseas.

Second Language Speaking Skills

A working knowledge of the local language is often crucial to effective intercultural communication. Even knowing a few phrases will help—if only by showing that you have made an effort. (For more detailed information, see Chapter 5, Learning a Foreign Language.)

OVERSEAS WORK EFFECTIVENESS TRAITS AND SKILLS

Whether you are applying for an administrative position, a technical or research job, a teaching job, or a job in the field, most employers want to see evidence of particular work skills. This chapter discusses skills that are vital to typical overseas assignments but less crucial to North American workplaces. As part of your job hunting strategy, let employers know you understand these skills. Outline them in your international resume and discuss them in interviews.

Work environments overseas vary widely. You may be working in an office tower in downtown Rio de Janeiro, trekking the dirt roads of India in a land rover, or treating patients in a rural African community with no electricity. Your placement may be in the urban slums of Jakarta or in the cosmopolitan atmosphere of Hong Kong. Your primary contacts may be with the rural village market women in the Andes, the nomad herdsmen of the Sahara, senior government bureaucrats in Rwanda or fellow compatriots in an NGO office in San José.

Each of these overseas postings requires different combinations of skills. Some general skills are listed below. Please note that their relative importance varies from job to job.

Independence and Self-discipline

An overseas posting may be far removed from head office supervision. In many cases, you work totally on your own or with just one level of supervision. You will probably have a great deal of discretionary decision-making power, the flip-side of which is responsibility. To thrive in these conditions, you must be independent and self-disciplined. Employers look for people who can, in effect, be their own bosses.

Training Experience

The raison d'être for most expatriate jobs is to aid in the transfer of expertise to local workers. You may have successfully implemented a program; don't commit the common, albeit unforgivable, oversight of neglecting to train local people to take over when you leave. A project's long-term success depends on the effective training of people in your host country. Since more and more employers are recognizing this, it is useful to highlight in your international resume any training experience you possess.

Resourcefulness

You are unlikely to have the kinds of support networks you enjoy in North America. The photocopier repairperson is not around the corner—if you even have access to a machine. You may not have reliable telephone service. There will likely be no temporary employment agencies. Just ordering a supply of paper and envelopes may require you to fill out an astounding number of forms.

You will have to find your own solutions, build your own contacts, and solve problems without guidance and often without benefit of previous experience. Resourcefulness involves both coping in an unfamiliar environment and improvising new combinations of solutions. A resourceful problem-solver is someone who is imaginative, determined and flexible. International recruiters look for resourceful employees.

Versatility in Work

Many international jobs require that you work alone, without the aid of any specialists. You have an advantage if you are versatile and possess a range of skills. In developing countries, if you are in charge of an office, you should be proficient in some or all of the following: report writing, negotiation, personnel management, supervision of employees, training of employees, office management, computer skills, accounting, budgeting, procurement of supplies, inventory control, shipping and handling imported supplies, satellite phones and radio communication technology, car repair, carpentry, and gardening. This might seem like an odd collection of skills, but if you speak to anyone who has worked in such locales, they will tell you that versatility is of the utmost importance. While few people possess all of these skills, employers prefer to send versatile employees to difficult environments.

Persistence

In a culture you don't understand, it's easy to believe there's no solution to a problem. Don't be tempted to give up and become cynical, however. You may be exhausted from chasing an elusive form from an elusive government department. You may have waited four months for delivery of an important cement shipment only to be informed that the rail link to the cement factory has been shut down for repairs. Your landlord may have once again failed to fix the plumbing. Instead of throwing up your hands in frustration and defeat, be persistent! Your future employer will want to know how you react to such common aggravating situations. Enthusiasm and persistence are necessary parts of the makeup of a successful overseas employee. Be sure to discuss with your potential employer situations in which you exhibited persistence.

Organizational and People Skills

These two important skill sets are discussed in Chapter 26, Interviewing for an International Job.

Leadership

As the person in charge of a project, you will be required to provide leadership. Some common leadership tasks are motivating a group, assigning duties, following up on work in progress, avoiding and solving conflict, building consensus around an objective, giving rewards and providing feedback. Impress upon a recruiter that you possess leadership skills. Outline your past accomplishments and give examples of instances where you took the lead.

Management styles can change as you cross cultural boundaries. In some places, locals may interpret your use of the North American participatory approach as a sign that you are a weak manager. A more authoritarian approach may be appropriate. Discipline and motivational methods also vary widely. In certain African countries, trying to motivate an employee by offering a promotion and salary increase can sometimes backfire: the promotion could be associated with extending the employee's family responsibilities to more people in his or her extended family, which might not be appreciated. In this situation, a different form of motivation would have to be used. Your skills in sizing up a situation will have a lot to do with your ability to provide leadership in the workplace.

Energy

An employer will be looking for energy to complement your resourcefulness. Let the recruiter know you won't allow fatigue or cynicism to get to you in a situation where it may be very hot, noisy, frustrating or demanding. If you're going to be a successful overseas worker, you need energy. Describe your success at meeting deadlines and overcoming constraints. Talk about your need for challenge, how you don't give up until the job is done.

Calm Demeanour

As North Americans we often value a public display of emotion or an admission of a personal vulnerability. This perspective is contrary to that in most cultures of the world, in which a greater emphasis is placed on maintaining a calm, stoic composure. The ability to remain cool-headed in stressful situations is essential for success in overseas work. As an outsider, you will be watched more closely than at home, and you must be able to stay composed under close public scrutiny and criticism. This is important for career success, and also for maintaining your mental health while overseas. The ability to respond to change spontaneously and quickly will also help you a great deal in overseas work; you will likely need to use your best decision-making skills in unexpected or new situations.

Project Planning Skills

As most international work is based on implementing projects, it is important to understand the fundamentals of project management. Do you know how to break a project down into phases? Can you track projects through a project life cycle? Are you familiar with how to write a project plan? Do you know about the nine project management knowledge areas? Whether you're graduating in international affairs, economics or microbiology, learn to speak of projects in terms of phases and learn how to write project plans. Take an on-line course in project management and easily learn the fundamentals—and ably impress your international employers.

Writing Skills

Most overseas jobs demand good writing skills, as extensive report writing is often required to keep head office informed. As a general rule, there is a correlation between the size of the company and the amount of report writing required. Smaller organizations tend to put more emphasis on the operational side of their work. Whatever your international field, you can be assured that international employers place much greater emphasis on strong writing skills than what is generally expected here in North America. North American students, even graduate students, should note that we often have much lower writing skills than university educated professionals elsewhere in the world, and certainly in comparison to Europe.

Verbal Communication Skills

As a representative of your institution abroad, you will meet many people and even be called upon to speak publicly. You are likely to find that the people you deal with overseas put greater emphasis on verbal skills. Many societies cultivate the art of conversation to a greater extent than we do; Westerners are often at a disadvantage in this respect. Your hosts will expect you to be polite and articulate. Don't let your verbal communication skills slide!

Diligence and Dedication

Because of its inherent challenges, overseas work requires a high degree of commitment. In order to succeed, you might need to be willing to undergo discomfort or take unusual measures. You will certainly need to persist and surmount what seems like a thousand absurd or mundane obstacles. You will be much more successful if you possess an ability to stick with a task until it is done and if you're unusually committed to your work. Your future employers know that this is required and you will need to prove your worth in this area.

Loyalty

Overseas employers demand greater loyalty than is normally required in a domestic job. Your terms of employment will place restrictions on your behaviour, both at work and in social situations. You will be expected to socialize with co-workers and their families. You will also have to respect local customs and observe local laws.

As many employers take on the responsibility of providing for your housing and your children's schooling, this opens the door to a much wider range of grievances against your employer. Despite their commitment to making your life overseas as pleasant as possible, there are bound to be disappointments. You will have to face these and sustain your loyalty to your employer.

One of the most common reasons for failure at working abroad has nothing to do with job performance but with a loss of trust and support from headquarters. Communication must be kept open and fluid or your superiors could become suspicious. In this respect, there is a certain career risk to going overseas, because it is harder to show the results of your work. You could lose credibility at home if you can't explain what you are accomplishing overseas. Time zone differences, lack of telephone service and widely differing expectations can contribute to tensions between personnel at head office and abroad. Let potential employers know you recognize this reality and are prepared to deal with it.

Diplomacy and Tact

Experienced international employees are very aware of how their own behaviour can affect others. They are careful and they give thought to the consequences of all their actions. In your new work environment, you may encounter greater formality in day-to-day operations. Try always to observe local customs and avoid thoughtless, potentially offensive remarks. For example, never forget to be sensitive about money while in less affluent societies. Don't make flippant comments to officials in your host country, or to everyday workmates. Be tactful at all times!

Philosophical Commitment to Field of Work

In North America, making money is a major concern for many people. In international work, however—especially with the UNITED NATIONS, the NGO community and in government sponsored programs—be careful about asserting the making of money as your goal. Most international employers are looking for employees who are committed to a broader cause. International employees often have a deep sense of mission. They believe they are making a contribution to human-kind. International employers may be looking for these qualities, especially if you are young and just starting your career (the UN is a good example). Do not, however, overstate your case. Employers are not looking for zealots or international "do-gooders." A brief discussion of your commitment will suffice. Reserve your longer discussion for describing your organizational and people skills.

A LAST WORD

The international employer is looking for someone who has a high international IQ. This is a person who understands the skills that are important for succeeding in any overseas environment. These skills are not just about learning to deal with the Japanese, negotiate with Columbians or converse with Arabs. They are not just culturally specific skills or knowledge. The sets of skills we speak about in this chapter are portable and transferable from culture to culture. They can be learned in South Africa and applied in the Philippines. From the streets of Mexico to offices in Moscow, as a knowledgeable international employee you must be able to interact and adapt quickly to whatever new environments you find yourself in.

An open mind, a taste for adventure, an interest in other cultures, a strong self-concept and a sense of humour—all are essential ingredients for the successful overseas worker. Landing that international job means you are about to experience drastic changes in your day-to-day life. Accept the changes, meet the challenges—and above all, enjoy yourself!

RESOURCES

This chapter contains the following Resources sections: Cross-Cultural Skills; Cross-Cultural Business Skills; Periodicals to Raise Your International IQ; and Book Distributors.

CROSS-CULTURAL SKILLS

These books are for anyone living overseas, including the accompanying spouse, the businessperson, the community development worker, the intern and the government official. If you are new to the international job market, you'll quickly acquire a knowledge base that will broaden your understanding of other cultures and highlight the subtleties of cross-cultural communication. Most of these resources are practical and easy to read. The companion to this list of cross-cultural resources is the Cross-Cultural Business Skills list of resources also found in this chapter. Much more has been written about American cultural traits; we've listed these resources after the section "United States" in Chapter 27, Jobs by Regions of the World. These books make very good reading for Canadians interested in learning how North Americans interact in the overseas workplace. Also consult the Resources sections in the following chapters: for the more practical aspects of living overseas see Chapter 3, Living Overseas and Chapter 12, Cross-Cultural Travel; and, finally, for country-specific advice on social and business customs, see the Resources section in Chapter 27, Jobs by Regions of the World.

American Ways: A Guide for Foreigners 📖

2002, Gary Althen, Intercultural Press, 328 pages ➤ Masters & Scribes Bookshoppe, 9938 - 81 Ave., Edmonton, AB T6E 1W6, Canada, www.mastersandscribes.com, $27.50 CDN; Credit Cards; 800-378-3199, fax 780-439-6879 ◆ This resource means to help foreigners understand the American culture and psyche. With sections on individualism and "Ways of Reasoning," it is one of the best-organized and clearest basic presentations of American thought process to date. Filled with case studies and helpful observations, this book covers the basic needs of the foreign student or businessperson. From understanding American society to making one's way in daily life, this book should help anyone interested in learning more about the world's most lucrative overseas job market. [ID:2009]

The Art of Crossing Cultures 📖

2001, Craig Storti, Intercultural Press, 144 pages ➤ Masters & Scribes Bookshoppe, 9938 - 81 Ave., Edmonton, AB T6E 1W6, Canada, www.mastersandscribes.com, $24.50 CDN; Credit Cards; 800-378-3199, fax 780-439-6879 ◆ This book explains why so many expatriates fail—where they go wrong and what to do about it. Extensively rewritten, in the new edition you will find new insights, expanded chapters on country and culture shock, new examples of cross-cultural misunderstanding and a new emphasis on the workplace. Storti's core model of cultural adjustment has also been refined and expanded. The fresh collection of quotations, alone, are worth the price of the book. [ID:2008]

Asia Pacific Country Backgrounders 📖 🖥

2002, 15 pages each ➤ Asia Pacific Foundation of Canada, Suite 666, 999 Canada Place, Vancouver, BC V6C 3E1, Canada, www.asiapacific.ca, Free on-line; VISA, MC; 604-684-5986, fax 604-681-1370 ◆ A series of booklets on 14 Asia Pacific countries and Canada's economic relationship with each of them. Includes key facts and figures, economic and trade statistic comparisons, Canada's ranking among major trading partners, imports and exports, main sectors of opportunity for Canadian business and more. Recommended for entrepreneurs and others seeking quick, dependable facts on Canada's Asian trade partners. [ID:2166]

Background Notes Series 📖

Annual ➤ Department of State, CA/PA, US Government Printing Office, Room 5807, Washington, DC 20520-4818, USA, www.access.gpo.gov/su_docs, $55 US/set; VISA, MC; 202-512-1800, fax 202-512-2250 ◆ Background Notes are factual publications containing information on all the countries of the world with which the United States has relations. They include facts on the country's land, people, history, government, political conditions, economy, and its relations with other countries and the United States. Helpful primers for Canadians working overseas. [ID:2076]

Barnga 📖

1990, Sivasailam Thiagarajan, Barbara Steinwachs, Intercultural Press, 80 pages ➤ Masters & Scribes Bookshoppe, 9938 - 81 Ave., Edmonton, AB T6E 1W6, Canada, www.mastersandscribes.com, $43.50 CDN; Credit Cards; 800-378-3199, fax 780-439-6879 ◆ This game simulates the effect of cultural differences on human interaction. Players learn that they must understand and reconcile these differences if they want to function effectively in a cross-cultural group. [ID:2205]

Being Abroad 💻
www.beingabroad.com ◆ Packed with links to information on all the usual topics related to living overseas: language acquisition, culture shock and teaching abroad, as well as some you wouldn't expect such as travelling with pets, skiing, snowboarding and motorcycling abroad. Also distributors of printed publications on living and working overseas. [ID:2463]

Canadian Foreign Service Institute (CFSI) 👬
Canadian Foreign Service Institute (CFSI), Lester B. Pearson Bldg. A4-235, 125 Sussex Drive, Ottawa, ON K1A 0G2, Canada, www.dfait-maeci.gc.ca/cfsi-icse, 613-944-0011, fax 613-996-4381; Fr ◆ The Canadian Foreign Service Institute (CFSI) is the part of Foreign Affairs Canada (FAC) that is responsible for providing the learning tools designed to foster more effective international relations. The CFSI provides training to FAC employees, as well as offering a series of courses to other Canadians that allow them to acquire practical knowledge and skills for living and working on assignments abroad. If you are a professional or a youth planning on going overseas, you should consult the course calendar to see which courses you might benefit from attending. [ID:2699]

Centre for Intercultural Learning (CIL) 👬
Foreign Affairs Canada (FAC) Canadian Foreign Service Institute, Centre for Intercultural Learning, 15 Bisson Street, Gatineau, QC J8Y 5M2, Canada, www.dfait-maeci.gc.ca/cfsi-icse/cil-cai/menu-en.asp, 800-852-9211, fax 819-997-5409; Fr ◆ The CIL seeks to help professionals and organizations develop the intercultural competencies essential for success in the international realm. CIL's philosophy is that intercultural learning accelerates the pace of adaptation, enhances performance and helps the learner recognize and manage culture shock. CIL resources help you learn how business is done in foreign countries, as well as helping you to adopt appropriate perspectives, develop intercultural communication skills, cultivate professional relationships and practice diplomacy and persistence. [ID:2310]

Communication Between Cultures 📖
2003, Larry A. Samovar, Richard E. Porter, 352 pages ➤ Thomson Wadsworth, P.O. Box 6904, Florence, KY 41022-6904, USA, www.wadsworth.com, $68.95 US; Credit Cards; 800-354-9706, fax 800-487-8488 ◆ Gives readers an understanding and appreciation of different cultures and helps develop practical skills for improving communication with people from other cultures. Packed with the latest research and filled with numerous compelling examples that force readers to examine their own assumptions and cultural biases. An excellent resource for those desiring to improve their ability to communicate in an intercultural environment. [ID:2168]

The Cross-Cultural Adaptability Inventory 📖
1993, Colleen Kelley, Judith Meyers, Pearson Assessments ➤ Pearson Reid London House, Suite 1600, 1 North Dearborn, Chicago, IL 60602-4331, USA, www.pearsonreidlondonhouse.com, $6.50 US; Credit Cards; 800-922-7343 ext. 4261, fax 312-242-4400 ◆ This self-assessment tool helps individuals and groups identify their current strengths and weaknesses within four skill areas that are critical for effective cross-cultural communication and interaction. Provides insight into your ability to adapt to new situations, interact with people of different cultures from your own, tolerate ambiguity and maintain a sense of self in new or different surroundings. Excellent tool for pre-departure self-exploration. [ID:2098]

Cross-Cultural Collaborations 📖
1995, Daniel Kealey, David Protheroe, Centre for Intercultural Learning, Canadian Foreign Service Institute, 65 pages ➤ Masters & Scribes Bookshoppe, 9938 - 81 Ave., Edmonton, AB T6E 1W6, Canada, www.mastersandscribes.com, $14.95 CDN; Credit Cards; 800-378-3199, fax 780-439-6879 ◆ This book clarifies why so few development assistance personnel are successful overseas by examining the individual, organizational and contextual factors at play in success or failure. It also discusses how the field of technical cooperation is evolving and how new forms of collaboration are emerging in fields such as diplomacy, peacekeeping and business. Recommended reading for both development workers and their managers. [ID:2683]

Cross-Cultural Dialogues 📖
1994, Craig Storti, 150 pages ➤ Masters & Scribes Bookshoppe, 9938 - 81 Ave., Edmonton, AB T6E 1W6, Canada, www.mastersandscribes.com, $28.95 CDN; Credit Cards; 800-378-3199, fax 780-439-6879 ◆ A collection of brief conversations between North Americans and people of other countries and cultures. Each dialogue has within it at least one, and usually several, breaches of cultural norms which the reader is challenged to recognize. An excellent learning resource for those planning international careers. [ID:2103]

Cross-Cultural Effectiveness: A Study of Canadian Technical Advisors Overseas 📖
2001, Daniel Kealey, 70 pages ➤ Foreign Affairs Canada (FAC) - Centre for Intercultural Learning, 125 Sussex Drive, Ottawa, ON K1A 0G2, Canada, www.dfait-maeci.gc.ca/cfsi-icse/cil-cai/menu-en.asp, $18.95 CDN; 800-267-8376; ₣r ◆ This study's findings challenge commonly held beliefs about what it takes to be effective in living and working in a new culture. Defines the interpersonal skills and pre-departure attitudes which are predictive of overseas success and links these to the practical issues of selection and training. A must read for anyone interested in an international and intercultural job experience. [ID:2031]

Cultural Profiles Project 💻
www.settlement.org/cp/english ◆ Citizenship and Immigration Canada, in association with the AMNI Centre of the Faculty of Social Work at the University of Toronto, has developed this excellent Web site profiling the life and customs of 102 countries worldwide. Select the country you are interested in and then navigate the information on landscape, family life, health care, education, religion and the arts, just to name a few. This is a good, reliable starting point for exploring the cultural information of your overseas destination, with each country page listing links to more in-depth information on the Web or in print. [ID:2655]

Culture Shock! Series 📖
Graphic Arts Center Publishing Company, 3019 NW Yeon, Portland, OR 97210, USA, www.gacpc.com, $13.95 US each; 503-226-2402, fax 503-223-1410 ◆ There are now 42 country guides available in this, making it one of the most successful and long-standing reference sources on international social and business customs. [ID:2104]

Culture Smart! Series 📖
Graphic Arts Center Publishing Company, 3019 NW Yeon, Portland, OR 97210, USA, www.gacpc.com, $9.95 US each; 503-226-2402, fax 503-223-1410 ◆ A new travel series focusing on cultural familiarization. Contains easy-to-access cultural and etiquette information and stuffs into your backpack. The series includes titles on Australia, Britain, China, France, Germany, India, Ireland, Japan, the Netherlands, Russia, Spain and Thailand. Break yourself into a lifelong journey toward cultural learning with these entertaining books. [ID:2537]

Culturgrams: The Nations Around Us 📖
Annual, David M. Kennedy Center for International Studies, four volumes: 730 pages ➤ David M. Kennedy Center for International Studies, Brigham Young University, 280 HRCB, Provo, UT 84602, USA, http://kennedy.byu.edu, $129.99 US; Credit Cards; 800-528-6279, fax 801-378-7075 ◆ Culturgrams are four-page summaries containing highlights of 181 cultures throughout the world. They cover customs, manners, lifestyles and other specialized information for those with a big interest but little time. Comes in looseleaf or bound edition and includes a free CD-ROM. An excellent quick reference tool. [ID:2025]

Developing Intercultural Awareness: A Cross-Cultural Training Handbook 📖
1994, L. Robert Kohls, John M. Knight, Intercultural Press, 158 pages ➤ Masters & Scribes Bookshoppe, 9938 - 81 Ave., Edmonton, AB T6E 1W6, Canada, www.mastersandscribes.com, $31.50 CDN; Credit Cards; 800-378-3199, fax 780-439-6879 ◆ This book features outline designs of one- and two-day cultural awareness workshops, and training materials that include simulation games, case studies, and exercises on values and ice-breaking. Designed for intercultural educators and trainers, and useful to anyone wishing to expand his or her general training or teaching repertoire. [ID:2102]

Doing Business with Japanese Men: A Woman's Handbook 📖
1993, Christalyn Brannen, Tracey Wilen, 176 pages ➤ Stone Bridge Press, P.O. Box 8202, Berkeley, CA 94707, USA, www.stonebridge.com, $9.95 US; Credit Cards; 800-947-7271, fax 510-524-8711 ◆ One of the only books that looks at the uniquely delicate situation that confronts the Western businesswoman, whether she is travelling to Japan or meeting Japanese clients at her home office. Includes practical discussions, background, do's and don'ts of decorum and seating charts etc. [ID:2107]

Do's and Taboos Around the World 📖
1993, Roger E. Axtell, 208 pages ➤ John Wiley & Sons, 22 Worcester Road, Etobicoke, ON M9W 1L1, Canada, www.wiley.ca, $16.95 CDN; Credit Cards; 800-567-4797, fax 800-565-6802, canada@wiley.com ◆ In a lively blend of tips, facts and cautionary tales, this fascinating guide tells travellers how to dress, exchange gifts, deal with unusual food, pronounce names and interpret body language in 96 countries. [ID:2006]

Encountering the Chinese: A Guide for Americans 📖
1999, Hu Wenzhong, Cornelius L. Grove, Intercultural Press, 230 pages ➤ Masters & Scribes Bookshoppe, 9938 - 81 Ave., Edmonton, AB T6E 1W6, Canada, www.mastersandscribes.com, $30.95 CDN; Credit Cards; 800-378-3199, fax 780-439-6879 ◆ This book is tailored to the overseas job seeker interested in China. Analyzes basic Chinese values, cultural norms and modern market mindsets. Presents insights into how to interact with Chinese people and identifies the cross-cultural factors that can lead to failed business negotiations, embarrassing faux pas and disruptive misunderstandings between Westerners and the Chinese. This edition includes an update on the modern Chinese market mentality and a special section for North American women working in China. [ID:2099]

European Journal for Intercultural Communication 🖥
Steven Dahl ➤ http://intercultural.at, Free on-line ◆ This UK-based Web site is the future home of an on-line peer review journal geared toward a general audience on the Web. Available for free and printed in English, this journal will be an interdisciplinary discussion forum for cross-cultural issues, education and training. Looks to be an amazing source of information for those wishing to go a little deeper in understanding intercultural issues. Check it out. [ID:2652]

Exploring the Greek Mosaic: A Guide to Intercultural Communication in Greece 📖
1996, Benjamin J. Broome, Intercultural Press, 192 pages ➤ Masters & Scribes Bookshoppe, 9938 - 81 Ave., Edmonton, AB T6E 1W6, Canada, www.mastersandscribes.com, $28.90 CDN; Credit Cards; 800-378-3199, fax 780-439-6879 ◆ Examines the cornerstones of Greek culture—community, family and religion—and their part in daily life. A frank discussion of the images Americans and Greeks have of each other. [ID:2204]

French Fun: The Real Spoken Language of Québec 📖
2000, Steve Timmins, 168 pages ➤ John Wiley & Sons, 22 Worcester Road, Etobicoke, ON M9W 1L1, Canada, www.wiley.ca, $14.95 US; Credit Cards; 800-567-4797, fax 800-565-6802, canada@wiley.com ◆ Through lively illustrations, hilarious literal translations and a listing of the most colourful contemporary Quebecois expressions, this book introduces the reader to the rich distinctness of the language of modern Quebec. [ID:2189]

French or Foe? 📖
2003, Polly Platt, 292 pages ➤ Distribooks International, $16.95 US, www.pollyplatt.com ◆ Designed primarily for people who will be living or working in France for extended periods, this book illuminates nuances in the manners, attitudes, and culture of the French people that are helpful to both the international job seeker and the occasional visitor. [ID:2147]

From Nyet to Da: Understanding the Russians 📖
2003, Yale Richmond, Intercultural Press, 228 pages ➤ Masters & Scribes Bookshoppe, 9938 - 81 Ave., Edmonton, AB T6E 1W6, Canada, www.mastersandscribes.com, $28.95 CDN; Credit Cards; 800-378-3199, fax 780-439-6879 ◆ Illuminates the dynamics of traditional Russian culture in the framework of contemporary events. Enlightening reading on virtually every aspect of Russian life.

Suitable for international job seekers, business executives, educators, students, governmental officials and russophiles generally. [ID:2013]

Gestures: The Do's and Taboos of Body Language Around the World 📖
1997, Roger E. Axtell, John Wiley & Sons, 256 pages ➤ Masters & Scribes Bookshoppe, 9938 - 81 Ave., Edmonton, AB T6E 1W6, Canada, www.mastersandscribes.com, $26.50 CDN; Credit Cards; 800-378-3199, fax 780-439-6879 ◆ Full of amusing anecdotes and helpful information, this book is a country-by-country exploration of gestures and intercultural rules of decorum. [ID:2001]

Good Neighbours: Communicating with the Mexicans 📖
1997, John C. Condon, Intercultural Press, 104 pages ➤ Masters & Scribes Bookshoppe, 9938 - 81 Ave., Edmonton, AB T6E 1W6, Canada, www.mastersandscribes.com, $24.95 CDN; Credit Cards; 800-378-3199, fax 780-439-6879 ◆ With penetrating insight, the author examines how Mexicans and Americans perceive themselves and each other, and how their behaviour, based on these perceptions, often leads to cross-cultural misunderstanding. Also helpful for Canadians interested in working in Mexico. [ID:2011]

Intercultural Communication Institute 💻
www.intercultural.org ◆ This Portland-based Web site belongs to a non-profit organization that seeks to promote an awareness and appreciation of cultural differences internationally and locally. While some might be interested in taking a Master's degree or attending summer professional certification courses, if you're simply looking for information on raising your cultural awareness, then this site is a good place to start. The resources section has excellent bibliographies of intercultural communication texts and there are links to Web sites with related topics. There is even an exercise section where you can download seminar exercises and explore your own, or those in your organization's intercultural awareness. [ID:2650]

Intercultural Communication: A Reader 📖
2003, Larry A. Samovar, Richard E. Porter, 480 pages ➤ Thomson Wadsworth, P.O. Box 6904, Florence, KY 41022-6904, USA, www.wadsworth.com, $77.95 US; Credit Cards; 800-354-9706, fax 800-487-8488 ◆ A broad-based, highly engaging resource that introduces readers to the theoretical and practical aspects of intercultural communication. An excellent primer for working in international environments. [ID:2093]

Intercultural Press On-line Catalogue 💻 ♦
Intercultural Press Masters & Scribes Bookshoppe, 9938 - 81 Ave., Edmonton, AB T6E 1W6, Canada, www.mastersandscribes.com, Credit Cards; 800-378-3199, fax 780-439-6879 ◆ This US publisher is the most comprehensive source for cross-cultural books available anywhere in the world. Numerous invaluable resources on intercultural training, international business, diversity, overseas living and community development. Most titles are available to the international job seeker on-line from the Canadian distributor, Intercultural and Community Development Resources (ICDR). [ID:2178]

Intermundo: The Culture Network 💻
http://intermundo.net ◆ This Web site is an on-line network for those interested in intercultural issues. Membership is free and gives you access to articles, Web discussion forums on intercultural topics and book reviews. You can watch Internet-streamed reports, interviews, discussions and lectures on intercultural topics while chatting with a subscriber in Poland about whether or not you'll need to bring your hiking boots for March in Krakow. [ID:2651]

International Journal of Intercultural Relations 📖
Quarterly ➤ Customer Service Department, Elsevier, 11830 Westline Industrial Drive, St. Louis, MO 63146, USA, www.elsevier.com/wps/find/homepage.cws_home, $175 US; Credit Cards; 800-460-3110, fax 314-453-7095, usbkinfo@elsevier.com ◆ An International scholarly journal, published quarterly and dedicated to advancing knowledge and understanding of theory, practice and research in intergroup relations. [ID:2072]

Japan's Cultural Code Words 📖
2004, Turtle Publishing, 352 pages ➤ Raincoast Books, 9050 Shaughnessy Street, Vancouver, BC V6P 6E5, Canada, www.raincoast.com, $24.95 CDN; VISA, MC; 800-663-5714, fax 800-565-3770 ◆ A must for Western business travellers to Japan, this book is the fastest way to understand the emotional/rational dualities of Japanese attitudes and behavour. Comprises 234 essays offering personal insight into the dynamics of Japanese society. [ID:2536]

Journal of Intercultural Studies 📖
3 issues/year ➤ Carfax Publishing: Taylor and Francis Group: Journals, Taylor & Francis Group, Suite 800, 325 Chestnut Street, Philadelphia, PA 19106, USA, www.tandf.co.uk, $130 US; Credit Cards; 800-354-1420, fax 215-625-8914 ◆ Provides a vital forum for research and debate related to intercultural issues arising out of the increased fluidity of borders, expanded communication technologies and the globalization of cultures and identities. Available on-line or in print. Look for it at your university library. [ID:2448]

Learning Across Cultures 📖
1994, Gary Althen, 200 pages ➤ National Association for Foreign Student Affairs, 8th Floor, 1307 New York Ave. N.W., Washington, DC 2005-4701, USA, www.nafsa.org, $15 US; Credit Cards; 800-836-4994, fax 202-737-3657 ◆ In this US volume, experts in international education provide a vital overview of cross-cultural communication and a detailed, yet accessible, deconstruction of cultural barriers. Still a good intercultural resource. [ID:2167]

Library of Congress Portals to the World 💻
www.loc.gov/rr/international/portals.html ◆ This is one of the single best Web portals available for cross-cultural and country information on the Internet. Produced by the Library of Congress, it is comprehensive, easy-to-use and up-to-date. Simply select the country you are interested in and navigate to reliable links to culture, history, education, business, commerce and economy, religion, government and politics, and recreation, just to name a few. You'll be hard pressed to find dead links on these pages. Rather, you'll surf a plethora of informative and high-quality Web resources on which you're bound to find the answers you seek and a whole lot more. Mark this as a favourite and start journeying from your father's rickety old office chair. [ID:2654]

Masters & Scribes Online Catalogue 💻 👬
Masters & Scribes Bookshoppe, 9938 - 81 Ave., Edmonton, AB T6E 1W6, Canada, www.mastersandscribes.com, Credit Cards; 800-378-3199, fax 780-439-6879 ◆ Hands down, this Edmonton distributor boasts the most comprehensive selection of cross-cultural resources available in Canada. Their product line includes books by the Intercultural Press and other respected US, Canadian and international publishers. Highly recommended for international IQ building resources. The Web site makes ordering from their extensive publications list easy. (For more information, see their ad in the sponsor section at the end of this guide.) [ID:2337]

A Practical Guide to Living in Japan 📖
2003, 256 pages ➤ Stone Bridge Press, P.O. Box 8202, Berkeley, CA 94707, USA, www.stonebridge.com, $16.95 US; Credit Cards; 800-947-7271, fax 510-524-8711 ◆ Whether you're teaching, travelling or doing business in Japan, there is something in this book for you. Includes facts on banking, immigration and insurance, plus daily-life tips on renting an apartment, utilities, transportation, using the post office and shopping for furniture. You'll get insider advice on how to find a job, learn Japanese and make new friends, as well as basic information on etiquette and customs. Packed with strategies, charts and simple how-to instructions. [ID:2540]

A Profile of the Interculturally Effective Person 📖
2001, Thomas Vulpe, Daniel Kealey, David Protheroe, Doug MacDonald, Foreign Affairs Canada (FAC) - Centre for Intercultural Learning, 65 pages ➤ Masters & Scribes Bookshoppe, 9938 - 81 Ave., Edmonton, AB T6E 1W6, Canada, www.mastersandscribes.com, $35.95 CDN; Credit Cards; 800-378-3199, fax 780-439-6879 ◆ This study moves beyond vague characteristics like "adaptability," "tolerance" and "sensitivity" to a more concrete description of the actual behaviours

exhibited by the interculturally effective person. This is a comprehensive intercultural competency profile that is valuable for those looking toward an international career. [ID:2556]

Spain Is Different 📖
1999, Helen Wattley Ames, Intercultural Press, 152 pages ➤ Masters & Scribes Bookshoppe, 9938 - 81 Ave., Edmonton, AB T6E 1W6, Canada, www.mastersandscribes.com, $23 CDN; Credit Cards; 800-378-3199, fax 780-439-6879 ◆ Although written for a US audience, Canadians can benefit from the book's focus on the uniqueness of both the Spanish people and their culture. It examines what effects the differences have on the way Spaniards and Americans relate to and interact with each other. Readers explore certain aspects of Spanish culture important in cross-cultural interactions: society and the individual, relationships, language and communication, and work and play. Each chapter contains helpful and humorous anecdotes to illustrate its thesis. Recommended. [ID:2012]

Survival Kit for Overseas Living 📖
2001, L. Robert Kohls, Intercultural Press, 181 pages ➤ Masters & Scribes Bookshoppe, 9938 - 81 Ave., Edmonton, AB T6E 1W6, Canada, www.mastersandscribes.com, $19.95 CDN; Credit Cards; 800-378-3199, fax 780-439-6879 ◆ This indispensable handbook provides the reader with straightforward information on the challenges of moving to a new country: culture shock, stereotyping, misperceptions and misunderstandings. Provides tools for overcoming cross-cultural obstacles and preparing for a rewarding and successful experience. This trusted guide has withstood the test of time as one of the best resources for international job seekers. [ID:2052]

Transitions Abroad 📖
Bimonthly, Clay Hubbs ➤ Department TRA, Transitions Publishing, P.O. Box 745, Bennington, VT 05201, USA, www.transitionsabroad.com, $32 US/year; Credit Cards; 802-442-4827, fax 802-442-4827 ◆ An excellent periodical. Required reading for students and globe trotters planning to travel, study or work abroad. Promotes learning through direct involvement in the daily lives of peoples of host countries. Describes publications, information sources, organizations, and programs offering study opportunities, entry-level jobs and living arrangements abroad. Highly recommended. (For more information, see their ad in the sponsor section at the end of this guide.) [ID:2074]

Understanding Arabs: A Guide for Westerners 📖
2002, Margaret Kleffner Nydell, 264 pages ➤ Masters & Scribes Bookshoppe, 9938 - 81 Ave., Edmonton, AB T6E 1W6, Canada, www.mastersandscribes.com, $28 CDN; Credit Cards; 800-378-3199, fax 780-439-6879 ◆ Introduces the complexities of Arab culture and Islam in an evenhanded, unbiased style. The book covers such topics as beliefs and values, religion and society, the role of the family, friends and strangers, men and women, social formalities and etiquette and communication styles. This edition includes a completely revised appendix on 17 Arab countries. [ID:2014]

We Europeans 📖
2002, Richard Hill, 432 pages ➤ Europublic SA/NV, P.O. Box 504, Uccle 5, Brussels, B-1180, Belgium, www.europublic.com, €17.25; VISA, MC; (32) (0) 2-343-77-26, fax (32) (0) 2-343-93-30 ◆ This European book provides a penetrating and entertaining analysis of the attitudes and behavioural traits of each European nationality and continues with inter-country comparisons covering such aspects as value systems, attitudes to health, day-to-day living, spare-time preferences and communication habits. Helpful background information for preparing for your overseas work experience in Europe. [ID:2169]

The Whole World Guide to Culture Learning 📖
1994, J. Daniel Hess, Intercultural Press, 280 pages ➤ Masters & Scribes Bookshoppe, 9938 - 81 Ave., Edmonton, AB T6E 1W6, Canada, www.mastersandscribes.com, $43.50 CDN; Credit Cards; 800-378-3199, fax 780-439-6879 ◆ A guide for sojourners learning about other cultures. [ID:2106]

The Yin and Yang of American Culture: A Paradox 📖
2001, Eun Y. Kim, Intercultural Press, 252 pages ➤ Masters & Scribes Bookshoppe, 9938 - 81 Ave., Edmonton, AB T6E 1W6, Canada, www.mastersandscribes.com, $36 CDN; Credit Cards;

800-378-3199, fax 780-439-6879 ◆ This book takes an Eastern view of American culture and places it in the context of Asian value sets. Based on decades of conversations and interactions with Americans and Asians, the author presents American virtues and vices from an Asian perspective, using the unique Asian concepts of yin and yang. A helpful resource for anyone planning to live and work in the US. [ID:2550]

CROSS-CULTURAL BUSINESS SKILLS

Being knowledgeable about how people of other nationalities react to us is as important as knowing how we react to others. No matter what country you travel to, at least a basic understanding of the cultural differences is crucial to the success of your venture. Judging by the number of international business resources available, you might think the art of doing business internationally is difficult to master. You will find, however, that the skills of cross-cultural communication are portable, whether applied to business, diplomacy, or friendship. Moreover, once you learn to do business with the Japanese, you can easily apply much of your knowledge to doing business with Indonesians or Brazilians. Many of the following resources pertain to international business negotiations, but don't back away from this material if you are not a business person; all international employees need cross-cultural negotiation skills. Supplementing this list of cross-cultural resources is the Cross-Cultural Skills section, also located in this chapter. Canadians share many cultural traits with Americans. Helpful books describing American cultural traits are listed after the section, "United States", in Chapter 27, Jobs by Regions of the World. For the more practical aspects of living overseas, see the resources in Chapter 3, Living Overseas and Chapter 12, Cross-Cultural Travel. For books on the practice of international business (such as how to import and export) see the International Business Resources in Chapter 21, Resources for the International Job Search.

Business Chinese 📖
2002 ➤ China Books & Periodicals Inc., 2929 - 24th Street, San Francisco, CA 94110, USA, www.chinabooks.com, $14.95 US; Credit Cards; 415-282-2994, fax 415-282-0994 ◆ This introductory text focuses on learning spoken Chinese for business. Lessons focus on real-life business situations, with exercises and up-to-date business terms. A good primer for a successful business trip. [ID:2480]

Canada Year Book 📖
2001, Statistics Canada, 563 pages ➤ Renouf Publishing Co. Ltd., Unit 1, 5369 Canotek Road, Ottawa, ON K1J 9J3, Canada, www.renoufbooks.com, $65 CDN; Credit Cards; 888-767-6766, fax 613-745-7660; Fr ◆ This book is published every two years by Statistics Canada and serves as a vital reference resource. It provides an up-to-date picture of the social, economic and cultural life of Canada. It's a great book to bring as a gift or as a handy reference for all the questions your overseas friends will ask you when you travel overseas. Also available in French. [ID:2365]

Centre for Intercultural Learning (CIL) ⅲ
Foreign Affairs Canada (FAC) Canadian Foreign Service Institute, Centre for Intercultural Learning, 15 Bisson Street, Gatineau, QC J8Y 5M2, Canada, www.dfait-maeci.gc.ca/cfsi-icse/cil-cai/menu-en.asp, 800-852-9211, fax 819-997-5409; Fr ◆ The CIL seeks to help professionals and organizations develop the intercultural competencies essential for success in the international realm. CIL's philosophy is that intercultural learning accelerates the pace of adaptation, enhances performance and helps the learner recognize and manage culture shock. CIL resources help you learn how business is done in foreign countries, as well as helping you to adopt appropriate perspectives, develop intercultural communication skills, cultivate professional relationships and practice diplomacy and persistence. [ID:2310]

Competitive Frontiers: Women Managers in a Global Economy 📖
1994, Nancy J. Adler, Dafna Izraeli, 414 pages ➤ Blackwell Publishers, 350 Main Street, Malden, MB 02148, USA, www.blackwell.com, $55.95 US; Credit Cards; 781-288-8200, fax 781-338-8210, mbarilla@bos.blackwellpublishing.com ◆ This book examines the changing nature of world business and its impact on women managers. [ID:2134]

Craighead's International Business Travel and Relocation Guide to 84 Countries 📖
2004, 4 volumes ➤ Thomson Gale, 835 Penobscot Bldg., 645 Griswold Street, Detroit, MI 48226-4094, USA, www.gale.com, $775 US; Credit Cards; 800-877-4253 ext. 1330, fax 800-414-5043; Available in large libraries ◆ Now covering 84 countries, this authoritative four-volume set is designed specifically to meet the needs of individuals who require in-depth information about doing business and living and working in the countries most important to international business. Craighead's provides data necessary to understand and evaluate the political, economic and business environment and everyday living conditions of foreign destinations. [ID:2040]

The Cultural Dimension of International Business 📖
2001, Gary P. Ferraro, Pearson: Prentice Hall Canada, 214 pages ➤ Masters & Scribes Bookshoppe, 9938 - 81 Ave., Edmonton, AB T6E 1W6, Canada, www.mastersandscribes.com, $46.95 CDN; Credit Cards; 800-378-3199, fax 780-439-6879 ◆ Demonstrates how the theory and insights of cultural anthropology can positively influence the conduct of international business. Explores general concepts about culture, the nature of communication and value systems. A good read with insights bound to improve your cross-cultural business skills. [ID:2105]

Culture Shock! Succeed in Business 📖
Graphic Arts Center Publishing Company, 3019 NW Yeon, Portland, OR 97210, USA, www.gacpc.com, $13.95 US; 503-226-2402, fax 503-223-1410 ◆ In this guide the international entrepreneur will learn to see beyond the stereotypes and misinformation that often precede business travel to foreign lands. Whether you plan to stay for a week or a year, you'll benefit from such topics as understanding the rules of driving and monetary systems, building business relationships and the particular intricacies of setting up an office. [ID:2538]

Cultures and Organizations: Software of the Mind 📖
2004, Geert Hofstede, McGraw-Hill Ryerson Ltd., 300 pages ➤ Masters & Scribes Bookshoppe, 9938 - 81 Ave., Edmonton, AB T6E 1W6, Canada, www.mastersandscribes.com, $42.95 CDN; Credit Cards; 800-378-3199, fax 780-439-6879 ◆ This book shows that effective intercultural cooperation is possible. Deals with differences among opinion leaders, their followers, and national cultures, and with the popular notion of organizational cultures and how these develop and change. Outlines ways of learning intercultural cooperation by applying these ideas to various situations in the world where cultures meet—such as education, migration and business. Dispells many myths about organizational cultures. [ID:2094]

Developing Global Organizations: Strategies for Human Resource Professionals 📖
1993, Robert T. Moran, William G. Stripp, Gulf Publishing, 318 pages ➤ Masters & Scribes Bookshoppe, 9938 - 81 Ave., Edmonton, AB T6E 1W6, Canada, www.mastersandscribes.com, $47.95 US; Credit Cards; 800-378-3199, fax 780-439-6879 ◆ Discover various cross-cultural training and education strategies aimed at developing global organizations and managers who are able to conduct business successfully in world markets. Combines a theoretical foundation with practical information and suggestions that show how to become an agent of change in creating a high-performance workforce that is ready to capitalize on all international and intercultural opportunities that arise. Still a good resource for the international manager. [ID:2199]

Doing Business Internationally: The Guide to Cross-Cultural Success 📖
1995, Terence Brake, Danielle Walker, Princeton Training Press, 256 pages ➤ Masters & Scribes Bookshoppe, 9938 - 81 Ave., Edmonton, AB T6E 1W6, Canada, www.mastersandscribes.com, $59.95 CDN; Credit Cards; 800-378-3199, fax 780-439-6879 ◆ Provides executives and managers with the knowledge and skills they'll need to compete in today's gigantic, multicultural marketplace. Starting with an overview of six cultural regions: Africa, Asia, Latin America, Europe, the Middle

East, and North America, the authors build a framework for organizing cross-cultural experiences and identifying and working with key cultural differences. Designed to be used by an individual or group, this participant workbook leads the reader through the process of: analyzing key global trends and their impact on current business practices; recognizing the impact of cultural differences on business relationships; identifying and overcoming intercultural communication barriers in order to achieve greater effectiveness and synergy; and, adapting key business skills to maximize effectiveness when working across cultures. The book is divided into four modules: Global Business Thinking, Cross-Cultural Awareness, Cross-Cultural Communication and Working Across Cultures. [ID:2197]

Do's and Taboos Around the World for Women in International Business 📖
1997, Roger E. Axtell, 272 pages ➤ John Wiley & Sons, 22 Worcester Road, Etobicoke, ON M9W 1L1, Canada, www.wiley.ca, $19.95 CDN; Credit Cards; 800-567-4797, fax 800-565-6802, canada@wiley.com ◆ Draws on experiences of 100 women to offer advice on body language, health concerns, dress, balancing family life with work abroad, and more. [ID:2218]

Ecotonos 📖
1997, Dianne Hofner-Saphiere, Nipporica Associates, Intercultural Press ➤ Masters & Scribes Bookshoppe, 9938 - 81 Ave., Edmonton, AB T6E 1W6, Canada, www.mastersandscribes.com, $282.75 CDN; Credit Cards; 800-378-3199, fax 780-439-6879 ◆ An excellent simulation tool for engaging groups in problem solving and decision-making where power issues, cultural assumptions and expectations are at issue. Methods and processes of decision-making are examined in four contexts: monocultural groups, multicultural groups, groups where one culture is in the majority and groups evenly balanced in cultural representation. Used successfully in the US and Japan in business, education, cross-cultural counselling and community development. For 12 to 50 participants. Designed for participants with no prior multicultural experience and those interested in expanding their understanding. [ID:2206]

Euromanagers & Martians: The Business Cultures of Europe's Trading Nations 📖
2002, Richard Hill, 264 pages ➤ Europublic SA/NV, P.O. Box 504, Uccle 5, Brussels, B-1180, Belgium, www.europublic.com, €17.25; VISA, MC; (32) (0) 2-343-77-26, fax (32) (0) 2-343-93-30 ◆ Looks closely at the business and management cultures of Europe. Identifies those areas where cultures collide, comparing management styles and negotiating strategies, and analyzing the implications of cross-frontier strategic alliances, multicultural teamwork and "New Age" management techniques. [ID:2200]

From Boston to Beijing: Managing with a World View 📖
2002, 304 pages ➤ Thomson South-Western, 5191 Natorp Blvd., Mason, OH 45040, USA, www.swlearning.com, $22.95 US; Credit Cards; 513-229-1000 ◆ International entrepreneurs in every industry can benefit from the advice this book contains on how to manage in a multicultural environment. It illustrates how countries vary and how people recognize, manage and effectively use cultural variance. In addition to information on working with colleagues across the globe, the book contains information on culture shock, spousal transition and returning home after an overseas stint. [ID:2549]

Going to Japan on Business: Protocol, Stategies & Language for the Corporate Traveler 📖
2002, Christalyn Brannen, 176 pages ➤ Stone Bridge Press, P.O. Box 8202, Berkeley, CA 94707, USA, www.stonebridge.com, $14.95 US; Credit Cards; 800-947-7271, fax 510-524-8711 ◆ This US book includes tips for first-time and seasoned business travellers, all in a handy form for quick reference and on-the-spot use. Includes information on preparing for your trip, getting around, making introductions, conducting business meetings, socializing, sounding good in Japanese, and much more. Essential reading for those with business interests in Japan. [ID:2142]

Graybridge International Consulting Inc. ⚑
Graybridge International Consulting Inc., 76 Rue Hotel-De-Ville, Gatineau, QC J8X 2E2, Canada, www.graybridge.ca, 800-259-4482, fax 819-776-6491, success@graybridge.ca ◆ This Canadian

consulting firm has over 10 years' experience delivering a wide range of activities linked to international training and overseas management services. Offers cross-cultural and overseas effectiveness training, organizational development training, professional skills development training and international / domestic event coordination. (In June 2004, Graybridge was about to merge with Malkam Consultants Ltd.) [ID:2341]

International Business Case Studies for the Multicultural Marketplace 📖
1999, Robert T. Moran, David Braaten, John Walsh, Gulf Publishing, 416 pages ➤ McGraw-Hill Ryerson Ltd., 300 Water Street, Whitby, ON L1N 9B6, Canada, www.mcgrawhill.ca, $42.95 CDN; Credit Cards; 800-565-5758, fax 800-463-5885 ◆ This US book presents specific, real-life examples of the strategies and tactics used by some of the world's most successful international businesses and organizations to excel in the global marketplace. A comprehensive collection of more than 30 case studies of such critical international business issues as globalization and marketing. Good reading for those aspiring to careers in international business. [ID:2171]

International Business Etiquette: Latin America 📖
2000, Anne Marie Sabath, 224 pages ➤ Career Press, P.O. Box 687, 3 Tice Road, Franklin Lakes, NJ 07417, USA, www.careerpress.com, $14.99 US; Credit Cards; 800-227-3371 ◆ This quick-reading US book shares the do's and don'ts of interacting with individuals in all the major commercial countries of Latin America. Each chapter is devoted to a specific country and begins with the top 10 reasons why people do (or should do) business in this country. What follows are countless tips for knowing what to do and when to do it, whether you are meeting someone for the first time or the tenth time. Each chapter closes with tips for avoiding the most commonly made country-specific faux pas. Interesting and informative. [ID:2382]

Japan's Cultural Code Words 📖
2004, Turtle Publishing, 352 pages ➤ Raincoast Books, 9050 Shaughnessy Street, Vancouver, BC V6P 6E5, Canada, www.raincoast.com, $24.95 CDN; VISA, MC; 800-663-5714, fax 800-565-3770 ◆ A must for Western business travellers to Japan, this book is the fastest way to understand the emotional/rational dualities of Japanese attitudes and behavour. Comprises 234 essays offering personal insight into the dynamics of Japanese society. [ID:2536]

Managing Cultural Differences 📖
2004, Robert T. Moran, 624 pages ➤ Customer Service Department, Elsevier, 11830 Westline Industrial Drive, St. Louis, MO 63146, USA, www.elsevier.com/wps/find/homepage.cws_home, $69.95 US; Credit Cards; 800-460-3110, fax 314-453-7095, usbkinfo@elsevier.com ◆ Completely updated to reflect many recent global phenomena: globalization, SARS, AIDS, the handover of Hong Kong. Contains plentiful region and country descriptions, demographic data, graphs and maps. Zeroes in on cultural education as the crucial dimension of a successful international career. [ID:2053]

Managing Cultural Diversity in Technical Professions 📖
2003, Lionel Laroche, Elsevier, 236 pages ➤ Masters & Scribes Bookshoppe, 9938 - 81 Ave., Edmonton, AB T6E 1W6, Canada, www.mastersandscribes.com, $48.95 CDN; Credit Cards; 800-378-3199, fax 780-439-6879 ◆ Technology is one of the fastest-growing employment sectors worldwide, and this European book provides managers of technical professionals with clear and tested strategies to improve communication and increase productivity among culturally diverse technical professionals, teams and departments. Outlines the differences in education and training, career expectations, communication styles and management expectations in countries around the world. Recommended. [ID:2553]

Mind Your Manners: Managing Business Cultures in Europe 📖
2003, John Mole, Nicholas Brealey Publishing, 286 pages ➤ Masters & Scribes Bookshoppe, 9938 - 81 Ave., Edmonton, AB T6E 1W6, Canada, www.mastersandscribes.com, $36 CDN; Credit Cards; 800-378-3199, fax 780-439-6879 ◆ The standard guide to European business cultures for over a decade. Now it covers 33 different business cultures, including the 13 countries—from Bulgaria to Turkey—joining the new and enlarged EU as well as non-EU countries such as Norway, Switzerland, Russia and America. Recommended for international entrepreneurs. [ID:2198]

Mindsets: The Role of Culture and Perception in International Relations 📖

1997, Glen Fisher, Intercultural Press, 228 pages ➤ Masters & Scribes Bookshoppe, 9938 - 81 Ave., Edmonton, AB T6E 1W6, Canada, www.mastersandscribes.com, $34.75 CDN; Credit Cards; 800-378-3199, fax 780-439-6879 ◆ This non-technical book is ideal for the international job hunter desiring a better understanding of how socialized preconceptions about cultural differences affect intercultural relations and international affairs. Chapters touch on the roles these notions play in international political relations, development and technical assistance, global economic and business affairs, and ethnic conflict. [ID:2092]

The Rice Paper Ceiling 📖

2000, Rochelle Kopp, 272 pages ➤ Stone Bridge Press, P.O. Box 8202, Berkeley, CA 94707, USA, www.stonebridge.com, $19.95 US; Credit Cards; 800-947-7271, fax 510-524-8711 ◆ What can the non-Japanese employee of a Japanese company do to advance his or her career prospects? This US book presents a readable and detailed analysis of the "rice-paper ceiling" and "breakthrough" strategies for overcoming it. Includes techniques for improving working relationships and career prospects, as well as insights into the profound differences between Japanese and American work styles and cultures. [ID:2208]

Riding the Waves of Culture: Understanding Diversity in Global Business 📖

1998, Fons Trompenaars, 274 pages ➤ Masters & Scribes Bookshoppe, 9938 - 81 Ave., Edmonton, AB T6E 1W6, Canada, www.mastersandscribes.com, $57.95 CDN; Credit Cards; 800-378-3199, fax 780-439-6879 ◆ Revealing seven key dimensions of business behaviour and ways in which they combine to form four basic types of corporate culture: the Family (Japan, Belgium), the Eiffel Tower (France, Germany), the Guided Missile (US, UK) and the Incubator (Silicon Valley), this book outlines strategies for management success in the new international marketplace. [ID:2196]

Sharks and Custard: The Things that Make Europeans Laugh 📖

2001, Richard Hill, 189 pages ➤ Europublic SA/NV, P.O. Box 504, Uccle 5, Brussels, B-1180, Belgium, www.europublic.com, €12.95; VISA, MC; (32) (0) 2-343-77-26, fax (32) (0) 2-343-93-30 ◆ English humour is an important component of international business life—a life that needs to be handled with tact and understanding. At best it can defuse the difficult moments of a major negotiation, at worst it can ruin a relationship! This is a great guide to a deeper understanding of your European business partners. [ID:2551]

Transcultural Leadership: Empowering the Diverse Workforce 📖

1999, George Simmons, Carmen Vazquez, Phillip Harris, Gulf Publishing, 260 pages ➤ McGraw-Hill Ryerson Ltd., 300 Water Street, Whitby, ON L1N 9B6, Canada, www.mcgrawhill.ca, $63.50 CDN; Credit Cards; 800-565-5758, fax 800-463-5885 ◆ Interns and young professionals can benefit from this discussion of the modern global reality of cultural and gender diversity in the workplace. [ID:2170]

When Cultures Collide: Managing Successfully Across Cultures 📖

1999, Richard D. Lewis, Intercultural Press, 468 pages ➤ Masters & Scribes Bookshoppe, 9938 - 81 Ave., Edmonton, AB T6E 1W6, Canada, www.mastersandscribes.com, $28.50 CDN; Credit Cards; 800-378-3199, fax 780-439-6879 ◆ This book explores cultural socialization, the relationship between language and thought, and the importance of foreign language learning for true cultural understanding. The reader is then taken on a journey to fifteen individual countries, explaining the cultural underpinnings of people's behaviour and giving practical advice on how to minimize friction with each group. A good resource for those wishing to expand their intercultural awareness in preparation for an overseas career. [ID:2194]

Wiley Publishers and Distributors Catalogue 💻 ⋔

John Wiley & Sons, 22 Worcester Road, Etobicoke, ON M9W 1L1, Canada, www.wiley.ca, Credit Cards; 800-567-4797, fax 800-565-6802, canada@wiley.com ◆ North America's largest professional book distributor and publisher. The Web site features their wide selection of business books, many pertaining to international subjects. [ID:2181]

Women in Management Worldwide: Facts, Figures and Analysis 📖
2004, 370 pages ➤ Ashgate Publishing Company, Suite 420, 101 Cherry Street, Burlington, VT 05401-4405, USA, www.ashgate.com, $89.95 US; Credit Cards; 802-865-7641, fax 802-865-7847 ◆ A genuinely cross-cultural assessment of women's progress in management throughout the world. Each chapter of the book focuses on one of twenty countries worldwide. Chapters follow the same format, so direct comparisons are easy. Key issues arising from the statistics are discussed, trends analyzed and best practices recommended. An informative and essential sourcebook for international job seekers concerned about the progress of women in management worldwide. [ID:2527]

PERIODICALS TO RAISE YOUR INTERNATIONAL IQ

The following is a list of resources to help you improve your international IQ. While there's no shortage of good material available, we think this list includes a few of the best sources of information and news about the world around us, and represents a diversity of perspectives. Developing an international IQ is an important part of your international job search strategy. If you haven't already begun this process, start yesterday! For more information on building your cross-cultural communication skills while abroad, consult the following Resources sections: Chapter 1, The Effective Overseas Employee, offers material focused on general cross-cultural skills required by all international employees; Chapter 3, Living Overseas, has resources that discuss the more practical aspects of living overseas; Chapter 27, Jobs by Regions of the World, lists books that provide country-specific advice on social and business customs.

Canada World View 📖
Quarterly ➤ Enquiries Service, Foreign Affairs Canada (FAC), 125 Sussex Drive, Ottawa, ON K1A 0G2, Canada, www.fac-aec.gc.ca, Free; 800-267-8376, fax 613-996-9709; Fr ◆ Provides an overview of Canada's perspective on foreign policy issues and highlights the Government of Canada's international initiatives and contributions. A good primer. [ID:2485]

Culturgrams: The Nations Around Us 📖
Annual, David M. Kennedy Center for International Studies, four volumes: 730 pages ➤ David M. Kennedy Center for International Studies, Brigham Young University, 280 HRCB, Provo, UT 84602, USA, http://kennedy.byu.edu, $129.99 US; Credit Cards; 800-528-6279, fax 801-378-7075 ◆ Culturgrams are four-page summaries containing highlights of 181 cultures throughout the world. They cover customs, manners, lifestyles and other specialized information for those with a big interest but little time. Comes in looseleaf or bound edition and includes a free CD-ROM. An excellent quick reference tool. [ID:2025]

Current History 📖
9 issues/year ➤ Current History, 4225 Main Street, Philadelphia, PA 19127-9989, USA, www.currenthistory.com, $40.75 US/year; VISA, MC, AMEX; 215-482-4464, fax 215-482-9197 ◆ This is the oldest US publication dedicated exclusively to world affairs. It is useful for its region-by-region annual summaries. Each issue focuses on one region or country, providing annual coverage on China, the former Soviet Union, the Middle East, Latin America, Africa and South and Southeast Asia. It also has a country-by-country "Month in Review" feature. Excellent if you're about to travel to a region and need a quick overview of its current political trends; order back issues or visit the indexed Web site. [ID:2373]

The Economist 📖
Weekly, The Economist ➤ www.economist.com, $189 US/yr ◆ One of the best magazines around for keeping up-to-date on the economic and political situations in both developed and developing countries, as well as for classified ads for senior management jobs. [ID:2136]

Far Eastern Economic Review 📖
Weekly ➤ Subscription Department, Far Eastern Economic Review, P.O. Box 160, General Post Office, Hong Kong, China, www.feer.com, $220 HK/year; Credit Cards; (800) 522-2714, fax (413) 592-4782 ◆ With a circulation of over 100,000 in Hong Kong, Malaysia and Singapore, this news weekly is Asia's premier business magazine. Reports on politics, business, economics, technology and social and cultural issues throughout Asia, with a particular emphasis on both Southeast Asia and China. Sign up on-line for a one-, two- or three-year subscription. [ID:2141]

Financial Times 📖
Daily ➤ Customer Service, Financial Times, P.O. Box 1329, Newburgh, NY 12551-9970, USA, www.ft.com, $498 US for one-year subscription; 800-628-8088, fax 845-566-8220; Available at international newsstands ◆ A world-renowned daily paper that provides excellent international coverage. [ID:2159]

The Guardian Weekly 📖
Daily, Guardian Publications Ltd. ➤ Manchester Guardian Weekly, P.O. Box 2515, Champlain, New York, NY 12919-2515, USA, www.time.ca, $2.50 US/issue; VISA, MC; 514-630-1106, fax 514-697-3490, gwsubsna@time.ca ◆ A weekly newspaper with excellent coverage of international events and issues including international job postings. [ID:2160]

Le Monde 📖
Daily ➤ Le Monde, 21 bis, rue Claude-Bernard, Paris Cedex 05, 75242, France, www.lemonde.fr, $2.25 US/issue; (33) (1) 40-65-25-25, fax (33) (1) 49-60-34-90; 𝐅𝐫 ◆ Journal quotidien français renommé pour ses articles internationaux ; la section Emplois présente de nombreux postes disponibles en France. [ID:2161]

Mondial: Journal of the World Federalist Movement of Canada 🖥
Quarterly ➤ World Federalist Movement of Canada, Suite 207, 145 Spruce Street, Ottawa, ON K1R 6P1, Canada, worldfederalistscanada.org, Free on-line; VISA, MC; 613-232-0647, fax 613-563-0017 ◆ This interesting Web magazine touches on issues surrounding global governance. A good primer for the curious internationalist. [ID:2526]

The New Internationalist 📖
Monthly ➤ Subscription Office, New Internationalist, Unit 17, 35 Riviera Drive, Markham, ON L3R 8N4, Canada, www.newint.org, $44/year; Credit Cards; 905-946-0407, fax 905-946-0410 ◆ The magazine reports on issues of world poverty and inequality and seeks to focus attention on the unjust relationship between the powerful and the powerless in both rich and poor nations. Acts as an insightful forum for debate and campaigns for global change so that the basic material and spiritual needs of all humans can be met. A great alternative to mainstream coverage of the international issues often encountered when living and working overseas. (For more information, see their ad in the sponsor section at the end of this guide.) [ID:2060]

New York Times 📖
Daily ➤ New York Times Co., 229 West 43rd Street, New York, NY 10036, USA, www.nytimes.com, Credit Cards; 800-631-2500, fax 201-342-2539; Available at international newsstands ◆ One of the largest US dailies. Excellent international coverage. Register as a member and enjoy the coverage for free. Boasts a great job board for the US region. [ID:2158]

Wall Street Journal 📖
Daily ➤ Wall Street Journal, Suite 200, 2 Summit Park Drive, Independence, OH 44131, USA, www.dowjones.com, $79 US on-line or $198 US/52 weeks; Credit Cards; 800-369-2834, fax 212-597-5600 ◆ Bills itself as the world's most trusted news source. Good coverage, but with a bit of a business leaning. [ID:2157]

World Press Review 🖥
Monthly ➤ World Press Review, P.O. Box 228, Shrub Oak, NY 10588-0228, USA, www.worldpress.org, Free on-line; 212-889-5155 ◆ This monthly new magazine draws upon publications around the globe, and a network of correspondents in dozens of countries to illuminate

the issues ignored in the mainstream US press, translating, reprinting, analyzing and contextualizing the best of the international press from more than 20 languages. Published by the Stanley Foundation as a non-profit educational service to foster the international exchange of information. [ID:2372]

WWW Virtual Library: International Affairs Resources 🖳
www.etown.edu/vl ◆ This excellent Web site is a section of the WWW Virtual Library system and presents over 2,600 annotated links to a wide range of international affairs, international development, international studies and international relations Web sites. Browse for resources organized by media sources, organizations, regions and countries, and topics. An excellent source of information on international affairs. Also, if your career interest is in international affairs or international development, you can canvass potential organizations using this list. A great resource. [ID:2761]

BOOK DISTRIBUTORS

One of the most amazing things about working overseas is the richness of the surrounding sensory experiences—the dazzling sights as well as the chorus and aroma of life. The following is similarly interesting—a list of book publishers and distributors specializing in overseas living and other international subjects.

Apex Press Catalogue 📖 🖳 ♔
Annual ➤ Council on International and Public Affairs, Apex Press, P.O. Box 337, Croton-on-Hudson, NY 10520, USA, www.cipa-apex.org, Credit Cards; 800-316-2739, fax 800-316-2739 ◆ The catalogue for this specialized distributor of books on human rights, grassroots activism, sustainable development, peace and security, Third World politics, social change, and international education is now available on the distributor's Web site. [ID:2123]

Book Passage Travelers' Bookshelf ♔
Book Passage, 51 Tamal Vista Blvd., Corte Madera, CA 94925, USA, www.bookpassage.com, Credit Cards; 800-999-7909, fax 415-924-3838, messages@bookpassage.com ◆ One of San Francisco's coolest bookstores offers a mail-order travel book and map service. Also a great Web site with information on all their cross-cultural publications listed by region: Northern Europe, Southern Europe, Mexico, Latin America, the Caribbean, East Asia and the South Pacific. If you can't visit in person, at least check out the home page! [ID:2404]

Impact Publications Catalogues 🖳 ♔
Annual ➤ Impact Publications, Suite N, 9104 North Manassas Drive, Manassas Park, VA 20111-5211, USA, www.impactpublications.com, Credit Cards; 703-361-7300, fax 703-335-9486 ◆ Impact Publications is a US organization that produces a number of catalogues together, comprising the best mail-order source for career books in North America (including many international career books). Be sure to check out their Web site. [ID:2179]

Intercultural Press On-line Catalogue 🖳 ♔
Intercultural Press Masters & Scribes Bookshoppe, 9938 - 81 Ave., Edmonton, AB T6E 1W6, Canada, www.mastersandscribes.com, Credit Cards; 800-378-3199, fax 780-439-6879 ◆ This US publisher is the most comprehensive source of cross-cultural books available anywhere. Numerous invaluable resources on intercultural training, international business, diversity, overseas living and community development. Most titles are available to the international job seeker on-line from the Canadian distributor, Intercultural and Community Development Resources (ICDR). [ID:2178]

Kumarian Press Catalogue 🖳 ♔
Kumarian Press Inc., 1294 Blue Hills Ave., Bloomfield, CT 06002, USA, www.kpbooks.com, Free; VISA, MC; 800-289-2664, fax 860-243-2867 ◆ This excellent US publisher of independent scholarly works has replaced its catalogue with an excellent Web site featuring a large selection of books relating to international affairs and development. [ID:2016]

Lynne Rienner Online Catalogue 💻 ♔

Annual ➤ Lynne Rienner Publishers, Suite 314, 1800 30th Street, Boulder, CO 80301, USA, www.rienner.com, Credit Cards; 303-444-6684, fax 303-444-0824 ◆ With a foundation of 20 years of experience in independent publishing, this on-line catalogue is an excellent source for academic resources related to international affairs. [ID:2336]

Masters & Scribes Online Catalogue 💻 ♔

Masters & Scribes Bookshoppe, 9938 - 81 Ave., Edmonton, AB T6E 1W6, Canada, www.mastersandscribes.com, Credit Cards; 800-378-3199, fax 780-439-6879 ◆ Hands down, this Edmonton distributor boasts the most comprehensive selection of cross-cultural resources available in Canada. Their product line includes books by the Intercultural Press and other respected US, Canadian and international publishers. Highly recommended for international IQ building resources. The Web site makes ordering from their extensive publications list easy. (For more information, see their ad in the sponsor section at the end of this guide.) [ID:2337]

PACT Publications Catalogue 💻 ♔

Semi-annual ➤ PACT Publications, Suite 350, 1200 18th Street N.W., Washington, DC 20036, USA, www.pactpublications.com, Free on-line; Credit Cards; 202-466-5666, fax 202-466-5669 ◆ Pact Publications is an integrated publishing house that facilitates the design, production and distribution of innovative and progressive development materials. The Catalogue offers development professionals the most appropriate educational materials and training tools available. Available on-line in PDF format. [ID:2065]

Renouf Catalogue 💻 ♔

Renouf Publishing Co. Ltd., Unit 1, 5369 Canotek Road, Ottawa, ON K1J 9J3, Canada, www.renoufbooks.com, Credit Cards; 888-767-6766, fax 613-745-7660 ◆ This Web site is produced by the North American specialty distributor Renouf, which features the publications of international and governmental organizations such as the United Nations, governments of Canada, US and the EU. The list of titles is extensive. Highly recommended. Visit the Web site to contact their US distribution office. [ID:2180]

Taylor & Francis Social Sciences Journals 📖 💻 ♔

www.tandf.co.uk/journals/listings/soc.asp#top ◆ So, now you know where you're being deployed. You've read all the books from Chapters and surfed all the Web sites you can find on your region. But you want something a little more in-depth. Here's your next stop. Taylor & Francis publishes of a surprising variety of scholarly journals, for example, "The Journal of Israeli History," "Ethnomusicology Forum" or "African Identities." Find them by region and head to the library. Better yet, many have free on-line sample copies. Happy research! [ID:2782]

United Nations Publications Catalogue 💻 ♔

Annual ➤ United Nations Publications, Sales and Marketing Section, Room DC2-853, Department I004, New York, NY 10017, USA, www.un.org/Pubs/sales.htm, Free on-line; Credit Cards; 800-253-9646, fax 212-963-3489 ◆ This UN Web catalogue is a compendium of the all the United Nations' publications. Also available on CD-ROM. [ID:2790]

Westview Press Catalogue 💻 ♔

Annual ➤ Perseus Books Group: Westview Press, 5500 Central Ave., Boulder, CO 80301-2877, USA, www.westviewpress.com, Free; 800-386-5656, fax 720-406-7336 ◆ Now part of the US Perseus group, the Westview Press Web site contains a comprehensive selection of quality titles relating to development and regional studies. [ID:2121]

Wiley Publishers and Distributors Catalogue 💻 ♔

John Wiley & Sons, 22 Worcester Road, Etobicoke, ON M9W 1L1, Canada, www.wiley.ca, Credit Cards; 800-567-4797, fax 800-565-6802, canada@wiley.com ◆ North America's largest professional book distributor and publisher. The Web site features their wide selection of business books, many pertaining to international subjects. [ID:2181]

CHAPTER 2
Myths & Realities

This chapter looks carefully at the cold realities of overseas life. If you find these points discouraging, do not despair. There are overwhelming benefits to living and working overseas as well. Moreover, most of us who have already worked overseas had no forewarning of these realities, but we nonetheless endured, adapted to and enjoyed overseas life. If you are new to the international arena, just keep in the forefront of your mind your ability to adapt. Then you'll have a good chance of overcoming the pitfalls listed in this chapter.

ARE YOU READY FOR LIFE OVERSEAS?

Reality overseas may not always measure up to expectations. This is a fact of life that applies to any new endeavour.

The idea of a job in Geneva may sound inviting, but only if it's right for you. Be careful not to base your idea of working abroad on glamour. While living overseas may seem like a full-time touring opportunity, the realities of daily living and working must be taken into consideration before you even begin your job search, let alone sign that contract and get on the plane!

Thus, before taking the plunge and perhaps making a costly mistake in your career and personal life, here are some questions you should answer before deciding to look for work overseas:

- Are you prepared for major adjustments in your home and work life?
- Are you prepared to be separated from your family, loved ones and friends?
- Are you prepared to live in a country where you don't understand the language?
- Are you prepared to give up all the services and facilities you take for granted at home—medical, legal, financial?
- Are you willing to try new foods? Perhaps do without television? Your daily newspaper? Even a telephone?

- Are you prepared to live with new security considerations, possible political instability, crime, corruption, and major class differences?
- Are you prepared to live in a different climate?
- Are you prepared for living in a culture very different from your own, with customs and attitudes you have never encountered before?
- Are you prepared to be patient in a way you never had to be at home?
- Are you prepared to frequently misunderstand and be misunderstood?
- Are you prepared to put in storage or divest yourself of your belongings?
- Are you capable of dealing with the tremendous contrast of poverty and wealth existing side by side in developing countries?

Answering carefully the above questions should give you some idea of your suitability for an overseas career.

MYTHS ABOUT LIVING OVERSEAS

There are many misconceptions about living overseas. Often, if we talk to friends or acquaintances with overseas experience, they only mention the good (or bad) things about their lives. Or, on the other hand, we sometimes only hear what we *want* to hear. Consider some of the following points.

"International living is exciting and exotic."

It can be, but it can also be boring. After eating a few local dishes and attending a few cultural events, the novelty of a new culture can wear off. Many expatriates complain about the lack of recreation, movies, television, radio, and especially, long-time friends and family.

"Living overseas will allow me a life of leisure."

It is true that many expatriates have domestic help, but life overseas can be hectic. It takes a lot of work to supervise a cook, maid, gardener and guard. Everything from shopping to cooking to cleaning takes more time because of the lack of modern conveniences and our lack of familiarity with the culture.

"International work involves a lot of socializing with very interesting people from around the world."

Your friends may well be other expatriates. Since there will be fewer people to befriend, friendships will likely be broader than at home with less regard for age or work background. This may differ from your expectations.

"International work involves a lot of travel with time to explore new cultures."

Rarely do international jobs require lots of travel once you arrive at your posting. Even if your job does require travel, you usually have little time to explore during business travel.

"Living overseas is dangerous and involves substantial health risks."

While it's true that terrorism and anti-American or anti-Western sentiments have increased in some parts of the world, actual occurrences of violence against foreigners remain localized and relatively uncommon. Theft and automobile accidents are often greater risks.

"My employer will solve all my housing problems and guarantee my safety."

Your employer can solve some of your problems, but don't expect him or her to solve all of them. You have to make do with your own initiatives and sometimes just learn to live with your predicaments.

"The work I find frustrating at home will be more interesting overseas."

Whatever the view from the office window, work is work. The frustrations of an international working environment are usually even greater than those you find at home.

"I can escape my problems by moving overseas."

Are you having marital, emotional or drug problems? Attempting to start anew by heading for an overseas assignment usually does not work. For example, it is generally known that strong marriages become stronger overseas and weak marriages often fall apart. Personal problems tend to worsen when you have no familiar support systems to rely on. The stress of life in a new culture will put strains on even the best relationships and the hardiest of personalities.

"International development work is very rewarding and I will make a difference in the country I work in."

If you are going overseas full of zeal to impart your knowledge to improve the lives of the poor, you will be disappointed. The process of economic development is a slow one. It can take decades before you see changes in the lives of whole communities. Moreover, with the eyes of a foreigner, you may be hard pressed to recognize important changes in a culture that is not your own. The practice of giving assistance to developing countries is an imprecise science, and development projects can and do fail!

MYTHS ABOUT WORKING OVERSEAS

There are many misconceptions about how to find international work. The international field is a whole new ball game compared to the domestic job market. The misconceptions that abound are partly due to the mystique surrounding the international scene. The following may clear up some of these.

"International jobs pay extremely well and I will save much of my salary."

Few people go overseas to become rich. Even if the salary is higher than at home (and often it isn't), the hidden costs of moving, travelling, living overseas and re-entry all add up. You'll spend more on travel during holiday periods. You'll probably not recoup the full cost of furnishings, cars, etc., when it comes time to leave your overseas posting. And there are many hidden costs involved in setting up a household when you return home. Be prepared to come back richer in experience but not necessarily better off financially.

"I need international work experience to find an overseas job."

Not necessarily, but it certainly helps. With or without experience, however, what you really need is an international IQ (a concept discussed throughout this book). Luck is, of course, a factor. Persistence is vital.

"There are few international jobs. Only the most qualified professionals get jobs."

An estimated 50,000 to 100,000 Canadians are working overseas. Most international recruiters will tell you how difficult it is to find qualified individuals who are willing to give up their personal lives to travel abroad. International recruiters are always looking for people who have good technical skills as well as an international IQ. With this combination, the opportunities abound, not just for university-educated people, but for tradespeople as well.

"All I need to do is show employers that I am willing to sacrifice myself to help the poor of the world."

Sorry, international work is no longer a place for do-gooders, as it may have been in the 1960s. If you want to contribute to improving the world, develop a skill and build your international IQ.

"I need to study something 'international' to find international work."

International studies in no way guarantees a start in an international career. You have to develop yourself and experience a lot more before an employer will consider you. International studies are invaluable, however, when they are used to complement an already existing base of skills and experience.

"It is easier to find an international job while living or travelling overseas."

Not usually. You probably won't find a salaried position that actually pays a good wage in this way. Remember that most countries place severe restrictions on employment of non-nationals, and local pay scales tend to be far lower than what you would be paid if you signed an international contract. You may be able to find work while travelling if you are looking for grassroots volunteer experience and are willing to ignore local employment laws. An innovative person with a good skill base can often find volunteer overseas employment on the spot.

"I need connections to break into the international job market."

No, what you need is a networking and job search plan. Then, you must stick to it tenaciously and work at finding an international job. Of course, connections help!

"Large multinational corporations are good places to find overseas work."

Rarely, and if a job is available, corporations usually transfer recruits from within their firm.

"The job search process is the same for a domestic job as it is for an overseas job."

Not at all. You have to be able to uncover jobs and describe your skills in terms of international work. Read this book to see how each step of the process is different.

A LAST WORD

You should look at both the positive and the negative aspects of living overseas. Two things are of paramount importance in your self-assessment before you begin to look for overseas employment. First, you should have a solid grasp of who you are. Second, give a lot of consideration to your ability to adapt. Think carefully about living abroad.

CHAPTER 3
Living
Overseas

People choose to live overseas for a variety of reasons. Some go to improve the quality of their lives while others go to leave the rat race behind. Whatever the reason, you've just accepted an overseas posting: your contract is signed, your passport updated and you've done some research on your host country. In short, you're counting the days till you leave your home here in North America—until you're face to face with the challenges of your new environment. But do you really know how you'll react to the unfamiliarity of another language, the different work ethics of your new colleagues, the frequent shortages of electricity, water and telephone service? You can only hazard a guess. Everyone reacts differently to new experiences.

This chapter outlines a few common scenarios and draws upon the cross-cultural experiences of others. If you have never lived overseas, this chapter will help you understand the intercultural awareness sought by international employers. It must be stressed however, that conditions vary from continent to continent, community to community. Remember—in taking an overseas posting, you are not only adjusting to a new country, but uprooting yourself from your own culture and identity.

For those of you who don't have the benefit of a formal briefing before departure, or are just reading this chapter to build up your international IQ, we strongly advise you to increase your knowledge by consulting the numerous resources suggested at the end of this chapter.

RESEARCHING YOUR HOST COUNTRY

Briefings

Briefings are invaluable to newcomers, and it's usually assumed that a country briefing will be provided by your new employer. However, these are sometimes crossed off an agenda because of time constraints. Staff veterans often overlook the importance of psychological preparation of new recruits.

A briefing can be drawn from in-house expertise or from alternative sources, and usually summarizes the socio-economic conditions of a country, its politics, history, living conditions, culture and customs.

For those Canadians whose overseas positions are partially or fully funded by the CANADIAN INTERNATIONAL DEVELOPMENT AGENCY (CIDA), you are eligible to attend a briefing session on your country of posting. For information, contact the CENTRE FOR INTERCULTURAL LEARNING (CIL), listed in the Resources section at the end of this chapter. You could also arrange a briefing through GRAYBRIDGE INTERNATIONAL CONSULTING, a private firm based in the Ottawa/Gatineau region that provides a wide range of cross-cultural and international training services. (For more information on Graybridge, see the Profiles section in Chapter 35, Private Sector Firms in Canada.) If you're going abroad as a family, attempt to have everyone attend the pre-departure briefing. As a single person, you may invite a family member or friend to help discover the country that will be your new home. A volunteer wrote: *"I took my mother and we both found it an educational experience. She began to view Zimbabwe as a civilized and more familiar place than a dot on the map."* Having the company of another person also helps lessen the feeling of being the odd one out in a room full of families and couples. Feel free to ask questions, no matter how silly they may seem. That's the purpose of a briefing.

Brief Yourself

During the period between when you are offered the position and your departure, consume as much information about your new country as possible. (For more information, see the Country Guides & Reports Resources in Chapter 27, Jobs by Regions of the World.) The Canadian government's Consular Affairs Web site has excellent up-to-date country information. (See the Foreign Affairs Canada Resources in Chapter 37, Canadian Government.) Public and university libraries are also useful resources for country research. Mail-order videos and on-line archives of radio programs will also lead you to shows about your new host country. Try also to preview aspects of your new country through restaurant dining, craft shops, museums, or the ethnic music section of a record store.

Meet a Host National

Make a few friends, or at least acquaintances, from the country where you'll be working. The foreign students' association and the registrar's office at a university or college is a good starting point. For example, the University of Manitoba's International Centre for Students has a Welcome Family program that provides an opportunity for new international students to stay with a local family for a few days after they arrive in Winnipeg. (To contact the international students office in your area, see the institutional profiles for the larger universities listed in Chapter 15, International Studies in Canada.) Many Canadian agencies will also arrange cross-cultural postings. For example, CANADIAN CROSSROADS INTERNATIONAL and CANADA WORLD YOUTH both have programs for hosting representatives from other countries for short-term visits to Canada. (For more information, see Chapter 11, Hosting Programs.) Ethnic communities are another source of information, as expatriates of the country you're going to can provide information you won't find in fact sheets and tourist guides. Look for community associations in your area, or try non-profit organizations that assist immigrants—newcomers to your home country.

Connect with Other Expatriates

The Internet is a powerful tool. With little effort, you should be able to directly e-mail fellow expatriates who are already living in your host country. Contact North American organizations working in your host country and ask to be put in touch with their employees overseas. Better yet, research and join the thousands of expatriate networking clubs already on-line. (See the Expatriate Networking Resources at the end of this chapter.) Fellow expatriates can provide a flood of information for the newcomer, from settling in to job search advice.

Keep in Touch

Involve your family and friends as much as possible. Remember, an adventure for you could be a sorrowful parting for them. No matter how hackneyed it sounds, remind them that they will see you again on home leaves and at the end of your contract. And encourage them to visit.

There are other ways to keep in touch while you're overseas. Postcards and letters, while slower than e-mail, make good souvenirs of your trip. Letters home can also serve as a travel journal. We know of one American abroad whose mother diligently saved and printed all her e-mails, and had them bound in a book as a gift upon her return. An Internet journal or "blog" (short for "Web log") is an easy way to let large numbers of friends and family stay up to date with what you're doing. A cheaper-model digital camera can be a great investment for helping family and friends to feel close to you. You can e-mail your pictures home, and there are also several Web sites that will allow you to post photos for free.

While you're getting settled in, also keep in mind that mail can be forwarded temporarily to a Canadian consulate or an American Express office in the capital of the country to which you are posted. Most countries now have excellent telephone linkages with North America, allowing you to call home. People abroad and family members at home should look into pre-paid phone cards. These can be purchased in increments of $5 to $20 in convenience stores and pharmacies. They are often the best deals for phoning between Canada and a specific country. Prices are competitive, so be sure to compare different cards; we've heard of rates as low as five cents a minute between Canada/US and Asia.

Lastly, you will want to be diligent in collecting addresses of the people you meet while travelling—other foreigners or host country nationals. Start an address book for each trip you make abroad. Collect the "permanent" mailing addresses of dear friends (for example, their parents' address). In your later years, and once you become a seasoned traveller, you will be very happy to sort through your old address books and re-kindle contact with long lost friends.

CULTURE SHOCK

You've probably heard the term "culture shock," but you might not think it will happen to you. In fact, everyone goes through a painful process of adapting to a new culture, and your reaction can range from mild irritation to extreme trauma. Canadian

Jim Shannon had a good dose of it when he arrived in Zimbabwe. The following is an excerpt from an article by him in the *Ottawa Citizen*:

"I was teaching and living in a rural school in Zimbabwe and it was one of the most interesting and stimulating times of my life. Learning to live without a car, telephone, television or movies was a broadening experience. Some would call it cultural deprivation. I call it the opportunity to savour the delights of a new culture and, at the same time, stand back and take a good look at 'things Canadian.'

"To say that I came to prefer the lifestyle of an expatriate teacher in the African bush would be, perhaps, simplistic. After all, being without power for 24 hours after you've done your weekly grocery shopping trip—by the slowest bus imaginable to the nearest town 60 kilometres away—is no joke. And having to negotiate several days in advance to hitch a ride to Harare on the back of a school lorry can be frustrating...

"There's also the isolation. And the lack of privacy. And the intense heat. And the hopelessly overcrowded and under-equipped classrooms... And the underlying racial tension.

"I cannot say I adapted right away. But I'm glad I adjusted to the culture shock I experienced when I got off the plane one stiflingly hot night, hungry, tired and angry because the Kenyan airline on which I was travelling was 10 hours late. The long, bumpy ride in the back of a truck through the pitch-black night to the school in the bush did not help...

"Yet I found life there to be more 'hands on,' more real and simple than what I had left behind in Canada. I came to appreciate the warmth of the local people, to learn to 'make do.' Evenings also became social events... talking well into the night..."

Look at culture shock as a rite of passage. When you enter a new culture, the cues and clues you normally rely on are gone. It's like having the rug pulled out from under you! In India, you'll have to get used to the fact that nodding your head doesn't necessarily mean "yes." In Muslim countries, you must never pass anything to anyone with your left hand. As a woman, you can't drive or travel alone in some Middle Eastern countries. You may walk into a shop and not recognize a single product on the shelves, let alone the lettering on the packages. The lack of privacy will also take getting used to. You'll be crushed and pushed in markets and buses, your children will resent having their hair stroked for the umpteenth time, and you may be asked highly personal questions. All in all, you may become so depressed you'll want to return home!

Culture Shock or Culture Fatigue—What Is It?

Overseas employees must learn to deal with the stress brought on by changes in:

- home
- friends
- job
- cultural environment
- food, climate, security, transportation, etc., etc., etc.

"Culture shock" is a term used to describe the stress brought on by all these changes. It can involve any of the following areas of life: manners, customs, beliefs, ceremonies and rituals, social institutions, myths and legends, values, morals, ideals, accepted ways of behaviour, ideas and thought patterns, laws, language, and arts and artifacts. The differences threaten your own belief systems and habits. The term "culture shock" has a negative connotation for some, and for this reason experts believe "culture fatigue" is a more apt term to describe a person's response to the process of cultural adjustment. Others refer to the reaction to sudden immersion in a radically different environment as "cultural disorientation" or "change shock." What you're really doing is taking apart your own frame of reference in order to understand another culture. Because your own frame of reference has become inappropriate, naturally you feel confused, disoriented, frustrated and anxious. And unlike other health disorders, you can't get an inoculation for this one!

Like every expatriate worker, we're sure you'll devise imaginative ways to cope. Culture shock is actually a positive, necessary part of the cultural adjustment process.

STAGES OF CULTURE FATIGUE

Sociologists, anthropologists and psychologists have divided the culture shock or fatigue phenomenon into stages. They say the intensity of culture fatigue varies; it is cumulative and sometimes difficult to understand.

Experts speak of four stages: the honeymoon stage, anxiety stage, rejection or regression stage, and the adjustment stage.

The Honeymoon Stage

You're finally overseas after much preparation and anticipation. You just can't wait to see, feel, taste, experience *everything!* People seem friendly (not pushy), laid back (not inefficient), they enjoy the simple things. This is the world through the honeymooners' eyes. You have great expectations and a positive outlook. This period may last from a week or two to a month, but inevitably the letdown comes.

The Anxiety Stage

In this stage, the need to build a new social structure to replace the one you've left behind takes precedence. You react to small difficulties as if they were major catastrophes. You may seek out compatriots to reinforce your "we–they" attitude.

At this crisis stage, you may suffer varying degrees of some of the following symptoms:

- homesickness
- boredom
- withdrawal (for instance, spending excessive amounts of time reading; only seeing other Westerners; avoiding contact with host nationals)
- need for excessive amounts of sleep
- loss of appetite
- compulsive eating
- compulsive drinking
- irritability
- exaggerated cleanliness

- marital stress
- family tension and conflict
- chauvinistic or patronizing behaviour
- stereotyping of host nationals
- hostility towards host nationals
- loss of ability to work effectively
- uncontrollable weeping
- physical ailments

The Rejection or Regression Stage

Your anxiety is compounded by constantly having to face problems you cannot define. Things don't work—your shipment of belongings hasn't arrived. Local help has proven unable to follow instructions. Things are constantly breaking down and repairs are shoddy. The streets don't coincide with the maps. You are still having language difficulties (why can't they speak English properly?). The children miss cable television. Nothing seems right. Tension and anxiety build up. Your new friends from the first few weeks have disappeared, carrying on with their lives. Eventually you reject what you had so enthusiastically embraced in those first few weeks, and long for the way things are done at home.

Some people manifest antisocial behaviour, such as rudeness or excessive drinking. Others seek a "safe haven"—an international club for example. Some people never get beyond the regression stage, even if they live overseas for years. Others leave during this stage. There is no shame in going home with the satisfaction that you gave it your best.

The Adjustment Stage

Gradually, you recover. You begin to feel less isolated in your surroundings. Gone is the feeling of hopelessness. You're able to greet someone in the local language, hail a taxi, haggle with the merchants. Before they were cheating you, now they're merely trying to earn a living.

You experience a measure of biculturalism, of acceptance of the differences between two societies. No one expects you to totally assimilate or to approve of harmful practices such as bribery or the exploitation of women. Instead, you find a middle ground you're comfortable with.

How Long Does Culture Fatigue Last?

It has been observed that there are actually two low points, which stretch out according to the length of your assignment. This also depends on your resilience. But once your first low is over, remember that you'll have another, and it may be more severe. Keep in mind, however, that the ultimate usually happens—you reach glorious stage four, and adjust!

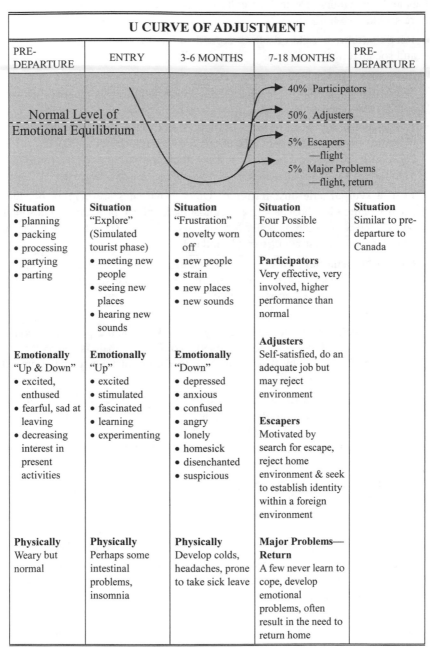

U CURVE OF ADJUSTMENT				
PRE-DEPARTURE	ENTRY	3-6 MONTHS	7-18 MONTHS	PRE-DEPARTURE
Situation • planning • packing • processing • partying • parting	**Situation** "Explore" (Simulated tourist phase) • meeting new people • seeing new places • hearing new sounds	**Situation** "Frustration" • novelty worn off • new people • strain • new places • new sounds	**Situation** Four Possible Outcomes: **Participators** Very effective, very involved, higher performance than normal **Adjusters**	**Situation** Similar to pre-departure to Canada
Emotionally "Up & Down" • excited, enthused • fearful, sad at leaving • decreasing interest in present activities	**Emotionally** "Up" • excited • stimulated • fascinated • learning • experimenting	**Emotionally** "Down" • depressed • anxious • confused • angry • lonely • homesick • disenchanted • suspicious	Self-satisfied, do an adequate job but may reject environment **Escapers** Motivated by search for escape, reject home environment & seek to establish identity within a foreign environment	
Physically Weary but normal	**Physically** Perhaps some intestinal problems, insomnia	**Physically** Develop colds, headaches, prone to take sick leave	**Major Problems—Return** A few never learn to cope, develop emotional problems, often result in the need to return home	

Originally conceived by Clyde Sargeant, with subsequent revision by Daniel Kealey.

How to Deal with Culture Fatigue

Experts say half the battle with culture fatigue is knowing what's happening to you. When you find yourself being judgmental, simply try to accept the differences in values and behaviours in your host culture. Here are a few pointers for coping with culture shock:

- **Participation:** Instead of sitting around reflecting on your sorry state, go out and socialize with the locals. Try to learn all about your new country.

- **Tolerance:** Undoubtedly, many things will appear strange to you in the beginning. So stop over-examining the local people's behaviour and habits. You'll drive yourself bonkers.

- **Language:** It always helps to understand, if not speak, the language. Who cares if your grammar and pronunciation are muddled? Your efforts will be appreciated by the local people and you'll feel less like an outsider. (See Chapter 5, Learning a Foreign Language.)

- **Find a sympathetic host national:** Other expatriates are helpful, but they're usually in the same boat as you are. A host national can provide a good sounding board. And what could be better for your overall experience than having a friend who knows your new country inside and out?

- **Gather information:** Never lose your curiosity. It will give you insight into why people behave as they do. An interest in history, geography, politics, religion and cultural norms will help you appreciate and adjust to your new environment.

- **Take a break:** Treat yourself to a day off, bake an apple pie, take a long hot bath. Do something just for yourself, something that is typically North American. Find a hobby that allows you to escape or take regular time off to indulge in your own culture.

- **Maintain contact with family and friends back home:** Writing home about your experiences and problems can help you deal with them. Be cautious, however, about alarming your relatives about situations they cannot understand or act on. Some people have learned to wrestle with culture shock by keeping a diary of their thoughts and feelings.

- **Be imaginative in finding solutions:** One returning overseas employee recalls West African village life:

    "When we moved to Ghana, we discovered that the front door was only closed at night before going to bed. To do otherwise was inhospitable to visitors and the whole community. We finally got around this problem by advising our neighbours that we occasionally had to shut our door to pray. This turned out to be an acceptable excuse when we needed some down time."

Some of the above research on culture shock was excerpted with permission from the excellent book by Robert L. Kohls, *Survival Kit for Overseas Living.* (For a detailed annotation, see the Cross-Cultural Skills Resources in Chapter 1, The Effective Overseas Employee.)

Useful Skills for Daily Life Overseas

Some people adapt to new cultures better than others. Cross-cultural experts agree that certain skills play a key role in cultural integration. Besides the skills for coping with culture shock—tolerance, open-mindedness, empathy, flexibility, adaptability, curiosity and self-reliance—there are some other useful skills that will help you survive daily life overseas:

- **Sense of humour:** The ability to laugh, particularly at yourself, is your best weapon against despair.

- **Low goal- or task-orientation:** North Americans abroad, or their superiors back home, often set tasks that are unrealistic. An unattainable goal can contribute to failure and frustration. From studies of Americans living overseas, results show that those who are less goal-oriented or task-driven are more likely to be relaxed and effective in their work, and derive more enjoyment from their experiences. (For more information, see Kellee Ngan's article, "Adjusting to a Slower Pace of Work" in Appendix 7a on the CD-ROM.)

- **Coping with failure:** If failure is unfamiliar to you, be aware that it is almost certain you will fail at something overseas. Your dinner party may be a disaster because the food in your refrigerator has gone bad due to a power outage. Your dinner guests may have to dine on tinned sardines by candlelight. Try to look on the bright side and adapt to the fact that this will likely happen again.

SPECIAL CONCERNS FOR COUPLES AND FAMILIES

Your family should be involved in your decision to move overseas. If it isn't a joint decision, you can expect trouble! Life overseas can add stress to family life and contribute to divorce and the breakdown of the family unit. On the other hand, members of a family can become more reliant on each other for companionship and strength.

Male Employee and Spouse

The dissatisfaction of a non-working spouse is cited as the main reason for failure and early returns from overseas assignments. Think about it! The working husband has the structure of a job and the camaraderie of colleagues to rely on. Children have the routine of school. Chances are the female, non-working spouse has given up her career, friends, family and social activities for the stay-at-home life overseas. Her interactions may be largely confined to dealing with domestic help or locals catering to other household needs. She may have to face her frustrations alone while her working husband sits in his office commiserating with colleagues in English.

From past experiences, here are some of the difficulties faced by non-working wives:

- **Lack of preparation:** Many wives arrive not knowing what to expect. Reactions may vary from surprise and excitement to bewilderment and anxiety.

- **Culture fatigue:** Levels of frustration can be quite high in certain conditions, such as dealing with domestic help who do not speak English, an undependable power and water supply, a telephone that never works, and trying to understand the local goods and services available.

- **Language problems:** The employed partner may work in English and have little need for competency in the local language, but the stay-at-home spouse will certainly need language lessons. Unfortunately, many organizations offer language training only to employees, with spouses left to their own devices.

- **Loneliness:** It's common to feel loneliness and depression after you've left family and friends behind. Someone once said, "When you've lived abroad and suffered deep loneliness, you become your own best friend." Sometimes loneliness is compounded by the isolation of being the stay-at-home spouse.

- **Loss of identity:** One of the hardest things about moving abroad as the dependent wife of a working husband is the loss of identity and individuality. You are viewed merely as a wife, not as someone with her own interests and talents.

- **Boredom:** Although it may sound like bliss to have hired help doing much of the housework and childcare, having too much time on your hands can be a real problem, particularly after a hectic North American life juggling job, housework and family. Sometimes the boredom is compounded by local restrictions that prevent foreign dependants from competing with locals in the job market.

- **The absentee husband—lack of support:** The man may work long hours, thereby increasing the woman's sense of isolation. A vicious circle can develop, in which the working spouse feels guilty over his non-working partner's emotional state, and spends even less time at home.

Female Employee and Spouse

This kind of couple is no longer a rarity in international employment situations. The problem for non-working male spouses is that they cannot resolve their loneliness by joining a women's social group or informal network. Furthermore, other working male acquaintances will be inaccessible during the day. As a stay-at-home male spouse, you may feel resentment and may even object to your wife's elevated professional status. Domestic responsibilities such as grocery shopping and childcare can lead to unfavourable reactions and misunderstanding on the part of local men and women, and possibly even your own compatriots. On the other hand, you may find yourself inundated with requests to repair things, or act as a chauffeur or gofer.

A sampling of data from Zimbabwe shows a fairly high number of male spouses accompanying wives employed by the DEPARTMENT OF FOREIGN AFFAIRS AND INTERNATIONAL TRADE. Six men, who had left positions ranging from senior administrative and professional posts to small business owners, had to adjust to the role of male stay-at-homes. They reported that it took three to six months to adjust to their new roles. Some had high expectations of doing work similar to what they had left behind, but were thwarted by local employment regulations. Others found moderate satisfaction in doing odd jobs. Remarked one male spouse, *"I now realize I was crazy to think I could land here and pick up from where I'd left off back home."* They all found dealing with household staff and repair people to be frustrating.

There are many strategies you can employ to ensure that your marriage makes a smooth transition overseas. Experts assert that planning and lots of communication are the way to avoid problems. (For more information, see Robin Pascoe's article, "Moving Your Marriage" in Appendix 3b on the CD-ROM. Also see *A Moveable Marriage: Relocate Your Relationship without Breaking It* and other excellent books by Robin Pascoe in the Children and Families Overseas Resources at the end of this chapter.)

The Single Person Overseas

Singles face many of the same problems as married couples. The loneliness, however, can be more painful. You may already feel that the world is biased in favour of couples and families. In traditional societies, where marriage and the number of children you have determine social status, you may be made to feel incomplete if you are a childless woman "of a certain age," meaning over 21! It is a good idea to bring photos of your parents, siblings, and cousins just to prove that you "belong" to a family. Expect your photos to be pored over for family resemblance. A West African triumphantly remarked to one Canadian about a photograph of a family member, "you look like two tomatoes!," his variation of the "peas in the pod" expression.

Sentimental belongings help maintain your sense of identity and continuity. You should bring along reading and writing material, sports equipment or a musical instrument to help you pass the time and remind you of home.

Your social life will be what you make it. Flexibility and working at socializing are important. As a single you will be more free to mix and travel.

Lesbians, Gays and Bisexuals

Many expatriate gays thrive in the overseas environment, creating their own social support network to make it easier to adapt. Homosexuals can almost always find a distinct gay subculture overseas. Initially, however, you may have no support structure for being open with friends, and meeting others in the lesbian, gay and bisexual (LGB) community. It's no surprise that for the women and men who have gone through the process of coming out, working overseas can seem like a return to the closet. You will have to gauge whether to come out to your fellow workers.

In many countries, homosexuals are invisible in mainstream society. You may not be able to locate bars, community centres or gay and lesbian associations at your destination, particularly if you are in a rural area. But it is fair to say that in almost every city in the world there is a specific place to meet other gays and lesbians. As a foreigner, you may be relatively free of social customs that inhibit local gays. But exercise caution, because in most countries the law is not on your side. Canada is one of only a handful of countries to prohibit discrimination on the basis of sexual orientation, whereas open and often violent discrimination is still the norm globally. Similarly, while same-sex marriages and partnerships are increasingly recognized at home, this is often not the case around the world, and you will likely find it difficult to access many of the benefits afforded to heterosexual partners.

You can prepare yourself for the prevalent social attitudes wherever you're going. Before departure, talk to returnees from your host country, dig through international gay guides, make contact with international LGB organizations. Many NGOs actively support lesbian, gay and bisexual rights, as well as human rights in general.

Government departments such as CIDA, Foreign Affairs Canada (FAC), and Citizenship and Immigration Canada (CIC) have adopted practices that accommodate the family life of lesbian and gay staff working and travelling overseas. Being open about your sexual orientation is no longer deemed a national security risk; nor is it an impediment to promotion. While officially accepted by many international employers, you may still be required to have a "private" lifestyle because of local prejudices when living overseas.

Women Overseas

A separate chapter discusses the issues facing women working overseas (see Chapter 6, Women Living & Working Overseas). If you are the spouse of a working partner overseas, you may want to consider freelancing while abroad (see Chapter 34, Spousal Employment & Freelancing Abroad).

Children Abroad

As a parent, it is hard to predict how your child will react to living in a strange country with different customs and language. Some children have a delayed reaction to separation from family and friends, while others are too young to appreciate the geographic move or to articulate their feelings. Parents have found that looking at photographs and writing letters to friends and family members left behind can be therapeutic for their children.

When contemplating moving overseas, the single most important issue facing families with children between the ages of 6 and 16 is education. Local school systems abroad are often so different from your home country education system that re-integration can be very difficult. The most common solution for expatriate families living abroad is to enrol students into the worldwide English-language network of international schools. This system uses the Canadian and US model of education, and allows children to move from country to country (including back to Canada/US) without leaving the regular grade system. The French government also promotes a similar worldwide system. (For more information, see the Educating Your Children Resources at the end of this chapter.)

If no adequate schooling exists, some North American families place their children in boarding schools, either in Canada/US or in capital cities abroad. But this is less common for North Americans than, say, British families. In some cases, if the housebound spouse feels able, he or she may tutor the children using widely available correspondence course material. If your overseas employer has more than eight school-age children in a remote area, it may become feasible to hire a full-time North American teacher.

As mentioned previously, a spouse's or family's happiness will affect the success of the overseas employee in his or her assignment. So it follows that children require special consideration. They should be part of the whole decision-making process. School-aged children must participate in discussions about the kind of school they will attend or the form their education will take. Young children can be assigned such tasks as choosing toys and mementoes to pack, and selecting clothes. Older children and teenagers should take part in selecting information from libraries and other sources, and arranging travel routes or holiday destinations.

As stated, it is difficult to predict a child's reaction to moving. Factors such as personality, stage of development, and previous experiences with moving will have an impact. But research has shown that children of anxious parents have a harder time adjusting; therefore, try to downplay your own anxiety. There are many positive aspects to family life abroad. Apart from a tighter emotional bond, children learn tolerance and respect for other cultures.

Mindful of the fact that children must return to North American living, experts suggest children maintain their share of household duties. So don't assign all chores to the domestic help, should you have that option.

Too Much Free Time

Chances are there will be many occasions when you have too much free time on your hands. How do you and your family pass the time in a country without cable television or video rental outlets? Here are some tips that other expatriates have found useful.

- **Shape up:** Develop an exercise routine alone or with others.
- **Exercise the mind or learn a new skill:** Pursue your interests through a local college, correspondence or find a tutor. The US INFORMATION SERVICE and the BRITISH COUNCIL provide good English library services in most foreign cites.
- **Quality family time:** Finally, you can spend more time with your family.
- **Volunteer:** Your diplomatic office, local NGOs, or other expatriates may provide a list of ideas of useful volunteer work you can do.
- **Travel:** Tour your host and neighbouring countries to learn about their history, culture and language. There's nothing like the thrill of discovering new terrain.

THE WESTERNER OVERSEAS

The Expatriate Ghetto

There is a hazard of becoming too attached to the expatriate ghetto in your overseas posting. It has been said that sharing complaints is a way of forming a community, and nowhere is this more true than when expatriates get together. They can quickly become a community of complainers. Somehow, being together triggers the impulse to criticize "these people," or "this place" and encourages the us-against-them response. If you find yourself falling into this pattern, perhaps you should review why you are really there.

To rectify this problem, or avoid it completely, make a conscious decision to choose friends who are inspired by the challenges and intrigue of the local culture. Avoid expatriates who are always complaining. The choice is yours.

The Person in the Mirror

You may discover aspects of yourself that aren't admirable. One researcher noted that Americans, on the whole, are offended by the practice of bribery and the habit of spitting in some countries. On the other hand, certain aspects of our behaviour, such as a man and a women holding hands in public, direct eye contact, our casual attire and posture, and our straightforward way of "getting down to business" can be offensive to foreigners. As a North American abroad, think of yourself as an ambassador for your country. Try to be accepting and open-minded. Think twice before indulging in North American habits that could be distasteful to others. There's nothing worse than leaving a lasting negative impression.

Lifestyle and Work

It's difficult to separate your work from your lifestyle overseas. In much of North America, we find it convenient to separate our professional life from our personal life. We often look upon international travel as an incentive, reward or vacation in relation to our jobs. International jobs, however, generate lifestyles in which one's job and personal life merge into a unique form of worklife. A teacher posted at a rural boarding school in Kenya, for example, can hardly leave his or her job behind in the evening or on the weekend; a doctor working in a clinic in Thailand will always be identified as "the doctor," even while out for an evening stroll. Let's face it, in many overseas environments, you are indeed a "visible minority." You'll be identified in terms of your work to a much greater extent than in North America—and your spouse and children will be similarly identified. This fact has both positive and negative ramifications. It's a matter of how you adjust to your new environment.

As an international worker, you will likely have more responsibility than you would have in a similar job back home. This can be a real challenge, offering you the chance to use your creativity along with your interpersonal skills. There will probably be fewer rules and regulations—less red tape to deal with.

On the other hand, you may encounter barriers to getting things done that you never dreamed of. Many developing countries have incredibly inefficient, bureaucratic systems rife with corruption. Different customs, currency fluctuations, broken promises—all will tax even the most easy-going overseas worker.

Still, most international workers are motivated by a certain degree of restlessness, the desire for something different, a need to change a stale work environment, a commitment to a cause or an idea. They are career risk-takers, concerned more with new challenges than with how much money they will make or how many conventional creature comforts they can acquire. They are usually seeking a particular lifestyle rather than a particular job or career. However, a careful, professional self-assessment will enhance your chances of having a satisfying overseas experience, and will serve you well in developing long-term career strategies. (For an insider view of how work life and family life mesh together, see Steven James's article, "Letter from an Expat Family" in Appendix 3a on the CD-ROM.)

SECURITY AND POLITICAL CONCERNS

The recent rise in terrorism since 9/11 has brought new concerns about safety and security for those working overseas. The best general advice for dealing with these issues is to stay aware: keep abreast of the news in your host country and surrounding area, and regularly check in with your consular office or embassy to find out about travel warnings or changes to procedures in the event of political unrest or disaster.

The Consular Affairs Bureau of FOREIGN AFFAIRS CANADA (FAC) produces travel reports for individual regions and countries; these can be found on the Internet or accessed by telephone. They also publish a weekly travel bulletin highlighting current "hot spots" and issues. You can subscribe to the bulletin by e-mail. The American government provides similar information for its citizens. (Contact information for both Canadian and American security reports are listed in the Country Guides & Reports Resources in Chapter 27, Jobs by Region of the World.)

If you plan to be away for more than three months, it is essential that you register with your home embassy upon arrival in your host country. This process can be completed on-line and it takes only a few minutes.

If you will be working in a high-risk area, you should discuss evacuation procedures with your prospective employer. They should agree to cover the costs of emergency evacuation. In some cases, you may even be able to get provisions in your contract for severance pay should your work term be cut short due to political unrest or natural disaster. It's important to be prepared, as your home country government is

not necessarily obligated to cover the costs of evacuation, and emergency accommodation or last-minute travel arrangements can be expensive.

Travel Arrangements

Increased security measures have changed international travel. Wait times for
crossing borders have increased, as has the time needed to check in for airline flights.
Allow extra time for crossing borders, and when flying, always contact your carrier
to find out how early you need to arrive and adjust your schedule accordingly. Also
check to find out what items are prohibited in carry-on and checked luggage, as these
can vary among airlines.

Short trips to surrounding areas can be one of the most satisfying parts of
working overseas. When you travel, someone in your host country should know
where you are and when you intend to be back. This person should also have contact
information for friends or family in your home country. In general, it's a good idea
for your friends or family at home to have an emergency contact in your host country
in case they are unable to get a hold of you.

CRIME AND PERSONAL SAFETY

Before leaving home, you should explore the issue of crime in your new country so
you'll be prepared and not unduly alarmed. There are three categories of crime that
affect foreigners:

- household intruders
- street incidents
- ongoing political violence

The topic of crime should be covered in your briefing session; if it isn't, then
you should raise it. Foreigners are vulnerable to crime because foreign nationality is
often equated with wealth. But situations vary from country to country. Apart from
registering at your nearest diplomatic mission, here are some other precautions you
can take.

Household Intruders

Normal precautions should be taken, as well as additional ones relevant to the
country you are in. This again varies from urban to rural locations. In developing
countries, many expat homes are surrounded by high walls and have ornate
protective grilling on doors and windows. Homeowners may also employ a guard or
have watchdogs. Although regulations regarding weapon ownership may be lenient, it
is unwise to possess a gun. Instead, favour burglar bars, alarms, or other electronic
devices for your home and vehicle. Don't forget to insure your belongings when you
arrive. You must understand that you are now a potential target for theft. Because of
the lack of foreign currency for importing Western goods such as televisions, CDs,
and even clothing and food, your possessions are desirable commodities. However,
don't let paranoia cripple you to the point that you view every local face as a
potential robber. As in North America, the criminal element is only a small sector of
society. After taking the necessary precautions, it is futile to expend further energy on
the situation.

Street Crime

This form of crime is on the increase worldwide. Advice here is simple—don't wander alone in areas that are unfamiliar to you. Don't invite temptation by displaying excessive jewelry, cameras or large handbags. If driving alone, ensure that all passenger doors are locked, including the trunk. In the event that you are robbed on the street, never tackle the robber single-handedly or put up strenuous resistance. He or she may be armed. You're better off to shout "thief" and try to attract a crowd to intercept on your behalf.

It goes without saying that you should never ship irreplaceable or costly items. Theft, minor and major, is commonplace in poor countries.

I can recall the case of one US missionary who was repeatedly robbed by his house staff in Zaire. When confronted with their crime, they asserted that white people were like hens, and their possessions were like a hen's eggs: if you took them away, they simply replaced them! However, the thefts stopped after the priest explained the fallacy of their thinking and threatened to use part of their workers' salaries to replace missing items.

Political Violence

Political violence is an issue for many, though it is difficult to predict where or how it will strike you. If you believe you could become a target, your concern should be raised with in-country diplomats. Other precautions you could adopt should the situation arise are as follows:

- Vary your route and schedule to and from work.
- Travel with car windows closed; use air conditioning if necessary.
- Avoid demonstrations and street scenes, and observe such rules as curfews. Keep abreast of news and possible evacuations.
- If there are demonstrations, accompany your children to school or stay home.

In countries where access to foreign currency or luxury goods is restricted, you may find yourself befriended by opportunists or wheeler-dealers pursuing imported items. Let common sense prevail. Helping someone is fine, but where foreign currency is restricted, never become involved in any money dealings! Often there are stiff penalties for both supplier and receiver.

Most of you will enjoy trouble-free assignments as far as these sorts of problems are concerned, but, hackneyed as it may sound, "forewarned is forearmed!"

PERSONAL MATTERS

Driving in Your New Country

Don't forget to pick up an international driver's licence from the CANADIAN AUTOMOBILE ASSOCIATION (CAA) before leaving Canada or the AMERICAN AUTOMOBILE ASSOCIATION (AAA) before leaving the US. At some point your host country may require that you obtain a local license. Make such inquiries at the time of your arrival. Be sure to learn the local rules of the road. Apart from possibly having to adjust to driving on the other side of the road, you will have to decipher and memorize foreign road signs to determine whether an ox or your car has the right of way, etc. As a pedestrian, observe street rules and keep well away from traffic by walking on sidewalks or as far to the side of the road as possible, particularly in rural areas. Don't assume drivers will go out of their way to avoid you! Cyclists should take similar precautions and bring such protective gear as helmets, bike pumps, lights, reflectors, and repair kits.

Car Accidents

When travelling to developing countries, you should be more concerned about traffic accidents. Traffic accidents are a major cause of death for travellers in developing countries. This is due to faulty vehicles, bad driving habits, and poor roads. Drunken driving is another hazard, as regulations are often less stringent than in North America. Check out insurance practices and liability laws before you decide to drive. In many countries, responsibility for accidents is determined differently than in Canada or the US, and a fender-bender could leave you in debt.

Health Concerns

Always carry adequate medical insurance. In most cases your provincial health plan will not totally cover your medical expenses while overseas (this is usually dependent on the number of consecutive days you are away, the country you are in and the reason why you are overseas). When dealing with an insurance company, find out the specifics: whether or not you have to pay medical fees upfront, how long it takes to receive health claims, whether or not pre-existing conditions are covered, the type of drug coverage, emergency coverage and so on. Read all the print on your insurance policy, especially the fine print where hidden conditions might cost you later. Costs for treatment can be astronomical, even in developing countries. We know of one case where the cost of air evacuation from an African country to Belgium was $174,000! When faced with a life-threatening emergency, you don't want the added worry of such expenses.

Several months before departure, contact your local travel medical centre for specific information about your country of destination. (In Canada, see for example HEALTH CANADA's excellent Web site *Travel Medicine Program,* listed in the Health Overseas Resources at the end of this chapter.) Vaccinations and other precautions should definitely be taken against tropical diseases. A visit to your local travel health clinic can usually provide you with the necessary precautions.

A critical factor in many illnesses is stress, which lowers your body's resistance. Treat every infection and illness seriously. Don't let an illness run too long in the hopes that it will go away. Often times when you are ill you aren't thinking rationally. You therefore need to have a buddy where you work or live who knows your blood type, your wishes in the event of an accident and emergency contacts back home just in case. Also contact your provincial healthcare provider about the regulations regarding your healthcare coverage once you return home. Ask how long the waiting period is before your health insurance plan is active again; waiting periods vary depending on which province you live in and how long you are away. Remember that many illnesses picked up from living abroad may linger in your body and cause difficulty months later back home in North America.

The issue of HIV/AIDS cannot be ignored, particularly in developing countries, where medical standards are often inadequate or non-existent. Forget about "high-risk groups"—everyone is at risk. You may want to adopt the defensive measure of packing an HIV/AIDS kit, which includes sterile needles and syringes to be used in the event that you require medical treatment while abroad.

Finances, Currency Exchange, Budgeting

Try to settle your financial matters before leaving your home in Canada or the US. Appoint a Power of Attorney to look after any financial matters arising during your absence. Although you may end up in a cash-only society, you should have at least one credit card with you, kept in an imaginative and safe place.

To avoid paying Canadian taxes, Canadians can look into the non-resident status with REVENUE CANADA. The non-resident status is not for everyone, and there are many restrictions and ramifications. (For more information on the Canadian non-resident status, see the article by Garry Duncan and Elizabeth Peck, "Canadian Income Taxes & Non-Resident Status" in Appendix 3c on the CD-ROM.)

Where the black market is active, the host government normally demands that you keep an accurate record of all financial transactions during your stay. As stated earlier, avoid all dealing!

In many developing countries, your household expenses will probably be far lower than in North America. However, you may incur other expenses, such as customs clearing fees, money for your staff's unexpected needs, etc. The cost of fuel is also extremely high in some countries. You should keep an emergency fund handy in case of hospitalization or evacuation.

Domestics

A domestic worker is a perk for many North Americans. Apart from providing employment to the local labour market, it may seem like a perfect step up. But having someone in your home seven or eight hours a day, or living on your property, can be a loss of privacy which takes getting used to. Many expatriates experience frustration in the training and monitoring of household help.

Check with local sources to determine the wage scales, work hours, expected duties, bonuses, holidays, etc. Some countries have unions for domestic workers and may provide information and references, and monitor complaints for both parties.

Food

Be both experimental and cautious. Keep in mind that your digestive system isn't accustomed to the new foods. And don't forget to pack your favourite foodstuffs, no matter how mundane. You've no idea how good macaroni and cheese can taste when you have a craving for "North American" food or you're simply feeling homesick.

A LAST WORD

Not all of us are cut out for overseas living. If you find you're unable to cope with the situation and have to come home, look upon it as a learning experience, not a failure. After all, there are many different ways to make a contribution to society.

But chances are you'll thrive in your new environment. An exciting experience awaits you!

APPENDIX ON THE CD-ROM
3a. "Letter From an Expat Family," by Steven James
3b. "Moving Your Marriage," by Robin Pascoe
3c. "Canadian Income Taxes & Non-Resident Status," by Garry Duncan &
   Elizabeth Peck

RESOURCES
This chapter contains the following Resources sections: Health Overseas; Children &
Families Overseas; Educating Your Children; Relocating Abroad; and Expatriate
Networking Sites.

HEALTH OVERSEAS
Life overseas involves potentially being exposed to health risks not normally
encountered in North America. Fortunately, most of the health issues you will run
into living abroad can be avoided if you arm yourself with information on health
risks, including prevention and treatment. Having one or two of these books is a must
for long-term travel or when moving to a developing country. Don't forget to contact
your local travel health clinic several months prior to your departure and keep in
mind that health risks vary greatly from country to country. If you're interested in
working in international health, see the Resources section for health careers in
Chapter 33, Health Careers Abroad.

Canadian Society for International Health (CSIH) ⚕
Canadian Society for International Health, 1 Nicholas Street, Suite 1105, Ottawa, ON K1N 7B7,
Canada, www.csih.org, 613-241-5785, fax 613-241-3845, csih@fox.nstn.ca; Fr ◆ This is a great
Web site with numerous resources relating to overseas health careers and travellers' health. The
CSIH is a network that extends across Canada and around the world, linking individuals and
organizations from all health sectors. The CSIH maintains the International Health Human
Resources Registry, which is open to health and health-related professionals experienced in
working in developing countries or with expertise that is applicable internationally. Add your name
to the roster through the CSIH Web site and check out the overseas health job board. Or if you want
to do an internship in international health, you can choose from Ethiopia, Malawi, Mali, Paraguay
and Thailand, to name a few. New site features include a direct link to the Student University
Network for International Health and great information on CSIH projects in Bolivia, the Caucuses,
Ukraine, Russian Guyana and the Philippines. Find travellers' health information and a list of
contact information for every travellers' health clinic in every major centre in Canada. Their
publication "Synergy Online" will keep you connected to events around the network. A great hit for
aspiring overseas health professionals. [ID:2258]

Don't Drink the Water: The Complete Traveller's
Guide to Staying Healthy in Warm Climates 📖
2000, Dr. J.S. Keystone, Canadian Public Health Association & Canadian Society for International
Health ➤ Canadian Public Health Association (CPHA), Suite 400, 1565 Carling Ave., Ottawa, ON
K1Z 8R1, Canada, www.cpha.ca, $19.95 CDN; VISA, MC; 613-725-3769, fax 613-725-9826
◆ Travelling can involve exposure to significant health hazards, the majority of which are
preventable. This book has been written with a minimum of "medicalese" for the lay public and
contains all the information that travellers would receive from health care providers on how to stay
healthy while travelling abroad. [ID:2032]

Get Ready! Hints for a Healthy Short-Term Assignment Overseas ▢

2001 ➤ CUSO, Suite 500, 2255 Carling Ave., Ottawa, ON K2B 1A6, Canada, www.cuso.org, $7 CDN; 613-829-7445, fax 613-829-7996; *Fr* ◆ Available in French under the title "Á votre santé!" This booklet can be used by both the experienced and inexperienced Canadian traveller going to a developing country for a period of six months or less. It provides health information and advice in an easy-to-read and accessible manner. [ID:2100]

Health Advice for Living Overseas ▢

1999 ➤ CUSO, Suite 500, 2255 Carling Ave., Ottawa, ON K2B 1A6, Canada, www.cuso.org, $17 CDN; 613-829-7445, fax 613-829-7996; *Fr* ◆ Written for Canadians planning to live or work in a developing country for a period of six months or more. It provides up-to-date health information for preparation and living overseas. Available in French as "Vivre en santé à l'étranger." [ID:2172]

Health and Wellness for International Students, Scholars and Their Families ▢ ▤

2002, 16 pages ➤ National Association for Foreign Student Affairs, 8th Floor, 1307 New York Ave. N.W., Washington, DC 2005-4701, USA, www.nafsa.org, Free on-line; Credit Cards; 800-836-4994, fax 202-737-3657 ◆ This brochure is concise and comprehensive and provides foreign students and scholars with information on the US health care system and payment structure, staying healthy during their stay, finding medical care, necessary immunizations, personal hygiene, sexual health and family planning, mental health, dental health and a personal health checklist for students. [ID:2557]

Health Canada Travel Medicine Program ▤

www.TravelHealth.gc.ca; *Fr* ◆ Health Canada's Travel Medicine Program boasts a fantastic Web site with current information on international disease outbreaks, immunization recommendations for international travel, general health advice for international travellers and disease-specific treatment and prevention guidelines. Highly recommended! [ID:2647]

International Society of Travel Medicine ▢ ▤

www.istm.org ◆ This Georgia-based Web site is directed at health professionals specializing in the area of international travellers' health, but is also an excellent resource for anyone interested in the latest information about overseas health. Not only can you search for travellers' health clinics all around the world, but you can access the latest breaking overseas health information on the newsletter "NewsShare." The ISTM's "Responsible Traveller" initiative can provide you with information on how to lessen your public health impact when visiting other countries. And, if you're really keen, you can order the "Journal of Traveller's Health" on-line or in print for about $125.00 US per year. A great source of information and links for staying healthy overseas. [ID:2649]

International Travel and Health by CPHA ▢

Annual, World Health Organization, 205 pages ➤ Canadian Public Health Association (CPHA), Suite 400, 1565 Carling Ave., Ottawa, ON K1Z 8R1, Canada, www.cpha.ca, $31.50 CDN; VISA, MC; 613-725-3769, fax 613-725-9826 ◆ Geared toward health professionals, this resource was completely redesigned in 2002 to reflect better knowledge about the risks travellers face and the precautions needed to protect their health. The book offers guidance on the full range of health risks likely to be encountered at specific destinations and associated with different types of travel—from business, humanitarian and leisure travel to backpacking and adventure tours. Navigate to CPHA's Health Resources Centre and check out the HRC Catalogue to view a description and order the book. [ID:2124]

The International Travel Health Guide ▢

Annual, Stuart Rose ➤ Travel Medicine Inc., Suite 312, 351 Pleasant Street, Northampton, MA 01060, USA, $12.95 US; Credit Cards; 413-584-0381, fax 413-584-6656, www.travmed.com; ◆ This US book offers the latest information on how to stay healthy abroad, including insect bite prevention, water filtration and purification, and how to prepare and use oral rehydration solutions to treat dehydration caused by traveller's diarrhea. The World Medical Guide section of the book provides extraordinarily detailed information on health risks and diseases in over 200 countries plus listings of many foreign hospitals. An excellent resource for overseas workers. Order on-line or download individual PDF chapters for free. [ID:2075]

Staying Healthy While Living in Canada 📖
1994, 102 pages ➤ CUSO, Suite 500, 2255 Carling Ave., Ottawa, ON K2B 1A6, Canada, www.cuso.org, $15 CDN; 613-829-7445, fax 613-829-7996; 𝐹𝑟 ◆ Provides health information and advice for students coming to Canada from developing countries to study or work for six months or more. Addresses such issues as accessing the Canadian health care system, depression, stress, winter health issues and Canadian culture as it affects physical and mental well-being. Available in French under the title "Visa-santé pour le Canada." [ID:2173]

Travel Immunization Record 📖
Canadian Public Health Association (CPHA), Suite 400, 1565 Carling Ave., Ottawa, ON K1Z 8R1, Canada, www.cpha.ca, $2.50 CDN; VISA, MC; 613-725-3769, fax 613-725-9826; 𝐹𝑟 ◆ Developed in partnership with Health Canada, the "Travel Immunization Record" is a practical booklet that helps you keep track of information concerning both routine and specialized immunizations. It has been designed as a companion piece for the new Yellow Fever Certificate of Vaccination and its convenient size makes it easy to carry along with your passport or other travel documents. An excellent way to manage an often overlooked detail of living and working overseas. Bilingual. [ID:2440]

Traveller's Health Services 👫
www.cha.ab.ca/travellers ◆ These Edmonton clinics offer pre-travel services for those who want to stay healthy and enjoy their journey. The latest information on regional health risks and illness prevention is easily accessible on the Web site. Find information on required and recommended vaccines, make appointments for prescriptions for afflictions such malaria, altitude illness and travellers' diarrhea and, for those in the Edmonton region, off-site presentations to groups of more than 10 travellers. [ID:2788]

Where There Is No Doctor: A Village Health Care Handbook: Revised Edition 📖
2003, David Werner, Carol Thuman, Jane Maxwell, Hesperian Foundation, 632 pages ➤ Masters & Scribes Bookshoppe, 9938 - 81 Ave., Edmonton, AB T6E 1W6, Canada, www.mastersandscribes.com, $20 US; Credit Cards; 800-378-3199, fax 780-439-6879 ◆ Trans-lated into over 90 languages, this US publication is considered the most accessible and widely used community health care manual in the world. This revolutionary health care "bible" has saved millions of lives around the world by providing vital information on diagnosing and treating common medical problems and diseases, and giving special emphasis to prevention. Includes sections detailing effective examination techniques, home cures, correct usage of medicines and their precautions, nutrition, caring for children, ailments of older individuals and first aid. [ID:2048]

World Health Organization: International Travel and Health 🖥
www.who.int/ith ◆ The World Health Organization International Travel and Health Web site provides up-to-date traveller's health information. Research by health issue or by the region you'll be going to and find out what vaccinations are required and what infectious diseases are currently a concern. A great resource from a trusted international source. [ID:2646]

CHILDREN & FAMILIES OVERSEAS

For children, the benefits of living overseas are immense. They adjust to new environments and learn languages at a rate that adults can only envy. Still, for children, moving will involve many of the same stressors as those experienced by adults. A few simple tips: stay upbeat and enjoy your move to a new culture and so will your children. Involving them in the logistics of your move will make them feel that they have an important role in the changes you all will face. These books will aid you in helping your children adapt to your new home overseas. We've also included resources on adoption, relationships and cross-cultural marriage.

Culture Shock! A Parent's Guide 📖

1999, Robin Pascoe, Times Books International, 269 pages ➤ Graphic Arts Center Publishing Company, 3019 NW Yeon, Portland, OR 97210, USA, www.gacpc.com, $13.95 US; 503-226-2402, fax 503-223-1410 ◆ Raising happy, well-adjusted children is always a challenge for parents, regardless of where they live. But overseas, parenting issues take on a whole new dimension. Of particular importance are reducing the stress of relocation and ensuring your child's overseas cross-cultural experience is a positive one, filled with healthy growing experiences. This book contains sound advice on achieving these goals as well as helpful information on how to ensure your child's special needs are looked after in an international school environment, and how you can help your child make a healthy adjustment to a new environment. [ID:2086]

Culture Shock! A Wife's Guide 📖

2002, Robin Pascoe, 212 pages ➤ Graphic Arts Center Publishing Company, 3019 NW Yeon, Portland, OR 97210, USA, www.gacpc.com, $13.95 US; 503-226-2402, fax 503-223-1410 ◆ Written by a Canadian, the book is easy to read, and provides useful advice for the wife going overseas for the first time, especially if her husband is with Foreign Affairs or an international agency. Chapters on maids, entertaining and home leave may be off-putting, but after you've lived in Pascoe's shoes, they may seem pertinent. Has a useful chapter on getting a job or freelancing overseas. [ID:2085]

Expat Expert 💻

www.expatexpert.com ◆ This Canadian site is designed for relocating expatriate spouses and families and written by the author Robin Pascoe. Many well-written articles on the challenges faced by families while living overseas. [ID:2567]

Guardian Angel: How To Be a Supportive Parent or Guardian
When Your Young Adult Decides to Work or Study Abroad 📖 💻

1999, Jeffrey Holmes, Canadian Bureau for International Education (CBIE), 30 pages ➤ www.destineducation.ca, Free on-line ◆ This practical, easy-to-read Canadian guide is chock full of advice for the parent/guardian of a young person embarking on a first international adventure. The author highlights opportunities for young people to participate in exchange programs and examines how to assist before, during and after the young adult goes abroad. Health issues, academic issues, visiting and re-entry are some of the topics touched upon. This guide is an essential resource for parents/guardians and the work/study abroad adviser. [ID:2792]

Homeward Bound: A Spouse's Guide to Repatriation 📖

Robin Pascoe, Expatriate Press Limited, 194 pages ➤ Chapters Indigo Books, www.chapters.indigo.ca, $16.95; Credit Cards ◆ Homeward Bound captures the emotional upheaval experienced by many returning spouses as they face the challenges of re-entry. Drawing on her personal experience, Pascoe takes the reader step by step through the repatriation process. She addresses and offers advice to such re-entry challenges as professional reinvention, coping with re-entry shock, settling in the children and suppressing a natural anger and rage against the working partner. Health issues are also discussed—notably, fatigue and depression. [ID:2833]

Intercultural Marriage: Promises and Pitfalls 📖

2001, Dugan Romano, 244 pages ➤ Intercultural Press, P.O. Box 700, 374 US Route One, Yarmouth, ME 04096, USA, www.interculturalpress.com, $16.95 US; VISA, MC; 800-372-5168, fax 207-846-5181, interculturalpress@internetmci.com ◆ A resource for couples either in or contemplating an intercultural marriage. Examines the impact of cultural differences on marriage and offers practical guidelines on how to deal with the complexities and problems involved. Anecdotes and interviews highlight the joys of an intercultural marriage, from both overcoming cultural challenges and embracing cultural differences. [ID:2091]

A Moveable Marriage: Relocate Your Relationship Without Breaking It 📖

Robin Pascoe, Expatriate Press Limited, 206 pages ➤ www.amazon.com, $16.95 US ◆ In this book, Pascoe takes stock of her life and offers an irreverent, quirky and just plain hilarious look at modern-day marriage and the quagmires and pitfalls that lie ahead when you and your marriage hit the road. With candid talk about the stress on relationships created by children, careers, money, sex and infidelity, this book is for couples who know that moving isn't all about furniture. [ID:2832]

Talking With Youth About War and Crisis 💻

2001, 2 pages ➤ Office of Overseas Schools (A/OS), US Department of State: Office of Overseas Schools, Room H328, SA-1, Washington, DC 20522-0132, USA, www.state.gov/m/a/os, Free on-line; 202-261-8200, fax 202-261-8224, OverseasSchools@state.gov ◆ Working overseas with children can involve the risk of immediate exposure to trauma or second-hand trauma in a post-conflict zone. The impact of this on the lives of children can be significant. These resources are intended to serve as a guideline for communicating with and helping children through the stresses of living overseas in an environment less stable than home. A must for families stationed in post-conflict zones. From the Office of Overseas Schools Web page, access these resources using the "Additional Information" index to the right. [ID:2515]

Transitioning to an Overseas Assignment with a Special Needs Child 💻

2003, 24 pages ➤ Office of Overseas Schools (A/OS), US Department of State: Office of Overseas Schools, Room H328, SA-1, Washington, DC 20522-0132, USA, www.state.gov/m/a/os, Free on-line; 202-261-8200, fax 202-261-8224, OverseasSchools@state.gov ◆ Designed to help families think through the decisions involved in living and working overseas with a special needs child. Focused on choosing the most appropriate school setting possible. Very useful PDF document available on-line. [ID:2514]

Travel With Children 📖

2002, Cathy Lanigan, Lonely Planet, 280 pages ➤ Raincoast Books, 9050 Shaughnessy Street, Vancouver, BC V6P 6E5, Canada, www.raincoast.com, $14.95 US; VISA, MC; 800-663-5714, fax 800-565-3770 ◆ This practical book is an inspiration for every parent planning an overseas experience. With vital pre-departure advice, your young family will be the best travelling companions you'll ever have. Discover how travel can be the greatest education as your kids explore different cultures, meet local families and answer the age-old riddle, "Are we there yet?" Contains practical guidance on breastfeeding, pregnant travel and on-the-road health as well as useful information on packing, planning and preparing for your trip and detailed country profiles with the best in kid-friendly sights. And yes, lots of travel games to amuse your little trekkers for hours. [ID:2081]

When Abroad Do As Local Children Do 📖

2002, Xpat Media, 112 pages ➤ The Interchange Institute, 11 Hawes Street, Brookline, MA 02446, USA, www.interchangeinstitute.org, $18.95 US; Credit Cards; 617-566-2227, fax 617-277-0889 ◆ This book reaches out to international mobile families with children between 8 and 12 years old. The activities and assignments in the book encourage the taking of initiatives in exploring the opportunities connected with the new environment. Great resource for those moving the whole family to take an overseas job. [ID:2555]

Where in the World Are You Going? 📖

1996, Judith M. Blohm, Intercultural Press, 64 pages ➤ Masters & Scribes Bookshoppe, 9938 - 81 Ave., Edmonton, AB T6E 1W6, Canada, www.mastersandscribes.com, $17.25 CDN; Credit Cards; 800-378-3199, fax 780-439-6879 ◆ An entertaining activity book for children ages five to ten which will make any overseas move more manageable. Encourages readers to express their excitement, fears, questions and hopes about the move, and leads them through activities that will help them say goodbye to their old home and embrace the new one. [ID:2203]

EDUCATING YOUR CHILDREN

Okay, so you've decided to move overseas with your children. Where can you find schools? What if your kids have special needs? These resource books will help get you started.

Adult Education Resources 🖳
www.teleeducation.nb.ca ◆ Distance education is sometimes a faceless risk. Enter New Brunswick's excellent on-line learning support Web site. Access information on distance learning such as on-line courses available, admissions and transferral of credits. Check out listings of accrediting agencies and unaccredited institutions to avoid fly-by-night diploma mills. The "Learner Resources" section contains job postings and information on starting a business. [ID:2348]

American-Sponsored Elementary and Secondary Schools Overseas Fact Sheets 🖳
Annual ➤ Office of Overseas Schools (A/OS), US Department of State: Office of Overseas Schools, Room H328, SA-1, Washington, DC 20522-0132, USA, www.state.gov/m/a/os, Free; 202-261-8200, fax 202-261-8224, OverseasSchools@state.gov ◆ A directory of all State Department supported overseas schools for dependents of US citizens. Each fact sheet lists contact information and school information. From the State Department home page, navigate to the Office of Overseas Schools via the "History, Education and Culture" tab. Once there, you can search for schools by region. A quick and comprehensive starting point for your overseas teaching job search. [ID:2064]

The Handbook of Private Schools 📖
2000, Daniel P. McKeever, 1,408 pages ➤ Porter Sargent Publishers Inc., Suite 1400, 11 Beacon Street, Boston, MA 02108, USA, www.portersargent.com, $95 US; Cheque or Money Order; 617-523-1670, fax 617-523-1021 ◆ One of three American books in a series designed to help readers make appropriate educational choices based on a child's particular needs, this book lists private schools by state. [ID:2389]

The ISS Directory of Overseas Schools 📖
2004, 533 pages ➤ International Schools Services (ISS), P.O. Box 5910, Princeton, NJ 08543, USA, www.iss.edu, $45.95 US; 609-452-0990, fax 609-452-2690, edustaffing@iss.edu ◆ The ISS Directory of International Schools is a comprehensive guide to American and International schools around the globe with over 500 listings of address, phone, fax, e-mail and chief school officer for each school. ISS also has a very useful Web site with lots of information related to education abroad. [ID:2050]

Schools Abroad of Interest to Americans 📖
2003, 544 pages ➤ Porter Sargent Publishers Inc., Suite 1400, 11 Beacon Street, Boston, MA 02108, USA, www.portersargent.com, $45 US; Cheque or Money Order; 617-523-1670, fax 617-523-1021 ◆ Authoritatively describes 700 elementary and secondary schools in 150 countries that accept English-speaking students. Written for the educator, personnel advisor, student and parent, as well as for diplomatic and corporate officials, this unique guide is also a useful reference for the overseas teaching job seeker. [ID:2067]

Transitioning to an Overseas Assignment with a Special Needs Child 🖳
2003, 24 pages ➤ Office of Overseas Schools (A/OS), US Department of State: Office of Overseas Schools, Room H328, SA-1, Washington, DC 20522-0132, USA, www.state.gov/m/a/os, Free on-line; 202-261-8200, fax 202-261-8224, OverseasSchools@state.gov ◆ Designed to help families think through the decisions involved in living and working overseas with a special needs child. Focused on choosing the most appropriate school setting possible. Very useful PDF document available on-line. [ID:2514]

RELOCATING ABROAD

Moving is always a challenge, but what exactly are you up against when you pick up and move to another country? These resources will help you with the logistics as well as researching the cost of living overseas. We've also included resources on financial planning, which is an important but little understood topic on everyone's mind when relocating overseas. If you're interested in what expatriates say about the country that you're relocating to, consult the Expat Networking Sites Resources below.

Border Guide: A Canadian's Guide to Investing, Working, and Living in the United States 📖

2004, Robert Keats, Self-Counsel Press, 320 pages ➤ Chapters Indigo Books, www.chapters.indigo.ca, $19.95; Credit Cards ◆ In this informative guide, noted financial planner and columnist Bob Keats teaches you everything you need to know about cross-border financial planning. [ID:2836]

Canada Year Book 📖

2001, Statistics Canada, 563 pages ➤ Renouf Publishing Co. Ltd., Unit 1, 5369 Canotek Road, Ottawa, ON K1J 9J3, Canada, www.renoufbooks.com, $65 CDN; Credit Cards; 888-767-6766, fax 613-745-7660; Fr ◆ This book is published every two years by Statistics Canada and serves as a vital reference resource. It provides an up-to-date picture of the social, economic and cultural life of Canada. It's a great book to bring as a gift or as a handy reference for all the questions your overseas friends will ask you when you travel overseas. Also available in French. [ID:2365]

Canadian Foreign Post Indexes 💻

Monthly, Statistics Canada ➤ www.statcan.ca, Free on-line; Fr ◆ Statistics Canada researches and publishes these post indexes on a monthly basis in order to calculate the approximate cost of living in various overseas cities. Post indexes are based on price comparisions of family expenditures such as food consumed at home, meals in restaurants, household maintenance and supplies, domestic help, clothing, transportation, health and personal care, reading and recreation. Post indexes are relative to the cost of living in Ottawa, which is assigned an index of 100. A city with a post index of 120 would have a cost of living 20 per cent higher than that in Ottawa. From the index, click the "Products and Services" menu, then navigate to "Prices and Indexes" through the "Free" publications link. [ID:2259]

Canadian Representatives Abroad 💻

Foreign Affairs Canada (FAC), www.dfait-maeci.gc.ca/world/embassies/cra-en.asp, Free on-line; Fr ◆ This is a bilingual directory of Government of Canada diplomatic and consular missions overseas, as well as a resource for finding Canada-based staff at those missions. You can search the directory, choose a region on the map below or access a list by city, country or surname. Finally, access a list of Canadian Missions to international organizations. This is an excellent tool to use if you want to learn about the size of a mission abroad. For embassies, note that many can be found just by entering the name of a city or country within www.***.gc.ca (e.g., www.losangeles.gc.ca, www.london.gc.ca, and www.india.gc.ca). Good luck in your search! [ID:2027]

Canadians Resident Abroad 📖

2002, Garry R. Duncan, Elizabeth Peck, 304 pages ➤ Thomson Carswell, One Corporate Plaza, 2075 Kennedy Road, Scarborough, ON M1T 3V4, Canada, www.carswell.com, $26.95 CDN; Credit Cards; 800-387-5164, fax 416-298-5094, cra@inforamp.net ◆ This book is especially for Canadians working abroad, regarding the tax consequences of leaving Canada, taxation as a non-resident and returning home. It provides a review of tax law and real-life situations dealing with non-resident issues, including emigration, departure tax, non-resident status, non-resident taxes, RRSPs, RRIFs, LIFs, treaties, overseas employment tax credit, moving expenses and relocation benefits, health insurance, immigration, foreign property reporting rules, Canadian tax forms and much more. Highly recommended. Remember: a balanced plan for working overseas includes financial management and reduces stress while abroad and after returning home. [ID:2146]

Canadians Resident Abroad Magazine 🖳

Quarterly ➤ Canadians Resident Abroad, Suite 600, 100 York Blvd., Richmond Hill, ON L4B 1J8, Canada, www.canadiansresidentabroad.com, Free on-line; 905-709-7911, fax 905-709-7022 ◆ Canada's first e-zine designed specifically for Canadians who are currently living abroad, who have done so in the past or who are contemplating an out-of-country sojourn in the future. Subscribe on-line and join Canadians in 129 countries around the world in receiving sound and timely information on everything from investment and taxation, offshore employment, vacation/travel and international real estate to country profiles, medical/insurance matters and education options for your children. This site is run by an international financial planner. [ID:2442]

Centre for Intercultural Learning (CIL) 🏛

Foreign Affairs Canada (FAC), Canadian Foreign Service Institute, Centre for Intercultural Learning, 15 Bisson Street, Gatineau, QC J8Y 5M2, Canada, www.dfait-maeci.gc.ca/cfsi-icse/cil-cai/menu-en.asp, 800-852-9211, fax 819-997-5409; Fr ◆ The CIL seeks to help professionals and organizations develop the intercultural competencies essential for success in the international realm. CIL's philosophy is that intercultural learning accelerates the pace of adaptation, enhances performance and helps the learner recognize and manage culture shock. CIL resources help you learn how business is done in foreign countries, as well as helping you to adopt appropriate perspectives, develop intercultural communication skills, cultivate professional relationships and practice diplomacy and persistence. [ID:2310]

Consular Affairs: Information and Assistance for Canadians Abroad 🏛

www.voyage.gc.ca, fax (800) 575-2500; Fr ◆ The Canadian government produces this great Web site, featuring essential travel, including country and regional reports, travel updates, maps, pre-departure information, and emergency contacts. Check out the weekly travel bulletin on safety "hot spots" for the most current information. [ID:2756]

Escape from America 🖳

www.escapeartist.com ◆ This site stems from the book version by the same name. The site provides resources for people wanting to move to "safe havens" such as New Zealand, Australia, Belize and Costa Rica. The focus is on real estate, international investing, retirement and finding a country with a low-cost comfortable overseas lifestyle. While not focused on cultural sensitivity issues or adaptation, the site is well-organized and has a lot of useful information about overseas living. Worth noting is the extensive archives of the free monthly magazine "Living Overseas." A new magazine "Offshore Quarterly" is in the works. [ID:2364]

The Expatriate Group Inc. 🏛

The Expatriate Group Inc., Suite 280, 926 - 6th Ave. S.W., Calgary, AB T2P 0N7, Canada, www.expat.ca, 403-232-8561, fax 403-294-1222, expatriate@expat.ca ◆ This site offers peace of mind to Canadian expatriates through financial planning and tax services, ensuring that your overseas move is successful. Few companies emphasize the integrity, technology, trusted service, tax efficiencies and investment risk reduction that the Expat Group offers. [ID:2360]

The Expert Expatriate: Your Guide to Successful
Relocation Abroad: Moving, Living, Thriving 📖

Melissa Brayer Hess, Nicholas Brealey Publishing, 271 pages ➤ Chapters Indigo Books, www.chapters.indigo.ca, $19.95; Credit Cards; ◆ This book not only covers the practical aspects of relocating; it enters new territory, laying emotional and cultural groundwork to help the expatriate thrive. [ID:2834]

FGI's Global Relocation Services 🏛

FGI's Global Relocation Services, Suite 200, 10 Commerce Valley Drive E., Thornhill, ON L3T 7N7, Canada, www.fgiworld.com, 905-886-2157, fax 905-886-4337 ◆ For 20 years, this Canadian company has provided a wide range of services related to living and working overseas to Canadian companies, employees and their families in over 100 countries worldwide. With offices in all major centres across Canada, you can access services such as cross-cultural business training and general cross-cultural skills, international security briefings, recovery and repatriation services. [ID:2367]

International Living 📖 💻
www.internationalliving.com, $129 US/year ◆ This American site and monthly magazine focus on travel, retirement, real estate and investment. Back issues available on-line free. [ID:2572]

Live and Work Series 📖
Vacation Work, 9 Park End Street, Oxford, OX1 1HJ, UK, www.vacationwork.co.uk, £10.99; Credit Cards; (44) (0) (1865) 24-1978, sales@vacationwork.co.uk ◆ This book series is unique in its comprehensive treatment of living overseas. Part One deals with the practicalities of living in a particular region: schooling, health, transport, property and retirement. Part Two covers all aspects of employment: availability of work, salaries, hours and holidays and starting a business. [ID:2547]

Moving Your Family Overseas 📖
1992, Rosalind Kalb, Penelope Welch, Intercultural Press, 135 pages ➤ Masters & Scribes Bookshoppe, 9938 - 81 Ave., Edmonton, AB T6E 1W6, Canada, www.mastersandscribes.com, $28.50 CDN; Credit Cards; 800-378-3199, fax 780-439-6879 ◆ Details the basic steps involved in this big decision: deciding to go, preparing to leave, arriving and settling in, working through culture shock and adaptation, living in the expatriate community and returning home. Good general advice, detailed suggestions and careful examination of issues such as informing the children, assisting them in adapting, taking look-see trips, settling into new living quarters, dealing with servants, finding social outlets in the host country, keeping the family functioning as an effective unit and, of course, coping with re-entry upon returning home. An excellent resource for the internation job seeker with a family. [ID:2090]

Out Post: Expatriate Information Centre 💻
www.outpostexpat.nl ◆ Maintained by volunteers to provide information to Shell expatriates and their families. Information is country-specific to more than 100 Shell locations around the world. A well-organized and useful resource for expatriates at pre-departure and for settling in. [ID:2573]

Vehicle Exports 💻
www.mapsupport.com ◆ Mission and Project Support is a Montreal firm helping expatriates with worldwide vehicle exports. Also includes information about driving while overseas. [ID:2343]

EXPATRIATE NETWORKING SITES

These resources will help you network with expats already living overseas. They can be an important source for job information, specific country information and companionship when you arrive in a new country. Since these expats are already on the ground and most likely well settled in, they know the job market and can help you with leads. Whether you are doing a country-specific job search, or have arrived in a new country as a traveller or an accompanying spouse, don't pass up on these valuable networking leads.

Back To My Roots 💻
www.backtomyroots.com ◆ This site is for young expatriates such as exchange students and interns. It displays two lists of useful links—one from your home country and one from the country in which you are residing in. Also offers Web-based e-mail, discussion forums and your own private photo album. [ID:2574]

The Canada Post 📖
Monthly ➤ The Canada Post, P.O. Box 46249, London, W5 2YN, UK, www.canadapost.co.uk, £20/12 issues or free on-line; (44) (0) (2088) 40-9765 ◆ "The Canada Post" is a free monthly

newspaper for the 200,000 Canadians living in the UK. Circulation is 23,000 copies, serving a readership of 50,000-plus. Keep up with news and events from a Canadian perspective. [ID:2265]

Canadians Resident Abroad Magazine 💻

Quarterly ➤ Canadians Resident Abroad, Suite 600, 100 York Blvd., Richmond Hill, ON L4B 1J8, Canada, www.canadiansresidentabroad.com, Free on-line; 905-709-7911, fax 905-709-7022 ◆ Canada's first e-zine designed specifically for Canadians who are currently living abroad, who have done so in the past or who are contemplating an out-of-country sojourn in the future. Subscribe on-line and join Canadians in 129 countries around the world in receiving sound and timely information on everything from investment and taxation, offshore employment, vacation/travel and international real estate to country profiles, medical/insurance matters and education options for your children. This site is run by an international financial planner. [ID:2442]

Expat Boards 💻

www.expatboards.com ◆ Message boards and country-specific information for expats in Western Europe. Includes topics on education, health, social life and taxes. [ID:2565]

Expat Expert 💻

www.expatexpert.com ◆ This Canadian site is designed for relocating expatriate spouses and families and written by the author Robin Pascoe. Many well-written articles on the challenges faced by families while living overseas. [ID:2567]

Expat Focus 💻

www.expatfocus.com ◆ This UK site is a Web-based meeting place and information centre for expats worldwide. Focus is on investments. [ID:2570]

Expat Forum 💻

www.expatforum.com ◆ Expatriates get together on 24 country-specific chat sites including the Netherlands, Switzerland and the US. The site also provides an expat bookstore and links. [ID:2568]

Expat Network 💻

www.expatnetwork.com, £72/year membership ◆ A UK site for overseas jobs and contract news, country profiles, expatriate health care, gift service, expatriate bookshop, expat forum, and articles on issues which affect expatriates. [ID:2569]

Expat World 📖 💻

10 issues/year ➤ www.expatworld.net, $30 US on-line; $89.95 US print ◆ A newsletter delivered to expatriates, travellers, business people and other internationals. Issues cover topics like investing for your retirement, taxation matters and global travel. [ID:2711]

ExpatAccess 💻

www.expataccess.com ◆ Practical country information for people moving to Belgium, Germany, France, the UK, Italy, Spain, the Netherlands and Switzerland. News, tools, community and free classifieds. [ID:2564]

Expatexchange.com 💻

www.expatexchange.com ◆ Largest of the general expat sites, it offers tons of country-specific information and services of interest to expats, country-specific expat forums, and a free weekly e-newsletter. There is even a country list of expat hangouts. [ID:2566]

Expatica 💻

www.expatica.com ◆ Detailed site for the English-speaking expatriate community in Belgium, France, Germany and the Netherlands. The site features local and international news, community activities and services relevant to expatriates, as well as popular discussion boards. [ID:2571]

CHAPTER 4

What Expats Say About Living Abroad

In writing this book, we talked to or surveyed dozens of men and women with overseas experience. The following is a sampling of what they told us about their experiences. (CUSO and PEACE CORPS also generously provided quotations from their cooperants and volunteers.) While there's no way of foretelling what you will encounter abroad, we hope you'll find their comments helpful, interesting and entertaining.

BENEFITS OF OVERSEAS LIFE

An overseas job provides variety and job satisfaction that you don't get in a large corporation at home, according to an accountant who volunteered for CUSO in Zimbabwe.

"In a big organization, an accountant is usually stuck in one department, but here I'm dealing with the whole works. There is a lot of satisfaction in teaching accounting skills here because the people take so much interest in learning."

Many overseas jobs allow you to have a greater impact than you would at home, writes this American NGO worker in Costa Rica.

"Here, I see the effects of my work every single day. When fundraising efforts provide money for scholarships, when kids come to our community centre for homework help, even just on the bus home when I happen to chat with a curious local. I can see that I'm having an impact here, and that's very rewarding."

Living overseas provides a much richer experience than merely travelling abroad or taking an extended vacation, as this PEACE CORPS volunteer from New Jersey discovered.

"Personally, I was given the opportunity to live within a culture. I was not a tourist and I was not living in a bubble away from the community. I knew the community members and they knew me. We shared meals and laughed together, and we shared moments of sorrow and cried together. Regardless of the realities of our economic environments and our cultural differences, we came to know each other as people with specific personalities and dedications."

It can be easier overseas to move among social classes. A CUSO cooperant in Africa reflects on the wide cross-section of people she met.

"Hitching from Accra to New Tafo several months ago, I found myself the sole passenger with the Secretary to the Ambassador of Liberia. For the next two hours I was chauffeured in style—enjoying fine music, air-conditioning and political small talk. I alighted, much to my chagrin, at the Bunso junction—about 20 kilometres from New Tafo—only to be picked up a few minutes later by a rattling, windowless Datsun, already well-packed with four passengers and all their gear. For the next two hours (we suffered mechanical problems en route) I bounced along, assuring the driver I could survive the heat, while trying to convince the young man next to me that my husband was back home looking after our children."

It can take time and patience to make friends abroad. One private sector consultant—a woman—has the following suggestions for getting to know local colleagues.

"Mingle with local staff. Participate in staff weddings and funerals, when invited and when appropriate. Also try the odd custom from home. I had a shower for a young bride-to-be and it was a success and enjoyable to do. The stories of wives at that afternoon shower were fascinating and revealed a lot about local customary marriage and how donors' ideas of 'women-in-development' will be years in realizing."

Other expats can provide rich opportunities for friendship, as this American university professor in Northeast Asia has found.

"People here have been wonderful to me. I've made good friends among the local population, and also among other expat workers. In fact, I have more in common with the Americans, Australians, and Canadians I've met here than I ever did with my colleagues at home. My expat friends here are adventurous, politically savvy, and very culturally sensitive."

Living abroad helps you appreciate life at home and recognize real priorities for a productive and contented life, says one CANADIAN CROSSROADS INTERNATIONAL volunteer, after returning from a short work-term in Africa.

"After having learned to eat the same foods twice a day, every day, for four months, I realized that people don't require 10 different items for each meal. Back home, we have such a warped notion about what constitutes adequate nutrition. We do not need a wide array of 30,000 food items in our supermarkets. People all over the world live happy, productive, and healthy lives with very basic foodstuffs. I will never again complain or worry about the future if I have access to bread, milk, rice, fish and one or two vegetables."

WORKING IN A FOREIGN COUNTRY

Management styles vary throughout the world. That's one of the first things you will notice when you work overseas, according to one UNITED NATIONS employee based in a regional office in Africa.

"The most important thing to remember is that it does not function like a North American office. The management style is top-down and unparticipatory, stemming in part from its isolation from North American management theory... For another, shortages in office supplies such as paper for photocopying or typewriter ribbons, and local staff who suffer from low levels of training, make office efficiency a fraction of what it is in North America."

You will have to adapt to the workplace conditions you find. A CANADIAN CROSSROADS INTERNATIONAL volunteer taught in Ghana despite major problems.

"The school often runs out of money so we close it down for one or two weeks and contract out the students' labour. We dug out a fish pond for a good profit three months ago. Then we made cement blocks and built walls for a local person. We are currently thinking of building a pig barn for someone. While these projects have their practical applications and make the students proud of their school, it really throws a cog into our efforts to give the students an ongoing, logically planned education."

Basic resources that you take for granted at home are not available in many parts of the world, says a CUSO volunteer working as a teacher at a paramedic school in Sierra Leone.

"The job came with some difficulties and frustrations. The school runs out of paper, pens and chalk regularly. The hospital is functioning on practically nothing. This makes it difficult to teach simple lessons, for example—taking a temperature without a thermometer. Maintaining hygienic procedures is almost impossible with no running water. At the end of the dry season one bucket of water must do a 33-bed paediatric ward for a day. With time one forgets all the shortcomings and adapts and makes use of what little resources one has."

Be prepared to wait, and wait, and wait to get things done, according to a manager with a large engineering firm working in West Africa.

"The typical office day for a management expatriate in the private sector is from about 7:30 a.m. to 7 p.m. You must work long hours to compensate for time lost during the day on items not related to your actual job. Things like personnel problems, equipment problems, long waits for meetings, and long and unnecessary meetings. You get your actual work done before 9 a.m. and after 4 p.m."

Workplaces can be much more hierarchical, warns this American ESL teacher after a stint in Northeast Asia.

"Back home, we tend to maintain an illusion of equality in the workplace—we talk to the doorman the same way we talk to our boss. So I was unprepared for office politics when I first arrived. I really had to learn to use the appropriate signs of respect with my supervisors, including body language. I had to learn

that I couldn't just bring my habits from home with me and expect everyone to understand me."

Many Westerners overseas take their job too seriously and miss out on other aspects of their stay, says one CUSO volunteer in Sierra Leone.

"I am still learning to draw the line with regard to my work. I think that most cooperants are extremely serious about their work, and, if not careful, they can often 'burn out' by forgetting that work is just one part of life and they are here not only to perform professional duties but to learn about people, places and much more."

Many Westerners overseas try to carry out all the work themselves for the sake of efficiency. In the long run that's a mistake, says a CUSO volunteer in Nigeria.

"Development workers often have personal ambitions. Over time they can develop 'realistic' attitudes (about local people) which can be patronizing, culturally aggressive, and cynical... At my workplace this (attitude) is sometimes translated into excessive reliance on expatriate skills and judgment, and very little consultation with people who were to 'benefit' from all this good work."

A CIDA project officer in the Philippines stresses respectful human relationships at work above "efficiency" in an office abroad.

"Office work overseas can be deceptively like office work at home. The competent and efficient secretaries further that impression. However, human and social relationships nearly always are more important than at home. Greater sensitivity is generally called for overseas.

"You must make your priority human dignity and respect. Loss of face by colleagues and those one supervises is to be avoided whenever possible. When a conflict cannot be responsibly side-stepped, it should be dealt with privately... There is no such thing as brutal honesty. Skills of mediation, compromise and quiet authority are respected."

A boss is a boss is a boss. No matter where you go in the world, your boss will make or break your job according to one Junior Professional Officer with the UNITED NATIONS who is based in Africa:

"The experience you have in the UN could depend on the office you have been assigned to and, to an extent, the boss you have been sent to work with. And like any other workplace, your boss can turn the job of your dreams into the job of your lifetime, or into a daily nightmare."

You must learn to accept the work pace and habits overseas if you want to adapt, says the regional director for Nigeria and Ghana of a large engineering firm.

"The major differences in work habits are the lack of urgency to get anything done and the lackadaisical approach to quality of work. These two items are enough to drive you crazy if you do not adapt mentally to the situation... You can try to change this, but it is a long, slow process and you must recognize this.

"Try to get a local interface between workers and expatriate management. As long as you stay you will never be as good as a local administrator for certain tasks. Recognize the administrator's limitations and try to upgrade him or her."

Be prepared for a learning experience, says one UN employee.

"As an international civil servant, so much can throw your work off. You've got elections, government and organizational bureaucracy, office politics, cyclones and screw-ups. Patience, and lots of it, is what you need, as well as lower expectations... You can't avoid mistakes, especially when you first arrive. You are very vulnerable emotionally, socially and professionally. Therefore, make your mistakes and learn from them."

Learn from your environment, suggests one Junior Professional Officer with the UNITED NATIONS in Africa:

"An international bureaucracy is a great training ground for life... Life here is too often built on an exchange of smiles and daggers. Working in a different and difficult cultural milieu in two foreign languages, and getting things done, is no small piece of cheese either."

Working overseas can increase your confidence and provide you with an opportunity to develop skills that you simply wouldn't get at home. One young American who volunteered in Uzbekistan writes:

"I think you acquire skills as a Peace Corps Volunteer that you can't possibly get from any job in America... You become tremendously creative and flexible. I honestly believe I could do anything after this. Any boss could ask me to do anything, and I could take the most minuscule materials and do anything with them."

Host nationals may expect Westerners to boost the economy by employing local people.

"Every time we park the car we hire a watchman, even if it is only for ten minutes. This tends to be a customary practice and many small boys depend on it for a living. Shopping excursions always include one or two hired helpers to tell us where to buy the things we want (it isn't easy to find things in the maze of the market), and to carry cartons. Washing clothes takes a full day, and if you are working there is no time for it... the same goes for cooking. It may sound very imperialistic and I must confess to a certain degree of guilt. Nonetheless, it is the only way of getting things done, and it puts money in peoples' pockets which they otherwise would not receive."

Overseas business deals take more time and patience to firm up, according to an environmental consultant who has worked throughout the world.

"Doing business overseas is much more difficult and can be frustrating if a person is not extremely patient. People overseas often promise a lot but seldom deliver... Be prepared to entertain a lot. If a client is with you for over a year with no results, politely dump them."

PREPARATION AND CULTURE SHOCK

Make every effort to speak to others who have lived in the country where you will be stationed, suggests one manager working for a consulting company in Africa.

"Before you leave, make every effort to speak to another family—husband, wife, kids—who have lived in the country. Prepare for this interview well, list all

your questions, concerns, fears, no matter how silly they may seem. Preferably, speak to someone not in your own organization, to avoid any bias. And if you are in the private sector DO NOT speak to a diplomat. They have no concept of what real life is like in these countries. They live in an isolated environment protected by special concessions made for the diplomatic corps."

Give some thought to the possessions you take overseas, advises one CUSO volunteer in Malaysia.

"After dragging luggage around on my way here, paying excess baggage and storage charges, I'm convinced that volunteers should be encouraged to bring nothing which cannot be carried in a small backpack. Much of what I brought with me proved to be either useless, unsuitable, or could be bought cheaper or of a more suitable design or materials. The exception might be cotton underwear. That small backpack would easily hold a year's supply, your photo album, a change of clothing, and a few small gifts for special friends you make."

Once you arrive, absorb as much information as you can about your host country, says one CUSO cooperant.

"When you get to your country, read the newspaper. Read the whole newspaper—the ads, the classified, letters to the editor, obituaries. You'll quickly find out what is important and start getting a sense of where people are at."

Don't expect everything to be covered in official orientations, says a CUSO volunteer in Africa.

"The separation of black and white and underlying hostility towards white expats... was completely ignored in an official orientation. I am only now beginning to see the joyful side of (the local) culture, by spending much more time with the local people... I have certainly been made aware of latent racist tendencies in myself which would never have surfaced in Canada. This has also heightened my awareness of outspoken racism in others."

All overseas workers and volunteers experience culture shock. This CUSO volunteer in Malaysia had a clear case shortly after she arrived.

"Personally, I found life in Malaysia difficult to adjust to. My senses were offended by the smells of open sewers, exhaust fumes, garlic prawn paste, smelly toilets, by the sound of traffic, Michael Jackson singing 'Beat It,' the oft-heard male greeting 'Hello miss, want to sleep with me?' and by the sights of garbage-strewn streets, open sewers, mouldy buildings and poor imitations of western shopping centres.

"The traffic rules, or rather lack of them, left me wondering why I had left Canada to be run down by a bus or taxi driver. The physical aspects simply compounded the emotional problems caused by loneliness, lack of privacy, and my inability to deal with racial and sexual discrimination and harassment."

Keep in mind that culture shock passes, and you can help yourself through it by being attentive to your surroundings. An American teacher in Korea describes the process.

"In the beginning, it seemed like every day held new confusion and devastating faux pas. As time passed, however, I began to make sense of what was going on, and soon many aspects of my new host country's culture even

seemed preferable to my own. It just took time, patience, and most importantly, a sense of humour."

Some countries give new meaning to the word "bureaucracy," as a CANADIAN CROSSROADS INTERNATIONAL volunteer in Ghana explains.

"Upon arrival I was granted a 14-day visa, which had to be renewed with the government in order to get a resident visa. The problem is, the passport office referred my request to the Ministry of Culture and Sports to see if they had any information on my organization. No reason was given for this procedure. This ministry has since been split into two separate ministries and no one knows which one has the letter, who is responsible to answer it, who the letter was addressed to, or even where the new offices are located. The Passport Office now refuses to act on the matter until they get an answer and they say it is my responsibility to track it down."

Many people are surprised at their own clichéd ideas of other cultures, as a CUSO volunteer in Malaysia discovered.

"I suppose, like most North Americans, I had the stereotypical view of the East as an ancient land of exotic mystery. This has in some ways turned out to be true, but in many ways Malaysia has surprised me with its modernity. The old and new meet head-on. Open-air markets compete with air-conditioned shopping malls. Rickshaws and bicycles share the road with Mercedes, Mazdas, Fords. Haute cuisine mixes with hamburgers and hot dogs. If someone tells you that 'everything' is available here, believe them."

Manners vary from country to country. One CUSO cooperant in Southeast Asia explains how these differences can contribute to culture shock.

"There are times when the famous politeness and refinement of character will grate on your nerves, seeming like cowardice, hypocrisy, ignorance or any combination thereof, and you will gnash your teeth in a fury of impotent rage. There will be times while teaching when you hear your voice being mimicked aloud by someone in the next room and you want to stalk out of the class and throttle the damn fool... There will be times when your patience will be paper thin as you stagger through, for the umpteenth dozen time, the gauntlet of 20 questions regarding your social, sexual, marital, dining habits... I've found it's usually better to ignore, if possible, what you find negative in the foreign culture and concentrate on what you find positive."

SPOUSE, FAMILY AND SOCIAL RELATIONS

Life can be tough for a non-working spouse overseas. The spouse of a CIDA employee in Harare, Zimbabwe had the following advice for adjustment.

"Have realistic expectations. You probably will not find paid employment and if you do, it may be considerably lower paying than in Canada. Why not focus on meaningful volunteer work which could lead to a new or continued career in Canada? Get involved in something in the local community, preferably an activity in your field of interest. It's by talking to people that you hear of opportunities.

"Imagine that you won't find a job and plan for that situation. Think of doing correspondence courses. Arrange to do research in your field. Create your own job. For example, if you have a counselling degree, why not advertise among the other foreign missions and start your own practice out of your house or apartment?."

A woman who was a UNITED NATIONS employee in Africa suggests that men who accompany their partners abroad must be prepared for pressures.

"When we went to Zaire together it wasn't because he got a job, it was because I got a job. I was really proud of my husband because he's quite a novelty. But it was very difficult for him. He is a translator with a master's degree in translation and he is quite skilled at what he does. But there was no work. He tried to get contracts here and there but it wasn't very consistent... And he felt societal pressures.

"He's got to work, he's a man. I think it does put a lot of pressure on a marriage if the spouse is unhappy and wants to work and makes you feel like he is doing you a big favour by being there."

Life can be tough for the spouses of private company employees who work overseas, according to this manager of a consulting firm.

"In management the long hours affect your home life. Your wife must be happy or your life will be hell and you will have to leave. So, even if the company does not provide for it, spend some of the money you are making to ensure your family is comfortable, safe and occupied. Most problems come from bored spouses."

On the other hand, a stint overseas can provide opportunities for couples to become closer, like this American couple who volunteered with the PEACE CORPS in Armenia.

"We spent more time communicating with one another than we ever had before. We also enjoyed working together on activities, like coaching the girls' soccer team and taking kids on environmental hikes."

Living and working overseas has its down side, says a UNITED NATIONS employee stationed in Africa.

"The requirements of living like a gypsy and moving every two or three years prevents you from putting down roots and confines your peer group to a bunch of maladapted diplomats.

"Your position as a rich foreigner makes it very difficult to integrate into the local community and instead privileges you as a member of an isolated ruling class. Some people may enjoy the instant respect you get and the easy life with chauffeurs and servants. Others who grew up with North American egalitarian values may be disgusted by the whole thing."

Your social life may be quite different from at home, according to two CUSO cooperants in Sierra Leone.

"As we live on a Seventh Day Adventist compound, we are fairly isolated and our lifestyle is conservative. We have both purchased our own Honda 70's to make the 10-mile trip to the nearest town once a week, to shop and get a beer."

In some cultures you may feel like nationals want to know everything about you, as one CUSO volunteer in Indonesia discovered.

"You may well find people here frightfully honest by Western standards, depending on the subject matter. There will be no hesitation in discussing the three kilos you recently lost or gained and you will find yourself answering very personal questions from people who seek to understand how it is that you are so different."

Likewise, trying to find out everything you can about your host culture can only enhance your experience, as this VSO CANADA volunteer discovered.

"Although I brought a new language and a different culture to share, I also immersed myself in the Mongolian way of life. Many Mongolians were surprised and pleased at this, and it reinforced the idea that I was there to work together with them. My Mongolian friends, colleagues and students brought ideas and energy to the process of development, working towards improving the future on their own terms without sacrificing their own values."

Life in an African village can be full of social activities, says a CUSO volunteer in The Gambia.

"I'll barely have finished supper before visitors start arriving. Every evening, beginning at 7 p.m., I have anywhere from 6 to 20 visitors. First it is young boys, then a couple of girls, finally a few young men and women. It can be pretty loud and lively at times. Conversation between the villagers and me is usually pretty limited, but there's lots of laughter. At 9 o'clock I politely explain that I want to write in my book and they all get up, shake my hand, and leave."

The impact of a high crime rate and poverty affected one UN employee's ability to meet people in a large urban centre in Africa.

"(The high rate of crime) was difficult because it caused me to be mistrustful of people immediately. I made one local friend, a woman who is very independent, works in an office, makes a good salary, and was definitely not interested in me because I was white and come from a developed country and had money. But other than this person we were not able to make any local friends because people were not interested in us."

Many people experience loneliness and feelings of isolation during their stay overseas. One CUSO volunteer in Africa describes her experience.

"I felt socially isolated and found this quite discouraging. I had perhaps unrealistic expectations of friendships with Sierra Leonians, especially women. I wonder how much of this is due to barriers I've erected myself, how much to the fact that my cultural and background experiences are so different from those of the people I've met?"

On the other hand, Living near to neighbours in an apartment block helped this PEACE CORPS couple to connect with their host community.

"Some of the greatest times were spent with our neighbours. We shared all of our new experiences with them, and they helped us to communicate more easily with other people."

Learning a local language can help to break down some of the barriers between people, says a CUSO volunteer in the Solomon Islands of the South Pacific.

"A gradual introduction into the world of dances and night life has polished my Pidgin, though it may have tarnished my reputation... I'd like to reiterate what was wisely repeated to us a number of times at orientation. Different language is the biggest barrier between two people. Shared language is the sweet bridge over it."

WOMEN OVERSEAS AND
WOMEN IN DEVELOPING COUNTRIES

A woman working overseas does not have the same experiences as a man, explains a consultant who works throughout Africa.

"The most surprising treat of working overseas as a woman consultant was the pure pleasure of being able to focus my attention completely on my work, relieved of my at-home roles of wife and mother. The most difficult aspect of working overseas as a woman and a consultant is the loneliness. When the work day was over, I was often trapped in my hotel, too restrained by cultural taboos and lack of familiarity with the locale to venture far alone."

Sometimes cultural rules that apply to local women will be waived for North American women, explains a private consultant working in Africa.

"As a North American woman, I was able to work effectively with men in Muslim countries as I was not expected to conform to the cultural practices of local women. As a middle-aged woman, I commanded more respect from both women and men than younger female consultants would have."

But many women are unprepared for the advances of men or harassment in other cultural settings, as a CUSO cooperant in Malaysia explains.

"Every day I rode to language class in a minibus in which people were packed like sardines. In fact, some of the braver souls swung on the door as the bus skidded around 90-degree corners for 20 to 30 minutes. This was traumatic because it marked the beginning of another day of being stared at. Language classes were tolerable by comparison to the rest of the day.

"The worst part of the day was the walk through the shopping complex in which the language school was located—the male school drop-outs, aged 16–20, leered and made comments. After one particularly trying day, when a person followed me into the language school, I decided I would stay for only six months. This was a compromise between leaving immediately and staying for two years."

Many women find themselves able to come to an understanding of culture-based gender differences, like this American PEACE CORPS volunteer.

"After about six months, something magical happened. I started to feel as if Tunis was my home. Somehow, somewhere along the way, I began to win the war of stares and stopped letting the comments chip away at my personality. I stopped feeling as though every incident was a personal attack in a war waged solely against me. I discovered it was pointless to let these occurrences bother me. A Western woman is fair game and rules don't apply. These exceedingly annoying and overconfident flirtations were just attempts to capture my attention,

and my interest. They were also completely harmless. In fact, I was far safer in Tunis than I was in Detroit."

An American relief worker with experience throughout Africa recommends caution when approaching gender politics.

"When you first arrive, it can be difficult to interpret what you see around you, especially relationships between people. Don't automatically assume that, as an outsider, you know the role of women in a community, or what changes women need. Take as much time as you can to listen and observe before making comments, let alone suggesting projects or plans."

A private sector development consultant argues that women play such a large role they should not be ignored in the planning and execution of development projects.

"Don't forget that women constitute 50 per cent of the population, and include women in all projects from the start to end."

Sometimes the host of issues facing women in developing countries may seem overwhelming to North American women, says one CUSO health educator at a women's centre in Peru.

"Our health team has focused on women's reproductive health, treating items such as birth control, maternal death, cervical cancer and problems with illegal abortions. I feel we are striving for so many social justices: the right for a woman not to be beaten by her husband, the right to decent medical services, the right for women and men to have honest information about birth control and access to all methods available, the right to organize against discrimination and racism in health services and the right to fair and affordable health care."

In the name of North American "efficiency," many disadvantaged groups, including women, don't get as involved as they should, according to a CUSO volunteer in Nigeria.

"In my own work the need to get things done often overrode the needs and aspirations of the disabled and the poor. Disabled people often work more slowly than able-bodied people, so it was easier to hire strong, young men. The poorest are often the least knowledgeable and lack hope. It was easier to work with those who understood English, had some education, and had hope that translated into ambition. Women had family responsibilities that made them less reliable in their attendance, especially widows who had less extended family support. They also tend to be less educated, speak less English, be less physically strong and complain less about drudgery. It was easier to educate the men and keep the women working."

DAY-TO-DAY LIVING OVERSEAS

One Crossroader shares his reluctance to try the Indonesian method for everything.

"The WCs have no toilet paper. A shock for Westerners, but people use their hands and water or a washcloth and then wash up. They would regard our way as unhygienic, but most of us are grateful to use the familiar western commode. We regrettably are passing up on another cultural experience—squatting over a ceramic basin set in the tile floor."

We take many products for granted that are used and reused in other parts of the world, says one CANADIAN CROSSROADS INTERNATIONAL volunteer in Africa.

"Ghanaians are starved for books and papers. We bring all of our papers to the life-guard at the beach. From there it seems paper reading parties materialize, with everyone reading and sharing the material. It is amazing to see 10 people all huddled under a palm hut on the beach, reading and reading, not a word being said. There is so little reading material in this country and with such a high literacy rate everyone is starved for something new or current to read. This makes me realize how much we take even daily newspapers for granted in Canada."

Coping with a lack of supplies can be very instructive, as this American woman found while working with an NGO in rural Costa Rica.

"At home in Boston, I always thought I was a great environmentalist. Since coming here I've learned that I could still be a lot less wasteful. The women in this community find ways to reuse everything—food, cloth, plastic, scraps of metal. It's amazing to see, and it's taught me a lot about how I operate back in America."

You may be offered odd foods while living and working in another country—as one Crossroads volunteer living in South America writes to friends:

"Now that I have eaten the local delicacy—roast guinea pig—a total of three times, I feel I am ready for almost anything. It's quite good, once you get over the shock."

Commuting can become, well, something of a nightmare as this Crossroads volunteer describes.

"Traffic has brought city problems to a village society. Indonesians believe that the other guy sees you and will give way... Scooter riders have to swerve around a clumsy Westerner, when usually they just turn a bit and whip by, braking only at the last minute.

"Traffic is an instinctive organism here, none of our slow, linear logic. People tailgate, honk, blink, yell and gesture to say 'watch out, I'm coming, don't pass, OK you can pass now' or 'I'm just glad I'm still alive.' Streamlined Mercedes buses with gutted exhausts belch by swarms of tiny motorcycles with gutted exhausts, as a steady flow of vehicles avoids imminent collision. There is no enforcement of safeguards or pollution controls. Even the helmet law is quite casual. People put their helmets on unstrapped to get through policed intersections."

Prepare for the climate to be quite different from the four seasons you know in Canada. One CUSO volunteer in Malaysia comments on the conditions.

"No one told us about the rain before we came to Sarawak. This seemed strange because Sarawak is wetter than the Sahara is dry... In Sarawak it is always raining, has always rained and will always rain... And it isn't just how it rained but when it rained... Oh sure, the monsoons are now over... but life is always wet (even on Sundays)... In the happy reminiscences of a selective memory this will all be forgotten. Is this why they never told us about the rain?"

A tropical climate can bring additional visitors to your home, says one CUSO cooperant to Indonesia.

"While much of nature lives outside the walls of my home, the inside is nonetheless resplendent with things that fly, crawl, hop, run, swim and grow... The lizards which crawl about the walls and ceilings are likely to provide the greatest amusements to newcomers to Indonesia. These guys eat their weight in insects and should not be the objects of fear and loathing.

"Every once in a while a tree frog, either the large green variety or its smaller brown cousin, manages to get in and goes nuts, bouncing off the walls in a crazed attempt to get out of my restful abode...

"Insects are the mainstay of my menagerie. While mosquitoes are constantly soliciting blood donations, it is the ants who literally threaten the foundations of my existence. There are many different kinds, the dishwashers, the musclemen, the carpenters...

"Another occasional visitor is the cockroach. These like to live in dark places and during occasional fits of frenzy and passion, take to the sky. Like everything else here, they only come in a large size."

A LAST WORD

We hope you've found these comments helpful, interesting and entertaining. From the many varied shared experiences, there is no doubt that living overseas is always intellectually interesting and most of the time enticingly exciting!

RESOURCES

PERSONAL STORIES OF LIFE OVERSEAS

This is a mixed bag of stories about living overseas, some humorous, some serious. This list of references will be of interest to anyone seeking anecdotes and insights into how others have thrived or survived living overseas.

Graveyard For Dreamers: One Woman's Odyssey in Africa 📖
2002, Joan Baxter, 224 pages ➤ Potter's Field Press, 83 Leslie Road, East Lawrencetown, NS B2Z 18P, USA, www.pottersfieldpress.com, $16.95 CDN; VISA; 800-646-2879, fax 888-253-3133 ◆ A Canadian's personal and colourful account of living, travelling and reporting on coups and customs in seven West African countries. Baxter grew up in Nova Scotia and lived in four West African countries. A well-written and entertaining read. [ID:2293]

Letters From Afghanistan 📖
2003, 176 pages ➤ Branden Publishing, P.O. Box 812094, Wellesley, MA 02482, USA, www.branden.com, $14.95 US; VISA, MC; fax 781-790-1056 ◆ A Peace Corps volunteer's letters home, reflecting on life in Afghanistan, the land and the people. [ID:2763]

Mobility International USA 🖥
www.miusa.org ◆ This US Web site describes hundreds of opportunities for people with challenges to mobility in international educational exchange programs, work camps and volunteer positions. Includes first-person accounts of travel and learning experiences. [ID:2626]

Once Again at Forty 📖
1995, Jim Shannon, 134 pages ➤ General Store Publishing House Inc., 1 Main Street, Burnstown, ON K0J 1G0, Canada, $16.95 CDN; Credit Cards; 800-465-6072, fax 613-432-7184, www.amazon.ca ◆ An entertaining, inspiring account of 10 years of work and travel undertaken by

the author after he quit a successful, 20-year college teaching career. If you are contemplating a change but still wondering if you can or should do it, this book could persuade you. [ID:2162]

Outpost Magazine - Travel for Real 📖
Quarterly ➤ www.outpostmagazine.com, $20 for 6 issues; VISA, MC ◆ Outpost Magazine is Canada's own sophisticated travel magazine—Winner of Canada's top magazine award - The Presidents Medal. You needn't subscribe in order to access travel articles and information, but after reading the free stuff, you just might want to! (For more information, see their ad in the sponsor section at the end of this guide.) [ID:2338]

A Rich Broth: Memoirs of a Canadian Diplomat 📖
1993, David Chalmer Reese, 231 pages ➤ McGill-Queen's University Press, 3430 McTavish Street, Montreal, QC H3A 1X9, Canada, www.mqup.mcgill.ca, $19.95 CDN; VISA, MC; 514-398-3750, fax 514-398-4333 ◆ A witty autobiography containing a mix of insight and humour based on a 38-year career in the Canadian foreign service. [ID:2095]

Serving America Abroad 📖
2003, Irwin Rubenstein, 335 pages ➤ Xlibris, 11th Floor, 436 Walnut Street, Philadelphia, PA 19106-3703, USA, http://www1.xlibris.com, $45.23 US; Credit Cards; 888-795-4274, fax 215-923-4685 ◆ "Real-Life Adventures of American Diplomatic Families Overseas." New anthology of American Diplomats' experiences, edited by a retiree from the foreign service. [ID:2770]

Tales From a Small Planet: The Literary and Humour Magazine for Expatriates Everywhere 💻
www.thesun.org ◆ Written unofficially by US State Department employees and their families, this site is somewhat like an underground newsletter. It has "honest" country reports written by people who live there. The site has all types of excellent articles, links and a message board. You can even sign up for a free weekly e-mail newsletter. [ID:2575]

They Only Laughed Later 📖
1997, 216 pages ➤ Europublic SA/NV, P.O. Box 504, Uccle 5, Brussels, B-1180, Belgium, www.europublic.com, €14.95; VISA, MC; (32) (0) 2-343-77-26, fax (32) (0) 2-343-93-30 ◆ This collection of essays is the product of a series of "Women On the Move" conferences, which brought together expatriate women from over 20 countries. Their concerns were mutual: to share experiences in meeting the challenges that confront women who move to strange lands in pursuit of their own or their husbands' careers. A fabulous account of the unique perspectives of women living and working overseas. [ID:2552]

Travel That Can Change Your Life: How to Create a Transformative Experience 📖
1997, Jeffrey A. Kottler, 180 pages ➤ Wiley: Jossey-Bass Publishers, 10475 Crosspoint Blvd., Indianapolis, IN 46256, USA, www.josseybass.com, $23.45 US; Credit Cards; 877-762-2974, fax 800-597-3299 ◆ An inspiring look into the deeper significance of travel. It reveals how travelling provides an ideal opportunity for personal change and the chance to take an inner journey and reflect on spiritual needs. This book explores the reasons why we travel, identifies problems we encounter and goals we often set for a trip, and describes how to plan a journey that can inform, enlighten and bring about life changes. An excellent resource for those embarking on their first overseas experience. [ID:2143]

Verge Magazine 📖
Quarterly ➤ Verge Magazine Inc., 1517 B Schutt Road, Palmer Rapids, ON K0J 2E0, Canada, www.vergemagazine.ca, $10.95 for 3 issues; VISA; 613-758-9909, fax 613-758-9914, editor@vergemagazine.ca ◆ Verge is Canada's magazine for people who travel with purpose. Exploring opportunities to work, study, volunteer and travel overseas, Verge Magazine provides tips, expert advice, program profiles and loads of information to send you packing. Broaden your horizons - see the world! (For more information, see their ad in the sponsor section at the end of this guide.) [ID:2843]

CHAPTER 5
Learning a Foreign Language

It should come as no surprise that a good working knowledge of a foreign language is often a prerequisite to landing an overseas job. In fact, the ability to speak a second, third and even fourth language is so important to your international career that it deserves special attention. You can't function effectively in a situation where you are unable to communicate directly with taxi drivers, store clerks, office staff, and perhaps most important of all, your clients. While you needn't engage in complicated debates about world affairs or local politics, you will need to ask simple questions, give instructions, order a meal in a restaurant, introduce yourself or have a friendly conversation.

You'll be of more value to your employer—and gain more from the experience yourself—if you can help bridge the gap between Canada and your host country. This requires, among other things, facility with the local language.

Employment advantages are not the only reason for learning a new language, however. Your effort to speak the local tongue sends out an important message to your hosts. It tells them you have come, not to impose North American customs and standards on them, but to learn about their culture and meet them on their own terms. When you take this approach, you open yourself up to a world of new ideas and attitudes. Certainly your work overseas is important, but so is your chance for enjoyment and personal growth.

THE SECOND LANGUAGE ADVANTAGE

US citizens are fortunate that it is easy to learn and practice Spanish in most areas of the US, given the increasing influence of Spanish-speaking US citizens. Even if you do not go abroad, there are strong incentives to learn Spanish for home use. If you want to launch an international career, US citizens should take advantage of the nation's multilingual strength—its strong links to Spanish culture.

Canadians are particularly fortunate to have the opportunity to learn two important international languages: English and French. The federal government's policy of official bilingualism has strongly influenced Canada's international reputation. After three decades of promoting acquisition of one of our official languages as a second language, many Canadians are now functionally bilingual.

As for other languages, Canadians interested in developing countries tend to focus on Latin America and parts of the Caribbean, where Spanish predominates. As a result, the third most common language used by Canadians abroad is Spanish. In recent times, however, concern for the Pacific Basin has resulted in an increased demand for Asian languages. In other parts of the world, where finding work often hinges on your ability to provide skills to locals, familiarity with less common languages such as Swahili, Arabic, Hungarian or Portuguese can be a real asset.

Even when the languages you are familiar with are not specifically required in a posting, the fact you know them will still impress employers. It suggests you have an aptitude for languages and are open to learning new ones. However, unless you are a translator or interpreter, knowing other languages will not guarantee you an overseas job; your international career must be grounded in technical or professional expertise. Foreign language proficiency is just one of many secondary elements in your total skills inventory, albeit an important one. Such proficiency makes you harder to replace, and thus provides you with greater job security.

LEARNING THE LOCAL LANGUAGE

If you are going to a country where French or English is commonly used (such as Cameroon, Côte d'Ivoire, India, Malaysia, the Netherlands, Nigeria, Togo or the United Kingdom), you can probably get by without learning the local language. In countries where very little English or French is spoken (as in Indonesia, Chile, or Mozambique), you will be in trouble if you can't speak the local language. When you can't communicate with the people around you, you are likely to become frustrated and suffer from feelings of isolation.

Learning a foreign language is not a simple task, and for some people it may seem impossible. However, most of us do, in fact, have the capacity to learn another language. And there's no better place to do this than where the language is spoken.

With a little humility on your part, everyone in your new country is a potential teacher. Whether you're a teacher, engineer, nurse or economist, you will have to set aside your status as the educated foreigner and ask locals to help you say "I need a haircut," or "Do you have this shoe in a larger size?" People will appreciate your efforts and will want to help you. As you open yourself up to learning a new language, you'll find that your effectiveness on the job is enhanced, you'll feel more at home in your new community, and the local people will begin to accept you.

Let's face it, though. Along with all the other demands of cultural adjustment, the stress of learning a new language may be more than some of us can bear. Fear of failure can impair our ability to learn and be more damaging than our inability to speak the new language. If you fall into this category, and decide not to learn the local language, concentrate on becoming involved in the local culture in other ways.

Your experience will be richer, however, if you can greet your hosts in their own tongue and speak at least a few common phrases. So go ahead and try, and don't underestimate the value of your efforts. They demonstrate that you recognize and respect your new country's culture. With that in mind, why not set yourself the goal of learning a few new words or phrases every day?

PRACTICE MAKES PERFECT

Have you wondered why, after a minimum of five years' classroom instruction in French, very few anglophone high school graduates can speak French? Well, the one fundamental truth about learning languages is that formal classroom instruction is not enough.

Learning a second language is not unlike learning your first language. As children, we add new words to our vocabularies as we need them and in this way are able to absorb them. When we come to learn a second language, we quickly find we learn best by carrying out our daily routines and responsibilities in the new language. The tired, old truism, "necessity is the mother of invention" has yet to be proven wrong! Start with the basics, such as exchanging greetings and buying food in the market. As you improve, you'll feel more comfortable with the people and culture around you. You'll quickly be immersed in the local scene by going to restaurants, shopping, attending social events and talking to people on the street. By the same token, if you don't practice every day, you'll find it almost impossible to pick up the new language.

Full summer immersion courses now help Canadians function in their second language in less than three months. Motivation is necessary, of course, but the key is practice, practice, and more practice.

FOUR RULES FOR LEARNING A NEW LANGUAGE

Begin Immediately

When you reach your post, start learning the new language right away. Experience shows that if you put it off, you probably won't get around to it.

Be Humble

Your phrasing will be rudimentary at first, but no matter how awkward you feel, keep at it. Learn to laugh and accept help. People will be delighted with your efforts.

Immerse Yourself

Take every opportunity to speak the language. You cannot learn a second language by memorizing it, so don't spend too much time on books and formal classroom instruction. Concentrate on human interaction. Socialize in your new language. Better yet, why not try living your new life in the new language? Whatever you do, remember that practice is the key, whether you're bartering at the market, participating in local events, or negotiating with bureaucrats.

Listen Carefully

In the beginning you'll understand little of what you hear, but do not tune it out. Study facial expressions and gestures and listen for familiar words. Gradually your comprehension will grow. You might not catch every word, but you'll soon understand the overall ideas.

OTHER PRACTICAL TIPS

While Overseas

Always carry a notebook with you, to record new words and phrases and helpful information. Begin with common phrases, such as greetings, and add a few new words every day. Label every item in your new house in the new language. Put lists of common phrases on your bulletin board or fridge (if you have one!).

Find yourself a tutor. Trying to learn another language without an instructor is like trying to learn to swim without water.

Contact the CANADIAN EMBASSY or HIGH COMMISSION, the US PEACE CORPS or other large foreign institutions in your overseas country. They may offer orientation programs that include language training; they may also be able to assist you with materials and tutors.

Face it—you're not likely to write a great novel in your new language, so just concentrate on being able to carry on a good conversation. And don't become overly stressed about learning the language. Slow down, enjoy yourself!

Before You Leave

Search out the appropriate ethnic communities in your area and participate as much as possible in their events and activities. The more exposure you get to the new language and culture before you leave, the better.

Tape programs in your new language and play them back repeatedly. At first, the dialogue will seem impossibly fast, but you can stop, rewind and listen again. You'll be amazed at what you pick up the second or third time around!

Try to arrange at least 20 to 30 hours of language lessons before you leave home. Listen to language tapes while you drive, on walks, or making dinner.

Read children's books in the new language. The pictures, story lines and simple words will help you learn the basics.

If you have the time, and are able, find a job in your new language environment. Working in a local Japanese or Latin American restaurant, for example, is a great idea. Better yet, try to arrange a job in a restaurant in Québec or France (or Spain, Mexico, or Japan). Or best of all, volunteer with, say, a French NGO in francophone West Africa.

An excellent method for learning French or English is to take a one-year university program in one or the other language. Many large Canadian universities allow you to write your exams in either official language. This means that an anglophone who wants to become more fluent in French could move to Québec City, take classes in French, and still write their essays and exams in English. The International Studies and Modern Languages Program at the University of Ottawa, for example, trains students in both of Canada's official languages and requires students to gain proficiency in at least one other modern language. (For more information on the University of Ottawa, Faculty of Social Sciences, see the sponsor section at the end of this guide. Also, for a description of their international studies programs, see Appendix 15a, "Profiles for Chapter 15: International Studies in Canada" on the CD-ROM.) Other possibilities include taking conversational French classes, attending a French college at an anglophone university or, as mentioned earlier, taking an immersion program.

Learning a Language in Canada

There are numerous public and private schools in Canada that specialize in language training. Consult the *Yellow Pages* under "Schools – Language" for detailed listings, or call your local college or university. If you want information on where to learn French in Canada or abroad, contact CANADIAN PARENTS FOR FRENCH listed in the Resources section below.

A LAST WORD

How you go about learning a foreign language depends on you, and on your destination overseas. If you are just beginning to develop long-term career strategies, your agenda will differ from that of an experienced engineer heading out on his or her third posting. One thing is certain: the more languages you are familiar with, the better you will fare in the international arena. Remember, once in your overseas posting, take advantage of every opportunity to learn about the new culture. Understanding the local language will help you in this process.

APPENDIX ON THE CD-ROM

5a. "Kids Adjusting to a New Language & Culture," by Lori Wolfe

RESOURCES

This chapter contains the following Resources sections: Learning a Foreign Language and Language Careers.

LEARNING A FOREIGN LANGUAGE

While many books on this subject are theoretical, the following have been chosen for those wishing to learn another language on their own. For related resources, consult the "Language Careers" section in this chapter.

Business Chinese 📖
2002 ➤ China Books & Periodicals Inc., 2929 - 24th Street, San Francisco, CA 94110, USA, www.chinabooks.com, $14.95 US; Credit Cards; 415-282-2994, fax 415-282-0994 ◆ This introductory text focuses on learning spoken Chinese for business. Lessons focus on real-life business situations, with exercises and up-to-date business terms. A good primer for a successful business trip. [ID:2480]

Canadian Parents for French 👫
Canadian Parents for French, 176 Gloucester Street, Suite 310, Ottawa, ON K2P 0A6, Canada, www.cpf.ca, 613-235-1481, fax 613-230-5940, cpf@cpf.ca; Fr ◆ This is a national organization that provides excellent information on French second language programs available in Canada and overseas. Their focus is on programs for young Canadians, but they can provide information on adult programs as well. [ID:2342]

Center for Language Acquisition 🖥
http://language.la.psu.edu/index.php ◆ This is the Web site of the Penn State Center for Language Acquisition. It's an excellent site for the links it offers to various technological and linguistic resources organized by language. Links take you to on-line foreign language dictionaries, language-specific search engines and directories, and native language media sites, including television and newspaper. Recommended for linguists! [ID:2266]

China Books & Periodicals Inc. (On-line Catalogue) ▣

China Books & Periodicals Inc., 2929 - 24th Street, San Francisco, CA 94110, USA, www.chinabooks.com, Credit Cards; 415-282-2994, fax 415-282-0994 ◆ Probably the single best source for China-related job-search books. Choose from among hundreds of resources on Chinese language, culture, history, business, arts, literature and living in China. [ID:2035]

Cours de français langue étrangère et stages pour professeurs. Répertoire des centres de formation en France. ◫ ▣

Ministère des Affaires Étrangères Sous-Direction de la politique linguistique et éducative, 153 pages ➤ Service Culturel, Ambassade de France, 464 Wilbrod Street, Ottawa, ON K1N 6M8, Canada, http://culturel.org, Gratuit; 613-238-5711, fax 613-238-7884, ambafr@culturel.org; *Fr* ◆ Ambassade de France à Ottawa : répertoire des centres de formation en France, informations sur le système d'éducation, échanges et cours de français langue étrangère. [ID:2023]

Foreign Language Learning Homepage ▣

www.foreignlanguagehome.com ◆ This German Web site provides free language learning software, in addition to tips for learning new languages and a database where you can search for language schools worldwide. [ID:2769]

French Fun: The Real Spoken Language of Québec ◫

2000, Steve Timmins, 168 pages ➤ John Wiley & Sons, 22 Worcester Road, Etobicoke, ON M9W 1L1, Canada, www.wiley.ca, $14.95 US; Credit Cards; 800-567-4797, fax 800-565-6802, canada@wiley.com ◆ Through lively illustrations, hilarious literal translations and a listing of the most colourful contemporary Quebecois expressions, this book introduces the reader to the rich distinctness of the language of modern Quebec. [ID:2189]

French or Foe? ◫

2003, Polly Platt, 292 pages ➤ Distribooks International, $16.95 US, www.pollyplatt.com ◆ Designed primarily for people who will be living or working in France for extended periods, this book illuminates nuances in the manners, attitudes, and culture of the French people that are helpful to both the international job seeker and the occasional visitor. [ID:2147]

How to Be a More Successful Language Learner ◫

1994, Joan Rubin, Irene Thompson, Heinle & Heinle, 120 pages ➤ Thomson Nelson Canada, 1120 Birchmount Road, Scarborough, ON M1K 5G4, Canada, www.nelson.com, $42.95 CDN; Credit Cards; 800-268-2222, fax 800-430-4445 ◆ Incorporates the contemporary linguistic thought about learner strategies and language learning. [ID:2059]

I Love Languages ▣

www.ilovelanguages.com ◆ I Love Languages is a comprehensive catalogue of language-related Internet resources. The more than 2,000 links at I Love Languages have been hand-reviewed to bring you the best language links the Web has to offer. Whether you're looking for on-line language lessons, translating dictionaries, native literature, translation services, software, language schools, or just a little information on a language you've heard about, I Love Languages can help you in your overseas adventure preparation. [ID:2562]

International Language Schools ⌘

EF International Language Schools, Suite 405, 60 Bloor Street W., Toronto, ON M4W 3B8, Canada, www.ef.com, VISA; 800-387-1463, fax 416-927-8664, ilscan@ef.com ◆ This program offers language courses abroad, in France, Spain, Ecuador, Italy, and Germany, for students and adults of all ability levels. Check out their site for detailed information. [ID:2263]

Japanese for Professionals ◫

1998, Association for Japanese Language Learning, 288 pages ➤ Kodansha International, www.kodansha-intl.com, $34.95 US ◆ A comprehensive course for people who need to use Japanese in business. [ID:2219]

Language Acquisition Made Practical (LAMP) 📖

1989, Elizabeth Brewster, 384 pages ➤ Lingua House, 135 North Oakland Ave., Pasadena, CA 91182, USA, www.instantweb.com/l/linguahouse, $14.95 US; VISA, MC; 626-584-5276 ◆ An excellent book on how to learn a foreign language. This is an easy- and fun-to-use manual that shows you how to learn any language, anywhere—if you live where the language is spoken and are motivated to learn it through involvement with the people. LAMP is a methodology involving a Daily Learning Cycle, with ideas of learning activities you can do, step by step, each day. An accompanying audio cassette tape explicitly demonstrates all these activities. It is loaded with ideas that can lead you to full professional competence in the new language. [ID:2057]

Language Resource Center, American University ♔

www.american.edu/academic.depts/cas/lfs/lrc/home.HTML ◆ This Web site is the home page of American University's Language Resource Center. Boasts an excellent links page portal to resources for learning languages, such as on-line newspapers, dictionaries, news groups, cultural studies and job sites. [ID:2264]

Self-Guided Language Courses: The Foundations and Breakthrough Series 📖

2004, Brian Hill, 256 pages + cassette ➤ Palgrave Macmillan, 175 Fifth Ave., New York, NY 10010, USA, www.palgrave-usa.com, £39.99-£59.99; Credit Cards; 212-982-3900, fax 212-777-6359; ℱr ◆ This excellent series offers cost-effective ways to acquire a second language quickly. Working through these self-guided books is a great way to develop a base you can build upon when you immerse yourself later. There's also lots of invaluable cultural knowledge in the books that'll actually stick, because you learn it along with the language. Both series are available in different media depending on your preferences. Available only for the major European languages: French, German, Italian and Spanish. [ID:2211]

Spanish Study Holidays 💻

www.spanishstudyholidays.co.uk ◆ Gain overseas travel experience and learn Spanish. [ID:2773]

Teach Yourself Series 📖

Annual, 320 pages + cassette ➤ International Sales Dept., Teach Yourself, Bookpoint, Bldg. 130, Milton Park, Abingdon, OX14 4SB, UK, www.teachyourself.co.uk, $15-$35 US; (44) (0) (1235) 40-0573, fax 01235-861038 ◆ Excellent crash courses for language beginners. Covering almost any language you can think of, from Afrikaans to Zulu, this series will have the book you need for an excellent working knowledge of the local language of your overseas posting. Well written and easy to use, these courses are among the best on the market. Highly recommended. Find them at your local bookseller. [ID:2212]

Total Physical Response 💻

www.tpr-world.com ◆ Total Physical Response (TPR), created by Dr. James J. Asher, is a stress-free approach to acquiring another language. Based in California, TPR's Web site offers details about the organization, comments from around the world, an on-line bookstore and ordering information. [ID:2290]

LANGUAGE CAREERS

The following is a smattering of the many resources available for linguists, translators and interpreters looking to use their talents overseas. For advice on teaching English overseas, consult Chapter 29, Teaching Abroad.

Bilingual-Jobs.Com 💻

www.bilingual-jobs.com ◆ This free Internet job directory is especially designed for English-speaking job hunters with fluency in a second language. Allows you to search jobs by language and location. [ID:2235]

Careers in Foreign Languages 📖

2001, Blythe Camenson, 256 pages ➤ Chapters Indigo Books, www.chapters.indigo.ca, $21.95 CDN; Credit Cards ◆ Both first-time job hunters and those looking to change careers will benefit from exploring the rewarding paths outlined in this US book. Includes detailed overviews of careers in the field of foreign languages, outlines job options and shows how to plan and prepare for a successful career using your foreign language skills. [ID:2767]

European Personnel Selection Office 🖥

http://europa.eu.int/epso/competitions/news_en.cfm ◆ EPSO organizes open competitions in various fields to select personnel for various European institutions. Lots of jobs for linguists, administrators, clerical assistants and skilled employees. Citizenship requirements are clearly indicated in job descriptions and competition timetables. [ID:2665]

LatPro 🖥

www.LatPro.com ◆ Lat Pro is a job board for employees bilingual in English and Spanish or Portugese. There are international and US-based jobs and company listings which can be searched by profession and location. The site contains great resources including immigration information and links to sites in other countries for local news, magazines, recruiters and search engines. Bonus: the site offers free subscriptions to over 70 engineering publications! [ID:2824]

multilingualvacancies.com 🖥

www.multilingualvacancies.com ◆ Focused on multilingual jobs in Europe, this Web site links job seekers with employers from across the continent. Job seekers can search for openings via language, location and industry. The site also maintains a small directory of companies and a notice board where users can post their details. [ID:2768]

Ohio State University: Careers In Foreign Languages 🖥

www.flc.ohio-state.edu/FLC_pages/careers_website ◆ This helpful US Web site includes information for job seekers with foreign language skills. Breaking resources down by job category, you can find links relating to language careers in education, business, travel and tourism, law, media and much more. It also includes a section with tips for conducting job searches and resume and cover letter writing. [ID:2766]

The Translator's Handbook 📖

2002, 500 pages ➤ Schreiber Publishing, P.O. Box 4193, Rockville, MD 20849, USA, www.schreiberpublishing.com, $35.95 US; VISA, MC; 800-822-3213, fax 301-424-2336 ◆ This US book is a resource for translators and for anyone who is interested in joining the field. The fourth edition includes nearly 500 pages of essential information covering topics such career options, how to freelance, translator education (in the US) and translation techniques. [ID:2781]

CHAPTER 6

Women Living & Working Overseas

International professional opportunities for women have never been better. With fewer formal and informal barriers, women are receiving recognition internationally as decision-makers, managers, and policy-makers. No longer is a woman overseas simply viewed as "the wife" or the "trailing spouse" of her working partner.

This chapter is written for the professional woman already established in her international career and for the woman just beginning to explore the endless international possibilities that promise to open up a global career. It explores the benefits and disadvantages facing women managers, examines the best employers for women, describes the academic credentials and skills required in today's work environment and provides tips on how to work effectively in an overseas environment while keeping yourself healthy, safe and sane.

WOMEN AS MANAGERS

Professional women face many challenges in the overseas job market. Although women have made considerable inroads on international assignments, and they currently assume positions of authority in governmental, non-governmental and international organizations, their actual numbers, especially in the private sector, remain significantly lower than men's. Studies on women expatriates conducted within the past five years reveal that organizations still assume that women are not interested in working overseas and that they do not want to become international managers. This research also shows that organizations continue to believe that women are not well received or respected by foreign hosts, suggesting that women might not be successful overseas. Fortunately, these false and outdated perceptions are slowly being outweighed by success stories that prove otherwise.

While it is true that in some countries professional women abroad are treated differently than their male counterparts, cross-cultural experts say that foreign prejudice is exaggerated. It is often more a product of the minds of North Americans at office headquarters than the reality of women working overseas. Expatriate women are viewed as foreigners, and repressive standards that control local women are often not applicable—although there are some exceptions, as in Saudi Arabia. In fact, being a woman in some cases can prove to be an advantage, especially in Asian countries. Women tend to possess personal characteristics that positively affect their overseas assignments, such as being flexible and adaptable as well as sensitive and empathetic with a heightened awareness of nonverbal communication. These are all essential skills that are needed for survival in a different culture and that will assist in fostering cross-cultural relationships. Women bring these skills to their work in ways that help them succeed in new cultures.

Women have proven themselves to be extremely competent overseas. In fact, a 1990 CANADIAN INTERNATIONAL DEVELOPMENT AGENCY (CIDA) study shows women rated higher than men on many of the skills and attitudes associated with overseas effectiveness. Major differences include the following:

- Women are generally less concerned about status and advancement, while men tend to place great value on upward mobility.

- Prior to departure, women express a greater desire for contact with the local culture, and while overseas they are more involved in the culture.

- Women place more value on and devote more time to learning the local language.

- Women express more liberal attitudes toward development and are seen by peers as more caring of others.

In some cultures you will be given immediate respect because you are a woman, the assumption being that if your employer sent a woman in a "man's" place, you must be the best. This is true, to some degree. The women who preceded you had to be the best of the best just to get there!

In addition, because there are so few professional women overseas, the ones who are there tend to be highly visible. This can be an advantage if you are in sales, marketing or business negotiations, or if you are simply trying to get your foot in the door. Chances are you will be better remembered than your male counterpart.

It cannot be ignored that females working abroad have unique difficulties with foreign colleagues and clients. To ease cultural tensions, women managers are often required to renounce some of their authority. An international development officer in charge of aid programs in Bangladesh realized soon after being posted there that she would have to relinquish much of her command in meetings and negotiations. The male government officials and male villagers refused to take instructions from a woman. They dealt instead with her male subordinates.

One woman manager deals with this problem by strategizing with her male North American colleagues prior to any meeting with foreign clients. In order for her to appear as non-threatening as possible, they divide up the agenda so that all members seem equal. This exercise helps the foreign client feel more at ease and, in addition, sensitizes her male North American colleagues to the problem. Criticism from them could be disastrous as the foreign client might be waiting for any excuse to discredit her.

How successful a woman is overseas can therefore depend a great deal on how much support she is provided by her home organization. Foreign colleagues and clients might at first be confused about her status and role. Will she do the same job as her male predecessor? What is her level of authority? If her position is backed by her organization, she will have the necessary authority to properly carry out her responsibilities. If, on the other hand, her company limits her professional opportunities by restricting, for example, the scope of her job or the extent of her travel, or by criticizing her openly, she will lose credibility.

Despite some of the difficulties faced by women managers, an overseas posting provides most with opportunities they would not normally have in Canada. Many state that they are given greater responsibility in their work, receive better work experience and are promoted faster.

THE BEST EMPLOYERS

Economics, information technology, law, business, marketing, engineering and science are all growth areas in which women are increasingly finding international employment. The technology industry has created an information explosion, opening up a plethora of jobs around the world for programmers, software designers and other highly computer-literate individuals.

Financial service firms such as banks and insurance companies have branch offices or subsidiary operations abroad and send many women overseas. These organizations generally have policies and practices to provide equal opportunity for women. Free trade and globalization have also been boons to the fields of advertising, publishing, market research and sales. In addition, human resource development with an emphasis on cross-cultural training is a high-growth area, and one favoured by women.

Many women are attracted to the field of international consulting because it offers a flexible working environment. Contracts are short-term, with international travel usually lasting less than a month at a time; much consulting work can be done out of the home. The number of women involved in consulting work has increased dramatically in the last few years.

Government and other international organizations are offering women the chance to advance in their international careers through equal opportunity employment policies. In addition, affirmative action policies are in place in many organizations. The UNITED NATIONS, for example, is attempting to reach an equal gender representation for professional and high-level positions. In the 1990s, women accounted for approximately 35 per cent of staff in the professional category. CIDA is aiming for increased representation and distribution of women in its workforce. In the late 1990s, women accounted for 41 per cent of the agency's total professional staff at headquarters and 32 per cent of the professionals on field postings.

However, a difference still exists between men and women in earning and promotion practices. For example, in the late 1990s, women made up only 17 per cent of the executive category at CIDA and 15 per cent in the high-level categories at the UN.

Many organizations with gender and development policy concerns look for employees who, along with an area of expertise, are sensitive to gender issues. The UN has a number of agencies with active women in development programs. In addition, the UN has a number of women's organizations that report on social and economic issues affecting women. They include the UNITED NATIONS INTER-

NATIONAL RESEARCH AND TRAINING INSTITUTE FOR THE ADVANCEMENT OF WOMEN (INSTRAW). Main projects include credit, data on the informal sector, statistics, environment, and financial and institutional arrangements for women. Another UN women's organization is UNITED NATIONS DEVELOPMENT FUND FOR WOMEN (UNIFEM). Its main programs include development projects addressing women's issues, especially water, sanitation and agriculture projects. (For more information, see Chapter 41, United Nations and Other IGOs.)

ACADEMIC CREDENTIALS AND SKILLS

To advance in your international career, you must have the necessary academic credentials and skills. According to Nancy Adler, in her book *Competitive Frontiers*, a survey of expatriate women managers revealed that almost all held graduate degrees (MBAs being the most common), had extensive international interests and experience, and spoke, on average, two or three languages.

Without appropriate academic credentials, it is very difficult to progress in your career. In the past, women went overseas as nurses or healthcare workers, teachers or administrators and, after several postings, advanced into positions managing field programs. Today, this way of getting ahead is much less common and not nearly as profitable.

NETWORKING

Networking is a means of gaining important business information. Informal networking most commonly takes place after work, over a few drinks, or during business socializing. Formal networking takes place in business seminars or conferences.

This traditional type of "old boys" network can be closed to women due to responsibilities at home, or simply because they are excluded due to their gender. As a woman, foreigner or not, there is a good chance your overseas male colleagues will exclude you from their network. The nature and location of the networking session (such as golf at a men's club) often leave women out of the loop.

Women have developed their own type of networking in which information is shared, issues common to women are discussed, and careers are supported. It normally occurs through professional organizations and local women's groups, or during sports, arts, cultural or children's events.

Studies have shown, however, that for women to advance in their careers, they must network with *both* men and women. The challenge both for employees (men and women) and for organizations is to facilitate this type of networking so that it is effective for everyone involved.

Mentoring is another way to gain support in your career and social development. Having an alliance with a role model can provide greater job mobility and recognition and ultimately assist you in breaking into both male and female networks.

FAMILY MATTERS

Spousal satisfaction and overall family concerns have consistently been documented as the greatest cause of international assignment failure for both men and women. Overseas postings where little is offered in the way of spousal support and assistance can leave you with more challenges than you bargained for. Make sure to look into your organization's career support services for your spouse and children when you decide to go; there are many ways to ensure a more satisfied and better-adjusted family. (For more information on relocating your spouse and children, see Robin Pascoe's article, "Moving Your Marriage" in Appendix 3b, and Lori Wolfe's article, "Kids Adjusting to a New Language & Culture" in Appendix 5a on the CD-ROM.)

YOUR SOCIAL LIFE

An overseas posting is a great opportunity to meet a wide variety of people. Within the expatriate community, friends are made quickly because, like yourself, everyone is there for a short period of time and is receptive to meeting new people. If you are open to and accepting of the local culture, you will be embraced by your hosts. The unfortunate side of many overseas friendships is that they are often temporary. People come and go and you often lose contact with people you were once close to.

It is important to understand the social etiquette of the local culture in which you are living. In some countries, social protocol calls for the segregation of women and men, and in others it is forbidden to consume alcohol in public or eat with your left hand. Depending on the country and your host, rules can sometimes be bent, but often they are unavoidable. If you are in such a situation, don't fight it. It is important to respect the local customs.

You will find that, overseas, more of your free time must be given to business-related social events. Remember, business entertaining abroad is like business entertaining at home in the sense that you cannot truly relax or let your guard down. You should avoid giving too much personal information about yourself, even if you are urged to do so. What you might consider very normal, such as having a boyfriend or drinking alcohol, is often shocking to people in other cultures.

In social situations, professional women are often assumed to be dependent spouses. This is to be expected, however, as many Western women overseas *are* wives of working male expatriates.

You might suffer resentment from local women envious of your freedom to travel without your husband's or father's permission, or to pursue a professional career. North American women are often viewed as overly independent and you may also be resented out of fear that you will impose your Western feminism.

For single women, an overseas posting can be a lot of fun and a time to meet many interesting people. Within the diplomatic circle, however, there tends to be a focus on couples and families, and being a single woman can be socially awkward and at times extremely isolating. Special effort to socialize within this circle is required as it is much harder for single women to socialize alone without any stigma placed upon them. Some local cultures will look upon you with pity if you are unmarried. They will perceive you as a woman who is working because you cannot attract a marriage partner. Some single women on overseas assignments invent husbands or fiancés to avoid comments about their single status.

Expect less freedom and privacy on an overseas posting. Complete strangers may accost you with personal questions or may ridicule you as you walk by. You will be stared at, or even pinched, on the street. "I can't go anywhere without getting bothered" is the lament of one expatriate woman living in West Africa. Experienced women travellers state that it is important not to be paralyzed by this attention. A Canadian woman had this response for the forward men of the Ivory Coast who frequently asked, "When are you going to go to bed with me?" Her comic reply, "The day it rains frogs!" defused the situation through laughter.

WHAT TO WEAR

Many countries put great emphasis on appearance, especially for women. No matter how polite you are, if your dress offends, chances are you will be ignored or mistreated. It is therefore very important to dress according to the culture and weather conditions of your host country. If you are working in the Middle East, it is wise to avoid body-hugging clothes, T-shirts and shorts. Some Muslim countries have such strict dress codes that failure to comply can result in deportation. A brochure at a hotel in Saudi Arabia advises that "Women shall wear long dresses with long sleeves. Men shall not wear open shirts, tight trousers or chains."

Another reason to minimize your sexuality with regard to dress and conduct is because people in foreign countries invariably carry stereotypes and misconceptions of Westerners, particularly women. This is often fuelled by pornography. You may find yourself being observed to see if you fit the stereotypes. It is in your best interest to dress conservatively!

Buy good quality clothes that are easy to care for. Do not take clothes that require dry-cleaning. Your best choice in hot climates is cotton, silk or linen blends. Synthetic fabrics may not wrinkle but they retain heat. Cotton underwear and bras are essential in the tropics. For shorter trips, take silk/cotton combination blouses that can be washed in hotel sinks and hung to dry. A small travel iron can be useful. Many women swear by long, wide cotton skirts which are cool, comfortable and convenient.

HEALTH IN BRIEF

Health concerns and considerations in developing countries are not specifically gender-based. Although immunizations, vaccines and thorough medical examinations should be part of anyone's pre-departure preparations, women must be aware that there may be no diagnostic facilities and a limited range of treatment options available overseas. In the areas of reproductive technology, diagnosis of breast cancer and endometriosis, treatment of recurrent vaginal infections, alternative birth control methods, and complications arising out of pregnancy, there may be few facilities and resources.

Medical care abroad is often at odds with Canadian standards. For this reason, seek out country-specific information before leaving Canada. Contact organizations and clinics that specialize in tropical medicine and request current material on the status of health care in the countries where you will be travelling. If you require medical treatments in a developing country, be very selective and ensure that the hygienic standards are acceptable.

Consult your family physician before departing. Your doctor should be informed of your travels in the event that you require ongoing medication or immediate access to your health records while you are overseas.

If you require medication, it is wise to buy it in Canada before you leave or to have it sent to you. Prescription drugs are available over the counter in developing countries at greatly reduced prices, but pharmaceutical standards for drugs vary from country to country. In addition, your doctor can explain side-effects and recommend precise dosages. Self-diagnosis can create further problems; for example, yeast infections can be caused by taking high doses of antibiotics.

Prepare a customized health kit according to your destination. It needn't be elaborate, but should include feminine hygiene products such as tampons, which can be hard to purchase or outrageously expensive overseas. Treatments for yeast and urinary track infections are essential, as many women are prone to infection while in the tropics. If you use over-the-counter medications for colds and flu, pack these as well. Take a good supply of contraceptives with you. Many countries now manufacture their own but the quality of condoms and birth control pills can be substandard.

Keep in mind that many developing countries have high incidences of HIV, the virus that leads to AIDS. It is important to protect yourself from infection by ensuring that only new needles are used when you require an injection, and that you practice safe sex, which includes the use of condoms. (For more information on health-related issues, see the Health Overseas Resources at the end of Chapter 3, Living Overseas.)

SAFETY TIPS

The following are a few tips to bear in mind while living and travelling overseas.

- Be alert. Remember, you are in a foreign country and do not fully understand the culture. It is best to remain vigilant and aware of your surroundings at all times.

- Avoid speaking loudly in English. Unfortunately, the stereotype of the loud obnoxious North American is still alive around the world. Speaking English is often associated with having money and might identify you as a potential target.

- Avoid walking alone. When you don't have an alternative, walk purposefully on well-travelled streets or walk in the middle of the road rather than on the sidewalk.

- Avoid walking the streets after dark. In some places it is unsafe, even in a group.

- Avoid isolated areas such as beaches and parking lots. Don't go to bars alone.

- Avoid pulling out a map and looking lost. Always make sure you know where you are going and map out your travels ahead of time.

- Don't wear flashy jewellery on the street. In some areas, even an inexpensive watch should be kept in your pocket.

- Ensure your valuables are safely stored. Carry them only when necessary and use a money belt. Hotel safes are not always the safest! And don't leave jewellery and money out for maids or household help to be tempted by.

- Ensure hotel windows and doors are secure. For extra protection, put a stopper in windows or sliding doors. Portable door alarms can be great to have on hand.

- Don't invite strangers into your hotel room or give your address and phone number too readily to someone you've just met.

- Use an established taxi company, especially if you are riding alone. Don't be afraid to turn down a taxi driver if you do not feel comfortable. Always make sure the meter is running.

- Keep your car doors locked and windows up when driving in crowded streets. In some countries, thieves will reach into an open car window and grab your purse, necklace or earrings.

- Depending on the country of posting, your single status may imply that you are an easy mark. It is not uncommon for single women to invent a spouse or fiancé. Some single women find wearing a wedding ring cuts down on harassment.

- Most importantly, use your common sense. Exercise all the safety precautions you use at home, with added prudence.

If you are harassed, be assertive—say "no" or "leave me alone." Don't be afraid to ask for help. To remove yourself from dangerous situations, go into a store or office building. If need be, shout or yell. If you are mugged, hand over your possessions. They are not worth your life.

A LAST WORD

There are tremendous professional and personal rewards for women working internationally. Professionally, you will be given greater responsibilities and put on the "fast track" in your career. Personally, you will gain a unique, and humbling, insight into other cultures.

It is important to remember when working overseas that you can be accepted and can succeed as a professional simply by showing competence and professionalism. Often in male-dominated societies, it is important to respect the positions of local men and women in their culture, including their notions of feminism. Remember, many men aren't used to working with women, especially a woman boss!

A woman manager from Telecom worked out her approach long ago. She plays both sides. She lets businessmen in any culture know that she expects to be treated like anyone else there on business, but she also creates a comfort level by abiding by their customs whenever possible. For example, at an evening reception in India, she noticed that women were moving to one side and congregating there, while the men were moving to another side to talk business. She spent an appropriate amount of time networking with the men and then moved over to the women. In this way she acknowledged the barriers that exist, and showed her respect for the way they do things, but also demonstrated that she had broken through them enough to get her business done.

RESOURCES

WOMEN LIVING & WORKING OVERSEAS

Most international job search books have sections on the special concerns of women living and working in cross-cultural environments. There are now a number of Web sites dedicated exclusively to this topic. Our short list deals with resources specifically focused on the issues facing women living and working overseas. For references more broadly related to women living and working overseas, see also the Children & Families Overseas Resources in Chapter 3, Living Overseas.

Association for Women's Rights in Development (AWID) ⚏

www.awid.org/jobs ◆ Each week a list of job openings around the world is posted on AWID's "Resource Net" e-mail digest. Click the "Find a Job" link and browse opportunities by viewing the "Resource Net" issues. As the name of the resource indicates, the jobs are focused on women's human rights and gender issues. An excellent collection of overseas jobs for those interested in this field. [ID:2584]

Competitive Frontiers: Women Managers in a Global Economy 📖

1994, Nancy J. Adler, Dafna Izraeli, 414 pages ➤ Blackwell Publishers, 350 Main Street, Malden, MB 02148, USA, www.blackwell.com, $55.95 US; Credit Cards; 781-288-8200, fax 781-338-8210, mbarilla@bos.blackwellpublishing.com ◆ This book examines the changing nature of world business and its impact on women managers. [ID:2134]

Culture Shock! A Wife's Guide 📖

2002, Robin Pascoe, 212 pages ➤ Graphic Arts Center Publishing Company, 3019 NW Yeon, Portland, OR 97210, USA, www.gacpc.com, $13.95 US; 503-226-2402, fax 503-223-1410 ◆ Written by a Canadian, the book is easy to read, and provides useful advice for the wife going overseas for the first time, especially if her husband is with Foreign Affairs or an international agency. Chapters on maids, entertaining and home leave may be off-putting, but after you've lived in Pascoe's shoes, they may seem pertinent. Has a useful chapter on getting a job or freelancing overseas. [ID:2085]

Directory of Financial Aids for Women 2003-2005 📖

2003, 580 pages ➤ Reference Service Press, Suite 4, 5000 Windplay Drive, El Dorado Hills, CA 95762, USA, www.rspfunding.com, $45 US; Credit Cards; 916-939-9620, fax 916-939-9626, fiindaid@aol.com ◆ This US resource details nearly 1,600 funding programs—representing billions of dollars in financial aid set aside specifically for women who are interested in areas such as athletics, engineering, chemistry and biological sciences. Includes an annotated bibliography of the key directories that identify even more financial-aid opportunities and a set of indexes that let you search the directory by program title, sponsoring organization, geographic coverage, subject field and application deadline. [ID:2539]

Doing Business with Japanese Men: A Woman's Handbook 📖

1993, Christalyn Brannen, Tracey Wilen, 176 pages ➤ Stone Bridge Press, P.O. Box 8202, Berkeley, CA 94707, USA, www.stonebridge.com, $9.95 US; Credit Cards; 800-947-7271, fax 510-524-8711 ◆ One of the only books that looks at the uniquely delicate situation that confronts the Western businesswoman, whether she is travelling to Japan or meeting Japanese clients at her home office. Includes practical discussions, background, do's and don'ts of decorum and seating charts etc. [ID:2107]

Do's and Taboos Around the World for Women in International Business 📖

1997, Roger E. Axtell, 272 pages ➤ John Wiley & Sons, 22 Worcester Road, Etobicoke, ON M9W 1L1, Canada, www.wiley.ca, $19.95 CDN; Credit Cards; 800-567-4797, fax 800-565-6802, canada@wiley.com ◆ Draws on experiences of 100 women to offer advice on body language, health concerns, dress, balancing family life with work abroad, and more. [ID:2218]

Graveyard For Dreamers: One Woman's Odyssey in Africa 📖

2002, Joan Baxter, 224 pages ➤ Potter's Field Press, 83 Leslie Road, East Lawrencetown, NS B2Z 18P, USA, www.pottersfieldpress.com, $16.95 CDN; VISA; 800-646-2879, fax 888-253-3133 ◆ A Canadian's personal and colourful account of living, travelling and reporting on coups and customs in seven West African countries. Baxter grew up in Nova Scotia and lived in four West African countries. A well-written and entertaining read. [ID:2293]

International Centre for Research on Women ⋔

www.icrw.org ◆ ICRW is a US NGO with a mission to improve the lives of women in poverty, advance women's equality and human rights and contribute to the broader economic and social well-being of women. This Web site contains an excellent collection of resources on gender issues, human rights and development. Join on-line discussion forums and share your thoughts with others interested in these issues. Highly recommended! [ID:2225]

A Journey of One's Own: Uncommon Advice for the Independent Woman Traveler 📖
2003, Thalia Zepatos, 268 pages ➤ The Eighth Mountain Press, 624 SE 29th Ave., Portland, OR
97214, USA, $14.95 US; Cheque; 503-233-3936, fax 503-233-0774, www.amazon.com ◆ A great
compilation of personal travel essays by women, interspersed with chapters on practical matters
such as travelling alone, finding a compatible travel companion, planning an itinerary, sexual
harassment, and staying safe and healthy. Includes a list of resources that covers a variety of topics,
from travel books and magazines to Internet service providers and socially/environmentally
responsible travel opportunities. [ID:2190]

Journeywoman 💻
www.journeywoman.com ◆ Finally, an on-line travel resource just for women! This Canadian site
has a mandate to inspire women to travel safely and well, and to connect with each other
internationally. Though it's not very graphically appealing, you'll find resources on just about any
topic related to women travelling. In particular, it shines in providing helpful information and tips
on travel planning, recommendations for restaurants and accommodations abroad. Of special note
are the sincere travel stories from women contributors who've gone their own way. Keep connected
by signing up for a monthly on-line newsletter. If you're really into it, follow the link to
HERmail.net, where you can access secure Web-based e-mail services that allow women to connect
and swap travel stories and information from anywhere on the planet. [ID:2751]

They Only Laughed Later 📖
1997, 216 pages ➤ Europublic SA/NV, P.O. Box 504, Uccle 5, Brussels, B-1180, Belgium,
www.europublic.com, €14.95; VISA, MC; (32) (0) 2-343-77-26, fax (32) (0) 2-343-93-30 ◆ This
collection of essays is the product of a series of "Women On the Move" conferences, which brought
together expatriate women from over 20 countries. Their concerns were mutual: to share
experiences in meeting the challenges that confront women who move to strange lands in pursuit of
their own or their husbands' careers. A fabulous account of the unique perspectives of women living
and working overseas. [ID:2552]

Women in Management Worldwide: Facts, Figures and Analysis 📖
2004, 370 pages ➤ Ashgate Publishing Company, Suite 420, 101 Cherry Street, Burlington, VT
05401-4405, USA, www.ashgate.com, $89.95 US; Credit Cards; 802-865-7641, fax 802-865-7847
◆ A genuinely cross-cultural assessment of women's progress in management throughout the world.
Each chapter of the book focuses on one of twenty countries worldwide. Chapters follow the same
format, so direct comparisons are easy. Key issues arising from the statistics are discussed, trends
analyzed and best practices recommended. An informative and essential sourcebook for
international job seekers concerned about the progress of women in this field. [ID:2527]

CHAPTER 7

The Canadian Identity in the International Workplace

Imagine arriving at the New Delhi office of a senior Indian executive for an appointment and finding him surrounded by relatives. Or, weeks after completing what seemed to be very successful verbal negotiations with a Malaysian businesswoman, you still have not received a contract. Or, consider the West African businessman caught by surprise when you actually show up on his doorstep in response to his dinner invitation. Each of these situations points to a clash between your Canadian culture-bound attitudes about business relations and the attitudes of those from other countries.

From culture to culture there exists a wide range of attitudes about appropriate business practices. To succeed in a cross-cultural work environment, we must be aware of our own culturally based business practices and acknowledge that each of us brings our own cultural baggage along on overseas assignments. The more aware we are, the more successful our overseas assignments will be. How do we as Canadians think in the workplace? How do our practices fit with those of other cultures? Any seasoned international employee will tell you this knowledge is crucial to success in the international realm.

"It is essential to understand the cultural dimensions of the environment in which you want to work. I have found it useful to explain to my Moroccan business associates some Canadian cultural characteristics, in particular those of Canadian business people. They then have a better understanding of where I am coming from and why I react in certain ways. It takes time, but I find it helpful."

This chapter deals with the most common culturally influenced behaviours of Canadians in business situations. We include quotes from senior international consultants who reveal how these behavioural traits clash in the vastly different business cultures of other countries.

109

Generalizing about Canada's cultural business practices is difficult as we are a country with a complex cultural mosaic and an increasingly rich ethnic diversity. While recognizing our cultural diversity, we do acknowledge that there are some dominant cultural practices in Canada. It is therefore the premise of this chapter that whether you are a Jewish Torontonian or an outport Newfoundlander, your work habits and attitudes toward business protocol will likely bear some similarity. We will attempt to describe these similarities and explore their relevance to a cross-cultural, overseas employment framework.

HOW ARE WE PERCEIVED ABROAD?

Canadians have forged a good reputation in the international workplace. We are seen as non-threatening and known as generous aid-givers throughout the developing world. We are recognized worldwide as international peacekeepers who promote a standard of fairness. The fact that we have neither invaded, nor attempted to colonize, other countries is an important factor in how we are perceived internationally.

Thanks to our multicultural heritage, we are known to have an affinity with other ethnically diverse nations. We tend to be a little more conservative than our US or European counterparts. We are often seen as self-deprecating, which contrasts with the boastfulness attributed to Americans.

The Canadians who preceded you to your foreign destination have probably helped to optimize the reception you will receive when you step off the plane. We hope this chapter will help you to maintain, and indeed improve upon, Canada's already solid international image.

OUR GENERAL ATTITUDE TOWARD WORK

The following is an attempt to analyze the Canadian work ethic. Quotes from international consultants will help situate the various elements in a cross-cultural work context.

Goal-Oriented and Hard-Working

Canadians tend to be goal-oriented and to place high value on achievement, both in our professional and personal lives. This is evident in our respect for hard work and commitment to a given task. We believe hard work will bring reward, and if financial recognition is not immediately forthcoming, our work is nonetheless worthy of respect.

We tend to value organizational skills and a goal-oriented, orderly work style. We greatly value timeliness, efficiency and progress. Even in leisure time many of us pursue a hobby or personal interest with similar concentration, setting goals and aiming for a certain level of competence.

"I once read in a magazine that a birdwatchers' association was organizing a weekend trip, during which a contest would be held. The prize would go to the person with the highest number of bird sightings! Even while we enjoy nature, we feel the need for concrete achievement."

We value upward mobility, self-improvement and professional success attained through discipline, hard work and playing by the rules. We tend to be action-oriented, "doers" rather than "thinkers," so concerned are we with tangible evidence of work having been performed. Canadians are so committed to this pursuit of concrete results that recent surveys show a large number of us feel we neglect our personal lives for our careers. Even in social situations conversation revolves around what we do for a living, and our social status is, to a large extent, determined by the positions we hold.

"I, as a Canadian, have worked hard all my life—literally day in and day out. I am now married to a Pakistani and living in an extended family in Pakistan. Almost all disagreements stem from my work habits, as I am still work-driven and do not allow myself time to enjoy my life and my family. We Canadians are like robots when it comes to relaxing and enjoying what life offers."

As a consequence, Canadians overseas tend not to put enough energy into developing personal relationships with business colleagues, which in many cultures must precede going after results. In fact, we are sometimes perceived as pushy in our determination to complete our tasks. By not establishing trust with our overseas partners through personal relationships, many Canadians have also proven ineffectual in their work.

"In talking with my Indian counterpart about key elements for a briefing to Canadian contractors on establishing partnerships in India, my counterpart emphasized the following: 'business people in Canada must recognize that they are task-oriented while we Indians are relationship-oriented. Canadians need first to relax their task orientation in order to build the trust that is the foundation of a good working relationship in India. The task will follow in its own good time.

"When I first started doing business in Morocco, I was impatient with my partner because he wanted me to spend more time socializing with his family than discussing our joint venture. I came to realize, however, that, in his view, getting to know me and having me get to know him and his family was a pre-condition to doing business. After I accepted this, things moved along just fine!"

Law-Abiding

Canadians' ethical and moral values tend to be conservative and, as peace lovers, we are, mostly, a law-abiding nation. We draw a rather hard line between right and wrong and are not easily swayed from our judgments. This makes it difficult for Canadians to accept different sets of values in other countries. For instance, hiring a close relative is a common and even desirable practice in many countries, but is regarded as a serious impropriety (nepotism) by many Canadians.

"As a participant on a committee reviewing applications to bring exchange students from an Asian country to Canada, we were concerned that our Asian counterparts were recommending a work colleague. Our high moral ground seemed clear until someone pointed out that two of our own committee members were related, and one of us had just arranged to have a relative's tree nursery business take a foreign student. We realized that we looked upon our own initiatives as generous and appropriate while regarding with suspicion similar decisions made by the overseas selection committee!"

Corruption in the business place is considered a part of normal business operations in many countries. Bribes often account for one-third of the value of a contract and fall directly into civil servants' pockets. When you work in a developing country, sooner or later you will face the dilemma of giving into corruption or not. Canadian business people are uncomfortable with some foreign business practices and will often walk away from a deal rather than pay a bribe. Business people from other countries consider us naive. There are many platitudes and excuses offered for corruption, but no matter how it is presented, or who is involved, we agree with the following experts: corruption is wrong.

"It is possible to live and do business abroad without getting involved in corruption. Not condoning or becoming involved does not make us naive. There are always ways around it. It may come as a surprise that in an institutional culture where corruption seems pervasive, most people find it just as distasteful as you or I, but have learned to work around it.

"By paying your first bribe, you can get caught in a spiral of corruption from which it is difficult to escape. I once paid a bribe to the downtown traffic cops, though I had been stopped for dubious reasons. Since I was late for a meeting, I decided to slip the officer a few bills rather than take the time to argue. From that day on, I had to pay a bribe each time I crossed the city business district. The only way out was to call their bluff and insist on being arrested. After that I was no longer bothered, and have learned an important lesson on bribery."

Separate Work and Personal Lives

As Canadians, we make a clear distinction between our professional and personal lives. We carefully protect our privacy and keep our work life separate from our home life. Interruptions at work by friends or family members are generally frowned upon. It is also common to disapprove of a colleague who uses office time to deal with family matters. In other cultures the interaction between personal and professional life flows far more naturally. Canadians posted in countries where such behaviour is the cultural norm have identified this lack of separation as a major source of stress, mostly because they use a lot of energy trying to maintain their own barriers.

"I volunteered to help develop a business plan for a dynamic Somali immigrant to Canada who had started up a professional-looking community newspaper. Despite the long volunteer hours he put in, and the obvious benefits of his work to the Somali community, I felt uncomfortable when I realized he was using his volunteer work to help start up his own graphic design business. Everyone benefited from this young man's initiative, so why the mistrust? It really struck me how much Canadians mistrust crossovers from work, volunteer activities and family, not to mention religion or politics. Canadians segment everything. Integrated spheres of activity are suspect.

"I had a very close African friend who was also a senior government official. Whenever I visited him at his house, it seemed like he was holding court, as there were always people waiting to see him. When I asked how he could put up with his personal life being so disrupted, he stated that he gathered more support for his programs at home than at his office, but most importantly, this was expected from an official at his level."

We also avoid doing business with friends or relatives for fear of ruining our personal relationships or creating conflicts of interest.

"As a project manager on an African assignment, I was very wary of engaging local professionals who were close friends of my local sub-consultant. It was explained to me, however, that in West Africa this was not only acceptable, but preferable, as it ensures loyalty. While Canadians derive loyalty from a pay package, Africans' loyalties are based on tribal or cultural traditions, or on social obligations. This is practical given the limited pool of resources in Africa and the fact that most educated Africans have studied together at the higher education levels.

"As a Canadian I am sometimes shocked at the number of relatives and friends of one ethnic group or 'tribe' being brought into the government. Appointments within the government often pay for favours, a currency in its own right. This is the world's most common form of barter and the essence of protecting one's position and family—and in many cases, the only way of getting ahead."

Entwining professional and personal lives however, can have detrimental effects in the workplace.

"A World Bank project in which I work is collapsing. After a year and a half of researching the reasons behind the project's failure we have just begun to understand. The local project director brought the project to a standstill because of a family feud between the wife of his superior and the wife of the chief minister. The bank plans to close the multimillion dollar project, which was designed to aid the rural poor."

Polite but Not Necessarily Friendly

Canadians are seen as reserved and rather serious. We are often perceived by foreigners as cold and not particularly outgoing, polite but not necessarily friendly. Moreover, Canadians are generally considered humourless, unable to tell a good story or a joke. In many countries, humour and tactful frankness not only help in closing business deals, but often keep them going.

"I was involved in a very lucrative project in Asia that became unravelled when a Canadian firm sent in a group of humourless professionals to manage the project after the deal was signed. No further contracts were forthcoming, as all of the goodwill gained during negotiations was lost by the unfriendly implementation team."

Lacking in General Cultural Knowledge

North Americans are known as culturally ignorant for our common inability to discuss art, literature, politics and history. Unlike other countries where interest in these topics is widespread and encouraged, our work ethic, and in the case of Canadians, fear of treading on controversial ground, often prevent us from enjoying art and appreciating knowledge for its own sake.

"I remember being amazed in France by the level of knowledge of plumbers and other tradesmen. They were far better at discussing politics and literature than I, despite my master's degree. Our education simply does not put enough emphasis on general cultural knowledge."

Our omnipresent concern with work leaves other parts of our lives under-developed. Conversation is a rare art in our society. For many of us, our most meaningful exchange of ideas occurs at work. By avoiding discussion of such imprecise subjects as the arts, we deprive ourselves of growth into new fields of knowledge.

"When I first arrived in India I was overwhelmed by the diversity of this culture whose history spanned more than 5,000 years! When I admitted this to my host, he was both sympathetic and delighted to introduce me to his particular religion and region. He talked at length about Sikhism, his extended family in his home state of Punjab, and about the religious and political conflicts in that region. After our workday was over, he spent hours showing me the historical monuments in and around Delhi."

Canadians tend to avoid discussion of controversial subjects. We prevent embarrassing encounters by making politics, philosophy and spirituality taboo when socializing with co-workers. Some of us think it is inappropriate or irrelevant to discuss such things with colleagues, while others feel simply that we have nothing to contribute. We tend to be suspicious of co-workers who display expertise or even simple interest in areas unrelated to the work at hand. Moreover, Canadians are not very inquisitive in conversation, perhaps because they prefer to be in control, making statements rather than asking questions.

"Very early in my overseas career, I was confronted by a senior African official who, halfway through a three-hour dinner, berated me for being so unresponsive to conversation. He was right. I was trying so hard not to get into any controversial issues. In a gentle way, he explained that the most rewarding aspect of an overseas career was learning about other cultures. Being overly guarded in cross-cultural oral interchanges was keeping me from understanding the new culture."

We generally drop a conversational item if we discover that our friends have strongly differing views from our own. We don't want to point out significant value differences for fear of creating a breach in our relationship.

"What a thrill it was to be in France and to have tremendous arguments at dinner parties over communism, capitalism and the Pope, knowing full well that we would all still be close friends when the evening was over. I couldn't help wondering why we can't be like that in Canada."

By taking an interest in local arts and music in their overseas work, Canadians not only develop a greater appreciation of the culture, but gain respect from their hosts and a better understanding of the business environment.

"The best piece of advice I received, and fortunately it came early in my first assignment in Africa, was that if you really want to understand the dynamics of the place, find out a little about the local music, theatre, art, media and history. In addition to situating my business activities in a useful way, the interest I expressed was rewarded by a number of rich personal relationships."

BUSINESS PROTOCOL

In the business environment we adhere to entrenched norms. The following section examines how we as Canadians conduct our daily business activities and how these activities contrast with those of other countries.

The First Contact

In a business setting, Canadians use the handshake as their primary form of greeting. It is not uncommon among French Canadians to precede business between well-established contacts by exchanging hugs and kissing each other on both cheeks. In general, however, a reserved demeanour and a strong handshake accompanied by direct eye contact is the norm.

> *"Many cultures are different from Canada with regard to eye contact. Canadians tend to look people in the eyes a lot. In many cultures, women do not look men in the eyes, as this can be taken as a sign of sexual interest. Old people are shown deference in most cultures, and this can include not looking them in the eyes and, in some cases, not touching them.*
>
> *"In Pakistan, the practice between male friends is to hug and immediately afterwards hold hands. This is a wonderful way to break barriers, far better than the crushing handshake!*
>
> *"When I began working in Tanzania, I was initially bemused by the time-consuming practice of shaking hands and exchanging pleasantries with everyone in the room before and after a meeting. It was only after returning to Canada that I realized how much I missed this formality and how important it had become to me. Having your presence and individuality continuously acknowledged is rare in our Canadian culture."*

Getting Down to Business

Because of the lines we draw between our professional and private lives, we tend to get down to business quickly, leaving little time to socialize or get acquainted with new colleagues. In many cultures, socializing with business associates is an opportunity for people to get to know their partners on a personal basis, thereby building trust, the essential ingredient in mutually satisfactory arrangements.

> *"I had to sit through interminable meetings in African villages, most consisting of long periods in which participants inquired about each other's health and my family's history. In the beginning I thought we were getting nowhere, until I realized this practice was helpful in building consensus and trust among group members."*

We Canadians delude ourselves into thinking that time spent establishing interpersonal relationships will detract from our professional performance. It is said that when Canadian projects fail, it has less to do with lack of technical expertise than with breakdowns in communication and failure of Canadian counterparts to take the time to familiarize themselves with the culture.

Establishing a good interpersonal relationship can lead to successful, long-term work partnerships and friendships.

"When I worked in eastern Africa I quickly adapted to the ritual of sharing tea and biscuits with my host, regardless of the time of day. This was a time that was never rushed, when pleasantries were exchanged. In my early years in Kenya and Malawi, I learned to attach much importance to these rituals. Now, years later, many of the officials with whom I drank tea and chatted prior to 'getting down to business' are senior members of the public service. They are not only colleagues, but also friends who have helped me overcome obstacles and provided me with assistance when I returned to work in their countries on other projects.

"You might be surprised to learn that in places like Africa your business partners see the work relationship as long-term, a potential friendship."

Giving and Receiving Hospitality

Canadians are accustomed to putting their professional lives ahead of their personal lives in business situations. We tend not to spend time inquiring about our colleagues' families or home environments. When faced with out-of-town business guests, we are hospitable to the extent that we ensure they are comfortable and have all the resources necessary to perform their given mission.

Canadians working abroad, however, are frequently treated with tremendous hospitality. Hosts take extraordinary amounts of time to welcome us and show us around. So when foreigners visit us in Canada, we have great difficulty reciprocating. Our jobs and compartmentalized lives make it extremely hard to take days or entire weeks to show visitors around, and we have no relatives willing to do the job for us. We feel unable to live up to the standards of our foreign hosts.

"I remember when our first exchange teacher arrived from Kenya. It was a very busy time of year, with many pressures on my staff and myself. I recall making a very conscious effort to allow plenty of time to greet our Kenyan associate, inquire about his trip, his family, the colleagues I knew at his home institution in Kenya, the political situation in Kenya, etc. I know that some of my Canadian staff felt I took too much time, under the circumstances, to welcome our visitor. However, I had learned from working in Kenya that putting his needs and concerns aside to tend to what I considered the more pressing details of his program, would only impede his progress later on. To this day, I recall the stress of trying to balance our institutional and cultural perspectives on time and priorities with those of our exchange teachers from Africa."

Egalitarian Relationships

Canadian society is not so rigidly stratified as some other societies. We enjoy a high degree of social mobility and it is common for us to mix with people of different social classes and both genders. Because of this, Canadians are often seen to be disrespectful of local power structures, and overseas hosts sometimes find this aspect of our behaviour embarrassing. Indeed, our overseas hosts and business colleagues are often bemused or offended by the lack of distinction we make between subordinates, peers and superiors. We appear to treat everyone equally, even when their status differs from ours.

"When we were in East Africa we had a 'maid.' As salaries were so low and people needed jobs, it seemed like a good idea. We wanted her to eat with us at

the table, but while we were very comfortable with this idea, she was not. No amount of discussion could persuade her otherwise."

Unlike countries where the class system is more firmly entrenched, we value personal experience and expertise over family origins. Belief in the concept of equality is an integral part of the Canadian identity. In cross-cultural situations, both work-related and social, we tend to be insensitive to or even offended by overtly hierarchical structures. Canadian organizations are "flatter" and function with less hierarchy. Thus, subordinates have easier access to senior levels of management.

Canadians tend to question authority. We require that our superiors "earn" our respect, while in most other societies, authority is granted by status and rarely challenged.

"Canadians respect youth and not age. This is inverted in most of the world. Abroad, it is better to have grey hair and be older, as you are accorded prestige and seen as wise. Many other cultures have great difficulty understanding our obsession with youthfulness."

Respect for Space

Canada is, geographically, the second-largest country in the world and has a disproportionately small population. It is therefore hardly surprising that Canadians place a high value on large homes and ample working space. The need to maintain sufficient physical distance from colleagues is an important aspect of our business protocol. It is a factor while we are talking with others, in meetings and in our individual workplaces. We neither expect nor welcome violations to our territory.

"I didn't realize how important our personal space or 'bubble' is to us until I started to work in China. For whatever reasons, the Chinese don't throw up as wide a psychic screen around themselves as we Canadians do. In crowds and even in normal work situations, I initially found myself reacting against what I perceived as violations of my personal space."

The typical Canadian office reflects this need for personal space and is designed to provide individual privacy for its occupants and reduce unintentional contact. In fact, we place such importance on space that the size of our office reflects our status within the company. Some advice for the confused foreigner: if you can't tell who the boss is by the way we talk to each other, you can find her or him in the large corner office with the window!

As mentioned, our need for personal space is further reflected in how closely we stand to each other. Canadians tend to stand about one metre apart while conversing. In many other cultures people stand much closer together; we find this disconcerting.

"I remember one evening in Nigeria where, at a cocktail party, I ended up in a corner surrounded by Nigerians all standing very close to me. I felt so uncomfortable. It was only later that I realized my discomfort stemmed from the clash of the Nigerian custom of standing very close to the person they are speaking with and the Canadian custom of keeping your distance."

Canadians also place a high priority on privacy and a controlled environment free of extraneous noise.

"During a field mission to Tanzania, I asked my local partner for a quiet place to write. There were a few empty offices around, so I thought it would be easy to accommodate me. To my dismay, I was given a space next to the reception area, the busiest of all spots, with heavy office traffic, and noise and smells from the street. When I asked for the quiet office at the end of the hall, I discovered I had been given the most desirable place of all. He said the other office was not a good place to work as I would not be able to see other people."

Blind Individualism

In business situations we focus on the task at hand and pay little attention to the context. Because we are individualistic, we tend to be impatient with group efforts, preferring to work on our own toward concrete goals. This sometimes involves cutting through red tape to improve efficiency. Superiors from other cultures may be offended by our neglect of the consultative process. It is not uncommon for Canadians to be unaware of what their colleagues are doing, even when they are members of the same team.

"On a recent consultation in South Asia, I was monitoring an institutional cooperation project. The ministry of labour and planning, in partnership with Canadians working on the project, were to be involved in deciding which experts were needed to run training programs. The ministry and the Canadians were to jointly decide, on a case-by-case basis, whether the qualified local resource people could be hired at considerably less cost, or whether it was necessary to select Canadians for the job.

"The Canadian partners established a pattern of seeking the ministry's approval only after they had selected the personnel they felt were suitable for the job. Predictably, they were always Canadians. The Canadian staff were trying to prove they could get the job done and keep the project 'on target.' They thought they were being helpful by relieving the overloaded ministry of time-consuming work reviewing applications and selecting resource people. While ministry officials were initially too polite to object to decisions made without their consultation, they became increasingly upset. They felt project resources were being wasted on Canadians when they should have been directed to local personnel. They began refusing to cooperate on other aspects of the project. The arrival of the monitor brought this issue to light. Finally the partners met to work out an acceptable approach, and the consultative process described in the management plan was resurrected."

COMMUNICATING

Canadians trust the written word and expect straight answers to questions. But while this may be comfortable for us, it is not the norm in many cultures. The next section explores the ways in which Canadians communicate and how our communication style is interpreted in the international arena.

Formal Communication and Belief in the Written Word

The way we compartmentalize our lives creates a need for formal communication systems. We tend not to be effective at verbal communication, except in structured settings such as meetings. Therefore, while many cultures place a higher value on verbal business agreements, Canadians trust the written word. To us, signing a contract is the beginning of a business liaison. This is clearly different from other cultures, where the contract is viewed merely as an outcome of an already-established relationship.

"When I began working in China, the Canadians I was with expressed frustration at the inordinate amount of time spent eating and touring prior to getting down to business and signing formal partnership agreements. However, for the Chinese to reach this point in the business relationship meant that the deal was already complete. They had accepted the Canadian partners and for them the rest was pure mechanics."

While we use formal methods of communication, such as memos, structured meetings, minutes of meetings and letters, we tend to view verbal exchanges as not only inefficient, but unreliable. With our respect for the documented word, we can feel left out of the action in some overseas work environments. While our local colleagues are doing business through the grapevine and assuming we are abreast of recent developments, we are sitting in the dark, waiting for the memos to come through!

"In many instances, both written and verbal communication is inadequate. It is accepted that trust is strongest in the extended family and between old classmates from university. Otherwise, anything goes. The written word is a way of trying to get everything on top of the table but there is usually a lot more going on beneath."

Clear and Assertive Communication Style

Canadians strive for and respect a direct communication style. We look for straight answers to our questions and tend to discuss issues in a blunt way. This bluntness can be hurtful to someone coming from a culture where saving face is crucial. By ignoring the subtleties of human communication we miss non-verbal messages, which can be an integral part of the picture. Therefore, we must be careful not to be so honest as to humiliate others whose cultural communication styles differ from our own.

It is important to understand that every culture employs certain means of communication which are further refined by individual organizations within that culture. A good reading of your environment can dramatically increase your chances of communicating effectively with others. For instance, once you know that Southeast Asians dread offending others by expressing opposition directly and will therefore say "yes" when they mean "no," you can adjust your behaviour in the workplace to be less confrontational, more subtle.

"As a foreigner meeting high-ranking officials, I was cautioned against asking any questions for fear they would be unable to answer them and become embarrassed. Asking questions in that context is considered impolite and disrespectful. At first I was shocked and wondered how anyone up and down the ladder communicated. Now I realize that hierarchy and respect for one's 'superiors' is the glue that holds things together and without it, anarchy threatens."

CONDUCTING BUSINESS

The way we arrange our schedules, make decisions and achieve results affects how we interact with our foreign colleagues. The following section examines how we as Canadians structure our business lives.

"Time Is Money"

For most Canadians, "time is money." We value punctuality and regard it as an expression of respect toward others. We hate to waste our own and other peoples' valuable time. We conceive of time as a precious resource to be used, divided and assigned to particular projects and activities. Accordingly, our days are carefully sliced up into periods, each reflecting time allocated to a particular activity. We prefer to approach each task separately and to move on to the next only when the first is complete. Dealing with unplanned events creates stress.

> *"For a while I felt really lost in this environment. Meetings never started on time. We would have a meeting and agree on steps to be taken and several days later I would realize that nothing had been done. Priorities had changed and the duration of the project had lengthened without my being informed. I was really frustrated.*
>
> *"On a research project in Ecuador, I had carefully planned structured interviews of 250 farmers to correspond to my financial and time resources. I forgot to consider the questions the farmers would have for me, not to mention the drinks to be consumed in celebration of the friendship between Canada and Ecuador!"*

Assessing the Facts

Our favourite approach to problem solving is the step-by-step, linear model: we identify the facts and where they originate from, thereby constructing a cause-and-effect chain for gathering, sharing and analyzing information. In this process, intuition is not valued at all and emphasis is on hard facts. Canadians have little tolerance for ambiguity and will eliminate it rather than attempt to understand it.

Canadians approach business opportunities in the same cautious manner, ensuring they have all the facts before making a decision. As mentioned, we are known as conservative people who avoid unnecessary risks.

> *"In my 20 years of business travel, one comment I have received over and over is 'We really respect Canada and Canadians, but why are they so conservative and unwilling to take risks? A little assertiveness would also help.'"*

Making Decisions

In Canada, we value managers who take immediate, decisive action after a problem-solving exercise. We admire those who can make decisions quickly and take responsibility for the consequences. We like to see action, work in progress and evidence that things are moving.

> *"Forget all your Canadian approaches to decision-making, as they are rarely used in developing countries. In China, for example, managers were taught for 40 years not to make decisions. This is changing, but basic managerial skills are*

still severely lacking and responsibility for making decisions is often passed onward and upward."

Increasingly however, Canadian business, institutions, and management training schools are promoting decision-making processes that involve both the manager and staff. This approach does not come easily to the individualistic Canadian, but it is now considered good policy to consult the people who will be affected by a decision. Based on the idea that employees know best what their needs are, supervisors are offering support to employees and allowing them to search for solutions, rather than providing ready-made answers.

This approach can be disconcerting to non-Western societies, where employees are used to a more hierarchical process. For someone accustomed to taking orders, a supervisor's belief that an employee is equipped to solve her or his own problem might suggest incompetence on the part of the supervisor. A boss is supposed to be all-knowing!

"I spent my first few months in Zaire trying to involve my staff in all levels of decision-making. They ignored me. I decided I had to become more autocratic. I was more decisive, made most decisions unilaterally and requested more service from staff. I had the office boy bring me coffee rather than serving myself and always used the driver instead of driving myself. Things greatly improved. My staff liked my autocratic behaviour and, in their eyes, I was assuming my responsibilities as a boss."

Getting Results

Ours is a rational attitude aimed at eliminating problems. Once a decision is made, we want it carried out immediately. Delay generates anxiety. Because we tend to design courses of action which focus on results, little attention is paid to the process.

"While conducting a training course on international negotiations in Colombia, we sometimes felt we were forcing conclusions on our students. They preferred a much longer period of exploration than we had anticipated.

"In many countries the process is more important than the product. For example, when checking in at the airport in Karachi, one goes through an intricate series of steps from checking, double-checking and triple-checking paper tags tied to hand luggage. The process is so full of holes it would be easy to slip an illicit bag on board. But the process gives 15 police officers something to do and allows them to be seen by the elite. And it gives a sense of security to the passengers, even if it is false. It is the process that matters the most."

WHAT WE NEED TO IMPROVE ON

Our interview research shows Canadians need to improve in certain key areas if they are to be comfortable, and therefore successful, in cross-cultural work situations. Some useful suggestions follow.

Be Culturally Sensitive

Canada is made up of people from a wide range of cultures, but our daily lives take place in fairly homogeneous communities. Even if we live in large cities, our lives are compartmentalized and present little opportunity for contact with people from other cultural backgrounds. Our limited exposure to cross-cultural situations differs dramatically from regions such as Asia or West Africa, where a variety of cultures and languages interact on a daily basis.

Learning to successfully integrate into a new cultural environment means using a combination of hard facts and intuition, the latter being quite a challenge for the logically minded Canadian. We must remember, however, that beneath apparent chaos, there is always order, and this order is understandable in culturally specific terms. You are thus confronted with a dual learning challenge: the organizational and the societal. It is crucial that you carry out your responsibilities while respecting the values of those you encounter in your cross-cultural experience.

Have Realistic Goals

In planning, we often assume we have complete control over our time and environment. We do not anticipate our work being disrupted. Planning is oriented toward quantifiable results and objective, rather than intuitive, consideration of all the options. This rigid approach can create frustration on a cross-cultural posting where unexpected factors can be brought into play at any time. You must be knowledgeable about your new environment to plan your work realistically.

It is important to bear in mind potential logistical constraints when planning your work in developing countries. Can you imagine the impact that a shortage of fuel, the rainy season or sudden inflation can have on a project? Even a lack of paper and pens at the local office supply store has been known to frustrate implementation of a project. What was a realistic expectation in your Canadian work environment could be totally unrealistic in a cross-cultural context.

Think Long-Term

Canadian society is oriented toward the future. Our government reflects this in its long-term strategic planning, but even at an individual level we attempt to conduct our professional and personal lives in a strategic way. We like having one activity lead to the next in a logical manner, with our future well-being in mind.

Unfortunately, projects conducted in developing countries sometimes lack this comprehensive focus. This is often the result of the short time Canadians spend in a particular country, in combination with poor technology transfers to our overseas counterparts. Without long-term, comprehensive development strategies, there is little continuity from one project to another. It is important for Canadians to reverse this trend and promote long-term sustainable growth.

A LAST WORD

Many of the world's cultures are thousands of years old and steeped in history and traditions. Our tendency to focus on facts and results often leads us to ignore the subtleties of these cultures and to misunderstand their business practices. We highly recommend you learn as much as you can about the corporate culture of the organization you will be working with, as well as the shared beliefs and values of the country you are going to.

APPENDIX ON THE CD_ROM

7a. "Adjusting to a Slower Pace of Work," by Kellee Ngan

CHAPTER 8
Re-Entry

Phew! At last you're home—cozy, safe, predictable, surrounded by familiar faces. You've anticipated your homecoming with a mixture of feelings, from elation to regret. Your incredible journey—across waters and within yourself—is over. Or is it?

You're about to enter the final, and perhaps most difficult, phase of your overseas experience. This is the *re-entry stage*, and its impact on you is at least as profound as the cultural adaptation stage.

Here are some returnees' thoughts on this period.

"You've enjoyed your homecoming; you're starting a new job, resuming your studies or setting up housekeeping. You're surprised at how easily you're settling in, and then all of a sudden you're overtaken by an acute sense of malaise, of 'otherness,' of 'what on earth am I doing here?' You scoffed at the idea of reverse culture shock, but now you just don't feel right and you can't seem to shake it. You're suffering from re-entry shock!"

One young woman described the experience of returning home from Africa as coming back to anonymity.

"Abroad, I had a strong sense of myself. My skin colour was different, my language was different, and I was the centre of attention even when I was buying groceries at the local market. Now I'm back home, busily carrying out my responsibilities. My fabulous tan has faded; my T-shirt from Senegal is hidden under layers of winter clothing; no one seems interested in the three amazing years I spent in a tropical paradise. No one knows (or apparently cares) how much I've changed, how much I've seen, how much I've grown!"

Another traveller returning from six months in Mali and Burkina Faso felt contempt for his fellow Canadians.

"To my surprise, the first thing I noticed when I arrived was how pale and unappealing all these white people looked. They seemed so undignified—they dressed sloppily, slouched, spoke too loudly. Overseas, I had grown accustomed to certain rituals around mealtimes. I was dismayed to find my family still watching TV while they ate, or eating alone, sometimes straight out of the fridge! At work, my fellow employees ate while they talked on the phone, while they walked, or even while they ran. I felt like an outsider observing a society with no culture."

In many ways, coming home can be more painful than leaving. The "weirdness" of home, its different pace and social pressures—and people's lack of interest in your mind-altering experience—can make you feel like a stranger. This chapter gives an overview of the phases of re-entry and makes suggestions on how you can cope with anxieties, problems and frustrations caused by *re-entry shock*.

THINGS TO EXPECT AS PART OF RE-ENTRY SHOCK

If you are in the re-entry stage, you are probably dealing with feelings of frustration and rejection and a sense of being out of step with the people around you. Here is a list of symptoms you may experience on your return:

- **Feeling let down:** You have a peculiar sense of disappointment very much at odds with the joy you expected to feel when you got home. A young woman who worked for an NGO in China for several years describes her reaction. Keep in mind that hers is not a solitary experience—most returnees feel the same way!

   "My thoughts about being back ranged from how great it would be to see my family and friends, to 'At last! A decent cup of coffee.' I looked forward to returning to a democratic society, to having a say in the things that affect me— as an individual, as a woman, as a consumer. Well, all that was mine when I returned—and I drank a lot of coffee in these great new coffee bars—but that old song kept playing in my head: 'Is that all there is? Is that all there is?'"

- **You feel disconnected from your community:** You don't fit in any more. You feel like you changed while everything at home stayed the same, or maybe everything at home changed while you were away. You miss the community you just left. Sometimes you're overwhelmed with nostalgia. You feel abnormal.

- **Your relationships with family and friends are strained:** Nobody seems interested in your overseas experience. Some people didn't even notice you were gone! People around you seem boring and narrow-minded. It's hard to hide your disappointment. You withdraw from your friends and family and, not surprisingly, you feel isolated.

- **Your emotional state is in flux:** You feel disoriented. You sleep a lot, but your dreams are disturbed. You feel out of control, even aggressive. You're angry one minute, sad the next. You try to deny the importance of your experience abroad. You're restless, forgetful, petulant. Your unpredictability begins to take its toll on your family and friends.

- **Your life skills are gone:** You look the wrong way when you cross the street. You leave your gloves at home in the middle of winter. You buy powdered milk, like you did in Mozambique, because the array of milk choices at the corner store is overwhelming. The things you do without thinking are often inappropriate. You feel overwhelmed by the tasks of everyday life.

- **Your health deteriorates:** You catch a lot of colds and other viruses; you get headaches; your appetite fluctuates. You're irritable, lethargic, even depressed.

For more accounts of returnees' experiences with re-entry shock, see the "Individual Circumstances" section later on in this chapter. In the meantime, let's look a little closer at re-entry.

RE-ENTRY SHOCK VERSUS CULTURE SHOCK

For many of you, re-entry shock is very different from the culture shock you experienced abroad. Far from home, you were motivated to adapt because you were an outsider, and even at the worst of times you knew you would go home one day. Now that you're back, you feel you ought to fit in, you know the territory, and you shouldn't need to make adjustments. But being home doesn't feel right, and since, for some of us, returning home is forever, the stakes are much higher.

Re-adapting to your home culture can follow a similar pattern to the "U-Curve of Cultural Adaptation" described in Chapter 3, Living Overseas. Like adaptation, re-entry has three stages: euphoria ("the tourist high"), shock, and adjustment. There are differences, however.

- The shock of re-entry can set in faster and be more intense than culture shock.

- Every person adapts differently.

- The phases of re-entry do not follow a standard pattern and may blend into one another. You may experience symptoms of a stage you thought you'd finished long ago.

- Overseas adaptation, according to the experts, takes about one-third of the duration of your stay. When you come back, however, your stay could be forever. Many people find it takes the repetition of a season to make them feel comfortable back home.

In the words of one freelance writer who returned after a six-year absence:

"It was six months since I'd returned. I had lived abroad two other times and therefore hadn't given re-entry shock much thought this time around. When the first wave of depression hit me, I was taken completely off guard—I was angry, overly sensitive, and short with my co-workers, who seemed to go merrily about their little lives. They seemed faster than me, more efficient, technically able— and a little boring.

"Eventually I had to admit that my sense of disconnectedness, and even hostility, was caused by reverse culture shock. I also had to concede that I was struggling to adjust to the time and effort required to look after myself—to do laundry, ironing, dishes. We had two maids in our house overseas! I'd gone from a four-bedroom house with attached guest house, swimming pool, and hired help to a two-bedroom apartment with noisy radiators. Overseas, my skills were highly valued; now I faced unemployment. It took more than 18 months for the most obvious symptoms of re-entry shock to disappear."

In the next few sections, you'll find descriptions of a variety of reactions to the re-entry process. If you don't recognize your own experiences, however, don't worry! Just about any reaction is normal and none of them last forever. Remember that adaptation is a process, not a single event.

Now, let's take a closer look at the three phases of re-entry shock, and what you can expect, why it happens and what to do to ease the process.

THE PHASES OF RE-ENTRY

The re-entry process is a phase of your overseas experience—and is itself divided into three parts: euphoria (the above-mentioned "tourist high"), shock and adjustment.

PHASE I: EUPHORIA OR THE TOURIST HIGH

Most returnees experience the "tourist high." During this phase you feel very optimistic and tend to focus on the positive, such as reuniting with loved ones, returning to a familiar culture, and for some, Tim Hortons doughnuts! This euphoria helps sustain you through any initial problems. You avoid difficult situations and convince yourself that everything is wonderful. You downplay or ignore anything that unsettles you. You don't allow yourself to miss your life overseas.

You may actually achieve a lot during this phase, as you are quite focused and highly motivated. You accomplish immediate tasks easily, partly because you have lots of energy, enthusiasm and the odd surge of adrenaline. Others may find you a bit high-strung or even overbearing.

In this first phase, you're generally glad to be home. You've missed your family, the seasons, your old neighbourhood, and people are happy to see you back. Here's how one lawyer felt when he returned home after taking part in South Africa's transition to democracy.

> *"I really felt like a distinguished visitor, almost a hero. People were very interested in the dramatic changes that had occurred in South Africa, and in my role in them. Dinner parties were organized to celebrate my return. I was even asked to make a presentation at a Canadian Bar Association event, and was interviewed on the local university radio station. I had a period of a month or two of really being in demand, of feeling like a celebrity, and then it tapered off. Soon, people just wanted to talk about the last movie I'd seen rather than the last few years I'd lived. Well, it was kind of tough just being 'Mr. One-of-us' again!"*

The euphoria phase of re-entry is cathartic. You've been anticipating your homecoming for months, and as your overseas adventure concludes, you reflect on it, comparing your original expectations with the outcome. Often it has turned out much better than you expected, and you may be revelling in this feeling!

PHASE II: SHOCK!

You've changed, your friends, family and co-workers have changed; indeed, home itself has changed, and you have no choice but to adjust. This realization puts you into shock.

Re-entry shock makes us feel we don't belong in the place that is supposed to be our home; it makes us wonder where we do belong.

There are a lot of factors at play in the shock phase of re-entry. We describe them as follows to help clarify the process.

You Don't Expect Change on Your Home Turf

Because it is unexpected, re-entry shock, sometimes called reverse culture shock, catches many travellers and international workers by surprise. As mentioned, the process of readjusting to home bears some similarity to that of adjusting to a foreign culture—it's just that you feel like you shouldn't have to adjust!

One way of summing up the experience of re-entry shock is that *home culture seems foreign*. Truly, as hard as this may be to fathom, the shock of re-entry is in part due to the feeling that home isn't home any more. The more immersed you were in the culture overseas, the more adjusting you'll have to do when you leave.

It is helpful to think of culture as being all of the things you take for granted in everyday life—that's everything from which way to look when you cross the street, to the importance of religion in daily decision-making. When you adapt to life overseas, you actually *change* your culture. Upon arriving home, you find that you no longer take for granted the same things other Canadians or Americans do. The stress of re-entry shock (and culture shock) is largely due to this fact. If you cannot take anything for granted, you cannot relax.

You Have Changed

Your experiences and adventures overseas have changed forever how you perceive the world. You adjusted to a new lifestyle, made different friends, did business in different ways, prepared and ate different food, and perhaps even functioned in a different language. Now you're home and people expect you to carry on as you did before. But as you try to settle into your old routines—or even new ones—you become acutely aware of changes in your outlook, and even in your sense of self. You must acknowledge these changes, and allow for them. Some are for the better and will be worth preserving. And there are changes you will have to make to survive.

Virtually every returnee feels like an outsider, like he or she is observing life rather than participating in it. Here's how one traveller describes it:

"I found my perceptions had changed, I'd adjusted to a new lifestyle, with its different set of joys and stresses, and of course I'd learned to say a few words in several different languages. Yet others around me—and even I—expected that when I returned I would carry on as I had before I left. As if I was the same old me—but I felt nothing like the me who'd left all that time ago."

No One is Interested in Hearing about Your Life Abroad

Whereas the people you return to may appear not to have changed, there are bound to be discernible differences, as everyday life *does* carry on without you. Children grow up, old people die, neighbours move. Governments change, the economy ebbs and flows. Your relationships with people close to you are affected by the very fact of your absence. You may not have met certain of their expectations, such as caring for elderly parents. Friendships may have suffered, either from lack of contact or because someone else filled your place. You come back expecting to slip into the seat you thought they were saving for you.

But they haven't saved you a place, and worse, they don't seem to care where you've been. As ridiculous as it seems, they don't want to hear about your experiences. They'd rather talk about last night's game or who's getting a promotion. Even close family and friends may show only passing interest in your travels and may have difficulty relating to the new you.

Routine existence goes on at home while you pack a lifetime of experiences into each day overseas. Or so it seems...

Even an international traveller who'd written on the subject of re-entry was taken aback by her friend's behaviour. While anticipating limited interest among the general populace, she believed *her* set of friends, many of them writers and international travellers, would want to see her photos of Africa at a reunion dinner. *"Oh, maybe after dinner,"* one friend said. *"Bring them into the office,"* said another, to her utter astonishment.

Life at Home Changed While You were Abroad

Your return will require you to adjust to a variety of things, from the pace of life, attitudes, consumer habits, language and food to the sense of personal space and even the climate.

Where considerable changes took place while you were away—in your town, the economy, technology, your family, or in other ways—you can count on being confused, especially if these are unexpected changes.

Sometimes it's the small changes that throw you off. For instance, one man returned to Ontario after several years to find a multitude of long-distance telephone companies offering their services. After three years in Africa with no phone at all, he was bewildered by the choices.

"I was going crazy, signing up with one company for a few weeks, then switching when a seemingly better deal came along. Finally it struck me that I was doing most of my long-distance communicating by e-mail—and I stopped fretting about trying to find the best deal. It took a while after I got back to understand what my needs really were—and to stop being flustered by the heap of choices!"

You are Critical of Home

Now that you've stopped taking home for granted, you can see the flaws in your own society in a way you couldn't before. It's far more difficult to forgive your own culture's flaws than to accept another's, because you feel partly responsible for them.

"I was staggered by the materialism in our society. I found it hard to readjust, even though I'd only been in Russia for six months. Now, a year later, I'm still trying to maintain a "live with less" attitude—but it's a real challenge."

You find yourself being critical of others. Their lifestyles seem self-indulgent, decadent and irresponsible. They seem callous, self-involved and unfriendly... You're lonely. It seems you'll never reconnect with your old friends, or make new ones... You're bored. You've done all the things you'd planned to do. Nothing interests you. You're fed up with moving and everything associated with it...

You may worry that you'll never like home again, that it's no longer your real home. You may quit trying to get along here. When people are friendly to you, you may respond with indifference. You rack your brains for ways to get back to the country you left, or just to get away from home. In short, you resist adaptation.

You Miss Your Overseas Friends and Lifestyle

Your life abroad seems like a fantasy now. There was always something new and exciting and being a visitor kept you removed from the more mundane aspects of life overseas. While you were away, your letters home made you a local celebrity. Now that you're back, however, you're just like everyone else. And your standard of living may have dropped substantially.

People at home seem uninteresting, uninspired. You miss the exciting discussions you had with your new friends overseas. You find people's preoccupations small-minded and boring.

You may have romanticized North American efficiency while you were away. Now the smallest lineup or delay infuriates you. And you can never get through to anyone on the telephone! The tyranny of voice mail is a common complaint, even among those who are accustomed to it. It's particularly agitating when you've been somewhere with minimal or no telephone service!

"The phone system in Zimbabwe drove me crazy—not just because of the many technical problems, but because people wouldn't answer telephones, or if they did, they wouldn't pass on messages. The telephone was at the root of several of my missed deadlines. Now that I'm back, however, I resent the incredibly efficient phone service. It prevents any chance of spontaneity—invariably, you're expected to call ahead and announce your intentions! And several days in advance, if you please!"

You Feel Vulnerable, Powerless

You may feel overwhelmed by your seeming inability to find a job, or by a general sense of personal failure.

"I didn't have a job, our belongings hadn't been unpacked because we hadn't yet found suitable accommodation, and we were living with relatives. All of us were sick of living out of suitcases and not being able to find anything. There was no more household help to call on, our savings were being eroded, and everyone in the family was suffering from adjustment problems I couldn't solve."

Dwindling finances often contribute to this sense of powerlessness. The cost of living may be much higher at home or the lifestyle you'd grown accustomed to might be beyond your budget. Resettlement expenses can make re-entry financially draining—you have to pay for everything, from new winter coats to a new car.

Much has been said about returning to your home and your old life, but you may, in fact, be returning to very *different* personal or professional circumstances. You may be coming back to a different job or to live in a different part of the country. You may have developed a long-term personal relationship while you were abroad, or a relationship at home may have ended. You may have to relocate soon after you return, or you may not even have a home to return to.

Summary: Why Re-Entry Shock Happens

You may be surprised to learn you are experiencing some of the symptoms of the *grieving process*. Specifically, you are suffering from the anxiety associated with separation and loss. For very good reasons:

- Change is difficult.
- You have left a significant part of yourself behind.
- There are no guarantees you will ever go back.

HOW TO EASE RE-ENTRY SHOCK

We would like to have called this section "Cures for Re-entry Shock"—but there are none! So, expect re-entry shock. No matter how seasoned a world traveller you are, you're unlikely to get through the re-entry process unscathed. When you live so far from home, in such a different culture, and for such a long time, home begins to seem less and less real. Many people idealize Canada or the US, and are horrified by the real thing. So come back with your eyes open: you've changed, home has changed, the country has changed. Be prepared to adapt.

Practical And Easy Tips

- **Enjoy phase one, the tourist high:** Take a break when you get back, before you return to work or start looking for a job. Plan a "welcome home" party.
- **Get organized:** Make lists of specific tasks you need to accomplish and keep track of your priorities, emotional as well as practical. Don't make snap decisions, however tempted you are to settle things quickly. You'll need to make some decisions, but keep in mind long-term consequences.
- **Take good care of yourself:** You may be particularly susceptible to illness, so a healthy lifestyle is crucial. Recognize that this is an extremely stressful time, both physically and emotionally. If you experience unusual symptoms, make sure your doctor knows *where* you were posted overseas, particularly if it was a tropical area. Doctors may not automatically check for malaria or bilharzia.
- **Take breaks:** Schedule some downtime; forget about the outside world and do something you enjoy.
- **Treat yourself to something you enjoyed overseas:** Food is the best example. Plan to cook some of your favourite dishes once you get home. Make sure you bring the right spices with you.
- **Maintain your sense of humour:** Remember how important this aspect of cultural adaptation was overseas? The same applies here—maybe twice over!

Reflect on Your Experience Abroad

- Choose which parts of the experience you value and which you will let go.
- Keep in mind that you have adapted before.
- Use the adaptation skills you learned overseas.
- Try to see North American people and events within a North American context.

Start Building a Community

- **Five simple ideas to get you started:** First, work on building your confidence. Second, join in, get involved. Third, search for and get to know other returnees. Fourth, look for others (not just returnees) who share common ground (e.g., other job seekers, new immigrants). And fifth, stay in touch with your overseas friends.

- **Rekindle old friendships:** Prepare yourself for your friends' indifference, and try to be understanding. Some will seem unable, or worse, unwilling, to discuss your overseas experiences. This can be particularly galling for international development or aid workers, who've devoted themselves to humanitarian causes and lived in poor conditions among the world's most desperate peoples. Effective communication skills will help ease the transition and make the difference between a bad case of re-entry shock and a relatively mild one. If you can express yourself clearly and in a way that doesn't offend, your friends will benefit from the insights you share with them, and you will benefit from their support. The following points are worth keeping in mind.

- **Decide which parts of your experience you're going to talk about:** Try to distinguish what is important to your audience—whether it's your grandmother or the local Rotary Club—and what detracts from making your point.

- **Choose your audience carefully and be respectful of them:** Make sure your audience is interested before you launch into a long story about life overseas. Be mindful of their attention span. Listen to their questions. Know when to change the subject. Be especially careful about who hears you express your frustrations about home. Other returnees will be sympathetic, but even they have limited tolerance for complaining.

- **Think before you speak:** Try to be inclusive. Don't start every sentence with "When I was in Harare/Paris/Bangalore," or people will feel excluded. Try to make your comments relevant to the situation at hand.

- **Don't get too attached to your celebrity status:** Remember, most people are only interested in the five-minute version of your trip, and even that won't last.

- **Show interest in others:** Don't assume that what you've done is more interesting or exciting than what they've done. Ask questions. Be a good listener.

PHASE III: ADJUSTMENT

This is where the "U Curve of Adjustment" (see Chapter 3, Living Overseas) begins to swing upward. During this period, you start to fit in.

- **You actually like it here at home:** Go on, admit it. You respect the people around you. You participate in everyday life, in work, in your community. You're not angry any more. You feel competent and effective. Some days you even have fun.

- **You develop routines:** You remember garbage day. You watch regular television programs and enjoy them.

- **You begin to appreciate the canadian or american perspective:** You are able to talk about your experiences in a way that your friends and family can understand.

- **Your sense of humour is revived:** You begin to talk about your experiences of re-entry—poking some fun at yourself as you regain perspective.

- **Your life has continuity:** You begin to see the long-term value of your experiences abroad. You find ways to use the skills you gained overseas in your everyday life at home.

- **Your health improves:** You sleep better, you don't get as many colds, and you have more energy. You can focus on the people and things around you.

Adaptation is hard work, but it's a natural process, a human survival skill. Think about it—if human beings weren't good at adapting, we wouldn't live in such a complex, technologically advanced world. And you wouldn't have gone overseas in the first place!

What's Good About the Re-Entry Experience?

Re-entry is not an entirely negative experience. Through your struggle, you will uncover and develop a number of skills and insights.

- Not only did you have the privilege of learning about a new culture overseas, but you also gained a fresh perspective on your own culture.

- You are more adaptable and open to new ideas. You have developed greater sensitivity in interpersonal communications, especially as they relate to the traumas of crossing cultures.

- You appreciate value structures other than your own.

- You emerge a stronger, more resourceful person, with deeper insights into the human condition.

Suggestions for the Long Term

You have learned a great deal from your overseas experience *and* from going through the re-entry process. You can apply this knowledge in very useful ways.

- **Set Goals:** Figure out which aspects of your overseas experience are relevant at home and how you can integrate them into your work or home life. Set a course of action now, before you fall into hard-to-break habits. Here's a lesson from a teacher who has worked in many different countries:

    "From Finland to Japan, I keep coming across the same saying: 'Every ending is a new beginning.' You've probably heard it before, but it may be particularly meaningful for you now, while you're unfettered by old habits and inflexible patterns. This is your chance to do some of the things you've been meaning to do all your life!"

- **Give Back:** You have useful information to impart. Why not offer a slide show about your overseas community to a local group—Scouts, Rotarians, your neighbours? Are there particular skills you could pass on? Who needs your help? Could you offer your support to more recent returnees still in the grips of re-entry shock? Do you have something to offer new immigrants?

INDIVIDUAL CIRCUMSTANCES

Everyone has different things to manage depending on their age, personality, professional, personal and family circumstances. This part of the chapter outlines experiences common to specific groups.

Unaccompanied Travellers

If you went overseas alone, you probably had a more intense experience than you would have if you'd gone with other people. You may have been involved in projects that were humanitarian or idealistic in their goals. You may have worked in circumstances that others would consider dangerous, or been expected to work under poorer conditions and for longer hours than your colleagues with immediate family obligations. Such experiences can be very exciting and rewarding, but also isolating. You may now be continents away from others who shared your experience, who know what it was like, and who may be struggling with similar re-entry problems. If you travelled or worked with a group of other unaccompanied travellers, the relationships you formed were likely very close, but not necessarily permanent. Such relationships depend more on your common purpose than on your interest in each other as individuals.

Unaccompanied travellers with personal as well as professional expectations of their overseas assignments may have difficulty coming to terms with them. There is a double pressure to succeed: you feel you should have advanced your career or fulfilled certain obligations, but you also feel you should have developed your personal life.

You may, in fact, be returning home with a new partner, in which case you will feel responsible for their adaptation while you deal with your own re-entry. The pressure of a new relationship, in a new environment, combined with the weight of your own expectations and those of your family and friends, may seem more than you can bear.

Whatever your circumstances, the key is to find a balance between your obligations to family, friends and community and your need for support and independence. Spending time with others who have had similar experiences is very helpful, therefore. You may already have such contacts, but if you're stuck, there are resources available to help you.

Employees

Whether you have a job or a job search waiting for you, you will have to re-adapt to the workforce. This can be frustrating, but it can also be an excellent opportunity to restructure your life, set short-term tasks and long-term goals, and take stock of your career.

Remember, though, that returning to jobs with comparatively little influence or autonomy can be hard on your self-esteem. On top of that, not everyone is interested in, or sees the value of, international experience. Don't be surprised if your employer or prospective employer dismisses your overseas career development.

Your best allies will be curiosity and the ability to translate your experiences into meaningful discussions with prospective employers, co-workers or clients. If you are looking for a job, be thorough. Do your research and relearn the ropes, if necessary. At the same time, be open–minded. Do a thorough investigation of your field and the social and political factors affecting it. What are employers in your field looking for? Assume they need help to appreciate the relevance of your overseas experience. Present it in a non-threatening, inclusive manner. Once you start work, you will have to learn the politics and hierarchies of your workplace. You may have to work in environments that you thought you'd escaped forever!

Above all, be sensitive and attentive to other people. They can be sources of information and good advice, sometimes without realizing it. One returnee describes a meeting where the colleague to his right turned to him and said, "If you mention Sarajevo or Beirut one more time, I'm going to break your nose." Once he'd recovered from the rudeness of her outburst, the returnee was grateful: if she hadn't said something, he might have alienated the whole group. He stopped dropping names of foreign cities and immediately found his colleagues more receptive to his ideas. (For more details about managing professional re-entry, see Chapter 28, Job Hunting When You Return Home.)

Accompanying Spouses

As an accompanying spouse, you probably had more exposure to the culture of your overseas home than your employed partner did, and you probably had to work harder to adapt. You went overseas in support of your spouse's career and had no employment structure to rely on when you arrived. If you worked while you were abroad, it may have been for a local organization. Or perhaps you joined or developed a local network. Your cultural experiences were likely richer and more enduring because of this.

You are now faced with similar circumstances at home. You are under the same pressure as your spouse to rejoin the community and re-establish your occupation (in the workforce or at home), but you may still lack control over your life. You may be the only member of the family without a built-in community to return to. You may have to spend more time at home than your spouse and children, who have work and school to occupy their days. If you are a homemaker accustomed to a comfortable life abroad, you may find the drop in your standard of living difficult. Your family's financial situation may require you to work outside the home. You may blame your spouse for your unhappiness and feel resentful that your life has been disrupted for the sake of someone else's job.

Your best strategy is to develop some structure in your life. Find something outside the home that you can do independently, or offer your services to an organization in need. At first, any kind of activity will help, whether it's working out at the local Y or going to the art gallery. Eventually, though, you will want to find ways to integrate your overseas experience into your life at home.

One accompanying spouse reports that she never experienced the tourist high stage of re-entry, mainly because it was immediately apparent that she had lost touch with her old network. One friend told her, "I'd love to get together in a couple of months, after I've finished my PhD thesis." How could she tell them she needed company right away? Things improved for this person, however, when she contacted an international organization and volunteered to help with pre-departure briefings for overseas employees.

The section entitled "Employees," above, will likely be useful to you, as will the Resources section at the end of this chapter. (Also see Part Five, International Career Directories, at the end of this book.)

Children

Young children tend to have the least difficulty during re-entry because their senses of security and identity are so closely linked to their families.

They do, however, notice and respond to the anxiety of their parents and older siblings. They may revert to behaviour they have outgrown, such as bedwetting, thumb-sucking or fear of the dark. They may be particularly fussy, clingy, temperamental or prone to tears. Fortunately, these symptoms are normal and temporary, and will decrease as you establish routines. Young children adapt quickly.

It may be a good idea to visit your children's school before they begin, and to advise their teachers that they have been overseas for the last while. On buying the right clothes—sometimes it's good to "check out what the other kids are wearing" before re-outfitting your kids. And the revived popularity of second-hand clothes takes some of the pressure off the budget.

Remember, too, that returning home often means returning to extended family networks, which can be a source of pleasure for both children and family. When one little girl learned they would soon return home, she told her parents she wanted to live next door to her grandmother. She planned to build a ladder over the fence and into her grandma's yard so she could visit whenever she wanted.

Teenagers

As a young adult between 12 and 18, you perhaps stand to gain the most from living overseas. You're very flexible, able to adapt to almost anything, and you're probably a very good problem solver. *But*—teenagers also tend to have the hardest time during re-entry. As you are already coping with an adaptation process—of trying to define yourself and establish some independence from your family—an international move can be an added and very unwelcome pressure at this stage in your life.

Here are a few tips on what to expect:

- Your old friends have changed and so have you.
- All the social rules are different.
- You're a celebrity for a day, then people lose interest in you.
- School work is different.
- You are forced to spend time with your family.
- You blame your parents for everything.
- You are lethargic and bored.
- You're rebellious, have a harder time obeying rules.

You probably feel alone, like no one else is going through what you're going through. In fact, there are lots of people in similar situations. Try to find someone around your age who has made an international move. It's a huge relief to talk to someone who knows how you feel. Find out from your parents whether any of their co-workers are returnees with kids your age. Ask around at school, too—the guidance counsellor might know someone.

Here are some suggestions put together by a group of returnees between the ages of 12 and 18:

"Be yourself. Get out of the house. Go for walks, get fresh air. Relax. Think, read, meditate, listen to music. Take a bubble bath. Get a part-time job. Go shopping. Observe others—their actions, dress and interactions. Accept them for

what they are. Try to meet people. Go back to the place you came from for a visit, if you can. Keep your opinions to yourself. Be outgoing, friendly. Don't judge people before you get to know them. Don't be racist, sexist, etc. Go to concerts. Be sociable. Be cooperative at home. Don't compromise your values just to be accepted. Organize or go to parties. Try to meet someone before school starts. Join sports teams, bands and clubs. And finally, keep a sense of humour."

Families

One family of returnees (let's call them the Smiths) tell a story about choosing a telephone for their new house. They all got excited by the pamphlet Dad picked up from the phone centre on the way home from work. Mom, a freelance consultant, felt she needed a telephone in her study. Jason, 16, wanted his own number and voice-message service so his parents couldn't listen to his messages. He also really "needed" an extension in his room. Dad pointed out that it would be useful to have at least one handset in the hallway. Mom told Jason he could choose either his own handset or his own number, and he could forget about the voice-message service. Dad mentioned that most of the handsets on display were ugly and suggested a rotary dial phone would be more attractive in the hallway. Jason said there was no way he was having a rotary dial phone because "they're totally useless." At this point, Emma, who was nine, burst into tears and said the only thing she had ever wanted in her whole life was a phone in the shape of a coke bottle... Two days later, they got one modern handset with no special features and plugged it into the jack in the kitchen. End of story!

The challenge for families is to find ways to convert torture into quality time. Everyone's nerves are frayed, you've seen more than enough of each other, and you all wish you had friends to complain to. On any given day, Mom is on cloud nine because she got a job offer, Dad is frustrated because the dog has to stay in quarantine for another three weeks, and older brother is threatening to stow away on a plane back to Nairobi. Each family member seems to be working against the other.

Don't allow things to get worse by pretending there's no problem. There will be lots of conflict. Parents should be prepared for their children to be angry about having to move. There will be tension about money. Everyone will feel impatient, frustrated and rebellious, and for good reason. You all need to talk about how you feel and to understand how everyone else feels.

Spend quality time together, and make sure you choose activities everyone can enjoy. You may need to be creative. For example, if you decide to go on an outing, some of you can ride bicycles, others may skateboard, and still others can rollerblade. Try to find common goals or projects that allow each person some self-expression.

Use each other for support. Complain about home. Appreciate that your family may be the only ones who will listen to this stuff.

High-Risk Situations

Re-entry is very stressful. Combined with other pressures, it may become impossible to manage without support. If you experienced particularly dangerous or threatening circumstances while you were abroad, such as natural disasters, accidents, robberies, personal assaults or terrorist attacks, your symptoms of shock and stress may be delayed until you return home. You may benefit from professional counselling. One woman who was physically assaulted during an assignment in Africa coped very well until she returned home, where she found herself afraid to leave her apartment. Short-term counselling proved very helpful to her for managing the combined stresses of the assault and her return home.

Major life changes, such as the illness or death of someone close to you, the end of a long-term relationship, or the loss of work, can also cause excessive stress when combined with an international move. Similarly, if you have been forced to come home early for any reason, re-entry can be particularly difficult. One family cut short their posting to care for a terminally ill parent who died soon after their return. Three months later, the young son was still having difficulty adjusting to school and feeling very angry. The mother and father were depressed. The members of this family would have been good candidates for short-term counselling intervention.

We have described a few scenarios that can lead to excessively high levels of stress. Needless to say, there are countless more. As a rule, symptoms generally last a few weeks and should not be overly debilitating. However, if your symptoms continue for more than a few weeks, or if you are having difficulty managing the re-entry process, do not hesitate to contact a professional counsellor.

If you seek counselling, try to find a professional familiar with re-entry and adaptation issues. The Resources section at the end of this chapter provides a preliminary list of contacts that can refer you to someone in your area.

A LAST WORD

Where in the world do I belong? Everyone who has lived or worked overseas has asked this question. We face an unusual challenge in trying to create a sense of home and community without the benefits of a stable location or even a common language. It is frighteningly easy to lose all sense of home.

We must find alternative ways to develop roots. We can create continuity in our lives through objects we carry with us from place to place, activities we can enjoy anywhere in the world and rituals meaningful to us in any context. We must find ways to maintain friendships with people all over the world who we may not see for long periods of time. Most of all, we need to allow ourselves time to settle between moves.

Remind yourself that technology is advancing and the community of international travellers is expanding. Remember also that human beings have adapted to change throughout history. Ultimately, the events you experience, the cultures you encounter and the people you meet are a rich reward for the effort of adaptation.

ABOUT THE AUTHOR

This chapter was written by Betty-Ann Smith, with the assistance of her daughter, Jennifer. Elizabeth Smith has adapted it for THE BIG GUIDE TO LIVING AND WORKING OVERSEAS.

Betty-Ann Smith (MSW) is a counsellor specializing in psychological and emotional aspects of adjustment to international mobility. She has 21 years of experience conducting seminars for business, governmental and non-governmental organizations. She and her family have lived in Europe and the Middle East as well as in several Canadian cities. (For contact information, see the listing for Re-Entry Counselling Services in the Resources section below.)

RESOURCES

RE-ENTRY

Those of you who have done it know that coming home can be as difficult as moving abroad. More and more is being written about this important topic, and most resources dealing with culture shock discuss this topic, at least briefly. See also the Resources sections in Chapter 1, The Effective Overseas Employee, and Chapter 3, Living Overseas.

The Art of Coming Home 📖
1997, Craig Storti, Intercultural Press, 216 pages ➤ Masters & Scribes Bookshoppe, 9938 - 81 Ave., Edmonton, AB T6E 1W6, Canada, www.mastersandscribes.com, $24.50 CDN; Credit Cards; 800-378-3199, fax 780-439-6879 ◆ An examination of the issues faced by people returning from living and working overseas. This often overlooked but serious phenomenon is broken into four stages and examined through the use of anecdotes. Readers learn what to expect, and also receive helpful suggestions for overcoming the financial and emotional challenges arising from reintegration. A pre-emptive must for the overseas job seeker. [ID:2195]

Graybridge International Consulting Inc. 👯
Graybridge International Consulting Inc., 76 Rue Hotel-De-Ville, Gatineau, QC J8X 2E2, Canada, www.graybridge.ca, 800-259-4482, fax 819-776-6491, success@graybridge.ca ◆ This Canadian consulting firm has over 10 years' experience delivering a wide range of activities linked to international training and overseas management services. Offers cross-cultural and overseas effectiveness training, organizational development training, professional skills development training and international / domestic event coordination. (In June 2004, Graybridge was about to merge with Malkam Consultants Ltd.) [ID:2341]

Homeward Bound: A Spouse's Guide to Repatriation 📖
Robin Pascoe, Expatriate Press Limited, 194 pages ➤ Chapters Indigo Books, www.chapters.indigo.ca, $16.95; Credit Cards ◆ Homeward Bound captures the emotional upheaval experienced by many returning spouses as they face the challenges of re-entry. Drawing on her personal experience, Pascoe takes the reader step by step through the repatriation process. She addresses and offers advice to such re-entry challenges as professional reinvention, coping with re-entry shock, settling in the children and suppressing a natural anger and rage against the working partner. Health issues are also discussed—notably, fatigue and depression. [ID:2833]

People Development Ltd. 👯
People Development Ltd., 2050 Gottingen Street, Halifax, NS B3K 3A9, Canada, www.peopledevelopment.ns.ca, 902-425-6800, fax 902-423-7214 ◆ People Development re-entry programs include elements of cross-cultural adaptation, but the primary focus is on how to "come home and be home." Many returnees go through a period of "grieving." These programs focus on how to adjust and move beyond the grieving process by establishing support systems, creating self-care systems, developing objectives to establish equilibrium, and accepting losses and emotions. The program methodology is rooted in the principles of adult education. The experiences of both the program facilitators and the returnees involved are used to their fullest as resources for the participant group. [ID:2340]

Re-Entry Counselling Services 👯
Re-Entry Counselling Services ◆ We have selected the following counselling resources because of their familiarity with re-entry issues. Re-entry counselling is offered to individuals, couples and families and is usually short-term and solution focussed. ◆ Betty-Ann Smith, Vatican City, Rome, Italy, (39) 06-700-8250. ◆ FGI, Suite 200, 10 Commerce Valley Drive East, Thornhill, Ontario, L3T 7N7; 905-886-2157, fax 905-886-4337. (See their profile in the Moving Abroad Resource section of Chapter 2, "Living Overseas".) ◆ Allan Greenwood, 1685 136th Street, White Rock, BC V4A 4E3; 604-586-4227, awg123@telus.net. [ID:2366]

PART TWO

Acquiring International Experience

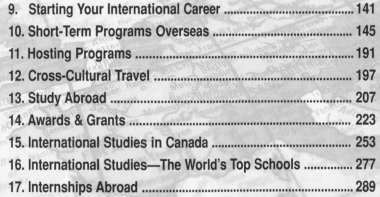

CHAPTER 9

Starting Your International Career

Gaining international career experience—building your international IQ—is a long-term endeavour. No single experience in itself will get you an international job. Rather, it is the cumulative effect of your many efforts that makes your international IQ credible and marketable to employers.

This chapter introduces you to a range of long-term strategies for developing international awareness and building career experience. Subsequent chapters offer more information and greater detail on these subjects.

Part Two of this guide, Acquiring International Experience, is divided into non-academic and academic chapters. Non-academic chapters comprise the first set, providing information on how to gain international experience outside of the university setting. (See Chapter 10, Short-Term Programs Overseas; Chapter 11, Hosting Programs; and Chapter 12, Cross-Cultural Travel, and see Larissa Brown's article, "My Experience Preparing for an International Career", in Appendix 18a on the CD-ROM.) The next set groups academic chapters together, providing important information for building your international career within the university and college setting. (See Chapter 13, Study Abroad; Chapter 14, Awards & Grants; Chapter 15, International Studies in Canada; Chapter 16, International Studies – The World's Top Schools and Chapter 17, Internships Abroad.)

Gaining international work experience is always a Catch-22 situation. You need experience to get that first job, but, how do you get experience if you haven't worked in the field before? The advice in this and the following chapters will help you build international experience and launch you into your first international job (most likely an internship)—your first stepping stone toward a paying international career.

International careers are not launched overnight. They are carefully built over a period of time. Your first international job will most likely provide you with on-the-job training—and the pay may be less than you desire. You may be required to do mundane work, perhaps even in harsh, remote areas of the world. As you gain experience, however, you will be rewarded with more responsibility, better pay and easier living conditions.

One last thing about this long path toward landing your first international job— the path is a fun and creative one, full of wonderful experiences. And the best part: you can jump off at any time and still have a lifetime of satisfying memories and experiences that will serve you well, no matter where you work.

HELPING CHILDREN BECOME INTERNATIONAL

An international IQ is best started in adolescence, or even earlier. If children are encouraged to explore and appreciate new cultures, learn languages and develop a sense of adventure and curiosity about the world, they will get a head start in developing a strong international IQ. As adults, it is our responsibility to encourage children to have a worldly outlook, to be tolerant of people with different cultural backgrounds and to have a healthy curiosity about the many peoples who inhabit this planet.

How do you encourage an international outlook in children? To start, recognize that children often take up the interests of their parents. If you are interested in other cultures, so, very likely, will your children. If you demonstrate tolerance and curiosity in the unknown, your children will probably follow suit. Children learn best by direct exposure, so travelling with offspring and immersing them in different cultures will broaden their outlook, particularly when they are old enough to appreciate the contrasts. If you are travelling without your children, involve them in preparations for your trip. Give them a world map to chart your route, or find books for them on the places you plan to visit. Once away, send them postcards describing foods, animals, toys, buildings, religions, etc. Suggest to your school board that it provide global education courses. Go to ethnic restaurants with your kids. Befriend people from other cultures living in Canada and encourage your children to do the same at school and in your neighbourhood. Encourage your kids' curiosity in children from other cultures by purchasing books on the subject. Promote conversation about the pleasures of cross-cultural friendships. Help children learn a second language or enrol them in early immersion schools.

Above all, remember that children can detect their parents' joy and anxieties. If you are enthralled with the challenges and rewards of cross-cultural interaction, this is likely to positively influence your children.

HIGH SCHOOL AND UNIVERSITY STUDENTS

For the high school and university student, the most important thing is to work hard in school. Read magazines and listen to international news coverage. There are excellent programs that allow you to spend a high school year living with a family in a foreign country (see Chapter 10, Short-Term Programs Overseas and Chapter 11, Hosting Programs). For university students, there is a plethora of international study programs at Canadian universities (see Chapter 16, International Studies – The World's Top Schools) and an enormous number of opportunities for internships (see Chapter 17, Internships Abroad). As learning a second language is essential for many international careers, it is important to start early (see Chapter 5, Learning a Foreign Language). There are also a host of exchange programs for young people that provide international experience (again, see Chapter 10, Short-Term Programs Overseas).

While at school, join international clubs and make friends with people from other cultures living in Canada. Socialize with them, taste their food, exchange views on the world. The closer you are to graduating from university, the more important it is to match your international education with cross-cultural volunteer and work experience. Become a leader/organizer in international groups, travel to international conferences, volunteer for professional internship positions. Start reading books on cross-cultural business skills—being able to articulate and discuss the cross-cultural work environment with others will be a crucial part of your international portfolio of skills.

Finally, don't be overwhelmed by the vast amount of information and range of approaches suggested in this book. Genuine curiosity and good humour are often the most useful qualities for a career of meeting and dealing with people from other cultures.

CHANGING CAREERS

If you are currently employed but wish to change careers, there are still many ways to increase your international IQ. Your challenge with international employers is to reshape the knowledge and experience you have of the Canadian workplace and translate it into the cross-cultural environment.

How can you do this when you haven't been overseas? The possibilities are endless, and are described in detail throughout this book. As a first step, work at becoming an expert on the international aspects of your field of work. Look for opportunities to meet people with international responsibilities whose work is similar to yours. Read books on doing business abroad. Sign up for university courses or attend seminars on international subjects relevant to you. Organize a group or conference around an international theme, or volunteer your services at international conferences in your area. Subscribe to international journals. Join the international branch of the CHAMBER OF COMMERCE. Start a local chapter of a national organization involved in international affairs. Become a member of a trade organization that has an international branch. Call the mayor's office to see what international visitors, delegates or trade missions are coming to your area and volunteer your talents to host them. Research your community's links to international trade. Talk to your local trade development council for information on its international efforts. Become familiar with intercultural groups and join intercultural commissions and studies at provincial and municipal levels. Participate in ethnic events. Join refugee and immigrant support groups. Become a volunteer on short-term programs overseas. Set up your own mid-career international internship. And, the easiest way to jump into the international world: teach English abroad to the over one billion people in the world who want to learn, and use this teaching experience as a stepping stone to other international careers.

Remember, it is never too late to seek the pleasures of international work, travel and friendship.

INTERNSHIPS

The importance of participating in internship programs is paramount. While the US has a long history of promoting internships to jump-start careers, Canada has only been whole-heartedly endorsing this system since the mid-1990s. There are thousands of internship opportunities. Internships are usually short-term professional positions ranging in length from two months to one year. While internship positions offer little or no salary, they can provide invaluable training and professional experience. And did we mention that they are plentiful? Most organizations in this book, from non-governmental organizations to private sector firms, have informal or formal internships. Canadians should not overlook that the federal government's international internship programs offer an astonishing 1,340 internships annually. (For internship leads, check out Chapter 10, Short-Term Programs Overseas; and Chapters 35 to 41 in Part Five, International Career Directories. For a description of the Canadian Government International Internship Programs, see Chapter 17, Internships Abroad.)

VOLUNTEERING

Many people start their international careers by volunteering for international organizations. Thousands of organizations around the world offer internationally-related volunteer positions. (See Chapter 10, Short-Term Programs Overseas; Chapter 38, NGOs in Canada; Chapter 39, NGOs in the US; and Chapter 40, NGOs in Europe & the Rest of the World.) As with any job, you must earn your volunteer position. If you live in a small town, you can begin your international volunteer work by starting a local committee of any one of the numerous NGOs with a local committee structure for volunteers. Remember, making money is not the most important factor—acquiring international experience is.

The best way to learn about an organization is to be proactive and find an innovative way to offer your services. Rather than announcing that you're looking for work (guaranteed to put some people off), look for opportunities to volunteer in your general area of expertise. A good volunteer is one who does not expect to be waited on. Most organizations find it difficult to manage volunteers, so it may be up to you to manage yourself. And it is your responsibility to overcome the frustrations and institutional roadblocks you encounter.

While you are lucky if you find work in a specific field, don't be overly concerned with targeting a precise area in which to volunteer. Take a long-term view by making yourself useful and getting involved anywhere you're needed in the international field. A generalist approach will help you acquire many essential skills and introduce you to the broader international community.

A LAST WORD

International work is a fascinating way to live and see the world. Whether you decide to live abroad for a short or long time, the insights you acquire—the wonders of other cultures, people, food and geography—will forever fill your thoughts and bring a deeper appreciation for life, wherever you live. Good luck with your international career and have a happy journey!

CHAPTER 10
Short-Term Programs Overseas

This chapter contains important information not only for those who want to enhance their chances of landing a job overseas, but also for individuals who are simply seeking personal growth through cultural travel. There are 108 mainly Canadian profiles in this chapter. Note that the information in this chapter overlaps with that provided in Chapter 17, Internships Abroad. Both chapters should be read to appreciate the full breadth of the advice we have to offer.

SHORT-TERM PROGRAMS FOR LONG-TERM GAIN

Participating in short-term placements and internships overseas is often the only way to begin an international career. Although these programs generally combine hard work with minimal financial compensation in the short-term, they can be a source of long-term gain, providing relevant job experience or a "foot in the door" with a Canadian organization engaged in international activities. Your willingness to participate in short-term programs will demonstrate to future employers your commitment and initiative.

Short-term placements overseas offer brief and invaluable experience. Challenging your skills, they allow you to demonstrate your strengths. Giving up the comfort and security of your home for unfamiliar languages, cultures, climates and accommodations can, after all, require courage, enterprise and adaptability. And as an opportunity to experience overseas work on a temporary basis, a placement can help you decide if an international career is for you!

Many people feel that working abroad should involve work in a field directly related to their studies. Though study-related work has obvious benefits, it is important to recognize that any kind of work abroad adds to one's maturity, ability to adapt and function effectively outside of Canada, and international career profile. As one placement officer put it, *"Experience working as a waiter in a pub in London or as a lifeguard in Sydney can impress a potential employer offering a career position."*

WHAT KINDS OF PROGRAMS ARE THERE?

A wide variety of short-term programs are available, but not all will be appropriate for you. Although the majority of short-term programs are less than a year in duration and are geared to individuals with little or no previous experience, some programs are more career-oriented and last up to two years. Qualifications vary. While some programs have few limitations regarding who may participate, others have age, nationality and educational restrictions. Respect the restrictions rather than manipulating your skills and background into a specific category. For example, it is best only to apply for missionary work if you are committed to its doctrine. Remuneration for most short-term placements is generally low, but gains in cross-cultural knowledge can be invaluable.

The 108 short-term programs overseas profiled in this chapter are divided into the following six categories: youth exchange, internship, professional exchange, teaching abroad, work and learn, and independent work and travel.

Youth Exchanges

There are a number of popular international exchange programs open to youth. These programs, which operate in a variety of industrialized and developing countries, are usually geared toward young people between 15 and 30 years of age, or toward a target age group within this range. Some are true exchanges—meaning that for every person or group sent overseas, a person or group comes to Canada—while others operate differently. Be sure to understand the terms of the exchange and its time frame, as some are designed for the summer and others for the school year.

A number of group exchanges are coordinated by provincial boards of education and non-profit organizations with limited funds. Group fundraising is common in many of these programs. While the organizations cover the costs of administering the program, participants are required to cover a large portion of the cost and are expected to help with fundraising efforts before or after the trip.

Keep in mind that youth exchanges are not study abroad programs that offer students academic credit. For such programs, see Chapter 13, Study Abroad; Chapter 15, International Studies in Canada; and Chapter 16, International Studies – The World's Top Schools.

Internships

This section covers opportunities for recent graduates or youth interested in gaining international work experience in their fields. Internship programs allow young Canadians to live and work in another country, gain valuable skills and make international contacts that will benefit their future careers, whether in Canada or abroad. Some internships do involve cost to the intern. When salaries are paid, they are usually only sufficient to cover living and travel expenses, and in some cases interns are provided with room and board in exchange for volunteer service. Again, the idea of short-term experience for long-term gain applies to internships, and the experience and exposure you can get from internships is second to none.

During the past 10 years, internship programs have become increasingly important. Internships are actually displacing other programs, often because they are directly linked to career building. There are so many internship programs that we have only listed a selected few here. More specifically, we have not described the numerous programs financed by the Canadian federal government and its hundreds of partner organizations. These programs provide approximately 1,500 international internships per annum. This is an enormous number in comparison to the size of the Canadian job market. All these internships have an international component and are invaluable for young people wanting to "go international." (For more information on the Canadian Government International Internship programs, see the Profiles section in Chapter 17, Internships Abroad. The programs listed in this chapter actually overlap with those in Chapter 17, Internships Abroad. Both chapters should be read for the general advice offered and for the profiles listed.)

Professional Exchanges

The professional exchanges listed in this chapter are offered through non-governmental organizations. Professional exchanges are geared toward the participant's area of expertise, and usually require at least a few years of relevant experience. They vary in length, but usually last one year. Salaries often only cover travel expenses and a stipend for living, but the professional rewards usually surpass monetary compensation. These exchanges offer first-hand experience with other cultures and lasting personal and business contacts.

Teaching Abroad

Teaching abroad is an excellent way to see and experience a new area of the world. Your daily interaction with students will give you unparalleled exposure and insight into your host countries. The length of programs varies, but a commitment of at least one year is usually required. Usually travel expenses are covered and a stipend is provided. Most provincial school boards facilitate teaching abroad experiences for their teachers. Requirements vary. Although some programs require a teaching certificate or university degree, many require no prior experience. (For more information, see Chapter 29, Teaching Abroad.)

Work and Learn

These programs are seldom professional work opportunities. They usually, but not always, offer an opportunity to volunteer with a community work project or development organization. Most offer a combination of work, scheduled events and free time. These projects can offer useful opportunities for studying a foreign language or immersing yourself in another culture. Lodgings are usually provided, but not travel expenses. Salaries are sometimes offered.

Independent Work and Travel

Several countries issue working holiday visas to youth for a period ranging from six months to two years. Working holiday programs are designed to allow youths to extend the length of their overseas holiday by engaging in short-term casual employment. Finding employment is usually the responsibility of the visa holder. Check embassy Web sites to find out specific information regarding working visa conditions. One of the best-known working holiday programs is SWAP (the Student Work Abroad Programme), which is more broad in program offerings than many other work and learn programs. (For more information on SWAP, see Dave Smith's article, "The Value of SWAP", in Appendix 10a on the CD-ROM; see the SWAP profiles at the end of this chapter; and see SWAP's ad in the sponsor section at the end of this guide.)

APPLYING TO PROGRAMS

Many short-term programs don't require much international experience or any professional skills. Instead, they depend upon mature, committed and enthusiastic individuals who can work well in groups and in situations that require hard work and initiative.

Having leadership, entrepreneurial or organizational skills, coupled with a demonstrated history of involvement in other projects or organizations, is beneficial; don't panic if your resume shows little volunteer experience. Many programs are designed for inexperienced participants. Some organizations look for commitment to their ideals and aims, and it's a good idea to discuss with them how your participation will help further their goals. Your involvement may, for example, increase your own community's awareness of global issues.

Begin your search for short-term overseas programs well in advance of your intended departure date. Application dates vary widely, and it is important to leave yourself enough time for applying and preparing for departure. With some organizations you can expect to wait 18 months before departure, and most require that you apply at least 6 to 8 months in advance.

If you are turned down by the selection committee, don't hesitate to appeal. Participants often cancel at the last minute, giving rejected applicants a second opportunity to be considered. It is important to maintain contact with the selection committee and to show continued enthusiasm for the programs you are interested in. If all else fails, reapply the following year.

MAKE YOUR VOLUNTEER EXPERIENCE PROFESSIONAL

Altruistic impulses, often the motivation for volunteer work, can also help your career. Volunteering for a project, even a project unrelated to your career field, may enhance your chance of securing overseas work at a later date. Whatever volunteer work you do, show initiative, work hard and put yourself in positions of responsibility. These traits will not go unnoticed. For example, help your program leader with administrative work and look for similar opportunities with organizations in your host country. You could also extend your visit by volunteering with an organization and living with a host family or by creating your own internship with a local organization. Don't forget to ask supervisors and managers for letters of recommendation. It's much harder to contact them after the program has ended and you have returned to Canada.

It goes without saying that it is important to expand your international experience by travelling around your host country. It's worthwhile to discover new areas and to see the country from outside the formal structure of your work program. The well-travelled individual gains a greater sensitivity to other people, and is more comfortable and effective in cross-cultural work situations.

WHAT TO EXPECT FROM THE ORGANIZATION

Most short-term overseas programs are not heavily structured and many organizations will not give you a lot of guidance. You will be expected to be independent and to cope on your own. Being in an unfamiliar place and trying to obtain access to basic services overseas can sometimes be a daunting experience, to say the least. You will probably surprise yourself with your own tenacity, enterprise and ability to survive. Be prepared to be challenged, and be patient. (For complementary advice, make sure you read Chapter 3, Living Overseas.)

A LAST WORD

There are a number of points to consider when comparing short-term overseas programs. The first considerations are cost, availability of a work or activity schedule, travel arrangements, health insurance, and orientation programs or materials. You should then consider the location of the program and the political stability of the region. Educate yourself by reading newspapers and checking current embassy security updates on areas of the world to avoid. On a more philosophical level, consider the purpose of the program and whether or not you are comfortable with the ideals and objectives of the organization. Lastly, look at the track record of the program or organization. Ask the organization to put you in touch with former participants. They will be an invaluable source of information and can give you advice on how to apply, what to expect and what resources to bring.

APPENDIX ON THE CD-ROM

10a. "The Value of SWAP," by Dave Smith

RESOURCES

SHORT-TERM PROGRAMS OVERSEAS

This list covers a wide range of short-term opportunities overseas, primarily focusing on summer and young adult volunteer programs. They usually require little skill, but demand hard work, enthusiasm and initiative. These programs are an invaluable first step for anyone wishing to bank overseas experiences for future, paid international employment. At this stage, your focus should be on learning about yourself, and building cross-cultural communication and intercultural understanding skills. Refer also to the Resources sections in Chapter 12, Cross-Cultural Travel; Chapter 13, Study Abroad; Chapter 15, International Studies in Canada; Chapter 16, International Studies – The World's Top Schools; and Chapter 17, Internships Abroad.

University of Alberta International Centre ♔
www.international.ualberta.ca ◆ The University of Alberta International Centre has an excellent Web site that offers a database of opportunities for study abroad, summer study programs, volunteering abroad and working overseas. Simply enter your regional preference and browse the opportunities available. Even if you are not a U of A student, there is lots of information available to assist non-students in their search for overseas experience. [ID:2216]

The Au Pair & Nanny's Guide to Working Abroad 📖
2002, Susan Griffith, Sharon Legg, Vacation Work, 320 pages ➤ Globe Pequot Press, P.O. Box 480, 246 Goose Lane, Guilford, CT 06437, USA, www.globepequot.com, $17.95 US; VISA, MC; 888-249-7586, fax 800-820-2329 ◆ This British book is for anyone looking for short- or long-term

work abroad as an au pair, nanny or mother's help. Highlights how to find the thousands of vacancies in Europe and worldwide and what experience or training is necessary. Includes a directory of 286 agencies and regional guides to the opportunities in 24 countries. Special features on cooking, first aid, games and entertainment for children. [ID:2108]

The Back Door Guide to Short-Term Job Adventures 📖
2002, 436 pages ➤ Ten Speed Press, P.O. Box 7123, Berkeley, CA 94707, USA, www.tenspeed.com, $31.95 US; Credit Cards; 800-404-4446 ◆ Tempted to chuck your 9-to-5 job to be a whitewater rafting guide in Alaska? Always wanted to spend your summer restoring a medieval castle in the south of France? This one-of-a-kind guide contains more than 1,000 opportunities to work, play, learn, help, create, experience and grow. [ID:2684]

Canada Corps 🏛
www.CanadaCorps.gc.ca; *Fr* ◆ At the time of printing, the Canadian government made a commitment to create Canada Corps under Foreign Affairs Canada (FAC). Canada Corps will enhance linkages among existing Canadian efforts and explore new partnerships with other levels of government and the private sector. The initiative will harness the energy and experience of Canadian experts, volunteers and young professionals to deliver international assistance in the areas of governance and institution building. Keep an eye on their Web site for exciting developments about this new initiative. [ID:2839]

Centre d'Information sur le Volontariat International 🖥
www.civiweb.com/default.asp?action=offres; *Fr* ◆ Centre d'Information sur le Volontariat International : site français avec des offres de volontariat à travers le monde et conseils pour devenir volontaire. [ID:2676]

Courrier international 🖥
www.courrierinternational.com; *Fr* ◆ Hebdomadaire français d'information internationale avec une section Emplois internationaux, incluant différents stages et une rubrique d'informations ayant pour titre « S'expatrier » (informations sur différents pays, conseils, études sur les niveaux de salaire des jeunes diplômés dans le monde et sur les différents modes de recrutement en Europe). [ID:2704]

The Directory of Work & Study in Developing Countries 📖
1997, Robert Miller, 256 pages ➤ Vacation Work, 9 Park End Street, Oxford, OX1 1HJ, UK, www.vacationwork.co.uk, £9.99; Credit Cards; (44)(0)(1865) 24-1978, sales@vacationwork.co.uk ◆ For those who wish to experience life in a developing country as more than a tourist. Thousands of short- and long- term opportunities for work and study with over 400 organizations in Africa, the Middle East, Asia, the Far East, the Pacific, Latin America and the Caribbean, including health care, engineering, disaster relief, agriculture, business, teaching, archaeology, economics, oil, irrigation, etc. [ID:2047]

Exchanges Canada 🖥
Department of Canadian Heritage, www.exchanges.gc.ca, exchanges@pch.gc.ca; *Fr* ◆ Exchanges Canada is a Government of Canada initiative that creates opportunities for young Canadians to gain a better understanding of their country, to connect with one another and to experience the diversity of Canada's communities, languages and cultures. The Web site has an excellent list with which job seekers can search international exchanges by destination, exchange name, area of interest and delivery organization. Teachers: don't miss the Fulbright Teacher Exchange Program profiled in the exchange listings. [ID:2441]

Focus 🖥
Quarterly ➤ Canadian Executive Service Organization (CESO), Suite 700, 700 Bay Street, Toronto, ON M5G 1Z6, Canada, www.ceso-saco.com, Free on-line; 416-961-2376, fax 416-961-1096 ◆ This newsletter features articles about the organization's worldwide activities. CESO is a non-governmental voluntary agency that sends Canadians with professional, technical and managerial skills to be volunteer consultants to business organizations in Canadian aboriginal communities and in developing countries. [ID:2030]

Foreign Policy Association 🖳
Foreign Policy Association, www.fpa.org ◆ International job postings categorized by development assistance, education, environment, humanitarian relief, health and population, research, youth and other. Also a great listing of internships and volunteer opportunities. Highly recommended. [ID:2579]

Get Ready! Hints for a Healthy Short-Term Assignment Overseas 📖
2001 ➤ CUSO, Suite 500, 2255 Carling Ave., Ottawa, ON K2B 1A6, Canada, www.cuso.org, $7 CDN; 613-829-7445, fax 613-829-7996; ℱ ◆ Available in French under the title "Á votre santé!" This booklet can be used by both the experienced and inexperienced Canadian traveller going to a developing country for a period of six months or less. It provides health information and advice in an easy-to-read and accessible manner. [ID:2100]

Go Abroad Fair ⋔
www.goabroadfair.ca ◆ Every year, young Canadians pack their bags to experience the world. With limitless choices about where to study, travel or work overseas, they have some big decisions to make. The Go Abroad Fair gives students and youth interested in going abroad a chance to meet exhibitors from cultural and educational organizations, study abroad programs, universities, colleges, institutes of technology, travel agencies, as well as work and volunteer abroad programs. It's the most comprehensive fair of its kind in Canada and admission is free! The Go Abroad Fair takes place every October in Toronto. (For more information, see their ad in the sponsor section at the end of this guide.) [ID:2838]

Great Learning Vacations.Com 🖳
www.greatlearningvacations.com ◆ A site dedicated to travellers who crave "hands on" learning experiences, from tours with award-winning photographers, to cooking courses in Tuscany, watercolour painting weekends in the Canadian wilderness or even astronaut training camps in the USA. Created by award-winning travel journalist Lucy Izon, the site acts as an information gateway, providing feature stories, news, helpful trip-planning links and a worldwide 22-category directory of learning opportunities for travellers. The site is designed to stimulate readers with suggestions for experiential learning opportunities that they may not have previously considered. [ID:2753]

Green Volunteers 📖
2003, Fabio Ausenda, Universe Books, 256 pages ➤ Vacation Work, 9 Park End Street, Oxford, OX1 1HJ, UK, www.vacationwork.co.uk, £10.99; Credit Cards; (44) (0) (1865) 24-1978, sales@vacationwork.co.uk ◆ This leading source of conservation volunteering opportunities lists almost 200 projects and organizations through which you can volunteer without previous experience and work throughout the year with marine mammals, sea turtles, primates and a wide range of wildlife in National Parks, rain forests and a variety of unusual locations. Contains information on projects lasting from one to three weeks, but also highlights projects lasting an entire year. Great for finding thesis and research opportunities and starting your green international career. [ID:2544]

Guardian Angel: How To Be a Supportive Parent or Guardian
When Your Young Adult Decides to Work or Study Abroad 📖
1999, Jeffrey Holmes, Canadian Bureau for International Education (CBIE), 30 pages ➤ www.destineducation.ca, Free on-line ◆ This practical, easy-to-read Canadian guide is chock full of advice for the parent/guardian of a young person embarking on a first international adventure. The author highlights opportunities for young people to participate in exchange programs and examines how to assist before, during and after the young adult goes abroad. Health issues, academic issues, visiting and re-entry are some of the topics touched upon. This guide is an essential resource for parents/guardians and the work/study abroad adviser. [ID:2792]

Le guide des jobs pour changer d'air 📖
2002, Dakota Éditions, 160 pages ➤ Les Éditions Ulysse, 4176 rue St-Denis, Montréal, QC H2W 2M5, Canada, www.guidesulysse.com/cc/main_achat.htm, $17.95 CDN; Cartes de crédit; 514-843-

9447, fax 514-843-9448; *Fr* ◆ Ouvrage qui propose des centaines d'emplois tous plus dépaysants les uns que les autres, 120 fiches employeurs du monde entier détaillées, des pistes surprenantes et différentes destinations. [ID:2717]

Le Guide du Routard Expat 📖
2002, Philippe Gloaguen, 500 pages ➤ Éditions Hachette Tourisme, 43 quai de Grenelle, Paris Cedex 15, 75905, France, www.hachette.com, €7.90; (33) (1) 43-92-30-00; *Fr* ◆ Le Guide de l'expatrié nous brosse un portrait des secteurs qui embauchent à l'étranger (incluant entreprises et organismes) et nous conseille sur les marches à suivre pour l'expatriation. [ID:2720]

Guides du Job-Trotter au Canada, en Espagne et en Grande-Bretagne 📖
2002, Dakota Éditions, 200 pages ➤ Les Éditions Ulysse, 4176 rue St-Denis, Montreal, QC H2W 2M5, Canada, www.guidesulysse.com/cc/main_achat.htm, $22.95 CDN; Credit Cards; 514-843-9447, fax 514-843-9448; *Fr* ◆ Ces trois guides nous éclairent sur la situation de l'emploi au Canada, en Espagne et en Grande-Bretagne. On dresse une liste d'adresses d'employeurs dans tous les domaines, sites Internet et organismes qui fournissent emplois & stages, formalités pour décrocher un permis de travail, un logement, une protection sociale, etc. [ID:2719]

Host Family Survival Kit: A Guide for American Host Families 📖
1997, Nancy King, Ken Huff, Intercultural Press, 215 pages ➤ Masters & Scribes Bookshoppe, 9938 - 81 Ave., Edmonton, AB T6E 1W6, Canada, www.mastersandscribes.com, $23 CDN; Credit Cards; 800-378-3199, fax 780-439-6879 ◆ This US guide promotes an understanding of the exchange experience by bringing to life the joys and challenges of hosting. The book examines the role the exchange student plays in the host family and the skills needed for host parenting. It also provides an insightful examination of cultural differences. [ID:2088]

International Centre, Queen's University 🏛
www.queensu.ca/quic/home.htm ◆ This site is well organized and offers a variety of services geared toward securing overseas placements. The resource library contains videos and printed resources on issues like cultural adaptation and re-entry. The links section is extensive and puts you in touch with a number of placement and job search organizations. [ID:2220]

The International Directory of Voluntary Work 📖
2002, David Woodworth, Vacation Work, 320 pages ➤ Globe Pequot Press, P.O. Box 480, 246 Goose Lane, Guilford, CT 06437, USA, www.globepequot.com, $19.95 US; VISA, MC; 888-249-7586, fax 800-820-2329 ◆ This UK guide profiles over 750 organizations around the world seeking volunteers. Covers short-, medium- and long-term possibilities in Europe and around the world. Opportunities for both skilled and unskilled workers of any age group to work in conservation, development, medicine, education, archaeology, and agriculture as well as with refugees, orphans and other populations. [ID:2044]

International Youth and Young Workers Exchange Programs 🏛
www.dfait-maeci.gc.ca/english/culture/youthex.html; *Fr* ◆ This directory, maintained by Foreign Affairs Canada (FAC), is designed for the use of Canadians between the ages of 18 and 35 who are seeking employment abroad. It lists opportunities by region and describes ways of gaining access to employment markets around the world. [ID:2241]

InternationalStudent.com 💻
www.internationalstudent.com ◆ This Web site provides comprehensive information to international job seekers and students, including advice on work-permit applications and applying for jobs in the US, the UK, Europe, Canada and Australia; studying abroad; scholarships; grants and other information to assist students in their quest to study abroad. [ID:2627]

Invest Yourself: The Catalogue of Volunteer Opportunities 📖
Annual, Susan Angus, 280 pages ➤ Commission on Voluntary Service and Action, Suite 902, 1 Union Square W., New York, NY 10003, USA, $10 US; Credit Cards; 646-486-2446, www.amazon.com ◆ Comprehensive listings of full-time volunteer positions offered through North American nonprofit organizations. Placements are located in North America and overseas and range

from a few weeks to a summer to a few years. International opportunities are not listed separately, but are indexed. Order directly from Publisher. [ID:2017]

Kibbutz Volunteer 📖

2000, John Bedford, 224 pages ➤ Vacation Work, 9 Park End Street, Oxford, OX1 1HJ, UK, www.vacationwork.co.uk, $17.95 US; Credit Cards; (44) (0) (1865) 24-1978, sales@vacationwork.co.uk ◆ The comprehensive guide to Kibbutz life that not only gives full details of 200 Kibbutzim and conveys their special atmosphere but also covers other short-term work in Israel including the Moshav movement, conservation, archaeological digs, fruit picking, au pair and hotel work, etc. Detailed information on Israel itself, including customs, the main sites, where to stay, hitch-hiking, weather, beaches, bargaining, travelling, and holy days, make this an essential overseas job search resource for those interested in Israel. [ID:2111]

La mission des fonctionnaires internationaux ᛃᛃ

www.france.diplomatie.fr/mfi; 𝐹𝑟 ◆ Site du Ministère des affaires étrangères en France: informations générales, listes des avis de vacances de postes des organisations internationales, postes spécifiques pour jeunes professionnels, stages, etc. [ID:2705]

Mobility International USA 💻

www.miusa.org ◆ This US Web site describes hundreds of opportunities for people with challenges to mobility in international educational exchange programs, work camps and volunteer positions. Includes first-person accounts of travel and learning experiences. [ID:2626]

Outpost Magazine - Travel for Real 📖

Quarterly ➤ www.outpostmagazine.com, $20 for 6 issues; VISA, MC ◆ Outpost Magazine is Canada's own sophisticated travel magazine—Winner of Canada's top magazine award - The Presidents Medal. You needn't subscribe in order to access travel articles and information, but after reading the free stuff, you just might want to! (For more information, see their ad in the sponsor section at the end of this guide.) [ID:2338]

Peace Corps ᛃᛃ

www.peacecorps.gov ◆ This is the Web site of the United States Peace Corps, one of the world's most successful and respected development organizations. Peace Corps sends volunteers overseas to work in development-related, 27-month projects. The organization also hires overseas and domestic program administrators, so be sure to check out those opportunities! [ID:2625]

Planning Your Gap Year 📖

2003, Nick Vandome, 188 pages ➤ How To Books Ltd., 3 Newtec Place, Magdalen Road, Oxford, OX4 1RE, UK, www.howtobooks.co.uk, $22.96 US; Credit Cards; (44) (1752) 202-301, fax (44) (1865) 202-331 ◆ This British guide to taking a year off includes topics such as preparation, deciding when to go, staying healthy and overcoming the pitfalls and problems of travel. Over 220 contact organizations are listed while personal accounts from people who've been there and done it provide useful advice. Lots of good information for university graduates as well. [ID:2398]

Summer Jobs Abroad 2004 📖

Annual, David Woodworth, Vacation Work, 304 pages ➤ Globe Pequot Press, P.O. Box 480, 246 Goose Lane, Guilford, CT 06437, USA, www.globepequot.com, $17.95 US; VISA, MC; 888-249-7586, fax 800-820-2329 ◆ This British guide to summer jobs abroad contains details of over 30,000 vacancies in over 50 countries, from Austria to Costa Rica, for sports instructors, bar staff, holiday company reps, kibbutz volunteers, English teachers, tour guides, farm hands, archaeologists and fruit pickers etc. Includes full details of who to apply to, period of work, what qualifications are needed and how to go about acquiring work permits and visas. [ID:2058]

Summer Jobs in Britain 2004 📖

Annual, David Woodworth, Andrew James, 304 pages ➤ Globe Pequot Press, P.O. Box 480, 246 Goose Lane, Guilford, CT 06437, USA, www.globepequot.com, $17.95 US; VISA, MC; 888-249-7586, fax 800-820-2329 ◆ In this guide you'll find everything you need to land that summer job in

Britain including where the jobs are; details of wages; experience needed; regional prospects; info on taxes; minimum wage rates; tips on applying and the essentials of preparation. Explore a huge range of opportunities, find something suited to you and kick-start your international resume. [ID:2545]

Summer Jobs in Canada 📖

Annual, Kevin Makra ➤ Sentor Media Inc., Suite 1120, 388 Richmond Street W., Toronto, ON M5V 3P1, Canada, www.sentormedia.com, $24.95 CDN; VISA, MC; 416-971-5090, fax 416-977-3782 ◆ Provides an exhaustive list of employers and organizations that offer the best summer jobs in the country. Have you ever considered being a camp counsellor, painter, landscaper or web technician? These and many other exciting summer positions are available to you! Each job profile contains: contact name and address, website, employer description, job information, types of positions, and how to apply. In addition you'll find: How to find a summer job, How to get your Social Insurance Number (SIN), Job search tips throughout, and job safety in the workplace. Whether you are a high school, college or university student, this is the first and only book providing essential information on Summer Jobs in Canada! (For more information, see their ad in the sponsor section at the end of this guide.) [ID:2801]

Summer Jobs Search 💻

www.summerjobs.com/index.html ◆ This is a relatively small database with limited counselling and other job-related services. However, it is unique in that it provides a listing of short-term and summer employment opportunities throughout the world. Worth a glance as it may be the place to find a summer adventure. Very easy to use. [ID:2244]

Summer Jobs USA 📖

Annual, 390 pages ➤ Thomson Peterson's, P.O. Box 2123, Princeton, NJ 08543-2123, USA, www.petersons.com, $18.95 US; Credit Cards; 800-338-3282, fax 609-243-9150 ◆ This US publication lists more than 55,000 summer jobs for students with nearly 800 employers in the US, Canada and overseas. Data profiles include general information about the employer, location, setting and features; a profile of summer employees (number of employees, ages, gender, education level, geographic residence); job information (number of positions, background and requirements, pay, application procedures); benefits and pre-employment training; and contact information. Employers are listed alphabetically by state and country. A great resource for looking for work in the US. [ID:2128]

Summer Study Abroad 📖

2003, 800 pages ➤ Thomson Peterson's, P.O. Box 2123, Princeton, NJ 08543-2123, USA, www.petersons.com, $29.95 US; Credit Cards; 800-338-3282, fax 609-243-9150 ◆ This US book is ideal for students looking for a shorter overseas experience. It is the summer program counterpart to "Study Abroad 2004" and presents readers with updated descriptions of more than 1,700 once-in-a-lifetime summer academic, volunteer and foreign language programs. In addition to eligibility requirements, living arrangements and financial aid, it also offers special advice for students interested in non-traditional destinations. [ID:2444]

Taking a Gap Year 📖

2003, Vacation Work, 448 pages ➤ Globe Pequot Press, P.O. Box 480, 246 Goose Lane, Guilford, CT 06437, USA, www.globepequot.com, $19.95 US; VISA, MC; 888-249-7586, fax 800-820-2329 ◆ This is the definitive handbook for all those students who want to travel or work before or after they begin university. Gives details on companies that arrange special gap year programs, work experience, voluntary work, seasonal jobs and languages. Includes country information on opportunities to be found all over the world. A great resource! [ID:2543]

Taking a Year Out 📖

2002, Nick Vandome, 176 pages ➤ How To Books Ltd., 3 Newtec Place, Magdalen Road, Oxford, OX4 1RE, UK, www.howtobooks.co.uk, £9.34; Credit Cards; (44) (1752) 202-301, fax (44) (1865) 202-331 ◆ This British guide to taking a year out includes topics such as preparing before you go, deciding when to go, staying healthy, and overcoming the pitfalls and problems of travel. [ID:2507]

Teaching and Projects Abroad 🖳
www.teaching-abroad.co.uk ◆ This is a fabulous British Web site that caters to anyone wishing to use their skills to teach abroad. By no means limited to teaching English, this site allows you to explore teaching opportunities in the fields of medicine, conservation, journalism, veterinary medicine, business and archaeology to name just a few. Alternatively, the site offers a portal through which you can organize electives and placements with other teachers in your field in other countries. Highly recommended! [ID:2693]

Tourisme jeunesse ⛺
Tourisme jeunesse www.tourismej.qc.ca/images/boutiques5.html; Fr ◆ Un organisme sans but lucratif qui regroupe les détenteurs québécois de la carte internationale des auberges de jeunesse; leur site regroupe des informations touristiques pour la jeunesse incluant, sous la rubrique Voyages, une liste de ressources pour dénicher des emplois saisonniers et temporaires, carrières professionnelles et universitaires à l'étranger ainsi que des bourses d'études. [ID:2182]

Transitions Abroad 📖
Bimonthly, Clay Hubbs ➤ Department TRA, Transitions Publishing, P.O. Box 745, Bennington, VT 05201, USA, www.transitionsabroad.com, $32 US/year; Credit Cards; 802-442-4827, fax 802-442-4827 ◆ An excellent periodical. Required reading for students and globe trotters planning to travel, study or work abroad. Promotes learning through direct involvement in the daily lives of peoples of host countries. Describes publications, information sources, organizations, and programs offering study opportunities, entry-level jobs and living arrangements abroad. Highly recommended. (For more information, see their ad in the sponsor section at the end of this guide.) [ID:2074]

United Nations Volunteers (UNV) 🖳
www.unv.org ◆ This program offers mid-career professionals the opportunity to volunteer overseas in a humanitarian effort. Every year some 5,000 UN Volunteers from more than 150 different nationalities take part in the programs of the United Nations itself as well as UN funds, programs and specialized agencies. This informative and user-friendly site has all the information you need to become a UN Volunteer and gain international experience. [ID:2153]

Verge Magazine 📖
Quarterly ➤ Verge Magazine Inc., 1517 B Schutt Road, Palmer Rapids, ON K0J 2E0, Canada, www.vergemagazine.ca, $10.95 for 3 issues; VISA; 613-758-9909, fax 613-758-9914, editor@vergemagazine.ca ◆ Verge is Canada's magazine for people who travel with purpose. Exploring opportunities to work, study, volunteer and travel overseas, Verge Magazine provides tips, expert advice, program profiles and loads of information to send you packing. Broaden your horizons - see the world! (For more information, see their ad in the sponsor section at the end of this guide.) [ID:2843]

VFP International Workcamp Directory 🖳
Annual ➤ International Workcamps, Volunteers for Peace (VFP), 1034 Tiffany Road, Belmont, VT 05730, USA, www.vfp.org, Free on-line; Credit Cards; 802-259-2759, fax 802-259-2922 ◆ Updated frequently, this is a directory of over 2,400 short-term volunteer programs around the world. The directory is accessible for free, but registration as a volunteer costs $20.00 US, with actual placements in workcamps ranging from $200-400 US dollars each. This fee covers the full cost of room and board during your work camp experience. An excellent chance to test the overseas working waters. [ID:2078]

Vivre à l'étranger 🖳
www.vivrealetranger.com; Fr ◆ Site français sur la mobilité internationale : articles et dossiers sur différents pays, guide pratique de l'expatriation (stages, volontariat, préparation, déménagement, santé, assurances). [ID:2707]

What in the World is Going On? 🖳
2001, Alan Cumyn, Canadian Bureau for International Education (CBIE), 40 pages ➤ www.destineducation.ca, Free on-line; Fr ◆ This Canadian guide is geared both toward

professionals beginning their careers and those winding it down who want a different and challenging overseas work or study experience. If you want to go abroad for an extended period and settle in the country, then this guide is an excellent first resource intended to get you on the right track. Recommended. [ID:2702]

Work Abroad: The Complete Guide to Finding a Job Overseas 📖
2002, Clay Hubbs, 224 pages ➤ Transitions Abroad, P.O. Box 745, Bennington, VT 05201, USA, www.transitionsabroad.com, $15.95 US; Credit Cards; 802-442-4827, fax 802-442-4827, publisher@TransitionsAbroad.com ◆ A comprehensive US guide to all aspects of international work, including work permits, short-term jobs, teaching English, volunteer opportunities, planning an international career, starting your own business and much more. [ID:2262]

Work Your Way Around The World 📖
2003, Susan Griffith, 576 pages ➤ Globe Pequot Press, P.O. Box 480, 246 Goose Lane, Guilford, CT 06437, USA, www.globepequot.com, $19.95 US; VISA, MC; 888-249-7586, fax 800-820-2329 ◆ Includes details on pre-trip preparation, red tape, visas and tax, getting a job before you go and how to make speculative and opportunistic applications. Find information on how to travel around the world for free, very cheaply or even get paid for your voyage. Read descriptions of different types and areas of work including tourism, agriculture, teaching English, childcare, business and industry, volunteering and many more. Vivid first-hand accounts from working travellers give a flavour of what the work is actually like. [ID:2046]

World Volunteers 📖
2003, Universe Books, 256 pages ➤ Vacation Work, 9 Park End Street, Oxford, OX1 1HJ, UK, www.vacationwork.co.uk, $14.95 US; Credit Cards; (44) (0) (1865) 24-1978, sales@vacationwork.co.uk ◆ A UK-based guide for anyone who wants to get involved worldwide in helping those who suffer. Includes details on finding the most suitable project to match your interests and abilities and becoming a volunteer in a developing country. Highlights projects from one month to several years in a variety of settings: from work camps to internships. [ID:2546]

World Wildlife Fund Canada 🖥
www.wwfcanada.org ◆ WWF Canada is part of the international WWF network, which seeks to stop degradation of the planet's natural environment and to build a future in which humans live in harmony with nature by conserving the world's biological diversity, ensuring that the use of renewable resources is sustainable and promoting the reduction of pollution and wasteful consumption. Check this Web site out to find program information as well as career and volunteering sections that are regularly updated. [ID:2344]

Worldwide Volunteering 📖
2004, 628 pages ➤ How To Books Ltd., 3 Newtec Place, Magdalen Road, Oxford, OX4 1RE, UK, www.howtobooks.co.uk, £17.99; Credit Cards; (44) (1752) 202-301, fax (44) (1865) 202-331 ◆ This UK text is an A-to-Z directory focusing on volunteer projects. It covers over 800 organizations and over 250,000 annual placements throughout the UK and in 200 other countries. It is indexed by both project and country. A fabulous resource for planning your overseas short-term program. [ID:2508]

Profiles of Short-Term Programs Overseas

There are a total of 108 short-term programs overseas (SPOs) listed in this chapter. These programs have been divided into six categories. There are 32 youth exchanges; 16 internships; 14 professional exchanges; 12 teaching abroad programs; 20 work and learn programs; and 14 independent work and travel programs.

Participating in a short-term overseas program is an important step in expanding your global horizons and building ties across cultures. For many, it is also the initial step required for launching an international career.

AFS Interculture Canada (AFS)
1425 boul.Rene-Levesque ouest, Montreal, QC, H3G 1T7, Canada;
514-288-3282, fax 514-843-9119, info-canada@afs.org, www.afscanada.org ▭ *Fr*

YOUTH EXCHANGE ◆ AFS Interculture Canada's (AFS) core programs immerse Canadians from ages 15 to 18 in a foreign cultural and linguistic environment. Students can choose a year, semester or summer term in one of more than 40 countries. AFS also provides placements in Canada for some 250 foreign students from 36 countries, to attend high school and live with volunteer families. Participants must be in good health and mature enough to handle the challenges of adapting to a new way of life. AFS also offers adult programs for participants over 18 years of age. The programs currently offered are: Dialogue Across The Americas and Internship and International Community Service. (For more information on AFS, see Chapter 11, Hosting Programs and Chapter 38, NGOs in Canada.) [ID:7100]

Aga Khan Foundation Canada (AKFC)
FELLOWSHIP IN INTERNATIONAL DEVELOPMENT MANAGEMENT
Suite 1220, 350 Albert Street, Ottawa, ON, K1R 7X7, Canada;
613-237-2532, fax 613-567-2532, info@akfc.ca, www.akfc.ca

INTERNSHIP ◆ Aga Khan Foundation Canada (AKFC) offers two nine-month fellowships in international development that send recent graduates and young professionals overseas to learn first-hand about development. The Fellowship in International Development Management (IDM) offers a four-week management seminar in Ottawa followed by an eight-month work placement with a non-governmental organization in Asia or Africa. Up to 15 fellowships are awarded each year. The Fellowship in International Microfinance and Microenterprise (FIMM) offers an intensive four-week training course in Ottawa, in which participants receive a solid grounding in the latest microfinance and mircoenterprise concepts followed by an eight-month placement with an NGO in Asia or Africa. Up to 10 fellowships are awarded each year. These programs are aimed at young Canadians with a clear commitment to international development who are seeking to build their professional careers. During the program, participants undertake a practical research project in conjunction with their host organization.

Applicants must be Canadian citizens or landed immigrants, between 18 and 29 and hold, at a minimum, an honours bachelor's degree or professional designation (master's degree preferred). Return air fare and a living allowance are provided. Participants are expected to contribute $1,000. (For more information on AKFC see, Chapter 38, NGOs in Canada.) [ID:7101]

Agence Québec Wallonie Bruxelles pour la jeunesse
300, rue du St-Sacrement, Bureau 320, Montreal, QC, H2Y 1X4, Canada;
514-864-6028, fax 514-873-1538, lagence@aqwbj.org, www.aqwbj.org

PROFESSIONAL EXCHANGE ◆ L'Agence Québec Wallonie Bruxelles pour la jeunesse permet annuellement à près de 350 jeunes québécois âgés de 18 à 30 ans de vivre une expérience d'immersion, de prospection, de coopération ou de travail-formation en Wallonie et à Bruxelles, en Belgique francophone. Les meilleurs projets individuels ou de groupe sont retenus par les membres d'un jury indépendant et les stages se déroulent généralement sur une période de 14 jours. Les frais d'inscription individuels de 400$ donnent droit à une bourse de 700$ applicable au transport aérien et, dans la plupart des cas, à un forfait de séjour de 125 euros (environ 200$) par personne. Le but des programmes est de faciliter l'accès au milieu francophone international et de mettre en place des réseaux durables entre partenaires dynamiques de tous les secteurs. [ID:7259]

Alberta Learning - Learning Network Educational Services
STUDENT LANGUAGE DEVELOPMENT EXCHANGE, EDUCATOR EXCHANGE PROGRAMS
University of Alberta, 832 Education S., Edmonton, AB, T6G 2G5, Canada;
780-492-0395, fax 780-492-0390, learnnet@ualberta.ca, www.learning-network.org

YOUTH EXCHANGE ◆ Alberta Learning (the Alberta Ministry of Education) sponsors exchanges for high school students studying second languages through Learning Network Educational Services. Alberta students alternate between hosting and living with their partners as well as attending school in both locations. The program's focus is on developing language, cross-cultural, coping and interpersonal skills. Programs take place in Quebec, Germany, Japan, Mexico and Spain. The total exchange period for the Quebec and Germany programs is six months while the Japan and Spain exchange programs are four months. Students spend half of their time in Alberta and half in their host country.

Alberta Learning also offers Educator Exchange Programs which are job and home swaps with teachers in Australia, Germany, New Zealand, the UK, US or other provinces in Canada. Teachers are paid by their Alberta school jurisdiction, and return to their own teaching position after the year is over. Short-term exchanges (approximately six weeks) are also available. [ID:6889]

Amigos de las Americas (AMIGOS)
5618 Star Lane, Houston, TX, 77057, USA; 713-782-5290,
fax 713-782-9267, info@amgioslink.org, www.amgioslink.org ▢ *Sp*

INTERNSHIP ◆ Amigos de las Americas (AMIGOS) provides summer volunteer service in Brazil, Costa Rica, Dominican Republic, Honduras, Mexico, Nicaragua, Panama or Paraguay. AMIGOS has a Correspondent Volunteer Program where participants live with a host family and work in close collaboration with community members, defining and implementing service projects and facilitating local youth on topics such as: community health and education, youth leadership development, ESL, computer literacy, environment and team work. Programs last four to eight weeks, June to August, and are usually completed in teams of two or three members. The participation fee is $3,625 US which includes international airfare, food and lodging. Successful volunteers are ages 16 to 25, have studied at least one year of Spanish or Portuguese, appreciate diversity and are motivated, enthusiastic individuals. Training is provided. For an application, visit the AMIGOS Web site. [ID:7023]

ASSE - International Student Exchange Programs
INTERNATIONAL STUDENT EXCHANGE PROGRAMS
Coordinator, Suite 204, 7, De La Commune Street W., Montreal, QC, H2Y 2C5,
Canada; 514-287-1814, fax 514-281-1525, assecanada@asse.com, www.asse.com ▢ *Fr*

YOUTH EXCHANGE ◆ ASSE International Student Exchange Programs offer qualified students, aged 15 to 18, from Western Europe, North America, Australia, New Zealand, Japan and Thailand, the opportunity to spend a high school year abroad with a host family in another one of these countries. Applicants must have a B average over the previous two years. ASSE also offers a six-week summer homestay program in Europe during June and July, as well as a four-week language program with instruction and other activities in France, Germany and Spain. Program costs range from $2,000-$3,600 US for the summer program, to $3,600-$7,500 US for the school-year program. A limited number of school-year program scholarships are available. Applicants are screened for character and proficiency in the English language. [ID:7024]

Association of Universities and Colleges of Canada (AUCC)
FINNISH CAREER DEVELOPMENT EXCHANGE PROGRAM
Suite 600, 350 Albert Street, Ottawa, ON, K1R 1A4, Canada; 613-653-3961,
fax 613-563-9745, postmaster@accc.ca, www.aucc.ca/programs/intprograms/cimo/index_e.html ▢ *Fr*

PROFESSIONAL EXCHANGE ◆ The Finnish Career Development Exchange Program is designed for young Canadian workers who have backgrounds in areas such as information technology, forestry, agriculture and horticulture, northern studies, business, teaching English and French as a foreign language, hospitality and tourism, international trade, architecture and design, environment and sustainable development, social sciences and the humanities.

Applications in other fields such as the pure sciences, may also be considered. Applications of those meeting the eligibility requirements are sent to the Finnish government's Centre for International Mobility (CIMO), who matches the applicants with jobs for which they are qualified. Trainees will not be admitted to Finland unless authorities are satisfied that the remuneration offered meets the going rate in Finland for the type of job and region concerned, and that the terms of employment meet Finnish standards and will be respected. Participants may stay in Finland for up to 18 months. Once the internship ends, trainees may not remain in Finland to look for work or to hold a job unless they are expressly authorized to do so.

To be eligible, you must be over 18; have a working knowledge of English, Finnish, Swedish or German; and have completed at least one year at an Association of Universities and Colleges of Canada (AUCC) member institution or have graduated from a member of institution within the last two years. Trainees are responsible for making their own travel arrangements and for travel costs and are not entitled to enter Finland without a residence permit. You are strongly advised to wait until you receive your work permit before leaving for Finland. Applications are accepted throughout the year. (For more information on AUCC, see Chapter 14, Awards & Grants and Chapter 38, NGOs in Canada.) [ID:7136]

Association Québec-France
Maison Fornel, 9, place Royale, Quebec, QC, G1K 4G2, Canada;
418-643-1616, fax 418-643-3053, assquefr@quebecfrance.qc.ca, www.quebecfrance.qc.ca

WORK AND LEARN ◆ Association Québec-France est un programme d'échanges pour les étudiants canadiens âgés de 18 à 30 ans qui résident au Québec. Le programme permet aux participants de travailler dans une municipalité française durant l'été ou d'obtenir un permis de travail d'une durée de trois mois s'ils présentent une offre de travail écrite. Un autre programme propose aux personnes de 18 à 35 ans de participer aux vendanges. [ID:7260]

AYUSA International
2226 Bush Street, San Francisco, CA, 94115, USA;
800-727-4540, fax 415-674-5232, info@ayusa.org, www.ayusa.org

YOUTH EXCHANGE ◆ AYUSA International offers programs for high school students, aged 15 to 18, to participate in an academic year, semester or summer homestay abroad. Programs varying in length from summer, semester or academic year are available depending on individual needs. Students live with host families and attend local schools. Some programs require two years of high school language coursework. Cost to participants ranges from $1,900 to $6,000 US, including international airfare and insurance. Scholarships are available and announced throughout the year. (For more information on AYUSA, see Chapter 11, Hosting Programs.) [ID:7027]

British Columbia - Germany International Student Exchange Program
Suite 320, 3680 East Hastings Street, Vancouver, BC, V5K 2A9,
Canada; 604-298-4526, fax 604-298-4503, www.bchla.org

YOUTH EXCHANGE ◆ The British Columbia - Germany International Student Exchange includes approximately 60 students from many areas of British Columbia. Students must be between 15 and 18 years of age at the time of participation and must have some German language ability, either through classroom instruction, alternative learning programs or through family. It is recommended that students participate during their grade 10 or 11 year. Although grade 12 students are not excluded, it is best to take part earlier due to final exams and other year-end activities. Once applications have been received in both British Columbia and Germany, matching is finalized and students and their families are notified by early April. The German students spend three months in BC in the fall and BC students travel to Germany to spend three months the following spring of the same school year. As this is an academic exchange, both BC and German students attend and participate in school and host family-initiated activities. [ID:6957]

British Columbia - Spain International Student Exchange Program
Suite 320, 3680 East Hastings Street, Vancouver, BC, V5K 2A9,
Canada; 604-298-4526, fax 604-298-4503, www.bchla.org 💻 *Fr*

YOUTH EXCHANGE ◆ British Columbia - Spain International Student Exchange Program participants must be between 15 and 18 years of age at the time of the program and must have some Spanish language ability, either through classroom instruction, alternative learning programs or through family. It is recommended that students participate during their grade 10 or 11 year. Although grade 12 students are not excluded, it is best to take part earlier if possible, due to final exams and other year-end activities. Once applications have been received in both British Columbia and Spain, matching is finalized and students and their families are notified by March. The Spanish students spend approximately 10 weeks in BC in the fall and BC students travel to Spain to spend approximately 10 weeks the following February of the same school year. As this is an academic exchange, both BC and Spanish students attend school and participate in both school and host family-initiated activities. [ID:6850]

British High Commission
GREAT BRITAIN WORKING HOLIDAY MAKER SCHEME
Program Officer, 80 Elgin Street, Ottawa, ON, K1P 5K7, Canada;
613-237-2008, fax 613-232-2533, www.britainincanada.org 💻 *Sp*

INDEPENDENT WORK AND TRAVEL ◆ The Great Britain Working Holiday Maker Scheme provides opportunities for Commonwealth citizens aged 17 to 30 to take a vacation in the UK while undertaking work for a period of up to two years. Participants pay for all expenses, including the cost of the Working Holiday Maker entry clearance of $94 (price is subject to change). Commonwealth citizens who have close connections with the UK through birth, marriage or ancestry may be eligible for admission without any restriction on the length of their stay or freedom to take employment. For further information please refer to their Web site. [ID:6936]

Canada Council for the Arts
CANADA COUNCIL PROGRAMS
P.O. Box 1047, 350 Albert Street, Ottawa, ON, K1P 5V8, Canada;
613-566-4414, fax 613-566-4390, info@canadacouncil.ca, www.canadacouncil.ca 💻 *Fr*

PROFESSIONAL EXCHANGE ◆ The Canada Council for the Arts is a national arm's-length agency that provides grants and services to professional Canadian artists and arts organizations in dance, media arts, music, theatre, writing and publishing, interdisciplinary work and performance art, and visual arts. Much of the artistic work that the council supports involves exchange in a broad sense. In some cases, individual artists may use grants for travel within Canada or to seek professional development abroad. There are also grants available for activities such as touring or the staging of travelling exhibitions. For a detailed listing of grants and services available, visit the Canada Council for the Arts Web site. (For more information on the Canada Council for the Arts, see Chapter 14, Awards & Grants.) [ID:6851]

Canada World Youth (CWY)
3rd Floor, 2330 Notre-Dame Street W., Montreal, QC, H3J 1N4, Canada;
514-931-3526, fax 514-939-2621, cwy-jcm@cwy-jcm.org, www.cwy-jcm.org 💻 *Fr*

YOUTH EXCHANGE ◆ Canada World Youth (CWY) has programs offering youth a cultural exchange experience for four to seven months, depending on the program. There are four programs administered: 1) The Core Program is CWY's longest running program for those between the ages of 17 and 24. They are six- to seven-month exchanges in which participants spend half their time living and working as volunteers in a host community in Canada, and the other half in a country in Africa, Asia, Latin America, the Caribbean or Eastern Europe. 2) Overseas Internships provide youth from 18 to 29 years of age with an opportunity to participate in international cooperation and development through volunteer work placements overseas, in partnership with host-country organizations. Although it does not have a Canadian phase, the volunteers undertake public awareness activities before and after their programs. 3) Customized Programs meet the needs of specific clientele or partners, or are designed around a specific theme. They respect the underlying philosophy of CWY's educational programming while customizing the structure, components and form to fit the specific project. 4) Academic and Community Partnerships are responsive in nature. CWY works with representatives of high schools, colleges, universities and youth groups who want to organize their own short-term immersion project for youth in a developing country. The CWY Web site offers a complete list of all programs and their specific qualifications. (For more information on CWY see Chapter 38, NGOs in Canada.) [ID:6937]

Canadian 4-H Council
W. GARFIELD WESTON FOUNDATION
4-H UNITED KINGDOM EXCHANGE
Central Experimental Farm, 930 Carling Ave., Bldg. #26, Ottawa, ON, K1A 0C6, Canada; 613-234-1112, fax 613-234-4448, www.4-h-canada.ca/international_programs.html ▭ Fr

YOUTH EXCHANGE ◆ The W. Garfield Weston Foundation 4-H United Kingdom Exchange allows five deserving senior 4-H members to represent their province and Canada as ambassadors abroad, participating in the Canadian 4-H Council's most prestigious travel program. Fully funded by the W. Garfield Weston Foundation, this international exchange allows delegates to spend six weeks living with various host families throughout the United Kingdom, learning about their agriculture, sharing and acquiring knowledge, experiencing a new and different cultural environment and forming lasting international friendships. There are opportunities to work on family farms, tour local attractions and attend Young Farmer club meetings. The primary objective of the program is to provide delegates with the opportunity to gain a more global knowledge of agriculture, food and natural resources, as well as the importance of technology transfer. Applicants must be at least 18 years of age. [ID:6852]

Canadian Crossroads International (CCI)
Crossroads Placement Programs, Suite 500, 317 Adelaide Street W., Toronto, ON, M5V 1P9, Canada; 416-967-1611, fax 416-967-9078, ontario@cciorg.ca, www.cciorg.ca ▭ Fr

WORK AND LEARN ◆ Canadian Crossroads International (CCI) works in partnership with community-based organizations in Guatemala, Suriname, St. Vincent and the Grenadines, Bolivia, Mali, Senegal, Côte d'Ivoire, Burkina Faso, Togo, Niger, Ghana, Kenya, Swaziland, Zimbabwe and India. It has over 20 long-term partnership projects. Individual volunteer work placements take place in the context of these longer-term projects and are designed to increase the capacity inherent in the developing partner organizations. Volunteer job descriptions vary widely by project. For more information, see www.cciorg.ca/volunteer.html. Frequent requests include people with related work experience in HIV/AIDS, microcredit, community economic development, organizational development, information technology, education, social development, finance and accounting, fundraising, rural development and the environment.

Residents of Quebec may also apply to a program called Initiation to International Cooperation. Each year, groups of seven to 10 people aged 18 to 30 contribute to local initiatives in West Africa. Groups develop a wide range of concrete professional skills while gaining both an enriching personal experience and meaningful work experience in international development. Fluency in French is required.

Volunteers must meet skill criteria required for the project. Some positions require fluency in English, Spanish or French. Applicants must be 19 or older and Canadian citizens or landed immigrants. Youth internship applicants must be between the ages of 18 and 30. All applicants must have demonstrated cultural sensitivity, adaptability and tolerance. Postings usually last four to 12 months. Participants live with host families while overseas. All participants are asked to raise funds in support of CCI's program and CCI provides support for fundraising. Modest living allowances are provided. (For more information on CCI, see Chapter 11, Hosting Programs and Chapter 38, NGOs in Canada.) [ID:6949]

Canadian Education Exchange Foundation (CEEF)
CANADIAN EDUCATOR EXCHANGES: PROVINCE OF ONTARIO, NEW BRUNSWICK AND BRITISH COLUMBIA
250 Bayview Drive, Barrie, ON, L4N 4Y8, Canada;
705-739-7596, fax 705-739-7764, info@ceef.ca, www.ceef.ca

PROFESSIONAL EXCHANGE ◆ The Canadian Education Exchange Foundation (CEEF) arranges exchanges for educators at the elementary, secondary and in some cases college levels. The basic exchange program assumes that a Canadian teacher will exchange his or her teaching position (and residence or provide appropriate living accommodation) with an educator in another country or province for a period of one year. Canadian educators continue to be employed and paid by their home school boards and all benefits and seniority are retained. To qualify as a potential exchange candidate, a teacher must have a minimum of five years' experience; obtain formal approval from his/her principal/school board; and meet the criteria established by the exchange country to which he/she wishes to apply.

CEEF offers interprovincial exchanges for British Columbia, Ontario and New Brunswick teachers with counterparts from all other Canadian provinces, except Quebec. Destinations for international teacher exchanges are: Australia, Denmark, France, Germany, the Netherlands, New Zealand, Spain, Switzerland, the Republic of Ireland, the UK (including England, Scotland, Wales and Northern Ireland) and the US. [ID:6861]

Canadian Film and Television Production Association (CFTPA)
CFTPA NATIONAL MENTORSHIP PROGRAM
CFTPA National Mentorship Program, Suite 605, 151 Slater Street, Ottawa, ON,
K1P 5H3, Canada; 613-233-1444, fax 612-233-0073, ottawa@cftpa.ca, www.cftpa.ca ▣ *Fr*

INTERNSHIP ◆ The Canadian Film and Television Production Association (CFTPA) is a non-profit trade association representing almost 400 Canadian production companies involved in television, film and interactive media. The CFTPA National Mentorship Program includes the Young Professionals International Program, funded by Foreign Affairs Canada (FAC) and International Trade Canada (ITCan) as part of the Government of Canada's Youth Employment Strategy. This initiative gives young Canadians aged 18 to 30 a comprehensive understanding of domestic and international markets through international placements in the film and television industry. Placements focus on production, marketing, international distribution, administration and communication activities. Participants can be placed abroad or domestically with a mentor company for a minimum of 26 weeks (foreign placements would include eight weeks of work outside Canada). Applicants must not be enrolled in any full-time academic program or have any immediate plans to return to school; have a genuine interest in permanently entering the workforce and launching an international career; and the placement must be the first paid career-related international work experience. For more details contact the CFTPA National Mentorship Program. [ID:6884]

Canadian Government International Internship Programs
YOUTH INTERNATIONAL INTERNSHIPS PROGRAM
Human Resources Development Canada, Phase IV, 140 Promenade du Portage,
Gatineau, QC, K1A 0J9, Canada; 800-935-5555, fax 613-941-5992, www.hrdc-drhc.gc.ca ▣ *Fr*

INTERNSHIP ◆ (For a detailed description of this great program, see the Canadian Government International Internships profile in Chapter 17, Internships Abroad.) [ID:7123]

Canadian International Development Agency (CIDA)
JUNIOR PROFESSIONAL OFFICER PROGRAM (JPO)

Human Resources Division, Personnel and Administration Branch, 200 Promenade du Portage, Gatineau, QC, K1A 0G4, Canada; 819-997-5006, fax 819-953-6088, info@acdi-cida.gc.ca, www.acdi-cida.gc.ca ▣ Fr

INTERNSHIP ◆ The Junior Professional Officer Program (JPO) is administered under the auspices of the United Nations. Its primary objectives are to provide experience in managing a development program, support the UN through JPO services, place Canadians in the UN, and repatriate knowledge gained from assignments. General duties of a JPO include the administration and coordination of projects and liaising between local authorities, regional offices and headquarters. Through the Canadian International Development Agency (CIDA), Canada sponsors several JPOs annually in the following UN Agencies: United Nations Development Program (UNDP), United Nations International Children's Fund (UNICEF), United Nations High Commissioner for Refugees (UNHCR) and the World Food Program (WFP).

Candidates should be under 32 years of age and possess a completed master's degree in a relevant discipline. Knowledge of a third language is an asset and work experience (paid or voluntary) is becoming increasingly important as placements become more competitive. Contracts are for a period of one year with the possibility of a one-year extension.

Information about the JPO program, application forms and UN agency office contacts are available on CIDA's Web site. (For more information on the JPO program, see the Canadian Government International Internships profile in Chapter 17, Internships Abroad.) [ID:7124]

Canadian Summer School in Germany (CSSG)
CANADIAN SUMMER SCHOOL IN GERMANY

Director, Augustana University College, Suite 4901, 46th Ave., Camrose, AB, T4V 2R3, Canada; 780-679-1162, fax 780-679-1590, www.cssg.ca ▣ Fr

WORK AND LEARN ◆ The Canadian Summer School in Germany (CSSG) offers unique and intensive immersion in university-level language and culture studies in Kassel. Courses are offered at the intermediate and advanced level. For a period of approximately six and a half weeks, students participate in a full course (approximately 85 hours of classroom instruction) and in numerous additional activities: lectures at various museums, visits to theatres and operas, excursions to cities with cultural and historical significance, and a three-day trip to Berlin. The main feature of the program, though, is the students' rapid progress in linguistic skills, enhanced mainly by the fact that they are immersed in German life, culture and civilization. [ID:6938]

Canadian Teachers' Federation (CTF)
PROJECT OVERSEAS

Director of International Programs, 2490 Don Reid Drive, Ottawa, ON, K1H 1E1, Canada; 613-232-1505, fax 613-232-1886, info@ctf-fce.ca, www.ctf-fce.ca ▣ Fr

TEACHING ABROAD ◆ Project Overseas is a joint endeavour by the Canadian Teachers' Federation (CTF) and its members to give professional assistance to fellow teachers in developing countries. Project Overseas is held during the months of July and August. Established in 1962, with one in-service program in Nigeria, Project Overseas has now assisted teacher organizations in over 50 countries in Africa, Asia, the Caribbean and the South Pacific. As many as 60 volunteers are sent to approximately 15 countries each summer. Applicants should be in excellent health, flexible and demonstrate mature judgment. Academic or administrative specialization is an asset. Travel and living expenses are paid, but no salary is offered. Applicants must possess an appropriate teachers' certificate, have a minimum of five years' teaching experience, and belong to a provincial or territorial teachers' organization that is a member of CTF. In addition to Project Overseas, CTF does offer a variety of other opportunities for teachers to volunteer abroad. See their Web site for more details. (For more information on CTF, see Chapter 38, NGOs in Canada.) [ID:6953]

Carrefour de solidarité internationale (CSI)

165, rue Moore, Sherbrooke, QC, J1H 1B8, Canada;
819-566-8595, fax 819-566-8076, info@csisher.com, www.csisher.com

YOUTH EXCHANGE ◆ Le Carrefour de solidarité internationale (CSI) offre un programme de stages outre-mer au Mali, en Haïti, au Pérou, au Nicaragua ou en République dominicaine, pour des jeunes de 18 à 29 ans. Ces stages comprennent une phase de préparation-formation, un séjour à l'étranger et des activités de sensibilisation au retour. (Voir aussi leur profil dans le chapitre 38, NGOs in Canada.) [ID:7276]

Chantiers jeunesse

C.P.1000, succursale M, 4545, ave. Pierre-De Coubertin, Montreal, QC,
H1V 3R2, Canada; 514-252-3015, fax 514-251-8719, cj@cj.qc.ca, www.cj.qc.ca ▣*En*

WORK AND LEARN ◆ Chantiers jeunesse est un organisme sans but lucratif qui vise à favoriser le développement de jeunes citoyens actifs et engagés, à appuyer le développement d'une communauté en offrant des milieux d'apprentissage et de formation en collaboration avec des partenaires d'ici et d'ailleurs, et ce, dans un esprit de solidarité et de respect des différences. Les projets sont offerts aux jeunes de 16 à 30 ans. Les projets court terme, les chantiers de jeunes bénévoles, regroupent 12 jeunes de différents profils et pays pendant environ trois semaines, dans une action concrète d'appui au développement local (environnement, patrimoine, rénovation, culture) dans différentes régions du Québec et dans plus de 25 pays en Europe, Europe de l'Est, Amérique du Nord et Asie. Des projets moyen et long terme de volontariat ou de stage à l'étranger sont aussi offerts ainsi que le développement de projets spéciaux comme des chantiers familles et des projets sociaux. Environ 500 jeunes participent annuellement à des projets. [ID:7275]

Children's International Summer Villages (CISV)

5 Dunvegan Road, Ottawa, ON, K1K 3E7, Canada;
613-749-9680, fax 613-749-9680, ottawa@ca.cisv.org, www.cisv.ca

YOUTH EXCHANGE ◆ Children's International Summer Villages (CISV) Canada promotes global peace education Canada-wide. In addition to its Canadian activities, CISV offers four main overseas programs to youth aged 11 to 19. Through International Villages (age 11), Interchanges (ages 12-13, 13-14 and 14-15), Summer Camps (ages 13, 14 or 15), and Seminar Camps (ages 18 and 19), delegations from a number of countries around the world meet for a period of approximately three or four weeks in a host country. In some cases delegations stay in their home country. The programs are designed to promote cross-cultural awareness and understanding. Participants spend four weeks with a host family overseas, and in turn host their billet the following year for a period of four weeks. Cost to participants varies by local chapter and program. Opportunities are available for youth aged 16 and 17 to work as junior counsellors, and individuals over 21 can become program leaders. Leaders and counsellors are provided with valuable leadership and emergency first-aid training. Those interested in learning more about CISV should contact their local chapter or contact the Secretary of CISV Canada. (For more information on CISV see Chapter 11, Hosting Programs.) [ID:6930]

Class Afloat

851 Tecumseh, Dollard Des Ormeaux, QC, HB9 2L2, Canada; 514-683-9052,
fax 514-683-1702, discovery@classafloat.com, www.classafloat.com ▣*Fr*

WORK AND LEARN ◆ With Class Afloat students take a semester of high school while sailing around the world and earning credits. Each fall and spring semester, 48 high school juniors and seniors board the S.V. Concordia to study and work as crew as they sail around the world. Academic programs aboard ship are tailored to the needs of serious college preparatory students. Their studies are enhanced by hands-on experiences in over 40 countries worldwide. Credits for study are earned through West Island College, a Canadian high school, or Marie Victorin, a Quebec-based junior college. Official transcripts are issued by either the Alberta or Quebec Ministry of Education. This is a once-in-a-lifetime opportunity. Not only do Class Afloat students learn and grow in an exceptional setting, they acquire unique experience, skills and friendships that will serve them throughout their lives. [ID:6853]

Commonwealth Games Canada
Suite 215, 720 Belfast Street, Ottawa, ON, K1G 0Z5, Canada; 613-244-6868, fax 613-244-6826, cslc@commonwealthgames.ca, www.commonwealthgames.ca, www.jeuxcommonwealth.ca ⌨ *Fr*

INTERNSHIP ◆ Commonwealth Games Canada's (JCGC) mission is to strengthen sport within Canada and throughout the Commonwealth through participation in the Commonwealth Games and to use sport as a development tool. International internships use sport as a vehicle to develop individual and organizational capacity-building, basic education, basic nutrition and health, child protection, and HIV/AIDS awareness. Positions are open to recent Canadian university and college graduates who have been positively influenced by sport and are prepared to share their experience and expertise while working in partnership with JCGC's international partners. Internships are considered volunteer; however, all expenses related to training, debriefing, immunizations, insurance and international flights are covered. Interns also receive a monthly living allowance to cover modest accommodations, food and transportation to work. Commonwealth Games Canada maintains an active database for application packages. For more information on programs, application procedures and past participants, visit their Web site. (For more information on JCGC, see Chapter 38, NGOs in Canada.) [ID:6899]

Cross-Cultural Solutions
2 Clinton Place, New Rochelle, NY, 10801, USA; 914-632-0022, fax 914-632-8494, info@crossculturalsolutions.org, www.crossculturalsolutions.org

WORK AND LEARN ◆ Cross-Cultural Solutions is a non-profit, international volunteer-sending organization headquartered in New Rochelle, New York, with an office in Brighton, UK. Cross-Cultural Solutions operates 18 programs out of 11 countries, with more than 250 staff members in 15 offices worldwide. Programs are open to foreigners and, to date, the organization has brought more than 7,000 participants to countries around the world. A partnership formed between Cross-Cultural Solutions and CARE (a non-governmental organization) gives individuals interested in international development the chance to go into the field and work with CARE.

Cross-Cultural Solutions offer two types of programs: Volunteer Programs and Insight Programs. Volunteer Programs focus on cultural immersion through volunteering and cultural learning opportunities, and are year-round, normally ranging from two to 12 weeks. Programs are based in Brazil, China, Costa Rica, Ghana, Guatemala, India, Peru, Russia, Tanzania and Thailand. The Insight Program, which also focuses on cultural immersion but without the volunteering component, is Insight Cuba. The fees for these programs start at $2,175 US and include lodging, meals, travel medical insurance, ground transportation, in-country perspectives programming, language assistance, professional locally-based staff, informational documents, local phone calls, incoming international phone service, and a toll-free emergency hotline in the US. For more information and to register for one of their programs check out their Web site. [ID:6862]

Directorate of Cadets (DND)
INTERNATIONAL AIR, ARMY AND ROYAL
SEA CADETS INTERNATIONAL EXCHANGES
All of Canada Directorate of Cadets 4-5, 101 Colonel By Drive, Ottawa, ON, K1A 0K2, Canada; 613-992-3995, fax 613-996-1618, www.cadets.forces.gc.ca/about-nous/echange_e.asp ⌨ *Fr*

YOUTH EXCHANGE ◆ International Air Cadet Exchange, International Army Cadet Exchange and Royal Canadian Sea Cadet International Exchanges are all reciprocal cultural exchanges, allowing Canadian Cadets to train with international counterparts in a variety of countries. Age requirements vary from 12 to 18. Exchanges occur all over the world and last usually one to three months. Cadets apply through their unit using the appropriate application forms. Additional eligibility information for this exchange is available from Cadet Administrative and Training Orders (CATO). [ID:6859]

Earthwatch Institute

P.O. Box 75, Suite 100, 3 Clock Tower Place, Maynard, MA, 01754, USA;
978-461-0081, fax 978-461-2332, info@earthwatch.org, www.earthwatch.org

WORK AND LEARN ◆ The Earthwatch Institute offers a unique opportunity to join ongoing scientific research projects in Canada, the US and 49 other countries worldwide. Participants are volunteers on expedition sites, and assist scholars and scientists in field research. Projects of one to three weeks are coordinated in small groups. Participants must pay travel and living costs, ranging from $800 to $3000 US, which includes all expenses except airfare to the site. As Earthwatch is a non-profit organization, these costs, along with annual membership fees of $35 US, directly support research efforts. Earthwatch currently has over 100,000 supporters and about 4,000 volunteers from 79 countries each year. Volunteers gain hands-on experience in over 15 fields of study, including archaeology, ornithology, marine mammalogy, ecology and public health. Applicants are 16 and older, open-minded, curious to learn about other cultures and in good physical condition. (For more information on the Earthwatch Institute, see Chapter 41, United Nations & Other IGOs.) [ID:6946]

Échanges «Go» Échanges

Ministère des affaires étrangères et du commerce international, 3140, rue Boisclair, Brossard, QC,
J4Z 2C2, Canada; 450-462-0547, fax 450-462-4679, www.dfait-maeci.gc.ca/123go/go_echanges-fr.asp

YOUTH EXCHANGE ◆ Le programme Échanges « Go » Échanges permet aux jeunes de 18 à 30 ans de vivre une expérience culturelle d'un à douze mois et d'acquérir de nouvelles compétences pour compléter leur formation ou leur expérience de travail. Les échanges touchent essentiellement les secteurs agricole et agroalimentaire tels que la production agricole, l'agronomie, les produits agro-alimentaires et l'horticulture maraîchère et ornementale. Les échanges peuvent avoir lieu dans des pays comme la France, la Belgique, la Suisse, la Suède, le Luxembourg, les Pays-Bas, les États-Unis et l'Australie. La rémunération varie selon les dispositions législatives de chacun des pays. Pour participer à ce programme, les candidats doivent être citoyens canadiens et posséder des connaissances et une expérience de travail suffisantes dans le domaine agricole. Le programme est accessible à longueur d'année. Les départs se font selon les disponibilités d'accueil dans les différents pays. [ID:7229]

EDUC INTER

4, rue Saint-Joachim, Pointe-Claire, QC, H9S 4P1, Canada; 514-695-9846,
fax 514-695-4445, educintl@point-net.com, www.educinter.com/fra.htm 🖳*Sp* 🖳*En*

INTERNSHIP ◆ EDUC-INTER, un centre d'éducation international, est actif dans le domaine de l'éducation et de la formation internationales depuis 1997. Depuis son siège social de Montréal, le personnel spécialisé d'EDUC-INTER (trois employés permanents et quatre consultants) assure différents services dans un contexte dominé par l'économie du savoir. Les activités de cette organisation s'orientent autour de la gestion de projets, de la recherche, des échanges éducatifs ainsi que des séminaires et conférences. EDUC-INTER offre également des stages aux citoyens canadiens âgés de 18 à 30 ans, dans le cadre du programme des jeunes professionnels. Ces stages professionnels sont concentrés en Amérique latine et en Amérique du Nord. Ils permettent aux candidats d'acquérir des compétences stratégiques, de maîtriser l'anglais et une troisième langue, soit l'espagnol et,ou le portugais et de saisir le fonctionnement de l'économie et de la politique d'un autre continent. [ID:7293]

Embassy of Austria
CANADA-AUSTRIA INTRA- AND PARTNER COMPANY TRAINING

445 Wilbrod Street, Ottawa, ON, K1N 6M7, Canada; 613-789-1444,
fax 613-789-3431, Ottawa-OB@BMaA.gv.at, www.austro.org/e/ExchPgms/ExchPgms_frames.html

PROFESSIONAL EXCHANGE ◆ The Canada-Austria Intra- and Partner Company Training program seeks to support Canadian and Austrian firms in developing business links together by facilitating intra- and partner-company training. Canadian and Austrian workers can travel to either country to receive or provide training, which could include skills upgrading, familiarization with current business practices and, in some cases, formal classroom training. Either the Embassy of

Austria or an Austrian consulate in Canada issues a residence permit. This may be a transfer licence valid for four months, or a clearance certificate valid for up to 36 weeks. To participate, you must: possess a Canadian passport valid for a period of three months beyond the termination of activities under the program; be 18 to 30 years of age at the time of application (except in those cases where the authorities of both countries decide to raise the maximum age to 35 years or higher); possess sufficient funds to purchase a round-trip airplane ticket and to meet your needs during your stay in Austria; be prepared to pay a visa fee or program participation fee; and undergo a medical examination before starting the training if this is required by law for the specific training or activity in question. (For more information on the Embassy of Austria's training program, see Chapter 10, Short-Term Programs Overseas.) [ID:6961]

Embassy of Austria
CANADA-AUSTRIA YOUNG WORKERS' EXCHANGE PROGRAM
445 Wilbrod Street, Ottawa, ON, K1N 6M7, Canada; 613-789-1444,
fax 613-789-3431, Ottawa-OB@BMaA.gv.at, www.austro.org/e/ExchPgms/ExchPgms_frames.html

PROFESSIONAL EXCHANGE ♦ The Canada-Austria Young Workers' Exchange Program allows exchanges of young Canadian and Austrian workers so that they can obtain the practical experience necessary for professional training in tourism, agriculture and forestry. A visa is valid for six months. To be eligible, you must possess a Canadian passport valid for a period of three months beyond the termination of the practical training in Austria, and must be a resident of Canada; be 18 to 30 years of age at the time of application for admission (except in cases where the responsible authorities of both countries decide to raise the maximum age to 35 years); be a graduate of a recognized university or similar institution or hold a post-secondary diploma or certificate from a teaching institution in the field of tourism, agriculture or forestry; have no accompanying dependants; possess a return airplane ticket or sufficient funds to purchase such a ticket; and have sufficient funds to meet your needs during the first part of your stay in Austria. (For more information on the Embassy of Austria's Exchange Program, see Chapter 10, Short-Term Programs Overseas.) [ID:6960]

Embassy of France
CANADA-FRANCE YOUNG WORKERS' EXCHANGE PROGRAM
42 Sussex Drive, Ottawa, ON, K1M 2C9, Canada;
613-562-3751, fax 613-562-3790, www.ambafrance-ca.org ▭*Fr*

PROFESSIONAL EXCHANGE ♦ The Canada-France Young Workers' Exchange Program allows Canadian workers to upgrade their career skills as trainees by undertaking an internship in France. Trainees are not admitted to France unless the authorities are satisfied that the remuneration offered meets the going rate in France for the type of job and region concerned, and that the terms of employment meet French standards. Trainees receive the same treatment as French nationals in all matters concerning the application of laws, regulations and practices regarding health and working conditions. Generally, an internship permit is granted for a maximum of one year (in certain cases the permit may be extended up to 18 months).

To be eligible, you must be a Canadian citizen; be a graduate of a university or equivalent institution, or have a post-secondary diploma or certificate from an institute of technology or equivalent educational institution; have some work experience directly related to your degree or diploma; undertake an internship in your own trade or profession; be 18 to 35 years of age in good health; as well as have a working knowledge of French. You must also obtain a written job offer from a prospective employer in France or one of its territories stating the terms of employment (type of work, period for which you will be employed, wages, hours of work per week, and welfare benefits if any). Successful applicants are responsible for making their own travel arrangements and for travel costs. [ID:7137]

Embassy of France - Toronto Consulate
FRANCE'S WORKING HOLIDAY PROGRAM
Cultural Service, 130 Bloor Street W., Toronto, ON, M5S 1N5, Canada; 416-925-8041,
fax 416-925-2560, culturel@consulfrance-toronto.org, www.consulfrance-toronto.org ⬛*Fr*

INDEPENDENT WORK AND TRAVEL ◆ France's Working Holiday Program allows young Canadians to visit France for a maximum of 12 months and to supplement their funds by taking temporary employment. Work may be part- or full-time. However, the main purpose of the visit should be to holiday and travel. Participants are not permitted to remain with any one employer for more than three months. They also may not enrol in a course of studies while in France. To be eligible, you must be a Canadian citizen aged 18 to 30. See your closest consular office for more details. [ID:7131]

Embassy of Germany
CANADA-GERMANY YOUNG
WORKER'S EXCHANGE PROGRAM (YWEP)
Coordinator, 1 Waverley Street, Ottawa, ON, K2P 0T8, Canada; 613-232-1101,
fax 613-594-9330, germanembassyottawa@on.aibn.com, www.germanembassyottawa.org

INDEPENDENT WORK AND TRAVEL ◆ The Canada-Germany Young Worker's Exchange Program (YWEP) is designed for candidates aged 18 to 35 who have graduated in disciplines related to industry, science and technology or commerce. Applicants must have one year of work experience directly related to their academic degree or diploma as well as a working knowledge of German. Applications meeting the eligibility requirements are sent to the German government, which begins a job search based on the applicant's qualifications. Applicants may not enter the country until they have found employment and are in possession of a work permit and/or visa. Exchanges may last up to 18 months. Send your application directly to: Bonn-ZAV.aussereuropaeische-laender@arbeitsamt.de or International Placement Service (ZAV), Zentralstelle für Arbeitsvermittlung, Villemombler Str. 76, 53123, Bonn, Germany. Other exchange possibilities to Germany include the Working Holiday Program, Pen Pals and Au Pair Organizations, Working Holiday Program for German Language Students and University to University Exchange. For full details check out their Web site. [ID:7018]

Embassy of Germany
GERMANY'S WORKING HOLIDAY PROGRAM
1 Waverley Street, Ottawa, ON, K2P 0T8, Canada;
613-232-1101, fax 613-594-9330, www.germanembassyottawa.org

INDEPENDENT WORK AND TRAVEL ◆ Germany's Working Holiday Program enables college and university students to expand their travel experience by working in Germany. Work does not have to be study related. Participants receive the same treatment as German nationals in all matters concerning the application of laws, regulations and practices regarding health and working conditions. The normal working holiday exchange is up to three months. To be eligible, you must be a Canadian citizen, aged 18 to 30 and enrolled at a post-secondary institution. You must also be able to demonstrate a working knowledge of German, and a written job offer from an employer in Germany is required before leaving Canada. The German Embassy and Consulates in Canada can help you with your job search. Students are responsible for their own travelling costs and expenses in Germany. In some cases, board and lodging are provided by the employer. Visa applications must be made directly through the Zentralstelle für Arbeitsbeitsvermittlung (ZAV). Deadline for applications is March 1 of each year. Please contact the ZAV for application forms at: Bonn-ZAV.info-auslaendische-studenten@arbeitsamt.de or Zentralstelle für Arbeitsvermittlung (ZAV), Studentenvermittlung 21.11, D-53107 Bonn, GERMANY. Visit their Web site at www.arbeitsamt.de/zav. [ID:7132]

Embassy of Japan
JAPAN EXCHANGE AND TEACHING PROGRAMME (JET)
JET Desk, Information and Cultural Section, 255 Sussex Drive, Ottawa, ON, K1N 9E6,
Canada; 613-241-8541 ext. 134, fax 613-241-4261, infocul@embjapan.ca, www.ca.emb-japan.go.jp

TEACHING ABROAD ◆ The Japan Exchange and Teaching Programme (JET) is a government exchange program that promotes international understanding of Japan through foreign language education and international exchange activities. One-year placements are available to assist in teaching English in the public school system. Applicants must be Canadian citizens under the age of 40, have a university degree, show strong interest in both Japan and teaching, and have excellent English language skills. They should also be well-rounded in terms of work, study and volunteer experience. Placements are also available with local governments in the area of international relations for applicants with strong Japanese language skills. One-year contracts beginning in late July or early August are renewable up to five years and have a salary of 3.6 million yen (at time of printing) after Japanese taxes (exempt from Canadian taxes). Return airfare is included. Applications are available for download in September with a deadline in mid- to late November or by contacting your local Embassy or Consulate General of Japan. (For more information on JET, see Chapter 10, Short-Term Programs Overseas.) [ID:6964]

Embassy of Japan
JAPAN WORKING HOLIDAY PROGRAM
Program Officer, Visa Section, 255 Sussex Drive, Ottawa, ON, K1N 9E6, Canada;
613-241-8541, fax 613-241-9831, consul@embjapan.ca, www.ca.emb-japan.go.jp 🖳𝓕𝓻

INDEPENDENT WORK AND TRAVEL ◆ The Japan Working Holiday Program is an opportunity for Canadian citizens aged 18 to 30 to work in Japan for an initial period of up to six months, and a possible extension of an additional six months. The working holiday visa is designed for youth who intend primarily to holiday in Japan for a specific period, and who may take on casual employment during their stay. Participants cover all costs. General information is located on their Web site; however, for specifics, interested applicants must contact the Japan Embassy or any one of the consulates located in Toronto, Vancouver, Montreal and Edmonton. (For more information on the Japan Working Holiday Program, see Chapter 10, Short-Term Programs Overseas.) [ID:6965]

Embassy of Netherlands
CANADA-NETHERLANDS YOUNG WORKERS' EXCHANGE PROGRAM
Suite 2020, 350 Albert Street, Ottawa, ON, K1R 1A4, Canada;
613-237-5030, fax 613-237-6471, www.netherlandsembassy.ca

PROFESSIONAL EXCHANGE ◆ The Canada-Netherlands Young Workers' Exchange Program is designed for Canadians who wish to expand their overseas travel experience by living and working in the Netherlands. The program targets the following employment sectors: industry, commerce, science and technology, tourism, and agriculture and horticulture. Only those applicants wishing to work in agriculture or horticulture receive assistance in finding a job. Placement services are available only to students in a university program (either full-time or part-time) in agriculture or horticulture, or graduates from such a program or an equivalent college program. To be eligible, you must be 18 to 30 years of age; a Canadian citizen or landed immigrant; and enrolled at a university, college, institute of technology or equivalent educational institution, or have graduated from such an institution within the last year. Also, for experienced agricultural/horticultural workers, the Stichting Uitwisseling, an agency for youth exchange and agricultural study tours in the Netherlands, coordinates placements at suitable farms and companies. A detailed resume is required. Participants who find employment in the agricultural/horticultural sector on their own will be paid at a rate that reflects supply and demand. [ID:6958]

Embassy of Netherlands
NETHERLANDS WORKING HOLIDAY PROGRAM
Suite 2020, 350 Albert Street, Ottawa, ON, K1R 1A4, Canada;
613-237-5030, fax 613-237-6471, www.netherlandsembassy.ca/passport.html

INDEPENDENT WORK AND TRAVEL ◆ The Netherlands Working Holiday Program is designed for Canadian young adults who wish to travel and work on an incidental basis in the Netherlands. Application for the program is made at the Netherlands Embassy or consulates in Canada. In order to qualify, the primary intention of your visit must be to holiday, and it must be made clear that work is only an incidental reason for your visit. The embassy or consulate will issue an authorization for temporary stay, valid for six months from the date of issue. You do not have to be enrolled as a student in order to participate in the program. Applicants wishing to work in agriculture or horticulture can receive assistance in finding a job. See their Web site for specific details on visas. [ID:7134]

Embassy of Sweden
SWEDEN WORKING HOLIDAY PROGRAM
Mercury Court, 377 Dalhousie Street, Ottawa, ON, K1N 9N8, Canada;
613-241-8553, fax 613-241-2277, www.swedishembassy.ca 💻*Fr*

INDEPENDENT WORK AND TRAVEL ◆ The Sweden Working Holiday Program allows students and non-students to expand their travel experience by living and working in Sweden. A working permit must be issued from the Swedish Embassy or a Swedish Consulate in Canada and is valid for up to 12 months. Employment in Sweden is not limited to only one employer, place or particular field. To be eligible, you must be between 18 and 35 years old and have an adequate knowledge of Swedish or English. Applications must be submitted at least six weeks before the intended date of arrival in Sweden. You are responsible for making your own travel arrangements and for international insurance plan coverage for medical and hospital expenses. [ID:6933]

Embassy of the Republic of Korea
REPUBLIC OF KOREA'S WORKING HOLIDAY PROGRAM
150 Boteler Street, Ottawa, ON, K1N 5A6, Canada; 613-244-5010,
fax 613-244-5034, manager@emb-korea.ottawa.on.ca, www.emb-korea.ottawa.on.ca

INDEPENDENT WORK AND TRAVEL ◆ The Republic of Korea's Working Holiday Program promotes understanding, cooperation and closer cultural ties between Canada and Korea. The program allows young Canadians to visit Korea for an extended holiday and to cover their travel expenses through temporary employment. The working holiday visa is valid for an initial six months and may be extended for another six months. To be eligible, you must be 18 to 30 years of age; be a Canadian citizen residing in Canada at the time of application; possess a valid passport and a round-trip ticket, or sufficient funds to purchase such a ticket; and have enough funds to cover expenses, including possible medical expenses, during the initial period of your stay in Korea. Applications can be found on their Web site. [ID:6956]

Embassy: Australian High Commission
AUSTRALIA'S WORKING HOLIDAY MAKER PROGRAM
Suite 710, 7th Floor, 50 O'Connor Street, Ottawa, ON, K1P 6L2, Canada;
613-236-0841, fax 613-236-4376, dimia-ottawa@dfat.gov.au, www.immi.gov.au

INDEPENDENT WORK AND TRAVEL ◆ Australia's Working Holiday Maker Program aims to provide an opportunity for young people to holiday in Australia and to supplement their funds through incidental work. To receive the appropriate visa you must be a citizen of an agreement country and must be at least 18 years old and no older than 30 years old at the time of application. Further information on the program's policy is available from the Web site of the Australian Department of Immigration and Multicultural and Indigenous Affairs (DIMIA) under the subject, "Working Visas." Applications may be completed on-line at www.immi.gov.au or through the Australian High Commission in Ottawa, Canada. [ID:7025]

Expérience-Jeunesse International
PROGRAMME D'ÉCHANGES DE
JEUNES TRAVAILLEURS CANADA-SUISSE
12, Le Ber, Gatineau, QC, J9H 1C5, Canada; 819-684-9212,
fax 819-684-5630, suisse@experience.ca, www.experience.ca

YOUTH EXCHANGE ◆ Expérience-Jeunesse International propose un programme d'échanges de jeunes travailleurs entre le Canada et la Suisse. Ce programme est destiné aux Canadiens qui désirent parfaire leurs connaissances linguistiques et acquérir des compétences professionnelles reliées à leur domaine d'études en Suisse. Quels que soient le métier ou la profession, un permis de travail d'une durée de quatre à dix-huit mois leur est accessible par le biais de ce programme officiel entre le Canada et la Suisse. Pour participer au programme, les candidats doivent avoir la citoyenneté canadienne et détenir un diplôme universitaire ou un diplôme d'études postsecondaires d'un collège, cégep ou institut de formation spécialisée. À défaut de ces qualifications scolaires, les candidats doivent avoir une expérience professionnelle de travail d'au moins 2 ans. Ils doivent être âgés de 18 à 35 ans et posséder une connaissance suffisante du français, de l'allemand ou de l'italien.

Dans le cadre de ce programme, les participants doivent effectuer eux-mêmes les démarches pour rechercher un emploi en Suisse. Expérience-Jeunesse International (EJI) fournit cependant une aide dans ces démarches. À la suite de son adhésion au programme, EJI fournit aux candidats divers outils pour la recherche d'emploi. Une assistance est également accordée lors des démarches visant l'obtention du permis de travail. Les participants doivent organiser eux-mêmes leur voyage et assumer leurs frais de déplacement. [ID:7239]

Foreign Affairs Canada (FAC)
YOUTH PROGRAMS
Enquiries Service (SXCI), 125 Sussex Drive, Ottawa, ON, K1A 0G2, Canada; 613-944-4000,
fax 613-996-9709, enqserv@dfait-maeci.gc.ca, www.dfait-maeci.gc.ca/123go/menu-en.asp 🖳 Fr

YOUTH EXCHANGE ◆ Foreign Affairs Canada (FAC) offers a general Web site that lists information about its International Youth Programs. The programs give young Canadians, primarily between the ages of 18 and 30, the opportunity to obtain new skills and training to help them compete in the global economy and broaden their exposure to foreign cultures. Some of the International Youth Programs are managed by foreign embassies, high commissions or consulates in Canada, while others are administered by private sector Canadian organizations.

Three out of four of FAC's programs are listed in this chapter under Working Holiday Programs; Student Work Abroad Program (SWAP); and the Young Workers' Exchange Programs; their Co-op Education Programs are not listed. (For more government program information, see the Canadian Government International Internship Programs in Chapter 17, Internships Abroad.) [ID:6934]

Friends of World Teaching and Nursing
Director, P.O. Box 301994, Escondido, CA, 92030-1994, USA; 619-224-2365,
fax 619-224-5363, teachinginfo@fowt.com, nursinginfo@fowt.com, www.fowt.com

TEACHING ABROAD ◆ Friends of World Teaching is affiliated with more than 1,000 English language schools and colleges in 100 countries worldwide. The organization offers teaching and administrative opportunities to American and Canadian educators. Positions exist in most subject areas and at most levels, from kindergarten to university, and are filled throughout the year, including summer terms. Not only teachers, but also counsellors, librarians, coaches, school nurses, school administrators, special educators, audio-video media specialists and school secretaries are needed. Qualifications are similar to those in North America, and foreign language knowledge is usually not required. Salaries vary from country to country and, in most cases, are adequate for overseas living.

Another branch of this organization, Friends of World Nursing, assists American and Canadian RNs in securing international assignments. For more information check out their Web site for specific job postings worldwide. [ID:6935]

Frontiers Foundation Inc.
419 Coxwell Ave., Toronto, ON, M4L 3B9, Canada; 416-690-3930,
fax 416-690-3934, frontiersfoundation@on.aibn.com, www.frontiersfoundation.org

PROFESSIONAL EXCHANGE ◆ Frontiers Foundation Inc. is a voluntary service organization that works in partnership with requesting rural, low-income communities across northern Canada. The foundation works with these groups (and with occasional projects in Bolivia and Haiti) for the purpose of community advancement. Volunteers must be at least 18 years of age to work on housing construction and recreation projects which last a minimum of 12 weeks. Skills in carpentry, plumbing and electrical work are preferred. Volunteers will be provided with accommodation, food and transportation within Canada. A limited number of volunteer tutors are also needed for Arctic educational placements that entail a commitment of at least five months. If you are willing to become part of an international team, have the spirit of adventure, and are able to endure trying conditions, Frontiers Foundation is looking for you! [ID:7076]

German Academic Exchange Service (DAAD)
19th Floor, 950 Third Ave., New York, NY, 10022, USA;
212-758-3223, fax 212-755-5780, daadny@daad.org, www.daad.org 🖳 *Fr*

WORK AND LEARN ◆ The German Academic Exchange Service (Deutscher Akademischer Austauschdienst - DAAD) offers young lawyers the opportunity to gain insight into the structure and function of German law during an eight-month program in Germany, from late October to June. The first part of the program consists of a two-month course in German legal terminology. The following six months comprise courses and seminars in German law and conclude with a legal internship. In general, applicants must have a JD or LLB degree and have passed the bar examination. An excellent command of German is necessary. In addition to tuition and fees, the scholarship includes a monthly allowance, travel subsidy and health insurance. (For more information on other programs that DADD offers, see Chapter 14, Awards & Grants). [ID:6858]

Global Change Game
Volunteer Coordinator, P.O. Box 1632, Winnipeg, MB, R3C 2Z2,
Canada; 204-783-2675, gcg@mts.net, www.mts.net/~gcg 🖳 *Fr*

WORK AND LEARN ◆ The Global Change Game is an international development education program which visits high schools, universities and community groups during regional tours each year, teaching about world issues in a fun and innovative way. Each year, eight to 12 volunteers travel with a team for periods of six to12 weeks. All costs are covered. To apply, you must be a high school graduate over 18 years of age, and a non-smoker. You also must have some knowledge of environmental and development issues, and the curiosity to learn more. You don't have to be an expert, but you must be able to discuss complicated issues in clear and simple language, and be good at creative problem solving and thinking quickly and logically. [ID:7118]

Heart-Links
P.O. Box 443, 1486 Richmond Street, London, ON, N6A 4W1,
Canada; 519-432-3781 ext. 227, info@heart-links.org, www.heart-links.org

WORK AND LEARN ◆ Heart-Links was founded in 1994 and is managed in London, Ontario by an active board of 12 directors and numerous volunteers. It has no paid staff. Heart-Links works closely to support two grass-roots organizations in Northern Peru, primarily the Women's Center based in the coastal valley of Zaña and the Asociación Red de Bibliotecas Rurales, a network of over 600 rural libraries in the Andean department of Cajamarca.

Heart-links offers two-week annual Work/Awareness trips. Selected participants pay their own expenses for the trip. Participants gain first-hand knowledge of the community development initiatives in the fields of education, nutrition and health, and income generation projects that promote self-sufficiency. [ID:7142]

HOPE International Development Agency
214 Sixth Street, New Westminster, BC, V3L 3A2, Canada; 604-525-5481,
fax 604-525-3471, hope@hope-international.com, www.hope-international.com

WORK AND LEARN ◆ HOPE offers an education program for Canadians interested in international development. A group of 15 to 20 people spend five months, part-time, preparing in Canada, followed by one month working in a developing country at the community level. (For more information on HOPE, see Chapter 38, NGOs in Canada.) [ID:6939]

HorizonCosmopolite
3011, Notre-Dame ouest, Montreal, QC, H4C 1N9, Canada; 514-935-8436,
fax 514-935-4302, info@horizoncosmopolite.com, www.horizoncosmopolite.com 💻*En*

YOUTH EXCHANGE ◆ HorizonCosmopolite a pour mission de rapprocher les gens de cultures différentes et de développer une solidarité durable entre les peuples. L'organisme propose différents stages et programmes d'échange qui favorisent l'apprentissage de nouvelles aptitudes, connaissances et habiletés afin d'encourager l'essor d'une société juste, harmonieuse et respectueuse de son environnement. Une équipe constituée de cinq personnes à temps plein assure les services qui se traduisent par l'appui à la gestion de programmes internationaux (promotion, formation et recrutement), la formation (prédépart et retour), les programmes de groupes en immersion linguistique, culturelle ou professionnelle (institutions d'enseignement ou autres), les stages individuels (près de 40 programmes dans plus de 25 pays sur tous les continents) et la gestion de stages pour jeunes professionnels de la stratégie emploi jeunesse du gouvernement du Canada (ACDI, DRHC, Patrimoine canadien). [ID:7273]

IAESTE (Canada) - International Association for the Exchange of Students for Technical Experience
INTERNATIONAL STUDENT EXCHANGE
P.O. Box 1473, Kingston, ON, K7L 5C7, Canada; 613-533-2030,
fax 613-545-6869, Canada@iaeste.org, www.queensu.ca/iaeste 💻*Fr*

YOUTH EXCHANGE ◆ International Association for the Exchange of Students for Technical Experience (IAESTE) is an international exchange program providing on-the-job training experience for students in their own field of study. Over 6,500 Canadian students have benefited from the program, which includes over 90 member countries. A modest salary is paid to cover living costs but generally does not cover the costs of travel. Students of engineering, science and related technologies can apply each fall for a placement to start the following summer. Placements are from a minimum of six weeks to a maximum of 52 weeks. Applicants must be full-time students and have completed at least two years of post-secondary study, preferably with some practical experience. Costs include an application fee, which is partially refunded if a suitable placement is not found. Students who are interested in an IAESTE placement abroad must apply through the IAESTE committee in their home country. Application information and forms are available on their Web site. [ID:6962]

International Agricultural Exchange Association (IAEA)
AGRIVENTURE
Suite 105, 7710 5th Street S.E., Calgary, AB, T2H 2L9, Canada;
800-263-1827, fax 403-255-6024, post@agriventure.com, www.agriventure.com

WORK AND LEARN ◆ Agriventure, run by the International Agricultural Exchange Association, offers opportunities for Canadians aged 18 to 30 to travel and gain first-hand agricultural work experience in Europe, the United Kingdom, Japan, Australia and New Zealand. This unique program is open to agricultural/horticulture students or individuals with practical farming or horticulture experience. Individual exchange programs range in length from four to 12 months. For more information please visit their Web site or call them directly. [ID:6955]

International Association for Students of Economics and Commerce (AIESEC)

Suite 602, 30 Duncan Street, Toronto, ON, M5V 2C3, Canada;
416-368-1001, fax 416-368-4490, info@ca.aiesec.org, www.aiesec.org

YOUTH EXCHANGE ◆ AIESEC—International Association for Students of Economics and Commerce—is an independent, non-political, student-run, non-profit organization of business, economics and computer science students, which organizes an international exchange program. Each year, more than 5,000 students gain vast experience from these traineeships in over 85 countries. The program attempts to bridge the gap between theory-based university education and the practical business world. It also helps to develop internationally educated managers who can be effective in various economic environments in Canada and abroad.

Participants can stay from eight weeks to 18 months. To be eligible, students must be studying primarily in the business disciplines of economics, accounting, marketing, finance, business administration or computer science. Students must also have been members of AIESEC at any time during their studies, either before or after obtaining their degree. Participants pay for all travel, insurance and in-country accommodation and are paid as permanent employees. An administration fee for processing is applicable. Please see their Web site for more details. [ID:6864]

International Development Research Centre (IDRC)

Centre Training and Awards Program, P.O. Box 8500, Ottawa, ON, K1G 3H9,
Canada; 613-236-6163 ext. 2098, fax 613-563-0815, cta@idrc.ca, www.idrc.ca 💻 *Fr*

INTERNSHIPS ◆ The International Development Research Centre (IDRC) offers three types of internships in its effort to support scientific research in Africa, Asia, Latin America, and the Caribbean as it relates to social, economic and environmental problems.

The IDRC's internships involve a program of work and research responding to its three core programming areas: social and economic equity, environmental and natural resources management, and information and communication technologies for development. Internships range in duration from four months to one year at the IDRC headquarters in Ottawa or in a regional office. Positions in Canada are remunerated at a rate of between $32,391 and $37,523 per year. Travel and research expenses up to $10,000 may also be provided. Salaries for interns in regional offices will vary according to regional conditions. Candidates should have at least some training at the master's level. Application forms are available from the IDRC Training and Awards Unit, Special Initiatives Program, Corporate Services Branch.

The IDRC Gender Unit also offers internships as professional development awards given to individuals to develop their expertise in gender and development research management by working on IDRC program issues. Interns normally have several years of work experience. Duration and compensation varies depending on the individual and his or her experience and qualifications. Candidates must have completed their master's degree or be working toward a doctorate. Proposals can be submitted year-round.

In addition to these internships, IDRC offers a variety of awards and fellowships oriented toward graduate-level student training and research. Application forms for most programs can be downloaded on-line at the IDRC Web site. [ID:5641]

International Rural Exchange (IRE)

P.O. Box 111, Elgin, MB, R0K 0T0, Canada; 204-769-2448,
fax 204-769-2177, irecanada@shaw.ca, www.ire.org.au

INTERNSHIP ◆ International Rural Exchange (IRE) is a non-profit organization based on volunteer work around the world. The IRE programs are designed to give young adults the opportunity to learn about the agriculture, horticulture and customs of other countries while living and working with host families in those countries. IRE provides a combination of work and study programs in Scandinavia, Western Europe, Australia and the United States. The exchange operates both incoming and outgoing programs of which four types are possible. 1) Agricultural Trainee:

Applicants should have general knowledge and practical experience in agriculture and be prepared to participate in all general farm operations. 2) Home Management Trainee: Applicants should have a good general knowledge of household duties and be interested in child care and gardening. 3) Agri-mix Trainee: Designed for those who have limited knowledge or practical experience in agriculture and good overall knowledge of household management. Time is evenly divided between the two areas. 4) Horticulture Trainee: Applicants should have good general knowledge and practical experience in horticulture and be prepared to participate in all general horticultural operations.

IRE matches qualifications and interests with a suitable farm or horticulture operation and gives participants an orientation seminar on arrival in the host country. IRE also provides supervision at the training facility. A monthly allowance is paid, as well as room and board. [ID:6963]

International Student Exchange - Ontario
Suite 486, 65 Cedar Pointe Drive, Barrie, ON, L4N 9R3, Canada;
705-722-9440, fax 705-722-9441, info@iseontario.on.ca, www.iseontario.on.ca ▢ Fr

YOUTH EXCHANGE ◆ International Student Exchange - Ontario offers opportunities for Ontario elementary and secondary school students to discover and explore exciting places and cultures, improve or develop new language skills, and make lifelong friendships. Exchange countries include: Belgium, Costa Rica, France, Germany, Italy, Quebec, Spain and Switzerland. Participants are between 12 and 17 years of age, and exchanges are 10 days to one year in duration. To participate, you must be a resident of Ontario, Manitoba or Quebec. See their Web site for on-line applications and more details. [ID:6840]

International Youth Experience
CANADA-SWITZERLAND YOUNG WORKERS' EXCHANGE PROGRAM
12 Le Ber, Gatineau, QC, J9H 1C5, Canada; 819-684-9212,
fax 819-684-5630, switzerland@experience.ca, www.experience.ca ▢ Fr

PROFESSIONAL EXCHANGE ◆ The Canada-Switzerland Young Workers' Exchange Program is designed for Canadians who wish to upgrade their language skills and gain professional expertise in their field of study in Switzerland. Internships of four to 18 months are available under this official government program. To be eligible, you must be a Canadian citizen; be a graduate of a university or other post-secondary institution; wish to undertake an internship in a trade or profession directly related to your studies; have an adequate knowledge of French, German or Italian; be 18 to 35 years of age; and you must find a job in Switzerland that you could hold under a career development program or internship contract. The last requirement means that you have to find an internship by yourself although International Youth Experience can help you do so provided that you meet all the eligibility requirements. Participants are responsible for their own travel arrangements and transportation costs. As the Swiss government will not issue work permits on Swiss territory, you are strongly advised to wait until you receive a work permit before making travel arrangements. [ID:6959]

InterUniversity Centre Canada
Department of Political Studies, University of Guelph, Guelph, ON, N1G 2W1,
Canada; 519-824-4120, fax 519-824-4120, info@interuniversity.com, www.interuniversity.com

INTERNSHIP ◆ InterUniversity Centre Canada is a private corporation active in study abroad and international development, as well as business support and training with reference to the USSR successor states and Eastern Europe. It seeks to contribute to Canadian capabilities in order to understand developments in the region as well as to work there. InterUniversity Centre Canada also facilitates cooperation among North American universities with educational and research institutions in its target area.

For students, it organizes Russian language training in Moscow, St. Petersburg and Kharkov, as well as full-semester programs in English in Russia, Estonia and the Czech Republic. Short summer courses in Russia are also available on business and agriculture, as well as ecological field trips and folklore expeditions. The full-semester programs can be combined with English teaching, work internships and directed research. InterUniversity Centre Canada maintains a database of internships that are either volunteer, subsidized or self-arranged. There is a $500 US fee for internships placements. See their Web site for specific details. [ID:6894]

INTO Canadian Cultural Exchange Foundation
INTO CANADIAN CULTURAL EXCHANGE
Suite 408, 170 The Donway W., Don Mills, ON, M3C 2G3, Canada;
416-447-0612, fax 416-447-5902, contact@intoexchange.org, www.intoexchange.org

YOUTH EXCHANGE ◆ The INTO Canadian Cultural Exchange Foundation's mission is to promote peace and understanding of international cultures by offering Canadian students quality educational travel and exchange programs abroad. The INTO Canadian Cultural Exchange offers a full cultural immersion experience for Canadian students to live with a host family and attend a foreign high school. International students also benefit when they attend a Canadian high school and live with a Canadian family. Exchange countries include Australia, Austria, Belgium, Brazil, Denmark, France, Germany, Holland, Italy, Mexico, South Africa, Switzerland and the US. Students interested in participating must be between 15 and 18 years of age, demonstrate maturity, good character, flexibility and be prepared to spend a semester overseas. They must also possess a keen interest in learning about another culture/language, a willingness to represent and share Canadian culture, as well as attain a C average in overall academics. Some prior language skills or willingness to attend language camp depending on destination is required. [ID:6841]

Junior Professional Officer Program (JPO)
Human Resources Division, Personnel and Administration Branch, Canadian
International Development Agency (CIDA), 200 Promenade du Portage, Gatineau, QC,
K1A 0G4, Canada; 800-230-6349, fax 819-953-6088, http://w3.acdi-cida.gc.ca ☐ *Fr*

INTERNSHIPS ◆ The Junior Professional Officer Program (JPO) is administered under the auspices of the United Nations. Its primary objectives are to provide experience in managing a development program, support the UN through JPO services, place Canadians in the UN, and use knowledge gained from assignments. General duties of a JPO include the administration and coordination of projects and liaising between local authorities, regional offices, and headquarters.

Through the Canadian International Development Agency (CIDA), Canada sponsors several JPOs annually in the following UN agencies: United Nations Development Programme (UNDP), United Nations Children's Fund (UNICEF), United Nations High Commissioner for Refugees (UNHCR), the World Food Programme (WFP) and the United Nations Population Fund (UNFPA). Each organization recruits its own JPOs, therefore candidates must fill in an application form for each organization of interest. Contracts are for a period of one year.

Candidates should generally be under the age of 32 and possess a master's degree in a relevant discipline. Knowledge of two of the UN's three working languages and prior work experience (paid or voluntary) in a developing country is a definite asset. Information about the JPO program and application forms are available on CIDA's Web site. [ID:5633]

Katimavik
Suite 2160, Wing 3, Port of Montreal Bldg., Cité du Havre, Montreal, QC, H3C 3R5,
Canada; 519-868-0898, fax 519-868-0898, info@katimavik.org, www.katimavik.org ☐ *Fr*

YOUTH EXCHANGE ◆ Katimavik offers young Canadian men and women aged 17 to 21 an opportunity to acquire valuable personal and professional skills through volunteer work service. The Katimavik program is based on the concept of service learning—learning through volunteer work on community projects to which participants make a significant contribution. Katimavik incorporates five strategic learning programs: leadership, official languages, cultural discovery, environmental protection and adoption of a healthy lifestyle. For nine months, participants live in groups of 11 anglophones and francophones originating from all over the country in three regions of Canada, of which one is French-speaking. Katimavik covers the costs of accommodation, food, transportation and program-related activities. Participants receive a $3 CDN per day allowance and a $1,000 CDN bursary upon completion of the program. Applications to the program are completed on their Web site. [ID:6896]

Latin America Mission (Canada) Inc. (LAM)

Unit 14, 3075 Ridgeway Drive, Mississauga, ON, L5L 5M6, Canada;
905-569-0001, fax 905-569-6990, info@lamcanada.ca, www.lam.org

YOUTH EXCHANGE ◆ Latin America Mission (Canada) Inc. has a Spearhead Program whereby participants are involved in real, front line ministry activities. Participants serve as part of a team, learning leadership skills, studying language and culture while sharing faith and ministering with a local church. In the summer program, participants between ages 19 and 30 are expected to share their Christian faith through development and evangelism projects. Intensive Spanish language classes and the study of Mexican life, culture and history are also an integral part of the program. A $1,495 US fee covers room and board. Participants are responsible for travel expenses. A similar program is also facilitated in Honduras. Long-term career mission opportunities are also available. Visit the Canadian Web site to request application forms. [ID:6966]

Manitoba International Education Branch
MANITOBA GERMAN EXCHANGE PROGRAM

Suite 330, 800 Portage Ave., Winnipeg, MB, R3G 0N4, Canada; 204-945-4034,
fax 204-945-1792, education-exellence@gov.mb.ca, www.education-excellence.ca

YOUTH EXCHANGE ◆ The Manitoba Council for International Co-operation (MCIC) is an umbrella organization that supports the international development efforts of a number of Manitoban NGOs. It coordinates information and resources among its members and promotes public awareness and engagement of international development issues in Manitoba by holding workshops, sponsoring speakers and distributing literature. It also administers the Manitoba Government Matching Grant Program.

MCIC employs two permanent staff in Canada. MCIC seeks team players with good interpersonal, oral, writing and word processing skills, as well as experience in international development. While MCIC does not arrange overseas employment, it does act as an information resource for those interested in becoming involved in any of its member agencies, which operate throughout the developing world. [ID:6967]

Medical Ministry Canada Inc.

Suite 301, 15 John Street N., Hamilton, ON, L8R 1H1, Canada;
905-524-3544, fax 905-524-5400, mmican@mmint.org, www.mmint.org

PROFESSIONAL EXCHANGE ◆ Medical Ministry Canada Inc. provides one-week and two-week opportunities for volunteers to work in medical, dental, surgical and eye clinics in developing countries. Every year, approximately 1,600 North American participants go on over 70 missions to more than 25 developing countries. Volunteers come from a variety of denominational traditions and backgrounds. Most projects are in surgery, general medicine and dentistry. Eye projects may involve surgery only, as well as teams that include ophthalmology, optometry, opticians, nurses, techs, anaesthesia, general helpers and teens. Participants' donations cover travel and living expenses. Applications are processed on a first-come-first-served basis, and project size is determined by project directors and the number of physicians or dentists registered. [ID:6948]

NACEL Canada Inc.

Suite 208, 8925 - 82nd Ave., Edmonton, AB, T6C 0Z2, Canada;
780-468-0941, fax 780-465-7583, can@nacel.org, www.nacel.org/canada

YOUTH EXCHANGE ◆ NACEL Canada Inc. offers a variety of opportunities for students aged 13 to 18 to travel abroad. The majority of NACEL's programs are language based and involve a family homestay element. NACEL offers semester and year-long academic programs in France, Quebec, Spain, Mexico, Ireland and Australia. Students aged 15 to 18 may choose to spend a semester or school year in France, Germany, Spain, Mexico, Japan, Australia, the US, or Quebec. NACEL Canada also offers a limited number of scholarships opportunities for qualified applicants.

In addition, NACEL also has Discovery Tours that offer teachers and students the chance to travel and experience the world. Visit the NACEL Web site for further details. (For more information on NACEL, see Chapter 11, Hosting Programs.) [ID:7122]

NetCorps Canada International
3rd Floor, 2330 Notre-Dame Street W., Montreal, QC, H3J 1N4, Canada; 514-931-9306, fax 514-939-2617, secretariat@netcorps-cyberjeunes.org, www.netcorps-cyberjeunes.org ▣*Fr*

INTERNSHIP ◆ NetCorps Canada International offers exciting volunteer internships in developing countries for people aged 19 to 30 with appropriate skills in information and communication technologies (ICT). These internships, of approximately six months, are implemented by members of the NetCorps Coalition, which includes some of Canada's largest volunteer-sending international development organizations in partnership with Industry Canada. By building on the comparative strengths of the members, the coalition provides effective management and support to the program while adding valuable shared and collective services for interns. NetCorps Canada International is currently delivered by the following nine coalition members: Canada World Youth, Alternatives, CUSO, Canadian Crossroads International, the Canadian Society for International Health, Human Rights Internet, Oxfam-Québec, VSO, and the International Institute for Sustainable Development. (For more information on these organizations, see Chapter 38, NGOs in Canada.) [ID:6898]

Office Franco-Québecois pour la Jeunesse
Directrice de programme, Bureau 100, 11, boul. René-Lévesque est, Montreal, QC, H2X 3Z6, Canada; 514-873-4255, fax 514-873-0067, info@ofqj.gouv.qc.ca, www.ofqj.gouv.qc.ca

INTERNSHIP ◆ L'Office franco-québécois pour la jeunesse (OFQJ) contribue au rapprochement de la jeunesse française et québécoise. L'OFQJ participe par ailleurs aux grandes orientations de la coopération franco-québécoise et initie des activités vers des pays tiers ou des organisations internationales. L'OFQJ soutient les séjours professionnels ou pédagogiques outre-Atlantique de jeunes adultes de 18 à 35 ans. Chaque année, sous l'égide de l'OFQJ, des milliers de jeunes de France et du Québec réalisent dans l'autre communauté des activités en lien avec leur formation. Ils sont étudiants ou travailleurs, artistes, entrepreneurs ou en démarche d'insertion à l'emploi.

Les projets prennent diverses formes : stage en entreprise, mission commerciale, tournée de spectacles, immersion prolongée dans le monde du travail, chantier de travail, participation à un colloque ou à un séminaire spécialisé, université d'été, sessions d'études et autres événements spéciaux.Les candidats qui désirent participer à un stage doivent être âgés de 18 à 35 ans et habiter au Québec depuis au moins un an. Lorsqu'un projet est sélectionné, les coûts d'inscription sont de 450 $. Les participants reçoivent en retour les conseils d'une équipe chevronnée pour le développement de leur projet, le transport international, une assurance médicale et rapatriement, ainsi que la première nuitée à Paris. [ID:7322]

Pan American Health Organization (PAHO)
INTERNATIONAL HEALTH EXCHANGE PROGRAM
Office of the Director of Program Management, Human Resources Development Unit, Area of Strategic Health Development, 525 Twenty-third Street N.W., Washington, DC, 20037-2895, USA; 202-974-3592, fax 202-974-3612, www.paho.org ▣*Fr*▣*Sp*

PROFESSIONAL EXCHANGE ◆ The Pan American Health Organization (PAHO) promotes leadership in public health through their Training Program on International Health. The program enables participants to develop a broader vision of international and regional health trends, and a more profound understanding of technical cooperation in this field. Participants are engaged in the work of PAHO for a period of 11 months. Minimum requirements include a graduate degree in public health or in the social sciences related to health; two years' experience directing programs or projects in education or in health research; and a working knowledge of Spanish. Participants receive a non-taxable subsistence stipend of $2,194 US per month. (For more information on PAHO, see Chapter 41, United Nations and Other IGOs.) [ID:6952]

The Pangea Partnership (Pangea)

239 Bradley Ave., Ottawa, ON, K1L 7E8, Canada;
613-747-9185, info@PangeaPartnership.org, www.PangeaPartnership.org

WORK AND LEARN ◆ The Pangea Partnership (Pangea) is a small development assistance group employing 10 part-time staff and volunteers in Ottawa. Pangea's core focus is on public engagement and education. The project scope is global with an emphasis on Latin America.

Pangea's model of public engagement, involving Canadians directly in development initiatives, offers educational, participatory work experiences with the aim of exposing many Canadians to issues of global consequence while fostering cultural and environmental awareness. Participation is open to the general public.

The Pangea Partnership conducts workshops in developing countries that connect travellers with local youth. They teach participants how to construct healthy, ecological and economic buildings such as homes, schools and medical clinics that are essential to a community's well-being. Their workshops bring together travellers visiting host countries with locals who will take what they learn back to their communities to assist others. Workshops teach straw bale construction and complementary alternative technologies. Pangea's Web site lists workshops and schedules. [ID:7140]

Pearson Peacekeeping Centre (PPC)
PPC INTERNSHIP PROGRAM

P.O. Box 100, Clementsport, NS, B0S 1E0, Canada; 902-638-8611,
fax 902-638-8888, internship@peaceoperations.org, www.peaceoperations.org 🖳 *Fr*

INTERNSHIP ◆ The Pearson Peacekeeping Centre (PPC) Internship Program provides 30 opportunities per year to young professionals who are beginning a career in peace operations or international relations. Internships are offered in Cornwallis, Montreal and Ottawa, lasting four months, with a possibility of extension. The program operates throughout the year, with sessions usually beginning in January, May/June and September/October. The deadline for applications is three months before the start of a new session. Interns are directly involved with the Centre's programs, usually supporting the development and delivery of courses, exercises and other activities. In addition, interns at Cornwallis meet regularly for discussion and presentation of research papers, and develop their own personal research topics under the direction of the Director of Research and Program Development. Interns working at the Cornwallis campus, have room and board provided, as well as a per diem allowance to cover incidentals. Interns working at the Montreal or Ottawa centres are responsible for their own accommodation—however, the Centre provides a living allowance to help offset the higher costs of living expenses. (For more information on PPC, see Chapter 38, NGOs in Canada.) [ID:6895]

Province of Alberta
EDUCATOR EXCHANGE PROGRAMS

National and International Education Branch - Alberta Education,
The Learning Network, 832 Education S., Edmonton, AB, T6G 2G5, Canada;
888-945-5500, fax 780-492-0390, learnnet@ualberta.ca, www.learning-network.org

TEACHING ABROAD ◆ Educator Exchange Programs provide an international professional development opportunity in which participants exchange assignments but remain in the service of their regular employers, maintaining salary and benefit status. Programs are available in the United Kingdom, the US, Germany, Australia and other Canadian provinces. General criteria for the exchange programs include a permanent professional teaching certificate, a tenured teaching position, two years of successful teaching/administration experience, as well as recommendation and approval from the superintendent of the schools. Educators must also be in good health and be able to assume the financial commitment (travel and living costs) associated with participation in the programs. Alberta educators must request information packages and applications from their school jurisdiction. Additional information may be obtained from The Learning Network; see their Web site. [ID:6843]

Province of Manitoba
MANITOBA TEACHER EXCHANGE
Professional Certification Unit -Teacher Exchange, P.O. Box 700,
Russell, MB, R0J 1W0, Canada; 204-773-2998, fax 204-773-2411,
certification@gov.mb.ca, www.edu.gov.mb.ca/ks4/profcert/teachexchg.html 💻*Fr*

TEACHING ABROAD ◆ The Manitoba Teacher Exchange has exchange opportunities available in Australia, the United Kingdom, the United States, Germany (teachers must be fluent in German) and other Canadian provinces. Applicants must have a minimum of five years of teaching experience in Manitoba and must hold a valid Permanent Professional teaching certificate. Applicants must also possess permanent employment as well as obtain support for their application from the receiving school principal and school division/district. Teachers should be genuinely interested in participating in the exchange and flexible enough to adapt to new conditions and environments. The deadline for all applications is November 30, of the current year. Applications received for exchange to Australia are for January to December, while applications to other exchange countries are for the September to June school year. [ID:6846]

Province of Newfoundland and Labrador
TEACHER EXCHANGE
International Education Division, Department of Education, 4th Floor, West Block,
Confederation Bldg., St. John's, NL, A1B 4J6, Canada; 709-729-7430, fax 709-729-7481

TEACHING ABROAD ◆ Province of Newfoundland and Labrador Teacher Exchange Programs are administered with the USA, Australia, and Great Britain. It can also arrange exchanges to most provinces, but has a formal agreement with Ontario only. To qualify for the program, the person has to be in a continuing contract with a school board and must be at least 25 years of age.

Teachers submit an application form to their home province and their jurisdiction forwards it to the other provinces. In the application, the applicant identifies a preference or preferences. If a suitable match is available, it is proposed to the teacher's employer. If the employer is satisfied with the proposed match, the teacher can participate in the program. [ID:6860]

Province of Nova Scotia
NOVA SCOTIA TEACHER EXCHANGE
Registrar, Nova Scotia Department of Education - Teacher Exchange,
P.O. Box 578, 2021 Brunswick Street, Halifax, NS, B3J 2S9, Canada;
902-424-0511, fax 902-424-0511, certification@EDnet.ns.ca, www.exchanges.gc.ca

TEACHING ABROAD ◆ The Nova Scotia Teacher Exchange program provides opportunities for Nova Scotia teachers to gain teaching experience in other provinces and countries and for their counterparts to share their knowledge and skills with students and teachers in Nova Scotia. Exchanges are carried out with all other Canadian provinces, the United Kingdom, Germany, the United States and certain states in Australia (Queensland, Victoria, New South Wales and Canberra). Participants must be certified teachers with at least five years public school experience in Nova Scotia and members of the Nova Scotia Teachers Union. [ID:6848]

Province of Prince Edward Island
PRINCE EDWARD ISLAND TEACHER EXCHANGE PROGRAMS
Office of the Registrar - Teacher Exchange Program, P.O. Box 2000, Charlottetown, PE,
C1A 7N8, Canada; 902-368-4651, fax 902-368-6144, registrar@gov.pe.ca, www.gov.pe.ca 💻*Fr*

TEACHING ABROAD ◆ The Prince Edward Island Teacher Exchange Programs offer exchanges between PEI teachers and those in other Canadian provinces, US states or Commonwealth countries. Requirements include being a licensed teacher with five years of teaching experience; a permanent teaching position in order to exchange with another teacher; as well as approval from one's principal and school board. Some individuals trade places for a year while other exchanges are group study tours of a shorter duration. Individuals interested in participating in an exchange should contact the Office of the Registrar. Applications are processed as they are received. [ID:6849]

Province of Québec
MINISTÈRE DE L'ÉDUCATION DU QUÉBEC
1035, rue De La Chevrotière, 28e étage, Quebec, QC, G1R 5A5,
Canada; 418-643-7095, fax 418-646-6561, www.meq.gouv.qc.ca ▯*En*

TEACHING ABROAD ◆ Le Ministère de l'éducation du Québec offre peu de programmes d'échanges à l'extérieur du pays. Le seul programme offert s'adresse aux professeurs de langue seconde qui désirent se perfectionner. Pour y participer, les enseignants doivent demander à la direction de leur établissement de rédiger une lettre officielle au Ministère. Le Ministère rembourse les frais de transport et frais d'inscription à des cours de langue dans un établissement hors Québec. Une indemnité forfaitaire est également versée à chaque stagiaire.

Par ailleurs, la Fédération des commissions scolaires du Québec conseille aux enseignantes et enseignants qu'un échange intéresse de s'adresser à Éducation internationale, une coopérative de services de développement et d'échanges en éducation. Voici l'adresse du site Internet de cet organisme : www.education-internationale.com. [ID:7340]

Province of Saskatchewan
SASKATCHEWAN TEACHER EXCHANGE
Officer-in Charge, Saskatchewan Learning - Teacher Services, 1500 4th Ave., Regina, SK, S4P 3V7,
Canada; 306-787-6085, fax 306-787-1003, www.sasked.gov.sk.ca/student_records/teachexchange.html

TEACHING ABROAD ◆ Saskatchewan Learning - Teacher Services acts as the official agency for arranging the Saskatchewan Teacher Exchange. Destination locations include Germany, Ireland, Scotland, Wales and the US. Exchanges are available for teachers who are employed by a public school division in Saskatchewan and who have at least five years of teaching experience. Teachers must also have the approval of their employer in order to participate. Application forms can be requested from Teacher Services and must be completed before November 30. [ID:6845]

Provincial Programs for British Columbia, New Brunswick, Ontario
CANADIAN EDUCATOR EXCHANGE FOUNDATION (CEEF)
Canadian Education Exchange Foundation (CEEF), 250 Bayview Drive, Barrie, ON,
L4N 4Y8, Canada; 705-739-7596, fax 705-739-7764, info@ceef.ca, www.ceef.ca

TEACHING ABROAD ◆ Canadian Educator Exchange Foundation (CEEF) provides teachers from British Columbia, New Brunswick and Ontario with the opportunity to gain teaching experience in other countries and provinces while teachers from other countries share their knowledge and skills with students and teachers here in Canada. Exchanges are available to individuals who have a minimum of five years' teaching experience. Teacher exchanges in these provinces are administered by the Canadian Education Exchange Foundation (CEEF). Interested educators should contact the CEEF directly for complete information and application instructions. (For more information on CEEF, see their profile in this chapter.) [ID:6844]

Rotary International
ROTARY YOUTH EXCHANGE
One Rotary Center, 1560 Sherman Ave., Evanston, IL, 60201, USA; 847-866-3000,
fax 847-866-3251, youthexchange@rotaryintl.org, www.rotary.org/programs/youth_ex/index.html

YOUTH EXCHANGE ◆ Rotary International is a worldwide organization of business and professional leaders that provides humanitarian service, encourages high ethical standards in all vocations, and helps to build goodwill and peace in the world. Approximately 1.2 million Rotarians belong to more than 31,000 Rotary clubs located in 166 countries. Rotary International offers a broad range of humanitarian, intercultural and educational programs and activities designed to improve the human condition and advance the organization's ultimate goal of world understanding and peace.

Rotary administers its Youth Exchange program through individual districts, and potential applicants must contact their local district or club to begin the application process. There are more than 32 separate districts in Canada but no one central office. (For more information on Rotary International's programs, see Chapter 11, Hosting Programs.) [ID:6865]

Routes to Learning Canada
4 Cataraqui Street, Kingston, ON, K7K 1Z7, Canada;
613-530-2222, fax 613-530-2096, information@routestolearning.ca, www.routestolearning.ca

WORK AND LEARN ◆ Routes to Learning Canada (formerly Elderhostel Canada) is Canada's first and largest learning-travel organization. It offers innovative programs that give rare opportunities to learn by experience through adventure, exploration, and discovery. Routes to Learning Canada's network of over 250 educational and cultural institutions provide access to places that most people don't even know about. Experienced field staff provide first-hand knowledge and thought-provoking activities. Travel with people like yourself and grow and learn from each other's experiences. As a non-profit organization, Routes to Learning Canada's first commitment is providing a high-quality learning experience. Each year 10,000 participants join 300 exciting learning adventures in Canada and around the world. For more information or to receive a Routes to Learning Canada catalogue free of charge, contact the National office at 1-866-745-1690, or visit their Web site. [ID:6947]

Séjours Internationaux de Travail en Entreprise (SITE)
Ministère des affaires étrangères et du commerce international, C.P. 160,
succursale NDG, CDG - Conseil, Montreal, QC, H4P 3P5, Canada; 514-482-6453,
fax 514-879-8423, cdg.conseil@qc.aira.com, http://www.dfait-maeci.gc.ca/123go/siteprg-fr.asp

PROFESSIONAL EXCHANGE ◆ Le programme SITE est proposé aux entreprises qui désirent offrir à leurs employés un séjour à l'étranger, dans un but de formation, de motivation ou de récompense. Puisqu'il s'agit d'un programme d'échange, l'entreprise canadienne est jumelée à une entreprise française de son secteur d'activité. Chaque entreprise accepte d'accueillir des employés de l'autre organisation en nombre équivalent. L'entreprise paie les employés qu'elle accueille en suivant la politique de rémunération en vigueur pour son personnel. Les organisations peuvent ainsi donner à de jeunes citoyens canadiens de 18 à 35 ans la possibilité d'acquérir des compétences professionnelles et de vivre une expérience humaine tout en étant exposés à la culture du pays d'accueil. La durée du séjour de travail est de deux à douze mois et les séjours peuvent avoir lieu à toute période de l'année. Pour adhérer à ce programme, les candidats doivent être à l'emploi d'une entreprise qui participe au programme SITE. Ils doivent compléter une demande de participation et la faire approuver par l'employeur, posséder un passeport en règle et acquitter les frais requis d'analyse de dossier. [ID:7230]

Shastri Indo-Canadian Institute (SICI)
SHASTRI YOUTH INTERNSHIP PROGRAMME
Coordinator, University of Calgary, Education Tower 1402, 2500 University Drive N.W.,
Calgary, AB, T2N 1N4, Canada; 403-220-7467, fax 403-289-0100, sici@ucalgary.ca, www.sici.org ▢*Fr*

INTERNSHIP ◆ The Shastri Youth Internship Programme provides young professionals with opportunities to work in India for six months. The Shastri-Indo-Canadian Institute (SICI) delivers the program in partnership with different universities, private institutes and non-governmental organizations in Canada and India. The internships bridge the gap between academic study and career-related international work experience with the aim of enhancing the intern's employability skills for the Canadian labour market. Each internship will usually have a one- to two-month training period in Canada followed by a five- to six- month overseas assignment in India. Funds will be paid to the young professional in the form of an educational stipend of $8,000 CDN.

Candidates must be between 19 and 30 years of age; not currently enrolled in an educational program; and a recent graduate from a formal post-secondary education program. They must also be available for the duration of the internship (minimum six months) and must not have not participated in a previous international internship program funded by the Government of Canada, or have previous paid career-related international work experience. [ID:6968]

Société Mer et Monde
340, rue St-Augustin, Montreal, QC, H4C 2N8, Canada;
514-495-8583, fax 514-937-7652, info@monde.ca, www.monde.ca

PROFESSIONAL EXCHANGE ◆ La Société Mer et Monde a comme objectif principal d'appuyer le travail des ONG qui œuvrent auprès des personnes démunies au Canada et dans les pays en voie de développement. Mer et Monde suscite les occasions de contacts, d'échanges et de partenariat entre les gens du Sud et du Nord. La société collabore avec les organisations qui s'engagent dans diverses activités de coopération au Honduras ou au Sénégal en santé, éducation, intervention sociale et environnement. Mer et Monde offre des stages pour adultes d'une durée de 6 à 12 semaines et propose quelques semaines de découverte aux jeunes de 15 à 19 ans. Mer et Monde emploie quatre personnes à Montréal pour les programmes de stage, en plus d'une équipe de formation de quatre personnes. À l'étranger, Mer et Monde emploie deux personnes à temps plein au Sénégal, et deux au Honduras; un personnel occasionnel s'ajoute selon les besoins. [ID:7160]

SWAP
IRELAND WORKING HOLIDAY PROGRAM
Working Holiday Program, Suite 100, 45 Charles Street E., Toronto, ON, M4Y 1S2,
Canada; 416-966-2887, fax 416-966-6644, swapinfo@travelcuts.com, www.swap.ca

INDEPENDENT WORK AND TRAVEL ◆ SWAP's Ireland Working Holiday Program allows students and non-students to expand their travel experience by living and working in Ireland. The working permit is valid for up to 12 months. Employment is not limited to only one employer, place or particular field. To be eligible, you must be registered as a full-time, post-secondary student; be 18 to 35 years of age; and apply at least six weeks before departure. Pre-departure and arrival orientation, job information and ongoing support are provided. You are responsible for making your own travel arrangements. Visit the SWAP Web site for application information. (For more information, see their ad in the sponsor section at the end of this guide.) [ID:7133]

SWAP
NEW ZEALAND WORKING HOLIDAY PROGRAM
Working Holiday Program, Suite 100, 45 Charles Street E., Toronto, ON, M4Y 1S2,
Canada; 416-966-2887, fax 416-966-6644, swapinfo@travelcuts.com, www.swap.ca

INDEPENDENT WORK AND TRAVEL ◆ The New Zealand Working Holiday Program offered by SWAP permits young Canadians to holiday in New Zealand and to take temporary employment as needed to cover the expenses of their visit. Participants may stay up to 12 months. To be eligible, you must be a Canadian citizen who is 18 to 30. There is no student status requirement. Participants must cover the costs of their travel, room and board. This is a year-round program and applications must be submitted in person at least four weeks prior to departure at any Canadian Travel CUTS/Voyages Campus office. Pre-departure and arrival orientation, job info and ongoing support are provided. Visit their Web site for application information. (For more information, see their ad in the sponsor section at the end of this guide.) [ID:7135]

SWAP
SOUTH AFRICA WORKING HOLIDAY PROGRAM
Working Holiday Program, Suite 100, 45 Charles Street E., Toronto, ON, M4Y 1S2,
Canada; 416-966-2887, fax 416-966-6644, swapinfo@travelcuts.com, www.swap.ca ☐*Fr*

INDEPENDENT WORK AND TRAVEL ◆ SWAP South Africa offers, for the more adventurous types, flexible departures down to spectacular Cape Town where you can enjoy a working holiday of up to one year. This program is open to Canadians aged 18 to 30 who are full-time post-secondary students and/or graduates of the year in which they are applying. Applications should be made at least six weeks prior to departure. Upon arrival in South Africa, SWAP presents a comprehensive seven-day orientation package in Cape Town, including tours and work and safety information. If you are an experienced and confident traveller with the desire to gain experience in an evolving country, SWAP South Africa is for you. South Africa is also a great jump-off point to extend your travels into other parts of Africa. Visit the SWAP Web site for more details. (For more information, see their ad in the sponsor section at the end of this guide.) [ID:7036]

SWAP
SWAP TEACH/WORK GHANA WORKING HOLIDAY PROGRAM
SWAP Ghana Coordinator, Working Holiday Program, Suite 100, 45 Charles Street E., Toronto, ON,
M4Y 1S2, Canada; 416-966-2887, fax 416-966-6644, swapinfo@travelcuts.com, www.swap.ca ▯*Fr*

WORK AND LEARN ◆ SWAP Teach/Work Ghana is a pre-placement program that offers adventurous Canadians the opportunity to teach for a period of three months to one year in a primary and/or secondary school setting. Other placements include teaching adults about subjects such as banking in a financial setting, building homes, current health matters, safety and sanitation. Many schools are located in extremely rural areas, and both living and teaching conditions are very basic with limited resources. Participants live with a local host family for the duration of their stay. The work placements are unpaid and participants must therefore have adequate funds prior to departure. However, the cost of living and travelling in Ghana is very low, so money should go a long way. To qualify, Canadians must be at least 19 years of age (there is no maximum age limit) and no student status is required. Applications are processed in Toronto and are not accepted at Travel CUTS/Voyages Campus offices. Previous teaching experience is an asset, but not required. All applicants will be interviewed as part of the application process. Visit their Web site to download an application pack. (For more information, see their ad in the sponsor section at the end of this guide.) [ID:7037]

SWAP
SWAP USA AND SWAP USA INTERNSHIP PROGRAMS
Working Holiday Program and Internship Program, Suite 100, 45 Charles Street E, Toronto, ON,
M4Y 1S2, Canada; 416-966-2887, fax 416-966-6644, swapinfo@travelcuts.com, www.swap.ca ▯*Fr*

INDEPENDENT WORK AND TRAVEL ◆ SWAP USA allows you to head south of the border (or north to Alaska!) for a summer work term. SWAP USA is one of the few ways that Canadian students can legally work in the US. In order to participate, Canadians must be 18 and over and be full-time students. Participants are able to work for up to four months between the beginning of May and the beginning of October. It is encouraged that participants try to pre-arrange an offer of employment. Visit the SWAP Web site for a rapidly growing database of US employers and direct links to a range of US employment-oriented Web sites. Apply early for this program at your local Travel CUTS/Voyages Campus, The Adventure Travel Company, or Odyssey Travel office, as it is in high demand. The complete SWAP USA application pack can be downloaded from their Web site.

SWAP also offers internship programs in the US where Canadians aged 20 to 40 can train for periods of one to 18 months. Programs are available to both students and non-students. Visit the "USA Internship" page on their Web site for information and application procedures. (For more information, see their ad in the sponsor section at the end of this guide.) [ID:7038]

SWAP Working Holiday Programs
Coordinator, Suite 100, 45 Charles Street E., Toronto, ON, M4Y 1S2, Canada;
416-966-2887, fax 416-966-6644, swapinfo@travelcuts.com, www.swap.ca ▯*Fr*

INDEPENDENT WORK AND TRAVEL ◆ SWAP Working Holiday Programs (SWAP), Canada's largest international exchange program, with over 3,000 participants annually, arranges work permits and provides extensive pre-departure and arrival guidance for Canadian youth, aged 18 and older, who are interested in work opportunities while travelling abroad. SWAP offers programs in 12 international regions including Australia, Austria, Britain, France, Germany, Ireland, Japan, New Zealand, South Africa, Ghana, the South Pacific and the United States. Services vary by country, but all offer a welcome orientation and ongoing advice and assistance regarding employment and accommodation.

The minimum age for participation is 18, and the maximum age limit varies by country (generally most countries are 30, France and Ireland are 35; a number of countries have no age limit as long as you are a student). Participants are responsible for conducting their own job search, but the SWAP overseas hosting organizations assist participants by providing employer contacts and information regarding resumes and job strategies. Applications are accepted on a year-round basis, and the processing time takes approximately four to six weeks. SWAP is an excellent, affordable way for young people to gain experience by working with another culture. It also provides participants with a great deal of flexibility to travel at their leisure. Brochures and further information are available at local student association offices, campus placement/career centres and any of the 70 travel offices of Travel CUTS/Voyages Campus/The Adventure Travel Company located across Canada. (For more information, see their ad in the sponsor section at the end of this guide.) [ID:6950]

L'Union des producteurs agricoles (UPA)

555 boul. Roland-Therrien, Longueuil, QC, J4H 3Y9, Canada;
450-679-0530 ext. 8387, fax 450-463-5202, upa@upa.qc.ca, www.upa.qc.ca

YOUTH EXCHANGE ◆ L'Union des producteurs agricoles (UPA) est une organisation représentant l'ensemble des producteurs et productrices agricoles. Son mandat principal et ses actions sont basés sur les valeurs suivantes : respect de l'individu, solidarité, action collective, justice sociale, équité et démocratie. L'UPA offre aux résidants du Québec la possibilité d'effectuer un stage en France. Les participants doivent être âgés de 18 à 30 ans et posséder une expérience adéquate d'au moins 6 mois dans le domaine agricole. Les stages varient d'une période de 3 à 6 mois. Le stagiaire plus expérimenté sera rémunéré au salaire minimum incluant les frais de logement et de nourriture. Moins expérimenté, il recevra une gratification mensuelle incluant le logement et les repas.

UPA Développement international (UPA DI) est un organisme sans but lucratif, propriété de l'UPA. Il réalise des projets de coopération internationale, principalement en Afrique. À ce titre, l'organisme est parfois à la recherche de personnes issues du domaine de l'agroalimentaire qui peuvent participer à des mandats de courte et longue durée à l'étranger. Les personnes intéressées doivent faire parvenir leur curriculum vitae par courriel à l'adresse suivante : upadi@upa.qc.ca [ID:7318]

United Nations Volunteers (UNV)

Postfach 260 111, Bonn, D-53153, Germany; (42) (228) 815-2000,
fax (49) (228) 815-2001, information@unvolunteers.org, www.unv.org 🖵*Fr* 🖵*Sp*

INTERNSHIP ◆ The United Nations Volunteers (UNV) program supports global human development by promoting volunteerism and mobilizing volunteers. Administered by the United Nations Development Programme (UNDP), UNV operates amidst the growing recognition that volunteerism makes important economic and social contributions that build more cohesive societies and forge relationships based on trust and reciprocity. Every year 5,500 UN volunteers from more than 150 different nations actively support the programs of the United Nations and many UN funds, programs and specialized agencies.

Job vacancies for postings all over the world are listed on-line. Currently, UNV seeks qualified specialists in policy (health, governance, education), natural heritage protection, human resources development, environmental coastal zones, volunteerism, HIV/AIDS, micro-credit, participatory development, and crisis prevention. They also seek medical doctors with various specializations. Applicants must be at least 25, have a minimum of five years' work experience and good working knowledge in at least one of the following languages: Arabic, English, French, Portuguese, Russian or Spanish. Assignments usually last 24 months; however, assignments of six to 12 months are increasingly common. Benefits include a settling-in-grant; a volunteer living allowance (VLA) intended to cover basic living expenses (paid monthly); travel expenses; health insurance; annual leave; and a resettlement allowance. New arrangements making it easier for Canadians to participate in the work supported by the UNV program were formalized in 2004 with the Canadian International Development Agency (CIDA), the Canadian Centre for International Studies and Cooperation (CECI), and the World University Service of Canada (WUSC).

Visit the UNV Web site regarding further volunteer opportunities, such as on-line volunteer positions and internships at headquarters in Bonn, Germany. The site includes on-line application forms and a "Volunteer Voices" section where past and present volunteers share their experiences as they work for peace and sustainable development around the globe. (For related information on working with the UNV, see Chapter 17, Internships Abroad and Chapter 41, United Nations and Other IGOs.) [ID:6863]

Up with People
THE WORLDSMART LEADERSHIP PROGRAM
Admissions, Office of Admissions, Suite 1460, 1675 Broadway, Denver, CO, 80202,
USA; 303-460-7100 ext. 108, anarans@upwithpeople.org, www.worldsmart.org ▭*Fr* ▭*Sp*

YOUTH EXCHANGE ◆ The WorldSmart Leadership Program, Up with People's global education program, is a semester-long study abroad program for international youth, aged 18 to 29. The goal of the program is to develop, inspire and transform young people into future leaders and global citizens. WorldSmart provides students with invaluable skills and experiences needed for our increasingly global and multicultural environment. Students from more than 20 countries travel together throughout the program. The group spends one week in each city they visit, learning first-hand from their host families, classmates, instructors and the unforgettable people they meet and places they experience along the way. See their Web site for more specifics. [ID:6931]

Veterans Affairs Canada
STUDENT GUIDE PROGRAM IN FRANCE
Coordinator, Veterans Services, P.O. Box 7700, Charlottetown, PE, C1A 8M9, Canada;
902-566-8363, fax 902-566-8534, newfoundland_memorial@vac-acc.gc.ca, www.vac-acc.gc.ca ▭*Fr*

WORK AND LEARN ◆ The Student Guide Program in France is a unique program open to bilingual, Canadian, post-secondary students. Students from across Canada live and work in France for a period of four months as interpretive guides at memorial sites including the Canadian National Vimy Memorial, and the Newfoundland Beaumont-Hamel Memorial. Applicants are expected to have some knowledge and interest in the history of the battle of Vimy Ridge and the role of the Canadian/Newfoundland forces in the First World War. They should also have some tour guide, interpreter or public relations experience. This work involves giving guided tours in battlefield terrain and in underground tunnels, sometimes in adverse weather conditions. It also involves providing operational support to visitors' centres on site. The current rate of pay is $11.41 CDN (2004), plus an additional allowance is given to the participant. Students must assume the costs of their accommodation, meals, and health care (basic dorm style accommodation is available at a reasonable cost). Applications are made through the Federal Student Work Experience Program (FSWEP) and guides are hired for the following periods: January to May, April to August and August to November. Visit their Web site for more information. [ID:6932]

Visions in Action
2710 Ontario Road N.W., Washington, DC, 20009, USA; 202-625-7402,
fax 202-588-9344, visions@visionsinaction.org, www.visionsinaction.org

WORK AND LEARN ◆ Visions in Action is an international non-profit organization based in Washington, DC. The organization is dedicated to achieving social and economic justice in the developing world. Volunteers are placed with non-profit development organizations, research institutes and the media in Uganda, Tanzania, South Africa and Mexico for six or 12 months. There is also a summer program available. Volunteers work in various fields based on experience, interest and the needs of the organizations. Program fees, including housing, health insurance, orientation and staff support range from $3,500 to $6,200 US. Applicants must be at least 20 years of age for long-term programs and have a college degree or equivalent experience. Prior work overseas and cross-cultural experience is preferred. Program applications and further information is available on their Web site. [ID:6940]

Volunteer Abroad
Coordinator, 186 Princess Street, Kingston, ON, K7L 1B1, Canada;
613-549-3342, fax 613-548-1787, info@volunteerabroad.ca, www.volunteerabroad.ca ⌨ *Fr*

YOUTH EXCHANGE ◆ Volunteer Abroad allows Canadians over 18 years of age to see the world and become involved in international and global issues. Many volunteers are students who are looking to combine their volunteer experience with their academic program, while some participants are retired individuals who wish to offer their skills and knowledge to those who need it. Volunteers from around the world give two to four weeks of their time to a variety of environmental, archaeological or community service projects. Projects include working on a reforestation project in Borneo's rainforest, teaching in Thailand or building porter shelters in Nepal's Mount Everest region. Other countries where you can volunteer include: Costa Rica, Ecuador, Guatemala and Peru. Also, regardless of study discipline, there is often an opportunity to gain credit through an educational institution for work abroad. Volunteer Abroad seeks people with a generous spirit and an interest in working with others. The first step to volunteering is to fill out an on-line application. Fundraising before departure is expected. Check out their Web site for more details. [ID:6951]

Volunteers for Peace
43 Tiffany Road, Belmont, VT, 05730-0202, USA;
802-259-2759, fax 802-259-2922, vfp@vfp.org, www.vfp.org

YOUTH EXCHANGE ◆ Volunteers for Peace offers approximately 2,500 volunteer positions annually, in order to promote goodwill through people-to-people exchanges and community service. Volunteers cooperate with locals on host community projects in many different work areas, including archaeology, social sciences, natural resources, construction, agriculture and the environment. Positions are available in over 90 countries worldwide. Most programs are from May to September, with a few in winter and spring. Room and board are provided, but travel expenses are not paid. Specific details are noted on their Web site. [ID:7019]

World Learning
EXPERIMENT IN INTERNATIONAL LIVING
P.O. Box 676, Kipling Road, Brattleboro, VT, 05302-0676, USA;
802-257-7751, fax 802-258-3248, eil@worldlearning.org, www.worldlearning.org

YOUTH EXCHANGE ◆ World Learning is the only international organization with both academic and project capabilities dedicated to promoting international education, social justice and world peace. World Learning's summer exchange program immerses high school students in another culture in one of over 20 countries. Through homestays, language training, community service, peace studies and ecological projects, these cross-cultural adventures challenge stereotypes, reduce xenophobia and celebrate diversity.

Experiment in International Living programs are located in 26 countries around the globe, immersing participants in the daily life of another culture. For three to five weeks, Experimenters focus on themes such as community service, language study, ecology, travel or the arts, as they enjoy life with their host families and participate in activities with their group. Program fees include round-trip international transportation (except for programs in Mexico and the Navajo Nation); orientation; guidance by a skilled group leader; placement with a host family; all meals and lodging; host-country transportation; admission to program-related events; health and accident insurance; and baggage insurance. Financial assistance is available to a limited number of participants. Group leader positions are also sought. Experience working with young people, as well as cross-cultural experience and language competency are required. For catalogue and application forms visit their Web site. [ID:6941]

World University Service of Canada (WUSC)
P.O. Box 3000, Stn. C, 1404 Scott Street, Ottawa, ON, K1Y 4M8, Canada;
613-798-7477, fax 613-798-0990, wusc@wusc.ca, www.wusc.ca 💻*Fr*

YOUTH EXCHANGE ◆ World University Service of Canada (WUSC) attempts to provide as many opportunities as possible for Canadians to work in the field of international development both in Canada and overseas, in the belief that Canadians have an important contribution to make to international understanding and that a broadened world view should be a defining Canadian characteristic. Opportunities with WUSC include everything from highly expert positions to internship experiences for recent graduates.

WUSC recruits Canadian volunteers and technical experts for capacity-building programs and projects in selected African, Asian and South American countries. It also has approximately 60 staff at its secretariat office in Ottawa and field offices in six countries abroad. Through its volunteer and public engagement programs, the organization fields approximately 100 volunteers and students overseas each year. Assignments vary in length from six weeks to two years. Refer to WUSC's Web site for more details on how to apply on-line.

In 2004, WUSC began working with the Canadian Centre for International Studies and Cooperation (CECI) to administer a joint volunteer program. At the same time, CECI joined WUSC as the Canadian cooperating agency for the United Nations Volunteers Programme (UNV), handling the recruitment process for Canadians and permanent residents on behalf of UNV headquarters in Bonn. UNV offers mid-career professionals the opportunity to volunteer overseas in humanitarian efforts. Thousands of people from more than 100 countries volunteer as specialists and field workers. Consult the UNV Web site at www.unv.org. (For more information on WUSC, see Chapter 38, NGOs in Canada.) [ID:6942]

World Vision Canada
INSIGHT TRIPS
The Life Change Network Department, 1 World Drive, Mississauga, ON, L5T 2Y4,
Canada; 905-565-6100, info@worldvision.ca, www.destinationlifechange.com

WORK AND LEARN ◆ World Vision Canada is a Christian humanitarian relief and development agency, working in partnership with communities in more than 100 countries. The Life Change Network department currently offers short-term Insight Trips that allow Canadians the opportunity to see development work in action. These trips offer a balance between lending a hand to help with the ongoing community development work and a strong educational element to help Canadians see how child sponsorship works first hand. The goal upon return is for participants to share their experience and new knowledge with others and to become an advocate on behalf of the children.

Programs range from two to three weeks in length and are open to anyone 18 or older. Applicants must have an open mind and demonstrate a positive outlook, flexibility and sensitivity to the customs and traditions of other cultures. There is a varying project cost associated with each program location, which covers accommodation and some living expenses. Participants are responsible for covering their own travel expenses. Contact World Vision's Life Change Network for current opportunities. [ID:7120]

WorldTeach Inc.
Director of Recruiting and Admissions, c/o Centre for International Development,
Harvard University, 79 John F. Kennedy Street, Cambridge, MA, 02138, USA;
617-495-5527, fax 617-495-1599, info@worldteach.org, www.worldteach.org

TEACHING ABROAD ◆ WorldTeach is a well-established international volunteer program based at the Center for International Development at Harvard University. The organization has nearly two decades of experience training, placing and supporting volunteers as teachers in developing countries. Every year, WorldTeach places approximately 250 volunteers, in both long-term (six to 12 months) and summer programs, in countries that have requested assistance throughout the world. At the time of publication, program countries include Chile, China, Costa Rica, Ecuador, the Marshall Islands, Namibia and Poland. Applications are accepted year-round. Participants in long-term programs must have a bachelor's degree, while summer program participants must be at least

18 years of age. No previous language or teaching experience is required. Check their Web site for the latest program updates. [ID:6943]

YMCA International
INTERNATIONAL CAMP COUNSELLOR
PROGRAM AND WORK IN BRITAIN PROGRAM

2nd Floor, 5 West 63 Street, New York, NY, 10023-9197, USA;
212-727-8800 ext. 119, fax 212-727-8814, ips@ymcanyc.org, www.ymcainternational.org

WORK AND LEARN ◆ YMCA International offers both the International Camp Counsellor Program and the Work in Britain Program to Canadians. The International Camp Counsellor Program offers four- to eight-week positions for summer camp counsellors around the world in Asia, Africa, South America and Europe. Requirements include a high school diploma and previous experience with the YMCA. In some cases special educational, language or athletic skills may be required. Applicants should be between 21 and 30, flexible, and possess organizational and leadership skills. Program fees are $155 US, which covers insurance and continual support staff. Room, board, and other expenses are usually provided, but travel costs are the responsibility of the participant. For additional details, check out www.ymcaiccp.org.

YMCA International also offers Work in Britain, a student exchange employment program, open to currently enrolled full-time college students and recent graduates. The British Universities North America Club (BUNAC) provides a Blue Card that will allow employment for up to six months in Great Britain, while the International YMCA can find you employment at a YMCA in Great Britain. If YMCA work is unavailable, BUNAC will provide a catalogue of job listings for other organizations that you can apply to. Positions with YMCAs include child care, health & fitness, and Housekeeping. Participants are responsible for airfare, an application fee of $275 US (includes BUNAC application fee), and all living expenses (rent, meals, leisure activities, etc.). These expenses should be covered by the salary earned. [ID:6944]

Youth Challenge International (YCI)

Suite 305, 20 Maud Street, Toronto, ON, M5V 2M5, Canada;
416-504-3370, fax 416-504-3376, generalinfo@yci.org, www.yci.org ▄*Fr*

WORK AND LEARN ◆ Youth Challenge International (YCI) promotes global youth development and believes youth driven solutions are a critical component to their work. YCI provides young Canadians with the opportunity to implement overseas development programs in engagements of five weeks to eight months in a team-based environment. Young Canadians learn project management and implementation skills and develop an understanding of global issues. At the same time, youth in developing countries receive education on HIV/AIDS and basic employability skills. YCI sends up to 160 Canadian volunteers who directly impact roughly 4,000 youths from developing countries every year through workshops, modules and activities. These programs are managed by five full-time staff in the Toronto office and by up to 30 overseas staff in YCI's partner organizations. One notable success has been the establishment and development of indigenous and independent partner organizations in Guyana, Costa Rica, Vanuatu and Australia, through seed funding and ongoing institutional capacity-building and support. (For more information on YCI, see Chapter 38, NGOs in Canada.) [ID:6974]

Youth for Understanding Canada (YFU-Canada)

690 Fountain Street N., Cambridge, ON, N1T 1N9, Canada;
519-653-0550, fax 519-653-5792, go@yfu.ca, www.yfu.ca

YOUTH EXCHANGE ◆ Youth For Understanding Canada (YFU-Canada) is a non-profit, volunteer-based international exchange organization. Established in 1951, YFU has successfully exchanged more than 200,000 students worldwide. Students can choose an academic year, semester or summer exchange in one of over 50 countries. YFU also provides placements in Canada for foreign students to attend high school and live with a host family. Students applying should be open-minded, flexible and willing to adapt to and show interest in a different culture. Program fees start from $6,485 CDN. For application forms or more information you can contact the office directly or visit their Web site. [ID:6975]

Youth International
92 Grenadier Road, Toronto, ON, M6R 1R3, Canada; 416-538-0152,
fax 416-538-7189, info@youthinternational.org, www.youthinternational.org

YOUTH EXCHANGE ◆ Youth International is an experiential education program that focuses on international travel and intercultural exchange, adventure, community service and homestays. Teams of up to 14 people between the ages of 18 and 25, along with two group leaders, travel together to different regions of the world for a three-and-a-half month semester. Youth International offers three separate trips. One travels to Asia (Vietnam, Thailand and India); the second travels to Africa (Kenya, Tanzania, Botswana, and Namibia); the third program travels to South America (Bolivia, Peru and Ecuador). All three trips are offered twice a year once in the fall semester, which runs from early September to mid-December and once in the spring semester, which runs from early February to late May. [ID:6890]

CHAPTER 11
Hosting Programs

It is possible to gain a unique cross-cultural experience without actually making a trip abroad simply by hosting visitors from overseas. Sharing your home and lifestyle with someone from another culture offers many benefits to both the host and the guest. Most host families are surprised by how much they learn, not only about the guest's culture, but also themselves and the subtleties of Canadian culture they had never questioned in the past.

The profiles you find at the end of this chapter are by no means an exhaustive listing of North American hosting programs (only 11 profiles are listed). They offer examples of both short- and long-term possibilities that may be suited to your interests. Keep in mind that hosting options often arise through informal channels, so personal initiative may be the best way to get involved.

TYPES OF PROGRAMS

There are a variety of different hosting experiences that may be appropriate for you. You may wish to take someone from another culture into your home for a period of time, ranging from four months to a year. Youth and student exchanges are examples of longer-term hosting possibilities. You can contact any of the organizations profiled in this chapter, or call your local university or college's International Centre and English as a Second Language department to find out what opportunities they offer. Working with refugees or landed immigrants is another option. This type of host experience is certainly both very challenging and very rewarding. Working couples— with or without children—single parents, or empty nesters can participate in a hosting program. For longer-term hosting programs, families are usually interviewed by the organization for suitability. Your efforts can provide a strong, long-lasting friendship and a relationship of trust between you and your guest.

If you are unable to commit to the length of time and amount of energy necessary for a long-term host experience, it is possible to take a brief glimpse into the lifestyle of others by hosting guests for a few days, or even one evening. A short-term encounter opens your eyes to new people and world views. Individuals from overseas will appreciate any time you spend assisting them in getting accustomed to Canadian culture. Greeting someone at the airport or helping her get settled in her new location eases the pressure of arriving in a foreign place. Helping familiarize a newcomer to Canada with the city's transportation system or the daily want-ads makes him feel welcome, confident and independent. Entertaining people in town on business for an evening provides a welcoming atmosphere and makes their stay in Canada more pleasant and memorable. If you think short-term hosting is for you, contact organizers of international conferences, local organizations with a focus on new immigrants, professors, and international student services of universities. They often look for volunteers willing to assist international arrivals and visitors.

REWARDS OF HOSTING

All cross-cultural experiences have both benefits and challenges; hosting is certainly no exception. Perhaps one of the most obvious benefits is the opportunity it provides to broaden your international outlook. Hosting sensitizes you to other cultures and allows you to understand how people interpret events from their own cultural perspective. It is also an excellent start in your quest for information about what life will be like overseas.

Through the daily contact that hosts have with their international guests, they begin to understand the cultural attitudes and norms that govern each society or community. Cultural attitudes and norms exert a strong influence over the way people live, and are unique to every culture. Dress, body language, ways of expressing happiness, love, anger or disagreement, sense of humour, behaviour associated with food and alcohol, and concepts of space are key areas around which cultures differ. Living with someone from overseas offers exposure to these differences, and forces you to examine elements of Canadian culture that you may not have considered in the past. This process enables you to become more attuned and flexible to different perspectives on world issues, and more accepting of other cultures. This type of awareness is crucial to a successful experience overseas.

CHALLENGES OF HOSTING

It is important to recognize the demands that subtle cultural differences place on hosts and guests alike. Particularly in the initial stages of hosting, both parties will be uncertain about what constitutes appropriate behaviour. You will likely be faced with awkward situations with your guests because of limited communication and cultural differences. What may seem like a polite gesture to you might actually be received very negatively by someone with a different cultural perspective. Take for example Canadians' concept of space. Many Canadian families place importance on personal, private space in the home. As a result, providing children or guests with their own bedroom is highly valued. However, a guest from a more communal culture in which shared accommodation is the norm may be insulted, or feel isolated or abandoned in a private room. The guest might misinterpret this situation as a sign that he is considered an outsider by the host family. Misunderstandings such as these are inevitable, but not insurmountable.

With time, patience, an open mind and lots of discussion you can work through these challenges. Be prepared to spend many hours communicating with your guest. This is a necessary component of hosting, and will make your host experience all the more worthwhile. Keep in mind that learning to communicate with someone from another culture can be a lot of fun, a way of sharing humour and happy times. Not only will both parties learn more about the intricacies of each other's culture, but a strong and potentially long-lasting relationship can develop.

A LAST WORD

Set realistic goals for your host experience. Don't expect to solve the world's problems during your guest's stay, and certainly don't expect to change the way your guest sees the world. Instead, think of hosting as a way to situate yourself in a complex and interdependent world. Listening to what others have to say is the first step towards a more just and equitable social order.

RESOURCES
HOSTING PROGRAMS

Whether you are hosting someone on a brief visit for international business purposes or taking someone in (perhaps a student) for a longer period of time, at least one of these resources should be appropriate for you.

AYUSA International ᛟ
www.ayusa.org ◆ AYUSA is a non-profit educational and cultural exchange organization with headquarters in San Francisco, California that promotes global learning and leadership through high school exchange programs. Since 1980, AYUSA has provided opportunities for more than 37,000 students from the US and around the world to live and study overseas. [ID:2214]

Host Family Survival Kit: A Guide for American Host Families 📖
1997, Nancy King, Ken Huff, Intercultural Press, 215 pages ➤ Masters & Scribes Bookshoppe, 9938 - 81 Ave., Edmonton, AB T6E 1W6, Canada, www.mastersandscribes.com, $23 CDN; Credit Cards; 800-378-3199, fax 780-439-6879 ◆ This US guide promotes an understanding of the exchange experience by bringing to life the joys and challenges of hosting. The book examines the role the exchange student plays in the host family and the skills needed for host parenting. It also provides an insightful examination of cultural differences. [ID:2088]

NACEL International 💻
www.nacel.org ◆ This UK Web site has information on the academic exchange, internship, work placement and homestay programs offered by the organization. [ID:2210]

Staying Healthy While Living in Canada 📖
1994, 102 pages ➤ CUSO, Suite 500, 2255 Carling Ave., Ottawa, ON K2B 1A6, Canada, www.cuso.org, $15 CDN; 613-829-7445, fax 613-829-7996; Fr ◆ Provides health information and advice for students coming to Canada from developing countries to study or work for six months or more. Addresses such issues as accessing the Canadian health care system, depression, stress, winter health issues and Canadian culture as it affects physical and mental well-being. Available in French under the title "Visa-santé pour le Canada." [ID:2173]

Profiles of Hosting Programs

The following is a selection of 11 hosting programs. This is only a short list which includes the largest hosting program organizations. There are however thousands of opportunities to host foreign nationals. Try contacting local NGOs in your areas, or better still, offer to host a foreign student studying at a local educational institution. Enjoy the experience!

AFS Interculture Canada (AFS)
1425 Rene-Levesque W. Blvd., Montreal, QC, H3G 1T7, Canada;
514-288-3282, fax 514-843-9119, info-canada@afs.org, www.afscanada.org ☐*Fr*

HOSTING PROGRAM ◆ AFS Intercultural Canada's Hosting Program welcomes any type of family—single-parent families, couples with children and couples without children. Hosting periods range from four weeks to 11 months, and AFS assumes responsibility for the welfare and safety of the participant. Orientation camps and social activities are organized by AFS volunteers. (For more information on AFS, see Chapter 10, Short-Term Programs Overseas and Chapter 38, NGOs in Canada.) [ID:6945]

Alliances Abroad
Suite 250, 1221 S Mopac Expressway, Austin, TX, 78746, USA;
512-457-8062, fax 512-457-8132, www.alliancesabroad.com

HOSTING PROGRAM ◆ Alliances Abroad is the only company of its kind designing and delivering customized programs for individuals and groups around the globe who want to learn about other cultures by studying or working abroad. They have helped thousands of people travel abroad for the experience of a lifetime - from two weeks to one year, in over 50 cities around the world. Alliances Abroad is also a resource for companies around the US as they offer several programs which bring students, young professionals and seasonal workers to the US for three- to 12-month work programs. For most overseas programs, Americans, Canadians and Australian citizens are eligible; but, be sure to verify the requirements of each program before applying. After you've decided on the program you want, you can download their application on-line. [ID:6000]

Bowers Homestay and Educational Services of Canada
34 Moorcrest Drive, Aurora, ON, L4G 3R4, Canada; 905-726-2629,
fax 905-726-3966, info@canadahomestay.com, www.canadahomestay.com

HOSTING PROGRAM ◆ Bowers Homestay and Educational Services of Canada believes that providing an international student with a safe and comfortable place to live and learn provides a unique opportunity to learn about people from around the world. Bowers brings students of all ages from several countries to Canada for at least a four-week period.

Canadian families must provide their host student with a private and furnished room and two meals a day. The cost to the student for this service is $680 CDN. Host families must also include their host student in family activities on a regular basis. Honorariums for host families are provided. The most important criteria that Bowers looks for in a host family is the desire to share their time and interests with an international student. Visit the Bowers Homestay and Educational Services of Canada Web site for full details. [ID:7121]

Canadian Crossroads International (CCI)
Suite 500, 317 Adelaide Street W., Toronto, ON, M5V 1P9, Canada;
416-967-1611, fax 416-967-9078, ontario@cciorg.ca, www.cciorg.ca ☐*Fr*

HOSTING PROGRAM ◆ Canadian Crossroads International (CCI) is an international development agency with over 20 partnership projects in 15 countries. As part of these projects, volunteers and staff from partners in developing countries participate in work placements with Canadian partner organizations.

While in Canada, volunteers (Crossroaders) stay with host families. Becoming a host family is a great way to learn about the social and cultural life of another country while at home. CCI provides a small allowance to cover costs of food and accommodation. To find out how to become a host family, visit their Web site or contact the CCI office in your region. (For more on CCI, see Chapter 10, Short-Term Programs Overseas and Chapter 38, NGOs in Canada.) [ID:6926]

Canadian Relief Fund for Chernobyl Victims in Belarus

190 Bronson Ave., Ottawa, ON, K1R 6H4, Canada;
613-567-9595, fax 613-567-9971, crfcvb@cyberus.ca, www.crfcvb.ca

HOSTING PROGRAM ♦ The Canadian Relief Fund for Chernobyl Victims in Belarus was created with the aim of helping the Belarussian people cope with the fallout of the April 1986 Chernobyl explosion. The fund is involved in a variety of medical and educational projects in Canada. Each year the Canadian Relief Fund invites children from the contaminated areas of Belarus to Canada for several weeks of life in a clean environment. Knowledge of a Slavic language is helpful but not necessary. Families interested in hosting a child should e-mail the organization. Check out their Web site to find out the contact organization in your region. [ID:7022]

Children's International Summer Villages Canada (CISV)

5 Dunvegan Road, Ottawa, ON, K1K 3E7, Canada;
613-749-9680, fax 613-749-9680, cisvcan@allstream.net, www.cisv.ca

HOSTING PROGRAM ♦ Children's International Summer Villages Canada (CISV) promotes global peace education. CISV offers overseas programs geared to youths aged 11 to 19. Through its Interchange Program, a Canadian delegation of 10 youths, aged 12 to 15 and a delegation from another country (countries vary by interchange) meet for approximately three to four weeks for two consecutive summers. Delegations engage in a variety of activities which promote cross-cultural awareness and international understanding. Each Canadian participant is matched to a participant in the host country. Participants spend four weeks with the host family of their billet, and in turn host their billet the following year for the same period of time. Cost to participants varies by local chapter. Families interested in hosting through this program must have a child participating in the interchange. For more information on hosting, contact your local CISV chapter or contact the CISV Canada Secretary. (For more information on CISV, see Chapter 10, Short-Term Programs Overseas.) [ID:6927]

University of Manitoba International Centre for Students

ICS Program Coordinator, University of Manitoba, 541 University Centre, Winnipeg, MB, R3T 2N2, Canada; 204-474-8880, fax 204-474-7562, ics@cc.umanitoba.ca, www.umanitoba.ca/student/ics

HOSTING PROGRAM ♦ The University of Manitoba's International Centre for Students has a Welcome Family program that provides an opportunity for new international students to stay with a Welcome Family for a few days after they arrive in Winnipeg. Welcome Families are volunteers who are interested in meeting and helping students. International students are placed with a family for three to five days, at no cost, to give them an opportunity to recover from travel, adjust to a new culture, find accommodations and register at the university. Students who request a Welcome Family can look forward to meeting and getting to know typical Canadian families. Welcome Families are not necessarily language or culture specialists, but people interested in broadening their horizons by befriending individuals from around the world. [ID:6929]

NACEL Canada Inc.

Suite 208, 8925 - 82 Ave., Edmonton, AB, T6C 0Z2, Canada;
780-468-0941, fax 780-465-7583, can@nacel.org, www.nacel.org

HOSTING PROGRAM ♦ NACEL Canada Inc. is dedicated to coordinating quality educational experiences for both host families and exchange students. NACEL Canada Inc. is an associate of

NACEL International, which has served close to 300,000 participants since 1957. Host families have the opportunity of welcoming an international exchange student into their home for a period of four weeks to one year. Students are between 13 and 18 years of age, have two to six years of English study and are individually matched with their host family's interest. Successful host family applicants are of various ages and family size, but all are warm, welcoming, open-minded and interested in learning about a new culture. Visit the NACEL Web site for further details, applicant requests, and to have any questions answered via e-mail. (For more information on NACEL, see Chapter 10, Short-Term Programs Overseas.) [ID:7026]

Rotary International
One Rotary Center, 1560 Sherman Ave., Evanston, IL, 60201, USA; 847-866-3000,
fax 847-866-3251, youthexchange@rotaryintl.org, www.rotary.org/programs/youth_ex/index.html

HOSTING PROGRAM ◆ Rotary International has youth exchanges with more countries than any other exchange organization; therefore, you can consider hosting a student from 163 different countries in your home. Participating in this program provides an unforgettable service to a student from abroad, as well as an educational experience for your family. Rotary Youth Exchange is the most affordable program of its kind, and is run entirely by dedicated volunteers. As such, students are not required to pay any kind of placement fee to participate in the program. This enables financially disadvantaged students and students from developing countries to share in the exchange experience.

Each year, local Rotary districts and clubs worldwide arrange thousands of international exchanges for high school-aged students. The primary goal of the program is to foster world understanding by way of intercultural exchange. The two principal types of exchanges are long-term and short-term. Long-term exchanges usually last one academic year, during which students live with more than one host family (usually three families for three months at a time) and attend school. Short-term exchanges vary from a few weeks to three months. They often take place when school is not in session and usually do not include an academic program. Short-term exchanges usually involve a homestay experience with a family in the host country, but can also be organized as international youth camps and tours that bring together students from many countries. (For more information on Rotary International's programs, see Chapter 10, Short-Term Programs.) [ID:7138]

SERVAS Canada
canada@servas.org, www.canada.servas.org ▢*Fr*

HOSTING PROGRAM ◆ Present in over 130 countries, SERVAS is a non-profit, non-political, inter-faith and interracial system of hosts and travellers, whose goal is to promote peace and understanding between people by providing opportunities for deeper, more personal contacts between different cultures. It offers approved travellers of all ages the opportunity to meet and/or have short stays (normally two nights) with people in the country they're visiting. Do not expect luxury accommodation, or to be entertained, but to share in the everyday life of the host. Each participating country has a list of hosts, and the traveller arranges his or her own visits directly with the hosts. You can choose the hosts whose interests and beliefs are most interesting to you. You can also become a host and welcome travellers into your home. Participants are sincerely interested in learning about other cultures and have an adaptable personality. An interview and references are required, and there is a participation fee. [ID:6928]

Youth for Understanding International Exchange (YFU)
Suite 100, 6400 Goldsboro Road, Bethesda, MD, 20817, USA;
240-235-2100, fax 240-235-2104, admissions@yfu.org, www.yfu.org ▢*Fr*▢*Sp*

HOSTING PROGRAM ◆ Youth For Understanding (YFU) is a non-profit educational organization offering opportunities for young people in over 50 countries around the world to spend a summer, semester or year with a host family in another culture. Their Web page allows you to select your home country to find out about the specific programs available to you. In addition to providing excellent information on exchanges, each home country site also has its own employment page where you can look at jobs and review summer staffing and internship opportunities with YFU. [ID:5786]

CHAPTER 12
Cross-Cultural Travel

You don't have to wait for a professional job or a volunteer posting to get international experience. You can increase your international IQ by travelling overseas on your own. Cross-cultural travel has little in common with *tourist travel*. It does not have much to do with lounging on beaches, eating in restaurants with other tourists, shopping for souvenirs or touring the sights. Cross-cultural travel can involve living with a local family or volunteering your services to an indigenous organization. It is about integrating yourself into a different culture.

Imagine herding sheep to market, 150 kilometres across mountains, with a Mongolian caravan. How about living with a Syrian family for a few weeks? Working for a few months in an Indonesian manufacturing plant, teaching software applications and living in the workers' quarters? Maybe you would like to visit Bombay's well-developed financial district and spend three weeks meeting with bankers, attending conferences, and researching the bond market and stock exchange? All these enriching cross-cultural travel experiences are available to you *and* they can help in your international career.

Successful cross-cultural travel experiences will help you develop a stronger international IQ. You will learn about cultural differences, cross-cultural communications, culture shock, other languages, travel logistics, and world geography. You will come to know your levels of tolerance, your limitations and your strengths, and you will begin to develop your observation skills. These are precisely the skills sought by international employers. Of course, the other benefit to cross-cultural travel is *fun*.

DESCRIBING YOUR TRAVEL EXPERIENCE

It is important to learn to describe your travel skills in a professional way. International employers hire people who, along with their technical expertise, have the capacity to integrate into and accept local cultures. If you have travelled extensively overseas, especially in developing countries, you will have some of the cross-cultural skills employers are looking for.

Let's look at two ways to describe your international travel skills: casually, when talking to friends, and professionally, when speaking to a prospective employer.

First, describing your travel experiences to your friends:

"I love travelling and meeting new people. Being surrounded by a foreign culture, the smells, the colours, the noise, is exciting. The food is great—I even like eating with my fingers... It can be difficult at times, even a little scary—like the time I was pulled into the police station for no reason. I got out of it without paying a bribe... I was sick a few times but, like everything else, people were kind to me and helped me out. I got over it... The line-ups! I would stand for hours at the bank rubbing shoulders with the locals. It turned out to be a great way to make friends and find out about the local scene. I loved to haggle for hours with the market mamas... Travelling is such a wonderful, life-enriching experience!"

Second, describing the same travel experiences as professional skills, to potential employers:

"I am culturally sensitive, able to communicate effectively with people from other cultures. I am aware of differences in approaches to decision-making in various parts of the world. I have a good understanding of the cross-cultural environment. I appreciate the importance of tact and diplomacy and understand the subtleties of cross-cultural negotiations. I am able to cope under stress and I thrive in conditions of uncertainty. I enjoy change and am mobile and/or willing to relocate."

THE SUCCESSFUL CROSS-CULTURAL TRAVELLER

Cross-cultural travel usually means spending most of your trip in one country, or in one region of a large country. Hopping through 12 countries on a three-month vacation is not cross-cultural travel. One traveller advises, "Use the three weeks or three visits rule. Stay in one place for three weeks, or return to a place where you have made good friends three or four times for short visits during your stay."

To make contact with the local culture, you need a vehicle that allows you to interact. Sitting on beaches, visiting tourist sites, or dancing in nightclubs won't work. You need a reason to become involved for longer than one week. Try volunteer work, professional networking, and/or living with a family.

Volunteering your services to an organization is one of the best ways to integrate into a community. You can approach a local NGO for work, offer to give a talk about Canada to a local school, teach English at an adult learning centre, or assist at a local orphanage. Offer to give a presentation to a local professional association. Try networking with businesses operating in your area of expertise.

The possibilities are endless for both volunteer work and professional networking. The best approach is to find an organization that you are interested in and speak to the person in charge. Explain that you are travelling and will be staying in this village/town/city for the next few weeks and would like to offer your services. Call it what you want: research, interest in the culture, searching for experience, providing a service, sharing your expertise, learning the language. Don't expect accommodation or food, but feel free to accept it when offered. Once you commit yourself to an organization, respect the agreement! By not following through, you not only make yourself look bad but spoil things for the foreign travellers who follow you.

If you are invited to stay in someone's home, you should participate in their family activities and show respect and interest in their daily lives. Until you become familiar with your host, a cross-cultural friendship can be an emotional roller-coaster ride, so remember to sit back and observe carefully. Don't jump to any conclusions, as you probably don't understand what is going on around you. You are there to learn. Talk and ask questions. Enjoy being with your host family.

When you live with a host family, you have to give up some of the freedom you had while travelling. You can't always retire to your room and close your door, or come and go as you please. In addition, you probably won't be involved in the family's decision-making processes, and will be unsure about what plans are being made. You might find yourself wondering, "Where are we going? Who are we meeting? When is supper?" An experienced cross-cultural traveller will sit back, observe the drama unfolding before them, and fight the need to know "the plan." It is best just to accept what comes your way.

OTHER WAYS TO MAKE
CONTACT WITH LOCAL PEOPLE

Other ways to make contact are:

- striking up conversations while waiting in long lines at banks or in post offices;
- speaking with fellow passengers while travelling by bus, train or plane;
- talk to people about their children; admire and play with the child;
- registering at a foreign university, or just visiting and attending lectures;
- taking up offers to visit other people's friends or relatives, or just visiting friends living abroad.

Learning a new language is another excellent way to make new friends. Always carry a small notepad in your pocket to record new words and phrases. In addition to guidebook phrases, such as "Where are the restaurants? Where is the toilet?" you will want to learn things that link you to people. These include daily greetings, the names for family members, "thank you," "the food is delicious," "this is beautiful," "I enjoy this." Learn also the numbers from 1 to 10, the months of the year, and names of the most common foods. With a vocabulary of as few as 20 or 30 words, you will be able to interact with local people, and your efforts will be appreciated.

Should you travel alone, with a friend, or with a partner? It is easiest to integrate into another culture if you are travelling alone. Your potential hosts will find it difficult to accommodate groups of people. Two females, or two males travelling together is the next best travel arrangement. A female and male travelling together have the hardest time integrating, especially into traditional cultures. Mixed couples are difficult for hosts to accommodate. Most cultures in the world, including our own, segregate women from men. This is relevant when you are looking for venues to meet people across cultures. Platonic, same-sex relationships are the easiest: men can meet other men, women can befriend other women. In many cultures, it is difficult for men and women from different cultures to connect professionally. Romance is usually implied.

SAFETY TIPS

Developing cross-cultural friendships while travelling implies a certain amount of risk. This can be minimized, however, by using your common sense and street smarts. Here are a few tips to help keep you safe:

- Avoid making friends with people who approach *you*. It is generally safer if you initiate a cross-cultural friendship. People you approach are likely to be genuine, interested more in your friendship than in your pocket book.

- Never befriend someone who approaches you at a beach, bus stop, train station or airport. Be careful about making friends where there are many tourists. There are con artists everywhere you find tourists.

- Be prepared to flee the company of anyone who makes you feel physically threatened, who shows erratic behaviour, disregard or lack of compassion for others, who participates in illegal activities, or who exhibits uncontrolled behaviour. (You might also cut short friendships where the culture gap is just too great or the person is just plain boring!)

- Be careful and alert with a host family until you feel secure. You will know you are in a trusting cross-cultural relationship when your host takes care of you, is considerate of your needs, inquires if you are hungry or have slept well, and protects you from making mistakes. Good cross-cultural friendships offer companionship and a sense of security.

- If you are travelling to a country with a history of instability and/or violence, contact the INQUIRIES SERVICE at FOREIGN AFFAIRS CANADA (FAC) AND INTERNATIONAL TRADE CANADA (ITCan) or the nearest Canadian mission close to your departure date. They provide excellent short page travel reports concerning the political climate, high-risk areas, and other precautionary measures.

REST DAYS

Travelling, visiting, touring, talking, sharing, absorbing, analyzing, adapting, searching, discovering, appreciating, liking and loving can be exhausting. Give yourself time to rest. Full days away from the demands of a foreign culture are necessary from time to time. They will refresh you and make you once again enthusiastic, curious, and open to new things.

TRAVEL AND HUMAN RIGHTS

You may want to consider the political ramifications of your cross-cultural travels. In some instances, travelling to a country may lend support to, or help finance, an oppressive government. Whatever your choice, a conscientious reflection on human rights can be a useful guide in deciding where you travel and spend your hard currency.

EXPANDING YOUR EXPERIENCE

Sending postcards home and sharing your experiences through letters will widen the cross-cultural impact of your trip. Send post cards to extended family and friends, especially children, from each of your destinations. Send your family a tourist map so they can follow your route. Mail cards from all your stops to one address, so when you return home you can retrace your trip through the postcard collection. You might even send cards to a classroom in Canada, so the children can follow your travels.

Describe where you are as you write—a train station, a café overlooking a busy street. Describe what you see, eat, smell, the conversations you have. Talk about the religion, the festivals, the animals of the country. Write about the *marvels* of this new culture. Choose postcards that depict the daily life, such as markets, foods, festivals, modes of transportation.

RE-ENTRY CONCERNS

You will likely experience re-entry shock upon your return to Canada. The familiar may have become unfamiliar. Thus, instead of peace, relaxation and familiarity, your exploration may continue—you will observe your own country with a fresh perspective. You may, for the first time, understand what it means to be "Canadian!"

A LAST WORD

Cross-cultural travel is a deeply rewarding experience. It takes more time, effort, patience and trust than regular tourist travel. My experience is that despite the many challenges, I was rewarded with kindness, friendship, hospitality and new insights. It is an opportunity you shouldn't miss. Enjoy!

APPENDIX ON THE CD-ROM

12a. "Taking a Gap Year," by Jeff Minthorn

RESOURCES

CROSS-CULTURAL TRAVEL

Many of these books are published as part of various travel guide series. Besides tips on travel destinations, they often provide excellent insights on the local culture. For more information on building your cross-cultural communication skills, consult the following Resources sections: Chapter 1, The Effective Overseas Employee; Chapter 27, Jobs by Regions of the World; and Chapter 3, Living Overseas. If you want to combine travel and study, consult the following: Chapter 13, Study Abroad; Chapter 14, Awards & Grants; Chapter 15, International Studies in Canada; Chapter 16, International Studies – The World's Top Schools; Chapter 17, Internships Abroad; and Chapter 10, Short-Term Programs Overseas.

All Hotels on the Web 💻
www.all-hotels.com ◆ Planning to scout out your new job in Venezuela? With this site you can search through lists of the world's finest hotels and connect directly to their home pages. Many hotels will even allow you to make on-line reservations. This is a well-designed, easy-to-use site. [ID:2277]

Altapedia Online 💻
www.atlapedia.com/index.html ◆ Provides facts, figures and statistical data on geography, climate, people, religion, language, history, economy, maps on just about any place on earth. [ID:2772]

The Alternative Travel Directory 📖
2000, Clay Hubbs, 262 pages ➤ Department TRA, Transitions Publishing, P.O. Box 745, Bennington, VT 05201, USA, www.transitionsabroad.com, $30.95 US; Credit Cards; 802-442-4827, fax 802-442-4827 ◆ A comprehensive and up-to-date guide for working, studying, living and

travelling abroad. Reviews hundreds of international work, study, and travel books and organizations. Over 2,000 descriptive, country-by-country listings detail specialty travel tours, study programs, and resource information for independent travellers, seniors, families, and high school and college students. Packed full of Web links to hard-to-find travel resources. An excellent springboard for the international job search. [ID:2186]

The Back Door Guide to Short-Term Job Adventures 📖

2002, 436 pages ➤ Ten Speed Press, P.O. Box 7123, Berkeley, CA 94707, USA, www.tenspeed.com, $31.95 US; Credit Cards; 800-404-4446 ◆ Tempted to chuck your 9-to-5 job to be a whitewater rafting guide in Alaska? Always wanted to spend your summer restoring a medieval castle in the south of France? This one-of-a-kind guide contains more than 1,000 opportunities to work, play, learn, help, create, experience and grow. [ID:2684]

Being Abroad 🖥

www.beingabroad.com ◆ Packed with links to information on all the usual topics related to living overseas: language acquisition, culture shock and teaching abroad, as well as some you wouldn't expect such as travelling with pets, skiing, snowboarding and motorcycling abroad. Also distributors of printed publications on living and working overseas. [ID:2463]

Bon Voyage, But... 📖 🖥

2004, 83 pages ➤ Enquiries Service, Foreign Affairs Canada (FAC), 125 Sussex Drive, Ottawa, ON K1A 0G2, Canada, www.fac-aec.gc.ca, Free; 800-267-8376, fax 613-996-9709; *Fr* ◆ A handy reference booklet that contains travel tips, important phone numbers and the addresses of Canadian government offices around the world. Preparation is the key to a successful trip, and Bon Voyage, But... will help Canadian travellers to plan ahead and minimize the risk of accidents, illnesses, legal problems and linguistic and cultural difficulties. Access online as a PDF document or order online. [ID:2039]

Book Passage Travelers' Bookshelf 👬

Book Passage, 51 Tamal Vista Blvd., Corte Madera, CA 94925, USA, www.bookpassage.com, Credit Cards; 800-999-7909, fax 415-924-3838, messages@bookpassage.com ◆ One of San Francisco's coolest bookstores offers a mail-order travel book and map service. Also a great Web site with information on all their cross-cultural publications listed by region: Northern Europe, Southern Europe, Mexico, Latin America, the Caribbean, East Asia and the South Pacific. If you can't visit in person, at least check out the home page! [ID:2404]

CIA World Factbook 🖥

www.cia.gov/cia/publications/factbook ◆ Easy-to-use, well-organized and relatively authoritative, this Web site is a great source of information on almost every country in the world. You'll find updated maps and information on geography, political systems, climate, economy, population demographics and culture. A good place to start your research. [ID:2278]

Consular Affairs: Information and Assistance for Canadians Abroad 👬

www.voyage.gc.ca, fax (800) 575-2500; *Fr* ◆ The Canadian government produces this great Web site, featuring essential travel, including country and regional reports, travel updates, maps, pre-departure information, and emergency contacts. Check out the weekly travel bulletin on safety "hot spots" for the most current information. [ID:2756]

Cultural Profiles Project 🖥

www.settlement.org/cp/english ◆ Citizenship and Immigration Canada, in association with the AMNI Centre of the Faculty of Social Work at the University of Toronto, has developed this excellent Web site profiling the life and customs of 102 countries worldwide. Select the country you are interested in and then navigate the information on landscape, family life, health care, education, religion and the arts, just to name a few. This is a good, reliable starting point for exploring the cultural information of your overseas destination, with each country page listing links to more in-depth information on the Web or in print. [ID:2655]

Europrail International 💻
www.europrail.net ◆ North America's leading source for European rail passes such as Eurail, Eurail Flexipass, Eurail Saver Pass, Eurail Youth Pass and BritRail. [ID:2355]

Fielding's: The World's Most Dangerous Places 📖
2003, Robert Young Pelton, Coskun Aral, Wink Dulles, Harper Collins: Harper Resource, 1,088 pages ➤ Chapters Indigo Books, www.chapters.indigo.ca, $35.95 CDN; Credit Cards ◆ This unusual travel guide features ratings of the most dangerous countries in the world to visit, exclusive first-person reports, thousands of hard-to-find contacts, Web sites, e-mails, survival tips, travel ideas, adventures and even safety schools for war journalists. No walls, no barriers, no bull. Take it with a grain of salt. [ID:2359]

Foreign Affairs Canada (FAC) ⚏
www.fac-aec.gc.ca; *Fr* ◆ FAC's Web site provides information on international trade and the countries and regions that make up the international system within which Canada exists. Authoritative fact sheets, population data and highlights of special issues complement the usual political and economic information available. A good source of trustworthy information. [ID:2267]

Great Learning Vacations.Com 💻
www.greatlearningvacations.com ◆ A site dedicated to travellers who crave "hands on" learning experiences, from tours with award-winning photographers, to cooking courses in Tuscany, watercolour painting weekends in the Canadian wilderness or even astronaut training camps in the USA. Created by award-winning travel journalist Lucy Izon, the site acts as an information gateway, providing feature stories, news, helpful trip-planning links and a worldwide 22-category directory of learning opportunities for travellers. The site is designed to stimulate readers with suggestions for experiential learning opportunities that they may not have previously considered. [ID:2753]

Hostelling International ⚏
Hostelling International, Suite 400, 205 Catherine Street, Ottawa, ON K2P 1C3, Canada, www.hihostels.ca, 613-237-7884, fax 613-237-7868 ◆ Hostelling International—Canada is a network of 80 hostels from coast to coast offering budget accommodation for travellers of all ages. Reservations can be made by calling the hostel direct. Membership is required and can be purchased at any Hostelling International—Canada office and at most hostels. Provides access to 5,000 hostels in 70 countries worldwide. [ID:2137]

A Journey of One's Own: Uncommon Advice for the Independent Woman Traveler 📖
2003, Thalia Zepatos, 268 pages ➤ The Eighth Mountain Press, 624 SE 29th Ave., Portland, OR 97214, USA, $14.95 US; Cheque; 503-233-3936, fax 503-233-0774, www.amazon.com ◆ A great compilation of personal travel essays by women, interspersed with chapters on practical matters such as travelling alone, finding a compatible travel companion, planning an itinerary, sexual harassment, and staying safe and healthy. Includes a list of resources that covers a variety of topics, from travel books and magazines to Internet service providers and socially/environmentally responsible travel opportunities. [ID:2190]

Journeywoman 💻
www.journeywoman.com ◆ Finally, an on-line travel resource just for women! This Canadian site has a mandate to inspire women to travel safely and well, and to connect with each other internationally. Though it's not very graphically appealing, you'll find resources on just about any topic related to women travelling. In particular, it shines in providing helpful information and tips on travel planning, recommendations for restaurants and accommodations abroad. Of special note are the sincere travel stories from women contributors who've gone their own way. Keep connected by signing up for a monthly on-line newsletter. If you're really into it, follow the link to HERmail.net, where you can access secure Web-based e-mail services that allow women to connect and swap travel stories and information from anywhere on the planet. [ID:2751]

Let's Go 💻

www.letsgo.com ◆ Discover the secrets of affordable international travel. Check out articles by researchers and access information on safety concerns from a great travel library. You can also make hostel reservations and research travel destinations. Get your cross-cultural travel plans in gear. [ID:2619]

Let's Go Guides 📖

Annual ➤ St. Martin's Press, 175 5th Ave., New York, NY 10010, USA, www.stmartins.com, $14-$30 US; 212-674-6132, fax 212-674-6132 ◆ Now offering a total of 45 well-researched guides. Excellent source of country-specific information for the international job seeker or the budget-minded overseas experience seeker. [ID:2117]

Library of Congress Portals to the World 💻

www.loc.gov/rr/international/portals.html ◆ This is one of the single best Web portals available for cross-cultural and country information on the Internet. Produced by the Library of Congress, it is comprehensive, easy-to-use and up-to-date. Simply select the country you are interested in and navigate to reliable links to culture, history, education, business, commerce and economy, religion, government and politics, and recreation, just to name a few. You'll be hard pressed to find dead links on these pages. Rather, you'll surf a plethora of informative and high-quality Web resources on which you're bound to find the answers you seek and a whole lot more. Mark this as a favourite and start journeying from your father's rickety old office chair. [ID:2654]

Lonely Planet 📖 💻

www.lonelyplanet.com ◆ This Web site offers much more than simply a method of purchasing guide books. There are extensive maps, a newsletter, travel forums, travelogues, advice on healthy and safe travelling, and a great links page to some of the best travel sites on-line. A fabulous informative site from the publishers of the best travel guides on the market. [ID:2280]

Martindale's "The Reference Desk" 💻

www.martindalecenter.com ◆ This is a great directory, which contains an "International Countries" section with links to 272 country, territorial and municipal pages on-line. An excellent resource for learning about your next exotic posting. [ID:2362]

On a Shoestring Guides 📖

Annual, Lonely Planet ➤ Raincoast Books, 9050 Shaughnessy Street, Vancouver, BC V6P 6E5, Canada, www.raincoast.com, $25-$42 US; VISA, MC; 800-663-5714, fax 800-565-3770 ◆ Covering a continent or selected region, these guides are perfect for overseas workers with small budgets and big travel dreams. [ID:2118]

Outpost Magazine - Travel for Real 📖

Quarterly ➤ www.outpostmagazine.com, $20 for 6 issues; VISA, MC ◆ Outpost Magazine is Canada's own sophisticated travel magazine—Winner of Canada's top magazine award - The President's Medal. You needn't subscribe in order to access travel articles and information, but after reading the free stuff, you just might want to! (For more information, see their ad in the sponsor section at the end of this guide.) [ID:2338]

Planning Your Gap Year 📖

2003, Nick Vandome, 188 pages ➤ How To Books Ltd., 3 Newtec Place, Magdalen Road, Oxford, OX4 1RE, UK, www.howtobooks.co.uk, $22.96 US; Credit Cards; (44) (1752) 202-301, fax (44) (1865) 202-331 ◆ This British guide to taking a year off includes topics such as preparation, deciding when to go, staying healthy and overcoming the pitfalls and problems of travel. Over 220 contact organizations are listed while personal accounts from people who've been there and done it provide useful advice. Lots of good information for university graduates as well. [ID:2398]

Rough Guides 📖

www.travel.roughguides.com ◆ For independent budget travellers, these guides are written with a political awareness and a social and cultural sensitivity that makes them unique. You don't have to buy the books to access an abundance of information found on their web site. Register for their on-line club and post your travel journals on-line. There are excellent photo essays of selected travel destinations as well as health and safety advice, advisories and chat forums. [ID:2618]

Round-the-World Travel Guide 📖
www.travel-library.com ◆ Find travel advice on topics like transportation, accommodation, health and safety, and money matters. [ID:2352]

Tourism Offices Worldwide Directory 💻
www.towd.com ◆ This Web site consists of a searchable directory of over 1,400 tourist offices worldwide. A great resource for planning your overseas adventure. [ID:2351]

Tourisme jeunesse ⋔
Tourisme jeunesse www.tourismej.qc.ca/images/boutiques5.html; 𝐹𝑟 ◆ Un organisme sans but lucratif qui regroupe les détenteurs québécois de la carte internationale des auberges de jeunesse; leur site regroupe des informations touristiques pour la jeunesse incluant, sous la rubrique Voyages, une liste de ressources pour dénicher des emplois saisonniers et temporaires, carrières professionnelles et universitaires à l'étranger ainsi que des bourses d'études. [ID:2182]

Transitions Abroad 📖
Bimonthly, Clay Hubbs ➤ Department TRA, Transitions Publishing, P.O. Box 745, Bennington, VT 05201, USA, www.transitionsabroad.com, $32 US/year; Credit Cards; 802-442-4827, fax 802-442-4827 ◆ An excellent periodical. Required reading for students and globe trotters planning to travel, study or work abroad. Promotes learning through direct involvement in the daily lives of peoples of host countries. Describes publications, information sources, organizations, and programs offering study opportunities, entry-level jobs and living arrangements abroad. Highly recommended. (For more information, see their ad in the sponsor section at the end of this guide.) [ID:2074]

Travel CUTS ⋔
Travel CUTS, 187 College Street, Toronto, ON M5T 1P7, Canada, www.travelcuts.com, 888-359-2887, fax 416-979-8167 ◆ Owned and operated by the Canadian Federation of Students (CFS), and with 40 offices in Canada and one in the UK, Travel CUTS serves the travel needs of over 250,000 students each year. Offers student-class airfares to domestic and international destinations, and comprehensive "Bon Voyage" travel insurance. Also offers working holidays through its Student Work Abroad Program (SWAP), and volunteer opportunities through its Volunteer Abroad program. Their International Student Identity Card (ISIC), offers discounts and student rates in 70 countries worldwide. [ID:2174]

Travel Finder 💻
www.travel-finder.com ◆ This specialized search engine is designed to help you find Web sites with country information, as well as travel service providers by country. It contains 8,000 sites in its database, and you can add your favourite travel-related site. [ID:2281]

Travel That Can Change Your Life: How to Create a Transformative Experience 📖
1997, Jeffrey A. Kottler, 180 pages ➤ Wiley: Jossey-Bass Publishers, 10475 Crosspoint Blvd., Indianapolis, IN 46256, USA, www.josseybass.com, $23.45 US; Credit Cards; 877-762-2974, fax 800-597-3299 ◆ An inspiring look into the deeper significance of travel. It reveals how travelling provides an ideal opportunity for personal change. This book explores the reasons why we travel, identifies problems we encounter and goals we often set for a trip, and describes how to plan a journey that can inform, enlighten and bring about life changes. An excellent resource for those embarking on their first overseas experience. [ID:2143]

Treasures and Pleasures...The Best of the Best Series 📖
2003, Caryl Krannich, Ronald Krannich ➤ Impact Publications, Suite N, 9104 North Manassas Drive, Manassas Park, VA 20111-5211, USA, www.impactpublications.com, $14.95-$19.95 US each; Credit Cards; 703-361-7300, fax 703-335-9486 ◆ A travel series exploring the major regions and exotic countries of the world. Includes information on the fascinating worlds of artisans, and craftspeople, shopkeepers, as well as on fine hotels, restaurants and sightseeing. Country- and

region-specific guides include the Caribbean, China, Hong Kong, Indonesia, Italy, France, Singapore, Thailand and more. [ID:2188]

Verge Magazine 📖
Quarterly ➤ Verge Magazine Inc., 1517 B Schutt Road, Palmer Rapids, ON K0J 2E0, Canada, www.vergemagazine.ca, $10.95 for 3 issues; VISA; 613-758-9909, fax 613-758-9914, editor@vergemagazine.ca ◆ Verge is Canada's magazine for people who travel with purpose. Exploring opportunities to work, study, volunteer and travel overseas, Verge Magazine provides tips, expert advice, program profiles and loads of information to send you packing. Broaden your horizons - see the world! (For more information, see their ad in the sponsor section at the end of this guide.) [ID:2843]

Work Your Way Around The World 📖
2003, Susan Griffith, 576 pages ➤ Globe Pequot Press, P.O. Box 480, 246 Goose Lane, Guilford, CT 06437, USA, www.globepequot.com, $19.95 US; VISA, MC; 888-249-7586, fax 800-820-2329 ◆ Includes details on pre-trip preparation, red tape, visas and tax, getting a job before you go and how to make speculative and opportunistic applications. Find information on how to travel around the world for free, very cheaply or even get paid for your voyage. Read descriptions of different types and areas of work including tourism, agriculture, teaching English, childcare, business and industry, volunteering and many more. Vivid first-hand accounts from working travellers give a flavour of what the work is actually like. [ID:2046]

World of Maps 🏛
World of Maps, 1235 Wellington Street, Ottawa, ON K1Y 3A3, Canada, www.worldofmaps.com, Free on-line; Credit Cards; 800-214-8524, fax 800-897-9969 ◆ This Canadian map and travel guide retailer ships products anywhere in the world. The catalogue contains maps from every imaginable locale. Visit the Web site to order and start planning your next adventure. [ID:2177]

CHAPTER 13

Study
Abroad

No matter what your career path, studying abroad can benefit you and enrich your life in a number of ways. As an overseas student, you will gain important insights into international issues and acquire new skills and sensibilities. The whole experience will improve your international IQ, giving you a necessary edge in an increasingly internationalized world.

Students returning from overseas study will be the first to tell you that learning is not restricted to the classroom. Experiencing day-to-day living in a foreign environment gives you a deeper understanding of life outside Canada and forces you to examine your own cultural values as you become sensitive to those of your host country. Studying abroad also allows you to come away with a better understanding of the people and politics of the country in which you are studying. This will impress a potential employer and prove to her that you are willing to live overseas and are able to adapt to new surroundings.

Studying abroad also gives you the chance to learn a new language or brush up on your existing language skills. In fact, for those embarking on an international career, proficiency in a second, and often third, language is usually mandatory. Stories abound about people losing out on the perfect job opportunity because they weren't able to speak a second language, such as Spanish, French or Japanese. Even if the language you are proficient in is not the one required by an overseas employer, it demonstrates that you are capable of learning another language. "Learn a second language" is a recurring piece of advice given to job seekers by North American businesses with international operations. (For more information, see Chapter 5, Learning a Foreign Language.)

WHO CAN STUDY OVERSEAS?

For years, the opportunity to travel and enjoy overseas education was restricted to the wealthy. However, times have changed. International educational traffic has risen exponentially thanks to the relative ease of international travel, a growing appreciation for the practical value of international education, and a huge increase in international study programs. These days, almost any student, in any given subject area, with interests in any region of the world, can find an appropriate study program. Because of the number and variation of study programs out there, researching the program that best serves your interests and objectives is important.

If you make a commitment to study abroad, seek out the situation that is right for you, and face it with a spirit of adventure and independence. The benefits you will derive from an international education will be enormous and will pay big dividends in your future international career.

Let's look at the profiles of two people who chose to study abroad.

• Ted is dedicated to improving the international environment. A master's student in Ottawa, he has a particular interest in governments and organizations in the European community that stress environmental issues. Feeling that his Ottawa program lacked a hands-on element, he looked into spending a year studying in Europe. His decision to live in Scotland and study at the UNIVERSITY OF EDINBURGH has had a lasting effect on his life, personally and professionally, giving him an invaluable preparation for his international career. He has now travelled throughout the United Kingdom, as well as Europe and Russia. Because of his determination to study abroad, Ted has gained a good understanding of issues and cultures in the European community, especially as they relate to the environment. He has made friends and contacts and has already been back to attend student conferences.

• Fiona wanted to improve her French and take a break after a demanding year in her graduate program in Alberta. She applied for one of many short-term language study programs through EUROCENTRES (see www.eurocentres.com). Although the program was relatively expensive, all the arrangements and details were taken care of as part of the package. Fiona enrolled in three weeks of intensive language instruction and lived with a family in Amboise (located in the scenic Loire Valley), who provided accommodation and meals. Above all, the program provided a wonderful opportunity to live in a French milieu and practice the language every day. Although three weeks was not a long enough period to become fluent, Fiona's French improved considerably. Equally important, she met students from around the world and travelled in France and Britain after she completed her course. Apart from the linguistic and cultural benefits, she found that studying abroad and travelling on her own gave her a strong sense of independence and made her more self-reliant and confident.

WHAT KINDS OF PROGRAMS ARE AVAILABLE?

Educational programs vary in length, price, academic rigour, course type, student mix, etc. In general, there are the following three categories of overseas educational programs.

Undergraduate Study Abroad: Academic Year or Semester Abroad

Most Canadian universities and colleges have established exchange programs or formal exchange agreements that allow students to accumulate academic credits overseas. Some schools, such as UNIVERSITÉ LAVAL, have made exchanges a priority, with the objective of encouraging a large proportion of their students to study abroad for at least one semester. It is possible to spend an entire year abroad. Sometimes, programs are restricted to specific countries and particular universities. Opportunities vary widely from university to university.

Most academic advisors suggest that in terms of academic planning, most students find it easiest to study abroad during their third year in a four-year program. We think that any year is a good year, so make the leap and explore the possibilities. Once abroad, your outlook on life will be forever changed and you will be able to face life's challenges differently—with much more acumen, vitality and courage.

Contact your institution's international centre to explore the options available to you. You should also investigate study abroad programs in your field of study that are offered by other Canadian colleges and universities, as several institutions accept students from other schools, and credits are usually transferable. Some foreign universities offer programs designed specifically for visiting students. These are usually in the arts and humanities, and emphasize language training. It may be more difficult to acquire academic credit at your university for this type of study abroad, but credit or no credit, this is a great way to learn a language and immerse yourself in another culture.

Graduate Study Abroad

Overseas universities openly welcome non-nationals who already possess undergraduate degrees. There is an advantage here because many more scholarships and bursaries are open to graduate than undergraduate students. A number of resources listed at the end of this chapter, and elsewhere in this section, will provide further information on foreign universities and scholarship programs. Another source of information is professors in the faculty of your chosen field of study. Seek them out: many professors will have studied or taught abroad themselves. Keep in mind that every university has its own guidelines and procedures for accepting international students.

Even if you are enrolled in a Canadian university for your graduate degree, opportunities to study abroad are numerous. Programs vary in length, formality and structure. Again, your university's international centre and the faculty within your department are the best places to make inquiries.

Summer and Short-Term Programs for International Students

This is a popular route for those who may not wish to pursue a complete university degree or academic credit, and for students who prefer not to interrupt their academic year. Entrance requirements are usually more lenient, and short-term cultural programs and intensive language courses can be squeezed into the summer or combined with holidays. However, the classes are usually comprised of North Americans like yourself and, hence, may not be as beneficial from a cross-cultural point of view. For information on such programs, see the resources at the end of this section. Embassies and high commissions located here in Canada are another source of information.

Free Style—Studies in Developing Countries

You may be the type of person who wants to backpack around the world. You may be considering taking a four-month study program to learn French or Spanish in another country. What if you tried an unconventional route and started your world tour by enrolling in a developing world university, learning French while studying business in the Comores Islands or in Togo? Try registering for political science courses in Venezuela while learning Spanish. Imagine living in Ghana, West Africa, attending the University of Kumassi. In all of these scenarios, you would likely live in a university dorm and be surrounded by one hundred other warm and attentive fellow students. You would be one of the few foreign students on campus. The cross-cultural experience would be outstanding. You could visit the local countryside, partake in the culture, learn the local language, and you would even have time to make career building contacts with other expatriates who live and work in this foreign land. The objective in all these scenarios is not to gain university credit but to gain life credits—an understanding and perspective on one of the world's peoples. And an added benefit is that it usually costs very little to live at and be enrolled in a developing country's university. It provides an expensive experience with a guarantee that you will be surrounded by friends. This is a much easier and enriching experience than backpacking around the world without support (although we encourage this also).

LIMITATIONS AND OPTIONS

For the most part, enrolling in a formal exchange program at a Canadian university is fairly easy; applicants should be in good academic standing and be able to demonstrate the relevance of a particular program to their area of study. Acquiring credit for these programs is usually part of the deal, so this isn't an issue. However, regardless of the reality, some Canadian universities perceive academic standards in some countries—particularly the developing countries—as less rigorous than those in Canada. This may create problems in having the courses you complete recognized for full academic credit when you return home. If getting academic credit for your program overseas is a priority, then it is a good idea to discuss these sorts of issues with the appropriate administrators before you embark upon your overseas learning experience. In some cases it is possible to arrange for academic credit in advance of your departure, often by enrolling in a special topics or self-directed reading course offered through your department. If your department doesn't offer these types of courses, ask around to find out which departments or professors are inclined to support a similar arrangement.

Even if you are forced to forgo academic credit, your experience of studying abroad can still be worthwhile, especially if you are planning an international career. And keep in mind that you don't always have to be enrolled at a Canadian university to qualify for study abroad programs.

Another key aspect to consider before studying abroad is financing. Scholarships and bursaries can be difficult to come by, and are often reserved for nationals. Getting assistance in Canada can also be tricky. It will take an extra effort to have the CANADA STUDENT LOAN PROGRAM cough up the additional money for studies overseas. (For suggestions on how to secure funding and financial support, see Chapter 14, Awards & Grants; for tips on financial planning and on saving money while abroad, see the article by Murray Baker, author of *The Debt-Free Graduate*, "Financing Travel & Study Abroad" in Appendix 13a on the CD-ROM.)

Language can also be a barrier, not only for studying, but also for living in your host country. If your program doesn't include language training, then language lessons beforehand, to learn at least the basics, are a good idea.

Be sure to choose your living arrangements carefully. You want to ensure that you don't surround yourself solely with Canadians and other English-speakers. One of the best ways to maximize your study abroad experience is by living with a host family. You will get insight into the culture and improve your language skills considerably. We encourage you to live with a host family; there can be pitfalls but there are many, many rewards when you are truly connected with the locals in this way.

An academic contact in the country you're planning to visit is also another asset. Find out which professors at your university are engaged in overseas projects or research, and ask them to link you up with a college or friend in the country to which you are heading. A helpful and friendly voice in an otherwise confusing and daunting environment, especially at first, will be most welcome.

Apart from considering how much time you're willing to devote to an international study program, you should also look at the viability of a particular program. Determine whether the institution has adequate resources and facilities. What is the status of the library and how are the laboratories equipped? Does it have computer facilities? If you are planning to live on campus, the conditions of the living quarters and who and how many share accommodations are important questions to ask. You might also want to consider the social aspects of university life: are there any athletic or social clubs? Does the university provide counselling services to foreign students? All of these elements are important factors in a successful overseas educational experience and should be taken into account throughout the planning process.

PREPARATION

Taking the time to select an overseas study program is important. If you decide on a short-term summer study program, it usually won't entail a lot of complicated planning or take a lot of preparation. But if you are planning a long-term academic exchange or a year abroad, you will have to start thinking ahead at least 9 to 12 months prior to the date of your intended departure. Most applications must be submitted by early January. Scholarship programs also usually require completed applications, accompanied by letters of reference, by January or February. If you are applying for graduate studies, you may have to write relevant subject exams, and probably a Graduate Records Exam (GRE), in the summer or fall.

The International Student Identity Card is available from the VIA RAIL or TRAVEL CUTS offices located in most large Canadian cities. This card offers internationally recognized proof of student status and is available to full-time students aged 12 and up. To get the card you will have to provide proof of your student status along with a passport size photo and your student card. At less than

$20, the card is well worth the price; you can receive discounts for lodging, restaurants, museum admissions and even transportation.

For many destinations, you will also require various immunization shots. Receiving these shots can take several weeks, so don't leave them until the last minute. Contact your provincial health department, or HEALTH CANADA, to find out about requirements for particular countries. And also be sure to arrange for medical and other insurance coverage.

Lastly, don't arrive in ignorance. Read up on the history, culture and current political-economic climate of the country you will be visiting. It's also a good idea to read up on culture shock and its effects.

A LAST WORD

The most important thing to remember in planning a study abroad program is to just go ahead and do it. It takes a little courage, and you may need to work while overseas to finance your studies and/or save for a semester before going. But do not pass up the opportunity to study abroad. It is perhaps the most critical aspect in starting to build an international career—there is no easier way to get started. Match your needs and interests with the program you choose. Consider what length of time you are willing to spend studying abroad, how rigorous a program you want, and whether you want to receive academic credit at your home university or college.

You also have to realize that certain trade-offs may be involved. You may have to forego academic credit in exchange for the cultural benefits you will receive. A long-term program may interrupt your program of study at your Canadian university and will require a long separation from family and friends. Short-term programs, while unlikely to interrupt your study program and living pattern, may allow you only to scratch the surface of a foreign culture, and only rarely provide enough time to learn another language. If you also want time to travel, your study time will likely be further limited. Similarly, while living with a host family might take some adjusting to at first, it will enrich your overseas experience immeasurably.

In general, you should study in a country or a region of the world that you find interesting or would like to get to know better. And, as always, consider how the experience is going to help you along your chosen path—a career in the international arena.

APPENDIX ON THE CD-ROM

13a. "Financing Travel & Study Abroad," by Murray Baker

RESOURCES

STUDY ABROAD

Many of these books focus on US study abroad programs that are usually open to Canadians. The programs range from leisurely, vacation-oriented study to serious, degree-oriented academic study. Whatever your field, make sure you broaden your experience by learning the local language and culture.

Academic Year Abroad 📖
Annual, Sara Steen ➤ Publication Service, Institute of International Education, P.O. Box 371, Annapolis Junction, MD 20701-0371, USA, www.iie.org, $46.95 US; VISA, MC; 800-445-0443, fax 301-206-9789 ◆ This US publication has over 2,900 semester and academic-year programs

offered by US and foreign universities and private organizations. Key information on application procedures and requirements, academic credit, contact addresses, e-mail, phone, fax, costs, fields of study, language of instruction, housing, travel and orientation. Introductory section on planning international study. An excellent resource for planning your international study abroad experience. Much of this excellent information is available on IIE's great Web site. [ID:2051]

University of Alberta International Centre ♔

www.international.ualberta.ca ◆ The University of Alberta International Centre has an excellent Web site that offers a database of opportunities for study abroad, summer study programs, volunteering abroad and working overseas. Simply enter your regional preference and browse the opportunities available. Even if you are not a U of A student, there is lots of information available to assist non-students in their search for overseas experience. [ID:2216]

The Alternative Travel Directory ▱

2000, Clay Hubbs, 262 pages ➤ Department TRA, Transitions Publishing, P.O. Box 745, Bennington, VT 05201, USA, www.transitionsabroad.com, $30.95 US; Credit Cards; 802-442-4827, fax 802-442-4827 ◆ A comprehensive and up-to-date guide for working, studying, living and travelling abroad. Reviews hundreds of international work, study, and travel books and organizations. Over 2,000 descriptive, country-by-country listings detail specialty travel tours, study programs, and resource information for independent travellers, seniors, families, and high school and college students. Packed full of Web links to hard-to-find travel resources. An excellent springboard for the international job search. [ID:2186]

AYUSA International ♔

www.ayusa.org ◆ AYUSA is a non-profit educational and cultural exchange organization with headquarters in San Francisco, California that promotes global learning and leadership through high school exchange programs. Since 1980, AYUSA has provided opportunities for more than 37,000 students from the US and around the world to live and study overseas. [ID:2214]

Back To My Roots ▭

www.backtomyroots.com ◆ This site is for young expatriates such as exchange students and interns. It displays two lists of useful links—one from your home country and one from the country in which you are (temporarily) residing. Also offers Web-based e-mail, discussion forums and your own private photo album. [ID:2574]

Canadian Bureau for International Education ♔

www.cbie.ca; Fr ◆ The Canadian Bureau for International Education (CBIE) is an umbrella non-governmental organization comprised of 200 colleges, universities, schools, school boards, educational organizations and businesses across Canada. Nationally, CBIE engages in policy development, research, advocacy and public information. Internationally, CBIE engages in cooperative projects in capacity building, institutional strengthening and human resource development. CBIE works in partnership with educational institutions, community-based organizations and governments in Africa, the Middle East, Asia, the Americas, the Former Soviet Union, and Central and Eastern Europe. The organization offers grants and scholarships for study abroad and publishes an interesting e-zine called the "Internationaliste." [ID:2145]

Canadian Internationalist ▭

Quarterly, variable ➤ Canadian Bureau for International Education (CBIE), Suite 1550, 220 Laurier Ave W., Ottawa, ON K1P 5Z9, Canada, www.cbie.ca, Free on-line; VISA; 613-237-4820, fax 613-237-1073; Fr ◆ This is the CBIE's quarterly news bulletin covering events, publications and opinions in the world of international education. Informative articles on studying abroad for Canadians and international project opportunities are featured. [ID:2438]

Commonwealth Universities Yearbook ▱

Annual, 2,600 pages ➤ Association of Commonwealth Universities, 36 Gordon Square, London, WC1H 0PF, UK, www.acu.ac.uk, £220; VISA, MC; (44) (0) 20-7380-6700, fax (44) (0) 20 7387 2655, acusales@acu.ac.uk; Available in large libraries ◆ This two volume set is a key resource on every aspect of higher education—senior staff, general facilities, degree programmes and research strengths—at over 700 universities throughout the Commonwealth. Includes institutional data and contact details, as well as profiles of the programs of study. The higher education schemes of the 36 members countries of the ACU network are explained, giving you reliable insight into studying in Africa, Asia, Australasia, Europe, Canada and the Caribbean. [ID:2024]

Council on International Educational Exchanges ▥

www.ciee.org ◆ This is the Web site of the US organization, Council on International Educational Exchange. With programs designed for students, faculty and administrators, CIEE's respected and extensive listing of international academic programs will help you choose the international experience that is right for you. Highly recommended. [ID:2482]

Cours de français langue étrangère et stages pour professeurs. Répertoire des centres de formation en France. ▦ ▤

Ministère des Affaires Étrangères Sous-Direction de la politique linguistique et éducative, 153 pages ➤ Service Culturel, Ambassade de France, 464 Wilbrod Street, Ottawa, ON K1N 6M8, Canada, http://culturel.org, Gratuit; 613-238-5711, fax 613-238-7884, ambafr@culturel.org; ℱr ◆ Ambassade de France à Ottawa : répertoire des centres de formation en France, informations sur le système d'éducation, échanges et cours de français langue étrangère. [ID:2023]

The Debt-Free Graduate ▦

2003, Money$marts, 308 pages ➤ www.debtfreegrad.com, $16.95 US; Cheque or Money Order ◆ A successful international career begins with your post-secondary education. Unfortunately, university and college degrees cost a fortune these days. Never fear, in this excellent Canadian book (and accompanying Web site) you'll learn how to manage your finances so that you can achieve your career goals. It's filled with simple measures on how to stay out of debt, including tips on finding the best summer jobs, making your money go further, living cheaply, eating and entertaining on a shoestring, finding hidden sources of free money, cutting the costs of school supplies, travelling cheap and avoiding being "had" by the banks. Turn your student status into a financial advantage. Check out the Web site for more great advice. Both highly recommended! [ID:2787]

DestinEducation ▤

Canadian Bureau for International Education (CBIE) www.destineducation.ca; ℱr ◆ Maintained by the Canadian Bureau for International Education (CBIE), this Web site contains a wealth of information and planning tools about international education from a Canadian perspective. The site is divided into three sections catering to Canadians who want to study or work abroad; those outside of Canada interested in studying here; and professionals in Canada and abroad who are involved in international aspects of education. Recommended. [ID:2701]

The Directory of Work & Study in Developing Countries ▦

1997, Robert Miller, 256 pages ➤ Vacation Work, 9 Park End Street, Oxford, OX1 1HJ, UK, www.vacationwork.co.uk, £9.99; Credit Cards; (44)(0)(1865) 24-1978, sales@vacationwork.co.uk ◆ For those who wish to experience life in a developing country as more than a tourist. Thousands of short- and long- term opportunities for work and study with over 400 organizations in Africa, the Middle East, Asia, the Far East, the Pacific, Latin America and the Caribbean, including health care, engineering, disaster relief, agriculture, business, teaching, archaeology, economics, oil, irrigation, etc. [ID:2047]

Economics Departments, Institutes and Research Centres Around the World ▤

http://edirc.repec.org/index.html ◆ There is now an amazing number of economics institutions on the Web. Currently, 7,899 institutions in 217 countries and territories are listed on this University of Connecticut Web site. Links are indexed by country and field. Included are economics departments, research centres and institutes in universities, as well as finance ministries, statistical offices, central banks, think tanks and other non-profit institutions which employ mainly economists. Each institution is hyperlinked, making this a very useful site. Get a head start on researching your post-graduate studies, or on a systematic search of organizations around the world that just might be hiring an economist! [ID:2347]

Education UK ▣

Education UK, www.educationuk.org ◆ This site, produced by the British Council answers all questions about studying and living in the UK. With a database of degree programs and a wealth of information on scholarships, living accommodation and study advice, this site is a must for anyone seriously considering pursuing studies in the UK. [ID:2780]

EduPASS ▣

www.edupass.org ◆ Information on what students need to know when planning to study in the US including admissions, financing, visa requirements and cultural differences. [ID:2777]

Exchanges Canada ▣

Department of Canadian Heritage, www.exchanges.gc.ca, exchanges@pch.gc.ca; Fr ◆ Exchanges Canada is a Government of Canada initiative that creates opportunities for young Canadians to gain a better understanding of their country, to connect with one another and to experience the diversity of Canada's communities, languages and cultures. The Web site has an excellent list with which job seekers can search international exchanges by destination, exchange name, area of interest and delivery organization. Teachers: don't miss the Fulbright Teacher Exchange Program profiled in the exchange listings. [ID:2441]

Financial Aid for Research & Creative Activities Abroad: 2002-04 ▥

2002, Gael Ann Schlachter, R. David Weber, 398 pages ➤ Reference Service Press, Suite 4, 5000 Windplay Drive, El Dorado Hills, CA 95762, USA, www.rspfunding.com, $45 US; Credit Cards; 916-939-9620, fax 916-939-9626, fiindaid@aol.com ◆ Want to go abroad to write, paint, sculpt, teach, travel or conduct research? This directory highlights more than 1,200 funding opportunities covering every major subject area, in practically every country and region of the world. Geared toward US citizens, this book contains awards open to all segments of the population and is a good starting point for funding research. [ID:2135]

Go Abroad Fair ⛣

www.goabroadfair.ca ◆ Every year, young Canadians pack their bags to experience the world. With limitless choices about where to study, travel or work overseas, they have some big decisions to make. The Go Abroad Fair gives students and youth interested in going abroad a chance to meet exhibitors from cultural and educational organizations, study abroad programs, universities, colleges, institutes of technology, travel agencies, as well as work and volunteer abroad programs. It's the most comprehensive fair of its kind in Canada and admission is free! The Go Abroad Fair takes place every October in Toronto. (For more information, see their ad in the sponsor section at the end of this guide.) [ID:2838]

Health and Wellness for International Students, Scholars and Their Families ▤ ▣

2002, 16 pages ➤ National Association for Foreign Student Affairs, 8th Floor, 1307 New York Ave. N.W., Washington, DC 2005-4701, USA, www.nafsa.org, Free on-line; Credit Cards; 800-836-4994, fax 202-737-3657 ◆ This brochure is concise and comprehensive and provides foreign students and scholars with information on the US health care system and payment structure, staying healthy during their stay, finding medical care, necessary immunizations, personal hygiene, sexual health and family planning, mental health, dental health and a personal health checklist for students. [ID:2557]

Institute of International Education ⛣

www.iie.org ◆ This excellent US Web site has sections for students and scholars with information on financial aid, Fulbright Fellowships and academic exchanges. You can also access two excellent areas, called "Academic Year Abroad" and "Short-Term Study Abroad" which are useful resources for researching study-abroad opportunities. [ID:2656]

International Council for Canadian Studies ⛣

www.iccs-ciec.ca; Fr ◆ If you're thinking about studying abroad or doing graduate work abroad in the area of Canadian Studies, this Web site has an excellent listing of awards and grants available to budding Canadianists. [ID:2010]

International Directory of Canadian Studies ▣
Didier Cencig, Christian Pouyez ➤ International Council for Canadian Studies, Suite 908, 75 Albert Street, Ottawa, ON K1P 5E7, Canada, www.iccs-ciec.ca, VISA, MC; 613-789-7834, fax 613-789-7830; ℱr ◆ An excellent Web directory listing more than 300 Canadian Studies Centres and Programs around the world. Your complete information source for contact information, library holdings in Canadiana, course offerings, research areas and linkages with Canadian universities. Navigate to the "Canadian Studies Centres" link from the ICCS-CIEC home page. [ID:2054]

International Handbook of Universities ▢
2001, 3,000 pages ➤ Palgrave Macmillan, 175 Fifth Ave., New York, NY 10010, USA, www.palgrave-usa.com, $300 US; Credit Cards; 212-982-3900, fax 212-777-6359; Available in large libraries ◆ This is an indispensable and up-to-date US guide to over 7,300 higher education institutions in 175 countries. Based on data collected by the International Association of Universities, the information is both accurate and current, making this one of the most detailed and authoritative guides to worldwide higher education institutions available. [ID:2138]

International Studies in the UK ▣
www.internationalstudies.ac.uk ◆ This UK Web site offers an excellent list of international relations and global politics programs offered by UK universities, complete with detailed descriptions of programs offered, degree titles, contact data and hyperlinks. Simple, easy-to-access layout makes your search for international studies programs in Britain easy. [ID:2658]

International Support Services ▣
www.isservices.biz/students.htm ◆ International Support Services is an independent, professional organization, specialising in the care, safety and welfare of international visitors to Australia. This Web site is specifically for those studying in Australia and includes valuable pre-departure information. [ID:2716]

International Youth and Young Workers Exchange Programs ▥
www.dfait-maeci.gc.ca/english/culture/youthex.html; ℱr ◆ This directory, maintained by Foreign Affairs Canada (FAC), is designed for the use of Canadians between the ages of 18 and 35 who are seeking employment abroad. It lists opportunities by region and describes ways of gaining access to employment markets around the world. [ID:2241]

InternationalStudent.com ▣
www.internationalstudent.com ◆ This Web site provides comprehensive information to international job seekers and students, including advice on work-permit applications and applying for jobs in the US, the UK, Europe, Canada and Australia; studying abroad; scholarships; grants and other information to assist students in their quest to study abroad. [ID:2627]

Learning Across Cultures ▢
1994, Gary Althen, 200 pages ➤ National Association for Foreign Student Affairs, 8th Floor, 1307 New York Ave. N.W., Washington, DC 2005-4701, USA, www.nafsa.org, $15 US; Credit Cards; 800-836-4994, fax 202-737-3657 ◆ In this US volume, experts in international education provide a vital overview of cross-cultural communication and a detailed, yet accessible, deconstruction of cultural barriers. Still a good intercultural resource. [ID:2167]

Medical Insurance for International Students, Scholars and Their Families ▣
2002, 12 pages ➤ National Association for Foreign Student Affairs, 8th Floor, 1307 New York Ave. N.W., Washington, DC 2005-4701, USA, www.nafsa.org, Free on-line; Credit Cards; 800-836-4994, fax 202-737-3657 ◆ This pamphlet is directed at foreign academics and explains the often confusing and sometimes intimidating US health care system. Topics included are an overview of the types of medical insurance plans available, how to evaluate policies, why insurance is needed, how to use the insurance plan, suggestions for keeping medical care costs manageable, as well as a very useful glossary of definitions and explanations of medical insurance terms. Helpful information for Canadians studying in US. [ID:2558]

NAFSA's Guide to Education Abroad for Advisors and Administrators 📖
2004, Joseph Brockington, William Hoffa, Patricia Martin, 700 pages ➤ National Association for
Foreign Student Affairs, 8th Floor, 1307 New York Ave. N.W., Washington, DC 2005-4701, USA,
www.nafsa.org, $55 US; Credit Cards; 800-836-4994, fax 202-737-3657 ◆ This Guide is used by
universities to build and shape their study-abroad programs. Contains full details on faculty roles,
non-traditional locations, health, safety and legal issues, credit, financial aid, work abroad,
marketing, demographics, advising, budgeting and assessment, research on outcomes, resident
directors abroad and much more. Invaluable for those interested in the profession of education
abroad. Though written for advisors, this book and Web site are great resources for researching
study abroad programs. [ID:2130]

Short-Term Study Abroad 📖
Annual ➤ Publication Service, Institute of International Education, P.O. Box 371, Annapolis
Junction, MD 20701-0371, USA, www.iie.org, $46.95 US; VISA, MC; 800-445-0443, fax 301-
206-9789 ◆ Over 2,700 programs offered by US and foreign universities, schools, museums,
associations and organizations—on land and at sea, in Western and Eastern Europe, Asia, Africa,
the Middle East, Oceania and the Americas. US education abroad for pre-college students, graduate
students, teachers, professionals, senior citizens and other adult learners—as well as US
undergraduates. Learning options that range from classwork and intensive language immersion to
work study, internships, student teaching, field research and volunteer service. Indexes on costs,
credit, fields of study, scholarships and program duration make finding the right program for you a
snap. [ID:2512]

Spanish Study Holidays 🖳
www.spanishstudyholidays.co.uk ◆ Gain overseas travel experience and learn Spanish at the same
time. [ID:2773]

Sports Scholarships and College Athletic Programs in the USA 📖
1999, 872 pages ➤ Thomson Peterson's, P.O. Box 2123, Princeton, NJ 08543-2123, USA,
www.petersons.com, $39.95 US; Credit Cards; 800-338-3282, fax 609-243-9150 ◆ Both male and
female athletes can explore scholarships worth more than $500 million at more than 1,700 two- and
and four-year US colleges. [ID:2129]

Study Abroad 📖
2003, 992 pages ➤ Thomson Peterson's, P.O. Box 2123, Princeton, NJ 08543-2123, USA,
www.petersons.com, $29.95 US; Credit Cards; 800-338-3282, fax 609-243-9150 ◆ A
comprehensive book geared toward adventurous US college students hoping to see the world and
get credit for it. Introduces readers to fact-filled profiles of more than 1,800 semester and full-year
programs located all over the world. Access helpful advice and articles on getting credit for study
abroad, paying for study abroad, the essentials of studying abroad (passports, visas, ID cards,
money and more), non-traditional destinations, international internships, volunteering abroad,
exchange for people with disabilities, and travelling smart: staying on budget, drinking the water
and safety. Also includes searchable indexes by field of study, program sponsors, host institutions
and internship programs. [ID:2443]

Study Abroad Web Site 🖳
www.petersons.com/stdyabrd ◆ An amazing Web site by an American leader in study abroad
program resources. Includes informative articles about culture shock, issues encountered by
minorities and African-Americans studying abroad, as well as travel health and safety. Search a
huge database of overseas programs by subject and view helpful and succinct results. A great place
to start researching study programs abroad. [ID:2445]

Study Abroad: 2004-2005 📖
Annual, UNESCO, 600 pages ➤ Renouf Publishing Co. Ltd., Unit 1, 5369 Canotek Road, Ottawa,
ON K1J 9J3, Canada, www.renoufbooks.com, $29.95 US; Credit Cards; 888-767-6766, fax 613-
745-7660 ◆ Provides essential information on post-secondary study opportunities, scholarships and

financial assistance opportunities offered by degree-granting institutions in over 130 countries and territories around the world. Includes over 2,000 entries concerning education and training in all academic and professional fields, and the information is valid for the years 2004 and 2005. Each entry provides the reader with the full address (including Web site addresses where available), courses by subject offered, scholarships available, admission requirements, application deadlines, tuition fees, living expense information and possible work opportunities for the students. Includes three indexes: Index of International Organization Scholarships; Index of National Institutions (by country) and Index to Subjects of Study. [ID:2070]

Study Abroad: How to Get the Most Out of Your Experience 📖
2002, Michele-Marie Dowell, Kelly P. Mirsky, 208 pages ➤ Pearson: Prentice Hall Canada, 26 Prince Andrew Place, Toronto, ON M3C 2T8, Canada, www.pearsoned.ca, $30.95 CDN; Credit Cards; 800-567-3800, fax 800-563-9196 ◆ This self-directed workbook guides students through five distinct strands of development, all of which are necessary to capitalize fully on their study abroad experience. Topics include personal development, learning about one's own culture, learning about another culture, professional development and learning a language. Each is addressed at the three crucial phases of the experience: before, during and after the sojourn. One major goal of the text is to offer a purposeful agenda to help students move from being the conventional tourist to an explorer who truly acquires an authentic view of another culture. Excellent advice for the overseas student. [ID:2511]

StudyAbroad.com 🖥
www.studyabroad.com ◆ This US site has information on all aspects of studying overseas. Great surf appeal: navigable, up-to-date and well-organized, country-specific information and study program information for college, high school and non-US students. Browse boundless opportunities by country, education level and field in a surprising number of countries. You can even sign up for a free weekly newsletter called "EXPRESS!" which delivers the best study-abroad program information, including special offers and financial information. Highly recommended! [ID:2673]

Summer Study Abroad 📖
2003, 800 pages ➤ Thomson Peterson's, P.O. Box 2123, Princeton, NJ 08543-2123, USA, www.petersons.com, $29.95 US; Credit Cards; 800-338-3282, fax 609-243-9150 ◆ This US book is ideal for students looking for a shorter overseas experience. It is the summer program counterpart to "Study Abroad 2004" and presents readers with updated descriptions of more than 1,700 once-in-a-lifetime summer academic, volunteer and foreign language programs. In addition to eligibility requirements, living arrangements and financial aid, it also offers special advice for students interested in non-traditional destinations. [ID:2444]

Taking a First Degree at Commonwealth Universities 🖥
2001, 5 pages ➤ Association of Commonwealth Universities, 36 Gordon Square, London, WC1H 0PF, UK, www.acu.ac.uk, Free; VISA, MC; (44) (0) 20-7380-6700, fax (44) (0) 20 7387 2655, acusales@acu.ac.uk ◆ The ACU Web site generally is a good source of information on scholarships, contact information and studying at university members of its 36 country network of commonwealth universities. The virtual library is accessible from the home page by clicking on "Yearbook and Publications" and offers a number of links and documents in PDF format that are free of charge and very helpful to those interested in study abroad. One in particular is "Taking a First Degree" which can answer many of those burning questions about studying in a Commonwealth country for the first time. [ID:2403]

Teaching and Projects Abroad 🖥
www.teaching-abroad.co.uk ◆ This is a fabulous British Web site that caters to anyone wishing to use their skills to teach abroad. By no means limited to teaching English, this site allows you to explore teaching opportunities in the fields of medicine, conservation, journalism, veterinary medicine, business and archaeology to name just a few. Alternatively, the site offers a portal through which you can organize electives and placements with other teachers in your field in other countries. Highly recommended! [ID:2693]

Transitions Abroad 📖
Bimonthly, Clay Hubbs ➤ Department TRA, Transitions Publishing, P.O. Box 745, Bennington, VT 05201, USA, www.transitionsabroad.com, $32 US/year; Credit Cards; 802-442-4827, fax 802-442-4827 ◆ An excellent periodical. Required reading for students and globe trotters planning to travel, study or work abroad. Promotes learning through direct involvement in the daily lives of peoples of host countries. Describes publications, information sources, organizations, and programs offering study opportunities, entry-level jobs and living arrangements abroad. Highly recommended. (For more information, see their ad in the sponsor section at the end of this guide.) [ID:2074]

Who's Who of Executive Heads 2003 📖
2003, 150 pages ➤ Association of Commonwealth Universities, 36 Gordon Square, London, WC1H 0PF, UK, www.acu.ac.uk, £25; VISA, MC; (44) (0) 20-7380-6700, fax (44) (0) 20 7387 2655, acusales@acu.ac.uk ◆ A compilation of detailed entries for some 500 university officials and members of national inter-university bodies in the 36 Commonwealth countries that have universities. Navigate quickly around the publication with indexes conveniently sorted by country, university or organization. A good source of reliable and up-to-date information on institutions around the world. [ID:2400]

World List of Universities and Other Institutions of Higher Education 📖
2002, International Association of Universities (IAU), 1,772 pages ➤ Palgrave Macmillan, 175 Fifth Ave., New York, NY 10010, USA, www.palgrave-usa.com, $200 US; Credit Cards; 212-982-3900, fax 212-777-6359; Available in large libraries; ℱr ◆ Since 1952, this publication has provided a concise directory including approximately 15,000 universities and other institutions worldwide. An invaluable information resource on higher education worldwide, it is prepared by the International Association of Universities (IAU) and the UNESCO Information Centre on Higher Education. Institution listings include contact information as well as a listing of faculties, departments and major subject areas. Available in French. IAU's Web site is also excellent, with many on-line resources to assist you in your search for international studies programmes. [ID:2776]

Youth Link 🖳
Human Resources and Skills Development Canada, www.youth.gc.ca, Free on-line; ℱr ◆ Not to be confused with the Canadian government's Web site, YouthPath, Youth Link is publication that includes more than 250 programs, services and resources for youth between the ages of 15 and 30. It is also a valuable resource for career counsellors, parents, educators, employers and community groups. From the YouthPath index, navigate to "Publications" and search for Youth Link. [ID:2703]

YouthPath 🖳
Human Resources and Skills Development Canada, www.youth.gc.ca, Free on-line; ℱr ◆ A Web site resource for Canadian youth seeking work and study opportunities in Canada or abroad. Lists hundreds of Government of Canada youth programs, services and resources. You can learn about Canada's role internationally or about how you can get involved by clicking the "International" tab on the index. Navigate to the "Opportunities" page and explore external links and government-sponsored exchange, volunteer and internship programs, such as internships with CIDA. If you want to gain international experience, this is an excellent place to start your research. [ID:2191]

Selected Opportunities

The following is a description of nine selected opportunities for studying abroad. Chosen from universities across Canada and representing a variety of academic fields, these opportunities send students all over the world. These programs are described here because we want to whet your appetite to study abroad and expand your mind.

University of Alberta
NANYANG TECHNOLOGICAL UNIVERSITY – UNIVERSITY OF ALBERTA EXCHANGE

Education Abroad Program, International Centre, 172 HUB International, University of Alberta, Edmonton, AB, T6G 2E1, Canada; 780-492-2692, fax 780-492-1134, global.options@ualberta.ca, www.international.ualberta.ca/studyabroad

CREDIT PROGRAM ◆ The Nanyang Technological University (NTU) - University of Alberta Exchange allows students in all faculties, especially those studying science and engineering at the University of Alberta to spend a term or full academic year studying in Singapore. A central feature of the exchange is NTU's ultra-modern campus with 'intelligent' facilities for teaching and research, as well as ample residential and recreational facilities for students. As classes are in English, it is an excellent opportunity for students wanting an Asian experience without having to be concerned about a second language. Another unique aspect of this exchange is the opportunity to participate in a four-month internship for academic credit. Students can study and/or work while experiencing the cultural richness of Asia and living in one of the cleanest, greenest and safest cities in the world.

Once accepted as an exchange student, tuition and fees are paid at the University of Alberta. The equivalent costs incurred in Singapore are waived by NTU. Students are responsible for their accommodation and meals, return airfare, books, supplies and other miscellaneous expenses. Exchange students are eligible for Canada and Alberta Student Loans. Students that remain registered at the University of Alberta for the duration of the exchange are also eligible for University of Alberta scholarships and awards. [ID:5060]

University of Calgary
CREDIT TRAVEL STUDY PROGRAM IN GHANA

Credit Travel Study Office, International Student Centre, Room 275, MacEwan Student Centre, University of Calgary, Calgary, AB, T2N 1N4, Canada; 403-220-8922, fax 403-210-3869, crdttrvl@ucalgary.ca., www.ucalgary.ca/cted/specialsessions/travel

CREDIT STUDY TOUR ◆ The Credit Travel Study program in Ghana offered through the University of Calgary immerses students both physically and intellectually in a developing society. Ghana provides a unique opportunity to explore the African landscape as it encompasses significant socio-cultural, political, historical and economic elements that reflect the continental picture. Students stay in local communities thereby providing an intensive cross-cultural and ethnographic experience. The program offers three credit courses: Field Studies in Africa, Political History of Ghana and Women in African Literature, and also includes two travel excursions in addition to extended stays in the Ashanti and Volta Regions. It is six weeks in duration and gives participants an opportunity to undertake independent research projects on a topic of their choice. [ID:5486]

Dalhousie University
INTENSIVE RUSSIAN LANGUAGE PROGRAM

Coordinator, Russian Studies Program, Department of Russian Studies, Dalhousie University, Halifax, NS, B3H 4P9, Canada; 902-494-3473, fax 902-494-7848, www.dal.ca/%7Erusswww/russinte.html

CREDIT PROGRAM ◆ Dalhousie University's interdisciplinary Intensive Russian Studies Program, the first of its kind in Canada, allows students to undertake Russian language studies at St. Petersburg University in Russia during the Spring term (end of January to the end of May). Students are encouraged to attend the Intensive Fall Term Study Program at Dalhousie University beforehand. Students must have a minimum of two years to four semesters of Russian, or the equivalent, with a standing of B or better. The cost of the program (which includes round-trip airfare, visa fee, travel insurance, tuition and accommodation) is $4,375.00. [ID:5457]

University of Guelph
INTERNATIONAL AGRICULTURAL PROGRAM
Coordinator, OAC Dean's Office, Ontario Agricultural College, University of Guelph, Guelph, ON, N1G 2W1, Canada; 519-824-4120 ext. 56518, fax 519-824-0813, oacinfo@oac.uoguelph.ca, www.oac.uoguelph.ca

CREDIT PROGRAM ◆ The Agriculture program at the University of Guelph provides undergraduate students with the opportunity to attend a two-week field trip to Costa Rica during spring break. This field course is designed to introduce students to corporate and individual farms, university and government research stations, and familiarize students with tropical agricultural production systems. Through site visits and group discussions, students learn about the ecological, economical and social issues facing agriculture in Costa Rica. Students interested in attending must be enrolled at the University of Guelph but do not have to be Agriculture students. The approximate cost of the field trip is $1800 (all inclusive) and there is a maximum of 20 participants annually. Upon completion of the field course, students receive a graded credit. For more information on this opportunity visit the Web site listed above. [ID:5363]

McGill University
MCGILL MANAGEMENT SUMMER SCHOOL ABROAD PROGRAM
Faculty of Management, 1001 Sherbrooke Street W., Montreal, QC, H3A 1G5, Canada; 514-398-4068, fax 514-398-3876, bcom.mgmt@mcgill.ca, www.management.mcgill.ca/dynamik/gak.php?node=88

CREDIT PROGRAM ◆ The McGill Summer School Abroad Program offers business students from the university and from abroad the unique opportunity to earn credits from the McGill Faculty of Management while learning about business and experiencing life in another country. The program is four weeks in length and gives participants at both the undergraduate and graduate level credit in two courses. The summer school combines formal class time (lectures, guest speakers and visits to surrounding area businesses) with informal learning as students study, live and work together while abroad. The Faculty of Management offers two summer schools each year in two different locations, usually taking place on foreign university campuses. At the time of publication, students will be embarking to Spain and Brazil, while in past years programs have been held in Cuba, the Czech Republic, England, France, Greece, Germany, Italy, Scotland and Vietnam. Participation is usually limited to 25 students per group and McGill tuition fees apply. Costs for airfare, housing, meals and personal expenses are paid directly by the student. [ID:5487]

Simon Fraser University
SOUTHEAST ASIA FIELD SCHOOL
SFU International, MBC 1200, 8888 University Drive, Simon Fraser University, Burnaby, BC, V5A 1S6, Canada; 604-291-4494, fax 604-291-5880, fieldschools@sfu.ca, www.sfu.ca/international

CREDIT STUDY TOUR ◆ The Department of Sociology and Anthropology at Simon Fraser University hosts the Southeast Asia Field School for 12 weeks beginning each year in May. The first week of the field school takes place in Singapore and then moves throughout southern and northern Thailand for six weeks. Students also spend a few days in Laos and the remainder of the time in northern Vietnam. Consisting of three courses totalling 12 credit hours, the program provides an overview of society in Singapore, Thailand and Vietnam with particular reference to minority peoples and traditional arts. It includes lectures, tutorials and trips to museums, archaeological and historical sites, and rural communities. Admission is by application and participants are selected by a steering committee. Applicants must be in good academic standing, as well as have completed an introductory anthropology or sociology course. The cost is approximately $6,500 CAD per student and covers tuition, return airfare from Vancouver, visas, basic health insurance, shared accommodation and field trips. In addition to the Southeast Asia Field School, the university runs several other field schools in other disciplines and places, including in China, Fiji, the Islands of Tonga, Ghana, the Czech Republic, France, Greece, Italy and Spain. [ID:5460]

University of Waterloo
INSTITUTE OF PEACE AND CONFLICT
STUDIES INTERNSHIP PROGRAM
Internship Program for Students of Peace and Conflict Studies, Conrad Grebel
University College, 140 Westmount Road N., Waterloo, ON, N2L 3G6, Canada;
519-885-0220, fax 519-885-0014, congreb@uwaterloo.ca, http://grebel.uwaterloo.ca

CREDIT PROGRAM ◆ The Institute of Peace and Conflict Studies, located within Conrad Grebel College at the University of Waterloo, sends approximately 12 students overseas annually. Students must have completed at least two PACS courses. The internship is offered in all three semesters and covers a four-month period. A stipend of up to $1,500 is available to approved candidates and additional support comes from the hosting agencies overseas. There is no set fee for the program. However, if the cost is not covered through program funding, the remainder is the student's responsibility. The program covers all regions of the world. Visit the University of Waterloo's Web site for program information and course descriptions offered at the institute. (For more information on the Peace and Conflict Studies Program, see Chapter 15, International Studies in Canada.) [ID:5464]

University of Winnipeg
UNIVERSITÉ MICHEL DE MONTAIGNE
BORDEAUX 3, FRANCE EXCHANGE PROGRAM
French Studies and German Studies, 515 Portage Ave.,
University of Winnipeg, Winnipeg, MB, R3B 2E9, Canada; 204-786-9107,
fax 204-774-4134, french.studies@uwinnipeg.ca, www.uwinnipeg.ca/web/faculty/french

CREDIT PROGRAM ◆ Through a partnership between the University of Winnipeg and the Université Michel de Montaigne Bordeaux 3 in Bordeaux, France, undergraduate students have a unique opportunity to study at either institution for up to two semesters with their tuition fees waived by both institutions. This innovative study abroad program was launched in 2002 and allows students to choose from a variety of humanities courses offered at Bordeaux 3, a world class institution. Courses range from literature, history, journalism and world languages including Chinese, Greek and German, in addition to the school's intensive French language program (offered through the Département d'Etudes de Français Langue Etrangère (DEFLE)). Students from any area of the university are eligible to apply for the program after completion of their first year of studies. As many as four students per year are selected to participate and credits will be transferred upon return to the University of Winnipeg. Note that tuition fees are waived but students are still responsible for room and board, transportation and minimal registration fees. For more information contact the Department of French Studies and German Studies. [ID:5001]

York University
SUMMER STUDIES IN ITALY
Department of Languages, Literatures and Linguistics, Room S561,
Ross Bldg., 4700 Keele Street, York University, Toronto, ON, M3J 1P3, Canada;
416-736-5016, fax 416-736-5483, http://momiji.arts-dlll.yorku.ca/italian/abroad.htm

CREDIT PROGRAM ◆ York University and its exchange partner, the University of Bologna (l'Università degli Studi di Bologna), offer two six-credit Italian language and culture courses: one at the intermediate level and one at the advanced level. Offered in both Italian and English, both courses start at the beginning of May on the York University campus for a period of four weeks and then continue in Bologna for three weeks in June. Italian courses cover language structures and functions, vocabulary and topics on Italian culture and civilization, while lectures focus on Bologna as a centre of academia, culture and civilization from its origins to the present. The coursework is complemented with visits to four important cities: Ferrara, Florence, Ravenna and Venice. These courses can accommodate majors, non-majors and students interested in a Certificate of Proficiency in Italian. They are also open to any applicant who meets the general admissions requirements for degree studies at York. Interested students from other degree granting institutions should request a letter of permission from their home institution to ensure that credits can be applied to their program of study. [ID:5002]

CHAPTER 14

Awards & Grants

Going overseas to study can be an expensive proposition. To offset these costs, however, you can apply for awards, scholarships and grants. Finding the appropriate awards will involve background research, careful planning and lots of follow-up. This chapter lists 80 awards and grants to help you get started on finding funds for that exciting year of study abroad.

WHERE TO START

The most obvious place to research is on the World Wide Web. But due to the sheer amount of information available on-line, Web research can become overwhelming, especially if you don't know where to start. Begin your search by getting a general idea of what is out there before you find yourself inundated with too much information. Great places to start are Web sites like StudentAwards.com or ScholarshipsCanada.com. (See the Resources section at the end of this chapter.) These sites allow you to search for multiple awards and scholarships, including those available for international study. You can customize your search according to criteria such as school, area of study, level of study and so on. Search results display names of awards, as well as descriptions, eligibility criteria and links to more specific information. These sites also allow you to save your search results so you can return to them at a later date. You can even update your saved list of favourites when new awards become available.

Universities

There are also many resources available at universities, colleges or public libraries. Most of these institutions have a selection of guidebooks providing details on awards. Helpful staff are on-hand to provide advice. Because guides can sometimes be out of date, follow up your initial research by visiting the Web site and then directly contacting the institution that administers or disburses a particular award. Make sure all your information is up to date and that you are aware of deadlines.

Some awards have a higher public profile than others. While these tend to be the ones of significant value, they also tend to be awarded on a very general, nationwide or even worldwide basis. As a result, they not only attract the most applicants but also have very rigid selection criteria and procedures, as well as inflexible deadlines. Consider looking for less prominent awards in your area of interest. Almost every university and college calendar lists internal awards available to students attending that university. There are literally hundreds of these awards at each school, and many of them are available for overseas study. Be sure to check out the resources at your university's international centre, or better yet speak to staff. It can also be worthwhile to ask your graduate association, your department or your professors about awards and grants of which they may be aware. Also, consider expanding your search to other schools besides your own. Often opportunities for international funding and scholarships are not restricted to students of a particular university, and are detailed on the Web sites of the international centres, faculties and departments of other institutions.

Whenever you find an award, note the restrictions before you apply. Some awards are available only to candidates nominated by faculty, professional associations or employers.

Canadian Government

Many federal, provincial and territorial government departments have specialized award programs. In addition, the Canadian government provides considerable amounts of money to universities and colleges for research. Most federal research funds are channelled through three granting councils: the CANADIAN INSTITUTES OF HEALTH RESEARCH (CIHR), the SOCIAL SCIENCES AND HUMANITIES RESEARCH COUNCIL (SSHRC) and the NATURAL SCIENCES AND ENGINEERING RESEARCH COUNCIL (NSERC). All of these councils have a variety of awards programs for overseas study. Some of these are attached to specific research areas, but in many cases, the councils have general funds available to applicants who submit a proposal for a specific project. Check out their Web sites to find out exactly what is available. (For more information, see the Profiles section at the end of this chapter.)

The CANADA STUDENT LOANS PROGRAM also supports overseas study. These funds are available only if your school and program of study is approved by the Student Assistance Office in your home province or territory. Restrictions vary; you may have to demonstrate that the study abroad program is relevant to your academic objectives and that a comparable program is not available in Canada. Provincial loans generally cannot be used outside the province from which they originate. However, your post-secondary institution may offer courses overseas in conjunction with other institutions, in which case you could be eligible for loans. Contact your university awards officer to find out which ones you are eligible for and how they apply to your program.

Other Leads

Before you go overseas, contact the embassy of the country in which you intend to study. Embassies sometimes administer programs, and they have information on organizations and institutions that offer awards to foreign students. You can also contact professional associations, national foundations, international organizations and private corporations that offer specialized awards for overseas study. A surprising number of employers offer scholarships to their employees' children, so be sure to find what is available at your parents' places of work.

A LAST WORD

It is crucial that you start your search early. The deadline for many applications is six months to one year before the award is granted. We speak from experience when we say that there is nothing worse than finding a scholarship for which you fit all the criteria, only to discover that the deadline has passed. When filling out applications for awards, scholarships and grants, start the process well in advance of the deadline. This cannot be stressed enough: many applications require extensive documentation, carefully written project proposals, letters of reference, resumes, and in some cases, short essays. These requirements put demands on your time, as well as the time of others. Don't underestimate how long it will take to properly complete an application.

RESOURCES

AWARDS & GRANTS

Researching awards and grants can be a slow, painstaking process. That's why we've tried to do as much of the work for you as possible! This list of resources will help you find a program tailored to your particular international interest. For more help, consult Chapter 10, Short-Term Programs Overseas; Chapter 13, Study Abroad; Chapter 15, International Studies in Canada; Chapter 16, International Studies – The World's Top Schools; and Chapter 17, Internships Abroad.

After Latin American Studies: A Guide to Graduate Study,
Fellowships, Internships, and Employment for Latin Americanists 📖
2000, Shirley A. Kregar, Jorge Nallim, 142 pages ➤ University Center for International Studies, Center for Latin American Studies, 4E04 Wesley West Posvar Hall, University of Pittsburgh, Pittsburgh, PA 15260, USA, www.ucis.pitt.edu/clas, $15 US; US Cheques or Money Orders; 412-648-7392, fax 412-648-2199 ◆ Provides information on graduate study, research and internships. For graduate as well as undergraduate students, opportunities in the private sector, and career opportunities in the US government and in international organizations. An essential resource for anyone with career or scholarly interests in the region. [ID:2037]

Association of Universities and Colleges of Canada ⅲ
www.aucc.ca ◆ AUCC and its 93 member universities have carried out more than 2,000 international development projects in the past 30 years. The focus is on international opportunities that enhance other countries' resources and lead to improvements in their living standards. AUCC also administers more than 150 scholarship, fellowship and internship programs on behalf of governments, foundations and private sector companies. Each year more than 3,500 scholarships are delivered to young people interested in pursuing higher education. The site is well-designed; searching for scholarships or university programs is a breeze. [ID:2148]

Awards, Honors and Prizes 📖
2004 ➤ Thomson Gale, 835 Penobscot Bldg., 645 Griswold Street, Detroit, MI 48226-4094, USA, www.gale.com, $575 US; Credit Cards; 800-877-4253 ext. 1330, fax 800-414-5043; Available in large libraries ◆ This international directory describes awards given for achievements in virtually

every field of endeavour, listed alphabetically by the name of the administering organization, followed by alphabetical listings and descriptions of each of the awards it offers. Each volume contains organization, award, and subject indexes for quick reference. This reference now includes e-mail addresses and URLs. [ID:2494]

The British Council: UK Scholarships Database 🖳
http://ukscholarshipsdatabase.britishcouncil.org ◆ Produced by the British Council, this is a comprehensive database detailing sources of funding for international students who wish to study in the UK. You can search by country of origin, level of study, subject or host institution. [ID:2779]

Canada-US Fulbright Program 🖳
www.fulbright.ca ◆ This site provides information on the Canada-U.S. Fulbright exchange program, which is a joint, binational program supported by the Government of Canada through the Department of Foreign Affairs and International Trade and the Government of the United States through the United States Department of State. It strives to enhance understanding between the two nations by providing grants to the best Canadian and American graduate students, faculty, professionals and independent researchers to conduct research, study or lecture in the other country. [ID:2349]

Canadian Bureau for International Education 🏛
www.cbie.ca; *Fr* ◆ The Canadian Bureau for International Education (CBIE) is an umbrella non-governmental organization comprised of 200 colleges, universities, schools, school boards, educational organizations and businesses across Canada. Nationally, CBIE engages in policy development, research, advocacy and public information. Internationally, CBIE engages in cooperative projects in capacity building, institutional strengthening and human resource development. CBIE works in partnership with educational institutions, community-based organizations and governments in Africa, the Middle East, Asia, the Americas, the Former Soviet Union, and Central and Eastern Europe. The organization offers grants and scholarships for study abroad and publishes an interesting e-zine called the "Internationaliste." [ID:2145]

Canadian Directory to Foundations and Grants 📖 🖳
Annual ➤ Canadian Centre for Philanthropy (CCP), Suite 700, 425 University Ave., Toronto, ON M5G 1T6, Canada, www.ccp.ca, Members: $350 on-line, $275 print version; Credit Cards; 416-597-2293, fax 416-597-2294; Available in large libraries ◆ CCP's Canadian Directory to Foundations and Grants contains current, reliable and thoroughly researched profiles and grant information on over 1,700 foundations that are actively granting in Canada. Profiles include contact information, application procedures, deadlines and even a list of previous grantees. Each Directory subscription or purchase comes with a free copy of Building Foundation Partnerships, a foundation fundraising resource manual. Available in two formats: a searchable on-line version (available by one-year subscription) and a print edition. [ID:2028]

CanLearn 🖳
www.canlearn.ca; *Fr* ◆ This Canadian government Web site provides information on everything you need to know about post-secondary education in Canada including program, school and scholarship searches. It details how to plan and finance your education as well as helps you explore career possibilities. It also includes the National Student Loans Service Centre, where you will find the information you need about applying for student loans. [ID:2774]

Commonwealth Universities Yearbook 📖
Annual, 2,600 pages ➤ Association of Commonwealth Universities, 36 Gordon Square, London, WC1H 0PF, UK, www.acu.ac.uk, £220; VISA, MC; (44) (0) 20-7380-6700, fax (44) (0) 20 7387 2655, acusales@acu.ac.uk; Available in large libraries ◆ This two volume set is a key resource on every aspect of higher education—senior staff, general facilities, degree programmes and research strengths—at over 700 universities throughout the Commonwealth. Includes institutional data and contact details, as well as profiles of the programs of study. The higher education schemes of the 36 members countries of the ACU network are explained, giving you reliable insight into studying in Africa, Asia, Australasia, Europe, Canada and the Caribbean. [ID:2024]

The Debt-Free Graduate 📖
2003, Money$marts, 308 pages ➤ www.debtfreegrad.com, $16.95 US; Cheque or Money Order;
◆ A successful international career begins with your post-secondary education. Unfortunately, university and college degrees cost a fortune these days. Never fear, in this excellent Canadian book (and accompanying Web site) you'll learn how to manage your finances so that you can achieve your career goals. It's filled with simple measures on how to stay out of debt, including tips on finding the best summer jobs, making your money go further, living cheaply, eating and entertaining on a shoestring, finding hidden sources of free money, cutting the costs of school supplies, travelling cheap and avoiding being "had" by the banks. Turn your student status into a financial advantage. Check out the Web site for more great advice. Both highly recommended! [ID:2787]

Directory of Financial Aids for Women 2003-2005 📖
2003, 580 pages ➤ Reference Service Press, Suite 4, 5000 Windplay Drive, El Dorado Hills, CA 95762, USA, www.rspfunding.com, $45 US; Credit Cards; 916-939-9620, fax 916-939-9626, fiindaid@aol.com ◆ This US resource details nearly 1,600 funding programs—representing billions of dollars in financial aid set aside specifically for women who are interested in areas such as athletics, engineering, chemistry and biological sciences. Includes an annotated bibliography of the key directories that identify even more financial-aid opportunities and a set of indexes that let you search the directory by program title, sponsoring organization, geographic coverage, subject field and application deadline. [ID:2539]

Fellowships in International Affairs: A Guide
to Opportunities in the United States and Abroad 📖
1994, Women in International Security, 196 pages ➤ Lynne Rienner Publishers, Suite 314, 1800 30th Street, Boulder, CO 80301, USA, www.rienner.com, $10 US; Credit Cards; 303-444-6684, fax 303-444-0824 ◆ A handy reference guide that takes the guesswork out of finding and applying for research support. Clarifies qualifications, deadlines and conditions for each grant or fellowship listed. Organized alphabetically by granting institution, the entries are also indexed by geographic focus, academic and career qualifications, and grant name. [ID:2113]

Financial Aid for Research & Creative Activities Abroad: 2002-04 📖
2002, Gael Ann Schlachter, R. David Weber, 398 pages ➤ Reference Service Press, Suite 4, 5000 Windplay Drive, El Dorado Hills, CA 95762, USA, www.rspfunding.com, $45 US; Credit Cards; 916-939-9620, fax 916-939-9626, fiindaid@aol.com ◆ Want to go abroad to write, paint, sculpt, teach, travel or conduct research? This directory highlights more than 1,200 funding opportunities covering every major subject area, in practically every country and region of the world. Geared toward US citizens, this book contains awards open to all segments of the population and is a good starting point for funding research. [ID:2135]

Institute of International Education 🏫
www.iie.org ◆ This excellent US Web site has sections for students and scholars with information on financial aid, Fullbright Fellowships and academic exchanges. You can also access two excellent areas, called "Academic Year Abroad" and "Short-Term Study Abroad" which are useful resources for researching study-abroad opportunities. [ID:2656]

International Awards 2001+ 📖
2001, 396 pages ➤ Association of Commonwealth Universities, 36 Gordon Square, London, WC1H 0PF, UK, www.acu.ac.uk, £40; VISA, MC; (44) (0) 20-7380-6700, fax (44) (0) 20 7387 2655, acusales@acu.ac.uk ◆ This British guide to funding opportunities for international students and researchers contains over 950 detailed entries that will help you match your requirements with the award schemes offered by international, US and European sponsors, as well as by many Commonwealth universities. Awards are available for all levels of post-secondary study all over the world, and are both for long- and short- term periods of study. The award profiles cover residency requirements, deadlines and other eligibility requirements, making your application process a little easier. [ID:2401]

International Council for Canadian Studies ♔

www.iccs-ciec.ca; *Fr* ◆ If you're thinking about studying abroad or doing graduate work abroad in the area of Canadian Studies, this Web site has an excellent listing of awards and grants available to budding Canadianists. [ID:2010]

InternationalStudent.com 💻

www.internationalstudent.com ◆ This Web site provides comprehensive information to international job seekers and students, including advice on work-permit applications and applying for jobs in the US, the UK, Europe, Canada and Australia; studying abroad; scholarships; grants and other information to assist students in their quest to study abroad. [ID:2627]

University of Manitoba Faculty of Graduate Studies Awards Database 💻

http://webapps.cc.umanitoba.ca/gradawards ◆ An amazing Web resource, featuring an extensive searchable database of awards for study both in Canada and abroad. Users can search according to keyword, area of study and/or citizenship, and browse awards. Recommended. [ID:2714]

Natural Science and Engineering Research
Council of Canada (NSERC) – International Relations ♔

www.nserc.ca ◆ NSERC supports approximately 16,000 undergraduate, post-graduate and post-doctoral students every year with research scholarships and fellowships in science and engineering. The Web site offers a section on international cooperation detailing NSERC's projects and programs, including bilateral relations and exchanges. Contains searchable databases of opportunities and links to other organizations offering similar support for scientists and engineers. [ID:2217]

Policy Library 💻

www.policylibrary.com ◆ Policy Library Web site is a social, economic and foreign policy resource—updated daily with the latest jobs, research and events. An annual membership costs $70 CDN and allows access to hundreds of jobs, internships and scholarships from all around the world. A good resource for policy buffs. [ID:2644]

ScholarshipsCanada.com 💻

http://scholarshipscanada.com ◆ Canada's most comprehensive scholarship portal. Search through our extensive database to find scholarships, student awards, bursaries and grants. You'll also find information about student loans, applications and budget planning. [ID:2713]

Sports Scholarships and College Athletic Programs in the USA 📖

1999, 872 pages ➤ Thomson Peterson's, P.O. Box 2123, Princeton, NJ 08543-2123, USA, www.petersons.com, $39.95 US; Credit Cards; 800-338-3282, fax 609-243-9150 ◆ Both male and female athletes can explore scholarships worth more than $500 million at more than 1,700 two- and and four-year US colleges. [ID:2129]

Studentawards.com 💻

www.Studentawards.com, Free ◆ This flashy US-Canada Web site is a scholarship search service that is free to registered users. Canadian users can navigate to a Canadian version of the site. Not only can you search existing scholarships, bursaries, grants and other assistance, but registration makes you eligible for awards available only through Studentawards.com. Add this to your favourites if you are thinking about continuing your post-secondary studies. [ID:2402]

Study Abroad: 2004-2005 📖

Annual, UNESCO, 600 pages ➤ Renouf Publishing Co. Ltd., Unit 1, 5369 Canotek Road, Ottawa, ON K1J 9J3, Canada, www.renoufbooks.com, $29.95 US; Credit Cards; 888-767-6766, fax 613-745-7660 ◆ Provides essential information on post-secondary study opportunities, scholarships and financial assistance opportunities offered by degree-granting institutions in over 130 countries and territories around the world. Includes over 2,000 entries concerning education and training in all academic and professional fields, and the information is valid for the years 2004 and 2005. Each entry provides the reader with the full address (including Web site addresses where available), courses by subject offered, scholarships available, admission requirements, application deadlines, tuition fees, living expense information and possible work opportunities for the students. Includes three indexes: Index of International Organization Scholarships; Index of National Institutions (by country) and Index to Subjects of Study. [ID:2070]

Taking a First Degree at Commonwealth Universities 🖳
2001, 5 pages ➤ Association of Commonwealth Universities, 36 Gordon Square, London, WC1H 0PF, UK, www.acu.ac.uk, Free; VISA, MC; (44) (0) 20-7380-6700, fax (44) (0) 20 7387 2655, acusales@acu.ac.uk ◆ The ACU Web site generally is a good source of information on scholarships, contact information and studying at university members of its 36 country network of commonwealth universities. The virtual library is accessible from the home page by clicking on "Yearbook and Publications" and offers a number of links and documents in PDF format that are free of charge and very helpful to those interested in study abroad. One in particular is "Taking a First Degree" which can answer many of those burning questions about studying in a Commonwealth country for the first time. [ID:2403]

Tourisme jeunesse ⅲ
Tourisme jeunesse www.tourismej.qc.ca/images/boutiques5.html; Fr ◆ Un organisme sans but lucratif qui regroupe les détenteurs québécois de la carte internationale des auberges de jeunesse; leur site regroupe des informations touristiques pour la jeunesse incluant, sous la rubrique Voyages, une liste de ressources pour dénicher des emplois saisonniers & temporaires, carrières profession-nelles et universitaires à l'étranger ainsi que des bourses d'études. [ID:2182]

Profiles of Awards & Grants

The following section lists 80 awards and grants for international studies. To help you speed-read, we have identified each profile with a combination of the following field types: Undergraduate, Graduate, Doctoral, Professional and All Levels.

Academia Sinica
TAIWAN INTERNATIONAL GRADUATE PROGRAM (TIGP)
Admissions Office, 128, Academia Road Sec. 2, Nankang, Taipei 115, Taiwan;
(886) (2) 2789-8050, fax (886) (2) 2789-8045, tigp@gate.sinica.edu.tw, www.tigp.sinica.edu.tw

DOCTORAL ◆ Founded in 1928, Academia Sinica is a prominent academic institution with two basic missions: conducting scientific research in its own institutes, and raising academic standards in Taiwan. In cooperation with the top universities in the country, they offer the Taiwan International Graduate Program (TIGP) for PhD students. Programs are focused in the sciences and courses are conducted in English. Fellowships are granted for applicants who receive admission. The stipend levels are about $11,000 US per year. Additionally, the support will be extended to two more years for students who perform well academically. The deadline for applications is March 31. [ID:5168]

Association of Universities and Colleges of Canada (AUCC)
DEPARTMENT OF NATIONAL DEFENCE SECURITY
AND DEFENCE FORUM SCHOLARSHIPS AND INTERNSHIPS
Coordinator, Suite 600, 350 Albert Street, Ottawa, ON, K1R 1B1, Canada;
613-563-1236, fax 613-563-9745, awards@aucc.ca, www.aucc.ca 🖳 Fr

GRADUATE & DOCTORAL ◆ The Department of National Defence offers three scholarships and an internship, which are administered by the Association of Universities and Colleges of Canada. Successful applicants of all awards are involved in studies relating to current and future Canadian national security and defence issues, including their political, international, historical, social, military, industrial and economic dimensions. There are eight master's scholarships valued at $8,000 each, four doctorate scholarships valued at $16,000 each and three post-doctoral scholarships valued at $35,000 each. Study must be undertaken in Canada. Three one-year internships worth $32,000 each are also awarded annually, and are undertaken at a Canadian non-governmental organization or private firm. Deadline for all applications is February 1. Visit the AUCC Web site for details and application forms. [ID:5338]

Association of Universities and Colleges of Canada (AUCC)
FRANK KNOX MEMORIAL FELLOWSHIP PROGRAM
Coordinator, Suite 600, 350 Albert Street, Ottawa, ON, K1R 1B1, Canada;
613-563-1236, fax 613-563-9745, awards@aucc.ca, www.aucc.ca ▣ *Fr*

GRADUATE ◆ The Frank Knox Memorial Fellowship is awarded to three graduate students annually to enable them to pursue one year of studies at Harvard University. The program is open to Canadian citizens or permanent residents who are graduate students in the fields of arts and sciences (including engineering), business administration, design, divinity studies, education, law, public administration, medicine, dental medicine and public health. Students presently studying in the US will not be considered. Applicants must have graduated from an AUCC-affiliated university. The fellowship is valued at $18,500 US, plus tuition fees and student health insurance. Deadline for application is December 31st. Visit the AUCC Web site for details and application forms. [ID:5339]

Association of Universities and Colleges of Canada (AUCC)
INTERNATIONAL SPACE UNIVERSITY SUMMER PROGRAM
Suite 600, 350 Albert Street, Ottawa, ON, K1R 1B1, Canada;
613-563-1236, fax 613-563-9745, awards@aucc.ca, www.aucc.ca ▣ *Fr*

GRADUATE & PROFESSIONAL ◆ The Association of Universities and Colleges of Canada administers the International Space University Summer Program on behalf of The Canadian Foundation for the International Space University (CFISU), a private, non-profit charitable organization which promotes the International Space University Program in Canada. This intensive summer program covers the principal space-related fields, both technical and non-technical, and its interdisciplinary curriculum emphasizes international cooperation, giving students broad new perspectives on the world's space activities. Areas covered include space and society, space business and management, space policy and law, space engineering, satellite applications, and space information technology. The program takes place from June to August and the location changes each year. At the time of publication, it was taking place at universities in Australia. Tuition, travel, and room and board are covered with a grant of approximately $25,000. The competition is open to graduate students, graduate degree holders and practicing professionals from all disciplines. Practicing professionals are eligible provided they have not been in the work force longer than five years. Candidates must also be conversant in English and in a second language, preferably French. Visit AUCC's Web site for more detailed information about application procedures. The deadline is usually at the end of January. [ID:5054]

Association of Universities and Colleges of Canada (AUCC)
PAUL SARGENT MEMORIAL SCHOLARSHIP FOR
FOREIGN LANGUAGE STUDIES
Suite 600, 350 Albert Street, Ottawa, ON, K1R 1B1, Canada;
613-563-1236, fax 613-563-9745, awards@aucc.ca, www.aucc.ca ▣ *Fr*

GRADUATE ◆ The Association of Universities and Colleges of Canada (AUCC) administers the Paul Sargent Memorial Scholarship for Foreign Language Studies on behalf of the Communications Security Establishment (CSE). Two recruitment scholarships valued at $12,000 are awarded to candidates studying at the master's level and are renewable for one academic year. Applicants must hold a major or minor bachelor's degree in an Asian, Middle Eastern or Eastern European language (a consistent A- in language courses is required) and be entering or continuing a master's language program. The award is tenable at any Canadian university which is a member, or affiliated with a member, of AUCC. (Check AUCC's Web site for their member list.) Applicants must also be willing to work at CSE in Ottawa during the interim summer of the master's program, at a pro-rated, monthly salaried rate, and for 2 years following the completion of their degree. [ID:5055]

Association of Universities and Colleges of Canada (AUCC)
PUBLIC SAFETY AND EMERGENCY PREPAREDNESS CANADA RESEARCH FELLOWSHIPS PROGRAM

Coordinator, Emergency Preparedness Canada Research Fellowship, Suite 600, 350 Albert Street, Ottawa, ON, K1R 1B1, Canada; 613-563-1236, fax 613-563-9745, awards@aucc.ca, www.aucc.ca ▣ Fr

GRADUATE ♦ The Public Safety and Emergency Preparedness Canada Research Fellowships Program in honour of Stuart Nesbitt White, seeks to encourage PhD research in two areas of the department's mission, which is to enhance the safety and security of Canadians in their physical and cyber environments. Fellowships are related to disaster and emergency management and physical critical infrastructure studies. Therefore it is preferred that applicants have a background in disciplines such as urban and regional planning, geography, sociology, economics, engineering, environmental sciences and/or areas such as risk assessment and modelling. Multidisciplinary studies are also encouraged. Fellowships are also awarded in the area of cybersecurity, relating to critical infrastructure protection, preferably geared towards those in disciplines such as computer/software/electrical/mechanicalengineering, computer science and/or areas such as systems science, and risk modelling and management. In total, four awards are offered at a value of $13,500 each and are tenable at any accredited university in Canada or abroad. The deadline is March 31. [ID:5408]

British High Commission
CHEVENING TECHNICAL ENTERPRISE SCHOLARSHIPS (CTES)

Economic, Science and Trade Section, 80 Elgin Street, Ottawa, ON, K1P 5K7, Canada; 613-237-1530, stcanada@fco.gov.uk, www.ctesnet.com

GRADUATE & DOCTORAL ♦ The Chevening Technical Enterprise Scholarships (CTES) are designed and run by the UK's Centre for Scientific Enterprise. Focused in the international technology field, this program is aimed at enabling non-EU students to study in the UK. Its goal is to deliver the skills to allow participants to be effective at technology transfer and the commercialization of innovation, combining technology and business training with specific commercialization projects. Participants, known as CTES Fellows, will be hosted by renowned British university departments, all of which are world-leaders in the field of technology education. In order to be eligible, candidates should have a first degree in a relevant science or technology discipline, a PhD or equivalent technology-related qualifications. More information about the program is available on the CTES Web site. [ID:5163]

Brookings Institution
FOREIGN POLICY AND GOVERNANCE STUDIES PREDOCTORAL FELLOWSHIP PROGRAMS

Coordinator, Foreign Policy Studies or Governance Studies Program, 1775 Massachusetts Ave. N.W., Washington, DC, 20036-2103, USA; 202-797-6000, fax 202-797-6004, www.brook.edu

DOCTORAL ♦ The Brookings Institution awards a limited number of resident fellowships for policy-oriented doctoral research in US foreign policy and governance studies. Only candidates nominated by graduate departments can be considered for these fellowships; applications from individuals not nominated cannot be accepted. The fellowships carry a stipend of $20,000 US, payable on a 12 month basis, for 11 months of research in residence at Brookings and one month of vacation. The institution will also provide supplementary assistance for support services, research requirements and research related travel, plus access to a personal computer and the Institution's main server and networks.

Essential criteria for the scholarships are evidence that the research will be facilitated by access to the Institution's resources or to federal government agencies and Washington-based organizations. Research for the Foreign Policy Studies Predoctoral Fellowship Program should be relevant to contemporary US foreign policy and/or post-Cold War international relations. The Governance Studies Predoctoral Fellowship Program focuses on political institutions and public management in the US, and on the broader challenge of governance, including the role played by the private, NGO, and philanthropic sectors; the changing relationships among federal, state, and local bodies; and the evolution of the international economic architecture. See their Web site for eligibility, application procedures and the specifics of each fellowship. [ID:5469]

Brucebo Fine Art Scholarship Foundation of Gotland, Sweden
BRUCEBO FINE ART SCHOLARSHIPS

Liaison Officer, Associate Dean's Office, Faculty of Fine Art, 1455 Maisonneuve Blvd. W., Concordia University, Montreal, QC, H3G 1M8, Canada; 514-398-7437, www.swedishembassy.ca 💻Fr

ALL LEVELS ◆ The Brucebo Fine Art Scholarship Foundation has two scholarship programs, both offered annually: the Brucebo Fine Art Summer Scholarship and the W.B. Bruce European Fine Art Travel Scholarship. Valued at 25,000 SEK each, the scholarships are offered to young, talented, graduating Canadian artists, presently in their final year of an accredited BFA or MFA study program, or in the early years of a professional fine art career. Initiated in 1972, the scholarship program commemorates the Canadian-Swedish artist couple, sculptress Caroline Benedicks (1856 - 1935) and painter W.B. Bruce (1859 -1906), residents at Gotland, Sweden and owners of the Brucebo estate, from which the funding of the scholarships have evolved. Applications should be postmarked no later than January 31. For more details about the scholarship program please contact the Canada-based Liaison Officer at jan.lundgren@mcgill.ca. [ID:5003]

Cambridge University
CAMBRIDGE COMMONWEALTH TRUST SCHOLARSHIPS

Admissions Office, Board of Graduate Studies (BGS), P.O. Box 338, Cambridge, CB2 1YP, UK; (44) (1223) 760606, fax (44) (1223) 338723, admissions@gradstudies.cam.ac.uk, www.admin.cam.ac.uk/univ/gsprospectus/funding/overseas

GRADUATE & DOCTORAL ◆ In collaboration with various trusts, foundations, corporations, organizations and individuals, the Cambridge Commonwealth Trust offers a number of scholarships to Canadian students wishing to pursue doctoral studies at Cambridge University. Awards include the Canada Cambridge Commonwealth Trust, which is awarded to up to five Canadian students annually, and the William and Margaret Brown Cambridge Scholarship awarded to a Canadian doctoral student in Engineering, Natural Sciences, Physical Sciences or Political Sciences. There is also the Pegasus Cambridge Scholarship, eligible to students pursuing their Master of Law Degree, and the Tidmarsh Cambridge Scholarship, tenable at Trinity Hall, Cambridge. Other scholarships include the UK Commonwealth (Cambridge) Scholarships, the C.T. Taylor Studentship, and the CIALS Cambridge Scholarships which is offered annually in collaboration with the Canadian Institute for Advanced Legal Studies. Lastly, there is also the Gates Cambridge Trust eligible for candidates from every country in the world (except the UK) who are pursuing a course of study leading to a second undergraduate degree, master's or PhD. All applicants should normally be under the age of 30, must be in high academic standing and must have been successful in winning an ORS award, which pays the difference between the home and overseas rate of the University Composition Fee. Application deadlines vary according to awards. (For more information on the ORS Award Scheme, see the profile in this Chapter.) [ID:5456]

Canada Council for the Arts
INTERNATIONAL RESIDENCIES PROGRAM IN VISUAL ARTS

Visual Arts Section, P.O. Box 1047, 350 Albert Street, Ottawa, ON, K1P 5V8, Canada; 800-263-5588 ext. 5060, fax 613-566-4390, info@canadacouncil.ca, www.canadacouncil.ca 💻Fr

PROFESSIONAL ◆ The International Residencies Program in Visual Arts Grants contribute towards subsistence, travel, production costs, accommodation and residency fees for professional Canadian visual artists to participate in one of the following international residencies: La Cité Internationale des Arts (Paris), Caribbean Contemporary Arts (Trinidad), International Studio and Curatorial Program (New York), Künstlerhaus Bethanien (Berlin) or SPACE (London). These residencies may be used to pursue creative work for a period of three months to one year. A grant of $24,000 or less to cover subsistence and travel expenses is provided. [ID:5092]

Canada Council for the Arts
J.B.C. WATKINS AWARD
Endowment and Prize Unit, P.O. Box 1047, 350 Albert Street, Ottawa, ON, K1P 5V8, Canada; 800-263-5588 ext. 4116, fax 613-566-4430, info@canadacouncil.ca, www.canadacouncil.ca ▣ Fr

PROFESSIONAL ◆ A bequest from the estate of the late John B.C. Watkins, this award provides fellowships of $5,000 to professional Canadian artists in music, architecture or theatre who are pursuing graduate studies, and who are graduates of a Canadian university, post-secondary art institution or training school. Preference is given to those who wish to carry out their post-graduate studies in Denmark, Norway, Sweden or Iceland, but applications are accepted for study in any country other than Canada. Post-graduate schools include post-secondary institutions or training schools, whether or not these are degree-granting institutions. [ID:5476]

Canada Council for the Arts
PRIX DE ROME IN ARCHITECTURE
Visual Arts Section, P.O. Box 1047, 350 Albert Street, Ottawa, ON, K1P 5V8, Canada; 800-263-5588 ext. 5060, fax 613-566-4390, info@canadacouncil.ca, www.canadacouncil.ca ▣ Fr

PROFESSIONAL ◆ The Canada Council for the Arts Prix de Rome in Architecture recognizes the work of an individual or an architectural firm who is actively engaged in the field of contemporary architecture, whose career is well underway and whose work shows exceptional talent. In addition to a grant of $34,000 for subsistence, travel and working expenses, the winner has the use of an apartment studio in the Tratevere district of Rome for one year. The Prix de Rome is not an academic award; rather, it is intended to enable the winner to pursue independent work in architecture and to make an original contribution to the development of the discipline through extended contact with the architectural culture of Rome. The winner is chosen by a peer assessment committee for the Canadian Council Creation/Production Grants. [ID:5093]

Canada Council for the Arts
TRAVEL GRANTS TO PROFESSIONAL ARTISTS
Information Officer, P.O. Box 1047, 350 Albert Street, Ottawa, ON, K1P 5V8, Canada; 800-263-5588 ext. 5060, fax 613-566-4390, info@canadacouncil.ca, www.canadacouncil.ca ▣ Fr

PROFESSIONAL ◆ The Travel Grants to Professional Artists assist professional Canadian artists to travel on occasions important to the development of their artistic practice or career. Specific details on the Travel Grants for the various fields of art funded by the Canada Council (dance, music, theatre, media arts, visual arts, writing and inter-arts) are available by contacting an Information Officer at the phone number listed above. [ID:5458]

Canada Millennium Scholarship Foundation
CANADA MILLENNIUM SCHOLARSHIPS
Suite 800, 1000 Sherbrooke Street W., Montreal, QC, H3A 3R2, Canada; 877-786-3999, fax 514-985-5987, millennium.foundation@bm-ms.org, www.millenniumscholarships.ca ▣ Fr

UNDERGRADUATE ◆ Established in 1998 with an endowment of $2.5 billion from the Government of Canada, the Canada Millennium Scholarship Foundation administers awards programs which include: the Millennium Bursary Program, and the Millennium Excellence Award Program. Both programs require students to be completing their degree at a Canadian post-secondary institution, although students who are studying abroad for a semester or an academic year may still be eligible, providing they are participating in an academic exchange through a Canadian post-secondary institution and continue to meet the program's eligibility criteria.

Students pursuing an undergraduate post-secondary degree, diploma or certificate are automatically considered for the Millennium Bursary Program when they apply for financial assistance in their province or territory of residence. Those who meet the foundation's eligibility criteria, which includes prior completion of at least 60 per cent a year of post-secondary study, and are assessed with the highest levels of financial need in their province or territory are awarded a millennium bursary. The Millennium Excellence Award Program offers two awards: entrance awards distributed to students entering post-secondary studies for the first time, and national in-course awards given to students entering the upper years of their undergraduate post-secondary study. Candidates are assessed according to the following criteria: leadership, community involvement, innovation and academic achievement. The application deadline for the entrance awards is in January, and during the spring for the in-course awards. See the foundation's Web site for more info. [ID:5144]

Canada Student Loans Program (CSLP)
CANADA STUDENT LOANS PROGRAM
Contact your provincial government's student aid branch
for specific address, fax and e-mail., www.canlearn.ca ⌨ *Fr*

ALL LEVELS ◆ The Government of Canada offers full-time loans to students with demonstrated need to achieve their lifelong learning goals and overcome financial barriers. Students studying outside Canada should contact their provincial or territorial student financial assistance office to determine if their school is a designated post-secondary educational institution and to obtain a loan application form. Some students who apply for and receive student loans may also be eligible to receive study grants, non-repayable forms of assistance. Visit the CanLearn Web site for more on loans, grants and student financial assistance office contact information. [ID:5127]

Canadian Bureau for International Education (CBIE)
INTERNATIONAL LEARNING GRANTS (ILG)
Suite 1550, 220 Laurier W., Ottawa, ON, K1P 1Z9, Canada;
613-237-4820 ext. 243, fax 613-237-1073, info@cbie.ca, www.cbie.ca ⌨ *Fr*

UNDERGRADUATE ◆ The International Learning Grants (ILG) promote international education and international relations careers. Application is open to Canadian citizens and permanent residents who are enrolled full-time in an undergraduate program at a CBIE member educational institution. Students must be aged 16 or older at the time that the international program commences. Applicants must be undertaking an exchange program organized by their home institution. College and undergraduate university programs are eligible. Secondary school exchange programs also have the opportunity to participate. [ID:5051]

Canadian Bureau for International Education (CBIE)
J. ARMAND BOMBARDIER INTERNATIONALIST FELLOWSHIPS
Suite 1550, 220 Laurier Ave. W., Ottawa, ON, K1P 5Z9, Canada;
613-237-4820 ext. 234, fax 613-237-1073, info@cbie.ca, www.cbie.ca ⌨ *Fr*

UNDERGRADUATE & GRADUATE ◆ This program is administered by the Canadian Bureau for International Education (CBIE) on behalf of the J. Armand Bombardier Foundation. This program offers 25 fellowships a year valued at $10,000 each to Canadian university graduates who wish to pursue advanced academic study or a combination of study, research and/or work abroad. The objective is to build the knowledge, skills, linguistic ability and cultural awareness of Canadian students, thereby preparing them to play a leading role in international endeavours. University graduates (undergraduate degree required) from all disciplines of study are eligible to apply. The program abroad must be of one academic year and it can be undertaken anywhere in the world outside Canada. Applications are reviewed in annual competitions. The deadline is usually in mid-March. Visit CBIE's Web site for program details and application forms. [ID:5052]

Canadian Bureau for International Education (CBIE)
LUCENT GLOBAL SCIENCE SCHOLARS PROGRAM
Suite 1550, 220 Laurier Ave. W., Ottawa, ON, K1P 5Z9, Canada;
613-237-4820 ext. 243, fax 613-237-1073, info@cbie.ca, www.cbie.ca 💻Fr

UNDERGRADUATE ◆ The Lucent Global Science Scholars Program selects top students to represent Canada among the world's best and brightest science and technology undergraduates. Winners will receive a $5,000 US award, visit the world-renowned Bell Labs in New Jersey and tour New York for a weekend. Students must be in their first year of undergraduate study in: computer science, computer engineering, electrical engineering, or a specialized technical communications major such as wireless engineering. Visit their Web site for details and application forms. [ID:5053]

Canadian Centennial Scholarship Fund (CCSF)
CANADIAN CENTENNIAL SCHOLARSHIP FUND (CCSF)
c/o Canadian Women's Club, 1 Grosvenor Square, London, W1K 4AB, UK; (44) (207) 258-6637,
fax (44) (207) 258-6344, canadian.women's@virgin.net, www.canadianscholarshipfund.co.uk

GRADUATE ◆ The Canadian Centennial Scholarship Fund (CCSF) is funded by the Maple Leaf Trust, a UK charity. Scholarships are available to Canadian citizens who are already studying in the UK at the graduate level. Application forms are available on the Web site and the deadline for applications is March 15, for scholarships which will be awarded the following September. Scholarships range from £500 to £2,500. Between 12 to 15 scholarships are normally awarded each year. [ID:5128]

Canadian Consortium on Human Security (CCHS)
HUMAN SECURITY FELLOWSHIP PROGRAMME
Project Coordinator, Human Security Fellowship Programme, Center of International
Relations, Liu Institute for the Study of Global Issues, 6476 N.W. Marine Drive, University
of British Columbia, Vancouver, BC, V6T 1Z2, Canada; 604-822-1877, cchs.hq@ubc.ca

DOCTORAL & PROFESSIONAL ◆ The Human Security Fellowship Programme is administered by The Canadian Consortium on Human Security (CCHS). Intended to foster innovative research and policy development on a range of human security issues, the program is funded by FAC and ITCan. This program reflects Canada's human security agenda, which recognizes that international security can only be achieved by ensuring that all citizens of the world enjoy personal security. Approximately five to seven doctoral dissertation, post-doctoral and non-academic fellowships are awarded to individuals that demonstrate the potential to advance the human security agenda in national policy in regional and global contexts. The fellowships last between six and 12 months and carry annual stipends of $10,000 to $45,000. (For more information on CCHS, see Chapter 38, NGOs in Canada.) [ID:5069]

Canadian Federation of University Women (CFUW)
CANADIAN FEDERATION OF UNIVERSITY
WOMEN FELLOWSHIPS AND AWARDS
CFUW Fellowships Chair, Suite 600, 251 Bank Street, Ottawa, ON, K2P 1X3,
Canada; 613-234-8252, fax 613-234-8221, cfuwfls@rogers.com, www.cfuw.org 💻Fr

GRADUATE & DOCTORAL ◆ Founded in 1919, The Canadian Federation of University Women (CFUW) is a voluntary, non-profit, self-funded bilingual organization of over 10,000 women university graduates. Since it established its first fellowship in 1921, CFUW has continued to award more than $800,000 to Canadian women who have obtained a first degree. Applicants for these fellowships must be Canadian citizens, full-time students and possess an undergraduate degree. Study may take place in Canada or abroad. Among the fellowships that the CFUW presently administers are the Margaret McWilliams Pre-Doctoral Fellowship ($11,000); the Dr. Marion Elder Grant Fellowship ($10,000); the CFUW Memorial Fellowship ($6,500) for master's study in science, math or engineering; the Alice E. Wilson Awards (three awards at $5,000) for those returning to study after at least three years; and the 1989 Polytechnique Commemorative Award ($2,800). The period of study for these awards is one academic year. Applications are posted on or before May 31 and the deadline is November 1. Visit CFUW's Web site to download the application form, guidelines and instructions. [ID:5126]

Canadian Institute of Ukrainian Studies
LEO J. KRYSA FAMILY UNDERGRADUATE SCHOLARSHIP
Scholarships Officer, 450 Athabasca Hall, University of Alberta, Edmonton, AB,
T6G 2E8, Canada; 780-492-2972, fax 780-492-4967, cius@ualberta.ca, www.cius.ca

UNDERGRADUATE ◆ The Krysa Undergraduate Scholarship, is awarded to an undergraduate student about to enter their final year of study in the faculties of Arts or Education. The applicant's course of study must emphasize Ukrainian and/or Ukrainian-Canadian Studies, through a combination of Ukrainian and East European or Canadian courses in one of the above areas. The scholarship is for an eight-month period of study at any Canadian university and is non-renewable. Its value cannot exceed $3,500 in any given year. The deadline for application is March 1. Visit the Canadian Institute of Ukrainian Studies' Web site to download an application form and to find out more about other scholarship programs they offer. [ID:5263]

Canadian Institute of Ukrainian Studies
MARUSIA AND MICHAEL DOROSH MASTER'S FELLOWSHIP
Fellowships Officer, 450 Athabasca Hall, University of Alberta, Edmonton, AB,
T6G 2E8, Canada; 780-492-2973, fax 780-492-4967, cius@ualberta.ca, www.cius.ca

GRADUATE & DOCTORAL ◆ The Dorosh Master's Fellowship (one fellowship for up to $10,000) and the Helen Darcovich Memorial Doctoral Fellowship (one fellowship for up to $12,000) are awarded in the fields of education, history, law, humanities, arts, social science, women's studies and library sciences. The awards aid students in the completion of their theses on a Ukrainian or Ukrainian-Canadian topic. The fellowships are awarded only in the thesis year of the academic program for thesis work. Canadian citizens or permanent residents studying at any institution of higher learning in Canada or elsewhere are eligible. The deadline for applications for both fellowships is March 1. [ID:5266]

Canadian Institutes of Health Research (CIHR)
DOCTORAL RESEARCH AWARDS
Program Coordinator, Program Delivery Division, Address Locator 4209A, 9th Floor, 410 Laurier Ave. W., Ottawa, ON, K1A 0W9, Canada; 613-954-1963, fax 613-954-1800, www.cihr-irsc.gc.ca 🖳 *Fr*

DOCTORAL ◆ The Canadian Institutes of Health Research (CIHR) Doctoral Research Awards are intended to provide special recognition and support to students who are pursuing a doctoral degree in a health-related field in Canada or abroad. Candidates are expected to have an exceptionally high potential for future research achievement and productivity. Doctoral Research Award recipients will receive an annual stipend of $20,000 for awards held inside Canada and $25,000 for awards held outside Canada. Doctoral Research Award recipients will receive a yearly research allowance of $500. The maximum period of support is three years and the award is not renewable. The program is open to Canadian citizens and permanent residents of Canada who are engaged in full-time research training in a graduate school. At the time of application, candidates must have completed at least 12 months of graduate study at the master's or PhD level, and have been registered for no more than 26 months as a full-time student in a doctoral program. The closing date for receipt of applications is October 15. [ID:5132]

Canadian Institutes of Health Research (CIHR)
FELLOWSHIPS
Address Locator 4209A, 410 Laurier Ave. W., Ottawa, ON, K1A 0W9, Canada;
613-954-1964, fax 613-954-1800, info@cihr-irsc.gc.ca, www.cihr-irsc.gc.ca ☐ 𝑓𝑟

GRADUATE & DOCTORAL ◆ Fellowships offered by the Canadian Institutes of Health Research (CIHR) provide support for highly qualified candidates to add to their experience by engaging in health research either in Canada or abroad. The objectives of the fellowships are to provide recognition and funding to academic researchers early in their career and to provide a reliable supply of highly skilled and qualified researchers. The program is open to both Canadians and citizens of other countries. Candidates must hold or be completing a PhD or a health professional degree (or equivalent). The health professional degree must be in a field such as medicine, dentistry, pharmacy, optometry, veterinary medicine, chiropractic, nursing or rehabilitative science. The closing dates for receipt of applications are February 1 and October 1. See the CIHR Web site for more detailed eligibility requirements and application procedures. [ID:5133]

Canadian Institutes of Health Research (CIHR)
INTERNATIONAL SCIENTIFIC EXCHANGES
Program Director, International Scientific Exchanges, 410 Laurier Ave. W.,
Ottawa, ON, K1A 0W9, Canada; 613-941-4640, fax 613-954-1800, www.cihr-irsc.gc.ca ☐ 𝑓𝑟

PROFESSIONAL ◆ The Canadian Institute of Health Research (CIHR) participates in seven distinct programs, which are intended to foster collaboration between scientists in Canada and those in Argentina, Brazil, China, France and Italy. Candidates must be Canadian scientists. Recipients receive a living allowance from the host-country agency and a travel allowance from CIHR. Application deadline is October 1 for all programs. Visit their Web site for further details and an application form. [ID:5349]

Canadian Institutes of Health Research (CIHR)
JAPAN SOCIETY FOR THE PROMOTION OF
SCIENCE (JSPS) INVITATION FELLOWSHIPS
Address Locator 4209A, 410 Laurier Ave. W., Ottawa, ON, K1A 0W9, Canada;
888-603-4178, fax 613-954-1800, info@cihr-irsc.gc.ca, www.cihr-irsc.gc.ca/e/services/7369.shtml ☐ 𝑓𝑟

PROFESSIONAL ◆ The Japan Society for the Promotion of Science (JSPS) conducts two invitation fellowship programs (short- and long-term). The programs permit researchers employed in Japan to invite researchers from other countries to participate in cooperative activities. Applications for these programs must be submitted to JSPS by the inviting scientist in Japan through the head of his/her institution. JSPS does not accept applications submitted directly by foreign scientists or through diplomatic channels. Foreign scientists wishing to participate in either of these programs are advised to establish contact with a Japanese/foreign resident researcher in their field and to ask him/her to submit an application to JSPS. The short-term program is 14 to 60 days, while the long-term program is from six to ten months. For further information on the Invitation Fellowships, visit the CIHR's Web site and the JSPS Web site at www.jsps.org. [ID:5005]

Canadian Institutes of Health Research (CIHR)
JAPAN SOCIETY FOR THE PROMOTION OF SCIENCE (JSPS)
POST-DOCTORAL FELLOWSHIPS FOR FOREIGN RESEARCHERS
Address Locator 4209A, 410 Laurier Ave. W., Ottawa, ON, K1A 0W9, Canada;
888-603-4178, fax 613-954-1800, info@cihr-irsc.gc.ca, www.cihr-irsc.gc.ca/e/services/7369.shtml ☐ 𝑓𝑟

PROFESSIONAL ◆ The Japan Society for the Promotion of Science (JSPS) offers post-doctoral fellowships to promising young researchers from overseas to allow them to conduct research in Japan. The JSPS will support Canadian scientists for a minimum of 12 months and up to a maximum of 24 months for health research training in Japan. Candidates must hold a doctorate degree when the fellowship goes into effect (the doctorate must have been received within six years prior to April 1, 2001). Candidates must also have arranged a research plan in advance with his/her Japanese host researcher who is employed at a Japanese university or research institution. The Canadian Institutes of Health Research (CIHR) is responsible for selecting Canadian nominees for these fellowships, but the JSPS reserves the right to make final decisions on suitable candidates. CIHR deadlines for receipt of applications are November 1 and April 1. The CIHR is also prepared to support a third year of funding in a Canadian laboratory for JSPS fellowship recipients who have held the JSPS award for the 24 month maximum based on satisfactory progress in that period. For further information visit the Web site listed above and the JSPS Web site at www.jsps.org. [ID:5260]

Canadian-Scandinavian Foundation (CSF)
CSF STUDY GRANTS
CP 5150, succursale Maison de la Poste, Montreal, QC, H3B 4B5,
Canada; studygrants@canada-scandinavia.ca, www.canada-scandinavia.ca

ALL LEVELS ◆ The Canadian-Scandinavian Foundation (CSF) administers CSF Study Grants to approximately 17 students a year. The CSF was established in 1950 as a national, non-profit organization with the purpose of providing assistance and support to qualified and talented young Canadians of university age planning a study or a research visit to one or more of the Nordic countries (Denmark, Iceland, Finland, Norway or Sweden). The CSF believes that Canadians and Canada as a whole can benefit greatly from the Nordic experience in many fields such as public policy and planning, technology and engineering, resource management, the arts, and sciences. The CSF Study Grants vary from $500 to $2,000 and the duration of tenure can be any where from one semester to a full degree. Application deadline is March 15. [ID:5467]

Centre for International Mobility (CIMO)
SCHOLARSHIPS FOR ADVANCED STUDIES OF FINNISH
International Programs in Finnish Higher Education, P.O. Box 343, Hakaniemenkatu 2, FIN-00531
Helsinki, Finland; (358) (9) 7747-7033, fax (358) (9) 7747-7064, cimoinfo@cimo.fi, http://finland.cimo.fi

UNDERGRADUATE & GRADUATE ◆ The Centre for International Mobility (CIMO) is a governmental organization whose expertise is geared to the promotion of cross-cultural communication and international mobility with focus on education and training, work, and young people. CIMO grants scholarships for degree students of Finnish language and literature from universities outside Finland (not older than 35). Preference is given to applicants who are working on their master's thesis and the grant should be applied at least 3 months before the intended scholarship period. Before applying, the applicant should establish contact with the receiving university department. Currently, the monthly allowance is €725. Application forms are available at Finnish embassies, consulates, cultural and scientific institutes abroad, and from CIMO. CIMO also offers courses for university students of Finnish language or linguistics. Some scholarships will be granted for these courses, primarily for full-time students who would not otherwise be able to participate. Check out CIMO's Web site for more information, including a searchable database that provides information on nearly 400 study programs taught in English offered by Finnish universities and polytechnic institutions. [ID:5407]

Embassy of France
CHATEAUBRIAND SCHOLARSHIP
PROGRAM RESEARCH GRANTS TO FRANCE
Scientific Affairs Section, 464 Wilbrod Street, Ottawa, ON, K1N 6M8, Canada; 613-593-7412,
fax 613-593-7430, assistant.science@ambafrance-ca.org, www.ambafrance-ca.org/hyperlab 💻 *Fr*

DOCTORAL ◆ The Chateaubriand Scholarship Program for Pure and Applied Sciences, Engineering, Medicine and Social Sciences is available to Canadian citizens currently completing a PhD or who have completed a PhD in the last three years. The scholarships are awarded by the government of France and are tenable at a French university, engineering school or private laboratory. Scholarships are available for periods of six to 12 months with a stipend of €2,055 per month. Health insurance and the cost of travel to and from France is covered. The deadline for applications is January 31. Visit the Embassy's Web site for details. [ID:5465]

Embassy of Italy
SCHOLARSHIPS FOR CANADIAN CITIZENS
Scholarships Officer, Suite 2100, 275 Slater Street, Ottawa, ON, K1P 5H9, Canada;
613-232-2401, fax 613-233-1484, ambital@italyincanada.com, www.italyincanada.com 🖳 *Fr*

ALL LEVELS ◆ The Italian government offers scholarships to Canadian citizens wishing to pursue studies in Italy. They are intended for students, professionals, teachers and artists who meet the necessary requirements for enrolment in Italian post-secondary institutions and who would like to attend specialized courses or conduct research in specific fields. For Italian language study, the scholarships are awarded for specific programs at the Universities for Foreigners in Perugia, Siena and Roma Tre, or at other recognized institutions authorized to issue certification of Italian as a second language. The short-term scholarships consist of a three-month period to be used in the summer and are reserved primarily for courses in Italian language and culture. The long-term scholarships consist of a nine- to a 12-month period, beginning in the fall. They are awarded for specific research or specialized courses at public post-secondary institutions in any area of study. Applicants must possess a high school diploma entitling the applicant to enrol in university; for those wishing to study or conduct research at the post-graduate level, the minimum requirement is a master's degree. Elements taken into consideration by the Selection Committee include the applicant's curriculum studiorum and vitae; proposed program of study and letters of reference from Canadian or Italian academics. Visit their Web site for more details. The deadline is the end of March. [ID:5350]

Embassy of Japan
JAPANESE GOVERNMENT (MONBUKAGAKUSHO) AWARDS
Information and Culture Section, 255 Sussex Drive, Ottawa, ON, K1N 9E6, Canada;
613-241-8541, fax 613-241-4261, infocul@embjapan.ca, www.ca.emb-japan.go.jp

ALL LEVELS ◆ Through the Ministry of Education, Science and Technology, and Culture and Sport, the Japanese government offers Monbukagakusho Scholarships to Canadian students who wish to study at Japanese universities as research students. Research can take place in a wide variety of disciplines including the humanities, social sciences, and the pure and applied sciences. Separate awards are available to undergraduate and graduate level candidates, all of whom must be, or intend to become, fluent in Japanese. Recipients of this scholarship will receive a monthly allowance, return airfare, university fees, and a housing allowance. For more information please write to the Information and Culture Section of the Embassy of Japan. Applications will not be accepted via fax transmission or e-mail. [ID:5478]

Embassy of the People's Republic of China
CHINA/CANADA SCHOLARS EXCHANGE PROGRAM
Second Secretary and Program Manager, Education Office, 80 Cobourg Street, Ottawa, ON, K1N 8H1, Canada; 613-789-6312, fax 613-789-0262, edoffice@buildlink.com, www.chinaembassycanada.org 🖳 *Fr*

ALL LEVELS ◆ The China Scholarship Council offers approximately 20 awards to Canadian scholars and students who wish to study and/or do research in subject areas related to China in Chinese universities. Applicants should be faculty members at Canadian institutions of higher learning or students who have a bachelor's degree or are enrolled in a graduate program. Valid for four to 12 months, the award consists of a basic living allowance, payment of tuition fees, on-campus accommodation, basic medical coverage, as well as necessary teaching and research material. Foreign Affairs Canada/International Trade Canada (FAC/ITCan) will cover the cost of return transportation. The application form is usually available in December and January. [ID:5466]

Endeavour International Postgraduate Research Scholarships (IPRS)
ENDEAVOUR INTERNATIONAL
POSTGRADUATE RESEARCH SCHOLARSHIPS (IPRS)
Australian Government, Department of Education, Science and Training, GPO Box 9880,
Canberra Act 2601, 16-18 Mort Street, Canberra Act 2600, Australia; (61) (2) 6240-8892,
fax (61) (2) 6240-8093, scholarships@dest.gov.au, www.dest.gov.au/highered/scholars

GRADUATE & DOCTORAL ◆ The Endeavour International Postgraduate Research Scholarships
(IPRS) provide 330 new scholarships each year enabling international students to undertake a post-
graduate research qualification in Australia and gain experience with leading Australian
researchers. Scholarships are open to international students of all countries (except New Zealand)
and are available for a period of two years for a master's research degree or for three years for a
doctorate research degree. The scholarship covers tuition fees and health costs for scholarship
holders, and health costs for their dependents. Applications for a scholarship should be made
directly to a participating institution. Each institution has responsibility for determining the
selection process by which scholarships are allocated to applicants. Interested applicants should
consult the institutions they wish to attend for more information. [ID:5255]

Fondation Desjardins
BOURSES GIRARDIN-VAILLANCOURT
1, complexe Desjardins, C.P. 7, succursale Desjardins, Montreal, QC, H5B 1B2, Canada;
514-281-7171, fax 514-281-2391, fondation.desjardins@desjardins.com, www.desjardins.com/fondation 🖳*En*

GENERAL ◆ La Fondation Desjardins s'acquitte de sa mission de soutien à l'éducation en
recueillant des fonds et en distribuant les revenus sous forme de bourses d'études, de primes à la
créativité et à l'esprit d'entreprise des jeunes,et de reconnaissances de l'action bénévole. Reconnue
comme la Fondation privée qui offre le plus de bourses universitaires au Québec, elle aura
distribué, en 2004, une somme totale de plus d'un demi-million de dollars à quelque 350 jeunes.
Depuis sa création, c'est près de huit millions de dollars qui ont été versés en soutien à l'éducation.
La Fondation Desjardins emploie quatre personnes, dont deux, à temps partiel. Tous ses
programmes sont disponibles sur le site www.desjardins.com/fondation. [ID:7323]

Foreign Affairs Canada (FAC)
CULTURAL PERSONALITIES EXCHANGE
AND BANK OF MISSIONS PROGRAMS
International Academic Relations, 125 Sussex Drive, Ottawa, ON,
K1A 0G2, Canada; 613-996-4527, fax 613-995-3238, ace@dfait-maeci.gc.ca,
www.dfait-maeci.gc.ca/culture/iear/academic_relations/cultural-en.asp 🖳*Fr*

ALL LEVELS ◆ The Bank of Missions Program offers exchanges between Canada and other
countries with which bilateral cultural agreements have been reached. The program is intended to
reward outstanding Canadians who do not meet the eligibility criteria of other existing programs.
Applications from all cultural, social and academic fields are considered, and Canadian Studies
abroad is emphasized. The receiving country normally pays a per diem, while the Canadian
government pays the least expensive round trip airfare. Length of stay is limited to 21 days.
Applicants must submit a full proposal of their project and upon return are required to complete a
report. For full details, visit the Web site. (For information on their international internships, see the
Canadian Government International Internships profile in Chapter 17, Internships Abroad.)
[ID:5108]

Foreign Affairs Canada (FAC) and International Trade Canada (ITCan)
INTERNATIONAL NOTEBOOK
125 Sussex Drive, Ottawa, ON, K1A 0G2, Canada; 613-944-0489,
fax 613-992-2432, www.dfait-maeci.gc.ca/culture/int_notebook-en.asp 🖳*Fr*

UNDERGRADUATE & GRADUATE ◆ As part of the Media Outreach Program, International
Notebook gives Canada's future journalists the opportunity to meet with some of the country's

foreign policy makers and learn about the mandate of Foreign Affairs Canada (FAC) and International Trade Canada (ITCan). International Notebook annually brings 15 students, representing Canada's geographic and linguistic diversity, to Ottawa for an intensive week of press briefings, usually held at the beginning of February.

Participants receive a plane or train ticket, a grant to cover the costs of accommodation, and a per diem for meals and transportation within the city. The selection process is two-fold, the first selection being done by the journalism schools in early November. Students must submit an application form and a one-page letter highlighting their interests and experience with regards to foreign affairs and international trade, as well as explaining why they should be chosen for the program (more details and the application form are available on their Web site). Each school can nominate up to three candidates—note that the program will only accept applicants recommended by their school. A committee of journalists will review the letters and select the 15 final participants. [ID:5147]

Foundation for Educational Exchange
between Canada and the United States of America
CANADA-US FULBRIGHT PROGRAM
Program Officer, Suite 2015, 350 Albert Street, Ottawa, ON, K1R 1A4, Canada; 613-688-5513, fax 613-237-2029, info@fulbright.ca, www.fulbright.ca ☐ Fr

ALL LEVELS ◆ Established with a mandate to enhance mutual understanding between the two countries, the Foundation's awards programs offer Canadian and US students and scholars a unique opportunity to explore contemporary issues relevant to Canada and the United States and their relationship to each other. While the competition for Canada-US Fulbright awards is "field open," candidates in the following areas of study are especially encouraged to apply: comparative public policy, Canada-US relations, international trade, North American integration, communications, culture, ecology and the environment, indigenous issues, law, border issues, public health, Canadian studies and American studies.

The awards offered by the program include the Canada-US Fulbright Student Awards, intended for Canadian and American graduate students, prospective graduate students, graduating seniors and junior professionals who wish to study or conduct research at an American or Canadian institution for one academic year; the Canada-US Fulbright-Migration Policy Award, which offers Canadian graduate students and junior professionals a unique opportunity to explore contemporary migration policy issues at one of the leading think-tanks on migration in the United States; and the Fulbright-OAS Ecology Initiative Award, available to Canadians interested in regional ecology and environmental issues who wish to pursue graduate degrees in the fields of natural science, social science or public policy in the US. Visit the Canada-US Fulbright Program's Web site for more detailed information on these awards and application instructions. [ID:5470]

Foundation for Educational Exchange
between Canada and the United States of America
KILLAM FELLOWSHIPS PROGRAM
Suite 2015, 350 Albert Street, Ottawa, ON, K1R 1A4, Canada; 613-688-5513, fax 613-237-2029, info@killamfellowships.com, www.killamfellowships.com ☐ Fr

UNDERGRADUATE ◆ The Foundation for Educational Exchange between Canada and the United States of America is a joint, bi-national treaty-based organization created to encourage mutual understanding between Canada and the United States through academic and cultural exchange. The Killam Fellowships Program provides exceptional undergraduate students from select universities in Canada and the US with the opportunity to spend either one semester or a full academic year as an exchange student during the third year of their undergraduate career. Interested applicants should submit their application to their home institution and are evaluated based on their proposed program of study, personal statement, record of academic achievement and letters of reference. Visit the Killam Fellowships Program Web site for more details on eligibility and application procedures. [ID:5448]

German Academic Exchange Service (DAAD)
GERMAN ACADEMIC EXCHANGE SERVICE SCHOLARSHIPS (DAAD)
871 United Nations Plaza, New York, NY, 10017, USA; 212-758-3223, daadny@daad.org, www.daad.org

ALL LEVELS ◆ The German Academic Exchange Service (Deutscher Akademischer Austauschdienst - DAAD) is a private, publicly-funded, self-governing organization of the institutions of higher education in Germany. DAAD has the function of promoting international academic relations with mobility programs for students and faculty around the world interested in studies or academic research in Germany. DAAD offers fellowships for residents of Canada and the US who are enrolled or employed full-time at a Canadian or American institution of higher education and who would like to study or conduct academic research in Germany.

The programs include the Graduate Scholarships for master's or PhD study and/or research in Germany, as well as the German Studies Research Grants, available to undergraduates and graduate students studying contemporary German affairs (tenable in either in North America or Germany). DAAD also provides support for language study in Germany with the University Summer School Program (three to four weeks) and the Grants for Intensive Language Courses (two months). Lastly, they offer a unique eight month program for young lawyers to study and gain practical training in Germany and become familiar with the structure and function of German law. Each of these programs has varying application and eligibility requirements, check out DAAD's Web site for up-to-date information. (For more information on DAAD, see Chapter 10, Short-Term Programs Overseas.) [ID:5164]

Griffith University
GRIFFITH UNIVERSITY POSTGRADUATE RESEARCH SCHOLARSHIPS (GUPRS)
Postgraduate Scholarships Officer, Nathan, Brisbane, QLD, 4111, Australia;
(61) (7) 3875-6596, fax (61) (7) 3875-3885, rhd-schol@griffith.edu.au, www.griffith.edu.au/postgrad

GRADUATE ◆ The Griffith University Postgraduate Research Scholarships (GUPRS) are intended to attract high-quality applicants from both Australia and overseas in a wide range of research disciplines. The awards provide financial assistance for students enrolling in a Master or PhD of Philosophy. They are tenable at Griffith University and include a living stipend, relocation allowance and thesis allowance. The scholarships are available for up to two years for a master's and three years for a PhD. The requirement for eligibility is a bachelor's degree with first class honours or a master's degree of equivalent standing. [ID:5300]

Harvard Academy for International and Area Studies
ACADEMY SCHOLARS PROGRAM
Harvard Academy for International and Area Studies, 1033 Massachusetts Ave.,
Cambridge, MA, 02138, USA; 617-495-2137, fax 617-384-9259, www.wcfia.harvard.edu/academy

DOCTORAL ◆ The purpose of the Academy Scholars Program is to identify outstanding scholars who are at the start of their careers and whose work combines disciplinary excellence in the social sciences and history with an in-depth grounding in particular countries or regions outside the United States, Canada and Western Europe. Selected scholars are given time, guidance, access to Harvard's facilities, and substantial financial assistance as they work for two years conducting either dissertation or post-doctoral research in their chosen fields. Pre-doctoral scholars will receive an annual stipend of $25,000 and post-doctoral scholars will receive an annual stipend of $40,000. This stipend is supplemented by funding for conference and research travel, and some health insurance coverage. The deadline for application is October 15. See the Centre for International Affair's Web site for more information and application procedures. [ID:5302]

Institut Universitaire des Hautes Études Internationales
Secretary General, C.P. 36, 132 rue de Lausanne, CH 1211, Genève 21, Switzerland;
(41) (22) 731-1730, fax (41) (22) 738-4306, info@hei.unige.ch, http://heiwww.unige.ch ▭ Fr

GRADUATE ◆ The Institut Universitaire des Hautes Études Internationales is a teaching and research establishment devoted to the scientific and interdisciplinary study of contemporary international relations. This plural approach draws upon the methods of history and political science, and of law and economics. Between 15 and 20 scholarships are awarded each year on the basis of both academic performance and the financial status of applicants. Amount of support is 15,000 Swiss francs per year. Candidates for admission must address an application to the organization on forms obtained from the secretariat. The application must reach the institute by March of the preceding academic year. [ID:5348]

International Council for Canadian Studies
FOREIGN GOVERNMENT AWARDS PROGRAM
Program Officer, Suite 90875, St. Albert Street, Ottawa, ON, K1N 7G2, Canada;
613-789-7828, fax 613-789-7830, general@iccs-ciec.ca, www.scholarships-bourses-ca.org ▭ Fr

GRADUATE & PROFESSIONAL ◆ As part of the implementation of international cultural agreements, the governments of Canada, Chile, Colombia, France, Germany, Italy, Japan, Korea, Mexico, the Netherlands and Spain will offer a number of awards to Canadian graduate students. These awards are intended to help Canadian students further their studies or conduct research abroad at the MA, PhD and post-doctoral level, and usually cover a period of at least six months. Most countries offer awards in a wide selection of disciplines. Although all of the awards are similar, the value of each award is determined by the offering country. Complete details on each award are contained in the Foreign Government Awards Handbook which is available from all Graduate Studies Offices or Student Awards Offices at any university or by consulting the International Council for Canadian Studies Web site. [ID:5468]

International Council for Canadian Studies
THE COMMONWEALTH SCHOLARSHIP PLAN
Program Officer, Suite 908, 75 Albert Street, Ottawa, ON, K1P 5E7, Canada;
613-789-7828, fax 613-789-7830, general@iccs-ciec.ca, www.scholarships-bourses-ca.org ▭ Fr

GRADUATE & DOCTORAL ◆ The Commonwealth Scholarship Plan is available to master's and PhD students who want to study or conduct research in India, Jamaica, Malaysia, New Zealand, Sri Lanka, Trinidad, Uganda or the UK, and occasionally Cameroon, Fiji and Ghana. Scholarships are granted by the awarding country and the value of the scholarships and deadlines for applications vary. Consult the Web site listed above for further information and application forms. [ID:5341]

International Council for Canadian Studies
ORGANIZATION OF AMERICAN STATES FELLOWSHIP PROGRAM
Program Officer, Suite 908, 75 Albert Street, Ottawa, ON, K1N 7G2, Canada;
613-789-7828, fax 613-789-7830, general@iccs-ciec.ca, www.scholarships-bourses-ca.org ▭ Fr

GRADUATE ◆ The Organization of American States (OAS) offers fellowships to graduate students wishing to pursue study or research in an OAS member state. Those in the fields of medical sciences and languages are not considered. Applications must be postmarked by January 23 to be considered for the following September. Consult the Web site above for further information and application forms. [ID:5340]

International Development Research Centre (IDRC)
AGROPOLIS: INTERNATIONAL GRADUATE
RESEARCH AWARDS PROGRAM IN URBAN AGRICULTURE
P.O. Box 8500, Ottawa, ON, K1G 3H9, Canada; 613-236-6163 ext. 2040,
fax 613-567-7749, AGROPOLIS@idrc.ca, www.idrc.ca/awards 💻 *Fr*

GRADUATE & DOCTORAL ◆ AGROPOLIS is an international research awards program in urban agriculture that seeks to promote the advancement of knowledge and inform interventions in critical areas of (peri-)urban agriculture (UA). This program supports innovative master's and doctoral field research, designed and implemented jointly with international, national or local research users. Two-thirds of all awards are granted to applicants from a developing country, while the other third may be granted to citizens or permanent residents of a developed country. The award covers field research expenses to a maximum of $20,000 CDN per year. Award tenure corresponds to the period of field research, normally no less than three months and no more than 12 months. Up to 14 awards will be granted annually, with at least five awards supporting field research at the master's level. The AGROPOLIS Program also offers up to two post-doctoral awards to promising researchers who have obtained a PhD in urban agriculture or in a related field and who wish to specialize further in their field. Of particular interest are applications focusing on any of the following themes: health and environmental impacts of urban agriculture, economics of urban agriculture, and technology development and its use for efficient urban agriculture. Contact the IDRC either by e-mail or mail for more information. [ID:5141]

International Development Research Centre (IDRC)
THE BENTLEY FELLOWSHIP
Centre Training and Awards Program, P.O. Box 8500, Ottawa, ON, K1P 6M1, Canada;
613-236-6163 ext. 2098, fax 613-563-0815, cta@idrc.ca, www.idrc.ca/awards 💻 *Fr*

GRADUATE & DOCTORAL ◆ The Bentley Fellowship provides assistance to Canadian or developing country students or researchers with a university degree in agriculture, forestry or biology, to undertake post-graduate applied on-farm research in a developing country with cooperating farmers. Projects should evaluate and/or promote the use of fertility enhancing plants such as leguminous forages, cover crops and grain legumes in subsistence tropical agriculture. Projects planned and executed in cooperation with an International Agricultural Research Centre or with a developing country institution involved in agricultural research and training, and which has an applied on-farm orientation will receive preferential consideration. The candidate's host research institution will be expected to certify that the research protocol has been reviewed by a qualified statistician and that it meets an internationally high standard in terms of experimental and survey designs used. The proposal must demonstrate that the research results have the potential to improve the lives of farming households and to preserve or enhance the capacity of their lands to sustain agriculture. Deadline for application is October 1. [ID:5137]

International Development Research Centre (IDRC)
CANADIAN WINDOW ON INTERNATIONAL DEVELOPMENT AWARDS
Centre Training and Awards Program, P.O. Box 8500, Ottawa, ON, K1G 3H9, Canada;
613-236-6163 ext. 2098, fax 613-563-0815, cta@idrc.ca, www.idrc.ca/awards 💻 *Fr*

GRADUATE & DOCTORAL ◆ The Canadian Window on International Development Awards Program offers two awards. The first is for doctoral research that explores the relationship between Canadian aid, trade, immigration and diplomatic policy, international development, and the alleviation of global poverty. A second award will be granted for doctoral or master's research into a problem that is common to First Nations or Inuit communities in Canada and a developing region of the world. The awards offer a maximum of $20,000 per year for the duration of research (usually 3 to 12 months). Deadline is April 1st. See the International Development Research Centre's Web site for more information on how to apply. [ID:5143]

International Development Research Centre (IDRC)
ECOSYSTEM APPROACHES TO HUMAN HEALTH TRAINING AWARDS
Centre Training and Awards Program, P.O. Box 8500, Ottawa, ON, K1G 3H9, Canada;
613-236-6163 ext. 2098, fax 613-563-0815, cta@idrc.ca, www.idrc.ca/awards ⬛ℱ𝓻

GRADUATE & DOCTORAL ◆ The Ecohealth Training Awards encourage graduate-level students to examine the relationships between the environment, human health and development from a holistic perspective through field research that contributes to understanding these relationships as interrelated. At the time of publication, the focus of the competition is health in an urban context. Applicants are asked to submit proposals that use ecosystem approaches to human health to analyze the links between human health and urban ecosystem conditions, as well as to identify potential intervention strategies based on better natural resource management that improves human health and ecosystem sustainability. Deadline for receiving applications is May 15. [ID:5138]

International Development Research Centre (IDRC)
GENDER UNIT INTERNSHIPS
P.O. Box 8500, Ottawa, ON, K1G 3H9, Canada;
613-236-6163 ext. 2098, fax 613-563-0815, cta@idrc.ca, www.idrc.ca/awards ⬛ℱ𝓻

PROFESSIONAL ◆ The International Development Research Centre's (IDRC) Gender Unit Internships are professional development awards given to individuals to develop their expertise in gender and development research management by working with staff on IDRC program issues. Interns normally have several years of work experience and are therefore able to contribute their knowledge and skills to IDRC's program of work. At the same time, the internship is used to refine expertise and widen experience in a chosen research area. Candidates must either be Canadian citizens/permanent residents or developing country nationals. Interested individuals should consult IDRC's Web site for more information on application procedures. [ID:5142]

International Development Research Centre (IDRC)
IDRC DOCTORAL RESEARCH AWARDS (IDRA) PROGRAM
Centre Training and Awards Program, P.O. Box 8500, Ottawa, ON, K1G 3H9, Canada;
613-236-6163 ext. 2098, fax 613-563-0815, cta@idrc.ca, www.idrc.ca/awards ⬛ℱ𝓻

DOCTORAL ◆ IDRC Doctoral Research Awards are intended to promote the growth of Canadian capacity in research on sustainable and equitable development from an international perspective. Applications are accepted for research at the doctoral level in three areas of focus: Social and Economic Equity,
Environment and Natural Resource Management, and Information and Communication Technologies (ICTs) for Development. Normally, such research is conducted in Latin America, Africa, the Middle East or Asia. Award tenure corresponds to the period of field research. In general, this will be between three and 12 months. The number of awards varies and covers justifiable field research expenses to a maximum of $20,000 per year. Deadlines are April 1 and November 1. [ID:5136]

International Development Research Centre (IDRC)
IDRC INTERNSHIP AWARDS
P.O. Box 8500, Ottawa, ON, K1G 3H9, Canada;
613-236-6163 ext. 2098, fax 613-563-0815, cta@idrc.ca, www.idrc.ca/awards ⬛ℱ𝓻

PROFESSIONAL ◆ The IDRC Internship Awards provide exposure to research for international development through a program of training in research management and grant administration under the guidance of IDRC program staff. Under the mentorship of a Program Officer, the intern will undertake a program of research on the topic submitted when competing for the internship, and will be trained in the techniques of research management through hands-on experience with the IDRC's policies and practices for grant administration. Candidates can be Canadians (or permanent residents) or citizens of developing countries, and should have some training at the master's level.

Candidates need not be affiliated with an institution but they may participate in internships as part of an academic requirement. Internships will be considered for a program of training and research responding to IDRC's research priorities. IDRC's research activities focus on three program areas: Social and Economic Equity, Environmental and Natural Resources Management, and Information and Communication Technologies for Development. The deadline for applications is September 12. [ID:5148]

International Development Research Centre (IDRC)
INTERNATIONAL DEVELOPMENT JOURNALISM AWARDS
Senior Program Officer, P.O. Box 8500, 250 Albert Street, Ottawa, ON, K1G 3H9,
Canada; 613-236-6163, fax 613-238-7230, cta@idrc.ca, www.idrc.ca/awards 💻*Fr*

GRADUATE ◆ The International Development Journalism Awards grants are made to five Canadian institutions: Carleton University (Department of Journalism), Concordia University (Department of Journalism), The University of Western Ontario (Faculty of Information and Media Studies), Université Laval (Département d'information et de communication) and University of British Columbia (School of Journalism). The competition is organized by the appropriate department in university.

Awards are granted to full-time graduate students who are currently enrolled in, or are graduates from the preceding academic year of an MA or Graduate Diploma program in Journalism, and are based on academic achievement. The recipient of the award spends approximately four to ten months in a developing country to enhance his/her knowledge of international development and international reporting issues. The award of up to $20,000 covers living, research, equipment and travel expenses while undertaking field research in the developing country. For additional information, please visit the Web sites of the five universities which grant these awards. Candidates are advised to contact the universities directly. [ID:5299]

International Development Research Centre (IDRC)
JOHN G. BENE FELLOWSHIP
Centre Training and Awards Program, P.O. Box 8500, 250 Albert Street, Ottawa, ON, K1P 6M1,
Canada; 613-236-6163 ext. 2098, fax 613-563-0815, cta@idrc.ca, www.idrc.ca/awards 💻*Fr*

GRADUATE ◆ The John G. Bene Fellowship provides assistance to Canadian graduate students undertaking research on the relationship of forest resources to the social, economic, cultural and environmental welfare of people in developing countries. The award must be used, at least in part, to help fund field research in a developing country. The successful candidate will be the one whose work most benefits the lives of less privileged people in the developing country. Open to Canadian citizens and permanent residents registered at a Canadian university. Deadline is March 1. [ID:5479]

The Japan Foundation Toronto
THE JAPAN FOUNDATION FELLOWSHIP PROGRAM
Fellowship Officer, Suite 213, 131 Bloor Street W., Toronto, ON, M5C 1R1, Canada;
416-966-1600 ext. 233, fax 416-966-9773, info@jftor.org, www.japanfoundationcanada.org

ALL LEVELS ◆ The Japan Foundation Fellowship Program is designed to provide outstanding overseas scholars and researchers, artists and other professionals with opportunities to conduct research or pursue creative projects in Japan. The awards are administered by the Japan Foundation (established in 1972) which introduces Japanese culture overseas and promotes cultural exchanges between Japan and other countries. An applicant's field of study must be in the humanities or social sciences and must have a link to Japanese studies. Doctoral candidates should have completed all degree requirements except their dissertation prior to commencing the four- to 14-month fellowship. Artists in the fields of literature, plastic artists, performing and audiovisual arts, as well as specialists in the administration of cultural organizations and/or exchange programs and the restoration/preservation of cultural properties are eligible to apply for a two- to six-month program. The foundation also has a Short-Term Research Fellowship Program for scholars and researchers who need to conduct intensive research in Japan anywhere from 21 to 60 days. See the Japan Foundation's Program Guide on their Web site for more information and guidelines. [ID:5477]

The Japan Foundation Toronto
JAPANESE LANGUAGE PROGRAM
Suite 213, 131 Bloor Street W., Toronto, ON, M5S 1R1, Canada;
416-966-1600 ext. 224, fax 416-966-9773, info@jftor.org, www.japanfoundationcanada.org

GRADUATE & DOCTORAL ◆ The Japanese Language Program for Researchers and Post-Graduate Students is available for the intensive study of Japanese at the Japan Foundation Japanese-Language Institute, Kansai. To be eligible, applicants must be engaged in research/study in the social sciences or humanities as they relate to topics relevant to Japanese Studies. There are three courses of study ranging from two, four and eight months in duration. The grant covers all necessary expenses for participation in the program including lodging (single room is provided), food and other incidental living expenses (note that airfare is not included). See the Japan Foundation Program Guide (available on their Web site) for information updated yearly. [ID:5447]

John Simon Guggenheim Memorial Foundation
GUGGENHEIM FELLOWSHIPS
Coordinator, Guggenheim Fellowships, 90 Park Ave., New York, NY, 10016,
USA; 212-687-4470, fax 212-697-3248, fellowships@gf.org, www.gf.org ☐*Sp*

PROFESSIONAL ◆ The Guggenheim Foundation offers fellowships to further the development of scholars and artists by assisting them to engage in research in any field of knowledge and creation in any of the arts under the freest possible conditions. Fellowships are awarded to men and women who have already demonstrated exceptional capacity for productive scholarship or exceptional creative ability in the arts. Appointments are generally made for one year. The value of the grants depends on the applicant's need, and the purpose and scope of the applicant's plans. In 2004 the foundation awarded 185 fellowships in the US and Canada, for a total value of $6,912,000 (the average grant was $37,362). The deadline for applications is October 1. [ID:5301]

Lady Davis Fellowship Trust
Executive Secretary, Hebrew University, Givat Ram, Jerusalem, 91904, Israel;
(972) (2) 651-2306, fax (972) (2) 566-3848, LDFT@vms.huji.ac.il, http://ldft.huji.ac.il

DOCTORAL & PROFESSIONAL ◆ The Lady Davis Fellowship Trust offers fellowships to visiting professors, post-doctoral researchers and doctoral students at the Hebrew University of Jerusalem and at the Technion, Israel Institute of Technology in Haifa. Over the past 25 years, fellowships provided by the Trust-Developing Research Network have allowed nearly 1,400 distinguished scholars to spend three months to one year at these institutions, teaching and enjoying a young, world-class, academic environment in a fascinating country. This unique program is offered to superior scholars of any age, in any field and from any region. Please consult their Web site for further information. [ID:5262]

Mackenzie King Scholarship Trust
MACKENZIE KING OPEN SCHOLARSHIP
Chair, Mackenzie King Scholarship Selection Committee, Curtis Bldg., 1822 East Mall,
University of British Columbia, Vancouver, BC, V6T 1Z1, Canada; 604-822-4564,
fax 604-822-8108, mkingscholarships@law.ubc.ca, www.mkingscholarships.ca

GRADUATE ◆ The Mackenzie King Open Scholarship is made available annually for a graduate of a Canadian university who intends to pursue post-graduate study (master's level or higher) in any country, including Canada, in any discipline. In recent years the award typically has a value of $7,500 CDN, but the amount is subject to change. Applications must be submitted by February 1 to the Faculty of Graduate Studies of the Canadian university from which the applicant received or expects to receive his or her most recent Canadian degree. Full details and application forms are available on the Web site given above. [ID:5264]

Mackenzie King Scholarship Trust
MACKENZIE KING TRAVELLING SCHOLARSHIP
Chair, Mackenzie King Scholarship Selection Committee, Curtis Bldg., 1822 East Mall,
University of British Columbia, Vancouver, BC, V6T 1Z1, Canada; 604-822-4564,
fax 604-822-8108, mkingscholarships@law.ubc.ca, www.mkingscholarships.ca ▱ Fr

GRADUATE ◆ One or more Mackenzie King Travelling Scholarships are made available annually
for graduates of a Canadian university who intend to pursue post-graduate study (master's level or
higher) in the US or UK in the fields of international or industrial relations. Recently four
scholarships of $10,000 CDN each have been awarded annually, but the number and the amount is
subject to change. Applications must be submitted by February 1 to the Faculty of Graduate Studies
at the Canadian university from which the applicant received or expects to receive his or her most
recent Canadian degree. Full details and application forms are available on their Web site. [ID:5265]

University of Manitoba
JW DAFOE GRADUATE FELLOWSHIP
Awards Officer, Faculty of Graduate Studies, 500 University Centre, Winnipeg, MB,
R3T 2N2, Canada; 204-474-9836, fax 204-474-7553, http://webapps.cc.umanitoba.ca/gradawards

GRADUATE ◆ The J.W. Dafoe Graduate Fellowship is designed to encourage the study of
international relations at the graduate level and to promote international understanding. The
fellowship has a value of $17,000 and is tenable at the University of Manitoba. The award is open
to graduates of any recognized university who possess an honours BA, or its equivalent, and who
intend to pursue a higher degree in the fields of international studies, political studies, economics or
history. Applications should be directed to the awards officer at the Faculty of Graduate Studies.
Visit their Web site for information on this and other scholarships, fellowships, bursaries and
awards. [ID:5480]

McEuen Scholarship Foundation Inc.
MCEUEN ST. ANDREWS SCHOLARSHIP
Secretary, Suite 1100, 100 Queen Street, Ottawa, ON, K1P 1J9,
Canada; 613-237-5160, fax 613-230-8842, www.mceuenscholarship.com

UNDERGRADUATE ◆ The McEuen Scholarship Foundation provides scholarships to Canadian
students who wish to obtain an undergraduate degree at St. Andrews University in St. Andrews,
Scotland. The scholarship is tenable for three years (ordinary degree) or four years (honours degree)
and comprises full tuition and residence fees plus a book allowance. One scholarship is awarded
annually to a Canadian citizen residing in Canada who attends or is qualified to attend a university
in Canada. Applicants must not be older than 21 years of age on December 31 of the year preceding
the award of the scholarship. Closing date is January 31. [ID:5267]

McGill University
OSLER MEDICAL AID FOUNDATION
Coordinator, Bursaries and Scholarships, McGill International Health Initiative (MIHI), 3655 Drummond
Street, Montreal, QC, H3G 1Y6, Canada; 514-398-3520, fax 514-398-3595, www.medicine.mcgill.ca/mss/mihi

UNDERGRADUATE ◆ The Osler Medical Aid Foundation, in cooperation with the McGill Centre
for Tropical Diseases, provides three to four scholarships to undergraduate students currently
enrolled in the Faculty of Medicine at McGill to help finance an elective in a developing country.
All second year students are eligible to apply. The elective must be at least six weeks in duration.
The scholarship covers travelling expenses and a living allowance for the duration of the stay, up to
a maximum of $1,500. Please direct your inquiries to the coordinator of bursaries and scholarships
at McGill University. [ID:5482]

Natural Sciences and Engineering Research Council of Canada (NSERC)
JAPAN SOCIETY FOR THE PROMOTION
OF SCIENCE FELLOWSHIPS (JSPS)

JSPS Fellowships, Scholarships and Fellowships Division, 350 Albert Street, Ottawa, ON, K1A 1H5,
Canada; 613-944-6241, fax 613-944-6250, schol@nserc.ca, www.nserc.ca and www.jsps.go.jp ☐Fr

DOCTORAL ◆ The Japan Society for the Promotion of Science (JSPS) has established Post-
doctoral and Invitation Fellowships for Foreign Researchers to conduct research in Japan. The
program allows for collaborative research at Japanese universities and other institutions, helping
visiting researchers advance their own work while stimulating the research activities of the host
institution. Fellowships are awarded for a period of two to 24 months, and include round-trip
airfare, a monthly stipend and health insurance. Allowances for moving, settling-in and language
training are also provided. Approximately 25 fellowships per year are granted to Canadian citizens
and permanent residents.

Applicants in the fields of humanities, social sciences, natural sciences and engineering, and
medicine are considered. Applicants must hold a doctoral degree and have made prior arrangements
on their research plan with a Japanese host researcher. The Natural Sciences and Engineering
Research Council of Canada is responsible for selecting Canadian nominees for JSPS Fellowships.
Candidates may also apply directly to the JSPS via their proposed host researcher. (For more
information on JSPS, see the profiles listed under the Canadian Institutes of Health Research in this
chapter.) [ID:5261]

Natural Sciences and Engineering Research Council of Canada (NSERC)
POSTGRADUATE SCHOLARSHIPS

Scholarships and Fellowships Division, 350 Albert Street, Ottawa, ON, K1A 1H5,
Canada; 613-996-2009, fax 613-996-2589, schol@nserc.ca, www.nserc.ca ☐Fr

GRADUATE & DOCTORAL ◆ The Natural Sciences and Engineering Research Council of
Canada (NSERC) usually awards Postgraduate Scholarships (PGS) for research at Canadian
universities, but will approve a limited number of PGS on a competitive basis for tenure at
universities outside Canada. In these cases, the selection committee takes into consideration the
unavailability of a suitable program of research or the required facilities at a Canadian university
(the availability of the program will be considered, not simply whether or not the specific thesis
project can be carried out in Canada); and the benefits to the applicant of studying abroad (for
example, the unique opportunity to train in a world-class laboratory). The Postgraduate
Scholarships provide financial support to high-calibre scholars who are engaged in master's or
doctoral programs in the natural sciences or engineering. This support allows scholars to fully
concentrate on their studies and to seek out the best research mentors in their chosen fields. Visit
NSERC's Web site for more detailed information. [ID:5135]

Natural Sciences and Engineering Research Council of Canada (NSERC)
SUMMER PROGRAM IN JAPAN OR TAIWAN

Scholarships and Fellowships Division, 350 Albert Street, Ottawa, ON, K1A 1H5, Canada;
613-944-6241, fax 613-944-6250, schol@nserc.ca, www.nserc.ca and www.jsps.go.jp ☐Fr

GRADUATE ◆ The Summer Program in Japan or Taiwan provides approximately 15 graduate students in science and engineering with first-hand research experience, and an introduction to the
university research system, as well as the culture and language of the respective country. The
program's goals are to introduce students to Japanese or Taiwanese science and engineering in the
context of a research laboratory, and to increase the potential for future collaboration. The program
usually lasts from June to August. The results of the competition are announced in April. [ID:5134]

ORS Awards Scheme
OVERSEAS RESEARCH STUDENTS AWARDS SCHEME
ORS Office, Universities UK, Woburn House, Tavistock Square,
London, WC1H 9HQ, UK; (44) (20) 7419-5499, fax (44) (20) 7383-4573,
ors_scheme@universitiesuk.ac.uk, www.universitiesuk.ac.uk/ors

GRADUATE ◆ The Overseas Research Students Awards Scheme (ORS) was established in 1979 to provide awards for full-time graduate research students registered at an institution of higher learning in the UK. Approximately 850 awards are disbursed annually on a competitive basis and cover the difference between tuition fees for UK graduate students and fees for overseas students. ORS awards do not cover maintenance expenses. All applications for the awards should be made to the academic institution where the student has been accepted. Outstanding academic merit and research potential are the only criteria for selection. For details see the ORS Web site. [ID:5483]

Rhodes Scholarship Secretariat
RHODES SCHOLARSHIP
General Secretary for Rhodes Scholarships in Canada, Suite 4700, Toronto-Dominion Bank Tower, Toronto Dominion Centre, Toronto, ON, M5K 1E6, Canada; 416-601-7500, fax 416-868-0673, www.rhodesscholar.org

UNDERGRADUATE & GRADUATE ◆ The Rhodes Scholarship is designed for Canadian citizens or permanent residents who are between the ages of 18 and 24, and have at least three years of university training. Qualities of both character and intellect are the most important requirements for the Rhodes Scholarships and these are what the selection committees will seek. Recipients study at the undergraduate or graduate level at the University of Oxford, UK. Eleven Canadians are accepted annually. Each scholarship is worth £7,000 plus tuition annually for two to three years. Application deadline is October 24. [ID:5112]

Rotary Foundation Ambassadorial Scholarships
ROTARY FOUNDATION AMBASSADORIAL SCHOLARSHIPS
For further information contact your local Rotary Club or The Rotary Foundation,
847-866-4459, fax 847-866-0934, scholarshipinquiries@rotaryintl.org, www.rotary.org 💻 *Fr* 💻 *Sp*

ALL LEVELS ◆ The Rotary Foundation Ambassadorial Scholarships were created to further international understanding and friendly relations among people of different countries. The program sponsors several types of scholarships for undergraduate and graduate students as well as for qualified professionals pursuing vocational studies. The awards allow candidates to complete study or training in a country where Rotary Clubs are located. The most common type of scholarships offered are the Academic-Year Ambassadorial Scholarships which provide funding for one academic year of study in another country and help cover round-trip transportation, tuition, fees, room and board expenses, and some educational supplies for $25,000 US. The Multi-Year Ambassadorial Scholarships are for two years of degree-oriented study in another country. A flat grant of $12,500 US or its equivalent is provided per year to be applied toward the costs of a degree program. The Cultural Ambassadorial Scholarships are for either three or six months of intensive language study and cultural immersion in another country and provide funds to cover round-trip transportation, language training expenses, and homestay living arrangements up to $12,000 US and $19,000 US, respectively. Note that some Rotary districts may only offer one type of scholarship (or none at all) so applicants must check with the local club regarding availability as well as application procedures and due dates. Consult Rotary International's Web site to find out more general information about the scholarships and to locate a club near you. [ID:5113]

Royal Military College of Canada (RMC)
REGULAR OFFICER TRAINING PLAN (ROTP)
P.O. Box 17000, Station Forces, Royal Military College of Canada,
Kingston, ON, K7K 7B4, Canada; 866-762-2672, liaison@rmc.ca 💻 *Fr*

UNDERGRADUATE & GRADUATE ◆ The Royal Military College of Canada (RMC) located in Kingston, Ontario is a bilingual institution offering an education that is unique in Canada. Students are accepted to RMC, enrol in the Regular Officer Training Plan (ROTP) in the rank of Officer Cadet and become members of the Canadian Forces. The Department of National Defence (DND) pays for tuition, uniforms and books, and provides free medical and dental care. Officer Cadets live on campus, and costs for accommodation and meals are deducted from a monthly salary. The curriculum at RMC is broad and interdisciplinary, and both the undergraduate and graduate offerings reflect the military context. Programs with an international focus include: Military and Strategic Studies, Political and Economic Science, as well as War Studies. Upon graduation, Officer Cadets are awarded a degree from RMC, granted an Officer's commission and must serve in the Canadian Forces for a minimum of five years. Note that the ROTP is extremely competitive and only one in ten applicants are accepted. For more information, consult RMC's Web site. [ID:5488]

Royal Society of Canada
KONRAD ADENAUER RESEARCH AWARD
Konrad Adenauer Research Award Committee, 283 Sparks Street, Ottawa, ON,
K1R 7X9, Canada; 613-991-6990, fax 613-991-6996, adminrsc@rsc.ca, www.rsc.ca 🖳𝐹𝑟

DOCTORAL ◆ The Konrad Adenauer Research Award, established in 1988, is disbursed annually to a Canadian scholar engaged in research in the humanities and social sciences. The award is administered by the Alexander von Humboldt Foundation in Germany, in cooperation with the Royal Society of Canada and the University of Toronto, and aims to promote academic relations between Germany and Canada. An amount of up to DM$100,000 is made to a qualified Canadian scholar whose work has brought them international recognition and who belongs to a group of leading scholars in their area of specialization. Candidates should be nominated by their university. Dossiers must be received at the Royal Society of Canada no later then January 31. [ID:5481]

Royal Society of Canada
NATO COMMITTEE ON THE CHALLENGES
OF MODERN SOCIETY FELLOWSHIP
NATO Fellowships Committee, 283 Sparks Street, Ottawa, ON, K1R 7X9,
Canada; 613-991-6990, fax 613-991-6996, adminrsc@rsc.ca, www.rsc.ca 🖳𝐹𝑟

DOCTORAL & PROFESSIONAL ◆ The NATO Committee on the Challenges of Modern Society (CCMS) was created in 1969 by the North Atlantic Council with the initial aim of addressing problems affecting the environment of the nations and the quality of life of their peoples. The CCMS sponsors a small fellowship program, which makes modest grants to a number of scholars each year, to encourage research linked to the committee's ongoing pilot projects. CCMS pilot studies are designed to achieve a better understanding of the adverse effects of our technology-intensive way of life on the natural and social environment and to stimulate governments to take remedial action. Their objective is to find practical solutions to specific problems and to make recommendations to national regulatory agencies and/or other international organizations. Applications are due by February 28 of each year. Please note that this fellowship is not designed for students to obtain a diploma but rather more for senior researchers. [ID:5268]

Royal Society of Canada
NATO MANFRED WÖRNER FELLOWSHIP
283 Sparks Street, Ottawa, ON, K1R 7X9, Canada;
613-991-6990, fax 613-991-6996, adminrsc@rsc.ca, www.rsc.ca 🖳𝐹𝑟

DOCTORAL & PROFESSIONAL ◆ Since 1996, NATO has granted the Manfred Wörner Fellowship, endowed with a value of €20,000. Offered annually, the purpose of the fellowship is to honour the memory of the late Secretary General of NATO in the transformation of the Alliance, including efforts at extending NATO's relations with Central Eastern European countries and promoting the principles and image of the transatlantic partnership. It is aimed at senior academics, think-tanks or research centres of established academic excellence, and representatives of the media. It is granted on the merit of a proposal for future work to be completed within one year after the awarding of the fellowship on a topic of particular interest to the Alliance. Applicants' research projects must relate to the subjects within the areas listed in the brochure NATO-Manfred Wörner Fellowship Programme of the year for which the application is submitted. Refer to their Web site for more information. The deadline for applications is December 31. [ID:5034]

Shastri Indo-Canadian Institute (SICI)
ARTS FELLOWSHIP
Programme Officer, 1402 Education Tower, 2500 University Drive, University of Calgary, Calgary, AB, T2N 1N4, Canada; 403-220-7467, fax 403-289-0100, sici@ucalgary.ca, www.sici.org 💻 ℱr

ALL LEVELS ◆ The Arts Fellowships are for visual and performing artists who are: i) recognized and emerging practitioners of an Indian art form and wish to undergo training or engage in related activity in India to improve their skills or expand their repertoire, or ii) not practitioners of an Indian art form but wish to undergo training in India in an Indian art form to develop their own work in new, interesting and creative ways. [ID:5114]

Shastri Indo-Canadian Institute (SICI)
SHASTRI LANGUAGE TRAINING FELLOWSHIP
Programme Officer, 1402 Education Tower, 2500 University Drive, University of Calgary, Calgary, AB, T2N 1N4, Canada; 403-220-7467, fax 403-289-0100, sici@ucalgary.ca, www.sici.org 💻 ℱr

ALL LEVELS ◆ The Shastri Indo-Canadian Institute's Language Training Fellowship is intended to assist anyone who would like to improve their knowledge of an Indian language. The award provides financial assistance for fellows and senior scholars in the humanities and social sciences and will support research initiatives that are between three months and a year in length. Applicants must have a BA or MA and some prior training in an Indian language. [ID:5115]

Social Science Research Council (SSRC)
SSRC FELLOWSHIPS
810 Seventh Ave., New York, NY, 10019, USA; 212-377-2700, fax 212-377-2727, info@ssrc.org, www.ssrc.org

ALL LEVELS ◆ The Social Sciences Research Council offers a variety of fellowships to support researchers for international study. Most programs target the social sciences, but many are also open to applicants from the humanities and the natural sciences. Most support from SSRC goes to pre-dissertation, dissertation and post-doctoral fellowships, while some programs offer summer institutes, advanced research grants and grants for professionals and practitioners to conduct research. Check out their program on Global Security & Cooperation or the Berlin Program for Advanced German and European Studies. Other grants offered are for study in and/or about Asia, Africa, the Near and Middle East, Latin America, East Europe and the former Soviet Union. See SSRC's Web site for specific awards offered, eligibility requirements and how to apply. [ID:5162]

Social Sciences and Humanities Research Council of Canada (SSHRC)
SOCIAL SCIENCES AND HUMANITIES
RESEARCH COUNCIL FELLLOWSHIPS
Director, P.O. Box 1610, 350 Albert Street, Ottawa, ON, K1P 6G4, Canada; 613-992-0530, fax 613-992-1787, fellowships@sshrc.ca, www.sshrc.ca 💻 ℱr

DOCTORAL ◆ The Social Sciences and Humanities Research Council offers doctoral and post-doctoral fellowships that can be used for overseas study. Candidates must be Canadian citizens or permanent residents. The current value of a doctoral fellowship is $20,000 CDN per year, and post-doctoral fellowships are valued at $35,028 CDN per year. Further details on eligibility criteria and application procedures are found on the council's Web site at www.sshrc.ca. [ID:5116]

CHAPTER 15

International Studies in Canada

This chapter is a unique inventory of 349 international studies programs; there exists no other list like it. By choosing one of the many programs described here, you will greatly enhance your international career prospects. The following types of study programs are included in this chapter: area studies, development studies, intercultural studies, international business, international education, international health, international law, international sciences, international studies (including international affairs/relations) and peace/conflict studies. We have also written 28 *university international profiles* which detail those universities that have a significant international focus.

These profiles are too numerous and comprehensive to include in the printed pages of the book. Instead, we have provided an index of programs at the end of the chapter, and you will find the actual profile descriptions on the companion CD-ROM. (See Appendix 15a, "Profiles for Chapter 15: International Studies in Canada" on the CD-ROM.)

Good luck with your international studies; you are headed towards the launch of an exciting and rewarding career path. (For related information, see also Chapter 13, Study Abroad and Chapter 16, International Studies – The World's Top Schools.)

WHY INTERNATIONAL STUDIES?

Much of Canada's wealth comes from our interaction with other countries. We derive 38 per cent of our gross national product (GNP) from the export of goods and services. International trade supports one-third of all Canadian jobs, and, as the North American Free Trade Agreement (NAFTA) extends south into Latin America, projections for the future indicate that Canada will increasingly rely on international trade to sustain long-term economic growth. As the world continues to become more interdependent, there is an increasing demand for managers, policy-makers and professionals familiar with the international community. While the need for intercultural skills and overseas experience grows, many educators refer to practical knowledge of international fields as "the new literacy."

Virtually all Canadian universities and colleges include as part of their mandates "the internationalization of their campus and curriculum." Since this chapter first appeared in our guide, we have witnessed a strong and steady increase in the internationalization of campuses across Canada. What began as a list of 210 profiles in the Second Edition (1995) grew to 314 profiles in the Third Edition (1998) and has now reached 349 in this Fourth Edition (2004).

As this chapter clearly shows, there isn't a university in Canada that doesn't offer some kind of international study program, whether it's a diploma, degree or a coordinated area of specialization. There is an abundance of expertise in international subject areas on campuses across the country (including some college campuses). The programs offered vary dramatically in rationale, scope, breadth and rigour. Whether you are interested in politics, history, education, business, environmental studies, law or rural planning, most programs integrate international perspectives into their curriculum.

WHAT SKILLS WILL YOU DEVELOP?

International programs increase your awareness and appreciation of other cultures and help you develop cross-cultural communication skills. As a student just starting university, you have probably had little or no real exposure to the world outside of Canada. By *internationalizing* your education through the study of other languages, legal systems, cultures, politics and economies, you will become conversant with the international scene and gain insight into the global community. A university education in any of these areas demonstrates that you have developed breadth and flexibility in your thinking, analytical writing and verbal skills, the ability to take and defend a position, and so on. Your increased knowledge base, plus these skills, makes you attractive to recruiters from international agencies and businesses. Of course, completing a semester or year of study abroad or an overseas internship will make you all the more appealing in today's competitive job market.

CHOOSING THE RIGHT PROGRAM

Selecting a program can be an intimidating prospect. It is a choice that can affect the rest of your life; so taking the time and effort to research your options is very important. You should start by reading the list of programs in this chapter. Once you've selected some schools, visit their Web sites for program and course descriptions, entry requirements and special attributes. During our research, we discovered that some programs are not adequately documented on the Web. So, once you have established a serious interest in a particular program, contact the program administrators directly for more detailed information.

Whether you are beginning a first degree or moving on to graduate work, there are a number of practical factors to consider in selecting a program: duration, location, cost, funding available, reputation of the program, and a variety of crucial intangibles. The two most common considerations for evaluating a program are the reputation of its faculty and the selectivity of its admissions policy. A program with a tough admissions policy, a limited enrolment and a prestigious faculty is likely one that provides graduates with excellent employment prospects.

Once you've found a program that appeals to you, set up an informational interview with a faculty representative. Prepare questions and topics for discussion so that you get the maximum benefit from the meeting. What are the goals of the program? What courses are offered? Seek out graduates and current students as well.

Next, find out if the program has internships with international agencies, government or non-governmental organizations in Canada. Practical experience of this sort is invaluable, and it will help you make contact with people who can assist you with your employment search once you have completed your studies. The NORMAN PATERSON SCHOOL OF INTERNATIONAL AFFAIRS at CARLETON UNIVERSITY, for example, offers practical, unpaid internships with a variety of government departments and agencies, public institutions, private firms and non-governmental organizations in Ottawa. And, as part of the MBA program at DALHOUSIE UNIVERSITY in Halifax, a foreign studies mission course sends students to Europe to explore trade opportunities for Nova Scotia companies. Additionally, the University of Ottawa's International Development and Globalization Program provides a co-op option that allows students to work with NGOs and government agencies in Canada and abroad. Past co-op placements in this program have included working with the Canadian Border Securities Agency, CIDA, FAC and Public Safety and Emergency Preparedness Canada, as well as various Canadian Embassies abroad. (For more information on the University of Ottawa, Faculty of Social Sciences, see the sponsor section at the end of this guide. Also, for a description of their international studies programs, see Appendix 15a, "Profiles for Chapter 15: International Studies in Canada" on the CD-ROM.)

Another important question to ask is whether there are opportunities for overseas studies as part of the program. This component allows you to make valuable contacts abroad and gives you the chance to improve your foreign-language and cross-cultural skills. Such opportunities are commonplace with most international studies programs, especially business programs. (See Chapter 13, Study Abroad.) Most international business programs have an overseas option. As a requirement of the Bachelor of International Business (BIB) honours degree at CARLETON UNIVERSITY in Ottawa, students must spend one year of study at a university abroad.

Find out what percentage of students accepted into the program are foreign nationals. Obviously, the higher the number of students from other cultures and countries, the greater your opportunity for exposure to different attitudes and traditions. Many US schools list the percentage of foreign nationals (as well as women, members of visible minorities, etc.), but most Canadian universities, and particularly specific programs, do not. Befriending foreign students will help you gain the cross-cultural experience employers are looking for, but it is ultimately up to you to seek out these experiences, regardless of the numbers of foreign students on your campus.

You should also inquire about language requirements for graduation from the program. An increasing number of undergraduate degrees have language stipulations; for graduate programs, proficiency in a second language is usually a requirement. Language training is an important consideration at any level because few employers will hire someone for an international position without a second and possibly a third language. Starting language training at the beginning of your university career will allow you time to build proficiency gradually, instead of cramming it into your last year of undergraduate or first year of graduate studies. Over time, this strategy is definitely more effective, and may allow you to learn a third or fourth language as well. (See Chapter 5, Learning a Foreign Language.)

Finally, find out about the rate of placement for graduates. How many have found work? How many of those working are in jobs related to the program? How many are working in the international arena? What sort of jobs do they have and in what sectors?

The information from this interview, plus prior research, should help you decide if this is the right program for you. The interview should help you clarify what sort of program you really need, and you may decide to go elsewhere or continue your search. There are a lot of options out there, and the more you know, the more discerning you can be.

Undergraduate vs. Graduate Degrees

With very few exceptions, undergraduate degrees are now considered a minimum in the workforce. In most fields, students must have completed graduate studies to be considered for international positions. International studies should be the focus of your master's degree, regardless of whether or not your undergraduate degree has an international focus. In today's world you almost always need a master's degree to be taken seriously in your international career; a graduate degree will not guarantee you an overseas job, but it will certainly increase your chances of getting an interview.

In many disciplines, a PhD renders you overqualified unless you plan to teach at the university level. Economics and some sciences are exceptions: for example, a PhD in economics can lead to jobs with international organizations under the umbrella of the UNITED NATIONS.

College vs. University Programs

Another consideration when assessing international study programs is whether to attend a college or university program. Many colleges offer programs of university quality for considerably less cost. Moreover, many college credits are transferable to university, so taking your first years at the college level and then continuing at university is a path some students follow. Some colleges also have post-graduate diplomas, especially in business-related areas, which are highly specialized and reputable. As with any international studies program, it is important to ensure the quality of the program, that the program matches your needs, and that credits are transferable to the university level. In the final analysis, however, most professional international positions require a university degree at the master's level.

WHAT SHOULD YOU DO BESIDES STUDY?

In this day and age, a formal education alone isn't sufficient to interest a prospective employer. In addition to the skills needed for the actual job, three other things are important: fluency in *at least* one other language, the ability to travel and move often, and experience working in stressful or unfamiliar situations. Finding an overseas job depends as much on practical experience as academic preparation.

To gain experience, develop extracurricular interests that not only complement your academic record, but also demonstrate your interest, initiative and ability to work cooperatively. Get involved on campus: join a club with an international focus, volunteer at your international student centre, make friends with international students and get involved in their activities. Tutor someone in English. Such activities bolster your international IQ and are personally rewarding. Help organize international conferences at your university, and, if possible, attend conferences elsewhere. Offer to volunteer or intern at research centres on campus or at non-governmental organizations in the community. Apply for summer jobs with the international affairs departments of private companies.

Apply for scholarships to study overseas. (See Chapter 14, Awards & Grants and Chapter 16, International Studies – The World's Top Schools.) Arrange a summer internship with an international organization. (See Chapter 17, Internships Abroad.) Take a vacation, working holiday or a gap year abroad to expose yourself to other peoples and cultures. (For more information about gap years, see Jeff Minthorn's article, "Taking a Gap Year" in Appendix 12a on the CD-ROM.) Get involved in research projects that require meeting representatives of Canadian international development agencies, international non-governmental organizations, foreign diplomats, etc. These are important initiatives to pursue in order to add a hands-on element to your academic career. (For more information on skills required to enter the job market, see Chapter 18, Your Career Path & The Ideal International Profile.)

JOB PROSPECTS AFTER GRADUATION

You have just completed six years of post-secondary study. You need a job. The question is, where do graduates with an international specialization find work?

If you are studying international affairs (or related subjects) you should visit the Web site of the NORMAN PATERSON SCHOOL OF INTERNATIONAL AFFAIRS (NPSIA) at CARLETON UNIVERSITY to see an excellent list and descriptions of the varied types of jobs held by NPSIA graduates. (For the specific web address, see the "NPSIA Work Career Futures" resource at the end of this chapter.) This site is useful for students in all types of international study programs as it demonstrates how you can transform international academic credentials into a wide variety of international jobs.

A survey of firms in the private sector showed that they want to hire graduates with master's degrees or MBAs that include an international specialization or concentration. According to a survey prepared by the CORPORATE HIGHER EDUCATION FORUM, 16 per cent of the private sector's overseas positions are filled by recent university graduates. Canadian companies generally hire new graduates for entry-level positions in Canada. After they have proven themselves at home, they are rewarded with overseas postings. New graduates interested in careers in the private sector should approach smaller companies experiencing rapid growth. These organizations tend to move new employees into overseas positions more quickly. Alternatively, your job search can focus on companies or agencies based overseas. This generally works for entry-level positions where wages are lower.

Graduates with a master's degree in economics are recruited by banks, big business and government. As mentioned, those with PhDs often find work in international agencies such as the INTERNATIONAL MONETARY FUND (IMF), the WORLD BANK or the UN. An MA in International Relations or Political Science qualifies you for positions in government departments, think tanks and some NGOs. Entry-level job opportunities in international law are generally rare in the private sector and slightly more common in the public sector. (See Chapter 31, International Law Careers.)

HOW TO KEEP YOUR FIRST JOB

The most common reason for losing your first job is failure to come to grips with office politics. During your first months, focus your energies on learning people-skills. In cross-cultural work, as in many other fields, good people skills are often more important than technical knowledge. (For strategies and advice, read the section "Surviving Your First Professional Job" in Chapter 17, International Internships. See also the article from acclaimed workshop facilitator and speaker Eric Glanville, "Maximizing Your First Year on the Job" in Appendix 17c on the CD-ROM.)

A LAST WORD

Growing up in rural New Brunswick, I had no role models to lessen the fear of unknown places and exotic peoples. Aside from an aunt living in Peru, I knew no one who had lived abroad. It was the university environment that allowed me to challenge my assumptions, mix with a diverse group of people and develop my interest in working overseas. I learned that the international realm is populated by interesting people from many backgrounds. So, to my fellow small-town readers I say, *go for it*! Now is the time to explore and to broaden your world view.

RESOURCES

INTERNATIONAL STUDIES

This list of resources will help you decide where to study all things international, both in Canada and the US. Included are program-specific university directories and international studies associations. A word to the wise: much of this study is theoretical and academic. A large part of the skills and knowledge you need to be successful overseas is practical and functional, so complement your academic studies with work experience. Also read books describing actual development projects, international business success stories or the personality skills required to manage overseas contracts. This kind of information expressed at the right time during an interview will help make up for a lack of overseas work experience. To help you with your international studies, consult Chapter 13, Study Abroad; Chapter 14, Awards & Grants; and Chapter 17, Internships Abroad.

Association of Canadian Community Colleges (ACCC) Ⅲ
www.accc.ca; *Fr* ◆ This national organization was created in 1972 and represents colleges and institutes throughout Canada. On their Web site, you will find a database where you can search full-time programs available at ACCC's 150 member colleges and institutes. You can also find out about ACCC's international projects and browse through their education resources. [ID:2775]

Association of Professional Schools of International Affairs Ⅲ
www.apsia.org ◆ This US site allows you to search for information on APSIA's 29 member schools of international affairs located in the Americas, Asia and Europe. It provides information on degree programs, requirements and contacts. Also lists career resources in international affairs. [ID:2757]

British International Studies Association Ⅲ
British International Studies Association, www.bisa.ac.uk ◆ Founded in 1975, this UK organization is the professional association for academics and practitioners of international relations in Britain. BISA promotes the study of international relations and related subjects at UK universities and abroad. If you are thinking about international studies in Britain, this is a good place to start. BISA's Web site allows you to start searching a directory of programs offered by UK universities in the area of international studies. [ID:2657]

CanLearn 💻

www.canlearn.ca; *Fr* ◆ This Canadian government Web site provides information on everything you need to know about post-secondary education in Canada including program, school and scholarship searches. It details how to plan and finance your education as well as helps you explore career possibilities. It also includes the National Student Loans Service Centre, where you will find the information you need about applying for student loans. [ID:2774]

Council on International Educational Exchanges 🏛

www.ciee.org ◆ This is the Web site of the US organization, Council on International Educational Exchange. With programs designed for students, faculty and administrators, CIEE's respected and extensive listing of international academic programs will help you choose the international experience that is right for you. Highly recommended. [ID:2482]

DestinEducation 💻

Canadian Bureau for International Education (CBIE) www.destineducation.ca; *Fr* ◆ Maintained by the Canadian Bureau for International Education (CBIE), contains information and planning tools about international education from a Canadian perspective. Divided into three sections: Canadians who want to study or work abroad; those outside of Canada who want to study here; and professionals in Canada and abroad involved in international education. Recommended. [ID:2701]

Directory of Canadian Universities 📖

Annual, Association of Universities and Colleges of Canada (AUCC), 500 pages ➤ AUCC Publications Office, Suite 600, 350 Albert Street, Ottawa, ON K1R 1B1, Canada, www.aucc.ca, $39.95 CDN; Credit Cards; 613-563-1236, fax 613-563-9745; *Fr* ◆ A comprehensive, bilingual guide to higher education in Canada. Provides information about campuses, facilities, admission requirements, programs, degrees, financial assistance, and student life and services. [ID:2101]

Directory of Canadian Universities Database 💻

www.aucc.ca/can_uni/search/index_e.html; *Fr* ◆ The Web site of the Association of Universities and Colleges in Canada (AUCC) has a comprehensive on-line Directory of Canadian Universities Database where you can search undergraduate and graduate programs offered by Canadian Universities. Saves time because you don't have to browse all the Web sites of Canadian universities. Contains over 10,000 search records, from which you can navigate directly to the more detailed program information on the university Web sites. [ID:2628]

Fellowships in International Affairs: A Guide to Opportunities in the United States and Abroad 📖

1994, Women in International Security, 196 pages ➤ Lynne Rienner Publishers, Suite 314, 1800 30th Street, Boulder, CO 80301, USA, www.rienner.com, $10 US; Credit Cards; 303-444-6684, fax 303-444-0824 ◆ A handy reference guide that takes the guesswork out of finding and applying for research support. Clarifies qualifications, deadlines and conditions for each grant or fellowship listed. Organized alphabetically by granting institution, the entries are also indexed by geographic focus, academic and career qualifications and grant name. [ID:2113]

Global Directory of Peace Studies Programs 📖

Annual, The Peace and Justice Studies Association, 180 pages ➤ www.peacejusticestudies.org, $45 US ◆ This is a comprehensive annotated guide to peace studies and conflict resolution programs at colleges and universities worldwide. Profiles over 500 undergraduate, master's and doctoral programs and concentrations in over 40 countries. Describes the programs' philosophies and goals, examples of course offerings, key course requirements, degrees and certificates offered, and complete contact information. A great resource for this growing field of international study. [ID:2325]

International Development Studies Network 🏛

www.idsnet.org ◆ Maintained by the Canadian Consortium of University Programs in International Development Studies (CCUPIDS), this site is a great resource for Canadians studying, researching and working in international development. It provides links to and information about international development studies programs in Canada and opportunities for study abroad, as well as links to organizations that have work, internship and volunteer opportunities in the field. [ID:2778]

University Affairs 📖
10 issues/year, Association of Universities and Colleges of Canada (AUCC) ➤ AUCC Publications Office, Suite 600, 350 Albert Street, Ottawa, ON K1R 1B1, Canada, www.aucc.ca, $39 CDN/year or $3.75 CDN per issue; Credit Cards; 613-563-1236, fax 613-563-9745; *Fr* ◆ This bilingual magazine, published 10 times a year, is of general interest to Canadian students and academic staff. It contains articles on many topics and trends related to Canadian universities and colleges, and posts job openings at affiliated member institutions as well as at educational institutions around the world. Visit the publisher's Web site, www.aucc.ca, for ordering information. [ID:2237]

University Telephone Directory 📖
Annual, Association of Universities and Colleges of Canada (AUCC), 230 pages ➤ AUCC Publications Office, Suite 600, 350 Albert Street, Ottawa, ON K1R 1B1, Canada, www.aucc.ca, $54.95 CDN; Credit Cards; 613-563-1236, fax 613-563-9745; *Fr* ◆ This extensive list of Canadian academic and administrative contacts is updated yearly, saving you time and trouble in staying connected and keeping your networking on track. Also available in French. [ID:2374]

Indexes of International Studies in Canada

This chapter is so comprehensive that due to space limitations, we are only printing one index to International Studies in Canada. Descriptions for each of the university programs as well as the other index (Index by Program Type) are available on the companion CD-ROM. (See Appendix 15a, "Profiles for Chapter 15: International Studies in Canada" on the CD-ROM.) We hope the information in this chapter will help you find the program best suited to your career objectives. (For related information, see Chapter 13, Study Abroad and Chapter 16, International Studies – The World's Top Schools.)

Index by University

This index is sorted alphabetically by university or college name. (For example, the University of Alberta is sorted under "A," the University of Toronto is under "T", and so on.) After being sorted by name, the profiles are then sorted by program name.

There are three types of profiles in this chapter: international study programs, international academic research centers, and university international profiles. We have listed 349 programs that meet the following criteria:

- Certificate, diploma and degree programs that are exclusively international in their orientation and are noted as such on official transcripts.
- Established international programs (concentration or specialization) supervised and coordinated by faculty.
- Doctoral programs with a designated international focus.

The official name of the credential as awarded by its issuing institution is indicated in uppercase and written in parentheses. All other related information, such as program minors/ concentrations/options/etc., is presented in lowercase.

The 67 *academic research centres* are listed because they have a strong international focus and in most cases enhance a corresponding international study program. These centres raise the profiles of their departments and offer academic support, research opportunities, internship programs and job possibilities to students.

The 28 *university international profiles* are included for those universities with significant international activity. These profiles detail the universities' international strengths and expertise, their student population and percentage of foreign students, language programs, and the international offices on campus.

Canada's Most Internationally Oriented Campuses

Canadian Universities (sorted by number of international study programs)	International Study Programs in THE BIG GUIDE	Size of Student Body	% of Foreign Students
Carleton University	22	22,535	8.2%
University of Toronto	19	63,109	7.0%
York University	18	50,000	6.4%
University of British Columbia	17	40,945	10.0%
McGill University	16	30,500	11.5%
Université de Montréal	16	54,465	9.5%
Université du Québec à Montréal	14	41,200	8.2%
Queen's University	13	19,702	4.7%
University of Alberta	13	37,844	4.0%
University of Ottawa	10	30,175	5.6%
University of Calgary	9	28,419	3.7%
Simon Fraser University	8	21,968	10.0%
Dalhousie University	7	15,190	7.4%
Université Laval	7	38,000	8.7%
University of New Brunswick	7	13,200	5.0%
University of Victoria	7	19,110	6.9%
HEC Montréal	6	11,000	9.1%
University of Guelph	6	15,710	5.5%
University of Manitoba	6	25,000	8.0%
University of Waterloo	6	24,897	6.2%
Trent University	5	7,350	9.0%
Brock University	4	15,527	6.0%
Concordia University	4	32,000	10.0%
McMaster University	4	22,280	7.0%
University of Western Ontario	4	32,083	6.2%
University of Winnipeg	4	8,500	4.0%
Université de Moncton	3	5,027	4.9%

Descriptions for each of the 349 university programs indexed here are available on the companion CD-ROM. (See Appendix 15a, "Profiles: International Studies in Canada" on the CD-ROM.)

This index to Canadian international studies and academic research centres is first sorted alphabetically by university or college name, then by program type, and lastly by program name.

ACADIA UNIVERSITY

INTERCULTURAL STUDIES

Fred C. Manning School of Business Administration
BBA: major in French, Spanish or German [ID:5117]

INTERNATIONAL STUDIES/AFFAIRS

International Relations Program
BA & MA IN POLITICAL SCIENCE: specialization in International Relations [ID:5118]

UNIVERSITY OF ALBERTA

INTERNATIONAL PROFILE
[ID:5428]

AREA STUDIES

Canadian Institute of Ukrainian Studies
RESEARCH CENTRE [ID:5198]

Department of East Asian Studies
BA, BA (Honours), BA: minor & MA IN EAST ASIAN STUDIES; BA (Combined Honours) IN CHINESE AND EAST ASIAN STUDIES or IN JAPANESE AND EAST ASIAN STUDIES [ID:5239]

Middle Eastern and African Studies Programme (MEAS)
BA, BA: minor & CERTIFICATE OF SPECIAL INTEREST IN MIDDLE EAST & AFRICAN STUDIES [ID:5472]

Prince Takamado Japan Centre for Teaching and Research
RESEARCH CENTRE [ID:5484]

Wirth Institute for Austrian and Central European Studies
RESEARCH CENTRE [ID:5199]

INTERCULTURAL STUDIES

The Dimic Research Institute
RESEARCH CENTRE [ID:5453]

INTERNATIONAL BUSINESS

Centre for International Business Studies (CIBS)
RESEARCH CENTRE [ID:5076]

School of Business
MBA: specialization in International Business [ID:5462]

Undergraduate Business Program
BComm IN INTERNATIONAL BUSINESS: specialization in East Asian Studies, European Studies or Latin American Studies [ID:5241]

INTERNATIONAL EDUCATION

Theoretical, Cultural and International Studies in Education (TCI)
MEd or PhD IN THEORETICAL, CULTURAL AND INTERNATIONAL EDUCATION STUDIES [ID:5240]

INTERNATIONAL HEALTH

Centre for the Cross-Cultural Study of Health and Healing
RESEARCH CENTRE [ID:5471]

International Nursing Centre (INC)
RESEARCH CENTRE [ID:5200]

INTERNATIONAL STUDIES/AFFAIRS

Department of Political Science
PhD IN POLITICAL SCIENCE: concentration in International Relations [ID:5077]

COLLÈGE D'ALFRED DE L'UNIVERSITÉ DE GUELPH

DEVELOPMENT STUDIES

Agriculture et développement international
CERTIFICAT EN DÉVELOPPEMENT INTERNATIONAL [ID:7277]

INTERNATIONAL EDUCATION

Agriculture et développement international
DIPLÔME COLLÉGIAL EN AGRICULTURE ET DÉVELOPPEMENT INTERNATIONAL [ID:7255]

CÉGEP ANDRÉ-LAURENDEAU

INTERNATIONAL EDUCATION

Baccalauréat international
D.E.C. EN SCIENCES DE LA NATURE et EN SCIENCES HUMAINES [ID:7313]

AUGUSTANA UNIVERSITY COLLEGE

DEVELOPMENT STUDIES

Prairies/Mexico Rural Development Exchange
DIPLOMA IN INTERDISCIPLINARY STUDIES [ID:5450]

BISHOP'S UNIVERSITY

INTERNATIONAL BUSINESS

Division of Business Administration
BBA: concentration in International Business [ID:5412]

BRITISH COLUMBIA INSTITUTE OF TECHNOLOGY

INTERNATIONAL BUSINESS

International Trade and Transportation Program
DIPLOMA IN INTERNATIONAL TRADE AND TRANSPORTATION [ID:5250]

UNIVERSITY OF BRITISH COLUMBIA

INTERNATIONAL PROFILE
[ID:5429]

AREA STUDIES

Centre for Asian Legal Studies
RESEARCH CENTRE [ID:5095]

Department of Asian Studies
BA, MA & PhD IN ASIAN STUDIES [ID:5326]

Institute of Asian Research
RESEARCH CENTRE; MA IN ASIA-PACIFIC POLICY STUDIES (MAPPS) [ID:5096]

Latin American Studies
BA & BA: minor IN LATIN AMERICAN STUDIES [ID:5035]

Modern European Studies Program
BA IN MODERN EUROPEAN STUDIES [ID:5097]

DEVELOPMENT STUDIES

Centre for Human Settlements (CHS)
RESEARCH CENTRE [ID:5352]

Institute for Resources, Environment and Sustainability (IRES)
CERTIFICATE IN WATERSHED MANAGEMENT [ID:5354]

School of Community and Regional Planning
MA, MSc & PhD IN PLANNING: concentration in International Development Planning [ID:5098]

INTERNATIONAL BUSINESS

Centre for International Business Studies
RESEARCH CENTRE [ID:5196]

Sauder School of Business
BComm: option in International Business [ID:5327]

INTERNATIONAL HEALTH

Centre for International Health
RESEARCH CENTRE [ID:5174]

INTERNATIONAL LAW

International Centre for Criminal Law Reform and Criminal Justice Policy (ICCLR)
RESEARCH CENTRE [ID:5328]

INTERNATIONAL SCIENCES

Food and Resource Economics Group
BSc (Agr) & MSc: specialization in International Trade and Resource Management [ID:5413]

Global Resource Systems Program
BSc IN GLOBAL RESOURCE SYSTEMS [ID:5139]

INTERNATIONAL STUDIES/AFFAIRS

Centre of International Relations (CIR)
RESEARCH CENTRE [ID:5353]

International Relations Program
BA & BA: minor IN INTERNATIONAL RELATIONS [ID:5145]

Liu Institute for Global Issues
RESEARCH CENTRE [ID:5146]

BROCK UNIVERSITY

INTERNATIONAL PROFILE
[ID:5430]

INTERNATIONAL BUSINESS

Faculty of Business
BBA: concentration in International Business [ID:5119]

INTERNATIONAL STUDIES/AFFAIRS

Centre for International Studies
BA: minor in International Studies [ID:5414]

Department of Political Science
BA & MA IN POLITICAL SCIENCE: concentration in International Relations [ID:5120]

International Political Economy Program
BA (Honours) IN INTERNATIONAL POLITICAL ECONOMY [ID:5215]

UNIVERSITY OF CALGARY

INTERNATIONAL PROFILE
[ID:5409]

AREA STUDIES

Department of French, Italian & Spanish
BA: minor in Italian Studies [ID:5232]

Faculty of Communication and Culture
BA & BSc: minor in African, East Asian, Latin American or Central and East European Studies [ID:5355]

DEVELOPMENT STUDIES

Faculty of Communication and Culture
BA & BA (Honours) IN DEVELOPMENT STUDIES [ID:5356]

Faculty of Social Work
MSW: International concentration [ID:5233]

INTERNATIONAL BUSINESS

Haskayne School of Business
MBA: Global Energy Management and Sustainable Development Specialization (GEMS), specialization in Environmental Management/Sustainable Development (EM/SD), or customized specialization in International Business [ID:5205]

Haskayne School of Business
BComm: concentration in International Business (IBUS) [ID:5202]

INTERNATIONAL EDUCATION

Graduate Division of Educational Research
GRADUATE CERTIFICATE, GRADUATE DIPLOMA, MEd, MA, MSc, EdD, and PhD IN EDUCATION: International focus [ID:5359]

INTERNATIONAL STUDIES/AFFAIRS

Centre for Military and Strategic Studies (CMSS)
RESEARCH CENTRE; MA & PhD IN STRATEGIC STUDIES [ID:5204]

International Relations Program (IR)
BA IN INTERNATIONAL RELATIONS [ID:5203]

UNIVERSITY COLLEGE OF CAPE BRETON

INTERNATIONAL STUDIES/AFFAIRS

Centre for International Studies
RESEARCH CENTRE [ID:5238]

CAPILANO COLLEGE

AREA STUDIES

McRae Institute of International Management
POST GRADUATE DIPLOMA IN INTERNATIONAL MANAGEMENT [ID:5130]

CARLETON UNIVERSITY

INTERNATIONAL PROFILE
[ID:5432]

AREA STUDIES

Centre for European Studies (CES)
RESEARCH CENTRE [ID:5089]

Centre for Research on Canadian-Russian Relations (CRCR)
RESEARCH CENTRE [ID:5234]

East-West Project (EWP)
RESEARCH CENTRE [ID:5235]

Institute of European and Russian Studies (EURUS)
RESEARCH CENTRE [ID:5122]

Institute of European and Russian Studies (EURUS)
BA & BA (Honours) IN EUROPEAN AND RUSSIAN STUDIES; MA IN CENTRAL/EAST EUROPEAN AND RUSSIAN AREA STUDIES; DIPLOMA IN EUROPEAN INTEGRATION STUDIES [ID:5121]

Institute of Interdisciplinary Studies
BA & BA (Honours) IN DIRECTED INTERDISCIPLINARY STUDIES: concentration in Aboriginal Studies, African Studies, Asian Studies, Latin American and Caribbean Studies, Environmental Studies, Third World Studies or United States Studies [ID:5123]

DEVELOPMENT STUDIES

Centre for Development Research and Training (CDRT)
RESEARCH CENTRE [ID:5088]

Development Administration Program
MA IN PUBLIC ADMINISTRATION: specialization in Development Administration [ID:5149]

Research Resource Division for Refugees (RRDR)
RESEARCH CENTRE [ID:5150]

INTERNATIONAL BUSINESS

Centre for the Study of Training, Investment and Economic Restructuring (CSTIER)
RESEARCH CENTRE [ID:5152]

International Business Study Group (IBSG)
RESEARCH CENTRE [ID:5153]

Sprott School of Business
BACHELOR OF INTERNATIONAL BUSINESS (BIB); BCom: concentration in International Business [ID:5151]

INTERNATIONAL LAW

Centre for Trade Policy and Law (CTPL)
RESEARCH CENTRE; CERTIFICATE IN TRADE POLICY AND COMMERCIAL DIPLOMACY
[ID:5084]

INTERNATIONAL SCIENCES

Ottawa Carleton Earthquake Engineering Research Centre
RESEARCH CENTRE [ID:5085]

INTERNATIONAL STUDIES/AFFAIRS

Arthur Kroeger College of Public Affairs
Bachelor of PUBLIC AFFAIRS AND POLICY MANAGEMENT: specialization in Development Studies, Human Rights or International Studies
[ID:5059]

Canadian Centre of Intelligence and Security Studies (CCISS)
RESEARCH CENTRE [ID:5070]

Centre for Security and Defence Studies (CSDS)
RESEARCH CENTRE [ID:5072]

Department of Economics
PhD IN ECONOMICS: specialization in Economic Development, Economics of the Environment or International Economics [ID:5154]

Human Rights Program
BA (Combined Honours) IN HUMAN RIGHTS
[ID:5086]

Institute of Political Economy
MA IN POLITICAL ECONOMY [ID:5155]

Norman Paterson School of International Affairs (NPSIA)
MA IN INTERNATIONAL AFFAIRS; MA IN INTERNATIONAL AFFAIRS & LLB [ID:5156]

PEACE/CONFLICT STUDIES

Centre for Negotiation and Dispute Resolution (CNDR)
RESEARCH CENTRE [ID:5071]

CHAMPLAIN LENNOXVILLE

INTERNATIONAL STUDIES/AFFAIRS

International Studies Program
CERTIFICATE IN INTERNATIONAL STUDIES
[ID:5452]

CONCORDIA UNIVERSITY

INTERNATIONAL PROFILE
[ID:5431]

AREA STUDIES

Department of Religion
BA & BA: minor IN SOUTHERN ASIA STUDIES
[ID:5236]

INTERNATIONAL BUSINESS

Centre for International Business
RESEARCH CENTRE [ID:5347]

John Molson School of Business
BComm & BAdmin: minor in International Business
[ID:5157]

MBA Program
MBA: concentration in International Business
[ID:5158]

CONFEDERATION COLLEGE OF APPLIED ARTS AND TECHNOLOGY

INTERNATIONAL BUSINESS

Faculty of Business
DIPLOMA IN INTERNATIONAL BUSINESS AND INTERNATIONAL BUSINESS MANAGEMENT
[ID:5225]

DALHOUSIE UNIVERSITY

INTERNATIONAL PROFILE
[ID:5433]

AREA STUDIES

Department of Russian Studies
BA & BA (Honours) IN RUSSIAN STUDIES
[ID:5307]

DEVELOPMENT STUDIES

Department of Economics
MA IN DEVELOPMENT ECONOMICS [ID:5160]

Department of International Development Studies
BA (Major & Double Major), BA (Honours & Combined Honours) & MA IN INTERNATIONAL DEVELOPMENT STUDIES [ID:5159]

INTERNATIONAL BUSINESS

Centre of International Business Studies (CIBS)
RESEARCH CENTRE [ID:5165]

School of Business
MBA: concentration in International Business
[ID:5161]

INTERNATIONAL STUDIES/AFFAIRS

Centre for Foreign Policy Studies
RESEARCH CENTRE [ID:5449]

Department of Political Science
BA (Honours), MA & PhD IN POLITICAL SCIENCE: specialization in International Politics, Foreign Policy or International Development
[ID:5166]

ÉCOLE NATIONALE D'ADMINISTRATION PUBLIQUE (ENAP)

INTERNATIONAL BUSINESS

Administration internationale
D.E.S.S. EN ADMINISTRATION
INTERNATIONALE [ID:7282]

Administration publique
M.A. ADMINISTRATION PUBLIQUE, option pour
gestionnaires, concentration management international
[ID:7285]

INTERNATIONAL STUDIES/AFFAIRS

Administration publique
MAÎTRISE EN ADMINISTRATION PUBLIQUE,
option pour analystes, concentration administration
internationale [ID:7267]

FIRST NATIONS UNIVERSITY OF CANADA

INTERNATIONAL STUDIES/AFFAIRS

**Indigenous Centre for
International Development**
CERTIFICATE IN INDIGENOUS
MANAGEMENT: International emphasis [ID:5281]

FLEMING COLLEGE

INTERNATIONAL BUSINESS

International Education Office
DIPLOMA IN INTERNATIONAL TRADE
[ID:5287]

COLLÈGE FRANÇOIS-XAVIER-GARNEAU

INTERNATIONAL STUDIES/AFFAIRS

Baccalauréat international
DIPLÔME D'ÉTUDES COLLÉGIALES [ID:7253]

GEORGE BROWN COLLEGE

INTERNATIONAL BUSINESS

International Trade Program
INTERNATIONAL TRADE CERTIFICATE
[ID:5224]

GRANT MACEWAN COLLEGE

AREA STUDIES

Canada Ukraine Research Team (CURT)
RESEARCH CENTRE [ID:5033]

INTERNATIONAL BUSINESS

**Applied International Business &
Supply Chain Management Program**
BACHELOR OF APPLIED INTERNATIONAL
BUSINESS & SUPPLY CHAIN MANAGEMENT
[ID:5032]

Asia-Pacific Management Program
DIPLOMA IN ASIA-PACIFIC MANAGEMENT
[ID:5485]

UNIVERSITY OF GUELPH

INTERNATIONAL PROFILE
[ID:5434]

AREA STUDIES

European Studies Program
BA (Honours) IN EUROPEAN STUDIES
[ID:5087]

Scottish Studies Program
MA & PhD IN SCOTTISH STUDIES [ID:5308]

DEVELOPMENT STUDIES

**Collaborative International Development
Studies Program (CIDS)**
BA, BA (Honours), MA & MSc IN
INTERNATIONAL DEVELOPMENT STUDIES
[ID:5361]

Department of Political Science
BA & MA IN POLITICAL SCIENCE: focus on
Comparative/International Development; Participant
in Collaborative PhD in Rural Studies Program
[ID:5362]

**Don Snowden Program for Development
Communication**
RESEARCH CENTRE [ID:5194]

**School of Environmental Design & Rural
Development (SEDRD)**
, PhD & GRADUATE DIPLOMA IN
INTERNATIONAL RURAL PLANNING AND
DEVELOPMENT [ID:5364]

HEC MONTRÉAL

INTERNATIONAL PROFILE
[ID:7317]

INTERNATIONAL BUSINESS

Administration internationale
Ph. D en administration internationale [ID:7232]

Centre d'études en administration internationale (CETAI)
CENTRE DE RECHERCHE [ID:7298]

Commerce international
CERTIFICAT EN COMMERCE INTERNATIONAL [ID:7257]

Gestion internationale
B.A.A. spécialisation en gestion internationale [ID:7256]

Gestion internationale
MSc profil gestion internationale [ID:7247]

Gestion internationale
M.B.A. profil gestion internationale [ID:7231]

HUMBER COLLEGE INSTITUTE OF TECHNOLOGY AND ADVANCED LEARNING

DEVELOPMENT STUDIES

International Project Management Postgraduate Program
POSTGRADUATE CERTIFICATE IN INTERNATIONAL PROJECT MANAGEMENT [ID:5172]

INTERNATIONAL BUSINESS

International Marketing Postgraduate Program
POSTGRADUATE CERTIFICATE IN INTERNATIONAL MARKETING [ID:5426]

LAKEHEAD UNIVERSITY

INTERNATIONAL STUDIES/AFFAIRS

Department of Political Science
BA & BA (Honours) IN POLITICAL SCIENCE: minor in International Politics [ID:5410]

LANGARA COLLEGE

AREA STUDIES

Latin American Studies Program
DIPLOMA & ASSOCIATE OF ARTS (AA): concentration IN LATIN AMERICAN STUDIES [ID:5403]

Pacific Rim Studies Program
DIPLOMA IN PACIFIC RIM STUDIES [ID:5253]

INTERNATIONAL BUSINESS

Department of Business Management
DIPLOMA IN INTERNATIONAL BUSINESS [ID:5251]

PEACE/CONFLICT STUDIES

Peace and Conflict Studies Program
DIPLOMA & ASSOCIATE OF ARTS (AA) IN PEACE AND CONFLICT STUDIES [ID:5252]

UNIVERSITÉ LAVAL

INTERNATIONAL PROFILE
[ID:7333]

AREA STUDIES

Centre d'études nordiques
CENTRE DE RECHERCHE [ID:7290]

Centre interdisciplinaire de recherches sur les activités langagières (CIRAL)
CENTRE DE RECHERCHE [ID:7300]

Études russes
CERTIFICAT OU MICROPROGRAMME EN ÉTUDES RUSSES [ID:7289]

INTERNATIONAL BUSINESS

Gestion internationale
M.B.A. concentration en gestion internationale [ID:7291]

INTERNATIONAL STUDIES/AFFAIRS

Institut québécois des hautes études internationales
[ID:7297]

Journalisme international
DIPLÔME D'ÉTUDES SUPÉRIEURES EN JOURNALISME INTERNATIONAL (2e cycle) [ID:7299]

Relations internationales
M.A. EN RELATIONS INTERNATIONALES [ID:7296]

LESTER B. PEARSON COLLEGE OF THE PACIFIC

INTERNATIONAL STUDIES/AFFAIRS

International Baccalaureate Program
INTERNATIONAL BACCALAUREATE [ID:5461]

UNIVERSITY OF LETHBRIDGE

INTERNATIONAL BUSINESS

Faculty of Management
BMgt: major in International Management [ID:5370]

UNIVERSITY OF MANITOBA

INTERNATIONAL PROFILE
[ID:5435]

AREA STUDIES

Asian Studies Centre
BA & BA: minor IN ASIAN STUDIES [ID:5371]

**Central and Eastern
European Studies Program**
BA IN CENTRAL AND EASTERN EUROPEAN
STUDIES [ID:5372]

Latin American Studies Program
BA: minor in Latin American Studies [ID:5373]

INTERNATIONAL BUSINESS

I.H. Asper School of Business
BComm (Honours) IN INTERNATIONAL
BUSINESS [ID:5242]

INTERNATIONAL STUDIES/AFFAIRS

Centre for Defence and Security Studies
RESEARCH CENTRE [ID:5309]

Global Political Economy Program
BA & BA (Advanced) IN GLOBAL POLITICAL
ECONOMY [ID:5243]

McGILL UNIVERSITY

INTERNATIONAL PROFILE
[ID:5436]

AREA STUDIES

Centre for East Asian Research
RESEARCH CENTRE [ID:5175]

East Asian Studies Program
BA (Honours & Joint Honours), BA: minor, MA &
PhD IN EAST ASIAN STUDIES [ID:5167]

Institute of Islamic Studies
MA & PhD IN ISLAMIC STUDIES [ID:5176]

**Latin American and Caribbean
Studies Program**
BA & BA (Honours) IN LATIN AMERICAN AND
CARIBBEAN STUDIES [ID:5177]

Middle East Studies Program
BA & BA (Honours, Joint Honours, Joint Major) IN
MIDDLE EAST STUDIES [ID:5178]

North American Studies Program
BA & BA: minor IN NORTH AMERICAN
STUDIES [ID:5179]

DEVELOPMENT STUDIES

**Centre for Developing-Area
Studies (CDAS)**
RESEARCH CENTRE [ID:5181]

**Centre for Society, Technology and
Development (STANDD)**
RESEARCH CENTRE [ID:5191]

**International Development
Studies Program**
BA, BA (Honours & Joint Honours) & BA: minor IN
INTERNATIONAL DEVELOPMENT STUDIES
[ID:5180]

School of Architecture
MArch IN MINIMUM COST HOUSING IN
DEVELOPING COUNTRIES [ID:5405]

INTERNATIONAL BUSINESS

**Centre for International
Management Studies**
RESEARCH CENTRE [ID:5183]

Faculty of Management
BCom: option in International Management
[ID:5197]

Faculty of Management
MBA: concentration in International Business
[ID:5182]

INTERNATIONAL LAW

Institute of Air and Space Law
RESEARCH CENTRE; GRADUATE
CERTIFICATE, LLM & DCL IN AIR AND SPACE
LAW [ID:5189]

Institute of Comparative Law (ICL)
LLM: concentration in International Business Law,
Human Rights or Cultural Diversity; GRADUATE
CERTIFICATE IN COMPARATIVE LAW
[ID:5184]

INTERNATIONAL STUDIES/AFFAIRS

Department of Political Science
MA & PhD IN POLITICAL SCIENCE:
specialization in Comparative Government and
Politics in Developing Countries or International
Politics [ID:5190]

McMASTER UNIVERSITY

INTERNATIONAL PROFILE
[ID:5437]

AREA STUDIES

Japanese Studies Program
BA (Combined Honours) & BA: minor IN
JAPANESE STUDIES [ID:5310]

INTERNATIONAL STUDIES/AFFAIRS

Department of Political Science
MA & PhD IN POLITICAL SCIENCE: concentration
in International Relations or Comparative Politics
[ID:5192]

**Institute on Globalization and
the Human Condition (IGHC)**
RESEARCH CENTRE; MA in GLOBALIZATION
STUDIES [ID:5201]

PEACE/CONFLICT STUDIES

Centre for Peace Studies
BA (Combined Honours) & BA: minor IN PEACE
STUDIES [ID:5193]

MEMORIAL UNIVERSITY OF NEWFOUNDLAND

INTERNATIONAL BUSINESS

Centre for International Business Studies
RESEARCH CENTRE [ID:5311]

UNIVERSITÉ DE MONCTON

INTERNATIONAL PROFILE
[ID:7235]

INTERNATIONAL BUSINESS

Centre de commercialisation internationale (CCI)
CENTRE DE RECHERCHE [ID:7250]

Commerce international
B.A.: concentration commerce international
[ID:7249]

INTERNATIONAL LAW

Études de la common law
CENTRE INTERNATIONAL DE LA COMMON LAW (CICLEF), DIPLÔME D'ÉTUDES EN COMMON LAW (D.E.C.L.), M.A. EN DROIT, FORMATION MÉDIATISÉE [ID:7234]

UNIVERSITÉ DE MONTRÉAL

INTERNATIONAL PROFILE
[ID:7331]

AREA STUDIES

Centre canadien d'études allemandes et européennes
CENTRE DE RECHERCHE, MINEUR EN ÉTUDES EUROPÉENNES (1er CYCLE), DIPLÔME COMPLÉMENTAIRE EN ÉTUDES ALLEMANDES DANS LE CONTEXTE EUROPÉEN (CYCLES SUPÉRIEURS) [ID:7236]

Centre d'études de l'Asie de l'Est
CENTRE DE RECHERCHE, B.A., MAJEUR, MINEUR EN ÉTUDES EST-ASIATIQUES
[ID:7304]

Études arabes
MINEUR EN ÉTUDES ARABES (1er cycle)
[ID:7251]

Études italiennes
MAJEUR & MINEUR EN ÉTUDES ITALIENNES
(1er cycle) [ID:7302]

Études latino-américaines
MINEUR EN ÉTUDES LATINO-AMÉRICAINES
(1er cycle) [ID:7252]

Langue et littérature allemande
MINEUR, MAJEUR, B.A., M.A. EN ÉTUDES ALLEMANDES [ID:7307]

Langue et littérature espagnole
MINEUR, MAJEUR, B.A., M.A. EN ÉTUDES HISPANIQUES [ID:7308]

Langue et littérature portugaises
MINEUR EN LANGUE PORTUGAISE & CULTURES LUSOPHONES (1er cycle) [ID:7309]

DEVELOPMENT STUDIES

Gestion urbaine pour les pays en voie de développement
DIPLÔME D'ÉTUDES SUPÉRIEURES SPÉCIALISÉES EN GESTION URBAINE POUR LES PAYS EN VOIE DE DÉVELOPPEMENT
[ID:7301]

Centre d'études ethniques des universités montréalaises (CEETUM)
CENTRE DE RECHERCHE [ID:7324]

INTERCULTURAL STUDIES

Groupe de recherche ethnicité et société
GROUPE DE RECHERCHE [ID:7330]

INTERNATIONAL EDUCATION

Éducation comparée et internationale
DIPLÔME D'ÉTUDES SUPÉRIEURES SPÉCIALISÉES EN ÉDUCATION COMPARÉE ET INTERNATIONALE [ID:7262]

INTERNATIONAL SCIENCES

Unité de santé internationale
CENTRE DE RECHERCHE [ID:7237]

INTERNATIONAL STUDIES/AFFAIRS

Centre de recherche sur les transports
CENTRE DE RECHERCHE [ID:7326]

Centre international de criminologie comparée (CICC)
CENTRE DE RECHERCHE [ID:7325]

Sciences économiques
MSc ÉCONOMIQUE: options économie du développement ou économie et finances internationales [ID:7303]

MOUNT ALLISON UNIVERSITY

AREA STUDIES

American Studies Program
BA & BA (Honours) IN AMERICAN STUDIES
[ID:5312]

Japanese Studies Program
BA: minor in Japanese Studies [ID:5455]

INTERNATIONAL STUDIES/AFFAIRS

International Relations Programme
BA & BA (Honours) IN INTERNATIONAL RELATIONS [ID:5040]

NEW BRUNSWICK COMMUNITY COLLEGE - ST. ANDREWS

INTERNATIONAL BUSINESS

International Business: Latin American Studies Program
DIPLOMA IN INTERNATIONAL BUSINESS: LATIN AMERICAN STUDIES [ID:5131]

UNIVERSITY OF NEW BRUNSWICK

INTERNATIONAL PROFILE
[ID:5438]

AREA STUDIES

Russian and Eurasian Studies Program
BA & BA: minor IN RUSSIAN AND EURASIAN STUDIES [ID:5313]

DEVELOPMENT STUDIES

International Development Studies Program
BA (Joint Major & Joint Honours) & BA: minor IN INTERNATIONAL DEVELOPMENT STUDIES; BA IN THIRD WORLD STUDIES [ID:5342]

INTERNATIONAL BUSINESS

Centre for International Business Studies
RESEARCH CENTRE [ID:5344]

Faculty of Administration
BBA & MBA: concentration in International Business [ID:5343]

Faculty of Business
MBA: concentration in International Business [ID:5223]

INTERNATIONAL STUDIES/AFFAIRS

Military and Strategic Studies Program
Undergraduate and Graduate Courses [ID:5039]

PEACE/CONFLICT STUDIES

Centre for Conflict Studies
RESEARCH CENTRE [ID:5345]

NIPISSING UNIVERSITY

DEVELOPMENT STUDIES

Faculty of Arts and Sciences
BA IN GEOGRAPHY OF REGIONAL PLANNING AND INTERNATIONAL DEVELOPMENT [ID:5314]

UNIVERSITY OF NORTHERN BRITISH COLUMBIA

INTERNATIONAL STUDIES/AFFAIRS

International Studies
BA & MA IN INTERNATIONAL STUDIES [ID:5325]

COLLÈGE COMMUNAUTAIRE DU NOUVEAU-BRUNSWICK BATHURST

DEVELOPMENT STUDIES

Technologie du commerce international
DIPLÔME EN TECHNOLOGIE DU COMMERCE INTERNATIONAL [ID:7265]

UNIVERSITY OF OTTAWA

INTERNATIONAL PROFILE
[ID:5439]

DEVELOPMENT STUDIES

International Development and Globalization Program
BSocSc (Honours) IN INTERNATIONAL DEVELOPMENT AND GLOBALIZATION [ID:5212]

Sociologie du développement
M.A. EN SOCIOLOGIE: spécialisation en sociologie du développement [ID:7248]

INTERNATIONAL BUSINESS

Faculty of Administration
BComm: option in International Management [ID:5297]

INTERNATIONAL LAW

Centre for Trade Policy and Law (CTPL)
RESEARCH CENTRE [ID:5056]

Human Rights Research and Education Centre (HRREC)
RESEARCH CENTRE [ID:5346]

INTERNATIONAL STUDIES/AFFAIRS

Department of Economics
PhD IN ECONOMICS: specialization in International Economics and the Economics of Natural Resources and the Environment [ID:5374]

Global Studies Program
BSocSc: concentration in Global Studies [ID:5214]

Governance and Public Policy
BSocSc: concentration in Governance and Public Policy [ID:5061]

International Relations and Global Politics
BSocSc: concentration in International Relations and Global Politics [ID:5017]

International Studies and Modern Languages Program
BSocSc (Honours) IN INTERNATIONAL STUDIES AND MODERN LANGUAGES [ID:5213]

UNIVERSITY OF PRINCE EDWARD ISLAND

INTERNATIONAL EDUCATION

Faculty of Education
BEd: specialization in International Education
[ID:5459]

UNIVERSITÉ DU QUÉBEC À CHICOUTIMI

AREA STUDIES

Études régionales et développement régional
M.A. EN ÉTUDES RÉGIONALES et Ph. D. EN DÉVELOPPEMENT RÉGIONAL [ID:7288]

INTERCULTURAL STUDIES

Chaire d'enseignement et de recherche interethniques et interculturels (CERII)
CENTRE DE RECHERCHE [ID:7315]

UNIVERSITÉ DU QUÉBEC À MONTRÉAL

INTERNATIONAL PROFILE
[ID:7332]

DEVELOPMENT STUDIES

Centre interuniversitaire Paul-Gérin-Lajoie de développement international en éducation (CIPGL)
CENTRE DE RECHERCHE [ID:7280]

Chaire Unesco-Bell en communication et développement international
CENTRE DE RECHERCHE [ID:7278]

INTERCULTURAL STUDIES

Immigration et relations interethniques, Module de sociologie
CERTIFICAT EN IMMIGRATION ET RELATIONS INTERETHNIQUES [ID:7287]

INTERNATIONAL BUSINESS

Bureau de la coopération internationale du Département des sciences administratives
CENTRE DE RECHERCHE [ID:7286]

École des sciences de la gestion
B.A.A. ADMINISTRATION, concentration gestion internationale, concentration carrière internationale [ID:7284]

Programme de M.B.A. Recherche
M.B.A. avec spécialisation en gestion internationale [ID:7306]

Sciences de la gestion, commerce international
CERTIFICAT EN COMMERCE INTERNATIONAL [ID:7305]

INTERNATIONAL STUDIES/AFFAIRS

Centre d'études internationales et mondialisation
CENTRE DE RECHERCHE [ID:7279]

Institut d'études internationales de Montréal
CENTRE DE RECHERCHE [ID:7263]

Relations internationales
B.A. EN RELATIONS INTERNATIONALES ET DROIT INTERNATIONAL [ID:7264]

Sciences politiques
M.A. SCIENCE POLITIQUE concentration Relations internationales, politique étrangère, coopération et développement / concentration politique internationale - droit international [ID:7281]

PEACE/CONFLICT STUDIES

Centre d'études des politiques étrangères et de sécurité (CEPES)
CENTRE DE RECHERCHE [ID:7310]

Chaire Raoul-Dandurand en études stratégiques et diplomatiques
CENTRE DE RECHERCHE [ID:7314]

Groupe de recherche sur l'industrie militaire et la sécurité
GROUPE DE RECHERCHE [ID:7316]

UNIVERSITÉ DU QUÉBEC À RIMOUSKI

DEVELOPMENT STUDIES

Développement régional
M.A. et Ph. D. EN DÉVELOPPEMENT RÉGIONAL, DIPLÔME DE DEUXIÈME CYCLE EN ADMINISTRATION PUBLIQUE RÉGIONALE [ID:7283]

INTERNATIONAL STUDIES/AFFAIRS

Gestion de projet
D.E.S.S., M.G.P. ou M.Sc. EN GESTION DE PROJET [ID:7329]

Maîtrise en gestion des ressources maritimes
D.E.S.S. et M.Sc. EN GESTION DES RESSOURCES MARITIMES [ID:7312]

Océanographie
CENTRE DE RECHERCHE, M.Sc. et Ph. D. EN OCÉANOGRAPHIE [ID:7233]

QUEEN'S UNIVERSITY

INTERNATIONAL PROFILE
[ID:5444]

AREA STUDIES

**Department of German
Languages and Literature**
BA, MA & PhD IN GERMANIC LANGUAGE AND
LITERATURE [ID:5415]

Jewish Studies Program
BA & BA (Honours): minor IN JEWISH STUDIES
[ID:5185]

DEVELOPMENT STUDIES

Development Studies Medial
BA (Honours) IN DEVELOPMENT STUDIES
[ID:5298]

INTERNATIONAL BUSINESS

School of Business
BComm: concentration in International Business
[ID:5237]

INTERNATIONAL HEALTH

**International Centre for the
Advancement of Community-Based
Rehabilitation (ICACBR)**
RESEARCH CENTRE [ID:5451]

INTERNATIONAL LAW

Faculty of Law
LLM: concentration in International Legal Studies
[ID:5269]

**International Law Program
(International Study Centre)**
CERTIFICATE OF COMPLETION IN
INTERNATIONAL BUSINESS LAW;
CERTIFICATE OF COMPLETION IN PUBLIC
INTERNATIONAL LAW [ID:5258]

INTERNATIONAL STUDIES/AFFAIRS

Centre for International Relations
RESEARCH CENTRE [ID:5271]

Department of Political Studies
MA & PhD IN POLITICAL STUDIES: concentration
in International Politics or Comparative Politics
[ID:5270]

**Institute of Intergovernmental
Relations (IIGR)**
RESEARCH CENTRE [ID:5208]

International Studies
CERTIFICATE IN INTERNATIONAL STUDIES
[ID:5206]

International Study Centre (ISC)
FIRST-YEAR & UPPER YEAR PROGRAM
[ID:5254]

School of Policy Studies
MPA IN PUBLIC ADMINISTRATION: optional
concentrations in Defence Management, Health
Policy, the Third Sector, Social Policy or Global
Governance [ID:5207]

UNIVERSITY OF REGINA

INTERNATIONAL PROFILE
[ID:5445]

INTERNATIONAL EDUCATION

**Centre for International
Education and Training (CIET)**
RESEARCH CENTRE [ID:5454]

INTERNATIONAL LAW

Department of Justice Studies
BA IN HUMAN JUSTICE; BA, MA &
ADVANCED CERTIFICATE IN JUSTICE
STUDIES [ID:5375]

CÉGEP DE RIVIÈRE-DU-LOUP

DEVELOPMENT STUDIES

Programme Coopérant-Volontaire
ATTESTATION D'ÉTUDES COLLÉGIALES EN
COOPÉRATION INTERCULTURELLE [ID:7254]

ROYAL MILITARY
COLLEGE OF CANADA

PEACE/CONFLICT STUDIES

Faculty of Arts
MA IN WAR STUDIES [ID:5279]

SAINT MARY'S UNIVERSITY

AREA STUDIES

Asian Studies Program
BA & BA: minor IN ASIAN STUDIES;
CERTIFICATE IN CHINESE AND JAPANESE
STUDIES [ID:5187]

DEVELOPMENT STUDIES

International Development Studies (IDS)
BA, BA (Honours), MA & GRADUATE DIPLOMA
IN INTERNATIONAL DEVELOPMENT STUDIES
[ID:5280]

INTERNATIONAL BUSINESS

Sobey School of Business
BComm: major in Global Business Studies
[ID:5188]

UNIVERSITY OF SASKATCHEWAN

INTERNATIONAL BUSINESS

Centre for International Business Studies
RESEARCH CENTRE [ID:5376]

INTERNATIONAL STUDIES/AFFAIRS

International Studies Program
BA & BA (Honours) IN INTERNATIONAL STUDIES: emphasis in Development Studies, International Cooperation and Conflict, Latin American Studies or Slavic and East European Studies [ID:5377]

UNIVERSITÉ DE SHERBROOKE

DEVELOPMENT STUDIES

IRECUS - Gestion du développement des coopératives et des collectivités et Institut de recherche et d'enseignement pour les coopératives de l'Université de Sherbrooke
CENTRE DE RECHERCHE et M.Sc. EN GESTION DU DÉVELOPPEMENT DES COOPÉRATIVES ET DES COLLECTIVITÉS [ID:7266]

INTERNATIONAL BUSINESS

Gestion internationale
M.A. EN ADMINISTRATION, cheminement gestion internationale [ID:7311]

SHERIDAN COLLEGE

INTERNATIONAL BUSINESS

Post-Graduate International Business Program
POST-GRADUATE DIPLOMA IN INTERNATIONAL BUSINESS [ID:5427]

SIMON FRASER UNIVERSITY

INTERNATIONAL PROFILE
[ID:5446]

AREA STUDIES

Faculty of Arts
CERTIFICATE IN CHINESE STUDIES [ID:5283]

Latin American Studies Program
BA (Joint Major), BA: minor or extended minor & MA IN LATIN AMERICAN STUDIES [ID:5282]

INTERCULTURAL STUDIES

David Lam Centre for International Communication
NON-CREDIT PROGRAM IN EAST ASIAN LANGUAGES [ID:5284]

Department of Sociology and Anthropology
CERTIFICATE IN ETHNIC AND INTERCULTURAL RELATIONS [ID:5285]

INTERNATIONAL BUSINESS

Faculty of Business Administration
BBA & MBA: concentration in International Business [ID:5286]

INTERNATIONAL LAW

International Centre for Criminal Law Reform and Criminal Justice Policy (ICCLR)
RESEARCH CENTRE [ID:5246]

INTERNATIONAL STUDIES/AFFAIRS

Centre for Global Political Economy
RESEARCH CENTRE [ID:5245]

Department of Political Science
MA & PhD IN POLITICAL SCIENCE: focus in Comparative Politics and International Relations [ID:5063]

ST. FRANCIS XAVIER UNIVERSITY

AREA STUDIES

Department of Celtic Studies
BA IN CELTIC STUDIES [ID:5186]

DEVELOPMENT STUDIES

Development Studies Program
BA (Joint Major or Joint Advanced Major) & BA: minor IN DEVELOPMENT STUDIES [ID:5062]

UNIVERSITY OF TORONTO

INTERNATIONAL PROFILE
[ID:5078]

AREA STUDIES

African Studies Program
BA, BA (Honours & Specialist) & BA: minor IN AFRICAN STUDIES [ID:5378]

American Studies Program
BA & BA: minor IN AMERICAN STUDIES [ID:5381]

Centre for Russian and East European Studies (CREES)
RESEARCH CENTRE; MA, MA/MBA & MA/JD IN RUSSIAN AND EAST EUROPEAN STUDIES [ID:5379]

Collaborative Master of Arts Program in Asia-Pacific Studies
MA IN ASIA-PACIFIC STUDIES [ID:5064]

Collaborative Program in South Asian Studies
COLLABORATIVE MA & PhD IN SOUTH ASIAN STUDIES [ID:5380]

Department of East Asian Studies
BA, BA (Specialist), BA: minor, MA & PhD IN EAST ASIAN STUDIES [ID:5337]

Department of Italian Studies
BA (Honours & Specialist), BA: minor, MA & PhD
IN ITALIAN STUDIES [ID:5099]

**Department of Near & Middle
Eastern Civilizations**
BA, MA & PhD IN NEAR EASTERN STUDIES
[ID:5382]

Institute for European Studies
BA IN EUROPEAN STUDIES [ID:5124]

Jewish Studies Program
BA, BA (Honours) & PhD IN JEWISH STUDIES
[ID:5100]

DEVELOPMENT STUDIES

International Development Studies (IDS)
BA & BSc: specialization in International
Development Studies (Cooperative Program); BA &
BA: minor in INTERNATIONAL DEVELOPMENT
STUDIES [ID:5226]

INTERNATIONAL EDUCATION

**The Comparative, International and
Development Education Centre (CIDE)**
MA, MEd, EdD & PhD: specialization in
Comparative, International or Development Education
[ID:5195]

INTERNATIONAL HEALTH

Centre for International Health
RESEARCH CENTRE [ID:5058]

INTERNATIONAL STUDIES/AFFAIRS

Centre for International Studies (CIS)
RESEARCH CENTRE [ID:5057]

Department of Political Science
BA, MA & PhD IN POLITICAL SCIENCE:
specialization in Development Studies, Comparative
Politics, Environmental Studies or International
Relations [ID:5227]

**International Relations
Collaborative Programme**
MA, MSc & COMBINED MA/JD IN
INTERNATIONAL RELATIONS [ID:5125]

International Relations Programme
BA, BA (Specialist) IN INTERNATIONAL
RELATIONS [ID:5229]

Munk Centre for International Studies
Various Degrees [ID:5129]

PEACE/CONFLICT STUDIES

**Trudeau Centre for Peace
and Conflict Studies**
BA IN PEACE AND CONFLICT STUDIES
[ID:5228]

TRENT UNIVERSITY

INTERNATIONAL PROFILE
[ID:5079]

AREA STUDIES

**Department of Modern
Languages and Literature**
BA & BA (Honours) IN HISPANIC STUDIES
[ID:5423]

German Studies
BA & BA (Honours) IN GERMAN STUDIES
[ID:5422]

DEVELOPMENT STUDIES

**International Development
Studies Program (IDS)**
BA, BA (Honours, Joint Honours & Joint Major) IN
INTERNATIONAL DEVELOPMENT STUDIES
[ID:5288]

INTERNATIONAL STUDIES/AFFAIRS

Department of Political Studies
BA & BA (Honours) IN POLITICAL STUDIES:
concentration in Global Politics [ID:5000]

Global Studies
BA (Honours): special concentration in Global
Studies; BA (Joint Honours): Globalization:
Communities and Identities; BA (Joint Honours): IN
INTERNATIONAL POLITICAL ECONOMY
[ID:5018]

VANIER COLLEGE

AREA STUDIES

Jewish Studies Program
DIPLOMA IN JEWISH STUDIES [ID:5386]

INTERNATIONAL STUDIES/AFFAIRS

International Studies Program
MAJOR IN INTERNATIONAL STUDIES
[ID:5387]

UNIVERSITY OF VICTORIA

INTERNATIONAL PROFILE
[ID:5080]

AREA STUDIES

Centre for Asia-Pacific Initiatives (CAPI)
RESEARCH CENTRE [ID:5393]

Department of Hispanic and Italian Studies
BA & BA: minor IN ITALIAN STUDIES; MA
(Combined) IN HISPANIC AND ITALIAN
STUDIES [ID:5424]

Department of Pacific and Asian Studies
BA, BA (Honours) & BA: minor IN PACIFIC
STUDIES [ID:5392]

INTERNATIONAL BUSINESS

Faculty of Business
MBA: specialization in International Business
[ID:5425]

Faculty of Business
BComm: concentration in International Management
[ID:5394]

INTERNATIONAL STUDIES/AFFAIRS

Centre for Global Studies
RESEARCH CENTRE [ID:5244]

PEACE/CONFLICT STUDIES

Institute for Dispute Resolution
RESEARCH CENTRE; MA IN DISPUTE
RESOLUTION (MADR) [ID:5103]

UNIVERSITY OF WATERLOO

INTERNATIONAL PROFILE
[ID:5081]

AREA STUDIES

Waterloo Centre for German Studies
RESEARCH CENTRE [ID:5091]

DEVELOPMENT STUDIES

**Local Economic Development
Program (LED)**
MAES IN LOCAL ECONOMIC DEVELOPMENT
[ID:5090]

INTERNATIONAL BUSINESS

Department of Economics
BA & BA (Honours and/or Co-op) IN ECONOMICS:
specialization in International Economics [ID:5463]

Department of Economics
BA (Honours): Arts and Business Co-op
specialization in International Trade [ID:5395]

INTERNATIONAL STUDIES/AFFAIRS

International Studies Program
ALL FACULTIES: option in International Studies
[ID:5396]

PEACE/CONFLICT STUDIES

**Peace and Conflict Studies
Program (PACS)**
BA & BES (General, Honours & Joint Major): option
in Peace and Conflict Studies; ALL FACULTIES
(Honours): minor in Peace and Conflict Studies;
DIPLOMA IN PEACE AND CONFLICT STUDIES
[ID:5397]

UNIVERSITY OF WESTERN ONTARIO

INTERNATIONAL PROFILE
[ID:5082]

AREA STUDIES

Centre for American Studies
RESEARCH CENTRE; BA (Honours) & BA: minor
IN AMERICAN STUDIES [ID:5209]

INTERNATIONAL BUSINESS

Richard Ivey School of Business
HBA & MBA: specialization in International Business
[ID:5398]

INTERNATIONAL STUDIES/AFFAIRS

**Centre for the Study of International
Economic Relations (CSIER)**
RESEARCH CENTRE [ID:5211]

Department of Sociology
MA & PhD IN SOCIOLOGY: specialization in
Social Demography [ID:5210]

WILFRID LAURIER UNIVERSITY

INTERNATIONAL STUDIES/AFFAIRS

Global Studies Program (GS)
BA, BA (Combined Honours) & BA: minor IN
GLOBAL STUDIES [ID:5041]

UNIVERSITY OF WINDSOR

INTERCULTURAL STUDIES

Multicultural Studies Program
BA IN MULTICULTURAL STUDIES [ID:5104]

INTERNATIONAL BUSINESS

Odette School of Business
BComm & MBA IN INTERNATIONAL BUSINESS
[ID:5111]

INTERNATIONAL STUDIES/AFFAIRS

**International Relations and
Development Studies Program**
BA (Honours) IN INTERNATIONAL RELATIONS
AND DEVELOPMENT STUDIES; MA IN
POLITICAL SCIENCE: specialization in
International Relations [ID:5399]

UNIVERSITY OF WINNIPEG

INTERNATIONAL PROFILE
[ID:5083]

DEVELOPMENT STUDIES

International Development Studies
BA IN INTERNATIONAL DEVELOPMENT
STUDIES [ID:5400]

INTERNATIONAL SCIENCES

Environmental Studies/ Urban Studies Program
BA & BSc IN ENVIRONMENTAL AND URBAN STUDIES [ID:5105]

INTERNATIONAL STUDIES/AFFAIRS

Department of Political Science
BA & BA (Honours) IN POLITICAL SCIENCE: concentrations in: Global Politics, Canadian and Comparative Politics [ID:5401]

PEACE/CONFLICT STUDIES

Conflict Resolution Studies Program
BA IN CONFLICT RESOLUTION STUDIES [ID:5402]

YORK UNIVERSITY

INTERNATIONAL PROFILE
[ID:5107]

AREA STUDIES

African Studies Program
BA (Honours) IN AFRICAN STUDIES [ID:5404]

Centre for Jewish Studies
RESEARCH CENTRE [ID:5106]

Centre for Research on Latin America and the Caribbean (CERLAC)
RESEARCH CENTRE; GRADUATE DIPLOMA IN LATIN AMERICAN AND CARIBBEAN STUDIES [ID:5230]

East Asian Studies Programme
BA, BA (Specialized Honours, Honours, Honours Double Major) & BA: minor IN EAST ASIAN STUDIES [ID:5231]

European Studies Program
BA (Honours & Honours Double Major) & BA: minor IN EUROPEAN STUDIES [ID:5173]

Jewish Studies Program
BA IN JEWISH STUDIES [ID:5222]

Latin American and Caribbean Studies Program
BA (Honours) & BA (Honours): minor IN LATIN AMERICAN AND CARIBBEAN STUDIES [ID:5219]

York Centre for Asian Research (YCAR)
RESEARCH CENTRE [ID:5170]

DEVELOPMENT STUDIES

Centre for Refugee Studies
RESEARCH CENTRE; GENERAL CERTIFICATE & GRADUATE DIPLOMA IN REFUGEE AND MIGRATION STUDIES [ID:5221]

Faculty of Environmental Studies (FES)
BES, MES & PhD IN ENVIRONMENTAL STUDIES [ID:5220]

International Development Studies
BA, BA (Specialized Honours, Honours, Honours Double Major), BA (Honours): minor IN INTERNATIONAL DEVELOPMENT STUDIES [ID:5171]

INTERNATIONAL BUSINESS

Schulich School of Business
INTERNATIONAL MBA (IMBA) [ID:5385]

Schulich School of Business
INTERNATIONAL BACHELOR OF BUSINESS ADMINISTRATION (iBBA) [ID:5169]

INTERNATIONAL LAW

Osgoode Hall Law School
LLB: concentration in International, Comparative and Transnational (ICT) Law [ID:5406]

INTERNATIONAL STUDIES/AFFAIRS

Department of Political Science
BA (Specialized Honours) IN GLOBAL POLITICAL STUDIES [ID:5065]

Department of Political Science
BA (Honours), MA & PhD IN POLITICAL SCIENCE: concentration in International Relations; BA (Specialized Honours) IN GLOBAL POLITICAL STUDIES [ID:5473]

International Studies Programme (ISP)
BA (Honours, Combined Honours, Specialized Honours & Double Major) IN INTERNATIONAL STUDIES [ID:5474]

PEACE/CONFLICT STUDIES

York Centre for International and Security Studies (YCISS)
GRADUATE DIPLOMA IN STRATEGIC STUDIES [ID:5475]

CHAPTER 16

International Studies – The World's Top Schools

Are you interested in studying international law, international affairs, international business, international health or other programs in international studies? If so, this chapter is for you. We have documented a selection of the 119 world's top international studies programs to assist you in your selection of an overseas university. The programs listed here are recommended by academics and professionals and are located at schools around the world that have solid reputations and that include English as a language of instruction. The programs are grouped under eight areas of study, representing the most popular international disciplines. We have strived to list a variety of programs in order to make the list representative of the wider world. For example, the inclusion of US schools and programs is by no means exhaustive since we have made an attempt to balance their representation with those outside of the US.

A LAST WORD

This list will provide you with a starting point to investigate the exciting world of international studies overseas. For a more detailed description of why you should pursue international studies, read the introductory text and consult the Resources section in Chapter 15, International Studies in Canada. For general advice about studying in another country, see Chapter 13, Study Abroad.

A Selection of the World's Top Schools

This list documents 119 selected international studies programs from around the world. The list is in alphabetical order and is divided into the following eight areas of study: development studies, 16; intercultural studies, 7; international business, 21; international education, 11; international health, 11; international law, 13; international studies (such as international affairs/relations), 30; and peace/conflict studies, 10. Note that the Canadian schools in this list are fully profiled in Appendix 15a, "Profiles to Chapter 15: International Studies in Canada" on the CD-ROM.

Thirty-seven universities are based in the US, 28 in the UK, 6 in Australia and New Zealand, 5 in Canada, 8 in Japan, 13 in Western Europe and the remaining 17 are spread across Africa, Asia, the Caribbean, the Middle East and the Pacific region. Degrees or courses from abroad may not always be recognized by Canadian universities (particularly those from developing countries). However, we've included them to encourage you to gain invaluable cross-cultural experience.

Development Studies

AUSTRALIAN NATIONAL UNIVERSITY
School of Archaeology and Anthropology

BA IN DEVELOPMENT STUDIES ◆ Faculty of Arts, AD Hope Bldg., Australian National University, Canberra, ACT 0200, Australia; (61) (2) 253498, fax (61) (2) 252711, admin.arch&anth@anu.edu.au, www.anu.edu.au [ID:5277]

CORNELL UNIVERSITY
College of Agriculture
and Life Sciences (CALS)

MASTERS OF PROFESSIONAL STUDIES (MPS) IN INTERNATIONAL DEVELOPMENT ◆ Academic Programs Director, International Programs/CALS, 33 Warren Hall, Cornell University, Ithaca, NY, 14853-4203, USA; 607-255-3037, mpsid@cornell.edu, ip.cals.cornell.edu [ID:5304]

UNIVERSITY OF EAST ANGLIA
School of Development Studies

BA, MA, MRes, GRADUATE DIPLOMA, MPhil & PhD IN DEVELOPMENT STUDIES; MA IN DEVELOPMENT ECONOMICS, GENDER ANALYSIS IN DEVELOPMENT, RURAL DEVELOPMENT; MSc IN ENVIRONMENT AND DEVELOPMENT; MRes IN DEVELOPMENT STUDIES ◆ Undergraduate Admissions or Post-graduate Admissions, School of Development Studies, University of East Anglia, Norwich, NR4 7TJ, UK; (44) (1603) 592807, fax (44) (1603) 451999, dev.general@uea.ac.uk, www.uea.ac.uk/dev [ID:5216]

UNIVERSITY OF GUYANA
Institute of Development Studies

POST-GRADUATE DIPLOMA IN DEVELOPMENT STUDIES ◆ Faculty of Social Sciences, University of Guyana. P.O.Box 101110, Turkeyen, Greater Georgetown, Guyana; (592) 222-4184, www.uog.edu.gy [ID:5291]

INSTITUTE OF SOCIAL STUDIES
Institute of Social Studies

MA & PhD IN DEVELOPMENT STUDIES ◆ P.O. Box 29776, 2502 LT, The Hague, Netherlands; (31) (70) 426-0460, fax (31) (70) 426-0799, student.office@iss.nl, www.iss.nl [ID:5101]

INTERNATIONAL INSTITUTE
FOR POPULATION SCIENCES
International Institute for Population Sciences

MA & MPhil IN POPULATION STUDIES ◆ Director, International Institute for Population Sciences, Govandi Station Road, Deonar, Mumbai, 400 088, India; (91) (22) 2556 3254, fax (91) (22) 2556 3257, diriips@vsnl.com, www.iipsindia.org [ID:5247]

INTERNATIONAL
UNIVERSITY OF JAPAN
International Development Program

MA IN INTERNATIONAL DEVELOPMENT ◆ Office of the Graduate School of International Relations, International University of Japan, Yamato-machi, Minami Uonuma-gun, Niigata, 949-7277, Japan; (81) (257) 79-1200, fax 81 (257) 79-1187, admgsir@iuj.ac.jp, www.iuj.ac.jp [ID:5321]

KOBE UNIVERSITY
Graduate School of
International Cooperation Studies

MA IN ECONOMIC DEVELOPMENT AND POLICIES, INTERNATIONAL COOPERATION POLICY STUDIES, REGIONAL COOPERATION POLICY STUDIES ◆ 2-1 Rokkodai, Nada-ku, Kobe, Hyogo, 657-8501, Japan; (81) (78) 803-7267, www.kobe-u.ac.jp/en [ID:5276]

LONDON SCHOOL OF ECONOMICS
AND POLITICAL SCIENCE
Development Studies Institute (DESTIN)

MSc IN DEVELOPMENT STUDIES, DEVELOPMENT MANAGEMENT, ENVIRONMENT AND DEVELOPMENT, ANTHROPOLOGY AND DEVELOPMENT, GENDER AND DEVELOPMENT, POPULATION AND DEVELOPMENT ◆ Director, Development Studies Institute (DESTIN), London School of Economics and Political Science, Houghton Street, London, WC2A 2AE, UK; (44) (20) 7955-7425, fax (44) (20) 7955-6844, www.lse.ac.uk/Depts/destin [ID:5335]

UNIVERSITY OF LONDON
Department of Development Studies

BA, MSc, MPhil & PhD IN DEVELOPMENT STUDIES; MSc IN DEVELOPMENT STUDIES: special reference to Central Asia; MSc IN VIOLENCE, CONFLICT & DEVELOPMENT ◆ Registrar, School of Oriental and African Studies, Thornhaugh Street, Russell Square, London, WC1H 0XG, UK; (44) (20) 7637-2388, fax (44) (20) 7436-3844, study@soas.ac.uk, www.soas.ac.uk [ID:5322]

UNIVERSITY OF MANCHESTER
Institute for Development Policy
and Management (IDPM)

MA, MSc, MPhil & PhD IN INTERNATIONAL DEVELOPMENT ◆ Institute for Development Policy and Management (IDPM), Harold Hankins Bldg., Precinct Centre, Booth Street W., Manchester, M13 9QH, UK; (44) (161) 275-2800, fax (44) (161) 273-8829, idpm@man.ac.uk, idpm.man.ac.uk [ID:5021]

MOSCOW STATE UNIVERSITY
Institute of Oriental and African Studies

BA & MA IN PHILOLOGY; BA & MA IN HISTORY AND SOCIO-ECONOMICS ◆ Dean, International Students Office, A-812a, Main Bldg., Moscow State University, Leninskie Gory, Moscow, 119992. GSP-2, Russia; (7) (095) 203-939-3510, fax (7) (095) 938-0165, admission@rector.msu.ru, www.ied.msu.ru [ID:5323]

NATIONAL UNIVERSITY OF SINGAPORE
Faculty of Arts and Social Sciences

MSc IN INTERNATIONAL STUDIES: specialization in Development Studies ◆ Office of Programmes, Faculty of Arts and Social Sciences, National University of Singapore, Shaw Foundation Bldg., AS7, Level 2 , 5 Arts Link, 117570, Singapore(65) 6874-5276, fax (65) 6773-3291, opis@nus.edu.sg, www.fas.nus.edu.sg/oop [ID:5110]

UNIVERSITY OF READING
International and Rural
Development Department (IRDD)

MSc IN APPLIED DEVELOPMENT STUDIES, DEVELOPMENT POLICY, PRACTICE AND PROCESS, ENVIRONMENT AND DEVELOPMENT, DEVELOPMENT FINANCE; MPhil & PhD IN DEVELOPMENT STUDIES ◆ P.O. Box 237, Reading, RG6 6AR, UK; (44) (118) 378-8119, fax (44) (118) 926-1244, ird@lists.reading.ac.uk, www.rdg.ac.uk/IRDD [ID:5020]

UNIVERSITY OF SUSSEX
Development Studies

BA (Joint Degree) & BA: minor IN DEVELOPMENT STUDIES; MA & POST-GRADUATE DIPLOMA IN ENVIRONMENT, DEVELOPMENT & POLICY; MA IN GENDER, DEVELOPMENT & POLICY; MA IN RURAL DEVELOPMENT; MSc IN SOCIAL RESEARCH METHODS (DEVELOPMENT STUDIES) ◆ Culture, Development and Environment Centre (CDE), Arts C, University of Sussex, Brighton, BN1 9SJ, UK; (44) (1273) 678261, fax (44) (1273) 623572, www.sussex.ac.uk/development [ID:5420]

YOKOHAMA NATIONAL UNIVERSITY
Department of
International Development Studies

PhD IN INTERNATIONAL DEVELOPMENT STUDIES: concentrations in Economics, Business Administration or Cooperation ◆ Administration Department, International Graduate School of Social Sciences, 79-1 Tokiwadai, Hodogaya-ku, Yokohama, Japan; (81) (45) 339-3602, int.somu@nuc.ynu.ac.jp, www.igss.ynu.ac.jp [ID:5324]

Intercultural Studies

ANTIOCH UNIVERSITY
Individualized Liberal and
Professional Studies Department (ILPS)

MA IN INTERCULTURAL STUDIES ◆ Student &
Alumni Services Office, Antioch University McGregor,
800 Livermore Street, Yellow Springs, OH, 45387, USA;
937-769-1818, sas@mcgregor.edu, www.mcgregor.edu
[ID:5296]

CLAREMONT GRADUATE UNIVERSITY
Cultural Studies Department

MA & PhD IN CULTURAL STUDIES ◆ Admissions
Coordinator, Cultural Studies Department, Center for the
Arts and Humanities, 121 E. Tenth Street, Claremont
Graduate University, Claremont, CA, 91711, USA;
909-607-1278, fax 909-607-1221, Humanities@cgu.edu,
www.cgu.edu/hum/cul [ID:5360]

INTERNATIONAL
UNIVERSITY OF JAPAN
International Relations Program

MA IN INTERNATIONAL RELATIONS: concentration
in Comparative Culture and Society ◆ Office of the
Graduate School of International Relations, International
University of Japan, Yamato-machi, Minami Uonuma-
gun, Uonuma-gun, Niigata, 949-7277, Japan;
(81) (25) 779-1200, fax (81) (25) 779-1187,
admgsir@iuj.ac.jp, www.iuj.ac.jp [ID:5318]

KOBE UNIVERSITY
Faculty of Cross Cultural Studies

BA IN INTERCULTURAL STUDIES ◆ Dean,
Faculty of Cross Cultural Studies, Kobe University,
Tsurukabuto, Nada-ku, Kobe, Hyogo, 657-8501, Japan;
(81) (78) 803-7530, fax (81) (78) 803-7539,
www.kobe-u.ac.jp [ID:5319]

LESLEY UNIVERSITY
Intercultural Relations Program

MA IN INTERCULTURAL RELATIONS;
CERTIFICATE OF ADVANCED GRADUATE STUDY
(CAGS) IN INTERCULTURAL RELATIONS ◆ Office
of Admissions, Graduate and Adult Baccalaureate
Programs, 29 Everett Street, Lesley University,
Cambridge, MA, 02138-2790, USA; 617-349-8300,
info@mail.lesley.edu, www.lesley.edu [ID:5306]

UNIVERSITY OF MALAYA
Academy of Malay Studies

MA IN MALAY STUDIES ◆ Dean, Institute of Post-
graduate Research, University of Malaya, Kuala Lumpur,
50603, Malaysia; (60) (3) 7967-4623,
fax (60) (3) 7956-6634, unitmas@um.edu.my,
www.um.edu.my [ID:5257]

SCHOOL FOR
INTERNATIONAL TRAINING
School for International Training

MA IN SOCIAL JUSTICE AND INTERCULTURAL
RELATIONS ◆ P.O. Box 676, Kipling Road,
Brattleboro, VT, 05302-0676, USA; 802-258-3510, fax
802-258-3500, info@sit.edu, www.sit.edu [ID:5389]

International Business

BOCCONI UNIVERSITY
SDA Bocconi

MBA: specialization in International Economics and
Management; MA IN INTERNATIONAL HEALTH
CARE MANAGEMENT ECONOMICS AND POLICY;
INTERNATIONAL MA IN MANAGEMENT, LAW
AND HUMANITIES OF SPORT ◆ Via Bocconi 8,
201 36, Milan, Italy; (39) (2) 5836-6605, fax (39) (2)
5836-6638, www.sdabocconi.it [ID:5043]

BOND UNIVERSITY
Faculty of Business

BA & MA IN INTERNATIONAL BUSINESS
◆ Academic Adviser, Bond University, Gold Coast,
QLD, 4229, Australia; (61) (7) 5595-2266, fax (61) (7)
5595-1160, business@bond.edu.au, www.bond.edu.au
[ID:5293]

BRANDEIS UNIVERSITY
The Lemberg Program in
International Economics and Finance

MA IN INTERNATIONAL ECONOMICS AND
FINANCE ◆ Admissions Officer, International Business
School (IBS), Mail Stop - MS 032, Sachar International
Cente, 415 South Street, Brandeis University, Waltham,
MA, 02454, USA; 781-736-2250, fax 781-736-2267,
admission@lemberg.brandeis.edu
<admission@lemberg.bran [ID:5303]

ERASMUS UNIVERSITY ROTTERDAM
Rotterdam School of Management

INTERNATIONAL MBA; INTERNATIONAL MA IN
BUSINESS INFORMATICS (MBI) ◆ Burgemeester
Oudlaan 50, J-Bldg., 3062 PA Rotterdam, Netherlands;
(31) (10) 408-2222, fax (31) (10) 452-9509,
info@rsm.nl, web.eur.nl/english [ID:5421]

ESADE
ESADE

MBA; EMBA; PhD IN MANAGEMENT SCIENCES
◆ MBA Office, ave. d'Esplugues, 92-96, 08034
Barcelona, Spain; (34) (93) 495-2088, fax (34) (93) 495-
3828, mba@esade.edu, www.esade.edu [ID:5044]

HELSINKI SCHOOL OF ECONOMICS
Helsinki School of Economics

INTERNATIONAL MBA ◆ International Center, MBA Program, P.O.Box 1210, 00100 Helsinki, Finland; (358) (9) 4313-8631, fax (358) (9) 4313-8841, www.mbahelsinki.net [ID:5441]

IMD (INTERNATIONAL INSTITUTE FOR MANAGEMENT DEVELOPMENT)
International Institute for Management Development

MBA & EMBA IN INTERNATIONAL MANAGEMENT ◆ MBA Program, P.O. Box 915, Chemin de Bellerive 23, CH-1001, Lausanne, Switzerland; (41) (21) 618-0298, fax (41) (21) 618-0615, info@imd.ch, www.imd.ch [ID:5333]

INSEAD
MBA and International Marketing Programmes

MBA; INTERNATIONAL MARKETING PROGRAMME (IMKP) ◆ MBA Information Office, boul. de Constance, Fontainebleau Cedex, 77305, France; (33) (1) 60-72-40-05, fax (33) (1) 60-74-55-30, mba.info@insead.edu, www.insead.edu [ID:5008]

INTERNATIONAL UNIVERSITY OF JAPAN
Graduate School of International Management

MBA ◆ Admissions Committee, MBA Program, Yamato-machi, Minami Uonuma-gun, Niigata, 949-7277, Japan; (81) (25) 779-1500, fax (81) (25) 779-1187, admgsim@iuj.ac.jp, ibs.iuj.ac.jp [ID:5109]

UNIVERSITY OF LONDON
London Business School

MBA; Global EMBA; PhD IN STRATEGIC AND INTERNATIONAL MANAGEMENT ◆ Regent's Park, London, NW1 4SA, UK; (44) (207) 262-5050, fax (44) (207) 724-7875, www.london.edu [ID:5042]

MOSCOW STATE INSTITUTE OF INTERNATIONAL RELATIONS
International Business Administration Programme

INTERNATIONAL MBA ◆ Dean, International Student Education, Moscow State Institute of International Relations, 76 Vernadsky Prospect, Moscow, Russia; (7) (095) 434-0089, fax (7) (095) 434-9061, www.mgimo.ru [ID:5443]

UNIVERSITY OF NAVARRA
IESE Business School

MBA; EMBA; GLOBAL EMBA; PhD IN MANAGEMENT ◆ Barcelona Campus, Avenida Pearson, 21, 08034 Barcelona, Spain; (34) (93) 253-4200, fax (34) (93) 253-4343, info@iese.edu, www.iese.edu/en [ID:5045]

NEW YORK UNIVERSITY
Leonard N. Stern School of Business

MBA: concentration in Global Business, International Finance; GLOBAL EMBA ◆ MBA Admissions, NYU Stern School of Business, Suite 6-70, Henry Kaufman Management Center, 44 West 4th Street, New York, NY, 10012, USA; 212-998-0600, sternmba@stern.nyu.edu, www.stern.nyu.edu [ID:5315]

NYENRODE UNIVERSITY, THE NETHERLANDS BUSINESS SCHOOL
Faculty of International Business

INTERNATIONAL MBA ◆ Universiteit Nyenrode, c/o Program Information Center, Straatweg 25, 3621 BG Breukelen, Netherlands; (31) (34) 629-1291, fax (31) (34) 629-1450, www.nijenrode.nl [ID:5440]

UNIVERSITY OF OXFORD
Saïd Business School

MBA; EMBA ◆ Park End Street, Oxford, OX1 1HP, UK; (44) (1865) 288800, fax (44) (1865) 288805, enquiries@sbs.ox.ac.uk, www.sbs.ox.ac.uk [ID:5047]

UNIVERSITY OF PENNSYLVANIA
The Wharton School

BS IN ECONOMICS: concentration in Global Analysis; MBA; EMBA; PhD IN MANAGEMENT: specialization in International Business ◆ Office of MBA Admissions and Financial Aid, University of Pennsylvania, Room 420 Jon M. Huntsman Hall, 3730 Walnut Street, Philadelphia, PA, 19104.6340, USA; 215-898-6183, fax 215-898-0120, mba.admissions@wharton.upenn.edu, www.wharton.upenn.edu [ID:5075]

ROTTERDAM SCHOOL OF MANAGEMENT
Erasmus School of Business

INTERNATIONAL MBA; GLOBAL EMBA; MBA; EMBA ◆ Rotterdam School of Management, P.O. Box 1738, 3000 DR Rotterdam, Netherlands; (31) (10) 408-2222, fax (31) (10) 452-9509, admissions@rsm.nl, www.rsm.nl [ID:5046]

STOCKHOLM SCHOOL OF ECONOMICS
Institute of International Business

MSc IN INTERNATIONAL ECONOMICS AND BUSINESS; MSc IN BUSINESS ADMINISTRATION: specialization in International Management ◆ P.O. Box 6501, 113 83 Stockholm, Sweden; (46) (8) 736-9000, fax (46) (8) 318-186, info@hhs.se, www.hhs.se [ID:5442]

THUNDERBIRD, AMERICAN GRADUATE SCHOOL OF INTERNATIONAL MANAGEMENT
American Graduate School of International Management

MBA & EMBA IN INTERNATIONAL MANAGEMENT ◆ Admissions Office, 15249 N. 59th Ave., Glendale, AZ, 85306-6000, USA; 602-978-7100, fax 602-439-5432, admissions@t-bird.edu, www.t-bird.edu [ID:5320]

UNIVERSITY OF WESTERN ONTARIO
Richard Ivey School of Business

HBA & MBA: specialization in International Business
◆ Admissions Director, 1151 Richmond Street N.,
University of Western Ontario, London, ON, N6A 3K7,
Canada; 519-661-3206, fax 519-661-3485,
HBA@ivey.uwo.ca, www.ivey.uwo.ca [ID:5038]

YORK UNIVERSITY
Schulich School of Business

INTERNATIONAL BACHELOR OF BUSINESS
ADMINISTRATION (iBBA); INTERNATIONAL MBA
(IMBA) ◆ Undergraduate Programs Unit / International
MBA Program, 4700 Keele Street, York University,
Toronto, ON, M3J 1P3, Canada; 416-736-5060,
fax 416-650-8174, undergrad@schulich.yorku.ca or
imba@schulich.yorku.ca, www.schulich.yorku.ca
[ID:5019]

International
Education

THE UNIVERSITY OF BIRMINGHAM
School of Education

EdD IN INTERNATIONAL EDUCATION,
MANAGEMENT AND POLICY ◆ University of
Birmingham, Edgbaston, Birmingham, B15 2TT, UK;
(44) (121) 414-4866, fax (44) (121) 414-4865,
education@bham.ac.u, www.education.bham.ac.uk
[ID:5013]

UNIVERSITY OF
CALIFORNIA AT LOS ANGELES
Graduate School of Education
and Information Studies

MA, PhD IN CULTURAL STUDIES IN EDUCATION;
MA & PhD IN COMPARATIVE AND
INTERNATIONAL STUDIES IN EDUCATION
◆ Department Head, Social Sciences & Comparative
Education Division (SSCE), Box 951521, Moore Hall,
405 Hilgard Ave., Los Angeles, CA, 90095-1521, USA;
310-825-8326, info@gseis.ucla.edu,
www.gseis.ucla.edu/ded [ID:5330]

COLUMBIA UNIVERSITY
Teachers College

MA, EdM, PhD IN COMPARATIVE INTERNAT-
IONAL EDUCATION; MA, EdM & EdD IN INTER-
NATIONAL EDUCATIONAL DEVELOPMENT
◆ Program Coordinator, International & Transcultural
Studies, 357 Grace Dodge Hall, Box 211, 525 West
120th Street, Columbia University, New York, NY,
10027, USA; 212-678-3947, fax 212-678-8237,
www.tc.columbia.edu [ID:5010]

FLORIDA STATE UNIVERSITY
International/Intercultural
Development Education Program

MS, EDS & PhD IN INTERNATIONAL/ INTER-
CULTURAL DEVELOPMENT EDUCATION
◆ Program Coordinator, 114 Stone Bldg, Tallahassee,
FL, 32306-4452, USA; 850-644-7777, fax 850-644-
1258, www.fsu.edu/~elps/iide [ID:5015]

HARVARD UNIVERSITY
International Education
Policy Program (IEP)

MA IN INTERNATIONAL EDUCATION POLICY
◆ IEP Program Coordinator, Harvard Graduate School of
Education, 4th Floor Gutman, 6 Appian Way, Cambridge,
MA, 0213, USA; 617-495-4845, fax 617-496-3095,
iep@gse.harvard.edu, www.gse.harvard.edu [ID:5016]

UNIVERSITY OF HONG KONG
Comparative Education
Research Centre (CERC)

MEd IN COMPARATIVE EDUCATION ◆ Faculty of
Education, Room 408C, Hui Oi Chow Bldg., Pokfulam
Road, University of Hong Kong, SAR China, Hong
Kong(852) 2517-4737, fax (852) 2857-8541,
cerc@hkusub.hku.hk, www.hku.hk/cerc [ID:5004]

UNIVERSITY OF LONDON
School of Lifelong Education
and International Development

MA IN COMPARATIVE EDUCATION; MA IN
EDUCATION AND INTERNATIONAL DEVEL-
OPMENT: Health Promotion ◆ Institute of Education,
20 Bedford Way, University of London, London, WC1H
0AL, UK; (44) (207) 947-9516, fax (44) (207) 612-6632,
school.leid@ioe.ac.uk, http://ioewebserver.ioe.ac.uk/ioe
[ID:5012]

UNIVERSITY OF PITTSBURGH
Social and Comparative
Analysis in Education Program

MA, MEd & PhD IN INTERNATIONAL AND
DEVELOPMENTAL EDUCATION ◆ University of
Pittsburgh School of Education, Student Service Center,
5K Wesley W. Posvar Hall, University of Pittsburgh,
Pittsburgh, PA, 15260, USA; 412-648-2230,
www.education.pitt.edu [ID:5011]

STANFORD UNIVERSITY
School of Education

MA & PhD IN INTERNATIONAL COMPARATIVE
EDUCATION; MA IN INTERNATIONAL EDU-
CATIONAL ADMINISTRATION AND POLICY
ANALYSIS ◆ 485 Lasuen Mall, Stanford University,
Stanford, CA, 94305-3096, USA; 650-723-2109, fax
650-725-7412, info@suse.stanford.edu,
http://ed.stanford.edu/suse [ID:5009]

UNIVERSITY OF TORONTO
The Comparative, International and Development Education Centre (CIDE)

MA, MEd, EdD & PhD: specialization in Comparative, International or Development Education ◆ Director, Room 10-136, Ontario Institute for Studies in Education of the University of Toronto, 252 Bloor Street West, University of Toronto, Toronto, ON, M5S 1V6, Canada; 416-923-6641 ext. 2361, fax 416-923-4749, cide@oise.utoronto.ca, http://cide.oise.u [ID:5022]

YORK UNIVERSITY
Department of Educational Studies

MA IN CITIZENSHIP AND GLOBAL EDUCATION ◆ The Higher Degree Co-ordinator, Department of Educational Studies, University of York, Heslington, York, YO10 5DD, UK; (44) (1904) 433455, fax (44) (1904) 433459, educ15@york.ac.uk, www.york.ac.uk/depts/educ [ID:5014]

International Health

UNIVERSITY OF BIELEFELD
Bielefeld School of Public Health

MA IN PUBLIC HEALTH ◆ Faculty of Health Sciences, P.O. Box No.10 01 31, University of Bielefeld, Bielefeld, D-33501, Germany; (49) (521) 106-4380, aaa@uni-bielefeld.de, www.uni-bielefeld.de/gesundhw [ID:5007]

BOSTON UNIVERSITY
Center for International Health

MASTER OF PUBLIC HEALTH (MPH) & DOCTOR OF PUBLIC HEALTH (DrPH): concentration in International Heatlh; International Health Certificate Programs ◆ Chair, Center for International Health, 715 Albany Street, T-4 West, Boston, MA, 02118, USA; 617-638-5234, fax 617-638-4476, ih@bu.edu, www.bumc.bu.edu/sph [ID:5358]

UNIVERSITY OF CALIFORNIA AT LOS ANGELES
School of Public Health

MASTER (MPH) & DOCTOR (DrPH) IN PUBLIC HEALTH ◆ Dean's Office, 16-035 Center for Health Sciences, Box 951772, Los Angeles, CA, 90095-1772, USA; 310-825-6381, fax 310-825-8440, info@ph.ucla.edu, www.ph.ucla.edu [ID:5351]

UNIVERSITY OF COPENHAGEN
Department of International Health

MASTER OF INTERNATIONAL HEALTH (MIH); MASTER OF PUBLIC HEALTH (MPH) ◆ Institute of Public Health, Panum Institute, University of Copenhagen, 3 Blegdamsvej, Copenhagen N, DK-2200, Denmark; (45) 35 32 77 36, www.ku.dk/english [ID:5050]

ERASMUS UNIVERSITY ROTTERDAM
Netherlands Institute for Health Sciences (n i h e s)

MSc & DSc EPIDEMIOLOGY, CLINICAL EPIDEMIOLOGY, MEDICAL INFORMATICS, & HEALTH SERVICES RESEARCH; MASTER OF PUBLIC HEALTH (MPH) ◆ Director, Netherlands Institute for Health Sciences (n i h e s), Erasmus MC, P.O. Box 1738, 3000 DR, Rotterdam, Netherlands; (31) (10) 408-8158, fax (31) (10) 408-9382, info@nihes.nl, www.nihes.nl [ID:5329]

THE HEBREW UNIVERSITY OF JERUSALEM
Hadassah School of Public Health and Community Medicine

INTERNATIONAL MASTER OF PUBLIC HEALTH (MPH) ◆ Office of Academic Affairs, Hadassah School of Public Health and Community Medicine, P.O. Box 12272, Jerusalem, 91120, Israel; (972) (2) 677-7117, fax (972) (2) 643-1086, www.cfhu.org [ID:5274]

JOHNS HOPKINS UNIVERSITY
Bloomberg School of Public Health

MASTER OF HEALTH SCIENCES (MHS); PhD, ScD & DOCTOR OF PUBLIC HEALTH (DrPH) IN INTERNATIONAL HEALTH ◆ Academic Program Office, Department of International Health, 615 N. Wolfe Street, Baltimore, MD, 21205, USA; 410-955-3734, IHInfo@jhsph.edu, www.jhsph.edu/Dept/IH [ID:5316]

UNIVERSITY OF LIVERPOOL
Liverpool School of Tropical Medicine

MA & CERTIFICATE IN COMMUNITY HEALTH; MA IN TROPICAL MEDICINE; DIPLOMA IN REPRODUCTIVE HEALTH IN DEVELOPING COUNTRIES ◆ Director, Liverpool School of Tropical Medicine, Pembroke Place, Liverpool, L3 5QA, UK; (44) (151) 708-9393, fax (44) (151) 705-3370, imr@liverpool.ac.uk, www.liv.ac.uk/lstm [ID:5365]

UNIVERSITY OF LONDON
London School of Hygiene & Tropical Medicine

MSc: concentrations in Demography and Health, Epidemiology, Public Health, Public Health in Developing Countries, and Tropical Medicine and International Health ◆ Department Head, London School of Hygiene & Tropical Medicine, Keppel Street, University of London, London, WC1E 7HT, UK; (44) (20) 7636-8636, fax (44) (20) 7436-5389, registry@lshtm.ac.uk, www.lshtm.ac.uk [ID:5317]

UNIVERSITY OF MALAYA
Faculty of Medicine

MASTER OF PUBLIC HEALTH (MPH) ◆ Dean, Faculty of Medicine, University of Malaya, Kuala Lumpur 50603, Malaysia; (60) (3) 7950-2102, fax (60) (3) 7956-8841, unitmas@um.edu.my, www.um.edu.my [ID:5275]

**VICTOR SEGALEN
BORDEAUX 2 UNIVERSITY
Institut de Santé Publique, d'Epidémiologie
et de Développement (ISPED)**

MA IN EPIDEMIOLOGY AND INTERVENTION IN
PUBLIC HEALTH ◆ Université Victor Segalen
Bordeaux 2, 146 Rue Léo Saignat, Bordeaux Cedex,
33076, France; (33) (5) 57-57-13-93, fax (33) (5) 56-99-
13-60, sec.isped@isped.u-bordeaux2.fr, www.isped.u-
bordeaux2.fr [ID:5049]

International Law

**UNIVERSITY OF
CALIFORNIA, BERKELEY
Boalt Hall School of Law**

JD: specialization in International Law ◆ Director,
Boalt Hall School of Law, 209 Boalt Hall, University of
California, Berkeley, Berkeley, CA, 94720-7200, USA;
510-642-8074, fax 510-642-3728, www.law.berkeley.edu
[ID:5272]

**UNIVERSITY OF CAMBRIDGE
Faculty of Law**

DIPLOMA IN INTERNATIONAL LAW ◆ Director,
Lauterpacht Research Centre for International Law,
10 West Road, Cambridge, CB3 9DZ, UK;
(44) (1223) 330033, fax (44) (1223) 330055,
enquiries@law.cam.ac.uk, www.law.cam.ac.uk
[ID:5273]

**COLUMBIA UNIVERSITY IN
THE CITY OF NEW YORK
Columbia Law School**

LLM IN INTERNATIONAL, FOREIGN &
COMPARATIVE LAW; HUMAN RIGHTS LAW
◆ Graduate Legal Studies Office, Columbia University in
the City of New York, 435 West 116th Street, Mail code
4036, New York, NY, 10027-7297, USA; 212-854-2655,
fax 212-854-9742, gls@law.columbia.edu,
www.law.columbia.edu [ID:5259]

**UNIVERSITY OF ESSEX
Department of Law**

LLM IN INTERNATIONAL HUMAN RIGHTS
LAW; LLM IN INTERNATIONAL TRADE LAW
◆ University of Essex, Wivenhoe Park, Colchester,
CO4 3SQ, UK; (44) (1206) 872587, fax (44) (1206)
873428, www2.essex.ac.uk/law [ID:5416]

**UNIVERSITY OF EXETER
Department of Law**

LLM IN INTERNATIONAL BUSINESS LAW; LLM IN
INTERNATIONAL AND COMPARATIVE PUBLIC
LAW ◆ Post-graduate Secretary, Department of Law,
University of Exeter, Amory Bldg., Rennes Drive, Exeter,
EX4 4RJ, UK; (44) (1392) 263380, fax (44) (1392)
263196, law-pgadm@exeter.ac.uk, www.exeter.ac.uk
[ID:5417]

**GRADUATE INSTITUTE OF
INTERNATIONAL STUDIES, GENEVA
International Law Section**

PhD IN INTERNATIONAL LAW ◆ Admissions,
Graduate Institute of International Studies (HEI), 132 rue
de Lausanne, Case postale 36, CH-1211, Geneva 21,
Switzerland; (41) (22) 908-5720, fax (41) (22) 908-5710,
info@hei.unige.ch, heiwww.unige.ch [ID:5048]

**UNIVERSITY OF LONDON
Institute of Advanced Legal Studies**

LLM: (various study options available); MPhil & PhD IN
COMPARATIVE LAW, HUMAN RIGHTS ◆ Charles
Clore House, 17 Russell Square, London, WC1B 5DR,
UK; (44) (207) 862-5800, ials@sas.ac.uk, ials.sas.ac.uk
[ID:5068]

**McGILL UNIVERSITY
Faculty of Law**

LLM: concentration in International Business Law,
Human Rights or Cultural Diversity; GRADUATE
CERTIFICATE, LLM & DCL IN AIR AND SPACE
LAW; GRADUATE CERTIFICATE IN COMPAR-
ATIVE LAW ◆ Graduate Programs Coordinator, Faculty
of Law, 3661 Peel Street, McGill University, Montreal,
QC, H3A 1X1, Canada; 514-398-3544,
fax 514-398-8197, gradadmissions.law@mcgill.ca,
www.law.mcgill.ca [ID:5006]

**NEW YORK UNIVERSITY
School of Law**

LLM: specialization in International Legal Studies; JD/
LLM IN INTERNATIONAL LAW; LLM/JSD IN
INTERNATIONAL LAW ◆ Office of Admissions,
161 Avenue of the Americas, 5th Floor, New York, NY,
10013-1205, USA; 212-998-6060,
law.llmadmissions@nyu.edu, www.law.nyu.edu
[ID:5066]

**UNIVERSITY OF NOTTINGHAM
School of Law**

LLM IN HUMAN RIGHTS LAW, INTERNATIONAL
LAW, INTERNATIONAL COMMERCIAL LAW,
INTERNATIONAL CRIMINAL JUSTICE AND
ARMED CONFLICT, MARITIME LAW AND PUBLIC
INTERNATIONAL LAW ◆ LLM Admissions Secretary,
Law & Social Sciences Building, University of
Nottingham, University Park, Nottingham, NG7 2RD,
UK; (44) (115) 951-5694, llmphd@nottingham.ac.uk,
www.nottingham.ac.uk [ID:5419]

**UNIVERSITY OF SYDNEY
Faculty of Law**

MA & GRADUATE DIPLOMA IN INTERNATIONAL
LAW; MA IN INTERNATIONAL BUSINESS AND
LAW; GRADUATE DIPLOMA IN INTERNATIONAL
BUSINESS LAW; MA IN INTERNATIONAL
TAXATION ◆ The Information Desk, Level 12, 173-175
Phillip Street, Faculty of Law, University of Sydney,
Sydney, NSW, 2000, Australia; (61) (2) 9351-0351,
info@law.usyd.edu.au, www.law.usyd.edu.au [ID:5249]

UNIVERSITY COLLEGE OF WALES
Department of Law

LLM IN INTERNATIONAL BUSINESS LAW ◆ Director of Post-graduate Studies, University of Wales, Aberystwyth, Hugh Owen Bldg., Penglais, Aberystwyth, SY23 3DY, UK; (44) (1970) 622712, fax (44) (1970) 622729, law-enquiries@aber.ac.uk, www.aber.ac.uk/law [ID:5102]

YALE UNIVERSITY
Yale Law School

JD; LLM; MSL; JSD ◆ Yale Law School Admissions Office, P.O. Box 208215, New Haven, CT, 06520-8329, USA; 203-432-4995, admissions.law@yale.edu, www.law.yale.edu [ID:5067]

International Studies/Affairs

AMERICAN UNIVERSITY
School of International Service

BA, BA: minor IN INTERNATIONAL STUDIES; MA IN INTERNATIONAL AFFAIRS; PhD IN INTERNATIONAL RELATIONS ◆ Dean, School of International Service, American University, 4400 Massachusetts Ave. N.W., Washington, DC, 20016-8071, USA; 202-885-1600, sisgrad@american.edu, www.american.edu/sis [ID:5366]

AUSTRALIAN NATIONAL UNIVERSITY
Graduate Studies in Political Science and International Relations

MA & GRADUATE DIPLOMA IN INTERNATIONAL AFFAIRS; MA & PhD IN INTERNATIONAL RELATIONS; MA IN STRATEGIC STUDIES ◆ Director of Studies, Australian National University, Canberra, 0200, Australia; (61) (6) 6125-4643, fax (61) (6) 6125-5550, graduate.int@anu.edu.au, www.anu.edu.au [ID:5217]

BILKENT UNIVERSITY
Department of International Relations

MA & PhD IN INTERNATIONAL RELATIONS; MA IN INTERNATIONAL AFFAIRS AND PUBLIC POLICY ◆ Faculty of Economics, Administrative and Social Sciences, Bilkent University, Bilkent 06800, Ankara, Turkey; (90) (312) 290-1249, fax (90) (312) 266-4326, ir@bilkent.edu.tr, www.bilkent.edu.tr [ID:5292]

UNIVERSITY OF CALIFORNIA, SAN DIEGO
Graduate School of International Relations and Pacific Studies (IR/PS)

MA IN PACIFIC INTERNATIONAL AFFAIRS; PhD IN INTERNATIONAL AFFAIRS ◆ Robinson Bldg. Complex, 9500 Gilman Drive, La Jolla, CA, 92093-0520, USA; 858-534-5914, fax 858-534-1135, irps-apply@ucsd.edu, www-irps.ucsd.edu [ID:5384]

CARLETON UNIVERSITY
Norman Paterson School of International Affairs (NPSIA)

MA IN INTERNATIONAL AFFAIRS; MA IN INTERNATIONAL AFFAIRS & LLB ◆ Administrator, 1401 Dunton Tower, 1125 Colonel By Drive, Carleton University, Ottawa, ON, K1S 5B6, Canada; 613-520-6655, fax 613-520-2889, international_affairs@carleton.ca, www.carleton.ca/npsia [ID:5023]

CENTRAL EUROPEAN UNIVERSITY, BUDAPEST
Department of International Relations and European Studies

MA & PhD IN INTERNATIONAL RELATIONS AND EUROPEAN STUDIES ◆ Department Coordinator, Central European University, Nador u. 9, 1051 Budapest, Hungary; (36) (1) 327-3017, fax (36) (1) 327-3243, ires@ceu.hu, www.ceu.hu/ires [ID:5073]

UNIVERSITY OF CHICAGO
Committee on International Relations

MA IN INTERNATIONAL RELATIONS ◆ Dean of Students, Division of the Social Sciences, Foster Hall 108, 1130 E. 59th Street, Chicago, IL, 60637, USA; 773-702-8415, cir@uchicago.edu, cir.uchicago.edu [ID:5391]

COLUMBIA UNIVERSITY
School of International and Public Affairs

MA IN INTERNATIONAL AFFAIRS ◆ Office of Admissions and Financial Aid, School of International and Public Affairs, Mail Code 3325, Room 408, 420 West 118th Street, New York, NY, 10027, USA; 212-854-6216, sipa_admission@columbia.edu, www.sipa.columbia.edu [ID:5367]

GEORGE WASHINGTON UNIVERSITY
Elliott School of International Affairs

BA & MA IN INTERNATIONAL AFFAIRS ◆ Office of Graduate Admissions, George Washington University, Suite 301, 1957 E Street N.W., Washington, DC, 20052, USA; 202-994-7050, fax 202-994-9537, esiagrad@gwu.edu, www.gwu.edu [ID:5368]

GEORGETOWN UNIVERSITY
Edmund A. Walsh School of Foreign Service

BSc & MSc IN FOREIGN SERVICE ◆ Graduate Admissions, 301 InterCultural Center, 37th & O Streets, N.W., Washington, DC, 20057, USA, 202-687-5696, fax 202-687-1431, gradmail@georgetown.edu, www.georgetown.edu/sfs [ID:5369]

GRADUATE INSTITUTE OF INTERNATIONAL STUDIES, GENEVA
Graduate Institute of International Studies (HEI)

DES IN INTERNATIONAL RELATIONS
♦ Admissions, Graduate Institute of International Studies (HEI), 132 rue de Lausanne, Case postale 36, CH-1211, Geneva 21, Switzerland; (41) (22) 908-5720, fax (41) (22) 908-5710, info@hei.unige.ch, heiwww.unige.ch [ID:5332]

HARVARD UNIVERSITY
John F. Kennedy School of Government

MA IN PUBLIC ADMINISTRATION ♦ Office of Admissions, John F. Kennedy School of Government, Harvard University, 79 JFK Street, Cambridge, MA, 02138, USA; 617-495-1155, fax 617-496-1165, KSG_Admissions@harvard.edu, www.ksg.harvard.edu [ID:5305]

INTERNATIONAL UNIVERSITY OF JAPAN
Graduate School of International Relations

MA IN INTERNATIONAL RELATIONS ♦ Office of the Graduate School of International Relations, International University of Japan, Minami Uonuma-gun, Niigata, 949-7277, Japan; (81) (25) 779-1200, fax (81) (25) 779-1187, admgsir@iuj.ac.jp, www.iuj.ac.jp [ID:5248]

JAWAHARLAL NEHRU UNIVERSITY
School of International Studies

MA IN POLITICS: specialization in International Studies; MPhil & PhD IN INTERNATIONAL POLITICS ♦ Director, Admissions, Jawaharlal Nehru University, New Mehrauli Road, New Delhi, 110067, India; (91) (11) 2671-7676, director_admissions@mail.jnu.ac.in, www.jnu.ac.in [ID:5278]

JOHNS HOPKINS UNIVERSITY
Paul H. Nitze School of Advanced International Studies (SAIS)

MA & PhD IN INTERNATIONAL RELATIONS ♦ Dean of Admissions, The Nitze Bldg., 1740 Massachusetts Ave., N.W., Washington, DC, 20036, USA; 202-663-5600, fax 202-663-5656, admissions.sais@jhu.edu, www.sais-jhu.edu [ID:5334]

KEELE UNIVERSITY
School of Politics, International Relations and the Environment (SPIRE)

MA IN DIPLOMATIC STUDIES; MA IN GLOBAL SECURITY; BA, MA, MPhil & PhD IN INTER-NATIONAL RELATIONS ♦ Keele University, Keele, Staffordshire, ST5 5BG, UK; (44) (1782) 583452, fax (44) (1782) 583592, www.keele.ac.uk/depts/spire [ID:5036]

UNIVERSITY OF LEEDS
School of Politics and International Studies

BA & MA IN INTERNATIONAL STUDIES ♦ School of Politics and International Studies, University of Leeds, Leeds, LS2 9JT, UK; (44) (113) 343-6843, fax (44) (113) 343-4400, polispg@leeds.ac.uk, www.leeds.ac.uk/polis [ID:5418]

LONDON SCHOOL OF ECONOMICS AND POLITICAL SCIENCE
International Relations Department

BSc, MSc, MPhil & PhD IN INTERNATIONAL RELATIONS; MSc in POLITICS OF THE WORLD ECONOMY, THE PRACTICE OF INTERNATIONAL AFFAIRS, GLOBAL POLITICS ♦ Graduate Admissions, International Relations Department, London School of Economics & Political Science, Houghton Street, London, WC2A 2AE, UK; (44) (20) 7955-7404, fax (44) (20) 7955-7446, www.lse.ac.uk/Depts/intrel [ID:5388]

MONTEREY INSTITUTE OF INTERNATIONAL STUDIES
Graduate School of International Policy Studies

BA IN INTERNATIONAL STUDIES; MA IN INTERNATIONAL POLICY STUDIES; MA IN INTERNATIONAL TRADE POLICY ♦ Admissions Office, 460 Pierce Street, Monterey, CA, 93940, USA; 831-647-4123, fax 831-647-6405, admit@miis.edu, www.miis.edu [ID:5256]

UNIVERSITY OF OXFORD
Department of Politics and International Relations

MPhil, MLitt & DPhil IN INTERNATIONAL RELATIONS; MSc IN POLITICS AND INTER-NATIONAL RELATIONS RESEARCH; MPhil IN POLITICS: specialization in Comparative Government ♦ University Offices, Wellington Square, Oxford, OX1 2JD, UK; (44) (1865) 270059, fax (44) (1865) 270049, Graduate.Admissions@admin.ox.ac.uk, www.politics.ox.ac.uk [ID:5074]

UNIVERSITY OF THE PHILIPPINES
Department of Political Science

MA IN INTERNATIONAL STUDIES ♦ Graduate Program Coordinator, Department of Political Science, College of Social Sciences and Philosophy, Faculty Center 3135, University of the Philippines, Diliman, Quezon City 1101, Philippines; (63) (2) 924-4875, polisci@kssp.upd.edu.ph, web.kssp.upd. [ID:5290]

PRINCETON UNIVERSITY
Woodrow Wilson School of Public and International Affairs

MA & PhD IN PUBLIC AFFAIRS: concentration in International Relations ♦ Assistant Dean of Graduate Admissions, Admissions, Princeton University, Robertson Hall, Princeton, NJ, 08544-1013, USA; 609-258-4800, fax 609-258-2095, wwswww@princeton.edu, www.wws.princeton.edu [ID:5336]

QUAID-I-AZAM UNIVERSITY
Department of International Relations

MSc, MPhil & PhD IN INTERNATIONAL
RELATIONS ◆ Admissions Office, P.O. Box 1090,
Quaid-I-Azam University of Islamabad, Islamabad,
45320, Pakistan; (92) (51) 287-4041, www.qau.edu.pk
[ID:5289]

UNIVERSITY OF
SOUTHERN CALIFORNIA
School of International Relations

BA & MA IN INTERNATIONAL RELATIONS; PhD IN
POLITICS AND INTERNATIONAL RELATIONS
◆ Graduate Advisor, Admissions, 3518 Trousdale
Parkway, VKC 330, University Park, Los Angeles, CA,
90089-0043, USA; 213-740-2136, fax 213-742-0281,
sir@usc.edu, www.usc.edu/dept/LAS/ir [ID:5411]

UNIVERSITY OF SYDNEY
School of Economics and Political Science

MA IN INTERNATIONAL STUDIES ◆ Post-graduate
Coursework Coordinator, Room 259, H04 Merewether
Bldg., The University of Sydney, Sydney, NSW 2006,
Australia; (61) (2) 9351-4075, fax (61) (2) 9351-3624,
esiagrad@gwu.edu, www.usyd.edu.au [ID:5294]

TUFTS UNIVERSITY
The Fletcher School of Law and Diplomacy

MA & PhD IN LAW AND DIPLOMACY ◆ The
Fletcher School Office of Admissions and Financial Aid,
160 Packard Ave., Tufts University, Medford, MA,
02155, USA; 617-627-3040 ext. 2410,
fax 617-627-3712, FletcherAdmissions@tufts.edu,
http://fletcher.tufts.edu [ID:5390]

VICTORIA UNIVERSITY
OF WELLINGTON
Political Science and International Relations

DIPLOMA & MA IN INTERNATIONAL RELATIONS
◆ School of History, Philosophy, Political Science and
International Relations, P.O. Box 600, Victoria University
of Wellington, Wellington, New Zealand;
(64) (4) 463-5351 ext. 8682, fax (64) (4) 463-5414,
www.vuw.ac.nz/pols [ID:5295]

UNIVERSITY OF WALES,
ABERYSTWYTH
Department of International Politics

BA, MA & PhD IN INTERNATIONAL POLITICS
◆ Undergraduate or Post-graduate Secretary, Department
of International Politics, University of Wales, Penglais,
Aberystwyth, Wales, SY23 3DA, UK; (44) (1970)
622702, fax (44) (1970) 622709, interpol@aber.ac.uk,
www.aber.ac.uk/interpol [ID:5218]

UNIVERSITY OF WARWICK
Department of Politics
and International Studies

BA IN POLITICS AND INTERNATIONAL STUDIES;
MA IN GLOBALISATION AND DEVELOPMENT; MA
IN INTERNATIONAL POLITICS AND EAST ASIA;
MA IN INTERNATIONAL POLITICAL ECONOMY;
MA INTERNATIONAL RELATIONS ◆ University of
Warwick, Coventry, CV4 7AL, UK; (44) (2476) 523302,
fax (44) (2476) 524221,
www2.warwick.ac.uk/fac/soc/pais [ID:5037]

UNIVERSITY OF ZIMBABWE
International Relations Program

MSc IN INTERNATIONAL RELATIONS
◆ Coordinator, P O Box MP167, University of
Zimbabwe, Mount Pleasant, Harare, Zimbabwe;
(263) (4) 303-211 ext. 1251, fax (263) (4) 732-828,
www.zimweb.com/Education.html [ID:5140]

Peace/Conflict Studies

AMERICAN UNIVERSITY
School of International Service

MA & PhD IN INTERNATIONAL PEACE AND
CONFLICT RESOLUTION; MA IN ETHICS AND
PEACE; GRADUATE CERTIFICATE IN
PEACEBUILDING ◆ Dean, School of International
Service, American University, 4400 Massachusetts Ave.
N.W., Washington, DC, 20016-8071, USA; 202-885-
1600, sisgrad@american.edu., www.american.edu/sis
[ID:5028]

UNIVERSITY OF BRADFORD
Department of Peace Studies

BA, MA & POST GRADUATE DIPLOMA IN PEACE
STUDIES; MA, POST-GRADUATE DIPLOMA, MPhil
& PhD IN CONFLICT RESOLUTION ◆ Head of
Department, Department of Peace Studies, Pemberton
Bldg., University of Bradford, West Yorkshire, BD7 1DP,
UK; (44) (1274) 235 235, fax (44) (1274) 235 240,
enquiries@bradford.ac.uk,
www.bradford.ac.uk/acad/peace [ID:5357]

EUROPEAN UNIVERSITY
CENTER FOR PEACE STUDIES (EPU)
European University Center
for Peace Studies (EPU)

MA IN PEACE AND CONFLICT STUDIES; POST-
GRADUATE CERTIFICATE IN PEACE AND
CONFLICT TRANSFORMATION ◆ Rochusplatz 1, A-
7461, Stadtschlaining, Austria; (43) (3355) 2498, fax (43)
(3355) 2381, epu@epu.ac.at, www.aspr.ac.at [ID:5029]

GEORGE MASON UNIVERSITY
Institute for Conflict Analysis
and Resolution (ICAR)

BA, BS, MS & PhD IN CONFLICT ANALYSIS AND
RESOLUTION ◆ Office of Admissions, 4260 Chain
Bridge Road, Fairfax, VA, 22030, USA; 703-993-1300,
fax 709-993-1302, www.gmu.edu/departments/ICAR
[ID:5026]

UNIVERSITY OF
KENT AT CANTERBURY
Department of Politics
and International Relations

BA IN CONFLICT, PEACE AND SECURITY; MA,
MPhil and PhD IN INTERNATIONAL CONFLICT
ANALYSIS ◆ Rutherford College, University of Kent,
Canterbury, Kent, CT2 7NX, UK; (44) (1227) 823678,
fax (44) (1227) 827033, www.kent.ac.uk/politics
[ID:5094]

UNIVERSITY OF NOTRE DAME
Joan B. Kroc Institute for
International Peace Studies

BA & MA IN PEACE STUDIES ◆ Joan B. Kroc
Institute for International Peace Studies, P.O. Box 639,
100 Hesburgh Center for International Studies, University
of Notre Dame, Notre Dame, IN, 46556-0639, USA;
574-631-6970, fax 574-631-6973, krocinst@nd.edu,
kroc.nd.edu [ID:5025]

UNIVERSITY FOR PEACE
University for Peace

MA IN ENVIRONMENTAL SECURITY AND PEACE;
MA IN GENDER AND PEACE BUILDING; MA IN
INTERNATIONAL PEACE STUDIES; MA IN PEACE
EDUCATION ◆ Office of the Dean for Academic
Administration, P.O. Box 138-6100, University for
Peace, San José, Costa Rica; (506) 205-9000, fax (506)
249-1324, acadmin@upeace.org, www.upeace.org
[ID:5024]

UNIVERSITY OF ULSTER
Peace and Conflict Studies

MA & POST-GRADUATE DIPLOMA IN PEACE AND
CONFLICT STUDIES ◆ University of Ulster, Magee
Campus, Northland Road, Londonderry, Co.
Londonderry, BT48 7JL, UK; (44) (8) 700-400-700,
online@ulst.ac.uk, www.ulster.ac.uk [ID:5031]

THE UNITED NATIONS UNIVERSITY
United Nations University
International Courses (UNU/IC)

CERTIFICATE OF COMPLETION FOR PEACE AND
GOVERNANCE ◆ Training Assistant, United Nations
University Centre, The United Nations University
Headquarters, 5-53-70 Jingumae, Shibuya-ku, Tokyo,
150-8925, Japan; (81) (3) 3499-2811, fax (81) (3) 3499-
2828, www.unu.edu [ID:5331]

UPPSALA UNIVERSITY
Department of Peace and Conflict Research

BA & PhD IN INTERNATIONAL CONFLICT
STUDIES ◆ Box 514, Uppsala University, SE 751 20
Uppsala, Sweden; (46) (18) 471-0000, fax (46) (18) 695-
102, info@pcr.uu.se, www.pcr.uu.se [ID:5027]

CHAPTER 17

Internships
Abroad

Internships are one of the surest routes into the international job market. Why? Because they help you overcome one of your biggest obstacles—a lack of professional international work experience. Even with years of schooling and language training, you may find doors closed and few opportunities available. For this reason, interning is a popular and effective way to gain practical training, build a network of contacts and launch your international career.

International internships have become so important and widely popular that merely one chapter on the subject will not do it justice. If you want to be an intern abroad, you need career advice and you need to find contacts to locate your best placement.

What advice do you need? Internships are professional endeavours—just like real jobs. If you want to intern, you will need to review the advice found in Part Three of this book, The International Job Search. You will need to know how to research employers (the same process for finding internships), sell your international skills, write an international resume and prepare for an interview. This chapter provides supplemental advice only—describing additional tips and tricks specific to interns. (For more specific job hunting advice, see Chapters 18 to 28 in Part Three, The International Job Search.)

What contacts are required to locate an internship? Almost every type of organization profiled in this book has a formal or informal internship program. For this reason, we have not profiled an exhaustive list of organizations at the end of this chapter—they are just too numerous. To research Canadian internships you should read the profiles in this book. (See Chapter 10, Short-Term Programs Overseas; Chapter 38, NGOs in Canada; and Chapter 35, Private Sector Firms in Canada. Also see the US profiles in Appendix 39a, "Profiles for Chapter 39: NGOs in the US," and Appendix 36a, "Profiles for Chapter 36: Private Sector Firms in the US".)

To broaden your perspective on what internships are available beyond Canadian and US organizations, this chapter profiles 39 hard-to-research internships, those with international organizations engaged in research and policy development. There are many opportunities in this sector and we want to encourage you to be bold and take the plunge with an internship sponsored by an international organization. (For information on internship strategies in international organizations, see Chapter 41, United Nations & Other IGOs, and Chapter 40, NGOs in Europe & the Rest of the World.)

For Canadian readers, this chapter also profiles one internship program that is worth noting—the Canadian Government International Internship Programs. This program is so large and important for Canadian university graduates that it is profiled in this chapter and also has its own section below (see the "Canadian Government International Internship Programs" section and the Profiles section at the end of this chapter).

Finally, Canadian readers should also consult the many internships that are profiled in Chapter 10, Short-Term Programs Overseas.

WHAT IS AN INTERNSHIP?

There is no simple answer to this question. Generally speaking, it refers to the exchange of work for knowledge, and in this way, is similar to an apprenticeship. A good internship allows you to work on a specific project of interest and to build on your academic specialization or previous work experience. You may not receive a stipend as an intern, but typically the sponsoring organization will invest some time and money in structuring your internship and making it a beneficial training experience for you. Being new to the field and to the organization, your work will likely be monitored by a supervisor or mentor. The underlying principle of an internship is to provide both knowledge and practical experience in exchange for your labour and low salary/living allowance.

Internships are often organized by universities or NGOs—they'll help you find a placement with an international employer. Motivated applicants can be creative and find internships directly with employers themselves. (See more on this below in the section "Creating Your Own Internship".)

Whatever type you choose, completing an internship before you begin an international career is now becoming standard.

TYPES OF INTERNATIONAL INTERNSHIPS

There are many different types of international internships. Some conform to an established structure while others are tailored to meet the needs of the individuals and organizations involved. Internships range in duration from a few months to a year. Often, they are available for an academic semester or summer term. They may vary in terms of financial support and the degree of independence accorded interns.

The international organizations that offer internships are diverse and numerous. They generally look for highly skilled and motivated people to work in research, advocacy, communications or public policy. In many cases, internships are designed for students or recent graduates.

Here are a few examples of typical international internships:

- An honours political science student, focusing on human rights and development studies, successfully applies to the Young Professional International program sponsored by FOREIGN AFFAIRS CANADA (FAC) and INTERNATIONAL TRADE CANADA (ITCAN) to work with a human rights organization in Bosnia and Herzegovina. The internship is managed by CANADEM, a Canadian NGO based in Ottawa. It begins with a week of orientation in Canada, five to six months working with the organizations overseas, and ends with a follow-up session in Canada upon return.

- An international MBA student with export trade and business planning skills receives a modest stipend for a summer internship with a Mississauga, Ontario firm studying the feasibility of exporting to Latin America.

- A recent law graduate works with the UNITED NATIONS COMMISSION ON INTERNATIONAL TRADE LAW (UNCITRAL) in Vienna on legal policy related to the illicit drug trade.

- An urban planning student, funded by his academic institution, spends eight months in Nairobi developing a social housing project with the UN CENTRE FOR HUMAN SETTLEMENTS.

- An inexperienced journalist gets quality reporting jobs while interning with a national news magazine in New York for six months.

- The INTERNATIONAL DEVELOPMENT RESEARCH CENTRE (IDRC) provides $28,000 for a biology intern who uses the funds to study theories and issues of alternative medicine for one year in Ottawa.

- An Ottawa-based student, enrolled in Central/East European and Russian-area studies, arranges a two-day per week internship during the winter school term with the RUSSIAN EMBASSY.

Canadian Government International Internship Programs

No Canadian university student should pass on applying to one of these programs. The five programs are managed by seven federal government departments—in total they offer 1,340 internships a year. If you have just graduated from university, and are under the age of 30 (eligibility varies), you are eligible to apply and, with a little determination, your chances of landing an internship are very good. Each program is managed by partner organizations located across the country. With a combined total of over 130 partner organizations, there is no shortage on where to apply or the number of applications you can submit.

The five programs are listed under one heading in the profiles at the end of this chapter—Canadian Government International Internships:

- FOREIGN AFFAIRS CANADA (FAC) and INTERNATIONAL TRADE CANADA'S (ITCAN) Young Professionals International program. Annually, approximately 400 internships are administered by 50 partner organizations (mainly NGOs) located across Canada.

- CANADIAN INTERNATIONAL DEVELOPMENT AGENCY'S (CIDA) International Youth Internship program. Annually, approximately 400 internships are administered by 57 partner organizations (mainly NGOs) located across Canada.

- INDUSTRY CANADA's NetCorps Canada International program. Annually, approximately 250 internships are administered by nine partner organizations (Canadian NGOs) with offices located across Canada

- CANADIAN HERITAGE and PARKS CANADA'S Young Canada Works Internships program. Annually, approximately 160 internships are available through one partner organization.

- ENVIRONMENT CANADA's International Environmental Youth Corps program. Annually, approximately 130 internships are available through one partner organization.

WHY INTERN?

You probably won't hear of people embarking on international internships to make loads of cash. But internships do pay off. Why? Because they provide invaluable international work and life experience. Surprisingly, the skills you acquire as an intern are often greater than those you would gain with the same organization in an entry-level position. Often, your sponsoring organization will take the time to train you, precisely because you are unpaid. Internships also provide more challenges. Usually they are project-based and offer responsibilities that are broader in scope than those required for the day-to-day operations of an organization. If you are assigned to an internship overseas, you will also acquire essential cross-cultural living and working experience. So, while an internship may not appear financially attractive in the short term, it usually pays off!

Moreover, if you prove your reliability and competence as an intern, you are likely to be first in line for a job with that organization. Some estimates of interns who find employment with their sponsoring agencies are as high as 60 per cent. Many employers state that they *"appreciate the initiative and diligence of interns. Interns tend to work hard and show a keen interest in learning about the business."* Even internships that do not lead directly to employment can still be extremely valuable. The diverse array of professional contacts you make as an intern will help tremendously with your job search. Contacts can give you the inside scoop on jobs in your field, and if your work has been valued, your supervisor can provide you with a strong recommendation.

FINDING THE RIGHT INTERNSHIP

While many internships are available, not all will correspond to your needs and interests. You will have to do some preliminary research to locate the one that's right for you. The first step in evaluating any internship is to consider whether the experience will be worth the time and effort required. For example, you should consider whether it matches your career goals; or, if you have little or no overseas experience, consider that gaining this experience may be more important than acquiring specific career training. This is true even if the assignment is unstructured (and many of them are). The cross-cultural living and working experience you gain will make it worthwhile!

If you already have previous international living experience, you might want to consider working for a Canadian-based international internship, such as an NGO or the international branch of a private firm or government department. Gaining international experience at home can be equally valuable and just as essential to your resume as your international experience abroad. For Canadian-based internships, it is best to work out in advance the substance of the internship assignment, the terms of participation and the organization's expectations. Pay close attention to the organization's description of an intern's duties. This will help you determine whether your own needs will be met. Most internships involve some combination of administrative work and substantive projects, and you will want to know in advance that the balance between the two will enable you to meet your personal learning needs. If possible, contact former interns and arrange information interviews in person or over the telephone. Once these steps have been taken, you will be in a much better position to determine whether a position suits you. Be as selective as your previous experience dictates, and find the internship that best matches your skills and aspirations. (For more and similar advice, see the article by Geoff Owen, "Choosing the Right Internship Organization," in Appendix 17a on the CD-ROM.)

RESEARCHING INTERNSHIPS

Once you've decided on the type of internship you want, you can focus your research. In what field of work are you interested? Are you prepared to work in a non-paying internship? With what type of organization do you want to intern—an NGO, international agency or private firm? In what city, country or region of the world would you like to work—urban or rural, advanced economy or developing country? When reviewing internship possibilities on the Web, be sure to note any eligibility requirements that might disqualify you from applying, such as age restrictions or field of study criteria.

Begin your research well in advance of your availability. Six to eight months of lead time is a safe bet for a formal internship program with an international organization or for a self-directed internship. For example, for a summer internship, start your research in early fall and begin making direct contact with organizations by December. For FAC/ITCAN and CIDA internships, the application process is shorter, with recruitment generally beginning in early spring for departures in June and September.

Be a vigilant researcher—since many internships are posted on Web sites, the early bird researcher has the best chance of finding the ideal match.

Do not limit yourself to a simple search of organizations based in your country. The following story shows how you can harness the power of the Internet to scan for internships from around the world. This is not really an Internet story, however; it is a story about the type of determination that will eventually lead you to a full-time, professional, well-paying job abroad.

> *"I was in my third year of a four year Bachelors in Biochemistry, and was looking for a co-op job. I was fairly easygoing about location—just eager to leave Canada and get some experience in my field at the same time. Having exhausted all of the usual job search channels at my university, I was determined to maintain my resolve and be resourceful. I started doing extensive Internet searches looking for international job postings in my field or programs that sent Canadians overseas. After many late nights on Google, I found something that looked like maybe it might be of interest. The posting was in German and appeared to be from a Japanese company. Being a pure Anglophone, I couldn't decipher either the German or the Japanese. I tried viewing the page with a few*

different on-line translators (Google, babelfish) and managed to figure out that it was a job posting on a German Web site for interns at a Bayer research centre in Japan. I sent a resume and cover letter to the contact address, had a phone interview within a few weeks and found myself in Japan a few months later!"

TACTICS FOR APPLYING

The selection process for internships can be highly competitive and is much like applying for a job. You will need to use all the common strategies. Young professional interns should know that international internships are about understanding the applicant's personality. The problem with our Internet-driven world is that e-mail correspondence is not conducive to conveying personality. Below are a few strategies for standing out in the crowd of applicants.

Your first telephone call to an organization is a good opportunity to request background information that may help you score extra points for a highly competitive internship. Ask the intern recruiter what types of applicants were successful in the past, what were their qualifications, etc. When you are preparing a cover letter or statement of interest, the more you know about an organization the better. Browsing an organization's Web site is the quick and easy way to gather this type of information, but it is also good to phone or meet former interns.

Getting into a good internship program can be a competitive process and you will have better results if you can clearly show what you will bring to an organization. In your application, therefore, it is important to highlight experiences and qualities that demonstrate how well your interests and skills suit the needs of the organization. Have your resume ready before you begin contacting organizations. Give serious thought and effort to developing a skills inventory. Prepare an elevator pitch to summarize your top skills and experience. You will also need a good covering letter, and in many cases, a written proposal for your internship. (For more information, see Chapter 23, Selling Your International Skills; Chapter 24, International Resumes and Chapter 25, Covering Letters.)

If you are making cold calls, make sure that you have a phone strategy. For example, you may be calling to set up your own internship. (See the section below, "Creating Your Own Internship.") In this case, you would generally ask to speak with someone in your area of expertise to discuss the possibility of arranging an internship. Example: *"Good afternoon. I would like to speak to a manager in your international finance department."* After reaching the person you requested, begin your inquiry with a brief profile of yourself (your elevator pitch) and describe your internship plan. *"Hello my name is Joan Landry. I am an MBA student with a specialization in international finance. I have a strong interest in selling mutual funds stock portfolios from the South. I am looking for a three-month work internship starting next April. Who should I speak with to discuss the possibility of arranging this?"* You may also use this approach when writing to someone via e-mail; however, don't discount the value of a phone call. E-mail is not the best medium when you want to impress someone and convey your professional personality. Phoning, especially long-distance phoning, will serve you well. (For more information on the use of these tactics, see Chapter 22, Phone Research Techniques.)

The basic application and selection criterion for applying to an internship is the written word—the cover e-mail, the cover letter, the resume and the application form.

If there is a formal application form, the organization likely takes its form seriously, so fill it out carefully. There is much anecdotal evidence to suggest that 80 per cent of the applicants to any large program submit poor applications, dull resumes and mediocre cover letters. The cover e-mails accompanying these documents are even more poorly written. If you assess that an internship is critical to your long-term career plans, then you should work hard at producing a perfect application package. There is no doubt that you need outside help for this. There are lots of resume writing workshops at universities, colleges and career centres. Or better still, find a mentor to help you with your application. Some of you are lucky and have professional parents to rely on. For others, you will need to put in some time as a mentee to a mid-career professional who will help you craft your application package. Five full days of work on your part is normal. Find a writer and proofreader to review your work—this is essential.

When you send your application by e-mail, follow up with a telephone call to ensure that all your materials were received. Use this opportunity to make personal contact with the organization and help ensure that you are remembered when the applications are being evaluated. Many Web sites today ask that applicants not contact the company by phone or e-mail. However, depending on the application instructions and your personality, you may still choose to contact the company to gather more information and follow up.

Here is a little known but very effective strategy when applying for internship positions: offer yourself as a fill-in candidate to replace other interns who drop out of the program at the last moment. This strategy is effective if you were previously rejected, if you missed the application deadline or if you find yourself available just prior to the departure dates. Consider the predicament of an organization that has funding for 24 internship positions and two or three of their candidates withdraw a few weeks prior to their scheduled departure. This always happens. Imagine if you are in touch with the intern recruitment officer, you are congenial on the phone, you have a good resume and you state that you are open and available to leave on short notice—you might actually get yourself that internship! You could even go so far as to offer to participate in the pre-departure training with no guarantee that there will be a position for you, and that you agree to be the fill-in candidate if a vacancy appears on short notice.

CREATING YOUR OWN INTERNSHIP

It is important to understand that while many organizations have formal internship programs, just as many, or more, do not. This doesn't mean they won't take an intern—rather, it may mean they will take one on an ad hoc basis if the person can contribute something valuable to the organization. From an organization's perspective, a proposal from an enthusiastic applicant offering services at little or no cost, is alluring.

There are many ways to create your own internship. Here are a few approaches:

- Prepare an internship proposal. Send it to the international office you are targeting for your internship. Generally, one page will suffice for a private firm; two or three pages for an NGO or international organization. The proposal should include a summary of your internship idea, your area of interest and motivation, your availability, suggested terms and your contact address and phone number. Of course, include a cover letter and your resume.

- Decide on a target at the beginning of your search. Do your research. For example, read international news magazines and target those organizations that are making headlines. Focus on an organization in your area of expertise and contact their international offices directly—choose the head office as well as branch offices in the countries of your choosing. In a small organization, contact the executive director. For large organizations, contact the department head in the unit that interests you. For a country-specific search, contact the country director overseas. Research specific names and e-mail addresses by looking at the company Web site or by calling the general number. Call ahead (even if you are calling overseas) to impress, to make personal contact and to ask if they would consider receiving an internship proposal.

- Tailor your university course load and research to match the work of an organization you are targeting for an internship or summer job. University research centres, especially those specialized in business or area studies, can also provide leads to organizations interested in hosting interns.

- If you have family or professional friends living overseas, target them to help arrange an internship.

- Take a gap year and consider going on a job hunting internship vacation. For example, you could arrive in Bangkok with the express purpose of looking for an internship. Have a business suit, resume and internship proposal ready. Rent a cell phone and get access to the Internet, and start conducting your search while staying at an inexpensive hotel. Check out the student work abroad programs that allow you to work on a student visa; don't use these programs just to be a barmaid—use them to set up professional internships. (For more information on the 30 countries offering Canadians student work visas, see the SWAP Programs in the Profiles section in Chapter 10, Short-Term Programs Overseas.)

- It is worth noting that some of the sponsoring organizations of the Canadian government's international internship programs allow interns to go out and make their own arrangements. These programs generally cover up to $12,000 of your costs for a six- to eight-month internship. You will be particularly desirable to an organization if, in addition to volunteering your services, you are already receiving a basic salary at no cost to them.

Don't let long-distance telephone charges or the time it takes to write an e-mail message stand in your way. This is especially important if you live outside the hub of large cities. If you live in small-town New Brunswick and want to intern for an NGO in Washington, DC, contact its managers directly. These efforts will go a long way toward establishing the personal contacts that are necessary to create a self-directed, international internship.

NEGOTIATING SALARY AND BENEFITS

An internship requires a substantial investment. Not only will it involve a great deal of your time and energy, but the costs of travel and your living expenses for the duration of the assignment will not be insignificant. So, while you may not be able to negotiate a salary, it is important to know that many "unpaid" interns do manage to negotiate some benefits.

You can broach the subject by asking if there is a possibility of being paid an *honorarium*—a salary that covers very basic living costs. It can be as low as $25 per day to cover transportation and food, or $350 per week to subsidize accommodation.

If you travel abroad for the internship, most organizations will agree to pay for accommodation. If they don't do this, ask about being billeted with an employee's family. Many organizations will also cover airfare or agree to a departure payment equivalent to airfare. It is also important to discuss health coverage and, if necessary, make alternative arrangements.

You may be able to get funding for your internship from a sponsoring institution, such as your school's faculty of graduate studies or your academic department. With some scholarships or awards, a portion can be used for research undertaken during an internship. If you are submitting a proposal for a scholarship, factor the cost of an internship into your budget.

The cost of an internship may seem prohibitive, especially if you are just finishing a degree and have large student debts. However, if you compare the cost of one term at university with the benefits of an opportunity abroad, you will see that your internship is really a short-term expense for long-term gain.

SURVIVING YOUR FIRST PROFESSIONAL JOB

An internship may be your first professional job. In order to succeed, there are a host of fundamental work habits and skills that you will need to master. First, realize that professional work is all about communicating. In today's workplace, great value is placed on being able to communicate simple ideas to a wide and varied audience. Often universities do not fully prepare students for this reality because university education is traditionally theory-based and focus is placed on retaining knowledge, not on application and building communication skills. However, communicating in the international workplace is particularly important, since these environments tend to be more formal with a greater emphasis placed on good writing. There's also the added complexity of fellow employees from all corners of the world who often communicate in ways different from you. So, it really is essential that international interns exhibit good communication skills.

There are two aspects to communicating in the workplace: first, you should focus on planning and organization skills. And second, focus on people skills. Based on feedback and experiences of hundreds of recent graduates, some of the following tips will help you succeed in your first professional work placement:

- **Always maintain a well-organized to-do list.** When an action comes to mind, write it down immediately. When your manager asks you to do something, he or she wants to see you writing it down. There are two types of to-do lists. One is required for managing a running list of items (and this should not be a series of papers with scribble notes or a wall of post-it notes). A second is required for organizing various projects—this second system comprises lists that itemize by project and that are separate from general to-do lists. For all types of to-do lists, have a method for flagging or prioritizing important items.

- **When organizing a meeting always write an agenda ahead of time.** Make two copies, one for yourself and one for the colleague with whom you are meeting.

Group similar items together under separate headings and sort items from most to least important. Number each item and sub-item to promote clearer discussions. When attending meetings, always have a note pad and write down important points that are discussed. Take time immediately after a meeting to notate the outcome and communicate this to colleagues who attended the meeting.

- **When writing, always write perfectly.** Learn to write grammatically perfect e-mails, letters and reports. Look for the top writers in your department—savour and emulate their skills. Learn when to send an e-mail (to communicate facts) and when to pick up the phone (to communicate an opinion, provide feedback, negotiate). You may already believe that, because of your university education, you are a good writer. Take note, however, that—by world standards—many believe that North Americans are poor writers. From day one, you should concentrate on consistently producing clear and effective writing. Your career will benefit greatly.

- **Get organized and create systems to manage work.** At least 10 per cent of your day should be devoted to filing and organizing such things as hard-copy files, to-do lists, agendas, project plans and status reports. Learn how to organize your pending e-mails and completed e-mails. Develop and adhere to a consistent electronic file-naming procedure. Stay on top of paper filing. Develop audit tables to track the progress of your work. Look for repetitive processes and document them. Seek out formal methodologies and let these guide your work. Write and adhere to procedures manuals. Write evaluation/closing reports on all mid-sized and large projects. Manage your systems to perfection. Design your systems to allow your successor to step in seamlessly.

- **Become familiar with project planning techniques.** For all your projects, whether they are a two-hour or a two-month piece of work, write project plans before they become active. Have the plan pre-approved by your manager. There is nothing more impressive than an intern following up after an initial project discussion with a short project plan broken into phases. It's easy to become proficient with the fundamentals of project management—simply take an on-line course.

- **Learn to answer the phone professionally and make effective phone calls.** Learn how to place someone on hold politely, to answer two calls at the same time or to ask who is calling before passing the call on to your manager. For some international jobs, you will need a similar set of skills for short wave radio communications. When making phone calls, learn to devise a strategy before making the call. Write down the specific outcome you want to achieve and jot down the points you want to make.

- **Manage your time with the boss.** Ask questions, but organize them first. Tell your boss when you successfully finish a project. Always present your work in a professional manner. If you must absolutely be late for a deadline, let your boss know well ahead of time so that she or he can prepare. If your boss is not organized, or is too busy, help your boss be organized—write the meeting agenda and action items, offer to file, edit, bring the car around or pick up a sandwich to save time during lunch.

- **Your people skills are the most important of all your skills.** Many university graduates learn a hard lesson in their first full-time, salaried position. The most common reason for losing your first job is failure to come to grips with office politics. Natural enthusiasm and hard work only take you so far. You must focus on learning people-skills *first*. Be respectful of your supervisor's position and responsibilities. Practice tact at meetings, and find ways to recognize the accomplishments of co-workers. Master the imprecise arts of listening, and taking and giving constructive criticism. Understand the value of compromise, work to build consensus, learn to mediate, and practice motivating others. In cross-cultural work, as in many other fields, good people skills are at least as important as technical knowledge and personal ambition.

- **Thank your boss and colleagues regularly.** You may have graduated at the top of your class and won out over dozens to attain your internship. You may also believe that four to six years of university study entitles you to special treatment, especially since you are practically volunteering your valuable time as an intern. The fact of the matter is, however, interns require a lot of handholding and demand great amounts of energy from managers. You may not realize this since you are leaving an education system where everyone is devoted to serving you, the student. Experienced managers know that it takes long hours and patience to provide an intern with directions and feedback. Many managers are reluctant to accept interns because of the time it takes to train them, and then see this investment evaporate when the intern leaves. So no matter what level of service you get as an intern (and no internship is without its problems), you should regularly take the time to thank your boss and colleagues. There are many gracious ways to say thanks to the managers who are shepherding you at the start of your career path. Bravo to them!

- **Read pertinent articles.** A good place to start is Eric Glanville's article, "Maximizing Your First Year on the Job," in Appendix 17c on the CD-ROM.

A FEW SPECIFIC LESSONS FROM THE FIELD

Search out past interns who have gone abroad. They have experienced first-hand the excitement and challenges of working in a cross-cultural work environment. Here are some tips and a random selection of what some interns have to say about interning abroad.

- **Many interns find placements with large international organizations.** They may find the bureaucracy frustrating, old fashioned, hierarchical and be shocked when colleagues do not necessarily share their humanitarian ideals. Interns who are successful in large organizations learn quickly that it is futile to try to beat or change the bureaucratic system. They understand that their job is to make the system work; they learn the system and then take delight in making it work for them. Recognize that there is such a thing as a "good bureaucrat"—someone who knows the ins and outs and understands the politics. Seek out these people as coaches and mentors.

- **Many international interns are given wide latitude in choosing projects.** Interns come with fresh ideas, and they quickly identify many areas that can be improved. The experience of past interns suggests that their enthusiasm may lead them to promise too much at the start. They suggest that new interns should be cautious and not over-promise. Choose small projects and finish them professionally.

"When I started my internship with a large NGO in Bangladesh, I soon realized that the organization's Web site was in shambles. I enthusiastically volunteered to redesign the whole site as a side project to my regular work. In

hindsight, the task was much too big and required the coordination of too many stakeholders. I would have been much better off first volunteering to redesign a smaller section of the site, and then completed this smaller project with 100 per cent satisfaction."

- **Be patient in your analysis and critique, especially when you first arrive at a placement.** Don't let your enthusiasm overtake you or jump to conclusions about what you first observe.

   "Part of the learning curve as an intern with a small NGO in the northern region of Togo required that I sit back and observe without jumping to conclusions. When I first arrived, the office looked like it was in shambles, only two computers for a staff of seven, no one showed up on time for meetings, I was given little or no direction. As time passed, I came to appreciate the level of professionalism of the Togoleese outreach workers. They were skillful in dealing with villagers and running community meetings and they worked long and hard when making their rounds visiting our partner organizations. In the end, I decided that we were in fact a highly effective NGO."

- **Take time to socialize, it is not all about work.** Interns who spend personal time with work colleagues, learn a bit of the local language and share in local food, are much appreciated. North Americans are very *results-oriented* but most of the world is *process-oriented*. While we often measure our success with *what we accomplish*, we often give little regard for *how we accomplished it*. The rest of the world is much more concerned with how things were done or how the needs of work colleagues were attended to. Was each person treated according to his or her credentials? Was the hierarchy respected? Take time to ensure that the people-equation is part of your formula in how you accomplish work.

- **Expect problems.** International internships are by definition fraught with a series of small and large challenges. Your host organization may not measure up. Your sponsoring organization back home will not always meet your expectations. The work you are given may be boring and job descriptions may change. You may feel justified in lashing out. In reality, this rarely helps or heals the situation. You will be much better off if you expend your energies in finding solutions, being flexible and rolling humorously with the punches. If an internship is really not working, then negotiate a transfer. Generally, however, do not simply analyze work issues solely in terms of how you are affected—your manager will appreciate it if you see your role as a small part in the larger picture.

   "As project manager in Vietnam, we had an unfortunate incident with one intern. She was bright and worked hard on her assignment, conducting field research as part of a large report for a new commercial venture. Three quarters of the way through her assignment, senior management decided that they did not need her research and her work was to be struck from the final report. She was so disappointed that she left her internship on the spot and did not even submit a final report. This intern was doing a good job, but she failed to realize that the needs of the firm were more important than her own."

JOB HUNTING DURING YOUR INTERNSHIP

Here are a few important career-building strategies to ensure that your internship experience will help you improve your long-term international job prospects. The overall objective is to score as many points as possible, thus building experience for your resume prior to graduating with a master's degree. Don't be overwhelmed; adhering to only a few of the suggestions below will put you in a much better position to land a paying international job once you graduate.

- **Be bold in your job hunting tactics.** Most entry-level job offers are found through the back door. Keep your eyes open for any potential jobs and take quick action on them when they arise.

- **Be curious during your internship.** Make friends in other departments and organizations. Make networking contacts and attend every conference and meeting outside of your department. Travel on short job hunting trips in your region of the world. Search out managers and leaders in your field of interest. Track names and addresses of all international colleagues for future job networking. Maintain an old-fashioned address book.

- **Work hard.** Internships are often viewed by employers as testing periods for selecting permanent hires. You will need to impress. Go beyond your job and volunteer with whomever needs you, especially to gain professional experience. Offer services that are in short supply: editing, translation, computer work, Internet set-up. Work hard and enjoy yourself—have fun at work.

- **If a paying job opportunity arises, consider leaving your internship.** You need to be gracious and honourable when negotiating your departure. Your new employer should be flexible on start dates in order for you to give full consideration to your internship hosting organization.

- **Score extra resume points during your internship.** While interning abroad, look at how you can add one or two other professional experiences so that you can score extra points on your resume. Teach a computer class at a local high school or for local NGOs. Produce a radio program on a development-related topic. Present a seminar to a professional group or university class on your area of expertise. Participate in organizing an event, any event, outside of your workplace. Write a quick-reference card on the cultural norms of your host country which will help you cleverly promote your cross-cultural skills when you give it to other expats and show it to international employers. Design and deliver an orientation program for new expatriates entering the country. Teach business English part-time. Edit a manuscript for a professional in your field of expertise. Over one weekend, use Quicken software to design the accounting system for a small NGO. The ideas are endless. Any of these suggestions can be done fairly easily to score big career building points on your resume.

- **Continue traditional job hunting techniques while you are abroad.** This is a very potent job hunting technique. There is nothing more impressive for an international employer than to receive a job application from a young organized intern based overseas. The Internet makes doing so quite easy. Whether you are applying to a North American or an international organization, employers will take notice when they receive, for example, an application from a North American currently interning in Taiwan. You are much more impressive if you are job hunting abroad than if you are at home sitting jobless on your couch looking for international work! (See the article by Tanissa Martindale, "Job Hunting During Your Internship," in Appendix 17b on the CD-ROM.)

- **Plan for two internships while studying for a master's degree.** Consider doing two international internships during your university studies, one after your undergraduate degree, and another after or during your master's. The premise is that you will be completing a master's degree to qualify for an international position. (Also read the ideas outlined in the section "The Ideal International Profile" in Chapter 18, Your Career Path & The Ideal International Profile.)

- **Find a short-term consulting contract abroad after your internship.** This is perhaps the most important advice in this whole chapter. There is nothing more important than trying to extend your stay as an intern abroad for an extra month to work in a professional job with another organization. With a one-month consultancy, you double the value of your professional international work experience on your resume.

  - It will never be easier to grab an international contract. The key concept here is that you are abroad, you are able to make contacts and you are bathing in a soup called *the international job market*. There is no other more effective strategy in building your international resume than looking for international work while you are interning abroad. The task of finding international work will get harder when you return home to North America. So seize the moment.

  - Go abroad with the express purpose of extending your stay. You need this mindset to envision that you will be staying longer than your six-month internship. Remember, this is an important career move for you and you should realize the potency of your decision to extend your stay. If you don't envision it, then it likely will not happen.

  - Start with a plan that begins when you first arrive in your host country as an intern. For a six-month internship broken into two-month phases—Phase One: work hard to impress your host organization; Phase Two: begin researching potential employers outside of your workplace, begin a series of information-gathering interviews and network, network, network; Phase Three: actively approach potential employers.

  - Who are these potential employers that can offer you a one- or two-month consulting contract? Here is a list of possibilities: other NGOs, IGOs or INGOs; embassies (and not just your own); other international consultants who are always hanging out at the local high-end hotel; international firms operating in your country; your host organization might transpose your internship into a paying contract; and, field offices of all the above types of organizations located inside your host country or in nearby countries.

  - Why would these employers be interested in you? Firstly, you are already on the ground and you know the ropes. In comparison to any other international consultant, you cost very little in salary and travel costs. You know the geography of the city and the country, you probably have a smattering of local language skills and you certainly have the cross-cultural experience to work in tandem with local staff. You can quickly respond to an employer's needs. You probably also have good contacts with other expats and their international employers. Moreover, you are skilled—university educated with talent and enthusiasm. Bravo, what an irresistible combination for an employer with temporary staffing needs.

- Off-the-wall research techniques. Have a c.v. ready—one clearly stating that you are looking for a short-term, one- or two-month contract at the end of your current internship. Create a small half-page ad and post it everywhere expatriates hang out: the embassies, the expat clubs, the local bars. Have business cards printed to facilitate all manners of networking. Socialize at the spousal clubs that exist in most capitals—it is often easier to network through them than directly with their working spouses. Go to as many expat parties as you can. Offer to work for free and to provide country orientation for incoming consultants—pick them up at the airport and hand them your resume while driving into town (this works). Speak to commercial officers at embassies and ask for private sector contacts from firms based in your home country and operating in your host country. Do your own freelance consulting—submit proposals directly to international organizations in your region. Offer to work as a low-paid assistant to busy international professionals living in-country—do this even in exchange for room and board (save money and reside in their home) and with the express purpose of building experience. Offer to be an administrative assistant (and driver) to an international consultant who is in town on a short mission. Find a second short-term internship with another organization—make it project specific to your field of interest.
- Be flexible, seize any opportunity to extend your stay after your internship to gain more international experience and build up your resume.
- **Other strategies to extend your stay abroad after an internship.** There are hundreds of ways to stay abroad and continue to build international experience. Here is a list of tactics, and use your diplomatic prowess and entrepreneurial imagination to find more. (For other suggestions, see also Chapter 9, Starting Your International Career; Chapter 12, Cross-Cultural Travel; Chapter 14, Awards & Grants and Chapter 18, Your Career Path & The Ideal International Profile.)
  - Consider teaching at a Third World university for a semester if you have a master's and like to teach.
  - Consider teaching English abroad as a stepping-stone to other jobs.
  - Consider doing international refugee or relief work.
  - Continue to travel, but make it a job hunting vacation. Show up on the doorsteps of international employers.
  - Extend your stay to learn a new language and job hunt while doing so.
  - Volunteer as an editor with non–English speaking experts.
  - Keep up your correspondence with international colleagues.
  - Write directly to experts in your field and volunteer your services.

A LAST WORD

International internships can provide fascinating professional experiences and are an excellent means of launching your international career. So, remember to take your internship seriously, but also keep a good sense of humour—no internship is perfect. Think of your placement as a "real job" that carries importance for the organization you're serving. The value you place on your internship will translate into value placed on your skills by your sponsoring organization—and could even lead to an offer of paid employment. Don't be overwhelmed by the many suggestions found in this chapter. Choose only a few, and make a professional go at it without being over-serious. Good luck and enjoy your internship!

APPENDIX ON THE CD-ROM

> 17a. "Choosing the Right Internship Organization," by Geoff Owen
> 17b. "Job Hunting During Your Internship," by Tanissa Martindale
> 17c. "Maximizing Your First Year on the Job," by Eric Glanville

RESOURCES
INTERNATIONAL INTERNSHIPS

Here's a list of books and resources to help you find that first job and get you started on your international career. Remember that most organizations in this book have indicated that they provide formal and ad hoc internships within their organizations; so, contacting them directly is a good start. You should also consult the numerous Resources sections in this guide related to job searching and volunteering.

Back To My Roots 🖳
www.backtomyroots.com ◆ This site is for young expatriates such as exchange students and interns. It displays two lists of useful links—one from your home country and one from the country in which you are (temporarily) residing in. Also offers Web-based e-mail, discussion forums and your own private photo album. [ID:2574]

Canada Corps ﷼
www.CanadaCorps.gc.ca; *Fr* ◆ At the time of printing, the Canadian government made a commitment to create Canada Corps under Foreign Affairs Canada (FAC). Canada Corps will enhance linkages among existing Canadian efforts and explore new partnerships with other levels of government and the private sector. The initiative will harness the energy and experience of Canadian experts, volunteers and young professionals to deliver international assistance in the areas of governance and institution building. Watch their Web site for news about this initiative. [ID:2839]

CANADEM ﷼
www.canadem.ca; *Fr* ◆ Canadem maintains a national roster of Canadians skilled in human rights, peace building, democratization, admin-logistics, security, reconstruction and other international field experience. One way it achieves this goal is by administering the Junior Professional Consultant Program, which is one of the best-run internship programs around. Each year approximately 30 young Canadians are deployed to a number of host organizations (OSCE, IOM, UNDP to name a few) in Africa, Eastern Europe and Central Asia. Pre-departure training is excellent, as is post-deployment support. [ID:2616]

Canadian International Development Agency (CIDA): International Internships ﷼
www.acdi-cida.gc.ca/internships ◆ This Web site lists internships by country, title, sector and organization and presents information on how to apply and what to expect. Internships are available in both official languages. [ID:2623]

Courrier international 🖳
www.courrierinternational.com; *Fr* ◆ Hebdomadaire français d'information internationale avec une section Emplois internationaux, incluant différents stages et une rubrique d'informations ayant pour titre « S'expatrier » (informations sur différents pays, conseils, études sur les niveaux de salaire des jeunes diplômés dans le monde et sur les différents modes de recrutement en Europe). [ID:2704]

Directory of International Internships: A World of Opportunities 📖
2003, Charles Gliozzo, Vernicka Tyson, Adela Pena, Bob Dye, 176 pages ➤ Attn: International Placement, Michigan State University, Career Services and Placement, 113 Student Services Bldg., East Lansing, MI 48824, USA, www.csp.msu.edu, $45.95 US; VISA, MC; 517-355-9510 ext. 371, fax 517-353-2597 ◆ This excellent US directory contains 170 pages of information on how to obtain an international internship as well as listings of international internships sponsored by educational institutions, government agencies and private organizations. Topics covered include subject areas, number of internships, objectives, description, location, duration, financial data, eligibility, stipulations, guidelines, and contact information including name, address, telephone, fax, e-mail and Web site. The directory is indexed by countries and topic, which are organized to provide easy access to international internship information. [ID:2110]

Employment Resources on the Internet 🖥
www.cco.purdue.edu/asp/JobWeb/View.asp, Free on-line ◆ This US University job search page is a good starting point for your job search on the Web. Contains a good list of links to dozens of career sites, organized in easy-to-use categories such as job fields, internships, recruiters, geographic locations and classifieds. [ID:2243]

Foreign Policy Association 🖥
Foreign Policy Association, www.fpa.org ◆ International job postings categorized by development assistance, education, environment, humanitarian relief, health and population, research, youth and other. A great listing of internships and volunteer opportunities. Highly recommended. [ID:2579]

Human Rights Education Associations 🖥
www.hrea.org/erc/Links/indcx.html ◆ This Dutch Web site has an incredible links page to human rights organizations all over the world. A great place to start researching jobs in this field. [ID:2624]

International Mode D'Emploi 🖥
www.insert-export.com/index/indexoffre.htm; ℱ𝓇 ◆ L'International Mode d'Emploi est un site français regroupant diverses offres d'emploi et stages à l'étranger. On nous propose aussi des conseils et informations pour travailler à l'extérieur. À noter: pour avoir accès aux postes offerts, il faut s'inscrire comme membre et débourser des frais. [ID:2708]

International Youth and Young Workers Exchange Programs ⛺
www.dfait-maeci.gc.ca/english/culture/youthex.html; ℱ𝓇 ◆ This directory, maintained by Foreign Affairs Canada (FAC), is designed for the use of Canadians between the ages of 18 and 35 who are seeking employment abroad. It lists opportunities by region and describes ways of gaining access to employment markets around the world. [ID:2241]

InternJobs.com 🖥
www.internjobs.com ◆ This is a US national database of internships for students and recent graduates. Search our database by keywords or location. Employers can post internships and entry-level jobs for free. [ID:2648]

Internships 2004 📖
Annual, 744 pages ➤ Thomson Peterson's, P.O. Box 2123, Princeton, NJ 08543-2123, USA, www.petersons.com, $26.95 US; Credit Cards; 800-338-3282, fax 609-243-9150 ◆ Whether you're searching for work experience during the academic year, during the summer or immediately after graduation, you will find this fact-filled directory useful. Complete information on getting the most out of the internship experience including the value of internships, choosing the right internship and the application process. Includes profiles of nearly 50,000 paid and unpaid internship opportunities at thousands of corporations and organizations all over the world. Great for anyone looking for entry-level experience in a new career too. [ID:2015]

Internships for Dummies 📖
2001, 312 pages ➤ John Wiley & Sons, 22 Worcester Road, Etobicoke, ON M9W 1L1, Canada, www.wiley.ca, $21.99 CDN; Credit Cards; 800-567-4797, fax 800-565-6802, canada@wiley.com

◆ This books provides criteria for deciding which internship and industry is right for you. Includes helpful tips on preparing your resume, interviewing effectively and building a successful career after your internship. [ID:2390]

Job/Internship Vacancy Links & Resources to Research Employers 💻
www.ub-careers.buffalo.edu/career/oco/cpp/student/internat.shtml ◆ This extensive list of links is brought to you by the University of Buffalo. This page is a great portal to thousands of international job hunting resources on the Internet. [ID:2254]

Jobs et stages autour du monde 📖
2002, Dakota Éditions, 544 pages ➤ Les Éditions Ulysse, 4176 rue St-Denis, Montréal, QC H2W 2M5, Canada, www.guidesulysse.com/cc/main_achat.htm, $24.95 CDN; Cartes de crédit; 514-843-9447, fax 514-843-9448; *Fr* ◆ Ce guide offre des milliers d'emplois et de stages sur les cinq continents. On y recense 300 fiches employeurs détaillées et des dizaines de témoignages. De nombreuses informations et astuces nous sont données pour décrocher un permis de travail et rédiger un bon curriculum vitae en langue étrangère. [ID:2718]

La mission des fonctionnaires internationaux 👬
www.france.diplomatie.fr/mfi; *Fr* ◆ Site du Ministère des affaires étrangères en France : informations générales, listes des avis de vacances de postes des organisations internationales, postes spécifiques pour jeunes professionnels, stages, etc. [ID:2705]

Monster Trak 💻
www.monstertrak.monster.com ◆ This US site is directed toward recent and future post-secondary graduates seeking internships and jobs. Requires registration and allows uploading of your resume to their database and checks internships and job postings daily. [ID:2434]

Policy Library 💻
www.policylibrary.com ◆ Policy Library Web site is a social, economic and foreign policy resource—updated daily with the latest jobs, research and events. An annual membership costs $70 CDN and allows access to hundreds of jobs, internships and scholarships from all around the world. A good resource for policy buffs. [ID:2644]

Russian and Eastern European Institute Employment Opportunities 💻
www.indiana.edu/~reeiweb/indemp.html ◆ This Web site is produced by Indiana University and contains links to job hunting resources, internships and non-academic opportunities for those with an interest in Russia and Eastern Europe. [ID:2363]

Transcultural Leadership: Empowering the Diverse Workforce 📖
1999, George Simmons, Carmen Vazquez, Phillip Harris, Gulf Publishing, 260 pages ➤ McGraw-Hill Ryerson Ltd., 300 Water Street, Whitby, ON L1N 9B6, Canada, www.mcgrawhill.ca, $63.50 CDN; Credit Cards; 800-565-5758, fax 800-463-5885 ◆ A discussion of the modern global reality of cultural and gender diversity in the workplace. [ID:2170]

United Nations Volunteers (UNV) 💻
www.unv.org ◆ This program offers mid-career professionals the opportunity to volunteer overseas in a humanitarian effort. Every year some 5,000 UN Volunteers from more than 150 different nationalities take part in the programs of the United Nations itself as well as UN funds, programs and specialized agencies. This informative and user-friendly site has all the information you need to become a UN Volunteer and gain international experience. [ID:2153]

Vivre à l'étranger 💻
www.vivrealetranger.com; *Fr* ◆ Site français sur la mobilité internationale : articles et dossiers sur différents pays, guide pratique de l'expatriation (stages, volontariat, préparation, déménagement, santé, assurances). [ID:2707]

WetFeet 💻
www.wetfeet.com ◆ This is a very well-designed US Web site with an excellent international job and internship search page accessible from the index under "Find a Job." The "Internship Search

Engine" database contains hundreds of internships listed by location and job category. In addition, you'll find heaps of helpful advice on finding and making the most of your internship experience, written by insiders. Many articles are field specific; others tackle subjects like "Creating Your Own Internships" and "Turning Your Internship Into a Job." The job-search page is also comprehensive and easy to use. Add this one to your favourites. [ID:2428]

YouthPath 🖳
Human Resources and Skills Development Canada, www.youth.gc.ca, Free on-line; ᶠr ◆ A Web site resource for Canadian youth seeking work and study opportunities in Canada or abroad. Lists hundreds of Government of Canada youth programs, services and resources. You can learn about Canada's role internationally or about how you can get involved by clicking the "International" tab on the index. Navigate to the "Opportunities" page and explore external links and government-sponsored exchange, volunteer and internship programs, such as internships with CIDA. If you want to gain international experience, this is an excellent place to start your research. [ID:2191]

Profiles of International Internships

There are so many international internship possibilities that we cannot profile them all in this chapter. Some internships have been profiled in Chapter 10, Short-Term Programs Overseas while others can be arranged with most of the organizations profiled in this book. With the exception of the first profile, the following 37 internships are all hosted by international organizations, which are sometimes difficult to research. The first profile is one that Canadians should absolutely take note of.

Canadian Government International Internship Programs
Youth International Internships Program, Human Resources Development
Canada, Phase IV, 4th Floor, Place du Portage, Gatineau, QC, K1A 0J9,
Canada; 800-935-5555, fax 613-941-5992, http://youth.hrdc-drhc.gc.ca 🖳ᶠr

---

INTERNSHIPS ◆ The resources that follow offer programs that are fantastic for gaining international experience. The Government of Canada's Youth Employment Strategy (YES) annually offers approximately 1,340 international work experiences in a wide range of fields including communications, international development, international trade and the environment. The program gives young college or university graduates the opportunity to gain work experience in the private, non-governmental, and non-profit sectors for up to one year. Individuals interested in participating in these international work experiences generally must be between the ages of 15 and 30, and must have a college diploma or university degree. Under the Youth Employment Strategy's Career Focus program, international work opportunities are available through the following departments: Foreign Affairs Canada (FAC), the Canadian International Development Agency (CIDA), Industry Canada, Canadian Heritage, Parks Canada and Environment Canada.

Application procedures vary for each program. For example, programs administered by CIDA and FAC require candidates to apply directly to the partner organizations that these departments have chosen. For others, including those administered by Canadian Heritage and Industry Canada, candidates can apply using on-line applications found on the department's Web site. In some instances, individuals have set up their own internship with a company and arranged for a government-sponsored partner to fund them. These internships are an invaluable opportunity to get your international career started—take advantage of them!

FOREIGN AFFAIRS CANADA (FAC) AND INTERNATIONAL TRADE CANADA (ITCAN) Young Professionals International (YPI) provides a career-related international work experience that furthers the objectives of Canada's foreign policy, specifically the promotion of prosperity and employment, peace and global security, and the projection of Canadian values and culture abroad. Approximately 400 placements are awarded per year. (For more information on this department, see the Foreign Affairs Canada (FAC) and International Trade Canada (ITCan) profile in Chapter 37, Canadian Government.) Visit www.dfait-maeci.gc.ca/ypi-jpi for further details.

The CANADIAN INTERNATIONAL DEVELOPMENT AGENCY (CIDA) **International Youth Internship Program (IYIP)** offers recent graduates the opportunity to gain work experience in an international development setting. Internships fall under at least one of CIDA's six programming priorities: basic human needs; women in development; infrastructure service; human rights, democratic development and good governance; private sector development; and environment. Approximately 400 internships are awarded per year. (For more information, contact the Government of Canada Youth Info line at (800) 935-5555, or consult CIDA's Web site at www.acdi-cida.gc.ca/youth.) (For more information on this department, see the Canadian International Development Agency (CIDA) profile in Chapter 37, Canadian Government.)

INDUSTRY CANADA, **in partnership with** NETCORPS CANADA INTERNATIONAL, annually offers approximately 250 exciting volunteer internships in developing countries for people 19 to 30 years of age with appropriate skills in information and communication technologies (ICT). These internships are implemented by some of Canada's largest volunteer-sending international development organizations. NETCORPS CANADA INTERNATIONAL is currently delivered by the following nine coalition members: CANADA WORLD YOUTH, ALTERNATIVES, CUSO, CANADIAN CROSSROADS INTERNATIONAL, THE CANADIAN SOCIETY FOR INTERNATIONAL HEALTH, HUMAN RIGHTS INTERNET, OXFAM-QUÉBEC, VSO, and THE INTERNATIONAL INSTITUTE FOR SUSTAINABLE DEVELOPMENT. Information on the program may be obtained by visiting www.netcorps-cyberjeunes.org.

CANADIAN HERITAGE AND PARKS CANADA'S **Young Canada Works (YCW)** internships are an enriching experience on all counts. You can choose an internship focused on building your linguistic capabilities, or one entirely dedicated to culture and heritage. Approximately 160 internships are available each year. These internships help you make contacts in the workplace, perfect your professional skills in your chosen field and improve your career options by working in Canada or abroad. For more information, visit www.pch.gc.ca/ycw-jct.

ENVIRONMENT CANADA'S **International Environmental Youth Corps (IEYC)** creates and provides employment opportunities and work experience though internships with Canadian ex-porters of environmental products and services. Approximately 130 internships are awarded per year. The IEYC is managed by Environment Canada and delivered by THE CANADIAN COUNCIL FOR HUMAN RESOURCES IN THE ENVIRONMENT INDUSTRY (CCHREI). For more information and an application package, consult Environment Canada's Web site at www.ec.gc.ca or the CCHREI's Web site at www.cchrei.ca. You may also phone CCHREI at (403)233-0748. [ID:5657]

Canadian Mission to the European Union
Coordinator, Canadian Mission to the European Union, B-1040, Avenue de Tervuren 2,
Brussels, Belgium; www.dfait-maeci.gc.ca/canadaeuropa/EU/menu-en.asp ⌨ℱr

INTERNSHIPS ◆ The Canadian Mission to the European Union Internship Program is intended to offer Canadian citizens an opportunity to improve their understanding of Canada-Europe relations and European integration, while contributing to the Mission's objectives. By participating in the work of the Mission, under the supervision of one of the Mission's counsellors, participants gain practical insight into the conduct of Canadian diplomacy in Europe and the issues at stake in the Canada-Europe relationship. Applicants for the Mission Internship Program should be Canadian citizens who have recently graduated from university with at least a bachelor's degree. Deadlines for applications usually fall in late May. [ID:5601]

Economic and Social Commission for Western Asia (ESCWA)
Internship Programme, P.O. Box 11-8575, Riad el-Solh Square, Beirut, Lebanon;
(961) (1) 981-301, fax (961) (1) 981-510, webmaster-escwa@un.org, www.escwa.org.lb

INTERNSHIPS ◆ The Economic and Social Commission for Western Asia's (ESCWA) internship program offers three- to six-month unpaid internships to outstanding young students and professionals under 30 years of age who specialize in fields relevant to ESCWA's work, such as agriculture, computer science, demography, economics, engineering, environment, finance, international relations, journalism, mass media, public administration, sociology, statistics, and translation and terminology.

Successful applicants will be graduate students or holders of a first university degree who intend to study further or to work in a field relevant to the ESCWA work program. Preference will be given to candidates pursuing a graduate degree. Applicants must submit copies of their university diplomas and grades, and write an essay explaining how the internship will contribute to the candidate's overall academic or professional goals. The deadline for applications is two months before the starting date. Applicants should be fluent in Arabic, English or French. (For more information on ESCWA, see Chapter 41, United Nations & Other IGOs). [ID:5660]

The European Union Internship Program
Internship Coordinator, Delegation of the European Commission to the United States, 2300 M Street N.W., Washington, DC, 20037, USA; 202-862-9500, fax 202-429-1766, www.eurunion.org

INTERNSHIPS ◆ The Delegation of the European Commission offers internship positions at its offices in Washington, DC, New York City, Brussels and Luxembourg. Internships are intended to provide college and university students and recent graduates with the opportunity to acquire knowledge of the European Union, its institutions, activities, law and statistics. The internships in Washington are offered exclusively on a volunteer basis only. The Commission Internship and The Economic and Social Committee (ESC) Internships are offered in Brussels and at the European Parliament in Luxembourg. Internships are usually offered on a volunteer basis and a working knowledge of French is useful, but not essential. Deadlines vary according to position. Visit the European Union Web site for specific information and application forms. [ID:5644]

Inter-American Development Bank (IADB)
Junior Professional Program, Employment and Scholarships Section,, 1300 New York Ave. N.W., Washington, DC, 20577, USA; 202-623-1000, fax 202-623-3096, pic@iadb.org, www.iadb.org 📖 Fr 📖 Sp

INTERNSHIPS ◆ The Inter-American Development Bank's (IADB) Junior Professional Program (JPP) is a starting point for careers at the bank. Assignments are available for those with skills in economics, finance, engineering, business management, public administration, health, computer science or law, or in emerging areas such as trade, labour, modernization of the state, governance, the environment and women in development.

The number of internships available varies annually according to budgetary allocations, but generally there are between five and 10 junior professionals on board at any one time. The duration of the program is 24 months, with two 12-month assignments in different departments. Junior Professionals are treated as full-fledged staff members with specific responsibilities and may be assigned to country offices as part of the Program. Participants are generally hired as regular staff members during the course of their program.

To be considered, candidates must be citizens of a member country of the bank, have at least a master's degree, and be under the age of 32. Applicants should also have at least one year of professional-level experience, be fluent in English and Spanish and have a working knowledge of an official third language.

The bank also offers other seasonal internship programs for those who wish to gain practical experience in the operational and administrative activities of the bank. IADB will accept up to 10 interns in these activities at any time for two to three months. Operational and administrative Interns must be enrolled in an undergraduate university program and be returning to their studies. (For more information about IADB see Chapter 41, United Nations & Other IGOs.) [ID:5640]

International Atomic Energy Agency (IAEA)
Division of Personnel, P.O. Box 100, Wagramerstrasse 5, A - 1400 Vienna, Austria; (43) (1) 2600-0, fax (43) (1) 2600-7, official.mail@iaea.org, www.iaea.org

INTERNSHIPS ◆ The International Atomic Energy Agency (IAEA) offers a limited number of unpaid internships each year to students specializing in areas relevant to the agency's programs.

Opportunities arise according to the needs and resources of individual divisions within the secretariat.

Successful applicants will be under the age of 32 and come from a member state country. Internships are flexible in scope and range in duration from one month to one year. Applicants must have an excellent knowledge of spoken English and be able to write in English. (For more information on the IAEA, see Chapter 41, United Nations & Other IGOs). [ID:5645]

International Fund for Agricultural Development (IFAD)
Via del Serafico 107, 00142 Rome, Italy; (39) (6) 54591,
fax (39) (6) 504-3463, internships@ifad.org, www.ifad.org

INTERNSHIPS ◆ The International Fund for Agricultural Development's (IFAD) internship exposes interns to a wide range of development issues including small-scale rural development, agricultural extension projects, sustainability, project development and financing. As a rule, internship assignments will not exceed six consecutive months.

IFAD has an ad hoc recruiting scheme, and draws from different university programs in various countries in filling the up to 25 intern positions each calendar year. Successful candidates will be upper-level undergraduates or graduate students who are 30 years of age or younger and have excellent analytical and writing abilities. Interns may offer to volunteer their services without compensation or can be paid the equivalent of an all-inclusive lump sum amount of $600 US per month, less any payment received from a sponsor. (For more information on IFAD, see Chapter 41, United Nations & Other IGOs). [ID:5639]

International Monetary Fund (IMF)
Summer Internship Program, Recruitment Division, 700 19th Street N.W., Washington, DC,
20431, USA; 202-623-7000, fax 202-623-4661, recruit@imf.org, www.imf.org ▣ *Fr* ▣ *Sp*

INTERNSHIPS ◆ The International Monetary Fund (IMF) offers a Summer Internship Program to provide interns with an opportunity to familiarize themselves with the operations of the IMF. Opportunities are in the fields of monetary economics, public finance, international trade and finance, and econometrics.

Each summer, IMF offers approximately 40 internships to graduate students to carry out a research project under the supervision of an experienced economist for 10 to 13 weeks. Candidates within one or two years of completing their doctoral program in macroeconomics or a related field, and those with outstanding backgrounds in economics, will be considered.

Interns receive a salary of approximately $4,500 US per month and round-trip airfare to Washington, DC from their university. Applicants should submit a completed IMF employment application and include a list of economics courses taken and grades obtained at the university level. All applications for employment with the IMF must be made via its on-line application form on the IMF Web site. (For more on the IMF, see Chapter 41, United Nations & Other IGOs.) [ID:5638]

International Telecommunications Satellite Organization (Intelsat)
Summer Intern Program, Human Resources Division, Box 24 INT, 3400 International Drive, N.W.,
Washington, DC, 20008, USA; 202-944-6800, fax 202-944-7898, www.intelsat.com

INTERNSHIPS ◆ The International Telecommunications Satellite Organization (Intelsat) owns and operates the world's most extensive global communications satellite system. Their Summer Intern Program is designed to provide an opportunity for students to obtain practical work experience in an international, high technology environment.

Intelsat offers a couple of 12-week summer internship programs for university students pursuing degrees in business, marketing, sales, engineering, finance, accounting, law or other related areas. Preference is given to international students studying in the US. Information and application procedures for the program are available on Intelsat's Web site. (For more information on Intelsat, see Chapter 41, United Nations & Other IGOs.) [ID:5655]

International Trade Centre (ITC)

Human Resources Section, Division of Programme Support, 54-56 rue de Montbrillant, CH 1211, Geneva,
Switzerland; (41) (22) 730-0111, fax (41) (22) 730-0803, itcreg@intracen.org, www.intracen.org ⌨*Fr* ⌨*Sp*

INTERNSHIPS ◆ The International Trade Centre's (ITC) internship program is intended to promote among participating students a better understanding of matters related to trade promotion at the international level. The ITC seeks students specializing in fields such as economics, trade promotion, market development and international trade law, to work with the Centre for a duration of two to six months. Successful applicants will be enrolled in a graduate-level degree program and should be no more than 30 years of age. Internships are unpaid and interns are responsible for all costs. (For more information on the ITC, see Chapter 41, United Nations & Other IGOs.) [ID:5659]

International Tribunal for the Law of the Sea (ITLOS)

Am Internationalen Seegerichtshof 1, 22609 Hamburg, Germany;
(49) (40) 35607-227, fax (49) (40) 35607-245, press@itlos.org, www.itlos.org ⌨*Fr*

INTERNSHIPS ◆ The International Tribunal for the Law of the Sea (ITLOS) internship program gives participants the opportunity to gain an understanding of the work and functions of the Tribunal. ITLOS seeks candidates specializing in fields such as the law of the sea, public international law, international organizations and international relations, political science, public information, publications and library science, and translation. Internships are unpaid and usually last two to six months.

Successful applicants will be in a graduate degree program and 35 years of age or younger. A good command of English and/or French is essential; an interest in international law, specifically in international law of the sea, international affairs or international institutions and organizations, is an asset. Applicants must submit a resume, with grade transcript or list of courses taken, and if available, a brief sample of research work in English or French. Applications should be submitted between three and eight months before the start of the internship. (For more information on ITLOS, see Chapter 41, United Nations & Other IGOs.) [ID:5658]

Joint United Nations Programme on HIV/AIDS (UNAIDS)

Human Resources Management (Interns), 20 Avenue Appia, CH 1211, Geneva,
Switzerland; (41) (22) 791-3666, fax (41) (22) 791-4187, hrm@unaids.org, www.unaids.org

INTERNSHIPS ◆ The Joint United Nations Programme on HIV/AIDS (UNAIDS) has internship opportunities for graduate students at the secretariat in Geneva, Switzerland. The duration of internships ranges from six weeks to three months.

Successful candidates will be enrolled in a graduate program and be fluent in English. Working knowledge of a second language (French or Spanish) would be desirable. Internships are unpaid, and interns are responsible for all related expenses. At the time of publishing, the 2004 UNAIDS Internship Programme was temporarily interrupted. (For more information on UNAIDS, see Chapter 41, United Nations & Other IGOs.) [ID:5665]

Office of the United Nations High Commissioner for Human Rights (OHCHR)

Internship Coordinator, Internship Programme - Administrative Section, 8-14 Ave. de la Paix, 1211 Geneva 10,
Switzerland; (41) (22) 917-9000, fax (41) (22) 917-9024, personnel@unhchr.ch, www.unhchr.ch ⌨*Fr* ⌨*Sp*

INTERNSHIPS ◆ The Office of the UN High Commissioner for Human Rights (OHCHR) Internship Programme aims to increase interns' understanding of current human rights issues at the international level and to give them an insight into the work of the UN and of the OHCHR in particular. Interns may be involved in researching human rights issues, drafting analytical papers and reports, providing substantive and technical servicing of meetings, underwriting fact-finding and technical cooperation activities as well as field operations.

Successful applicants are graduate students and holders of graduate level degrees in disciplines such as international law, political science, history, social sciences with a good command of at least two of the six official languages of the UN. Drafting ability in either English or French is required. The OHCHR accepts up to 24 interns, and are selected twice a year: in May/

June for summer and fall internships, and in November/December for the following year's winter and spring internships. Internships are between three and six months in duration, and are unpaid. (For more information on OHCHR, see Chapter 41, United Nations & Other IGOs.) [ID:5666]

The Population Institute
107 2nd Street N.E., Washington, DC, 20002, USA; 202-544-3300 ext. 121,
fax 202-544-0068, web@populationinstitute.org, www.populationinstitute.org

INTERNSHIPS ◆ The Population Institute's Future Leaders of the World Program (FLW) provides students interested in international relations and development in the non-profit sector, the opportunity to work on the issue of population growth. Six to eight university graduates and graduate students per year intern at the institute. In FLW, one media coordinator, one to three public policy assistants, one field coordinator, and one world population awareness week coordinator are hired for one year.

Interns earn $24,000 US per year, plus benefits. Applicants must be able to demonstrate leadership qualities, international experiences and perspectives, a good academic record and strong oral and writing skills. Knowledge of a foreign language is a must. Applicants must also have completed two years of university and be between the ages of 21 and 25. To apply, send a resume, cover letter, three recommendations (two from academic sources) and an official transcript. [ID:5634]

Preparatory Commission for the
Comprehensive Nuclear-Test-Ban Treaty Organization
P.O. Box 1200, Vienna International Centre, A - 1400 Vienna, Austria;
(43) (1) 26030-6200, fax (43) (1) 26030-5823, info@ctbto.org, www.ctbto.org

INTERNSHIPS ◆ The Preparatory Commission for the Comprehensive Nuclear-Test-Ban Treaty Organization (CTBTO Preparatory Commission) offers a limited number of unpaid internships each year. Interns usually work on projects such as limited research or studies. Opportunities for internships become available as needs arise and resources become available in individual divisions within the secretariat.

Internships are unpaid and are usually between three and six months in duration. Successful candidates will be under 30 years of age and have a university degree (or be advanced in their university studies). Applications are accepted on an ongoing basis and are reviewed as positions become available. (For more information on the CTBTO Preparatory Commission, see Chapter 41, United Nations & Other IGOs). [ID:5490]

United Nations Children's Fund (UNICEF)
Training and Staff Development, UNICEF Internship Programme, 3 United Nations Plaza,
New York, NY, 10017, USA; 212-303-7915, fax 212-303-7984, www.unicef.org ❏*Fr*❏*Sp*

INTERNSHIPS ◆ The United Nations Children's Fund (UNICEF) advocates the protection of children's rights to help meet their basic needs and to expand their opportunities to reach their full potential. Six to 16-week internships are offered to exceptional graduate- or post-graduate-level students in fields related to international or social development, child survival or development, or management.

Successful applicants will be fluent in English and one other UNICEF working language (i.e., French or Spanish). Internships are unpaid, and responsibility for all expenses must be borne by the applicant or sponsoring institution. Applications are accepted on an ongoing basis, and internships are available during three periods: January to May, June to August, and September to December. (For more information on UNICEF, see Chapter 41, United Nations & Other IGOs.) [ID:5664]

United Nations Commission on International Trade Law (UNCITRAL)
Ad-hoc Internship Programme, P.O. Box 500, Human Resources
Management Section, UNOV, A - 1400 Vienna, Austria; (43) (1) 26060-4061,
fax (43) (1) 26060-5813, uncitral@uncitral.org, www.uncitral.org ❏*Fr*❏*Sp*

INTERNSHIPS ◆ United Nations Commission on International Trade Law (UNCITRAL) on occasion accepts interns with law degrees. Interns are assigned specific tasks in connection with projects being worked on in the branch, and are expected to be able to communicate in English. Internships begin with an initial period of three months and may be extended to one year. Candidates must be sponsored by an organization, university, or a governmental agency, and should apply at least six months before their desired internship period as admission to the program is very competitive. (For more on UNCITRAL, see Chapter 41, United Nations & Other IGOs). [ID:5651]

United Nations Development Fund for Women (UNIFEM)
Chief, HR/Administration, Internship Programme, 15th Floor, 304 East 45th Street,
New York, NY, 10017, USA; 212-906-6400, fax 212-906-6705, unifem@undp.org, www.unifem.undp.org

INTERNSHIPS ◆ The United Nations Development Fund for Women's (UNIFEM) Internship Programme offers graduate-level students direct exposure to UNIFEM's work, and is designed to complement studies with practical experience in various aspects of multilateral technical cooperation. Every attempt is made to match the interests of the intern with the needs of the organization.

Internship vacancies are not posted, but submitted applications are retained and reviewed as needs arise within UNIFEM. All assignments are unpaid and vary in length according to the availability and academic requirements of the intern, as well as the needs of UNIFEM. (For more information on UNIFEM, see Chapter 41, United Nations & Other IGOs.) [ID:5652]

United Nations Development Programme (UNDP)
1 United Nations Plaza, New York, NY, 10017, USA;
212-906-5558, fax 212-906-5364, hq@undp.org, www.undp.org ▭ *Fr* ▭ *Sp*

INTERNSHIPS ◆ The United Nations Development Programme's (UNDP) Internship Programme is designed to complement development-oriented studies with practical experience in various aspects of multilateral technical cooperation, but also complements other international studies, including law. Internship assignments are unpaid and vary in length according to the availability and academic requirements of the intern, as well as the needs of UNDP. Interns are responsible for all related costs.

Successful applicants will be enrolled in a graduate-level degree program in a development-related field, have a demonstrated interest in the field of development, and written and spoken proficiency in at least two of the three working languages used by UNDP: English, French and Spanish. Internships may be either in a UNDP country office or in the organization's headquarters in New York. Since selection for internships is fully decentralized within UNDP, applicants should forward their application directly to the bureau/country office of interest to them. (For more information on UNDP, see Chapter 41, United Nations & Other IGOs). [ID:5635]

United Nations Economic and Social
Commission for Asia and the Pacific (ESCAP)
Human Resources Management Section, Office 1508A, United Nations Bldg., Rajadamnern Ave., Bangkok,
10200, Thailand; (66) (2) 288-1234, fax (66) (2) 288-1000, escap-registry@un.org, www.unescap.org

INTERNSHIPS ◆ The United Nations Economic and Social Commission for Asia and the Pacific (ESCAP) offers an ad hoc internship program designed to meet the research interests of students in a diverse range of areas relevant to the commission, including development research and policy analysis, international trade and economic cooperation, industry and technology, environment and natural resources, rural and urban development, transport, communications and tourism.

Internships range in duration, and all costs must be borne by interns. Candidates must be sponsored by their academic institution. Interested applicants should submit a completed application form and an outline of their preferred research or work to be undertaken during the internship. (For more on ESCAP, see Chapter 41, United Nations & Other IGOs). [ID:5649]

United Nations Economic Commission for Europe (ECE)

Internship Coordinator, Office 366, Palais des Nations, CH - 1211 Geneva 10,
Switzerland; (41) (22) 9171234, fax (41) (22) 9170123, interns@unece.org, www.unece.org

INTERNSHIPS ◆ The United Nations Economic Commission for Europe (ECE) is one of the five regional commissions of the United Nations. Its primary goal is to encourage greater economic cooperation among its member states. ECE activities include policy analysis, development of conventions, regulations and standards, and technical assistance. The working languages of ECE are English, French and Russian.

ECE has an ad hoc, unpaid internship program offering opportunities as needs arise to graduate or post-graduate students with a specialization in a field relating to ECE programs. Fields of interest include economic analysis, environment and human settlements, industrial restructuring and enterprise development, standardization, statistics, sustainable energy, timber, trade and transport. Internships are normally three months in duration, and all costs associated with the internship must be borne by the intern. (For more information on the ECE, see Chapter 41, United Nations & Other IGOs). [ID:5643]

United Nations Economic Commission for
Latin America and the Caribbean (ECLAC)

Casilla de Correo 179-D, Vitacura, Santiago, Chile;
(56) (2) 210-2000, fax (56) (2) 208-0252, www.eclac.org 💻*Sp*

INTERNSHIPS ◆ The United Nations Economic Commission for Latin America and the Caribbean (ECLAC) exists for the purposes of contributing to the economic and social development of Latin America and the Caribbean region, coordinating actions directed towards these ends, and reinforcing relationships among the countries and with the other nations of the world. ECLAC has an unpaid ad hoc internship program for graduate students from the Latin American and Caribbean region who have specialized in a field related to its work. Internships are for a maximum of six months, and interns are expected to work full-time hours and to incur all related costs. (For more information on ECLAC, see Chapter 41, United Nations & Other IGOs). [ID:5646]

United Nations Educational, Scientific and Cultural Organization (UNESCO)

Bureau of Human Resources Management, Training and Career Development
Section, 7 place de Fontenoy, 75352 Paris 07 - SP, France; (33) (1) 4568-1000,
fax (33) (1) 4567-1690, bpiweb@unesco.org, www.unesco.org 💻*Fr*💻*Sp*

INTERNSHIPS ◆ The United Nations Educational, Scientific and Cultural Organization (UNESCO) offers interns the opportunity to develop a better understanding of UNESCO while working in an international setting. UNESCO accepts students from a wide range of disciplines, as well as researchers and national civil servants for one- to three-month internships at UNESCO headquarters. Intern responsibilities may relate either to the Organization's strategic activities or to administrative or technical functions.

Successful applicants will have already completed at least four years of full time studies at a university or equivalent institution towards the completion of a graduate degree, as well as be registered for a post-graduate degree (MA, DEA, DESS, Maestria or equivalent) at the time they submit their application, and for the duration of the internship. Successful applicants will also have excellent spoken and written knowledge of English or French, and a good knowledge of the other language. Interested applicants are encouraged to apply three to six months before the period requested for the internship. (For more information on UNESCO, see Chapter 41, United Nations & Other IGOs.) [ID:5662]

United Nations Environment Programme (UNEP)

Internship Programme, Staff Development and Training Unit Human Resource
and Management Service, United Nations Office at Nairobi, P.O. Box 67578,
Nairobi, Kenya; (254) (20) 624-730, fax (254) (20) 623-789, www.unep.org 💻*Fr*

INTERNSHIPS ◆ United Nations Environment Programme (UNEP) offers a number of unpaid internship opportunities each year at its headquarters in Nairobi, Kenya. Successful applicants must be upper-year undergraduate students or in a graduate program (MA or PhD), have a sponsoring institution, and be able to commit between three to six months to the internship. Detailed information regarding the application process is available on UNEP's Web site. At the time of publishing, an electronic application is under construction. (For more information on UNEP, see Chapter 41, United Nations & Other IGOs.) [ID:5663]

United Nations Framework Convention on Climate Change (UNFCCC)
Intern Focal Point, P.O. Box 260124, D-53153 Bonn, Germany;
(49) (228) 815-1000, fax (49) (228) 815-1999, secretariat@unfccc.int, http://unfccc.int ☐*Fr* ☐*Sp*

INTERNSHIPS ◆ The United Nations Framework Convention on Climate Change's (UNFCCC) internship program aims to provide graduate students with an opportunity to enhance their educational experience through practical work assignments. Interns are accepted throughout the year for periods of between two and six months in duration. The UNFCCC's internship program is unpaid, and interns are responsible for all costs related to the internship. Successful candidates will be enrolled in a graduate-level degree program, be fluent in English, and specialize in a field related to the work of the UNFCCC, such as economics, environmental sciences, international law, international relations, natural sciences, political science and public administration. (For more information on the UNFCCC, see Chapter 41, United Nations & Other IGOs). [ID:5610]

United Nations Headquarters Internship Programme
Internship Coordinator, Room S-2500J, United Nations, New York, NY, 10017, USA;
212-963-4437, fax 212-963-3683, OHRM_interns@un.org, www.un.org ☐*Fr* ☐*Sp*

INTERNSHIPS ◆ The United Nations Headquarters Internship Programme is designed to provide graduate and post-graduate students from diverse academic backgrounds an opportunity to enhance their educational experience through practical work assignments within various UN offices in New York City, in a variety of fields. Internships are offered in three two-month program periods throughout the year: mid-January to mid-March, early June to early August, and mid-September to mid-November. Applications must be submitted between four and 12 months prior to the desired commencement date. Interns are not paid, and the costs of travel and accommodation must be borne by the interns or their sponsoring institutions. [ID:5661]

United Nations Human Settlements Programme (UN-HABITAT)
P.O. Box 30030, UN Office at Nairobi, Nairobi, Kenya; (254) (20) 623-120,
fax (254) (20) 623-477, infohabitat@unhabitat.org, www.unhabitat.org

INTERNSHIPS ◆ United Nations Human Settlements Programme (UN-HABITAT) coordinates activities within the UN system principally related to housing, building, and planning. Internships are available on an ad hoc basis for students specializing in fields of study relevant to the organization. Internships range in duration and are unpaid. Applicants should be currently enrolled in at least the latter stages of their undergraduate degree and must be sponsored by their academic institution. UN-HABITAT has a formal application form for interested students. (For more information on UN-HABITAT, see Chapter 41, United Nations & Other IGOs). [ID:5648]

United Nations Industrial Development Organization (UNIDO)
Human Resource Management Branch, P.O. Box 300, Room D1667, Vienna International Centre, A - 1400 Vienna, Austria; (43) (1) 26026-4146 or 4147, fax (43) (1) 26026-6834, unido@unido.org, www.unido.org ☐*Fr*

INTERNSHIPS ◆ The United Nations Industrial Development Organization's (UNIDO) ad hoc internship program accepts for a period of three to six months a small number of unpaid interns who wish to obtain experience with UNIDO or to do research on items of direct relevance to UNIDO's program of work. Internships are available in a variety of areas, and are open to individuals who have completed an advanced university degree or are enrolled in the last year of such a program. Successful applicants must also be nominated by their national mission to the UN, or sponsored by their university. (For more on UNIDO, see Chapter 41, United Nations & Other IGOs). [ID:5489]

United Nations Institute for Disarmament Research (UNIDIR)
Internship Coordinator, Palais des Nations, CH - 1211 Geneva 10, Switzerland;
(41) (22) 917-1583, fax (41) (22) 917-0176, unidir@unog.ch, www.unidir.org ☐ *Fr*

INTERNSHIPS ◆ The United Nations Institute for Disarmament Research (UNIDIR) offers a limited number of unpaid internships. Successful applicants may be undergraduate or graduate students. They will be fluent in English or French, and demonstrate a strong interest in disarmament, security, arms control, peace studies or related issues. They will also have research and/or work experience in one of the following fields: international relations, political science, security studies, international law, economics, physics, nuclear physics, biology, chemistry, biochemistry, pharmacology, engineering, education or journalism. Internships are approximately two to three months in duration and are available from January-May, June-September, and October-December. Applications should be submitted at least three months before the desired start date. (For more information on UNIDIR, see Chapter 41, United Nations & Other IGOs.) [ID:5577]

United Nations International Research and Training Institute for the Advancement of Women (INSTRAW)
César Nicolás Penson 102-A, Santo Domingo, Dominican Republic;
(809) 685-2117, fax (809) 685-2117, comments@un-instraw.org, www.un-instraw.org ☐ *Fr* ☐ *Sp*

INTERNSHIPS ◆ The United Nations International Research and Training Institute for the Advancement of Women (INSTRAW) hosts an internship program at their headquarters in Santo Domingo, Dominican Republic. Interns assist in a variety of tasks including Internet research, database development, preparation of abstracts of books and articles, organization of chats and discussion forums, and correspondence with focal points and other networks.

Successful candidates will be recent university graduates or enrolled in a graduate-level program. They will have a demonstrated interest in research and training on gender issues and be fluent in English. Internships typically last two to three months, and are unpaid; interns are responsible for covering their own travel and living expenses. (For more information on INSTRAW, see Chapter 41, United Nations & Other IGOs.) [ID:5637]

United Nations Interregional Crime and Justice Research Institute (UNICRI)
Internship Coordinator, Viale Maestri del Lavoro, 10, 10127 Turin, Italy;
(39) (11) 653-7111, fax (39) (11) 631-3368, internship@unicrit.it, www.unicri.it ☐ *Fr* ☐ *Sp*

INTERNSHIPS ◆ The United Nations Interregional Crime and Justice Research Institute's (UNICRI) ad hoc internship program accepts a limited number of unpaid interns each year. The objective of the program is to enhance the educational experience of students through practical work assignments and on-the-job experience.

Successful candidates will be graduate students or holders of first university degrees who intend to study further or to work in a field relevant to UNICRI's activities, such as social and political sciences, particularly criminology; international and national law; or criminal, public, and comparative law. They will be fluent in at least one of English and French. The duration of internships will be between three and six months. (For more information on UNICRI, see Chapter 41, United Nations & Other IGOs.) [ID:5587]

United Nations Office at Vienna (UNOV)
Co-coordinator, Ad-Hoc Internship Programme, Human Resources Management
Section, P.O. Box 500, Vienna International Centre, A - 1400 Vienna, Austria;
(43) (1) 26060-0, fax (43) (1) 26060-5886, recruitment@unvienna.org, www.unvienna.org

INTERNSHIPS ◆ The United Nations Office at Vienna offers internships on an ad hoc basis in areas relevant to its activities, which include political sciences, psychology, economics, journalism, finance, information technology, accounting and international law. Internships are unpaid and range in duration from two to six months. Applicants must hold a university degree, be enrolled in a graduate program, and have their application endorsed by their educational institution or, in exceptional cases, by their respective Permanent Mission in Vienna. Application forms are available on UNOV's Web site and, when completed, should be accompanied by an official transcript and submitted between four and eight months before the desired start date. [ID:5653]

United Nations Population Fund (UNFPA)

Personnel Branch, 17th Floor, 220 East 42nd Street, New York, NY, 10017, USA;
212-297-5000, fax 212-297-4908, internship@unfpa.org, www.unfpa.org ▢ *Fr* ▢ *Sp*

INTERNSHIPS ◆ The United Nations Population Fund (UNFPA) Internship Programme offers a small group of outstanding graduate students the opportunity to acquire direct exposure to UNFPA operations. It is designed to complement development-oriented studies with practical experience in various aspects of technical assistance. Internships are primarily at the New York headquarters.

Successful candidates will have a strong interest in the field of development, and will have completed their first year of studies in a master's degree program or equivalent in a social science field, with a concentration in population studies. Written and spoken proficiency in English is required. Interns are not paid, and all costs must be borne by the intern or nominating institution. (For more information on UNFPA, see Chapter 41, United Nations & Other IGOs.) [ID:5636]

United Nations Research Institute for Social Development (UNRISD)

Graduate Student Programme (GSP), Palais des Nations, 1211 Geneva 10, Switzerland;
(41) (22) 917-3020, fax (41) (22) 917-0650, info@unrisd.org, www.unrisd.org ▢ *Fr* ▢ *Sp*

INTERNSHIPS ◆ The United Nations Research Institute for Social Development (UNRISD) has, in lieu of an internship program, a graduate student programme (GSP), through which graduate students from around the world can gain practical experience at UNRISD's Geneva headquarters. Placements are for a minimum period of three months, with the possibility of extension.

Successful candidates will hold a graduate degree or currently be enrolled in a graduate degree program, will have experience working for an intergovernmental or non-governmental organization in the development field; have a research interest in social development, poverty eradication, democratization, human rights, gender equity and environmental sustainability; and have an excellent working knowledge of English, French or Spanish. Application information is available on UNRISD's Web site, under FAQs. (For more information on UNRISD, see Chapter 41, United Nations & Other IGOs.) [ID:5656]

United Nations System Staff College (UNSSC)

Human Resources Unit, Viale Maestri del Lavoro, 10, 10127 Torino, Italy;
(39) (11) 653-5911, fax (39) (11) 653-5902, recruitment@unssc.org, www.unscc.org

INTERNSHIPS ◆ The United Nations System Staff College's (UNSSC) internship program provides opportunity for graduate students to be exposed to and participate in the work of the UNSSC. Internship assignments are available throughout the year and vary in length according to the needs of the UNSSC. Normally lasting up to six months, internships are unpaid. All internship-related expenses are the responsibility of the intern. Successful candidates will be enrolled in a graduate-level degree program in a development-related field of interest to the Staff College. They will have excellent written and spoken proficiency in English, an interest in developing training programs, as well as a desire to work with and gain the confidence and respect of people with different linguistic, national and cultural backgrounds. (For more information on UNSSC, see Chapter 41, United Nations & Other IGOs.) [ID:5650]

United Nations University (UNU)

Chair of the Internship Committee, 53-70, Jingumae 5-chome, Shibuya-ku, Tokyo 150,
Japan; (81) (3) 3499-2811, fax (81) (3) 3499-2828, mbox@hq.unu.edu, www.unu.edu ▢ *Fr* ▢ *Sp*

INTERNSHIPS ◆ The United Nations University's (UNU) internship program aims to promote interaction and dialogue between young scholars and the UNU. Successful candidates will have a university degree, as well as qualifications and expertise relevant to the UNU in one or more of its activities (environment and sustainable development, peace and governance, rector's office/ capacity-building, UNU Press, library). Applications are considered four times a year, at the end of

January, April, July and October. The duration of the internship will be between three and six months. Internships are unpaid, and all related expenses are the responsibility of the intern. (For more information on the UNU, see Chapter 41, United Nations & Other IGOs.) [ID:5632]

The World Bank
1818 H Street N.W., Washington, DC, 20433, USA; 202-473-1000,
fax 202-477-6391, opportunities@worldbank.org, www.worldbank.org ☐*Fr* ☐*Sp*

INTERNSHIPS ◆ The World Bank Internship Program provides approximately 150-200 internships every year for post-graduate students. The program is highly competitive and designed to attract outstanding young and motivated individuals from around the world. The internship program is open to nationals of the Bank's member countries who possess an undergraduate degree and are enrolled in a full-time graduate degree program. Generally, successful candidates have completed their first year of graduate studies or are already in PhD programs. The program often seeks candidates in economics, finance, human resource development, social sciences, agriculture, environment and private sector development. Fluency in English is required. The Bank pays interns an hourly wage and, where applicable, provides an allowance toward travel expenses. Most positions are located in Washington, DC, and are a minimum of four weeks in duration. Internship opportunities begin in both the summer and winter.

In addition to the Bank internships, the organization also offers a two-year Junior Professional Associates (JPA) Program for individuals under 28 years of age who are interested in gaining experience with the Bank; and, a 12 to 18 month Young Professionals (YP) Program, which is the starting point for a career with the Bank. (For more information on the World Bank see Chapter 41, United Nations & Other IGOs.) [ID:5654]

World Food Programme (WFP)
Human Resources and Administrative Services Division, Via C.G. Viola 68, Parco dei Medici,
00148 Rome, Italy; (39) (06) 65131, fax (39) (06) 6513-2840, intern@wfp.org, www.wfp.org

INTERNSHIPS ◆ The World Food Programme (WFP) accepts interns in order to promote a better understanding of the United Nations and of the operations of the World Food Programme. Interns are fully involved in the work of the division that selects them for an internship, and interns carry out their assignments under the supervision of a professional staff member.

Candidates must be currently enrolled in a university program or graduate school and have completed at least two years of undergraduate studies. Internships are unpaid and all costs are the responsibility of the intern. WFP places resumes on their internship roster via the WFP Intranet. Interested applicants can create their resume on the WFP Web site, and apply on-line. (For more on the World Food Programme see Chapter 41, United Nations & Other IGOs.) [ID:5642]

World Health Organization (WHO)
Division of Personnel (Interns), 1211 Geneva 27, Switzerland;
(41) (22) 791-2111, fax (41) (22) 791-4773, www.who.ch ☐*Fr* ☐*Sp*

INTERNSHIPS ◆ The World Health Organization (WHO) offers a number of internships at its Geneva headquarters with the goal of deepening interns' knowledge and understanding of WHO's goals, principles and activities. Only a limited number of internships are available and all assignments are health-related.

Candidates must be over 20 years of age and be a graduate or post-graduate university student engaged in a course of study related to health. The internships are available in WHO headquarters in Geneva and some regional offices; duration of internships range from six to 12 weeks. No financial assistance is available. Applications can be filled out on-line, be sent to human resources services in Geneva or to the specific regional office concerned. (For more information on the World Health Organization see Chapter 41, United Nations & Other IGOs.) [ID:5647]

PART THREE
The International Job Search

CHAPTER 18

Your Career Path & The Ideal International Profile

The phrase *international career* does not necessarily mean *working abroad*. A traditional international career usually implies a combination of work stints, some based in your home country and others based overseas. Alternatively, some international jobs do not require living abroad, and you are permanently based in North America.

This chapter highlights long-term career building activities and a few of the career planning decisions you will face. For those of you just starting out, pay close attention to the section "The Ideal International Profile" located in the last third of this chapter.

LONG-TERM SKILL BUILDING

More than in a domestic career, you must have a long-term strategy for building your international career, block by block. International careers are built on experience in various areas. When contemplating a new international job, therefore, salary and your place in the pecking order are not as important as they would be in the domestic market. Choose jobs that lead to new careers, or that are prerequisites to the job you eventually want.

An important consideration in your job strategy is to recognize how volatile the international job market is. Rapid changes occur due to shifts in trade, government policy and personal events, and you must always be willing to take advantage of changes as they occur and accept new paths in your career.

Remember that diversity and flexibility are the hallmarks of an international career. It is always a good idea to develop your experience in at least two broad work areas. Thus, if you are an overseas teacher, make sure you take on some extra administrative duties at your school. If you are a researcher, develop a sideline in computer skills. A mix of skills is often required: for example, business-minded people with experience in community work or engineers with social science training. And of course, attach language skills to all these scenarios.

There is one key factor to consider in your long-term skill-building strategies: your international IQ. An international employer can teach you about his or her business, but it is difficult, time-consuming and highly speculative to attempt to teach you the refinements of intercultural communication. Thus, no matter what your international career specialization, always maintain a parallel set of international IQ skills.

MIX OVERSEAS AND DOMESTIC EXPERIENCE

Keep the right mix in your inventory of international skills; that is, skills acquired abroad versus skills acquired at home.

In deciding your international career path, consideration must be given to the balance between the time you spend working overseas and the time you spend working domestically. A useful grid for assessing your "mix" is to look at your skills inventory in terms of future needs. First, ask yourself the question, "What international skills must be developed at home?" Second, "What skills must be developed overseas?" And third, "What skills can be developed in either setting?" By breaking your skills inventory into these three categories, you will be better able to assess where you should be working.

Some international jobs are based at home and do not require the same level of intercultural awareness skills. For example, most international departments have information officers whose sole job is to guide people through the maze of international publications and sources of information. And an international currency buyer need not have overseas experience. The skills required for these international jobs must be acquired at home.

If you are just starting an international career, most international jobs at home or abroad require some overseas experience. Even if you work in Canada or the US in an international job that doesn't require overseas experience, your credibility with colleagues in other departments will be dependent on your understanding of the overseas working environment. Thus, it is highly recommended that you have at least one intensive overseas experience early in your career. Do not postpone this crucial step. The longer you wait, the smaller your chances are of finding an opportunity. Married life, older children and, indeed, your ability to adapt to the rigours of some overseas environments will hinder your chance of being chosen for that all-important first overseas posting.

After four or five years of living abroad, most employees lose touch with the realities of home and their old way of doing things. While they may not notice it, people have a tremendous ability to adapt to new surroundings, and in a short time lose sight of old methods of work and communication. A return to work in North America will keep your work habits current as well as make you aware of the changing facts of life at home.

PUBLIC, PRIVATE OR NON-PROFIT SECTOR?

The differences between overseas work in the public, private and non-profit sectors illustrate the standard stereotypes: government jobs and intergovernmental organization (IGO) jobs tend to be bureaucratic, with less room to manoeuvre, and have slower, more rigid career paths; private firms offer more fast-track job opportunities with greater remuneration; non-profit careers, while providing adequate salaries, have much less of the dollar-value perks often attributed to overseas work; while non-profit jobs are often more hands-on, less bureaucratic. Job security is relatively high in public institutions, whereas overseas private employment can be particularly erratic and harsh. Working overseas for an NGO or as a private-sector employee certainly tends to allow for more creativity than working for government or a large IGO.

Overall, government jobs offer you wider international experience, whereas private firms concentrate on narrow, specialized fields. In most cases, government will give you greater exposure to the varied facets of other cultures, such as language training; varied programming in many different areas; and dealing with different levels of governments and populations abroad. However, this wider perspective is also available to employees with NGOs and some international consulting firms.

The business person's life overseas has many more built-in hazards than the government official's. Whereas a government official or NGO employee will get paid whether or not he or she closes a deal, a private business person must live with the consequences of failure when doing business overseas. Another factor is the difference in support systems. A private individual must face the overseas market alone. A government official has a massive support system whereby housing, medical, and transportation concerns are looked after by support staff and work problems are resolved by teams of experts.

A major advantage of working for a government agency (or, to a certain extent, an NGO) is the protection you have in foreign countries. Diplomatic status or close linkages to the diplomatic corps are an extra measure of security and insurance against all types of problems overseas. Whether you are suffering from foreign bureaucratic stonewalling, trying to work your way through customs, or have inadvertently brushed up against unknown foreign laws (or corrupt officials), having close diplomatic ties is very helpful in resolving these problems or insulating you from them in the first place. Governments and NGOs have such buffers—the private sector often does not.

While you may never work for the foreign service on a mission abroad, knowledge of their services and operations is important. Embassies, high commissions and consulates are a ready source of information on local economic and political situations. All governments at the federal level, and increasingly at the provincial/state level, are providing services overseas to facilitate trade and business abroad. Whatever your type of overseas employment, take the time to visit and research your foreign diplomatic missions abroad. (Canadians should look at the Resources and profile of FOREIGN AFFAIRS CANADA (FAC) and INTERNATIONAL TRADE CANADA (ITCAN) at the end of Chapter 37, Canadian Government.)

CHOOSING YOUR INTERNATIONAL WORK SETTING

If you decide to focus your job search on a specific country, know that your chances of being successful are much slimmer. You are better off instead to focus on larger regions of the world—Asia, Latin America, or Africa (see also the section, "Better Networking with Country Information" in Chapter 20, The Job Search & Targeting Your Research). Don't be too strict about your choice of countries when you are researching overseas job opportunities. International employees know that it is usually the employer who chooses what country you will live and work in. Experienced employees take advantage of the opportunities that arise, and often accept the choices made by their employers. You never really know what life will be like in a particular posting until you get there. And guess what? Most international employees, especially if they're in their first posting abroad, will fall in love with their newly adopted region of the world.

You can, however, make some concrete decisions about certain geographical work settings. For some, working in a developing country is too unsettling; for others, geographic isolation or climate is a major issue. You may have a preference for a rural or an urban setting. Everyone will give consideration to the level of political instability, although this is difficult to gauge. Over the long course of an international career, you can expect to be evacuated at least once from the country you are living in. Other considerations are terrorism, crime and perhaps even cultural isolation for women in certain Arab countries. When working with employers, you should negotiate your situation based on all the factors that matter to you.

CAREER PLANNING AND FAMILY CONSIDERATIONS

Many of the strategies in this book assume that you are a young professional in your mid- to late twenties and that you have few family responsibilities. Here is a list of basic ideas on how to deal with career planning while taking into consideration various family situations. Note that these are only suggestions to the typical career-related problems encountered by families; your particular circumstance may warrant different strategies. (For non-career advice, see Chapter 3, Living Overseas.)

- **Interns wanting to work abroad as a couple.** Internship-sponsoring organizations can rarely accommodate a couple. Your best bet is to try to be posted to the same city, adjacent cities or adjacent countries. Plan on visiting each other on weekends and you'll likely find that you're expanding the value of your internships. If only one of you lands an internship abroad, still consider going, and make arrangements to accommodate your relationship while away—such as planning to meet during a break, or to travel together after the internship. Alternatively, one spouse accepts the internship, and the other travels as a companion with the hope of finding work while abroad.

- **Volunteers to go abroad as a couple or with a young family.** If you are going abroad for a long-term volunteer position (one year or more), organizations generally make every effort to accommodate the professional needs of both partners as well as the needs of small families. Note that there will normally be a few perks for your child's education, such as private schools or paid vacations home.

- **Professionals, where both spouses want to work abroad.** When two people with professional qualifications want to go abroad and both have the intention of working, who should be looking for a job first? The easy answer to this question is that the spouse with the most specialized and most highly paid profession should be the first to find a job. The accompanying spouse (he or she may humorously refer to him/herself as the trailing spouse—the one without a job) should be the person with the most portable career, such as nursing, teaching or general management. Thus in the case of a couple with one spouse being an engineer and the other a teacher, it is the engineer who should first find the international job, since the teacher can easily find work when arriving in the host country.

- **Gay couple to work abroad.** Volunteer organizations will often accommodate a gay couple if they are attuned to the necessities and nuances in their country of posting. Mid-career professional couples have an easier time, since accommodating employers usually employ them. The accompanying spouse usually ends up being underemployed, however. Local norms in host countries will dictate how open couples are when accompanying spouses look for local employment.

- **Single person with child to work abroad.** If you are a young person with a child looking for an entry-level position, it is very difficult to find an employer willing to accommodate you. We have heard of a few rare exceptions, we have also heard of the odd parent successfully backpacking with a young child in developing countries and building international experience this way. The situation is much different for mid-career or internationally experienced professionals who are single parents. They find living overseas actually easier than in their home country since they often have recourse to inexpensive household staff. They can therefore concentrate more easily on their professional lives and still have plenty of quality time with their children. It is also often heard that single international professionals adopt children while abroad.

- **Work abroad with children.** If you are planning to live in developing countries, some families with children under the age of three decide to wait until the youngest child is slightly older. Families with high school–aged children often decide to spend these years in North America, providing a consistent environment for teens. Parents of university-aged children are free to roam the world, provided they do not have to deal with aging parents.

- **Mid-career couples go abroad with family.** Once established in your international career, it is a great life, with plenty of quality family time, good schools and great opportunities for family travel.

- **Fifty-plus couples abroad.** If nearing retirement, some couples go abroad as a pre-retirement career option. We have heard of long-time married couples in good relationships where one spouse will go abroad to teach for eight months. If you have the means, the options are endless for those nearing retirement and also those working part-time for interest. You can always go abroad to teach English; there are also opportunities for volunteer consultants.

WHAT TYPES OF JOBS ARE OUT THERE?

If you are studying in the social sciences, you may want to visit the Web site of the NORMAN PATERSON SCHOOL OF INTERNATIONAL AFFAIRS (NPSIA) at CARLETON UNIVERSITY to see an excellent list and descriptions of the varied types of jobs held by NPSIA graduates. (For the specific Web address, look up the resource, "NPSIA Work Career Futures," in the Index to Resources at the end of this book.) This site is useful because it demonstrates how you can transform international academic credentials into a wide variety of international jobs. For those of you just new to the international field, or if you are having a hard time envisioning what types of international jobs are out there, then of course, reading more of THE BIG GUIDE is the best place to start your search.

THE IDEAL INTERNATIONAL PROFILE

Here is a list of things you should be doing during your time as a university student to improve your odds of getting a full-time, professional international job after you graduate with a master's degree. Design strategies to help you acquire the international experience international employers are looking for. Building these skills is easy, and it is especially easy if you have a plan. Depending on the competition in your field of expertise (there is more competition in the social sciences than within engineering, for example), you should, upon graduating with an MA, possess 70 to 90 per cent of the qualities listed in the following ideal international profile. (Note that the advice below is heavily tied to Chapter 23, Selling Your International Skills; and Chapter 24, International Resumes.) As you'll discover, determination and unbending curiosity are important traits to the successful international employee. (Consult the excellent article by Larissa Brown, "My Experience Preparing for an International Career," in Appendix 18a on the CD-ROM.)

Academic Studies

- **An MA is a prerequisite for most international positions.** This is especially true in the social sciences, pure sciences and business. It may be less important in health careers, engineering and computer science. No matter what your field, include an international component directly by your choice of courses or indirectly in your subject matter choice for major research projects.

- **A BA in any field with outside electives to broaden your skills inventory.** For example, a science student should have four internationally focused social science courses; a history major should have four finance or management courses. Include language skills with all types of disciplines. Specifically target courses that require you to write essays (we know that it is easy to avoid these courses, but developing top notch writing skills is very important to your career.)

- **Other academic experience.** Attend or help organize a conference; participate in a professor-led research project; work as a teaching assistant; write a book review for an academic journal; apply for merit-based scholarships and awards; participate in academic competitions; become a tutor; make public presentations; actively seek to work on team projects and preferably team with foreign students.

Networking and Cross-Cultural Experience

- **Network with at least three experts in your field of interest.** For example, write essays that require you to speak directly to someone working internationally in your field of interest.

- **Guide foreigners who are new to your country.** You can act as a tour guide for visiting professors; assist with foreign student orientation; work with refugees; or, teach English as a second language. Another way of doing this is to get involved in programs at your university that allow you the opportunity to take on the role of an English conversation leader. In these programs, leaders are assigned a small group of foreign students with whom they plan small activities that enable the foreign students to practice their social language skills.

- **Befriend foreign students on your campus.** Join up with them in their social circles on campus; visit with them in their homes in Canada; become familiar with their food and social behaviour; try to pay a visit to them and their families in their home country (you will love it); actively participate in foreign student associations such as the Venezuelan Student Society with the specific objective of learning Spanish.

- **Become socially active and knowledgeable in a culture other than your own.** Hang out at ethnic social clubs; learn to dance to African or South American music; become knowledgeable in one or more fields of ethnic music; focus on the writing or history from one region or country; learn ethnic cooking; join an Internet club with foreign members.

- **Acquire an Internet pen pal.** Correspond, either as a friend or professional acquaintance, with someone living in another country.

Overseas Experience

- **International work experience for 2–6 months.** As an intern, co-op student or volunteer, preferably in your field of expertise. Try for two professional internships over the course of your six years of study. Strongly consider taking a gap year to gain any manner of international experience.

- **Cross-cultural travel for 2–6 months.** Try Africa, Asia, the Middle East, Eastern Europe, South and Central America rather than North America or Western Europe.

- **Study abroad for one or more semesters.** Study abroad in your field and/or to learn a new language.

Soft Skills

- **Organizing, people, and leadership skills.** Demonstrate these through work and/or volunteer experience, preferably with an international group, organizing an event or as an executive member of a committee.

- **Intercultural communications abilities.** Demonstrate these by being conversant in describing patterns of behaviour in cross-cultural work and social environments. Learn to professionally describe these real-life experiences. Read books like those produced by Intercultural Press. (See their profile in the Book Distributor Resources in Chapter 1, The Effective Overseas Employee.)

- **Coping and adapting abilities.** Demonstrate these with examples of how you coped when living away from your support structure of family and friends.

- **Entrepreneurial or self-actualization skills.** Demonstrate fortitude and the ability to work, plan and organize without supervision. Examples: Go abroad, run a business, supervise a team, launch an idea that requires support of others.

Hard Skills

- **Be functional in a new language.** Be able to speak and read a language other than your mother tongue. In Canada, consider learning French; in the US, consider learning Spanish. In all cases, be an active listener and learn to pick up 20 or 30 words in any country you visit for more than 2 weeks.

- **Economic and geographic knowledge of the world.** Have a solid knowledge of the political and social forces shaping the planet. Get a well-rounded start on this by regularly reading news magazines such as *The Economist*.

- **Writing and analytical skills.** Demonstrate these skills outside of course work by participating in a research project, writing a brochure, publishing an article in a magazine, or writing for a Web site.

- **Computer skills.** Acquire strong word processing skills (can you produce a table of contents, section breaks, footnotes, or use styles?); be comfortable using spreadsheets (can you produce a budget or sort a table of data?); be familiar with databases (can you explain the difference between a flat file and a relational database?); try to possess exceptional Internet research skills (can you find the phone number of a cheap Paris hotel in five minutes? What about the CIA country profile for Bhutan?).

- **Business skills.** The most sought-after employees are those with multi-disciplinary backgrounds, especially business backgrounds that include strong people skills. Employers seek scientists who can understand market research, engineers who can manage research teams and help commercialize products, and political scientists who can work in trade promotion. There is a need to assess the business aspect in almost every field, such as strategic planning, financial management and systems analysis. Do not assume that these essential skills are all acquired incidentally, through classroom or thesis work. You need to interact!

- **Other management skills:** project management, accounting, training, research, report writing, evaluating.

International Job Hunting Skills

- **Essentials for finding international work.** Experience has shown that those who are successful at finding international work have all done something extraordinary to land their first job. They have gone out on a limb, acted boldly (but politely), have been entrepreneurial, have sacrificed certainty and taken risks to gain international experience and land that first job. International employers are looking for individuals who are fully committed to international work and living, and your job hunting methods should reflect this.

A LAST WORD

International jobs require a long-term commitment—you need to invest in yourself to build an international IQ. This process eventually becomes a lifestyle, an outlook on life, a commitment to internationalism and cross-cultural learning. It is a very interesting and creative process, where the process itself becomes an end. Go forth—the world is your teacher. And have fun with the exploration!

APPENDIX ON THE CD-ROM

18a. "My Experience Preparing for an International Career," by Larissa Brown

CHAPTER 19
The Hiring Process

Finding a job overseas takes persistence, good qualifications, contacts and a measure of luck. You may be asked to leave "yesterday," or it may take 12 months to place you in your post once you have been offered a position. Compared to a job in North America, the verification process and pre-departure activities for an overseas posting may be lengthy, especially if your employer is situated overseas.

This chapter is about understanding the hiring process for traditional full-time, professional international positions. Do not read this chapter in isolation from the others that suggest specific strategies and many variations on how to break into the international job market. (See, for example, Chapters 29 to 34 in Part Four, The Professions.) University students and recent graduates in particular should be looking at the backdoor strategies suggested in other chapters. (See Chapter 10, Short-Term Programs Overseas and Chapter 17, Internships Abroad.) Backdoor and entrepreneurial strategies are the norm for landing your first job. For many, internships abroad are the catalyst for squeezing into a full-time international position.

LEAD TIMES FOR INTERNATIONAL WORK

The hiring process for overseas work follows a number of patterns, from "Can you leave for Kuala Lumpur in three days?" to "We have your resume on file from last year. Are you still available?" Don't be discouraged if you hear nothing or are told that your resume has been placed on file. Overseas job offers are often received a long time after the resume has been submitted. On the other hand, don't be surprised if you are asked to be packed and ready in one week.

Here are a few of the factors that affect lead times in the hiring decisions of international employers.

- **International job boards on the Internet have had a profound impact on the hiring practices of international employers.** Employers no longer have to plan for a three- to six-month search to find the right candidate. Because of the proliferation of hundreds of specialized international job boards on-line, employers and qualified applicants are finding each other much more easily. This means that in many instances, the hiring process, and especially the search phase of the hiring process, is much shorter. An international employer can decide on a Monday to post an international job, and on a Thursday, they can have 50 applicants to choose from. (For more information on how job boards are affecting the international employment scene, see Chapter 20, The Job Search & Targeting Your Research. Also, visit our Web site for "THE BIG GUIDE's Top 100 Jobs Boards" at www.workingoverseas.com.)

- **Lead time for international projects is both long and short.** Funding for many international projects is often awarded on a contract basis. To derive the maximum competitive bidding advantage, overseas employers maintain computerized data banks of qualified candidates. Having a readily available labour pool is an important part of being successful in the bidding process. When bidding on a project, a firm will consult its resume data bank for qualified candidates. If you are registered with it, you may be contacted at this time for permission to submit your resume with the proposal. Don't get your hopes up, since the decision to award a contract may take over a year. On the other hand, immediate hiring action is also common, as many of the candidates whose names were submitted with the proposal will have found other employment by the time the project is awarded.

- **Other instances that require immediate hiring action.** There are many scenarios: for example, the long-awaited decision to proceed with a new program is suddenly taken, creating an urgent need to fill several positions; a crisis situation arises overseas that requires immediate staffing; new monies are found at year-end budget time (especially with government contracts) and must be allocated; an overseas employee leaves before his or her contract expires (this situation occurs frequently).

- **Lead times for hiring some international positions are easier to predict.** For example, teachers should start applying for overseas positions a full year ahead of their planned departure date, just prior to the beginning of a new school year. For UNITED NATIONS positions, most candidates can plan on waiting a full year from the point of initial contact. Those who apply for positions that involve placement on a UN waiting list have been known to wait two or even three years. For business and other non-governmental organizations, you can usually plan on a minimum two-month hiring process from when the offer is first suggested and the time you start work. If you are applying to institutions or firms that are based overseas, the process is normally even longer.

- **Delays once the decision to hire you has been made**. There are many factors that can delay your departure. Verification processes and pre-departure activities can easily add six months to your waiting time. A strong word of caution goes out especially to those who have been tentatively offered a post. While your employer may be enthusiastic about getting you into the field as quickly as possible, there are numerous delaying factors that can impede (or prevent) your departure. Examples include cultural orientation sessions that may be used to assess your overseas aptitudes; security clearance, which can take several weeks; medical exams and their approval by in-house specialists; acceptance of your credentials by the overseas country representative or the foreign government paying your salary; visa procurement (not always assured); tedious delays as a result of bureaucratic stumbling and the multi-level approval process.

- **Keep on top of things while looking for international work.** This list is a short reminder of some of the many things you have to keep in mind when looking for international work.

  - Plan on accepting other work to put food on the table while you are looking for an international job.

  - Organize your affairs, so that you can leave on short notice when an opportunity knocks.

  - Do not make any irreversible decisions with regard to present conditions or personal affairs on the basis of a tentative job offer. Horror stories abound. Only a signed contract will do.

  - Contact employers not with the objective of finding out who is hiring, but to enquire, "Who may need my services over the next year?"

  - Don't give up: follow up regularly with past employer contacts; keep looking elsewhere (even when you have a tentative offer); and keep adding related international experiences to your dossier.

SAMPLE LEAD TIMES FOR FINDING A JOB

There are no standard lead times involved in an international job search, but it is safe to say you should buckle down and plan for a long haul. Here are the actions taken by one individual, a university graduate in her last year of a master's program.

September–January

Organized an extensive Internet search while consulting THE BIG GUIDE. Identified 100 organizations and 20 job boards in field of expertise. Studied job descriptions to evaluate career plans and decided on what types of jobs to target. Started speaking with friends and professionals in the field to get familiarized with the job market.

February

Underwent a skills analysis, then decided on a clear job objective and wrote an elevator pitch (short description of one's professional self). Made use of information collected during Internet research (job descriptions) to design a skill-based resume and compose cover letters, each targeting the employer's ideal profile. Rewrote elevator pitch three times and resume four times, making them perfect. (For more information, see Chapter 23, Selling Your International Skills and Chapter 24, International Resumes.)

March–June

Started an active phone campaign (three hours a day). Contacted 60 organizations, made 245 follow-up phone calls and an equal number of e-mails to international employers. Rewrote resume twice and composed three new cover letters to fit new information received during job search. Actively studied job openings (one hour each day) on a selected list of eight international job boards. Reviewed 15 other related job boards once a week. Conducted 6 information interviews with employers.

July–August

Accepted a six-week, part-time contract at minimum wage with an NGO to acquire more experience. Began "Plan B" to contact international consulting firms to look for a fall internship in a head office based locally. Continued active job search during this time. Follow-up phone calls elicited three or four good leads.

August

Received an offer for a permanent domestic position with an NGO. Immediately made follow-up calls to all other possible employers to inquire if other opportunities were imminent. Another NGO offered an overseas opportunity with departure in October. Accepted overseas position.

October

Departed for overseas.

This successful job search took approximately 12 months, but it could have been a lot shorter… or even longer.

WHO MAKES THE HIRING DECISION?

Contrary to what you might logically expect, the human resources department rarely makes the international hiring decision. International hiring decisions require in-depth knowledge of the position and an expertise in assessing the international IQ of job applicants. Most hiring decisions are therefore made by managers from the department with the job to offer. For this reason, it is a good rule to always contact the department most likely to need your services. Speak to the most senior person available—the department manager or the project officer who will be overseeing your work.

Depending on the organization, there are a number of places where you can begin your search for the person with the mandate to hire you.

Human Resources Department

When contacting corporations whose main interest is not international affairs, persist in your efforts to speak to someone who has international responsibilities. Do not accept being automatically directed to the human resources department. This will most often be a waste of time. Except for organizations involved exclusively in international affairs, the human resources department is rarely able to appreciate your international qualifications. If you are speaking to an organization expressly involved in international activities, follow a dual strategy of contacting the human resources departments as well as the manager who would be supervising your work.

International Division

International departments of North American institutions or firms often operate as separate, independent entities, existing alongside domestic operations. This structural observation is important to the job seeker as many of the personnel decisions related to international activities are considered so unique they are handled strictly by the international division, whereas the human resources office handles the domestic departments. Always start your job inquiries with the international department. If the international division is a small one, ask to speak to the director. If it is a very large department, ask to speak to the department head in charge of the area you are interested in.

Large International Firm, Government Department or Institution

If you are contacting an organization whose main purpose is international, it is best to have a two-tiered approach. First, focus on the specific department involved in your area of interest; second, contact the human resources department. Thus, a sales director would contact the international sales division director, an engineer would call the project leader, and a person specializing in Asian studies would speak to the chief analyst of the Asia department. Continue with a dual strategy, follow the normal procedures with the human resources department, and in parallel, contact the international division directly. This strategy is especially crucial with governments, UN agencies and other intergovernmental organization (IGOs).

Small International Firm or Non-Governmental Organization

In this case, you should speak directly to the chief executive officer (CEO) or the president of the firm. If you are unable to speak to the CEO, ask to speak to another senior person. If you are looking for a volunteer position with an NGO, do not contact the chief executive. As a volunteer, you can increase your chances by registering with the human resources department and, at the same time, contacting the specific country placement officer dealing with programs of your interest.

THE IDEAL SELECTION PROCESS

Depending on the sophistication of the company doing the international hiring and the level of the position you are applying for, you can assess a company's expertise in the international field by considering the thoroughness of their selection process. You should be wary of a firm that neglects standard international hiring procedures. They will likely also neglect their responsibilities to an overseas employee.

Here are some of the most important points to look for during the selection process:

- The job advertisement information should include a detailed description as well as give an honest indication of overseas living and working conditions. Employers should then follow up with detailed and truthful assessments of living and working conditions. Be wary of employers who paint too rosy a picture. Experienced international recruiters know that deception at this stage will lead to a high failure rate and mistrust of head office. They want candidates to deselect themselves. Everything should be truthful and transparent.

- Experienced international managers who have lived overseas should conduct the interview process. The employer should question you extensively in the following areas: your personality, your technical expertise, your career path now and upon return, your domestic or family situation, your spouse's willingness to move, your health and the health of your family, your understanding of overseas living conditions. (For more information, see Chapter 26, Interviewing for an International Job.)

- Orientation information on the country of posting should be provided on these essential areas: housing, social life, recreation, schooling, churches, health facilities, cost of living, local shopping conditions, transportation, security, current political and socio-economic situations, cultural norms and customs, language information and working conditions.

- Your spouse should always be interviewed and given a thorough orientation session. This is not paternalistic—pressure from family life accounts for over half of the failures in international appointments. Any firm in the international arena that fails to take a spouse into account is operating naively.

THE CONTRACT

Clarify beforehand all of the benefits associated with a contract. Knowing your industry's standards will go a long way in helping you to evaluate your employer's contract offer. For example, an NGO may provide only $2,500 in airfreight allowance, whereas a private firm may cover the full cost of your move up to a maximum of $20,000. Both conform to their different industry standards.

It is part of the employer's responsibility to see that a family can function well abroad. Such items as proper housing and adequate schooling are essential components of contract negotiations. Any employer that shrugs off its responsibility to an expatriate family is being short-sighted.

Many organizations are too small, or perhaps just too lax, to develop standard remuneration policies. In these cases, you will have to negotiate your remuneration package from scratch.

Compared to a domestic employment contract, an overseas contract may include some of the following benefits: a post adjustment to salary allowance (including protection against local inflation rates), payment in convertible currency; a severance allowance or political risks allowance; relocation time off and allowance (including a moving and set-up allowance); a return visit home and visit by children to the country of placement; a schooling allowance; medical insurance, including special evacuation insurance; a special housing and car allowance; warehousing costs for goods left at home and which extends a number of months beyond the contract end date; and sometimes even a paid visit to the country of posting by the candidate and his or her spouse in the final stages of the selection process before the appointment is made.

A LAST WORD

Since most international job assignments involve either competitive bidding on projects or political influencing to acquire work visas, no job is guaranteed unless you have signed a contract or letter of employment. Despite whatever verbal promises or guarantees are made to you, never take irreversible action before you have a signed contract in your hand. This cannot be over-stressed. There are countless horror stories of people leaving their jobs, selling their businesses and renting out their homes only to find that the overseas assignment did not materialize.

CHAPTER 20

The Job Search & Targeting Your Research

Before undertaking an active job search, you will require certain skills. While almost anyone can pursue an overseas job, successful candidates have a number of traits that lead them to success. In reading the following list, keep in mind that these job search skills are often the same ones required for the overseas work itself, and it is therefore to your benefit to demonstrate these skills to employers. Note also that this chapter is not the only source for job search information in THE BIG GUIDE. Such information is found throughout the book, and this chapter serves to highlight the general processes without getting into too many specific strategies. (For more detailed job search strategies, see Chapter 17, Internships Abroad, and all of Part Three, The International Job Search.)

EFFECTIVE INTERNATIONAL JOB SEARCH SKILLS

Below is a list of important qualities to help you land international work. It takes someone with a special character to find international work and then be successful at it. The important qualities are not hard to find; most of us have them innately in us. You will, however, have to put these attributes into high gear as you look for international work. Don't be shy about showing them off to employers; they're what employers are looking for, as you'll need them to make you successful while abroad. You'll need to show

- knowledge of the hiring process
- determination
- confidence
- entrepreneurial instinct
- verbal communication skills
- writing skills

Knowledge of the Hiring Process

People who find jobs are not necessarily those with the most job-related skills; rather, they are often the people most skilled in job search techniques. Therefore, you should practice interview and phone techniques with friends, write and rewrite your resume to make it the best possible, and research and understand the overseas job market by consulting books or the Internet on the subject. In short, plan on becoming an effective job seeker.

Determination

The single most vital factor in achieving success is determination. For example, we know of one successful candidate who visited Ottawa from Toronto five times over a four-month period and contacted over 60 organizations. Another candidate had a job washing floors in a hospital for one year while he pursued international job openings with the UNITED NATIONS. He remained active in the international community by writing articles for development journals. Another job seeker became the co-ordinator for a cross-cultural volunteer committee and vigorously searched for funding for a development project he had put together while unemployed. All of these candidates were successful and are now working in challenging jobs in Madagascar, Bangladesh, and for an NGO in Ottawa. The key to their success was determination, both long and short term.

There is another side to the importance of showing determination during your international job search. Employers want to see this trait because they know that moving overseas takes a lot of effort and requires the employee to make many sacrifices. International employees need staying power. Therefore, employers only want to hire employees who are determined to work internationally. So show your determination while looking for international work—international employers are looking for it.

Confidence

Be confident and persistent. Recruiters and friends can sometimes discourage you in your endeavour, and finding that overseas job is not easy! It's normal to have moments of doubt; to be successful, you have to be relentless.

Entrepreneurial Instinct

To be a successful international job hunter, you must be innovative, willing to take risks, and confident in putting yourself in the forefront of new, unknown challenges.

Many international job seekers have positioned themselves overseas in low-level jobs with the specific purpose of making contacts in the industry in which they want to work. For example, an English teacher took a low-paying job teaching English to businessmen in Hong Kong with the goal of becoming an executive assistant to a VP with business affairs in Canada. A tour guide made contacts during his excursions in Asia that helped him establish a craft import company in Ottawa. The key to success is to pursue aggressively a larger goal while working at a job you know you won't have forever. Make contacts, join clubs, research, and find out all there is to know about the field you wish to work in. This not only includes the specific field, but also the business climate, the people, the language and the politics of your targeted host country or culture.

Verbal Communication Skills

In undertaking a job search, you should have excellent communication skills. Whether speaking on the phone or in an interview, you should have a clear idea of what you want to say. You must be able to speak convincingly and enthusiastically about your skills and character traits. It is especially crucial to convey to employers what makes you valuable to them. For those of you with uncertainty about your ability to communicate effectively, be rest assured that you can learn. You will improve as your job search progresses.

Writing Skills

To conduct an international job search, you have to put serious thought into good writing. Write prospective employers with perfect e-mails, resumes and cover letters. Electronic communications dominate the front end of the selection process, and you won't get an interview unless you pass an employer's writing test. You will be judged by the e-mails you write—keep them formal and grammatically correct. Your cover letter has to be customized for each employer. Your resume has to be absolutely perfect and it must be an example of the most efficient writing that you have ever produced.

TARGETING YOUR JOB SEARCH

Nothing is more important to your job hunt than deciding on a specific search target. This theme is very important; it is the main idea discussed in two upcoming chapters: Chapter 23, Selling Your International Skills and Chapter 24, International Resumes. It is broken down as such: first, decide on what you would love to do in life; second, decide on a specific career objective; and third, write up your skills and job experiences to support your career objective. In this section, we want to show how targeting your research for an international job will be equally important. We are assuming that you have already decided on a specific career objective. (If you haven't, trick yourself and choose a target. You can always change your mind later.)

Imagine how much more effective you will be in your job research once you've decided on a target. Compare the prospects for the following two job candidates, each with the same qualifications.

Candidate A does no targeting and Candidate B targets precisely. Candidate A is looking for an international job as a general administrator for an organization with international activities. This person searches various Web sites for contacts with government, NGOs, private firms, and international organizations. The process is frustrating for Candidate A because he can't get a handle on any of these sectors—the contacts he makes in one group are of no help in networking with other groups. Candidate B, on the other hand, has decided to look specifically for a program officer position with an NGO based in the Toronto–Ottawa–Montreal triangle. Candidate B makes a list of the 56 NGOs in the area. She researches extensively the ideal profile for a program officer by looking at job descriptions on the Internet. She then divides the NGOs into groups based on their size (small, medium and large) and decides to target large NGOs as her choice employer. Then Candidate B searches the Internet to find out general information on what is happening in the NGO sector. She begins by calling small and medium-sized NGOs to "practice" networking conversations. By the time Candidate B begins calling large NGOs, she has information to share about the sector and is familiar with the terminology for this field of work. She can also mention exact names of other contacts in the NGO sector.

Obviously, Candidate B has something to offer when speaking to potential NGO employers and can easily impress. Candidate A has little or no information to share because he has cast such a wide net that the information collected is not as valuable. Candidate A is frustrated and dislikes making networking contacts. Candidate B is empowered as each networking contact becomes easier to obtain and she gains more and more information to share with prospective employers.

Clearly, a targeted job search is much more powerful.

THE THREE JOB SEARCH PHASES

You must approach the international job market with more acumen than if you were searching for a typical domestic job. You need a plan for each phase. Your first task will be self-evaluation. As discussed throughout this book, the key to the creative job search is to be able to identify and label your skills for employers. Your second task will be to target your efforts efficiently by researching your field to uncover potential employers. The third task involves direct contact with employers, from telephoning and searching the Internet to e-mailing and face-to-face interviews. You may be tempted to jump phase one or two and begin contacting employers immediately, but we recommend otherwise. Do not contact any employers until you have completed your self-evaluation and done your research. If you want to look your professional best and highlight all that you are worth, you can't give this three-phase approach the short shrift.

The Three Phases of an International Job Search

Phase One – SELF-EVALUATION: What do I have to offer?

- Assess your personal skills (see Chapter 23, Selling Your International Skills).
- Decide on a target job type.
- Write your first resume (see Chapter 24, International Resumes).

Phase Two – RESEARCH: Where do I look?

- Formalize your target. Focus on a specific sector, a list of organizations or a specific region of the world. Start with organizations profiled in THE BIG GUIDE.
- Search the Internet for more organizations and review their job pages.
- Select a group of Internet job boards and check these regularly.
- Network with people in your field and possibly contact executive search firms.
- Learn to speak about "your sector" of international work, know the organizations, the players and the types of jobs in your field.
- Search the Internet for formal job descriptions in your field. Rewrite your resume and skills inventory to match the ideal profile found in these descriptions.

Phase Three – APPLYING FOR THE JOB: How do I approach the employer?

- Always review an organization's Web site for current information so that you have something to talk about before contacting employers.
- Consider phoning employers to start building a professional relationship (see Chapter 22, Phone Research Techniques).

- Rewrite your resume using the language of your future work after speaking with employers about their ideal profile.
- Write your covering letter and e-mail (see Chapter 25, Covering Letters).
- Prepare for the job interview (see Chapter 26, Interviewing for an International Job).

SELF-EVALUATION

You should already have read Part One, Your International IQ. You are now preparing to find a new job overseas: making plans and organizing your affairs for that important move. You have been building up your international IQ. You know yourself. You know you have the personal traits to enjoy an international assignment and you know you have the right skills. You have, perhaps, acquired a second language, done volunteer work for a number of international organizations, travelled in a developing country for three months and even managed to swing a conference in, say, Belize. You know that within the next year your current job contract will be finished and, therefore, you are now ready to begin a serious job search for that overseas posting. But how and where do you start?

You have to put a marketing package together. You need to be ready to describe yourself to employers. You have to help employers by doing the analytical work for them; analyze and categorize your own sets of skills for them. Who are you? What are you good at? What makes you tick? How do you sell yourself to the employer? All of these good questions have been addressed in Chapter 23, Selling Your International Skills, and you should consult this chapter extensively. Essentially, the high-level advice we provide is that you need to

- learn to sell your skills,
- learn to focus on your primary skills,
- learn to describe your skills internationally.

RESEARCH

We have already underlined the importance of choosing a target for your job research. You can achieve this by focusing on one sector, one region or an area of expertise. Once you've decided, there are three basic categories of where and how to research for an international job:

- **Research organizations** by looking them up in books and on the Web.
- **Research international job openings** on job boards and in advertisements.
- **Network and make contacts** to reach individuals and to research the international aspects of your field of work.

Research Organizations

There are many ways to do this. Here is a list of approaches.

- **Review international job search books** such as THE BIG GUIDE. (See the resource list, International Job Search Books, in Chapter 21, Resources for the International Job Search.)
- **Surf the Internet** for the thousands of Web sites on job search techniques, international job boards, resume postings, lists of international employers and

much more. (All the resources in THE BIG GUIDE are helpful. See for example the resource list, International Job Hunting Services on the Internet, in Chapter 21, Resources for the International Job Search.)

- **Review directories that list organizations**. (For an initial list of directories to help you locate organizations, see the Job Search Directories in the Resource section at the end of this chapter.)

- **Review trade journals and newspapers** for articles on organizations doing international work in your field.

Research International Job Postings

With the advent of Internet job boards, applicants from one corner of the world are finding and seeking employment in another far corner of the planet—thousands of international jobs are popping up instantaneously on hundreds and hundreds of job boards and job seekers are being recruited just as fast. Internet job boards have created a vast pool of candidates, but there is an equally vast pool of jobs on offer to those who can sell their qualifications.

The new reality is that international employers no longer have to search far and wide for qualified candidates; and better still, candidates do not have to search as hard to find all the jobs that are available. The traditional hiring process is being displaced. Hiring times are being slashed. Everyone has more to choose from in this new environment. The playing field has been levelled for both employers and job applicants. If you have professionally packaged your international qualifications, you will rise to the top and be able to grab the best job first.

Here are a few tips to help you navigate the wild world of job boards.

- **Look for industry-specific job boards.** There are thousands of job boards out there, but you should look for those with an international focus and any industry-specific ones that match your specific field of interest. (THE BIG GUIDE has 22 lists of industry-specific international job boards; see the Index by Resource Subject at the back of this book.)

- **Job boards require that you be at your computer searching for newly posted jobs every day.** Timing is everything! Jobs are posted quickly, applicants apply quickly and hiring decisions are made quickly. As an applicant, you have a narrow window of opportunity to find the job and respond.

- **Where feasible, re-submit your resume to job boards at intervals of six weeks.** This will ensure that your resume is listed as a recently received one. Employers who search on-line resume databanks most often search only for the most recently posted resumes to ensure that they have a pool of candidates who are still available. So you need to play this game with a well-orchestrated planning calendar to track the numerous job boards that are out there.

- **Beware of the wild goose chase.** The Internet can be a wild goose chase if you don't know where to find the information you want. This means that you might sift through sites containing unreliable information, costing you time and money. Be aware also that time flies on the Internet, so it pays to think strategically on how best to use your valuable time.

- **Outdated postings.** Just as millions of Web sites are created or updated daily, many become out of date or abandoned. Responding to outdated job postings is another way to waste time. Therefore, it's best either to phone or e-mail the potential employer before you apply for a job. While Web site job postings are often faster to access than those in the print media, your chances of being the very first to hear about an opportunity are quickly diminishing as the Internet is rapidly becoming more accessible to greater numbers of people. Competition for jobs on the Internet is global in scope, rather than regional or national.

- **Search the job pages on organization Web sites.** Thousands of people get hired through job boards, but most organizations also post their openings directly on their own sites because it costs nothing and it is easy to manage. So, search the job pages of your targeted organizations regularly.

- **Keep up with the traditional job hunting techniques.** Make direct contacts with international employers (yes, this means making cold calls) and keep up with e-mail correspondence and networking.

- **Your resume is an ongoing project during research.** Update it constantly with new terminology. After updating your resume, re-send it to prospective employers who have shown interest in your qualifications, informing them that you have a new resume that better reflects your skills. This keeps your resume current and gives you an opportunity to touch base with employers every six weeks or so. (In general, you should be making intermittent contact with prospective employers every six weeks to let them know that you are still available.)

Job Advertisements

It is common knowledge that a large percentage of jobs are not found through job advertisements, but through personal networking. Responding to job ads is an easy way to research a job, but it is also the most competitive and, thus, most unlikely to succeed—especially for entry-level candidates or those trying to break into the field. If you have solid international credentials, the job advertisement is a good option. Entry-level job seekers should take note of the organizations advertising for mid- and senior-level international positions and contact these organizations directly. Whatever your situation, no research method should be discounted. We mention a few tips here.

Major North American newspapers and other international publications carry ads for highly specialized, middle- and senior-management positions. Examples: *The Economist*, *L'Express*, *The Washington Post*, *The Wall Street Journal* (New York), *The Globe and Mail* (Toronto), the *Financial Times* (London), *Le Monde* (Paris) and *The New York Times*. The Sunday editions of these publications usually have the best selection of such ads. Don't forget to read the financial section of newspapers for information on new foreign contracts—new contracts imply that new people will be hired.

Most professions have a trade magazine. Such magazines are an invaluable source of ideas on how to build your international experience. Many of them carry international job advertisements. International articles are featured in most issues and can be useful for uncovering job information. For example, if you read about a new international initiative in your industry, contact the source immediately to find out about international employment possibilities. Do not wait for formal job postings to appear.

Don't get hung up on formal, narrow job requirements when applying for international work. While domestic jobs have many specialized requirements, the breadth of skills for international jobs is so wide that recruiting officers are often very flexible in their hiring criteria. While the job advertisement may state otherwise, always remember this fact. Knowing what to do overseas, how to work and think in other cultures—this is the key to your mobility.

Don't let the term "expert" scare you. Despite what you may have heard, becoming an expert has lost its original meaning and now stands for "has experience."

Network and Make Contacts

Contacts are everything. Making international networking contacts is not easy. Internationally experienced people see themselves as having unique insights into how the world works and how cultures interact. They are attuned to world political and economic trends, and they understand the diplomatic dancing that is required to make cross-cultural communication easier. Such people can be quick to dismiss the efforts of rookies trying to enter the field. Thus, you face the problem of how to network with little international experience behind you. Here are a few pointers to help you decide on your networking style.

Approach each new aspect of your job search with curiosity. Curiosity is a trait appreciated and recognized as a legitimate vehicle for pursuing knowledge. Aggressive, pushy behaviour, on the other hand, is not appreciated in many cultures and would interfere with your success overseas.

What differentiates curious researchers from aggressive ones is that the curious have a passion for the process of discovery, while the aggressive are motivated solely by outcome. The curious take delight in the people and situations they meet in their discovery of a new culture.

Do everything you can to meet people in your field. We know of one individual who decided he wanted to work in disaster relief management. For one year he read, researched and wrote letters to people and organizations involved in this area. The objective of his research was not to uncover job openings, but to find out what was happening in the field. In the process, this person discovered which major international organizations were involved in disaster relief and what their links were to Canadian organizations. Later, when a Canadian job opportunity came up, he was interviewed for it. As he had knowledge of the field, he was hired and sent to work on a Colombian volcano disaster relief effort.

As the above example demonstrates, networking is not necessarily direct job searching. Your networking conversations may have different purposes, but all can lead to jobs. There is a strong case to be made for focusing on information gathering when you are searching for a job. Ask specific questions about the activities of a given organization. Information gathering thus becomes a process of elimination of where you apply for jobs.

Involve yourself in international affairs by getting to know the organizations, departments, periodicals and conferences that relate to your field. This does not mean going to a library to do research. Rather, go out and meet people, make contacts, network. Visit trade offices, subscribe to trade journals, attend conferences. Get a working knowledge of your area of expertise. Volunteer for any international committee that you can. Offer to set up meetings, do research or take tickets at the door during public events. Do anything that will allow you to make connections.

With these strategies, you will get to know people and find out what is going on in the international community, and you will be even more valuable to the employer who hires you for that overseas job.

When networking, make sure that you are armed with as much cross-cultural knowledge as possible. International contact persons want to know how you would solve problems overseas, how you make contacts, what your insights are on the cultural peculiarities that affect negotiations and administration, what you know about import and export regulations, and your knowledge of the organizations that dominate or stand out in your international field. This sort of concrete information will impress potential employers and your other contacts.

Don't make the common mistake of trying to impress your networking contact by discussing macroeconomic development policy, world injustices or liberation movements. Speak instead of your organizing techniques, your administrative skills in a cross-cultural context, your language abilities and accounting skills. Discussions of why you are successful in your field or your solid understanding of overseas environments are more impressive to employers than academic theorizing on political or economic processes.

Networking is not an activity to be saved for after you've graduated from university. It is worthwhile to begin while a student. At the beginning of the school year, for example, ask your professors about upcoming international conferences in your field. Go to the conference prepared. Study the list of presenters and their topics. Arrange to do an essay on a related topic. Produce your own business cards to hand out at the conference. Once at the meeting, make contacts. Network! Connect with participants whose professional interests are similar to yours. Afterward, follow up with a handwritten thank-you note or greeting. Another good way to make contacts toward creating your own internship is to volunteer as a conference coordinator. Needless to say, you're guaranteed to meet a lot of people!

If you are currently unemployed, or in the final stages of an overseas contract/internship, you should expose yourself to as many opportunities as possible. Check bulletin boards at local embassies and other international offices, volunteer to manage a project, research and write an article in your field, join and become active in the international activities of an association, learn a second or third language and make use of the contacts you develop in the process. Each of these tactics puts you in line to meet people and make contacts. (For a full discussion on how to find work while overseas, see Chapter 17, Internships Abroad.)

Wherever you work in the international field, you should be forging links with similar institutions or companies. Take the time and every opportunity to build relationships outside your office. Never lose interest in what others are doing. This continued interest should provide you with contacts when you are again actively searching for an international job, and will help you in your present job by broadening your understanding and exposure. From early on in your career, maintain an address book of professional contacts. As time passes, you will find it invaluable to search through that book to look up old friends or contact acquaintances to network for future employment.

Networking, as opposed to job hunting, is a long-term process. You are not actively soliciting people for jobs, but are rather seeking to benefit from their understanding of the job market. Don't ask, *"Do you have a job?"* but rather, *"What new developments or programs are starting up?"* and, *"How do people normally enter this field?"* and, especially, *"What does your organization do and how does it do it?"*

Network with Contacts

- University professors in your field who have international links.
- Researchers in all fields and types of organizations.
- Employees of internationally oriented organizations.
- Recent immigrants who have international ties.
- Foreign students and their parents overseas.
- Business executives working internationally.
- International consultants concerned with work trends.
- Government employees in international departments (as public servants, it's their role to be helpful, and most of them are when sought out by a bright, well-informed young international job seeker).
- People you meet at conferences, trade associations or while learning a second language.
- Returned overseas volunteers and their contacts.
- People you meet during international travel.
- Colleagues or friends of anyone on this list, especially if they are currently overseas while you are travelling in their country.

Network with Organizations

- All the organizations profiled or listed as resources in THE BIG GUIDE.
- Government trade officials or business development offices (those abroad, in Canada or the US).
- Foreign government trade officers (those abroad, in Canada or the US).
- Foreign embassies and consulates.
- Foreign associations in Canada.
- International branches or foreign offices of your chamber of commerce.
- Trade associations in manufacturing, etc.
- Large municipalities, the mayor's office, city twinning programs.
- Convention and tourism bureaus.
- University international centres (see Chapter 15, International Studies in Canada).
- Economic development agencies.

DISCOVERING WHERE THE JOBS ARE

This book is full of contact addresses, resources, and Web addresses of international employers and opportunities. Since research strategies are discussed in detail throughout our guide, we shall limit ourselves here to pointing out a few important sectors for the North American international job hunter.

Thousands of people work overseas for Canadian or US private sector firms that have expanded globally during the past few decades. Typically, firms that have found international markets for their products hire their own citizens for a select number of overseas positions. The majority of such firms are involved in the service industry, consulting, engineering, construction, oil, manufacturing, banking, finance and high tech.

An important untapped market for Canadians and Americans is to look for employment with each other's international organizations. For example, US firms have often hired Canadians for overseas work, and Canadian NGOs have similarly hired US citizens for overseas work. Given our cultural similarity, our mutually recognized professionalism, and our respective language advantages (Canadians speaking French, Americans speaking Spanish), Canadians are attractive to many US organizations and Americans are attractive to Canadian organizations. (See the chapters on US and Canadian firms and NGOs in Part Five, International Career Directories.)

Wherever English is in short supply, there are opportunities not only for teaching English, but also for skilled employees able to operate in English as well as the local language. Japan, Hong Kong and Korea are examples of places where many North Americans have found employment because of their language skills.

Canada has three main centres for finding international work. By far the largest is the Montreal–Ottawa–Toronto triangle. In almost every field represented, Canadian companies and organizations working abroad have their head offices in this region. Obviously, the federal government plays a major role here, as do international development organizations and private consulting firms (many concentrated in the Montreal area). In the western provinces, many international oil jobs are based in Alberta, although the oil job market is much smaller than it used to be. In Nova Scotia, education and trade partnerships with Cuba and Western Europe exist, and more partnerships are emerging. And lastly, there is the Vancouver area, with its natural resources and business links with the Pacific Rim countries. If you are not close to one of these areas, do not despair. Long distance phone calls to specifically targeted companies can be very effective and usually receive more attention than a local call.

The US has similar geographic centres for international work. The major concentration for internationally based employers is along the eastern and western seaboards. New York, Boston and Washington, DC are obvious venues for government and NGO work as well as for internationally active management consulting and finance firms. Texas is huge in the international oil industry. Florida has many organizations with ties to Latin America. Because of its sheer size, the US has a fairly even distribution of internationally active private firms and NGO sub-offices across the entire country. For most US citizens, there is an internationally active organization within driving distance from their home.

Better Networking with Country Information

Awareness of a country's cultural diversity and socio-economic background will enhance your job search and improve your chances of success at the interview stage. Knowing the current affairs of a country is essential for any international career seeker, and the Internet can help you stay informed. (For an excellent list of country-based information, see Country Guides and Reports as well as other resources in Chapter 21, Resources for the International Job Search.) Here is a list of ideas on what type of country information is available on the Internet:

- **Current affairs/news.** Internet on-line news services can help you find out about current affairs before they are posted in newsgroups, not to mention in newspapers and on television. Web sites such as CNN and Reuters provide minute-by-minute international news and headlines about politics, finance and weather. Such coverage is also more comprehensive than other sources, allowing you to follow events in countries generally ignored by the Western media.

- **Country profiles.** To broaden your knowledge base of a country, you can look at country profiles posted on the Web sites of FOREIGN AFFAIRS CANADA (FAC), INTERNATIONAL TRADE CANADA (ITCAN) or the US STATE DEPARTMENT. These provide a general overview of the social and political climate of countries around the world. Just a note of caution: pay close attention to who is writing the country profiles and try to understand their perspective. Almost all governments have official Web sites providing useful data such as its culture, current events, economy, geography, history, trade and tourism, as well as links to various government departments.

- **Business opportunities.** The Internet is a gold mine of resources for the entrepreneur. Some countries' Web sites contain government and trade association information on export/import ventures, financial markets and contacts to various government agencies and trade programs.

- **Embassy services.** Most people would not think of contacting the embassy of a foreign country for anything other than traditional services such as visas or travel permits. Yet, they provide a lot of information about culture, tourism, trade and investment.

- **Tourist/travel information.** Many governments and privately sponsored Web sites can help answer your inquiries about accommodations, weather, cultural events or other general travel questions.

- **Country-specific research *without* the Internet.** For the adventurous who wish to get off their computers, there are, of course, many non-cyber sources for country information. You can contact embassies and organizations directly by phone, fax or personally visiting their offices. And don't just visit the Web site, visit the country: a "job hunting vacation" in a desired country could be fruitful by targeting potential employers before and after you arrive.

DO SOMETHING EXTRAORDINARY

It is our experience that anyone who finds international work has done something extraordinary to land his or her first job. They have gone the limit and pushed the envelope in the job hunting process. Indeed, most successful entry-level international job seekers have gotten their first job through the back door—using unconventional tactics. They have gone to Washington or Ottawa for a two-week round of networking interviews; brazenly called the director of a large international department; maximized every opportunity while interning abroad (see Chapter 17, Internships Abroad); or they have done simple things that make them stand out. Examples of this last tactic are calling an employer directly in Bangkok; sending a c.v. by courier in an attractive package instead of attaching it to a nondescript e-mail; or, better still, delivering a c.v. in person and speaking briefly with the manager. They have certainly spoken to employers directly in networking meetings or on the phone. They have searched for contact names on employer Web sites and called them directly, perhaps ignoring advertisements saying "no phone calls." Others have catapulted themselves from a domestic job to an international one within the same firm by openly canvassing and selling their international skills. THE BIG GUIDE is filled with other suggestions for doing extraordinary things to land your first international job. Good luck with your endeavours; the world is yours if you grasp it.

A LAST WORD

Here is a checklist of what we think is required for an international job search.

- Have you worked hard at building your international IQ?
- Are you prepared to spend time and money on an active job search campaign?
- Do you have a clear idea of the type of international job you want? Can you do that job right now? Are you willing to work your way up, pay your dues?
- Do you know people working internationally in your field? Have you spoken to at least five people who have worked overseas?
- Does your resume highlight your international experience and awareness?
- Can you clearly explain to employers what you do well and enjoy doing? Can you explain this in the context of an overseas work assignment?
- Why would an employer hire you?
- Have you written a professional elevator pitch—a two-sentence and a two-paragraph description of yourself and your key qualifications to use when networking?
- Have you researched the international aspects of your field? Have you conducted research into the international job market to determine where you fit ?
- Do you have a good idea of what your skills are worth to potential employers? If not, do you know how to find out?
- Do you possess the skills required to carry out an effective job search (letter-writing techniques, phoning techniques, resume-writing skills, interview and communication techniques)?
- Are you knowledgeable about the international hiring process? Who to contact? Who makes the hiring decisions? How long an international job search takes?

If you answered no to any of these questions, read on. THE BIG GUIDE is here to help you.

RESOURCES

This chapter contains the following Resources sections: General Job Search; Student Job Search; and Job Search Directories.

GENERAL JOB SEARCH

You have to start somewhere, and it has to be here: get your resume done, figure out how to research your industry and find that job you always wanted. Job hunting is not all misery. It's the one time in your life when you get to look seriously at your professional self, talk to people who are doing what you want to do and learn all about who is doing what in your field of expertise. That sounds exciting! Get started. Good luck.

101 Dynamite Questions to Ask at Your Interview 📖
2001, Richard Fein, 134 pages ➤ Impact Publications, Suite N, 9104 North Manassas Drive, Manassas Park, VA 20111-5211, USA, www.impactpublications.com, $13.95 US; Credit Cards; 703-361-7300, fax 703-335-9486 ◆ This book identifies the type and quality of questions the job seeker should ask as an often overlooked ingredient in a successful job interview. Identifies 101 key questions touching on the job, company, industry or profession, as well as questions that should be avoided. [ID:2213]

175 High-Impact Cover Letters 📖
2002, Richard H. Beatty, 256 pages ➤ John Wiley & Sons, 22 Worcester Road, Etobicoke, ON M9W 1L1, Canada, www.wiley.ca, $14.95 US; Credit Cards; 800-567-4797, fax 800-565-6802, canada@wiley.com ◆ This book provides job seekers with an sample arsenal of highly effective and professional cover letters that can quickly be modified to fit a variety of different circumstances. [ID:2193]

The Best Résumés for $75,000+ Executive Jobs 📖
1998, William Montag, 293 pages ➤ John Wiley & Sons, 22 Worcester Road, Etobicoke, ON M9W 1L1, Canada, www.wiley.ca, $16.95 US; Credit Cards; 800-567-4797, fax 800-565-6802, canada@wiley.com ◆ A unique resume workbook aimed exclusively at executives making $75,000 or more, this book will greatly benefit and assist in the critical job search, self-marketing process. Features over 75 proven achievement-oriented and market-tested resumes, along with cover letters. [ID:2000]

Canada's Top 100 Employers 📖
2004, Richard W. Yerema, 432 pages ➤ Mediacorp Canada Inc., 21 New Street, Toronto, ON M5R 1P7, Canada, www.mediacorp.ca, $22.95 CDN; Credit Cards; 416-964-6069, fax 416-964-3202, ct100@mediacorp.ca ◆ Find out what it's like to work at the nation's best employers, including many with opportunities at international locations. Now in its 5th edition, this book lets you find the leading employers in almost every industry and includes restaurant-style ratings of their company benefits, vacation policy and community involvement. The Globe and Mail called this book "an instant bible to HR professionals and job-seekers". To find out more, visit the book's Web site at www.CanadasTop100.com. ((For more information, see their ad in the sponsor section at the end of this guide.) [ID:2375]

The Canadian Internet Job Search Guide 📖
2004, Kevin Makra, 478 pages ➤ Sentor Media Inc., Suite 1120, 388 Richmond Street W., Toronto, ON M5V 3P1, Canada, www.sentormedia.com, $29.95 CDN; VISA, MC; 416-971-5090, fax 416-977-3782 ◆ This book seeks to jump-start your employment search by profiling 400 of the most important Web sites relating to employment searches by Canadians. Includes national, regional and industry sites, along with job boards, topic-specific sites, classifieds, newsgroups, links and international sites all arranged alphabetically. Get started with a crash course on the basics of Internet job searching or go directly to the index at the back of the book and start looking for jobs on-line. (For more information, see their ad in the sponsor section at the end of this guide.) [ID:2528]

Career City 🖳
www.careercity.com ◆ This US site offers advice on a number of valuable job hunting skills such as writing resumes, interview strategies and the basics of job hunting. It has been redesigned and now includes an international job search function, but has few jobs in the database. [ID:2155]

The Career Directory 📖
Annual, Richard W. Yerema, Karen Chow, 480 pages ➤ Mediacorp Canada Inc., 21 New Street, Toronto, ON M5R 1P7, Canada, www.mediacorp.ca, $35.95 CDN; Credit Cards; 416-964-6069, fax 416)964-3202, ct100@mediacorp.ca ◆ Now in its 14th edition, this directory with accompanying CD-ROM lets job-seekers match their degree or diploma with companies hiring in their field. A good start for your general job search and a great way to find out which companies have overseas jobs in your industry. To directly inquire about this book, e-mail tcd@mediacorp.ca. (For more information, see their ad in the sponsor section at the end of this guide.) [ID:2376]

Career Resource Center 💻

www.careers.org ◆ An excellent launch pad into cyberspace, this site contains over 6,000 links to various job-related resources. The sites are organized into geographical divisions, by province, state and other international areas. There are also links to university career offices, job banks, government resources and career counselling services. This is a very good place to initiate an Internet job hunt, particularly if you have an idea of what you want to do and where you want to go. [ID:2236]

Change Your Job, Change Your Life: High
Impact Strategies for Finding Great Jobs in the '90s 📖

2002, Ronald Krannich, 336 pages ➤ Impact Publications, Suite N, 9104 North Manassas Drive, Manassas Park, VA 20111-5211, USA, www.impactpublications.com, $17.95 US; Credit Cards; 703-361-7300, fax 703-335-9486 ◆ The new edition of this acclaimed career book is designed for anyone entering or re-entering the job market as well as for those making a career change. It contains 18 chapters on the job search, negotiating contracts, alternative careers and keeping up with changes in the job market. [ID:2018]

Contact Point 💻

www.contactpoint.ca ◆ Contact Point provides resources on career counselling and job services. There is also an on-line discussion forum for career counselling. This site is primarily for career counsellors, but the information could be useful to any job seeker. [ID:2222]

The Guide to Internet Job Searching 📖

2004, Margaret Riley, Frances Roehm, Steve Oserman, 288 pages ➤ VGM Career Horizons, 4255 West Touwey Ave., Lincolnwood, IL 60646, USA, www.ntc-school.com, $23.95 US; Credit Cards; 800-323-4900, fax 847-679-2494 ◆ This US book is basically the printed version of the Riley Guide Web site. It contains thousands of annotated Web site URLs that are either job boards themselves or are links to job boards organized by field. Also includes up-to-date chapters on the Internet job search, on-line applications, international jobs and career planning. For its meticulous research, this resource is hard to beat! [ID:2192]

High Impact Resumes & Letters: How to
Communicate Your Qualifications to Employers 📖

2002, Ronald Krannich, W. Banis, 300 pages ➤ Impact Publications, Suite N, 9104 North Manassas Drive, Manassas Park, VA 20111-5211, USA, www.impactpublications.com, $19.95 US; Credit Cards; 703-361-7300, fax 703-335-9486 ◆ This book treats resumes and cover letters as key aspects of the larger career planning process. The guide provides step-by step guidance on understanding today's highly competitive job market, developing both conventional and Internet job search skills, selecting appropriate resume formats for maximum impact at every level of experience, producing striking letters, distribution channels and employer follow-up. [ID:2019]

Job Hunting on the Internet 📖

2001, Richard Bolles, 240 pages ➤ Ten Speed Press, P.O. Box 7123, Berkeley, CA 94707, USA, www.tenspeed.com, $13.95 US; Credit Cards; 800-404-4446 ◆ This compact US resource shows you how to integrate the Internet into a comprehensive job hunting strategy, helping you reap the best of what the Internet has to offer while staying mindful of the pitfalls of the Web. Hundreds of updated Web sites organized into three sections: job boards, resume posting sites and career services on the Internet. A helpful handbook that's highly recommended. [ID:2689]

Resumes That Work: How to Sell Yourself on Paper 📖

1992, L. Foxman, 128 pages ➤ John Wiley & Sons, 22 Worcester Road, Etobicoke, ON M9W 1L1, Canada, www.wiley.ca, $14.95 US; Credit Cards; 800-567-4797, fax 800-565-6802, canada@wiley.com ◆ Updated for the '90s job market, this book helps readers get the jobs they desire. The unique workbook format uses the latest time-tested strategies for developing attention-grabbing, professional resumes. Goals are defined, resume-writing do's and don'ts are explained, and effective use of employment resources is discussed. Order online at: www.wiley.ca. [ID:2007]

The Smart Interviewer 📖
1990, Bradford D. Smart, 224 pages ➤ John Wiley & Sons, 22 Worcester Road, Etobicoke, ON M9W 1L1, Canada, www.wiley.ca, $24.95 US; Credit Cards; 800-567-4797, fax 800-565-6802, canada@wiley.com ◆ A how-to course in selection interviewing. Presents a simple, elegant technique based on sound psychological and universal management principles. The step-by-step approach shows how to plan the interview, demonstrates the psychology behind interview questions, and explains how to interpret answers. Also discusses legal aspects of interviewing and how to prepare job descriptions and "person specifications." Order online at: www.wiley.ca. [ID:2005]

The Three Boxes of Life: An Introduction to Life Work Planning 📖
2000, Richard Bolles, 466 pages ➤ Ten Speed Press, P.O. Box 7123, Berkeley, CA 94707, USA, www.tenspeed.com, $27.50 US; Credit Cards; 800-404-4446 ◆ If you want to change careers during the next three years, or you're just not satisfied with your present job, but don't know what you want to do with your professional life, this book is for you. This classic book helps you understand and assess your skills. Looks at long-term strategies for life planning. Particularly useful for those planning career changes. Excellent book; highly recommended. [ID:2049]

**What Color Is Your Parachute? A Practical
Manual for Job Hunters and Career Changers** 📖
Annual, Richard Bolles, 411 pages ➤ Ten Speed Press, P.O. Box 7123, Berkeley, CA 94707, USA, www.tenspeed.com, $27.95 US; Credit Cards; 800-404-4446 ◆ For decades, this book has assisted career-changers and job-hunters in discerning new career paths with a detailed plan for identifying what skills they most enjoy using and where they would be happiest using them. The book then moves from career identification to job seeking and provides advice to readers on helpful topics such as interview questions and the answers employers are looking for, as well as salary negotiation strategies. This perennial job seeker's classic is highly recommended to those beginning their international careers. [ID:2073]

WinningTheJob.com 💻
2004, Impact Publications ➤ www.winningthejob.com, Free on-line ◆ Provides job seekers and employees, from entry-level to CEO, with sound advice on finding jobs and managing their careers in today's highly competitive job market and workplace. Offering numerous tips for success in the form of one- to three- page articles, it includes expert advice on everything from developing a career objective, writing resumes and letters, networking, interviewing and negotiating a compensation package for job seekers to career development, empowerment, assessment, communication, stress management and anger control for managing the day-to-day details of one's job. From finding to keeping a job, WinningTheJob.com is one of the most comprehensive resource centres for managing one's career. [ID:2407]

STUDENT JOB SEARCH

This list of books will be especially important if you are just graduating from university or if you have not recently looked for a job. Job search techniques have changed a lot during the past 15 years. In today's job market, greater emphasis is placed on having a solid understanding of your skill base. The Internet is your primary tool. If you have not already bought and spent a week studying the classic, What Color is Your Parachute, mentioned above, you should seriously think of doing so. Learning how to job hunt is a life-skill you'll need until you retire. Good luck and happy careering!

The Canada Student Employment Guide 📖
Annual, Kevin Makra, 504 pages ➤ Sentor Media Inc., Suite 1120, 388 Richmond Street W., Toronto, ON M5V 3P1, Canada, www.sentormedia.com, $30.95 CDN; VISA, MC; 416-971-5090, fax 416-977-3782 ◆ Use this excellent Canadian resource to help you put your job-search strategy on the right path. Contains a wide array of valuable information that will assist you in looking for

employment and launching your career. Part I of the book contains essential employment strategies and tips beneficial to job seekers generally. The real strength of the book is Part II, where you'll find the handy company, industry and geographical indexes that reference the over 900 company profiles in Part III. The profiles include addresses, firm descriptions, academic fields and skills the companies consider valuable, types of positions available, starting salaries and much more. Part IV includes college, university and chartered accountant indexes that highlight programs that firms consider important in assessing candidates' qualifications. Part IV also contains indexes of firms that hire part-time/summer students and offer co-op programs. Highly recommended starting point for your job search brought to you by an expert in the field. (For more information, see their ad in the sponsor section at the end of this guide.) [ID:2379]

Career Options in Business, Arts & Science 📖
2003, 56 pages ➤ Canadian Association of Career Educators and Employers (CACEE), Suite 300, 720 Spadina Ave., Toronto, ON M5S 2T9, Canada, www.cacee.com, Credit Cards; 866-922-3303, fax 416-929-5256; Fr ◆ With helpful articles related to finding jobs and industry profiles on the cultural sector, banking, the health industry, policing and publishing, this invaluable resource assists graduates in non-technical disciplines in their work searches. Also available in French. [ID:2405]

Career Options in Hi-Tech & Engineering 📖
2003, 56 pages ➤ Canadian Association of Career Educators and Employers (CACEE), Suite 300, 720 Spadina Ave., Toronto, ON M5S 2T9, Canada, www.cacee.com, Credit Cards; 866-922-3303, fax 416-929-5256; Fr ◆ Targeting recent graduates in technical disciplines such as computer science and engineering, this book assists students in understanding how to mix technical skills with people skills, research career options and find the best possible co-op programs and internships for developing their careers. Also available in French. [ID:2406]

Les carrières d'avenir 📖
Annuel, 388 pages ➤ Les Éditions Jobboom, 300 avenue Viger est, Montréal, QC H2X 3W4, Canada, www.jobboom.com/editions, $16.95 CDN; VISA, MC; 514-871-0222, fax 514-890-1456; Fr ◆ Cet excellent outil de référence réunit 150 formations qui offrent des ouvertures sur le marché du travail au Québec, en l'an 2004. Différents dossiers nous sont présentés : économie, emploi et démographie, salaire, réalité actuelle du marché du travail, programmes d'études prometteurs. Plus de 600 entrevues ont été réalisées auprès d'établissements d'enseignement, employeurs, économistes et organismes observateurs du marché du travail. Ces entrevues nous éclairent sur les secteurs d'emploi qui recrutent, les perspectives d'emploi en région et les diplômés les plus recherchés. [ID:2381]

First Job: A New Grad's Guide to Launching Your Business Career 📖
1992, Richard Fein, 240 pages ➤ John Wiley & Sons, 22 Worcester Road, Etobicoke, ON M9W 1L1, Canada, www.wiley.ca, $14.95 US; Credit Cards; 800-567-4797, fax 800-565-6802, canada@wiley.com ◆ Built around basic employment search principles applied by actual students, this book presents key elements for job search success, such as identifying your positive characteristics, developing resumes, writing cover letters, the principles of interviewing and how to use them, and a no-lose approach to negotiating your starting salary. Order on-line at: www.wiley.ca. [ID:2004]

The Gordon Group Home Page 🖥
www.gordonworks.com ◆ This US site is visually uninspiring, but don't be turned off! It actually contains one of the best job site resource lists around. Hundreds of links to job finding sites and career counselling services focusing on, but not exclusively devoted to, the North American job market. [ID:2242]

Job Futures 🖥
www.jobfutures.ca; Fr ◆ One of Canada's prime sources of labour market information. Job Futures provides Canadians with information on 226 occupational groups and 155 fields of study, including

the most promising jobs, education and skills requirements, what you can expect to earn and the experience of recent graduates. [ID:2825]

Jobboom 💻

www.jobboom.com; 𝐹𝑟 ◆ Registering at this Canadian Web site (in English or French) gives you access to numerous Jobboom services and access to on-line and print publications: 1) a career e-zine called "boomerang", which gives you the skinny on the latest developments in the job market; 2) "Careerconnection", which is an on-line newspaper with a career section with updated job postings; and 3) the "Top 100 Internet Sites for Learning and Employment;" The main Web site has hundreds of job postings searchable by region. [ID:2791]

Monster Trak 💻

www.monstertrak.monster.com ◆ This US site is directed toward recent and future post-secondary graduates seeking internships and jobs. Requires registration and allows uploading of your resume to their database and checks internships and job postings daily. [ID:2434]

National Graduate Register 💻

www.worklinkngr.com, Free on-line ◆ This national database is brought to you by Industry Canada and contains profiles of post-secondary students and recent graduates which can be matched to the job skills requirements of interested employers. [ID:2289]

Who's Hiring 📖

Annual, 608 pages ➤ Mediacorp Canada Inc., 21 New Street, Toronto, ON M5R 1P7, Canada, www.mediacorp.ca, $42.95 CDN; Credit Cards; 416-964-6069, fax 416)964-3202, ct100@mediacorp.ca ◆ Now in its 8th edition, this directory ranks Canada's 5,000 fastest-growing employers in 61 major occupations. This guide with its accompanying CD-ROM lets you target fast-growing employers in your field or region, including many that have created new jobs abroad. Employer listings include full contact information, a summary of the employer's operations and the jobs the employer created in the past 12 months. To directly inquire about this book, e-mail whos@mediacorp.ca. (For more information, see their ad in the sponsor section at the end of this guide.) [ID:2377]

YouthPath 💻

Human Resources and Skills Development Canada, www.youth.gc.ca, Free on-line; 𝐹𝑟 ◆ A Web site resource for Canadian youth seeking work and study opportunities in Canada or abroad. Lists hundreds of Government of Canada youth programs, services and resources. You can learn about Canada's role internationally or about how you can get involved by clicking the "International" tab on the index. Navigate to the "Opportunities" page and explore external links and government-sponsored exchange, volunteer and internship programs, such as internships with CIDA. If you want to gain international experience, this is an excellent place to start your research. [ID:2191]

JOB SEARCH DIRECTORIES

The following list of books and Web sites is included because each is a valuable tool for locating potential international employers.

American Employer Digest 📖

Mediacorp Canada Inc., 21 New Street, Toronto, ON M5R 1P7, Canada, www.mediacorp.ca, $39.95 CDN; Credit Cards; 416-964-6069, fax 416-964-3202, ct100@mediacorp.ca ◆ Now in its 2nd edition, this large directory profiles the 10,000 most-admired employers in the USA. Includes full contact information and is indexed by city and industry. Use the included CD-ROM to apply online to all the most-admired US employers in your field in a single afternoon. To find out more about this book, visit www.aedigest.com or e-mail info@aedigest.com. (For more information, see their ad in the sponsor section at the end of this guide.) [ID:2841]

Associations Canada 📖 💻

2004, Micromedia Proquest ➤ Renouf Publishing Co. Ltd., Unit 1, 5369 Canotek Road, Ottawa, ON K1J 9J3, Canada, www.renoufbooks.com, $325 CDN; Credit Cards; 888-767-6766, fax 613-

745-7660; Available in large libraries ◆ Provides detailed listings of more than 20,000 Canadian organizations, including budgets, founding dates, scopes of activity, licensing bodies, sources of funding, executive information, full addresses and complete contact information. Includes 11 handy indexes for quick reference. One of the most complete sources available for researching associations in Canada. Also available on the Web to subscribers through the Micromedia ProQuest Canada Information Resource Centre. [ID:2529]

Blue Book of Canadian Business 📖 🖥

Annual ➤ Canadian Business Resource, Suite 208, 8130 Sheppard Ave. E., Scarborough, ON M1B 3W2, Canada, www.cbr.ca, $189.95 CDN or $299.90 CDN on-line; VISA, MC; 888-422-4742, fax 888-422-4749 ◆ The most economical, straightforward and comprehensive source of Canadian business data available. Features include vCards for over 40,000 executives and directors, direct links to press releases, public corporate documents and up-to-the-minute stock information. Includes a database with directory information for over 2,750 Canadian companies plus excellent and 50 detailed profiles of leading Canadian firms. Also ranks firms according to a variety of criteria. [ID:2120]

Canada Post Corporation ▦

www.canadapost.ca; Fr ◆ Canada Post's Web site is well designed and allows easy and convenient access to Canadian postal codes, parcel rates, delivery confirmation and postal outlet locations. [ID:2331]

Canadian Almanac and Directory 📖

2004, Ann Marie Aldighieri ➤ Micromedia Proquest, 20 Victoria Street, Toronto, ON M5C 2N8, Canada, www.micromedia.ca, $275 CDN; VISA, MC; 800-387-2689, fax 416-362-6161; Available in large libraries; Fr ◆ Canada's national directory and sourcebook of current and accurate institutional information for over 155 years. An excellent resource for job seekers, this directory answers critical questions and gathers up-to-date information on Canadian organizations, institutions, government departments, law firms, school boards, media and much more. Also available on the Web to subscribers through the Micromedia ProQuest Canada Information Resource Centre. [ID:2530]

The Canadian Directory of Search Firms 📖

Annual, 462 Pages ➤ Mediacorp Canada Inc., 21 New Street, Toronto, ON M5R 1P7, Canada, www.mediacorp.ca, $79.95 CDN; Credit Cards; 416-964-6069, fax 416-964-3202, ct100@mediacorp.ca ◆ This excellent Canadian directory with CD-ROM profiles companies that are involved in the business of locating candidates for employers in various industries. These search firms are listed alphabetically and are indexed by industry and region. A fabulous resource that can be used to contact the headhunters who specialize in your field and region, or as or a research tool to help decide which types of firms are best suited for your needs. To directly inquire about this book, e-mail cdsf@mediacorp.ca. (For more information, see their ad in the sponsor section at the end of this guide.) [ID:2380]

The Canadian Job Directory: Ultimate Guide to Canada's Hidden Job Market 📖

Biennial, Kevin Makra, 504 pages ➤ Sentor Media Inc., Suite 1120, 388 Richmond Street W., Toronto, ON M5V 3P1, Canada, www.sentormedia.com, $30.95 CDN; VISA, MC; 416-971-5090, fax 416-977-3782 ◆ Designed to help you tap into the hidden job market, this book profiles top Canadian companies in Part I, listing contact information and firm descriptions. Part II contains a Canada-wide list of recruiters, with a brief description of each and their areas of specialization. Part III profiles professional industry associations in Canada. Parts IV, V and VI include, respectively, career sites on the Internet, useful trade directories and Human Resources Centres throughout Canada. The book also contains indexes of firms, recruiters and industries. This book is a highly recommended guide to help you focus your search on the unadvertised jobs. (For more information, see their ad in the sponsor section at the end of this guide.) [ID:2378]

Canadian Key Business Directory 📖

Annual ➤ D&B Canada Ltd., 5770 Hurontario Street, Mississauga, ON L5R 3G5, Canada, www.dnb.com, $459 CDN; Credit Cards; 800-463-6362, fax 905-568-6197; Available in large libraries ◆ An important source of information on the top 2 per cent of Canada's businesses. It provides more than 20,000 alphabetical listings of the largest companies in Canada. Contains over 60,000 key contact names. Available in print form, on CD-ROM or as a set. [ID:2122]

Connexions Online 💻

www.connexions.org, Free on-line; ◆ Connexions Online is produced by a non-profit organization working to connect individuals and organizations working for social change with each other, with information and ideas, and with the general public. The on-line directory lists and profiles thousands of organizations concerned with social justice and environmental alternatives, democratization, economic justice and the creation and preservation of community. Search by full or partial name or search organizations by subject. [ID:2036]

The Consultants and Consulting Organizations Directory 📖

2004, two volumes: 725 pages ➤ Thomson Gale, 835 Penobscot Bldg., 645 Griswold Street, Detroit, MI 48226-4094, USA, www.gale.com, $895 US; Credit Cards; 800-877-4253 ext. 1330, fax 800-414-5043; Available in large libraries ◆ More than 25,000 firms and individuals listed and arranged in subject sections under 14 general fields of consulting activity ranging from agriculture to marketing. More than 400 specialties are represented. [ID:2041]

Development Business 📖 💻

Weekly ➤ United Nations Publications, Sales and Marketing Section, Room DC2-853, Department I004, New York, NY 10017, USA, www.un.org/Pubs/sales.htm, $550 US/year; Credit Cards; 800-253-9646, fax 212-963-3489 ◆ This United Nations Department of Public Information publication is available only by subscription and is the single best way that suppliers and consultants can find the information needed to successfully win contracts generated from projects financed by development banks governments and the United Nations. Graphically and organizationally excellent, this site includes an on-line Business Directory with links to the Web sites of companies involved in international business, which can be used for job searches and to locate potential business partners. A great resource [ID:2083]

Directory of American Firms Operating in Foreign Countries 📖

1996 ➤ Uniworld Business Publications, 30 Mallard Lake Road, Pound Ridge, NY 10576, USA, www.uniworldbp.com, $355 US; Credit Cards; 212-496-2448, fax 508-376-6006; Available in large libraries ◆ Lists some 3,000 American companies with more than 36,300 subsidiaries and affiliates in 189 foreign countries. Part I features US firms with foreign operations and Part II is organized by countries in which US firms are operating. [ID:2079]

Directory of Executive Recruiters 📖

2004, Kennedy Center Publications, 1,176 pages ➤ Impact Publications, Suite N, 9104 North Manassas Drive, Manassas Park, VA 20111-5211, USA, www.impactpublications.com, $49.95 US; Credit Cards; 703-361-7300, fax 703-335-9486 ◆ The latest edition of this directory of executive recruiters lists 13,600 recruiters at 5,600 search firms in the US, Canada and Mexico. Includes indexes of management functions, industries, geography, key principles and 570 individual recruiter specialties. Listings include phone, fax, e-mail and Web addresses. [ID:2021]

Directory of Foreign Firms Operating in the US 📖

Annual, ➤ Uniworld Business Publications, 30 Mallard Lake Road, Pound Ridge, NY 10576, USA, www.uniworldbp.com, $250 US; Credit Cards; 212-496-2448, fax 508-376-6006; Available in large libraries ◆ Similar to its counterpart, "Directory of US Firms Operating in Foreign Countries." Individual country editions are available for $29-$99 US each. [ID:2248]

Employment Spot 💻

www.employmentspot.com ◆ This US-based Web site allows you to search for jobs in major US cities. If working in the US is not your cup of tea, this site also offers directories of on-line job search sites which are great starting points for your international job search. [ID:2425]

Encyclopedia of Associations: International Organizations 📖
2004, Linda Irvin, three volumes ➤ Thomson Gale, 835 Penobscot Bldg., 645 Griswold Street, Detroit, MI 48226-4094, USA, www.gale.com, $765 US; Credit Cards; 800-877-4253 ext. 1330, fax 800-414-5043; Available in large libraries ◆ This classic three-volume reference covers multinational and national membership organizations from Afghanistan to Zimbabwe, including US-based organizations with a binational or multinational membership. Entries provide the names of directors, executive officers or other personal contacts; telephone, fax, telex, electronic mail, Web sites and bulletin boards. Also presents the group's history, governance, staff, membership, budget and affiliations. Entries are arranged in general subject chapters allowing users to browse in sections that interest them. Three indexes—geographic, executive and keyword—help speed research. An invaluable resource for your international job search! [ID:2042]

Financial Services Canada 📖
2004 ➤ Micromedia Proquest, 20 Victoria Street, Toronto, ON M5C 2N8, Canada, www.micromedia.ca, print edition $299 CDN, web edition $800 CDN; VISA, MC; 800-387-2689, fax 416-362-6161; Available in large libraries ◆ Kick-start your international business job search with this up-to-date source on hard-to-find business information such as contacts for senior executives, portfolio managers, financial advisors, agency bureaucrats and elected representatives. Indexed by type of firm, geographic location, executive name, corporate Web site and listed alphabetically. Includes statistics for banks and branches, non-depository institutions, stock exchanges and brokers, investment managers, mutual funds, insurance companies, major accounting firms, government agencies, financial associations and more. Also available on the Web to subscribers through the Micromedia ProQuest Canada Information Resource Centre. [ID:2531]

Hoover's Handbook of American Business 📖
2004, 1,232 pages ➤ Hoover's Inc., 5800 Airport Blvd., Austin, TX 78752, USA, www.hoovers.com, $205 US; Credit Cards; 800-486-8666 ◆ This comprehensive US two-volume set contains in-depth profiles of 750 of America's largest and most influential companies. Unlike any other business resource on the market, Hoovers' examines the personalities, events and strategies that have made these enterprises successful. [ID:2688]

Hoover's Handbook of World Business 📖
2004, 486 pages ➤ Hoover's Inc., 5800 Airport Blvd., Austin, TX 78752, USA, www.hoovers.com, $175 US; Credit Cards; 800-486-8666 ◆ With this US directory, you have access to comprehensive corporate information on 300 of the most influential firms from Canada, Europe and Asia. [ID:2385]

Hoover's Online 🖥
www.hoovers.com ◆ This US Web directory delivers comprehensive company, industry and market information through a database of 12 million companies. The in-depth coverage of 40,000 of the world's top business enterprises is updated daily to bring visitors and subscribers the latest business information available. Company profiles indicate whether a company's client base is international, and if a company engages in overseas projects. You can create a short-list of company Web sites you're interested in for later visits, as well as find similar companies in the listing of the top three competitors for each company. Most of Hoover's Online is free; however, for a fee you can access more detailed information. A great source for information on potential employers. [ID:2279]

The International Directory of Importers 📖
2004, 5,200 pages ➤ International Directory of Importers, 1741 Kekamek N.W., Poulsbo, WA 98730, USA, www.importersnet.com, $1,345 US for complete set.; Credit Cards; 800-818-0140, fax 360-697-4696; Available in large libraries ◆ Published yearly, this nine-volume directory offers listings for more than 150,000 active importers from 178 different countries around the globe. Importers are listed alphabetically under relevant headings. Includes company demographics and business activity information as well as contact data. Overseas businesspersons interested in specific regions can buy those volumes individually. [ID:2055]

International Telephone Directory ▣
http://numberway.com/phone-numbers/1, Free on-line ◆ This Web site is frequently updated and features telephone and e-mail directories from almost every country in the world. Search either white pages for company and individual names or yellow pages for companies classified by business type. Make searching for contacts a little easier. [ID:2333]

Internet Public Library: Associations on the Net ▣
www.ipl.org/ref/AON ◆ A comprehensive US guide to Web sites of prominent organizations and associations, listed by sector. A great resource for background work for your job search. [ID:2412]

Lycos Network: WhoWhere ▣
http://whowhere.lycos.com; *Fr* ◆ Using this e-mail directory, you can look up e-mail addresses, phone numbers, conventional addresses, corporate homepages, and a number of other contact points. Service is also available in French. [ID:2283]

Mergent's International Manual ▢
Mergent, www.mergent.com, Available in large libraries ◆ This authoritative global reference gives you up to seven years of extensive business descriptions on more than 13,000 companies in nearly 100 countries, indexed by country, industry, product, stock exchange index and geographic location. In addition to corporate data, this resource provides country descriptions and maps, political and economic structures, and officer and director names and titles. Includes addresses, telephone and fax numbers. Great starting point for opportunities with international businesses. [ID:2532]

Le Québec International ▢
Annual, Denis Turcotte, 150 pages ➤ Les Éditions Québec dans le monde, C.P. 8503, Ste-Foy, QC G1V 4N5, Canada, www.quebecmonde.com, $49.95 CDN; VISA; 418-659-5540, fax 418-659-4143 ◆ Cet annuaire recense plus de 1000 intervenants internationaux québécois et partenaires étrangers. On y retrouve différents organismes publics, associations et organisations internationales, exportateurs, établissements, ambassades et consulats, organismes non gouvernementaux, bureaux de coopération et centres d'études. [ID:2563]

US Postal Service ♔
www.usps.gov/ncsc ◆ Similar to the Canada Post site, this will give you postal information for the US. You can look up zip codes and locations of postal outlets, and make parcel inquires. [ID:2332]

Yearbook of International Organizations 2003/2004 ▢
Annual, Union of International Associations (Geneva) ➤ Thomson K. G. Saur Verlag, Ortlerstrasse 8, Munich, 81373, Germany, www.saur.de, €1,498; (49) (0) 769-02-239, fax (49) (0) 89-769-02-250; Available in large libraries ◆ The most up-to-date and comprehensive reference work on international non-profit organizations. Profiles 25,979 of the most important organizations active in the world today, including 2,552 intergovernmental (IGOs) and 23,427 international non-governmental organizations (NGOs). An excellent job hunting resource. [ID:2056]

CHAPTER 21

Resources for the International Job Search

The hundreds of resources in this chapter are *directly* related to international jobs.

RESOURCES IN THIS CHAPTER

RELATED RESOURCES IN THIS BOOK

A LAST WORD

Good luck with your search!

RESOURCES

This chapter contains the following Resources sections: International Job Search Books; International Job Hunting Services on the Internet; Academic Job Boards; Consulting; Economic & Finance Job Boards; Government Job Boards Around the World; International Business; IT Job Boards; Private Sector Job Boards – All Categories; Science Job Boards; Tourism Industry Careers; and Other Careers.

INTERNATIONAL JOB SEARCH BOOKS

Let's face it: the Internet has taken over. Most of your international job hunting resources will either be published on the Web or will be accessible via the Web. However, there are still a lot of fantastic books produced on this topic and we've listed a few of the best below.

Careers in International Affairs 📖
2003, Maria Pinto Carland, Lisa A. Gihring, Georgetown University Graduate School of Foreign Affairs, 371 pages ➤ Scholarly Books, www.sbookscan.com, $39.53 US ◆ This US book is one of the best resources available for information on careers in international affairs. Provides a basic understanding of the different international career fields and what each offers, insights into the skills and requirements employers find necessary for success, heightened awareness of career options and broad guidelines for helping you make important career decisions. The book is painstakingly researched in conjunction with one of the oldest foreign affairs institutions in the US. Structurally, it starts with a well-written overview of the international affairs job market, followed by chapters on interview and Internet job hunting skills. Finally, you'll have a head start with hundreds of organizational profiles at your fingertips. An invaluable resource. Highly recommended! [ID:2043]

Careers in International Business 📖
2003, Ed Halloran ➤ Impact Publications, Suite N, 9104 North Manassas Drive, Manassas Park, VA 20111-5211, USA, www.impactpublications.com, $23.95 US; Credit Cards; 703-361-7300, fax 703-335-9486 ◆ This US book shows how to find and keep that job that's right for you. Covers a wide range of jobs, including contract work and entrepreneurial endeavours. Shows how to research international positions, acquire the necessary credentials, determine the best career alternatives, prepare an international portfolio, conduct business in different cultures and much more. Ideal guide for anyone planning a career in international business. [ID:2187]

The Directory of Jobs and Careers Abroad 📖
2002, Dan Boothby, 408 pages ➤ Vacation Work, 9 Park End Street, Oxford, OX1 1HJ, UK, www.vacationwork.co.uk, $19.95 US; Credit Cards; (44) (0) (1865) 24-1978, sales@vacationwork.co.uk ◆ Though aimed at UK citizens, this excellent reference book contains

information applicable to all international job seekers, from recent graduates to qualified professionals. Helpful sections with international job search tips, career-specific directories and country-specific career opportunities complement leads on voluntary opportunities abroad. A great start to your international job search. [ID:2045]

The Directory of Websites for International Jobs 📖

2002, 252 pages ➤ Impact Publications, Suite N, 9104 North Manassas Drive, Manassas Park, VA 20111-5211, USA, www.impactpublications.com, $20.96 US; Credit Cards; 703-361-7300, fax 703-335-9486 ◆ Assists international job seekers in sorting through the thousands of resources available on the Web. Provides sound advice on using the Internet as a job-hunting tool and identifies more than 1,400 top-notch Web sites to get you started. Highly recommended. [ID:2384]

The Economist 📖

Weekly, The Economist ➤ www.economist.com, $189 US/yr ◆ One of the best magazines around for keeping up-to-date on the economic and political situations in both developed and developing countries, as well as for classified ads for senior management jobs. [ID:2136]

Getting A Job Abroad 📖

2003, Roger Jones, 336 pages ➤ How To Books Ltd., 3 Newtec Place, Magdalen Road, Oxford, OX4 1RE, UK, www.howtobooks.co.uk, £11.04; Credit Cards; (44) (1752) 202-301, fax (44) (1865) 202-331 ◆ With over 1,100 Web sites, hundreds of recruitment agencies and lots of useful contacts, this British book tells readers where there are overseas jobs available, how to apply for them and how to evaluate the risks and rewards of expatriate living, whether on a temporary or permanent basis. Highly recommended. [ID:2399]

Getting a Job in Australia 📖

2004, Nick Vandome, 192 pages ➤ How To Books Ltd., 3 Newtec Place, Magdalen Road, Oxford, OX4 1RE, UK, www.howtobooks.co.uk, £9.34; Credit Cards; (44) (1752) 202-301, fax (44) (1865) 202-331 ◆ This British book provides a step-by-step guide to all aspects of finding permanent and casual employment in Australia. Explains the economic climate, where to look for work, what pay and conditions to expect and provides key information about tax, contracts, your rights at work and the Australian philosophy of employment. Includes details about Australian tax laws, pensions, Newstart allowances and economic conditions. Also includes useful Web sites to enable your job searching from outside Australia. [ID:2495]

Getting a Job in Europe 📖

2000, Mark Hempshell, 208 pages ➤ How To Books Ltd., 3 Newtec Place, Magdalen Road, Oxford, OX4 1RE, UK, www.howtobooks.co.uk, £8.49; Credit Cards; (44) (1752) 202-301, fax (44) (1865) 202-331 ◆ This British book aims at helping job hunters from any country and of all levels, and includes key contacts for each country. Provides an employment guide and information on how to find and apply for jobs; there's also information on living and working in Europe. [ID:2496]

Le guide des jobs pour changer d'air 📖

2002, Dakota Éditions, 160 pages ➤ Les Éditions Ulysse, 4176 rue St-Denis, Montreal, QC H2W 2M5, Canada, www.guidesulysse.com/cc/main_achat.htm, $17.95 CDN; Credit Cards; 514-843-9447, fax 514-843-9448; ℱr ◆ Ouvrage qui propose des centaines d'emplois plus dépaysants les uns que les autres, 120 fiches employeurs du monde entier détaillées, des pistes surprenantes et différentes destinations. [ID:2717]

Le Guide du Routard Expat 📖

2002, Philippe Gloaguen, 500 pages ➤ Éditions Hachette Tourisme, 43 quai de Grenelle, Paris Cedex 15, 75905, France, www.hachette.com, €7.90; (33) (1) 43-92-30-00; ℱr ◆ Le Guide de l'expatrié nous brosse un portrait des secteurs qui embauchent à l'étranger (incluant entreprises et organismes) et nous conseille sur les marches à suivre pour l'expatriation. [ID:2720]

Guides du Job-Trotter au Canada, en Espagne et en Grande-Bretagne 📖
2002, Dakota Éditions, 200 pages ➤ Les Éditions Ulysse, 4176 rue St-Denis, Montreal, QC H2W 2M5, Canada, www.guidesulysse.com/cc/main_achat.htm, $22.95 CDN; Credit Cards; 514-843-9447, fax 514-843-9448; *Fr* ◆ Ces trois guides nous éclairent sur la situation de l'emploi au Canada, en Espagne et en Grande-Bretagne. On dresse une liste d'adresses d'employeurs dans tous les domaines, sites Internet et organismes qui fournissent emplois & stages, formalités pour décrocher un permis de travail, un logement, une protection sociale, etc. [ID:2719]

Impact Publications Catalogues 📖 💻
Annual ➤ Impact Publications, Suite N, 9104 North Manassas Drive, Manassas Park, VA 20111-5211, USA, www.impactpublications.com, Credit Cards; 703-361-7300, fax 703-335-9486 ◆ Impact Publications is a US organization that produces a number of catalogues together, comprising the best mail-order source for career books in North America (including many international career books). Be sure to check out their Web site. [ID:2179]

International Job Finder: Where the Jobs are Worldwide 📖
2002, Daniel Lauber, 348 pages ➤ Planning/Communications, 7215 Oak Ave., River Forest, IL 60305-1935, USA, www.planningcommunications.com, $21.01 US; Credit Cards; 888-366-5200, fax 708-366-5280 ◆ Includes full information on on-line job databases, resume banks and databases of employers as well as "off-line" job sources for job seekers. It also guides readers to up-to-the-minute advice on visas, work permits, residency requirements and other inside tips—like avoiding international employment scams—to turn your international job search into a rousing success. Free on-line updates on the Web site. [ID:2396]

International Jobs 📖
2003, Nina Segal, Eric Kocher, 354 pages ➤ Basic Books, 12th Floor, 387 Park Ave., New York, NY 10016-8810, USA, www.basicbooks.com, $29.95 US; Credit Cards; 212-340-8100 ◆ A popular American handbook listing career opportunities around the world. The book also provides practical advice on researching job opportunities, preparing for your international career, and applying and interviewing for overseas jobs. Part 1 covers career development and job strategy; Part 2, the international job market in areas such as government, the UN, non-profit organizations, business, banking and teaching. Includes the former Soviet Union and Eastern Europe. Recommended reading for the overseas job seeker. [ID:2022]

Jobs et stages autour du monde 📖
2002, Dakota Éditions, 544 pages ➤ Les Éditions Ulysse, 4176 rue St-Denis, Montreal, QC H2W 2M5, Canada, www.guidesulysse.com/cc/main_achat.htm, $24.95 CDN; Credit Cards; 514-843-9447, fax 514-843-9448; *Fr* ◆ Ce guide offre des milliers d'emplois et de stages sur les cinq continents. On y recense 300 fiches employeurs détaillées et des dizaines de témoignages. De nombreuses informations et astuces nous sont données pour décrocher un permis de travail et rédiger un bon curriculum vitae en langue étrangère. [ID:2718]

Jobs for Travel Lovers: Opportunities at Home and Abroad 📖
2003, Caryl Krannich, Ronald Krannich, 232 pages ➤ Impact Publications, Suite N, 9104 North Manassas Drive, Manassas Park, VA 20111-5211, USA, www.impactpublications.com, $31.50 US; Credit Cards; 703-361-7300, fax 703-335-9486 ◆ This book identifies numerous jobs that enable individuals to travel both at home and abroad. Dispelling 54 myths, exploring key motivations and outlining effective job search strategies, it surveys hundreds of jobs in business, government and education, including the travel and hospitality industry, non-profit organizations, international organizations, education institutions and consulting. Written for anyone interested in combining travel with earning a living. [ID:2397]

Live and Work Series 📖
Vacation Work, 9 Park End Street, Oxford, OX1 1HJ, UK, www.vacationwork.co.uk, £10.99; Credit Cards; (44) (0) (1865) 24-1978, sales@vacationwork.co.uk ◆ This book series is unique in its comprehensive treatment of living overseas. Part One deals with the practicalities of living in a particular region: schooling, health, transport, property, daily life and retirement. Part Two covers

all aspects of employment: availability of work, salaries, women in work, hours and holidays and starting a business. [ID:2547]

NPSIA Works Career Futures ▤
Norman Paterson School of International Affairs (NPSIA), 1401 Dunton Tower, Carleton University, 1125 Colonel By Drive, Ottawa, ON K1S 5B6, Canada, www.carleton.ca/npsia, Free on-line; 613-520-6655, fax 613-520-2889 ◆ The Norman Paterson School of International Affairs (NPSIA) publishes this fantastic Web resource, recommended for anyone interested in working in international affairs. It is a compendium of careers that graduates of the NPSIA program have gone on to, presented as job titles and job descriptions organized by job field. Examples of fields include: academia, human rights and communications. Each field is introduced briefly, followed by job titles and descriptions. By locating the jobs you're interested in, you can easily get an idea of the qualifications and skill sets employers in those fields are looking for. An invaluable guide to planning your future career in international affairs, the usefulness of which cannot be understated! Check it out. [ID:2789]

Work Abroad: The Complete Guide to Finding a Job Overseas ▢
2002, Clay Hubbs, 224 pages ➤ Transitions Abroad, P.O. Box 745, Bennington, VT 05201, USA, www.transitionsabroad.com, $15.95 US; Credit Cards; 802-442-4827, fax 802-442-4827, publisher@TransitionsAbroad.com ◆ A comprehensive US guide to all aspects of international work, including work permits, short-term jobs, teaching English, volunteer opportunities, planning an international career, starting your own business and much more. [ID:2262]

Work Worldwide: International Career Strategies for the Adventurous Job Seeker ▢
2000, 232 pages ➤ Avalon Travel Publishing, 1400 65th Street, Suite 250, Emeryville, CA 94608, USA, www.travelmatters.com, 510-595-3664, fax 510-595-2516 ◆ Offers step-by-step guidance on how to land a successful career in a foreign country, starting with advice on researching and applying for an international job. Includes quizzes to help define goals, advice for long- and short-term assignments, tips on international protocol and explains the basics of moving to a foreign country. [ID:2391]

Working Abroad: Unravelling the Maze ▢
2003, 32 pages ➤ Enquiries Service, Foreign Affairs Canada (FAC), 125 Sussex Drive, Ottawa, ON K1A 0G2, Canada, www.fac-aec.gc.ca, 800-267-8376, fax 613-996-9709; Fr ◆ Preparation and careful planning go a long way to ensuring a safe and successful international work experience. The goal of "Working Abroad: Unravelling the Maze" is to provide the overseas job hunter with practical information to maximize the chances of a successful venture and advice on what to do if things don't work out as planned. [ID:2490]

INTERNATIONAL JOB HUNTING SERVICES ON THE INTERNET

For an international job search, target job searching entails knowing what type of job interests you, the names of contacts and companies involved in that industry, and the location of your job market. Fortunately, most of this information can be found on-line, thus streamlining your search and increasing your chances of discovering the right opportunity. The following Web sites provide services such as career counselling, resume posting and job search functions. Most are internationally oriented, free and updated regularly, so take advantage of the extensive information they provide.

Aboriginal Planet ▤
Monthly, Foreign Affairs Canada (FAC) ➤ www.dfait-maeci.gc.ca/latinamerica/aboriginal-en.asp, Free on-line; Fr ◆ This e-zine reports monthly on the Aboriginal Canadian events taking place around the world and on important international Aboriginal events taking place in Canada. The site

also provides tools for Aboriginal Canadians to break onto the world stage: check out the "International Opportunities" and "Business Centre" sections. [ID:2486]

Brilliant People 💻

www.brilliantpeople.com ◆ This US site has a great selection of jobs in the United States and abroad. Also features many career management features such as a resume doctor, a salary wizard, job agents, an on-line application and job seeker profiles. [ID:2432]

CareerFrames 💻

www.careerframes.com/links_main_intl/consulting_links.htm ◆ This is an amazing German Web site dedicated to helping people find jobs overseas, no matter where they reside. Easily navigable, you won't get lost in the international job news, job-search articles, links to job-search tools, salary surveys, and advice on interviewing and networking. Not only can you search jobs by location or profession, but you can look for internships and summer jobs too! Check out links taking you to country- and culture-specific Web sites, as well as pages dealing with health, housing, relocation and family issues. Start here to search consulting jobs, but be sure not to miss those in other fields as well. Great resource! [ID:2682]

CareerJournal.com 💻

http://cj.careercast.com ◆ This US site isn't the easiest to use, but it is run by the "Wall Street Journal" and has a huge database of international jobs for executives and managers. Here's some advice: if the advanced search does not work out, then simply type your search term in the top left hand corner of the home page and who knows, you could soon be trading equities on the London Stock Exchange or be an editor of Market News International in Germany! Well worth a glance. [ID:2642]

Careermag.com 💻

www.careermag.com ◆ A good US site with all the usual features: keyword searches, resume posting, salary wizard and e-mails notifications. [ID:2447]

Center for Career Opportunities 💻

www.cco.purdue.edu/student ◆ Maintained by Purdue University, this centre is an excellent gateway to the international Internet job search. Databases arrange job listings by country, region or professional field. There are also links to general employment servers that often offer career counselling and resume assistance. [ID:2257]

Dickenson College: Web Guide to International Employment 💻

www.dickinson.edu/career/student/international.html ◆ This US institution has one of the best Web pages around for international job seekers. An entire section of the career centre site is devoted exclusively to international employment. Surf and find excellent information on working overseas, getting ready to go, job search techniques and how to find the right international opportunity for you. Lots of up-to-date, country-specific information and links to short-term programs and international business opportunities. A great primer. [ID:2715]

Direct Employers 💻

www.directemployers.com ◆ This employment search engine focuses on the US market, but has an excellent international job search page. It is unique in that it is the only such site dedicated exclusively to employment and featuring the American National College Employment System. [ID:2416]

Employment Resources on the Internet 💻

www.cco.purdue.edu/asp/JobWeb/View.asp, Free on-line ◆ This US University job search page is a good starting point for your job search on the Web. Contains a good list of links to dozens of career sites, organized in easy-to-use categories such as job fields, internships, recruiters, geographic locations and classifieds. [ID:2243]

Espace emploi international 💻

www.emploi-international.org; *Fr* ◆ Espace emploi international : informations sur l'emploi à l'étranger, liste de sites Internet pour travailler dans le monde, actualités internationales, conseils juridiques, les emplois sont offerts uniquement aux ressortissants Français et aux étrangers en situation régulière en France. [ID:2674]

Flip Dog 💻
www.flipdog.com ◆ FlipDog.com sniffs the World Wide Web and links to job openings found on employer Web sites. Although it focuses on the US market, this site contains a comprehensive directory of jobs found outside the US searchable by country and sector. This is a great Web site with lots of jobs. Worth adding to your favourites! [ID:2418]

Getting a Job in America 📖
2003, Roger Jones, 240 pages ➤ How To Books Ltd., 3 Newtec Place, Magdalen Road, Oxford, OX4 1RE, UK, www.howtobooks.co.uk, £11.04; Credit Cards; (44) (1752) 202-301, fax (44) (1865) 202-331 ◆ Explains the employment possibilities open to non-US citizens and offers information and advice on how to make the most of them. It includes lists of major employers, recruitment agencies, Web sites and other useful addresses. [ID:2165]

Global Health Directory 📖 💻
2003 ➤ Global Health Council, Suite 600, 1701 K Street N.W., Washington, DC 20006-1503, USA, www.globalhealth.org, $50 US, free online; VISA, MC; 202-833-5900, fax 202-833-0075 ◆ For anyone interested in overseas health careers, this directory is a great starting point. It contains accurate and up-to-date information on hundreds of organizations worldwide working to improve global health. Includes contact information, mission statements, details on service focus, regions/countries served and target groups. Expanded indexes make the "Global Health Directory 2003-2004" a comprehensive, easy-to-use reference tool. Available on-line for free. [ID:2533]

The Gordon Group Home Page 💻
www.gordonworks.com ◆ This US site is visually uninspiring, but don't be turned off! It actually contains one of the best job site resource lists around. Hundreds of links to job finding sites and career counselling services focusing on, but not exclusively devoted to, the North American job market. [ID:2242]

INTERCRISTO, The Christian Career Specialists ⅲ
INTERCRISTO, The Christian Career Specialists, P.O. Box 33487, 19303 Fremont Ave. N., Seattle, WA 98133, USA, www.jobleads.org, 800-426-1342, fax 206-546-7375 ◆ This job referral organization assists Christians in finding job opportunities with Christian organizations. The "Jobs in a Flash" database matches job seekers' qualifications and regional preferences with those required by employers. Other services include resume posting, career assessment and salary comparison. Highly recommended site for those wishing to work overseas in a Christian environment. [ID:2230]

International Employment Gazette 💻
Biweekly, Robert L. Whitmore ➤ International Employment Gazette, 423 Townes Street, Greenville, SC 29601, USA, www.intemployment.com, $19.95 US/month; Credit Cards; 864-235-4444, fax 864-235-3369 ◆ Subcribe to this on-line employment newsletter and receive over 400 current and overseas job openings every two weeks. Job searches require a subscription to view results. Those looking for international work can take advantage of nine years of experience in publishing international jobs as well as access to helpful resources such as resume writing and circulation. [ID:2080]

International Employment Resources - University of San Francisco 💻
www.usfca.edu/career/Joblists/International.html ◆ This is a fabulous list of links from the University of San Francisco to job banks in Asia, Australia and Europe and several general resources that are global in scope. This is a good on-ramp to the information highway. [ID:2255]

International Job Search 💻
www.international-job-search.com ◆ This US Web site assists executives to access overseas job markets. Focused primarily on executives, this site allows job seekers to register and e-mail

resumes without an initial obligation. Includes market reports from various regions around the world. Jobs are upper level and not suitable for young professionals, but the market reports, though brief, may be of benefit to young professionals seeking work in the regions profiled. [ID:2455]

Job Bank USA 💻

www.jobbankusa.com ◆ One of the Internet's largest and best-known on-line recruiting sites. Provides services to over 5 million job seekers, hiring managers, recruiters and human resource professionals. Search jobs, post resumes, view recruiter lists and free sample cover letters and resumes. [ID:2436]

Job Search Engine 💻

www.job-search-engine.com ◆ Job Search Engine is not a job board per se, but rather a meta-job search engine dedicated to employment. It searches the most popular American and Canadian job boards in parallel and in real time. The one click will save you hours of searching through the job boards and career fairs individually. [ID:2415]

Job Sniper 💻

www.jobsniper.com ◆ This Web site focuses on Canada, the US and the UK and allows the user to create up to five customized "search agents" that search pre-selected target markets and job sites and send periodic reports to your e-mail address. Saves time on those mundane daily job site checks! [ID:2427]

Job/Internship Vacancy Links & Resources to Research Employers 💻

www.ub-careers.buffalo.edu/career/oco/cpp/student/internat.shtml ◆ This extensive list of links is brought to you by the University of Buffalo. This page is a great portal to thousands of international job hunting resources on the Internet. [ID:2254]

JobLine International 💻

www.jobline.net ◆ This International job search site offers a database of jobs accessible by country and industry. You can also post your resume here and follow links to other job search Web sites. [ID:2473]

JobWeb 💻

www.jobweb.com ◆ An excellent site brought to you by the US National Association of Colleges and Employers. Offers a variety of on-line job search services, including a searchable database of job postings, employer and salary information, job search advice, and listings of the best and worst jobs out there. The job board has a large number of international positions. You can also order one of their successful "Job Choices" magazines, which explore in more depth the various issues faced by today's job seekers at the outset of their careers. [ID:2250]

Jumbo Careers 💻

www.jumboclassifieds.com ◆ This US-based site has free job searching advice and access to the database. Registration and a fee allow access to other services such as a resume blaster, which does exactly what the name implies: gets your resume seen by as many employers as possible. [ID:2439]

Monster Working Abroad 💻

www.monster.com ◆ This is one of the most popular job hunting resources on the Internet. The site provides employer profiles and a user-friendly search engine for international jobs. Simply enter job search section of the Web site, then click Work Abroad and you can browse international postings by the country you want to work in. [ID:2251]

Nation Job 💻

www.nationjob.com ◆ This US Web site offers the standard searchable job postings and member newsletters, but is also part of a network of specialty sites dedicated entirely to specific employment categories, such as law, engineering, medical and education. Includes a great resource page offering a directory of on-line degree programs, as well as helpful services such as career counselling, resume critiques, a salary wizard for determining what others in your field and region are making, a reference-checking service and industry magazines. What sets this site apart is the search feature, which is one of the most specific, yet easy-to-use of its kind on the Internet. Bookmark this one. [ID:2409]

NetJobs 💻

www.netjobs.com, Free on-line ◆ This Canadian-based resource provides many of the services provided by the larger US job sites. Its easy-to-use search engine allows you to look for jobs by location; there are several international listings. As with other quality job sites, free registration allows access to career counselling services, corporate reviews and some useful links. [ID:2252]

Les pages emploi 💻

http://emploi.hrnet.fr; *Fr* ◆ Les pages emploi : site complet pour dénicher un emploi à l'étranger (on nous fournit les types d'emploi par pays et région). [ID:2675]

Recrutement-international 💻

www.recrutement-international.com; *Fr* ◆ Différents articles sont proposés pour aller travailler à l'étranger : le contrat de travail, la protection sociale, l'adaptation, profils détaillés de différents pays et des offres d'emplois internationales sont offertes. [ID:2706]

The Riley Guide 💻

www.rileyguide.com ◆ This well-known US guide is a directory of employment and career information resources and services on the Internet. Find instructions for job seekers and recruiters on how to use the Internet to your best advantage. Boasts an excellent links page, with links to job boards, internship and volunteer opportunities, organized by field. Note that jobs and resumes are not posted on this Web site. A great starting point! [ID:2411]

SIL International 💻

www.sil.org/sildc/ThinkTanks_DC.htm ◆ This US Web site provides a comprehensive list of hyperlinks to US research and policy-development think tanks. Recommended as a great starting point for anyone looking for employment in this sector. [ID:2664]

Topica Expat List 💻

http://lists.topica.com/lists/expat_list/read ◆ This US Web site isn't very sophisticated, specializing in e-mail services, but it makes up for it by posting an eclectic mix of interesting jobs all over the globe that you won't find on other job boards. [ID:2680]

Wanted Jobs 💻

www.wantedjobs.com ◆ This Canadian site has no international job search component, but has an extensive database of US-based job postings. Includes helpful links to career assessment sites and contains information on freelancing and targeting your job search. Easy to use. [ID:2449]

WetFeet 💻

www.wetfeet.com ◆ This is a very well-designed US Web site with an excellent international job and internship search page accessible from the index under "Find a Job." The "Internship Search Engine" database contains hundreds of internships listed by location and job category. In addition, you'll find heaps of helpful advice on finding and making the most of your internship experience, written by insiders. Many articles are field specific; others tackle subjects like "Creating Your Own Internships" and "Turning Your Internship Into a Job." The job-search page is also comprehensive and easy to use. Add this one to your favourites. [ID:2428]

WorkTree.com 💻

www.worktree.com ◆ A unique US Web portal linking you to the thousands of international job sites and resources on the Internet. Thousands of job sites and career resources have been pre-researched and indexed to save time. Links to numerous national job sites from which you can search for international jobs. [ID:2423]

ACADEMIC JOB BOARDS

For the academics among us, this list of international jobs in academia is a good start for finding overseas work. A related set of resources can be found in Chapter 29, Teaching Abroad.

Academic Careers Online 💻
www.academiccareers.com/cgi-win/JobSite/jobsrch.exe/ACO ◆ US-based outfit bills itself as the ultimate global job Web site of career opportunities in education and academia. It has an excellent database of job postings at institutions all over the world. Postings are comprehensive and professional, lending credibility to the site's claim. Check it out and set your overseas academic career on the right track. [ID:2639]

The Chronicle of Higher Education 💻
http://chronicle.com/jobs ◆ This US-based site features thousands of academic positions at American institutions. Browse well-organized and comprehensive faculty, research, administrative and management postings with details about how and where to apply. A fabulous resource. [ID:2638]

The Guardian 💻
http://jobs.guardian.co.uk ◆ This site contains a huge number of jobs in the UK and around the world. An international keyword search brings up teaching and academic postings. [ID:2599]

Jurist: University of Pittsburgh School of Law 💻
http://jurist.law.pitt.edu ◆ Jurist offers an exceptionally broad array of information on emerging legal issues. It also has one of the best sections listing opportunities for professors to teach law. [ID:2765]

NACEL International 💻
www.nacel.org ◆ This UK Web site has information on the academic exchange, internship, work placement and homestay programs offered by the organization. [ID:2210]

Naturejobs 💻
http://naturejobs.nature.com/js.php ◆ This Web site contains lots of international positions in science and academia. [ID:2697]

CONSULTING, ECONOMIC & FINANCE JOB BOARDS

This list, composed mainly of job boards, has been compiled for those looking for work in the fields of finance and economics. It also includes Web sites that can be searched for overseas consulting opportunities.

Accounting Jobs Worldwide 💻
2001, 192 pages ➤ Vacation Work, 9 Park End Street, Oxford, OX1 1HJ, UK, www.vacationwork.co.uk, £9.95; Credit Cards; (44)(0)(1865) 24-1978, sales@vacationwork.co.uk ◆ Gives all the information needed by anyone looking for accountancy work abroad including a section on recruitment agencies, descriptions of all the major international accountancy firms and information on the transferability of qualifications. [ID:2541]

CareerFrames 💻
www.careerframes.com/links_main_intl/consulting_links.htm ◆ This is an amazing German Web site dedicated to helping people find jobs overseas, no matter where they reside. Easily navigable, you won't get lost in the international job news, job-search articles, links to job-search tools, salary surveys, and advice on interviewing and networking. Not only can you search jobs by location or profession, but you can look for internships and summer jobs too! Check out links taking you to country- and culture-specific Web sites, as well as pages dealing with health, housing, relocation and family issues. Start here to search consulting jobs, but be sure not to miss those in other fields as well. Great resource! [ID:2682]

CareerJournal.com 🖳
http://cj.careercast.com ◆ This US site isn't the easiest to use, but it is run by the "Wall Street Journal" and has a huge database of international jobs for executives and managers. Here's some advice: if the advanced search doesn't work out, simply type your search term in the top left hand corner of the home page and who knows, you could soon be trading equities on the London Stock Exchange or be an editor of Market News International in Germany! [ID:2642]

Deloitte Careers 🖳
http://careers.deloitte.com/opportunities.aspx ◆ This is the Web site of one of the world's largest audit, tax and financial advisory organizations. Deloitte has offices all around the world. Postings are consolidated on this site, in one comprehensive, easy-to-search database. A fabulous resource for economists with overseas longings. [ID:2632]

Economics Departments, Institutes and Research Centres Around the World 🖳
http://edirc.repec.org/index.html ◆ There is now an amazing number of economics institutions on the Web. Currently, 7,899 institutions in 217 countries and territories are listed on this University of Connecticut Web site. Links are indexed by country and field. Included are economics departments, research centres and institutes in universities, as well as finance ministries, statistical offices, central banks, think tanks and other non-profit institutions which employ mainly economists. Each institution is hyperlinked, making this a very useful site. Get a head start on researching your post-graduate studies, or on a systematic search of organizations around the world that just might be hiring an economist! [ID:2347]

Executivesontheweb.com 🖳
www.executivesontheweb.com/uk/job_search ◆ This UK Web site focuses on international consultancies and management positions in the private sector. Search by level, sector, type of work and geographic location and apply on-line. [ID:2615]

Human Resources International (HRI) 🎎
Adecco ◆ Adecco is a subsidiary of ADECCO S.A. and is a nationally recognized executive search, consulting and contract staffing firm with a singular focus in Human Resources. Adecco operates nationally and internationally in the staffing and recruitment of highly-trained human resources professionals in almost every industry. [ID:2315]

Inomics 🖳
www.inomics.com/cgi/job?action=default ◆ This US Web site contains a fabulous list of international postings for economists. Subscribe if you want to receive a weekly job postings newsletter, but you don't need to to view job descriptions and contact information. If you're into economics and want to work abroad, this site is for you! [ID:2631]

International Financial Law Review 📖 🖳
Monthly ➤ Legal Media Group, 225 Park Ave., New York, NY 10003, USA, www.legalmediagroup.com, $825 US; Credit Cards; 212-224-3542, fax 212-224-3101; Available in large libraries ◆ "IFLR" has established itself as the world's leading magazine for in-house counsel and practitioners in the financial markets. Each issue includes comprehensive international news and analysis of recent international deals, reports on legislative changes, practice issues, latest techniques and best practice strategies. Covers the latest innovations in areas such as capital markets, banking, project finance, corporate governance, bankruptcy, litigation, fund management and M&A. Highly recommended for the international financial practitioner. Subscribe on-line. [ID:2721]

International Jobs Center 📖
www.internationaljobs.org, $46 US for 3 months or $149 US for one year ◆ By becoming a member, you get access to late-breaking job openings and will receive the "International Career Employment Weekly" newspaper in hard copy or by e-mail. Take advantage of a comprehensive database of international jobs for professionals, but includes development jobs and internships as

well. Noteworthy on this site are the listings of international health care, commerce and IT jobs. [ID:2583]

Jobserve 🖥
www.jobserve.com ◆ This site features over 20,000 IT sector jobs in UK and Australia, in addition to thousands of jobs in accounting, engineering, law and medicine. Subscribe to a mailing list and receive e-mail updates regularly. [ID:2356]

Vault 🖥
www.vault.com/jobs/jobboard/searchform.jsp ◆ Fabulous US Web destination for on-line insider company information, advice and career management services. Lots of international jobs in the private sector. It's possible to search jobs by profession. Loads of legal and project-management postings. Also includes a great list of internships. In addition to a job board and newsletter, this site has information on over 3,000 companies and 70 industries including company-specific message boards allowing employees and job seekers the opportunity to network and ask advice about company trends. Order career guides such as the "Vault Guide to the Top 100 Law Firms", "Vault Guide to Finance Interviews" and the "Vault Guide to the Top 50 Consulting Firms". [ID:2596]

The Wall Street Journal Career Journal 🖥
www.careerjournal.com ◆ The Internet's premier career site for executives, managers and professionals. Content comes from the powerful editorial resources of "The Wall Street Journal" and CareerJournal.com's editorial team. You'll find daily updates and thousands of archived articles detailing the news and trends that are critical to your job search and career advancement. The site offers a searchable database of job postings from top companies: positions featured include senior and general management, sales, marketing, finance, technology and a range of related fields. [ID:2421]

GOVERNMENT JOB BOARDS AROUND THE WORLD

These are mainly US government sites.

European Personnel Selection Office 🖥
http://europa.eu.int/epso/competitions/news_en.cfm ◆ EPSO organizes open competitions in various fields to select personnel for various European institutions. Lots of jobs for linguists, administrators, clerical assistants and skilled employees. Citizenship requirements are clearly indicated in job descriptions and competition timetables. [ID:2665]

The Politix Group 🖥
www.politixgroup.com/dcjobs.htm ◆ This site is for US citizens and internationals interested in a career in international politics. On this site, you'll find resources on working legally in the US and other countries, international political career resources, political and government internships in Washington. For a $10 US donation you can become a member and browse the political jobs offered in the US and UK. [ID:2593]

UK Department for International Development 🖥
www.dfid.gov.uk/Recruitment/frameset.htm ◆ This British government Web site is the main recruitment page of the UK DFID. Along with postings of current external vacancies, you can find information on the recruitment process, DFID-sponsored volunteer work, working with the UK Civil Service and European Commission. [ID:2666]

US Department of Defense 🖥
http://dod.jobsearch.org ◆ The Department of Defense (DoD) Job Search is an associate Web site of the US Department of Labor's (DoL) America's Job Bank. The Web site is designed to assist separating service members in their job search by providing an entry to America's Job Bank. This site and America's Job Bank are operated and maintained by the Department of Labour. [ID:2667]

US Department of Justice 🖥
www.usdoj.gov/oarm ◆ The US Department of Justice, the federal government's law firm and the world's largest legal employer, offers opportunities for law students, entry-level lawyers and

experienced lawyers in virtually every area of legal practice. Their Web site provides an overview of the many legal employment opportunities and benefits available at the Department of Justice. You will also find information about legal recruitment, including eligibility, the application process, the work of each department component, salaries, security clearances, citizenship requirements, the department's employment policies, incentive programs and answers to frequently asked questions. [ID:2612]

US Department of State Employment 🖳

www.state.gov/employment/index.htm ◆ The US Department of State recruits Americans for the civil and foreign service, as well as for the UN and other IGOs. There is a great section on student programs and internships with information on how to apply, benefits, fellowships, summer clerk programs and FAQs—all to help your international career take off! [ID:2629]

US Department of State International Vacancy Announcements 🖳

www.state.gov/p/io/rls/iva/2004/29546.htm ◆ This site is updated every two weeks and contains an extensive list of job openings at the United Nations and other international organizations. [ID:2588]

US Government Globus and National Trade Data Bank 🖳

www.stat-usa.gov ◆ This is a full-service Web site for US businesses conducting domestic and international trade. Divided into two parts, the site provides access to current and historical economic data on the US economy under the "State of the Nation" heading. Under "Globus & NTDB" you'll hit current and historical trade-related releases, international market research, trade opportunities, country analysis and the National Trade Data Bank, which is available by no-cost registration. A great resource for international entrepreneurs. [ID:2292]

USAID 👬

www.usaid.gov/careers ◆ This is the recruitment Web site of the US Government's overseas development assistance agency. USAID is the largest funding agency in the world, with job postings listed for US citizens interested in working in development. [ID:2668]

INTERNATIONAL BUSINESS

Occupational and cross-cultural knowledge are needed to succeed in international business. These resources will help you with the occupational and business research side of international business. For more related resources see the Cross-Cultural Skills Resources in Chapter 1, The Effective Overseas Employee. For resources describing the all important cross-cultural aspects of international business, consult the Resources sections in the following chapters: Chapter 1, The Effective Overseas Employee; Chapter 3, Living Overseas; Chapter 12, Cross-Cultural Travel; and Chapter 27, Jobs by Regions of the World.

Asia Pacific Country Backgrounders 📖 🖳

2002, 15 pages each ➤ Asia Pacific Foundation of Canada, Suite 666, 999 Canada Place, Vancouver, BC V6C 3E1, Canada, www.asiapacific.ca, Free on-line; VISA, MC; 604-684-5986, fax 604-681-1370 ◆ A series of booklets on 14 Asia Pacific countries and Canada's economic relationship with each of them. Includes key facts and figures, economic and trade statistic comparisons, Canada's ranking among major trading partners, imports and exports, main sectors of opportunity for Canadian business and more. Recommended for entrepreneurs and others seeking quick, dependable facts on Canada's Asian trade partners. [ID:2166]

Asia Pacific Review 📖

Annual, 72 pages ➤ Asia Pacific Foundation of Canada, Suite 666, 999 Canada Place, Vancouver, BC V6C 3E1, Canada, www.asiapacific.ca, $34.95 CDN; VISA, MC; 604-684-5986, fax 604-681-1370; Fr ◆ This annual survey examines Canada's relationship with Asia and the impact on business of major developments during the year. The report includes a Canada-Asia report card which examines in depth nine key areas of the Canada-Asia relationship, assigning letter grades to each performance indicator. The Review is also available in French. [ID:2393]

Asian Development Bank Business Opportunities 💻 👫
Monthly ➤ Central Operations Services Office, Asian Development Bank, P.O. Box 789, Manilla Central Post Office, 0980 Manila, Philippines, www.adb.org, $30 US/year; 632-632-4444, fax 632-636-2444 ◆ The ADB is based in Manila and funds development projects and programs in the Asian and Pacific Regions. The goal is to generate opportunities for the business communities of member countries. The Business Opportunities page of the site is found by navigating from the index to "Opportunities" and then to "Business Opportunities." It provides information on the requirements for goods, work and services of projects under consideration by ADB. [ID:2286]

Asian Outlook 📖 💻
Quarterly, variable ➤ Asia Pacific Foundation of Canada, Suite 666, 999 Canada Place, Vancouver, BC V6C 3E1, Canada, www.asiapacific.ca, Free; VISA, MC; 604-684-5986, fax 604-681-1370 ◆ Offers a concise survey of the latest political and economic trends in 14 Asia Pacific economies of interest to Canadian business. Includes a succinct listing of developments to watch for in the months ahead, including a tabulation of major economic indicators. [ID:2395]

Building an Import/Export Business 📖
2002, Kenneth Weiss, 320 pages ➤ John Wiley & Sons, 22 Worcester Road, Etobicoke, ON M9W 1L1, Canada, www.wiley.ca, $19.95 US; Credit Cards; 800-567-4797, fax 800-565-6802, canada@wiley.com ◆ Packed with the latest information on US government regulations, tax law, customs requirements and shipping procedures, this book provides authoritative and up-to-date guidance on every aspect of planning, launching and operating a successful import/export business. Great resource for your budding export business. [ID:2002]

Canada Business Service Centres 💻
www.cbsc.org; ℱr ◆ Designed to serve Canadian business people, the CBSC Internet site contains searchable collections of information on federal and provincial government services, programs and regulations. The site also allows the user to contact Business Information Officers by e-mail. This is an excellent site for those interested in government. [ID:2245]

Canada in Asia Series 📖
2003, 12 to 40 pages each ➤ Asia Pacific Foundation of Canada, Suite 666, 999 Canada Place, Vancouver, BC V6C 3E1, Canada, www.asiapacific.ca, Free; VISA, MC; 604-684-5986, fax 604-681-1370 ◆ This is a research series dealing with issues affecting Canada-Asia relations and their influence on business trade between Canada and selected countries. [ID:2394]

CanadExport 📖
Biweekly ➤ Enquiries Service, Foreign Affairs Canada (FAC), 125 Sussex Drive, Ottawa, ON K1A 0G2, Canada, www.fac-aec.gc.ca, Free; 800-267-8376, fax 613-996-9709; ℱr ◆ Foreign Affairs' primary publication for keeping the Canadian business community and exporters informed about key trade matters. A biweekly newsletter, it provides timely information on business opportunities, trade fairs and other related matters. [ID:2119]

The Canadian Trade Commissioner Service 👫
Foreign Affairs Canada (FAC), www.infoexport.gc.ca; ℱr ◆ On this Government of Canada Web site, you can find trade commissioner offices in Canada and abroad. Navigate by country or industry sector to the region you're interested in and find the latest trade information on market prospects, key local contacts, local company information, visitor information and market intelligence. The best feature of the Web site is the virtual trade commissioner. Register on-line at no cost and receive a personalized Web page containing market information and business leads that match your international business interests. You can also request services on-line from the Trade Commissioners responsible for your industry in the markets of interest to you and be notified of new information related to your industry and target markets as it becomes available. Also, information on your company will be available to the 500 Trade Commissioners in 140 overseas offices. An excellent resource for international business. [ID:2249]

Careers in International Business 📖
2003, Ed Halloran ➤ Impact Publications, Suite N, 9104 North Manassas Drive, Manassas Park, VA 20111-5211, USA, www.impactpublications.com, $23.95 US; Credit Cards; 703-361-7300, fax 703-335-9486 ◆ This US book shows how to find and keep that job that's right for you. Covers a wide range of jobs, including contract work and entrepreneurial endeavours. Shows how to research international positions, acquire the necessary credentials, determine the best career alternatives, prepare an international portfolio, conduct business in different cultures and much more. Ideal guide for anyone planning a career in international business. [ID:2187]

CIDA's Contracts and Agreements 📖
Quarterly, 100 pages ➤ Canadian International Development Agency (CIDA), Communications Branch, 200 Promenade du Portage, Gatineau, QC K1A 0G4, Canada, www.acdi-cida.gc.ca, Free; 819-997-5006, fax 819-953-6088; *Fr* ◆ This publication seeks to help individuals, small- and medium-sized businesses (SME), and other organizations to identify potential opportunities for subcontracting to organizations responsible for implementing programs and projects funded by the Canadian International Development Agency (CIDA). The information about current major CIDA projects, recipient countries and Canadian organizations involved in international development is an excellent starting point for an international job search. [ID:2383]

The Consultants and Consulting Organizations Directory 📖
2004, two volumes: 725 pages ➤ Thomson Gale, 835 Penobscot Bldg., 645 Griswold Street, Detroit, MI 48226-4094, USA, www.gale.com, $895 US; Credit Cards; 800-877-4253 ext. 1330, fax 800-414-5043; Available in large libraries ◆ More than 25,000 firms and individuals listed and arranged in subject sections under 14 general fields of consulting activity ranging from agriculture to marketing. More than 400 specialties are represented, including finance, computers, fundraising and others. [ID:2041]

The Consulting Skills Manual 📖
Annual ➤ Sequus International, 381 Churchill Drive, Winnipeg, MB R3L 1W1, Canada, www.sequus.org, $100 CDN; Credit Cards; 204-992-2410, fax 204-478-5390, btrump@infobahn.mb.ca ◆ Winnipeg's Sequus International produces this workshop manual. It is widely used even by organizations that have not participated directly in Sequus's workshops. Part One deals with all of the details of the consulting process that are common to all consultants. The second part consists of a custom-tailored toolkit relating to each step in a six-part consulting process that forms the structure for the workshop. A great starting point for clarifying the opaque waters of international consulting. [ID:2535]

Contracted Work 🖳
www.contractedwork.com ◆ This US-based Internet freelance market allows you to bid on contracts awarded in all sectors of the private marketplace: find the job that matches your skills, crunch your numbers and then post a bid. The lowest bid at the close of bidding wins the job. Browsing is free, but bidding costs. Bid from abroad and supplement your income while travelling! [ID:2621]

D&B WorldBase 🖳
Annual ➤ D&B Canada Ltd., 5770 Hurontario Street, Mississauga, ON L5R 3G5, Canada, www.dnb.com, Credit Cards; 800-463-6362, fax 905-568-6197 ◆ Thinking about expanding globally? This resource helps overseas business opportunists quickly and easily identify new business opportunities. D&B WorldBase is D&B's extensive and fastest growing information base, currently listing more than 57 million companies in over 200 countries. D&B WorldBase facilitates easy identification of members of a corporate family quickly and easily, including branches, subsidiaries, domestic parents and, more importantly, the global parent. [ID:2492]

Economic and Social Survey of Asia and the Pacific:
Economic Prospects - Preparing for Recovery 📖
2002, 268 pages ➤ United Nations Publications, Sales and Marketing Section, Room DC2-853, Department I004, New York, NY 10017, USA, www.un.org/Pubs/sales.htm, $65 US; Credit Cards; 800-253-9646, fax 212-963-3489 ◆ Reviews the efforts in the region to cope with the economic slowdown in Asia. Examines official development assistance, with a particular focus on economic and technical cooperation among developing countries in Asia and the Pacific. Helpful information for doing business in Asia. [ID:2525]

Economic Survey of Europe 📖
2002, 260 pages ➤ United Nations Publications, Sales and Marketing Section, Room DC2-853, Department I004, New York, NY 10017, USA, www.un.org/Pubs/sales.htm, $70 US; Credit Cards; 800-253-9646, fax 212-963-3489 ◆ A survey of current economic developments in Europe, the Commonwealth of Independent States (CIS) and North America. Aims at providing information and analysis to policy-makers and economists in government, research institutes and universities, as well as the private business sector. [ID:2524]

European Monetary Union and Capital Markets 📖
2001, 250 pages ➤ Customer Service Department, Elsevier, 11830 Westline Industrial Drive, St. Louis, MO 63146, USA, www.elsevier.com/wps/find/homepage.cws_home, $95 US; Credit Cards; 800-460-3110, fax 314-453-7095, usbkinfo@elsevier.com ◆ Considering an international business that operates in the European Union? This book can help. Considers effects on capital and goods markets of monetary union in general and European Monetary Union (EMU) in particular. Touches upon adjustments in goods and labour markets, adjustments in money and capital markets and institutional adjustments. The relation between monetary union and capital market integration is also highlighted. Great resource. [ID:2493]

Export Development Corporation 👪
www.edc.ca; 𝐹𝑟 ◆ The Export Development Corporation assists Canadians wishing to do business with foreign countries. Services include risk assessment, export insurance, credit profiles of foreign customers, market trends analysis, export readiness tools and financial management assistance. A fabulous service for the international entrepreneur. [ID:2285]

Export Services for Small- and Medium-Sized Enterprises 📖
2001 ➤ Enquiries Service, Foreign Affairs Canada (FAC), 125 Sussex Drive, Ottawa, ON K1A 0G2, Canada, www.fac-aec.gc.ca, 800-267-8376, fax 613-996-9709; 𝐹𝑟 ◆ This pamphlet explains the activities of the export services for the Small and Medium-Sized Enterprises Division (TSME) of the Canadian Trade Commissioner Service. [ID:2484]

Exporting from Canada: A Practical Guide to Finding and
Developing Export Markets for Your Product or Service 📖
2002, Gerhard Kautz, 192 pages ➤ Self-Counsel Press, 1481 Charlotte Road, North Vancouver, BC V7J 1H1, Canada, www.self-counsel.com, $21.95 CDN; VISA, MC; 800-663-3007, fax 604-986-3947, sales@self-counsel.com ◆ This book provides Canadian exporters and would-be exporters with easy-to-follow information and advice on the strategies and issues involved in doing business outside the country. Includes reference guides, Web sites, business contacts and practical pointers on visiting foreign countries. [ID:2125]

ExportSource.ca 🖥
www.ExportSource.ca; 𝐹𝑟 ◆ ExportSource.ca is a service for Canadians in international export development. Publications include a guide to locating opportunities for bidding on international contracts, searching for bidding partners, and developing and evaluating bid proposals. The Web site has links to on-line databases of business opportunities in Canada and internationally. [ID:2829]

Far Eastern Economic Review 📖
Weekly ➤ Subscription Department, Far Eastern Economic Review, P.O. Box 160, General Post Office, Hong Kong, China, www.feer.com, $220 HK/year; Credit Cards; (800) 522-2714, fax (413)

592-4782 ◆ With a circulation of over 100,000 in Hong Kong, Malaysia and Singapore, this news weekly is Asia's premier business magazine. Reports on politics, business, economics, technology and social and cultural issues throughout Asia, with a particular emphasis on both Southeast Asia and China. Sign up on-line for a one-, two- or three-year subscription. [ID:2141]

Financial Services Canada 📖
2004 ➤ Micromedia Proquest, 20 Victoria Street, Toronto, ON M5C 2N8, Canada, www.micromedia.ca, print edition $299 CDN, web edition $800 CDN; VISA, MC; 800-387-2689, fax 416-362-6161; Available in large libraries ◆ Kick-start your international business job search with this up-to-date source for key contacts and hard-to-find business information such as names and contact numbers for senior executives, portfolio managers, financial advisors, agency bureaucrats and elected representatives. Conveniently indexed by type of firm, geographic location, executive name, corporate Web site and listed alphabetically. Include statistics for banks and branches, non-depository institutions, stock exchanges and brokers, investment managers, mutual funds, insurance companies, major accounting firms, government agencies, financial associations and more. Also available on the Web to subscribers through the Micromedia ProQuest Canada Information Resource Centre. [ID:2531]

Hoover's Handbook of American Business 📖
2004, 1,232 pages ➤ Hoover's Inc., 5800 Airport Blvd., Austin, TX 78752, USA, www.hoovers.com, $205 US; Credit Cards; 800-486-8666 ◆ This comprehensive US two-volume set contains in-depth profiles of 750 of America's largest and most influential companies. Unlike any other business resource on the market, Hoovers' examines the personalities, events and strategies that have made these enterprises successful. [ID:2688]

Hoover's Handbook of World Business 📖
2004, 486 pages ➤ Hoover's Inc., 5800 Airport Blvd., Austin, TX 78752, USA, www.hoovers.com, $175 US; Credit Cards; 800-486-8666 ◆ With this US directory, you have access to comprehensive corporate information on 300 of the most influential firms from Canada, Europe, Japan and the Asian tiger economies. [ID:2385]

IDB Project and Procurement Information 💻
Inter-American Development Bank, 1300 New York Ave. N.W., Washington, DC 20577, USA, www.iadb.org, Free on-line; 202-623-1000, fax 202-623-3096 ◆ This is the main source of Inter-American Development Bank funded project procurement information. Navigate to the "Projects" section of the IADB home page and click on "Procurement." You'll find yourself at the "Project and Procurement Information" Web page table of contents. "Project Pipeline" is a database of projects under consideration for financing, which are tracked from initial identification until they receive official approval. "Approved Projects" provides the same information for those projects officially approved. Both provide continuously updated information on anticipated consulting and business opportunities. You'll also find procurement notices, contract award information, policies, procedures and standard form procurement documents, all intended to help you in your bid for a consultancy or supply contract. [ID:2287]

IFInet 💻
www.infoexport.gc.ca/ifinet/menu-e.htm, Free on-line ◆ The International Financing Information Network offers information designed to help Canadian companies prosper in the booming international development business market. IFInet can help you find out how to supply your goods and services to development and humanitarian projects; where to find project financing and guarantees for your investments in developing and transition economies; how other companies are thriving in this market, and who in the Trade Commissioner Service can best support your efforts. From the World Bank to the United Nations, from health sector reform to wastewater treatment, IFInet helps Canadian international entrepreneurs prosper in the international development market. [ID:2316]

The International Business Dictionary and Reference 📖

1991, Lewis Presner, 504 pages ➤ John Wiley & Sons, 22 Worcester Road, Etobicoke, ON M9W 1L1, Canada, www.wiley.ca, $49.95 US; Credit Cards; 800-567-4797, fax 800-565-6802, canada@wiley.com ◆ Uses an integrative approach stressing the cross- and interdisciplinary dynamics of international business. Visit the distributor's Web site at www.wiley.ca. [ID:2003]

The International Directory of Importers 📖

2004, 5,200 pages ➤ International Directory of Importers, 1741 Kekamek N.W., Poulsbo, WA 98730, USA, www.importersnet.com, $1,345 US for complete set.; Credit Cards; 800-818-0140, fax 360-697-4696; Available in large libraries ◆ Published yearly, this nine-volume directory offers listings for more than 150,000 active importers from 178 different countries around the globe. Importers are listed alphabetically under relevant headings. Includes company demographics and business activity information as well as contact data. Overseas businesspersons interested in specific regions can buy those volumes individually. [ID:2055]

Mastering Global Markets 📖

2004, Michael R. Czinkota, Ilkka A. Ronkainen, Bob Donath, 320 pages ➤ Thomson South-Western, 5191 Natorp Blvd., Mason, OH 45040, USA, www.swlearning.com, $49.95 US; Credit Cards; 513-229-1000 ◆ This US book is designed for business entrepreneurs who want to take their business overseas. Covers all aspects of entering global markets from strategic planning to tactical implementation. [ID:2548]

Mergent's International Manual 📖

Mergent, www.mergent.com, Available in large libraries ◆ This authoritative global reference gives you up to seven years of extensive business descriptions on more than 13,000 companies in nearly 100 countries, indexed by country, industry, product, stock exchange index and geographic location. In addition to corporate data, this resource provides country descriptions and maps, political and economic structures, and officer and director names and titles. Includes addresses and telephone and fax numbers. Great starting point for your canvass of opportunities with international businesses. [ID:2532]

Open Network Trade Resources Access (onTrac) 💻

www.ontrac.on.ca ◆ A Canadian information service provider helping small- and medium-sized enterprises around the world expand their markets through international and national trade. Lots of country-specific trade information and services just a mouse click away. [ID:2358]

Strategis 💻

http://strategis.ic.gc.ca, Free on-line; Fr ◆ Strategis is Canada's business and consumer Web site, through which Industry Canada innovatively disseminates business information intended to improve conditions for investment and promote economic growth among Canada's businesses. The site is a comprehensive collection of company directories, business information by sector, economic analysis and statistics, as well as information on financing, licences and consumer information. Entrepreneurs: bookmark this site!

Strategis also features a number of informative guides on subjects like starting a business, financing, exporting, e-commerce and researching markets. Of particular interest to international entrepreneurs is the Guide to Exporting, which is accessible by clicking "Exporting" from the menu of Strategis Guides on the home page.

Here you'll find eight excellent resources including "Trade Data Online," through which you can access information and statistics on new markets and existing competition for your products; "Trade Team Canada Sectors," which provides information about services and activities for the trade promotion of Canada's key industries; "International Trade Centres," regional bodies that provide export counselling services and market entry support; "Trade Shows," highlighting opportunities to showcase products abroad; "Export Your Services," which is a fabulous tool that walks you through the stages of exporting your product; "Services 2000," which contains information on the national and international trade agreements; and "Building Abroad," which is especially for the construction industry abroad. There's also a link to "ExportSource," which is included as a separate resource write-up. [ID:2317]

Trade and Development Report 2002: Developing Countries in World Trade 📖
2002, 208 pages ➤ United Nations Publications, Sales and Marketing Section, Room DC2-853, Department I004, New York, NY 10017, USA, www.un.org/Pubs/sales.htm, $39 US; Credit Cards; 800-253-9646, fax 212-963-3489 ◆ The "Trade and Development Report 2002" analyzes trends and outlooks for the world economy and focuses on export dynamism and industrialization in developing countries. Questions the conventional wisdom that export growth and foreign direct investment (FDI) automatically generate commensurate income gains and suggests that countries move into higher-value exports by upgrading technology and improving productivity. [ID:2521]

Tri-Service Solicitation Network Web 💻
http://tsn.wes.army.mil ◆ The Tri-Service Solicitation Network is an electronic bid solicitation Web site that provides links to US government agencies and Web sites providing international business opportunities. It is currently advertising solicitations on the Internet. [ID:2828]

US Government Globus and National Trade Data Bank 💻
www.stat-usa.gov ◆ This is a full-service Web site for US businesses conducting domestic and international trade. Divided into two parts, the site provides access to current and historical economic data on the US economy under the "State of the Nation" heading. Under "Globus & NTDB" you'll hit current and historical trade-related releases, international market research, trade opportunities, country analysis and the National Trade Data Bank, which is available by no-cost registration. A great resource for international entrepreneurs. [ID:2292]

World Investment Report 2002: Transnational Corporations and Export 📖
2002, 384 pages ➤ United Nations Publications, Sales and Marketing Section, Room DC2-853, Department I004, New York, NY 10017, USA, www.un.org/Pubs/sales.htm, $49 US; Credit Cards; 800-253-9646, fax 212-963-3489 ◆ This report is recognized worldwide as an authoritative source of information and analysis on foreign direct investment. This year's Report focuses on the role of transnational corporations (TNCs) in the export competitiveness of developing countries. It analyzes the latest trends in international trade, and identifies the countries and sectors in which TNCs have driven export performance. Relevant strategies and policy options for developing countries are presented to help attract export-oriented FDI and benefit from it. Excellent resource for your international business. [ID:2522]

World Trade Organization 💻
www.wto.org ◆ This is the WTO's official Web site. You'll find information on the organization and its constituent members, as well as trade policy and statistics, legal documents and research reports. There's also a job site and internship vacancies page. [ID:2288]

WorldClass 💻
http://web.idirect.com/~tiger ◆ The WorldClass supersite links you to over 1,025 of the world's best business sites in over 95 countries. From here you can obtain news of current business trends or research a potential employer. The site also offers an excellent opportunity to connect with important people in your field. [ID:2282]

IT JOB BOARDS

The Internet job sites in this list are either exclusively dedicated to IT jobs or are noteworthy for their IT job databases.

Career Options in Hi-Tech & Engineering 📖
2003, 56 pages ➤ Canadian Association of Career Educators and Employers (CACEE), Suite 300, 720 Spadina Ave., Toronto, ON M5S 2T9, Canada, www.cacee.com, Credit Cards; 866-922-3303, fax 416-929-5256; *Fr* ◆ Targeting recent graduates in technical disciplines such as computer science and engineering, this book assists students in understanding how to mix technical skills with people skills, research career options and find the best possible co-op programs and internships for developing their careers. Also available in French. [ID:2406]

Computing 🖳

www.computing.co.uk/Careers ◆ This UK site offers a large selection of computing jobs not only in the United Kingdom, but all over the globe. All the usual newsletter and resume posting services. A great start to your overseas IT career search. [ID:2633]

Dice 🖳

www.dice.com ◆ This US site focuses on the technology job market. Post your resume and make yourself available to employers recruiting to fill over 30,000 tech jobs. Access salary information and check out companies and job markets in US high-tech hotbeds. [ID:2451]

Elan 🖳

www.elanit.com/global_elan/vrs/search_results.asp ◆ This UK-based IT recruiter's Web site has thousands of international permanent and contract positions. Search by skill type and browse results. The database features jobs mostly from Europe. [ID:2635]

International Jobs Center 📖

www.internationaljobs.org, $46 US for 3 months or $149 US for one year ◆ By becoming a member, you get access to late-breaking job openings and will receive the "International Career Employment Weekly" newspaper in hard copy or by e-mail. Take advantage of a comprehensive database of international jobs for professionals, but includes development jobs and internships as well. Noteworthy on this site are the listings of international health care, commerce and IT jobs. [ID:2583]

IT webForum 🖳

www.it-webforum.com ◆ Search on-line jobs in the IT field around the world on this net community. [ID:2794]

Job & Career Sites at Rensselaer Polytechnic Institute (RPI) 🖳

www.rpi.edu/dept/cdc/student/careeropps.html ◆ Rensselaer Polytechnic Institute offers a variety of career services geared toward graduates in the fields of engineering, architecture, management and IT through their excellent Career Development Centre Web site. They've built an extensive collection of links to Web sites with information on international career opportunities in these fields. [ID:2712]

Jobserve 🖳

www.jobserve.com ◆ This site features over 20,000 IT sector jobs in UK and Australia, in addition to thousands of jobs in accounting, engineering, law and medicine. Subscribe to a mailing list and receive e-mail updates regularly. [ID:2356]

Jobsweb 🖳

www.jobsweb.com ◆ This no-nonsense site is a true portal for job searches on the Web. This site offers job boards for regions throughout the world, such as Africa, Asia and the Middle East. Contains a good section of IT job sites. [ID:2253]

Rent a Coder 🖳

www.rentacoder.com/RentACoder/default.asp ◆ This unique US Web site allows you to earn income using your programming and coding skills. "Rent a Coder" lets you locate and bid on coding projects and questions from around the world! By registering for free, you can publicize your skills in the on-line resume system and receive e-mails as new bid requests come in. Win the contract, do the job and earn money from anywhere in the world! [ID:2634]

PRIVATE SECTOR JOB BOARDS ALL CATEGORIES

The following Web sites are listed because they feature excellent general job boards with postings related to the private sector.

Career Flex 🖳

www.careerflex.com ◆ A general directory of job finding resources on the Net. Specially focused directories on starting a business, working as a consultant, nursing and education. [ID:2426]

CareerBuilder.com 💻

www.careerbuilder.com ◆ CareerBuilder.com offers a leading recruitment resource, especially for those searching for work in the United States. As a job-seeking user, you will have access to a huge database of job postings. Receive an e-mailed job-seeker tool kit with tips on job searching and targeting information, as well as a newsletter profiling the most popular jobs each month and periodic information on local career events in your region. [ID:2408]

Careerflex.com 💻

www.careerflex.com ◆ This Internet job site is useful for its extensive links to resources such as starting your own business, consulting and working from home. Searching international jobs from the home page turns up an excellent list of links to international job sites. [ID:2422]

DegreeHunter 💻

www.degreehunter.com ◆ Engineering jobs, nursing jobs, medical jobs, health care jobs, legal jobs, physician jobs, legal jobs and MBA jobs can be found at DegreeHunter. DegreeHunter is the career search service that helps graduate degree candidates and other certified professionals find employment with a new career opportunity by focusing on distinct professions, providing pre-screened positions and resumes, and enabling real-time and confidential communication between candidates and recruiters. [ID:2823]

DiversityInc 💻

http://diversityinc.careercast.com/js.php ◆ Thousands of searchable jobs in this database, mostly in the US, but some international positions featured. [ID:2597]

Escape Artist 💻

www.escapeartist.com/jobs/overseas1.htm ◆ This US Web site lists international jobs by category or region. Postings details are succinct and no direct contact information is given; instead you apply on-line using a convenient e-mail format, pasting your resume and adding any comments you have directly. [ID:2677]

EUROGRADUATE 💻

www.eurograduate.com/data.cfm?language=english ◆ The "Careers Database" features thousands of graduate opportunities in the private sector across Europe. You can search by any combination of industry, organization, type of occupation, degree/diploma qualification or country of employment. [ID:2608]

EUROPA 💻

http://europa.eu.int/index_en.htm ◆ This EU Web site is a great source of international jobs in the European Union. Part of a larger Web site that has great information on living and working in the EU, including political, legal and economic information. Search jobs by profession, location and keyword, narrow your search by experience, contract type and qualifications. Thousands of jobs listed in easy-to-read postings complete with contact information. If Europe is where you're at, then hitting this site is a must. From the index, click on "Working" under the "Living in the EU" heading. Then select "Find a Job" from the "Job Mobility Portal." [ID:2679]

Expats Direct 💻

www.expatsdirect.com ◆ This UK Web site stakes its claim as the best on-line employment service for working overseas and it delivers. Browse literally thousands of overseas jobs; however, if you want to apply to them, you have to join. Membership costs £55 per year. It might well be worth your money for access to engineering, health care, technical and managerial positions everywhere from Milan to Malaysia. [ID:2645]

Goinglobal 💻

www.goinglobal.com ◆ This US Web site offers a huge database of private sector jobs in the United States, with a few jobs listed with corporations around the world. [ID:2594]

The Guardian 🖳
http://jobs.guardian.co.uk ◆ This site contains a huge number of jobs in the UK and around the world. An international keyword search brings up teaching and academic postings. [ID:2599]

Harrison Jones Associates Jobs Network 🖳
International Recruitment Consultants, Harrison Jones Associates, Buckingham House East, The Broadway, Stanmore, Middlesex, HA7 4EB, UK, www.africajobs.net, (44) (0) (2083) 85-7881, fax (44) 20 8385-7882 ◆ This is part of a network of job search Web sites which has for 10 years specialized in recruiting Western expatriates for international positions. From the African region home page, you can search jobs in any region or you can navigate to other job pages focusing on Africa, Arabia, Europe, Asia and North and South America and search directly from there. Lots of professional positions available in all regions. [ID:2453]

International Employment Resources - Brandeis University 🖳
www.brandeis.edu/hiatt/international.html ◆ This site, maintained by Brandeis University, provides an excellent international employment section with links to resources in Western and Eastern Europe, and Asia. There are also links to international job listings by career. Special attention is given to education, journalism, environmental issues, government jobs and high-tech jobs. Links to other useful career centres are also helpful. [ID:2256]

International Job Link 🖳
www.internationaljoblink.com ◆ This site focuses on non-professional jobs in industries such as cruise, hotel, offshore oil, airline and modelling. There are a few jobs for engineers and geologists in the offshore oil section. Postings list requisite qualifications, salary grades and contract length. [ID:2460]

International Jobs Center 📖
www.internationaljobs.org, $46 US for 3 months or $149 US for one year ◆ By becoming a member, you get access to late-breaking job openings and will receive the "International Career Employment Weekly" newspaper in hard copy or by e-mail. Take advantage of a comprehensive database of international jobs for professionals, including development jobs and internships. Noteworthy on this site are the listings of international health care, commerce and IT jobs. [ID:2583]

International Mode D'Emploi 🖳
www.insert-export.com/index/indexoffre.htm; *Fr* ◆ L'International Mode d'Emploi est un site français regroupant diverses offres d'emploi et stages à l'étranger. On nous propose aussi des conseils et informations pour travailler à l'extérieur. À noter : pour avoir accès aux postes offerts, il faut s'inscrire comme membre et débourser des frais. [ID:2708]

Jobpilot 🖳
www.jobpilot.com/function/content/search/jobsearch.jhtml ◆ This German Web site lists jobs in Europe and around the world searchable by industry and type of work: freelance and contract, graduate entry-level or permanent. The site also boasts an excellent database of internships and student jobs, and great career tips. Positions are most often high quality postings at leading European corporations. You'll be Europe bound before you know it! [ID:2681]

Jobs DB 🖳
www.jobsdb.com ◆ On-line recruiter network with job databases for many countries in the South Pacific and Southeast Asia. Caters to those looking for work in professions such as accounting, IT, banking, sales and marketing. Postings are easy to read and offer the option of applying directly on-line. [ID:2477]

Jobsite 🖳
www.jobsite.co.uk ◆ This job site offers nearly 100,000 searchable postings in the UK, France, Germany, Ireland, Italy and Spain. This site is easy to use and frequently updated. You can also post your resume and access career advice. Jobs tend toward the fields of IT, engineering, sales and finance. [ID:2598]

JobStreet.com 💻

http://my.jobstreet.com ◆ Explore South and Southeast Asia's booming skilled job market with this Malaysian Web site. Private sector jobs of all fields are listed, with an emphasis on IT, engineering and marketing. Database is searchable by regions outside of Malaysia: Thailand, Singapore, Philippines, India, and Hong Kong etc. The site is easy to use and the job desriptions indicate nationalities that can apply. [ID:2601]

Jobsweb 💻

www.jobsweb.com ◆ This no-nonsense site is a true portal for job searches on the Web. This site offers job boards for regions throughout the world, such as Africa, Asia and the Middle East. Contains a good section of IT job sites. [ID:2253]

OverseasJobs.com 💻

www.internationaljobs.com / www.overseasjobs.com ◆ Part of a network called AboutJobs.com, this US site features international job opportunities for professionals, expatriates and adventure seekers. Easy to use and contains a good searchable database of jobs. [ID:2420]

PlanetRecruit 💻

www.planetrecruit.com ◆ This is a truly international job-search site, with an excellent international job-search feature. Based in the UK, this site allows you to create a profile, store and manage multiple resumes, receive e-mail job alerts and apply for jobs on-line via the site. Highly recommended, especially for those in IT, engineering and management. [ID:2429]

Vault 💻

www.vault.com/jobs/jobboard/searchform.jsp ◆ Fabulous US Web destination for on-line insider company information, advice and career management services. Lots of international jobs in the private sector. It's possible to search jobs by profession. Loads of legal and project-management postings. Also includes a great list of internships. In addition to a job board and newsletter, this site has information on over 3,000 companies and 70 industries including company-specific message boards allowing employees and job seekers the opportunity to network and ask advice about company trends. Order career guides such as the "Vault Guide to the Top 100 Law Firms", "Vault Guide to Finance Interviews" and the "Vault Guide to the Top 50 Consulting Firms". [ID:2596]

Yahoo Hot Jobs 💻

http://hotjobs.yahoo.com ◆ This job search site has thousands of jobs and lets you search by country and keyword. It is also possible to browse companies that offer jobs in the country of your choice. A great start to your overseas job search. Navigate to the "Job Search" section from the index. [ID:2419]

SCIENCE JOB BOARDS

Use these resources to start looking for international science jobs.

Earthworks 💻

www.earthworks-jobs.com ◆ This is an excellent Web site where scientists of every imaginable discipline can search for jobs. Search by discipline and find interesting jobs throughout the world. [ID:2696]

Naturejobs 💻

http://naturejobs.nature.com/js.php ◆ This Web site contains lots of international positions in science and academia. [ID:2697]

New Scientist 💻

www.newscientistjobs.com ◆ This job page is part of an excellent Web site brought to you by the same organization that publishes the magazine. Well-respected and comprehensive, the site allows you to post resumes, research employers and search hundreds of quality jobs in North America, Europe and Australasia by discipline, sector and education level. Apply on-line and save yourself time. A great resource for anyone in the physical or biological science disciplines who wants to work overseas. [ID:2671]

Science Careers 🖵
http://aaas.sciencecareers.org ◆ Science Careers is a US Web site that allows you to search the latest openings from hundreds of employers, post your resume and create job alert agents. Create an account for free and the system will store multiple resumes and cover letters that you can use to apply to jobs posted on Science Careers. It will also save the jobs you have responded to so you can easily track and manage your applications. The database has a huge number of postings from all around the world, making this one of the best sites around for searching for international careers in science. [ID:2643]

Science in Africa 🖵
www.scienceinafrica.co.za/Jobs/jobs.htm ◆ This free South African Web site offers access to current job postings. Small but constantly updated, the database is searchable by scientific discipline. Postings are primarily in South Africa. [ID:2636]

Science Jobs 🖵
www.sciencejobs.com ◆ Science Jobs includes listings for engineering jobs and company contact information in North America, Europe and Australasia. The site has a link to the "New Scientist Magazine" profiling international projects and expert resources. [ID:2819]

TOURISM INDUSTRY CAREERS

These are resources for finding work in the travel industry.

Career Opportunities in Travel and Tourism 📖
1996, John K. Hawks, 309 pages ➤ Impact Publications, Suite N, 9104 North Manassas Drive, Manassas Park, VA 20111-5211, USA, www.impactpublications.com, $18.95 US; Credit Cards; 703-361-7300, fax 703-335-9486 ◆ Full of information on more than 70 major jobs in the world's largest industry, from job requirements to rewards. Includes travel agents, packagers, planners, suppliers and support services. Identifies key educational programs, associations, national travel employers and travel recruiting firms. Visit the distributor's Web site at www.impactpublications.com. [ID:2184]

Careers for Travel Buffs & Other Restless Types 📖
2003, Paul Plawin, 208 pages ➤ Chapters Indigo Books, www.chapters.indigo.ca, $20.95 US; Credit Cards ◆ So you wanna travel and work, eh? You may be surprised at the number of ways you can earn a paycheque while exploring the world. This US book explains how you can go on location to report on a new resort, book trips for other travellers or go on the road with the band and make money while doing so! You'll find all the information you need on salaries, working conditions and opportunities for professional advancement. Fun and accessible, this book is great for those beginning to build their international experience. [ID:2185]

Jobs for Travel Lovers: Opportunities at Home and Abroad 📖
2003, Caryl Krannich, Ronald Krannich, 232 pages ➤ Impact Publications, Suite N, 9104 North Manassas Drive, Manassas Park, VA 20111-5211, USA, www.impactpublications.com, $31.50 US; Credit Cards; 703-361-7300, fax 703-335-9486 ◆ This book identifies numerous jobs that enable individuals to travel both at home and abroad. Dispelling 54 myths, exploring key motivations and outlining effective job search strategies, it surveys hundreds of jobs in business, government and education, including the travel and hospitality industry, non-profit organizations, international organizations, education institutions and consulting. Written for anyone interested in combining travel with earning a living. [ID:2397]

Tourism Training Institute 🏛
International Department, Tourism Training Institute, Suite 200, 1245 West Broadway, Vancouver, BC V6H 1G7, Canada, www.tourismti.com/home.html, 604-736-7008, fax 604-736-7723 ◆ The Tourism Training Institute offers diploma programs on travel, airline, hospitality management,

flight attendant, cruise hospitality and business management in tourism. On-the-job work experience is offered with selected programs. Graduates benefit from local training and are able to use their acquired skills to work internationally. [ID:2339]

Working in Ski Resorts - Europe & North America 📖
2003, Victoria Pybus, Charles James, Vacation Work, 352 pages ➤ Globe Pequot Press, P.O. Box 480, 246 Goose Lane, Guilford, CT 06437, USA, www.globepequot.com, $19.95 US; VISA, MC; 888-249-7586, fax 800-820-2329 ◆ A unique guide for anyone wanting to find a job in a ski resort in Europe, the US or Canada. Explains where the jobs are and how to get them, both pre-arranged and on the spot. [ID:2109]

Working on Cruise Ships 📖
2002, Sarah Bow, Vacation Work, 224 pages ➤ Globe Pequot Press, P.O. Box 480, 246 Goose Lane, Guilford, CT 06437, USA, www.globepequot.com, $16.95 US; VISA, MC; 888-249-7586, fax 800-820-2329 ◆ "Working on Cruise Ships" covers thousands of seasonal and career opportunities for men and women with cruise lines throughout the world. Includes information on over 150 different types of jobs at sea, contact data for the main maritime agents and hiring agencies, and an extensive directory listing details of 200 cruise liners with information on size of ship, date launched, nationality and number of crew. [ID:2221]

OTHER CAREERS

This is a list of various career-specific resources.

Aboriginal Planet 🖥
Monthly, Foreign Affairs Canada (FAC) ➤ www.dfait-maeci.gc.ca/latinamerica/aboriginal-en.asp, Free on-line; 𝐹𝑟 ◆ This e-zine reports monthly on the Aboriginal Canadian events taking place around the world and on important international Aboriginal events taking place in Canada. The site also provides tools for Aboriginal Canadians to break onto the world stage: check out the "International Opportunities" and "Business Centre" sections. [ID:2486]

Bowker Annual Library and Book Trade Almanac 📖
Annual, 900 pages ➤ Bowker, 630 Central Ave., New Providence, NJ 07974, USA, www.bowker.co.uk, €175; Credit Cards; 800-521-8110, fax 908-665-6688 ◆ This US almanac has a small section on overseas library jobs, exchange programs and jobs in non-library settings for librarians. [ID:2068]

CANPOL 👥
http://canpol.ca ◆ CANPOL is a division of CANADEM, a national roster of 5,000 Canadians skilled in human rights, peace building, democratization, rule of law, admin-logistics, security, reconstruction and other field expertise. CANPOL's 800 police and security sector reform experts have experience in over 60 countries. Practitioners of police craft and operational management, they help achieve sustainable police development through delivering programs and police services to clients worldwide. Registrants must have well-honed interpersonal skills: flexibility, teamwork, cultural and gender sensitivity, as well as the ability to think on their feet. Once registered, your skills profile and resume are used to determine whether you are the ideal match for positions that come available. Registration is free. If you are a police expert and interested in overseas work, this is your first stop. [ID:2750]

Cultural Survival 📖 🖥
Quarterly ➤ Cultural Survival Inc., 215 Prospect Street, Cambridge, MA 02139, USA, www.cs.org, $14.97 US/issue; VISA; 617-441-5400, fax 617-441-5417 ◆ Since 1972 Cultural Survival has helped indigenous peoples and ethnic minorities deal as equals with Western society. Cultural Survival is dedicated to maintaining the world's cultural diversity by developing new strategies for responding directly to the critical needs of the world's indigenous populations. This Web site is a great resource because of its links to similar international organizations working with indigenous

peoples. If this is your area of interest, start your overseas job search here! "Cultural Survival Quarterly" is a magazine that features articles on indigenous peoples worldwide. Before you run out and buy the magazine, check the Web site: the articles are available on-line. [ID:2140]

Environmental Career Centre 🖳
www.environmentalcareer.com/jobs.htm ◆ Searching jobs on this US environmental career Web site is free; however to apply on-line, you must register. The database includes a broad spectrum of environment-related careers ranging from lab technicians to field ecologists and program managers. Most of the postings are in the US, but there is the odd overseas job listed. A good starting place to your environmental career search. [ID:2637]

FreelanceWriting.com 🖳
www.freelancewriting.com ◆ This US Web site is geared toward the freelance writer. Hundreds of job postings advertised with information on how to respond and apply. Get your writing career going from a beach in Thailand! No fees to apply. [ID:2622]

International Careers in Urban Planning 📖
2001, 193 pages ➤ International Division, American Planning Association, Planners Book Service, Suite 1600, 122 South Michigan Ave., Chicago, IL 60603, USA, www.planning.org/international/publications.htm, $29.95 US; Credit Cards; 312-786-6344, fax 312-431-9985 ◆ This second edition changes the name and expands the focus of the 1994 edition: "Career Opportunities for American Planners". It is now directed at planning students and planners outside the US and includes over 30 interviews of planners who have worked overseas covering subjects such as education, career path, current employment and helpful advice. [ID:2387]

International Planning Directory 📖
2001 ➤ International Division, American Planning Association, Planners Book Service, Suite 1600, 122 South Michigan Ave., Chicago, IL 60603, USA, www.planning.org/international/publications.htm, $10 US; Credit Cards; 312-786-6344, fax 312-431-9985 ◆ A continuously updated compilation of more than 700 international planning agencies, associations, institutes and societies. Includes publications and e-mail addresses. [ID:2386]

CHAPTER 22

Phone Research Techniques

This chapter outlines some basic pointers on phoning techniques and also illustrates the importance of calling potential overseas employers.

You have a list of overseas employers: consulting firms, non-governmental organizations (NGOs), and international organizations. You don't know who to contact, their job titles or departments. You are probably unfamiliar with the companies' hiring procedures, what job openings are or will be available, or which professional qualifications are being sought. You may be unsure how to find out.

Surprisingly, this information is easy to come by! The simple solution is to telephone potential employers and directly ask these questions *before you send your resume.* Personnel officers are in the business of hiring, and are usually quite willing to answer many of your questions over the telephone. Sure, they are often portrayed as mean, horrible creatures who specialize in rejection, but this is usually not the case. Try calling the human resources department or personnel department of the company or organization you are pursuing.

The initiative you show in obtaining information on the company can kindle the employer's interest in you, and might even result in an interview. Phone research is especially important, as it allows you to insert specific new information into your covering letter and resume.

Human contact is another reason for using the telephone as a basic tool in your job search strategy. The telephone gives you access to the people on the inside. Follow-up phone calls are also a key element in sustaining and building contacts with potential employers. They help keep your dossier alive in their minds.

Although e-mail has become a common medium for professional communication, phone calls provide an element of human contact that can be really powerful in an international job search. Phoning can show your determination and your personality in a way that e-mail simply cannot do. And it sets you apart from hundreds of other applicants who don't take the trouble to find out who they should speak to in order to get hired.

GETTING ORGANIZED WITH THE CARD SYSTEM

Once you have completed the initial research stage of compiling a potential employer address list, you are ready to begin telephoning employers to gather information. The phone system proposed here is based on a follow-through planning technique facilitated by a card filing system for each employer. As you will be phoning many employers, speaking to many other people, and collecting a variety of information, the information should be assembled into an easy-to-read format. One method is to use large recipe cards (8" x 5"), organized like the one below.

This employer card system should focus information-gathering on three important areas:

- the people involved in hiring you
- key terminology used by potential employers
- follow-up information and reminders.

Employer Card Follow-Up System

NAME OF FIRM: WEB SITE:		
DATE	Contact Persons/Title/Phone/E-mail	Comments Follow-up Action
Keywords, Programs, Skills		Mailing Address of Personnel Department Date resume sent: Date resume acknowledged:

Keeping track of people with the employer card system

When making your contacts, it is important to note names and exact titles of everyone you reach—support staff and project officers, as well as recruiting officers.

Prior to being introduced to your speaker, you should request the proper spelling of his or her name and specific job title. If this is not possible, you may request this information at the end of the conversation, particularly if you have agreed to mail documents or other materials. Otherwise, call back and obtain this information from the receptionist or the person's secretary.

Treat each contact with professionalism. Make brief notes to trigger your memory of the conversation. People are impressed and responsive to personal details about themselves and will treat your dossier with similar consideration. For example:

"Hello, Ms. Jones. This is Philippe Roy calling from Calgary. We spoke on the phone a month ago regarding my application forms. It was just before your field trip to Indonesia."

"I'm the person who spoke to you about the Nigerian development program just prior to your vacation. I trust you had a relaxing holiday."

Keeping Track of Employer Terminology with the Card System

An employer card filing system should help you become familiar with, and keep track of, the particular language and terminology (jargon) used by each organization. You may want to use this information in your covering letter and resume, as well as during your interview and in future phone conversations. There are two important groups of words to listen for: skill identification words and specific in-house program jargon.

For example: a recruitment officer may emphasize that an overseas post is *"field-oriented, working with community-based organizations, at the grassroots level."* One of the job requirements might be, *"to liaise effectively with senior government officials overseas and have intercultural problem-solving skills."* Deciphering these phrases, and even using them yourself, can be critical in achieving success in your job search. Take advantage of these free verbal clues offered by employers. These new words can be adopted to describe the skills you have developed in your previous and current jobs.

Specific in-house jargon can be used to describe positions, programs, departments and processes. For example, words such as *field rep, program officer, field officer, cooperant, volunteer, and country representative* can all be used by different institutions to describe the same overseas position. By using the appropriate terminology with each firm, you will avoid verbal confusion and demonstrate your ability to adapt to that firm's corporate culture. This could well increase your chances of getting that job.

Keeping Track of Follow-Up Information with the Card System

The card system allows you to organize follow-up phone calls to inform prospective employers of your continuing interest. The follow-up process dictates that you call or write potential employers on a regular basis, such as every two or three months. This means that you should have the organization's name, address, and telephone number and the name of a contact person on record.

On ending a telephone conversation, always inquire about or suggest a suitable date for your next call, and make careful note of this date somewhere on the card. Examples of such calls:

"Hello Ms. Thompson? This is Dean Allen speaking from Kingston. We spoke a few months ago regarding an administrative posting in Bangkok..."

"I was just calling to reaffirm my interest in the posting if funding for the project does come through."

"I'm calling to inform you that I'll be out of the country for a month. Are there further developments regarding this project?"

"I just wanted to mention that I'm still very interested in keeping my dossier active with your firm. I'm currently enrolled in an upgrading course at Carleton University. Nevertheless, I'm available for full-time employment."

"I've just updated my resume. I wanted to call prior to e-mailing it to re-express my interest in working with your firm."

TIME AND COST OF A PHONE CAMPAIGN

You may need to contact as many as 40 or 50 firms within your targeted field. If you make six telephone calls in a four-hour period, you are using your time efficiently. On average, it could take three telephone calls per hour to make one direct contact.

Long distance telephone charges to overseas locations can be expensive, but this is still a small price to pay for direct contact with the right individual. (After all, the cost of being unemployed can be far greater.) When a potential employer sees that you're willing to spend money pursuing a position, it helps establish your credibility as a serious job candidate.

SELF-CONFIDENCE ON THE TELEPHONE

The most important factor in acquiring self-confidence on the telephone is believing in the importance of your call. Think of it as a perfect opportunity to speak to people who can help you in your job search.

It's not an easy task to make a good impression while bothering someone on the phone. But confidence comes from practice. If you're very nervous, practice by starting with those companies you are least interested in.

A sure-fire confidence-building technique is to arm yourself with a 2-sentence or a 20-second summary of your best points. A few prepared responses will not only give you a measure of confidence but will also add to your peace of mind as you dial those numbers. (For detailed information on how to create a brief summary of your strengths, see Chapter 23, Selling Your International Skills.)

DEALING WITH PEOPLE ON THE PHONE

Who should you talk to? Try to speak directly with a manager in one of the organization's international divisions. Failing that, an employment officer in an international division is also a good starting point. But keep in mind that hiring decisions are rarely made by personnel officers or the personnel department. These decisions are made by project officers and other executives.

You may have difficulty in getting past the administrative assistant or receptionist. He or she will likely ask such questions as: *"What is this in reference to?"* or *"May I help you?"*

Prepare yourself with a set of responses. Rather than answering, *"to discuss employment possibilities,"* or simply, *"no,"* a preferable response would be: *"I'm looking for information on your organization's African projects, specifically in relation to agricultural studies,"* or *"Yes, could you possibly connect me with the manager of your African projects?"* Chances are your call will be transferred to someone who can help you. If you are still having difficulty getting through to the right person, call the president's office, or the person at the top of the corporate hierarchy, and politely ask: *"Who would I speak to about (this field)?"*

Take the initiative. Be persistent in trying to make direct contact with a certain individual. Try not to leave your name and number, because you will wind up wasting valuable time sitting by the telephone waiting for a return call that could take days or never come at all.

In the course of tracking down the right person, you may be shuffled from one administrator to another. Each time you are transferred, reintroduce yourself by giving your full name, regardless of who you are speaking to, secretary or manager.

"Hello, my name is Paula Doucet. I'm calling long distance from Orillia, Ontario, and would like to speak to someone concerning your overseas junior professional officer program."

"Hello, my name is Nancy Vautour. I'm calling to inquire about overseas employment possibilities in the area of community health. Who would be best to talk to?"

"Could you direct me to someone with information on your international division in relation to urban development?"

If the objective of your call is to gather information, then it is polite to say, *"Do you have a few moments to spare? I have a few questions to ask about working overseas in your particular field."*

Once you have made contact with a desired manager, you should be candid about the purpose of your call. Otherwise, you will not only waste his or her valuable time but also weaken your professional credibility by beating around the bush. Some examples:

"Hello Mr. Devon? My name is Alain Keta. I spoke to Ms. Ricks, your director of human resources. She told me that you were the best person to speak to concerning your firm's upcoming contract with CIDA in Ghana."

"Hello my name is Francine Dugas. Mr. Kyle, your name was referred to me by the consultant, John Smith, who has worked with your firm. He mentioned that you could possibly provide me with some information on the type of overseas employment I'm interested in."

If you were referred by someone, then mention the name and title of your referral. This way, you are reducing the chance of rejection by your new contact. Example:

"Hello, my name is Carl Arthur. I was speaking with Glen Allard from SCN who told me that you could direct me to someone in your firm with information on overseas employment possibilities in industrial plant management."

Always acknowledge your contact's expertise or abilities before imposing demands upon his or her time.

"Mr. Dupont has told me that you're one of the most respected people in the industry."

"Ms. Robin mentioned that you've spent many years in the business."

"Ms. Petrella told me that you're very knowledgable in the field and understand how the system works."

From your telephone campaign, you should have accumulated a wealth of information regarding international organizations, such as the organizations that are hiring, hiring authorities, current trends and opinions in your field. This should put you in a good position to speak comfortably and knowledgably with recruitment and program officers. After all, recruitment and program officers are always interested in updating information about other firms in their industry. Mentioning names of other people you have spoken to could also improve your chances of landing a job. The international community is relatively small; many of the professionals know each other, or know of each other. For example:

"Mr. Bollack from WUSC has mentioned the same organization, and has recommended to me that I contact Mr. Ameh at Inter Pares. Do you know of him?"

Phrase your questions in a non-threatening manner. That is, do not pose questions that demand a commitment from the other party, or that directly show your self-interest. Save those for later. For example:

DO NOT ASK:

- *"When can I expect an answer from you?"*
- *"What would I expect to earn in such a position?"*
- *"Do you have a current job opening in my field?"*

INSTEAD ASK:

- *"Will a decision be made by the end of the month?"*
- *"Do you have any idea of the salary range for someone with my experience?"*
- *"Are you currently accepting resumes?"*

INQUIRING ABOUT THE OPPORTUNITY

Before you pick up the telephone, make a list of questions you want answered. As you become more familiar with a particular field, your knowledge and list of questions will also expand.

Sample Inquiry Questions

Here are some suggestions to help you develop a more specific list of questions geared to your field of work.

- *"What type of jobs would be suitable for someone of my skills and experience?"*
- *"How do people typically get hired for these types of positions?"*
- *"Do you have any overseas job descriptions that you could send me?"*
- *"What is the typical profile of someone hired in these types of positions?"*
- *"What types of skills and traits are required?"*
- *"What level of experience is required? Is Canadian work experience judged on an equal footing with overseas experience?"*

- *"Are there any volunteer possibilities within your Canadian international division that I could undertake to help me better understand your organization?"*

"Who Else Is Hiring?" Questions

Use the contact to network with others. Here are sample questions to pose:

- *"Are you aware of other organizations that offer similar entry-level positions?"*

- *"Thank you for the information on your firm. Are there other firms with new overseas contracts that you know about? Can you refer me to someone else? May I mention your name as having referred me?"*

- *"Do you know anyone who works in that department? What type of people do they recruit? What can you tell me about their hiring policies or work philosophy? Do you have any information about their overseas programs or their major field of interest?"*

- *"Is there anything else you could suggest for someone with my qualifications?"*

Word of Mouth

Talk to as many people as possible to discover how they obtained their overseas positions. Do they know of anyone who could offer you an introduction to a firm with an international branch? What about their suggestions of possible employers and locations of work?

DEALING WITH NEGATIVE ANSWERS

Remember that recruitment officers are not interested in hiring someone who seems unsure of his or her career path, or is uncommitted to working overseas. International employment officers are known to make the occasional disparaging remark about their particular field. Their pessimism stems from the fact that their business is often a frenetic mixture of hiring followed by long periods of quiet. They sometimes even encourage newcomers to seek other employment. Whenever you encounter a negative response to your telephone questions, persist. Show the recruiter you are determined to land a position. He or she will respect your persistence.

Here are some tactics you might try in response to negative answers:

EMPLOYER: *"We are not hiring."*

YOUR RESPONSE:

- *"Yes, I understand. Your receptionist mentioned this to me. Nonetheless, would it be possible to have my resume kept on file in case your organization needs someone on short notice? I expect to be available over the next six months."*
- *"If a job does open up, how would it be advertised?"*
- *"Is it possible to send in my resume for inclusion in your data bank?"*
- *"Is there anything coming up in the foreseeable future?"*

EMPLOYER: *"We only hire the most qualified candidates with five years' overseas experience."*

YOUR RESPONSE:

- *"Yes, I'm aware that there is a lot of competition, but I think my background demonstrates that many of my skills are transferable to an overseas work environment, and I would appreciate having you look at my resume."*

- *"I am aware of your organization's requirements but I believe that some of my qualifications, especially my experience in working in isolated environments, have prepared me for that type of work."*

An unreceptive secretary or receptionist can compound the discomfort of making "cold" calls. Still, they can be a wealth of information. Don't be daunted by their screening techniques or their standard response of "Send us your resume." You should persist with statements such as:

- *"I was hoping to speak to someone who could give me more information prior to sending in my resume. Is there someone I could speak to first?"*

- *"When would it be best to call back? I have some specific questions about your project in Zaire."*

- *"Would it be possible to speak to an information officer who could provide more information on your organization?"*

Persistence, a little charm, and genuine politeness will go a long way in making contact with the right person. If these tactics all fail, then address any written material to the assistant's or receptionist's attention, even though the covering letter and resume is directed to the boss. A follow-up phone call to confirm the spelling of a name will fix your name in the secretary's memory, and may improve the chances of having your resume singled out for the boss's attention. These tactics should help in future follow-up calls.

Negative answers are a familiar part of the job search, even for highly qualified candidates, so don't be discouraged.

FOLLOW-UP PHONE CALLS

Most job seekers neglect to follow up with a phone call once they have made an initial contact. To ignore the follow-up stage is to ignore the basic fact that many job opportunities appear "out of the blue." They often appear with little advance notice to the recruiter, and they are usually filled within a short time. Follow-up phone calls improve your chances of being in the right place at the right time. Moreover, they allow you to build a relationship with someone in that firm who could be crucial in your obtaining an overseas posting.

When should you make a follow-up telephone call?

- Three to seven days after sending a resume, or after an interview.
- One to three months after your last contact with an employer. (This is done whether or not potential job openings were mentioned.)
- When you have new information to add to your resume and wish to inform a potential employer.
- Two days after you have received a negative reply following an interview. As a candidate, you have the right to receive feedback on why you were not offered

the job. (Do not make this call while distraught. Wait until you are calm. You may find this a difficult call, but it is extremely important to assess your approach and to improve your chances the next time around.)

- When you have received a job offer.

This last situation is when most people stop their job search. Surprisingly, this is a mistake! Your search should move into high gear the moment you have an offer. You should phone every potential employer from whom you have had the slightest encouragement. If an employer is really interested in you, he or she may offer you a position. For example:

"Hello Mr. Smith. I'm calling to let you know that I've just received a job offer from another firm. But I'm still interested in your company, and I thought it prudent to call to see if there is anything available in your department at this time."

"Since you'd mentioned that I may be considered for any openings, and since I am particularly interested in your firm's line of work, I decided to call before accepting another offer."

In a follow-up phone call always mention the circumstance of your last call. For example: *"There were no postings at the time of our last conversation, but you had mentioned that some positions were possibly going to be advertised this spring."* Be forthright in your questions. For example: *"I'm calling to inquire about possible openings since our last conversation."*

You don't want to be perceived as a nuisance, but there is nothing to lose by asking permission to call back at a later date. *"May I check with you again next month? What time or date is best for you?"*

Your follow-up phone calls are a strong indicator of your interest, and they show that you have the motivation and drive to follow through on your job search.

SUMMARY OF PHONE TECHNIQUES

Why Phone?

- To find out what jobs are open, or will be open.
- To address your resume to the proper person.
- To make contacts and build relationships.
- To make yourself known.
- To find out what personality traits are being sought.
- To find out what skills are essential.
- To learn the special language (jargon) of your future field.
- To facilitate writing a resume patterned on employer expectations and needs.
- To follow up and keep your resume active.
- To uncover other sources of overseas jobs.
- To demonstrate and improve your communication skills.
- To learn about the overseas job market in general.

Phone Manners

- Always announce yourself by name.
- Always address the person by name.
- Always mention your referral.
- Always be polite, courteous and persistent.
- Always treat everyone with the utmost respect.
- Always be direct about the nature of your call.

Phone Techniques

- Use the card system to keep track of people.
- Use the card system to note the in-house language of the field.
- Use the card system to keep track of follow-up calls.
- Have a written list of questions before phoning.
- Directly ask employers what type of candidates are sought and the exact criteria.
- Phrase your questions with diplomacy, without forcing employers into a commitment.
- Treat everyone as an expert and acknowledge his or her expertise in your conversation.
- Approach each information-gathering exercise with enthusiasm and confidence.
- If you're unable to get past a secretary, pose your questions to him or her.
- First practice your phone techniques with employers of least interest to you.
- When calling long distance, mention this fact to the other party.
- Share your knowledge of the job market with recruitment officers.
- Persist with requests for information and in sending your resume, despite negative feedback.
- Ask for further information on other overseas employers.
- Send a thank-you note to those who have been particularly helpful.
- Make full use of follow-up phone calls.

A LAST WORD

In this Internet age, it can still be easier to impress employers if you pick up the phone and make personal contact. Good luck with your search!

CHAPTER 23
Selling Your International Skills

This is an exciting chapter to help you uncover your professional skills, particularly your international skills. This chapter will help you package your skills and sell them to employers. It will also prompt you to take stock of your professional self and to be proud of the qualifications you have. For most students and young professionals, the exercise of uncovering and organizing their professional skills into a marketable package can be somewhat agonizing. But persevere—it is well worth the effort!

This chapter is organized into four sections: The first section explains why you need to know your skills and how to go about uncovering them. The second section describes general strategies for selling yourself to employers. The third section describes the all-important "elevator pitch" strategy—a short description of your professional self to sell yourself to employers. And finally, the chapter concludes with an inventory of international and other professional skills that you can draw on.

WHO ARE YOU?

Whenever I walk through a crowd of university students interested in international careers, I always have the same question on my mind: *"Who are you?"* The students who attend my seminars are an interesting bunch. They have travelled, lived abroad, studied abroad, interned in exotic places. They are articulate, well read, analytical, and they are full of enthusiasm and inquisitiveness about international careers. Since I want to hear about student career aspirations and past experience, I often ask them to tell me about themselves. It is rare that I get a truly professional reply. It generally takes me a full 20 minutes before I begin to grasp the main components that make up the individual's professional profile.

The same scenario is true when I meet senior professionals. I often ask myself *"Who are they? What are they good at? What are they known for in their careers?"* I am curious about their professional personalities.

Whatever job you are searching for, no matter your level of entry, and whether you are an engineer, a financial analyst, an economist, or a summer intern, the question you will be answering for employers is, *"Who are you?"*

WHY YOU NEED TO KNOW YOUR SKILLS

• **To sell yourself in your resume, in the job interview and while networking.** Employers hire people for their skills. During the selection process, they will invest time and effort to try to uncover who you are. What if you helped them in this analysis? What if you guided them and showed them your strengths and how your skills sets fit the "ideal profile" that they are looking for? You can do this only if you have already constructed a professional inventory of your skills and organized them into skills sets. To speak knowledgably about yourself, you will need to have an elevator pitch, a skills-based resume and a career goal to tie everything together.

• **To understand your professional self, your skills sets and areas for improvement**. You are the only one who can complete the arduous task of creating a package of skills. A professional colleague can help you refine your lists of skills, but you will need to invest effort to come up with an authentic list that truly represents your character. There is no predisposed cookie cutter list for you to use. Your list of skills will be unique to you alone. In the end, your efforts will allow you to sell yourself, speak easily about your skills and be knowledgeable about what areas you need to improve on.

• **To survive in a project-based world.** In the past, employers and employees had relationships that lasted several years, or even decades. Employers were very familiar with employees' skills and took responsibility for assigning staff to appropriate jobs. With the fast pace of change in today's ever-changing global economy, the workplace has become more project based. In this environment, you will have many different employers/supervisors and colleagues. You will be asked to join teams or even lead teams, and then the teams will be disbanded and you will join new ones. To be effective and move ahead in this environment, you need to be able to explain your skills sets quickly to new team members and managers. So it is a valuable idea to become familiar with your skills and skill sets, and what better place to start than during the job search?

FOCUS ON YOUR PRIMARY SKILLS

Most international employees have a wide range of skills they bring to the workplace—linguistic, economic, political, technical and administrative. Whatever your background, you must arrange your skills to ensure that your primary skill dominates in your resume and interview, and not the complementary ones. For example, a business person must sell himself or herself first as business-oriented, with a complementary knowledge of economics, even though his or her education may include economics. You don't want to be perceived as an economist dabbling in business!

The objective, therefore, is to uncover your core skills, core interests and core values. Find out what drives you, what motivates you and what you like. In the final analysis, your professional description should have only two to three major components, and you should group your skills according to these components. *"A chemical engineer with project management expertise," "a communications officer who specializes in public health education,"* etc.

One good method for assessing and selling your skills is to think of them as separate components. Compartmentalize them into blocks. In conversations with employers, stay away from detailed lists that are difficult to grasp. For example, speak about your block of business skills, your block of language skills and your block of intercultural awareness skills. You may also have a block of administrative skills, project management skills, program management skills and computer skills. These components are your selling points to employers. Ignore any overlap within these skills blocks (and there always is overlap); treat each block as separate. In speaking of your abilities in this manner, you'll be able to paint a broad and definable picture of yourself. The use of components/skills blocks simplifies the analytical profiling that employers must do when hiring. And with their use, you will have the employer thinking about you the way you want him or her to!

SKILLS VS. EXPERIENCE

Skills are different from experience. When you tell an employer about your past job responsibilities, you are not communicating your skills. Skills describe your ability to perform a task—they are portable. Experience, on the other hand is usually expressed as a label attached to a specific job. Unless you are applying for a very similar job, your experience is not usually very portable, but your skills are! Students and young professionals are generally looking to launch new careers that are different from their past work experiences. Employers themselves are generally looking for skills, not experience, when recruiting recent graduates and young professionals. When you describe your skills to employers, you put yourself in a more powerful position. With a skills-based analysis, you harness the selection process. Put forth an analysis of *why* you were successful, not *what* you were successful at.

HOW TO UNCOVER YOUR SKILLS

Listing your skills and related character traits can be a difficult exercise for anyone, no matter what your level of experience. Here are a few tips to get you started.

- **Contact past employers and colleagues.** Ask yourself, *"If my work colleagues had to mention my best work-related attributes, what would they say?"* Or better yet, ask past employers and colleagues why they enjoyed working with you. These are very productive strategies; ask your colleagues or supervisors to evaluate and help you list your professional attributes.

- **Brainstorm a list.** Start with a free flow of ideas to build a long list of your skills. Group these skills into three to five categories. Sort and eliminate duplicates or similar ideas—be ruthless. Professionalize the wording of skills by converting family- or friend-oriented skills to professional skills. For example, change *"friendly"* to *"communicates well with peers and supervisors."* (For more examples of skills, as well as tips on how to group them, see the "Inventory of Cross-Cultural Skills" and the "Inventory of Professional Skills" sections at the end of this chapter).

- **Analyze something you enjoyed from your past.** Search your past for some project or event you enjoyed and then analyze why you enjoyed it. For example, *"I loved building a log cabin with my brothers. What did I enjoy? The camaraderie, work ethic, team managing the project, taking care of details and getting supplies delivered in proper order."* Convert this into a list of professional skills. *"Effective in project planning, logistics, scheduling, facilitating decisions in a team environment, able to manage detailed tasks."*

- **Identify key reference points that helped define your professional identity.** Deconstruct these events to uncover what drives you, what skills you're good at, and what values you adhere to. These memorable events do not have to be work related. For example: *"One memorable defining moment was in an advanced Grade 11 history class. The professor never gave a lecture. Students worked in teams to research history projects and then made presentations. I remember how exciting it was to work independently from the professor, to work in teams, to organize the work, to store research in a simple database. I was born to work independently and to be an organizer."*

- **Self-analyze.** Ask yourself about how you performed on a previous task. Most of us begin this exercise by concentrating time and effort to answer the questions, *"Where did I go wrong? What could I have done better?"* While you should be aware of areas requiring improvement, you will be more productive if you ask yourself, *"What did I do correctly?"* If you start with a positive question and a positive review of your skills, you will end up with a list of skills that you have developed. You will most likely then find a job that fits with your skills and you will shine! When you are preparing to describe yourself, tie your analysis to a professional situation. *"The meeting with my boss went well because I took the time to write a detailed agenda before the meeting and I followed up immediately after with a written summary of our decisions."*

- **Create a list of skills by auditing each position you had in the past.** Review your resume and carefully identify the skills you used for each job or major volunteer involvement. This may be time consuming, but experience has shown that we often forget major skills, and it is only when we finish writing a perfect resume that we can uncover the missing ones. And don't forget to use the language of your future job by crossing out any skills that are industry specific and replacing them with similar or equivalent skills in your new targeted sector.

- **Read related job ads for key words in your field of work.** This strategy is important—a must do! The first place to look is the Web site of large organizations hiring internationally. The career pages of these sites will provide you with a rich harvest of terms describing international skills and skills sets in your field of work. Even if the job is not exactly the one you want (for example, few entry-level jobs are described on these sites, senior and technical positions being posted most often), the job descriptions for the posted positions will give you clues for the job you want, even for entry-level jobs. Job ads in newspapers and trade magazines may also be a good start for picking up industry words and hints about the "ideal" profile in your field.

- **Phone employers directly and ask what skills are required.** This sounds too easy—because it is! Most employers will answer questions such as, *"What skills do you generally look for in assessing persons for this type of position?"*

TECHNIQUES FOR SELLING YOUR SKILLS

The following are a few suggestions to help you speak about your skills when conversing with employers after you have completed your self-analysis.

Describe Your Skills Internationally

Most job searchers, including students, make the mistake of portraying themselves according to their past experience. Thus, the graduate student with a specialization in Middle East economics portrays herself as a graduate student looking for work. The shipping clerk still refers to his work as clerking even though he has five years of experience with international customs clearance. The point here is that you must sell yourself under the label of your future work and not under the labels of the past. The student presents herself as an economist with Middle East expertise, and the shipping clerk must present himself as a trade agent in international shipping. If you want respect, and if you want to be treated as a professional, develop the language and attitude that demonstrate your confidence and reflect your international IQ. Match your background to the international job. Don't rely on an employer to do the matching analysis for you. Show the recruiter exactly how your skills and experience are compatible with the job.

Use Short Stories

Soft skills are effectively communicated through short stories. You should develop a small inventory of three or four international stories to explain your professional personality. With one short story, you can demonstrate a wide range of international skills.

"One important lesson I learned when working with the UN in the Congo was to be flexible about management styles. In the US, we work with a participatory decision-making process, and managers take steps to be seen as equals of their staff. In the Congo, my life as a junior manager improved for the better when I broke with US conventions and exercised my authority in a more public fashion in front of staff. I learned to ride in the back seat of the car instead of next to the driver. I learned the hard way to always present myself as the supervisor, to not wear shorts to the office and to put on a tie for meetings. These might seem like little things when working in a refugee camp, but they were good lessons to learn rapidly in order to become more effective." Here are a few other examples of how to begin a story that alludes to important international skills: *"When I first arrive in a new country, I enjoy overcoming the unknown and the challenge of navigating my way around in an unfamiliar surroundings"* or *"When I was in Spain, I learned that the most important thing in a new situation is to begin by observing carefully before making judgments or taking action..."*

How to Describe Your Skills to Employers

Most of us feel a little awkward when describing personal attributes to others. Here are a few starting phrases that may help you along. These phrases are sorted by three main techniques. Note also that all phrases should be concise and direct.

Describe yourself in terms of what others say about you:

- *My colleagues tell me that I have an ability to...*
- *My previous supervisor relied on me mainly to...*
- *If my co-workers had to sum up my management style, they would probably say...*
- *My co-workers say that I am very...*
- *I am particularly well known for my skills in...*
- *My managers have always appreciated...*

Describe yourself in terms of why you were successful. Point to a success you have had and describe the skills that underline this success.

- *I was successful as a project manager because...*
- *The team achieved its goals in part because I carefully managed the...*
- *I have been commended on my approach...*
- *I can attribute my successes to being able to...*
- *I have an aptitude for...*
- *The policy paper I co-wrote was well received by the board because...*

Describe how you do things. You can convey many skills by simply describing the general rules you apply when tackling work.

- *My general approach in these circumstances is always to...*
- *Whenever I start a task, I always...*
- *I find that I can best organize work by...*
- *I can attribute my adherence to deadlines to my project management skills and training....*
- *I have positioned myself to accept responsibility in...*
- *I always keep a running to-do list....*
- *When starting a project, I always begin by writing a detailed plan and working with fellow team members to keep the plan alive....*
- *When designing a new database for a client, I recognize that 50 per cent of the work is writing a thorough needs analysis....*

THE ALL-IMPORTANT ELEVATOR PITCH

Imagine that you are full-time job hunting. You are continuously coming into contact with employers through e-mail and phone conversations, during face-to-face meetings at conferences and chance meetings in lobbies or hallways, and perhaps even at dinner parties with friends. Potential employers will most certainly say to you, *"Tell me about yourself."* On a moment's notice, you must be prepared to say who you are and what skills you have. Time is short and you have to make an immediate impression.

For all of these job-hunting situations, you need to have a pre-arranged two-sentence and two-paragraph description of your professional self. The message has to be short, clear and articulate. This is your "elevator pitch," a short marketing message about yourself—short enough to be delivered during one elevator ride. Unless you are prepared with a personal elevator pitch (and most young professionals are not), you will miss out on the many door-opening opportunities that come up when you are searching for a job.

Imagine now that you are on the phone with an employer who asks you to tell him or her about yourself. You have done your homework and you have in your arsenal of job-hunting techniques a pre-arranged 30-second sound bite—a two-paragraph, professionally worded description of all that you are. The wording and ideas in these few sentences flows effortlessly. They are communicated with confidence. As the conversation progresses, your short description ties into the ideas you have developed in your longer resume and covering letter. You have labelled and compartmentalized your skills sets so that you can now list them, then elaborate on each. You demonstrate confidence because you know yourself and have the professional words needed for describing who you are in the workplace.

Et voilà! Because you have an elevator pitch, a succinct, professional description of yourself, you now have the ability to grab the attention of all the potential employers you contact during your job-hunting phase. Once you have a clear idea of who you are and how to express it, contacting employers gets easier and easier.

Why You Need an Elevator Pitch

You need a short description of your professional self for the following reasons:

- It helps you get focused in your job search.
- It forces you to figure out what your major skills are and therefore what makes you valuable.
- It helps you figure out what to emphasize in your resume.
- It helps you demonstrate your confidence and communication abilities when employers say, *"Tell me about yourself."*
- It grabs the attention of potential employers when you interact with them by phone, by e-mail and in person.

Your Elevator Pitch is Linked to Your Resume

You generally write your elevator pitch before writing your resume. The decisions you make while writing your two-sentence and two-paragraph description will help you decide what is important about you, and what to include in your resume.

Before you start, decide on a career objective. The elevator pitch must be written in a manner that supports your career objective. (For more information, see Chapter 24, International Resumes.)

The elevator pitch provides a footprint for structuring your resume. It will be especially important when you write the "Skills Summary" section of your resume since the elevator pitch will have helped you focus on your best skills—the ones that make you shine and the ones that attract employers.

Where to Start—Your Career Labels

Begin writing your elevator pitch by choosing two or three career labels that summarize who you are. Try to imagine what a recruitment officer would write about you when discovering your resume while quickly going through a pile of resumes. You are deciding here on a focus—a few labels that will sum you up and tell employers what your main interests and skills are. Hard skills are generally the easiest to insert here. Begin with your education or areas of career experience. Follow this with your most dominant soft skill, which characterizes your aptitude.

Examples of Career Labels

International Trade and Immigration, strong writer

MA International Relations, aptitude for policy and analytical work

BA History & Literary Studies, tri-lingual with language-learning skills

Agricultural Engineering, familiar with project management, world traveller

Finance and IT systems, cross-cultural negotiations

Strategies for Writing an Elevator Pitch

Many different formulas work, but there are generally two main ideas that need to be covered when composing your professional description. You need to mention your hard skills and your soft skills. The following paragraph gets these ideas across.

- **Write a two-sentence and a two-paragraph description.** In the first sentence or paragraph you discuss your hard skills. Highlight your professional qualifications such as work experience, field of expertise, language skills and education. In the second sentence or paragraph, you discuss your soft skills. Speak about the personal qualities that describe you in the workplace. Mention your reasons for success, what captivates you, what sparks your interest, what qualities you are known for, what attracts you to certain types of tasks. (See below, Example of a Two-Paragraph Elevator Pitch.)

- **Open with your three areas of expertise, then describe each.** This strategy works best if you already have at least a couple of years of work experience. Example: *"I have three areas of expertise and interest: Latin America, Community Health, and Information Technologies."* Alternatively, you can start by announcing, *"I have three areas of interest,"* and then follow with the first sentence, the second sentence and then the third sentence.

- **Start with a theme, and have that theme run through your description.** This method can be used effectively to tie together disjointed experiences. Examples of opening sentences:

  "As a science student, I have always been interested in writing and travelling."

  "I have always been interested in cross-cultural environments when studying or travelling abroad, as well as in the US when teaching ESL to new immigrants."

  "The common theme that runs trough all my experiences my project management abilities."

Example of a Two-Paragraph Elevator Pitch

First Paragraph, Your Hard Skills: This paragraph is a very succinct list describing the highlights of your professional experience and training.

"I am fully bilingual, having completed a Bachelor of Business Administration from the University of New Brunswick in English, and a Masters in Political Science from l'Université Laval in French. I have two years' management experience in the planning department at General Motors head office in Oshawa. I have four international areas of experience: as a volunteer English teacher in Ghana West Africa, as an assistant to the Director of the German Volunteer Service also in Ghana, four months of cross-cultural travel experience throughout Africa, and finally, four years of active volunteerism with international organization in Canada."

Second Paragraph, Your Soft Skills: This paragraph puts the above paragraph in perspective. It tells employers who you are, how you operate and why you are successful.

"I am especially known as an organizer and planner. I believe that I was successful as a manager in West Africa because I always applied a follow-up management style. I always confirmed each 'yes' or 'no' two or three times with different parties. My colleagues liked working with me because I retained a sense of humour under pressure, despite difficult socio-political and economic conditions. I am an ardent cross-cultural observer and have a definite career goal of becoming an administrative manager working with an NGO in Africa."

Writing Tips

It can be very difficult to write a good elevator pitch. Be cautious. Once completed, you will need to learn your elevator pitch by heart so that it flows from your mouth as a normal conversation. Here are a few tips and common mistakes to keep in mind when writing your elevator pitch.

- The most common error is to write your description using a formal writing style. Remember that you are creating a *speech*, not a written document. It has to flow like normal conversation, not be read as a covering letter or an academic paper. If you read it out loud and it sounds pretentious or wooden, you will need to rewrite it.

- While the sentences are written in a speaking style, the wording and ideas must be professional, not personal.

- To make your description less formal, use "I" in the sentence structure. Examples are *"I was known for…"* and *"Past employers mentioned that I …."*

- Don't forget to include international skills when applying for international work. These may be hard skills like actual work and travel experience, or soft skills, like abilities to cope, communicate or adapt in new environments.

- Speak in terms that support the employer, not in terms of what your activities and interests do for you. For example, instead of *"I like to travel,"* say *"My travel experience has taught me how to be both streetwise and diplomatic."*

- To give personality to your description, insert one phrase that says what you love: *"Throughout my career, I have been passionate about… languages / cross-cultural interactions / public health / engineering project management in development environments."*

- Don't rattle off a long list of employers, organizations or program names. Don't list dates either. These will confuse your listener. The emphasis is your skills and your personality.

- Cause and effect sentences ("I have done this; therefore I have these skills") are too lengthy for the conversational format of your profile. It's more effective to cut straight to who you are—what your strengths are. Keep all your sentences short and punchy.

- Unless you're going to be an academic or a policy wonk, steer clear of grand yet empty phrases related to theory (yes, we know that you have been studying theory for six years at university, but it is not important for most jobs). Focus more on practical aspects of work. Show employers how you administer, stay organized, promote ideas, manage report writing, etc.

- Minimize the use of adjectives and adverbs in your professional profile; they can make your claims seem weaker.

- Focus only on your most important skills. While you may have a long list of abilities, employers only want to know about the most important ones.

- Don't pump up your skills descriptions to a level beyond your actual experience or capabilities. You will only end up making yourself look deceitful if you attempt to give yourself more skills than your experience suggests you possess.

- You may want to close with a mention of your immediate career goal. Make the link between your experience, your soft skills and your career goals. *"My main career goal is to build my education and volunteer experience to become a project manager working on aid or refugee projects in Africa or Asia."*

- Finally, do not write in a style that you are not comfortable with. Some people can be boastful and carry it well, while for others it does not come naturally. Choose the style of writing that best represents who you are. Always put your best foot forward, but if you are not comfortable writing it, you will not be comfortable saying it.

More Elevator Pitch Examples

Here are examples from a group of interns specialized in Latin American studies. Note that each has been written for the purpose of being spoken out loud, and each description begins with a career label followed by the elevator pitch.

- **Administrator with broad international experience.** *"A common theme that runs through my professional profile is my attraction to cross-cultural/intercultural environments. I have just completed a BA degree in social anthropology from Saint Mary's University where I focussed on Latin American cultures. I have three international work experiences. I interned this past year for four months in Brazil with The Canadian Embassy as an assistant to a trade officer. I am also an experienced TESOL teacher, having taught foreign students in Halifax and also in Brazil. In 2003, I travelled to West Africa with Canada World Youth. I am interested in working as an administrator in a multicultural work environment. I* *like the challenge, the creativity and the intellect required to interact across cultures. I especially enjoy the cross-cultural interaction with my students. I like being organized, and my past employers tell me that they appreciate my attention to details."*

- **BA in International Relations with program experience**. *"I have a BA in International Relations, with strong language skills. I'm fully fluent in English, Italian and French, and functional in Spanish. I have worked and studied in three countries. As an intern in Argentina, I worked with a private sector firm developing marketing plans. As a student in France and Italy, I was active with international student associations, and I worked part time while improving my language and cross-cultural skills. I have also worked for the Federal Government in Ottawa as a junior policy analyst."*

  I am known as an organizer with excellent writing and interpersonal abilities. I have always been a keen observer in the workplace and have benefited from the advice of a few key mentors. My immediate career aspiration is to gain experience in ... so that I can work as a program manager for an international organization once I complete my master's degree."

- **Science graduate interested in general administration work**. *"As a Science graduate with a BA in ecology, I have a somewhat unconventional combination of interests in management, administration and the cross-cultural side of science. I enjoy the organizing people side of managing—keeping track of numerous tasks, somewhat like an entrepreneur. I also have a fair amount of cross-cultural experience, including a four-month internship with the OAC in Washington, volunteer experience with international organization in Canada, and six months of cross-cultural travel experience in Central America and the Caribbean. I am proficient in French and Spanish."*

- **Latin America specialist and ESL trainer looking for entry-level management experience**. *"I have a strong interest and broad experience in Latin American socio-political issues, with a BA in Latin American studies, a Washington-based four-month internship with the Organization of American States, and a number of research and volunteer positions. I also have strong language skills, being fluent in English, Spanish and Italian. I have gained valuable cross-cultural and training experience as an ESL instructor, first in Canada and then for two years in Japan."*

- **Latin American program officer with an international organization**. *"I have three years of multi-faceted work-experience dealing with Latin America. Always recognized for my organizing and communication abilities, I have worked for the OAC in Washington as a program-officer intern; as an administrative assistant on a Peruvian project with a Vancouver-based mining firm; as a media relations officer with the 1997 APEC conference in Vancouver; and as an executive bilingual secretary with the Consulate General of Peru, also in Vancouver. I have just completed a master's degree in International Studies from the University of Barcelona, Spain. I am an accredited Spanish translator and I am also functional in French and Catalan. My greatest goal is to work in public relations or communications, where I can make use of my writing and communication skills. I am a social person, and work especially well as part of a team."*

AN INVENTORY OF CROSS-CULTURAL SKILLS

Employers are looking for people who have cross-cultural experience and skills. It is especially important to demonstrate this knowledge if you are just starting out in your international career. You must prove that you can survive and be successful in a work setting while abroad. Tell employers where and how you acquired your international experience—some acquired domestically, and some abroad. Tell them that you are aware of the international skills required and that you enjoy the cross-cultural work environment. Include cross-cultural information in your resume but don't overdo it! Choose only three or four places that will have the greatest impact. When speaking directly to employers, mention cross-cultural skills during your conversations and use them within career stories.

Here is a short inventory of phrases to help you get started in identifying which cross-cultural skills are important in your personality.

Cross-Cultural Relations and Communications

- Positive attitude toward change and new environments.
- Recognize and respect people's diversity and individual differences.
- Enjoy working with diverse populations.
- Comfortable working with people from different cultures.
- Outgoing individual, personable, able to develop close relationships quickly.
- Adept in new environments and at understanding the motivations of others.
- Seek opinions of others when making decisions.
- Able to relate to and interact with people of differing personalities and backgrounds.
- Able to notice details that others might normally miss.
- Sensitive to economic considerations and human needs.
- Able to cope with constant change.
- Broad background and knowledge of world affairs and cultures.
- High degree of physical stamina; excellent and robust health.
- Able to adjust to and fit into different situations.
- Significant experience in and enjoyment of intensive cross-cultural environments.
- Maintain composure under close public scrutiny and criticism.

Organizational Effectiveness in a Cross-Cultural Environment

- Enjoy cross-cultural work environments.
- Adept and attracted to multicultural environments, both social and professional.
- Thrive in a culturally diverse workplace.
- Diplomatic skills and sensitivity to different management styles.
- Understanding of work within the culture of the group, including multicultural work groups.
- Sensitive to the dynamics of a cross-cultural workplace.
- Maintain effectiveness under difficult circumstances.
- Able to pursue goals when difficulties arise.
- Able to operate successfully in different settings and to adapt to a wide range of situations.

- Good listening, clarifying, questioning and responding skills.
- Remain focused on obtaining results when facing delays.
- Tolerant, curious and appreciative of different work patterns while remaining committed to deadlines.
- Think critically and act logically to evaluate situations, solve problems and make decisions.
- Able to respond quickly to changing circumstances.
- Maintain composure in stressful situations or when under pressure.
- Sensitive and aware of how one's actions may effect others.
- Open to different viewpoints, techniques and methods of operations.
- Able to organize and work in a sensitively with people from other cultures.
- Enjoy challenges and tasks that require a special or extra effort.
- Poised; do not easily lose composure or sense of purpose.

Sample Cross-Cultural Skills for an Internship Abroad
- Gained valuable knowledge and experience performing tasks in a multicultural work environment.
- Enjoyed communicating and managing processes in an environment very different than a Canadian workplace.
- Enjoyed the subtleties and mannerisms of the British work style.
- Was adept at making contacts with a wide range of players, from labourers to managers, inside and outside of my organization.
- Was known for my abilities to integrate into the local population and make friends quickly.
- Often acted as a bridge between field staff and senior managers.
- As the only Canadian on a Norwegian business team, I recognized that it was important to be sensitive to the Norwegian way of working.
- Keen observer of the various management styles emanating from this pan-European milieu.
- Working in New York gave me a clearer understanding of the regional differences found in the United States.

AN INVENTORY OF PROFESSIONAL SKILLS

Below is a selected list of professional skills that have been randomly sorted under functional headings. Use these examples to spark ideas, and adapt them to your personal requirements. The list is by no means exhaustive; it is just a starting point to spur you on.

Personal Qualities
- Demonstrate integrity and honesty.
- Positive attitude towards learning.
- Show initiative, energy and persistence to get job done.
- Take initiative.
- Learn independently.

- Exercise responsibility.
- Display drive, determination, enthusiasm and commitment.
- Broad background and knowledge.

Work Qualities

- Set goals and priorities in work and personal life.
- Recognize and suggest new ideas to get job done.
- Self starter; able to perform with minimal supervision.
- Work independently more than 90 per cent of the time.
- Accurate tracking of information; excellent memory for details.
- Ability to meet deadlines and work under pressure.
- Ability to follow directions; work alone or with others.
- Industrious; work hard.
- Developed good rapport with...
- Excellent generalist skills in...
- Experienced in all areas of...
- Very thorough.
- Follow all projects to completion.
- Accomplish numerous tasks in short time period.
- Ability to plan and to manage time, money and resources to achieve goals.

Management and Organizational Skills

- Able to generate options and solutions when solving problems.
- Able to analyze and solve problems.
- Proactive administrator with team-based management style.
- Problem solver, focused on solutions to keep project moving.
- Flexible; able to improvise, negotiate and mediate.
- Ability to manage multiple tasks and meet deadlines.
- Motivate, supervise and lead.
- Plan, coordinate, implement, follow up, schedule, administer, prioritize tasks.
- Implemented..., which enabled fellow team members to...

Team Player and People Skills

- Active interest in understanding and contributing to organizational goals.
- Recognize the importance of making decisions with others and of supporting outcomes.
- Recognize importance of exercising "give and take" to achieve group results.
- Seek a team approach where appropriate.
- Worked as part of a five-person team to complete rush projects.
- Cooperate with others.

Leadership Skills

- Lead when appropriate, mobilizing the group for high performance.
- Ability to motivate others, to take risks, to formulate and champion a vision.
- Assumed lead role in...

- Ability to accept public scrutiny and criticism.
- Good at organizing and following up on details while making arrangements for others.
- Observant and responsive to political and organization demands, especially those made on my managers.
- Able to follow directions and provide feedback.
- Ability to persuade and influence others.

Communications and Public Relations Skills

- Ability to explain concepts and strategies and to facilitate during meetings.
- Enjoy public speaking and making presentations to both senior managers and general public.
- Able to influence outcomes.
- Recognize importance of consulting broadly to make informed decisions; advise and inform.
- Articulate communicator.
- Strong interpersonal and telephone communications skills.

Research, Analytical and Policy Writing Skills

- Investigate, analyze, evaluate, research, problem solve, provide needs analysis, observe, conceptualize, forecast, categorize, compile, classify, design systems.
- Attentive to detail in the accurate completion of work and detailed reports.
- Careful attention to processes.
- Recognize the importance of procedures.
- Categorize, manage records, compile, classify, design systems.
- Ability to analyze, organize and interpret scientific data/large quantities of data.
- Aptitude for accuracy and details.
- Aptitude for abstract reasoning, observation and concentration.
- Ability to concentrate intensely and to work alone for long periods of time.
- Carry out tasks with thoroughness.

Writing Skills

- Able to translate complex concepts into easy-to-understand text.
- Careful editor.
- Experience interviewing and investigating; able to uncover...
- Creative; ability to generate and synthesize ideas.
- Excellent writing skills, as demonstrated by articles written for student newspapers, fundraising materials and essays.
- Ability to write effectively in the language in which business is conducted.
- Compose, edit and proofread correspondence, reports and Web page material.
- Excellent grammar and spelling.

A LAST WORD

Writing a professional description of yourself can be difficult and taxing. In the final analysis, you must be comfortable with the text—it must be truthful and must suit your personality. Don't get caught up in writing a complex description or a description that does not match who you are. Your description must be succinct, organized around a very short list of common themes, and must clearly align itself with your (professional) personality. Experience has proven that once you build a comprehensive and organized list of skills, you will sit back and view yourself with new admiration! You will be proud to portray yourself as the international professional that you really are—in a resume and during conversations with employers. Good luck with this task.

CHAPTER 24
International Resumes

This chapter will discuss the important differences between an international resume and a domestic one, and how you can demonstrate on paper that you have the required overseas skills and professional experience to qualify for an international job. This chapter is written specifically for people just starting out in their international career—those who have had some international exposure, but perhaps little or no professional work experience.

The problem in finding a suitable international posting is the same as it is in any line of work. That is, competition is fierce. Moreover, international recruitment officers are particularly concerned with personality profiling. Your resume should portray you as a capable and talented professional while also highlighting your personality in action. Thus, we develop herein a technique for writing an effective international resume. This resume style highlights your skills profile as it relates to your future international job. By focusing on your personality and your international skills, your resume will get you that precious interview. (Before reading this chapter, you should have read Chapter 23, Selling Your International Skills.)

INTERNATIONAL RESUMES LEAD TO INTERVIEWS

Imagine an overworked recruitment officer sifting through a pile of resumes, looking for the candidate that best matches his or her organization's ideal profile. The recruitment officer's task is to find someone with the right mix of occupational and personal skills. In an eight-hour workday, the recruiter's workload might consist of meetings, phone calls, interruptions, and scheduled appointments, along with the task of sorting through hundreds of resumes. Each candidate's resume gets a three-minute cursory glance. The majority of resumes will be dismissed for reasons such as poor visual presentation or apparent lack of qualifications. The resumes that pass first reading will likely undergo a second and more detailed reading to select candidates for interviews.

As the recruitment officer reviews your resume, a lot of analytical thinking will be brought to bear in assessing if you match the "ideal profile." The profile for an international job candidate is usually weighted heavily on personality traits, related cross-cultural skills and professional abilities. This is a complex bag of requirements. But traditional resumes generally omit character and personality traits in their format and tend to bury facts that demonstrate your international awareness. Recruitment officers have the task of searching your resume for clues to your suitability to the organization's ideal profile. Chances are many of your abilities and qualifications will be overlooked.

With an effective international resume you leave nothing to chance or misinterpretation: you do the analytical work for the recruiter. Employers will see you the way you want them to—with highlights of your best skills, achievements and experience. *Et voilà*, the recruitment officer pulls out your resume for a second serious read, your professional self-portrait is confirmed, and you will be accorded the all-important interview.

INTERNATIONAL RESUMES ARE DIFFERENT

International employers want to know that you will be effective in an international work environment. They want assurance that you will be able to communicate effectively and cope with cultural differences. There are numerous ways to let an employer know that you have all of these abilities. Here is a summary of the major strategies proposed in this chapter.

- Begin your resume with a precise career objective and then compose your entire resume to support this objective.

- Write a summary of your personal traits and professional skills. This is a powerful strategy to get employers thinking of you the way you want them to.

- Organize your work history to match the employer's ideal profile by grouping similar professional experiences together (jobs, volunteer work, internships related to international work all go together) and separating these from other experiences that do not directly support your career objective. Within each job description, group and sort your descriptions around themes that support your career objective and the employer's ideal profile. This writing strategy is very effective because you do the analytical work for the recruiter and guide them to think of you on *your* terms.

- Write your resume using the language and terminology of your future international profession. This includes cross-cultural skills, as well as the specific international job functions of your chosen position. To do this, go on-line and examine job descriptions from the employment pages of Web sites for leading organizations in your field.

- Include other information specifically required for international resumes such as: mobility, nationality, spouse's occupation, travel, language, and permanent addresses.

The body of an effective international resume usually consists of seven parts: Career Objective, Your Professional Skills and Personal Traits, Work History (grouped into international and professional experience), Education, Volunteer Work and Professional Hobbies, and Personal Data.

International resumes are longer than domestic resumes because they include more information about your personality as well as more analysis to help employers understand who you are. It is okay for an international resume to be three or four pages long. But your wording must be efficient and effective and everything must be formatted to promote speed-reading. We explain how to do this in the following sections.

YOUR CAREER OBJECTIVE

Before you begin writing your resume, you need to decide on a career objective. To do this, you must know what type of job you will be targeting. You should research your desired job position and determine the ideal profile of the international candidate. You should also ask yourself if you have the necessary qualifications and if you can organize your skill sets to match these qualifications. You need to choose a specific objective and interpret your past experience to support that objective.

To help you write, decide on an objective and explore your international work options. What jobs are out there? What skills are important to international employers? What terminology is used to describe those skills? What is the ideal profile for your targeted position? (For information on self-assessment and evaluating your skills, see Chapter 23, Selling Your International Skills.)

Write a Targeted Resume First

If you are like most job hunters, you will be tempted to dive into the job hunting process by first writing a "general" resume and then modifying the resume for each job application. This approach is simply not as effective as a targeted resume. The first resume you write should be the resume that matches the ideal job you are looking for, the perfect job you are qualified for, the job you want and are destined to have!

If you cannot decide on a specific job, you should temporarily choose one precise objective. You are not alone if you are having a hard time deciding. But for the purpose of writing a strong and effective "targeted" resume, you need to make a choice. You may be equally qualified for two distinct positions, and you can write two separate resumes, but you must write your best resume, for your best job, first!

Why a Career Objective is Important

The career objective is the most important part of your resume. Here are the reasons:

- A career objective is a fundamental statement about your personality. It states what you want to do and what you like to do, and therefore what you will most likely excel at.

- A career objective helps international employers match you to their ideal profile: the type of job, areas of expertise, level of entry, region (local or international posting), permanent or contract work, your main skills and your personality.

- A career objective establishes the "theme" for the resume. If you have no theme, you have no focus; you are gambling that the employer will find a match between you and the "ideal profile." A "themed" resume is written to ensure that the reader (i.e., the recruitment officer) has one reinforcing idea throughout the entire document. That idea is your international job objective.

- A career objective defines how everything is written and organized. Every choice you make on what to include in your resume, every list and every idea you organize, every job description—all are written to support your objective.
- Everything in your resume should be written to support the career objective. With a clear objective you are able to:
  - choose professional skills and personal traits to support the objective
  - select precise wording throughout the resume to support the objective
  - decide on what part of a job description to emphasis and what to minimize or ignore
  - group career information to support the objective

When you accept the power behind a resume written to support one career objective, you are throwing away the notion that the resume is a historical document. The resume is not about documenting your past. It is about reinterpreting your past to demonstrate that you are qualified for a specific career. In this scenario, your resume is a marketing document written to support your objective.

The Career Objective from an Employer's Perspective

International employers often recruit from a wide cross-section of employment categories. Moreover, because of the project-based nature of international business, international employers often rely on data banks of candidates. If you have a clearly defined career objective, you can be well assured that your resume will be placed in the right categories of the firms' data bank. Thanks to the Internet, thousands of people can now apply for a single international job posting. You will therefore have to work harder and more intelligently to stand out, and a clearly targeted resume with a career objective is going to be important.

From an employer's perspective, your career objective is a label used to sum up your field of work and level of expertise. A clear objective helps the recruitment officer focus on your most salient professional characteristics. The more clear and specific your objective is, the more convincing your resume will be.

While it is true that employers love the "generalist," they hire only "specialists." This is the age of specialization, and recruiters demand specific job skills from candidates. You would be incorrect to assume that a general or ambiguously worded objective (such as, "I'll do anything, anywhere.") will work in your favour or open any doors.

Your career objective should not only reflect your professional goals but should also be credible and supportive of your documented work experience and abilities. In other words, the body of your resume should demonstrate that you can do the job stated in your career objective.

THE "DO'S" OF A CAREER OBJECTIVE

Keep your objective under three lines; use wording that is clear and precise. The career objective in a resume is an immediate one, not a long-term goal. A career objective states your two-year plan only. Avoid disclosing your real long-term career objective if it does not correspond with the position that you are seeking.

As a general rule, an international career objective should address four points: geographic setting, field of work, level of entry and highlights of experience and skills. Other qualifiers may be included according to your particular circumstances.

Geographic Setting

Many international organizations hire for both domestic and overseas positions, and their data banks are often sorted on this basis. If you are applying to an international organization, and your intention is to travel or work abroad, this intention should be revealed from the outset. You may also mention your preference with reference to continent, region, and rural or urban locale. Note that you rarely get to choose a specific country, especially for entry-level positions. In the great majority of cases, the international employer chooses the country for you. (The one exception to this rule is perhaps teaching English.)

Field of Work

This is the most important part of the career objective, and it is often the hardest to write. Absurdly, it is also the part that is often forgotten. Are you a trainer, program manager, public health survey specialist or community development worker? Use the terminology of your future international employer when describing your field of work. If you are changing careers, you should mention your new field of interest, and don't dwell on your previous experience unless it corresponds to your new objective.

Level of Entry

It is important, particularly if you are an administrator, to state whether you are seeking a mid-level, senior or management position. If you are just starting out, you may wish to use such phrases as "entry-level position," "assistant or junior program officer," or "junior professional consultant." Stating an entry-level status often offers you a stronger point of entry to an international career since entry-level candidates are not competing in the same pool as mid-career candidates. By stating "entry-level" in your objective you are telling employers that you have just graduated and possess the most recent knowledge in your academic field, that you are enthusiastic and can be counted on to be earnest, and lastly, that you will not cost a lot in salary. All of these elements are enticing to employers and work in favour of the young professional.

Highlights of Experience and Skills

The career objective is an excellent way to begin introducing your main skill sets to the international employer. This is a series of short labels to describe you, so keep them brief. Focus only on your most worthy previous experience and one or two main skills. Ask yourself, "What are my two or three main selling points? You're looking for something like this: *"Entry-level policy officer with previous government work experience. Recognized for concise writing and understanding of quantitative analysis."*

Other Qualifiers

This is the place to mention crucial limiting factors or qualifiers such as whether you are willing to work as a volunteer or a salaried employee. Other qualifiers include preference for supervisory or research work, and availability for short- or long-term contract work. You may also include the environment in which you wish to work, such as "growing new project," "grassroots community-based urban organization," or "major international organization."

Career Objective Examples

Here are some examples of effective career objectives:

- **For a business graduate recently returned from an international internship.** *"Work in an internationally-oriented company with operations in Southeast Asia to develop my sales and management abilities. Functional in basic Mandarin and Cantonese; culturally adept 'street-smart' communication skills."*

- **For a recent graduate with an engineering degree.** *"Field engineer on water project in Africa with project management skills and international volunteer experiences in the Gambia and Ghana."*

- **For a mid-career finance professional.** *"Economist specializing in micro-credit policy and programming with two years' experience in Bangladesh and India."*

- **For a recent graduate with a translation degree.** *"Entry-level translator and interpreter (English, French and Spanish) to work on short-term contract with an international organization or multinational corporation based in Eastern Europe."*

- **For a mid-career teacher.** *"Secondary school teacher in an international school that will benefit from my administrative and sport management expertise."*

- **For a recent graduate with an English degree.** *"Entry-level communications officer with a development-related NGO in Los Angeles area. Proficient in writing, editing and Web site design."*

Once you have stated your objective, the rest of your resume should be devoted to supporting this objective. If you run into trouble or are unsure about how to represent some aspect of your experience, refer back to your objective. Ask yourself, "Does this information support my objective? Can I write it in a way that better supports my objective?"

THE "DO NOT'S" OF A CAREER OBJECTIVE

Don't confuse personal and professional objectives. That is, don't state your objective as: *"an opportunity to use my talents to further my five-year career plan."* Or, equally bad: *"a well-remunerated position with opportunities for frequent travel."* These objectives may be true, but to get the job you want, you need to concentrate on what you can offer a prospective employer. Rework your objective: *"to work in an international organization where I can apply my three years of management experience in finance and accounting."* or *"A performance-based sales position requiring commitment and availability for international travel."*

Avoid using flowery language such as, *"My objective is to obtain a challenging international public relations position where my highly developed skills and outstanding knowledge in project management will be recognized."* Most ideas in a resume are stronger without adjectives. The previous example can be reworked to say, *"International public relations position requiring administrative and project management abilities."*

If you are responding to an advertisement, do not duplicate the exact wording of the position being offered. This could convey the impression that parts of your resume are fabricated or fictitious.

Avoid an overly precise objective that may disqualify you from other job openings. For example, a recent political science MA graduate should not write: *"Human rights program officer in West Africa wanting to work in public advocacy addressing issues of poverty alleviation."* It is important to remain targeted without being overly precise. Here are two better and shorter examples: *"Program Officer in Africa with experience in human rights"* or *"Overseas Field Officer working for a Human Rights NGO in Africa."*

YOUR PROFESSIONAL SKILLS AND PERSONAL TRAITS

The objective and skills summary are the most important parts of an effective international resume. They summarize who you are and what you are capable of. Without this summary, a recruitment officer has to very carefully hunt through your resume (perhaps one of hundreds) and determine your professional and personal strengths to see if they match the company's ideal profile. Without a skills summary, much is left to chance and the recruitment officer will certainly miss some of your strengths.

The process of clarifying your major skills and traits is a difficult one that can take days of work. The end result, however, will be that you understand yourself better and can therefore explain your worth to employers while on the phone and during interviews. A self-appraisal will help you recognize strengths and weaknesses in your work and put you on a better footing for performing new tasks and searching for areas for improvement.

Some of you may be skeptical of the value of listing skills because you've seen lists that all sound the same: *"team player, able to follow directions or work independently, communicates well with others, etc."* The fact is, however, that these lists do not sound the same. There are perhaps a thousand skills traits in common use, and you can carefully choose ones that represent you and sound unique. By working hard at self-analysis, you are telling employers who you are and what you are good at. And you then authenticate the list with supportive job descriptions. This strategy is effective—it communicates your absolute best self to potential employers.

One word of caution: writing a skills-based resume is difficult. It needs to be done with care and precise wording. Each skill needs to be backed up with a concrete example in other parts of the resume. After completing the task, however, you will stand back and be amazed by the level of professionalism emanating from your resume.

Getting Started

Focus only on your strongest attributes. Keep your list short, usually no more than three or four main categories, and no more than six skills or traits for each category.

Mention only those skills applicable to the position you are applying for. In other words, promote yourself, but don't add extraneous information that has no bearing on your job objective.

Support *each* skill and trait with one or two concrete examples in other parts of the resume. If you can't support it, don't write it.

Be honest and choose your words carefully. During the interview, your credibility could be called into question if you are asked to defend each skill or accomplishment that you have listed. If you cannot provide evidence that you were *"an effective communicator,"* or *"an experienced computer trainer,"* or that you *"initiated a project"* or *"worked independently"* as a *"self-starter"* or *"a team leader,"* then it is probably not one of your strong assets, and is not worth mentioning.

For those of you who are changing careers, you should place the emphasis on your abilities rather than job experience. If you have had overseas volunteer experience or have travelled abroad, you could list aspects of overseas life you most enjoyed, and the skills you used in those situations. For example, if you enjoyed working as a teacher, you might wish to add: *"can communicate effectively in other cultures."* Or, if you enjoyed a degree of success in accomplishing tasks under difficult economic or political conditions, you might wish to add: *"able to maintain a sense of optimism under difficult socio-economic conditions."* Career changers should take careful note to demonstrate to a potential international employer how their previous work skills are relevant to the position sought.

Don't forget to include management skills in your professional qualifications. Almost all jobs involve some degree of management, and this is especially true for international jobs. You will want to include skills such as project planning, negotiating, follow-up management style, leadership, grassroots organizing skills, demonstrated skill in starting new projects, ability to motivate staff, ability to chair meetings, recruitment skills, past success in conflict resolution and mediation, ability to draw out the skills and talents of others, effectiveness in promoting a cordial, professional atmosphere among associates, and a systematic approach to identifying project inputs.

You should include international skills. For example: *intercultural group facilitation skills, sensitivity to people from other cultures, international development experience, theoretical understanding of the socio-political environments of developing countries, three years' experience managing programs with American and South Asian participants, facilitation of pre-departure orientation seminars for volunteers going to Africa, knowledge of the cultural and social sensitivities associated with international work.* (For a more detailed list of cross-cultural skills, see Chapter 23, Selling Your International Skills. For those of you who need assistance assessing your skills, there is an excellent book entitled *The Three Boxes of Life: An Introduction to Life Work Planning,* listed in the General Job Search Resources in Chapter 20, The Job Search & Targeting Your Research.)

Alternative Formats for Listing Skills and Traits

After having worked with hundreds of young professionals, it is clear to me that no two skills summaries can be alike. Different emphasis and alternative approaches ensure that each is unique. There are many different ways of organizing your skills summary. Here is an explanation describing alternative approaches.

For those of you who have more than a couple of years of professional work experience, you will be able to organize a full one-page skills summary. It may be broken into three or four subheadings that have been carefully chosen to support your career objective. Examples of headings: *Research and Analytical Skills; Management Expertise; Computer and Technical Skills; Cross-Cultural Communications Skills.* (For an example of this strategy, see the Robin Millar Resume at the end of this chapter.)

If you are in your early twenties and seeking an entry-level position, you may not have enough material or experience to write a full one-page summary. You could combine your professional and personal skills under a single heading or list them separately. If you list them under a single heading you may try one of the following titles: *Major Traits, Summary of Professional Qualifications (Skills), Professional Summary,* or *Professional Profile.*

Our preference is to separate *Personal Traits* from *Professional Skills.* (For example, see the Marc Doucet Resume at the end of this chapter.) These two categories have no clear delineation, and may overlap somewhat. Items may even change depending on your job objective. For example, being a "proficient communicator" is a personal trait for an administrator but would be a professional skill for a public relations expert. Whatever the final outcome of your analysis, it will help to categorize your qualities for the recruitment officer.

Personal traits tend to be "soft" skills—those you learned from your parents or from life experiences. Here is a list of examples: *self-starter, high energy, adaptability, initiative, tolerance, relate well to people from all walks of life, close attention to detail, able to focus on key result areas, pragmatic, committed, good sense of humour, creative, resourceful, team-oriented, demonstrated communication skills, cheerful under pressure, strong interpersonal skills, adaptable to difficult living and working conditions, enjoy the challenge of managing a demanding set of responsibilities.*

Professional qualifications tend to be "hard" skills—those learned in school or work. The obvious ones include professional qualifications such as accounting or engineering designations. Others may include skills you learned on your own or through professional experience: *adept in using software, proposal and report writing skills, analytical abilities, training experience in a particular field, ability to communicate with government officials, ability to develop policies and procedures, bilingual proficiency.*

Alternatively, you can increase the impact by presenting your skills summary by listing a few key adjectives about yourself under the main headings in your resume. In the following example of resume title headers, the resume section is written in upper case followed by the "skill" in title case.

- For a job working at a think tank: *INTERNATIONAL POLICY AND RESEARCH: Detail-Oriented, Methodical, Responsible.*

- For a job as a relief worker: *INTERNATIONAL MANAGEMENT: Calm Under Pressure, Efficient, Organized.*

- For a teaching job: *TEACHING EXPERIENCE: Enthusiastic, Strong Communicator, Administrator. VOLUNTEER EXPERIENCE: Demonstrated Leadership and Organizational Abilities.*

- For an engineer listing education: *EDUCATION: Engineering; Focused on Water Resources and Participated in Team Projects.* The same engineer would also list: *INTERNATIONAL ENGINEERING EXPERIENCE: Experienced in Rural Africa—Cross-Culturally Astute.* Alternatively, for domestic work this engineer would list: *EMPLOYMENT HISTORY: Recognized by Senior Engineers for Organization and Communication Abilities in the Field.*

The above examples demonstrate the effectiveness of highlighting top skills. This approach lets international employers know who you are by labelling your credentials. (For an example of this approach, see the Water Resources Engineer Resume in Appendix 24c on the CD-ROM.)

ORGANIZING YOUR WORK HISTORY

The goal when organizing jobs and job descriptions is to bring the employer's attention to your strengths and personality. If your jobs are grouped, organized and written to support a career objective, you are doing the analytical work for the recruiter, and steering them to think of you in terms that you have developed to match the employer's ideal profile.

One of the most powerful strategies when writing an international resume is to group similar experiences together and guide the reader to focus more on those items that support your objective. There are many ways to accomplish this. Here are a few important examples of how grouping similar experiences together greatly improves the impact of your past work experience. Don't hesitate to use these grouping techniques for organizing other sections of your resume—Education, Volunteer Experiences, Publications, Conferences, Foreign Travel, etc.

Group Professional and Summer Jobs Separately

Most students graduate with a wide range of job experiences and have difficulty synthesizing this experience to support one objective. The typical example is that of a recent graduate who has had seven jobs. Five of these are "McJobs," and only two are related to your future international work. In a traditional resume you would list all seven jobs in reverse chronological order and give each job a description. The recruiter would then weed through these jobs to uncover which ones relate to the job at hand. Instead, try this alternative strategy.

Of these seven jobs, only two clearly support your career objective. Highlight these jobs by listing them first under their own section with a separate heading such as *INTERNATIONAL EXPERIENCE—POLICY AND RESEARCH* or *INTERNATIONAL AND BUSINESS EXPERIENCE.* Since these are your only career-enhancing jobs, write these up in much greater detail than other jobs—a full half or third of a page for each, covering your achievements, major projects, and skills acquired. Don't hesitate to write up an internship or a professional volunteer position as a real job if it supports your career objective. (Do clearly state that the job was volunteer or an internship.)

The remaining five jobs, those that don't strongly support your objective, should be grouped together under a heading such as *OTHER WORK EXPERIENCE* or *SUMMER WORK EXPERIENCE*. By grouping your "McJobs" together under a single heading, you are telling employers that these are secondary in your skills profile.

For these jobs, don't waste valuable space by describing job responsibilities; instead, highlight one key learning experience for each job. Write what you learned at that job, or better yet, how the job supports your current objective. For example, you could say this about a job in a warehouse in a large urban centre: *STOCKING CLERK: Recognized by supervisor for communicating successfully in a multi-ethnic new-immigrant work environmen*t. Or surprise yourself with the value derived from this next job: *SHORT ORDER COOK* at *MCDONALD'S: Recognized the importance of training and procedures for the delivery of a consistent quality product to clients.* If you have had four separate positions as a sales clerk or a waiter, you can roll everything together into one description with no need to mention the separate exact dates or details: *SALES CLERK: WALMART, K-MART, SHOE-LAND – Six years' part-time work while attending university; maintained admiration of supervisors for punctuality and professional demeanour.* There is no need to elaborate any further; you have made your point.

Group International Experiences Together

This strategy is especially powerful for highlighting your international experiences when you are just starting your career or when changing careers. To demonstrate that you have a high international IQ, assemble all your international experiences under one heading such as *INTERNATIONAL EXPERIENCE & UNDERSTANDING* or *KNOWLEDGE OF DEVELOPING COUNTRIES.* The items to include are: international studies in your home country (list full degrees or a block of courses), study abroad, language abilities, international travel, volunteering with international student clubs, cross-cultural exposure in your home country, an international skills summary, and of course, your one or two jobs abroad—most likely an internship or volunteer placement. It is very powerful to group all these elements together; it distinguishes you as an "international person." By grouping your international experience under one section, you are increasing the impact and minimizing the chances that aspects of your international experience are missed. (For an example of this strategy, see the Marc Doucet Resume at the end of this chapter.)

Group Similar Jobs Together

Whatever your job history, you help the recruiter understand who you are and how you match their ideal profile when you organize your jobs under separate headings. If you want to be known as the science person with administrative abilities, organize your jobs into *TECHNICAL AND SCIENCE WORK EXPERIENCE* and *ADMINISTRATIVE WORK EXPERIENCE.* As you progress along your career path, you can begin to separate out your work into more categories. Example, *INTERNATIONAL EXPERIENCE* and *BUSINESS EXPERIENCE.* Example, *INTERNATIONAL PROGRAM MANAGEMENT EXPERIENCE* and *OTHER INTERNATIONAL EXPERIENCE.* (For an example of this approach, see the Program Manager Resume in Appendix 24b on the CD-ROM.)

It is very powerful to group your work experience into separate sections. This helps recruiters to understand your "career labels" and to quickly focus on important jobs and skim the less important ones. Even the length of your job descriptions should clearly indicate their level of importance in supporting your career objective. Important jobs are written in greater detail and less important jobs are written briefly. If a past job did not support your objective then do not write a lot of detail about it! List the most important jobs at the top, not necessarily the most recent ones.

WRITING JOB DESCRIPTIONS

The following strategies will help you with the mechanics of writing a job description. This section first discusses the job header (title, employer, dates, etc.) and finishes with the actual description.

The Job Header

Here is the standard order for listing information in a job description: the job title comes first and is discussed below. The next item is the name of the employer (this could be written in SMALL CAPS to promote speed-reading) followed by the city, province and country. The country is important in an international resume and should be written in UPPER CASE so that it stands out. Don't include supervisors' names, phone numbers, street addresses, or e-mail or Web addresses. This information is reserved for the *References* section. If your current employer is unaware that you are seeking other employment, you may wish to write *"in confidence"* next to the employer name to ensure that your employer won't be contacted without your consent.

Young professionals are often very concerned about employment dates on their resumes. Here are the basics: unless you have an impeccable and progressive career history, you may wish to avoid highlighting dates. Dates of employment should be on the right-hand side of the page. To further de-emphasize them, simply place job dates (inside parentheses) after the country name. Be consistent with date formats. Always include months, always use the four-digit year. Here are the standard formats: (Aug. 2003 to June 2004) or (08/2003 – 06/2004), (July 2004 to present), (Summers 2003/2004), (Fall 2004).

Sample job headers with functional job titles:

Program Officer Intern
AGA KHAN FOUNDATION CANADA, Ottawa, ON, CANADA (07/2003 – 08/2003)

Conference Organizer and Field Support Intern
COWATER INTERNATIONAL, Dhaka, BANGLADESH (08/2003 – 04/2004)

Water and Agricultural Project Engineer
CANADIAN INTERNATIONAL DEVELOPMENT AGENCY (CIDA) and THE ZAMBIAN MINISTRY OF AGRICULTURE, Ikelenge, ZAMBIA (07/2003 – 08/2003)

Functional Job Titles

Job titles deserve special attention. A good job title allows the reader to "see the work" when it is read. The problem is that official titles assigned by past employers are often vague and have no meaning outside of your old place of work. The solution; change your title to one that more clearly represents what you did! Develop functional job titles. This will give the reader a clear overview of your experience.

Here are some examples of how to write a functional job title. Replace *"Intern"* with *"Micro-Credit Intern"* or *"Teacher"* with *"Overseas English Teacher in Adult Learning Environment."* *"Teaching Assistant"* can be improved by writing *"Teaching Assistant in Macroeconomics."* The main idea is to improve clarity and match your work to support the career objective. Here are more examples. Replace *"Engineer Intern"* with *"Intern Assistant to the Director of Engineering."* Replace *"Field Researcher"* with *"Nutritional Health Researcher in Nepal."*

Some of you may be uncomfortable with changing an official title for a more functional title of your own creation. In our opinion, it is not deceptive if the new job titles better represents what you actually did. If you are still uncomfortable, retain the new functional titles in the job header, but begin your job descriptions with the official title. Example: *"As the OAC Standards Officer, I was responsible for ..."*

Big Ideas for Writing Job Descriptions

Do not write detailed descriptions about a task that does not support your objective. If you are trying to land a job as a program officer, and your last job was only 20 per cent programming and 80 per cent fundraising, write most of your job description about programming and describe fundraising only in the last sentence. Example: *"Responsible for public awareness programs, special events and donor relations."*

One of the key strategies in documenting your work experience is to describe jobs in terms of what you accomplished and how you accomplished it, rather than listing the positions you held and the duties you were assigned. The recruiter is interested in what you can do (your accomplishments) and not what you were responsible for. A monotone description of duties conveys little information to an employer. Talk about the problems you solved, what you achieved, why you were promoted and what programs you initiated.

For your most important jobs, consider creating functional categories within each job description. This is a very powerful technique that puts you in charge of how the recruitment office views your skills. For example, you could break down a job description into: *Marketing, Administration, Writing.* Make sure that there is a link between these functional categories and your skills summary on page one of your resume. With functional categories, you are promoting speed-reading; this is especially important for longer resumes. (For an example of this approach, see the Robin Millar Resume at the end of this chapter.)

It is very helpful for recruiters if you start important job descriptions with a one- or two-sentence employer introduction, providing background information on a past employer or project. The recruiter most likely does not know your past international employers and is therefore at a loss to judge the context of your experience. This employer introduction is located immediately after the job header and is often written in italics to differentiate it from the detailed description that follows. Example: *"This project was funded by NUTRICAN, a small Vancouver NGO focused on women's and children's health and working mainly in Central America."* (For examples of this strategy, see the Lily Wong Resume at the end of this chapter or the Education Policy Advisor Resume in Appendix 24d on the CD-ROM.)

Each important job in your resume should have one success story as part of the job description. Example: *"Was first to develop reliable survey format that...."* *"Recognized by employer for having successfully...."* *"Achieved success on this difficult project because...."* *" Appreciated by colleagues for having resolved...."* *"Successfully managed transition towards...."* Insert only one success story per job, and only for important jobs. Try to put the success story in the middle of the job description to ensure that reader has already absorbed the context of the job being described.

The Details for Writing Job Descriptions

Here are a few more tips for writing job descriptions within the international resume.

To help recruiters place your job description in its proper context, start job descriptions with a sentence about the scope and breadth of your responsibilities. For example, you could describe an overseas stint as Office Manager in a refugee camp this way: *"As part of a four-person executive team overseeing the settlement of 22,000 Angolan refugees, managed eight local professional staff and supervised the disbursement of $5-million for community projects."* Another example: Volunteer President of Campus International Development Week: *"Successfully led a 4-member executive team to organize 14 events attended by 1,800 participants, with 45 volunteers and a budget of $11,500."*

Sort items according to how well they support your objective. Don't make the mistake of listing tasks in historical order or by size. Instead, start with the tasks that best show how you match the employer's ideal profile.

Use the active voice and action verbs to emphasize your experience. Employers are interested in knowing *why* you were promoted or *why* you are successful. Here are a few examples of phrases that point to the why of your accomplishments: *"aptitude for,"* *"proficient in the use of,"* *"was recognized as,"* *"became known for,"* *"was identified as."*

Another effective strategy is to attach a major skill to a job description: *"Due to the nature of this project this position required flexibility and versatility."* Use this technique sparingly—overuse will diminish your credibility.

Quantify your accomplishments. Be specific: *"Increased membership by 30 per cent. Reduced turnover time by four weeks. Increased public inquiries tenfold."* Examine your previous positions, and try to measure your past successes.

If you held several positions with a firm, emphasize the progression by stating, *"Advanced from desk clerk to area supervisor in three months."* If you suffered a demotion, then simply mention the new skills you learned. Your future employer need not know that your most recent position carried less responsibility than your previously-held one.

A Note to Career Changers

Your resume should clearly convey the link between your past work experience and your overseas career objective. As described in the previous chapters, many jobs require certain skills or qualifications that may be applicable to an overseas assignment. Every attempt should be made to portray your past jobs in terms of the ideal profile being sought by international employers.

You should edit and rework your job descriptions to highlight only those experiences that are relevant to the position you are currently seeking. Draw attention to the international aspects of each of your experiences in terms of character traits, adaptability to new environments and cultural sensitivity. For example, if you previously worked as a career counsellor and are seeking a position in international development, you would emphasize those skills you possess in community liaison work and project design, rather than your skills in job creation and employment counselling.

Reinforce your new career objective by eliminating in-house jargon from your previous employer; instead, use the language of your potential international employer.

Professional Certification and Memberships

If you're a teacher, doctor or engineer, or if you work within a profession or trade where provincial certification is required, you should provide the full details of your licensing as well as an address where your credentials can be verified. Attach photocopies of your certificates, especially to employers based overseas. Never send original certificates.

Include only current affiliations relevant to the position you're seeking. Recent graduates should list all affiliations to demonstrate their level of participation and experience. If you don't belong to any professional association, you may wish to join one.

Professional Certification and Memberships can be listed as the first or last item in the Professional Experience section of the resume. Alternatively, it can be inserted in the Education or Personal Data sections—wherever it fits best to suit your logic and formatting restrictions.

YOUR EDUCATION

Younger professionals should write up their education experience more extensively, just as if it were a job. Since people now have up to seven years of post-secondary schooling, there is more to be said about your education than just mentioning your degree and university name. This section will point out a few tactics to help bring out your personality for international employers.

If you are a recent graduate, you may wish to list your education after your career objective. It is most likely your strongest asset. If you are mid-career or if you have relevant work experience but not an advanced or recent degree, then you are better off adding your academic credentials at the end of your resume. Start with your most recent degree and work backwards. List your degree before your university: *"Bachelor of Education, York University."*

One powerful method for telling employers who you are is to say what you focused on in your studies. For each university degree, list your *Areas of Interest* or *Course Specialization*. This tells employers much more about you. Imagine three commerce students: One lists marketing as an area of interest, another lists management and the third lists finance. It's the same degree, but the students all clearly have very different expertise and personalities.

Do not provide a running list of course names in your resume; instead explain your studies through a skill you acquired. For example, instead of *"courses in Spanish literature,"* try, *"focused on developing an understanding of Hispanic culture."*

You might also consider including a new subsection under your degree, named *"Significant Projects"* or *"Field Studies."* These extra categories give your degree more value in your resume and allow you the opportunity to highlight group work, management skills, specific areas of expertise or even cross-cultural experience. There are a host of categories to include under Education. The following provide some of the main examples for projects, competition, group work, committee work, awards and others.

- **Major Design Project:** *The Eco-Bicycle. As part of a four-person team, was responsible for writing all project information, making formal presentations to faculty and industry, managing project schedule, and designing the control systems for the bicycle.*

- **Marketing Competition:** *As part of a team of four, was key presenter, taking fourth place at the Canada-wide McGill International Marketing competition.*

- **Cross-Cultural Mentor and Tutor:** *Informally assisted new international students with scholastic, social and logistical aspects of life in Canada.*

- **Laboratory User's Council:** *Appointed as student liaison on committee of department faculty and staff to discuss issues such as funding, safety, equipment availability and communications.*

- **Teaching Assistant and Award Recipient:** *Received the George Hamilton Award for significant contributions to classroom teaching in Civil Engineering. Gave lectures, performed tutorials, assisted with laboratory classes, and graded exams for university undergraduate engineering classes.* (Note: If you are short on professional experience, list academic internships, teaching assistant jobs or important research work separately as jobs. They are jobs. Don't bury them in your education section.)

- **Team Leader and Presenter** *for numerous class projects where I coordinated work schedules, facilitated meetings, and acted as key software support person for Microsoft Excel and Microsoft Access.*

- **International Teams:** *Gained valuable cross-cultural experience by purposely choosing to work with international students throughout my degree. Successfully completed projects within a diverse multicultural student team.*

If your school is very well recognized, do not assume that this is common knowledge, especially where an international employer is concerned. Consider adding a sentence immediately after your degree such as, *"Recognized as the leading international relations program in Canada"* or *"One of the top engineering schools in the Northeastern US"* or *"Johns Hopkins University is recognized worldwide in the health field for its teaching and innovative research"* or *"Praised as Canada's best engineering school, the University of Waterloo is internationally recognized for its co-op program, which gives students two full years of practical experience during their degree."*

If your academic standing was "B+" or higher, by all means, include it in your resume! For example, you might wish to add *"consistent 85% average,"* *"dean's honour list,"* or *"graduated with honours."* If you managed any unusual challenges or obstacles during your studies, indicate this: *"maintained a B average while consistently holding a part time job and actively volunteering with numerous student groups."*

You may also list published works, theses and conferences you've attended if they are relevant to your overseas job search. If you have several of these, consider grouping them together in a separate section titled *PUBLICATIONS* or *CONFERENCES*.

If you're just about to graduate, state this clearly: *"graduating in December 200X."* If you're currently in an MA or PhD program, then state, *"MA in Political Science (course work completed, thesis scheduled for completion in August 200X)."* If you've taken courses leading to a degree, but didn't complete the program, then you can write *"Student of Middle Eastern Studies (six courses taken towards a BA); PhD (course work completed); MBA (in progress); Registered Dietician (certification in progress, estimated completion date January 200X)"*.

University graduates needn't mention their high school curriculum unless they wish to highlight a particular achievement— for example: *"voted student of the year"* or *"educated for six years in French immersion program."* Do include high school experiences if they have an international component. Example: *"KINDERGARTEN TO JUNIOR HIGH, INTERNATIONAL SCHOOLS IN PHILIPPINES. I attended international schools under the British curriculum while my father was an engineer with Shell Oil. As part of my experience, we travelled extensively, often in remote areas, throughout Southeast Asia."* Or: *EDUCATED AND RAISED IN KENYA: Lived in rural and urban settings with missionary parents working on development projects and distributing aid. Attended Rift Valley Academy, a boarding school in Kijave Kenya, accredited by the American Middle States Association of Colleges and Secondary Schools."* Be sure to list any childhood overseas living experience that lasted six months or longer.

Exchange programs, immersion programs, student government, debate teams, or activities like a model UN should all be included in your education section.

Non-academic courses should be included if they support your career objective. Example, *"St. John Ambulance First Aid Course, Car Maintenance Courses, Management Development Seminars, and Leadership Training."* These courses are best listed at the end of your resume and generally not with academic credentials.

International study, whether for credit or not, generally deserves special mention. Provide context; consider highlighting the cross-cultural experience or your level of involvement. Example: *"Active participant in on-campus student life. Travelled often with Swiss students to visit their families and participate in community events. Was known as most active foreign student involved in on-campus human rights organizations. Worked part time as an intern architectural assistant and gained valuable insights into the trans-European personality."*

List separately all *awards and scholarships* you've received, especially those earned during university. Many international employers look at these awards as initiative indicators and illustrations of important character traits. Don't neglect to mention leadership awards from service clubs and sport groups. When listing your awards and scholarships, always indicate what each award is for: *"Commonwealth award for best undergraduate paper in international relations."* If you are an overall top achiever, separate your awards into two categories under the headings *"Awards for Academic Achievement"* and *"Awards for Community and Sport Involvement."*

VOLUNTEER WORK AND PROFESSIONAL HOBBIES

Volunteer work can demonstrate that you possess leadership skills, the ability to work independently, and other attributes that are pertinent to an overseas posting. It is sometimes viewed as being on par with paid employment. If you have significant volunteer experience, by all means list it under work experience. Professional volunteer work should be written up exactly the same as a job.

If you have numerous volunteer experiences and professional hobbies, attempt to group them under logical headings to assist the recruiter in speed-reading. For example, you could categorize this way: *INTERNATIONAL VOLUNTEER EXPERIENCE* (domestic and abroad) and *CHORAL & PIANO VOLUNTEER EXPERIENCE.* As this last example suggests, you should group significant non-career supporting experience together. Other examples are athletics, political activities and social activism experiences. These will have more impact if they are grouped together under their own separate subheadings. It can also be helpful to write an introductory sentence to explain the breadth of your involvement before enumerating a list of accomplishments. Example: *"I have been actively involved with various choral groups for the past 8 years, including the executive team as treasurer and conference organizer for multiple events attended often by over 30 choirs and 1,200 participants."*

Always be aware of drawing out the cross-cultural aspects of each experience, even if the experience is domestic. Example: *"Gained valuable experience working in a multicultural environment with new immigrants."*

PERSONAL DATA

Personal data is best listed at the very end of your resume since these details can detract from the importance of your career objective, personal and professional skills, and work history. Many of the items often excluded from North American resumes (age, marital status and nationality) are often crucial to overseas recruiters. Overseas employers don't always follow the guidelines with regard to domestic employment laws. Consider including the following in a Personal Data section in your resume: *Date of Birth, Marital Status and Dependents, Spouse's Occupation, Mobility and Availability, Language, Nationality* (including in some instances, *Ethnicity and Religion*), *Security Clearance, Foreign Travel, Hobbies, Contact Information* and *References*.

Date of Birth

Age is often an important consideration in overseas positions. Despite overtones of discrimination, it is a reality that must be addressed. For example, young people between the ages of 24 and 30 are often automatically considered for entry-level positions. Young professionals in this age bracket may actually benefit by listing their date of birth. Young people are hired for enthusiasm, hardiness under difficult conditions, good health, and technology skills. And best of all, they don't cost as much as a mid-career professionals. People over 50 are rarely considered for hardship postings. Older applicants are automatically (though informally) favoured by many traditional organizations such as the UNITED NATIONS and foreign governments, where, contrary to Canadian norms, ability can take second place to age in assessing a person's capacity to manage a department.

Mobility and Availability

Availability is an important category in many instances. You may have a definite preference for certain countries, or you may wish to state, *"Availability: Immediate for worldwide employment."* Clearly state your availability date if you're currently employed overseas and still have to complete your current contract. Other examples are: *"Mobility: able and willing to undertake short-term travel. Single, no dependants."* or *"Available immediately for one- to three-year contract accompanied by spouse and one preschool-aged child."*

Marital Status and Dependants

International employers will be concerned with your family situation; housing, education, and benefits are crucial issues that must be addressed. Being single has its advantages: unaccompanied individuals are less costly to an employer. If you're single and applying for a hardship post where families are unlikely to be sent, it's to your advantage to inform a recruiter of your single status. On the other hand, if you're married but have worked out an arrangement with your family to work abroad, you may wish to state, *"Married, willing to consider* (or *available for*) *single status posting."* If you are married with no dependents, this should also be mentioned.

Children are often a crucial factor in the final hiring process; you may either wish to omit the subject of children in your resume or give brief mention to being *"married with two school-aged dependents."* Some candidates prefer to provide full details of their dependants: names, ages and schooling status. Either way, the topic of children will most certainly arise during the interview process, and the issue of placement and mobility will have to be addressed. Finding the right overseas school for high school students can be a difficult matter; this is sometimes resolved through placing them in a boarding school. University-aged children are usually considered independent.

Many employers insist on conducting interviews with the spouses of their employees; it's common knowledge that a spouse's enthusiasm (or lack of same) can impact one's effectiveness when working abroad.

Spouse's Occupation

If your spouse has intentions of seeking work overseas, you should briefly mention his or her occupation in the event that a work opportunity may arise. Many employers promote the idea of working couples and are often helpful with overseas employment opportunities. It is especially important to list your spouse's occupation if she or he has a mobile career such as nursing, teaching, writing, consulting and all forms of home training. Here is an example of a relevant description: *"Spouse: Mark Nurani, Canadian citizen. MSc Rural Extension Studies from the University of Chicago: specialized in Third World agriculture, adult education and community development. Possesses unique blend of science and social science experience. Resume available upon request."* (For information on job hunting strategies when going abroad as a couple, see Chapter 20, The Job Search & Targeting Your Research.)

Languages

List all the ones that you know, no matter how obscure. In most cases, knowledge of a second language is a prerequisite to working overseas. Even if the language is uncommon, second language proficiency is an indicator of your ability to learn other languages. You must rate your language proficiency in the areas of reading, writing, speaking/comprehension. To organize this section, you may have to set up a small table with three or more columns: Language, Speaking/Comprehension, Reading/ Writing. Common terms for describing language aptitude are *basic, beginner, functional, conversational, intermediate, fluent, advanced,* and *fully proficient.* Do not use *"poor writing ability,"* but rather *"beginner-level writing."* If it is not clearly visible, indicate which language is your first language, since employers often seek native speakers.

If you are fluent enough to work at a basic level in a second language, you should invest in a professionally translated resume. Put a note at the end of your resume saying, *"Resume also available in English/French/Spanish"* and always send both resumes together when approaching non-native English speaking employers.

If you are good with languages, you can note in your skills summary *"adept at learning languages"* or *"ability and interest in learning languages."* You can further increase the value of your language section with the following suggested sentences. *"Enjoy cultural interaction when learning a new language"* or *"Ability to pick up languages quickly while travelling for short periods in new countries."* If you are a language aficionado, say so: *"Lifelong interest in languages and learning about new cultures."*

Security Clearance

For work with federal governments and their contractors, you may have (or in the past have had) security clearance. Mention the clearance level along with the date obtained and other relevant information such as *"security clearance can be upgraded to X level."*

Nationality and National Origin

If you're forwarding your resume to an employer outside of your country, by all means mention your nationality. If you were born abroad, but have become a US or Canadian citizen or landed immigrant, you should indicate so. Many North American organizations look favourably upon their foreign-born citizens since these individuals often carry dual citizenship along with an understanding of another culture. If you think your religious or ethnic background will help you adjust to a particular overseas working environment, then it would be beneficial to mention this in your resume. This is one example of a US citizen living in Canada and looking for international work with Canadian or US private sector firms: *"Nationality: US citizen and Canadian landed immigrant (citizenship in progress); fully eligible for Canadian and US employment."*

Foreign Travel

You should include the dates and names of countries you've visited as evidence that you've been exposed to other cultures. Employers look favourably upon candidates who have shown an interest in exploring cultures other than their own. In fact, previous foreign travel is practically a prerequisite to international employment. A long list of overseas travel (even tourist travel) can add many points to your candidacy. Be creative. Title the section: *CROSS-CULTURAL TRAVEL.* Add sentences in conjunction with the list of countries visited. Example: *"Lifelong interest in cross-cultural living and work; enjoy interacting with other people and cultures. Travelled extensively in West Africa and South Asia. Lived often with local families and adapted well to varied social and economic conditions. Enjoy building a wide cross-section of relationships when travelling to meet clients all over Europe. Able to integrate and adapt under difficult political and socio-economic conditions. Enjoyed the challenges and rewards of cross-cultural communications while travelling throughout Asia and Africa."* Do not just copy from these sentences; search within yourself to find the best sentence to describe what motivates you and what you learn when travelling.

Hobbies

Hobbies can be contentious because they often do not support your career objective. On the other hand, they do provide a glimpse into your broader personality, which is often important to international employers. Listing hobbies may even lead to a personal connection with a recruiter. As such, our recommendation is to write a short list of hobbies without going into lengthy details. Look to reinforce a connection with your career objective where you can.

Personal Statement on Your Field of Work

This is a bold tactic designed to show your personality type. It is used by those young professionals who are entering a crowded field and are willing to take a risk with an unconventional format to score extra points in the resume.

The personal statement on your field of work is a carefully written paragraph outlining your personal beliefs about your area of expertise. This paragraph shows in a practical way how you apply your expertise in the workplace. This tactic is especially useful if you are short on professional international experience but have volunteer or travel experience which you can use to demonstrate how you put your academic training into action. This paragraph is generally inserted just before the Personal Data section, toward the end of the resume. (See the last page of the Marc Doucet Resume at the end of this chapter.)

Contact Information

Your name, address, phone numbers and e-mail should be prominently positioned in your resume. Our suggestion is that you include them on the last page since there is often no room on the first page because your career objective and skill summary take up all the space there.

Since international hiring often has long lead times, include both a personal contact address (current address) and a permanent contact address and phone number (your parents' address or some other fixed address that is very unlikely to change). It is especially important to have an e-mail address that won't change for at least three years. A recent survey of large non-governmental organizations showed that at least 20 per cent of the candidates who were listed in resume data banks couldn't be contacted because they left no forwarding addresses or their e-mail address no longer functioned. Many organizations keep their promising resumes on file for a year, and some organizations have been known to retain them for as long as three or four years.

Since your resume is often circulated overseas, you should include *"CANADA"* or *"USA"* in the address. To avoid confusion, all abbreviations in the address should be omitted. Area codes for telephone numbers should be included, and consider adding country codes if your resume is circulated overseas. Example: *1 (212) 596-1693.* Be sure to use a trustworthy mail service provider that gives you enough storage space so that your account will not become overloaded. If you use a free mail service such as hotmail or yahoo, make sure you log onto your account frequently enough to keep it from being deactivated. Finally, choose an e-mail address that closely resembles your name and is easy to remember. For professional purposes, avoid using cutesy email addresses such as *"yippeeboy@aol.com."*

You may also need to purchase an answering machine or subscribe to a voice mail service. Otherwise, it's imperative that you have a telephone number where you can be contacted at all hours of the day, or where messages are taken on your behalf. Keep your voice mail message professional and upbeat. Remember, employers are evaluating you at every level, especially if they are at the stage of phoning you.

To avoid confusion about your gender, consider writing *"Mr."* or *"Ms."* in parentheses and in a smaller font. Men may place *"(Mr.)"* after their names while women should place *"(Ms.)"* in front of their names, in order to avoid any confusion with *(MSc.),* Master of Science. You may hesitate about indicating your gender, but international employers want to know how to address you in correspondence, and in China they might not know that "Louise" is female, just as some Canadians might not know that "Shyam" is male.

References

Young professionals often have a narrow range when choosing references. You should develop a broad list. For example, do not list more than two professors in a list of four references since professors are generally seen by employers as less objective (i.e., they are always positive about their students). Try to choose professors only if you have an employment history together or have a long-term relationship. Past employers are your best option for a reference. If you have few reference options, an alternative option is a professional friend of the family or personal friend with a professional background. Ensure that you have a nicely formatted list of references at the ready; always indicate your relationship to the reference (examples: *past employer, thesis director, professional friend of family*) and include full contact information including e-mail address.

Don't list references in your resume. Complete your resume with the phrase *"References available upon request."* A good reason for not listing the names and addresses of references is that organizations sometimes verify these references indiscriminately by sending out lengthy evaluation questionnaires, regardless of job openings. To avoid fatiguing your references, you want to control the number of reference checks to ensure that only serious potential employers are calling your references.

Whenever you give a reference's name to a prospective employer, you should contact the reference to let them know. This is a matter of common courtesy, and more importantly, it lets you debrief your reference about the kind of questions the employer might ask. References need to know about the specific job requirements.

Does the job entail customer service abilities, writing, research, administration, independent thinking? Each job is different, and your reference will want to prepare in advance to speak effectively about your skills and the job at hand. There is nothing dishonest about coaching a reference—it is a smart move. Finally, it is important to always thank your references and to inform them when you are successful in finding work.

There are a number of situations in which it would be advantageous to supply reference letters along with your resume. Examples: where transit time is a consideration or if you want to expedite the application process. If you're just beginning your career after a stint of volunteer work overseas, references from overseas host employers who are difficult to reach by mail could also strengthen the credibility of your dossier.

THE "DO NOT MENTIONS"

You should delete all information that doesn't support your career objective or is irrelevant to the position you're seeking.

Don't give a reason for terminating a position in a resume. During the interview process, avoid detailed discussions of past controversies or conflicts. When they're brought up, keep your explanations brief. Avoid lengthy justifications of your behaviour and end the topic on a positive and non-vindictive note.

Omit salary expectations or past salary levels in your resume. This should be reserved for the interview.

Avoid the mention of political or religious affiliations. If you have extensive experience in religious or political groups, but your work experience is weak, then simply describe your role in the organization without mentioning its name. For instance, the *Young Men's Evangelical Society* could be described as a *Large religious organization*; a political party could be referred to as a *Large mainstream political party*. When the information is requested, mention the organization's name, but don't dwell on its religious or political aspects. By applying these tactics, you are showing that you are able to have boundaries around your political or religious beliefs and not bring them into the office of your future employer.

In some circumstances, it is best not to over-emphasize any *military experience* you have had. It may be frowned upon and you may wish to omit it altogether. Conversely, military experience is valuable in some international positions (examples: logistics, relief work, security work) and it can be mentioned. These questions revolve around the employer rather than the specific sector of employment.

Many international organizations require a photo, but don't include one unless it's requested. Send only passport photos or an equivalent (a picture taken from the shoulders up).

Don't list your passport, social insurance or social security numbers.

WRITING STYLE

Clear writing is essential in international job searches. The task of writing your resume can be quite arduous. It's perfectly reasonable to spend a total of three to five days over a three-week period working on the final copy of your resume. The following are important points to remember:

- Omit all information that doesn't support your career objective.

- Your resume needs to be the most efficient document you have ever written. After completing your resume, reread it from beginning to end with the intention of eliminating everything superfluous or imprecise.

- Be selective in using the creative tactics described throughout this chapter. List only your strongest skills and traits and keep this list short. Describe one career success story per job, and only for the two or three most important jobs. Scatter cross-cultural awareness information throughout your resume, but limit this information to four or six occurrences.

- Use the terminology of your chosen field. Find this by studying detailed job descriptions (often senior positions) posted on the Web sites of leading organizations in your field.

- Be efficient in your job descriptions. Generally keep your resume under four pages, but don't sacrifice valuable information about your expertise to save space.

- Be direct. Focus on what you did and the results that were achieved.

- Be clear. Use short words, short sentences, and short paragraphs. Use outline format. Stay away from narrative paragraphs in job descriptions.

- Be consistent. In listing your work history, use the same format and sequence of information for each job. Use the same verb format, dating style, and fonts and character styles.

- Be careful with the overuse of adjectives and adverbs; rely instead on precise wording. *"Organized"* is stronger than *"very organized."*

- Use professional terms when describing yourself; stay away from colloquial terminology. Tell employers that you have strong collaboration, people or management skills, not that you are friendly, fun or nice.

- Never use an acronym without first mentioning the full title. For example: *"Non-governmental Organization (NGO),"* or *"Canadian International Development Agency (CIDA)."* After you've mentioned the full title once, you can use the acronym in the remainder of your resume.

- Your resume must be grammatically correct. Punctuation and spelling must be perfect.

You should have your resume professionally evaluated for clarity, order, continuity, etc. Your friends may not be the best readers; a professional acquaintance may be better. In either case, make it clear that you are looking for honest, constructive feedback, not just a pat on the back.

Your venture into the international job market will heighten your sensitivity to the nature of the marketplace. Don't hesitate to make improvements to your resume format or to add to the content of the resume using the terminology appropriate to the international field.

Sell Yourself with the Active Voice and Action Verbs

Use the active voice and action verbs to animate your accomplishments throughout your resume. This writing style allows the reader to better envision you in action and to "see" the work being performed. For example, *"successfully managed," "independently designed and developed," "trained staff in two departments"* or *"cultivated relationships with NGO representatives and government officials"* all serve to describe and amplify your skills. The following list is grouped so that you can choose from a wide cross-section of desirable skill sets: *Organized/Takes Initiative; Creative; Analytical; Team Player; Leader; Personable; Successful; Skilled Communicator; Reliable/Responsible; Knowledgeable.*

Organized / Takes Initiative	Analytical	Leader
organized	devised	led
reorganized	defined	decided
coordinated	identified	directed
maintained	classified	supervised
implemented	assembled	executed
conducted	gathered	oversaw
converted	compiled	managed
restructured	searched	administered
constructed	researched	instituted
designed	manipulated	spearheaded
planned	analyzed	initiated
standardized	interpreted	guided
consolidated	assessed	emphasized
tracked	compared	regulated
monitored	evaluated	delegated
scheduled	diagnosed	assigned
programmed	tested	charged with
distributed	computed	motivated
filed	measured	negotiated
reduced the cost	calculated	consultant to
	estimated	
	generated	**Personable**
Creative		listened
created		facilitated
designed	**Team Player**	moderated
redesigned	assisted	convinced
developed	helped	sold
envisioned	collaborated	obtained
formulated	liaised	recruited
conceived	built/cultivated	enlisted
conceptualized	relationships with	supported
invented	interacted	encouraged
located	communicated	counselled
arranged	contributed to	taught
simplified	answered to	tutored
modified	united	trained
adapted	strengthened	mentored
repaired	involved in	instructed
introduced	consulted with	coached
	worked closely	presented
		cared for

Successful	Skilled Communicator	Reliable/ Responsible
succeeded	published	prepared
achieved	co-authored	responded to
delivered	composed	handled
completed	wrote	secured
accomplished	edited	served as
improved	copy-edited	dealt with
increased	reviewed	performed
resolved	revised	established
uncovered	retrieved	volunteered
earned award for	researched	maintained
recognized as/for	summarized	ensured
was known for	synthesized	specialized
was appreciated for	communicated	focused on
was first to	demonstrated	
accredited for	represented	**Knowledgeable**
elected to	spoke	adept
excelled in	advocated	experienced
chosen for	promoted	skilled
selected from/for	persuaded	equality skilled in
discovered	explained	expert
promoted	illustrated	qualifications in
named	perceived	demonstrated
awarded	outlined	competency in
	printed	
	produced	
	recorded	

FORMAT FOR INTERNATIONAL RESUMES

Your resume should be visually designed for speed-reading, especially if you follow the many suggestions in this chapter, which tend to lengthen resumes to three or four pages. The objective with formatting is to catch the recruiter's attention on the first reading with the aim of obtaining a second, more detailed reading. This means you should consistently format each section and subsection. Each position should begin with a functional job title (the most important summary of your work), followed by employer information, then the description. Use point form as much as possible.

Errors and poor formatting can seriously damage your chances of getting a job. It can take hours to perfectly format your resume, but it's worth the investment. A number of formatting styles can easily promote readability. For instance:

- Promote speed-reading with the consistent use of subcategories, functional job titles and headings, and consistent formatting.

- Ensure that blocks of information are easily recognizable. Subcategories should all be related to the main category they come under.

- Minimize the use of underline in favour of bold fonts, upper case, small caps, and changes in font size.

- Use narrow margins to insert more information without making the resume appear lengthy.

- Minimize the use of varied fonts and font sizes. Use a maximum of two different styles. Do not be overly creative in layout unless you are in sales or marketing.

- Do not use fancy symbols of any kind except bullets and dashes.

- In the header or footer, discreetly indicate your name, the page number and the total number of pages (e.g., page 3 of 4).

- Use the "show formatting" feature on your word processor to make sure your formatting is well done. A messy or inefficient use of formatting features tells employers a lot about your computer skills.

- Consider using yellow highlighting to emphasize the experience in your resume that corresponded with the formal job posting.

- Have your resume proofread by someone with a good eye for layout or consider employing a professional do the formatting work. Resumes are often unappealingly formatted, and with a very small investment, you can easily stand out.

E-MAIL RESUME TIPS

Since e-mailing resumes is now the norm, here are a few essential tips.

- Send your resume as an attachment. Do not paste your resume directly into the body of your e-mail where you have little or no control over formatting.

- Your cover letter should also be attached as a separate file. Treat it with the respect it deserves. Do not insert it in the body of the e-mail (where it cannot be formatted) and do not include it in the same file as your resume.

- It is acceptable to send attachments in MS Word format but not other word processing programs—the employer may not be able to read them. MS Word does have its problems, however, since the formatting is often modified when printed on another printer. The safest strategy is to send your resume using the pdf format since this platform guarantees that your resume will always print the same way, no matter what printer is used. Adobe software is the most common choice for creating pdf files.

- Give careful consideration to your file-naming convention. Your employer will appreciate receiving clearly labelled file attachments such as: *"Mark-Doucet-Resume-20040815.pdf"* and *"Mark-Doucet-Cover-20040815.pdf"*.

- The most overlooked aspect of e-mailing a resume and cover letter is the short text written in the accompanying e-mail—the "cover e-mail." Most job candidates treat this component lightly but it is clearly part of your application package. Use the cover e-mail to highlight your top skills. Entice the reader with a personable and professional message. Keep the message formal and professional. Write in full sentences.

- Pay close attention to creating an appropriate e-mail subject heading and insert a key skill. Here are three separate examples: *"Application for Policy Analyst position with previous policy experience." "Researcher with expertise in Access and Fox Pro." "Intern applicant with MA in International Relations and Mandarin language skills."*

- Consider sending a paper copy by mail a few days after sending your e-mail resume. A second copy will keep your resume alive in the minds of employers and will look more professional when it is sitting in a pile of 100 resumes sent by e-mail. Make your resume stand out by printing both the resume and cover letter on bond paper. Send by express mail with a printed label for a more professional look. If possible, put on a business suit and deliver by hand for even more impact.

Web Site and Multimedia Resumes

You can also feature your resume on your own Web site. Graphics, pictures, videos, sounds, hypertext links to your publications or photographs of your work, and direct e-mail are all features that can be incorporated. Be forewarned that these types of resumes are ideal mostly for those in the multimedia field. For the rest of us, simple, text-based resumes are appropriate because most employers are not going to actively look on the Internet for your Web site.

Scannable Resumes and the Importance of Keywords

Many large companies are increasingly using automated databases (applicant tracking systems) to select new employees from a pool of candidates. A computer will read your electronic resume before the human recipient, and if the computer cannot read it due to complicated formatting, your resume will be discarded. Employers may request scannable resumes in job advertisements; in general, it's a good idea to contact employers and ask whether or not a scannable resume is appropriate, and what their formatting requirements are.

Resumes can be submitted to an employer's resume database using a variety of methods. You can use e-mail, conventional mail, or fill in an on-line form on the company Web site. Wherever possible, send your resume electronically to avoid the possible mishaps of the scanning process. Consider sending two copies of your resume—a regular one with formatting, fonts, etc. and a scannable one labelled "for scanning."

Formatting Scannable Resumes

- Send original resumes. If you are not e-mailing your resume then send it by regular mail. Photocopies and faxed copies will degrade the text when it is scanned by the employer's scanning system.
- Use 8 ½″ x 11″ paper, printed on one side only.
- Use wide margins.
- Font should be Courier, Helvetica, or Arial; in these fonts characters are least likely to blend together and be misread by the scanner.
- Point size should be 10 to 14.
- Do not use tabs, columns, italics, underlining, bold or coloured text, brackets or parentheses.

- If you must use slashes (/), insert a space on either side to make sure the slash does not touch any letters, thereby making them confusing for the scanner.
- Do not use compressed lines of text.
- Resumes should not be folded.
- Do not use staples. They will not go through the scanners.
- Depending on the type of system the employer uses, you may be able to include a cover letter.

Keywords

Having the right keywords is vital to your resume's effectiveness. The computer searches for resumes that contain keywords describing the qualifications needed by the company. If it doesn't find the prescribed keywords in your resume, it will move onto the next candidate. Experts recommend adding a *"Keyword Summary"* to your scannable resume. This is simply a list of synonyms that describe your field of work, your skills, and your abilities. Here are some tips for choosing keywords for your resume:

- Use industry-specific nouns and phrases; avoid verbs if possible. (Employers don't usually use verbs because changes in tense make them hard to search.)
- Wherever possible, use the keywords listed in the job ad. If you don't have a specific job posting to work from, use terms that are common to the industry, companies or organizations that you were involved with.
- List your educational background including universities and colleges attended, major area of study, certificates and degrees.
- Examples of Keywords for Electronic Resumes: Accounts Payable, BA, Economics, Dalhousie University, Business Unit Manager, Cooperative, Coordinator, Cross-Cultural Communication, Demand Management, Detail-Minded, Distribution Network, Education, Grant Writing, Instructor, Interpersonal Skills, Java, Multi-Modal Analysis, Multi-Tasking, National Accounts Manager, Negotiator, Oracle, Oral Communication, Problem-Solving Abilities, Project Manager, Project Officer, Proposal Writing, Public Presentations, Public Relations, Representative, Sales Associate, Sales Manager, Teacher, Troubleshooting, Written Communication.

On-line Applications and Application Forms

It's often a practice with international organizations to have candidates complete a formal application form. The UNITED NATIONS "Personal History Form" is the best known of these forms as it is used widely by UNITED NATIONS agencies. These forms are taken very seriously by employers and it is important for you to carefully complete them with as much detail as possible.

On-line application forms are just as important as the traditional paper versions and should be completed with the same amount of care. On-line application forms do not have spell check capabilities, so be sure to check all of your spelling by writing the information in MS Word or a similar application first to verify your spelling. If you are unable to copy and paste into the form from another application, be sure to carefully check your spelling before submitting.

A word of caution about on-line application forms: inaccurate and/or incomplete question fields do not allow recruiters to fully consider the merits of the application, and make it difficult for them to proceed further. Do not leave a field blank. If it's left blank, recruiters wonder why it is blank and, as they probably receive many resumes, they will seldom take the time to probe for further information to fill in the blank.

Application forms ask for particular information from you that is important to the company; however, you may have relevant credentials or experience that do not fit into one of the form's designated fields. In this case, be sure to take advantage of comments boxes and other fields (often found at the bottom of a form) which allow you to provide the company with extra information.

RESUMES THAT WORK

The following sections provide background on the three resumes presented at the end of this chapter. The selection of resumes shows some different ways to apply the concepts presented in this chapter. Read all three resumes to retain a view of what might work for you. (To see how individuals from different fields can reinterpret the strategies presented in this chapter, see the four sample resumes on the CD-ROM. These items are also described below.)

The Marc Doucet Resume

The Marc Doucet resume is for an entry-level candidate with a master's degree in political science. This resume was used to acquire an entry-level position as a logistics officer with the UNITED NATIONS HIGH COMMISSION FOR REFUGEES (UNHCR). The candidate had only six months' overseas experience and had many interruptions in his professional and academic work history. Originally, he had written a traditional chronological resume, sending out forty copies to potential employers over a two-month period. He received no positive responses.

After spending six weeks on Internet research and direct phoning to international employers to build contacts, this job hunter compiled a very good picture of the ideal profile for his particular field. He rewrote his resume using the format laid out in this chapter, re-targeted his career objective with a supporting work history, and sent out his new version to the previously contacted 40 employers. Within two months, he received five job offers for work overseas!

Why did his second resume work? The candidate kept his occupational objective broad, but specific enough for entry-level positions. His major traits indicated that he had the personality to survive and be productive in his field. The grouping of experience into "Understanding of International Development" and "Business Expertise" matched the combination of skills most sought by the employer. The amount of overseas experience was stretched by emphasizing volunteer work in Canada along with a personal statement regarding his management philosophy. Many of his phrases and words were taken directly from conversations with his potential employers.

The Lily Wong Resume

This resume is for an entry-level candidate with a bachelor of science and an interest in nutrition. The resume employs most of the techniques outlined in this chapter, tailored for someone with a science background. It is especially unique in the way it uses the concepts of grouping to support the career objective and to assist the recruiter in the analysis of the candidate's suitability for international work. While it is a very densely packed, four-page resume, the grouping and functional titles allow the reader to speed-read the titles and grasp the essence of the candidate's experience with ease.

Careful attention was paid to the titles, subtitles and job titles, ensuring that all support the career objective. Note also the italicized introductions to many of the job descriptions and educational degrees—these descriptions provide important background information that help international recruiters understand the background or context.

The Robin Millar Resume

The Robin Millar resume is for a senior-level candidate wanting to work in policy. The candidate has just moved to Geneva with her husband and she has 20 years of experience.

Her resume combines the chronological and functional resume formats. While young professionals will be able to use many of the writing tactics shown in the resume, this document is more conservative. Robin Millar does not have to be as creative in presenting her skills since she already has a lot of experience. The challenge with a more senior resume is to organize a wide range of job experiences into a readable and understandable format. The most important (and challenging) part is the summary of professional skills on page one. This page summarizes a complicated but enticing set of skills. Note how the bold skills headings on the first page are reinforced by the underlined functional job headings on the second and third pages. The resume is clearly set up for speed-reading (potential employers can quickly get a sense of the candidate by scanning the resume and reading only bold and underlined phrases). Concise descriptions are available in one short paragraph at a time.

APPENDIX TO CHAPTER 24 ON THE CD-ROM

There are four sample resumes in the Appendix to Chapter 24 on the CD-ROM. These have been chosen because they represent different fields of expertise than the resumes shown in the print edition of THE BIG GUIDE, and they highlight how different people can re-interpret the ideas presented in this chapter.

- **Sample Resume – Ahmed Khan, Engineer with IT and Development:** Ahmed's entry-level resume does an excellent job of using the section heading to list his most important skills. He also concisely lists his cross-cultural abilities at the end of his resume. (See Appendix 24a on the CD-ROM.)

- **Sample Resume – Larissa Brown, Program Manager:** Larissa's entry-level resume is particularly good at drawing together her widely varied experiences into logical groups, thus helping recruiters see her complex experiences as a meaningful picture. Her short skills summary (*"Demonstrated Competencies"*) does the same. (See Appendix 24b on the CD-ROM.) Note also how this resume is oriented toward Larissa's program experience, and downplays her translation experience. You should also read the companion story of how Larissa spent 10 interesting years building international experience. (See Larissa Brown's article,

"My Experience Preparing for an International Career" in Appendix 18a on the CD-ROM.)

- **Sample Resume – Erin Anderson, Water Resources Engineer:** Erin's entry-level resume was a challenge since the international work aspect was weak in comparison to her professional experience. We re-balanced the resume by dividing it into three equal chunks: the Education section (one whole page, written like job descriptions); the International section (expanded to fill a whole page) and the Employment History section (limited to one page). This ensures that over 30 per cent of Erin's impressive accomplishments are now being presented as international experience. The *"Skills Summary for International Engineering"* on page 4 further underlines her international experience, but this page is really optional since Erin has highlighted her key skills in the subheadings. (See Appendix 24c on the CD-ROM.)

- **Sample Resume – Peter Makundi, Education Policy Advisor:** Peter's senior-level resume is densely written, but formatted to promote speed-reading with functional job descriptions. Check out the strategy on page 2, where *"Program Examples"* provide an alternative format for describing project work. (See Appendix 24d on the CD-ROM.)

A LAST WORD

International resumes are constructed to display your international skills and your personality. The resume is built to support one theme—your career objective. An effective international resume summarizes your key professional and personal skills. These match the qualities of a person successfully working overseas—the employer's ideal profile. Your work history is organized around a few key functions that relate to your future overseas working environment and lend support to your skills summary. Job descriptions highlight accomplishments rather than the duties performed. You've used the language of your future work and deleted information irrelevant to, or not supportive of, your objective. In short, an international resume is organized and written so that you do the analytical work for the recruiter, and nothing is left to chance.

Put your best foot forward! Writing a good resume is one of the few activities in your life that allows you to reflect on your professional self. Focus on your strengths and skills. Put aside modesty and take credit. Do not boast or make unfounded claims, but have pride in the results after working hard to uncover and describe your professional skills. When you sit back and assess your new international resume, you will be certain to speak with renewed confidence and assurance in all that you have accomplished.

RESUME

MARC J. DOUCET (Mr.)

Current Address:
45 Laurier Street
Ottawa, ON K1N 7Z2 CANADA
Tel: (613) 231-1774
mdoucet@home.com

Permanent Address:
804 O'Neil Avenue
Petit Rocher, NB E8J 1H6 CANADA
Tel (506) 333-9482
ljdoucet@nbnet.nb.ca

OBJECTIVE: Overseas field administrator.

PERSONAL TRAITS: Self-starter; high energy; proven administrative abilities; communicates effectively with people from other cultures; cheerful under pressure; follow-up management style.

PROFESSIONAL SKILLS: MA, political science; BA, business administration; fully bilingual, four years volunteer leadership experience in a cross-cultural environment; six months overseas management experience; proficient with business software for managing a large field office.

INTERNATIONAL DEVELOPMENT EXPERIENCE
Effective and Knowledgeable in the Cross-Cultural Work Environment

---

Masters in Political Science, *Université Laval*, Québec City, Québec, Canada
Specialization: development economics. Maintained a consistent B+ average while working part-time and taking a full course load. Skilled in organizing and defining concepts. Gained a firm understanding of the political and economic forces that operate in developing countries (May 2003).

Orientation Counsellor, *Canadian Crossroads International (CCI)*, Canada
Helped orient over 35 African and Canadian volunteers. Proficient in topics such as culture shock, health tips, West African and North American social customs, dealing with officials, foreign currency. Acquired three years experience recruiting and interviewing candidates for overseas volunteer placements (2000 – present).

Assistant to the Director, *German Volunteer Service (GVS)*, Ghana
Successfully organized 4-day conference for 60 participants under conditions of severe food and transportation shortages; liaised effectively with Ghanaian ministries for increased fuel rations and food supplies; organized the importation of trucks and equipment and handled customs clearances; gave country orientation to GVS volunteers, their families and other visiting GVS staff; handled daily office management and was in-house software expert to a staff of four (August – November 2000).

CCI Volunteer School Administrator, *Abetiffi Vocational Training Institute*, Ghana
Assisted German Volunteers in managing school, developed school accounting system using Quicken software, implemented student recruitment program, procured school supplies, equipment and food from government ministries for students while also teaching English part-time (May - July 2000).

Travel to Other Developing Countries
Togo, Burkina Faso, Côte d'Ivoire, 2000; visited Nigeria for four weeks in 1998.

BUSINESS EXPERTISE
Leadership and Organization Abilities

Bachelor of Business Administration, *University of New Brunswick*
Specialization in marketing and management. Maintained B+ average while active on executive of student business association. Awarded *J.D. Irving Memorial Scholarship* for on-campus volunteer work with students associations (May 1998).

Manager Trainee, *General Motors of Canada, Forward Planning Department, Parts Division.* Compiled and analyzed industry data for senior management; gained strong reputation for analytical abilities; was the first to develop a reliable manpower analysis. AC Delco Supplier Rep: Successfully resolved long-standing problems with rebuilt suppliers that led to the elimination of my position. Inventory Planner: Managed $2 million parts inventory (September 1998 – January 2000).

Computer and Systems Design Skills
Proficient (expert level) in Microsoft Office Suite: including Access database and accounting software (Quicken and MYOB). Set up accounting systems for three student groups to manage a small technical school while in Ghana. Designed with Access database a new *Survey of Enrolment and Teaching of Political Science in Canada*, which was very well received by the chair of the Canadian Political Science Association. Currently employed as the Resource Person in computer laboratory, Faculty of Social Sciences at Université Laval and developed an administrative workbook for the lab (2000 – present).

Small Business Consultant, *UNB School of Administration*
Assisted small- and medium-sized businesses in managing information flow; designed and implemented marketing strategies for two small businesses resulting in increased sales; organized major consumer telephone survey; developed accounting and cost-control systems (summer 1998).

Active Member, *Canadian Crossroads International*
National Finance and Fundraising Committee: involved in financial policy formulation, expense and revenue monitoring, revision of national fundraising campaigns; developed field project evaluation forms. Special Project Coordinator: national resource person for Care Package projects, developed local committee fundraising support material (see manuals below). Francophone Regional Representative: liaison for francophone committees; initiated and coordinated national bilingual program for all major documents (2000 – present). CCI Local Committee Fundraising Coordinator, Quebec City: developed several successful fundraising projects generating revenues of $38,000 per year, enabling the committee to increase the number of overseas volunteers from four to nine in three years (2000 – 2003).

President, *U.N.B. Business Society*
Initiated new freshmen-orientation programs and raised membership by 35 per cent (1997 – 1998).

Member of several high school and university committees. Enjoys organizing events and working with people. President of High School Graduation Committee and awarded *Most Active Student of the Year* (1994 – 1995). Class President (1994 – 1995). Troop Scout Leader (1993 – 1995).

MANUALS AND PUBLICATIONS

Graphic and Advertising Manuals for Crossroaders and Local Committees, (print and web editions), *Canadian Crossroads International (CCI) 2002, 98 pp.*

Local Committee Finance and Fundraising Manual, (print and web editions), CCI: First edition, 2001, second edition 2003, 64 pp.

Master's Thesis: *The Political Economy of State-Economic Relations in Ghana* Université Laval, 2003, 168 pp.

Parts Manual for Projecting Business Growth, Warehousing, Equipment, and Manpower Needs. General Motors of Canada, Forward Planning Department, Oshawa, 1999, 114 pp.

SHORT COURSES (*relevant for international development field-office work*)

Emergency First Aid, St. John Ambulance	1996
Technicians Guild General Motors of Canada	1999
Dealer Business Management General Motors of Canada	1999

PERSONAL MANAGEMENT PHILOSOPHY

I am a hands-on organizer who likes to stay in contact with the people and programs I manage. Since most administrative problems and opportunities are people-related, it is important to have a hands-on understanding of the issues and personalities that surround a project. Qualities such as follow-up, persistence and personal contact have helped me to maintain a consistent record of achievement in Africa as well as with the many volunteer organizations I have worked for in Canada. People who work with me say that I am an effective organizer because I have a good sense of humour and remain enthusiastic in the face of frustration.

PERSONAL DATA

DATE AND PLACE OF BIRTH: November 13th, 1978; Petit Rocher, New Brunswick
STATUS: Single, no dependents
MOBILITY: Available immediately for worldwide employment.
NATIONALITY: Canadian
LANGUAGES: Fully bilingual in English and French (native French speaker). Excellent reading, writing and oral skills in both languages.

(MS.) **Lily Wong**

Career Objective: Program officer working in international health and based in Canada with an NGO, government agency or consulting firm.

SUMMARY OF EXPERTISE
International Health, Nutrition and Program Management

International Health and Nutrition Experience

- Bachelor of Science degree *UNIVERSITY OF ALBERTA* with unique combination of science and social science education: Honours, Nutrition and Physiology; Major, Peace and Conflict Studies.
- Two years project coordinator introducing *Nutri Rice™ Technology in Venezuela* .
- Four months compiling health survey results for *UNICEF CONSULTATIVE GROUP*.
- CIDA independent research grant for a 10-month study of nutritional health status of Nepali women in remote regions of Nepal.
- Six-month researcher for *UNICEF NEPAL* to conduct survey to produce questionnaire for iron-compliance campaign for women of child-bearing age.
- Various Canada-based experiences as a trainer, facilitator and office administrator for front-line nutrition and health projects.
- Worked successfully with populations at risk for nutritional deficiencies: women of child-bearing age, preschool and school-aged children, and immigrant and refugee women.

Program-Management Skills

- Strong administrator. Excellent planning skills. Goal oriented. Ability to think and act strategically. Effective at multi-tasking and prioritizing.
- Recognized for ability to coordinate and liaise effectively among various stakeholders working in the areas of community health and nutrition, including scientific experts, NGO and government policy-administrators, and food industry representatives.
- Strong interpersonal and public communication skills. Effective in delivering workshops, technical training and one-on-one information sessions.
- Experienced in compiling and disseminating scientific data. Appreciated for abilities to interpret complex health issues appropriate for different audiences.
- Clear and effective writing, including correspondence, report and scientific writing.
- Organized. System oriented. Methodological. Designed centralized filing system, created scientific report templates, managed bookkeeping, budgets and cash flow. Proficient with computers.

Personal Traits

- Dedicated, committed, very hard worker. Strong sense of initiative. Seeks challenges.
- Ability to deal with changing and unstructured environments. Willingness to take on new tasks. Reputation for meeting deadlines and being prepared.
- Creative and effective in designing processes to stay organized. Careful and precise when presenting information. Intense during the learning process.
- Strong communicator with both peers and managers. Quick and thorough in responding to management requests. Friendly and approachable while maintaining professional demeanour.

Cross-Cultural Skills

- Strong cross-cultural communications skills. Ability to fit in and put people at ease. Reputation for building trust across cultures.
- Excellent health. Able to travel to remote areas.
- Excellent language-learning abilities. Fluent in Spanish within four months of arrival in Venezuela.

INTERNATIONAL HEALTH-PROGRAMMING EXPERIENCE

Project Coordinator – Venezuela *Oct. 2000 – Jan. 2003*
"Nutri Rice™ Technology in Venezuela" project funded by *RURAL ADVANCEMENT FOUNDATION INTERNATIONAL (RAFI)* and *FFC-WASHINGTON*, Maturin, North West Venezuela, Venezuela. *This project was contracted to FFC-CANADA, a small Vancouver-based NGO focused on women and children's health. Nutri Rice™ is a laboratory-made rice fortified with Vitamin A and mixed at a 1 per cent ratio with regular rice to promote optimal absorption in undernourished populations that are prevalent in most developing countries.*

- As the Country Team Leader, successfully supported a team of five Venezuelan nutritional experts and spearheaded this $300,000 project by working with government and industry to promote the long-term acceptance of Nutri Rice™ technology through a school lunch program for 180,000 children in the economically depressed city of Maturin, Northwest Venezuela.
- Coordinated five Venezuelan university-based experts to help with advocacy—a senior nutritionist, a nutrition biochemist and three technicians.
- Established and secured relationships with partners: *CITY OF MATURIN SCHOOL LUNCH PROGRAMS, FEDERAL UNIVERSITY OF MATURIN*, government experts and policy officials at the local and national level, non-governmental organizations, educators, Venezuelan food industries, *FFC-WASHINGTON*.
- Recognized for having quickly gained the support of government and industry officials who had misperceptions of Nutri Rice™ prior to my arrival. Worked closely and strategically to build support of opinion leaders.
- Led advocacy initiatives through organization of workshops, technical training sessions and by building personal contacts. Designed and wrote technical documents for training sessions.
- Ensured project and campaign accountability to donor partners through reports and frequent feedback. Recognized for research report on *The Rice Market in Venezuela* by *FFC-WASHINGTON* and *RURAL ADVANCEMENT FOUNDATION INTERNATIONAL (RAFI)* and consequentially this report was published for the 2004 FFC-CANADA AGM.
- Efficient and competent administrator with reputation for being organized. Managed bookkeeping, budgets, cash flow, filing and project reporting.

Nutrition Consultant – Vancouver *Sept. 2000 – Jan. 2001*
GLOBAL VITAMIN A INITIATIVE, UNICEF CONSULTATIVE GROUP and *FCC-CANADA*, Vancouver, British Columbia, Canada.
The "Global Vitamin A Initiative" surveyed the member governments of 12 developing countries to determine the cost effectiveness of Global Vitamin A Programs. FCC-CANADA was responsible for compiling the survey results that affected the health-policy approaches of several countries in the southern hemisphere.

- Successfully coordinated the retrieval of survey data from leaders of 12 international NGOs under very tight deadline. Effective and efficient while relying solely on e-mail correspondence and while working across cultures.
- Designed template for collecting data that was recognized for its clear presentation of complex scientific and socio-economic data.
- Recognized for careful collection of data and ability to analyze and interpret data without distortion.
- Conducted meticulous research and literature reviews for well-received report, "Cost Effectiveness of Vitamin-A Projects."
- Promoted from consultant to project coordinator position (described above). Recognized for hard and careful work, pragmatic work style. Promoted over other candidates who had MA degrees.

Nutritional-Health Researcher – Nepal   *Aug. 1999 – June 2000*
CANADIAN INTERNATIONAL DEVELOPMENT AGENCY (CIDA) and the *CANADIAN SOCIETY FOR INTERNATIONAL HEALTH (CSIH),* Kathmandu and Northwest Regions, Nepal.
"Independent Research Grants" are awarded to a limited number of interns on the basis of a written proposal and for securing Canadian and local NGO partners. Local partners in Nepal: DALIT, AJUWA (large Nepali NGOs working with health projects for rural women, especially untouchables). Canadian NGO partners: CENTRE CANADIEN D'ÉTUDE ET DE COOPÉRATION INTERNATIONAL (CECI), UNITARIAN SERVICE COMMITTEE (USC).

- Awarded an independent research grant to identify relationship between socio-cultural trends among Nepali women and their nutritional health status.
- Designed questionnaire, conducted interviews and compiled data on dietary intake of 180 village women using "24 Hour Dietary Recall" method.
- Overcame cross-cultural communication barriers. Established trust and open communications with survey respondents. Facilitated village-based workshops. Worked in very isolated and challenging locations.
- Established cooperative working relationship with local and Canadian NGO partners.

Nutrition and Social-Marketing Researcher – Nepal   *Jan. 2000 – June 2000*
DEPARTMENT OF NUTRITION – UNICEF-Nepal, Kathmandu, Nepal.

- Invited by UNICEF Head Nutritionist who sought out the "qualitative research" methods applied in my survey described in previous job description.
- Worked with UNICEF Nutritional Program Officers to conduct KAP survey (Knowledge, Attitude and Practice) on iron supplements and anemia, to produce appropriate questionnaires for iron compliance campaign for women of child-bearing age.
- Helped write and present research findings to *MINISTRY OF HEALTH – NEPAL* officials to affect national maternity-health policy on iron supplementation.
- Contributed in writing IEC materials (information, educational and curriculum) on iron and anemia.
- Recognized for writing clear and understandable survey materials appropriate for target populations.

Nutrition Course Designer and Trainer   *March 2004*
SAINT JAMESTOWN COMMUNITY HEALTH CENTRE, Calgary, Alberta, Canada.

- Lead instructor for "Cooking Healthy with Fresh Vegetables and Fruits" program, a practical low-cost cooking course for families participating in food basket programs.
- Designed and wrote course material in collaboration with dietician from *CALGARY PUBLIC HEALTH.*
- Organized and successfully maintained multilateral partnerships between *CALGARY PUBLIC HEALTH, SOUTH CALGARY HEART HEALTH NETWORK, GABLE COMMUNITY MINISTRIES, SOUTH CALGARY FOOD HARVEST FOOD BANK* and four local farmers.

Office Manager – Women's Health Centre   *Sept. 2003 – Aug. 2004*
IMMIGRANT WOMEN'S HEALTH CENTRE, Calgary, Alberta, Canada. *The health centre has a staff of 10 sex-health counsellors, serving 7,000 immigrant and refugee women a year in 10 languages.*

- Was first to create a centralized filing system (resolving a long-standing problem) that streamlined tasks and significantly improved the orderly functioning of the office.
- Established new and more effective financial systems in collaboration with accountant.
- Communicated sexual-health issues to a diverse group of women, often in Portuguese, and in a culturally sensitive manner.
- Assisted Mobile Health Unit Coordinator with respect to logistics and communications with partner agencies.
- Responsible for maintaining relationships with other community agencies and service providers, including appointments for external client-service referrals.

Peer Nutrition Assistant   *Nov. 2003 – present*
SOUTH PARK HEALTH CENTRE, Calgary, Alberta, Canada.

- Nutrition volunteer to low-income mothers in inner-city neighbourhood. Facilitated
  during meal-preparation classes in community kitchen. Taught how to economize on
  household food costs and how to prepare nutritional food for infants and toddlers.

Founding Member, Nutritional-Health NGO   *Oct. 2003 – present*
PARTNERSHIP IN HEALTH AND NUTRITION (PHN), Calgary, Alberta, Canada.
*PHN was founded in 2004 by five nutritionists with the aim of supporting the work of
national and international agencies dedicated to alleviating nutritional deficiencies among
populations at risk, especially women and children.*

- Responsibilities as founding member: Collaborated closely on writing a strategic plan,
  goals and mission statement. Initiated and facilitated strategy meetings among
  founding members and potential contacts (example, *CANADIAN FEED THE CHILDREN*).
  Networked and researched on NGO start-up strategies by contacting other NGOs.
- Current project: Negotiating contract to provide nutrition services in support of an
  HIV/AIDS health project organized by the *CITY OF CALGARY* and the *MINISTRY OF HEALTH*
  in Zambia.

BUSINESS WORK EXPERIENCE

Sales and Marketing Officer   *Jan. 2003 – Sept. 2003*
ENVIRONET COMPANY, Calgary, Alberta, Canada.

- Expanded company's client base significantly through outreach and product
  demonstrations. Wrote and designed brochures and media packages to enhance
  company image. Communicated with diverse client population. Established
  professional partnerships with suppliers and retailers of product.

Part-Time Work (while attending high school and university)   *1990 – 1999*

- Customer Service Representative: *ROYAL BANK OF CANADA*, 1997 – 1999
- Retail Assistant: *MCARTHUR BOOKSHOP*, 1990 – 1994

EDUCATION

Registered Dietician, Certification in progress, estimated completion *Jan. 2006*.
UNIVERSITY OF ALBERTA, Edmonton, Alberta, Canada.   *Part-time since Jan. 2003*
*This certification will help with future MA studies as well as facilitate collaborations with
senior nutritional experts while working as an international health-programming officer.
Courses completed while maintaining an A– average: Organizational Behaviour, Health
Promotion and Community Development.*

Bachelor of Science (Hons. BSc), *UNIVERSITY OF ALBERTA*, Edmonton, Alberta.   *1999*
Honours: **Nutrition and Physiology.** Major: **Peace and Conflict Studies.**
*The NUTRITION DEPARTMENT is part of the UNIVERSITY OF ALBERTA SCHOOL OF MEDICINE and is
renowned for its groundbreaking research. While studying science and social science
subjects, I was always interested in the social and cultural aspects of food consumption,
especially in developing countries.*

High School, Edmonton, Alberta, Canada.   *1991*

Kindergarten to Junior High: *INTERNATIONAL SCHOOLS* in Philippines and Indonesia
*I attended international schools under the British curriculum while my father was an
engineer with Shell Oil. As part of my experience, we travelled extensively, often in
remote areas, all through Southeast Asia.*

RELATED SKILLS

Languages:

- English: first language, fully functional.
- Portuguese: fully functional in comprehension, speaking and reading, intermediate writing. *Adept at learning languages; was functional in Spanish after only four months in Venezuela.*
- Nepali: Basic proficiency while living in Nepal. *Example: was able to monitor translators during interviews.*
- Bahasa Indonesian: functional in conversation.

Computer Skills: Microsoft Word, Excel and SPSS (statistical software). Excellent Internet research skills.

Train the Trainer HIV/AIDS for Educators *DEPARTMENT OF PUBLIC HEALTH, CITY OF CALGARY, Calgary, Alberta, Canada (June 2004). As a student in this train-the-trainer, three-day workshop: planned HIV/AIDS prevention education programs; incorporated Stages-of-Change into prevention programs; learned new teaching techniques and increased understanding of people living with AIDS.*

Travel: Brazil, Uruguay, Venezuela, Nepal, Thailand, Malaysia, Singapore, Indonesia and Philippines. *Enthused cross-cultural observer and participant while travelling.*

PERSONAL DATA

Citizenship: Canadian

Year and Place of Birth: 1975, Jakarta, Indonesia

Mobility: Able and willing to undertake short-term travel. Single, no dependants.

Current Address:
#111, 2816 11th St. NE
Calgary, Alberta T2E 7S7 Canada
Tel: 780-942-2322
E-mail: lwong1960@sympatico.ca

Long-Term Address:
c/o Mr. or Mrs. Thomas Wong
334 Buckingham Crescent
Oakville, Ontario L6J 1J3 Canada
Tel: 905-285-7743

References available upon request.

(MS.) **Robin Millar**

OBJECTIVE: Senior policy or program officer to work part-time or as a consultant for an international organization based in Geneva.

KEY QUALITIES: Team leader, experienced and effective in introducing new policies; adept at long-term institutional planning and program design; visionary, competent administrator; personable, good communicator; pragmatist; fluent in three languages.

PROFESSIONAL SKILLS

Policy

- Policy and strategic planning at the global, regional and country level.
- Astute in distilling key components of policy and steering teams of experts towards solutions.
- Aware of ethical and cultural issues as they develop over time and impact on policy.
- Sensitive to public attitudes and how they affect government policy.
- Six years of community development programming.
- Able to balance pure research, applied/field research and capacity building.

Program Management

- Thirteen years experience in international development project management (Tanzania, Sudan, Canada).
- Familiar with developing and monitoring all phases of projects from needs analysis, program designs, implementation plans, monitoring and evaluations.
- Numerous overseas field missions in direct collaboration with local populations and communities.

Administration

- Worked in the field and at headquarters, and in all facets of project administration.
- Organized international meetings, official visits, field missions, and development studies. Monitored the implementation of numerous programs and related projects.
- Competent organizer, experienced trainer and supervisor of staff.
- Effective writer. Adept in financial and office systems management.

SECTORS OF EXPERIENCE

Health, education, communications, human resources, social policy, gender and development, institutional development.

PROFESSIONAL ASSIGNMENTS

First Secretary and Head of CIDA Operations, Tanzania, Canadian High Commission, Canadian International Development Agency (CIDA), Dar es Salaam, Tanzania (2000 – present)

- Manager: Managed CIDA's development programs in Tanzania.
- Project Planner: Responsible for reviewing the project implementation and management activities related to bilateral, institutional cooperation and partnership program activities in Tanzania.
- Areas of Responsibility: Managed complex bilateral program consisting of four sub-programs and 20 projects; sectors included health, social policy, gender and development, and institutional development.
- Reports/Studies: Reported to headquarters on social, economic and political factors influencing program delivery: realities of hyperinflation and introduction of currency reforms and price/wage freezes; outbreak of HIV/AIDS and socio-economic disparities.
- Coordinator/Planner: Assumed overall responsibility for multi-disciplinary teams to plan third phase of CIDA's bilateral program in Tanzania.
- Negotiator: Developed and negotiated on behalf of CIDA a framework for a new bilateral technical cooperation program, valued at $10 million, with Tanzanian authorities in May 1996.
- Program Evaluator/Monitor: Monitored CIDA-sponsored non-governmental and institutional cooperation activities and analyzed new project proposals.

Sudan Bilateral Development Officer, Regional Program, Africa Branch, (CIDA) Headquarters, Ottawa/Gatineau, Canada (1995 – 2000)

- Strategic Planner: Participated in drafting the Regional Program Review, a five-year policy framework for CIDA's activities in Sudan.
- Program Review: Evaluated community development and educational programs. Developed project implementation framework of a vocational training project. Secured cooperation and support of senior management in Department of Employment and Immigration Canada.
- Negotiator: As team leader, developed Memorandum of Understanding for $10 million goods and services line of credit for Sudan.
- Project Manager: Managed day-to-day activities of three bilateral projects: Functional Literacy, Primary Health Care, and Human Resource Development.
- Advisor: Analyzed, within headquarters and in field, emergency balance-of-payment options and instruments specific to Sudan's development needs and prepared draft papers for senior management which outlined social, economic and political considerations of policy options.

Overseas Country Director (Sudan), Canadian Save the Children Fund, Khartoum, Sudan (1991 – 1995)

- Manager: Initiated Canadian Save the Children Fund in Sudan and held responsibility for all financial and operational matters of the program budgeted at $250,000. Established agency office, hired administrative and program staff, and initiated necessary management procedures. Set personnel policies: job descriptions, salary scales and office procedures.
- Negotiator: Identified and negotiated projects involving rural self-help schools and rural women's community training centres, and integrated community development. Projects involved both direct support to community groups and support to local Sudanese NGOs.
- Report/Studies: Reported to headquarters on social, economic and political factors influencing program delivery, outbreak of HIV/AIDS and socio-economic disparities between rural and urban populations.
- Personnel Manager: Supervised one Canada-based employee, two senior-level, locally engaged program assistants, and two administrative assistants.

Program Officer, Employment Development, Employment and Immigration Canada (EIC) Ottawa, Ontario, Canada (1988 – 1991)

- Project Manager: Development of community-based projects designed to alleviate unemployment, particularly for women, youth, minority groups and disabled persons.
- Monitor: Monitored financial audit for operating projects.
- Liaison: Liaised with elected Members of Parliament and community organizations. Chaired advisory boards composed of community and business leaders. Clients ranged from small voluntary ad hoc group and public sector groups to large multinational companies.
- Report/Studies: Produced reports and briefing materials detailing the socio-economic disparities existing in the country, the ongoing study of the social, political and economic climate of the area, analysis of proposals including relevant research and determination of financial feasibility.

JPO Program Officer, United Nations Development Program (UNDP), Jakarta, Indonesia (1986 – 1988)

- Advisor: Drafted position papers, speeches, briefing notes and correspondence for Resident Representative.
- Monitor: Monitored UNDP-assisted community development projects.
- Coordinator: Selection committee responsible for disbursing funds for community development projects.
- Negotiator: Project for the Government of Indonesia, the Indonesian Association of Voluntary Organization (IAVO) and the UNDP, which provided management training and management services for indigenous NGOs.
- Administrator: Responsible for day-to-day program management of UNDP projects.

Robin Millar

NGO VOLUNTEER EXPERIENCE

World University Service of Canada (WUSC)
Member of WUSC Board of Directors (1996 – 2000). Led a WUSC seminar on development in Costa Rica in 1989. In charge of selecting both professors and student participants for seminars in Haiti, Egypt and Thailand. Active on the University of Ottawa WUSC committee in recruiting seminar students and raising funds for refugee students.

Canadian World Youth (CWY)
Participant in Kenya (1982) and, later, group leader in Tanzania (1984). Active board member and volunteer (1984 – 1988).

Canadian Association of African Studies (CAAS)
Coordinated the successful 13th Annual Conference of the CAAS at Carleton University in 1989 with 300 participants.

EDUCATION

- **MA in International Affairs**, Norman Paterson School of International Affairs, Carleton University (1985)
- **BA in Political Science**, Carleton University (1983)

LANGUAGES	Oral	Comprehension	Written
English	Excellent	Excellent	Excellent
French	Good	Excellent	Intermediate
Spanish	Good	Excellent	Basic

PERSONAL

Nationality:	Canadian citizen
Foreign Travel:	Travelled extensively in Africa and Asia
Marital Status:	Married with two teenage children, both attending university
Mobility:	Able to travel on assignments
References:	Available upon request

Home Address	**Contact Address in Geneva**	**Permanent Contact**
In Geneva	International Labour Organization (ILO)	**in Canada**
68 Avenue Appia	Attention: Mr. Robert Millar	Attention:
1211 Geneva 27	4, route des Morillons	Mr. Jim Eastman
SWITZERLAND	1211 Geneva 22	40 Isabella Street
Tel: (41) (22) 352-2445	SWITZERLAND	Ottawa, Ontario K1S 8G8
rmiller@look.ca	Tel: (41) (22) 352-6387	CANADA
	Fax: (41) (22) 352-7315	Tel: +1 (613) 238-6189
	robin.miller@ilo.org	jeastmam240@rogers.com

CHAPTER 25

Covering Letters

This chapter discusses follow-up letters and covering (or cover) letters. These are important to the job search process because they are a visible part of your dossier as it is passed from one recruitment officer to the next.

Cover letters are also part of the e-mail world, and thus they are generally e-mailed as attachments rather then actually mailed or faxed. Do not include your cover letter in the body of your e-mail—send it as an attachment where it can be properly formatted.

The covering letter accompanies every resume. It is a one-page marketing tool used to draw an employer's attention to your particular set of skills and experiences. Its main purpose is to help you get that important interview.

There are three basic types of covering letters:

- the e-mail cover letter
- the letter of inquiry
- the application letter

E-MAIL COVERING LETTER

First, as mentioned above, do not include your actual cover letter in the body of the e-mail. It is difficult to format and the recruiter has a hard time managing the letter in this form.

You will, however, need to send a short e-mail message along with your two-attachment application package that includes your resume and cover letter. Most job applicants ignore the importance of the e-mail cover letter. Anecdotal evidence shows that many job applicants treat this e-mail message lightly. The most common mistake is using an informal writing style that includes poor sentence structure and poor grammar. These mistakes aside, job applicants are also missing an important opportunity to sell themselves within the body of this e-mail.

A proper e-mail cover letter should be formal and grammatically perfect. Begin with a formal opening: *"Dear Mr. Lavender"* and not *"Hi there, Mr. Lavender."* The body of the letter should be short and succinct: *"Attached please find my resume and cover letter for the position of..."* You should then very briefly highlight one of your attributes or write about how you heard about the position.

> *"I am applying for the position of researcher/writer as posted on your Web site. I have spoken to your assistant regarding the job description and I would welcome the opportunity to work on this edition of your book with you and your team. Please find my cover letter and resume attached. If you have any questions, I may be contacted by e-mail or phone. Thank you for your time and consideration."*

Consider adding one sentence that will help the recruiter remember who you are. This could be a mention of who referred you to the position or something that makes you or your circumstances special. For example, *"I'm currently in the final two weeks of a teaching contract at Cheju National University on Cheju Island, South Korea, where I coach trainee-interpreters in international resume and job interview skills and teach graduate seminars in cross-cultural business protocol."*

And don't forget the value of the e-mail subject heading. Include specific information here, to attract the recruiter's attention. Rather than writing *"Internship Applicant,"* write *"Intern with MA in International Affairs and six months travel in Africa."*

In summary, spend time and thought on your e-mail cover letter, and make it work for you. In fact all your e-mail correspondence should be professional and formal. Employers will notice. The care you give to e-mail communication during the recruitment process is a good indicator of the care you will deliver when employed.

LETTER OF INQUIRY

This type of letter is used to inquire about possible job openings, to determine application procedures and to register your name in a recruitment data bank. A letter of inquiry is often part of the research phase of the job search. In many instances, it is part of a mass mailing and is sent well in advance of your employment target-date because exchanges of information can take several months. (See the sample letter of inquiry at the end of this chapter.)

LETTER OF APPLICATION

Use this to respond to a specific job opening. If you are replying to an advertisement, tailor the information in your letter to fit with the employer's criteria.

CALL YOUR FUTURE EMPLOYER FIRST

Telephone the company before mailing your resume. After all, we know only too well what is done with unsolicited mail. (For a full discussion on this subject, see Chapter 22, Phone Research Techniques.)

In the pre-resume phone call, you should do the following:

- Obtain the exact name and title of the recruitment officer for inclusion in your covering letter.

- Inquire about the employer's ideal profile so that these important characteristics can be highlighted in your covering letter.

When you write your covering letter, make reference to the phone conversation. This serves to demonstrate your communication skills and to remind the employer of who you are.

Calling ahead will demonstrate your communication and planning skills, and will also help you build a relationship with a particular recruiter. If you are unable to speak to a recruitment officer, you can still create a link with the organization. For example: *"Further to my telephone conversation with your assistant, Ms. Moores, I'm forwarding my resume and application for the civil engineering position in Islamabad, Pakistan."*

WRITING AN EFFECTIVE COVERING LETTER

You simply must have an effective covering letter. It should demonstrate the clarity of your thoughts, and it must be a sterling sample of your writing abilities. Do not use humour, slang or any approach that does not reflect a serious professional attitude. It is not unheard-of to spend four or five hours composing a good covering letter to achieve the payoff of an interview.

The standard format should not exceed one page in length. It is as follows:

- The first paragraph states the purpose of your letter.
- The second and possibly third paragraph highlights your experience (one paragraph usually focuses on overseas or international experience).
- The last paragraph states desired follow-up action (usually to arrange an interview date or follow-up phone call), along with a closing affirmative sentence about yourself.

The Introduction

Keep this first paragraph short. The objective is to be precise and personable. As a courtesy, briefly mention how you became aware of the position. If you were introduced to the company through an employee, mention his or her name. This person could very well become a relevant networking contact for you and the recruitment officer. For example:

"Mr. Nemo, the information officer at the Canadian Council of International Co-operation (CCIC) suggested that I write to you regarding employment possibilities in overseas international education."

State the purpose of your letter in the first paragraph (that is, a letter of inquiry, an application for a specific job, or a follow-up to a phone conversation related to a specified issue). State the position you are applying for or your career objective (field, level of entry, geographic preference).

Be personable. Include something specific to arouse an employer's interest such as a reference to your previous phone conversation or a particular problem that you might be able to resolve for the company.

The Body of the Letter

Sell yourself! Reveal only your most outstanding skills and experience. Draw attention to your best qualifications with the objective of arousing the employer's interest.

Describe your work experiences from an employer's perspective rather than your own. *"I believe my grassroots overseas experience with the United Nations Development Program will allow me to make an effective contribution to your rural water management program in Ghana,"* rather than, *"I want to work overseas because I enjoy new experiences."* State how you can help the employer rather than how they can help you.

Highlight your accomplishments. Be specific. Use the active voice when possible. Examples:

- *"I developed a new program in…"* or *"I initiated a successful program in…"*
- *"My past successes demonstrate my ability to handle this kind of work."*
- *"My work with the Refugee Committee in Montreal and teaching secondary school in an ethnic neighbourhood in Toronto exposed me to the challenges of cross-cultural communication. I have the background experience and understanding needed to teach effectively in another culture."*

Mention how your past experiences relate to the international field or why you are qualified for the position. This should be a major theme in at least one of the paragraphs of your covering letter. Example:

"As the son of a military officer in the Canadian Armed Forces, I have lived and travelled in many countries. I recently spent four months in Africa with my parents, who are now posted in Kinshasa, Congo. These experiences, along with my master's degree in international relations, have given me a solid understanding of social and economic conditions in the developing world."

Draw attention to an overall trend in your career and tie this to an important skill. You should also make reference to material in your attached resume; for instance: *"As my resume shows, I seek leadership roles where motivation is the crucial factor."*

Turn your weaknesses into strengths! Don't say, *"While I have never worked overseas, my five years of work with visiting Chinese students at…"* It would be much better to say, *"Five years of working with visiting Chinese students at the Winnipeg Vocational Training School has provided me with a wealth of cross-cultural knowledge."*

You can also list career highlights in point form rather than in paragraphs. For example:

"The highlights of my career that qualify me for an overseas posting are:

- *A bachelor's degree specializing in international affairs with some courses in business administration;*
- *Two years as a CUSO volunteer school administrator in Guyana;*
- *Two years project programming experience with ABC Consultants;*
- *Active volunteer participation with the Oxfam Local Committee of Kingston."*

The Closing Paragraph

In the closing paragraph you should stress your interest in the employer's field of work and state that you will be in touch in the near future. You should suggest an interview in your letter of inquiry, though it would be inappropriate to mention a specific date. In the case of an advertised job opening, there is usually a pre-arranged recruitment schedule. A closing sentence might be:

- *"I look forward to hearing from you in the near future, and to discussing how my finance skills would best fit your organizational objectives."*

- *"I want to restate my interest in your Zimbabwe project. I look forward to discussing my possible contribution to this exciting work."*

In the case of a letter of inquiry: *"I understand that you are not currently in need of an office administrator, but I believe a short meeting would be beneficial to both of us, in light of your continuing overseas requirements."*

FOLLOW-UP LETTERS

Imagine the recruiting officer who has just received the company's request to hire an overseas employee for a contract in Nigeria. The recruitment officer immediately consults the company's data bank for suitable candidates. If you had recently called the organization, the recruitment officer would likely pull your file for a quick review. It would contain: the standard company evaluation form, your resume and covering letter, as well as one or two letters of continuing interest. One letter might mention your current short-term contract in a particular field; another might be addressed to the Nigeria project officer and discuss your particular interest in the company's upcoming contract. All letters should demonstrate enthusiasm for the organization and for overseas employment.

In many cases, recruitment officers rely on computerized data banks for candidates. An excellent method of keeping your file active is to send out periodic letters expressing continued interest.

Letters of Continued Interest

The objective of these types of letters is to keep your dossier active after sending in your resume, and before you have an interview:

- You should send letters every three to six months to employers who have your file on record.

- Follow your phone calls with a letter expressing interest or adding new information related to your conversation.

- Document any changes to your resume, such as new employment, new courses taken, a change of address or phone number.

- If you decide to accept a position overseas, inform other employers in writing of your change in job status. It is important to maintain good relationships and contacts. After all, you will probably be looking for another job at the end of your contract.

Follow-up Letters After an Interview

This is a crucial step that should be taken within hours of a formal interview or an information interview. There are a number of reasons this will strengthen your employment prospects.

A thank-you letter will differentiate you from other candidates and may make a difference in the hiring decision. Always express enthusiasm for the position offered in light of your discussion. For example:

"Thank you for taking the time to meet with me yesterday. I appreciated the opportunity to learn more about the Nigerian project, your management philosophy, and your aim of integrating Nigerians into the project. As my engineering background includes training experience, I am optimistic about being able to contribute to the success of your endeavours."

The follow-up letter should contain additional information related to your interview. For example:

"Further to our discussion yesterday, I am forwarding you an article which discusses the new program developments being implemented by... In light of our discussion, I wish to restate my enthusiasm for the position being offered."

A follow-up letter gives you the opportunity to clarify a point or correct an error. Errors should be dealt with immediately, either by phone or letter. For example:

"In reviewing our interview discussion of December 10 concerning desert irrigation systems, I find myself uncomfortable with a point I had made, and wish to elaborate on the subject a little further..."

FORMATTING NOTES

Never send photocopies. Letters to potential employers should be individually typed on a good typewriter or word processor. Remember, you are competing with people who have access to high-quality laser printers. *Never* handwrite a letter.

If you do not know, never assume a person's gender or title in the opening salutation. Rather than *"Dear Recruitment Officer,"* or *"Dear Superintendent,"* you should begin with *"Dear Sir/Madam."* (Your cause will be lost if you use *"To whom it may concern,"* *"Gentlemen,"* or *"Dear Friends."*) Similarly, if you are replying to an advertisement in which only the name or initials are given, and you have no knowledge of gender, simply address your inquiry to *"Dear J.C. Boyle."* If a PhD is indicated, address your letter to *"Dear Dr. Boyle."* If an appropriate title is given, use it in the salutation; for example *"Dear Minister Boyle,"* or *"Dear President Boyle."* If the recruitment officer is female and she does not identify herself during a conversation as *"Miss"* or *"Mrs.,"* you should use *"Ms."*

The full address is usually listed in the following order: name, title, department, organization name, postal box, street address, floor or suite number, town or city, country, and postal code. To avoid confusion in international correspondence, never use address abbreviations (P.O., St., Dr., Ave., Ont., AB.).

If a resume and other items are included, complete your letter with the lists of items enclosed by using the abbreviation "Encl." For example:

"Encl.: Resume, three reference letters, application form."

It is perfectly acceptable to increase your chances of employment by sending your resume to more than one person in the same agency. You must, however, inform both parties by including the abbreviation "cc." on the last line of your letter; example, *"cc. Mr. Jack Smith, Manager, International Finance."*

A LAST WORD

Covering letters are crucial to your job search. They should be revised as often as necessary. They may be the key to getting someone to send you an application form, study your resume, grant you an interview or even decide that you are the person for the job. Covering letters give you the chance to sell yourself. Don't minimize their importance!

SAMPLE LETTER OF APPLICATION

15 April 2004

Ms. Sandy Welsh
Personnel Director
Plenty Canada
R.R. 3
Lanark, Ontario K0G 1K0
CANADA

Dear Ms. Welsh,

Further to a recent conversation with your assistant, Ms. Debbie Wilson, I wish to apply for the position of Assistant Administrator – the Dominican Republic, as advertised in the March Job Bulletin of the Canadian Council for International Co-operation.

As the coordinator of volunteer services at the Williamson Memorial Regional Hospital, I supervised a staff of over 300 volunteers. I am also the volunteer treasurer of the Alberta Alliance for Peace, supervising the accounting of a $30,000 annual budget. My resume points out numerous other activities that attest to my ability to organize and administer a large staff operating within a tight budget.

I have a realistic understanding of overseas living and working conditions and possess strong cross-cultural communication skills. Since returning three years ago from Zaire, where I worked with Canada World Youth (CWY), I have been active with numerous volunteer groups in Medicine Hat, Alberta. Besides being a member of the local World University Service of Canada (WUSC) committee, I have remained especially active with CWY in the areas of volunteer recruitment and assessment. I also had the opportunity to travel extensively in Latin America for two months last year. I am fluent in Spanish.

Please note that I am available for an interview at your convenience. You may also contact me during regular office hours at my business. I look forward to hearing from you and to discussing how my organizational skills could make a strong contribution to the challenging post of administrative assistant in the Dominican Republic.

Yours truly,

Ms. Patty Carter
23-1334 Avenue Road
Medicine Hat, Alberta R9T 5G5
Canada
patty1334@shaw.ca

Encl.: Resume

SAMPLE LETTER OF INQUIRY

15 January 2004

Dr. Phil Kilpatrick
Superintendent
Seoul International School
4-1 Hwayang-dong
Sungdong-ku
Seoul 120
KOREA

Dear Dr. Kilpatrick,

I am writing you to inquire about teaching possibilities at the primary level during the 2004–05 school year. I have spoken to a number of people at Foreign Affairs Canada who have informed me that your international school is held in high regard by the families of Canadian diplomats who reside in Seoul.

Please find attached my resume and an open letter of recommendation from my current supervisor, Mr. Matthew Godin, Principal at St. Michael's school. I am enjoying my fourth year of teaching since graduating with honours from the University of New Brunswick in 2000. For the past two years I have been chairman of two provincial committees dealing with the introduction of new primary school teaching methods in mathematics and sciences. I have also been involved in coaching team sports, and I recognize the rewards of working with children outside of the classroom.

My overseas experience includes two extensive cultural visits through Southeast Asia during the summers of 2001 and 2003 with the New Brunswick Teachers Federation. In 2003, I was group leader in charge of coordinating meetings between our group and local government officials.

Please send me an application package and any information on possible openings in the upcoming school year. I have included a self-addressed envelope and three UNESCO international reply coupons. In speaking to other teachers who have worked abroad, and in reviewing my own experiences in Southeast Asia, I am confident of my abilities to contribute to your international school.

Sincerely yours,

Mr. Joe Eddie
13 O'Connor Street
Saint John, New Brunswick E2A 3B4
CANADA
506-934-9788
jeddie@nbtel.nb.ca

Encl.: Resume

SAMPLE LETTER OF CONTINUED INTEREST

15 October 2004

Bernard C. Perkins
Chief, CDRS
United Nations High Commissioner
for Refugees (UNHCR)
Case postale 2500
1211 Geneva 2 Dépot
SWITZERLAND

Dear Mr. Perkins,

Further to our recent phone conversation, I am including an updated copy of my resume, along with my completed Personal History form.

As I pointed out in my recent application for a position as a Junior Professional Officer, I believe my abilities and experience in intercultural, refugee, international development and community development fields, as well as my studies in sociology, make me suitable for a position with the HCR. I also believe I possess the spirit, determination and diplomatic skills, as well as the humanitarian commitment that are required for employees of the United Nations.

I wish to reaffirm my admiration for the work the UNHCR does in the international arena and to assure you of my continuing sincere interest in joining your organization. Thank you again for considering my candidacy. I look forward to hearing from you soon.

Yours sincerely,

Jonas C. Boudreau
254 Edith Drive
Toronto, Ontario M2B 5X1
CANADA
416-925-0467
jboudreau234@rogers.com

Encl.: Updated Resume and Personal History form

SAMPLE FOLLOW-UP LETTER AFTER INTERVIEW

11 July 2004

Ms. Linda Lim
Senior Visiting Recruitment Officer
United Nations High Commissioner
for Refugees (UNHCR)
280 Albert Street, Suite 401
Ottawa, Ontario K1P 5G8
CANADA

Dear Ms. Lim,

I wish to express my thanks for your interview of July 10. After this meeting, I am even more certain that UNHCR is an international agency for which I want to work. I believe my skills would be well-used and that I could make an important contribution to the work being done by your organization.

After hearing your description of work in a refugee camp, I am convinced that I possess the sound judgment, organizational and leadership skills, and intercultural understanding required of UNHCR employees in the field. This JPO opportunity would also give me valuable experience that I could later apply in my own region of Canada, where so much work with refugees has to be done.

Once again, thank you for considering me. I am excited about the prospect of joining UNHCR and look forward to hearing from you soon.

Yours sincerely,

Denise Haché
324 Rocheforte Drive
Apartment 511
Don Mills, Ontario M3C 1H5
CANADA
deniseh486@sympatico.ca
416-923-9984

SAMPLE LETTER OF APPLICATION FOR INTERNSHIP

14 July 2004

Mr. Christopher Lee
Executive Director
Citizens' Clearinghouse on Waste Management
3128 W 10th Avenue
Vancouver, BC V6K 2R6
CANADA

Subject: Internship Position

Dear Mr. Lee:

Further to our conversation of July 13, please find enclosed my resume outlining my qualifications for the Composting Internship position available with the Cooperative Community Composting Center Project in Mexico.

I am both a strong advocate and a practitioner of ecologically sound development. My bachelor's degree in biology broadened my understanding of ecology and our world environment. I apply the "Three R's" of waste reduction in my everyday life, by avoiding disposable items, reusing bags and various paper products, and purchasing many things at garage sales. I also compost leaves, grass clippings and food scraps.

As an adaptable and sociable person, I interact well with others. My previous jobs have provided me with the opportunity to work with a variety of people and to hold a considerable amount of responsibility. My resourcefulness and ability to work independently have helped me win the appreciation of employers and co-workers. My communication skills are also well developed and I am fluent in English, French and Spanish.

I believe I am ideally suited to this internship where cultural sensitivity, teamwork and resourcefulness are essential. In addition, my scientific background and language skills would contribute greatly to your program. I look forward to hearing from you in the near future.

Sincerely,

Sarah K. Singleton
88 Sunset Court
Calgary, Alberta T2X 1K8
CANADA
sarajsingleton@shaw.ca
(403) 284-8512

Encl.: Resume

CHAPTER 26

Interviewing for an International Job

You want to work overseas. You've spent a lot of time preparing. You have researched hundreds of possibilities and sent your resume and a cover letter to a multitude of organizations. You have been in contact with a number of potential employers and, finally, you've been invited to an interview for a specific job.

The interview is the most critical point in your job search. It is here that an employer assesses your suitability for overseas employment, based on their criteria. How closely do you match the employer's *ideal profile*? Do you have the qualifications? Do you and the company share similar management styles? Will you present a good company image abroad? Will you survive culture shock?

Most candidates are nervous at the prospect of an interview. They feel they have no control, they are at the mercy of a recruitment officer or an interview team. But is the process really that one-sided, skewed to the candidate's detriment? Does the employer have anything to lose? You probably have these and other questions on your mind as you contemplate the all-important interview. Let's first discuss the interview from the employer's point of view.

Imagine the recruitment officer who must select a candidate for an overseas position. There is a great responsibility resting on his or her shoulders. The recruiter's professional expertise is on the line. People are relying on him or her to come up with the right person for the position. The outfit is investing time and money to interview candidates from across the country. The cost of posting an employee overseas is high: airfare, moving, settling-in allowance, cost of dependants, housing, salary, etc. The price of failure is equally high, in terms of the firm's reputation abroad and finding a replacement candidate.

The stakes are high on both sides. Both parties are depending on the outcome of the interview. A helpful strategy, then, for overcoming your anxiety is to focus on cooperating with the selection committee. Help them with their difficult hiring decision. They will likely have an equally positive attitude toward you.

How do you go about preparing for the interview?

Prior to your interview, carry out a "profile analysis" by matching your skills to those specified in the overseas job description. (For detailed information on how to do this, see Chapter 23, Selling Your International Skills.) You must be able to discuss your professional work history in terms of specific skills that match the overseas position. Work on your elevator pitch and your overall sales presentation until you've got it down pat!

A Reminder to be Cautious

Some overly enthusiastic candidates ignore the negative aspects of living and working overseas and are then faced with discussing them in their interview. *Be careful not to hear only what you want to hear*. Assess carefully all the information. A wrong decision results in your failure to adjust overseas, and it leaves its mark on your work history.

Who Will Interview You?

An interview team often consists of a minimum of three people: a personnel officer, the overseas manager or in-house liaison officer, and another senior-level manager. On the other hand, only one or two people might interview you. To better prepare yourself, always ask ahead of time who will be interviewing you and inquire about the structure of the interview as outlined below.

How Long Will the Interview Last?

The interview process begins with your first telephone call. Remember, despite the impersonal nature of the exchange, the other party is assessing you. The interview itself can last from one hour to a full day. Private sector employers often prefer a day-long series of one-on-one interviews with managers of different levels. The preferred format for government institutions and NGOs is a formal interview with a three-person selection panel, usually lasting an hour.

Be prepared for a second interview for some overseas positions. Remember that interviews are usually done on a national scale, your first interview may be in person (the organization will pay to fly you in) and the second interview may be on the phone. If an offer is made, you will be given time to finalize all questions and negotiate the terms of the contract.

DIFFERENT INTERVIEW STYLES

It is important to recognize and react appropriately to different interviewing styles. Some interviewers talk non-stop while others expect you to take the initiative. Then there are those interviewers who treat the process as nothing more than an informal chat, barely discussing the job in question.

The Structured Interview

This type of interview is common for government positions. Screening is based on a candidate's education and work experience. Government interviews are often loaded with pre-written questions and you are judged in three critical areas: knowledge, ability, and personal suitability. With the CANADIAN INTERNATIONAL DEVELOPMENT AGENCY (CIDA) for example, you must obtain a minimum score of 60 per cent in each area and it is therefore crucial that you study the policies and structure of CIDA as they relate to your job area.

In most cases, there will be a Statement of Qualifications, which sets out the basic job requirements. Study the text and incorporate the buzzwords into your interview. A panel of three people often conducts government interviews. You should answer each question directly, without rambling, as your answers are measured and tabulated against a rating guide. The objective is to score as many points as possible. Don't indulge in elaborate details, just mention the highlights of your subject and move on. If you feel that the question is very important, begin with a high-level analysis and then let your interviewers know when you are expanding beyond the high level into more details.

Remember, your interviewers will offer you little feedback on your performance, as this can be seen as prejudicial. Your best tactic is to probe; for example, *"Would you like me to elaborate further?"*

The Informal Interview

The informal interview is the most popular interview style and the one that best lends itself to pre-interview preparation. In this setting, the candidate is expected to play an active role in the interview process. This is your opportunity to present yourself in the best possible light by steering the discussion to focus on your skills.

Let the interviewer lead the interview. Despite their personal and friendly tone, remember, the interviewer is probing for facts that will enable him or her to assess your suitability for the job. Remember also that the interview is a formal affair even if the interviewer is acting informally. Do not yourself become overly familiar or friendly—stay professional and sharp, but of course you can still be engaging. If the interviewer overextends into personal discussions, steer the conversation toward professional/business topics.

WHAT AN OVERSEAS EMPLOYER IS LOOKING FOR

Chapter 1, The Effective Overseas Employee, in THE BIG GUIDE discussed what skills are needed to succeed abroad. Employers may not directly mention these skills, but they will be looking for evidence that you possess these attributes. You will be questioned about the following:

- Are there limiting factors to your availability such as health, family or other extenuating circumstances?
- Do you have a realistic understanding of overseas living and working conditions?
- Do you have the technical skills? And the social competence (or soft skills) to work with colleagues of different nationalities?
- Will you fulfill the terms of your contract and demonstrate loyalty to the firm in the face of frustrations?

To explain these areas further:

Expect to be probed on your personal life and family situation: e.g., the willingness of your spouse to relocate; the number of school-aged children you have and their planned education; the health of family members. If an interviewer neglects to bring up these issues, the firm's credibility is suspect.

Major emphasis is placed on the character of the recruit. In a culturally foreign environment, you not only deal with unforeseen hardships, but also must work and live in close proximity to your colleagues. One of the recruiter's tasks is to probe for your feelings about these situations and judge your ability to survive in a different, perhaps difficult, setting.

Team effort is an important consideration in assessing your suitability for an overseas post. How will you respond to subordinates or superiors of different nationalities? In the interview, more emphasis will be placed on character evaluation than technical competence. If you have been invited to an interview, you can usually assume that your professional credentials have passed the test.

Fulfilling the terms of a contract is extremely important. Untimely departures are costly. An employer will look for tenacity, flexibility and tolerance. For example: Will you threaten to quit if your home is without running water for three months, or if the replacement part for your air conditioner does not arrive?

PREPARING FOR INTERVIEW QUESTIONS

The key to a successful interview is preparation. It is surprising how few people prepare for interviews, given that one chance is all you get.

A good method is to run through a practice session with a friend, from the first greeting to your departure. Have your (professional) friend ask questions from your resume, followed by suggestions for improvement. Then incorporate these improvements into another interview rehearsal with someone else.

TWO VERY IMPORTANT SETS OF SKILLS

Every employer, regardless of the position advertised, seeks people who possess organizational and interpersonal skills. Candidates often overlook these; yet if you can describe them well, employers can fairly easily distinguish you from other job seekers.

Organizational Skills

North American employers place great importance on efficiency, regardless of the field of work. Therefore, it is important to convey to employers that you can organize your work and manage your time. Elaborate on your workday. Do you compile a list of things to do? How do you establish priorities?

Interpersonal Skills

Employers are interested in knowing how you deal with people in different situations: Do you have problems with authority figures? How would you cope with a request for information that you couldn't fulfill? How do you handle rejection? Could you continue to work with someone who had disappointed or insulted you?

Interpersonal skills are better demonstrated through statements of opinion. For example:

"In an overseas situation, I'll be particularly attentive to the role played by different authority figures in influencing the success or failure of projects. Overseas communities seem to have a more developed local leadership structure than our highly mobile, unstructured society in North America. It is important to recognize this hierarchy by having community leaders endorse new projects."

TACTICS FOR ANSWERING QUESTIONS

The interview is one of the few times in your life when you are asked to speak about your professional self—your accomplishments, skills and strengths. You may feel uncomfortable "boasting." Here are a few suggestions to help make the task easier.

One of the best tactics is to discuss your skills through a third party. For example:

- *"My colleagues tell me the reasons they like working with me are..."*
- *"All my past employers have mentioned my enthusiasm..."*
- *"If my friends had to describe three important character traits I possess, they would probably say..."*

Another tactic is to mention the reasons for your success, or examples of your strengths:

- *"In my previous job I was particularly well known for..."*
- *"I always try to understand a situation from my adversary's point of view..."*
- *"The reasons I have been successful in developing new programs are..."*

Alternatively, you can develop an *opening theme* when answering questions. The objective here is to reinforce your personality profile—your career labels. For example, below is a response to the following question, *"What qualifications and skills do you possess that would make you an effective overseas project manager?"*

> *"Throughout my career, as an assistant country manager with the Peace Corps and in my numerous volunteer jobs, I have seen myself as a grassroots organizer—planning, making lists, and continually communicating with the people involved—these are my priorities. I think that these are the attributes that most make me effective in my work—especial while managing projects in Africa. Other skills that have helped me in my career are..."*

A response to the same question by a UN project assessment officer might be,

> *"I have a universal rule which allows me to identify the important facts quickly, regardless of the situation. I always approach new ideas with enthusiasm and this, people say, makes me approachable. I encourage others—I help them clarify their ideas. These approaches allow me to assess situations and acquire an understanding of what moulds the project. My writing and communication skills have also contributed to my effectiveness..."*

QUESTIONS AN INTERVIEWER MIGHT ASK

A thorough preparation for an interview means that you have researched each of the following questions. Don't forget that each answer, if possible, should have an international component.

General Interview Questions

- *"Tell me about yourself."*
- *"What are your major strengths/weaknesses?"*
- *"What would your colleagues say if they had to describe your working style?"*

Knowledge About the Employer

- *"What do you know about this organization?"*
- *"Why do you want to work with us and not an NGO (or government, private firm or as a consultant)?"*

Overseas Working Conditions

- *"Why do you want to work overseas?"*
- *"What qualifications/skills do you possess that will make you effective overseas?"*
- *"What working conditions do you anticipate will be different in another culture?"*
- *"Tell us about your previous overseas experience."*

Overseas Living Conditions

- *"Have you ever lived through a difficult situation? How did you cope?"*
- *"Have you been separated from your family or your loved ones for extended periods of time?"*
- *"Have you ever had to cope with loneliness?"*
- *"How would you occupy your spare time?"*
- *"How important is privacy for you? Have you ever lived in situations where you have not had a lot of privacy?"*

OPEN-ENDED ENQUIRIES

Most international interviews use open-ended enquiries, such as, *"Tell me about yourself,"* or *"What do you think of development?"* There is no right or wrong answer. Interviewers are really probing for bits of information they might not get through specific questions. It is therefore to your advantage to use these open-ended enquiries to emphasize your most important international, administrative and interpersonal skills.

SITUATIONAL QUESTIONS

One of the most interesting and challenging tactics used by international recruitment officers is the situational question. These usually concern a predicament you might encounter overseas. Trying to come up with a *right* answer can be quite unnerving.

There usually is no clear *right* answer. The recruitment officer is looking for sound judgment and analytical ability. Your worst mistake would be to make a hasty remark without first asking questions and considering the situation carefully. If you are unable to arrive at an answer, you can still score an excellent rating by presenting a carefully thought out, cautious approach to solving the problem. Here are a few tips to guide you in your answers.

Demonstrate your thinking process to the recruitment officer by *thinking out loud.* Outline important facts for serious consideration. An answer might go like this: *"In this situation it would be important to give serious consideration to (these factors). One would have to weigh the importance of (this fact) and see if it is crucial to the assessment. It is only after considering all of these factors that I would be able to make a proper decision."*

Explain how you would study a situation. For example, *"This is a very delicate situation. The first thing I would do would be to study the facts and then, depending on my findings, I would have a discussion with..."* Mention general principles of evaluation such as, *"In these circumstances it is best to proceed cautiously, record and investigate the facts. I would refrain from forming an opinion until all the information was compiled."*

You should, however, try to provide a concrete answer. State your assumptions prior to giving your assessment. For example: *"If one were to assume that (this situation) were true, and that the cultural traits of the society were (these), then it's possible the best approach to this problem would be to..."*

Try to prioritize the items for consideration. For example: *"It is clear that the major limiting factors in this situation are... and must be considered before looking at less important factors such as..."*

State your limitations, and how you would react in light of them. For example: *"Since I have never travelled to Southeast Asia and am unfamiliar with the social norms, I might be more cautious and sit and wait until my guide/interpreter returned before making a firm decision."*

If uncertain of the situation, make a comparison with a more familiar one. For example: *"While I am unfamiliar with the ethical standards binding a United Nations employee, I know that as an NGO employee I would pay a small bribe rather than have 10 volunteers spend the night sleeping at the border."*

Involve the recruitment officer in your answer by probing, but don't ask more than a few questions; the object is not to demonstrate your interrogation skills, but to show that you think before acting. For example: *"Would it be right to assume that..."* or, *"Are there any policies that would guide me in this situation?"*

In some situations the best answer is that you would seek someone else's advice. For example: *"If I am a new arrival in the country and am not yet aware of the social customs, I would seek out another expatriate who has had more experience with this situation."*

Examples of Situational Questions

- You are a Canadian project officer of a large funding organization, doing an evaluation tour overseas. At one of the projects, several employees tell you that the expatriate project manager is stealing funds. How would you handle this?

- You are a junior officer with the UNITED NATIONS DEVELOPMENT PROGRAMME (UNDP) posted in the capital city of a developing country. You are at the airport to meet a visiting expert sent by the FOOD AND AGRICULTURE ORGANIZATION (FAO). The expert has lost her passport and the local airport official insists on putting her in jail despite all pleas. It is late in the evening and you have exhausted every conceivable argument. Suddenly, the official asks for a $25 bribe to free the expert. Would you pay?

- As a teacher posted at a rural African school, you discover that another teacher is making sexual demands on students. How would you react?

- As an office manager, you have caught four labourers and one of your most trusted assistants stealing supplies from the warehouse. How would you handle this situation?

- As the manager of a worksite, one of your employees is asking for a loan and time off to visit a sick family member in another city. Would you grant the request?

- You have just been asked to accompany a very important dignitary on an official three-day visit of a provincial district. During these next three days, you must submit next year's financial requirements to head office. How would you handle this dilemma?

EXPERIENTIAL QUESTIONS

These are a relatively new type of interview question wherein the recruiter asks you to give proof of your skills with an example from your own experience. These questions can be tricky—to be ready for them, you should prepare a few short anecdotes that describe times when you have shown ingenuity, perseverance, cross-cultural savvy and other useful international skills.

Examples of Experiential Questions

- *"Describe a situation in which you demonstrated good leadership skills."*
- *"Tell us about a time when you had to cooperate with someone whose values were very different from yours."*
- *"Tell us about a time when you didn't have all the resources you needed to complete a task on time. How did you handle the situation?"*
- *"Describe a time when you used cross-cultural awareness to achieve a goal."*
- *"Outline for us a situation from your past where you were not as effective as you would like to have been when managing a project."*

THINGS TO DO BEFORE THE INTERVIEW

The interview and evaluation process actually begin with your first contact with an organization.

You should carefully research the organization. Find out some of the types of programs that they conduct in Canada and abroad, the basic structure of the organization, their annual budget, number of employees, and their mandate. Usually this information can be found in a company's annual report. If not, speak to someone who is familiar with the organization.

Do some research on the Internet or telephone ahead for a detailed job description (see Chapter 22, Phone Research Techniques). Plan your responses to standard questions based on a careful read of the job description. Try to contact a manager beforehand to find out more about the job. Speak to someone who has worked in a similar position overseas. Examples of an opening conversation:

"I'm calling to find out a little more about a job for which I'm scheduled to be interviewed."

"I am doing a little research prior to my interview to ensure that I have a good understanding of what the job entails."

Try beforehand to learn something about your interviewer(s). At the minimum, you should know their names and job titles. Ask if it will be a structured interview? How long is it likely to last? This information can probably be obtained from a secretary.

Write down at least 10 questions that you would like to ask. They should pertain to the company's major projects and your possible role with the company. Avoid questions and remarks about how the company might further your career goals.

Practice reciting out loud your personal and professional qualifications and experience that match the job you seek. (For more information, see Chapter 23, Selling Your International Skills.)

Dress professionally. Do not wear ethnic clothing even if you are applying for a rural job in a developing country. Men should wear a suit and tie. Women should dress conservatively. If two candidates are equal in ability (and this often happens), the final choice can rest on appearance.

Look organized and prepared. Carry a briefcase containing a pen, a notepad, a typed list of references, two extra copies of your resume and cover letter packaged in envelopes, and a few examples of your past work, such as reports or publications.

THINGS TO DO DURING THE INTERVIEW

You have probably heard the popular theory that interviewers make up their minds during the first five minutes of the interview. It is only human to pass judgment on others. Here are some helpful hints to create a good first impression.

Arrive 15 minutes early. Familiarize yourself with your surroundings, read company newsletters, the bulletin board or something of interest to mention during the interview. Double-check your appearance. Hang your coat, have your arms free when you enter the interview room.

Use a firm handshake when introducing yourself: *"Hello, my name is Francis Drummond."* If there is an interview team, extend your hand to each member. And, unless otherwise informed, use the titles *Ms.* or *Mr.* and their surnames. As simple as all of this may seem, experience has shown that many candidates are unable to carry this off with confidence. I would like to repeat this: as simple as all of this may seem, experience has shown that many candidates are unable to carry this off with confidence.

Sit with your pad and pen ready to make notes (but don't be too obvious about this). If it is in your character, use your pad to draw a diagram when answering an interview question. You may want to jot down contract terms, key ideas and any follow-up actions that may arise from the interview. Even if you don't make use of the pen and paper, you are showing your preparedness.

If you have printed materials or a portfolio of project material, bring it to the interview.

Be conscious of potentially damaging non-verbal communication, such as a nervous foot tapping or excessive laughter. Sit in a relaxed manner, hands out of your pockets, back straight. Lean back a little when thinking, and forward a little when speaking. Consciously make eye contact with each interviewer.

Be dynamic and project enthusiasm through your voice.

Approach the overseas job interview as a meeting ground in which both parties interview each other. Try to make the recruiter's job easier by feeding him or her information about yourself in logical order.

Allow the recruitment officer to set the pace. Always ask how long the interview will last. But if two-thirds of the interview time has elapsed and you feel the interview team has not covered your important skills (some interviewers are not great at their jobs), this is the time to take the initiative. Examples:

- *"I would like to take a few moments to elaborate on a few other relevant job experiences to allow you to better analyze my skills."*
- *"I would like to mention a few more factors in my background that could help you assess my qualifications."*
- *"Would you permit me to add a few words about some of my other skills?"*

You will have the confidence to execute the tactics above if you have taken the time to analyze your skill sets, taken stock of your skills inventory and written a functional, skill-based resume. All of your hard work will pay off during the interview. Afterwards, thank your interviewers by name while shaking their hands firmly:

"Thank you for your time and consideration. I appreciated this opportunity to learn more about your organization. You have an interesting program and I look forward to hearing from you."

And ask when you may expect an answer.

Things to Avoid During the Interview

- Do not dominate the conversation. The normal guide is to speak half the time.
- Don't linger on a topic for more than four to six minutes. Your answers should be short, preferably under three minutes.
- Do not overuse humour; the interview is a serious meeting.
- Don't be late. If there is a remote chance that you will be, mitigate the damage by phoning ahead to apologize and explain your delay.

THINGS TO DO AFTER THE INTERVIEW

At the first opportunity, jot down what you could have done better. Use each successive interview to improve your performance for the next.

Immediately send a written thank-you note to the interviewers. This demonstrates your continued interest in the job, and it also gives you an opportunity to mention any information that might have been missed in the interview. You can send this by e-mail, or for a bit more drama, fax a perfectly hand written note, or if longer—a typed letter.

Call the company at an appointed date to inquire about their decision to hire. If the answer is negative, it is appropriate to ask why you were not selected. If you are too emotional to ask, call back a day or two later.

"I'm calling to discuss the results of my interview. I would like to ask a few questions and get feedback about my interview..."

If the answer is positive, celebrate!

A LAST WORD

In most interview situations, the employer is interested in your thought processes, your flow of ideas and is not looking for right or wrong answers. Let the interview team see how you analyze information; don't just offer the results of your analysis. Be prepared. Be confident. Relax, and go for the job you've always wanted!

CHAPTER 27
Jobs by Regions of the World

You have probably pointed to a world map and said, "How can I find a job in Hong Kong... London... Los Angeles? How exciting that would be!" But is it really possible to focus your job search on a specific country? This chapter will try to answer this question by looking specifically at international job opportunities in seven regions of the world where private sector jobs for expatriates are most abundant. We have, therefore, concentrated most of our analysis on industrialized countries and emerging markets.

The regions covered are the United States, Mexico and Latin America, Western Europe, Eastern Europe and the former Soviet Union, the Middle East, Africa and Asia Pacific. In this chapter we focus mainly on private sector jobs and, to some extent, opportunities for self-starters and entrepreneurs. The intent is not to provide an exhaustive overview of each region, but rather to highlight current hot job markets and touch on some of the idiosyncrasies of finding work in different parts of the world. We will outline the prospects, strategies and skill requirements for each region.

TACTICS FOR REGIONAL JOB HUNTING

This is an excellent time to be thinking about an international career. Global trade and financial flows are expanding at unprecedented rates. Technological advances have made business communications both quicker and less costly. Alongside these developments, companies are increasingly expanding overseas, creating numerous opportunities for international jobs.

A manager with a Canadian telecommunications company who has responsibility for the Middle East says, *"I tell my son, who is going to university now, 'Don't focus on getting a job in North America. Broaden your horizons. The world is small. And from a resume point of view, it's very valuable to work a couple of years offshore.'"*

Be Bold

People who get overseas jobs in the private sector are not necessarily those with the best qualifications, but often they are the most determined. As you read the personal stories at the end of each section in this chapter, you'll find that the men and women who get jobs with international businesses are generally self-starters who have firm goals and make things happen. We all have various amounts of motivation. The lesson is to use all that you've got.

A Canadian lawyer in his 30s took a leave of absence from a large Toronto law firm to earn an MBA degree from the LONDON SCHOOL OF ECONOMICS. With the help of his Canadian law contacts, a Parisian law office hired him for the summer. But he returned to the Toronto law firm after several months of trying unsuccessfully to get a job in business, law or finance in Europe. He has not given up, and has this to say:

"The best advice, after having been through the whole process, is to have a dream and stick to it. The people that have been most successful in obtaining jobs overseas are single-minded people—not those who have a vague notion that they'd like to work abroad or maybe try something different. They are the people who say they know they want to work in finance in London and start early and make all the necessary applications and contacts."

Being Canadian

Being Canadian can be a tremendous advantage in international business. Even though Canada has a tiny population by world standards, it is well known as an active trader and member of the Group of Eight (G8) industrialized nations. Most importantly, Canada has an international reputation as a country that doesn't carry a great deal of ideological baggage. For that reason alone, many countries prefer to do business with Canadian firms. A partner in a large Toronto firm that practices commercial law all over the world put it this way:

"Being Canadian means you're not German or Japanese or American, and that is a remarkable advantage. I think too few Canadian companies understand the extent to which having that Canadian passport or flying that Canadian flag will give you an enormous advantage over your American, Japanese and German competitors...

"Many international firms would welcome a Canadian application. I know dozens of lawyers, accountants and MBAs who couldn't get jobs with Canadian firms. But Americans, Germans and Japanese are doing a megatrade in these new markets and the service industries are really keen to hire Canadians."

Although being Canadian can be an asset because our country is not a dominant one, it can also prove to be a liability for the same reason. In most societies, especially in the corporate world, which schools you studied at and which companies you've worked for are of great importance. Compounding this problem is the fact that neither our universities nor our companies (with a few notable exceptions) are well known abroad, and even these tend to be overshadowed by their larger American, European, and Japanese counterparts.

Canadian business acumen and university degrees are not inferior. In fact, in most cases they stand up extremely well to foreign scrutiny. For some fields, the problem lies in convincing potential overseas employers and clients who have never heard of the Canadian company or university. If it is any consolation, this is a handicap we share with job seekers from most small countries.

In your job applications, make sure you describe the position of your university ("one of the top three schools in Canada") or company ("market leader in..."). This should be mentioned directly in your resume or covering letter and certainly in your direct discussions with future employers. (For more information, see Chapter 24, International Resumes.) Also, consider the option to study abroad. A degree earned at a well-known institution, such as the LONDON SCHOOL OF ECONOMICS or HARVARD, will help pave the way for an international career. A prestigious school with an international reputation can certainly help its graduates find jobs.

Where to Work

So, you know you want a job overseas, but where in the world should you go? Many people are equally happy to find a job in Europe, Asia or Latin America. In this case, your job search should focus on regions where demand is strongest for your specific skills and experience. This can be a moving target. The country that was hot for computer programmers yesterday may be stone cold tomorrow.

A big key to success is to go where the action is, where business is booming and there are lots of opportunities. In the field of finance, for example, the action was in New York and London in the mid- to late 1980s. In the early 1990s, it moved to Eastern Europe and Japan. In 1993–1994, emerging markets in Asia Pacific and Latin America were attracting the most capital. Since 2000, Asian countries like India and China are still among the world's fastest growing economies, and the EU's recent expansion into Eastern Europe may jump-start countries like Poland. As world events evolve, nothing is certain. There may be finance jobs opening in Lebanon or Thailand, to name just two possibilities.

Big infrastructure projects such as airports, highways and electric power projects, for which Western expertise is frequently sought, tend to move around the world, chasing the healthier economies. Mining and oil and gas exploration follow the latest finds in fuels and minerals, according to a variety of other country- and commodity-specific variables.

Professions in Demand

Every career, every level of expertise has an international component where Canadians are finding work abroad. From the grape picker to the financial analyst, the English teacher to the heavy-duty mechanic, all professions are represented.

If you haven't yet made a definite career choice, ask yourself whether any of the following professions interest you: engineer, geologist, computer specialist, telecommunications expert. Our research shows that these professionals have the best chance of getting a job outside Canada. If none of these avenues appeals to you, what about opportunities in finance, law, the environment, agriculture, medicine, project management, consulting, teaching English, or human resource development? These professions are similarly in demand around the globe, although the choice of countries may be somewhat narrower.

Companies that move people abroad are looking for unique packages of skills that they are unable to hire locally. The strongest combination for an international career is probably engineering with an MBA or law degree, but any double-barrelled combination is a strong ticket.

In the legal services field, try applying to large worldwide firms like BAKER & MACKENZIE or foreign firms with exchange programs like FRESH FIELDS in London. Because Canadian jurisprudence is based on common law (with the exception of Quebec), it is relatively easy to qualify for work in the UK or any other Commonwealth country. (For more information, see Chapter 31, International Law Careers.)

Accounting is growing more and more international in scope, as a few large firms acquire and form partnerships with smaller firms around the world. KPMG LLP and PRICEWATERHOUSECOOPERS (PwC) are just two examples of international chartered accounting firms operating in Canada as well as in dozens of other countries. Another option is to work for the financial department of a large international company, such as ROYAL DUTCH SHELL, which moves accountants to overseas posts.

Engineers working in construction will want to try one of the large Canadian firms that have a substantial share of their business overseas, such as SNC-LAVALIN INTERNATIONAL INC. or GOLDER ASSOCIATES. (For more information on engineering, see Chapter 32, Engineering Careers Abroad. For more information on Canadian and US firms, see Chapter 35, Private Sector Firms in Canada and Chapter 36, Private Sector Firms in the US.)

Whatever your expertise, there are international jobs available. Just remember that determination, persistence, and the single-minded pursuit of your international objective are crucial.

Strategies

There are four principle ways of getting a private sector job overseas: you can apply to a North American company with international operations and try to get transferred abroad. Alternatively, you can go to the region where you want to work and try to get hired. You can also base yourself in Canada and go abroad on short- or long-term contracts as a consultant. Finally, you can start your own international business.

The first of these routes can be both the most comfortable and most secure. If you're successful in getting a transfer, the company will likely pay for the transfer of your family and household goods, and will take care of visas. The benefits often include a housing allowance, tax exemptions and private schooling for your children.

But it's a competitive route. There is often a long queue in the organization for a transfer. (If you have the necessary working papers for a foreign jurisdiction, they may give you the jump over others.) You will also be expected to work extremely hard—the days when a company moved you overseas to put in a 35-hour week are history.

Don't be too choosy about where you will go. The human resources manager with a large international oil company says everybody wants to move to London, but she can never staff all the company's open positions in Nigeria. If you do agree to take a posting in Nigeria, which is considered difficult and dangerous, you will most likely be offered a more attractive destination the next time around.

The second route is to move overseas, possibly as a student, and look for work from there. This path is more or less successful depending on the person and region in question, and will be discussed in greater depth later in the chapter. But a few general tips: cold calls from Canada do not work, nor do a rash of c.v.'s sent out to foreign companies—you have to go there. Some experienced overseas workers suggest you save enough for a two- or three-week exploratory trip where you meet with local officials, people in your field and Canadian trade officials. As one expert suggested, what you can learn about the market grows exponentially every day you spend there soaking up information.

The third route, to base yourself in Canada and go abroad on a short- or long-term contract, is typically open only to people who have built up a considerable network of good contacts and specialized expertise. International consulting work is competitive and expensive. There is an active grapevine among international companies and organizations, and consultants must work hard at establishing a reputation for quality.

The fourth and final route has become increasingly common among young graduates, especially in Asia Pacific and Eastern Europe. It is discussed at length in the applicable regional sections.

Visas

While a Canadian passport is well suited to an international career, having a second passport is always an asset. That's because those precious work visas—so important yet so hard to come by—are easier to get when you can claim citizenship in the country you're working in. If you have a relative from another country (no matter how distant), it is worth making inquiries with the appropriate consulate or embassy as to whether your distant roots might qualify you for citizenship or immigrant status.

Always verify visa information before heading to a foreign country. Work visas are almost always necessary to work legally at a full-time job in a foreign country. In a few countries, a work visa can be applied for locally, but more often you must have one before leaving Canada. By the same token, it is almost impossible to get a work visa without a firm job offer. If a large, international company hires you, the firm will take care of the bureaucratic paperwork and usually pay any expenses to do with visas. The importance of confirming visa requirements with embassies or consulates before leaving Canada cannot be stressed too strongly. Visa regulations change all the time, and the information in this book or any other book may well be out of date by the time you read it.

A few countries with high demand for skilled labour will allow you to arrive on a tourist visa, look for work, and then, when you have a firm job offer, leave the country briefly to apply for a work visa from a neighbouring country.

In addition to speaking with visa officials, it is always worth canvassing for practical advice from people who have lived in the regions where you want to work. Countries in Asia, Latin America and Eastern Europe, where English-language teachers are in great demand, may not require work visas, or may simply turn a blind eye to infractions. The same holds true for casual jobs in the service industry in some countries.

If you plan to travel to a foreign country to explore job possibilities or business opportunities, be wary about telling immigration officials that you are looking for work. You may not have the correct visa, and might be turned away. It's usually better to say that you're a tourist if you have no intention of working on a particular trip. A self-employed Canadian journalist who travels around the world writing about the banking industry for some 40 trade publications says he almost never tells officials that he is entering to do work.

Language and Culture

Speaking the local language is a valuable, if not crucial, skill for any type of overseas employment. In a few countries, however, including Singapore and the Netherlands, mastering the local language is not as important. While English is clearly emerging as the language of international business, almost all overseas employees have second-language skills. A word of warning, however, since English is increasingly valued, you might well encounter people who profess to speak it and actually don't. Never assume that copious nodding and a repeated "yes!" mean that someone understands you! (For more information on language skills, see Chapter 5, Learning a Foreign Language.)

Traditionally, some of the soft skills of international relations discussed elsewhere in this book have not been considered as important by the private sector. But this attitude is changing. Large international companies spend thousands of dollars training their overseas workers in cross-cultural skills, which are essential to effectiveness in an overseas environment. International MBA graduates are required to take courses in cross-cultural management and communications.

Clearly, an international skills set is increasingly crucial to landing international work. In some fields, such as oil exploration and computer software design, companies are looking for trained and experienced engineers for particular jobs they have to fill. But they assume you can quickly learn the "soft" skills of tolerance, patience and getting along with people of another culture. Even when these skills aren't yet considered critical for your work, it can't help but enhance your job prospects to refine them. At the very least, it will help you enjoy your posting.

A LAST WORD

The opportunities for Canadians around the world vary depending on one's skills, experience and the economic conditions of the region or country that is targeted. While some professions are constantly in demand (such as medical and oil industry personnel in the Gulf states), economic and political conditions change rapidly, and so does job demand. Your best preparation is to read the most up-to-date and solid information you can get your hands on and talk to as many knowledgeable people as you can, before targeting your job search. Much can be accomplished before you leave home, but in most cases, there is no substitute for spending a few weeks in the country of your choice on an exploratory mission. Best of luck!

RESOURCES

This chapter contains the following Resources sections: Country Guides & Reports; United States; Mexico & Latin America; Western Europe; Eastern Europe & Former Soviet Union; Middle East; Africa; and Asia Pacific.

COUNTRY GUIDES & REPORTS

These resources provide snapshot pictures of country conditions. Find factual information on politics, economy, geography and culture. Consult travel advisories and learn about local news. This type of information is important to acquire before an interview, when networking with employers prior to a consulting visit abroad or when you are moving for a new international assignment. For more country-specific information, see the Country Guides & Reports Resources in Chapter 27, Jobs by Regions of the World.

Altapedia Online 🖥
www.atlapedia.com/index.html ◆ Provides facts, figures and statistical data on geography, climate, people, religion, language, history, economy and maps on just about any place on earth. [ID:2772]

Asia Pacific Country Backgrounders 📖 🖥
2002, 15 pages each ➤ Asia Pacific Foundation of Canada, Suite 666, 999 Canada Place, Vancouver, BC V6C 3E1, Canada, www.asiapacific.ca, Free on-line; VISA, MC; 604-684-5986, fax 604-681-1370 ◆ A series of booklets on 14 Asia Pacific countries and Canada's economic relationship with each of them. Includes key facts and figures, economic and trade statistic comparisons, Canada's ranking among major trading partners, imports and exports, main sectors of opportunity for Canadian business and more. Recommended for entrepreneurs and others seeking quick, dependable facts on Canada's Asian trade partners. [ID:2166]

Background Notes Series 📖
Annual ➤ Department of State, CA/PA, US Government Printing Office, Room 5807, Washington, DC 20520-4818, USA, www.access.gpo.gov/su_docs, $55 US/set; VISA, MC; 202-512-1800, fax 202-512-2250 ◆ Background Notes are factual publications containing information on all the countries of the world with which the United States has relations. They include facts on the country's land, people, history, government, political conditions, economy, and its relations with other countries and the United States. Helpful primers for Canadians working overseas. [ID:2076]

Canadian Foreign Post Indexes 🖥
Monthly, Statistics Canada ➤ www.statcan.ca, Free on-line; Fr ◆ Statistics Canada researches and publishes these post indexes on a monthly basis in order to calculate the approximate cost of living in various overseas cities. Post indexes are based on price comparisions of family expenditures such as food consumed at home, meals in restaurants, household maintenance and supplies, domestic help, clothing, transportation, health and personal care, reading and recreation. Post indexes are relative to the cost of living in Ottawa, which is assigned an index of 100. A city with a post index of 120 would have a cost of living 20 per cent higher than that in Ottawa. From the index, click the "Products and Services" menu, then navigate to "Prices and Indexes" through the "Free" publications link. [ID:2259]

CIA World Factbook 🖥
www.cia.gov/cia/publications/factbook ◆ Easy-to-use, well-organized and relatively authoritative, this Web site is a great source of information on almost every country in the world. You'll find updated maps and information on geography, political systems, climate, economy, population demographics and culture. A good place to start your research. [ID:2278]

CNN Interactive 💻
www.cnn.com, Free on-line ◆ This site, created by one of the world's largest media giants, provides updated international headlines including news, weather, sports, science and health. Most of the news is related to the US and reflects what you can see in their television broadcast. [ID:2330]

Consular Affairs: Information and Assistance for Canadians Abroad 🏛
www.voyage.gc.ca, fax (800) 575-2500; ℱr ◆ The Canadian government produces this great Web site, featuring essential travel, including country and regional reports, travel updates, maps, pre-departure information, and emergency contacts. Check out the weekly travel bulletin on safety "hot spots" for the most current information. [ID:2756]

Craighead's International Business Travel and Relocation Guide to 84 Countries 📖
2004, 4 volumes ➤ Thomson Gale, 835 Penobscot Bldg., 645 Griswold Street, Detroit, MI 48226-4094, USA, www.gale.com, $775 US; Credit Cards; 800-877-4253 ext. 1330, fax 800-414-5043; Available in large libraries ◆ Now covering 84 countries, this authoritative four-volume set is designed specifically to meet the needs of individuals who require in-depth information about doing business, and living and working in the countries most important to international business. Craighead's provides data necessary to understand and evaluate the political, economic and business environment and everyday living conditions of foreign destinations. [ID:2040]

Cultural Profiles Project 💻
www.settlement.org/cp/english ◆ Citizenship and Immigration Canada, in association with the AMNI Centre of the Faculty of Social Work at the University of Toronto, has developed this excellent Web site profiling the life and customs of 102 countries worldwide. Select the country you are interested in and then navigate the information on landscape, family life, health care, education, religion and the arts, just to name a few. This is a good, reliable starting point for exploring the cultural information of your overseas destination, with each country page listing links to more in-depth information on the Web or in print. [ID:2655]

Culture Shock! Series 📖
Graphic Arts Center Publishing Company, 3019 NW Yeon, Portland, OR 97210, USA, www.gacpc.com, $13.95 US each; 503-226-2402, fax 503-223-1410 ◆ There are now 42 country guides available, making it one of the most successful and long-standing reference sources on international social and business customs. [ID:2104]

Culture Smart! Series 📖
Graphic Arts Center Publishing Company, 3019 NW Yeon, Portland, OR 97210, USA, www.gacpc.com, $9.95 US each; 503-226-2402, fax 503-223-1410 ◆ A new travel series focusing on cultural familiarization. Contains easy-to-access cultural and etiquette information, and stuffs into your backpack. The series includes titles on Australia, Britain, China, France, Germany, India, Ireland, Japan, the Netherlands, Russia, Spain and Thailand. Break yourself into a lifelong journey toward cultural learning with these entertaining books. [ID:2537]

Culturgrams: The Nations Around Us 📖
Annual, David M. Kennedy Center for International Studies, four volumes: 730 pages ➤ David M. Kennedy Center for International Studies, Brigham Young University, 280 HRCB, Provo, UT 84602, USA, http://kennedy.byu.edu, $129.99 US; Credit Cards; 800-528-6279, fax 801-378-7075 ◆ Culturgrams are four-page summaries containing highlights of 181 cultures throughout the world. They cover customs, manners, lifestyles and other specialized information for those with a big interest but little time. Comes in looseleaf or bound edition and includes a free CD-ROM. An excellent quick reference tool. [ID:2025]

Current History 📖
9 issues/year ➤ Current History, 4225 Main Street, Philadelphia, PA 19127-9989, USA, www.currenthistory.com, $40.75 US/year; VISA, MC, AMEX; 215-482-4464, fax 215-482-9197 ◆ This is the oldest US publication dedicated exclusively to world affairs. It is useful for its region-

by-region annual summaries. Each issue focuses on one region or country, providing annual coverage on China, the former Soviet Union, the Middle East, Latin America, Africa and South and Southeast Asia. It also has a country-by-country "Month in Review" feature. Excellent if you're about to travel to a region and need a quick overview of its current political trends; order back issues or visit the indexed Web site. [ID:2373]

Directory of EU Information Sources 📖
2001, 1,250 pages ➤ Euroconfidentiel SA., BP 29, Rixensart, B-1330, Belgium, €213; Credit Cards; (32) (2) 652 02 84, fax (32) (2) 653 01 80, www.amazon.com ◆ This directory is the most comprehensive compilation of contacts and published information on the European Union, providing access to over 12,500 information sources. Contains in-depth information on all the EU institutions and lists key personnel, databases, Web sites, publications, information networks and libraries specific to each institution. The publication further details press agencies and journalists, consultants and lawyers specializing in EU affairs, professional associations, universities offering post-graduate courses in European integration and EU grants and loans programs. Easy-to-use and clearly indexed, it is the ideal desktop companion for anyone whose business is Europe. [ID:2087]

Employment Conditions Abroad Ltd. (ECA) ♔
www.eca-international.com, Anchor House, 15 Britten Street, London, SW3 3TY, UK, (44) (171) 351-5000, fax (44) (171) 351-9396 ◆ ECA is an information and advisory service for companies worldwide that employ expatriates or local nationals abroad. Through easy access to country-specific costs of living, housing allowances, hardship compensation and taxation issues, the site assists members to administer international work assignments. ECA serves a wide range of industries including banking, pharmaceutical, drilling, software, manufacturing and engineering. ECA is not a recruitment agency for individuals seeking employment. ECA maintains a useful Web site, with links to its global offices that contain information on products and services. [ID:2215]

E-thologies 💻
www.e-thologies.com/menu-en.asp ◆ Produced by the Centre for Intercultural Learning (CIL), this informative and accessible Web site is a great source for country information on the Web. Select the country you're interested in from the pull-down menu and get up-to-date demographic information. Click the tabs for links and more detailed information relating to the history, politics, geography, culture, economy and media of your destination. A great place to start your country research. Recommended. [ID:2685]

Foreign Affairs Canada (FAC) ♔
www.fac-aec.gc.ca; Fr ◆ FAC's Web site provides information on international trade and the countries and regions that make up the international system within which Canada exists. Authoritative fact sheets, population data and highlights of special issues complement the usual political and economic information available. A good source of trustworthy information. [ID:2267]

Library of Congress Portals to the World 💻
www.loc.gov/rr/international/portals.html ◆ This is one of the single best Web portals available for cross-cultural and country information on the Internet. Produced by the Library of Congress, it is comprehensive, easy-to-use and up-to-date. Simply select the country you are interested in and navigate reliable links to culture, history, education, business, commerce and economy, religion, government and politics, and recreation, just to name a few. You'll be hard pressed to find dead links on these pages. Rather, you'll surf a plethora of informative and high-quality Web resources in which you're bound to find the answers you seek and a whole lot more. Mark this as a favourite and start journeying from your rickety old office chair. [ID:2654]

Living Abroad International Resource Center 💻
www.livingabroad.com ◆ This US and European Web site is a great resource for anything related to living abroad, especially country-specific information for international assignees and business travellers. [ID:2795]

Lonely Planet 📖 🖥

www.lonelyplanet.com ◆ This Web site offers much more than simply a method of purchasing guide books. There are extensive maps, a newsletter, travel forums, travelogues, advice on healthy and safe travelling, and a great links page to some of the best travel sites on-line. A fabulous site from the publishers of the best travel guides on the market. Recommended. [ID:2280]

Martindale's "The Reference Desk" 🖥

www.martindalecenter.com ◆ This is a great directory, which contains an "International Countries" section with links to 272 country, territorial and municipal pages on-line. An excellent resource for learning about your next exotic posting. [ID:2362]

Monthly Bulletin of Statistics 📖 🖥

2003, 288 pages ➤ United Nations Publications, Sales and Marketing Section, Room DC2-853, Department I004, New York, NY 10017, USA, www.un.org/Pubs/sales.htm, $60 US; Credit Cards; 800-253-9646, fax 212-963-3489; Fr ◆ Each issue gives you a closer look at economic and social statistics from more than 200 countries and territories, as well as providing quarterly statistics on industrial production. Written in French and English, each issue details over 70 subjects such as population, food, trade, production, finance and national income; it also presents special monthly features on topics including fuel imports, industrial output, world shipbuilding and civil aviation traffic. "MBS" is published in association with the Department for Economic and Social Information and Policy Analysis (DESIPA). Annual subscription to the "MBS" includes access to "MBS On-line". [ID:2520]

Reuters On-Line 🖥

www.reuters.com, Free on-line ◆ This news service is provided by the largest international multimedia news agency in the world. Extremely current and comprehensive. [ID:2318]

Taylor & Francis Social Sciences Journals 🖥 👬

www.tandf.co.uk/journals/listings/soc.asp#top ◆ So, now you know where you're being deployed. You've read all the books from Chapters and surfed all the Web sites you can find on your region. But you want something a little more in-depth. Here's your next stop. Taylor & Francis publishes a surprising variety of scholarly journals, for example, "The Journal of Israeli History," "Ethnomusicology Forum" or "African Identities." Find them by region and head to the library. Better yet, many have free on-line sample copies. Happy research! [ID:2782]

Tourism Offices Worldwide Directory 🖥

www.towd.com ◆ This Web site consists of a searchable directory of over 1,400 tourist offices worldwide. A great resource for planning your overseas adventure. [ID:2351]

Travel Finder 🖥

www.travel-finder.com ◆ This specialized search engine is designed to help you find Web sites with country information, as well as travel service providers by country. It contains 8,000 sites in its database, and you can add your favourite travel-related site. [ID:2281]

US Department of State 👬

www.state.gov ◆ On the Web site, you will find information about the Department, press releases, information for US travellers abroad, country-specific information, employment opportunities, business information and current international issues that the US government considers a priority. A great backgrounder before deploying internationally. Huge amount of funding for overseas projects comes from the US Department of State. Anyone interested in overseas development project work should familiarize themselves with the ins and outs of State's policies and projects. [ID:2319]

The World Guide 📖

Annual, 628 pages ➤ Subscription Office, New Internationalist, Unit 17, 35 Riviera Drive, Markham, ON L3R 8N4, Canada, www.newint.org, $59.95 CDN; Credit Cards; 905-946-0407, fax 905-946-0410 ◆ Provides a wealth of information on the countries of the world from a refreshing perspective, drawing on United Nations' and other mainstream data. Includes all the facts, history, political and economic analyses found in a conventional reference work, as well as information on the issues central to the lives of people in Africa, Asia, the Middle East, Latin America and the Caribbean. Global reports on global issues like HIV, terrorism and up-to-date statistics on literacy, health and public expenditure. An excellent source of country-specific information when researching your future posting overseas! [ID:2127]

The United States
STILL THE HIGH-TECH MECCA

Without a doubt, the United States offers the most opportunities for Canadian professionals who want to work in another country. This huge market of some 270 million people is right next door, the working language is English, and the customs, training and business culture are similar to our own.

Even before the North American Free Trade Agreement (NAFTA) was signed in 1989, Canada and the US were each other's largest trading partners. Since then, the opportunities for Canadian companies, entrepreneurs, consultants and professionals have never been better. US demand for university-educated, experienced workers in the high-tech field, especially the computer industry, looks insatiable at the moment.

In this chapter, international work in the US is different from that described for other countries in this book. Many Canadians who move to work in the US eventually settle there. US jobs offered to Canadians are often full-time and permanent. This contrasts with international work in other countries which tends to be for two- or three-year assignments.

It often seems Canadians find more to damn than to praise about the US. But keep an open mind. As similar as it is, the US is still a foreign country where you'll gain valuable experience—and we haven't even mentioned the better weather!

Where the Jobs Are

Despite recent turbulence, the computer industry remains a major employer of Canadians in the US. The North American Free Trade Agreement (NAFTA) has meant that Canadians are often regarded by high-tech companies in the same light as their US counterparts. That said, the growing trend toward "outsourcing" such work as software programming or data processing to new high-tech centres in the south of India has changed the job landscape in the US for Canadians. Still, for those who are persistent and have the right skills, there continues to be work in the US for network specialists, systems engineers, systems analysts, systems architects, or hardware designers. Intra-company transfers by multinational IT firms continue much as in the 1990s.

The Pacific Northwest, including Oregon and Washington, is now an important region for software design. Washington, DC and suburbs in Virginia are strong for hardware jobs, while New York City is growing in computer systems design, especially for financial applications. California's Silicon Valley, of course, remains a major centre for experienced programmers, attracting top talent from around the globe, including Canada. Salaries are often equal to those offered to Americans, and usually higher than what you'll get in Canada.

The emphasis is on experience. Like most other sectors, the computer industry wants workers with a few years of job experience under their belts. A management consulting firm in New Jersey that recruits Canadian "techies" says the minimum requirements are a college degree in math, computer science, physics or business administration and two years' experience in the industry.

Other Job Opportunities

Job demand is strongest in the most highly specialized and highly trained fields. If you're an experienced microbiologist, for example, you should have no trouble finding a job in the US.

Despite a recent glut of MBAs, experienced professionals in the finance and banking industries, including financial analysts, investment dealers and accountants, can often find US jobs. But the glut of MBAs does make finding your first job tougher than it once was. Lawyers with unique specialties should be able to tailor a career to meet US requirements. Specialized Canadian doctors are often wooed by US hospitals and clinics, and nurses can usually find work in some states, but nursing salaries tend to be lower than at home. Experienced teachers can often find work in private or public schools, but these are usually in states offering the lowest salaries.

To find out whether there is demand in the US for people in your trade or profession, check with the union or professional association in the state or city that you want to move to. The careers section of *The New York Times* and other large city newspapers will give you an idea of which professions are in demand and where.

International jobs with the UNITED NATIONS in New York or the IMF and WORLD BANK in Washington are open to Canadians. (For more information, see Chapter 41, United Nations & Other IGOs.)

The US is a huge job market and it's close by—it's likely that any job you can think of is filled by a Canadian somewhere south of the border.

NAFTA

The free trade pact has made life easier for members of some 60 professions who can now cross the Canada–US border to work for 1 to 2 years without applying for a visa. (See the list below for a partial list of those professions.)

If you fall into one of the lucky professions, all you need to do is present proof of Canadian citizenship, proof of your licence or degree, the contract with your US employer and filing fees of $56 to a US official at any border crossing. (Most professionals exempted under Chapter 15, Section 2 of NAFTA already had privileged access before 1989, but the process was more cumbersome, requiring proof of special expertise and several letters of reference.) If you qualify under the exempt-professions category, your spouse and children may accompany you but they won't be permitted to work. Children are allowed to attend public school.

The trade pact also eliminates the need for a labour market test when a company moves its staff south of the border. Instead of having to prove that a certain employee from Canada is the only one who can do the job, the firm merely has to show that she or he is an engineer, for example, and has a work contract in hand.

List of Select Professions Under NAFTA

- **GENERAL:** Accountant, Architect, Computer Systems Analyst, Economist, Engineer, Forester, Graphic Designer, Hotel Manager, Industrial Designer, Interior Designer, Land Surveyor, Landscape Architect, Lawyer, Librarian, Management Consultant, Mathematician, Range Conservationist, Recreational Therapist, Research Assistant, Technical Publications Writer, Vocational Counsellor

- **SCIENTIST:** Agriculturalist, Animal Breeder, Animal Scientist, Apiculturist, Astronomer, Biochemist, Biologist, Chemist, Dairy Scientist, Entomologist, Epidemiologist, Geneticist, Geologist, Geochemist, Geophysicist, Horticulturist, Meteorologist, Physicist, Plant Breeder, Poultry Scientist, Soil Scientist, Scientific Technician, Silviculturist, Urban Planner, Veterinarian, Zoologist

- **MEDICAL/ALLIED:** Dentist, Dietitian, Medical Laboratory, Technologist, Nutritionist, Physician, Physiotherapist, Psychologist, Occupational Therapist, Pharmacist, Pharmacologist, Registered Nurse, Social Worker

- **TEACHER:** College, Seminary, University

It's worth keeping in mind that NAFTA is really about *trade* and the free movement of capital. In contrast with the provisions of the European Union, which allows its citizens to seek work almost anywhere in their fellow EU member countries, NAFTA does not guarantee the free movement of labour. For most job seekers, the rules of employment haven't changed. And a Canadian won't find it any easier to get permanent residency status in the US, post-NAFTA.

But it *is* easier for Canadian companies and investors to do business and to trade in the US since the original Canada–US Free Trade Agreement took effect in 1989. Visitors who are on business for their Canadian employers find it simpler and less bureaucratic to travel back and forth. So do people who work for a Canadian company that conducts substantial trade in the US and those investing a substantial amount in an enterprise in the US.

Canadian companies, large and small, continue to benefit from low tariffs and easier access, as well as from a low Canadian dollar that makes Canadian exports more attractive (even with the recent fall of the US dollar against all major currencies). A 1994 study by Quebec's Caisse de dépôt pension fund showed that among Quebec's exports of high value, low tariff goods expanded 90 per cent in the 4 years following the signing of the NAFTA, while total Canadian exports in that sector grew 49 per cent.

Entrepreneurs and business people who are considering relocating to the US will need to conduct market research and have a business plan before making a move.

The Green Card and Other Types of Visas

There are several other US work visas available to Canadians. The rules change, so make sure you check with the US consulate before attempting to work in the US.

The famous green card signals permanent residency status and is extremely difficult to come by unless you marry an American. Unlike most countries, the US offers a fast-track route for permanent residency to people who are deemed truly unique, but you might have to be the CEO of a Fortune 500 company.

The US offers a yearly lottery for several thousand immigrant visas, or green cards, specifying each year what nationalities may apply. Canadians are rarely eligible because Canada is considered a high-admission state. Canadian residents of another nationality may be eligible—call the US consulate nearest you for further details. Beware of advertisements that occasionally run in Canadian newspapers offering legal help with the US lottery. You don't need a lawyer if you are an eligible nationality, and Canadians cannot apply anyway.

There is also a three-year visa with a possibility of extension available to the same professionals who qualify under NAFTA. From 2001 to 2003 only 195,000 of these visas were available worldwide, and in 2002, only 79,100 of these H-1B visas were actually issued. In 2004, the limit returned to the 65,000 originally permitted under the US's *1990 Immigration Act*, although high-tech employers are lobbying hard to increase this limit again.

A Canadian studying at a US university may apply for a visa to work on campus during the school year. You aren't supposed to work off campus, but some students do find off-campus jobs under the table.

There is another visa (known as the E2 or Treaty Investor Visa) for people interested in starting a small business in the US. Prospective applicants require a minimum $500,000 US capital investment in order to qualify. In other words, it's *not* awarded to individuals investing in small or marginal businesses solely to earn a living.

Finally, it is illegal to enter the US as a tourist and then look for work. Of course, many backpackers, students and other travellers do, but working for cash in the black market as an illegal immigrant is not the advised route.

Job Search Strategies

The job search process is pretty much the same in the US as in Canada. Resume styles, phone techniques, interview styles and professional skill profiling are exactly the same. Canadians, with their similar education systems and way of life, are often considered "the same as Americans" by US employers. However, you are probably unfamiliar with the US job geography and will therefore have to do a lot of researching and networking. Making contacts via your profession, and a job search holiday are good methods.

Besides a visa, two things are generally needed to work in the US: specialized training (usually including at least one university degree), and experience. But there are exceptions to every rule and Canadian students have found good jobs with US firms. (See the Personal Stories below.)

There are four main strategies to consider in looking for your US job. Some of these routes apply to all international job hunting strategies and have been touched on in the introduction to this chapter. (These are explored in more depth in Chapter 20, The Job Search & Targeting Your Research.)

One route is to apply directly to a US branch or subsidiary of a Canadian company. Another strategy is to get a job with a US, international or large Canadian company at home and let it be known that you'd like to transfer to the US when possible. Companies that consider themselves international are most likely to transfer employees around the world. If you're interested in moving south, it makes sense to research what specific skills and experience the company needs in the US branch.

Remember, it is most often you who must take the initiative. Do not expect your employer to work hard at transferring you to the US.

An increasingly successful route is to apply directly to a US employer. Obviously, this strategy works best when your sector is experiencing a boom, the way the computer industry was in the 1990s.

Some Canadian professionals are making a good living by commuting to contracts in the US from a home base in Canada. It's easiest when you're on the exempt-professions list under NAFTA (see the list above). Telecommunications engineers, computer trainers with specialized areas of expertise and systems designers are finding consulting work this way.

Students

The US is not a mecca for foreign student jobs, but every year some Canadian students manage to find work in their fields or in the service industry through ingenuity and persistence. Like everyone else, students must have a job offer before leaving for the US. There are also jobs for students available at international agencies and through various exchange programs. If you're graduating from a well-recognized engineering degree program, you could consider applying directly to US firms. Co-op university programs in either computer science or engineering, which include stints working in industry, are proving a useful ticket for graduates seeking jobs in the US. (See the Resources at the end of this section for more information.)

Lifestyle

Even though the US is similar to Canada, it *is* a different country. Experiences south of the border vary widely, depending on which region you live in and whether you work in a big city or small town. Except for high housing costs in many large cities and parts of California, Canadians tend to be enthusiastic about cheap housing, low taxes, rock bottom gas and food prices and the lower cost of living in general. American university education is also held in high esteem, although it's expensive. Canadians invariably praise the weather. On the other side of the scale, Canadians living there complain about the high crime rate in many parts of the US, more expensive health insurance and "too many fundamentalist religious types."

Personal Stories

• In 1993, four UNIVERSITY OF TORONTO law students finishing second-year studies were discussing what they would do for the summer, and decided then and there to apply to US law firms for summer work. After some research and the mailing of many c.v.'s, all four of them managed to get summer jobs in the US, and one had to choose between two offers, in California or New York City. He chose to work for a New York patent law firm, where he earned $22,000 US for the summer and was treated like royalty, with frequent lunches and dinners at company expense and limousine service home whenever he had to work after 9:00 p.m. The firm offered him a job after graduation, but agreed to wait a year while he articled in Toronto, so that he could qualify to practice law in Canada. At the age of 28, he's earning more than $100,000 US and loving his job and the city. A definite advantage: he had an engineering degree before deciding to become a patent lawyer. Patent law offices are eager to hire people with strong scientific backgrounds.

- A young financial analyst who specialized in the telecommunications industry for a large Toronto-based pension fund accepted a job offer with a small, high-tech company based in New York City that manufactured a crucial component for personal computers. He wrote an innovative business plan that managed to attract $5 million in investment and a takeover offer from the giant computer chip maker, Intel. He was hired by Intel as marketing manager for Europe and is now working for Intel out of Oxford, England. He plans to transfer to Singapore soon. He says, *"There are excellent opportunities in both financial analysis and computers in the US. The US is a mecca for computer work and it is very easy for talented engineers to get work permits. Financial analysis may be a little more difficult since there is a glut of MBAs."*

- A software engineer got a job with BELL-NORTHERN RESEARCH (BNR) in Ottawa and two years later transferred to BNR's offices in Richardson, Texas. She is enjoying her work in software analysis, design and development, as well as the lifestyle and climate. *"We live in the suburbs of Dallas,"* she writes. *"The lifestyle is comfortable, the cost of living is low, the crime rate is about five times that of Toronto!"* Her husband is not allowed to work without a degree and is attending university instead. They would like to stay a few more years and then possibly move somewhere else within the US. *"Come on down y'all—Richardson, Texas is the telecommunications corridor of the US and there are lots of opportunities,"* she adds.

- A man in his mid-40s, certified to teach a specialized computer science program, lives in Toronto with his family, but spends a lot of time stateside training computer systems people with US firms. *"One way to get started in this field is to work for a computer manufacturer or reseller and gain valuable training, and then strike out on your own,"* he advises. He warns that you must be prepared for the ups and downs of entrepreneurship. *"I had a pot of money, about $40,000, that I was prepared to sink into the business, and if it hadn't worked by the time I'd spent it, I would have had to get a job."* He had computer sales experience to fall back on. *"Your success depends on how well known you are in the industry. If you're known and respected, then you can get to travel,"* he adds. He advises anyone pursuing the consulting route that it's important to live near a large airport; otherwise you'll waste too much time travelling.

RESOURCES

UNITED STATES

The following is a list of resources to help you search for work in the world's largest economy. Most of these resources are Internet job boards—a few focus specifically on strategies for landing a job in the US. The list also includes excellent cross-cultural books to help understand and explain US culture. For similar cross-cultural books, where US culture is benchmarked and compared to other cultures, see Cross-Cultural Business Skills and Cross-Cultural Skills Resources in Chapter 1, The Effective Overseas Employee.

4 Work 🖥
www.4work.com ◆ Post a resume, seek career advice and search jobs in the US. [ID:2430]

American Preferred Jobs 🖳

www.preferredjobs.com ◆ Slick site with thousands of jobs in a database searchable by job category, keyword or state. The site also has a great job search directory that's a springboard to hundreds of other US job search sites. [ID:2687]

American Ways: A Guide for Foreigners 📖

2002, Gary Althen, Intercultural Press, 328 pages ➤ Masters & Scribes Bookshoppe, 9938 - 81 Ave., Edmonton, AB T6E 1W6, Canada, www.mastersandscribes.com, $27.50 CDN; Credit Cards; 800-378-3199, fax 780-439-6879 ◆ This resource means to help foreigners understand the American culture and psyche. With sections on individualism and "Ways of Reasoning," it is one of the best-organized and clearest basic presentations of American thought process to date. Filled with case studies and helpful observations, this book covers the basic needs of the foreign student or businessperson. From understanding American society to making one's way in daily life, this book should help anyone interested in learning more about the world's most lucrative overseas job market. [ID:2009]

America's Job Bank 🖳

www.jobsearch.org ◆ Job seekers can post their resumes where thousands of employers search every day, search for job openings automatically and find their dream job fast. Employers can post job listings on the nation's largest on-line labour exchange, create customized job orders and search resumes automatically to find the right people fast. [ID:2417]

Association Central 🖳

www.associationcentral.com ◆ A good American Web directory indexed by subject. On the navigation bar on the left, follow the search link to the "Job" section and find a directory of US job boards and employment agencies. [ID:2413]

Best Jobs USA 🖳

www.bestjobsusa.com ◆ A good general US job search site with a small international jobs section. [ID:2431]

Brilliant People 🖳

www.brilliantpeople.com ◆ This US site has a great selection of jobs in the US and abroad. Also features many career management features such as a resume doctor, a salary wizard, job agents, an on-line application and job seeker profiles. [ID:2432]

Career.com 🖳

www.career.com ◆ Register on this site and you can post multiple resumes and search for jobs in the US market. [ID:2435]

CareerJournal.com 🖳

http://cj.careercast.com ◆ This US site isn't the easiest to use, but it is run by the "Wall Street Journal" and has a huge database of international jobs for executives and managers. Here's some advice: if the advanced search doesn't work out, simply type your search term in the top left hand corner of the home page and, who knows, you could soon be trading equities on the London Stock Exchange or be an editor of Market News International in Germany! Recommended. [ID:2642]

Careermag.com 🖳

www.careermag.com ◆ A good US site with all the usual features: keyword searches, resume posting, salary wizard and e-mail notification. [ID:2447]

CareerShop 🖳

www.careershop.com ◆ This US site offers a list of hiring employers, a search function, automated job seeker and resume posting services. The focus is on the US market, but it does have a small searchable international job database. [ID:2433]

Direct Employers 🖳
www.directemployers.com ◆ This employment search engine focuses on the US market, but has an excellent international job search page. It is unique in that it is the only such site dedicated exclusively to employment and featuring the American National College Employment System. [ID:2416]

Employment Guide 🖳
www.employmentguide.com ◆ Another good job site focusing on the US region, it includes searchable jobs by location and employer and a special search for medical jobs. Resources include career advice pages, job fair locations, information on working from home and an on-line application service that matches your skills with employer postings. Create your own account and receive newsletters via e-mail. [ID:2410]

Employment Spot 🖳
www.employmentspot.com ◆ This US-based Web site allows you to search for jobs in major US cities. If working in the US is not your cup of tea, this site also offers directories of on-line job search sites which are great starting points for your international job search. [ID:2425]

Employment Wizard 🖳
www.employmentwizard.com ◆ Search US jobs posted in newspapers, by region or state. No need to go to the library and thumb through US dailies! No international job search component, but a good database of jobs in all fields in the US. [ID:2450]

Employment911 🖳
www.employment911.com ◆ Employment911.com is a search engine that puts millions of available jobs right at its users' fingertips. Not only are Employment911's job postings searched but currently over three million jobs in over 300 major career sites are also simultaneously searched. Results are easily viewed through their easy-to-use job search page. [ID:2424]

Encountering the Chinese: A Guide for Americans 📖
1999, Hu Wenzhong, Cornelius L. Grove, Intercultural Press, 230 pages ➤ Masters & Scribes Bookshoppe, 9938 - 81 Ave., Edmonton, AB T6E 1W6, Canada, www.mastersandscribes.com, $30.95 CDN; Credit Cards; 800-378-3199, fax 780-439-6879 ◆ This book is tailored to the overseas job seeker interested in China. Analyzes basic Chinese values, cultural norms and modern market mindsets. Presents insights into how to interact with Chinese people and identifies the cross-cultural factors that can lead to failed business negotiations, embarrassing faux pas and disruptive misunderstandings between Westerners and the Chinese. This edition includes an update on the modern Chinese market mentality and a special section for North American women working in China. [ID:2099]

Flip Dog 🖳
www.flipdog.com ◆ FlipDog.com sniffs the World Wide Web and links to job openings found on employer Web sites. Although it focuses on the US market, this site contains a comprehensive directory of jobs found outside the US searchable by country and sector. This is a great Web site with lots of jobs. Worth adding to your favourites! [ID:2418]

From Boston to Beijing: Managing with a World View 📖
2002, 304 pages ➤ Thomson South-Western, 5191 Natorp Blvd., Mason, OH 45040, USA, www.swlearning.com, $22.95 US; Credit Cards; 513-229-1000 ◆ International entrepreneurs in every industry can benefit from the advice this book contains on how to manage in a multicultural environment. It illustrates how countries vary and how people recognize, manage and effectively use cultural variance. In addition to information on working with colleagues across the globe, the book contains information on culture shock, spousal transition and returning home after an overseas stint. [ID:2549]

Getting a Job in America 📖
2003, Roger Jones, 240 pages ➤ How To Books Ltd., 3 Newtec Place, Magdalen Road, Oxford, OX4 1RE, UK, www.howtobooks.co.uk, £11.04; Credit Cards; (44) (1752) 202-301, fax (44) (1865) 202-331 ◆ Explains the employment possibilities open to non-US citizens and offers information and advice on how to make the most of them. It includes lists of major employers, recruitment agencies, Web sites and other useful addresses. [ID:2165]

Goinglobal 💻
www.goinglobal.com ◆ This US Web site offers a huge database of private sector jobs in the United States, with a few jobs listed with corporations around the world. [ID:2594]

Good Neighbours: Communicating with the Mexicans 📖
1997, John C. Condon, Intercultural Press, 104 pages ➤ Masters & Scribes Bookshoppe, 9938 - 81 Ave., Edmonton, AB T6E 1W6, Canada, www.mastersandscribes.com, $24.95 CDN; Credit Cards; 800-378-3199, fax 780-439-6879 ◆ With penetrating insight, the author examines how Mexicans and Americans perceive themselves and each other, and how their behaviour, based on these perceptions, often leads to cross-cultural misunderstanding. Also helpful for Canadians interested in working in Mexico. [ID:2011]

The Gordon Group Home Page 💻
www.gordonworks.com ◆ This US site is visually uninspiring, but don't be turned off! It contains one of the best job site resource lists around. Hundreds of links to job sites and career counselling services focusing on, but not exclusively devoted to, the North American job market. [ID:2242]

Job Bank USA 💻
www.jobbankusa.com ◆ One of the Internet's largest and best-known on-line recruiting sites. Provides services to over 5 million job seekers, hiring managers, recruiters and human resource professionals. Search jobs, post resumes, view recruiter lists and free sample cover letters and resumes. [ID:2436]

Jumbo Careers 💻
www.jumboclassifieds.com ◆ This US-based site has free job searching advice and access to the database. Registration and a fee allow access to other services such as a resume blaster, which does exactly what the name implies: gets your resume seen by as many employers as possible. [ID:2439]

Living and Working in America 📖
2004, Steve Mills, 304 pages ➤ How To Books Ltd., 3 Newtec Place, Magdalen Road, Oxford, OX4 1RE, UK, www.howtobooks.co.uk, £11.04; Credit Cards; (44) (1752) 202-301, fax (44) (1865) 202-331 ◆ Packed with US country-specific information on immigration, employment and living conditions, useful names, addresses and Web sites, this highly readable and informative book sets you up with all you need to search for jobs in the land of opportunity. [ID:2164]

Living in the USA 📖
1996, C. William Gay, Intercultural Press, 240 pages ➤ Masters & Scribes Bookshoppe, 9938 - 81 Ave., Edmonton, AB T6E 1W6, Canada, www.mastersandscribes.com, $28.90 CDN; Credit Cards; 800-378-3199, fax 780-439-6879 ◆ Packed with practical advice that makes American lifestyles comprehensible to the foreigner. Widely used in ESL classrooms and by corporations, international organizations, governmental and non-governmental agencies. Sprinkled with American idioms, this book is as enjoyable as it is useful for teaching and orienting the newcomer to US culture. [ID:2089]

Medical Insurance for International Students, Scholars and Their Families 💻
2002, 12 pages ➤ National Association for Foreign Student Affairs, 8th Floor, 1307 New York Ave. N.W., Washington, DC 2005-4701, USA, www.nafsa.org, Free on-line; Credit Cards; 800-836-4994, fax 202-737-3657 ◆ This pamphlet is directed at foreign academics and explains the often-confusing and sometimes intimidating US health care system. Topics included are an overview of the types of medical insurance plans available, how to evaluate policies, why insurance is needed, how to use the insurance plan, suggestions for keeping medical care costs manageable, as well as a

very useful glossary of definitions and explanations of medical insurance terms. Helpful information for Canadians studying in US. [ID:2558]

Net Temps 💻
www.net-temps.com ◆ This US site offers a resume writing service, newsletters, market information, interview tips, job searches, recruiter profiles and helpful information for job seekers in today's market. Very informative and easy to use, with lots of jobs in the United States. [ID:2437]

The Politix Group 💻
www.politixgroup.com/dcjobs.htm ◆ This site is for US citizens and internationals interested in a career in international politics. On this site, you'll find resources on working legally in the US and other countries, international political career resources, political and government internships in Washington. For a $10 US donation you can become a member and browse the political jobs offered in the US and UK. [ID:2593]

Prohire 💻
www.prohire.com ◆ Another good US site that allows you to post resumes and create and save your own repeated searches with e-mail notification. [ID:2446]

Quintessential Careers 💻
www.quintcareers.com ◆ Contains more than 1,900 pages of college, career and job search content to empower job seekers. This excellent resource includes job finding resources such as resume critiques, advice from experts and insightful articles. [ID:2414]

The Rice Paper Ceiling 📖
2000, Rochelle Kopp, 272 pages ➤ Stone Bridge Press, P.O. Box 8202, Berkeley, CA 94707, USA, www.stonebridge.com, $19.95 US; Credit Cards; 800-947-7271, fax 510-524-8711 ◆ What can the non-Japanese employee of a Japanese company do to advance his or her career prospects? This US book presents a readable and detailed analysis of the "rice-paper ceiling" and "breakthrough" strategies for overcoming it. Includes techniques for improving working relationships and career prospects, as well as insights into the profound differences between Japanese and American work styles and cultures. [ID:2208]

Summer Jobs USA 📖
Annual, 390 pages ➤ Thomson Peterson's, P.O. Box 2123, Princeton, NJ 08543-2123, USA, www.petersons.com, $18.95 US; Credit Cards; 800-338-3282, fax 609-243-9150 ◆ This US publication lists more than 55,000 summer jobs for students with nearly 800 employers in the US, Canada and overseas. Data profiles include general information about the employer, location, setting and features; a profile of summer employees (number of employees, ages, gender, education level, geographic residence); job information (number of positions, background and requirements, pay, application procedures); benefits and pre-employment training; and contact information. Employers are listed alphabetically by state and country. A great resource for looking for work in the US. [ID:2128]

Understanding Arabs: A Guide for Westerners 📖
2002, Margaret Kleffner Nydell, 264 pages ➤ Masters & Scribes Bookshoppe, 9938 - 81 Ave., Edmonton, AB T6E 1W6, Canada, www.mastersandscribes.com, $28 CDN; Credit Cards; 800-378-3199, fax 780-439-6879 ◆ Introduces the complexities of Arab culture and Islam in an evenhanded, unbiased style. The book covers such topics as beliefs and values, religion and society, the role of the family, friends and strangers, men and women, social formalities and etiquette and communication styles. This edition includes a completely revised appendix on 17 Arab countries. [ID:2014]

US Department of Defense 💻
http://dod.jobsearch.org ◆ The Department of Defense (DoD) Job Search is an associate Web site of the US Department of Labor's (DoL) America's Job Bank. The Web site is designed to assist

separating service members in their job search by providing an entry to America's Job Bank. This site and America's Job Bank are operated and maintained by the Department of Labour. [ID:2667]

US Department of Justice 🖳
www.usdoj.gov/oarm ◆ The US Department of Justice, the federal government's law firm and the world's largest legal employer, offers opportunities for law students, entry-level lawyers and experienced lawyers in virtually every area of legal practice. Their Web site provides an overview of the many legal employment opportunities and benefits available at the Department of Justice. You will also find information about legal recruitment, including eligibility, the application process, the work of each department component, salaries, security clearances, citizenship requirements, the department's employment policies, incentive programs and answers to frequently asked questions. [ID:2612]

US Department of State ⚕
www.state.gov ◆ On the Web site, you will find information about the Department, press releases, information for US travellers abroad, country-specific information, employment opportunities, business information and current international issues that the US government considers a priority. A great backgrounder before deploying internationally. Huge amount of funding for overseas projects comes from the US Department of State. Anyone interested in overseas development project work should familiarize themselves with the ins and outs of State's policies and projects. [ID:2319]

US Department of State Employment 🖳
www.state.gov/employment/index.htm ◆ The US Department of State recruits Americans for the civil and foreign service, as well as for the UN and other IGOs. There is a great section on student programs and internships with information on how to apply, benefits, fellowships, summer clerk programs and FAQs—all to help your international career take off! [ID:2629]

US Department of State International Vacancy Announcements 🖳
www.state.gov/p/io/rls/iva/2004/29546.htm ◆ This site is updated every two weeks and contains an extensive list of job openings at the United Nations and other international organizations. [ID:2588]

US Government Globus and National Trade Data Bank 🖳
www.stat-usa.gov ◆ This is a full-service Web site for US businesses conducting domestic and international trade. Divided into two parts, the site provides access to current and historical economic data on the US economy under the "State of the Nation" heading. Under "Globus & NTDB" you'll hit current and historical trade-related releases, international market research, trade opportunities, country analysis and the National Trade Data Bank, which is available by no-cost registration. A great resource for international entrepreneurs. [ID:2292]

US Immigration Resource for Canadians 🖳
www.americanlaw.com ◆ Look no further for basic US Tax and Immigration information than this Web site. [ID:2361]

US Postal Service ⚕
www.usps.gov/ncsc ◆ Similar to the Canada Post site, this will give you postal information for the United States. You can look up zip codes and locations of postal outlets, and make parcel inquires. [ID:2332]

USAID ⚕
www.usaid.gov/careers ◆ This is the recruitment Web site of the US Government's overseas development assistance agency. USAID is the largest funding agency in the world, with job postings listed for US citizens interested in working in development. [ID:2668]

Wanted Jobs 🖳
www.wantedjobs.com ◆ This Canadian site has no international job search component, but has an extensive database of US-based job postings. Includes helpful links to career assessment sites and contains information on freelancing and targeting your job search. Easy to use. [ID:2449]

Washingtonpost.com 💻
www.washingtonpost.com ◆ Good database of US-based jobs, especially in the DC region. Also features the usual search agents, resume posting and a skills survey to help you get your job search on track. [ID:2452]

The Yin and Yang of American Culture: A Paradox 📖
2001, Eun Y. Kim, Intercultural Press, 252 pages ➤ Masters & Scribes Bookshoppe, 9938 - 81 Ave., Edmonton, AB T6E 1W6, Canada, www.mastersandscribes.com, $36 CDN; Credit Cards; 800-378-3199, fax 780-439-6879 ◆ This book takes an Eastern view of American culture and places it in the context of Asian value sets. Based on decades of conversations and interactions with Americans and Asians, the author presents American virtues and vices from an Asian perspective, using the unique Asian concepts of yin and yang. A helpful resource for anyone planning to live and work in the US. [ID:2550]

Mexico & Latin America
FOR ENTREPRENEURS & LONG-TERM INVESTORS

Latin American countries offer similar opportunities to entrepreneurs as do other emerging markets, with certain advantages for Canadians. They share the same time zones as Canada and in many cases seem more familiar. The ratification of NAFTA has already spurred Canadian–Mexican trade and investment. Canada also has free trade agreements with Chile and Costa Rica, and more such agreements are expected with other Latin American countries over the next few years, possibly including a "Free Trade Area of the Americas" that would be a NAFTA-like treaty bringing together virtually all of North and South America. Since 1990, nearly every country in the region has embarked upon a dramatic political and economic transformation, creating a sense of stability and predictability. While countries like Argentina and Venezuela have experienced some difficulties since 2001, others like Mexico and Chile are well-positioned to continue enjoying a healthy growth in the foreseeable future. Brazil, with about half of Latin America's GDP and 40 per cent of its population, is emerging as a major world economic power, not unlike India or Russia. Canada's technological expertise, natural resources, and high-end services and products match Latin America's current import needs, creating many untapped trade and investment opportunities. Direct Canadian investment in the region has soared, and Canadian trade with Latin America and the Caribbean grew from $5.5 billion in 1988 to $12 billion in 1998.

Here are three pieces of advice that entrepreneurs will hear over and over from those who have tried to make inroads into Mexico and Latin America. One, get a local partner—even big companies cannot make it on their own. Two, don't underestimate the time and patience it will take to initiate, develop and maintain a business venture. Three, expect to put up most of the financing.

So why bother? Many Canadian companies do come to the conclusion that the time and effort are not worth it. But many others expect to reap the big rewards that come from entering a new market at the right time. Mexico's middle class—read, consuming class—is already as large as Canada's in absolute numbers and in terms of spending power, and is growing rapidly.

Mexico and Latin America are not as fertile for professionals seeking overseas work. For one thing, there is a growing indigenous pool of well-educated lawyers, engineers, doctors, technicians and so forth. And second, interested individuals hired by Mexican companies will, at least in the short term, earn considerably less than they would at home. But for those dedicated to discovering the culture and gaining work experience, there are a number of possibilities, especially for people with backgrounds in marketing, product development and management, and high-tech industries.

The Mexican Economy and NAFTA

The Mexican economy has undergone a radical transformation over the last 15 years, and in the process has lifted many trade and investment restrictions and initiated a widespread program of privatization. Foreign debt indicators have shown considerable improvement since the late 1980s and inflation is down dramatically (from 180 per cent in 1988). By 1994, foreign investment in Mexico had tripled to $71 billion US from $24 billion in 1988. Canadian trade with Mexico has increase dramatically thanks to NAFTA, with exports to Mexico growing 25 per cent between 1993 and 2003, and Mexican exports to Canada jumping an astonishing 200 per cent.

Since the end of one-party rule in Mexico in the 1990s and the start of real reforms in its economy, most observers are bullish on Mexico as a market for Canadian business. Mexico has built on NAFTA by negotiating similar treaties with many more countries, notably with the EU, turning Mexico into a major player in international trade and investment. The provisions of NAFTA have improved access to potential investors, especially in mining, construction, petrochemicals, agriculture, autos, financial and other professional services. Government procurement markets will be open to Canadian suppliers as investment laws continue to ease.

Visas in Mexico

Visa requirements have been relaxed for business visitors who qualify under the temporary entry provisions of NAFTA. Visas are available from airlines and at entry points, as well as from Mexican embassies and consulates. As always, visitors should check for up-to-date visa information before making a trip.

If you are hired by a Canadian firm and posted to Mexico or elsewhere in Latin America, the procedure is quite simple and requires little paperwork on your behalf. But if you arrive without a work visa, it is next to impossible to get one.

Business Opportunities in Mexico

Many Canadian companies are producing the capital goods currently needed in Mexico, such as equipment for bottling and packaging plants. This kind of equipment represents a large, one-off sale with a high value-added component—technical people and training are often part of the package. The most promising sectors for Canadian firms include agricultural equipment, chemicals, services and expertise, high technology, auto parts, beverage industry and equipment, construction and engineering, environmental industries—impact assessment, pollution control, waste management and water resources, mining and mining equipment, petrochemicals, telecommunications equipment, systems and services, banking and financial services, and transportation.

Strategies for Business People in Mexico

Mexico, although it shares a continent with Canada and the US, is a very different country, which becomes increasingly clear the longer you try to do business there. Most of the steps to making a successful business deal apply equally to other countries in Latin America.

The first step is to collect as much information as you can prior to making a visit. Fortunately, there are now plenty of resources available, from government reports and programs to specific books on Canadian–Mexican trade to seminars and private consultants who help make connections between Canadian and Mexican firms. INTERNATIONAL TRADE CANADA (ITCAN) has detailed market studies for several sectors that could cover a lot of your early footwork. Many US and Mexican government agencies and trade groups can provide additional information, as can the "Trade Talks" division of the MEXICAN EMBASSY in Ottawa. (See the Resources at the end of this section for more information.)

If the prospects look promising for your business, the next step is to make an exploratory visit with a view to establishing local contacts. The Canadian government has recently opened a business centre in Mexico City that should serve as an excellent meeting point for liaising with Mexican counterparts. Some Canadians suggest setting up a hospitality suite in a hotel room for a few days to meet as many local people as possible. But don't expect to make a deal or choose a partner on your first visit.

Use any Mexican business contacts available to you through government or personal sources. As you will hear more than once, forging business relationships is extremely important and you need time and patience to do so. Fluency in Spanish, although not mandatory, is a definite asset.

Finding a Mexican partner is crucial—it'll help you to overcome the many impediments to entry such as cultural factors, lack of familiarity with consumer taste, government regulations and corporate concentration. Partnering can take many forms depending on whether it is a case of technology transfer, an exchange of marketing rights or sharing product development costs. Common forms of partnership include joint ventures, licensing arrangements, co-manufacturing agreements, franchising and joint production. The handbook *Canada–Mexico: Partnering for Success* (see the Resources at the end of this section) offers a good introduction to the kinds of partnering arrangements available, and the preparation needed.

Poor choice of partners is one of the key reasons cited by managers for the disappointing performance of business ventures. Many business people underestimate the amount of time and resources it will take to find, let alone develop, a successful partnership. (See the Personal Stories.)

Once you have decided to make the plunge, you'll have to select a target market. Most Canadians select one of the three main business areas: Mexico City, Guadalajara or Monterrey. Increasingly, however, there are financial incentives to set up operations in less populous regions.

Entrepreneurs have another word of caution: if you need a partner with deep pockets, then Mexico is not the market for you. Most financing will have to come from your side, with the deal structured in such a way to benefit you further down the road. *"There really is no money there—you have to tailor the deal accordingly,"* says the Ottawa businessman.

Culture in Mexico

A number of books have been written advising North Americans how to do business in Mexico, and it is probably a good idea to read one or two.

Cultivate patience and be prepared for major delays. The culture of each Latin American country is unique, but they share a common attitude to time, which doesn't mesh with the stress Canadians put on scheduling and keeping appointments.

Mexicans are extremely polite, so it is important to keep asking questions and make sure you understand the nuances of the conversation—it's often said that Mexicans dislike saying no, even when that's what they mean.

Canadian business people often expect to sit down and quickly finalize a deal, but Mexicans view the art of doing business differently. They expect to develop a relationship with the person they may do business with—the process can take months, if not years. Patience is paramount.

"The primary thing down there is building relationships, and the longer you're down there the greater chance there is of building a relationship," says a Spanish-speaking Canadian businessman who has made several visits. *"But at the end, it doesn't necessarily mean they'll become buyers, it may just mean you'll be good friends."*

Mexicans, who are proud of their Aztec history and culture, take music, art and literature seriously. If you have some knowledge of Mexican culture, you'll have something to talk about at business lunches and cocktail parties. Mexican business people do not like to discuss business during a meal; they wait until the meal is finished before launching into production costs and markets.

If Canadians are popular in Mexico and Latin America, then Quebecers are especially so. Mexicans often think of Quebecers as their fellow Latins of North America. They seem to share an affinity with Mexicans and several other Latin American cultures, partly because of a similar language, classical education and the ways they enjoy life.

Mexico's business culture is more formal than Canada's, so err on the side of formality. Women, especially, are advised to dress conservatively, but this holds true for men as well.

Finally, the Latin *machismo* cannot go unmentioned. A woman who toiled as a lawyer in Mexico found the "constant come-ons" so annoying that she left after six months. Another woman, who reports happier experiences, says it is important to be professional and businesslike, to dress appropriately and to know your field.

"I sound very official and I always have agendas typed out for meetings, which I hand to my counterpart before starting. I wear expensive suits and expensive jewellery because they know the difference... (In Mexico) the rich are very rich and the poor are very poor, and if you want to play the rich man's game you have to act accordingly."

Expat Jobs in Mexico

For Canadian professionals fluent in Spanish who want to work in Mexico, your best bet is to apply to the large Canadian or US firms that are doing business there. BOMBARDIER, SHL SYSTEMHOUSE, and LABATT are a few Canadian names that have invested heavily in Mexico. In many fields, the prospects are slim because there are many well-educated Mexicans, and professional salaries in Mexico are low, even compared with many Asian countries.

But there is also something to be said for being on the ground, and Canadians who have found jobs in Mexico have often started this way. An experienced salesman advises bringing enough money for a few months or teaching English while you look for other work.

In many Latin American countries, the demand for English-language instruction is high, from exclusive schools to backstreet commercial institutes to tutoring. Experience isn't usually necessary to land a job teaching English on the spot. Often working papers won't be necessary. Jobs are sometimes available in the tourist industry, albeit at low wages. It is essential for anyone interested in working in Latin America, including students and backpackers, to appear neat and well groomed.

Latin America

While Canada's commercial ties with the rest of Latin America remain modest, they have expanded in recent years as economic and political reforms have been consolidated and a modicum of stability has been restored to the region.

The formation of several regional trading blocs has promoted the dismantling of trade barriers and has greatly enhanced prospects for intra-regional trade. These arrangements include the Andean Pact (Venezuela, Colombia, Bolivia, Peru and Ecuador); the MERCOSUR group (Argentina, Brazil, Paraguay and Uruguay) and the Central American Common Market (Costa Rica, El Salvador, Guatemala, Honduras and Nicaragua).

These groupings, along with a variety of other bilateral free trade agreements in the region, have paved the way for a proposed Free Trade Area of the Americas (FTAA), which the Organization of American States (OAS) had hoped would be concluded by 2005. The US had seen the FTAA as a broadening of NAFTA into a hemispheric trade zone. Individual bilateral free trade agreements among members of the OAS, like that between Canada and Chile, or Mexico and Bolivia, continue to be signed as FTAA negotiations hit stumbling points.

Brazil, Chile and Colombia are currently the countries of greatest interest to the Canadian business community. The most promising sectors include forestry, mining, oil and gas, telecommunications, power generation, machinery manufacturing, auto parts, agriculture and environmental industries. Throughout the region, Canadian companies are benefiting from the sweeping privatization programs and are actively buying formerly state-owned companies in the natural resources and communications sectors.

Canadians with Latin American roots caution that each country has a different culture. You can't assume that because you know Mexico, Colombia will come easily. Mexicans are welcoming, whereas Venezuelans are cool to foreigners, partly due to fallout from the last oil boom. Ecuador, Colombia and Peru are very formal and "European" in their business circles.

Chile

Canada is Chile's largest foreign investor, with mining (high quality ore deposits in particular) accounting for the lion's share of investment. In the mid-1990s, Canadian mining firms had over $2 billion invested in Chile alone, and it remains a hot spot for the foreseeable future. Pulp and paper, transportation, telecommunications, industrial machinery, mining equipment and service sectors also look good.

Moreover, Canada and Chile now have a free trade agreement. Chile continues to score well in the World Competitiveness Record's ranking of most competitive newly industrialized countries, after Singapore, Hong Kong, Taiwan and Malaysia, and its trade barriers are among the lowest in the world.

Argentina

Once Canada's third largest Latin American market, after Mexico and Brazil, Argentina is now going through a difficult period. Prior to its currency crisis of 2001, the Argentine government's moves to deregulate, privatize, fight inflation and control the deficit had reaped rewards: high growth rates, an influx of capital and a return of business confidence. Despite the dramatic devaluation of the Argentine peso in December 2001, after it was delinked from the US dollar, opportunities for Canadians still exist in oil and gas, mining, energy transmission, environmental technologies, telecommunications, and food processing and packaging equipment sectors.

Colombia

The most promising sectors for Canadian firms here are oil and gas, telecommunications and power generation. Despite Colombia's fairly healthy economy, Canadian businesses and citizens remain wary of Colombia because of the extremely high rate of violent crime. However, a businesswoman who travels frequently to Colombia describes Bogota as a city where she feels safe. With bilateral trade over $600 million in 1993, Colombia is Canada's third largest export market in South America after Brazil and Chile, and high-profile companies like Bata, McCain Foods and Enbridge have helped create an environment where Colombians want to do business with Canadian firms.

Personal Stories

• The owner of an Ottawa computer services company with annual sales of $8 million is just beginning a Mexican effort. It took three years of his time and more than $150,000 of his professional services to get to the first stage. *"I'd travelled there quite a bit,"* says the entrepreneur who is fluent in Spanish. *"My interest was piqued at a NAFTA conference, when I became aware their economy was booming while ours was flat. Then, having looked, we found we were going into a market without competition,"* he says. On his first visit down, he met with representatives of 12 companies in 2 days, all arranged by a Mexican friend of a friend. He explained the kind of service he offered—custom-designed software programs to help businesses meet specific needs—*"and the response I got was, 'Can we place an order today?'"*

After two more exploratory trips, the businessman selected Guadalajara as a target market and tried several avenues to find a partner, including the Canadian consul general's office in Guadalajara, the embassy in Mexico City and INTERNATIONAL TRADE officials in Ottawa. But the route that worked best was placing an ad in English in the local Guadalajara newspaper, which the company did three times. The first time, after months of negotiations with the front-runner, the company backed out for lack of capital. The second time, the chosen partner called things off when they were close to signing a deal. The third time—which was going to be the last try—the second company came forward again and went through with the deal, owing to a change in senior management. Now the deal is at the final approval stage, after which several Mexican personnel will come to Ottawa for training. Then Canadian technicians will spend upwards of 10 weeks training the staff in Guadalajara. *"Is it worthwhile? Yes. But if someone had said it's going to take three years and cost $150,000, I wouldn't have done it, so in a sense, maybe it's better not to know ahead of time."* The company plans to "spend a fortune" on direct marketing, and ultimately hopes to have offices in Mexico City and Monterrey before moving into other Latin American countries.

- An Ottawa consultant went to Mexico to perfect his Spanish and ended up with a job working for a US company that bought and sold aluminum. He had two university degrees, one of them in international affairs, plus sales experience: he had put himself through university as a Xerox salesman. By chance, he met the country manager of the firm (also a Canadian) and learned of an opening for an aluminum salesman, which he jumped at. *"I did almost all my work by phone, selling aluminum from Brazil and Venezuela to Volkswagen, Nissan and the like in Mexico."* Despite the phone work, developing personal bonds was important. His boss took him around to meet the buyers. *"There was a degree to the relationship, too. I was never seen in the same light as my boss, who had been there 10 years."* He says the job seeker who wants to work in Mexico is in a bind: the all-important working papers are easier to get if you're hired from Canada, but it's important to be there on the ground. Try both methods. *"Be prepared to earn, at the onset, considerably less than you'd earn in Canada."*

- A marketing consultant in telecommunications has worked on contract for Mexican and other telephone companies for five years, from a base in Guelph, Ontario. She currently spends two weeks a month in Mexico City, on contract for a Mexican version of UNITEL. With two master's degrees (one in English, the other in business administration), she began her career with "excellent training" in marketing at STANDARD BRANDS and an ad agency before joining NORTEL. When the company wanted to transfer her, she decided to strike out on her own. And she advises would-be consultants to get some hands-on business experience first. (Now she earns enough to fly her husband down to Mexico at least once a month for a long weekend—"a cost of doing business.") Though she works for Canadian, US and Hong Kong telecommunications companies, most of her work is in Latin America. *"I love it—I love the language, the food, the people, everything about it. Second, when you're recommended in Latin America, people place enormous store by that so it's easier for me to get work from one country to another. I've been asked to work in China, but I feel I'm building an expertise in Latin America... I see a lot of opportunity because most of these economies have been closed, so there is very little true marketing talent, especially in the high-tech areas... A problem is the great machismo, whether you're male or female. I might sit across from someone who says 'you don't know my market,' even though I have knowledge from five years in Mexico. I know Inegi (Mexico's department of statistics) better than I know Stats Canada, and I can throw back information in tremendous detail."* She adds that relationships are extremely important to doing business. *"It's not personal relationships the way we have them in Canada, it's more having a history with a company. There's a company I have yet to do business with, but we've been exchanging business information for three years. Maybe in five years we'll do business."*

- A young Canadian befriended a Mexican while on holiday, and invited him to visit Canada. Eventually, the Mexican became manager of a restaurant in a west coast Mexican city, and the Canadian graduate went back to visit (without any working papers). After a few weeks of teaching English at a language institute, his Spanish had improved enough that he was offered a job as a waiter in his friend's restaurant. The restaurant manager had "an arrangement" with the local immigration official who ate at the restaurant, so there were no questions asked about the Canadian employee, who continued to work there for three months. *"The other staffers weren't too happy about my working there. I had to earn their respect by working harder and being paid less than any of them. Earning their respect made all the difference and after several weeks I became one of the locals."*

RESOURCES

MEXICO & LATIN AMERICA

There are more and more jobs being posted in Latin America. The resources included here are intended to be a starting point for researching a career in this region.

After Latin American Studies: A Guide to Graduate Study,
Fellowships, Internships, and Employment for Latin Americanists 📖
2000, Shirley A. Kregar, Jorge Nallim, 142 pages ➤ University Center for International Studies, Center for Latin American Studies, 4E04 Wesley West Posvar Hall, University of Pittsburgh, Pittsburgh, PA 15260, USA, www.ucis.pitt.edu/clas, $15 US; US Cheques or Money Orders; 412-648-7392, fax 412-648-2199 ◆ Provides information on graduate study, research and internships. For graduate as well as undergraduate students, opportunities in the private sector, and career opportunities in the US government and in international organizations. An essential resource for anyone with career or scholarly interests in the region. [ID:2037]

Association of American Schools in South America (AASSA) ♔
Association of American Schools in South America (AASSA), www.aassa.com ◆ AASSA recruits teachers for 41 private American/International schools located throughout South America. In most cases, applicants must be certified teachers and have at least two years' experience teaching K-12. Be forewarned: on their Web site AASSA discourages applications from teachers with dependent spouses, favouring teaching couples and singles. Candidates may apply on-line or by traditional methods. If your application is assessed as eligible, a $25 US (for singles, $40 US for teaching couples) registration fee gets you a spot in AASSA's database and an invitation to the annual recruiting fair held in a US city in December. Job listings are also posted on AASSA's Web site. [ID:2297]

Good Neighbours: Communicating with the Mexicans 📖
1997, John C. Condon, Intercultural Press, 104 pages ➤ Masters & Scribes Bookshoppe, 9938 - 81 Ave., Edmonton, AB T6E 1W6, Canada, www.mastersandscribes.com, $24.95 CDN; Credit Cards; 800-378-3199, fax 780-439-6879 ◆ With penetrating insight, the author examines how Mexicans and Americans perceive themselves and each other, and how their behaviour, based on these perceptions, often leads to cross-cultural misunderstanding. Also helpful for Canadians interested in working in Mexico. [ID:2011]

International Business Etiquette: Latin America 📖
2000, Anne Marie Sabath, 224 pages ➤ Career Press, P.O. Box 687, 3 Tice Road, Franklin Lakes, NJ 07417, USA, www.careerpress.com, $14.99 US; Credit Cards; 800-227-3371 ◆ This quick-reading US book shares the do's and don'ts of interacting with individuals in all the major commercial countries of Latin America. Each chapter is devoted to a specific country and begins with the top 10 reasons why people do (or should do) business in this country. What follows are countless tips for knowing what to do and when to do it, whether you are meeting someone for the first time or the tenth time. Each chapter closes with tips for avoiding the most commonly made country-specific faux pas. Interesting and informative. [ID:2382]

JobintheSun.com 🖥
JobintheSun.com, http://jobinthesun.com ◆ JobintheSun.com is the premier resource for Caribbean jobs. Using a pro-active approach to getting listings, jobs are added everyday. This site is the resource for getting international employment in the Caribbean and then relocating abroad. forums, chat rooms, relocation guide, career advice, expert staff and hundreds of members helping each other in their job search. [ID:2799]

Latin American Weekly Report 📖 🖥
Weekly ➤ Intelligence Research Ltd., Latin American Newsletters, 61 Old Street, London, EC1 V9HX, UK, www.latinnews.com, $965 US/year; Credit Cards; (44) (0) (2072) 51-0012, fax (44) (0) 20 7253-8193; Available in large libraries ◆ The leading independent source of political, strategic, economic and business intelligence on Latin America for nearly 40 years. Required reading for top government officials, senior executives, media commentators, leading academics and anyone with a professional interest in Latin American affairs, including the international job seeker. The "Latin American Weekly Report" provides a behind-the-scenes analysis of the week's developments along with not-to-be-missed, early warning reports. Great resource. [ID:2176]

LatPro 🖥
www.LatPro.com ◆ LatPro is a job board for employees bilingual in English and Spanish or Portugese. There are international and US-based jobs and company listings which can be searched by profession and location. The site contains great resources including immigration information and links to sites in other countries for local news, magazines, recruiters and search engines. Bonus: the site offers free subscriptions to over 70 engineering publications! [ID:2824]

Trade Office for the Mexican Embassy 🏛
www.embamexcan.com ◆ Interested in doing business in Mexico? This Web site is available from the Embassy of Mexico in Canada home page by navigating to the economic section where you'll find information on Mexican economic policy, as well as on investing in and trading with Mexico. Also has a link to the Government of Mexico's Investor Relation Office. [ID:2154]

Tropic Jobs 🖥
www.tropicjobs.com/search.html ◆ If it's the Caribbean you are after, then the Tropic Jobs Web site is a good start. It focuses on the Cayman Islands, but lists positions elsewhere in the region. There aren't a lot of postings, but there is some helpful information on finding work in the Caribbean. [ID:2605]

Web Sites on Latin America and the Carribean 🖥
Web Sites on Latin Amerca and the Carribean ◆ If you have always wanted to go somewhere warm, these sites can help you get there. There is information on current events, job opportunities, and news related to trade and government activities. The listings below are only a few examples of what you can find on the Internet. ◆ Argentina, www.buenosairesherald.com ◆ Bahamas, www.bahamas-on-line.com ◆ Bermuda, www.bermudacommerce.com ◆ Bolivia, www.boliviaweb.com ◆ Brazilian Business Connection, www.brazilbiz.com.br/english ◆ Chile, www.prochile.cl ◆ Costa Rica, www.costarica.com/Home/l ◆ Cuba, www.cubaweb.cu ◆ Dominican Republic, www.dr1.com ◆ Ecuador, www.ecuadorexplorer.com ◆ Grenada, www.grenada.org ◆ Haiti, www.port-haiti.com/cgibin/search/port-haiti.cgi ◆ Guatemala, www.quetzalnet.com/default.html ◆ Jamaica,

www.exportjamaica.org ◆ Mexico, www.mexguide.net/monterrey/index-i.html ◆ Panama, www.panamainfo.com ◆ Peru, peru.gotolatin.com/eng/Info/Hbook/business.asp ◆ Trinidad and Tobago, www.trinidadexpress.com ◆ Venezuela, www.venezuelaonline.com/indice_e.htm [ID:2321]

Western Europe
MAINLY FOR STUDENTS & SELECTED PROFESSIONALS

Imagine flying into The Hague to work in an international scientific institute and setting up a new home along a canal. Or landing a job as a financial analyst in Britain and renting a flat near Hyde Park in London. Or working for UNESCO and living in the Latin quarter of Paris.

These are the real-life stories of determined individuals who have engaged in long-term planning and have taken the initiative as opportunities presented themselves. These are the stories of people who, 10 years ago, took a year off to work in Europe as grape pickers, hotel maids and nannies. Many Canadians with European jobs have also spent a year as poor students in Berlin, Lisbon or Oxford. In some instances, a European Union (EU) passport, acquired because of European-born relatives, eased entry into their European jobs.

The European Union

In order to understand the job market in Europe you must understand the EU. The 25 members of the powerful European Union have adopted a treaty of European Unity which commits all signatories to take up common foreign, security and immigration policies and, ultimately, to share a single currency—the "euro," which on January 1, 2002, became the official currency of Austria, Belgium, Germany, Greece, Spain, Finland, France, Ireland, Italy, Luxembourg, the Netherlands and Portugal. It is only a matter of time before other members of the EU also adopt the euro, although there is real doubt about how soon the UK will do so.

In 2003, the EU included Austria, Belgium, Denmark, Finland, France, Germany, Greece, Ireland, Italy, Luxembourg, the Netherlands, Portugal, Spain, Sweden and the United Kingdom. In a pivotal moment in European history, 10 new members joined the EU on May 1, 2004: Cyprus, the Czech Republic, Estonia, Hungary, Latvia, Lithuania, Malta, Poland, Slovakia and Slovenia. Ultimately, the EU may extend its borders as far eastward as Belarus, Moldova and the Ukraine. Turkey has also expressed a desire to join the EU, but controversy continues to surround its application. (Note that Iceland, Norway and Switzerland are three Western European countries that have opted not to join the EU.)

Visas and the European Union

Any EU citizen may obtain work permits for jobs in any of the member countries. The free movement of labour is already noticeable, as people are drawn to the stronger economies and seasonal work around Europe. This means a Canadian with a passport from any EU country may work in any of the member countries. With respect to professional jobs, the barriers are down in theory, but in practice it sometimes takes longer to harmonize qualifications for certain types of positions.

Many Canadians of European ancestry do not realize how easy it is to obtain an EU passport. For example, Canadians with a European-born parent often can apply for citizenship to that country. Canadians with an Irish-born grandparent are eligible to apply for Irish citizenship. *"The key point is you need all the original documents, including your grandparent's birth certificate,"* says a Canadian who is now an Irish citizen. *"Once you have all the documents, it takes about 10 or 12 months."* It is well worth your while to query an Irish consulate in Canada if you think you may be eligible, because an Irish passport will give you the entrée to work in any EU country.

Each member country has its own laws governing working visas for non-EU members. Most are exclusionary, but there are some exceptions. For example, under a Commonwealth program, a Canadian aged 17 to 26 may obtain a work-holiday visa to travel and work in the UK for up to two years. *Working Abroad Made Easy!* provides work and travel visa information specifically geared to Canadians (see the Resources at the end of this section), but remember to check with the appropriate embassy or consulate for up-to-date regulations.

What Professional Jobs are Available?

With the development of the European Union and the monumental changes in Eastern Europe, the continent is an exciting place to live these days. In the immediate run-up to the 1992 common market, Canadian companies made significant investments in the region. Excluding the United States, the EU is the second most favoured destination of outward direct investment, with Canadian companies having European assets well in excess of $20 billion. (See the Resources at the end of this section for guidance on how to contact these companies.)

Individuals with exotic backgrounds, specialized technical knowledge and "UN types" continue to find positions in Europe. Lawyers, scientists, MBAs, engineers, professors, accountants, financial analysts and computer experts are among the expatriates who are working in Europe in relatively large numbers. International agencies, including UN and NATO agencies, employ significant numbers of Canadians. (For more information, see Chapter 41, United Nations & Other IGOs.)

It is obvious that high unemployment and a highly skilled European workforce mean that Europe is not the easiest place for Canadians to find jobs, especially for those looking for jobs at the entry level or lower management level. Unlike many other parts of the world, there are few mid-level or trade jobs available on a contract basis. Most jobs are for senior managers or professionals on an assignment with an international corporation, as part of their long-term employment with them.

Strategies

Once again, the watchwords in your European job search are "Be bold!" and "Be persistent!"

Wherever you may be on the chain of career experiences, the strongest link between you and a European job is knowledge of the continent itself. Once you have acquired European experience through travel and study, additional resources that are most useful in your European job hunt are a valid working visa, good contacts, determination, qualifications from a recognized school or firm, languages and luck.

There are generally two main paths to a professional job in Europe: through a North American company with European operations, or directly with a European company. Long-term planning is required if you take the former route with a North American firm. The most crucial decision you make will be to choose the right firm during your job search and then work your way into a European posting. Finding work directly with a European firm entails greater risks and usually requires European contacts.

The established Western European capitals are sometimes considered saturated with those seeking professional jobs, but there are hundreds of Canadians working as professionals in Frankfurt, London, Paris, Rome and other Western European financial capitals. What is required is some basic research. The best sources of advice are members of your profession who are working in Europe or who have recently returned from a European stint. Almost invariably, you will have to go there to get a job, though you can do a lot of legwork before you leave Canada. What was discovered in our research interviews was that the network of people you know is of critical importance—word of mouth can get you in to see the right person at the right time.

Always make sure your credentials are impeccable and well documented. European firms are often more traditional in their resume style, favouring the formal chronological format.

Students and Backpackers

Even though Europe isn't the casual job mecca it was in the 1960s and 1970s, there are still opportunities for the determined traveller or student.

Opportunities include seasonal work such as fruit and vegetable picking, harvesting and other agricultural work, service jobs in tourism, working as an au pair or other childcare duties, and teaching English.

Although you won't get rich in any of these pursuits, they offer a wonderful way to extend a summer vacation into an affordable and unforgettable year in Europe. An advantage is that you will meet Europeans, share in their customs and learn or practice their languages. (When you stay exclusively in youth hostels, you'll mainly meet other North Americans and student travellers.) A Canadian editor now in his 40s says a summer spent picking grapes in Europe changed his life. He discovered good food and wine, made lifelong friends and realized he loved farming, which he now does on a part-time basis.

Young people who are determined to work in Europe should get an up-to-date copy of the best resource book in the field, *Work Your Way Around the World* by Susan Griffith. You should also consider subscribing to *Transitions Abroad*, a bimonthly magazine that offers articles on studying, travelling and working overseas. (See the Resources in Chapter 12, Cross-Cultural Travel.)

Studying in Europe is another invaluable experience that will serve you well later in your international career, especially if you follow a degree program. Several Canadian lawyers, professors and financial analysts have credited their European study programs as crucial in landing their first job in Europe. The EU offers a few scholarships and study visits to non-EU members, and Canadians are also eligible to apply for certain other university scholarships in European countries. (For more information, see Chapter 13, Study Abroad and Chapter 14, Awards & Grants.)

Personal Stories

- A 31-year-old with a BSc and a law degree from the University of Western Ontario is working for a financial advisory firm in London, involved in the privatization process in Russia. She travels to Moscow roughly once a month, where she works with government officials to help train Russians to become fund managers, stockbrokers and investment analysts and to understand their own capital system. *"There's a lot of travel in a finance job in London,"* she says, *"much more international exposure than in Toronto"* where she worked before. Her six months of travel in Asia was seen as important to European employers (she has been with three companies), *"but in Canada they look on it as a time-out."*

  She concedes that her dual citizenship (Canadian–British) was a big help in getting her a job, but insists that many others are doing it without work visas beforehand—only it's mostly Australians who talk themselves into jobs. *"There's a huge difference between Canadians and Australians,"* she says. *"Canadians see the restraints, look at all the opposition and give up. The Australians don't see it that way. The bottom line is that you can talk people into things in Britain, you can fight for it and show it can be done."* She advises professionals to make as many contacts as they can—and use them!

- A Canadian accountant charted an international career by joining the Canadian subsidiary of a US oil exploration company when he graduated from university in the 1970s. Eight years later he was offered his first foreign posting. *"It was a combination of persistence on my part and an opportunity that came up,"* he recalls. His first son was born in Trinidad and Tobago and his second in Denmark. He was then posted to the Netherlands for three years, before the family decided to return to Calgary to give their children a wider sense of family and a Canadian childhood. *"It was a big growth opportunity and one that I'm glad we took,"* he says. Since the accounting profession is becoming more global, he advises accountants to aim for jobs in international firms or with industrial companies that have foreign operations.

- A history major from Ottawa travelled in Europe for several summers and his experiences picking grapes (and savouring the results) helped direct him to his chosen profession as a wine importer. After university, he continued to cultivate his wine-tasting and sales skills and soon was hired by a major wine importer in Toronto. He moved up the company ladder, making contacts in Europe and Canada and saving money until he could follow his dream of starting his own wine import company. Now in his early 40s, he has just embarked on his own, specializing in the wines of Burgundy. (He says that in Burgundy, his fluency in French gives him an advantage over American wine buyers, whereas French fluency isn't so important in Bordeaux, where every wine producer has English-speaking sales representatives.) His first six months have been so successful that he wishes he had set out on his own years ago! Based in Toronto, he makes at least three trips to France every year, tasting and buying wines for sale to the Liquor Control Board of Ontario and directly to Ontario restaurants and hotels. *"I've always done what I wanted to do, at least to some extent. Before, it was 10 per cent of my time and now it's 80 per cent."*

RESOURCES

WESTERN EUROPE

The EU continues to be an excellent place to look for work. The following list includes a number of excellent guidebook series that highlight the countries in Western Europe, information directories, Internet job boards and cross-cultural information. Keep in mind that you can cultivate good international job prospects if you approach European organizations to work for them outside of Europe.

The Canada Post 📖
Monthly ➤ The Canada Post, P.O. Box 46249, London, W5 2YN, UK, www.canadapost.co.uk, £20/12 issues or free on-line; (44) (0) (2088) 40-9765 ◆ "The Canada Post" is a free monthly tabloid-sized newspaper for the 200,000 Canadians living in the United Kingdom. Circulation is 23,000 copies, serving an estimated readership of 50,000-plus. Keep up with news and events from a Canadian perspective. [ID:2265]

CharityJOB 🖥
www.charityjob.co.uk/seekers.asp ◆ This site bills itself as the most popular site in the UK for charity jobs. With over 800,000 hits, 900 organizations and 500 jobs each month, it's hard to debate the claim. Search jobs by category, salary range or location, or simply view the complete list of current vacancies. You can also join the subscription list and receive a weekly e-mail digest of job postings. A great site for jobs in the UK! [ID:2581]

Computing 🖥
www.computing.co.uk/Careers ◆ This UK site offers a large selection of computing jobs not only in the United Kingdom, but all over the globe. All the usual newsletter and resume posting services. A great start to your overseas IT career search. [ID:2633]

Courrier international 🖥
www.courrierinternational.com; Fr ◆ Hebdomadaire français d'information internationale avec une section Emplois internationaux, incluant différents stages et une rubrique d'informations ayant pour titre « S'expatrier » (informations sur différents pays, conseils, études sur les niveaux de salaire des jeunes diplômés dans le monde et sur les différents modes de recrutement en Europe). [ID:2704]

Directory of EU Information Sources 📖
2001, 1,250 pages ➤ Euroconfidentiel SA, BP 29, Rixensart, B-1330, Belgium, €213; Credit Cards; (32) (2) 652 02 84, fax (32) (2) 653 01 80, www.amazon.ca ◆ This directory is the most comprehensive compilation of contacts and published information on the European Union, providing access to over 12,500 information sources. Contains in-depth information on all the EU institutions and lists key personnel, databases, Web sites, publications, information networks and libraries specific to each institution. The publication further details press agencies and journalists, consultants and lawyers specializing in EU affairs, professional associations, universities offering post-graduate courses in European integration, and EU grants and loans programs. Easy-to-use and clearly indexed, it is the ideal desktop companion for anyone whose business is Europe. [ID:2087]

Economic Survey of Europe 📖
2002, 260 pages ➤ United Nations Publications, Sales and Marketing Section, Room DC2-853, Department I004, New York, NY 10017, USA, www.un.org/Pubs/sales.htm, $70 US; Credit Cards; 800-253-9646, fax 212-963-3489 ◆ A survey of current economic developments in Europe, the Commonwealth of Independent States (CIS) and North America. Aims at providing information and analysis to policy-makers and economists in government, research institutes and universities, as well as the private business sector. [ID:2524]

EUROGRADUATE 🖥
www.eurograduate.com/data.cfm?language=english ◆ The "Careers Database" features thousands of graduate opportunities in the private sector across Europe. You can search by any combination of

industry, organization, type of occupation, degree/diploma qualification or country of employment. [ID:2608]

Euromanagers & Martians: The Business Cultures of Europe's Trading Nations 📖
2002, Richard Hill, 264 pages ➤ Europublic SA/NV, P.O. Box 504, Uccle 5, Brussels, B-1180, Belgium, www.europublic.com, €17.25; VISA, MC; (32) (0) 2-343-77-26, fax (32) (0) 2-343-93-30 ◆ Looks closely at the business and management cultures of Europe. Identifies those areas where cultures collide, comparing management styles and negotiating strategies, and analyzing the implications of cross-frontier strategic alliances, multicultural teamwork and "New Age" management techniques. [ID:2200]

EUROPA 🖥
http://europa.eu.int/index_en.htm ◆ This EU Web site is a great source of international jobs in the European Union. Part of a larger Web site that has great information on living and working in the EU, including political, legal and economic information. Search jobs by profession, location and keyword, narrow your search by experience, contract type and qualifications. Thousands of jobs listed in easy-to-read postings complete with contact information. If Europe is where you're at, then hitting this site is a must. From the index, click on "Working" under the "Living in the EU" heading. Then select "Find a Job" from the "Job Mobility Portal." [ID:2679]

European Personnel Selection Office 🖥
http://europa.eu.int/epso/competitions/news_en.cfm ◆ EPSO organizes open competitions in various fields to select personnel for various European institutions. Lots of jobs for linguists, administrators, clerical assistants and skilled employees. Citizenship requirements are clearly indicated in job descriptions and competition timetables. [ID:2665]

The European Union 🖥
http://userpage.chemie.fu-berlin.de/adressen/eu.html ◆ For information on the European Union, this German site is a great starting point. Its extensive links take you to detailed information on the EU itself, the former European Community (EC), member states and EU political institutions, as well as centres established under the authority of the EU, such as the European Patent Office (EPO), European Central Bank and European Science Foundation. Highly recommended. [ID:2271]

Expat Boards 🖥
www.expatboards.com ◆ Message boards and country-specific information for expats in Western Europe. Includes topics on education, health, social life and taxes. [ID:2565]

Exploring the Greek Mosaic: A Guide to Intercultural Communication in Greece 📖
1996, Benjamin J. Broome, Intercultural Press, 192 pages ➤ Masters & Scribes Bookshoppe, 9938 - 81 Ave., Edmonton, AB T6E 1W6, Canada, www.mastersandscribes.com, $28.90 CDN; Credit Cards; 800-378-3199, fax 780-439-6879 ◆ Examines the cornerstones of Greek culture—community, family and religion—and their part in daily life. A frank discussion of the images Americans and Greeks have of each other. [ID:2204]

French or Foe? 📖
2003, Polly Platt, 292 pages ➤ Distribooks International, $16.95 US, www.pollyplatt.com ◆ Designed primarily for people who will be living or working in France for extended periods, this book illuminates nuances in the manners, attitudes, and culture of the French people that are helpful to both the international job seeker and the occasional visitor. [ID:2147]

Getting a Job in Europe 📖
2000, Mark Hempshell, 208 pages ➤ How To Books Ltd., 3 Newtec Place, Magdalen Road, Oxford, OX4 1RE, UK, www.howtobooks.co.uk, £8.49; Credit Cards; (44) (1752) 202-301, fax (44) (1865) 202-331 ◆ This British book aims at helping job hunters from any country and of all levels, and includes key contacts for each country. Provides an employment guide and information on how to find and apply for jobs; there's also information on living and working in Europe. [ID:2496]

Going to Live in France 📖
2003, Alan Hart, 208 pages ➤ How To Books Ltd., 3 Newtec Place, Magdalen Road, Oxford, OX4 1RE, UK, www.howtobooks.co.uk, £9.34; Credit Cards; (44) (1752) 202-301, fax (44) (1865) 202-331 ◆ A clearly written compendium of information and advice for all visitors to France that covers all areas of life, but especially financial, legal and commercial topics. It also includes information regarding recreational and retirement issues. Includes working in France. [ID:2497]

Going to Live in Italy 📖
2003, Amanda Hinton, 160 pages ➤ How To Books Ltd., 3 Newtec Place, Magdalen Road, Oxford, OX4 1RE, UK, www.howtobooks.co.uk, £9.34; Credit Cards; (44) (1752) 202-301, fax (44) (1865) 202-331 ◆ A guide to all aspects of doing business, studying or working in Italy. Packed with information such as what documents you need, what to take and how to get there. It also explains how the Italian health, welfare and education systems work. Great for people with Italian wanderlust. [ID:2499]

Going to Live in Spain 📖
2003, 288 pages ➤ How To Books Ltd., 3 Newtec Place, Magdalen Road, Oxford, OX4 1RE, UK, www.howtobooks.co.uk, £9.34; Credit Cards; (44) (1752) 202-301, fax (44) (1865) 202-331 ◆ Another great guide from this British publisher. This resource is contemporary and packed with valuable information for anyone relocating to Spain or dreaming about it. The book covers work, education, finances, retirement and lifestyle. [ID:2500]

The Guide to EU Information Sources on the Internet 📖
2000, 550 pages ➤ Euroconfidentiel SA., BP 29, Rixensart, B-1330, Belgium, €186; Credit Cards; (32) (2) 652 02 84, fax (32) (2) 653 01 80; www.amazon.ca, Available in large libraries ◆ Divided thematically, this guide of Web sites about the EU covers both institutional and non-institutional sites. Each entry is standardized and comprises site name, URL address, publisher's details, description of contents, languages, cost and currency of the information. A series of indexes based on site name, publisher and subject keywords ensures easy and effective consultation. You also get a quarterly newsletter, containing an in-depth focus on a select number of informative listings of newly launched sites, detailing changes to previously published web addresses and offering useful search hints and tips. An invaluable research guide for experienced and inexperienced Web surfers alike. [ID:2678]

How to Get a Job in Europe 📖
2003, Cheryl Matherly, Robert Sanborn, 496 pages ➤ Planning/Communications, 7215 Oak Ave., River Forest, IL 60305-1935, USA, www.planningcommunications.com, $22.95 US; Credit Cards; 888-366-5200, fax 708-366-5280 ◆ The essential guide to getting jobs in England, France, Italy, Germany, Spain, Greece, Holland, Turkey, and 18 other countries. Discover where to find the best jobs. Presents job seekers with a "Nine-Step Plan" strategy for looking for work. Learn the different approaches to resumes, cover letters and interviewing required in an international job search. Get paths to permanent employment as well as summer and temporary jobs, and internships. Learn how to cut red tape and obtain your working papers. Great kickstart to your European job search. [ID:2020]

IrishJobs.ie 🖳
www.irishjobs.ie ◆ This award-winning Web site has a searchable database of hundreds of jobs in the private sector of Ireland's booming economy and other regions outside of Ireland. Lots of professional positions from architecture to Web developer and everything in between. [ID:2609]

Jobpilot 🖳
www.jobpilot.com/function/content/search/jobsearch.jhtml ◆ This German Web site lists jobs in Europe and around the world and is searchable by industry and type of work: freelance and contract, graduate entry-level or permanent. The site also boasts an excellent database of internships and student jobs, and great career tips. Positions are most often high quality postings at leading European corporations. You'll be Europe bound before you know it! [ID:2681]

Jobsite 💻

www.jobsite.co.uk ◆ This job site offers nearly 100,000 searchable postings in the UK, France, Germany, Ireland, Italy and Spain. This site is easy to use and frequently updated. You can also post your resume and access career advice. Jobs tend toward the fields of IT, engineering, sales and finance. [ID:2598]

Living and Working in Britain 📖

2001, Christine Hall, 160 pages ➤ How To Books Ltd., 3 Newtec Place, Magdalen Road, Oxford, OX4 1RE, UK, www.howtobooks.co.uk, £8.49; Credit Cards; (44) (1752) 202-301, fax (44) (1865) 202-331 ◆ As a result of the increased importance of international trade, Britain, as a major financial and business centre worldwide, is becoming a major receiving nation for professionals working overseas. This is a comprehensive and readable guide to searching for work in the UK, with advice, helpful examples and case studies. [ID:2502]

Living and Working in France 📖

2002, David Hampshire, 560 pages ➤ Survival Books, 1st Floor, St James's Street, London, SW1A1ZN, UK, www.survivalbooks.net, £11.66; Credit Cards; (44) (0) (1937) 84-3523, fax (44) (0) (2074) 91-0605 ◆ A comprehensive and up-to-date source of practical information about everyday life in France. It's packed with over 450 pages of important and useful data, designed to help you avoid costly mistakes and save both time and money. [ID:2503]

Living and Working in Germany 📖

2001, Nessa Loewenthal, 176 pages ➤ How To Books Ltd., 3 Newtec Place, Magdalen Road, Oxford, OX4 1RE, UK, www.howtobooks.co.uk, £8.49; Credit Cards; (44) (1752) 202-301, fax (44) (1865) 202-331 ◆ This guide explains which visas and permits are required, the right way to apply and the best places to find jobs in Germany. It covers education, housing, shopping, socializing, and more. There are more than 300 contact addresses listed, with many Web sites for further information. An excellent resource if you're looking for work in Europe's largest economy. [ID:2501]

Living and Working in Paris 📖

2001, Alan Hart, 144 pages ➤ How To Books Ltd., 3 Newtec Place, Magdalen Road, Oxford, OX4 1RE, UK, www.howtobooks.co.uk, £11.66; Credit Cards; (44) (1752) 202-301, fax (44) (1865) 202-331 ◆ A comprehensive handbook for anyone relocating, studying, temping, working on contract or buying a second home in Paris. The book includes useful contacts and Web sites. Bon voyage! [ID:2504]

Living and Working in Portugal 📖

2002, Sue Tyson-Ward, 267 pages ➤ How To Books Ltd., 3 Newtec Place, Magdalen Road, Oxford, OX4 1RE, UK, www.howtobooks.co.uk, £9.34; Credit Cards; (44) (1752) 202-301, fax (44) (1865) 202-331 ◆ This guide offers necessary advice on everyday life in Portugal, and on how to rent and buy property, find a job and start a business. It covers health care, education and retirement, and includes a list of useful contacts and essential phrases for you to get started on the language. An invaluable resource for the international job seeker interested in Portugal. [ID:2506]

Living and Working in the Netherlands 📖

2001, Pat Rush, 128 pages ➤ How To Books Ltd., 3 Newtec Place, Magdalen Road, Oxford, OX4 1RE, UK, www.howtobooks.co.uk, £9.34; Credit Cards; (44) (1752) 202-301, fax (44) (1865) 202-331 ◆ This volume offers advice to people thinking of relocating to the Netherlands. Contains information on the many fundamental aspects that have to be dealt with, including visas and permit requirements, house buying/renting, health, welfare, tax, education and job opportunities. There are also tips and guidelines on getting around, customs and etiquette, driving, entertainment and shopping. Also includes a list of over 100 useful contact names and addresses. [ID:2510]

Mind Your Manners: Managing Business Cultures in Europe 📖

2003, John Mole, Nicholas Brealey Publishing, 286 pages ➤ Masters & Scribes Bookshoppe, 9938 - 81 Ave., Edmonton, AB T6E 1W6, Canada, www.mastersandscribes.com, $36 CDN; Credit

Cards; 800-378-3199, fax 780-439-6879 ◆ The standard guide to European business cultures for over a decade. Now it covers 33 different business cultures, including the 13 countries—from Bulgaria to Turkey—joining the new and enlarged EU as well as non-EU countries such as Norway, Switzerland, Russia and America. Recommended for international entrepreneurs. [ID:2198]

Sharks and Custard: The Things that Make Europeans Laugh 📖
2001, Richard Hill, 189 pages ➤ Europublic SA/NV, P.O. Box 504, Uccle 5, Brussels, B-1180, Belgium, www.europublic.com, €12.95; VISA, MC; (32) (0) 2-343-77-26, fax (32) (0) 2-343-93-30 ◆ English humour is an important component of international business life—a life that needs to be handled with tact and understanding. At best, it can defuse the difficult moments of a major negotiation, at worst it can ruin a relationship! This is a great guide to a deeper understanding of your European business partners. [ID:2551]

Spain Is Different 📖
1999, Helen Wattley Ames, Intercultural Press, 152 pages ➤ Masters & Scribes Bookshoppe, 9938 - 81 Ave., Edmonton, AB T6E 1W6, Canada, www.mastersandscribes.com, $23 CDN; Credit Cards; 800-378-3199, fax 780-439-6879 ◆ Although written for a US audience, Canadians can benefit from the book's focus on the uniqueness of both the Spanish people and their culture. It examines what effects the differences have on the way Spaniards and Americans relate to and interact with each other. Readers explore certain aspects of Spanish culture important in cross-cultural interactions: society and the individual, relationships, language and communication, and work and play. Each chapter contains helpful and humorous anecdotes to illustrate its thesis. Recommended. [ID:2012]

StepStone 💻
www.jobscape.be/home_fs.cfm ◆ This job site focuses on private-sector vacancies in Belgium, but the site also enables you to search for jobs elsewhere in Europe. Job postings are searchable by job category. [ID:2606]

We Europeans 📖
2002, Richard Hill, 432 pages ➤ Europublic SA/NV, P.O. Box 504, Uccle 5, Brussels, B-1180, Belgium, www.europublic.com, €17.25; VISA, MC; (32) (0) 2-343-77-26, fax (32) (0) 2-343-93-30 ◆ This European book provides a penetrating and entertaining analysis of the attitudes and behavioural traits of each European nationality and continues with inter-country comparisons covering such aspects as value systems, attitudes to health, day-to-day living, spare-time preferences and communication habits. Helpful background information for preparing for your overseas work experience in Europe. [ID:2169]

Web Sites on Western Europe 💻
Web Sites on Western Europe ◆ The following are only a fraction of what you can find concerning Western Europe. Information includes current local news, travel and trade information, and links to job opportunities. ◆ Austria, www.austria.info ◆ Belgium, www.belgium.be/eportal/index.jsp ◆ Denmark, www.um.dk/english ◆ Finland, http://virtual.finland.fi ◆ France, www.premier-ministre.gouv.fr/en ◆ Germany, www.germany-info.org/relaunch/index.html ◆ Greece, www.hri.org ◆ Iceland, www.icetrade.is/EN ◆ Ireland, www.itw.ie ◆ Italy, www.countryreports.org/italy.htm ◆ Luxembourg, www.gouvernement.lu/index.html ◆ Malta, www.aboutmalta.com ◆ Netherlands, www.cbs.nl/en ◆ Norway, www.ssb.no/www-open/english ◆ Portugal, www.portugal.org ◆ Spain, www.sispain.org ◆ Sweden, www.swedishtrade.com ◆ Switzerland, www.admin.ch ◆ United Kingdom, www.open.gov.uk. [ID:2323]

Eastern Europe & the Former Soviet Union

FOR LANGUAGE TEACHERS, STRONG-HEARTED INVESTORS & THE YOUNG

The indications are that Eastern Europe and the former Soviet Union will experience massive changes during the next generation. Indeed, with the recent expansion of the EU and Russia's joining the G8 (and soon the WTO), the line between Eastern and Western Europe is increasingly blurred. All these dramatic changes, while disruptive, have created many job opportunities for westerners, both inside and outside the new EU. The large cities in the western region of the former Soviet Union are now attracting numerous foreign job seekers. Large and small companies are trying to cash in on the void in capitalist know-how. Job seekers are cashing in on the massive demand for business expertise.

But the road from communism to capitalism has been difficult, and EU membership will not be a panacea for the economic problems of countries like Poland or Hungary. Governments in these countries continue to struggle with the transition to private ownership, and as recent elections have indicated, there remains a great deal of political uncertainty in certain areas. Because of this turmoil and the accompanying crime rate, the job search in Eastern Europe and the former Soviet Union is reserved mainly for strong-willed individuals. If you are young, a recent graduate with marketable skills, an aggressive entrepreneur or a seasoned professional who likes to take risks, there are numerous jobs to be had.

The Job Market

Despite the lower standard of living in Eastern Europe and the former Soviet Union, there are several qualities that distinguish these regions from countries in the south and make them ripe for growth and international work: the people are highly educated, the region's advanced military technology can be reapplied to other industrial sectors, advanced information systems and institutions already exist and they have a more or less sound infrastructure, except for outlying areas of Russia.

After the collapse of the Soviet Union, and the subsequent transition toward market-based economies, foreign investment poured into the region, providing both technology and expertise, and taking advantage of a number of new business opportunities. Although Russia has since seen some sharp economic reversals on its bumpy road to free enterprise, new EU members in particular are now seeing an influx of foreign capital and professionals, and not just from fellow EU members. Some former Soviet states of Central Asia continue to attract investment—some of it Canadian—in oil and mining.

In 1993, Canada's exports to Eastern Europe and the former Soviet Union totalled $865 million, and imports from the region were $744 million. No reliable figures on Canadian direct investment are available, but there has been a significant amount invested recently in the mining and petrochemicals sectors. (Job seekers in these sectors should know that Canadian petrochemical firms are mainly based in

Calgary and mining firms tend to be based in British Columbia, often with offices in Toronto and Vancouver.)

Experienced business people say that there are many job opportunities for those familiar with the business management practices of the region.

Strategies

Speaking the local language is often a necessity, rather than just an asset, in many Eastern European countries. German and Russian are more widely spoken than English. One expert says that an inexperienced engineer who speaks Polish or Russian or Czech will get a job with an international concern in the appropriate country before an experienced engineer without the language. Nevertheless, many young westerners have gone to Eastern Europe speaking only English and have landed jobs in banking, marketing, and related businesses. Having relatives or contacts prior to arriving can make getting started without language skills a less daunting prospect.

In all countries, the teaching of languages, especially English, is in demand. Both the Czech Republic and Hungary have had some bad experiences with untrained English teachers, and now require either a degree or previous teaching experience. Editors, writers, translators and other language experts should also find it relatively easy to get work. Your first enquiries can be made to the appropriate embassy, which can refer you to suitable teaching agencies and school boards.

Now, well over a decade since the collapse of the Berlin Wall, the major cities are saturated with foreign residents. Housing can be both expensive and difficult to find, particularly in Prague. Major cities are filled with young, predominantly US graduates who have opened English-language newspapers, restaurants and other businesses in the tourist industry. Hungary had more than 13,000 foreign companies by 1994, and tourism there will only expand with admission into the EU.

With this in mind, you may have to go farther afield to improve your chances of finding work or starting up a business. English-language newspapers published in the major Eastern European cities are a good place to go to start making contacts.

For Canadian businesses interested in investing in Eastern Europe and Canadian professionals seeking work, in addition to the relevant country desks of the INTERNATIONAL TRADE CANADA (ITCAN) TRADE COMMISSIONER SERVICE, a good place to start is CIDA's RENAISSANCE EASTERN EUROPE program, which provides funding on a matched basis up to a maximum of $100,000 for straight business proposals by companies looking to establish joint ventures. There is also a smaller program that helps individuals who want to work in Eastern Europe on a volunteer basis. Program funding might, for example, pay travel expenses and a cost of living supplement for Canadians in a variety of development-related fields. CIDA's aim is to reduce the risk of doing business in Eastern Europe, and so nurture investment in the region.

THE ASSOCIATION OF CANADIAN COMMUNITY COLLEGES places college teachers in Eastern Europe (as well as Latin America and Asia) for short stints, mainly as technical advisors. An association official advises interested teachers to be specific in the kinds of desired assignments. *"If you have a specific interest and you know of the demand in a particular country and you focus on skills that are relevant and that the people need, your chances of getting a second look are much better."*

Other sources that can help place qualified individuals include the CZECH–CANADA CHAMBER OF COMMERCE and the HUNGARIAN TRADE ORGANIZATION. These associations vary in the degrees to which they are helpful. The names and addresses of such organizations can be obtained from the appropriate embassy.

Russia and the Commonwealth of Independent States (CIS)

As the financial crisis of 1998 painfully illustrated, Russia is chaotic, difficult and sometimes dangerous. To work there, you will need a spirit of adventure and the ability to take things in stride, and not complain when your water is turned off—because it likely will be. You have to be extremely careful to avoid being a target for thieves and hucksters. There is a tremendous amount of business-related crime (extortion is common) and the judicial system is 10 paces behind the requirements of the free market business community. As one young Canadian business person operating in Russia says, *"it isn't a place for quitters."*

A partner in a Canadian law firm with an office in Moscow has this to say about danger and the need to be careful when settling in places such as Moscow:

> *"The lesson we have learned is that if you want to live and work overseas in new markets where there is a major transition going on towards a market economy, and there's a criminal element developing, as there was in the US in the 1920s, then you've got to be really careful not to make yourself too obvious. We have cases of people being robbed, pistol-whipped and shot, not just in Russia, but also in China and Latin America. The clue is to put to one side your enthusiasm to live like and with the locals. Ninety-nine per cent of the locals will be incredibly generous but that small criminal percentage will learn where you're living and will begin to target your apartment for break and enters, to steal your car, maybe worse. So live and work as much as you can in areas where you don't stand out."*

As underlined before, language skills are important in Warsaw, Budapest and Prague, but they are doubly important in Russia. Basic Russian is a minimum requirement for nearly all job seekers. With a good command of the language plus relevant business experience, you can command a high salary, as much as $250,000 a year with a big international company. At the other end of the scale, casual jobs teaching English will bring in about $300 a month (a subsistence wage).

It is very difficult to get organized in Russia, says one Russian-Canadian who travels there often, but once you are organized, *"success is guaranteed."* You can begin preparation before you leave, by meeting with people who have returned and perusing the Moscow newspapers for classified job ads in English. Recent editions have advertised for all kinds of engineers, as well as chartered accountants, copywriters, lawyers, tax managers, customs officers, property managers, information systems managers, salespeople, secretaries, interpreters and translators.

Some experienced hands advise that people avoid Moscow, which is saturated with up to 250,000 foreigners, and look to St. Petersburg, Kiev, Odessa and other large cities.

Although US companies have been the most willing to take the big risks involved in setting up in Russia, there are some notable Canadian adventurers, large and small. MCCAIN, for example, a processed food manufacturer, has operations in

Russia. GOWLINGS—a Canadian law firm, has an office with legal staff in Moscow. A Montreal group set up a medical service to treat expatriates and is also serving wealthy Russians. A group of Canadians opened the first General Motors dealership in Moscow by selling cars designed for the Iraqi market that were sitting in warehouses after the Gulf War. The list goes on.

In addition, there are dozens of young Canadian entrepreneurs who have set out on their own to open photocopy shops, courier businesses, muffin kiosks, or dry cleaning outfits. "*You name the business and there are young men and women with barely a BA who are doing it with one or two friends,*" says a Canadian lawyer who represents several of them in Moscow.

When forging business ties, relationships are more important than contracts. You should find a reliable business partner and build a relationship on trust. Your first contacts will probably be made through the Canadian embassy, which is extremely helpful to those seriously trying to start a business in Russia.

Personal Stories

• A 31-year-old Canadian lawyer and MBA graduate began his sojourn in Russia as a bar bet with a friend on whether *glasnost* and *perestroika* meant anything at all. That bet turned into a proposal to hold a debate in Russia on the topic of collective security versus liberty, which eventually went ahead on Russian television! He parlayed the experience into a job, bringing 22 MBA students to Russia to offer a very basic business course for arts and science students. The courses were full to overflowing. He urges Canadian graduates to learn basic Russian and go over "*with anything, even a contract to teach English. If you get there and you have a pre-arranged contract, you'll be looked after very well.*" It's not necessary to be young to work in Russia, "just young at heart. If the heat is turned off, you can put on a sweater," he says. "*You have to have language skills and you have to be pretty quick, then there is lots of opportunity. I went with the spirit that I'd try to give more than I got and if you do that you'll find Russians generous to a fault.*"

• A man from Vancouver, married to a Russian immigrant, went to Russia to promote his family business, which made safety equipment for boats. The Soviet Arctic fleet was very interested in buying equipment, but had no hard currency, so he accepted their rubles, which everyone told him he was a fool to do. Then he took the rubles and bought a tanning factory in the Ukraine that produces world-class leathers. He lined up a multi-year contract in Germany that pays him in marks and has already made his money back 50 times over—by ignoring conventional wisdom which says you only deal in hard currency.

• A 22-year-old Canadian student of Croatian descent flew to Split in Croatia in May 1992 to volunteer for the summer. She immediately landed work (at $80 US per month) with the office of the European Community, interpreting meetings between Croatian commanders and UN officials, sometimes crossing the confrontation line and interpreting particularly tense meetings involving ceasefire violations. After a few months, she started interpreting for television stations on location in Sinj, about an hour's drive north of Split, and eventually was hired by the BBC as a "fixer," which paid $160 US per day. In addition to interpreting, she had to find contacts, sniff out news stories, organize checkpoint crossings for the crew, and translate clips for the news. She says it was interesting to see how news is made, and how subjective the process is. *"It's a dangerous job and you have to have nerves of steel. There were shells falling and we got shot at, but it's an experience I wouldn't trade. It changed me forever, that's for sure—it changed my perspective as a Canadian and I wish more people could have this experience."*

RESOURCES

EASTERN EUROPE & THE FORMER SOVIET UNION

The economies of a number of these Eastern European countries are expanding so rapidly that they have overtaken many of the smaller EU member states. There is a wealth of opportunity in this region, and the following resources were selected as a starting point for your job search.

EUROPA 🖳
http://europa.eu.int/index_en.htm ◆ This EU Web site is a great source of international jobs in the European Union. Part of a larger Web site that has great information on living and working in the EU, including political, legal and economic information. Search jobs by profession, location and keyword, narrow your search by experience, contract type and qualifications. Thousands of jobs listed in easy-to-read postings, complete with contact information. If Europe is where you're at, then hitting this site is a must. From the index, click on "Working" under the "Living in the EU" heading. Then select "Find a Job" from the "Job Mobility Portal." [ID:2679]

From Nyet to Da: Understanding the Russians 📖
2003, Yale Richmond, Intercultural Press, 228 pages ➤ Masters & Scribes Bookshoppe, 9938 - 81 Ave., Edmonton, AB T6E 1W6, Canada, www.mastersandscribes.com, $28.95 CDN; Credit Cards; 800-378-3199, fax 780-439-6879 ◆ Illuminates the dynamics of traditional Russian culture in the framework of contemporary events. Enlightening reading on virtually every aspect of Russian life. Suitable for international job seekers, business executives, educators, students, governmental officials and russophiles generally. [ID:2013]

Mind Your Manners: Managing Business Cultures in Europe 📖
2003, John Mole, Nicholas Brealey Publishing, 286 pages ➤ Masters & Scribes Bookshoppe, 9938 - 81 Ave., Edmonton, AB T6E 1W6, Canada, www.mastersandscribes.com, $36 CDN; Credit Cards; 800-378-3199, fax 780-439-6879 ◆ The standard guide to European business cultures for over a decade. Now it covers 33 different business cultures, including the 13 countries—from Bulgaria to Turkey—joining the new and enlarged EU as well as non-EU countries such as Norway, Switzerland, Russia and America. Recommended for international entrepreneurs. [ID:2198]

Moscow Times Career Center 🖳
www.careercenter.ru ◆ If you are interested in working in Russia, then this site is for you. Browse jobs by category, most are private sector, but there is a section of non-profit jobs. Register, post your resume and receive job alerts. A good starting point for finding work in the former Soviet Union. [ID:2602]

Russian and Eastern European Institute Employment Opportunities 🖳
www.indiana.edu/~reeiweb/indemp.html ◆ This Web site is produced by Indiana University and contains links to job hunting resources, internships and non-academic opportunities for those with an interest in Russia and Eastern Europe. [ID:2363]

Web Sites on Eastern Europe and the Former Soviet Union 🖳
Web Sites on Eastern Europe and the former Soviet Union ◆ These are a sample of sites providing information on this region of the world. The sites include local news, travel, export-import information, and job opportunities. ◆ Bosnia-Herzegovina, www.gksoft.com/govt/en/ba.html

◆ Belarus, www.friends-partners.org/friends/community/lists/belarus.htmlopt-tables-unix-english ◆ Bulgaria, www.bulgaria.com ◆ Croatia, www.hr/index.en.shtml ◆ Czech Republic, www.czech.cz ◆ Estonia, www.riik.ee/en ◆ Latvia, www.lda.gov.lv/eng ◆ Lithuania, http://neris.mii.lt ◆ Poland, www.fuw.edu.pl/PHe.html ◆ Romania, www.romania.com ◆ Russia, www.ru/eng/index.html ◆ Serbia, http://serbia.net ◆ Slovakia, www.slovak.com ◆ Slovenia, www.uvi.si/eng ◆ Ukraine, www.gu.kiev.ua. [ID:2324]

The Middle East
STILL GUSHING

The Middle East has been a hot job market for 50 years and will continue to be a hot spot for the next 50 years or until the region runs out of oil. Most jobs in this region are in the Gulf oil states, with strong demand for skilled labour ranging from doctors and nurses to oil rig workers and telecommunications engineers. To be sure, nowadays job applications from the West outstrip the number of jobs available—but it remains a good place to look for work, despite the increasing risks involved. An advantage is that many agencies in the oil states hire westerners directly: a telecommunications engineer can apply directly to SAUDI TELEPHONE for a job.

Here is what the Middle East marketing vice-president with a large Canadian service company has to say:

> *"The Middle East is an exceptionally good market to aim at because it has the financial resources combined with a lack of skills and a recognition that the West has the skills it needs. It has the mindset—in the Emirates, Kuwait and Saudi— that 'we have the funds to buy technological slaves. We don't need to learn how to do this because the country has enough money to buy what it needs.' So they maintain their dependency on Western technologists. Asia is the opposite—they ask for help but it's restricted and boxed: 'We'll hire you to do this specific job but then you're gone.'"*

This section will focus mainly on job opportunities in the rich Persian Gulf states. The Gulf countries include Bahrain, Kuwait, Oman, Qatar, Saudi Arabia, the United Arab Emirates and Yemen. Other Middle Eastern countries are Egypt, Iraq, Iran, Israel, Jordan, Lebanon, Syria and Turkey. Egypt is the recipient of generous amounts of US funding (and thus job opportunities), and Israel has been a popular stop for travellers who want to experience kibbutz life. With the ongoing conflict in Iraq, there are many job opportunities and, of course, inherent risks. Yemen, which doesn't border on the Gulf waters, is among the 10 poorest countries in the world, and is not in the same class as the other Gulf states in terms of jobs and salaries. Turkey, on the other hand, is a member of NATO and, as noted in the discussion of Western Europe, is aiming for membership in an increasingly receptive EU.

The Middle East represents a not insignificant market for Canadian companies. In the mid-1990s, annual Canadian exports to the region approached $2 billion and imports were well over $1 billion. A recent federal government brochure points to attractive opportunities for Canadian companies in selected Middle Eastern markets, although how the evolving situation in Iraq will influence the region economically is still unclear. Rising oil prices imply there may be many fresh opportunities among all OPEC states in the region.

The Persian Gulf

In the Persian Gulf, there is demand for people who can fill professional, managerial, supervisory and highly skilled technical positions. The professions include nurses, doctors, teachers, engineers, computer specialists, geologists and oil project managers. While salaries for beginning teachers and nurses are no higher, or possibly lower, than what they could earn in Canada, the salaries are not taxed, which makes a huge difference to the bottom line. Holidays are generous and many people are provided with free housing. Tax-free salaries for pilots, engineers, and other skilled technical personnel are in the $80,000 to $120,000 range.

What's more—there *are* jobs. For example, a young Canadian who specialized in the computer design of highways won a couple of small contracts in Canada after graduation, but was basically out of work for three or four years because no one was building new highways. After sending out more than 300 resumes, mostly in Canada, he was offered a contract in Qatar with a North American firm, where he is now earning $80,000 tax-free. Although he is not enamoured of life in the Gulf, *"he likes it a lot better than sitting around Ottawa unemployed,"* says a close friend.

Unskilled or semi-skilled workers, however, face tough competition from migrants from India, Pakistan, and Yemen who are willing to work for very low salaries.

When applying directly for jobs in the Gulf, resumes should include certain information that might be considered illegal for employers to request in North America: sex, nationality, marital status, age and number of dependents. Jews who want to work in the Gulf will have to lie about their religion. Women will face restrictions that are more severe than those facing men, and may not be considered for traditionally "male" technical jobs, such as engineering. It is the usual practice to sign the job contract with a Gulf government once you've arrived, not before.

The oil states vary considerably in terms of lifestyle and restrictions that Western job seekers will encounter. Bahrain and the Emirates are freer, permitting Christian church services and the sale of alcohol. Saudi Arabia has lots of Western services and luxuries and pays the highest salaries, but it also has the most "do not's." These include no alcohol (though it is available illegally), no driving by women, and no dating (but unmarried men and women get around it by using a married couple as "chaperones"). Women must dress conservatively and cover themselves with an abaya in public. When people are caught breaking the laws, as happened to some Canadian nurses caught coming out of a party where alcohol had been served, the punishment can include a jail sentence and deportation. An old Middle Eastern hand says, *"You should know what you're doing and make the best of it. Don't try to beat the system. It certainly is a different world, and you can enjoy it if you come to recognize it for what it is."*

Israel

Israel has long been a popular destination for Canadians, Americans, Europeans and Australians who want to spend time on a kibbutz, working for several weeks in the fruit orchards or at another communal job. You will earn room and board and a little pocket money and learn a bit more about the Israeli way of life. It used to be that you could arrive at the airport in Tel Aviv and sign up for a kibbutz on the spot, but in recent years there have been more applicants than spaces, so it pays to book ahead of time. Obviously, increasing violence in the region is another factor to keep in mind, and you will want to pay careful attention as to exactly where a kibbutz is located and what risks are involved.

A unique cultural experience for the physically fit is to work as a volunteer on archaeological digs in Israel. See the Canadian student guidebook, *A World of Difference*, for more information.

RESOURCES
THE MIDDLE EAST

This region offers countless opportunities for skilled professionals in the healthcare, engineering and teaching fields. While there are increasing security concerns, there has always been an allure for expats to work in the Middle East.

Arabian Careers Limited 💻
www.arabiancareers.com/position.html ◆ Arabian Careers Limited recruits skilled healthcare professionals with vacancies in Saudi Arabia and the surrounding area. Doctors, dentists, nurses, midwives, pharmacists, hospital administrators and technicians will want to check out the benefits of a tax-free salary, free accommodations and an opportunity to explore the amazing Middle East in their free time! [ID:2603]

Bayt.com 💻
http://jobs2.bayt.com ◆ The Bayt Web site allows you to search for jobs in the Middle East and Arabic world generally. Thousands of professional private-sector postings from companies in Jordan, Kuwait, Saudi Arabia and the UAE. The site is easy to use, with postings presented in a clear format. One can apply on-line for each posting. Great site for Middle East buffs. [ID:2604]

CareerMidEast.com 💻
www.careermideast.com ◆ This is an excellent job search Web site focusing on the Middle East and northern Africa. Lots of job postings as well as helpful links related to career enhancement: marketing yourself, developing your skills, locating training centres and deciding on courses, plus the usual resume and interview tips. [ID:2458]

Egypt Today 💻
www.egypttoday.com ◆ This site offers great exposure to Egyptian popular culture. Interesting travel, business, government and political sections as well as features on art, film and music. If you're interested in working in this part of the world, then check out this excellent on-line and print magazine. [ID:2465]

Living and Working in Saudi Arabia 📖
2001, Rosalie Rayburn, Kate Bush, 144 pages ➤ How To Books Ltd., 3 Newtec Place, Magdalen Road, Oxford, OX4 1RE, UK, www.howtobooks.co.uk, £9.34; Credit Cards; (44) (1752) 202-301, fax (44) (1865) 202-331 ◆ Saudi Arabia is a country where time-honoured traditions exist side by side with cutting-edge technology. Designed for those seeking business opportunities or anticipating a move there, this guide covers all aspects of life and culture in Saudi Arabia. [ID:2115]

Understanding Arabs: A Guide for Westerners 📖
2002, Margaret Kleffner Nydell, 264 pages ➤ Masters & Scribes Bookshoppe, 9938 - 81 Ave., Edmonton, AB T6E 1W6, Canada, www.mastersandscribes.com, $28 CDN; Credit Cards; 800-378-3199, fax 780-439-6879 ◆ Introduces the complexities of Arab culture and Islam in an evenhanded, unbiased style. The book covers such topics as beliefs and values, religion and society, the role of

the family, friends and strangers, men and women, social formalities and etiquette and communication styles. This edition includes a completely revised appendix on 17 Arab countries. [ID:2014]

Web Sites on the Middle East 💻

Web Sites on Africa and the Middle East ◆ These sites contain trade information, local news, and general country information. Sites such as ArabNet provide quick reference information for almost any country in these fascinating parts of the world ◆ ArabNet, www.arab.net ◆ Egypt, www.egypt.com/default.php ◆ Israel Information Service, www.mfa.gov.il/mfa ◆ Morocco, www.morocco.com ◆ Tunisia, www.tunisiaonline.com [ID:2847]

Africa
FOR THE SOCIALLY COMMITTED

A decade of democracy in South Africa has brought with it economic opportunities. The country has maintained its economic prominence on the continent although it has little influence in North Africa, which continues to operate separately from sub-Saharan Africa. South Africa plays a leading role in mining. Canadian geologists and engineers have obtained work in the mining industry throughout Africa. (For more information, see Chapter 32, Engineering Careers Abroad.)

There are other bright spots on the continent. Angola's oil sector is cautiously expanding with prospects that the country and region will remain stable. Nigeria is still a major oil producer and maintains relative stability given its size and complex, ethnic north–south divide. Ghana remains democratic and stable. Libya is surprisingly opening up to the world and, with greater world acceptance, its oil reserves will generate much new economic activity in the region. Algeria's economic prospects are also on the rise as its political troubles now seem to be in its past. The overall message to outside investors from the continent can still be discouraging, however. Zimbabwe and the Côte d'Ivoire have been poor economic performers where once they were stable and the source of many international jobs. War in the Sudan and continuing instability in the former Zaire do not help the continent.

The major source for international job prospects on the continent remains in the field of international development. Africa continues to be a major recipient of foreign aid, and this generates international jobs. (For more information, see Chapter 30, Careers in International Development.) Unfortunately, the greatest increase in international job prospects is the field of HIV/AIDS. From medical personnel to community outreach workers and project managers, sub-Saharan Africa is awash in development projects aimed at combating this disease. (For more information, see Chapter 33, Health Careers Abroad.)

RESOURCES

AFRICA

The number of employment opportunities in this part of the world has risen dramatically since our last edition. There are a number of Web sites catering to seekers of employment in the expanding sectors of mining, and oil and gas, in addition to the traditionally strong field of international development.

Africa Centre 🖳

www.africacentre.org ◆ Established in the US in 2000, the Africa Centre is a non-profit organization dedicated to promoting social awareness and knowledge of Africa through providing trustworthy information, materials and services to the local and national community. Recommended. [ID:2456]

Africa Online 🖳

www.africaonline.com ◆ This Web site offers a wealth of news, job postings and information on African culture, economy, politics and geography. Navigate to the "Careers" section of the home page and then to "Job Vacancies" to get to the search page. Contains a good database of teaching, consulting, technical advising and project management jobs all over the continent. [ID:2457]

AfricaJobs.net 🖳

www.AfricaJobs.net ◆ This Web site is part of a network of job sites for this region of the world. Search jobs in Africa by location, type and position. Check out the latest African news headlines. [ID:2672]

Career Junction 🖳

www.careerjunction.co.za ◆ With services such as innovative on-line job hunting tools, on-line resume builder, job alerts via e-mail, on-line reference checking, career advice and newsletters, this site has grown into one of South Africa's best job sites. [ID:2468]

FindaJobinAfrica 🖳

Commonwealth Business Council, www.findajobinafrica.com ◆ Since its launch in 2000, this appealing and highly functional South African site has grown into an excellent resource for job seekers looking to ply their skills in Africa. Post your resume and search jobs by country or industry. With jobs ranging from development to banking to senior management positions, this excellent site presents opportunities for everyone! [ID:2454]

Harrison Jones Associates Jobs Network 🖳

International Recruitment Consultants, Harrison Jones Associates, Buckingham House East, The Broadway, Stanmore, Middlesex, HA7 4EB, UK, www.africajobs.net, (44) (0) (2083) 85-7881, fax (44) 20 8385-7882 ◆ This is part of a network of job search Web sites which has for 10 years specialized in recruiting Western expatriates for international positions. From the African region home page, you can search jobs in any region or you can navigate to other job pages focusing on Africa, Arabia, Europe, Asia, and North and South America, and search directly from there. Lots of professional positions available in all regions. [ID:2453]

Iafrica: Careers 🖳

http://careers.iafrica.com ◆ A good job search site focusing on jobs in South Africa and abroad. Lots of quality jobs updated daily, excellent descriptions, all with the option of applying directly on-line. All the usual career advice, notifications and resume posting services in an attractive and easy-to-use format. [ID:2471]

Jobfood.com 🖳

www.jobfood.com ◆ This South African Web site contains an excellent searchable database of professional jobs in the country and surrounding region. Lots of career services such as resume posting, chat rooms and articles. [ID:2617]

Jobs Maroc 🖳

www.jobmaroc.co.ma; *Fr* ◆ Offres d'emplois, stages et formations disponibles au Maroc. [ID:2466]

Jobs.co.za 🖳

www.jobs.co.za ◆ A well-organized and appealing South African site providing the ability to search jobs by keyword, industry, and whether the employer has an employment equity programme. Also has search filter, c.v. management, newsletter and other career resources. [ID:2469]

Mail & Guardian Online: Career Junction 💻

http://mg.careerjunction.co.za ◆ This South African site is Africa's first on-line newspaper and has an excellent career junction where over 4,000 jobs can be searched by keyword, industry, job type, level of experience and age. Tip: the job search feature takes a bit of practice because the keyword settings are very specific, but once you figure it out, you'll have access to over 5,000 jobs in and around the Horn. The home page link is also a great source for news and information about Africa. Check it out! [ID:2472]

Mbendi Information For Africa: The Employment Space 💻

www.mbendi.co.za ◆ This South African site contains a good database of overseas mining and energy jobs located in Africa. Lots of business information on trading with African companies. From the home page, follow the employment link located in the business section to "The Employment Space," where you can view employment notices by employment category, location and industry. [ID:2461]

Pnet Job Advertisements 💻

www.pnet.co.za ◆ Create resumes and search jobs within and outside of South Africa. Lots of jobs in all sectors, especially IT and the sciences. [ID:2470]

Science in Africa 💻

www.scienceinafrica.co.za/Jobs/jobs.htm ◆ This free South African Web site offers access to current job postings. Small but constantly updated, the database is searchable by scientific discipline. Postings are primarily in South Africa. [ID:2636]

Web Sites on Africa 💻

Web Sites on Africa and the Middle East ◆ These sites contain trade information, local news, and general country information. Sites such as Africa Online provide quick reference information for almost any country in these fascinating parts of the world. ◆ Africa Online, www.africaonline.com/site ◆ Egypt, www.egypt.com/default.php ◆ Gambia, www.gambia.com ◆ Ghana, www.ghanaweb.com ◆ Kenya, www.kenyaweb.com ◆ Malawi, www.malawi.com ◆ Morocco, www.morocco.com ◆ South Africa, www.southafrica.net ◆ Tunisia, www.tunisiaonline.com ◆ UAE, www.ecssr.ac.ae ◆ Uganda, www.government.go.ug. [ID:2322]

Asia Pacific
FOR THE HIGHLY EDUCATED, YOUNG OR MOBILE ADVENTURER

Although crystal ball gazing lies beyond the scope of this book, it is easy to believe that the coming century belongs to the Asia Pacific region. Even with the economic correction and sharp decline of some Asian currencies in late 1997, economic activity is expected to thrive for years to come. Countries that were developing nations a decade ago are now tigers of growth. China, with 1.2 billion people, has lifted many trade and investment restrictions, as has Vietnam. Places such as Hong Kong, Singapore, South Korea and, of course, Japan, support a standard of living comparable to that of many European countries.

Thanks to an expanding basic infrastructure, business also continues to evolve in many countries. In Thailand, a huge freeway system in Bangkok as well as two oil refineries have been built. The world's tallest office building is now in Kuala Lumpur, Malaysia. A frequent business traveller to Southeast Asia says he is reminded of what Canadian cities were like in the 1950s, with construction on every corner.

The term Asia Pacific commonly includes the following 12 countries: Australia, China (including Hong Kong), Indonesia, Japan, Malaysia, New Zealand, the Philippines, Singapore, South Korea, Taiwan, Thailand and Vietnam. It is a huge, populous and varied region. Some also include the countries of South Asia (that border on the Indian Ocean) in this term, especially India with its high-tech centres and sustained economic expansion over the last decade.

The region's markets, which now have approximately 60 per cent of the world's population, 50 per cent of global production and 40 per cent of total consumption, are of vital interest to Canada. Meanwhile, there are more new immigrants arriving from Asia Pacific than from any other region, making Vancouver the second-largest Chinese-speaking city on the continent, after San Francisco.

For Canadians with experience in finance, banking, engineering, mining, geology, and computers, there are good work opportunities in the Asia Pacific region. Similarly, young entrepreneurs (particularly MBA graduates) have enjoyed considerable success in selected markets. For those who speak Mandarin, Cantonese or another Asian language, the chances of finding good jobs are even better. Canadian and American firms doing business in Asia advertise regularly in *The Globe and Mail* and Vancouver newspapers. Some companies even recruit and hold interviews in Vancouver.

Many Canadian firms have a physical presence in India, from smaller high-tech firms like Alias with their own Bangalore office, to Bata's long-established, massive retail and manufacturing presence. The rapid growth of high-tech firms and call centres in Chennai and Hyderabad (nick-named "Cyberabad" thanks to all of its Internet companies) is quite amazing. Canadian firms in such diverse fields as banking, gas exploration and hydroelectric development have found India a profitable country in which to base Canadian staff, and more can be expected as India catches up with China as a preferred destination for foreign investors. Some Canadians have even established a good career working in Mumbai's dynamic film and television industry, both behind and in front of the camera.

There are two standard strategies for the professional seeking overseas work in the area. One is to apply from outside the region. If successful, you're likely to get a better job package than if you apply from inside the country, and your working papers will be taken care of. A Canadian management consultant working in Malaysia cautions that many good jobs in finance are recruited internationally, usually through London, which is where he was based when he received his offer.

Canadian graduates armed with little more than a business degree have been moving to Hong Kong and Singapore to find work, and have met with some success. A Toronto lawyer with foreign experience advises more experienced professionals to visit the country of their choice before actually moving there:

"Spend your own money to go there and make some local contacts. It's not just a case of faxing c.v.'s from Toronto. You have to pound the pavement a bit, get a sense of meeting people and not just at the embassy, to get a better picture of where the opportunities are. If you spend that $5,000 and two or three weeks in your destination of choice, it's amazing what you can accomplish. It's geometric: what you learned in Day 1 is 10 times more in Day 2 and 100 times more in Day 3. You've got to get over there. The rewards are surprising and extensive and not necessarily what you think they'll be."

Casual work can be found teaching English, especially in China, Indonesia, Japan, South Korea, Taiwan, Thailand and Vietnam.

China

Teaching English is in great demand in Beijing and elsewhere in China. A Vancouver student who spent 10 months learning Chinese at a Beijing university says he tutored a couple of students, but practically had to be rude as he turned others away because he didn't have the time. Other young westerners he met earned money editing and translating from "Chinglish" to English.

For those with an entrepreneurial bent, buying artifacts and silk for sale in Europe, Japan and North America is a popular route. Would-be traders should check out their home market for pricing and demand. (Sizes can be a problem—even large Chinese sizes are small by Canadian standards.) One couple brought clothing designs from Europe to have made into clothes in China and then sold the results in Japan for a killing. *"In Canada there are obvious channels to get things done, whereas in China it is a case of who you know,"* says the student. *"Once you have good connections, they will always help you."*

For professionals, China is not the best destination to seek a well-paid job. The president of a California database company that matches trades and professionals with overseas jobs says, *"China is a revolving door. China wants all the technology and investment it can get without having to commit itself to a lot of employment of foreigners. It has never been the large employment market many companies thought it would be, but we do have people working there on highways, airports, and oil-related projects."* A Canadian who has worked in China on development projects concurs, *"China is always on the lookout for people who are willing to come and work for next to nothing."*

Hong Kong

Hong Kong returned to Chinese rule in 1997, but it is governed as a distinct area within China and remains economically vibrant. Work opportunities for westerners are still comparatively good. Partly because of the strong interest in emigration, there remains a high demand for teachers of English. Foreign investment is still flowing into the country, taking advantage of its low tax rates and favourable disposition toward foreign companies. Its main industries are in the light manufacturing sector, especially textiles, electronics and plastics, and machinery, with most production destined for export. Tourism also occupies an important place in the economy. Infrastructure projects like a newly built airport have helped sustain the city's economic edge, although other economically dynamic coastal cities in southern China are catching up to it. As the financial hub of Southeast Asia, Singapore is now giving Hong Kong stiff competition.

In recent years, with poor job prospects at home, quite a few Canadians, fresh out of business schools, have moved to Hong Kong with their MBAs and a few thousand dollars, and within a few months have found jobs. (See Personal Stories below.) *The South China Morning Post*, especially the Saturday edition, is the newspaper to check for job ads.

Japan

Japan, with one of the world's strongest economies and highest standards of living, is an important trading partner for Canada. More than half of our trade with the Asia Pacific region is conducted there. Canadian companies currently have investments of $3 billion in the country.

Teaching English has long been the traditional avenue for westerners wanting to work in Japan, partly because such positions pay well and also because few other jobs have been open to foreigners. But this is changing for several reasons. First, the high cost of living in Japan means that salaries for English teachers offered in some neighbouring countries, such as South Korea, are increasingly competitive. Second, competition for such jobs has become more intense as westerners grow more familiar with Japan. And, in small but growing numbers, westerners are being hired for jobs that don't involve teaching—mostly working for foreign companies, but increasingly with Japanese companies. A CARLETON UNIVERSITY graduate who speaks some Japanese works full time for a building materials company, processing orders and dealing with foreign customers.

The English-language *Japan Times*, especially the Monday edition, is a good source for those interested in English teaching jobs. The JAPANESE EXCHANGE AND TEACHING PROGRAM annually hires roughly 400 Canadians who have university degrees and are 35 years old or under to teach English in the school system for one year. (For more information, see Chapter 29, Teaching Abroad.)

Australia and New Zealand

New Zealand and Australia have proven to be difficult places for professionals and backpackers alike to find work. In Australia, a temporary residence visa is available to someone with a firm job offer from an Australian employer who can prove that no Australian can do the job. If you have unique or very advanced skills in computer-related industries, you may be able to swing it. There is also a working holiday visa available for people 18 to 30 years of age, to be used "once in a lifetime." The visa allows young people to travel and see the country, and get jobs lasting not more than three months with one employer, harvesting fruit, waiting on tables, typing or the like.

New Zealand offers a similar working holiday scheme but temporary work visas are even more difficult to come by than in Australia. In both countries, one-year job exchanges are available with people in your profession who can switch jobs, homes, cars and everything else with you and your family. Used frequently by teachers, this system has also been tried by journalists and film producers, and can be a wonderful way to experience the country.

Personal Stories

- With zero job opportunities at home, a 29-year-old Canadian with an MBA from CONCORDIA UNIVERSITY moved to Hong Kong with some money, a suit and a resume. Within a month he had a job. He lived in a hotel for the first month, sent out dozens of resumes and knocked on dozens of doors, acting far more aggressively than he would in Canada. He soon got his first job with an industrial company. About a year later, with fluency in French, a North American business background, a bit of business experience and a smattering of Cantonese, he was hired by a French company trying to break into Asia. He now has the lofty title of Director of Operations for the pan-Pacific branch. He travels frequently to Europe and is earning good money, but he finds the lifestyle lonely and has to put up with things he wouldn't accept in Canada: for example, cramped living quarters. He rents a small apartment for $3,600 a month, and sublets 2 of the 3 rooms (one of the rooms is 2 by 3 metres). A friend says, *"I thought he was a little crazy going there but he has done really well. Like anywhere else, you have to make your own opportunities and he is really good at it. He's created his own chances in a very competitive, fast-paced market. You have to have a really good business sense and be willing to make deals."*

- A Vancouver man in his mid-30s had a small company that made a unique airproof product used as a sheath over decaying pylons to repair docks under water. The business in Vancouver employed five or six people, but wasn't doing terribly well, so he went to Australia to try to sell the product, with no success. On his way home, he stopped in Manila for a short holiday, asked some questions, and learned that the Philippine government had just received $500 million US, from the ASIAN DEVELOPMENT BANK to refurbish their docks over 10 years. He had found a buyer! A Canadian who spent time with him there says, *"He has 150 divers working for him and you can't imagine how well he is living in Manila. A big house, parties—a young millionaire. All he has to do is the paperwork and some diving when he feels like it. He is one happy camper, let me tell you."*

- An editor for the *Ottawa Citizen* with dreams of moving to Australia was able to live out his dream—at least for one year. He switched jobs, houses and cars with a copy editor at the *West Australian* and moved to Perth with his two children and journalist wife for a year. (She enjoyed her time learning to surf with a moms-and-tots group called Moms on Boards.) They loved their time in Australia and would have stayed, but, because of massive layoffs in the newspaper industry, they were unable to find permanent work.

- An American woman who taught business English in Taiwan was asked to give a seminar on table settings for some Chinese women who had to accompany their husbands on frequent business trips to Europe or North America: they knew not to spit the crab shells on the table, but needed help with which fork, spoon or glass to use at the proper moment. Figuring there would be 10 to 15 participants for a half-day seminar, she set the fee at $150 US each. A couple of weeks before the scheduled seminar, she was invited to have a look at the room where it would take place: she was shown the ballroom of a downtown hotel. Realizing more people had signed up than she'd bargained for, the teacher revised her plans. She had a large table set up on a stage that people could walk around, and used overheads with diagrams of the different utensils so that everyone could see. In the end, some 625 women showed up and even in the ballroom it was standing room only. It was the most lucrative transaction of her life—more than $90,000 US, for 4 hours of work!

RESOURCES

ASIA PACIFIC

The Asia Pacific region continues to boast a large number of job resources for expats. For other resources focusing exclusively on teaching in the Asia Pacific region, or for more cross-cultural information, see the Resources section in Chapter 29, Teaching Abroad.

Asia Net 🖳
www.asia-net.com ◆ Asia Net is a job board for candidates bilingual in English and Chinese, Japanese or Korean. Most jobs listings are for technical or engineering type jobs which can be searched by location. [ID:2814]

Asia Pacific Country Backgrounders 📖 🖳
2002, 15 pages each ➤ Asia Pacific Foundation of Canada, Suite 666, 999 Canada Place, Vancouver, BC V6C 3E1, Canada, www.asiapacific.ca, Free on-line; VISA, MC; 604-684-5986, fax 604-681-1370 ◆ A series of booklets on 14 Asia Pacific countries and Canada's economic relationship with each of them. Includes key facts and figures, economic and trade statistic comparisons, Canada's ranking among major trading partners, imports and exports, main sectors of opportunity for Canadian business and more. Recommended for entrepreneurs and others seeking quick, dependable facts on Canada's Asian trade partners. [ID:2166]

Asia Pacific Review 📖
Annual, 72 pages ➤ Asia Pacific Foundation of Canada, Suite 666, 999 Canada Place, Vancouver, BC V6C 3E1, Canada, www.asiapacific.ca, $34.95 CDN; VISA, MC; 604-684-5986, fax 604-681-1370; *Fr* ◆ This annual survey examines Canada's relationship with Asia and the impact on business of major developments during the year. The report includes a Canada-Asia report card which examines in depth nine key areas of the Canada-Asia relationship, assigning letter grades to each performance indicator. The review is also available in French. [ID:2393]

Asiaco 🖳
http://jobs.asiaco.com ◆ A truly international site for job seekers. A huge database of thousands of jobs searchable by country. Useful services and resources including resume writing, interview tips and links to other job search sites. [ID:2459]

Asian Development Bank Business Opportunities 🖳 🏛
Monthly ➤ Central Operations Services Office, Asian Development Bank, P.O. Box 789, Manilla Central Post Office, 0980 Manila, Philippines, www.adb.org, $30 US/year; (632) 632-4444, fax (632) 636-2444 ◆ The ADB is based in Manila and funds development projects and programs in the Asia Pacific regions. The goal is to generate opportunities for the business communities of member countries. The "Business Opportunities" page of the site is found by navigating from the index to "Opportunities" and then to "Business Opportunities." It provides information on the requirements for goods, work and services of projects under consideration by ADB. [ID:2286]

Asian Outlook 📖 🖳
Quarterly, variable ➤ Asia Pacific Foundation of Canada, Suite 666, 999 Canada Place, Vancouver, BC V6C 3E1, Canada, www.asiapacific.ca, Free; VISA, MC; 604-684-5986, fax 604-681-1370 ◆ Offers a concise survey of the latest political and economic trends in 14 Asia Pacific economies of interest to Canadian business. Includes a succinct listing of developments to watch for in the months ahead, including a tabulation of major economic indicators. [ID:2395]

Business Chinese 📖
2002 ➤ China Books & Periodicals Inc., 2929 - 24th Street, San Francisco, CA 94110, USA, www.chinabooks.com, $14.95 US; Credit Cards; 415-282-2994, fax 415-282-0994 ◆ This

introductory text focuses on learning spoken Chinese for business. Lessons focus on real-life business situations, with exercises and up-to-date business terms. A good primer for a successful business trip. [ID:2480]

Byron Employment ▣
http://employment.byron.com.au ◆ This Australian Web site lists primarily private sector, and professional positions, with some government and teaching positions available as well. Also contains information for overseas candidates on living and working in Australia. [ID:2600]

Canada in Asia Series 📖
2003, 12 to 40 pages each ➤ Asia Pacific Foundation of Canada, Suite 666, 999 Canada Place, Vancouver, BC V6C 3E1, Canada, www.asiapacific.ca, Free; VISA, MC; 604-684-5986, fax 604-681-1370 ◆ This is a research series dealing with issues affecting Canada-Asia relations and their influence on business trade between Canada and selected countries. [ID:2394]

Career One ▣
www.careerone.com.au ◆ This Australia-based international job board can be searched by location, expertise and employer. There are currently 1,670+ engineering jobs listed. Sign up for e-mail alerts. [ID:2822]

China Books & Periodicals Inc. (On-line Catalogue) ▣
China Books & Periodicals Inc., 2929 - 24th Street, San Francisco, CA 94110, USA, www.chinabooks.com, Credit Cards; 415-282-2994, fax 415-282-0994 ◆ Probably the single best source for China-related job-search books. Choose from among hundreds of resources on Chinese language, culture, history, business, arts, literature and living in China. [ID:2035]

Doing Business with Japanese Men: A Woman's Handbook 📖
1993, Christalyn Brannen, Tracey Wilen, 176 pages ➤ Stone Bridge Press, P.O. Box 8202, Berkeley, CA 94707, USA, www.stonebridge.com, $9.95 US; Credit Cards; 800-947-7271, fax 510-524-8711 ◆ One of the only books that looks at the uniquely delicate situation that confronts the Western businesswoman, whether she is travelling to Japan or meeting Japanese clients at her home office. Includes practical discussions, background, do's and don'ts of decorum and seating charts etc. [ID:2107]

Encountering the Chinese: A Guide for Americans 📖
1999, Hu Wenzhong, Cornelius L. Grove, Intercultural Press, 230 pages ➤ Masters & Scribes Bookshoppe, 9938 - 81 Ave., Edmonton, AB T6E 1W6, Canada, www.mastersandscribes.com, $30.95 CDN; Credit Cards; 800-378-3199, fax 780-439-6879 ◆ This book is tailored to the overseas job seeker interested in China. Analyzes basic Chinese values, cultural norms and modern market mindsets. Presents insights into how to interact with Chinese people and identifies the cross-cultural factors that can lead to failed business negotiations, embarrassing faux pas and disruptive misunderstandings between Westerners and the Chinese. This edition includes a special section for North American women working in China. [ID:2099]

Far Eastern Economic Review 📖
Weekly ➤ Subscription Department, Far Eastern Economic Review, P.O. Box 160, General Post Office, Hong Kong, China, www.feer.com, $220 HK/year; Credit Cards; (800) 522-2714, fax (413) 592-4782 ◆ With a circulation of over 100,000 in Hong Kong, Malaysia and Singapore, this news weekly is Asia's premier business magazine. Reports on politics, business, economics, technology and social and cultural issues throughout Asia, with a particular emphasis on both Southeast Asia and China. Sign up on-line for a one-, two- or three-year subscription. [ID:2141]

From Boston to Beijing: Managing with a World View 📖
2002, 304 pages ➤ Thomson South-Western, 5191 Natorp Blvd., Mason, OH 45040, USA, www.swlearning.com, $22.95 US; Credit Cards; 513-229-1000 ◆ International entrepreneurs in every industry can benefit from the advice this book contains on how to manage in a multicultural environment. It illustrates how countries vary and how people recognize, manage and effectively

use cultural variance. In addition to information on working with colleagues across the globe, the book contains information on culture shock, spousal transition and returning home after an overseas stint. [ID:2549]

Getting a Job in Australia 📖
2004, Nick Vandome, 192 pages ➤ How To Books Ltd., 3 Newtec Place, Magdalen Road, Oxford, OX4 1RE, UK, www.howtobooks.co.uk, £9.34; Credit Cards; (44) (1752) 202-301, fax (44) (1865) 202-331 ◆ This British book provides a step-by-step guide to all aspects of finding permanent and casual employment in Australia. Explains the economic climate, where to look for work, what pay and conditions to expect and provides key information about tax, contracts, your rights at work and the Australian philosophy of employment. Includes details about Australian tax laws, pensions, newstart allowances and economic conditions. Also includes useful Web sites to enable your job search from outside Australia. [ID:2495]

Going to Japan on Business: Protocol,
Stategies & Language for the Corporate Traveler 📖
2002, Christalyn Brannen, 176 pages ➤ Stone Bridge Press, P.O. Box 8202, Berkeley, CA 94707, USA, www.stonebridge.com, $14.95 US; Credit Cards; 800-947-7271, fax 510-524-8711 ◆ This US book includes tips for first-time and seasoned business travellers, all in a handy form for quick reference and on-the-spot use. Includes information on preparing for your trip, getting around, making introductions, conducting business meetings, socializing, sounding good in Japanese, and much more. Essential reading for those with business interests in Japan. [ID:2142]

Japanese for Professionals 📖
1998, Association for Japanese Language Learning, 288 pages ➤ Kodansha International, www.kodansha-intl.com, $34.95 US ◆ A comprehensive course for people who need to use Japanese in business. [ID:2219]

Japan's Cultural Code Words 📖
2004, Turtle Publishing, 352 pages ➤ Raincoast Books, 9050 Shaughnessy Street, Vancouver, BC V6P 6E5, Canada, www.raincoast.com, $24.95 CDN; VISA, MC; 800-663-5714, fax 800-565-3770 ◆ A must for Western business travellers to Japan, this book is the fastest way to understand the emotional/rational dualities of Japanese attitudes and behaviour. Comprised of 234 essays offering personal insights into the dynamics of Japanese society. [ID:2536]

JobStreet.com 🖳
http://my.jobstreet.com ◆ Explore South and Southeast Asia's booming skilled job market with this Malaysian Web site. Private sector jobs of all fields are listed, with an emphasis on IT, engineering and marketing. Database is searchable by regions outside of Malaysia: Hong Kong, India, Philippines, Singapore, and Thailand etc. The site is easy to use and the job descriptions indicate nationalities that can apply. [ID:2601]

Living and Working in New Zealand 📖
2003, Joy Muirhead, 288 pages ➤ How To Books Ltd., 3 Newtec Place, Magdalen Road, Oxford, OX4 1RE, UK, www.howtobooks.co.uk, £11.66; Credit Cards; (44) (1752) 202-301, fax (44) (1865) 202-331 ◆ Offers the international job seeker information and advice from making the decision to go to New Zealand, coping with the migration process, settling into your new home, employment or business, and starting out on a new life. [ID:2505]

Living in China: A Guide to Teaching and Studying in China Including Taiwan 📖
1997, R. Weiner, M. Murphy, A. Li, 284 pages ➤ China Books & Periodicals Inc., 2929 - 24th Street, San Francisco, CA 94110, USA, www.chinabooks.com, $19.95 US; Credit Cards; 415-282-2994, fax 415-282-0994 ◆ Cross-cultural guide with advice for teacher or tourist, student or businessperson. Complete listings of Chinese colleges and universities, in both the Peoples' Republic of China and Taiwan, which accept foreign teachers or students. The authors are amusingly frank about surviving, working and even dating in China. Great read! [ID:2034]

A Practical Guide to Living in Japan 📖

2003, 256 pages ➤ Stone Bridge Press, P.O. Box 8202, Berkeley, CA 94707, USA, www.stonebridge.com, $16.95 US; Credit Cards; 800-947-7271, fax 510-524-8711 ◆ Whether you're teaching, travelling or doing business in Japan, there is something in this book for you. Includes facts on banking, immigration and insurance, plus daily-life tips on renting an apartment, utilities, transportation, using the post office and shopping for furniture. You'll get insider advice on how to find a job, learn Japanese and make new friends, as well as basic information on etiquette and customs. Packed with strategies, charts and simple how-to instructions. [ID:2540]

The Rice Paper Ceiling 📖

2000, Rochelle Kopp, 272 pages ➤ Stone Bridge Press, P.O. Box 8202, Berkeley, CA 94707, USA, www.stonebridge.com, $19.95 US; Credit Cards; 800-947-7271, fax 510-524-8711 ◆ What can the non-Japanese employee of a Japanese company do to advance his or her career prospects? This US book presents a readable and detailed analysis of the "rice-paper ceiling" and "breakthrough" strategies for overcoming it. Includes techniques for improving working relationships and career prospects, as well as insights into the profound differences between Japanese and American work styles and cultures. [ID:2208]

Stone Bridge Catalogue 🎏

Stone Bridge Press, P.O. Box 8202, Berkeley, CA 94707, USA, www.stonebridge.com, Free on-line; Credit Cards; 800-947-7271, fax 510-524-8711 ◆ An extensive collection of resources on Japan and Japanese culture and language. Browse for books and software and order on-line. [ID:2209]

VietnamWorks 🖥

www.vietnamworks.com ◆ This British Web site is based in Ho Chi Minh City and dedicated to assisting those seeking work in Vietnam. The site is organized, sleek and functional. It's packed with career advice on networking, cover letters, resumes and interviews. Lists hundreds of jobs and gets thousands of hits. Recommended! [ID:2474]

Web Sites on Asia Pacific 🖥

Web Sites on Asia Pacific ◆ Many of these sites provide government and trade information concerning this rapidly developing region. There is country and travel information, local news, and a few site links to job opportunities. ◆ Asiadragons Web portal, www.asiadragons.com ◆ Asian Development Bank, www.adb.org ◆ Australia, www.gov.au ◆ China, www.chinatoday.com ◆ Hong Kong Trade Development Council, www.tdc.org.hk ◆ India, www.indiaworld.com ◆ Japan, www.jetro.go.jp ◆ Malaysia, www.tourism.gov.my ◆ New Zealand, www.newzealand.com ◆ Pakistan, www.pak.gov.pk ◆ Philippines, www.gov.ph ◆ Singapore, www.gov.sg ◆ Thailand, www.mfa.go.th/web/1.php ◆ Western Samoa, www.govt.ws [ID:2320]

The Yin and Yang of American Culture: A Paradox 📖

2001, Eun Y. Kim, Intercultural Press, 252 pages ➤ Masters & Scribes Bookshoppe, 9938 - 81 Ave., Edmonton, AB T6E 1W6, Canada, www.mastersandscribes.com, $36 CDN; Credit Cards; 800-378-3199, fax 780-439-6879 ◆ This book takes an Eastern view of American culture and places it in the context of Asian value sets. Based on decades of conversations and interactions with Americans and Asians, the author presents American virtues and vices from an Asian perspective, using the unique Asian concepts of yin and yang. A helpful resource for anyone planning to live and work in the US. [ID:2550]

CHAPTER 28

Job Hunting When You Return Home

So you and your family have just returned from a four-year posting in Islamabad, Pakistan. You arrive in Calgary after a two-month vacation in South Asia. The kids are about to start school, and you're unpacking your belongings after four years in storage. It now dawns on you that you face the job search process. What a daunting task! Where do you begin?

This chapter will advise "returnees" (those recently returned from long-term overseas assignments) on how to conduct their non-international job search. The focus will be on adjusting to the domestic job scene after a long stint abroad. Re-entry concerns, the new international skills you acquired, how to search for a job with employers who have no international experience will be discussed.

RE-ENTRY ADJUSTMENTS

You are probably finding returning home more difficult than you expected. (For more on this topic, see Chapter 8, Re-Entry.) On a personal level, you might find your old social life boring. No one is interested in world events. Talk revolves around the weather or gossip about in-laws. Social conversations seem trivial. You miss the blend of international friends you had. Everyone here seems to conduct their friendships by phone. No one drops by for a good face-to-face conversation, or a cup of tea. You even have to do your own dishes and laundry!

The worst part—let's face it, it's the most common re-entry problem—is that no one will take an active interest in your overseas experience. Not even your parents or your brothers or sisters are interested. They have perhaps looked at your slide show and asked a few polite questions at the time, but nothing more. You are bursting with stories, ideas, new insights, and they have closed the book on the last four years of your life. They are all very happy to see you and to have you safely at home, but no

533

one seems interested in your adventures or the incredible changes you have undergone.

Before losing your sense of purpose and becoming totally discouraged about finding a job and starting your new life back home, stop and consider some important aspects of your overseas experience.

Returning Home A Stronger You

Success in an international career often rests more on your personality than on your technical skills. Now that you are home, it is worthwhile to reflect on the strengths and new, non-technical skills you acquired overseas. Once you've done this, your job search will not seem so frightening.

Most people return from their trips abroad feeling empowered. You have probably learned to deal with enormous ambiguities. You feel able to meet almost any challenge. You have experienced bizarre, dangerous situations, intense heat, floods, and disease. You have even survived daily shopping in Southern markets! All of these challenges have strengthened you.

You have probably developed a better understanding of yourself. Most expatriates experience a sense of freedom living overseas, where you are free of the usual cultural and societal restraints. As a foreigner, you can do a pirouette in the street and no one will bother you. As a manager or stay-home spouse, you have had the freedom to hire and fire at will and to manage your affairs to your liking, without outside pressure. This freedom has allowed you to clarify your individual boundaries of behaviour. Thus you have pushed your limits and come to know yourself better. You have learned to behave according to your own ethics, not those enforced by convention or peer pressure. This understanding is empowering and you know you can face new situations on the strength of your own judgment.

THE IMPORTANCE OF UNDERSTANDING YOUR SKILLS

Throughout this book we stress the importance of having a firm understanding of your skills during the job search. Knowing your strengths and weaknesses, and being able to steer discussions with potential employers onto topics which demonstrate your suitability, are crucial parts of any job search. Unless you are good at talking about what you do well, why you do it well, and how you can bring knowledge from past work experience to benefit your new employer, you will have difficulty finding a good job in this competitive market. (For a refresher on how to market yourself, see Chapter 23, Selling Your International Skills.)

If you've been out of the country for a long time, or if you're changing careers, consider meeting with a career counsellor. In one or two short meetings you can get up to speed on changes to the search/hiring process, appropriate vocabulary/jargon for your skills and experience, and new developments in your field. Fees vary, but are usually around $100 CDN per hour.

If you are working for a large or an enlightened international firm, perhaps there was the foresight to set you up with a mentor—a successful repatriate who is based in your home country and is adapting well. This mentor would have best been assigned while abroad but, if not, perhaps you can ask for one now that you are home. The mentor can help with all manner of things, keeping you posted on changes in the home office, looking out for your interest, offering advice and counselling on all aspects of re-entry.

It is now time to look at some practical factors affecting your job search as a returnee from overseas. We will start with the most difficult.

WHY SOME EMPLOYERS AVOID RETURNING EXPATS

Employers with little or no international experience may have misconceptions about job seekers returning from postings abroad. While not all employers believe the following myths about returnees, you may want to keep them in mind.

EMPLOYERS' ASSUMPTIONS:

- **Returnees have emotional re-adjustment problems**. Because of the hardships they've encountered, expatriates have undergone personality changes and traumas. Their re-adjustment will be difficult and will adversely affect their work.

- **Returnees are not used to Western business customs**. Having adapted to a very different culture (they may even have "gone native"), returnees have lost sight of standard Western business practices. They lack finesse. They no longer fit the corporate mould.

- **Returnees are too exotic**. They have adopted alternative lifestyles and can't be team players. They are excessively individualistic and independent. Their differences are threatening.

- **Returnees are flighty**. They don't really want permanent jobs or long-term responsibilities. They will soon be off travelling again.

- **Returnees have health problems**. They may have strange tropical diseases. They may be contagious. They will require a lot of sick leave.

YOUR SOLUTIONS:

- **Do not overstate or dwell on your re-entry adjustment problems**. Stress positive aspects of your overseas experience and return home.

- **Do not say that you plan to return overseas.**

- **State that you are happy to be back.** This is your home. You are anxious to join your peers in the work world.

- **Demonstrate your business acumen**. Draw attention to your good work habits, adaptability to new technologies, willingness to be a team player, understanding of Western leadership style. Avoid wearing souvenir clothing or jewellery. Dress in smart, businesslike clothing. Focus on fitting in. Downplay your independence—you have already made this clear through your willingness to travel outside your own culture.

- **Show your attachment to home**. Mention your enthusiasm for things like home cooking, a particular university, or a sports team. Talk about the pleasures of finally reading home country newspapers again.

- **Mention the clean bill of health** you received for your recent physical.

HOW TO EXPLAIN YOUR INTERNATIONAL EXPERIENCE

You are already aware that, with the exception of others who have lived abroad, very few people are interested or able to understand your international work experiences. You must therefore be cautious when discussing them with prospective employers. Here are a few tips to help you down this delicate path.

- **Be professional in describing your overseas work responsibilities**. You are probably fairly animated about the challenges you faced when overseas. Practice rewording your description of job responsibilities in a more businesslike manner. Be formal. Be articulate.

- **Use the language of your future work.** You will have to give up the expatriate jargon that may have become second nature to you. In the following chart, the left-hand column features words that are unfamiliar, and therefore intimidating, to some employers. The right-hand column shows equivalent terminology better suited to the domestic work environment.

- **Speak in terms familiar to your audience**. Use titles to describe your overseas customers, not foreign names which are difficult to pronounce. Avoid detailed geographical descriptions. State what government departments you worked with; simplify the name of the department or use the Western equivalent. Examples of international terms and their North American equivalents:

AVOID International Terms	USE North American Terms
Mission/Field Missions	Business Trip
Field Staff, Field Offices	Regional Staff, Regional Office
Cooperant/Volunteer/Expert	Employee/Consultant
Counterpart/Homologue/Local Staff	Staff
Delegate	Outside Company Representative
Culture Shock	Adjustment
Cross-Cultural Adaptability	Able to Deal with Change
Cultural Sensitivity	Interpersonal Skills
Cross-Cultural Communication	Effective Listening Skills
Diplomacy	Political Astuteness
Protocol	Politeness/Tact

- **Speak of your successes, your accomplishments**. Do not discuss insurmountable challenges, or why you did not succeed at something. Employers with no international experience will be unable to judge the context and could form erroneous judgments on your capabilities.

- **Use concrete and measurable examples of your work**. How many employees? Size of budget? The number of warehouses, number of trucks, number of hectares? Describe the project's strategic and long-term work plans and management objectives.

- **Avoid shocking stories**. Don't go into the bizarre tales from hell. The harder the posting, the more cautious you should be talking about the difficulties you encountered.

- **Play down your love for adventure**, your need for change.

- **Network with other returnees:** Actively search out others who have recently returned from abroad and provide mutual support during your job search. Find these people on the Internet and through the organization that sent them overseas.

INTERNATIONAL SKILLS YOU SHOULD EMPHASIZE

As a returnee from abroad, you have brought back important skills that are readily transferable to domestic contexts. Despite some of the negative expectations mentioned at the beginning of the chapter, you can demonstrate to prospective employers that internationally experienced job candidates are more savvy, sophisticated, and in tune with office politics, with customers, and with the world at large. It is to your advantage to emphasize the intuitive side of your international awareness. Below is a list of skills usually attributed to internationally experienced personnel that are sought after at home.

- **Interpersonal Skills:** open-mindedness, sensitivity, tact, listening and observing skills, ability to deal with stress, sense of humour, awareness of office politics, protocol, loyalty and tenacity.
- **Professional Work Skills:** ability to take on challenging work, independence, self-discipline, training experience, flexibility, resourcefulness, ability to deal with change and the unexpected, persistence, writing and report writing.

SKILLS IN WHICH YOU MAY HAVE FALLEN BEHIND

Having adapted yourself to your overseas position, you may find that you need to work at those skills that were neglected, and adjust others to Western standards. The following incomplete list should help get you started.

- **Management Skills:** Western business protocol, business practices, the latest issues being discussed and applied in your field. North American practices around leadership, management and motivating colleagues and subordinates.
- **Personal Skills:** Self-reliance, operating without assistants, making your own coffee, driving your own car. Relying on domestic help to leave you free to do business and entertain clients.
- **Computer Skills:** Basic understanding of the most recent software applications in your field of expertise.
- **New Business Models:** An understanding of the new and emerging business models being shaped by the Internet that affect your industry and daily life.
- **New Training:** If there are any important skills that you are lacking or have fallen behind on, consider registering for a course so that you can list it on your resume as currently underway.

A LAST WORD

No matter what your career objectives are upon returning home, the task of finding a place for yourself will be scary. Jobs are out there, and internationally experienced personnel are respected for their broad and worldly view. As your first step, I strongly recommend you make the major effort of developing a detailed skills inventory, using Western business terminology. After reconfiguring yourself in a new skills-based resume, it is empowering to see how good your professional self looks on paper. The second step is to go out and, in a focused manner, research the job you want. Remember, job hunting can be just as exciting as going overseas!

PART FOUR
The
Professions

CHAPTER 29
Teaching Abroad

Whether you're a seasoned professional teacher or someone just finishing university studies, you've probably imagined yourself in a far-off land where the pace of life is slower, more relaxed, and where fresh discoveries await you at every turn: new foods, new smells and friendly people. These are more than dreams and fantasies for some; they are reality for thousands of Canadians who teach abroad.

Teaching remains one of the *biggest* areas of overseas employment for Canadians. Teachers of English are in especially high demand, with an estimated one billion people worldwide wanting to learn English.

The range of opportunities abroad for teachers and school administrators runs the gamut, from private English language schools, to international and American schools, NGO-sponsored positions, universities, technical institutions, multinational firms, professional organizations, religious schools, and teaching private lessons for a few weeks or months while travelling. Assignments range from a couple of months to three years or more. And while positions often require formal teaching qualifications, many do not—especially in the English language field, where one can find employment in virtually any country in which English is not the first language.

Indeed, there are few careers more portable than teaching. There are opportunities in every corner of the world, from Prague to Paris, Istanbul to Bangkok, and from Chicago to Sao Paulo. The field is wide open and waiting for you.

WHY TEACH ABROAD?

Educators are in the enviable position of being able to use work for travel-learning experiences. Going abroad may be a way to enhance your career or get into the education field, a chance to see a part of the world that has always appealed to you, have an adventure, make new friends, rejuvenate a career that has gone stale, do some humanitarian work or simply earn an honest living.

On a professional level, teachers who work overseas almost always find new enthusiasm and a fresh outlook on their subject area and their careers. A successful experience in another culture also results in greater confidence in your own teaching ability. And of course, many overseas postings present the opportunity to learn another language.

You can use teaching as a stepping-stone to other international careers. Once you have learned another language, the ins-and-outs of the local culture, and made some valuable contacts, you have cleared some of the biggest obstacles to finding international work. You are, in effect, an insider!

Facing Myths and Realities

While the overwhelming majority of educators find their stints overseas immeasurably rewarding, most have experienced some degree of surprise, frustration and disappointment.

For example, it is a mistake to expect that personal and professional difficulties will disappear with a change of scenery. A foreign career should not be used to run away from problems or undesirable situations. In most instances, depression, marital discord or romantic disillusionment, boredom or burnout are intensified by unfamiliar surroundings.

Professionally, an educator who is unhappy with her or his job at home will usually find similar or even greater frustrations abroad. As one teacher returning from Zambia said, *"The realities of an eight-to-three schedule and the daily regimen of lesson plans, student discipline, hall duty and the rest are much the same, whether the school is in Lusaka or Vancouver."*

As for getting rich teaching abroad, this is more myth than reality. While most teachers report their standard of living as equivalent to or higher than what they had been accustomed to at home, the expenses of travelling and sightseeing eat up any surplus. Many are surprised at the cost of automobiles, gasoline, housing, food and so on. In short, seeking a teaching job in order to "come home with a bundle" is usually a misguided notion.

You can avoid some of the pitfalls of teaching overseas if you heed some words of caution from experienced overseas teachers and administrators. We strongly recommend you speak to at least two such teachers before you leave.

The Qualities of a Teacher Working Abroad

Making the final decision takes courage and enthusiasm. For some, moving abroad can be tremendously disruptive. Experienced international teachers, on the other hand, think nothing of giving up their possessions, renting out their home for a year or two, and freeing themselves of the worries of retirement and savings. They have a realistic understanding of loneliness and homesickness. Overseas teachers see themselves as free spirits and risk-takers, able to pick up and move themselves and, in many cases, their families to each new posting with enthusiasm, anticipation and curiosity.

International teachers see themselves as patient, observant and curious about human relations. They are sensitive to individual differences and needs. International teachers set aside professional commitments to their field in Canada, and continue their professional interests overseas. They understand the cross-cultural classroom environment. They understand second language acquisition, and see the need for flexibility in their roles as teachers. They are more concerned with fitting in than introducing new teaching methods. They work hard at teaching, are not unnerved by unfamiliar surroundings, and can deal with low task accomplishment, frustration and failure. For them, the point of teaching abroad is the human experience. (For an insightful essay on what it takes to successfully teach English overseas, see the article by Victoria McGraw, "Tips for Teaching English Overseas" in Appendix 29a on the CD-ROM.)

WHAT RETURNING TEACHERS SAY

The following quotations will assist you in answering the question *"Am I the sort of teacher who could live and work overseas?"*

Generally, people who are independent, healthy and flexible, with a degree of interest in the foreign culture into which they will be immersed, whatever their motivations, return home singing the praises of their experience abroad. As one teacher returning from Japan said, *"Teaching abroad made me realize there is a world outside Canada. I gained the concept of internationalism. I saw first-hand the interaction of world politics and economics. Plus, I was able to travel during holiday periods, meet people of other nationalities, and, all in all, gain a broader perspective."*

Teaching overseas is often seen as an exchange, where you deepen your cross-cultural understanding as students learn skills. One VSO volunteer English teacher in Vietnam observes, *"I think that a volunteer teacher in this part of the world gains a lot of respect from people. Having the chance to learn, research and work together is a fantastic atmosphere in which to exchange ideas and cultures."*

After you take that first step and get your initial overseas teaching job, you may become "addicted," as one educator from Calgary says, *"Teaching in a new culture is like entering a new life; around each corner is an entirely different experience. I have taught in Thailand, Iran and now Austria, and it just keeps getting better."*

This is not to imply that you'll have only positive experiences. As a teacher from Sarnia, Ontario, put it after returning from a CUSO posting in Papua New Guinea: *"You really have to throw your old teaching methods out the window. The school I taught at had no lab facilities, no audiovisual equipment, and one text for every three students. Basically, I had a chalkboard and chalk. It was tough for the first few months."*

At the same time, highly motivated students can make your teaching experience deeply satisfying even without the resources you might have at home. A VSO volunteer English teacher in Ethiopia observes, *"I had 90 students crowded into each of my classrooms. They were so eager to learn in order to have a brighter future, and to improve the lives of their families. I was just one volunteer, but with so many motivated students, my teaching efforts went a long way."*

Good advice is offered by a Québec teacher recently returned from Turkey: *"Go into the overseas assignment with a completely open mind, with tolerance, and with curiosity, and wherever you go it will be a rewarding experience. Be willing to learn and be patient with yourself."*

A Toronto teacher, after a posting in an international school in Egypt, cautions against the tendency to confine yourself to the "known," the expatriate "ghetto," in your overseas community: *"Beware of participating in the bitch sessions, complaining about how the local shopping, customs, transportation and so on aren't up to Canadian standards. It's a way of short-changing yourself in your overseas experience."*

You may find more room for creativity, greater freedom to experiment, in your new teaching situation. A Vancouver professor recalls her experience at the University of Indonesia: *"I was given more responsibility, independence, and authority and had to attend fewer meaningless meetings than back home. I could even create my own teaching assignment—what classes I'd teach and what materials I'd use."*

Finally, some encouragement for the inexperienced, unqualified traveller cum teacher. An Ottawa woman returning from an extensive trip that included a six-month stint teaching English in Greece says: *"I ended up in a small Peloponnesian town with no experience, no teaching qualifications, no degree and no knowledge of Greek, and I had the most memorable experience of my life."*

TYPES OF TEACHING POSITIONS

A large and well-defined market exists for educators of all types—VSO Canada, for example, sends educational professionals overseas in the disciplines of TEFL, primary and secondary education, math and science, special education, curriculum development, education administration and teacher training. (For more information on VSO Canada, see their ad in the sponsor section at the end of this guide. Also, see Chapter 38, NGOs in Canada.) While anyone with a university degree can generally find work, especially teaching English, the best candidates are those with teacher certification and two years' experience. For administrative, library, and counselling positions, advanced degrees (minimum MA) are usually required. If you have such qualifications, by all means consider administrative jobs, as returning teachers have told us there is often a shortage of such personnel.

Since most formal teaching jobs are on a contract basis (usually two to three years in length) there is always a substantial staff turnover. Language schools have even shorter contracts (usually one year or less) and higher rates of staff turnover.

Because of the isolation and difficulty in adapting to new cultures, there is often a preference for singles and teaching couples without dependents. Couples with one non-teacher member may find the job search difficult. Competition is fierce in European schools, but there are opportunities for recent graduates in developing countries.

Teaching as a Volunteer in a Developing Country

Several NGOs recruit teachers at all levels for postings in developing countries. Contracts are usually for two or three years, and remuneration varies from subsistence to professional levels. Some NGOs accept only those with teacher training and relevant experience, while others require only a university degree. Most positions are in the local education systems rather than with private schools. School facilities are often sparse. Your housing will vary from comfortable to very basic. You will often be the only volunteer around, and your friends will be from the local population. A WUSC volunteer describes teaching in rural villages of Bhutan in this way: *"Each morning started with cooking bread on an open fire. I rarely could afford meat, but the sheer pleasure of getting to know local Bhutanese families made it all worthwhile."*

Teaching at an International School

International schools exist to serve the needs of expatriates—diplomats, missionaries, aid workers, military personnel, and international businesspeople—and host country nationals who want their children to learn English or have a diploma that is accepted at universities around the world. In fact, enrolment in international schools can range from all host country nationals to all expatriates, and many schools have both. A network of French and English international schools operates worldwide and offers curriculums comparable to "those back home." For example, many international schools use the International Baccalaureate program; you may want to familiarize yourself with its curriculum before you begin your job search.

These schools are usually certified by an agency in the US or Europe and are sponsored locally by parent associations, an international company, or a government body. Contracts for these jobs usually range from two to three years.

As a teacher in an international school, you and your family will be based in a large city, usually the capital. The school will usually be very well equipped, and will follow a well-developed standard international curriculum. Housing will be comfortable, and you will enjoy the company of many other expatriate teachers and the parents of the children you teach, (usually diplomatic staff, employees of large multinationals, and sometimes, local elites). You may, however be somewhat removed from the local population.

Schools in industrialized countries differ from developing countries: competition can be more fierce; jobs usually pay enough to offer a middle-class existence; and you have a more traditional employee–employer relationship where you are responsible for your own housing and travel.

The privately funded and operated network of international schools is spread over some 90 countries. Salaries and benefits vary depending on the size of the school, the location, and the cost of living in the community. Many corporations employing US, Canadian, British, Belgian, or French citizens pay the tuition for dependent children attending these international or American-sponsored schools. There are several umbrella organizations that provide staffing and other services to the international school community. The placement office of Queen's University's Faculty of Education maintains a list of useful international teaching links, including such organizations. The French system works under the ALLIANCE FRANÇAISE. (For more details, see the Resources section at the end of this chapter.)

While contracts at international schools are usually one to two years in length, we have recently heard about INTERNATIONAL SUPPLY TEACHERS, a service that provides emergency substitute teachers to international schools for periods as short as one month. If you have experience and strong credentials and are able to travel on short notice, this sort of arrangement might be ideal. (For more information, see the Resources section at the end of this chapter.)

Other Private Schools

A number of other independent boarding schools exist overseas for English-speaking students. These schools have been established by private citizens of the host country, citizens of the United States, Britain or Canada residing in the community, religious organizations, or other special interest groups. Information about these independent international schools can be found in a number of directories, for example the *ISS Directory of Overseas Schools* and *Peterson's Annual Guide to Independent Secondary Schools*. (For more details, see the Resources section at the end of this chapter.)

Private Tutoring as a Business Overseas

Are you following a spouse to a foreign land or have you rented an apartment in Madrid for six months? Do you have experience teaching music, English, French, computers, accounting? While it is generally illegal to set up your own business, small private tutoring contracts, especially amongst the expatriate community, are a good possibility and can help finance an extended stay abroad. The people you market yourself to can be embassy staff, employees of multinationals or local businesspeople.

University Teaching in Developing Countries

If you have a master's degree, a spirit of adventure, and initiative, you can often arrange your own job teaching at a university in many developing countries. Many people find work simply by writing a year ahead of time to a few far-flung universities and offering their services. Salaries are lower than for university instructors at home, but you can live comfortably and gain an incredible experience. If you have a PhD from a recognized Western university and have teaching experience, formal positions are advertised in professional journals, or in newspapers such as the *Chronicle of Higher Education,* the *New York Times,* the *Times Education Supplement,* and the *Globe and Mail* (see the Resources section at the end of this chapter). Large libraries will have many useful directories, such as *Commonwealth Universities Yearbook*, *International Handbook of Universities* and *World Guide to Universities*. Local embassies are also worth contacting.

STRATEGIES FOR DIFFERENT LEVELS OF EXPERIENCE

Depending on your level of experience (defined as a mix of teaching experience and international experience), a variety of opportunities are open to you. Beginners often teach in developing countries where salaries are lower. Alternatively, English-teaching positions in industrialized Asian countries such as Korea or Japan are a more lucrative starting point. A senior teacher with good international credentials can land a job in Rome teaching at an international school. University teaching varies, from developing countries accepting an MA and no experience, to industrialized countries where a PhD and other senior credentials are required.

- **Recent Graduates with No Teaching or International Experience.** Unless you want to teach English (see next section) you will have a difficult time finding work using the traditional method of resume and covering letter, without some specialized, sought-after skills or outstanding achievements (for example, a degree in agricultural sciences or medicine). Your best bet is to take some teacher training or take six months off and travel the world. Visit schools and language learning centres, and try to find a volunteer or short-term paid position.

- **Experienced Teachers with No International Teaching Experience.** You must demonstrate that you are familiar with and can excel in a multicultural environment. Have you travelled extensively and lived with local peoples? Have you participated in multiracial issues and activities here in Canada? Have you demonstrated true "excellence" in teaching? Can you put all the above together in a resume that demonstrates to international employers that you and your family will thrive in another culture? Are you prepared to teach overseas for a number of years in a row?

- **Two or More Years' Overseas Teaching Experience.** Hopefully you have taken every opportunity during your first international job to demonstrate leadership, initiative, commitment and your love of the cross-cultural teaching experience. You should also have glowing letters of reference from two or three officials. You are now ready to apply to almost any international school. You can participate in international recruitment fairs and respond to international job postings.

THE HIRING PROCESS

Obviously, perseverance and patience play a role in your search. Don't be easily discouraged. Experienced educators know that the international teaching market is a fragmented one. This can mean long or short lead times, where both luck and a planned, systematic approach play a part in landing a teaching position.

- **How Long Will It Take?** The search for the right job can take a full year. If you're aiming for a job for the coming September, you should begin an active search twelve months in advance. This said, you should be aware that many teachers and administrators find jobs in a matter of weeks, often near the time for departure. Last-minute cancellations by other teachers are frequent. So follow up with schools at the beginning of the school year to let them know you're still interested.

- **What Time of Year Should I Start?** To time your job search properly, call embassies to find out when the school year begins in their countries. Most international schools approximate the Canadian timetable (August to June). Some exceptions include the public schools of southern African countries, where the school year begins in February and ends in November; two big breaks happen during December–January, and June–July. And in the Philippines, the public system begins in June and goes until March.

- **Who Makes the Hiring Decisions?** When making initial contact with a school overseas, it is important to know who makes the hiring decisions. Many international schools send administrators to fairs to interview candidates, and then final decisions usually rest with principals, directors, or superintendents. Always call ahead, as the title of headperson varies among school systems.

THE JOB SEARCH

The First Step: Focus Your Job Search

The first rule before starting to look is to *focus* your job search. You should be clear about the exact kind of job you want and what part of the world you want to work in. Narrow your research to two or three countries. First, your choice should be based on where you are most likely to get a job; second, on personal contacts who can refer you to a school; and third, make sure your job experience and qualifications are appropriate to the positions you're applying for.

Personal Contacts and Networks

You may already be lucky enough to know someone in your community who has worked in the region you are interested in, and who can offer first-hand advice. If you haven't spoken to someone who has lived and taught overseas in circumstances similar to those you seek, you should. What you want is to impress potential employers with your strong understanding of the overseas living and working environment. A network of contacts can also be extremely useful for providing inside information on employment possibilities.

For example, contact with a teacher who has worked at a particular school in Singapore could result in a job there for you. Overseas administrators are cautious about who they hire, and are likely to favour someone they are familiar with. If you state the name of a personal contact in a letter of introduction or application, you immediately set your letter apart from the dozens of others the school receives.

Direct Inquiries

Only a small percentage of schools advertise in the foreign press. The vast majority depend on local advertisements, personal contacts and direct approaches. The best source of addresses is usually local directories. Go to the embassy or consulate of the country you are considering to consult telephone books. If you know someone who has taught English abroad and recommends a particular school, send a letter of inquiry there. A speculative job search is more realistic with EFL jobs than with most other areas of overseas employment.

Job Boards and Advertisements

For English language teaching jobs, the most popular on-line job board is Dave's ESL Café. Schools from all around the world post advertisements here, and it is also possible to post your resume. Internet job boards are fast becoming the dominant way to locate teaching positions abroad, and make contact with potential employers. Many jobs in international education are advertised in specialized magazines or newspaper supplements. Two of the very best are the *Times Educational Supplement* and the *International Educator.* The *TESOL Bulletin* is also worth checking. You'll sometimes find overseas teaching jobs advertised in the *Globe and Mail*, the *New York Times*, and the *Manchester Guardian* on Tuesdays. The latter two British newspapers carry a large number of English teaching ads, especially between March and July for jobs starting in September. A word of caution: do not be discouraged if most ads insist on formal TEFL qualifications: in practice they are not always essential. (For more information, see the Resources section at the end of this chapter.)

Recruiting Fairs and Agencies

Job fairs should rate at the top of your "must do" list if you are serious about finding a full time overseas teaching job. Job fairs bring together teachers and recruiters from overseas schools. Most are held in February, with some in June and September. Pre-registration is usually a must and some fairs even have pre-acceptance criteria. You will certainly have a golden opportunity to collect information, make comparisons, and talk to other teachers and administrators looking for overseas jobs. The Teacher's Overseas Recruiting Fair held annually at QUEEN'S UNIVERSITY, for instance, offers education professionals the opportunity to discuss placements with 50-60 international schools from 25-30 countries worldwide. (For more information on the Teachers' Overseas Recruiting Fair at QUEEN'S UNIVERSITY, see their ad in the sponsor section at the end of this guide.) Also, many of the best international schools won't hire without a face-to-face interview, so it is well worth your money to travel to attend a recruiting fair. (For more information, see the Recruiting Agencies and Job Boards Resources at the end of this chapter.)

While Living Abroad

Many teachers have obtained satisfying employment overseas without a preliminary job search in Canada. Spouses of international employees often find employment after settling into a community. If you expect to be in such a position, plan ahead by taking academic and professional credentials, copies of good assessments from previous jobs, your resume and letters of recommendation. Once abroad, survey the education scene and make your move!

While Travelling Abroad

If you're planning extensive travel or are travelling as a tourist for a few weeks, you may want to try visiting a school and arranging an interview.

A recently returned traveller reports finding a good job, on the spot, teaching math in a secondary school in Botswana. He was away six months longer than he expected, but avoided a Canadian winter and, incidentally, is now enthusiastically planning his next teaching venture overseas. Another successful and organized teacher credits getting a good teaching job in Turkey to a covering letter he sent prior to vacationing there. He got an interview, checked out the school and the city, and returned six months later to teach full time for two years.

THE APPLICATION PROCESS

You should begin by consulting schools' Web sites to find out their application procedures. If you are unable to find on-line information, send an initial letter of inquiry requesting application instructions, stating your general qualifications, and why you are interested in their school. Offer to send a more detailed package describing your credentials. To demonstrate your teaching abilities you may even want to offer to send them a teaching session on videotape (assuming you have one).

Your covering letter should contain three essential elements in addition to the regular advice given in Chapter 25, Covering Letters. First, explain why you are a good teacher; second, stress your commitment to extracurricular activities; and third, show that you understand and enjoy the challenges of the cross-cultural teaching environment.

Always send a follow-up letter after you've received a refusal letter. If you are turned down for a position after a seemingly successful interview, do not hesitate to write and offer your services on a standby basis. International recruitment is precarious. Recruits don't always show up, or they become unavailable for numerous reasons. Let recruiters know you can leave on short notice.

Don't forget to add "CANADA" to your address, and state clearly in your letter and at the top of your resume that you are a Canadian citizen. Use a minimum of 10- or 11-point font size for your correspondence and resumes for ease of reading when faxing, e-mailing and photocopying.

THE RESUME FOR TEACHING OVERSEAS

The following are a few pointers specific to teachers and not covered in Chapter 24, International Resumes.

- International resumes for teachers are longer than domestic ones. Being so far away, you want to make sure all your information is clear.

- Resumes for teachers tend to follow the traditional chronological format. You can still de-emphasize dates in your job description by stating *what* you did first, then indicating the date. Format of job description begins as: job title, school, year. Example, "Head of Social Studies Department, St. Patrick High School, September 1992 to March 1993." Always include the month to avoid confusion. Because school years are different, employers may assume you worked only one year, not two.

- Be careful with terms such as "Separate School Board," which may be confusing to a foreign reader. Use "Catholic School Board" instead. Simplify institution names where possible. Use "Toronto School Board" instead of "Toronto Public School Board." Do not use "Carleton Roman Catholic Separate School Board," but "Carleton Catholic School Board."

- Provide exact descriptions of courses taught, not just subject headings. Instead of "Grade 13 Geography" or "History," use "Geography—World Issues," or "History—Africa."

- Stay away from jargon. For example, in your covering letter, don't say "I taught development studies"; rather, explain what development studies means: "I taught an innovative program called development studies, which is a combination of African and international history, geography, politics and economics."

- If you have little experience, put your major student teaching experience under "Teaching Experience." However, don't try to pass off your student teaching as professional experience. Call your four-month student teaching job a "Queen's University Internship," for example.

- Include a section entitled "Professional Activities" in your resume, to cover extracurricular activities. If you have little experience and are a recent graduate, list your high school and university extracurricular activities. If you are currently a teacher, list your participation in all student activities outside the classroom. International schools expect you to devote a lot of your free time to student activities. The balance is important. Emphasize a blend of sports, international programs, music and academic pursuits. Underline events you organized to demonstrate initiative and leadership. If you are weak in extracurricular areas you can add, toward the end of your resume, a section called "Interests and Abilities" and "Volunteer Work."

- Don't put your Social Insurance Number in any resume.
- Because of great distances and short time frames in the recruitment process, some of our advice on references is different for teachers than for other international work. Put names of references directly on the resume (do not use the traditional "references available upon request"). Always include full mailing address, e-mail address and *both* a telephone and fax number for each reference. You may even include your letters of reference, along with copies of your degrees, teaching certificates and even transcripts.

THE INTERVIEW

Many international schools attend recruiting fairs to save on recruitment and interview costs. It is not unheard of, however, for a school to request that you come there for an interview, at your own expense. Fortunately, phone interviews are much more common. Standard questions for teachers may include the following.

Questions about the cross-cultural teaching environment:

- What qualities do you have that would make you a good teacher in a cross-cultural environment?
- Have you ever taught students whose mother tongue is not English?
- What is important when you first start teaching in a classroom where the cultural norms are different from yours?

General questions:

- What are the qualities of a good teacher?
- How do you view the role of the principal?
- What do you have to say about your current principal?

Questions about living overseas:

- Why do you want to teach overseas?
- What do you know about our country?
- Tell me about your previous travel experience.
- What do you think will be most difficult about moving here?

Your questions to employers that demonstrate knowledge of the overseas teaching environment:

- How is this school's environment different from a typical Canadian school? Inquire about teaching methods and discipline.
- Does the school's curriculum take into account reintegration of children into the US or Canadian systems? Ask which agency certifies the school program?

- About the students: How are they selected? Who generally pays the children's tuition: parents, sponsoring agency or scholarship? Are the students children of diplomats, foreign businesspersons, local elites, local population, high achievers?

THE CONTRACT

Try not to be carried away by the euphoria and, in some cases, anxiety that follows a successful job search. Remember to investigate the following: class size, available equipment, makeup of student body, number of teaching periods per day, support staff. Salaries, method of payment and contracts are additionally important. Be prepared for last-minute arrangements.

Working Conditions

You should be clear about how many classes and periods are involved, as well as how many students you'll face in each class. Find out also what methods are used to evaluate both students and teachers. Do students undergo standardized tests? By whom will you be evaluated as a teacher? You might also want to inquire as to whether you'll be paid for time spent preparing lessons, grading assignments, and supervising extracurricular activities. It's important, though, not to appear overly "fussy," as you are supposedly a flexible person, open to new experiences. Nevertheless, before signing a contract you should have some idea of such items as access to photocopying equipment and teaching aids such as film projectors, television sets/VCRs, overhead projectors, and even availability of chalk. Knowing in advance exactly when holidays are and for how long is also useful.

Contracts

All but the most informal of teaching arrangements involve signing a contract. It should spell out clearly the length of the agreement, your salary and method of payment, your duties and benefits. If housing is to be provided by the employer, or if you're to be allotted a housing allowance, the contract should stipulate exact responsibilities of each party for maintenance, services and utilities. The contract should also indicate the currency in which you will be paid (particularly important in countries with fluctuating economies), and whether or not your employer will cover any taxes you may be subject to.

In addition, return travel expenses, charges for shipment of belongings, provision for interim lodging, life insurance and health insurance (including provisions for sick pay) should be covered. If you are bringing your family, the cost of your children's schooling is also normally included. Some longer contracts include professional development funds that allow you to subscribe to journals or travel to conferences to keep abreast of developments in your field. The list of special benefits varies with the post. While you may not have much bargaining power, you can judge the seriousness of the school by the contract proposed to you.

GETTING READY

The period between signing the contract with a foreign school and the first day of work can be both exhilarating and exhausting. Sharing the news of your upcoming adventure with family, friends and colleagues, securing all your required documents, completing travel arrangements and organizing personal affairs will involve much time and effort. Most of you will have begun learning about your host country during your job search, but no teacher/administrator who has worked abroad has expressed regret about spending too much time learning the language (if applicable), history and culture of a new country. Many, however, have lamented their ignorance in these areas upon arrival overseas.

Learning the Language

Even if you don't need to know the local language in the classroom, your ability to communicate with locals will increase your enjoyment of your overseas experience many times over (see Chapter 5, Learning a Foreign Language). Daily tasks such as shopping will be easier and more enjoyable, as will chance meetings or social encounters with neighbours. If you have time before your departure, consider taking a conversation course at a local institution. Or try a self-study program using books and tapes.

Don't Burn Your Bridges

Among the multitude of pre-departure tasks, take time to develop a clear picture of what awaits you upon your return to Canada in one, two or three years' time. If you have arranged a leave of absence with an employer, make sure the terms are specified. You don't want to return home and find that the superintendent who "promised" you your old job back has moved to another town. One teacher who has regularly faced insecurity between international contracts recommends, *"Keep your options open. Before returning from overseas, I had already registered for a course, so when I walked off the plane, 'Bang,' I was in school. This helped me get over re-entry shock quickly. Always think about what you'll do if you don't get another overseas assignment immediately. Always have a Plan B. Fill in time with volunteer work or take an extra course."*

Finally, while it is important to take care of such things as pension plans, income tax, work visas, insurance, international driver's licences and so on, don't be discouraged by the seemingly endless list. You will get through it. This "preparation period" can be extremely fulfilling and exciting. Enjoy the anticipation!

WORDS OF WISDOM FOR WHEN YOU ARRIVE

The following are comments from teachers who have worked in Africa. Their advice should help you get off to a good start in your new job.

- *"To have a truly full experience, you must be 'captured' by the culture."*

- *"Stand back and listen for at least the first month and even up to one year. As a new teacher, you are usually very welcome. They are happy to have you. In the initial excitement, a new teacher will have lots of ideas, and will be eager to present them, but....you should take the time to see if your ideas are appropriate. You must get to know your students first. Find out what their needs are, how they learn best, what works for them."*

- *"Going slowly when you first arrive and being culturally sensitive does not imply relaxing your academic standards. Show that you are there for a good reason."*

- *"Get used to cultural practices that you cannot change, even when they go against the grain. I had a hard time accepting that students were beaten. My advice is to get used to it, but don't accept it."*

- *"Don't get caught up in heavy school politics. Avoid taking sides. There are cultural aspects that you don't yet understand. Try to stay neutral."*

- *"Reduce your expectations. Go with the changes as they happen. If they tell you to teach something you didn't expect, do it. As an outsider, you may not understand their rationale."*

- *"Get as involved as possible in school activities to show that you are an active participant, you want to share the load, and you want to learn from them."*

- *"In a rural or small community, get to know the parents of your students. I found that it was so easy to visit them you didn't even have to announce your visit. Getting to know the parents really helped me become accepted."*

- *"It is normal for students to visit teachers at home. This can be very enriching. Students like to see pictures of your family... they want to know you. In this way, you can teach outside the classroom. With all the discussion about the world, your house becomes a sort of external office."*

- *"Students often helped me with my household chores. This was a normal thing. At first I felt I was taking advantage of them, but when my conscience made me give a pen as payment, I was berated by the other profs. They said this was the students' role.... It is also quite normal to support a student. You don't have to do it, but quite often you do help out a needy student. The actual cost is low, but your help is invaluable to them."*

TEACHING ENGLISH OVERSEAS

It is accurate to say that you can get a job teaching English in any country in the world in which English is not the first language. The field is wide open, both for experienced English teachers (who, granted, will obtain the best paying jobs) and for the world traveller who can take advantage of one of the best ways of financing a sojourn abroad. In many countries English is taught from elementary school to the university level, and in large companies, private language schools and private homes.

For many reasons, English has become the world's dominant language. The newly liberated countries of Eastern Europe turned to English after they rejected Russian. Countries as far-flung as China, Japan and Namibia have made knowledge of English one of the focal points in their education systems. English is the international language of trade, science and air traffic control. Thus, English-speakers possess a much sought-after commodity: literally hundreds of millions of people are out there waiting to talk to them.

The General Market

It is almost impossible to think of anywhere in the world that is closed to English teachers. The market is wide open for instructing local students, hotel clerks, foreign embassy staff, foreign students coming to Canada, entrepreneurs, businesspeople, scientists, researchers, academics, and émigrés worldwide. Currently, the big markets are Eastern Europe, Turkey, Korea, Taiwan, Hong Kong, Thailand, Indonesia, China and Japan.

In Western European countries, you will encounter strict work visa laws. Nonetheless, there remains a high demand in Spain, Portugal and Greece, and many language schools continue to hire unqualified teachers. There are also opportunities for live-in private tutoring of children. And Turkey has an exceptionally high demand for qualified teachers.

In Eastern Europe, Hungary, Poland and Czechoslovakia are currently the most active in recruiting teachers, but this region suffers from acute accommodation shortages and low salaries. ESL-trained teachers are preferred, but untrained English-speakers are used in high schools when necessary.

Hong Kong, Korea, Taiwan and Thailand offer the greatest opportunities for teachers without official certification. There is also a consistent demand for highly qualified teachers in China and Japan.

And in Latin America, it is relatively easy to find work in private schools in Mexico, Costa Rica, Chile, Peru and Venezuela.

Who Can Teach?

There are more qualified EFL teachers out there than ever before. Many positions require qualified and experienced teachers. However, anyone who can speak English fluently and has a positive attitude has a chance of landing a job. That said, it is unwise to assume that fluency in English will make you an adequate EFL teacher. Most, if not all, English teachers have at least one university degree. And if you're serious about teaching English abroad, you should consider taking at least a short training program. (See the sub-section below, Training to Become an English Teacher.)

There are many fine teachers, however, who have carved solid niches for themselves, having learned to teach through practice rather than formal training. In some cases, for example, a strong background in business can serve you better than any diploma for landing a job teaching business English.

A post-graduate TESL certificate, an MEd or a BEd with ESL specialization are generally required for positions with overseas universities, international schools or multinational corporations. For smaller private language schools and private tutoring, requirements are less stringent and vary widely.

How Much Does It Pay?

Everyone has heard of people teaching English in Japan for an upward salary of $40,000 US with free board. Although not all teaching jobs pay as well, many North American graduates teach abroad to pay off their student debts. They work for a year or two, enjoy life, and are often able to pay off $20,000 US in their student loans. If your aim is to make money, many teachers find that they quickly progress up the salary scale after six or more months by taking on extra courses, moving to better paying schools and giving private lessons. This is true in Japan, Taiwan, Korea, Hong Kong and in almost every large city with a vibrant economy in Asia and increasingly in Latin America.

Qualities of a Good English Teacher

Above all, an ability to be creative will take you a long way. EFL teachers, perhaps more than other teachers going abroad, have to be performers, able to draw out students who are as insecure and shy as any of us would be learning a foreign language. And of course, you must enjoy teaching! Experienced teachers tell us it is not love of the subject matter that carries them through the school year, but a strong interest in their students. (For an insightful essay on what it takes to successfully teach English overseas, see the article by Victoria McGraw, "Tips for Teaching English Overseas" in Appendix 29a on the CD-ROM.)

Training to Become an English Teacher

Without academic certification in one of the following areas, your chances of landing a job, especially a well-paid job, are reduced.

Some basic definitions for TEFL, TESL and TEAL

TEFL: pronounced "tefel," stands for Teaching English as a Foreign Language. It refers to teaching English in countries where English is not the language of the indigenous culture.

TESL: stands for Teaching English as a Second Language. This term usually refers to situations where English is an official working language, e.g., teaching English to immigrants in Canada.

TEAL: stands for Teaching English as an Additional Language, i.e., teaching English to speakers of more than one other language. This term is usually used in multicultural societies.

Canadian Universities with Teaching ESL Programs

Several universities, colleges and private schools in Canada provide TESL/TEFL teacher training programs. The two main professional associations that provide accreditation services for TESL/TEFL teachers and training programs are TESL CANADA and TESL ONTARIO. Their Web sites provide lists of accredited training programs. (For more information, see the Resources section at the end of this chapter.)

Other Ways to Gain English Teaching Experience in Canada

Another way of compensating for a lack of formal EFL training is to volunteer as a tutor for local immigrants. Placing advertisements in local newspapers can also lead to paid tutorials or language exchange sessions. Assisting classroom teachers with these newcomers is another good possibility. Contact schools in your community. You will likely be welcomed with open arms!

Become a Teacher to Land Another Type of Job

If you want to work in international finance, or become a computer programmer, try contacting people in your field while travelling and offering your services as an English teacher specialized in their exact field. The contacts you make will help you better understand the international aspects of your field of work and perhaps lead to a job.

Teaching Materials to Take

Returning teachers at all levels, and in all types of schools, advise not to go to your new job empty-handed. Be sure to find out in advance what facilities the school has. Says one Saskatchewan teacher after returning from Swaziland: *"Any teaching aid that you find indispensable at home, you should bring—reference books, dictionaries, language books, paper, blank ditto sheets, pens, tapes, carbon paper, a small portable typewriter. You name it."* Make several copies of frequently used documents, or bring electronic or laminated copies because paper products don't fare as well in very humid or very dry climates.

For English teachers, after gathering all the useful materials at your disposal, visit the English-teaching section of a large bookstore, or perhaps a university bookstore. The following are materials recommended by experienced English teachers: a picture dictionary, tapes for listening and role-playing, blank tapes and a cassette recorder, a games and activities book, a map of Canada, a grammar exercise book, carbon paper and a collection of photos of your home environment. (These will be of great interest to your students, for whom Canada is as exotic as far-flung Asian or African countries may be for you.) If possible, ship bulkier items ahead. Remember: anything that encourages students to *talk* is invaluable!

A LAST WORD

Teaching abroad can be one of the most rewarding overseas experiences. Few professions or careers are so portable and offer such tremendous possibilities for immersion in foreign cultures, close relationships far from home and travel to places where no tourists go.

APPENDIX ON THE CD-ROM

29a. "Tips for Teaching English Overseas," by Victoria McGraw

RESOURCES

This chapter contains the following Resources sections: Teacher Recruiting Agencies & Job Boards, and Teaching Abroad.

TEACHER RECRUITING AGENCIES & JOB BOARDS

The recruiting business is not regulated in Canada and the quality of service can vary. On a positive note, there does not seem to be a lot of scamming in this industry. Some teachers have been disappointed with the conditions and service received when abroad. (It's a fact of life that when overseas, not everything is going to go smoothly.) Since there are so many recruiting agencies to choose from, check out references, ask to speak to former recruits, study their advertising material and documentation, and check out their Web site. The size of the firm is not always an indicator of the level of service; the satisfaction of former recruits is more important.

AEON Corporation ♨

AEON Corporation, Suite 2500, 120 Adelaide Street W., Toronto, ON M5H 1T1, Canada, www.aeonet.com, 416-364-8500, fax 416-364-7561 ◆ AEON is one of the largest and most diversified English educational organizations in Japan. For over 30 years they built a solid reputation recruiting teachers from all over the world for their classrooms in Japan. AEON now has over 290 branch schools throughout Japan, a total student enrollment of over 100,000, and a select foreign teaching staff of over 700 native-English speakers, all of whom have (at least) one university degree. To apply, submit a resume and a one-page essay titled, "Why I Want to Live and Work in Japan" to the recruitment office nearest you. (For more information, see their ad in the sponsor section at the end of this guide.) [ID:2296]

Association of American Schools in South America (AASSA) ♨

Association of American Schools in South America (AASSA), www.aassa.com ◆ AASSA recruits teachers for 41 private American/International schools located throughout South America. In most cases, applicants must be certified teachers and have at least two years' experience teaching K-12. Be forewarned: on their Web site AASSA discourages applications from teachers with dependent spouses, favouring teaching couples and singles. Candidates may apply on-line or by traditional methods. If your application is assessed as eligible, a $25 US (for singles, $40 US for teaching couples) registration fee gets you a spot in AASSA's database and an invitation to the annual recruiting fair held in a US city in December. Job listings are also posted on AASSA's Web site. [ID:2297]

English Teachers Overseas (ETO) ♨

English Teachers Overseas (ETO), 813-1330 Burrard Street, Vancouver, BC V6Z 2B8, Canada, 604-689-3677, fax 604-682-2905, eto@direct.ca ◆ English Teachers Overseas (a Canadian organization since 1989) recruits for ESL schools in Japan and Korea. These schools serve a variety of students from children, teens, and adults to corporate clients. All companies provide excellent living and working conditions with competitive salaries. The minimum qualification required is a BA. Those with a BEd, TESL, CELTA or teaching experience will receive priority placement. Apply by e-mailing your resume and a photo. Feedback is given to all enquiries and requests for information. [ID:2298]

European Council of International Schools ♨

European Council of International Schools, 21B Lavant Street, Petersfield, Hampshire GU32 3EL, UK, www.ecis.org, (44) (1730) 268244, fax (44) (1730) 267914, ecis@ecis.org ◆ The European Council of International Schools, a US non-profit corporation based in the UK, acts as a placement service for English-speaking teachers and administrators. ECIS works with over 450 international schools in Europe, the Middle East, Asia, the Americas and Africa, and provides information on hundreds of primary and secondary school vacancies annually. It conducts annual recruitment fairs in London (UK) in January and May, and in Vancouver in February. Their Web site advertises both teaching and senior administrative jobs on-line. [ID:2299]

Hess Language School of Taiwan ♨

Western Canada Recruiting, Hess Language School of Taiwan, 15113 - 104 Ave., Edmonton, AB T5P 4R1, Canada, www.hess.com.tw, 780-421-9121 ◆ This is Taiwan's largest English school, comprising over 100 language schools and 70 kindergartens across the country and employing over 600 native-English speakers. [ID:2300]

International Educators Co-operative Inc. ♨

International Educators Co-operative Inc., 212 Alcott Road, East Falmouth, MA 02536, USA, 508-540-8173, fax 508-540-8173 ◆ International Educators Co-operative Inc. recruits certified teachers from both Canada and the United States. Their focus is upon jobs in Mexico, Central America, the Caribbean, South America and Spain. The firm holds an annual "Overseas Teacher Recruitment Fair" each year in Houston Texas. Applicants with experience are preferred, but the firm is also successful in placing recent graduates. There is a fee to register for the recruiting fair, and spaces are limited, so contact them as soon as you decide to go. [ID:2301]

International Schools Services (ISS) ▥

International Schools Services (ISS), P.O. Box 5910, Princeton, NJ 08543, USA, www.iss.edu, 609-452-0990, fax 609-452-2690, edustaffing@iss.edu ◆ ISS is a private, non-profit organization founded in 1955 to serve American international schools overseas. Among other areas of activity, ISS establishes and operates international schools for which it recruits and places teachers and administrators. Each year the organization publishes the "ISS Directory of International Schools," which is a very helpful job search tool listing schools for American students worldwide. The Web site has a great links page to other educational organizations and resources, as well as all the information you'll need to apply. [ID:2302]

Michigan State University ▥

Career Services and Placement, Michigan State University, 113 Student Services Bldg., East Lansing, MI 48824-1113, USA, www.csp.msu.edu/index.cfm, 517-355-9510, fax 517-353-2597 ◆ Career Services and Placement at Michigan State University assists certified teachers to find placements in American and US Department of Defence schools throughout the world. Overseas experience is preferred but not required. The language of instruction is English. The annual Overseas Teacher Recruitment Fair is open to all qualified teachers. A registration fee applies ($75 US in 1998). Those who cannot attend the fair can have their resumes included in the resume book provided to employers attending the fair ($25 US in 1998). Details are available on the Career Services and Placement Web site, www.msu.edu/csp. [ID:2303]

Nova Group ▥

The Nova Group, Suite 700, 1881 Yonge Street, Toronto, ON M4S 3C4, Canada, www.teachinjapan.com, 416-481-6000, fax 416-481-1362 ◆ Nova Group's Web site is the main recruitment zone for the organization's network of 530 English language schools located across Japan. Find information about salaries, living arrangments, teacher training and much more. You can even apply on-line or visit the office nearest you to make yourself available for upcoming positions. If teaching English is something you're interested in, then check their site out. Highly recommended. [ID:2327]

Overseas Placement Services for Educators ▥

Overseas Placement Services for Educators, University of Northern Iowa, Cedar Falls, IA 50614-0390, USA, www.uni.edu/placemnt/overseas, 319-273-2083, fax 319-273-6998 ◆ Offering services since 1976, the University of Northern Iowa (UNI) Overseas Placement Service for Educators, a program area of the UNI Career Center, connects international K-12 schools with certified educators year round. Services offered include the UNI Overseas Recruiting Fair, credential and referral services, and related publications. UNI is home to the original international fair for educators. No placement fees are charged to candidates or recruiting schools. [ID:2304]

Search Associates ▥

Search Associates, RR 5, 632 Vermilyea Road, Belleville, ON K8N 4Z5, Canada, www.searchassociates.com, 613-967-4902, fax 613-967-8981 ◆ Search Associates places qualified teachers and administrators in international schools all over the world through a year-round placement service and a series of recruitment fairs held for registered users in various North American cities. Interested teachers should apply early in the academic year prior to the one in which they plan to go overseas. A three-year registration with Search Associates costs $100 US, and a further placement fee of $300 US is payable upon signing an overseas contract. Search Associates maintains an excellent Web site, listing more detailed information on services, registration and living overseas. Qualified teachers seeking jobs overseas in International Schools can take part as candidates in the annual International Teacher Recruitment fair held in Toronto each February under the auspices of Search Associates. This fair attracts about 50 international schools from all over the world, and each school (and candidate) is carefully pre-screened for suitability prior to attending.

For further information on what is required to become a candidate and register for this event check out the Web site. [ID:2306]

Teachers' Overseas Recruiting Fair ♔

Teachers' Overseas Recruiting Fair, Placement Office, Faculty of Education, Queen's University, Kingston, ON K7L 3N6, Canada, http://educ.queensu.ca/~placment, 613-533-6222, fax 613-533-6691, placment@educ.queensu.ca ◆ The Queen's Teachers' Overseas Recruiting Fair (TORF) is the original recruiting fair for Canadian teachers wishing to teach in international schools. It is held annually at Queen's University, usually in February. Registration is limited to about 300 teachers. On-line registration materials are available in September. Teacher certification and a minimum of two years of full-time teaching experience are the usual requirements although some places are reserved for beginning certified teachers. The fair typically attracts approximately 50—75 schools from dozens of countries. Certified teachers, with or without experience, can also register with the year-round International Teacher Placement Service (ITPS). There is a $100 fee to register for and attend the TORF, while the ITPS charges a $100 fee only if the applicant is placed in a school. The placement office's Web site is also an excellent compendium of resources useful to teachers in their overseas job search, including international and Canadian links. (For more information, see their ad in the sponsor section at the end of this guide.) [ID:2305]

TESOL Placement Service ♔

TESOL Placement Service, Suite 300, 1600 Cameron Street, Alexandria, VA 22314-2705, USA, www.tesol.edu, 703-836-0774, fax 703-836-7864, tesol@tesol.edu ◆ TESOL Placement Services is the place to go to find a job worldwide: Asia, Central America, the Middle East, North America and Europe. The monthly Placement Bulletin lists position openings for ESL/EFL teachers and administrators. The Resume Search Service maintains a list of resumes for recruiters requesting searches—many of these job openings are never advertised. This service is free to those who subscribe to the Placement Bulletin. The Employment Clearinghouse is an annual job fair where recruiters from around the world post hundreds of job announcements, and interview on-site. The job openings listed with TESOL are for qualified professionals with certification, an MA or a PhD in TESOL. Visit the Web site for more information or for valuable advice on becoming a TESOL professional. The site also lists a number of useful resources. [ID:2307]

TEACHING ABROAD

Teaching abroad is still one of the biggest areas of overseas employment for North Americans. Entry-level English language teaching positions are especially easy to come by. For all entry-level job seekers, these positions are important for building your international IQ and pole-vaulting you into other international careers. Consult related resources in Chapter 5, Learning a Foreign Language; Chapter 10, Short-Term Programs Overseas; Chapter 13, Study Abroad; and Chapter 14, Awards & Grants.

American-Sponsored Elementary and Secondary Schools Overseas Fact Sheets 🖳

Annual ➤ Office of Overseas Schools (A/OS), US Department of State: Office of Overseas Schools, Room H328, SA-1, Washington, DC 20522-0132, USA, www.state.gov/m/a/os, Free; 202-261-8200, fax 202-261-8224, OverseasSchools@state.gov ◆ A directory of all State Department supported overseas schools for dependents of US citizens. Each fact sheet lists contact information and school information. From the State Department home page, navigate to the Office of Overseas Schools via the "History, Education and Culture" tab. Once there, you can search for schools by region. A quick and comprehensive starting point for your overseas teaching job search. [ID:2064]

Asia Facts Unlimited ♔

http://asiafacts.kingston.net ◆ This Canadian organization recruits teachers for positions in Northeast and Southeast Asia. The Web site, while not flashy, contains an abundance of on-line information on recruitment, living and working conditions, as well as publications that can help you get your overseas teaching career headed in the right direction. [ID:2291]

Association of Canadian Teachers in Japan ⚇

www.actj.org/index.shtml ◆ Membership to ACTJ is open to anyone with an interest in Canada and in any kind of teaching in Japan. Sign up and receive a membership directory and access information on finding work and on professional development opportunities. Job vacancies are e-mailed to members. [ID:2350]

British Council 🖳

www.britishcouncil.org ◆ This great British Web site contains a wealth of information on teaching English, with links to resources for teachers and career information. Highly recommended. [ID:2690]

Cambridge EFL 🖳

www.cambridge-efl.org/teaching/index.cfm ◆ This site has information on EFL teacher-training certification, as well as a database of organizations offering Cambridge-certified EFL programs. [ID:2692]

Dave's ESL Café 🖳

www.eslcafe.com/joblist ◆ This popular US Web site has literally hundreds of current ESL jobs posted for positions all around the globe. Get the skinny on the latest teaching information by entering one of the many discussion forums. Access teacher resources, advice and information on training and certification programs. [ID:2669]

The Distance Delta 🖳

www.thedistancedelta.com ◆ Great collaborative site between the British Council and International House. Information on teacher-certification progams from this highly respected organization. [ID:2694]

Ed-U-Link Services On-line Recruiting Fair 🖳

Edu-U-Link Services, Inc., P.O. Box 2076, Prescott, AZ 86302, USA, http://edulink.com ◆ An Internet job fair for educators, with an on-line registry of positions available in Africa, Europe, the Middle East, Central and South Asia, Asia Pacific and the Americas. The site has a specific section for short-term postings. Navigate to the region you're interested in and get up-to-date information on school names, Web sites and e-mail addresses. [ID:2247]

Eduserv Vacancies 🖳

www.vacancies.ac.uk ◆ Eduserv is a UK-based Web site geared toward connecting teachers with overseas placements, primarily in Britain. [ID:2640]

English in Britain 🖳

www.englishinbritain.com ◆ This UK Web site is a good starting place for locating teaching opportunities at organizations offering EFL courses as well as EFL training courses. [ID:2691]

English Job Maze 🖳

www.englishjobmaze.com ◆ This British-Australian Web venture offers a fabulous selection of ESL job postings from all around the world. Easy-to-use, professional and comprehensive, this Web site allows you to apply for teaching jobs on-line, with no registration fees. [ID:2641]

The ESLoop 🖳

www.linguistic-funland.com/esloop ◆ ESLoop is a collection of sites relevant to English language teaching and learning on the Web. Each site is linked to the next, so that no matter where you start, you will eventually make your way around all the sites and end up back at the beginning. Offer teachers and students a way to browse the Internet for resources specific to English language teaching and learning. [ID:2371]

ESLworldwide.com 🖥

www.eslworldwide.com/search/job_search.asp ◆ This job board is part of an amazing Web site dedicated to teaching English as a second language worldwide. Thousands of jobs are listed in formated postings to which you can apply on-line or on you own. The site includes resume posting services, career resources and teaching statistics by country, which you can use as a basis for comparing information provided by employers with the industry standards. There's also information on travel accommodations, teacher training and insurance, as well as a bookstore, links page and anecdotes from the field. Highly recommended, add it to your favourites! [ID:2670]

Global Study: English Schools Around the World 🖥

www.globalstudy.com ◆ This directory of English language schools allows you to search schools by name or country. If you are interested in teaching in the US, UK, New Zealand, Ireland or Australia, then this site is a good way of finding schools to apply to. [ID:2758]

The Internet TESL Journal (For Teachers of English as a Second Language) 🖥

http://iteslj.org ◆ This monthly Web journal is made up of submissions from ESL/EFL teachers. Includes helpful articles, research papers, lesson plans, classroom handouts, teaching ideas and links to other ESL resources. A great resource. [ID:2369]

The ISS Directory of Overseas Schools 📖

2004, 533 pages ➤ International Schools Services (ISS), P.O. Box 5910, Princeton, NJ 08543, USA, www.iss.edu, $45.95 US; 609-452-0990, fax 609-452-2690, edustaffing@iss.edu ◆ The ISS Directory of International Schools is a comprehensive guide to American and International schools around the globe with over 500 listings of address, phone, fax, e-mail and chief school officer for each school. ISS also has a very useful Web site with lots of information related to education abroad. [ID:2050]

Japan's Cultural Code Words 📖

2004, Turtle Publishing, 352 pages ➤ Raincoast Books, 9050 Shaughnessy Street, Vancouver, BC V6P 6E5, Canada, www.raincoast.com, $24.95 CDN; VISA, MC; 800-663-5714, fax 800-565-3770 ◆ A must for Western business travellers to Japan, this book is the fastest way to understand the emotional/rational dualities of Japanese attitudes and behavour. Comprises 234 essays offering personal insight into the dynamics of Japanese society. [ID:2536]

Joy Jobs 🖥

www.joyjobs.com ◆ Access hundreds of overseas teaching positions for free or register for a member's package and receive insider tips and daily job posts and upload your resume for school recruiters to see. Join the discussion room for current information or post your question for the site administrator to answer. Lots of jobs for experienced teachers and helpful information for the teaching overseas neophyte. [ID:2462]

Living in China: A Guide to Teaching and Studying in China Including Taiwan 📖

1997, R. Weiner, M. Murphy, A. Li, 284 pages ➤ China Books & Periodicals Inc., 2929 - 24th Street, San Francisco, CA 94110, USA, www.chinabooks.com, $19.95 US; Credit Cards; 415-282-2994, fax 415-282-0994 ◆ Cross-cultural guide with advice for teacher or tourist, student or businessperson. Complete listings of Chinese colleges and universities, in both the Peoples' Republic of China and Taiwan, which accept foreign teachers or students. The authors are amusingly frank about surviving, working and even dating in China. Great read! [ID:2034]

O-Hayo Sensei 🖥

www.ohayosensei.com ◆ Now in its 11th year of twice-monthly publication, the free electronic newsletter "O-Hayo Sensei" reports the best currently available teaching (and other English language related) positions at conversation schools, universities, jukus, colleges, public schools and companies all across Japan. Gives job seekers the kind of detailed information they really need— about salaries, contracts, benefits, professional/educational requirements, visa requirements, application procedures, housing, training, contact people and specific job duties. An excellent resource for people interested in teaching English in Japan. [ID:2353]

Office of Overseas Schools 🖥
www.state.gov/m/a/os ◆ The US Department of State does not employ teachers directly for assignments abroad. However, by navigating to the "Teaching Overseas" section of the Web site, you will find a comprehensive list of organizations that provide teaching opportunities. [ID:2149]

Schools Abroad of Interest to Americans 📖
2003, 544 pages ➤ Porter Sargent Publishers Inc., Suite 1400, 11 Beacon Street, Boston, MA 02108, USA, www.portersargent.com, $45 US; Cheque or Money Order; 617-523-1670, fax 617-523-1021 ◆ Authoritatively describes 700 elementary and secondary schools in 150 countries that accept English-speaking students. Written for the educator, personnel advisor, student and parent, as well as for diplomatic and corporate officials, this unique guide is also a useful reference for the overseas teaching job seeker. [ID:2067]

Teachers of English as a Second Language of Ontario ⍟
Teachers of English as a Second Language of Ontario (TESL Ontario), Suite 405, 27 Carlton Street, Toronto, ON M5B 1L2, Canada, www.teslontario.org, 800-327-4827, fax 416-593-0164 ◆ Established in 1972, TESL Ontario is a non-profit organization consisting of over 3,200 member instructors and teachers. It offers ESL training programs and advocacy, an annual conference, a great Web job board and a certification program, which will give you an edge in competing for overseas ESL positions. [ID:2755]

Teaching and Projects Abroad 🖥
www.teaching-abroad.co.uk ◆ This is a fabulous British Web site that caters to anyone wishing to use their skills to teach abroad. By no means limited to teaching English, this site allows you to explore teaching opportunities in the fields of medicine, conservation, journalism, veterinary medicine, business and archaeology to name just a few. Alternatively, the site offers a portal through which you can organize electives and placements with other teachers in your field in other countries. Highly recommended! [ID:2693]

Teaching English Overseas 📖
2003, Jeff Mohamed, 224 pages ➤ English International, Suite 2301, 2929 Hirschfield Road, Spring, TX 77373, USA, www.english-international.com, $23.95 US; US Money Orders; EngIntSF@aol.com ◆ A key resource for North Americans who want to find an overseas job as an EFL teacher. Written by an expert with 32 years' experience, the book includes advice on teaching without training and choosing a TEFL training program. Surveys the current TEFL market and provides guidance on searching for jobs, writing TEFL resumes and conducting successful job interviews. Loaded with helpful tips on evaluating job offers, dealing with culture shock and the practical side of working overseas. Order forms available on the publisher's Web site. [ID:2392]

Teaching English Abroad 📖
2001, Susan Griffith, 544 pages ➤ Globe Pequot Press, P.O. Box 480, 246 Goose Lane, Guilford, CT 06437, USA, www.globepequot.com, $19.95 US; VISA, MC; 888-249-7586, fax 800-820-2329 ◆ Includes a directory of more than 380 TEFL courses lasting from a weekend to three years, as well as other information related to preparing for teaching abroad. Job-finding information is indexed by country and covers 87 countries with expanded sections on Germany, China, Brazil, Russia, Korea, Albania, Vietnam, Spain and many others. There is full information on: the prospects for qualified and unqualified teachers; private teaching; red tape; conditions of employment; and culture shock. It features 1,150 language school addresses to contact for jobs plus first-hand accounts from English teachers who have travelled and worked abroad. Highly recommended. [ID:2084]

Teaching English in Taiwan ⌨

2003 ➤ Enquiries Service, Foreign Affairs Canada (FAC), 125 Sussex Drive, Ottawa, ON K1A 0G2, Canada, www.fac-aec.gc.ca, Free; 800-267-8376, fax 613-996-9709; *Fr* ◆ On-line guide for Canadians considering teaching English in Taiwan. Contains updated information on living and working conditions, as well as Taiwanese society. A good primer on visa matters, contracts, housing, income tax and medical insurance. [ID:2488]

The Teaching Overseas Information Handbook 📖

Annual, Robert Barlas, 40 pages ➤ Search Associates, RR 5, 632 Vermilyea Road, Belleville, ON K8N 4Z5, Canada, www.searchassociates.com, $10.50 CDN; 613-967-4902, fax 613-967-8981 ◆ Written especially for teachers interested in furthering their careers overseas, either on a long- or short-term basis, The Teaching Overseas Information Handbook serves as a valuable complement to much of the information available on the Search Associates Web site. It also provides detailed answers to many of the myriad personal and professional questions which teachers usually want to ask before embarking on such a venture. The Handbook is now available as a Canadian or American edition, so specify which you prefer when you order. It can now be ordered only via e-mail and is delivered to you as an e-mail attachment. Make your cheque or money order out to Bob Barlas and mail at the same time you send your e-mail. [ID:2038]

TESL Canada ⚙

TESL Canada, P.O. Box 44105, Burnaby, BC V5B 4Y2, Canada, www.tesl.ca, 604-298-0312, fax 604-298-0312 ◆ TESL Canada is the national federation of English as a second language teachers, learners and learner advocates. The group is dedicated to advancing communication and coordinating awareness of issues for those concerned with English as a second language and English skills development. [ID:2754]

TESOL Online (Teachers of English to Speakers of Other Languages) ⌨

www.tesol.edu ◆ Whether you are trying to make a difference in the lives of your students, teaching newcomers to the field to be the best they can be, or conducting research in the field of ESL/EFL, TESOL connects you to a global community of professionals teaching English as a second or other language. Includes links to a job finder, ESL periodicals and teacher education programs. [ID:2370]

TIE Online ⌨

International Educator's Institute, P.O. Box 513, Cummaquid, MA 02637, USA, www.tieonline.com, Credit Cards; 508-362-1414, fax 508-362-1411 ◆ A directory of hundreds of overseas teaching positions. Subscribe on-line and get immediate access to prominent international English schools. Submit your resume and have it accessible to over 200 school headmasters. An excellent resource for the aspiring international overseas English teacher! [ID:2513]

What's Next: A Job Search Guide for Teachers 📖

Annual, Alan Travers, Daniel Lalonde ➤ Alan Travers, 950 Front Road, Kingston, ON K7M 4M1, Canada, $20 CDN; Cheque or Money Order; http://educ.queensu.ca/~placment/job.html ◆ This Canadian book, updated and revised annually by Alan Travers and Daniel Lalonde, is intended for education students and recent graduates of BEd programs. Includes job-search strategies, information on international teaching and applying across Canada, as well as Web sites, bibliographies and other information bound to make your international teaching job search a success. Send cheques or money orders directly to the author with your name and address. [ID:2695]

Work Abroad: The Complete Guide to Finding a Job Overseas 📖

2002, Clay Hubbs, 224 pages ➤ Transitions Abroad, P.O. Box 745, Bennington, VT 05201, USA, www.transitionsabroad.com, $15.95 US; Credit Cards; 802-442-4827, fax 802-442-4827, publisher@TransitionsAbroad.com ◆ A comprehensive US guide to all aspects of international work, including work permits, short-term jobs, teaching English, volunteer opportunities, planning an international career, starting your own business and much more. [ID:2262]

CHAPTER 30
Careers in International Development

The term *international development* commonly refers to aid programs directed towards developing countries. As Canada and the United States are active aid-donors, many of us work overseas in the field of international development. For example, an estimated 1,700 Canadians work on CIDA-funded projects; 1,700 Canadians are employed by the UN system. Countless North Americans work as consultants, volunteers, and business suppliers to CIDA or USAID, the UN and numerous other aid agencies in the world. There are a wide variety of employment possibilities involving the administration and implementation of these programs by international bodies, the federal government, educational institutions, NGOs and private firms.

TYPES OF OVERSEAS POSTINGS

While some international development careers bring individuals to several continents over the span of their working life, many international positions are not permanent overseas jobs. The following explains some of the many types of postings.

The Consulting Visit

Government departments, international bodies and consulting firms often hire independent, highly-qualified and sometimes retired professionals. The visit is usually a few weeks in duration, with hotel accommodation covered by the employer, and may include a tour of several countries in a region. The international visit (often called a "mission" in government circles) is usually a fact-finding evaluation visit.

The Business Visit

These are mostly in-house, temporary transfers by businesses or large UN agencies. Postings are usually up to six months in duration and generally involve training, application of a special skill, or temporarily assuming a position until a permanent replacement is found. Personal effects are not moved overseas. Housing arrangements are usually temporary, in a hotel or guesthouse.

The International Posting

These are long-term positions lasting from two to three years. Personal effects and family accompany the employee. The one- or two-year renewable contract is also often applied. The objectives may be: to fill a job for which the applicant is highly qualified; to provide international training for the employee which will benefit head office upon his or her return; or to complete a specific project for which the employee's skills are required.

Long-Term Volunteer Placement with an NGO

The normal length of time for volunteer placements with NGOs is two years, followed by one-year renewal contracts. The average age of volunteers is between 30 and 35 years. Volunteers must have specialized skills and some overseas experience. They generally work with local government agencies or local grassroots organizations. Salaries are basic; enough to provide a comfortable lifestyle by local standards and allow you some local, regional travel but leave you with little savings at the conclusion of your posting.

Cooperant positions are different from volunteer positions in that salaries are usually equivalent to the low-end salary scale for your field in Canada. This allows you to accumulate moderate savings during a two-year placement, or to purchase a car or motorcycle locally, for example. Technical specialization and previous work experience are usually a prerequisite.

International Intern

There are different types of internships, from formal structured internship programs sponsored by government and international organizations to formal self-directed internships available to the entrepreneurial candidate. Internships can be as short as one month; the most common is a four- to six-month posting. Internships can be unpaid or fully funded. The challenge with these positions is choosing the right program to augment your interests and goals, and then working hard at getting noticed, maximizing the level of professional experience you receive, and seizing opportunities as they arise

ADMINISTRATIVE JOBS IN DEVELOPMENT

The following job descriptions cover many of the standard administrative jobs available in development organizations. Regardless of your position overseas, most international jobs require that you also perform some or all of the following tasks: training local nationals, supervising personnel, working with local officials, general office administration, and budget and project management.

In-Country Program Coordinator

As the country representative of your agency overseas, you are responsible for a number of projects. You are somewhere between an entrepreneur and a diplomat. You must, above all else, be versatile and able to work effectively in the face of stress. You alone will manage an office in which your duties will include writing reports to the Canadian head office, financial budgeting, administration of local staff, and liasing with partners and logistics work.

Country representatives normally fall into two categories: those primarily concerned with supervising Canadian volunteers, and those supervising projects funded by your organization and administered by local organizations. Volunteer administrators must deal mostly with personnel issues. Project supervision requires, on the other hand, a good understanding of local customs and the ability to negotiate solutions with local staff and officials. The biggest headaches with these jobs are communicating effectively with the Canadian head office and managing a wide range of endeavours in your region under difficult economic and social conditions. A major plus is that you are your own boss and are able to influence in-country policies and programs. This enables you to see direct results from your efforts.

Project Director

As the on-site coordinator of a development project, you are often isolated from the capital region of the country. You may have a number of Canadian employees to supervise. You are responsible for overseeing all aspects of a particular project. As you are involved directly with implementing a program, you must be adept at problem solving. This suggests a need for well-developed interpersonal skills to solve problems and maintain motivation. You must also be able to resolve the conflict between outside supervision of your program (from visiting consultants or administrators from head office) and the realities faced by on-site workers. Given the difficulties of implementing new programs, there is often a high risk of failure in such jobs. As a hands-on coordinator, you have to exercise the full breadth of leadership.

Diplomatic Staff

Aid programs are increasingly supervised by Canadian diplomatic staff, many of whom are closely linked with the CANADIAN INTERNATIONAL DEVELOPMENT AGENCY (CIDA). Most overseas UN personnel have the status of diplomats and many of their positions are related to the administration of international development programs. Diplomatic staff don't usually work directly on development projects. Rather, they monitor programs or negotiate with the implementing agencies or operational partners such as the local government, a private firm or an NGO. Thus, diplomats are more involved with monitoring, writing policy or processing paper than doing hands-on work. Their skills are usually in writing and negotiating in a highly protocol-oriented environment. Thus, career paths tend to be more hierarchical and promotions come after longer periods of time.

Peacekeeping

Over many decades the peacekeeping sector at the UNITED NATIONS has grown and broadened its mandate, creating a large number of "multi-dimensional" career opportunities overseas. Peacekeeping, according to the UNITED NATIONS, is based on the principle that *"an impartial UN presence on the ground can ease tensions and allow negotiated solutions in a conflict situation."* The two expansive categories of personnel serving in UNITED NATIONS peacekeeping operations include members that are recruited by governments, such as military and civilian staff, and those hired by or from within the UNITED NATIONS. Each peacekeeping operation has a defined number of tasks, following the UNITED NATIONS' goal *"to alleviate human suffering and to create conditions and build institutions for self-sustaining peace."* In most cases, peacekeeping operations involve a military component and various civilian components covering a range of fields. Mission services include: management, trainers, military, electoral specialists, humanitarian affairs, political affairs, media relations and medical support, to name just a few.

It takes a special kind of professional to be "mission ready"—able to fly out at a moment's notice for mission service overseas. First and foremost you must be in good mental and physical shape and be willing to leave family obligations for six months, to work long hours, to make decisions that can have profound results, to live in sometimes adverse conditions with restricted communications and to endure daily security risks within a potentially hostile environment. As a UN recruiter says about peacekeeping, *"It is a very demanding, dynamic and rewarding experience."* Salary is usually determined according to on-the-ground professional experience and educational background. All internationally recruited staff receive a mission subsistence allowance in addition to their salary, which is designed to cover, among other expenses, the cost of food and lodging, local transportation and incidentals.

International Internship

In today's competitive world, an internship is an important prerequisite to launching an international development career, whether you aspire to work in the private, public or NGO sectors. There are many options. The Canadian government sponsors over 1,000 international internships a year and, of these, 400 are sponsored directly by the CANADIAN INTERNATIONAL DEVELOPMENT AGENCY (CIDA) for development projects overseas. Interns do a variety of types of work, from helping NGOs develop their own Web sites to working in refugee camps and managing various education and health programs. Interns usually gain front-line experience, living and working directly with local nationals, adapting to new cultures and making do with a subsistence living allowance. Most interns will experience unstructured work environments and will only shine if they take an entrepreneurial attitude towards their work placement and seize opportunities as they arise. The challenge for interns in these circumstances is to recognize and value the chance to acquire cross-cultural management experience for an international development career. A proactive work attitude and the ability to see a ripe opportunity could provide an excellent and unexpected opportunity for professional growth. For example, an environmental educator working in a rainforest may have the opportunity to produce media materials and create radio broadcasts for local farmers. So seize the moment, be willing to explore new areas of learning while on the job. For advice for interns who work with large international agencies, read the "Junior Professional Officer" section below. (For information on how to apply for an internship, see Chapter 17, Internships Abroad).

Junior Professional Officer (JPO)

These rare and highly competitive UNITED NATIONS posts are open to Canadians under 32 who have a master's degree. Written and spoken proficiency in two of the

UN's three working languages (English, French, Spanish) is an asset. The Canadian government sponsors these positions through various UN agencies so that young Canadians can acquire overseas experience with the UN. Jobs usually consist of monitoring UN-sponsored projects. Tasks include reviewing project proposals to ensure that they fit certain criteria, helping to push the proposals though the UN bureaucracy, and evaluating projects. These are desk jobs; they are certainly not hands-on positions. The major frustration mentioned by former JPOs is learning to work in the large, formal, slow-moving, impersonal UN system where you see few concrete results from your efforts. Positive aspects of this work are learning to manage "the system," seeing the international development scene in its widest perspective, learning writing skills, acquiring diplomatic skills, and meeting a variety of experienced leaders in the field of international development. (For information on how to apply, see Chapter 41, United Nations & Other IGOs.)

Overseas Volunteer

There are hundreds of volunteer positions available in almost every field imaginable. Contracts are usually for a two-year period and require a special skill or trade. As a volunteer, you will most likely live and work at the local grassroots level. Salaries and housing are modest, but usually adequate. While you won't be able to join the local polo club or eat in five-star hotels, you will have enough money to live well and travel within the country by local transportation. Volunteering is one of the best ways to acquire experience in your field and is often a prerequisite for a career in international development. With this experience, you will have the credibility and expertise to make further inroads into your field. There is an increasing trend in the NGO community to create cooperant positions, where pay scales lie somewhere between a volunteer position and a standard overseas salaried position. Inquire about this category when approaching NGOs.

Community Development or HIV/AIDS Worker

As the teaching of certain skills is a major objective in development work, having good group communication techniques is important for overseas development jobs. Community development work involves dealing with local groups or a counterpart, to forge links, facilitate, train, maintain continuity, motivate and help promote change. Because the exchange of skills is essential to your job, so too is learning the local language. Most large development projects employ a full-time community development officer, while many smaller projects employ only one person, whose main job responsibility is community development work. You should have a lot of experience in organizing local committees at the grassroots level and be adept at maintaining motivation in the face of frustration.

It is worth noting here the valuable role community development workers play in the fight against the HIV/AIDS pandemic. Every minute, 11 people are infected with HIV. More than 42 million people are living with HIV/AIDS around the world. The disease has deepened existing poverty and the vulnerability of the poor, particularly in Sub-Saharan Africa. It is not merely a health problem that can be "fixed" by medical intervention, but is a complex and multi-faceted issue. Community development workers have responded to this pandemic by working at all levels in society: businesses, unions, religious groups, schools, community leaders, women's groups, human rights organizations and government at all levels. They provide vital services including: medical support, reproductive health services, leadership training, age-appropriate education and peer counselling.

Office Manager, Accountant

Most overseas projects, especially country-wide programs, have an office in the capital that requires an office manager and an accountant or controller. These posts are mostly available from private sector firms that have contracts with CIDA. As in similar Canadian operations, you need to have the versatility normally associated with working in a small firm. With the trend towards "indigenisation," skilled local-hire staff are increasingly assuming positions normally given to overseas staff in developing countries, so many of these positions no longer exist for foreign personnel.

Logistician

In this job, you are the person responsible for transportation, warehousing, travel arrangements, communications, building maintenance, local purchases and vehicle maintenance. Above all, you are an organizer. Depending on the size of the program, you may specialize in emergency food stock warehousing for the INTERNATIONAL RED CROSS, or perhaps supervising the transportation of equipment that is imported or locally purchased for a development project. For this type of job, you should be street smart and have inside knowledge about where to purchase local products, acquire a visa quickly, obtain special forms from the local government, or deal with merchants and local staff. The difficulty with this job is the stress of being on the front line, having to complete concrete tasks in an atmosphere in which unforeseeable obstacles dominate. The great thing about this work is that you deal directly with the local population at all levels. It's very hands-on and includes non-bureaucratic problem solving and risk assessment.

Support Staff

These jobs include everybody from the secretary, the telephone or communications expert and the security guard, to the assistant administrator. While most overseas employers hire local people for this work, in some cases security reasons dictate that key diplomatic posts be held by Canadians. (For more information, see Chapter 37, Canadian Government.)

Project or Program Officer (in Canada)

Most staff in Canadian NGOs and many in CIDA are program officers. In this position, you provide the link between the field operations (overseas operations) and the Canadian administration. Your job is primarily to monitor the overseas program (usually specific to one country or one region) and to support overseas personnel. As a good organizer or administrator, you must be proficient in writing, communications and financial administration. The job usually involves travel several times a year to the program country. The position can be frustrating as it is bureaucratic, but it is often a stepping-stone to an overseas position or an opportunity for a seasoned overseas worker to take a break from living abroad. Emphasis is on learning the Canadian component of development administration.

OTHER JOBS IN DEVELOPMENT

Here is a sample of job areas recently advertised:

- **Agriservices/Natural Resource Management:** agronomist, aquaculturist, agroforester, veterinarian, livestock extension officer, Geographic Information Systems (GIS) analyst

- **Administration and Human Resources:** human resource manager, project manager, institution-builder, procurement manager, recruiter, conference coordinator, contract specialist

- **Business:** economist, rural development planner, finance analyst, micro-credit officer, micro-enterprise planner, marketer, statistician, trade officer, accounting, database analyst

- **Communications:** writer, editor, publisher, Web site designer, radio producer, announcer, media technician, translator, report writer, researcher

- **Community Development:** capacity building officer, home economist, small business consultant, proposal writer, fundraiser, cooperative manager, gender advisor, volunteer coordinator, intercultural briefing trainer

- **Education:** English teacher, language teacher, university teacher, literacy trainer, librarian, global diversity trainer, crisis counsellor

- **Health:** doctor, nurse, dentist, HIV/AIDS prevention educator, reproductive health specialist, nutritionist, physiotherapist

- **Human Rights:** attorney, mediator/negotiator, journalist, activist, human rights observers, child protection officer, judicial reform trainer

- **Peacekeeping/Humanitarian Services:** humanitarian coordinator, transport specialist, landmine specialist, security advisor, disaster relief manager, food distributor, policy analyst, peacekeeper, refugee coordinator, occupational stress counsellor, military person

- **Technical Assistance:** irrigation technician, land surveyor, mechanical engineer, waste engineer, network engineer, geo-thermal engineer

- **Trades:** carpenter, blacksmith, boat builder, mason, mechanic, millwright

A LAST WORD

Working in international development is a rewarding endeavour. You work with good people, your work is worthwhile, and you are often on the front lines of helping to create a better world. Good luck!

RESOURCES

This chapter contains the following Resources sections: NGO Job Boards; International Development Job Books; International Development & Global Education; and Social Action & Activism.

NGO JOB BOARDS

Job boards are the fastest way to find international work. Check these sites regularly.

AlertNet 💻
www.alertnet.org/thepeople/jobs/?via=lnav ◆ This site boasts an excellent database of jobs in the international humanitarian aid and relief field. Filter your search by country, salary, field of expertise or location, or simply browse all jobs by country. [ID:2595]

Association for Women's Rights in Development (AWID) 👫
www.awid.org/jobs ◆ Each week a list of job openings around the world is posted on AWID's "Resource Net" e-mail digest. Click the "Find a Job" link and browse opportunities by viewing the "Resource Net" issues. As the name of the resource indicates, the jobs are focused on women's human rights and gender issues. An excellent collection of overseas jobs for those interested in this field. [ID:2584]

Canada's Council to End Global Poverty 💻
www.ccic.ca ◆ This Canadian Web site is an excellent resource for searching jobs in international development and educating yourself on global poverty issues. There's a good job board that is frequently updated and worth checking periodically. The site offers an outstanding resources page containing an extensive collection of PDF documents on gender, ethics, peace building, trade and poverty, and Canadian foreign policy, to name just a few. Start networking with over 100 NGO member organizations all over Canada and find the development job you want! [ID:2630]

CANADEM-International Trends and Opportunities 👫
www.canadem.ca; *Fr* ◆ CANADEM is a national level roster of civilians with a broad range of skills including human rights, peacebuilding, democratization, admin-logistics, security and reconstruction. It serves primarily as a rapid reaction source of skilled Canadians for the UN, OSCE, other international organizations, NGOs and the Canadian government. CANADEM's Web page, "International Trends and Opportunities," provides a synopsis for international job hunters by monitoring all major UN field missions including the UN Department of Peacekeeping. For more information, see the specific mission updates on this excellent site. [ID:2837]

CANPOL 👫
http://canpol.ca ◆ CANPOL is a division of CANADEM, a national roster of 5,000 Canadians skilled in human rights, peace building, democratization, rule of law, admin-logistics, security, reconstruction and other field expertise. CANPOL's 800 police and security sector reform experts have experience in over 60 countries. Practitioners of police craft and operational management, they help achieve sustainable police development through delivering programs and police services to clients worldwide. Registrants must have well-honed interpersonal skills: flexibility, teamwork, cultural and gender sensitivity, as well as the ability to think on their feet. Once registered, your skills profile and resume are used to determine whether you are the ideal match for positions that come available. Registration is free. If you are a police expert and interested in overseas work, this is your first stop. [ID:2750]

Care Canada 👫
www.care.ca; *Fr* ◆ This site gives detailed job information not only about positions with Care Canada, but also about overseas work in general. In its "Job Centre" sub-directory, you will find information on the employment sectors Care is involved in, important characteristics for overseas work, current job openings, internship programs and overseas volunteer opportunities. You can submit your resume into a database and instantly be considered for upcoming job openings with this internationally respected organization. [ID:2223]

Careers Without Borders 🖳

Careers Without Borders, Suite 100, 9 Gurdwara Road, Ottawa, ON K2E 7X6, Canada, www.careerswithoutborders.com, 800-965-1830 ◆ This Ottawa site bills itself as the first central recruitment site devoted to assisting both development professionals seeking international jobs and development organizations seeking new recruits. It allows you to create your on-line profile and resume, after which the database is scanned regularly, matching development professionals to international jobs. You can also browse "Current Openings" and apply to as many as you like. Apply on-line and receive an automatic confirmation every time. A great new site with lots of features and advice that promises soon to be a fixture on international ID job seekers' favourites lists. (For more information, see their ad in the sponsor section at the end of this guide.) [ID:2762]

CharityJOB 🖳

www.charityjob.co.uk/seekers.asp ◆ This site bills itself as the most popular site in the UK for charity jobs. With over 800,000 hits, 900 organizations and 500 jobs each month, it's hard to debate the claim. Search jobs by category, salary range or location, or simply view the complete list of current vacancies. You can also join the subscription list and receive a weekly e-mail digest of job postings. A great site for jobs in the UK! [ID:2581]

CharityVillage 🖳

www.charityvillage.ca ◆ This is one of the best sites for looking for work in the not-for-profit sector. Browse and search jobs posted by over 5,000 organizations, register for e-mail alerts and access job seeker resources online. [ID:2357]

The Communication Initiative 🖳

www.comminit.com/vacancies.html ◆ This Canadian Web site is the main initiative of the Communications Initiative's (CI's) mandate to foster dialogue and debate on development issues. The job board is updated daily with interesting and challenging positions in the field of development that are not readily found elsewhere. Lots of postings for program managers, public health officials and technical support officers. If it's capacity-building development work you're after, look no further. [ID:2659]

Development Executive Group 🖳

www.developmentex.com/job_opportunities/opp_summary.asp ◆ A global membership organization serving firms, non-profit organizations, and individual professionals working in the international development market. The site provides an excellent job board that lets you search for numerous jobs in the field of international development. The job board is especially used to advertise jobs with US consulting firms working in the field. [ID:2660]

DEVJOBS 🖳

www.seadphil.com/devjobs/index.html ◆ DEVJOBS provides international job announcements on various development fields such as micro-finance, food security, health and agriculture. With hundreds of new announcements and updates four times weekly, you get access to jobs posted by over 400 development organizations in one convenient place. [ID:2578]

DevNet Jobs 🖳

www.devnetjobs.org ◆ This site is labled as a Gateway to International Development Jobs and Consultancy Assignments. Look up current job listings in international development, including engineering jobs. A subscription is required to post resumes; however, you can browse postings and receive job hunting newsletters for free. [ID:2826]

Dev-Zone 🖳

www.dev-zone.org/jobs ◆ This is the job board of an excellent New Zealand Web site that provides information services on development and global issues to NGOs, consultants, academia, community, government and businesses. Jobs are listed by sector and the descriptions are detailed and informative. Subscribe to three updates for free and receive weekly e-mails with the latest job postings and resource updates. Check it out! [ID:2661]

Eldis 💻

www.eldis.org/news/jobs.htm ◆ This great British Web site offers a number of useful services to the international development job seeker. In addition to an excellent list of job postings, you can also browse a selected list of links to other job Web sites or view current postings at selected development agencies. The site is highly recommended as easy-to-use, professional and comprehensive. [ID:2662]

Euro Brussels 💻

www.eurobrussels.com/index.php ◆ Find your perfect job in Brussels, EU institutions or international organizations. Euro Brussels bills itself as the number one site in the business of European affairs and international relations and it delivers. With 200,000 hits per month and literally hundreds of postings for some of the more obscure international jobs, searchable by category: international organizations, NGOs and political consultancies, EU institutions, law firms, academic and private think tanks, internships and industry associations. Many positions are high level, but there are some entry-level positions. Subscribe to their excellent newsletter. [ID:2607]

European Bank for Reconstruction and Development (EBRD) 🏛

European Bank for Reconstruction and Development (EBRD), One Exchange Square, London, EC2A 2JN, UK, www.ebrd.com, (44) (20) 7338-6000, fax (44) (20) 7338-6100 ◆ EBRD provides funding for development projects in Europe and Asia. It provides a list of current and proposed projects and links to press releases and related stories. [ID:2827]

Foreign Policy Association 💻

Foreign Policy Association, www.fpa.org ◆ International job postings categorized by development assistance, education, environment, humanitarian relief, health and population, research, youth and other. Also a listing of internships and volunteer opportunities. Highly recommended. [ID:2579]

ForeignAID.com 💻

www.foreignaid.com ◆ The ForeignAID.com International Funding Directory is a database of over 700 foundations and donors in the U.S., Europe, and worldwide that give over $1 billion per year in grants and scholarships to individuals and projects. Yearly subscription price is $499 US. [ID:2844]

German Development Service 🏛

www.ded.de ◆ The German Development Service (DED) is one of the leading European development services for personnel cooperation. It was founded in 1963; since then, more than 13,000 development workers have committed themselves to improving the living conditions of people in Africa, Asia and Latin America. Almost 1,000 development workers are currently working in approximately 40 countries. Search DED development job postings all over the world. [ID:2476]

Human Rights Education Associations 💻

www.hrea.org/erc/Links/index.html ◆ This Dutch Web site has an incredible links page to human rights organizations all over the world. A great place to start researching jobs in this field. [ID:2624]

Human Rights Internet 💻

www.hri.ca/jobboard/jobSearch.asp ◆ This excellent Ottawa-based Web site with a great job board includes postings by organizations focusing on human rights. Well-organized, often updated and used by job seekers all over the world. [ID:2577]

Idealist.org 💻

www.idealist.org/ip/idealist/Home/default ◆ Idealist.org connects 37,000 non-profit and community organizations in 165 countries around the world. Navigate to the "Jobs" section and search hundreds of job postings by region, area of focus or job category. [ID:2580]

International Federation of Red Cross and Red Crescent Network 🏛

www.ifrc.org ◆ This great Web site is your portal to everything you could want to know about the International Red Cross/Red Crescent. You'll find listings of national societies, an excellent job/volunteer board and access to a number of great on-line publications on humanitarian relief and community health care. [ID:2272]

OneWorld 🖳 ♔
www.oneworld.net/job/list/professional ◆ OneWorld's network of autonomous centres have partnerships with a wider community of more than 1,500 civil society organizations based in 90 countries. Partners include charities, human rights NGOs, grassroots community groups, UN and government agencies, university departments, environmental organizations, trade unions, research institutions, advocacy groups, feminist organizations and groups of all shapes and sizes. They have a great job board, on which you can search for jobs in human rights, the environment and sustainable development all over the world on this job site. It's part of an extensive worldwide network of affiliated country sites. The Canadian site profiles 100 Canadian partner organizations. Check out the Canadian site, www.oneworld.ca. [ID:2582]

Policy Library 🖳
www.policylibrary.com ◆ Policy Library Web site is a social, economic and foreign policy resource—updated daily with the latest jobs, research and events. An annual membership costs $70 CDN and allows access to hundreds of jobs, internships and scholarships from all around the world. A good resource for policy buffs. [ID:2644]

ReliefWeb 🖳
www.reliefweb.int/vacancies ◆ One of the top international job boards around. Search vacancies by date, location and organization. As the name indicates, most jobs tend toward the humanitarian and development sectors. One can also subscribe to the vacancies mailing list. [ID:2576]

World Service Enquiry ♔
World Service Enquiry, 233 Bon Marché Centre, 241-251 Ferndale Road, London, SW9 8BJ, UK, www.wse.org.uk, VISA, MC; (44) (0) (8707) 70-3274, fax 0870 770-7991 ◆ World Service Enquiry provides expert information and advice about the opportunities that exist to contribute to peace, justice and development in the Third World. Their excellent Web site is a portal through which World Service Enquiries' many excellent services are made available. One that can help a lot in your international development job search is their "Opportunities Abroad" monthly vacancy magazine of aid, development and mission jobs, which you can subscribe to in print or on-line. On average, it lists over 400 vacancies available overseas. Another is the "Guide to Working Overseas and At Home For Development", is a fabulous three-part publication containing guidance on how to become involved in the field and build your ID IQ; a directory of agencies for which you can volunteer overseas; and strategies for landing the ID job that's right for you, including information on the job search, NGOs, education routes, and much more. Note that the 2003 "Guide" is available on the Web site and, for the cost of postage, you can order the 2004 one in print. But this isn't all, World Service Enquiry also offers "life coaching" related to careers in development through "E>volve" - its unique e-mail course that aims to help people discern the pros and cons of working in development, to understand careers in international aid and development, and to create a plan to get where you want to be. If you're located in the UK, you can also take advantage of their "One-to-One" international development career counselling service. A great organization with a great Web site worth bookmarking! [ID:2771]

INTERNATIONAL DEVELOPMENT JOB BOOKS

For related resources, consult the Resources section for Canadian International Development Agency (CIDA) in Chapter 37, Canadian Government; Chapter 38, NGOs in Canada; Chapter 40, NGOs in Europe and the Rest of the World; and Chapter 41, United Nations & Other IGOs. For resources describing the all important cross-cultural aspects of international development, consult the Resources sections in Chapter 1, The Effective Overseas Employee; Chapter 3, Living Overseas; Chapter

12, Cross-Cultural Travel; and Chapter 27, Jobs by Regions of the World. Also check out the many related resources in Chapter 33, Health Careers Abroad.

Aid as a Peacemaker: Canadian Development Assistance and Third World Conflict 📖

1994, Robert Miller, 224 pages ➤ McGill-Queen's University Press, 3430 McTavish Street, Montreal, QC H3A 1X9, Canada, www.mqup.mcgill.ca, $19.95 CDN; VISA, MC; 514-398-3750, fax 514-398-4333 ◆ Does development by its nature produce conflict? Are there times when Canada should take sides in Third World conflict? Are there ways that Canadian aid can be used to promote peace? Experts in Third World development pursue answers to these questions. Still interesting as a primer on Canadian aid and the nexus between development and conflict. [ID:2163]

Canada's Council to End Global Poverty 🖳

www.ccic.ca ◆ This Canadian Web site is an excellent resource for searching jobs in international development and educating yourself on global poverty issues. There's a good job board that is frequently updated and worth checking periodically. The site offers an outstanding resources page containing an extensive collection of PDF documents on gender, ethics, peace building, trade and poverty, and Canadian foreign policy, to name just a few. Start networking with over 100 NGO member organizations all over Canada and find the development job you want! [ID:2630]

CIDA Publications 📖

Canadian International Development Agency (CIDA), Communications Branch, 200 Promenade du Portage, Gatineau, QC K1A 0G4, Canada, www.acdi-cida.gc.ca, Free; 819-997-5006, fax 819-953-6088; *Fr* ◆ CIDA publishes a wide array of documents in the form of policies, strategies and research papers. Topics covered include sustainable development, health, globalization, opportunities in international development, and gender equity, to name a few. CIDA operates a library that is open to the public, but for job seekers not living in the Ottawa region, these documents can be accessed on-line by following the link to "Resources" and then "Publications" from the home page. These documents are available free of charge and are excellent resources for those interested in Canada's role in overseas development assistance. [ID:2308]

Cross-Cultural Collaborations 📖

1995, Daniel Kealey, David Protheroe, Centre for Intercultural Learning, Canadian Foreign Service Institute, 65 pages ➤ Masters & Scribes Bookshoppe, 9938 - 81 Ave., Edmonton, AB T6E 1W6, Canada, www.mastersandscribes.com, $14.95 CDN; Credit Cards; 800-378-3199, fax 780-439-6879 ◆ This book clarifies why so few development assistance personnel are successful overseas by examining the individual, organizational and contextual factors at play in success or failure. It also discusses how the field of technical cooperation is evolving and how new forms of collaboration are emerging in fields such as diplomacy, peacekeeping and business. Recommended reading for both development workers and their managers. [ID:2683]

Development Business 📖 🖳

Weekly ➤ United Nations Publications, Sales and Marketing Section, Room DC2-853, Department I004, New York, NY 10017, USA, www.un.org/Pubs/sales.htm, $550 US/year; Credit Cards; 800-253-9646, fax 212-963-3489 ◆ This United Nations Department of Public Information publication is available only by subscription and is the single best way that suppliers and consultants can find the information needed to successfully win contracts generated from projects financed by development banks governments and the United Nations. Graphically and organizationally excellent, this site includes an on-line Business Directory with links to the Web sites of companies involved in international business, which can be used for job searches and to locate potential business partners. A great resource [ID:2083]

Development Dictionary: A Guide to Knowledge as Power 📖

1992, Wolfgang Sachs, 352 pages ➤ Zed Books, 7 Cynthia Street, London, N1 9JF, UK, www.zedbooks.co.uk, $25 US; VISA, MC; (44) (0) (2078) 37-4014, fax (44) (0) (2078) 33-3960 ◆ The world's most eminent development critics review the key concepts of international development in the last 50 years. Includes a guide to relevant literature. [ID:2207]

Development Experience Clearinghouse 💻

USAID Development Experience Clearinghouse, www.dec.org ◆ The Development Experience Clearinghouse (DEC) is the largest on-line resource for USAID-funded, international development documentation. The purpose of the DEC is to strengthen USAID's development projects, activities and programs by making these development experience documents available to USAID offices and mission staff, PVOs, NGOs, universities and research institutions, developing countries and the public worldwide. You are able to download USAID documents from the DEXS database that contains records for over 124,000 USAID technical and program documents with over 19,000 available for electronic download. [ID:2800]

Development: Journal of the Society for International Development 📖

Quarterly, Society for International Development ➤ Palgrave Macmillan, 175 Fifth Ave., New York, NY 10010, USA, www.palgrave-usa.com, £40/year; Credit Cards; 212-982-3900, fax 212-777-6359 ◆ This long-established and affordable journal explores the cutting-edge issues related to human-centred development. With alternative perspectives on civil society, development policy and community based strategies for livelihoods, gender and social justice, it keeps readers up to date on the challenging issues of today's rapidly changing world. [ID:2156]

Directory of Non-Governmental Organizations (NGOs) Active in Sustainable Development 📖

1998, 338 pages ➤ Organization of Economic Cooperation and Development (OECD), Suite 700, 2001 L Street N.W., Washington, DC 20036, USA, www.oecdwash.org, $67 US; Credit Cards; 202-785-6323, fax 202-785-0350 ◆ Contains information on 1,905 NGOs in six OECD Member countries: Australia, Canada, Japan, Korea, New Zealand and the United States. A great starting point for the international job seeker. [ID:2063]

Health, Population and Reproductive Health Resources 💻

www.jhpiego.jhu.edu/websites/index.htm ◆ Those interested in a career in international health should check out this page of links to organizations involved in public health. [ID:2227]

InterAction: American Council for Voluntary International Action 👥

InterAction: American Council for Voluntary International Action, Suite 701, 1717 Massachusetts Ave. N.W., Washington, DC 20036, USA, www.interaction.org, Credit Cards; 202-667-8227, fax 202-667-8236 ◆ InterAction is the largest alliance of US-based international development and humanitarian non-governmental organizations. Made up of more than 160 members operating in every developing country working to overcome poverty, exclusion and suffering by advancing social justice and basic dignity. Learn more by subscribing to their newsletter, "Monday Developments," or purchase one of their publications, "InterAction Member Profiles." Use their directory to learn more about work done by member NGOs and international development issues. [ID:2368]

International Careers in Urban Planning 📖

2001, 193 pages ➤ International Division, American Planning Association, Planners Book Service, Suite 1600, 122 South Michigan Ave., Chicago, IL 60603, USA, www.planning.org/international/publications.htm, $29.95 US; Credit Cards; 312-786-6344, fax 312-431-9985 ◆ This second edition changes the name and expands the focus of the 1994 edition: "Career Opportunities for American Planners". It is now directed at planning students and planners outside the US and includes over 30 interviews of planners who have worked overseas covering subjects such as education, career path, current employment and helpful advice. [ID:2387]

International Centre for Research on Women 👥

www.icrw.org ◆ ICRW is a US NGO with a mission to improve the lives of women in poverty, advance women's equality and human rights and contribute to the broader economic and social well-being of women. This Web site contains an excellent collection of resources on gender issues, human rights and development. Join on-line discussion forums and share your thoughts with others interested in these issues. Highly recommended! [ID:2225]

International Development Research Centre (IDRC) ♔

www.idrc.ca ♦ IDRC's mandate includes encouraging and conducting research on the problems of developing regions and on means for fostering their economic and social advancement. The IDRC Web site has both an excellent library and a comprehensive "Booktique" of development resources that can be ordered on-line. Research your topics using the IDRC Online catalogue "Biblio." Resources span topics such as economics, environment, agriculture, health, social and political science and development. An excellent Web site for those inclined toward development. [ID:2270]

Kumarian Press Catalogue 🖳 ♔

Kumarian Press Inc., 1294 Blue Hills Ave., Bloomfield, CT 06002, USA, www.kpbooks.com, Free; VISA, MC; 800-289-2664, fax 860-243-2867 ♦ This excellent US publisher of independent scholarly works has replaced its catalogue with an excellent Web site featuring a large selection of books relating to international affairs and development. [ID:2016]

Le miniAtlas du développement global 📖

2004, World Bank, 66 pages ➤ Les Éditions Saint-Martin, bureau 203, 5000 rue Iberville, Montreal, QC H2H 2S6, Canada, $11.95 CDN; VISA, MC; 519-529-0920, fax 519-529-8384, st-martin@qc.aira.com; *Fr* ♦ "Le miniAtlas du développement global" is the French translation of "The miniAtlas of Global Development published by the World Bank. It is a quick guide to the most pressing development issues facing the world. The pocket-sized book is based on the Bank's compilation of development data—the World Development Indicators—as well as the "Bank Atlas" and the "Little Data Book." It provides colourful and easy-to-read world maps, tables and graphs that highlight key social, economic and environmental data for 208 countries and territories. The "miniAtlas" is designed to serve as an introduction and quick reference to today's most urgent development challenges. . [ID:2785]

NPSIA Works Career Futures 🖳

Norman Paterson School of International Affairs (NPSIA), 1401 Dunton Tower, Carleton University, 1125 Colonel By Drive, Ottawa, ON K1S 5B6, Canada, www.carleton.ca/npsia, Free on-line; 613-520-6655, fax 613-520-2889 ♦ The Norman Paterson School of International Affairs (NPSIA) publishes this fantastic Web resource, recommended for anyone interested in working in international affairs. It is a compendium of careers that graduates of the NPSIA program have gone on to, presented as job titles and job descriptions organized by job field. Examples of fields include: academia, human rights and communications. Each field is introduced briefly, followed by job titles and descriptions. By locating the jobs you're interested in, you can easily get an idea of the qualifications and skill sets employers in those fields are looking for. An invaluable guide to planning your future career in international affairs, the usefulness of which cannot be understated! Check it out. [ID:2789]

The Oxfam Handbook of Development and Relief 📖

1995, OXFAM UK, 1,200 pages ➤ Renouf Publishing Co. Ltd., Unit 1, 5369 Canotek Road, Ottawa, ON K1J 9J3, Canada, www.renoufbooks.com, $78 US; Credit Cards; 888-767-6766, fax 613-745-7660 ♦ This three-volume set is still a valuable reference tool for development practitioners, planners, students and teachers of development. [ID:2150]

PACT Publications Catalogue 🖳 ♔

Semi-annual ➤ PACT Publications, Suite 350, 1200 18th Street N.W., Washington, DC 20036, USA, www.pactpublications.com, Free on-line; Credit Cards; 202-466-5666, fax 202-466-5669 ♦ Pact Publications is an integrated publishing house that facilitates the design, production and distribution of innovative and progressive development materials. The Catalogue offers development professionals the most appropriate educational materials and training tools available. Available on-line in PDF format. [ID:2065]

Review 🖳

3 issues/year ➤ North-South Institute, Suite 200, 55 Murray Street, Ottawa, ON K1N 5M3, Canada, www.nsi-ins.ca, Free on-line; Credit Cards; 613-241-3535, fax 613-241-7435 ♦ The North-South

Institute's newsletter features research updates, reviews of recent publications, and other news items on international development and Canada's foreign policy. PDF format. [ID:2261]

Southern Exposure 📖
2003, 384 pages ➤ Kumarian Press Inc., 1294 Blue Hills Ave., Bloomfield, CT 06002, USA, www.kpbooks.com, $25.95 US; VISA, MC; 800-289-2664, fax 860-243-2867 ◆ Using an issue-based approach and keeping questions of gender and culture at the fore, this book examines the changes brought about by globalization from the perspective of ordinary people in the Global South, such as small farmers in Kenya, cocoa growers in Bolivia or garment workers in Bangladesh, highlighting both the diversity of their experience and common themes. An excellent resource. [ID:2559]

Sustainable Times Webzine 🖥
CUSO, Suite 500, 2255 Carling Ave., Ottawa, ON K2B 1A6, Canada, www.cuso.org, 613-829-7445, fax 613-829-7996 ◆ This Web zine explores practical alternatives to the ways business is done. Featuring original articles from Canada and the Third World, the Sustainable Times Web zine is for those seeking down-to-earth answers to our most pressing problems. [ID:2483]

Third World Quarterly: Journal of Emerging Areas 📖
8 issues/year ➤ Carfax Publishing: Taylor and Francis Group: Journals, Taylor & Francis Group, Suite 800, 325 Chestnut Street, Philadelphia, PA 19106, USA, www.tandf.co.uk, $199 US; Credit Cards; 800-354-1420, fax 215-625-8914 ◆ The leading journal of scholarship and policy in the field of international studies. For more than two decades, it has set the agenda on development discourses of the global debate. As the most influential academic journal covering the emerging worlds, TWQ is at the forefront of analysis and commentary on fundamental issues of global concern. Both on-line and print versions are recommended! [ID:2139]

Trade and Development Report 2002: Developing Countries in World Trade 📖
2002, 208 pages ➤ United Nations Publications, Sales and Marketing Section, Room DC2-853, Department I004, New York, NY 10017, USA, www.un.org/Pubs/sales.htm, $39 US; Credit Cards; 800-253-9646, fax 212-963-3489 ◆ The "Trade and Development Report 2002" analyzes trends and outlooks for the world economy and focuses on export dynamism and industrialization in developing countries. Questions the conventional wisdom that export growth and foreign direct investment (FDI) automatically generate commensurate income gains and suggests that countries should move into higher-value exports by upgrading technology and improving productivity. [ID:2521]

Virtual Library on International Development 🖥
http://w3.acdi-cida.gc.ca/virtual.nsf ◆ The Virtual Library is published by CIDA and contains an excellent collection of links to international development-related sites and documents on the Internet. Organized by topic, country, region and organization, the site allows for easy and comprehensive searches. A great way to search for overseas jobs in your area of interest. [ID:2224]

Westview Press Catalogue ♯
Annual ➤ Perseus Books Group: Westview Press, 5500 Central Ave., Boulder, CO 80301-2877, USA, www.westviewpress.com, Free; 800-386-5656, fax 720-406-7336 ◆ Now part of the US Perseus group, the Westview Press Web site contains a comprehensive selection of quality titles relating to development and regional studies. [ID:2121]

Who's Who in International Development 📖
2003, 316 pages ➤ Canadian Council for International Cooperation (CCIC), Suite 300, 1 Nicholas Street, Ottawa, ON K1N 7B7, Canada, www.ccic.ca, $40 CDN or $25 CDN for CCIC members; VISA; 613-241-7007, fax 613-241-5302; Fr ◆ This book profiles over 100 Canadian NGOs, providing information on the overseas activities, regions of interests, publications, finances and affiliations of each. Includes addresses and personnel, as well as geographical and sector/program bibliographies. [ID:2238]

World Development 📖

Monthly ➤ Customer Service Department, Elsevier, 11830 Westline Industrial Drive, St. Louis, MO 63146, USA, www.elsevier.com/wps/find/homepage.cws_home, $286 US; Credit Cards; 800-460-3110, fax 314-453-7095, usbkinfo@elsevier.com; Available in large libraries ◆ Multi-disciplinary monthly journal of development studies. It seeks to explore ways of improving standards of living, and the human condition generally, by examining potential solutions to problems such as poverty, unemployment, malnutrition, disease, lack of shelter and environmental degradation. Students receive a significant discount! [ID:2175]

**World Economic and Social Survey: Trends and Policies in
the World Economy - Public-Private Interaction for Development** 📖

2002, 344 pages ➤ United Nations Publications, Sales and Marketing Section, Room DC2-853, Department I004, New York, NY 10017, USA, www.un.org/Pubs/sales.htm, $55 US; Credit Cards; 800-253-9646, fax 212-963-3489 ◆ This is the United Nations' annual analysis of current developments in the world economy and emerging policy issues. Contains a forecast of short-term global and regional economic trends and reviews major developments in international trade. Part One revolves around the economic recovery underway in some developed market economies. Part Two explores current social issues interlinked with economic development. Special attention is given to public-private cooperation. Includes statistical tables with standardized data on international trade and finance. Essential resource on global economic trends for decision-makers in international business. [ID:2523]

INTERNATIONAL DEVELOPMENT & GLOBAL EDUCATION

Global education teaches us about global issues and usually focuses on North–South relations. Issues such as poverty, human rights, social justice, sustainable development and the inequities of the global economic system are concerns of global education literature. The wide range of material listed here will help you to begin building your international IQ. The companion list to these resources is the Social Action and Activism Resources, which follows in this chapter. Also consult the Resources sections in the following chapters: Chapter 1, The Effective Overseas Employee; Chapter 3, Living Overseas; Chapter 12, Cross-Cultural Travel; and Chapter 27, Jobs by Regions of the World.

Barnga 📖

1990, Sivasailam Thiagarajan, Barbara Steinwachs, Intercultural Press, 80 pages ➤ Masters & Scribes Bookshoppe, 9938 - 81 Ave., Edmonton, AB T6E 1W6, Canada, www.mastersandscribes.com, $43.50 CDN; Credit Cards; 800-378-3199, fax 780-439-6879 ◆ This game simulates the effect of cultural differences on human interaction. Players learn that they must understand and reconcile these differences if they want to function effectively in a cross-cultural group. [ID:2205]

Canadian Development Report 2003 📖

Annual, North-South Institute, 112 pages ➤ Renouf Publishing Co. Ltd., Unit 1, 5369 Canotek Road, Ottawa, ON K1J 9J3, Canada, www.renoufbooks.com, $30 CDN; Credit Cards; 888-767-6766, fax 613-745-7660 ◆ This report looks at multilateral trade arrangements from the perspectives of both the North and the South. Highlights development issues such as those regarding market access and the WTO Intellectual Property Agreement. Includes up-to-date statistics and analyses related to social and economic indicators of developing countries along with statistics regarding the Canadian government's trade-related involvement with developing countries. A valuable reference tool for students and international job seekers with interests in development and trade. [ID:2260]

Canadian Human Rights Commission ⛨
www.chrc-ccdp.ca; Fr ◆ This is the official Web site of the Canadian Human Rights Commission, which seeks to ensure universal access to fundamental Human Rights by promoting public understanding and employer compliance with human rights standards. The site has an excellent resource section with publications and links to legislation and other information on human rights. [ID:2269]

CIDA Development Information Program ⛨
Canadian International Development Agency (CIDA), Communications Branch, 200 Promenade du Portage, Gatineau, QC K1A 0G4, Canada, www.acdi-cida.gc.ca, 819-997-5006, fax 819-953-6088; Fr ◆ Established by CIDA to encourage public understanding of international development issues, this program financially supports the development of mass media and education initiatives aimed at increasing awareness and understanding of international development and cooperation issues among Canadians. The DIP has three components: a mass-media initiative, which funds the production of media features targeting the Canadian public; a global classroom initiative, which supports the development and delivery of school-based global education activities and a journalism and development initiative, which provides support to Canadian journalists interested in gaining more professional experience in the international development field. Access the DIP Web site by following the link from CIDA's home page. [ID:2311]

CIDA International Development Photo Library (IDPL) ⛨
Canadian International Development Agency (CIDA), Communications Branch, 200 Promenade du Portage, Gatineau, QC K1A 0G4, Canada, www.acdi-cida.gc.ca, 819-997-5006, fax 819-953-6088; Fr ◆ IDPL is a resource of over 80,000 slides depicting life in the South, international development and Canada's role in it. Staff will provide photo editing/research services to the public for a nominal fee. Those living in the Ottawa area can schedule a time to view these photos in the photo library. Requests take five to 10 working days to complete. Contact 613-953-6530 for more information. [ID:2312]

Developing Intercultural Awareness: A Cross-Cultural Training Handbook 📖
1994, L. Robert Kohls, John M. Knight, Intercultural Press, 158 pages ➤ Masters & Scribes Bookshoppe, 9938 - 81 Ave., Edmonton, AB T6E 1W6, Canada, www.mastersandscribes.com, $31.50 CDN; Credit Cards; 800-378-3199, fax 780-439-6879 ◆ This book features outline designs of one- and two-day cultural awareness workshops, and training materials that include simulation games, case studies, and exercises on values and ice-breaking. Designed for intercultural educators and trainers, and useful to anyone wishing to expand his or her general training or teaching repertoire. [ID:2102]

Development Alternatives: Communities of the South in
Action - A Teacher's Guide for World Issues Courses 📖
1993, 130 pages ➤ Is Five Communications, Suite 200, 161 Eglinton Ave. E., Toronto, ON M4P 1J5, Canada, www.isfive.com, $49.95 CDN; Cheque or Money Order; 416-480-2408, fax 416-480-2546 ◆ Development Alternatives is a curriculum kit for secondary schools. This package of field-tested learning activities was designed and produced by Is Five Communications, based on original research in Asia, Africa and Latin America. This innovative publication emphasizes success stories from the South, and a spirit of mutual learning and information exchange between Southern and Northern communities. [ID:2133]

Global Change Game ⛨
2004 ➤ Global Change Game, P.O. Box 1632, Winnipeg, MB R3C 2Z6, Canada, www.mts.net/~gcg, 204-783-2675, fax 204-783-2680 ◆ The Global Change Game is an international development education workshop that visits highschool, university and community groups across Canada teaching about world issues in a fun and innovative way. It is a three-hour workshop, played on a hand-painted world map the size of a basketball court, in which players deal with challenges such as hunger, war, biodiversity, refugees and deforestation. If you are interested in having the Global Change Game come to your school, please contact the address above. [ID:2326]

Green Teacher Magazine 📖

Quarterly, 50 pages ➤ Green Teacher, 95 Robert Street, Toronto, ON M5S 2K5, Canada, www.greenteacher.com, $7.95 CDN/issue or $28.04 CDN/year; VISA, MC; 416-960-1244, fax 416-925-3474 ◆ Provides the inspiration, the ideas and the classroom-ready materials to help get you there. A magazine by and for educators to enhance environmental and global education across the curriculum at all grade levels. [ID:2131]

IISD Publication Centre 📖

International Institute for Sustainable Development (IISD), 6th Floor, 161 Portage Ave. E., Winnipeg, MB R3B 0Y4, Canada, www.iisd.org, Free on-line; 204-958-7700, fax 204-958-7710 ◆ IISD's Publication Centre has a mandate to spread the knowledge generated through its projects and initiatives, as well as scholarship and projects of others, to all individuals interested in sustainable development issues. The Centre has a wide range of publications covering a breadth of topics: business, investment and economic policy, indigenous peoples, poverty, climate change and environment. [ID:2240]

IISDnet 🖥

www.iisd.org ◆ IISDnet is the name of the Web site of the International Institute for Sustainable Development, headquartered in Winnipeg. It is an excellent site offering easy access to the latest thinking on sustainable development issues like climate change, natural resources and communities. There are also links to resources and other organizations working on sustainable development. You can also access IISD Linkages from the IISDnet home page. This multimedia resource for environment and development policy-makers is also useful for those interested in becoming more familiar with sustainable development issues. The site also has a small employment section. Add this invaluable resource to your favourites. [ID:2239]

It's Only Right: A Practical Guide for Learning
About the Convention on the Rights of the Child 📖

1993, Susan Fountain, 77 pages ➤ UNICEF Ontario, Suite 1100, 2200 Yonge Street, Toronto, ON M4S 2C6, Canada, www.unicef.ca, $15 CDN; Credit Cards; 416-487-4153, fax 416-487-8875 ◆ This guide, aimed at students grade 9 and up, helps young people recognise, respect and protect their rights and the rights of others around the world. Students learn through case studies, cooperative games, problem solving and positive action. [ID:2132]

Monthly Bulletin of Statistics 📖 🖥

2003, 288 pages ➤ United Nations Publications, Sales and Marketing Section, Room DC2-853, Department I004, New York, NY 10017, USA, www.un.org/Pubs/sales.htm, $60 US; Credit Cards; 800-253-9646, fax 212-963-3489; *Fr* ◆ Each issue gives you a closer look at economic and social statistics from more than 200 countries and territories, as well as providing quarterly statistics on industrial production. Written in French and English, each issue details over 70 subjects such as population, food, trade, production, finance and national income; it also presents special monthly features on topics including fuel imports, industrial output, world shipbuilding and civil aviation traffic. "MBS" is published in association with the Department for Economic and Social Information and Policy Analysis (DESIPA). Annual subscription to the "MBS" includes access to "MBS On-line". [ID:2520]

The Oxfam Poverty Report 📖

1995, Kevin Watkins, OXFAM UK, 240 pages ➤ Renouf Publishing Co. Ltd., Unit 1, 5369 Canotek Road, Ottawa, ON K1J 9J3, Canada, www.renoufbooks.com, $31.50 CDN; Credit Cards; 888-767-6766, fax 613-745-7660 ◆ Draws on Oxfam's experience of working in over 70 countries to examine the causes of poverty and conflict. It identifies the structural forces that deny people their basic rights through case studies from Africa, Asia and Latin America. [ID:2151]

Talking With Youth About War and Crisis 🖥

2001, 2 pages ➤ Office of Overseas Schools (A/OS), US Department of State: Office of Overseas Schools, Room H328, SA-1, Washington, DC 20522-0132, USA, www.state.gov/m/a/os, Free on-line; 202-261-8200, fax 202-261-8224, OverseasSchools@state.gov ◆ Working overseas with children can involve the risk of immediate exposure to trauma or second-hand trauma in a post-conflict zone. The impact of this on the lives of children can be significant. These resources are intended to serve as a guideline for communicating with and helping children through the stresses of living overseas in an environment less stable than home. A must for families stationed in post-conflict zones. From the Office of Overseas Schools Web page, access these resources using the "Additional Information" index to the right. [ID:2515]

UN Cyberschoolbus 🖥

www.cyberschoolbus.un.org/infonation/index.asp ◆ This fantastic and interesting Web site is part of the UN Global Teaching and Learning Project. Want to know the population of El Salvador? Better yet, want to know how its economy compares with others in Central America? This site allows you to select up to seven countries and then compare geographic, economic, population and social indicator data for each country. A reliable and quick source of information about your dream destination in an easy to use format. Great for teachers and students alike! [ID:2653]

Unicef's Teaching-Learning Resources Catalogue 🖥

Semi-annual ➤ UNICEF Ontario, Suite 1100, 2200 Yonge Street, Toronto, ON M4S 2C6, Canada, www.unicef.ca, Free on-line; Credit Cards; 416-487-4153, fax 416-487-8875 ◆ This catalogue contains teacher resources renowned for their quality and positive, age-appropriate approach to increasing children's awareness of global issues of interdependence, diversity, children's rights, global citizenship and conflict resolution. From the home page, navigate to "Global Schoolhouse" and then to the "Education and Development" PDF Catalogue. [ID:2560]

World Concerns and the United Nations: Model Teaching
Units for Primary, Secondary and Teacher Education 📖

192 pages ➤ United Nations Publications, Sales and Marketing Section, Room DC2-853, Department I004, New York, NY 10017, USA, www.un.org/Pubs/sales.htm, $19.95 US; Credit Cards; 800-253-9646, fax 212-963-3489 ◆ Provides model teaching units for primary and secondary teachers directly applicable to the classroom. In addition to dealing with the aims and activities of the United Nations and its system, the 26 model units in the collection follow a young person's development, progressing through the interests characteristic of each age. The units are particularly sensitive to youth's deep concern for justice, the environment, equal opportunities and full participation in the life of society. The book also includes reading lists and illustrations. An excellent resource for introducing your children to a new life as a UN overseas worker. [ID:2519]

The World Guide 📖

Annual, 628 pages ➤ Subscription Office, New Internationalist, Unit 17, 35 Riviera Drive, Markham, ON L3R 8N4, Canada, www.newint.org, $59.95 CDN; Credit Cards; 905-946-0407, fax 905-946-0410 ◆ Provides a wealth of information on the countries of the world from a refreshing perspective, drawing on United Nations and other mainstream data. Includes all the facts, history, political and economic analyses found in a conventional reference work, as well as information on the issues central to the lives of people in Africa, Asia, the Middle East, Latin America and the Caribbean. Global reports on global issues like HIV, terrorism and up-to-date statistics on literacy, health and public expenditure. An excellent source of country-specific information when researching your future posting overseas! [ID:2127]

The World in Your Kitchen 📖

1994, 176 pages ➤ Subscription Office, New Internationalist, Unit 17, 35 Riviera Drive, Markham, ON L3R 8N4, Canada, www.newint.org, £10.99; Credit Cards; 905-946-0407, fax 905-946-0410 ◆ This book is listed because of our belief that vegetarian diets are far less draining of the world's resources than non-vegetarian ones. Many global education programs recognize the value of vegetarianism. You might just find yourself deployed to a meatless culture, so eating meatless is a valuable and enriching skill to learn beforehand! Check it out! [ID:2126]

SOCIAL ACTION & ACTIVISM

These resources are for people who want to be on the front lines of social change in this small world of ours.

Apex Press Catalogue 📖 💻 ⛪

Annual ➤ Council on International and Public Affairs, Apex Press, P.O. Box 337, Croton-on-Hudson, NY 10520, USA, www.cipa-apex.org, Credit Cards; 800-316-2739, fax 800-316-2739 ◆ The catalogue for this specialized distributor of books on human rights, grassroots activism, sustainable development, peace and security, Third World politics, social change, and international education is now available on the distributor's Web site. [ID:2123]

Connexions Online 💻

www.connexions.org, Free on-line ◆ Connexions Online is produced by a non-profit organization working to connect individuals and organizations working for social change with each other, with information and ideas, and with the general public. The on-line directory lists and profiles thousands of organizations concerned with social justice and environmental alternatives, democratization, economic justice and the creation and preservation of community. Search by full or partial name or search organizations by subject. [ID:2036]

Cultural Survival 📖 💻

Quarterly ➤ Cultural Survival Inc., 215 Prospect Street, Cambridge, MA 02139, USA, www.cs.org, $14.97 US/issue; VISA; 617-441-5400, fax 617-441-5417 ◆ Since 1972 Cultural Survival has helped indigenous peoples and ethnic minorities deal as equals with Western society. Cultural Survival is dedicated to maintaining the world's cultural diversity by developing new strategies for responding directly to the critical needs of the world's indigenous populations. This Web site is a great resource because of its links to similar international organizations working with indigenous peoples. If this is your area of interest, start your overseas job search here! "Cultural Survival Quarterly" is a magazine that features articles on indigenous peoples worldwide. Before you run out and buy the magazine, check the Web site: the articles are available on-line. [ID:2140]

Directory of Social Movements 💻

World Forum for Alternatives (WFA), www.alternatives.ca/en ◆ Throughout the world, engaged citizens are meeting and mobilizing to promote human rights and social justice while reinforcing their opposition to commercialization, social regression, and economic and military aggression. Social movements are organizing in international and trans-thematic coalitions for maximum impact and greater power. The "Social Movements" directory is a World Forum for Alternatives (WFA) on-line initiative to make known, or improve knowledge of, these new global actors. It includes social movement profiles and analysis articles. A great resource for those wishing to work for social activist organizations. [ID:2784]

Fundraising for Social Change 📖

2000, Kim Klein, 416 pages ➤ Jossey Bass / John Wiley and Sons, Chardon Press, 10475 Crosspoint Blvd., Indianapolis, IN 46256, USA, www.chardonpress.com, $35 US; Credit Cards; 877-762-2974, fax 800-597-3299, consumers@wiley.com ◆ The nuts-and-bolts strategies all non-profit groups need to understand how to raise money. Learn how to motivate your board of directors; use direct mail techniques; plan and implement major gift campaigns, endowments and planned giving programs; and more. [ID:2033]

How to Change the World: Social Entrepreneurs and the Power of New Ideas 📖

2004, 320 pages ➤ Oxford University Press, 198 Madison Ave., New York, NY 10016, USA, www.oxfordonline.com, $39.95 US; 800-334-4249 ext. 6484, fax 212-726-6476 ◆ This US book is a collection of extraordinary stories about extraordinary people that highlights a massive transformation that is going largely unreported by the media: around the world, the fastest-growing segment of society is the non-profit sector, as millions of ordinary people—social entrepreneurs—are increasingly stepping in to solve problems where governments and bureaucracies have failed.

"How to Change the World" shows, as its title suggests, that with determination and innovation, even a single person can make a surprising difference. For anyone seeking to make a positive mark on the world, this will be both an inspiring read and an invaluable handbook! [ID:2793]

How to Lobby at Intergovernmental Meetings 📖
2004, Felix Dodds, Michael Strauss ➤ Stakeholder Forum, 7 Holyrood Street, London, SE1 2EL, UK, www.stakeholderforum.org, £15.95; Credit Cards; (44) (0) 20-7089-4306, fax (44) (0) 20 7089 4310 ◆ Organizations spend considerable resources taking staff to international meetings, often without understanding how these meetings work. "How to Lobby at Intergovernmental Meetings" is a unique guide on how to participate and be heard at intergovernmental meetings, whether as a stakeholder or a government official. This UK book is based on 10 years of lobbying at the international level and provides detailed advice on the preparation and presentation of ideas, the consultation and negotiating process and practical and logistical matters. Contains a wealth of essential reference material including tips for navigating the intergovernmental hot spots of New York and Geneva, lists of UN Commissions, conferences and permanent missions, contact details of key international organizations, NGOs and stakeholder groups and useful Web addresses. If you have never lobbied or just want to have a better understanding of how the intergovernmental governance process works, this book is the essential resource to make your work much easier. Recommended. [ID:2783]

How We Work for Peace 📖
1988, Christine Perringer, 446 pages ➤ Peace Research Institute, 25 Dundana Ave., Dundas, ON L9H 4E5, Canada, www.prid.on.ca, $15 CDN; 905-628-2356, fax 905-628-1830, newcombe-prid@hwcn.org ◆ Readable, offers ideas, advice and motivation. Somewhat dated, but still essential reading for peace activists or anyone wishing to get involved in the peace movement. Excellent material on working in groups, reaching the unconverted, peace activities and campaigns. [ID:2066]

International Human Rights Resources 💻
www.law.csuohio.edu/lawlibrary/international.html ◆ Links to legal resources relating to human rights and international law. [ID:2226]

Managing and Leading in the Non-Profit Sector 📖
Annual ➤ Sequus International, 381 Churchill Drive, Winnipeg, MB R3L 1W1, Canada, www.sequus.org, $100 CDN; Credit Cards; 204-992-2410, fax 204-478-5390, btrump@infobahn.mb.ca ◆ This three-ring binder is a manual for Sequus's workshops on managing a non-profit organization. If you can't afford to attend the seminars in person, this great resource might be a little easier on the job seeker's pocketbook. Some of the topics covered are as follows: strategic planning, managing and evaluating programs and projects, working with volunteers and boards, writing proposals, fundraising, marketing, as well as financial, change, time and stress management. [ID:2534]

The New Internationalist 📖
Monthly ➤ Subscription Office, New Internationalist, Unit 17, 35 Riviera Drive, Markham, ON L3R 8N4, Canada, www.newint.org, $44/year; Credit Cards; 905-946-0407, fax 905-946-0410 ◆ The magazine reports on issues of world poverty and inequality and seeks to focus attention on the unjust relationship between the powerful and the powerless in both rich and poor nations. Acts as an insightful forum for debate and campaigns for global change so that the basic material and spiritual needs of all humans can be met. A great alternative to mainstream coverage of the international issues often encountered when living and working overseas. (For more information, see their ad in the sponsor section at the end of this guide.) [ID:2060]

Raise More Money: The Best of the Grassroots Fundraising Journal 📖
2001, Kim Klein, 208 pages ➤ Jossey Bass / John Wiley and Sons, Chardon Press, 10475 Crosspoint Blvd., Indianapolis, IN 46256, USA, www.chardonpress.com, $29 US; Credit Cards; 877-762-2974, fax 800-597-3299, consumers@wiley.com ◆ A collection of the best articles from past 20 years of the "Grassroots Fundraising Journal" offering non-profit organizations a wealth of

tips, strategies and guidance on how to raise money. Part of a series which focuses on providing fundraising and organizational development tools for community-based and social change organizations. [ID:2478]

Selling Social Change (Without Selling Out):
Earned Income Strategies for Nonprofits 📖
2002, Andy Robinson, 256 pages ➤ Jossey Bass / John Wiley and Sons, Chardon Press, 10475 Crosspoint Blvd., Indianapolis, IN 46256, USA, www.chardonpress.com, $25.95 US; Credit Cards; 877-762-2974, fax 800-597-3299, consumers@wiley.com ◆ Want to start your own NGO? Or improve your marketability among not-for-profit organizations? Then this book is for you. An expert fundraiser explains how to initiate and sustain successful earned income ventures that provide financial security and advance an organization's mission. Step by step, this resource shows how to organize a team, select a venture, draft a business plan, find start-up funding and successfully market goods and services. Includes tax implications of earned income and pros and cons of corporate partnerships. A great primer for the ins and outs of fickle NGO finances. [ID:2479]

Youth Action Network ⛊
Youth Action Network, Suite 307, 176 John Street, Toronto, ON M5T 1X5, Canada, www.youthactionnetwork.org, 416-368-2277, fax 416-368-8354; 𝓕𝓻 ◆ Youth Action Network (YAN) is a fully independent non-profit organization committed to bettering our world. This means YAN confronts such issues as human rights, world peace, the environment and international development. Youth Action Network believes in the ability of youth to effect constructive change. The group understands the need for a stronger youth voice and for greater youth participation in local and global communities. The Network publishes the "Youth Action Forum" which is distributed across Canada. Youth Action Network also maintains a Resource Action Centre and sponsors Youth Week. [ID:2752]

CHAPTER 31
International Law Careers

Public international law (PIL) is one of the fastest growing areas of law in the world. Specially created international criminal courts dealing with the armed conflicts in Sierra Leone, the former Yugoslavia and Rwanda continue to actively recruit experienced lawyers to prosecute the world's most heinous crimes. Lawyers representing non-governmental organizations are busy lobbying governments to ratify the Kyoto Accord. Even corporations are getting into the act, pressuring governments to conclude international trade agreements that will give them rights to sue foreign governments that make it too difficult to extract profits from their investments. There are 61 profiles at the end of this chapter to help you launch your international law career.

HOW THIS CHAPTER IS ORGANIZED

The first half of the chapter explains what public international law (PIL) is and provides information you'll need to know to get a job in that field of law. Topics include a description of PIL, where to study it, career strategies for students and recent graduates and who is hiring PIL lawyers.

The second section of the chapter provides information to law students and lawyers who are interested in working for private sector law firms. It contains information about how to get into a firm that has a PIL practice group, as well as information on how you can find work with an overseas law firm.

The third section of the chapter is an extended profile of Canada's DEPARTMENT OF JUSTICE. The DOJ employs the bulk of Canada's public international law practitioners. The profile includes an overview of the legal sections that practice PIL and provides advice on how to get your foot in the door.

In the final section of this chapter, there are two distinct lists of profiles. The first is a list of 6 law schools teaching PIL in Canada. The second set of profiles lists an assortment of 55 organizations that hire PIL practitioners. This list includes organizations that span the public and private sectors and the globe. It includes US human rights organizations, Canadian and US law firms and intergovernmental organizations (IGOs). Remember, though, that almost all organizations need lawyers. So explore all the organizations contained in THE BIG GUIDE.

WHAT IS PUBLIC INTERNATIONAL LAW (PIL)?

Despite being the world's oldest legal system, many people do not understand that international law is mainly public international law. The managing partner of one of England's "magic circle" law firm's PIL groups had this to say about his encounter with Canadian lawyers:

> *"When I travelled to Canada to work on an oil concession agreement that was being negotiated with an African country's government, I was surprised to encounter so many lawyers that, like me, were international lawyers. As I prodded them on their international legal work I came to realize that these lawyers simply styled themselves 'international' lawyers because they worked on multi-jurisdictional transactions. These lawyers failed to recognize that public international law is an entirely independent legal system."*

International law is not just about domestic jurisdictions; it is mainly about public international law—an entirely distinct legal regime, the rules of which are derived from international treaties, customary law and general principles of international law.

A true "international lawyer" works on issues involving PIL. Traditionally, the overwhelming majority of PIL lawyers worked for governments and concerned themselves with the legal relations that existed between states, which for centuries were collectively the only facet of PIL.

Over the last 50 years, and especially the last 10, this situation has changed greatly and the line separating private and public law has been broken down. In today's global marketplace, there is an ever-growing demand by NGOs, IGOs and governments for international lawyers; that is, lawyers who are trained and can navigate the distinct legal regime of public international law.

The growth of PIL has also led the world's largest law firms to introduce PIL practice groups that provide specialized legal services to multinational corporations (MNCs) that are increasingly being accorded rights under PIL through government endorsed trade agreements and bilateral investment treaties (BITs).

Why Practice PIL?

Public international law is a fascinating field that, in many respects, both underpins and responds to the challenges posed by globalization. What attracts so many people to PIL is its close connection to international public policy. Should water be privatized? Can states attack others pre-emptively? How do we protect migratory birds? These are the types of important public policy issues that international lawyers must broach.

The result is that the competition among lawyers to practice PIL outstrips the number of jobs available. If you want one of these coveted jobs—whether it's with an NGO or a corporate law firm—you'll have to distinguish yourself from your legal colleagues. You will need to begin early in your academic training and may also have to spend several years building experience and knowledge after graduation before you can begin your career as an international lawyer.

PRACTICE AREAS GOVERNED BY PIL

The following list is meant to provide you with a sampling of the types of issues that fall under the purview of public international law (PIL). Remember that it is not exhaustive and you can be rest assured that if you name any international issue it is in some way affected by PIL. (For more information about the types of practice areas in PIL, see the Resources at the end of this chapter.)

International Economic Law (IEL)

International economic law refers to the international laws, regulations and institutional frameworks that underpin the international economic system. This is a rapidly expanding area of law that encompasses everything from the laws regulating the Bretton Woods institutions, international monetary law, investment guarantees against non-commercial risk and the laws of the WORLD TRADE ORGANIZATION (WTO) to the international regulation of debt and intellectual property rights.

International Trade and Investment Law

International trade and investment law falls under the broader category of IEL and includes the laws that regulate foreign investments and the international movement of goods and services. This is perhaps the most identifiable area of PIL because it includes the well-known international agreements that comprise WTO law and regional trade agreements like the North American Free Trade Agreement and the European Union. The European Energy Charter is an example of a sectoral agreement that falls under this category. There are also now more than 2,000 bilateral investment treaties (BITs) that accomplish the goals of the stillborn Multilateral Agreement on Investment.

International Commercial Arbitration

The business community prefers to settle disputes through arbitration. In the age of globalization, specialized lawyers have emerged who concern themselves with the rules of international arbitral bodies and the enforcement of arbitral decisions in domestic courts. For instance, most BITs allow MNCs to sue sovereign states in international arbitral bodies, especially the INTERNATIONAL CENTRE FOR THE SETTLEMENT OF INTERNATIONAL DISPUTES (ICSID). These arbitrations usually result from major infrastructure projects, problems arising from foreign investments and problems involving large telecommunications companies. The most prominent international arbitral body is the IRAN–UNITED STATES CLAIMS TRIBUNAL. The explosion of BITs dictate that this is an area of law that will be growing in leaps and bounds over the next decade.

International Criminal Law

On July 1, 2002, the INTERNATIONAL CRIMINAL COURT (ICC) officially began its operations, thereby becoming the world's first permanent international criminal court with jurisdiction over crimes against humanity, war crimes, genocide and, once a definition is agreed upon, the crime of aggression. The ICC is distinct from the international criminal tribunals that have jurisdiction over international crimes committed in the armed conflicts in the former Yugoslavia, Rwanda and Sierra Leone. The domestic implementation of the Rome Statute of the ICC means that this is an area of law that is also growing at the domestic level.

International Refugee Law

International refugee law is also, unfortunately, a growing area of law that deals with the approximately 11 million individuals who have been forced to flee their home countries. The large number of refugees poses a grave problem to states throughout the world, which are increasingly shirking their international legal obligation to provide these dispossessed people the protection and care they require. International refugee law revolves around the 1951 Geneva Convention Relating to the Status of Refugees that sets out the rights of refugees and the standards of treatment for countries that receive them. A related legal issue involves the international community's responsibilities toward internally displaced persons.

International Human Rights Law

International human rights law is concerned primarily with how human rights can be enforced within the international system. This is a very broad category of law that deals with literally hundreds of international human rights agreements encompassing the full spectrum of human rights—civil, political, economic, cultural and social. The European Court of Human Rights is the best example of a forum through which international human rights law is practiced. This broad field of law overlaps to some degree with virtually every practice area that falls under PIL.

International Environmental Law

International environmental law is practiced by a small but very committed number of lawyers, particularly in Europe. This area of law deals with numerous issues such as biodiversity and marine resources, climate change and sustainable development. The Convention on Biological Diversity and the United Nations Framework Convention on Climate Change and its Kyoto Protocol are examples of the type of international agreements that the community of nations has consented to over the past decade that fall into this area of law.

Laws of the Use of Force

The 2003 war in Iraq put the *jus ad bellum* (or laws of the use of force) at the centre of the international community's agenda. These are the laws that are designed to prevent states from going to war.

International Humanitarian Law (IHL)

Once in war, states are bound by the *jus in bello* (or justice in war), the laws of armed conflict or international humanitarian law (IHL). These laws are intended to humanize warfare. In particular, IHL prohibits the use of illegal weapons and seeks to protect civilians and captured or wounded combatants. The Ottawa Convention that prohibits anti-personnel mines as a legitimate weapon is an example of the type of agreement that constitutes part of IHL. The INTERNATIONAL COMMITTEE OF THE RED CROSS is known as the promoter and guardian of IHL.

CHOOSING THE RIGHT LAW SCHOOL

In law, the name of your school matters. In seven of the last eight years, the UNIVERSITY OF VICTORIA has been ranked as the best law school in Canada by *Canadian Lawyer* magazine. Despite this, if you want an international career, you are much better off going to a law school that has instant name recognition. In Canada this limits your options, as only MCGILL UNIVERSITY is instantly recognized throughout the world. The world's premier law firms in New York have been recruiting MCGILL students for years and only a small number of the elite firms have recently begun to include the UNIVERSITY OF TORONTO and YORK UNIVERSITY'S OSGOODE HALL in the recruitment trips they carry out every fall. If you aren't interested in corporate law, the choice of your law school doesn't matter as much, but don't underestimate the importance that people continue to attach to the international reputation of your school.

After considering the issue of name recognition, your focus should be on finding the law school that has the best PIL program. The first thing you should do is to simply look at how many PIL and comparative law courses the faculty offers. The array of course offerings range from just a few basic PIL courses to well over 20 relevant courses. Obviously, the more international and comparative law courses you can take, the better.

A course is often only as good as the professor teaching it, so your next step should be checking out the credentials of the PIL professors. Look at whether they are published in reputable legal journals—check out their professional backgrounds, too. For instance, the UNIVERSITY OF OTTAWA'S LAW FACULTY not only has many well-regarded, full-time professors, but also has seasoned PIL practitioners from FOREIGN AFFAIRS CANADA (FAC) teaching courses. You should also speak directly to students and ask how they would rate their PIL instructors. More than a few students have found that some highly regarded professors are often the worst teachers because they have little time or regard for their students.

Finally, take a look at all of the non-academic opportunities the law school offers that will enhance your international legal education. Most schools offer a variety of opportunities for students to gain international experience through internships, exchanges or summer programs. Increasingly, schools are also offering interesting joint degree programs. MCGILL and the UNIVERSITY OF OTTAWA, for instance, offer students the opportunity to gain degrees in both the common and civil law. This unique comparative legal education is highly advantageous to anyone who wants to practice overseas. Now, many schools have specialized programs on human rights or refugee law, also valuable for an international career.

Unfortunately, another issue that should factor into your decision when choosing a law school is the cost of tuition. This especially concerns law schools in Ontario that have been deregulated and are free to charge any tuition they want. Tuitions for Ontario law schools have skyrocketed and now average roughly $12,000, with the UNIVERSITY OF TORONTO leading the way and planning to raise its tuition incrementally to an astronomical sum (by Canadian standards) of $22,000 a year.

This poses no problem if you plan on working in corporate law, but has major repercussions if you want to work in the public interest. The deregulation of Ontario's legal education essentially requires all but the privileged to begin their careers practicing corporate law. Any ideas of using your legal skills in the public interest will have to be put on hold until you can get your substantial debt load under control. The added pressure of working for a corporate law firm also makes it much harder to gain international experience over your summers. Instead of possibly working overseas or for an NGO, you'll more likely have to spend your summers doing due diligence.

Profiles of Law Schools Teaching PIL in Canada

To help get you started in choosing a law school, we have considered many of the issues discussed above and compiled a list of six of Canada's top PIL programs. See Profiles of Law Schools Teaching PIL in Canada immediately after the Resources section at the end of this chapter.

CAREER STRATEGIES FOR LAW STUDENTS

So you've beaten out several thousand other applicants for a coveted spot in a law school and are determined to become a human rights lawyer. If this sounds familiar, it's because you're not alone. According to an associate dean at a major Canadian law school, over 90 per cent of law students write in their application package that they want to go to law school because they are committed to protecting human rights. Don't worry though; you won't have to beat out all of your colleagues for the few human rights jobs out there, as over 90 per cent of law graduates go directly to corporate law firms.

The other 10 per cent are destined for what in legal terms is considered an "alternative career." If you want to work in the field of PIL, you fall into this amorphous category. One of the reasons this is considered an alternative career is because there are few entry-level jobs in the field. So, if you're serious about becoming an international human rights or international environmental lawyer, you'll have to take steps to distinguish yourself in the highly competitive legal job market.

The first thing you should do as soon as you enter law school is make an appointment with your school's career development officer. This person's job is to give you advice about the exact experience and education you'll need to succeed. They should also be able to help you chart out a career plan.

After charting out a loose career plan, you can concentrate on building your knowledge of international law. Here are some suggestions that will help you succeed:

- **Get published.** The way to cement your reputation in PIL is to have as many publications under your name as possible. One trick is to start modestly. Look for 1 of the more than 50 US student-edited international law journals and submit a piece for publication. Ask your professors for guidance on the type of small-case commentary that these journals usually accept from students.
- **Spend a semester at another Canadian university.** Curricula at various Canadian law schools can vary greatly. Spending a semester at another law school is a great way to access new international and comparative law courses and to study under

different professors. This is an especially important option if you're at a smaller school that doesn't offer an abundance of PIL courses.

- **Work on the editorial staff of a law journal.** Most schools have student-run law journals. Working on the editorial staff helps sharpen your writing skills, while increasing your legal knowledge. Moreover, (although this is not as important in Canada) in the US, working on the editorial staff of a law journal is considered a prestigious position that legal employers look favourably upon.

- **Get your BCL degree.** A bachelor of civil law (BCL) is valuable since most of the world's countries are governed by civil law. As a result, if you can get both an LLB and a BCL and you will have a definite advantage in getting international legal jobs. In Canada, MCGILL UNIVERSITY and the UNIVERSITY OF OTTAWA allow students to obtain both degrees.

- **Become a joiner.** The one piece of advice that all experienced PIL practitioners give is for students to join as many internationally focused legal clubs or associations as possible. PIL is a dynamic area of law and belonging to clubs or associations will allow you to keep on top of developments and provide you with a forum to network with other interested students and professionals. If your school doesn't have an international law society, you should start one. The Web also offers you the chance to join on-line listservs and discussion groups.

- **Participate in international law moots.** Canadian schools regularly perform very well in international moots. These are great avenues to hone incipient legal skills and demonstrate that you have the tools to succeed. They are also a nice distraction from the regular grind of law school. The most prestigious of the international moots is the Jessup Moot Court Competition.

- **Work closely with a PIL professor.** One of the best ways to increase your legal knowledge is to write a paper for credit or do legal research for a PIL professor. This will not only improve your legal skills, but will allow you to form a personal relationship with a professor. This is invaluable, because you'll need letters of reference for every legal internship or job you apply to. There is nothing more awkward than having to call up a professor for a letter of reference and beginning with, *"You might not remember me, but I was in your international trade class two years ago..."*

- **Attend international law conferences.** There are numerous conferences that focus on PIL issues. Attending these conferences is a great way for you to increase your knowledge of the law while networking with students, practitioners and professors. Don't miss the CANADIAN COUNCIL OF INTERNATIONAL LAW's annual conference, which draws Canada's and some of the world's most eminent international legal minds. The conference schedule also includes a student job fair and forum.

- **Volunteer.** Spending an afternoon a week volunteering for an NGO will build your professional experience and allow you to see the type of legal work carried out by NGOs. The UN, IGOs, NGOs and the government seek to hire people who have a demonstrated commitment to working in the public interest.

- **Improve your French.** Your chances of getting a job with an IGO or NGO will be substantially improved if you are bilingual.

• **Read Parts One and Two of THE BIG GUIDE.** The advice given throughout THE BIG GUIDE TO LIVING AND WORKING OVERSEAS applies to law students as well as other students building international careers. The more international exposure you can gain as a student, whether it is through travel, study, language training or volunteer work, will help you in your international legal job search.

WHAT TO DO OVER THE SUMMER?

Employers want to hire individuals who already have legal skills and experience. You'll gain some of this experience in law school, particularly if you participate in moot competitions, but your greatest opportunity to gain legal experience comes over the summer. If you're interested in a career in PIL, the summer is also a time to gain overseas experience. Getting the right summer job could be the catalyst in putting you ahead of the hundreds of people who will typically apply for each available law position. This is especially important in today's legal job market, which legal recruiters indicate is the worst in over 50 years.

As it is for most law students, you'll have two summers to build up your legal experience before applying for articling positions. Of these, the second summer is crucial, because if you want to work for a corporate law firm, it is increasingly required that you spend a summer with one. This allows the law firm to make sure you fit into its culture. Even if you are hesitant to work for a corporate law firm, you should at least consider it, because the larger firms do offer excellent training and, perhaps more importantly, they offer articling positions, which are very difficult to find elsewhere. The very high salaries paid by law firms will also enable you to pay off some of your debt—this will help to free you up to explore international opportunities.

If you are interested in working in articling with a corporate law firm, you'll accordingly have to gain PIL or overseas experience over your first summer. Begin your search early, as most law jobs and internships are usually awarded at least six months before their start date.

In the following section I explain some of the places you can work over the summer and the chances of gaining PIL experience at each.

Corporate Law Firms

No matter what your long-term goals, working for a law firm over the summer is not a bad idea. You'll gain legal experience working under seasoned lawyers. Your summer job will probably also lead to an articling position. The exorbitant tuition prices being charged at Ontario law schools might also require you to spend time at a corporate law firm where you can earn as much as $1,300 a week in Toronto or $2,400 US a week in New York. You'll earn considerably less in other cities, but it'll be more than you can earn anywhere else.

The great drawback to working in law firms is that you likely won't gain any international experience and you won't work on PIL issues. If you look around, you can find a few law firms that will pay for you to complete internships overseas or offer you the opportunity to spend some time in an overseas office. Keep in mind though that these are simply incentives to attract top students who will be expected to become corporate lawyers.

NGOs

There aren't very many NGOs in Canada that focus on international law issues. Moreover, most NGOs consider only their current volunteers for summer positions. As a result, if you want to work for an NGO over the summer, you should identify the organization early in the school year and volunteer throughout the year. The level of direct legal experience you'll gain working for an NGO varies greatly. Even if you don't gain a lot of legal experience, it will demonstrate your commitment to working in the public interest. Most summer positions for NGOs are government funded and offer a reasonable salary.

Government

The government is a great place to toil over the summer, because you'll be able to work on international issues under experienced lawyers. If you're interested, you should contact departments directly. Make sure you do this early in the fall. For more information, see the detailed profile of the DEPARTMENT OF JUSTICE CANADA below.

International Summer Abroad Law Programs

There are at least 100 law programs located throughout the world where you can take courses for credits over the summer—they are normally 3- to 6-week sessions. Many of these are specialized programs that focus on international or comparative legal issues. The credits you earn at these courses are transferable and will be counted toward your degree.

Summer-abroad programs are rather pricey, but they do give you the opportunity to gain international experience and, in some cases, to study under some very impressive professors and practitioners. At the same time, you should be cautious about which program you attend, as some are nothing more than glorified summer vacations and, if you're serious about your education, you could be disappointed if you don't choose carefully. You can avoid disappointment by getting the contact info of former participants and asking your professors if they know of reputable programs.

THE HAGUE ACADEMY OF INTERNATIONAL LAW offers one of the best summer programs around—it is the Rosetta stone for comparing other programs.

IGO Internships

Most intergovernmental organizations (IGOs), including the UN, have summer internships that will allow you to gain invaluable international legal experience. This is an especially good option if you've identified a particular area of law in which you'd like to practice. Becoming a known quantity with a particular office of an IGO could lead to future employment.

The drawback to most, but not all, summer IGO internships is that they're unpaid. The financial burden is somewhat softened since most law schools will allow you to receive credits for your completed internship. Don't be fooled though, just because these internships are unpaid does not mean that they aren't competitive. Every year, hundreds of students apply for these positions, which should give you an idea of just how valuable they can be to your career.

CAREER STRATEGIES AFTER GRADUATION

Your long-term career goals, debt load, interests, age and any other number of factors will all enter into your decision on what you'll do after completing law school. If you're like most law students, your next step will be to complete your articling year that will qualify you as a lawyer. Where you'll article is a major decision that you've likely pondered well before completing your studies.

For most law students, the only articling-related decision is where to complete their articles. A number of you may even be undecided as to whether to article or not. My advice to those of you who are sitting on the fence is to bite the bullet and article immediately after finishing your law degrees. Why? Well, here are five reasons:

- Qualifying as a lawyer will open up numerous career options that would otherwise not be open to you.

- You might have absolutely no interest in practicing law now, but in 20 years you might realize that you would like to qualify as a lawyer, at which point passing the bar will be much more difficult. Put otherwise, do you really want to relearn property law?

- Pay scales for lawyers are often determined by the year they're called to the bar.

- Law firms expect you to apply for articling positions after second year and usually after working for them as a summer student. Law graduates don't fit into the law firm's recruitment schedule and it'll be much more difficult for you to find an articling position after you've graduated.

- In Europe, lawyers usually qualify by passing an exam following law school, much as medical students do in North America. If you've gone to law school, but aren't a lawyer, Europeans will often assume you've failed one of these relatively easy qualifying exams. The concept of someone who went to law school but is not a lawyer does not impress overseas.

If the thought of articling is simply too much, then you can also consider writing the bar exam in New York. If you pass, you are a lawyer.

If you don't want to article right away, there are still a few options open to you to enhance your PIL experience. The two best options, along with some general advice on articling, are explained below.

Articling

The vast majority of articling positions are with law firms, especially corporate law firms. As has been mentioned, if you are interested in articling with a firm, it is increasingly a requirement that you work as a summer student for that firm.

If you're not interested in articling with a firm, your choices are greatly limited. The government offers some excellent opportunities, but they are quite limited and very competitive due to the interesting nature of the work and the desire that many have to work in the public interest. If these options aren't available or attractive, you'll have to be creative and search out other articling opportunities. For help on finding these positions, consult your career development officer and attend the alternative career day at your faculty. You can also try contacting NGOs and other organizations to try and arrange your own articles.

An interesting option that is open to articling students of certain jurisdictions is to complete part of your articles overseas. In Ontario, for instance, an articling student can complete up to six months of his or her nine-and-a-half month articling term overseas. This offers students an excellent opportunity to gain invaluable international legal experience.

International Internships

Unless you had some excellent previous experience, your chances of walking into a job out of law school and practicing PIL are very slim. Getting your foot in the door, however, is relatively easy thanks to the Canadian government and its excellent international internship programs. (These internship programs are described in the profile, Canadian Government Internship Programs, in Chapter 17, Internships Abroad.)

The value of these internships for aspiring or young lawyers is that they will allow you to get a start at an international organization or to gain direct international legal experience working at the grassroots level. For example, CANADEM and the ATLANTIC COUNCIL both offer excellent internship opportunities with large international organizations, including the INTERNATIONAL CRIMINAL COURT, the SPECIAL COURT FOR SIERRA LEONE and several other IGOs where the interns carry out legal work. At the end of the other spectrum, the NATIVE LAW CENTRE and the CANADIAN BAR ASSOCIATION are among the Canadian organizations that place law graduates and young lawyers with local organizations in the developing world. Often these positions provide much-needed legal aid to local communities. As mentioned, these internships can sometimes be used to fulfill up to six months of your articling term. (For a first-hand account of one young Canadian lawyer's experience with the SPECIAL COURT FOR SIERRA LEONE, see James Pickard's article, "Launching an International Law Career" in Appendix 31a on the CD-ROM.)

Master of Laws

A Master of Laws (LLM) is a one-year program that will allow you to focus on a particular area of law. There are some excellent LLM programs that focus on PIL issues. Taking one of these specialized international law programs will enhance your credentials as a legal specialist and demonstrate to prospective employees that you are committed to a particular area of law and possess the capability to work in an intellectually demanding field of law.

An LLM is a prerequisite for anyone interested in a career in academia and increasingly for anyone wanting to work as a PIL practitioner with an IGO or an NGO. If you want to work for a law firm, an LLM is not necessary, although most elite PIL lawyers do have, at least, an LLM and many are also highly regarded professors.

It might seem like a bit of overkill to complete yet another degree, but while a law degree is usually a student's second or third degree in North America, in Europe it is usually the first. In some jurisdictions, like England for instance, students can also take a non-legal undergrad and then simply complete a one-year legal conversion course to qualify as a lawyer. As a result, most jobs in Europe will require at least an LLM.

There are a number of factors to consider when choosing an LLM program. First of all, no matter how good your school is, you should try to complete your LLM at another one. This will expose you to new professors and allow you to experience living in a different city and, likely, another country. Second, if you're interested in a particular area of law, look for a relevant program that will allow you to explore your area of interest. If this isn't helpful, simply seek out the best professors in your field of interest. In the end, the professors are the barometer for ranking LLM programs. Finally, look for programs in leading international legal centres such as London, New York, Geneva and The Hague. Living in these cities will allow you to immerse yourself in legal communities that aren't available in Canada.

CAMBRIDGE, the NEW YORK UNIVERSITY SCHOOL OF LAW, YALE and the UNIVERSITY OF LONDON stand out as institutions that offer exceptional LLM programs taught by leading academics and practitioners.

WHO'S HIRING PIL LAWYERS?

The increasing use of PIL to regulate everything from international commerce to the environment means that many of the 3,100 organizations profiled in THE BIG GUIDE TO LIVING AND WORKING OVERSEAS will employ lawyers whose work will involve aspects of PIL. In this section I'll explain the types of legal training and experience you'll need to begin a legal career involving PIL with the government, an NGO, an IGO, in academia or for a private company. (For an excellent first-hand account of one Canadian lawyer's extended career experience with IGOs, see Ken Roberts's article, "Careers in Public International Law" in Appendix 31b on the CD-ROM.)

A separate section follows that provides more detailed information for private lawyers who want to practice PIL with corporate law firms or those who are simply looking to continue their legal career overseas.

Government

Public international law was traditionally the legal regime that governed the relations of states. Over time, especially over the last decade, this has begun to change as private individuals, corporations and other entities have been accorded limited standing as subjects of international law. Despite this growth of legal subjects, PIL is still primarily the legal regime of states. As a result, if you want to practice PIL, your best bet is with the federal government. Provincial and municipal governments do hire lawyers, but generally they will not have the opportunity to delve into PIL.

In Canada, FOREIGN AFFAIRS CANADA (FAC) and INTERNATIONAL TRADE CANADA (ITCAN) alone have at least 10 legal sections employing more than 150 lawyers who practice PIL. In the US, the DEPARTMENTS OF DEFENSE and STATE are the largest employers of PIL lawyers, followed by the DEPARTMENT OF COMMERCE, which employs about 100 lawyers who work exclusively on international trade issues. Remember though, that every federal department will have a legal in-house division or a general counsel office. And as globalization takes hold, more and more government departments are delving into PIL matters. In Canada, lawyers can be found working on international boundary issues with the DEPARTMENT OF FISHERIES AND OCEANS (DFO), on the European Energy Charter at NRCAN or on international intellectual property issues at INDUSTRY CANADA. At the DEPARTMENT OF FINANCE CANADA, lawyers interpret the Articles of Agreement of the IMF, while colleagues from EXPORT DEVELOPMENT CANADA (EDC) provide Canadian businesses with legal advice about protecting their investments into emerging economies.

With government, you won't make the money you would in private practice, but you'll get the chance to work in the pubic interest and on some very interesting files. You'll also receive excellent training that will quickly be put to the test. Indeed, the greatest benefit of working for the government is the amount of responsibility that will be heaped upon you as a junior lawyer. Within a year, you can expect to be working on files that are in the headlines of the newspaper, or travelling overseas to represent your country in the negotiations of an international treaty on sustainable development. The combination of power and policy work is irresistible to lawyers who can't hide the fact that they're policy wonks.

The federal government actively recruits graduates and sometimes advertises for experienced lawyers on the home page of the DEPARTMENT OF JUSTICE CANADA. While there are no tricks to getting these jobs, do recognize that competition for them is fierce. For detailed information about the DEPARTMENT OF JUSTICE CANADA, see the profile that follows in this chapter.

Government lawyers are excellently trained and it is relatively easy to move from the government to a private practice, an NGO or an IGO.

NGOs

Non-governmental organizations are increasingly required to delve into PIL issues. Many are active lobbying governments to fulfill their international human rights obligations. Some want governments to hold corporations accountable for their actions, while others pressure governments to deregulate everything. Like in domestic politics, law is increasingly the catalyst for change in the international system.

While law is increasingly becoming a concern that all NGOs must take account of, some organizations focus extensively on international justice. HUMAN RIGHTS FIRST, AMNESTY INTERNATIONAL and HUMAN RIGHTS WATCH stand out as NGOs that place law at the centre of their work. Then there is the world's oldest NGO, the INTERNATIONAL COMMITTEE OF THE RED CROSS, a powerful promoter and defender of international humanitarian law. (See the Organization Index at the back of this book to locate profiles on each of these organizations.)

If you're a lawyer committed to using your legal training and skills in the public interest, then these are the types of organizations you're probably hoping to work with. You are not alone in having this goal. Finding work as a lawyer with an NGO, particularly one focused on international justice issues, is extremely competitive. There are very few entry-level positions and to be successful you should usually have several years of professional legal seasoning, a related LLM, international experience and a demonstrated commitment to working in the public interest.

There are a very limited number of entry-level legal positions with NGOs, but you'll have to seek them out and then beat out hundreds of other candidates. The amount of legal work you'll carry out at the entry level varies greatly. NGOs are perpetually understaffed and you'll have to perform a multitude of tasks, many of which can be mundane. If you want to succeed in this environment, leave your ego at the door.

While working for an NGO can be challenging, it can also be tremendously rewarding. Effective lobbying to change three words on legislation to provide cheaper prescription drugs to developing nations can literally help save millions of lives. Your legal skills could also be the catalyst in enabling a family of refugees to return to their home.

You'll never make the money that your old school friends working for law firms will, but the feeling of helping improve the world is reward enough for the many lawyers who forego corporate law and instead use their legal training to help bring justice and equality to disparate nations.

IGOs

Lawyers working for IGOs are generally specialists who have developed particular expertise in an area of law, often, but not always, involving aspects of PIL. Not surprisingly, the area of PIL practiced by individual IGOs usually depends upon the mandate of the organization.

As the types of law practiced by IGOs differ so greatly, there is no ideal background. A lawyer working for the IMF drafting the legislation that will be given to a developing country probably has a corporate law background and very little grounding in PIL. The international criminal tribunals seek out lawyers with criminal prosecutorial experience, and many UN agencies prize lawyers who have an understanding of public policy issues. In short, IGOs can differ greatly and the types of lawyers they need are likewise very different.

What all hold in common is that it is very challenging to find work as a lawyer with an IGO. Like NGOs, IGOs often attract individuals interested in working in the public interest. Other people are attracted by the chance to work on emerging policy issues. Then there are the benefits: the salaries with IGOs are quite competitive, paid in US dollars and often tax-free. You also don't have the pressure of working in a corporate environment, but do have the administrative support lacking with NGOs. On top of all that, you get six weeks of vacation. This helps explain why so many people are attracted to IGOs. (For two first-job stories about working with IGOs, see James Pickard's article, "Launching an International Law Career" in Appendix 31a, and Ken Roberts's article, "Careers in Public International Law" in Appendix 31b, on the CD-ROM.)

Most advertised positions with IGOs require a related LLM, several years of experience, bilingualism (usually in French and English) and direct legal experience related to the position. Most IGOs follow the guidelines of the UN, which has minimum standards for its positions that are based on qualifications and experience. P-1 is the entry-level position, but these are seldom, if ever, available. It now seems that the abundance of interns has essentially made this category redundant. As a result, most people will enter IGOs at the P-2 level. For entry at this level, you should have an advanced degree specializing in the relevant area of law and at least two years of related professional experience. The levels then advance according to experience, a P-3 requires five years of experience, a P-4 eight to twelve years, and so on.

There are very few, if any, entry-level positions and IGOs do not offer legal training programs. Most lawyers come to IGOs after having received initial training either with private firms, NGOs or their national governments. There are also positions that academics can step into.

If you're still in school or have recently graduated and you want to work for an IGO, but don't know how, or are interested in developing several years' experience, you should apply for an internship or clerkship with an IGO. All IGOs have internship programs that will allow you to gain invaluable experience. The drawback is that the vast majority are not funded, which is not a realistic option to most law graduates who are probably already carrying significant debt loads.

There is funding out there, though. For instance, a few law firms and law faculties do offer funding for summer internships. Your best bet, though—provided you are under 30 and a graduate—is to apply for a FOREIGN AFFAIRS CANADA (FAC) sponsored internship. In 2004, placements were available with the INTERNATIONAL CRIMINAL COURT (ICC), the SPECIAL COURT FOR SIERRA LEONE, the ORGANIZATION FOR SECURITY AND CO-OPERATION IN EUROPE (OSCE) and several other organizations that do significant legal work in fields, including human rights and refugee law. Often these internships lead directly to further employment. (For related advice, see Chapter 17, Internships Abroad.)

Academia

Public international law is closely intertwined with international public policy issues and attracts large numbers of academics. Moreover, because of the academic nature of this area of law, it is common for leading practitioners to double as academics. This is especially true in fields like energy law and international commercial arbitration, where publications help cement the reputations of practitioners. There is always room at law faculties for experienced practitioners who can bring first-hand knowledge of emerging trends in the profession.

Most individuals who want to become professors are interested in legal scholarship rather than practicing law. The credentials you'll require to land that first teaching position vary greatly and depend on the tier of school you're targeting. In Canada, there are roughly 20 law faculties where you could teach. This compares to the over 180 law faculties in the US that are unofficially divided into 4 tiers. At the top of the hierarchy are about 15 "national" law schools, while at the bottom, or the "4th tier," are regional schools that approach teaching as a profession, rather than as scholarship.

The credentials you'll require to become a professor vary according to the tier of school you want to teach at. For the top schools, you'll require a doctorate of law (JSD) or an LLM from a highly regarded law faculty, excellent academic credentials, service on a law review and preferably a prestigious judicial clerkship. In Canada, almost all full-time faculty have an LLM. Many regional schools in the US require only a JD (US equivalent to the LLB) and a few years of professional experience.

If you're just starting out, your best option is to aim for a position at one of the secondary tiers of schools, where you'll be able to gain teaching experience and begin publishing.

If you're considering being a professor, you should take a look at academic job boards—they will give you an idea of what is out there and the types of credentials you'll require for different schools. Applying for individual jobs offered is a possibility, but not the best avenue if you have no experience. Your best bet in finding an entry-level teaching position is to participate in the ASSOCIATION OF AMERICAN LAW SCHOOLS' (AALS) annual fall Faculty Recruitment Conference. Every year roughly 1,000 aspiring professors participate. For more information, check out www.aals.org.

Law faculties look at a variety of factors when hiring professors, but by far the one that will stand out is your publishing record. Law faculties want to hire scholars, and the only way to demonstrate your potential as a scholar is through publications. If you can publish a few articles, even small case comments, you'll be able to demonstrate that you are serious about scholarship and possess the necessary research and writing skills to succeed in academia.

There are also opportunities to teach law abroad. Many are advertised on academic job boards or you can try contacting established overseas law programs that teach in English directly. If you are a lawyer looking for a one-year adventure or would like to gain some teaching experience, you can contact smaller foreign schools and indicate your interest in teaching and, more importantly, your willingness to work for local wages. This is a great way to gain international experience while passing along much-needed legal skills.

The job market for legal academics is very fierce at the moment, but PIL is a growing area of law and many schools are actively recruiting professors in this field.

Consulting Firms

Consulting firms specializing in international rule of law and democratization are new entrants in the international legal market. Most are based in the United States and undertake contracts that are funded through USAID or the WORLD BANK. The projects they work on include legal reform, legislative and institutional strengthening, modernizing of the legal system and alternative dispute resolution training.

As is to be expected, consulting firms generally have small staffs and rely extensively upon consultants that are recruited through resume databanks that most maintain. Consultants should possess at least five years of relevant professional experience and strong cross-cultural skills.

PRIVATE LAW

This chapter has thus far been mostly concerned with explaining how to break into the field of public international law. Most lawyers, however, work on private law issues and for private law firms or as in-house counsel for private sector companies. This section is meant for these private lawyers who would like simply to continue practicing the same type of law, just overseas. It also offers advice to corporate lawyers who are interested in working for a firm on PIL issues.

The section begins by offering law students advice about the steps they will have to take to successfully land a job with a well-respected corporate law firm.

Private Firms and Career Planning in Law School

Only the world's elite law firms have PIL practice groups and overseas offices. As a result, if you're interested in practicing PIL or getting overseas you're going to have to start out at a large firm in a leading commercial centre. There are no tricks here; all you have to do is get a summer associate position at a law firm.

All law firms maintain excellent career pages that provide detailed information about the summer positions they offer and the type of individuals they seek out. Most go on about firm culture and their commitment to pro bono work and other similarly high-sounding ideals. In the end though, all corporate law firms look for the same thing: people who will work hard and succeed in a very conservative corporate culture.

Law firms receive hundreds of applications for every position and will first weed out applicants based on two objective criteria. First they'll look at your law school. Simply put, the firms with the best reputations only recruit from the schools with the best reputations. For instance New York firms only recruit from Ivy League schools. In Canada, they recruit from McGILL and to a lesser extent the UNIVERSITY OF TORONTO, YORK UNIVERSITY'S OSGOODE HALL and the UNIVERSITY OF BRITISH COLUMBIA. Second, the firms place a tremendous emphasis on your marks, especially in courses like contracts, tax, securities and business associations.

If you have the necessary objective qualifications you'll be invited for an interview. The fact that your interview will include lunches and dinners reveals that the firms aren't necessarily testing your legal knowledge; they're instead determining whether you have the social skills and temperament to succeed in a firm that is very hierarchical and works with corporate entities. The interview is not the time to display your individuality or discuss your long-term ambition to save the world. Remember they are determining whether to pay you hundreds of thousands of dollars. They don't want to hire people who are looking to make a quick buck and then move on.

Generally speaking, if you want to work for a corporate law firm you should take a high number of corporate law courses in your first and second year. Once you've landed a summer position, you'll be considered for an articling or first-year associate position, which you'll likely get provided you display the right attitude (i.e., you won't complain about working 70-hour weeks).

Once you've secured your position, you can delve deeply into your school's offering of PIL and comparative law courses.

Private Lawyers Practicing Public International Law

The private sector has increasingly looked to public international law as a tool to liberalize the global economy. Trade agreements provide access to markets, the IMF forces countries to adhere to its "Washington Consensus"-inspired dictates, international intellectual property rights protect the investments of pharmaceutical companies and sector-specific agreements like the European Energy Charter protect the investments of oil companies.

If you want to work for a private firm to help protect the environment, human rights or labour laws, take off your rose-coloured glasses. PIL practitioners work for the world's largest, most prestigious law firms, whose clients are almost exclusively the world's largest multinational corporations (MNCs) that necessarily work in their private interest. PIL practitioners are usually hired to help ensure that the foreign investments of MNCs into developing and transitional economies are protected. Usually the investments relate to the exploitation of natural resources and issues relating to major infrastructure projects. Examples of their work include representing a country before the INTERNATIONAL COURT OF JUSTICE on a boundary dispute or representing an MNC that is suing a developing country through the ICSID.

In Canada, there are very few lawyers who work on PIL. Indeed, as has been mentioned, most lawyers in Canada, even in the largest law firms, don't quite grasp what PIL is. The few who do work in PIL are mostly based in Ottawa and focus on trade issues, or are based in Calgary and deal with oil and gas issues. There are also a few firms on the coasts that delve into maritime law. For the most part, if you want to be a PIL practitioner you'll have to work for a firm based in New York or London.

Even if you manage to secure a job in New York or London, it'll probably be several years before you can delve into PIL issues. Before getting into this specialized field of law, you'll be expected to build up your general corporate law expertise. The rapid expansion of PIL to regulate international commerce means that these opportunities should expand every year.

Practicing Overseas

Securities markets, financial service actors and multinational companies that are based in, and therefore regulated by, US laws, dominate the world's economy. Even when operating abroad, US companies must be cognizant of stateside laws, particularly the ever-present *Foreign Corrupt Practices Act*. Moreover, when US companies conclude contracts they almost always choose stateside laws, particularly those of New York and Delaware, to be the governing laws of the contract. There is, then, a tremendous demand throughout the world for lawyers who have experience dealing with US law.

What is referred to as the Anglo-Saxonization of law is a facet of globalization that law firms have responded to by setting up offices throughout the world. This presence is particularly evident in commercial centres such as London, Paris, Frankfurt, New York, Milan, Hong Kong, Dubai and Tokyo, but can also be seen in locales as far afield as Almaty, Riyadh or Buenos Aires. It is through this expansion that US, and to a lesser extent British, law firms are coming to dominate the global legal market completely. The vast majority of lawyers who practice overseas will accordingly work in one of these overseas offices.

A few hardy souls do still set out to start their own overseas practices or work for smaller local firms. But be warned that these people must work tirelessly to establish themselves and generally possess an unflagging entrepreneurial spirit.

Getting Over There

There are two main paths to get a job in an overseas office of a private law firm. The easiest way is to work for a firm that has overseas offices and simply request to go overseas after a few years of domestic practice. This is surprisingly easy for younger associates, because lawyers (usually saddled with families) who are working toward a partnership are often unwilling to go overseas, and firms are hesitant to send senior associates with developed client relations overseas. The ideal time to look for overseas opportunities is when you're a junior associate.

If your firm doesn't have opportunities overseas, you'll have to seek out other avenues. If you have the time, you can look on job boards or on the career pages of other firms. A much easier avenue, however, is to use a legal headhunter service— headhunters are widely used in Europe. Your best bet is to contact a service based in London.

Having overseas experience, cultural sensitivity, language skills and knowledge of comparative law will help you find work overseas. But these skills will only help to a point. If a law firm wants you overseas, it's because of the specialized legal skills and knowledge you possess. Generally, legal positions overseas require a year of general corporate law training and at least two years of specialized experience with a well-established corporate law firm. The areas of law that are presently in demand include banking and capital markets; securitization; intellectual property; project financing; mergers and acquisitions; joint ventures; privatization; capital markets; leveraged acquisition finance; and financial services regulation. You don't necessarily need to be a US qualified lawyer to practice in these areas of the law, but it certainly does help to be qualified in the US. The easiest way to qualify in the US is simply to write the New York bar exam.

As a Canadian looking to go overseas, your best bet is London, which continues to rival New York as the world's leading financial city. Firms in the "City" actively recruit Canadian lawyers who have earned a reputation for being well trained and hard-working. Qualifying as an English solicitor is very easy for Canadian lawyers trained in the common law, who are simply required to write a professional conduct and accounts exam—a very easy ethics test.

Don't be overly concerned about qualifying overseas, though. If you get a job overseas, it is because you come equipped with honed legal skills and knowledge that are transferable. You'll seldom be expected to worry about the laws of the foreign jurisdiction. There will be an abundance of locally trained and licensed lawyers to deal with local laws.

Private In-House Legal Counsel

Another avenue to the overseas market is to work at an MNC as the in-house legal counsel—MNCs are increasingly establishing offices overseas and staffing them with experienced lawyers. Lawyers for these positions usually do not need to have a background in PIL, but should have a general knowledge of corporate law. In addition to their legal background, they should be culturally sensitive, have overseas experience and possess a very good understanding of international affairs. Language skills are helpful, but not essential.

Going in-house is an attractive option to lawyers who don't have time for the office politics and hyper-competitive nature of law firms. Women, who traditionally (and statistically) do not fare well in law firms, are particularly attracted to in-house practices. If you want to go overseas, you'll probably have to work for a few years in North America before being sent. If you have language skills, you might be able to bypass this by searching out opportunities on job boards or through headhunters. For example, fluency in an Asian language coupled with a minimum of one-year of legal experience should land you a good job in the region.

If you're already overseas, you might just have to pound the pavement to find an opportunity and then market your skills effectively. For example, a lawyer with 10 years of contract law experience who accompanied her husband on a 1-year overseas posting explains how she got her position with the country's largest corporation:

"At a social occasion I heard of the company's upcoming plan to expand in North America. The next day I had my husband arrange a meeting for me with the legal department where I presented a proposal concerning how my legal experience could benefit them. When the legal department realized that no one else could perform the tasks I presented, they hired me on the spot."

The following is another example of someone who was bold and willing to take a chance while overseas:

"Don't expect to get a job applying from Canada—based on experience, you need to show up on the ground with a good resume and a good attitude. When I showed up in Indonesia, at the height of the economic crisis, I didn't know the language, knew no lawyers and had no contacts at firms in the country. I looked through the Martindale Hubbell and called lawyers who were from my alma mater: Canadians, Americans AND Australians. Every lawyer that I called agreed to meet with me—many because they wanted to know why a young lawyer with no experience (I'd just written the NY bar but was not called) would want to work in Jakarta. From those meetings I received two offers and ended up choosing a firm that was run by four female Indonesian partners, had four foreign advisors (two Canadian and two US lawyers) and 30 fun and young Indonesian associates. The work was very interesting and the experience even more so. My time in Jakarta gave me experience and contacts that helped me get a job working as a legal advisor for the UN mission in East Timor for one year— another amazing experience that I would never have had if I'd applied from Canada."

Department of Justice Canada

Department of Justice Canada, 284 Wellington Street, Ottawa, K1A 0H8
613-957-4222; fax: (613) 954-0811; www.justice.gc.ca

The DEPARTMENT OF JUSTICE (DOJ) works to ensure that Canada's justice system is as fair, accessible and efficient as possible. With over 5,000 employees, the DOJ (or "Justice") is the largest legal organization in the country. More than half of its employees are non-legal professionals who are experts in policy development, the social sciences and communications, or paralegals and support staff. Vacancies for non-legal positions are posted on the Public Service Commission's (PSC) Web site. (For information on how to apply for these positions, see the PSC profile in Chapter 37, Canadian Government.)

Justice's 3,000 lawyers have a diversity of responsibilities and are involved in virtually every aspect of Canadian law. Roughly half of these are based in Ottawa. They work at Justice's Ottawa headquarters, providing support to the minister of justice in formulating and advancing policy relating to Canada's justice system, drafting legislation, providing legal advice on public law issues, such as constitutional and administrative law, human rights law, international law and information and privacy law. Justice lawyers also represent the minister in his capacity as the attorney general, the chief legal officer of the Crown. Lawyers are also spread throughout the legal service units attached to more than 40 federal departments and agencies providing legal advice and opinions to the federal government.

The remaining lawyers work in 13 regional and sub-regional offices across Canada, where they are actively involved in prosecuting federal offences, litigating civil cases on behalf of the Crown and providing direction and advice throughout the development of government bills, regulations and guidelines

Why Work for Justice?

If you are interested in a legal career that will allow you to work on some of the most important legal issues in the country, while maintaining a high quality of life, then Justice is probably your best choice in Canada. Justice prides itself on fostering a workplace atmosphere that accommodates a diverse range of opinions and enables its employees to find a healthy balance between their professional and personal lives. Facilitating this are the many benefits you'll enjoy working with the federal government, such as flexible work hours, job sharing, teleworking and a full year of maternity or paternity leave.

The opportunity to pursue a legal career and enjoy a life outside of work is itself a great drawing point, but Justice's main attraction is the opportunity to work in the public interest advancing the causes of justice, human rights and the rule of law. Justice lawyers can choose from a wide range of practice areas, including criminal law, civil litigation, policy development, immigration, human rights law and both private and public international law. As a lawyer with Justice, you'll be able to specialize in one of these areas of law, or you can choose to rotate through several specialties throughout your career.

As the government's law firm, Justice is also your best pathway to a career in public international law. Here are some examples of the type of work you could do with Justice:

- Litigating international investment disputes before the International Centre for the Settlement of International Disputes.

- Negotiating an international environmental treaty on behalf of the Canadian government.

- Ensuring that Canadian courts take account of international human rights standards in their decisions.

- Helping to negotiate a bilateral investment treaty with a Central Asian country.

- Advising the minister of foreign affairs about the legality of Canada's involvement in an armed conflict.

- Representing Canada before the INTERNATIONAL COURT OF JUSTICE.

Simply put, if you want to practice public international law in Canada, you should work with Justice. In the next sections I'll explain how you can join Justice as a summer or articling student. I'll then briefly profile several of their divisions that focus on public international law.

Opportunities for Law Students

Every year the DEPARTMENT OF JUSTICE CANADA hires anywhere from 20 to 50 summer law students, including first-year students. Summer students work all over the country on a variety of files and projects across the mandate of the department. Most are hired through the Federal Student Work Experience Program (FSWEP), although some divisions and offices, including the Ontario Regional Office (Toronto) and the Vancouver Regional Office, hire their summer law students directly.

If you want to spend your summer with Justice you should complete your FSWEP application very early in the year, as the selection process can begin as early as October. Keep in mind that the FSWEP program is basically a lottery system and there is no guarantee you'll be selected. Further, your chances of being selected to work in an international division are very slim, so make sure you have some other options if your goal for the summer is to gain international legal experience. Working for a corporate law firm or doing an international internship in law will certainly not hurt your prospects of joining Justice as an articling student.

Justice's Web site includes information about summer employment. You should also be aware that Justice does not have a formal co-op program, but will consider proposals on an individual basis.

THE LEGAL EXCELLENCE PROGRAM (ARTICLING)

The Legal Excellence Program is a three- to four-year professional development program that provides articling students and junior lawyers with the opportunity to develop the essential knowledge and experience for practicing law. Civil law and common law students and notaries are eligible for the program that takes place over two phases: the student-at-law phase and the junior lawyer phase. We'll explain both of these phases after giving an overview of how Justice selects its articling students.

The Selection Process

Each of Justice's 13 regional and sub-regional offices has different articling programs and application deadlines. Students apply directly to the regional branch, or branches, where they are interested in working. Justice's Web site provides extensive information about each of the articling programs, including rotation summaries and contact information.

The hiring process may vary slightly from region to region, based on the size of the office, the number of students and the type of practice in the particular office. What is common to all is the focus on attracting strong academic performers that are committed to the field of public law and working in the public interest. I'm going to provide information about the selection process of the NATIONAL CAPITAL REGION OFFICE, which not only offers the most articling positions, but also is the most relevant if you're interested in articling rotations with sections that practice public international law.

The deadline for applications to be received by the NATIONAL CAPITAL REGION OFFICE is the same as for other firms in the Ottawa area, which is set by the LAW SOCIETY OF UPPER CANADA (LSUC) and usually falls around the second week of May. Every year, the NATIONAL CAPITAL REGION OFFICE receives anywhere from 350–400 applications and offers roughly 15–25 civil and common law articling positions, depending on that year's hiring needs. Your application package should include a cover letter, resume, law school transcripts and two reference letters.

A committee screens the applications based on a number of factors, including your academic achievement in law, professional and volunteer work experience, non-legal education, non-work interests, demonstrated community involvement and communication skills. Justice also looks to see if applicants have taken steps to develop experience and knowledge in a particular area of law. In terms of tips,

Justice offers this simple advice: do your best to draw a clear link between your background, experiences and education and the work of Justice.

For instance, a student who wound up with an articling position detailed how his internship with the INTERNATIONAL CRIMINAL TRIBUNAL in Yugoslavia would contribute to the institutional knowledge of the Crimes Against Humanity and War Crimes Section or the Criminal Law Policy Section. Another successful applicant clearly explained why her first degree in economics and interest in public international law made her an ideal candidate to work with the International Trade Section.

Justice will invite roughly 25 per cent of applicants for interviews, which occur during the few days set out by the LSUC. A panel of two or three lawyers interviews all applicants. You'll have the chance to discuss thoroughly your candidacy—this will probably include an opportunity to explore a substantive law issue. Knowledge of the law and of the department, analytical skills, communication skills, interpersonal skills and judgment are assessed in the process of determining the successful candidates.

The Student-at-Law Phase

This is the articling phase of the program that includes your articling term and bar admission course. Your salary will depend on a number of factors, most notably the office you work with. Justice frequently reviews its salaries to ensure that they are reasonably competitive with the salaries paid by other legal employers in that region. If you article in major urban centres, you'll accordingly receive a higher salary that will be paid during your bar studies. Many Justice offices offer their articling students guaranteed hire-back, especially those in urban centres. Other offices have an excellent track record of hiring their articling students to fill any vacancies.

Each office has a different articling program, which depends on the areas of law that they practice. All are based on a rotation system, although you'll also be assigned a mentor who'll provide you with professional advice, guidance and support. Throughout your articles, expect to receive excellent training and to attend numerous professional development courses that are designed to enhance your advocacy skills and provide an overview of Justice's work.

The articling program at the NATIONAL CAPITAL REGION OFFICE offers the unparalleled opportunity for the student to choose any four rotations from a list of almost 70 possible legal sections. This includes numerous sections that work on public international law, ranging from the NAFTA Secretariat to the International Law Section. Students are also required to complete a rotation with one of Justice's in-house legal service units, including with FOREIGN AFFAIRS CANADA (FAC), INTERNATIONAL TRADE CANADA (ITCAN) or the CANADIAN INTERNATIONAL DEVELOPMENT AGENCY (CIDA). Some of the PIL-practicing sections that you can choose to do rotations with are profiled below.

Junior Lawyer Phase

The junior lawyer phase begins when you have completed your articles and been called to the bar. Most justice offices offer guaranteed hire-back and you'll be assigned to work with a department based on your personal preferences and Justice's operational needs.

Justice does its best to accommodate its lawyers, but not everyone will start their career in their section of first choice. Don't be discouraged by this though, as you'll be surprised how many practice areas will delve into aspects of PIL. And even if you aren't practicing international law, the legal experience and skills you develop in other sections will help you in working in the international law field in the future.

As a junior lawyer, you'll continue to benefit from Justice's professional development programs while simultaneously being offered the opportunity to work on some major files. This is where the advantages of working with Justice really become apparent. Justice prides itself on giving its junior lawyers significant and unmatched levels of responsibilities on their files. At the same time, senior lawyers work very closely with junior lawyers, ensuring they have the support and guidance to excel in their legal work. The chance to work on high-profile cases that are often on the front pages of national newspapers adds an element of excitement that you won't find anywhere else.

Lateral Hires

Justice posts vacancies for legal positions on its Web site. Appointments from outside the public service are normally made at the LA-1 and LA-2A levels, which is the equivalent of an associate in a private firm. The chance of finding work with an international section simply depends on Justice's hiring needs. Also remember to look on the PSC's Web site. For instance, as I am writing this, there are openings to work with INDUSTRY CANADA on the TRIPS Agreement, the United Nations, and the Human Rights and Humanitarian Law Section of FOREIGN AFFAIRS CANADA (FAC).

JUSTICE'S INTERNATIONAL LEGAL WORK

Justice has numerous sections with international responsibilities and also places a number of its lawyers in the legal service units of numerous departments or agencies where they work on international legal issues. Below I'll profile several of Justice's departments that have significant legal responsibilities and provide examples of the work they do. Note that you can do an articling rotation with all of these departments if you article in the NATIONAL CAPITAL REGION OFFICE.

The International Cooperation Group

The International Cooperation Group (ICG) has been described as the foreign aid arm of the DEPARTMENT OF JUSTICE. It is responsible for developing and implementing cooperation projects in support of the legal reform efforts of developing countries and countries in transition. Currently it has projects in Central and Eastern Europe, Asia Pacific and Africa. The ICG becomes involved in international projects through regional and international organizations, or by dealing directly with individual countries. It has roughly 20 members. The ICG seeks individuals who have experience working in various legal traditions, international experience and a strong commitment to international development.

Example of work: The ICG significantly contributed to the development and drafting of South Africa's 1996 constitution that was introduced by the post-apartheid government. The constitution includes a Bill of Rights that was largely based on Canada's *Charter of Rights and Freedoms*.

International Assistance Group

The International Assistance Group (IAG) is responsible for matters falling under the *Extradition Act* and the *Mutual Legal Assistance in Criminal Matters Act*. Working with international partners, including international criminal tribunals, the IAG is Canada's central authority for mutual legal assistance and extradition. It also represents Canada internationally in the negotiation of new treaties in the increasingly important field of international cooperation. The IAG has just fewer than 30 members, most of whom have significant experience in international and criminal law.

Example of work: The IAG assists the RCMP and the DEPARTMENT OF NATIONAL DEFENCE CANADA in their support to the investigations and prosecutions of the international criminal tribunals for Rwanda and the Former Yugoslavia.

International Law Section

Situated within the public law portfolio, the International Law Section (ILS) is responsible for providing legal advice on a broad range of public international law issues. The ILS is involved in international litigation files and coordinates international legal issues within the department. The ILS has seven members who work closely with colleagues in Justice, FAC, CIDA and other federal departments. ILS lawyers are general specialists in public international law.

Example of work: Over the next three years, member of the ILS will work with non-governmental legal experts to promote human rights and reform the justice system in Indonesia.

Human Rights Law Section

The Human Rights Law Section (HLS) provides legal advice to governments and litigation support to Crown counsel on human rights issues. As well as providing advice on the *Canadian Charter of Rights and Freedoms* and other Canadian laws, it is also responsible for international human rights law, primarily the domestic implications of treaty obligations and individual petitions to international bodies. The HLS has about 20 members who have significant backgrounds in human rights, constitutional and international human rights law. It is also one of the most difficult sections to land employment with, given the interesting work it carries out.

Example of work: Submits responses to complaints received by treaty bodies of the UN or by the INTER-AMERICAN COMMISSION OF HUMAN RIGHTS.

The Trade Law Bureau of ITCAN

The Trade Law Bureau of ITCAN is staffed by lawyers from the DEPARTMENT OF JUSTICE CANADA and from INTERNATIONAL TRADE CANADA (ITCAN). In all, it has about 60 members who advise the government of its rights and obligations under international trade and investment law. Members of the bureau represent Canada in the negotiation and implementation of multilateral, regional and bilateral trade agreements and represent Canada in dispute settlement proceedings initiated under these agreements.

Example of Work: Counsel from the bureau represented Canada before an INTERNATIONAL CENTRE FOR SETTLEMENT OF INVESTMENT DISPUTES (ICSID) panel for *United Parcel Service of America v. Government of Canada*, an investment disputes case.

The Crimes Against Humanity and War Crimes Section

The section's purpose is to participate in the investigation of allegations that individuals presently in Canada have engaged in the commission of the crimes enumerated in the *Crimes Against Humanity and War Crimes Act*, regardless of whether the alleged offences were committed in Canada or abroad. The section consists of about 20 members that represent an interesting mix of lawyers, analysts, historians and other team members who collectively work to ensure that individuals are held accountable for committing the world's most heinous crimes, including genocide, war crimes and crimes against humanity. Lawyers working in the section should have a background in the growing field of international criminal law. The section occasionally hires contract analysts and related experts on an ad hoc basis.

Example of work: The Section is currently very active assisting less developed countries draft domestic implementing legislation of the Rome Statute of the International Criminal Court.

A LAST WORD

Public international law is a specialized area of law that is growing every year. The demand for lawyers throughout the world means that it is no longer a fringe area of law practiced only by government lawyers and discussed only by professors. Intellectually demanding and ever changing, this area of law offers those who dare to delve into it an unparalleled opportunity to protect those who all too often don't have a voice in the world. This helps explain why public international lawyers seem to truly love their jobs. If you want to practice law, improve the world and live in various countries, then PIL is the field of law for you. Good luck!

APPENDIX ON THE CD-ROM

31a. "Launching an International Law Career," by James Pickard
31b. "Careers in Public International Law," by Ken Roberts

RESOURCES

This chapter contains the following Resources sections: International Law Job Boards and International Law Careers.

INTERNATIONAL LAW JOB BOARDS

The following is a list of job boards geared toward aspiring international lawyers.

ABA Career Counsel 💻

www.abanet.org/careercounsel/home.html ◆ ABA Career Counsel is the central source for on-line information on finding jobs and enhancing lawyers' careers. Visit the various areas of this site often for tips on finding the right job and maximizing your career, job postings, tools and links to career-related resources. The site includes a link to "Legal Postings and Alternative Careers for Lawyers at the ABA." [ID:2733]

ABA-UNDP International Legal Resource Center 🖥

www.abanet.org/intlaw/ilrc ◆ The American Bar Association and the UNDP have come together to offer this superb site that is designed to assist the United Nations Development Program (UNDP) Country Offices recruit legal and human rights professionals for positions focused on drafting of legislation, judicial reform, building of legal institutions including professional groups and associations, and other legal dimensions of governance. To find available positions, click on "UNDP Positions" under the ABA-UNDP menu. Great site, highly recommended. [ID:2732]

BAR-eX 🖥

www.bar-ex.com/barex/index2.jsp ◆ This Web site contains probably the best database of jobs available to legal professionals in Canada. Searchable by practice area, sector, location and experience level, the database also contains overseas jobs in the US, Latin America and Europe. Career search services require you to register for free, which gives you access to helpful articles with advice on finding the legal job you want. Highly recommended. [ID:2610]

Law.com 🖥

http://lawjobs.careercast.com ◆ This US site has a large database of jobs requiring no registration or membership fees. Includes a long list of internationally focused jobs that are searchable by country. You can also register and post your resume and access information on legal recruiters, firm directories and rankings. [ID:2613]

Totallylegal.com 🖥

www.totallylegal.com ◆ If you are interested in working for a law firm in Europe or overseas make sure you visit this UK-based site that bills itself as "the legal recruitment site." The site includes a job-search function and provides a wealth of information about the legal job search, such as how to write a legal resume. [ID:2740]

ZSA 🖥

www.zsa.ca/En ◆ This Canadian Web site allows legal professionals to search for jobs by province or internationally, which you can apply to on-line. What sets this site apart is the useful information on all aspects of the legal employer-employee relationship. You will find information on salaries in Canada and abroad as well as access good advice on everything from moving in-house to moving on to better things. Well worth a hit. [ID:2614]

INTERNATIONAL LAW CAREERS

The following is a list of resources geared toward aspiring international lawyers.

American Society of International Law ♕

www.asil.org ◆ The American Society of International Law's Web site offers a wide array of resources on many of the world's leading public international law issues. The site also offers numerous opportunities to network with practitioners of international law. [ID:2734]

Association of American Law Schools ♕

www.aals.org ◆ If you're interested in a career in legal education you should visit the AALS Web site. The AALS is a non-profit association of 166 law schools that works toward the improvement of the legal profession through legal education. Every year the AALS holds a Faculty Recruitment Conference that is the best way to put yourself out there if you are interested in a career in academia. [ID:2764]

University of Bologna Research Guide to International Law 🖥

www2.spfo.unibo.it/spolfo/ILMAIN.htm ◆ The University of Bologna has put together this superb Research Guide to International Law on the Internet. This is an indispensable resource for students and practitioners alike. [ID:2743]

Canadian Bar Association ⚒

Canadian Bar Association (CBA), Suite 500, 865 Carling Ave., Ottawa, ON K1S 5S8, Canada, www.cba.org, 800-267-8860, fax 613-237-0185 ◆ The Canadian Bar Association has a large and active international law section with its own Web page. It promotes conferences and seminars, releases publications, makes deputations to hearings and inquiries and has a student international law section. [ID:2786]

Canadian Council on International Law ⚒

www.ccil-ccdi.ca ◆ The Canadian Council on International Law is an association of academics and practitioners of international law. Its main activities are the organization of an annual conference, the publication of various international legal materials and the administration of a scholarship fund. The yearly conference is attended by a veritable who's who of international law in Canada. Students are welcome to attend and are offered a career information seminar. [ID:2749]

Canadian Legal Resources on the WWW 🖥

www.legalcanada.ca ◆ This excellent Web site provides a comprehensive list of the Canadian legal resources on the Internet. It includes links to hundreds of Canadian law firms. [ID:2730]

Careers in International Law 📖

2001, Mark W. Janis, 205 pages ➤ Publication Orders, American Bar Association, P.O. Box 10892, Chicago, IL 60610-0892, USA, www.abanet.org, $64.95 US; VISA, MC; 312-988-5522, fax 312-988-5568, info@abanet.org ◆ In this US publication, 16 international lawyers practicing in public and private international law present essays based on their experiences. Their observations help create a comprehensive picture of what it is like to practice international law and show how to become an international lawyer. Highly recommended reading for legal professionals wanting to work overseas. Order from ABA's publications page. [ID:2114]

Export Development Canada: Legal Links ⚒

www.edc.ca/corpinfo/csr/anti_corrup/related_e.htm; *Fr* ◆ Export Development Canada has put together a list of links to organizations that work on international corruption issues and corporate social responsibility. [ID:2728]

Inter-American Bar Association (IABA) ⚒

www.123arab.com/English.html ◆ This Web site represents a permanent forum for the exchange of professional views and information for lawyers to promote the rule of law and protect the democratic institutions in the Americas. The IABA Web site offers a wealth of legal information and provides an opportunity to network with practitioners and law students throughout the Americas. [ID:2731]

INTERIGHTS International Human Rights Law Database 🖥

www.interights.org ◆ This is a useful Web resource that allows you to search for recent decisions of tribunals applying international human rights law. Decisions are unanimous unless otherwise indicated. An excellent tool for identifying relevant human rights cases and summaries. Search both international and Commonwealth case law by navigating from it's home page menu. [ID:2739]

International Bar Association ⚒

www.ibanet.org ◆ Billing itself as the global voice of the legal profession, the International Bar Association can provide you with education, information, networking and strategy for the practice of law. With more than 60 specialist committees, it provides members with access to leading experts and up-to-date information as well as top-level professional development and network-building opportunities through high quality publications and world-class conferences. [ID:2725]

International Criminal Defence Attorneys Association (AIAD/ICDAA) ⚒

International Criminal Defence Attorney's Association, Suite P-206, 137 St-Pierre Street, Montreal, QC H2Y 3T5, Canada, www.hri.ca/partners/aiad-icdaa, 514-285-1055, fax 514-289-8590 ◆ The International Criminal Bar (ICB) is a vehicle for the legal profession to be heard at the International

Criminal Court (ICC) and other international criminal tribunals. The ICB enables lawyers to speak with a strong voice on issues of common concern, such as the independence of the legal profession, the right to a fair trial, "equality of arms," lawyer-client confidentiality and the structure and guiding principles of legal aid. [ID:2741]

International Financial Law Review 📖 🖥️

Monthly ➤ Legal Media Group, 225 Park Ave., New York, NY 10003, USA, www.legalmediagroup.com, $825 US; Credit Cards; 212-224-3542, fax 212-224-3101; Available in large libraries ◆ "IFLR" has established itself as the world's leading magazine for in-house counsel and practitioners in the financial markets. Each issue includes comprehensive international news and analysis of recent international deals, reports on legislative changes, practice issues, latest techniques and best practice strategies. Covers the latest innovations in areas such as capital markets, banking, project finance, corporate governance, bankruptcy, litigation, fund management and M&A. Highly recommended for the international financial practitioner. Subscribe on-line. [ID:2721]

International Human Rights Resources 🖥️

www.law.csuohio.edu/lawlibrary/international.html ◆ Links to legal resources relating to human rights and international law. [ID:2226]

International Law Dictionary & Directory 🖥️

www.august1.com/pubs/dict ◆ This Web site contains a listing of definitions of words and phrases used in private and public international law with linked cross-references to related words and phrases. It also contains descriptions of international organizations with links to their on-line home pages and to other important materials describing the organizations. [ID:2746]

Jurist Canada: The Legal Education Network 🖥️

http://jurist.law.utoronto.ca; Fr ◆ This is Canada's foremost source of information about law. You can find everything on this site from information about law schools to links to Canadian law firms. [ID:2747]

Jurist: University of Pittsburgh School of Law 🖥️

http://jurist.law.pitt.edu ◆ Jurist offers an exceptionally broad array of information on emerging legal issues. It also has one of the best sections listing opportunities for professors to teach law. [ID:2765]

Lexpert 🖥️ 🏛️

www.lexpert.ca ◆ Lexpert is Canada's leading source of news and information about the business of law. Publications and services include "Lexpert Magazine", the "Canadian Legal Lexpert Directory", the "Lexpert/American Lawyer Guide to the Leading 500 Lawyers in Canada", the "Lexpert/CCCA Corporate Counsel Directory and Yearbook", and "Lexpert Conferences". Its Web site offers ordering information and news on what is happening in Canada's legal community. [ID:2729]

Martindale-Hubbell 🖥️

www.martindale.com ◆ Martindale-Hubbell is the authoritative resource for information on the worldwide legal profession. The Martindale-Hubbell Legal Network is powered by a database of over one million lawyers and law firms in 160 countries. Use the database to track down lawyers or law firms around the world. [ID:2724]

NALP Directory of Legal Employers 🏛️

www.nalpdirectory.com ◆ NALP is a non-profit educational association established in 1971 to meet the needs of the participants in the legal employment process: legal employers, law schools, law students and graduates for information, coordination and standards. NALP's membership includes virtually every ABA-accredited law school and more than 800 of the US's largest legal employers. NALP is committed to providing leadership in the areas of legal career planning, recruitment and hiring and research related to the employment market for law graduates. In addition, NALP offers law schools and employers the option of membership in a professional association whose members gain direct, ongoing access to the latest information regarding legal recruitment and employment. [ID:2742]

Osgoode Hall Law School Web site 🖳

www.osgoode.yorku.ca/careers/resources_links_directories.htm ◆ Osgoode Hall Law School's Web site is indispensable for law students. Along with providing a very thorough and well-done links list, it provides specific career information for law students. Especially make sure you take a look at the "Career Stages" and "Career Advice" pages that offer you advice on the type of experience you should be gaining throughout law school to ensure you find the legal job of your choice. [ID:2727]

University of Ottawa's Common Law Section: Career Development Resource Centre 🖳

www.commonlaw.uottawa.ca/eng/student_services/career/index.htm ◆ The University of Ottawa's Common Law Section has put together an excellent Career Development Resource Centre. This site is extensive and provides all the information you will need to know ranging from how to build your legal experience, writing a legal resume to how to find a job in academia. [ID:2726]

Pepperdine University School of Law: International LLM Programs 🖳

http://law.pepperdine.edu/alumni/career ◆ Pepperdine provides a list of law schools around the world offering LLM programs in numerous areas of international law. The site is especially helpful if you are trying to research very narrow areas of law. Find these LLM programs by navigating to the "Services" link. [ID:2722]

Robert Half Legal ♁

www.roberthalflegal.com ◆ Located in major markets throughout the United States and Canada, Robert Half Legal is the premier provider of experienced project and full-time professionals for law firms and corporate legal departments. They place highly qualified candidates in a wide range of specialized positions within the legal field, including attorney, paralegal and legal support professional. [ID:2744]

Slomanson's Career Opportunities in International Law 🖳

http://home.att.net/~slomansonb/career.html ◆ This site isn't pretty, but it's perhaps the single best resource to find information on international legal careers. It includes lists of books, Web sites and other information. A good starting point for a law student trying to chart his or her path. Check it out. [ID:2748]

Stetson University College of Law Career Services 🖳

www.law.stetson.edu/Career/resumes.htm ◆ This helpful Web site provides detailed information about how to write law resumes and cover letters and has helpful guides and tips for interviewing and obtaining clerkships. Great resource! [ID:2738]

United Nations International Law Web Site ♁

www.un.org/law ◆ The United Nations International Law site is the central page that provides access to the UN's work on international law. From this site you can access documents or link to the Web sites of organs and committees of the UN working on international legal issues. [ID:2735]

Universal Jurisdiction Information Network 🖳

www.universaljurisdiction.info ◆ This Web site provides a central resource for existing information on universal jurisdiction. Once the site has been completed, you will be able to find virtually everything that exists electronically on universal jurisdiction, including introductory explanations, international and national laws and cases, publications, advocacy, legal reform initiatives, directories and contact information of people and projects working in support of universal jurisdiction, links to other sites and more. [ID:2736]

US Department of Justice 🖳

www.usdoj.gov/oarm ◆ The US Department of Justice, the federal government's law firm and the world's largest legal employer, offers opportunities for law students, entry-level lawyers and experienced lawyers in virtually every area of legal practice. Their Web site provides an overview of the many legal employment opportunities and benefits available at the Department of Justice. There is also information about legal recruitment, including eligibility, the application process, the work of each department, salaries, security clearances, citizenship requirements, the department's employment policies, incentive programs and answers to frequently asked questions. [ID:2612]

Vault 💻
www.vault.com/jobs/jobboard/searchform.jsp ◆ Fabulous US Web destination for on-line insider company information, advice and career management services. Lots of international jobs in the private sector. It's possible to search jobs by profession. Loads of legal and project-management postings. Also includes a great list of internships. In addition to a job board and newsletter, this site has information on over 3,000 companies and 70 industries including company-specific message boards allowing employees and job seekers the opportunity to network and ask advice about company trends. Order career guides such as the "Vault Guide to the Top 100 Law Firms", "Vault Guide to Finance Interviews" and the "Vault Guide to the Top 50 Consulting Firms". [ID:2596]

University of Washington School of Law Career Services Center ⚓
www.law.washington.edu/Career ◆ Step-by-step guide on how to write a legal resume. Includes helpful examples. Click on "Interview & Resume Tips" from the "Career Center" page. [ID:2737]

William & Mary School of Law: International Law Career Guide 💻
www.wm.edu/law/lawlibrary/research/careerguides/index.shtml ◆ William & Mary School of Law's International Law Career Guide provides a very extensive list of resources that can help you find information about international legal careers. It is especially useful in that it provides a list of law journal articles that would be of interest to students. Click on "International Law" from the Career Guide home page. [ID:2723]

Profiles for International Law

There are two sets of profiles in this chapter. The first, Profiles of Law Schools Teaching Public International Law (PIL) in Canada; the second, Profiles of International Law Organizations.

Profiles of Canadian Law Schools Teaching PIL

To help get you started in choosing a law school, we have compiled a list of six of Canada's top PIL programs. The profiles are written to accentuate the criteria written at the start of this chapter in the section "Choosing the Right Law School."

University of British Columbia Faculty of Law
1882 East Mall, University of British Columbia - Faculty of Law,
Vancouver, BC, V6T 1Z1, Canada; 604-822-3151, fax 604-822-8108, www.law.ubc.ca

LAW SCHOOL ◆ University of British Columbia Faculty of Law has a very good selection of international law courses. Where it truly excels, however, is in its unparalleled offering of comparative law courses, especially as it concerns Asian legal systems. Many of these courses form part of the curriculum of the joint LLB/MA in Asia Pacific Policy Studies program. The faculty also offers a Natural Resource Law program and is associated with several prominent research centres including the International Centre for Criminal Law Reform & Criminal Justice Policy. [ID:5494]

Dalhousie University Law School

6061 University Ave., Dalhousie Law School, Halifax, NS, B3H 4H9,
Canada; 902-494-3495, fax 902-494-1316, LAWINFO@dal.ca, www.dal.ca/law

LAW SCHOOL ◆ Dalhousie University Law School has the oldest law faculty in the Commonwealth outside of England. It offers a very broad selection of international law courses, including some unique courses on natural resources. It is particularly strong in maritime and environmental law, and students have the option of pursuing specializations in both these areas. Students are offered the opportunity to spend a semester abroad in an exchange programs. [ID:5495]

McGill University Faculty of Law

3644 Peel Street, McGill University - Faculty of Law, Montreal, QC, H3A 1W9,
Canada; 514-398-6666, fax 514-398-4659, info.law@mcgill.ca, www.law.mcgill.ca 🖳*Fr*

LAW SCHOOL ◆ McGill University Faculty of Law is the only university in the world where students study the common law and civil law in an integrated fashion that fosters a comparative understanding of the world's two major legal traditions. Students graduating from McGill's unique bilingual, trans-systemic program receive degrees in both the common and civil law. Students can extend their studies by half a year if they want to qualify for a legal major in International Governance and Development. Along with its unparalleled comparative legal education, McGill offers a very thorough selection of PIL courses. These courses are often attended by the many overseas students who spend time at McGill, including those from three affiliated research institutes that focus on PIL: the Institute of Comparative Law; the Institute of Air and Space Law; and the Institute for European Studies.

Every year numerous McGill students take the opportunity to spend a semester abroad at universities throughout the world. Over the summer a select number of students participate in the International Human Rights Internship Program that places students with organizations throughout the world defending fundamental human rights. One placement is with Human Rights Watch, one of the world's best human rights NGOs. Finally, McGill is the only Canadian university to participate in the International Court of Justice's clerkship program. [ID:5496]

University of Ottawa Faculty of Law

57 Louis Pasteur Street, University of Ottawa - Faculty of Law, Ottawa, ON,
K1N 6N5, Canada; 613-562-5794, fax 613-562-5124, www.commonlaw.uottawa.ca 🖳*Fr*

LAW SCHOOL ◆ University of Ottawa Faculty of Law is distinguished by its impressive selection of joint degree options including a program that allows common law students to obtain a LLB and JD, as well as a joint LLB/MA program offered in partnership with the highly regarded Norman Patterson School of International Affairs at Carleton University. Students of the National Program study the common law or civil law and may complement their training with a fourth year of study in the other system. The faculty is very qualified in offering students a comparative legal education and also boasts an impressive assortment of public interest law courses. Best of all, many of these courses are taught by practitioners, including some from Foreign Affairs Canada (FAC).

Being based in Ottawa allows the faculty to offer several very interesting internships, for example with the House of Commons Standing Committee on Foreign Affairs and International Trade, and the Department of Justice's War Crimes Section. The faculty also consistently does very well in moot competitions and encourages students to take advantage of its international exchange program. The Human Rights Research and Education Centre is affiliated with the Faculty of Law and houses an excellent human rights library. [ID:5498]

University of Toronto Faculty of Law

84 Queen's Park Crescent, University of Toronto - Faculty of Law, Toronto, ON,
M5S 2C5, Canada; 416-978-0210, law.admissions@utoronto.ca, www.law.utoronto.ca

LAW SCHOOL ◆ The University of Toronto Faculty of Law offers an impressive assortment of courses in international law although it is thin in comparative law courses. Its public interest law courses are taught by an impressive list of professors that the faculty has been able to attract thanks to its new-found financial resources.

Its International Human Rights Program offers 10 to 30 students the opportunity to spend part of their summer working with governmental, non-governmental and United Nations organizations on international human rights law issues. These internships are well funded by law firms or the faculty. The faculty offers some internationally focused combined degree programs and also has an international educational exchange program. [ID:5499]

Osgoode Hall Law School of York University

4700 Keele Street, York University - Osgoode Hall, Toronto, ON, M3J 1P3, Canada;
416-736-5030, fax 416-736-5736, admissions@osgoode.yorku.ca, www.osgoode.yorku.ca

LAW SCHOOL ◆ The international reputation of Osgoode Hall Law School of York University was raised after its first place showing in the 2004 Vis International Arbitration Moot. Beating the world's elite universities in this prestigious international moot demonstrates that Osgoode Hall provides its students with an excellent international legal education. Over half of Osgoode Hall's full-time faculty members are currently working on some aspect of international, comparative or transnational law, including the interaction of the forces of globalization with the development of domestic law.

The faculty offers a very impressive selection of international and comparative law courses. A specialized International, Comparative and Transnational (ICT) Law Program offers students the opportunity to pursue international legal studies taught by leading faculty in the field. The faculty also offers students the chance to participate in an exchange program and summer study abroad programs. [ID:5497]

Profiles of International Law Organizations

Virtually every organization profiled in THE BIG GUIDE TO LIVING AND WORKING OVERSEAS has a legal section or retains lawyers. Some organizations, however, stand out because of their focus on legal issues and we've assembled them here into one helpful list. A quick scan will show the various types of organizations that you could work for as a PIL practitioner.

The 55 organizations listed include 20 Canadian and US law firms, 19 International Non-governmental Organizations and then a scattering of various organizations and have an interest in international law. Be aware that this list is far from exhaustive and is meant to give you an idea of what is out there.

ActionAid

Hamlyn House, Macdonald Road, Archway, London, N19 5PG, UK;
(44) (0) 20-7561-7561, fax (44) (0) 20-7272-0899, mail@actionaid.org.uk, www.actionaid.org

RELIEF AND DEVELOPMENT AGENCY ◆ ActionAid is a large development organization that works directly with marginalized people in more than 40 countries in Africa, Asia, Latin America and the Caribbean. Its aim is to eradicate poverty by overcoming the injustice and inequity that cause it. The vast majority of ActionAid's 1,800 staff come from the developing countries they work in. Vacancies for international staff are posted on its Web site and generally require a three-year commitment. [ID:5615]

Adalah - The Legal Center for Arab Minority Rights
P.O. Box 510, Shafa'amr, 20200, Israel; (972) (4) 950-1610,
fax (972) (4) 950-3140, adalah@adalah.org, www.adalah.org

INTERNATIONAL NON-GOVERNMENTAL ORGANIZATION ◆ Adalah -The Legal Center for Arab Minority Rights is an independent human rights organization registered in Israel. Its goal is to achieve equal individual and collective rights for the Arab minority in Israel in different fields, including land rights, civil and political rights, cultural, social and economic rights, religious freedom, and women's and prisoners' rights. Adalah has a staff of 18 individuals, most of whom are lawyers. Internships and fellowships are offered to overseas students and recent graduates. [ID:5630]

Akin, Gump, Strauss, Hauer & Feld, LLP
Robert S. Strauss Bldg., 1333 New Hampshire Ave. N.W., Washington, DC, 20036,
USA; 202-887-4000, fax 202-887-4288, washdcinfo@akingump.com, www.akingump.com

LAW FIRM ◆ Akin, Gump, Strauss, Hauer & Feld, LLP is one of the world's largest firms. With offices across the US and in Brussels, London, Moscow and Riyadh, this firm is well positioned for practice in such things as antitrust, global security, public law and policy, international trade and transportation, among many others. One in every four Akin Gump lawyers is a litigator, and each of their offices provides full-service litigation capabilities. The firm's on-line recruiting page provides information for law students, lateral attorneys, paralegals and staff. The site allows you to search all jobs by office location. [ID:5505]

American Civil Liberties Union (ACLU)
18th Floor, 125 Broad Street, New York, NY, 10004, USA;
212-549-2664, HRJOBS@aclu.org, www.aclu.org 🖳*Sp*

INTERNATIONAL NON-GOVERNMENTAL ORGANIZATION ◆ The American Civil Liberties Union (ACLU) is the guardian of the liberty of citizens of the United States. The ACLU works in the courts, legislatures and communities to defend and preserve the individual rights and liberties guaranteed to all people living in the United States by its Constitution and laws. The ACLU maintains an excellent career opportunities page on its Web site that provides an extensive list of vacancies, internships and fellowships. [ID:5525]

Appleton & Associates
Suite 300, 1140 Bay Street, Toronto, ON, M5S 2B4, Canada;
416-966-8800, fax 416-966-8801, inquiry@appletonlaw.com, www.appletonlaw.com

LAW FIRM ◆ Appleton & Associates is a small boutique law firm that assists clients on a variety of international law and government relations issues. It is very well known for its pioneering efforts in international commercial arbitration under NAFTA, as well as for its legal work dealing with other agreements such as the WTO and numerous bilateral investment treaties. Appleton & Associates continues to be a leader in the Canadian legal community and is one of the only firms with experience providing dispute resolution services under the ICSID, and perhaps the only Canadian law firm that provides representation on the European Energy Charter. [ID:5516]

Arnold & Porter, LLP
555 Twelfth Street N.W., Washington, DC, 20004 - 1206,
USA; 202-942-5000, fax 202-942-5999, www.arnoldporter.com

LAW FIRM ◆ Arnold & Porter, one of Washington's largest law firms, offers a sophisticated legal practice. With almost 700 lawyers practicing in its US and international operations, the firm brings a valuable perspective and proven track record of experience to those clients whose business needs require either US or coordinated and integrated cross-border regulatory, litigation and transactional services. Offices are located in Washington, DC, New York, London, Brussels, Los Angeles, Century City, Northern Virginia and Denver. In their on-line career section, you will find information about career opportunities for associates, summer associates, staff, and London trainees. [ID:5504]

Asia Pacific Forum on Women, Law and Development (APWLD)

Santitham YMCA Bldg. 3rd floor, 11 Sermsuk Road, Soi Mengrairasmi, Chiangmai 50300, Thailand; (66) (53) 404-613-4, fax (66) (53) 404-615, apwld@apwld.org, www.apwld.org

INTERNATIONAL NON-GOVERNMENTAL ORGANIZATION ◆ The Asia Pacific Forum on Women, Law and Development (APWLD) is committed to enabling women to use the law as an instrument of social change for justice, peace, equality and development. The APWLD works primarily on human rights issues affecting women and promotes basic concepts of human rights in the region. Vacancies are posted on its Web site and are generally only open to individuals from the Asia Pacific region. It accepts interns and volunteers from around the world. [ID:5581]

Avocats Sans Frontières (ASF)

rue Royale, 123 Koningsstraat, B - 1000 Brussels, Belgium;
(32) (0) 2-223-3654, fax (32) (0) 2-223-3614, info@asf.be, www.asf.be 💻 Fr

INTERNATIONAL NON-GOVERNMENTAL ORGANIZATION ◆ Avocats Sans Frontières (ASF) is an international NGO of lawyers and jurists that was founded in 1992. The organization's activities are centred on medium- and long-term development projects in the areas of law and justice. Currently it has such projects in Burundi, the Democratic Republic of Congo, Rwanda and Timor Leste. ASF also intervenes in trials around the world where the right to defence or the right to a fair trial is in peril; provides legal advice, services and support to other international and national NGOs working in the fields of human rights, economic globalization and international criminal justice; and lobbies and undertakes technical advice activities around topics of international justice. Lawyers from around the world participate in the activities of ASF on a voluntary basis. Young lawyers or jurists can apply for an internship at the secretariat in Brussels and there are regular openings for professional and administrative staff to work on its medium- and long-term development projects. For more information visit www.asf.be. [ID:5580]

Baker & McKenzie

Suite 2500, One Prudential Plaza, Chicago, IL, 60601, USA;
312-861-8800, fax 312-861-8823, info@bakernet.com, www.bakernet.com

LAW FIRM ◆ The Baker & McKenzie practice spans the full range of local and international corporate and commercial work, including trade, finance, corporate, dispute resolution, employment, international communications, real estate and tax. The firm has 68 offices in 38 countries, 3,212 attorneys and a total staff of 8,275. Each year, for those seeking a true international experience, Baker & McKenzie awards two scholarships to law students who are about to complete their qualifications and who are interested in acquiring qualifications in the laws of the European Union. They also offer 20 international clerkships to law students and graduates interested in exploring international legal practice. [ID:5509]

Canadian Bar Association (CBA)

International Development Program (IDP), Suite 500, 865 Carling Ave., Ottawa, ON,
K1S 5S8, Canada; 613-237-2925, fax 613-237-0185, info@cba.org, www.cba.org 💻 Fr

CANADIAN NON-GOVERNMENTAL ORGANIZATION ◆ The Canadian Bar Association's (CBA) International Development Program (IDP) enhances the rule of law in democratizing countries through systematic change. Programs are currently being carried out in Cambodia, China, Central and Eastern Europe, Bangladesh, East Africa, South Africa and Vietnam. Each program is unique to the country's particular needs, but all incorporate a focus on institutional capacity building, law reform, substantive law and professional training. The IDP also administers a number of Foreign Affairs Canada (FAC) sponsored international internships. [ID:5521]

Canadian Lawyers for International Human Rights (CLAIHR)
57 Louis Pasteur Street, Ottawa, ON, K1N 6N5, Canada;
613-562-5800 ext. 3353, fax 613-562-5125, contact@claihr.org, www.claihr.org

CANADIAN NON-GOVERNMENTAL ORGANIZATION ◆ Canadian Lawyers for International Human Rights (CLAIHR) promotes human rights globally through legal education, advocacy and law reform. CLAIHR puts Canadian lawyers' experience and expertise to work to further civil, political, economic, social and cultural rights worldwide. It focuses on the situations of indigenous people, workers and women, particularly in Africa, Asia and Latin America. CLAIHR relies heavily upon its network of members who volunteer their time and expertise. [ID:5522]

Center for International Environmental Law (CIEL)
Suite 300, 1367 Connecticut Ave. N.W., Washington, DC, 20036,
USA; 202-785-8700, fax 202-785-8701, info@ciel.org, www.ciel.org

LAW FIRM ◆ The Center for International Environmental Law (CIEL) is a public interest, not-for-profit environmental law firm founded in 1989 to strengthen international and comparative environmental law and policy around the world. CIEL provides a full range of environmental legal services in both international and comparative national law, including policy research and publication, advice and advocacy, education and training, and institution building. It has 25 full-time staff members and posts vacancies on its Web site. [ID:5511]

The Center for Justice and International Law (CEJIL)
1630 Connecticut Ave. N.W., Suite 401, Washington, DC, 20009 – 1053,
USA; 202-319-3000, fax 202-319-3019, info@cejil.org, www.cejil.org 💻*Sp*

INTERNATIONAL NON-GOVERNMENTAL ORGANIZATION ◆ The Center for Justice and International Law (CEJIL) works to achieve the full implementation of international human rights norms in the member states of the Organization of American States (OAS) through the use of the Inter-American System for the Protection of Human Rights and other international protection mechanisms. CEJIL's mandate is fulfilled through work in three program areas: the Legal Defense Program, the Training and Dissemination Program and the Campaign to Strengthen the Inter-American System. The CEJIL has an internship program for law students who are committed to working in human rights and are proficient in Spanish. Its site is also an excellent resource that contains all of the Inter-American Court's latest judgments. [ID:5585]

The Center for Reproductive Rights (CRR)
120 Wall Street, New York, NY, 10005, USA; 917-637-3600,
fax 917-637-3666, info@reprorights.org, www.reproductiverights.org 💻*Fr* 💻*Sp*

INTERNATIONAL NON-GOVERNMENTAL ORGANIZATION ◆ The Center for Reproductive Rights (CRR), formerly known as the Center for Reproductive Law and Policy, is a legal advocacy organization dedicated to promoting and defending women's reproductive rights worldwide. It is the only group of human rights lawyers focused exclusively on reproductive rights. In addition to its domestic work, it uses international human rights law to advance women's reproductive freedom and has succeeded in strengthening reproductive health laws and policies around the globe. CRR has worked with more than 50 organizations in 44 nations including countries in Africa, Asia, East and Central Europe, Latin America and the Caribbean. CRR often has openings and also offers internships and several excellent fellowships for law students and young lawyers. For more information visit www.crlp.org. [ID:5582]

Central European and Eurasian Law Initiative (CEELI)
740 15th Street N.W., Washington, DC, 20005, USA;
202-662-1950, fax 202-662-1597, ceeli@abanet.org, www.abanet.org/ceeli

INTERNATIONAL NON-GOVERNMENTAL ORGANIZATION ◆ The Central European and Eurasian Law Initiative (CEELI) is a public service project of the American Bar Association that advances the rule of law by supporting the law reform process in Central and Eastern Europe and the former Soviet Union. CEELI has more than 20 offices throughout these regions which focus on legal education reform, gender issues, anti-corruption and public integrity, legal profession reform, conflict mitigation and post-conflict transition. The CEELI currently has almost 50 staff in Washington and more than 35 liaisons and long-term legal specialists working overseas. Vacancies are regularly posted on its Web site, as is information about the CEELI's year-long Fellowship Program for newer legal practitioners. Applicants for liaison and legal specialist positions should have at least five years' legal experience. [ID:5510]

Coalition for International Justice (CIJ)

2001 S Street N.W., 7th Floor, Washington, DC, 20009, USA;
202-483-9234, fax 202-483-9263, coalition@cij.org, www.cij.org

INTERNATIONAL NON-GOVERNMENTAL ORGANIZATION ◆ The Coalition for International Justice (CIJ) supports the international war crimes tribunals for Rwanda and the former Yugoslavia, and justice initiatives in Rwanda, East Timor, Sierra Leone and Cambodia. CIJ's small but committed staff initiates and conducts advocacy and public education campaigns, targeting decision-makers in Washington and other capitals, media and the public. Its Web site is an excellent source of information on the various international efforts to hold individuals accountable for the commission of international crimes. [ID:5586]

Coudert Brothers LLP

1114 Avenue of the Americas, New York, NY, 10036, USA;
212-626-4400, fax 212-626-4120, info@coudert.com, www.coudert.com

LAW FIRM ◆ Coudert Brothers LLP has for more than 150 years pioneered the practice of commercial law for the international community. It was the first US-based law firm to establish a European office in Paris and is currently a worldwide partnership of more than 650 lawyers in 29 offices in 18 countries. The firm is particularly well known for complex cross-border transactions and dispute resolution. More than half of their lawyers are European and Asian, and a large proportion of their lawyers have worked in several offices in the firm. In hiring, the firm looks to a record of high academic achievement, especially in law school, but also in college and other schools. On a subjective basis, they are particularly interested in lawyers who are international in outlook and who possess initiative, maturity and ingenuity. Other qualifications, such as language training, are listed on the company's Web site. Hiring details and resources for each office is also listed on the site. [ID:5503]

Davis Polk & Wardwell

450 Lexington Ave., New York, NY, 10017, USA; 212-450-4000, fax 212-450-3800, www.dpw.com

LAW FIRM ◆ Davis Polk & Wardwell ranks among the world's finest law firms across the entire range of their practice. The firm has represented many of the world's leading companies and financial institutions. The practice is organized into four departments: Corporate, Litigation, Tax, and Trusts and Estates. Davis Polk lawyers work in highly collaborative teams that span across their practice, and if necessary, around the world. Davis Polk & Wardell is a world leader in counselling government-owned entities as they make the transition to public ownership. Since 1990, the firm has worked on more than 75 privatizations of formerly government-owned companies in approximately 30 countries in Latin America, Canada, Europe, Asia and the Pacific Rim, including transactions in the airline, automobile, banking, electric power, insurance, oil and gas, railroad, steel, mining and telecommunications industries. Davis Polk & Wardell employs 606 lawyers. A careers page can be found on the firm's Web site, which details their hiring process. Summer associate opportunities are available, as well as branch rotations. [ID:5507]

DPK Consulting

Suite 800, 605 Market Street, San Francisco, CA, 94105, USA; 415-495-7772,
fax 415-495-6017, dpk@dpkconsulting.com, www.dpkconsulting.com ⌨*Sp*

INTERNATIONAL NON-GOVERNMENTAL ORGANIZATION ◆ DPK Consulting, a private firm, works in developing and transitional countries to modernize justice systems. The firm's substantive scope includes the rule of law and administration of justice, anti-corruption, local governance and urban management, planning and design of public sector systems, and automation of management information systems. It is especially active in Latin America, but also does work in the Middle East, the Balkans and Asia. DPK has numerous consulting opportunities for individuals with experience working on rule of law, judicial reform and related issues. Check its Web site to see what is available or e-mail your resume if you have relevant expertise. [ID:5527]

The European Council on Refugees and Exiles (ECRE)

103 Worship Street, London, EC2A 2DF, UK;
(44) (0) 20-7377-7556, fax (44) (0) 20-7377-7586, ecre@ecre.org, www.ecre.org

INTERNATIONAL NON-GOVERNMENTAL ORGANIZATION ◆ The European Council on Refugees and Exiles (ECRE) is an umbrella organization that facilitates cooperation between non-governmental organizations in Europe concerned with refugees. The ECRE currently has 76 member agencies in 30 countries. Its principal activities are summarized under four main headings: policy analysis and advocacy; legal analysis and networking; information and documentation; and capacity building in Central, Eastern and Southeastern Europe. The ECRE secretariat consists of an office in London with a staff of 14 people plus interns, and the Brussels office with a staff of two and interns. Vacancies and internship opportunities are posted on its Web site. [ID:5629]

Fasken Martineau

Toronto-Dominion Centre, 66 Wellington Street W., Toronto, ON, M5K 1N6, Canada;
416-366-8381, fax 416-364-7813, webmaster@mtl.fasken.com, www.fasken.com ⌨*Fr* ⌨*Sp*

LAW FIRM ◆ Fasken Martineau is a leading national business and litigation law firm in Canada. Its 560 lawyers work out of its six Canadian offices, as well as offices in New York, London and Johannesburg. Its Trade and Customs Law Group is just one of its many practice groups that is engaged in international legal work. Its Asia Pacific and Latin American Groups provide regional expertise in all areas of law. It is very experienced in project finance work throughout the world and has a Global Mining Group that provides specialist advice. Finally, Fasken Martineau's International Dispute Resolution Group is very experienced in representing clients in international commercial disputes around the world, including international commercial arbitrations, investment disputes under the NAFTA, bilateral investment treaties and international trade disputes. [ID:5513]

Global Rights

Suite 602, 1200 18th Street N.W., Washington, DC, 20036,
USA; 202-822-4600, fax 202-822-4606, www.hrlawgroup.org

INTERNATIONAL NON-GOVERNMENTAL ORGANIZATION ◆ Global Rights is a human rights advocacy group that partners with local activists to challenge oppressive ideologies and power structures, channel international pressure to secure human rights protections and amplify new voices within the global discourse. Working through 10 offices, its international staff promotes racial and gender equality and develops the skills of local activists that are essential to addressing human rights concerns and promoting justice, such as documenting and exposing abuses, conducting community education and mobilization, advocating legal and policy reform in countries and internationally, and using the courts to increase access to justice for disadvantaged populations. Global Rights posts vacancies on its Web site. Applicants for program positions should have a commitment to working in the human rights field, demonstrated by several years of experience in addition to legal education. [ID:5583]

Gowlings
Suite 2600, 160 Elgin Street, Ottawa, ON, K1P 1C3, Canada; 613-233-1781,
fax 613-563-9869, webmaster@gowlings.com, www.gowlings.com ▣*Fr*

LAW FIRM ◆ Gowlings has offices throughout Canada and a representative office in Moscow that enables the firm to represent clients in Russia, Eastern Europe and Central Asia. Gowlings is the largest firm in the Ottawa area with over 160 professionals. The expertise it has developed working on files related to government has led to its being awarded several very interesting World Bank contracts to introduce alternative dispute resolution to transitional countries. It also provides strategic and policy advice to countries and governments around the world. [ID:5520]

Harris & Moure
Suite 1000, 720 Olive Way, Seattle, WA, 98101, USA;
206-224-5657, firm@harrismoure.com, www.harrismoure.com

LAW FIRM ◆ Harris & Moure, pllc has grown quickly by providing top-flight representation to domestic and international clients in maritime, corporate and litigation matters. A number of the world's leading law firms choose Harris & Moure attorneys to assist on matters requiring expertise in overseas dispute resolution. The firm does not list job opportunities on its Web site, so interested candidates are advised to contact the firm directly to discuss possible employment. [ID:5500]

Human Rights First
333 Seventh Ave., 13th Floor, New York, NY, 10001 - 5004, USA; 212-845-5200,
fax 212-845-5299, communications@humanrightsfirst.org, www.humanrightsfirst.org

INTERNATIONAL NON-GOVERNMENTAL ORGANIZATION ◆ Human Rights First (formerly the Lawyers Committee of Human Rights) works in the United States and abroad to create a secure and humane world by advancing justice, human dignity and respect for the rule of law. Its work includes advocacy and representing clients throughout the world on a pro bono basis. Some of the issues it focuses on include international justice and the International Criminal Court, International Refugee Law and supporting the work of international human rights activists. It has 52 staff members and posts vacancy, fellowship and internship opportunities on its Web site. Most of its legal positions require at least five years of related professional experience. [ID:5584]

INTERIGHTS - The International Centre
for the Legal Protection of Human Rights
Lancaster House, 33 Islington High Street, London, N1 9LH, UK;
(44) (0) 20-7278-3230, fax (44) (0) 20-7278-4334, ir@interights.org, www.interights.org

INTERNATIONAL NON-GOVERNMENTAL ORGANIZATION ◆ INTERIGHTS, the International Centre for the Legal Protection of Human Rights is an international legal centre that develops and promotes the legal protection of human rights worldwide. It provides technical advice and assistance to strengthen capacity and develop jurisprudence in Africa, the Commonwealth, Central and Eastern Europe and South Asia. It also works to improve the legal protection of certain key rights worldwide through development of jurisprudence, strengthening relevant mechanisms and providing education and training. It has 15 full-time staff members and posts information about vacancies, internships and volunteering on its Web site. Its Web site is also an excellent resource on human rights as it contains an abundance of information on it. [ID:5631]

International Bar Association (IBA)
271 Regent Street, Hanover Square, London, W1B 2AQ, UK;
(44) (0) 20-7629-1206, fax (44) (0) 20-7409-0456, member@int-bar.org, www.ibanet.org

CANADIAN NON-GOVERNMENTAL ORGANIZATION ◆ The International Bar Association (IBA) maintains permanent relations and exchanges between 190 Bar Associations and Law Societies throughout the world, advances the science of jurisprudence, and promotes the administration of justice under law among peoples of the world. Sixteen thousand individual lawyers are also members of the IBA, through which they influence the development of international law reform and shapes the future of the legal profession.

The IBA has about 50 full-time staff members and hires part-time assistants as required. The IBA Web site provides useful links to related organizations. Legal specialists are frequently recruited to develop continuing legal education programs in countries where there is little or no training after qualification. The IBA's Web site is an essential resource for international lawyers seeking information about emerging legal trends. [ID:5593]

International Center for Not-for-Profit Law (ICNL)

Suite 400, 1126 16th Street, N.W., Washington, DC, 20036, USA;
202-452-8600, fax 202-452-8555, infoicnl@icnl.org, www.icnl.org

INTERNATIONAL NON-GOVERNMENTAL ORGANIZATION ◆ The International Center for Not-for-Profit Law (ICNL) facilitates and supports the development of civil society and the freedom of association. The ICNL assists in creating and improving laws and regulatory systems that permit, encourage and sustain voluntary, independent, not-for-profit organizations in countries around the world. It is particularly active in Eastern Europe and Central Asia. The ICNL has 31 staff members that work out of its offices in Washington, Almaty and Budapest. Employment and internship opportunities are posted on its Web site. Law students can also apply to be editors of the International Journal of Not-for-Profit Law. [ID:5524]

International Center for Transitional Justice (ICTJ)

33rd Floor, 20 Exchange Place, New York, NY, 10005, USA;
917-438-9300, fax 212-509-6036, info@ictj.org, www.ictj.org ▢*Fr* ▢*Sp*

INTERNATIONAL NON-GOVERNMENTAL ORGANIZATION ◆ The International Center for Transitional Justice (ICTJ) assists countries pursuing accountability for mass atrocities or systematic human rights abuses. The Center works in societies emerging from repressive rule or armed conflict, as well as in established democracies where historical injustices or systemic abuse remain unresolved. Its 31 staff provide comparative information, legal and policy analysis, documentation and strategic research to justice and truth-seeking institutions, non-governmental organizations, governments and others. The ICTJ offers internships and several interesting fellowships that are coordinated with partner organizations in developing countries. Visit its Web site for further information. [ID:5627]

International Centre for Settlement of Investment Disputes (ICSID)

1818 H Street N.W., Washington, DC, 20433, USA;
202-458-1534, fax 202-522-2615, www.worldbank.org/icsid

WORLD BANK GROUP ◆ The International Centre for Settlement of Investment Disputes (ICSID) is one of five organizations that constitute the World Bank Group. ICSID was designed to facilitate the settlement of investment disputes between governments and foreign investors. ICSID is the designated dispute settlement forum of choice in most bilateral investment treaties (BITs). In addition, ICSID carries out advisory and research activities relevant to its objectives and has a number of publications. The Centre also collaborates with other World Bank Group units in meeting requests by governments for advice on investment and arbitration law. Its Web site is an essential resource for anyone interested in BITs or doing research on international investment laws. ICSID vacancies are also posted on the World Bank's Web site. [ID:5699]

International Commission of Jurists (ICJ)

P.O. Box 216, 1219 Chatelaine/Geneva, Switzerland;
(41) (22) 979-3800, fax (41) (22) 979-3801, info@icj.org, www.icj.org ▢*Fr* ▢*Sp*

INTERNATIONAL NON-GOVERNMENTAL ORGANIZATION ◆ The International Commission of Jurists (ICJ) is a group of 60 eminent jurists dedicated to the primacy, coherence and implementation of international law and principles that advance human rights. The ICJ provides legal expertise at both the international and national levels to ensure that developments in international law adhere to human rights principles and that international standards are implemented at the national level. The 17 staff at the international secretariat is responsible for overseeing the work of the Commission and works closely with a network that includes 37 national sections and 45 affiliated organizations around the world. The ICJ seeks the involvement of judges, other legal professionals, legal academics and law students that are interested in the promotion and protection of human rights through legal means. The ICJ maintains an excellent "Get Involved" page on its Web site that provides information about internships, vacancies and other ways to become involved in its work. [ID:5625]

The International Court of Arbitration of
the International Chamber of Commerce
38 cours Albert 1er, 75008 Paris, France; (33) (1) 49-53-28-28,
fax (33) (1) 49-53-29-33, arb@iccwbo.org, www.iccarbitration.org 💻 *Fr*

INTERNATIONAL NON-GOVERNMENTAL ORGANIZATION ◆ The International Court of Arbitration of the International Chamber of Commerce is one of the world's leading international commercial arbitration bodies. Since its creation, the Court has administered over 13,000 international arbitration cases involving parties and arbitrators from more than 170 countries and territories on all continents. The workload of ICC's numerous dispute resolution services continues to grow at a rapid pace. Vacancies for positions with the secretariat of the ICC International Court of Arbitration and other ICC dispute resolution services are posted on the Court's Web site. Generally the Court seeks at least bilingual (English/French) lawyers with a post-graduate degree in private international law or commercial law. [ID:5626]

International Court of Justice (ICJ)
Peace Palace, 2517 KJ, The Hague, Netherlands; (31) (70) 302-2323,
fax (31) (70) 364-9928, information@icj-cij.org, www.icj-cij.org 💻 *Fr*

INTERNATIONAL COURT OF JUSTICE ◆ The International Court of Justice (ICJ) is the principal judicial organ of the United Nations. The court has a dual role: to settle in accordance with international law the legal disputes submitted to it by states, and to provide advisory opinions on legal questions referred to the ICJ by duly authorized international organs and agencies.

Both professional and general services vacancies with ICJ are posted on the ICJ Web site. Graduates from Yale, McGill, New York University, the University of Michigan and Strasbourg University are all eligible for the ICJ's clerkship program. [ID:5701]

International Criminal Court (ICC)
Maanweg, 174, 2516 AB, The Hague, Netherlands;
(31) (70) 515-8515, fax (31) (70) 515-8555, pio@icc-cpi.int, www.icc-cpi.int 💻 *Fr*

INTERGOVERNMENTAL ORGANIZATION ◆ The International Criminal Court (ICC) is an independent international organization that was established by the Rome Statute of the International Criminal Court on July 17, 1998. The ICC is the first permanent, treaty-based international criminal court established to promote the rule of law and ensure that the gravest international crimes do not go unpunished. Even though the Statute entered into force on July 1, 2002, it will take some time before the Court begins prosecuting cases.

The seat of the Court is The Hague. As a new organization, the ICC seeks creative, professional and highly-motivated individuals who are proficient in one of the working languages of the Court, which are English and French. The ICC seeks to fill posts by nationals of a State Party to the Statute of Rome, or of a state which has signed or acceded to the Statute and is engaged in the ratification process, but nationals from non-state parties may also be considered. Canadians are already well represented at the Court and there are still many opportunities for experienced professionals. The Court offers excellent clerkship and internship opportunities. It has an excellent Web site that contains detailed information about the various opportunities that the Court offers. Applications are maintained on an active roster for a period of one year. [ID:5693]

International Justice Mission (IJM)

P.O. Box 58147, Washington, DC, 20037 - 8147, USA;
703-465-5495, fax 703-465-5499, contact@ijm.org, www.ijm.org

INTERNATIONAL NON-GOVERNMENTAL ORGANIZATION ◆ The International Justice Mission (IJM) is a Christian agency led by human rights professionals that helps people suffering injustice and oppression who cannot rely on local authorities for relief. The IJM uses investigation strategies, legal expertise and cutting-edge technology to rescue individual victims of injustice and abuse around the world. Through its education initiatives, IJM provides people of faith with the training, mobilization tools and resources to translate their convictions into active engagement. IJM posts vacancies and overseas volunteer opportunities on its Web site. Every summer, it also deploys law students to serve in its overseas field offices. Information on IJM Canada can be found at www.ijm.ca. [ID:5526]

International Seabed Authority (ISA)

14-20 Port Royal Street, Kingston, Jamaica; (876) 922-9105,
fax (876) 922-0195, webmaster@isa.org.jm, www.isa.org.jm ▢*Fr* ▢*Sp*

INTERGOVERNMENTAL ORGANIZATION ◆ The International Seabed Authority is an autonomous international organization established under the 1982 United Nations Convention on the Law of the Sea (UNCLOS) and the 1994 Agreement relating to the Implementation of Part XI of UNCLOS. The Authority is the organization through which all states party to the Convention organize and control activities within national jurisdictions, particularly with particular focus on resource administration. The ISA Web site contains detailed information on the organs of the Authority and lists all vacancies as they arise. [ID:7343]

International Trade Centre (ITC)

54-56 rue de Montbrillant, CH 1211, Geneva, Switzerland; (41) (22) 730-0111,
fax (41) (22) 730-0803, itcreg@intracen.org, www.intracen.org ▢*Fr* ▢*Sp*

SPECIALIZED AGENCY ◆ The International Trade Centre (ITC) is the technical cooperation agency of the United Nations Conference on Trade and Development (UNCTAD) and the World Trade Organization (WTO) that works with developing countries to set up effective national trade promotion programs for expanding their exports and improving their import operations. In particular the ITC works very closely with these countries' private sectors.

ITC has its headquarters in Geneva where it employs a handful of Canadian professional and support staff, and offers an internship program. ITC maintains a consultant roster, occasionally bringing on consultants for short-term contracts.

All vacancies including consultancies and temporary secretarial posts are listed on the ITC's Web site on their "About ITC" page. (For ITC internship information, see Chapter 17, Internships Abroad.) [ID:5686]

International Tribunal for the Law of the Sea (ITLOS)

Am Internationalen Seegerichtshof 1, 22609 Hamburg, Germany;
(49) (40) 35607-0, fax (49) (40) 35607-245, itlos@itlos.org, www.itlos.org ▢*Fr*

RELATED UN AGENCY ◆ The International Tribunal for the Law of the Sea (ITLOS) is an independent judicial body established to adjudicate disputes arising out of the interpretation and application of the UN Convention on the Law of the Sea. The Tribunal is composed of 21 independent members, elected from among persons enjoying the highest reputation for fairness and integrity and of recognized competence in the field of the law of the sea. Pursuant to the provisions of its statute, the Tribunal has formed the following Chambers: the Chamber of Summary Procedure, the Chamber for Fisheries Disputes and the Chamber for Marine Environment Disputes.

Both professional- and service-level vacancies are posted on the ITLOS Web site; applicants must complete a United Nations Personal History Form. ITLOS also hosts an internship program. (For ITLOS internship information, see Chapter 17, Internships Abroad.) [ID:5676]

Jones Day

901 Lakeside Ave., Cleveland, OH, 44114-1190, USA; 216-586-3939,
fax 216-579-0212, office@jonesday.com, http://www1.jonesday.com

LAW FIRM ♦ Jones Day is an international law firm with offices in 29 cities in centres of business and finance throughout the world. With more than 2,200 lawyers, it ranks among the world's largest law firms. The firm has offices in the United States, Latin America, Europe and Asia. The firm's international practice is significant and growing. In addition to representing a large number of its US-based clients in international matters, Jones Day maintains a significant presence in the principal legal and regulatory capitals of the world. In Europe, approximately 400 lawyers are based in Brussels, Frankfurt, London, Madrid, Milan, Munich and Paris. In Asia, more than 140 lawyers are based in Beijing, Hong Kong, Shanghai, Singapore, Taipei and Tokyo. The firm also has an office in Sydney. The firm's international practice focuses primarily on mergers and acquisitions, joint ventures and other investment transactions; securities and finance matters; tax, labour, environmental, competition and other significant regulatory matters; and international litigation and arbitration. [ID:5506]

Department of Justice Canada

External Liaison Unit, Room 209, 239 Wellington Street, Ottawa, ON,
K1A 0H8, Canada; 613-952-8346, fax 613-941-4165, http://canada.justice.gc.ca 🖳 *Fr*

CANADIAN GOVERNMENT ♦ (See the multi page profile of the Department of Justice at the beginning of Chapter 31, International Law Careers.) [ID:7342]

Macleod Dixon

3700 Canterra Tower, 400 Third Ave. S.W., Calgary, AB, T2P 4H2,
Canada; 403-267-8207, fax 403-264-5973, www.macleoddixon.com

LAW FIRM ♦ Macleod Dixon is an international firm of more than 230 legal professionals that operates with a closely linked network of international offices in Calgary, Moscow, Toronto, Almaty, Atyrau, Caracas and Rio de Janeiro. The centrepiece of its practice is Energy law. Lawyers provide advice on the legal aspects of exploration, development, production, transportation and marketing of oil and natural gas. It has developed extensive expertise in international transactions in Russia, Central Asia, Latin America and other regions of the world. It is particularly active in the very interesting legal happenings concerning the Caspian Sea. Its lawyers are also active in international arbitrations and mediations. [ID:5515]

McCarthy Tétrault

Suite 4700, Toronto Dominion Tower, Toronto, ON, M5K 1E6,
Canada; 416-362-1812, fax 416-868-0673, www.mccarthy.ca 🖳 *Fr*

LAW FIRM ♦ McCarthy Tétrault has a significant presence in all major financial centres in Canada as well as in New York and London. With close to 800 practitioners, its lawyers regularly advise on many of the largest transactions and cases in Canada and around the world. The firm is actively involved in cross-border transactions and international projects. McCarthy Tétrault is consistently ranked among the leading Canadian law firms in the areas of corporate finance, mergers and acquisitions, banking, mining, oil and gas, power, technology, communications, competition, tax, litigation and real estate. [ID:5519]

McMillan Binch

Suite 4400, BCE Place, 181 Bay Street, Toronto, ON, M5J 2T3, Canada;
416-865-7000, fax 416-865-7048, info@mcmillanbinch.com, www.mcmillanbinch.com

LAW FIRM ♦ McMillan Binch provides a full range of business legal services to corporate and financial service clients in Canada, the United States and abroad. Its integrated International Business & Trade Law practice offers the full spectrum of legal services including resolving commercial, trade, transfer pricing and procurement disputes through arbitration, litigation and mediation. McMillan Binch is very active internationally, and its work includes representing clients in international commercial arbitrations. [ID:5517]

National Judicial Institute (NJI)

International Cooperation Group, 300-161 Laurier Ave. W., Ottawa, ON, K1P 5J2,
Canada; 613-237-1118, fax 613-237-6155, nji@judicom.gc.ca, www.nji.ca ▣ 𝓕𝓻

CANADIAN NON-GOVERNMENTAL ORGANIZATION ◆ The National Judicial Institute (NJI) is an independent non-profit organization that serves the Canadian judiciary by planning, coordinating and delivering judicial education dealing with the law, the craft of judging and social context. The NJI's International Cooperation Group (ICG) manages international development projects that are aimed at judicial reform and include a substantial judicial education component. The ICG also coordinates the participation of Canada's judges, judicial educators and courts in international projects, whether through their overseas work or by the reception in Canada of judges and judicial educators from overseas. The NJI has 35 staff members, 6 of whom work on international issues. [ID:5523]

Office of the Judge Advocate General (JAG)

General Office, Constitution Bldg., National Defence Headquarters, 305 Rideau Street, Ottawa, ON,
K1A 0K2, Canada; 613-992-6420, fax 613-995-3155, information@forces.gc.ca, www.forces.gc.ca/jag ▣ 𝓕𝓻

CANADIAN GOVERNMENT ◆ The Office of the Judge Advocate General (JAG) is the legal adviser to the Governor General, the Minister of National Defence, the Department of National Defence (DND) and the Canadian Forces (CF) in matters relating to military law. The Office of the JAG comprises 114 regular force legal officer positions and 64 reserve force legal officer positions. The regular force legal officers are employed throughout the CF, in Canada and abroad. Every year JAG hires between one and four articling students that are hired as civilian term employees. This offers civilians the unique opportunity to be trained in international humanitarian law. Unlike most articling positions, these are recruited late in the spring through the Public Service Commission (PSC) Web site. JAG also usually takes on anywhere from six to 12 summer students, but it will take on no students in 2004 because of budget cuts. For more information consult JAG's Web site or call for detailed information. [ID:5711]

Ogilvy Renault

Suite 1600, 45 O'Connor Street, Ottawa, ON, K1P 1A4, Canada; 613-780-8661,
fax 613-230-5459, ottawa@ogilvyrenault.com, www.ogilvyrenault.com ▣ 𝓕𝓻

LAW FIRM ◆ Ogilvy Renault is one of Canada's oldest law firms. It has offices in Canada's major cities and in London, UK. Its international trade law practice is based out of its Ottawa office and is one of the largest in the country. This practice group works on a variety of international trade and regulatory issues, including interpreting bilateral and multilateral trade agreements, litigating under trade laws and working on investment disputes. [ID:5512]

Osler, Hoskin & Harcourt

50 O'Connor Street, Suite 1500, Ottawa, ON, K1P 6L2, Canada;
613-235-7234, fax 613-235-2867, counsel@osler.com, www.osler.com ▣ 𝓕𝓻

LAW FIRM ◆ Osler, Hoskin & Harcourt is one of Canada's leading business law firms. It has offices in four cities in Canada as well as in New York. Based in its Ottawa office, its International Trade Group has acted in more proceedings than any other Canadian law firm before the Canadian International Trade Tribunal (CITT), Binational Panels under Chapter 19 of the NAFTA and the Federal Court of Canada. [ID:5514]

REDRESS

87 Vauxhall Walk, London, SE11 5HJ, UK; (44) (0) 20-7793-1777,
fax (44) (0) 20-7793-1719, redresstrust@gn.apc.org, www.redress.org

INTERNATIONAL NON-GOVERNMENTAL ORGANIZATION ◆ REDRESS helps torture survivors obtain justice and reparation. Its primary objectives are to make accountable all those who perpetrate or aid and abet acts of torture and to seek reparation for victims and their families anywhere in the world. It accomplishes its mission through a range of activities, including bringing legal challenges to promote the rights of victims in various national and international forums and to help them gain both access to the courts and redress for their suffering; promoting the development and implementation of national and international standards and institutions, which provide effective and enforceable civil and criminal remedies for torture and other serious violations of human rights and humanitarian law; and increasing awareness of the widespread use of torture and the plight of survivors through a range of comparative research and advocacy programs. It has a small staff of eight in London and relies extensively on interns and volunteers. Visit REDRESS's Web site for more information. [ID:5628]

Shearman & Sterling, LLP

599 Lexington Ave., New York, NY, 10022 - 6069, USA;
212-848-4000, fax 212-848-7179, www.shearman.com

LAW FIRM ◆ Shearman & Sterling, LLP is one of the few global law firms with more than 1,000 lawyers located in all of the world's financial capitals. The firm's practice is divided into five major areas: litigation, tax, executive compensation and employee benefits, private client, and antitrust. Areas with a strictly international focus include international arbitration, international trade and government relations. Although the firm maintains its principal offices in New York, the firm is also spread throughout Europe, Latin America and Asia. The recruitment page on the company Web site is very descriptive and provides lots of information about life at the firm, career opportunities, summer programs, associate initiatives, their global diversity initiative and professional development, among others. Shearman & Sterling encourages associates to take advantage of work opportunities throughout the firm's worldwide offices. [ID:5502]

Stikeman Elliott

Suite 1600, 50 O'Connor Street, Ottawa, ON, K1P 6L2, Canada;
613-234-4555, fax 613-230-8877, info@stikeman.com, www.stikeman.com ▣*Fr*

LAW FIRM ◆ Stikeman Elliot is a full-service firm with offices in five Canadian cities, New York, London, Hong Kong and Sydney. Its international legal work encompasses advisory services on a host of issues including the identification and mitigation of transaction risks, the structuring and negotiation of project finance, the negotiation of host government assurances, including the drafting and negotiation of appropriate legislation and tax and customs regimes, and the drafting and negotiation of transaction documentation. It is also recognized as having one of Canada's most experienced international trade law groups. [ID:5518]

United Nations Commission on International Trade Law (UNCITRAL)

P.O. Box 500, Vienna International Centre, Wagramerstrasse 5, A - 1400 Vienna, Austria;
(43) (1) 26060-4061, fax (43) (1) 26060-5813, uncitral@uncitral.org, www.uncitral.org ▣*Fr*▣*Sp*

GENERAL ASSEMBLY ◆ The United Nations Commission on International Trade Law (UNCITRAL) is the core legal body within the United Nations system in the field of international trade law, with the mandate to further the progressive harmonization and unification of international trade law. For employment as an entry level (P-3) legal officer, successful applicants will have an advanced university degree in law with particular emphasis on commercial, economic and comparative private law, as well as six years of professional experience in international trade law and a sound background in the experience of a particular legal system. An advanced degree (PhD or equivalent) may be substituted for two years of professional experience. The UNCITRAL secretariat also hosts an internship program for young lawyers.

UNCITRAL's Web site has no job page, but offers some employment-related information on the FAQs page. Vacancies are posted on the UN job page. (For UNCITRAL internship information, see Chapter 17, Internships Abroad.) [ID:5689]

United Nations Conference on Trade and Development (UNCTAD)
Palais des Nations, 8 - 14 ave. de la Paix, 1211 Geneva 10, Switzerland;
(41) (22) 917-1234, fax (41) (22) 917-0043, info@unctad.org, www.unctad.org ▣ *Fr* ▣ *Sp*

RELATED UN PROGRAM ◆ The United Nations Conference on Trade and Development (UNCTAD) has a few principal functions: it promotes international trade, particularly between countries at different levels of development, formulates and implements principles and policies on international trade and related problems of development, facilitates the coordination of activities of other institutions within the UN system in the field of trade, initiates actions for the negotiation and adoption of multilateral legal instruments in the field, and acts as a centre for the harmonization of trade and related development policies of governments and regional economic groups.

UNCTAD employs approximately 400 people. Vacancies in technical cooperation are listed on the UNCTAD Web site, while those for professional posts are available on the UN job page. UNCTAD's job page offers advice for job seekers at all levels interested in working with UNCTAD and other UN agencies. [ID:5674]

United Nations Framework Climate Change Convention (UNFCCC)
P.O. Box 260124, D-53153 Bonn, Germany; (49) (228) 815-1000,
fax (49) (228) 815-1999, secretariat@unfccc.int, http://unfccc.int ▣ *Fr* ▣ *Sp*

RELATED UN PROGRAM ◆ The United Nations Framework Climate Change Convention (UNFCC) secretariat supports cooperative action by states to combat climate change and its impacts on humanity and ecosystems. Guided by the parties to the Convention, the UNFCC secretariat provides organizational support and technical expertise to negotiations and institutions while facilitating the flow of authoritative information on the implementation of the Convention.

Located in Bonn, the working language of the UNFCC is English; therefore fluency in both written and spoken English is essential for employment with the organization. All current vacancies are listed on the UNFCCC job page under the "Secretariat" tab of their Web site, as is information regarding UNFCCC's internship program. (For UNFCCC internship information, see Chapter 17, Internships Abroad.) [ID:5675]

White & Case
1155 Avenue of the Americas, New York, NY, 10036 - 2787,
USA; 212-819-8200, fax 212-354-8113, www.whitecase.com

LAW FIRM ◆ White & Case has lawyers in the United States, Latin America, Europe, the Middle East, Africa and Asia. Their clients are public and privately held commercial businesses and financial institutions, as well as governments and state-owned entities involved in sophisticated corporate and financial transactions and complex dispute-resolution proceedings. International practice is the foundation of the firm and they have been involved in transactions in virtually every corner of the world. They have a critical mass of US, English and domestic lawyers throughout the world who are either native to, or fully integrated in, the regions where they are based. On the firm's Web site you will find PDF files with information about recruiting in the US, the UK, and for their International Lawyers Program. Their law student page also provides information about summer programs, associate life, non-US office internship and career positions and a wealth of other information that will help you determine which area is best fit for you. [ID:5501]

CHAPTER 32

Engineering Careers Abroad

North America is one of the top regions in the world for research, development and utilization of modern technology and our engineers are recognized for their expertise and international work. Canada and the United States are top exporters of engineering services worldwide. Export sales for consulting engineering services in Canada are a $1.4 billion industry. As economic globalization and international free trade create new employment, international engineering work will also continue to grow. This chapter introduces the field of international engineering and provides advice for those interested in breaking into the field. Engineering work described in this chapter refers not only to work performed by licensed engineers, but includes that of skilled technicians and other related professionals.

WHY ENGINEER ABROAD?

In addition to the perks of international travel and new cultural experiences, an international engineering career offers an opportunity for advancing professionally as well as participating in innovative, meaningful projects abroad. With globalization, an international assignment can be beneficial for long-term career gain. Many North American firms compete for international contracts, so engineers who show that they are competent in the international arena tend to be acknowledged by management.

A point of view prevalent among international consulting firms is that overseas work broadens an individual engineer's perspective and exposes him or her to situations that one rarely finds in Canada and the United States, where engineering work is more structured. Such exposure develops judgment, which is a highly sought-after skill among mid-career professionals.

In spite of this, some engineers have experienced that domestic firms not participating in projects outside of North America may not appreciate international engineering work experience, apart from the technical component. One engineer said,

"International engineering experience is not particularly valuable for one's career back in Canada or the United States. Generally, career building requires being close to the head office, preferably in it. Influencing one's bosses is an up front and personal effort and one tends to be out of sight and out of mind in overseas placements. Also, the type of work done abroad doesn't fit the style of work in a larger home office environment, where everything is much more structured."

You may encounter this perception upon returning to North America and should keep it in mind as you pursue international engineering work. The appeal of working abroad has to be intrinsic to the work itself because for the most part international engineering experience is recognized by firms doing international work. In any case, we have not heard an engineer regret taking an overseas position because it did not advance her or his career. Working overseas can help engineers to increase their professional skills while being exposed to new ideas.

Overseas jobs differ from the home front in that they require not only technical expertise, but also the ability to adapt to working within a foreign culture. This usually involves toiling long hours with local or other expatriate engineers. On some projects, local labour crews may do work that would typically be done with heavy machinery in North America. Highly technical equipment and materials may not be available locally, thus requiring innovative solutions and the ability to deal with inevitable delays. Engineers are usually provided with accommodation close to the job site, as they may be located in remote areas. Most jobs provide great opportunities for newcomers to interact with other cultures.

A word of caution: if you are entering the international engineering field because you want to be exposed to the latest techniques, you may be disappointed. The practice of international engineering is more about being skilled in cross-cultural management than dealing with new technologies. Experienced international engineers are most often motivated and find their sense of satisfaction from the stimulating challenges that a cross-cultural environment provides. International employers recognize this, and are often willing to hire a less technically qualified engineer who has the personality traits needed to do the job in a cross-cultural environment.

TYPES OF ENGINEERING POSITIONS ABROAD

North American engineers are currently working all over the globe for mining and transportation firms, consulting firms, power companies, government and international agencies and international development NGOs. The diversity of opportunity within the engineering profession creates a wide choice of careers for its graduates, from the public sector to the non-profit and private sectors. The field of international engineering is, however, clearly dominated by the private sector. Private sector firms that have contracts with government agencies most often employ engineers who undertake public sector work. There are few direct employment opportunities in engineering with the government, international agencies or NGOs.

Engineering contracts abroad typically fall into these categories:

- **The Consulting Visit.** Many firms, especially consulting engineering firms, send their engineers abroad on a regular basis for short-term assignments generally lasting from one to three weeks. These visits often provide monitoring services or expert advice on large and varied projects.

- **Three- to Six-Month Posting in Emergency Relief.** These interventions are generally for engineers working in disaster relief, peacekeeping or on refugee projects. People with no family obligations almost always staff these positions and are employed directly with international organizations. Some organizations, like RedR, actively recruit for such positions. (For more information on RedR, see the Profiles section in Chapter 38, NGOs in Canada.)

- **The International Posting.** These positions are generally two-year contracts with private sector firms, and may include one-year renewable extensions. Engineers may be accompanied by their families for the international posting and the project is usually located in a relatively secure area. Many of the projects may be in isolated locations, particularly if the work is in natural resource extraction.

- **Overseas Rotational Work.** These jobs involve a rotation such as 10 weeks abroad, 10 weeks back in North America. The engineer's family stays at home in Canada or the United States. Many kinds of projects require this type of international work schedule. The work may be geographically dispersed, as with building a pipeline through Chad or a power grid over the Andes. In some cases, the environment may be politically contentious and unsuitable for families or the location may be too remote. Engineers who are attracted to this type of work arrangement usually see it as a sacrifice of normal family life in order to save money. Some families actually become accustomed to the arrangement, especially if the stay-at-home spouse is highly independent. Some families also find that the mother or father employed in this capacity has more time to connect with children during the 10-week rotation at home.

- **Long-Term Volunteer Placement.** Many people have started their international engineering careers by volunteering with NGOs for six-month to two-year placements. Payment for these positions is usually in the form of a stipend in the neighbourhood of $1500—enough perhaps to cover travel expenses. There is almost always a fundraising component to cover additional expenses, and housing is sometimes provided for the length of the placement. However, the pay is not typically enough for saving money or supporting dependents. In lieu of the perks commonly associated with an international posting, work with NGOs offers a number of unique and career-building benefits. Work abroad with NGOs tends to offer a broader, more hands-on professional experience than what you might find within a private sector firm, allowing you to roll up your sleeves and try your hand at a number of projects. In these placements, you have an opportunity to engage intimately with the host culture, since NGO projects focused on sustainable development will usually involve the direct participation of locals. This will allow you to experience meaningful interaction and even integration into the community. One engineering intern said the following.

"I found NGO work to be much less structured than the private sector. With NGO work, it was difficult to plan projects ahead of time. Be prepared for drastic changes when you first arrive. My fellow engineering friends and I found that the engineering component of our projects was actually very low (10 or 20 per cent) when compared to the cultural aspects affecting the project. The work was rewarding and important, but not necessarily because of the engineering."

QUALITIES OF AN INTERNATIONAL ENGINEER

While engineering is a technical profession with substantial emphasis on "hard" skills, the success or failure of an international engineering project most often rests upon "soft" skills. Can you manage a project where language and cultural differences abound? Are you good at handling differences in approaches, values and expectations? The cross-cultural aspect of an engineering project may in fact be the single most defining factor in your success overseas. For this reason, international recruiters place a lot of importance on it when selecting from a pool of candidates.

The engineering profession is very collaborative and interactive. Whatever the focus of your project, you will need to be able to communicate effectively to a broad range of individuals from varying cultures and backgrounds, including local communities, other engineers and managers, and government officials. Even when working with seemingly similar cultures (for example, English and US), an international engineer should be aware of subtle cultural differences. International engineers know the value of looking for differences in corporate culture, technical jargon, measurement terminology and organizational communication, even when there is no language barrier.

Many engineers working internationally find themselves dealing with problems well outside their chosen discipline, and often outside the field of engineering itself. Some observers would point out that there are probably more engineers working abroad in non-engineering fields than those practicing pure engineering.

Leadership and Cross-Cultural Skills

In developing countries, a number of regions, including portions of Africa and Asia, are beginning to turn out highly skilled engineers. These countries have begun hiring local applicants rather than Canadian or other foreign engineers due to lower costs, fewer cultural and language issues, general proximity and the boost to the local economy. In many of these areas, however, leaders in the private and public sectors continue to seek international investment, and will bring on foreign project managers or consultants as part of a broader contract. Avoiding any sense of arrogance that can be associated with a North American engineering background can enhance good working relationships between local and expat engineers. In fact, being exposed to the expertise of local engineers is one of the benefits and skills that can be derived from an international posting.

Learning to be more effective in an international engineering environment means that you need to be sensitive to how host country nationals do the following:

- conduct meetings;
- write reports and make presentations;
- supervise staff and provide feedback;
- manage projects;
- interact with clients.

(For a more detailed review of cross-cultural business differences, see Chapter 7, The Canadian Identity in the International Work Place.)

Approaches to Problem Solving

Approaches used to solve engineering problems vary across cultures and regions, and are often reflective of a country's educational curriculum, its culture and its available resources. In parts of southern Europe, for example, engineers tend to emphasize mathematical and theoretical approaches, in contrast to North America, where engineers tend to favour experimental or trial-and-error approaches to technical problems. And since there is no absolute "right way" to approach technical problems, issues are bound to arise when engineers and technicians with different training and outlooks work together to solve them. Once they learn to work together effectively, however, engineers trained in different countries and cultures can complement one another extremely well professionally and form some of the most dynamic and innovative teams!

As is the case with many technical professions, globalization continues to have an undeniable impact on the nature of North American engineers' work. Whether working at home or abroad, our engineers are frequently in contact with international clients, suppliers and colleagues. So, whatever direction your engineering career takes—but especially if you work internationally—strong interpersonal and cross-cultural communication skills are as important to your success as a solid understanding of basic engineering principles.

A recently returned engineer said, *"The most important skill is adaptability, even more so than communication skills. Humility and being able to problem solve in stressful situations was also important when working on small development projects."* (For more cross-cultural information, see Chapter 1, The Effective Overseas Employee and Chapter 3, Living Overseas.)

THE NATURE OF ENGINEERING FIRMS

It is difficult to categorize the field of international engineering.

First, there is no clear division between private and public sector work. By their very nature, engineering projects are often public—roads, bridges, water and sanitation facilities, agricultural and irrigations projects all are public enterprises—but private firms execute the work. Moreover, the exacting nature of engineering work means the practice of engineering is executed in similar ways for the public or private sector. A water engineering firm might simultaneously work on a rural water supply development project in Africa and on a water treatment system for a tourism complex in Dubai.

As a job searcher, you are faced with a field where projects and players are constantly changing. There is little historical continuity in the lists of projects that exist today in comparison to what existed five years ago. Likewise, there is a proliferation of small and new firms. For example, there are more than 8,000 engineering consulting firms in Canada alone, and over 75 per cent of them have fewer than 50 employees. There is often no correlation between the size of the engineering firm and the level of expertise. Small and large engineering firms can be at the top of their fields, whereas only large accounting firms can be industry leaders. Lastly, engineering firms apply their craft in a wide breadth of geographical areas, often working in both domestic and international markets. In short, engineering firms come in all shapes and sizes and they are hard to categorize.

JOB HUNTING STRATEGIES

There are some aspects of international contract work that benefit the entry-level engineering job seeker, particularly junior engineers who are flexible in respect to mobility and are available to take international postings on short notice. This can be an advantage as contracts are awarded and jobs become available that need to be staffed quickly. In addition, jobs are often located in remote areas where senior engineers are reluctant to move. The project environment ensures that there are continuous streams of new jobs starting and ending that provide favourable environments for less experienced engineers. This is now balanced, however, by the trend toward recruiting local engineers and flying in North American senior consultants for shorter periods.

It is extremely important to be persistent when applying for these jobs, as senior engineers are often considered first for positions, thus making it difficult for junior people to break into the field. When bidding on international contracts, private consulting engineering firms often include the experience of personnel as part of the proposal. Therefore, sending less experienced engineers is a considerable risk in a competitive environment. As a junior engineer, you will have to convince management that you are worth the risk.

As a young engineer, you are mobile, available to leave on short notice, and willing to work under difficult circumstances for less pay. Your strategy is to cast a wide net when job searching and to keep your dossier alive when you are accepted as an applicant in a firm's resume databank. There are few other international fields where job hunters can benefit from such circumstances.

The following is a list of ideas that we used to research engineering firms in THE BIG GUIDE. It should be useful to you in tracking down firms that match your interests. (For specific contact information, see the Resources section at the end of this chapter.)

- Search the Web sites of engineering umbrella organizations for the list of members. These lists are usually driven by a database with search features enabling you to find members with international expertise. Read the profile of the firm to locate those with international interests.

- Search the Web sites of engineering umbrella organizations for other international contact information that will allow you network or gain international experience. Contact members of international committees. Study their list of international services.

- Check out trade magazines for articles about international engineering projects and contact the firms involved. Pay particular attention to projects in the start-up phase. This is one of the best methods to place your resume in the hands of those hiring.

- Search for engineering firms by going directly to the funding sources who employ their services. Private sector firms bidding on international contracts are often funded by Canadian or US governments, or by intergovernmental organizations, especially development banks.

- Job boards are a great place to look for international jobs. But do not limit yourself to engineering job boards; engineering jobs are posted on all types of job boards.

- Accept a domestic engineering position, especially if the firm does international projects. Once hired, work hard at getting noticed, and then apply for international postings within the company.

- If you are working for an engineering firm with no international contracts, you are still well positioned for finding international work, so keep looking. You are building your professional certification and gaining experience. You are very mobile (especially if you're single) and your salary expectations are still moderate. And just as importantly, you also have time on your side as you cast a wide net looking for international engineering work.

- The beauty of an international career is that it is rarely predictable and often surprising! So, be open to the various types of engineering career options abroad that may take you where you want to go or build the skills you need to get there. As you begin your international job search, do not limit your opportunities to the focus of your undergraduate degree! Investigate what areas and fields are most in demand abroad, and do a skills analysis to determine how you might fit in and benefit a project. As in most fields these days, engineers across North America have diverse work experiences throughout their careers; most make several career shifts within engineering.

- Overall, be as flexible as you can when you are job hunting. You will often find openings that must be filled immediately (sometimes because the person chosen for the job backed out at the last minute and the project must proceed). In circumstances like this, you can usually negotiate a highly attractive salary and benefits package.

- Make sure that you sell yourself first before discussing salary and benefits. Salary and benefits are negotiable and discussions regarding them should be postponed as long as possible. Don't be shy about asking for more than what they first offer.

ENGINEERING SECTORS

Engineering Work in International Development

Engineering has gained recognition over the past decade in North America as a profession attractive for international development projects. While the field of international development is not booming (with the exception of peacekeeping and post-conflict reconstruction), engineering opportunities within development work are on the rise. Whether consulting on an infrastructure project in the Middle East or volunteering on a water and sanitation project in Southeast Asia, engineers are taking the lead on development projects around the world.

This development has come with a renewed focus within professional engineering circles on the importance of the soft side of technology—the human face of engineering projects. Volumes are being written and organizations founded on the basic principle that it is not enough to design and construct a new sewage and clean water facility in a village; rather, engineers must teach the community to use, integrate and benefit from the new technology, and empower people to take ownership of change and technology.

Engineering is involved in every stage of international development projects, and with increased focus on the human, soft-skills side of engineering projects, culturally sensitive engineers have the unique opportunity to become leaders in sustainable development.

It is worth noting that international work funded by developed countries requires that the codes and practices of the funding country be followed regardless of where the work is being done. This allows engineers' work abroad to be recognized as technically sound and rigorous, which is of value upon reintegration to North America.

Here are some of the most common types of engineering going on in international development.

- **Water resource management**, including the areas of water supply and sanitation, remains a key field for North American engineers seeking to work abroad. There is a relatively steady stream of international projects in this area. The work varies from large infrastructure schemes to small-scale community projects to working in refugee camps.

- **Agricultural engineering** is an equally steady area. Though traditionally a smaller field internationally, agricultural engineering is on the rise, gaining more recognition (and in turn, funding) as the need becomes clear to address hunger and nutrition issues, including irrigation, food shortages and sustainable farming practices.

- **Forestry engineering** was booming 10 years ago, and while this field used to offer substantially more projects and jobs abroad, Canada continues to lead in the field and will always have a role to play in new research, design and implementation of new projects.

- **Electrical engineering and computer science** have a large presence internationally. The manufacturing industry requires continual updates of software and hardware to remain competitive in the global economy. Canada is recognized for its expertise in these areas, so there will be opportunities for engineers entering the international scene.

- **Large infrastructure projects**, including transportation, communications and electrical utilities are often undertaken by private sector firms, which are not reliant upon government funding for projects (although firms often rely on government contracts to establish connections with international partners). While public funding has decreased in this area in favour of more resource-related projects, many developing nations continue to undertake large projects to improve their infrastructure. A public–private partnership (PPP) model is becoming more prevalent in these initiatives. This is apparent in the increasing number of private sector toll roads and private ownership of public transit and municipal utilities around the world.

- **Environmental engineering** is another field where Canada has traditionally been very strong. Having carried its expertise and leadership abroad over the past few decades, Canada continues to grow stronger in this area. Engineers are being sought for implementation of the Kyoto Protocol and Rio and Johannesburg Earth Summits to reduce poverty and environmental degradation. These international agreements have reinforced the importance of environmental engineering projects that develop and implement practices for managing emissions, energy consumption and waste management. If this trend continues both domestically and internationally, increased funding will likely be made available for such projects, with substantial implications for environmental engineering professionals. Increased funding would provide new opportunities for engineers to work in research, design and implementation both at home and abroad. Canada will no doubt play a role. This is an area to watch.

Private Sector Jobs

Private sector jobs tend to require more specialized skills than NGO positions and they offer correspondingly higher salaries. Traditionally, Canadian engineers have needed 10 to 12 years' experience to obtain an international posting in the private sector. Many companies hire internally from their North American branches for overseas postings. While there are more and more exceptions to this practice, it still is the general rule. A good way to be considered for international work in this sector is to find a job locally with an engineering company involved in international projects of interest.

Private sector engineering firms offer positions in both developed and developing countries, in a wide variety of fields, from information technology in California to resource extraction in East Africa. Private sector work can range from building an airport in Hong Kong to working in remote and poor areas such as mining in Ghana, Zambia or Tanzania. Thanks to NAFTA, Canadian engineers currently have a large professional presence in the United States. Many engineering companies operate in both private and public sector fields, particularly in those countries with government-owned industry. Areas that are more specifically private include mining, oil and nuclear power. There is a more recent demand for engineers in telecommunications, infrastructure, information technology, industrial services (resource extraction), transportation and the environment.

Generally, NGO projects tend to be small, with the exception of disaster relief, while private firms take on larger projects. Since most private firms concentrate on specialized fields, they offer an international experience that differs significantly from NGOs, and may be more suited for engineers with a clear specialization or a desire to strengthen one skills set.

Consulting Engineers

According to Industry Canada, the country's consulting engineering industry consistently ranks fourth in the world in international billings. This industry is made up of skilled, experienced professionals who provide independent advice, project management, design and implementation of capital projects. Both domestically and internationally, consulting engineers have traditionally held a competitive advantage in resource extraction, energy, telecommunications, transport, environmental and infrastructure engineering. More recently, consulting in design services and project management have been among the most lucrative project areas.

In order to work as a consultant, engineers should have at least 10 years' professional experience. Most consulting firms hire junior and intermediate engineers who may not work on international projects immediately, but are able to develop their skills at the local level for future international project work. It is very important for junior personnel to indicate that they are interested in international work and to develop a plan with management to achieve this goal. International work opportunities rarely just fall into your lap and you must take a proactive role in developing your career toward this end.

To become a consulting engineer, you can work with one of the numerous engineering consulting firms (in Canada, the field is overwhelming, dominated by small firms with fewer then 50 people) or even create your own company and bid on individual government contracts independently. Many short-term contracts are available through CIDA; even international divisions of a number of other government agencies, such as Industry Canada and Environment Canada, are increasingly using consultants. Contracts are difficult to get, however, and require substantial knowledge, research and planning. If you succeed in a government competition (on average, 20 of each 2,000 applicants succeed), then you're set.

For more information on working as a consulting engineer, the Association of Consulting Engineers of Canada (ACEC) has an informative Web site that will be of interest to you. (See the Resources section at the end of this chapter.)

ADVICE FOR STUDENTS AND RECENT GRADUATES

Students

If you're a student interested in working abroad immediately after graduation, don't wait. You will need to build international experience while you are still a student. Future employers want to see that you have had international experience and that you know what you're getting into. You can start by joining international student organizations and spending time with foreign students. Join up with international students for course projects and learn about working in cross-cultural teams. Ensure that some of your courses have an international focus—for both engineering and non-engineering courses. Study one semester abroad and then travel for a semester. While abroad, build in an engineering component to your trip by visiting engineering sites, meeting local engineers, or participating in conferences. Learn another language and stand out among your engineering peers.

While a student you will need to take the greatest risks and show the most amount of determination when finding international summer internships, co-op placements or volunteer opportunities overseas. It's not impossible. Gaining overseas experience before graduation will give you a competitive advantage over those with the same designation but less relevant experience—you'll be demonstrating your ambition and initiative. As mentioned by one recent graduate, *"If engineering students are interested in international development they should focus on that while a student. They should get exposure to different issues by joining clubs, reading books, speaking to professors in the school who specialize in various areas of international development."*

Intern Abroad

An international internship is invaluable for new graduates with little or no professional experience. An internship can introduce new cultural and professional dimensions to your life, and provide you with the opportunity to network and gain valuable international work experience. It will also familiarize you with a specific region of the world.

Through an international internship, you can develop a broad knowledge of new technologies and processes around the world while building a professional network that will help ensure your success in the global knowledge-based economy. Internships also help you to acquire and improve soft skills such as cultural sensitivity, adaptability and communication. Interning allows you to join the growing international labour force early in your career, which can be a catalyst for new career opportunities.

Finding an international internship takes work, but rest assured that we have met many students who have been successful at arranging their own self-directed internships. Success stories range from finding internships while travelling to using the SWAP program to launch an internship (see Chapter 10, Short-Term Programs Overseas) to hooking up with a family friend working abroad.

While you are more likely to find an international internship with an NGO than you are with a private engineering firm, a number of private engineering firms have caught onto the trend. Internships with private firms tend to offer more in the way of financial compensation, and are targeted at current students as well as recent graduates. To begin your search for a private sector internship, see Chapter 35, Private Sector Firms in Canada. You can also find many more engineering firms by reviewing the membership lists of engineering umbrella organizations. (For information on these organizations, see the Resources at the end of this chapter.)

The CANADIAN INTERNATIONAL DEVELOPMENT AGENCY (CIDA) and FOREIGN AFFAIRS CANADA (FAC) often fund internships with NGOs. (For information on the Canadian Government International Internship Programs, see Chapter 17, Internships Abroad.) There are also international engineering internship opportunities with the INTERNATIONAL ASSOCIATION FOR THE EXCHANGE OF STUDENTS FOR TECHNICAL EXPERIENCE (IAESTE). (See the Profiles section in Chapter 10, Short-Term Programs Overseas.) Two NGOs in Canada are worth highlighting because of their engineering focus: ENGINEERS WITHOUT BORDERS (EWB) and REDR CANADA. These organizations offer recent graduates and seasoned engineers a variety of opportunities to apply their skills to relief and sustainable development projects abroad. Most positions are volunteer ones, although a few are paid. (See the Profiles section in Chapter 38, NGOs in Canada.)

Co-op or Work Placement

There are often opportunities to work abroad as part of your university program. The co-operative (co-op) program is the most common, but other programs, such as professional experience placement and work placements, offer similar opportunities. Much like internships, co-op placements are often easier to find, since your university will likely be connected with several employers. Universities arrange for employers to interview students on campus in person, by telephone or video conference. These opportunities are usually for one or two terms (four to eight months) and sometimes longer for international postings. Approximately 5 per cent of the co-op postings at the University of Waterloo are international, and many of those are in the United States. Although international opportunities for co-op are increasing, there is a much greater response of students seeking international co-ops.

This often leads to students finding their own international jobs and getting subsequent approval to apply them toward co-op.

International co-ops outside of North America should be considered primarily for their benefit in gaining international experience, as the technical quality and salaries are often lower due to local economics and language issues. When considering an international co-op, it is important to remember that there are responsibilities in addition to merely getting a job offer. Immigration issues, such as obtaining the proper visa, are the responsibility of the student. Procuring international health coverage and taking measures to demonstrate the relative security of the area you will be living and working in are also requirements for the position to be considered as a bona fide co-op. With a little planning, however, an international co-op can be a rewarding experience.

Volunteer Abroad

Through these organizations, Canadian engineers can invest their skills to help find solutions for the many challenges faced by developing communities, such as a lack of water, sanitation, energy, or food. By volunteering abroad, you can help establish positive, sustainable development outcomes in communities around the world. Many NGOs listed in this book periodically need engineers to work on their projects. These projects usually involve less specialized technical work and more grassroots development of appropriate technology, so a broader range of projects is open to you.

Professional Designation for New Graduates

In order to earn their professional engineer designation (PEng), Canadian and US engineers need to have up to six years of professional work experience under the supervision of a PEng. Successful completion of an approved university engineering program may satisfy a portion of this requirement.

While working toward this designation, university graduates may apply for Engineer-in-Training (EIT) status through the provincial or state organization responsible for regulating professional engineering status. This program assists young engineers and provides resources during the licensing process.

Engineering work performed overseas may also count toward the work experience requirement; however, there are strict regulations pertaining to supervision and technical elements. Working for North American companies overseas (or for international organizations whose standards meet those of North American jurisdictions) can be deemed acceptable, but you may have to show equivalence standards. With these rules, young engineers can take advantage of international work opportunities while fulfilling their professional licensure obligations; however, be advised that eligibility for licensure may be delayed for engineering graduates who go to work overseas immediately. Since licensure requirements vary somewhat among states and provinces, it is recommended that you contact the appropriate agency. (A list of agencies can be found on national engineering organization Web sites provided in the Resources section at the end of this chapter.)

PERSONAL STORIES

Here are a few stories that demonstrate how a determined individual can find an entry-level international engineering job.

- One recent engineering graduate advises, *"Don't get discouraged if it takes some time to find the international job you are looking for. Take advantage of volunteer opportunities which are rewarding in themselves."* As a civil engineering undergraduate student, Carmen had decided to pursue an international engineering career. With an entry-level resume and bachelor's degree, she contacted international private sector firms and NGOs to find out about their projects and apply for jobs. She quickly realized that she needed more international and engineering experience. Carmen took a job locally in air quality engineering to gain technical work experience and also capitalized on opportunities to develop the communication and organizational skills valued by international employers. After working for three years, she volunteered in an engineering capacity on two short-term international projects. Carmen also returned to university and completed a master's degree in civil engineering. While in university, she increased her international IQ by participating in ENGINEERS WITHOUT BORDERS and acting as a mentor for international students. As she begins her job search for an international engineering job in water resources, these experiences have made Carmen better equipped and helped her to gain international contacts.

- A successful engineering student landed his first job abroad by *"being bold and politely persistent."* Harry travelled the world as a backpacker for over a year while completing his studies as a civil engineer. His first job was with a mid-sized Seattle-based engineering firm. The work was domestic with no international responsibilities. After being with the firm for 18 months, Harry heard that his firm had just landed a 3-year international contract to install a water system for a palace owned by the Sultan of Brunei on the island of Borneo. Harry walked into the president's office and offered his services. He was flatly turned down. The firm was looking internally for a more experienced engineer. Over the next two months, Harry returned to the bosses on several occasions to profess his continuing interest in the position, each time taking care to draw attention to his adaptability, cross-cultural experiences and confidence in his ability to do the job. The firm was having problems recruiting an experienced engineer, and finally, after consulting with their client, the boss offered Harry the position. Harry went on to complete a fantastic three-year posting. He has now just returned home and is taking a one-year MBA course in preparation for landing his next international posting.

- Another engineer became interested in international issues during her undergraduate program in environmental engineering. By planning ahead, Laura developed her international skills in parallel with her other studies by taking elective courses in international development, politics and Spanish, and by tailoring her engineering design projects to international applications. Through her university's Centre for International Programs, she also participated in an engineering work exchange program in Thailand during her final year of study. The connections that Laura made with engineering faculty involved in international work led to her contract with the WORLD BANK after graduation. Laura later returned home to undertake a master's program with faculty advisors from engineering and rural planning and development—her thesis focused on field research conducted in Mexico. After successful completion of her master's program, she searched specifically for a company that participated in international and development projects, accepted a job as an environmental engineer at a consulting firm and has since worked in Nepal, China and Russia. Laura continues with her professional and personal development by attending international development seminars and conferences, improving her language skills (Mandarin and Spanish), holding memberships in international associations and volunteering for the RED CROSS.

• This REDR CANADA environmental engineer worked for six months in Afghanistan as a general project engineer. He has experience in water systems design, knowledge of multiple languages and significant travel in the developing world. He describes his experience as follows.

"The NGO I work for has a great track record in recruiting "first-timers" and Afghanistan could certainly use some extra engineers at the moment. The first three weeks in Afghanistan have been enjoyably chaotic. The combination of 24 years of war resulting in a complete breakdown in infrastructure and marketplaces has meant that the country is desperately poor. This has been compounded by drought and rapacious warlords who control everything from the roads, water allocation and also land rights. The broad description of my role is "livelihood security." The first project I have taken on is the construction of 48 water reservoirs for vulnerable communities in one of the arid northern provinces. This will allow villagers to harvest as much water as possible during the infrequent periods when the "warlord water kings" allow water to flow in their channels. In the next few months, my role will expand to shallow well development and the construction of kandas, which are storage areas constructed on rocky platforms on mountainsides.

The REDR training courses that I have attended have shown their worth immediately—specifically the security and communications course. We use VHF radios, HF radios and satellite phones daily and deal with roadblocks, security procedures, mine awareness and all the other useful security issues covered in the course."

(For more career stories, see the article by Susan Elias, "Eight Engineering Career Stories from REDR CANADA" in Appendix 32a on the CD-ROM and the article edited by Heather Harding, "Career Stories from ENGINEERS WITHOUT BORDERS" in Appendix 32b on the CD-ROM.)

A LAST WORD

International engineering careers can be launched as soon as you leave university, or you can even enter the field after a few years of North American experience. Young engineers should strongly consider internships, volunteer positions and active travel to help launch their careers. If your primary goal is to work overseas with a private sector engineering firm (and most engineers eventually work in the private sector), start by looking through Chapter 35, Private Sector Firms in Canada as well as Chapter 36, Private Sector Firms in the US. Look for companies that are friendly to recent graduates, either actively recruiting new graduates or encouraging them to apply. Best wishes for an exciting and enticing engineering career abroad!

APPENDIX ON THE CD-ROM

32a. "Eight Engineering Career Stories from REDR CANADA," by Susan Elias

32b. "Career Stories from ENGINEERS WITHOUT BORDERS," edited by Heather Harding

RESOURCES

This chapter contains the following Resources sections: Engineering Job Boards and Engineering.

ENGINEERING JOB BOARDS

Job boards are the fastest way to locate international engineering jobs.

Asia Net 🖥

www.asia-net.com ◆ Asia Net is a job board for candidates bilingual in English and Chinese, Japanese or Korean. Most jobs listings are for technical or engineering type jobs which can be searched by location. [ID:2814]

Career One 🖥

www.careerone.com.au ◆ This Australia-based international job board can be searched by location, expertise and employer. There are currently 1,670+ engineering jobs listed. Sign up for e-mail alerts. [ID:2822]

DegreeHunter 🖥

www.degreehunter.com ◆ Engineering jobs, nursing jobs, medical jobs, health care jobs, legal jobs, physician jobs, legal jobs and MBA jobs can be found at DegreeHunter. DegreeHunter is the career search service that helps graduate degree candidates and other certified professionals find employment with a new career opportunity by focusing on distinct professions, providing pre-screened positions and resumes, and enabling real-time and confidential communication between candidates and recruiters. [ID:2823]

DevNet Jobs 🖥

www.devnetjobs.org ◆ This site is labled as a Gateway to International Development Jobs and Consultancy Assignments. Look up current job listings in international development, including engineering jobs. A subscription is required to post resumes; however, you can browse postings and receive job hunting newsletters for free. [ID:2826]

Dice 🖥

www.dice.com ◆ This US site focuses on the technology job market. Post your resume and make yourself available to employers recruiting to fill over 30,000 tech jobs. Access salary information and check out companies and job markets in US high-tech hotbeds. [ID:2451]

Engineer 500 🖥

www.engineer500.com www.engineer500.com ◆ This is a comprehensive and functional site containing a database of thousands of engineering jobs abroad searchable by country and engineering specialty. A great start to your overseas engineering career search! Highly recommended. [ID:2831]

Engineering Central 🖥

www.EngineeringCentral.com ◆ The site lists 6,000+ high-end engineering jobs that are sorted by discipline with US locations. There is a link to company profiles; however, companies remain anonymous in the job listings. Post your resume for free. [ID:2820]

Engineering Jobs 🖥

www.engineeringjobs.com ◆ This Web site contains extensive listings and contact information for US-based recruiters and headhunters who provide services for engineering companies. Users can link their resumes to the site for free or post them directly for a cost. [ID:2816]

EngineerJobSearch 🖥

www.engineer500.com ◆ This is a comprehensive and functional site containing a database of thousands of engineering jobs abroad searchable by country and engineering specialty. A great start to your overseas engineering career search! Highly recommended. [ID:2467]

Engineers for a Sustainable World (ESW) 👬

Engineers for a Sustainable World (ESW), 170 Uris Hall, Ithaca, NY 14853, USA, www.esustainableworld.org, 607-255-8996, fax 607-254-5000, info@esustainableworld.org ◆ ESW is a US-based, non-profit organization for sustainable development highlighting student chapters, NGOs, government and industry partners. The Web site has a good list of domestic and international opportunities. There are excellent volunteering positions with stipends open to anyone, provided they can attend training in New York. [ID:2815]

Environmental Career Centre 🖥

www.environmentalcareer.com/jobs.htm ◆ Searching jobs on this US environmental career Web site is free; however to apply on-line, you must register. The database includes a broad spectrum of environment-related careers ranging from lab technicians to field ecologists and program managers. Most of the postings are in the US, but there is the odd overseas job listed. A good starting place to your environmental career search. [ID:2637]

Expats Direct 🖥

www.expatsdirect.com ◆ This UK Web site stakes its claim as the best on-line employment service for working overseas and it delivers. Browse literally thousands of overseas jobs; however, if you want to apply to them, you have to join. Membership costs £55 per year. It might well be worth your money for access to engineering, health care, technicial and managerial positions everywhere from Milan to Malaysia. [ID:2645]

Institute of Electrical and Electronics Engineers, Inc. (IEEE) 👬

Institute of Electrical and Electronics Engineers, Inc. (IEEE), 17th Floor, 3 Park Ave., New York, NY 10016-5997, USA, www.ieee.org, 212-419-7900, fax 212-752-4929 ◆ IEEE is a US-based organization that supports electrical engineering members and students in 150 countries. The site has a job board with national and international job listings by location and expertise. There are resources for students including scholarships and international links. [ID:2804]

Jobserve 🖥

www.jobserve.com ◆ This site features over 20,000 IT sector jobs in UK and Australia, in addition to thousands of jobs in accounting, engineering, law and medicine. Subscribe to a mailing list and receive e-mail updates regularly. [ID:2356]

LatPro 🖥

www.LatPro.com ◆ Lat Pro is a job board for employees bilingual in English and Spanish or Portugese. There are international and US-based jobs and company listings which can be searched by profession and location. The site contains great resources including immigration information and links to sites in other countries for local news, magazines, recruiters and search engines. Bonus: the site offers free subscriptions to over 70 engineering publications! [ID:2824]

ENGINEERING

Stay connected with engineering employment trends by checking the Web sites of Canadian and US professional associations; they can be great resources for jobs! Also, check out the Web sites of the largest engineering firms; these can also be great places to get started in your job search. The following resources will help you to research and network for engineering jobs.

American Institute of Chemical Engineers (AIChE) ⋔
American Institute of Chemical Engineers (AIChE), 3 Park Ave., New York, NY 10016-5991, USA, www.aiche.org, 212-591-7338, fax 212-591-8897 ◆ AIChE is a US-based organization providing resources and support to chemical engineers globally. The Web site has a job board with international postings and resources specifically for students and young engineers. [ID:2803]

American Society of Civil Engineers (ASCE) ⋔
American Society of Civil Engineers (ASCE), 1801 Alexander Bell Drive, Reston, VA 20191, USA, www.asce.org, 800-548-2723 ◆ ASCE is an organization supporting American civil engineers and companies that work internationally. ASCE profiles and awards firms for excellence in international engineering. The Web site has links to international conferences and national job listings with employer contact information. [ID:2808]

American Society of Mechanical Engineers (ASME) ⋔
American Society of Mechanical Engineers (ASME), 3 Park Ave., New York, NY 10016-5990, USA, www.asme.org, 800-843-2763, infocentral@asme.org ◆ ASME is an international organization promoting mechanical engineering worldwide with resources such as global career opportunities and news. ASME has members in 13 regions of the world and the Web site has links to international chapters. International sites have local newsletters and job opportunities. [ID:2830]

Association for Facilities Engineering (AFE) ⋔
Association for Facilities Engineering (AFE), Suite 125, 8160 Corporate Park Drive, Cincinnati, OH 45242, USA, www.afe.org, 513-489-2473, fax 513-247-7422, mail@afe.org ◆ AFE provides education, certification, technical information and other relevant resources for plant and facility engineering, operations and maintenance professionals worldwide. The Web site has a membership directory with contact information for global facilities. [ID:2806]

Association of Consulting Engineers of Canada (ACEC) ⋔
Association of Consulting Engineers of Canada (ACEC), Suite 616, 130 Albert Street, Ottawa, ON K1P 5G4, Canada, www.acec.ca, 613-236-0569, fax 613-236-6193, info@acec.ca ◆ ACEC has a task force on Canadian International Development Agency (CIDA) contracting. This task force publishes reports that will be of interest to all professional engineers interested in independent consulting work. The Web site provides links to national and international engineering associations and the 1,400+ member firms can be searched by international characteristics. [ID:2797]

The Canadian Council of Professional Engineers (CCPE) ⋔
The Canadian Council of Professional Engineers (CCPE), Suite 1100, 180 Elgin Street, Ottawa, ON K2P 2K3, Canada, www.ccpe.ca, 613-232-2474, fax 613-230-5759, info@ccpe.ca ◆ CCPE strives to promote rigorous international engineering standards and qualifications and to facilitate international mobility for Canadian engineers. CCPE negotiates mutual recognition agreements on behalf of the engineering profession in Canada that make it easier for Canadian engineers to work and be licensed as engineers in other countries. The Web site provides links to CCPE's provincial member associations. [ID:2812]

Canadian Federation of Engineering Students (CFES) ⋔
www.cfes.ca, info@cfes.ca ◆ CFES provides worldwide resources for engineering students and advice for employment seekers. The CFES magazine is available on-line and it profiles international student projects of interest to engineers planning on working abroad. [ID:2811]

The Canadian Society for Civil Engineering (CSCE) ⋔
The Canadian Society for Civil Engineering (CSCE), #201, 4920 de Maisonneuve W., Montreal, QC H3Z 1N1, Canada, www.csce.ca, 514-933-2634, fax 514-933-3504, info@csce.ca ◆ CSCE's Web site is a comprehensive job networking source. You can search and apply for hundreds of

engineering jobs with employers around the world as well as manage your resume and job applications on-line. There is a good international affairs site which provides information on current international projects and links to international corporate members. [ID:2813]

Career Options in Hi-Tech & Engineering 📖

2003, 56 pages ➤ Canadian Association of Career Educators and Employers (CACEE), Suite 300, 720 Spadina Ave., Toronto, ON M5S 2T9, Canada, www.cacee.com, Credit Cards; 866-922-3303, fax 416-929-5256; *Fr* ◆ Targeting recent graduates in technical disciplines such as computer science and engineering, this book assists students in understanding how to mix technical skills with people skills, research career options and find the best possible co-op programs and internships for developing their career. Also available in French. [ID:2406]

Engineering Institute of Canada (EIC) 🏛

Engineering Institute of Canada (EIC), 1295 Hwy 2 E., Kingston, ON K7L 4V1, Canada, www.eic-ici.ca, 613-547-5989, fax 613-547-0195, jplant1@cogeco.ca ◆ EIC promotes education standards and professional development. The Web site provides contact information for member firms, most of which have an international component. The site also has links to a comprehensive list of national and international engineering organizations. [ID:2796]

Engineering News-Record (ENR) 💻

www.construction.enr.com ◆ ENR is an Internet news magazine that is a subsidiary of US-based McGraw Hill Construction. ENR is an excellent resource for national and global company listings, primarily in construction. The site features international projects, stories and contact information for top contractors and construction firms. There is a link for career resources. [ID:2818]

Engineers Without Borders (EWB) 🏛

Engineers Without Borders (EWB), Suite 201, 188 Davenport Rd, Toronto, ON M5R 1J2, Canada, www.ewb.ca ◆ EWB is a charitable organization committed to development work through international internship opportunities. It provides resource lists for engineering students interested in pursuing international activities. (For more information, see their ad in the sponsor section at the end of this guide and their profile in Chapter 38, NGOs in Canada.) [ID:2817]

EPC Global 🏛

www.epcglobal.com ◆ EPC Global is an international staffing solutions company with US- and UK-based databases that specializes in servicing the engineering and construction industry. You can browse excellent job descriptions or submit a profile that is automatically matched with employment opportunities. [ID:2821]

European Bank for Reconstruction and Development (EBRD) 🏛

European Bank for Reconstruction and Development (EBRD), One Exchange Square, London, EC2A 2JN, UK, www.ebrd.com, (44) (20) 7338-6000, fax (44) (20) 7338-6100 ◆ EBRD provides funding for development projects in Europe and Asia. It provides a list of current and proposed projects and links to press releases and related stories. [ID:2827]

Focus 💻

Quarterly ➤ Canadian Executive Service Organization (CESO), Suite 700, 700 Bay Street, Toronto, ON M5G 1Z6, Canada, www.ceso-saco.com, Free on-line; 416-961-2376, fax 416-961-1096 ◆ This newsletter features articles about the organization's worldwide activities. CESO is a non-governmental voluntary agency that sends Canadians with professional, technical and managerial skills to be volunteer consultants to business organizations in Canadian aboriginal communities and in developing countries. [ID:2030]

International Association for the Exchange of Students for Technical Experience (IAESTE) 🏛

International Association for the Exchange of Students for Technical Experience (I.A.E.S.T.E), P.O. Box 1473, Kingston, ON K7L 5C7, Canada, www.iaeste.org ◆ IAESTE is an international organization with offices in many countries that offers traineeships in engineering, technical sciences and applied arts for students enrolled in technical programs. There is a list of 70 member countries and contacts. (See IAESTE's profile in Chapter 38, NGOs in Canada.) [ID:2802]

International Environmental Consulting Practice:
How and Where to Take Advantage of Global Opportunities 📖
1998, Peter Sam, 320 pages ➤ John Wiley & Sons, 22 Worcester Road, Etobicoke, ON M9W 1L1, Canada, www.wiley.ca, $160 CDN; Credit Cards; 800-567-4797, fax 800-565-6802, canada@wiley.com ◆ A guide to environmental consulting opportunities and growth worldwide. Incorporates relevant information on culture, socio-economics and politics within the context of building a successful international career in environmental engineering. [ID:2798]

Job & Career Sites at Rensselaer Polytechnic Institute (RPI) 🖥
www.rpi.edu/dept/cdc/student/careeropps.html ◆ Rensselaer Polytechnic Institute offers a variety of career services geared toward graduates in the fields of engineering, architecture, management and IT through their excellent Career Development Centre Web site. They've built an extensive collection of links to Web sites with information on international career opportunities in these fields. [ID:2712]

Managing Cultural Diversity in Technical Professions 📖
2003, Lionel Laroche, Elsevier, 236 pages ➤ Masters & Scribes Bookshoppe, 9938 - 81 Ave., Edmonton, AB T6E 1W6, Canada, www.mastersandscribes.com, $48.95 CDN; Credit Cards; 800-378-3199, fax 780-439-6879 ◆ Technology is one of the fastest-growing employment sectors worldwide, and this European book provides managers of technical professionals with clear and tested strategies to improve communication and increase productivity among culturally diverse technical professionals, teams and departments. Outlines the differences in education and training, career expectations, communication styles and management expectations in countries around the world. Recommended. [ID:2553]

National Society of Professional Engineers (NSPE) 👥
National Society of Professional Engineers (NSPE), 1420 King Street, Alexandria, VA #22314-2794, USA, www.nspe.org, 703-684-2800, fax 703-836-4875 ◆ NSPE is a US-based engineering society with resources including a job board with national and international job opportunities and student internships. The on-line newsletter profiles international projects and information. There is also a list of national and international member firms. [ID:2805]

RedR Canada (Registered Engineers for Disaster Relief) 👥
RedR (Registered Engineers for Disaster Relief), Suite 102, 9 Gurdwara Road, Ottawa, ON K2E 7X6, Canada, www.redr.ca, 613-232-9999, fax 613-226-5991, info@redr.ca ◆ RedR Canada (Registered Engineers for Disaster Relief) is a humanitarian agency which mobilizes skilled engineers and technicians worldwide to work with NGOs on the front lines of disaster relief. Engineers and technicians apply their skills, experience and practical savvy to provide water, sanitary facilities, shelter and supplies to refugee camps. RedR looks for both men and women with resourcefulness, understanding and compassion, an ability to work on their own with limited resources and the ability to cope in very challenging environments. RedR members must adapt quickly to new cultures and harsh conditions that create the requirement for relief. They must work independently within a system yet remain flexible within highly demanding work situations. (For more information, see their ad in the sponsor section at the end of this guide and their profile in Chapter 38, NGOs in Canada.) [ID:2809]

Science Jobs 🖥
www.sciencejobs.com ◆ Science Jobs includes listings for engineering jobs and company contact information in North America, Europe and Australasia. The site has a link to the "New Scientist Magazine" profiling international projects and expert resources. [ID:2819]

Water Environment Federation (WEF) ⛪

Water Environment Federation (WEF), 601 Wythe Street, Alexandria, VA #22314-1994, USA, www.wef.org, 800-666-0206, fax 703-684-2492 ◆ WEF is a non-profit technical and educational network of water quality professionals in 35 countries with a mission to preserve the global water environment. Membership offers extensive job listings, technical journals and newsletters as well as world water news. Check out their Student Central resource for students and young professionals. [ID:2807]

Water for People ⛪

www.waterforpeople.com ◆ Water for People is a non-profit organization that promotes the use of appropriate technology and local labour to provide clean drinking water, increased sanitation and health in developing countries. The Web site lists funding sponsors and includes links to many technical organizations with an international vision. The organization profiles international projects primarily for fundraising. [ID:2810]

CHAPTER 33

Health
Careers
Abroad

The healthcare field is considered a growth area worldwide. Whether you're a student or a seasoned professional, more and more opportunities exist for those interested in leaving their own country to practice their skills. The vitality and strength of any country is very much dependent on the health and welfare of its individuals, and the prevention, care and treatment of illness is valued in most societies. However, there are often inadequate financial and human resources to meet those needs. Even countries that have well-developed healthcare systems frequently lack enough skilled professionals to do the work.

International involvement in health is constantly increasing. A wide range of health professionals is required for services attached to hospitals, companies, non-governmental organizations (NGOs), humanitarian organizations and multilateral organizations. Non-medical personnel can also be needed to bring support to health infrastructures and programs.

This chapter is intended for university or college graduate ready to embrace her or his first job, as well as for the experienced professional looking to change career direction. The information offered here will help guide you in your job search and long-term career building strategy.

The primary emphasis here is on health careers in developing countries. The chapter centres on the specific character traits required to adapt to new cultures and to work effectively in health care abroad. When assessing candidates' suitability for international health work, recruiters are interested not only in professional experience but also personal attributes. The information provided here is critical for applicants during their job hunt—both for those just starting out and those who are building on previous professional work experience. (Note that you should also consult other chapters in this book, especially the chapters in Part Three, The International Job Search.)

We do not focus on private sector health careers here—look elsewhere for information on working for a private hospital in Switzerland or Saudi Arabia, or for a private corporation elsewhere. Much of this type of information is available on the Web and we have therefore listed private sector Web resources in the Resources section at the end of this chapter. Readers interested in private sector careers will, however, still benefit from the cross-cultural advice provided here, which allows individuals to reflect on key elements of cross-cultural adaptation regardless of their specific place of work. But the skills sets described are especially helpful for those of you who, for example, want to work in a refugee camp in the Sudan or Somalia, or who want to work for an NGO in Nepal. There are also 20 profiles at the end of this chapter describing international health training programs around the world. All readers will benefit in some way from this chapter. Good luck with your search!

WHY GO ABROAD?

As a healthcare professional, you may have a variety of reasons for wanting to go abroad. You may be looking for a single life-changing experience—a short-term contract in a new and challenging environment. Or you may have a long-term career plan of many short- and long-term contracts abroad. Your motivation may be that there is little or no work in your areas of training in your home country, or you may be looking to increase your experience and expertise by working abroad. Many professional are attracted to the challenge of practicing their profession outside a conventional Western environment. Another common reason for going overseas is an interest in humanitarian efforts. Examples of such efforts are work that's done in war zones, within refugee camps and alongside peacekeepers to alleviate a famine, or in rural health or HIV/AIDS clinics in developing countries. Such professional possibilities are usually combined with a healthcare provider's desire to travel and experience different cultures and adventures. Whatever your specific reasons or interests are, your underlying motivations need to be reviewed and included in the equation—you need to understand why you want to go abroad.

Experienced health professionals say that to pursue an international health career you need a philosophical commitment in order to succeed and to overcome the many challenges of working in a new culture. They also say that you should envision a threefold objective: the opportunity to strive to offer patients the best possible care and treatment; the possibility to point out and influence the root causes of the patient's problems; and the benefits of sharing international health expertise with your medical community back home.

Your awareness, credibility and motivation will become key assets in working toward the achievement of these objectives. International recruiters want to know what makes you tick, what motivates you and what understanding you have of your own motivations. Obtaining international work may require patience and perseverance, depending on your area of interest. You may need to look in a number of different directions before you find success. However, most people find that the eventual rewards are well worth the effort.

WHAT TYPES OF JOBS ARE OUT THERE?

There are two broad categories of international health jobs: those with the private sector and those with NGOs. We begin here with a brief description of work in the private sector. The rest of the chapter is devoted to describing international health work with NGOs.

PRIVATE SECTOR HEALTH JOBS

The worldwide shortage of healthcare professionals means that just about every country is recruiting. Looking to the private sector for work may be a good choice if you are interested in living in another country but have less interest in working in a developing country or in doing international humanitarian work in which living conditions are more challenging. Or maybe you've just always wanted to live in a certain desirable location and are seeking job opportunities that will allow you to live there. Perhaps you want to work in a healthcare system in which you will have opportunities to increase your knowledge and skills while working in an environment that is technologically comparable to that of North America. The private sector offers many opportunities for both short- and long-term assignments, often with excellent incentives (relocation assistance, housing, immigration support, etc.). Working for the private sector is a great way to see if living overseas is right for you. This type of work can be ideal if you are a recent graduate who is adventurous but needs to gain experience and wants to work in an environment similar to where you trained.

Private sector jobs are often located in more stable environments than are NGO jobs. The country is most likely on an economic footing similar to North America's, and projects are developed with the aim of improving an existing healthcare system. Likely posting locations include Australia, the Bahamas, Britain, Ireland, Saudi Arabia, Switzerland and other industrialized countries.

Researching the Private Sector

You'll have no problem accessing the huge variety of private sector opportunities that are available. The Internet is an easy way to link to all the possible options. You may want to start your search by visiting www.medhunters.com, which provides an extensive menu of international medical work opportunities in Western countries. Another Internet resource is www.healthcareerscanada.com. Professional journals, magazines and job fairs are also sources commonly used by potential employers and job applicants.

There are a large number of recruiting firms that match job seekers with employers quickly and easily. Recruiters will do all the sweating to obtain work permits or visas. They can also help you decide where you'd like to go and what type of work you want to do. Recruiters can even ensure that housing is provided, along with very competitive salaries. One nurse had this to say about obtaining her job through a recruiter: *"I joined a travelling nursing agency because there weren't many jobs when I graduated. I loved it. A friend and I went to the Bahamas together. The agency helped arrange everything. I received a good orientation at the hospital I was sent to. We had a great apartment. The pay was good and I was able to get the experience I needed that helped me get a job when I came back to Canada."*

Recruiting firms are frequently linked to opportunities in the US, Canada, the UK, Australia and the United Arab Emirates. (For more information on recruiters, private sector job boards and other helpful Web sites, see the Resources section at the end of this chapter.)

NGO SECTOR HEALTH JOBS

When someone talks about going overseas to work in some aspect of health care, we usually have an image of a small mission hospital in a developing country. While that is where some people might go to work, international health work can in fact be much more varied.

The major employers tend to be non-governmental organizations (NGOs). These vary in size and are located throughout the world. Very large NGOs that have their funding base in a Western country are also referred to as international non-governmental organizations (INGOs). Job applicants, especially those with experience, can also find work in intergovernmental organizations (IGOs) and with most Western governments. (See Chapter 41, United Nations & Other IGOs.)

Historically, nurses and physicians have filled most health jobs that are abroad—having a background in one of these professions is still an advantage. However, the combination of increasing world health crises, such as HIV/AIDS, and the lack of qualified health practitioners worldwide, means that more opportunities now exist for other allied health professionals. The healthcare workers who are being recruited include health administrators, pharmacists, social workers, counsellors, health educators, nutritionists, mental health specialists, mid-wives, physical occupational and respiratory therapists; lab technologists and others.

Overseas health positions are often created to help maintain medical infrastructures/programs or set up new ones; to improve health programs; or to manage emergencies in response to people's needs. The following is a non-exhaustive list of the international positions most often available.

Doctors and Other Health Personnel

- medical doctors, (family, emergency, internal medicine, pediatrics)
- surgeons (general, orthopaedic, plastic)
- anaesthesiologists
- epidemiologists
- laboratory technologists
- obstetrician-gynecologists
- psychologists

Nurses and Related Practitioners

- community health nurses
- emergency room nurses
- intensive care nurses
- mental health nurses
- midwives
- nurse managers
- nurse practitioners
- operating room nurses
- pediatric nurses

Non-Medical Personnel to Support Health Projects

- construction managers
- electricians
- engineering staff—water resources and sanitation
- finance and accounting personnel
- humanitarian affairs officers
- information technology staff
- management—health program development and implementation
- managers, staff supervision
- mechanics
- project managers
- protection officers, human rights officers
- radio communications experts
- researchers—anthropology
- security personnel
- training officers
- transport/logistics experts

Policy Work with IGOs

Finally, some senior health professionals may be interested in seeking international involvement at the policy development level, which usually focuses on strengthening, developing and advocating for the medical or nursing profession. This area is typically multilateral—in other words, it is supported by many countries and is not accountable to any single country. Health professionals can get involved in many organizations, such as Canadian and US NGOs; international organizations such as the PAN AMERICAN HEALTH ORGANIZATION, the WORLD HEALTH ORGANIZATION and UNITED NATIONS agencies. The UN has many regional offices that perform roles from consultancy to policy advising to active involvement in a program.

Working in War Zones or in Disaster Relief

The context of working abroad has changed significantly since the early 1990s, elevating risk to real danger for medical aid and relief workers worldwide. Events from the 1991 Persian Gulf War to the 1994 Rwanda genocide to the 2001 terrorist attacks in the US changed the face of international medical and relief aid. So, whatever your destination—an industrialized or a developing country—the security situation is never completely certain. Security concerns can change quickly anywhere on the planet.

Before making the decision to go overseas, you must feel comfortable with the job offered and its program context. Prior to your departure, you must inquire about the security situation surrounding the project you will be joining. Check that you will be receiving a security briefing upon your arrival and updates on a regular basis. It is, for example, important to know who is directly in charge of security at your site. There are a host of other considerations, and each organization should have well-developed security plans.

Working in War Zones with the ICRC or MSF

Well-known international humanitarian NGOs like the INTERNATIONAL COMMITTEE OF THE RED CROSS (ICRC), MÉDECINS SANS FRONTIÈRES (MSF), and MÉDECINS DU MONDE (MDM) offer a wide range of work opportunities, including some in higher-risk areas. To offer a perspective on international healthcare delivery and to give you an institutional overview, we describe here two of these organizations: ICRC and MSF.

INTERNATIONAL COMMITTEE OF THE RED CROSS (ICRC): The role of the ICRC is to ensure the application of international humanitarian law (IHL) and thus the protection of people caught in conflict zones. This organization works exclusively in contexts of war and unrest. IHL is made up of international legal provisions (the Geneva Conventions of 1949 and the Additional Protocols of 1977) ensuring respect for the individual in armed conflict—specifically for wounded and sick armed forces in the field; wounded, sick and shipwrecked members of armed forces at sea; prisoners of war; and civilians (including humanitarian medical and relief personnel). ICRC medical activities, among other protection activities, are provided to victims of wars, including feeding programs, primary health care, surgical activities and visits to people in prisons in wartorn countries. The ICRC has a right of initiative to become operational in countries at war worldwide. To work with the ICRC, you should apply through your country's National Red Cross Society.

MÉDECINS SANS FRONTIÈRES (MSF): MSF brings medical assistance to populations in danger via a broad array of medical activities, including therapeutic and supplementary feeding centres; vaccination programs; basic health care; mother and child health care; mobile clinics in remote areas; water and sanitation provision; specialized programs for diseases such as tuberculosis, sleeping sickness and malaria; antiretroviral treatment and care for HIV/AIDS and AIDS-related opportunistic infections; social and psychological health care and reproductive health care. Populations in danger that are assisted by MSF are affected by famine, epidemics, a lack of health infrastructures, conflicts and sexual violence. Victims are often forgotten and marginalized refugees or displaced persons. MSF makes every effort to reach out to any population in distress. MSF principles are neutrality, independence, impartiality, volunteerism, proximity and respect for medical ethics. To work with MSF, you should apply through the MSF office in your country.

Both the ICRC and MSF are neutral and independent organizations; they act as witnesses to the populations they assist and advocate on their behalf. The ICRC acts on the basis of its legal mandate; MSF implements action on the basis of the needs of populations most in distress. Both organizations offer intensive training prior to departure and have extensive experience in security management. They often are the last organizations to remain in acute emergency situations when all others have left. Both organizations offer a wide range of medical and non-medical positions in the field.

To be able to work with the ICRC or MSF, you must agree to work in non-conventional settings and with colleagues from around the world and locally hired staff from the countries of operations. Expatriate teams are highly multicultural and work and live together in the field. Stress can often be extreme and work schedules very chaotic. Precautionary evacuations can be part of your routine life.

The ICRC offers healthcare professionals an international experience in war zones, combining involvement in protection activities, medical activities and advocacy. As a medical expatriate working with the ICRC in the field, you are at the heart of the application of international humanitarian law. The ICRC is not a medical organization, but it does offer medical assistance to victims of wars as part of its protection mandate.

MSF provides an international experience in emergency public health that offers involvement in a great variety of medical activities, as well as the opportunity to speak out on behalf of the populations that the organization medically assists. MSF is exclusively a medical organization working with populations in need of health care, with a primary emphasis in Africa. MSF is fighting the war against diseases and it promotes access to medication and health care worldwide.

Critical programs involving the ICRC and/or MSF may include, among others, postings in Afghanistan, Algeria, Angola, Burundi, Chad, Colombia, Democratic Republic of Congo, Haiti, Indonesia, Iran, Iraq, Kenya, Liberia, Mozambique, Nepal, Nigeria, North Caucasus, North Korea, Pakistan, the Palestinian Territories, the Russian Federation, Rwanda, Somalia, the Sudan, Yemen and Zimbabwe.

This list highlights the main distinctions between the ICRC and MSF:

- MSF's primary mandate is to provide medical assistance to populations experiencing danger that is not necessarily due to war. The ICRC's is to work only in situations of conflict or war.

- MSF is not responsible to ensure the application of international humanitarian law. The ICRC's primary responsibility is the application of international humanitarian law.

- MSF primarily provides medical care and, through its medical work, protects the human rights to life, security, fulfillment, basic health care and medical treatment. The ICRC undertakes protection activities on the basis of international humanitarian law and thus can provide medical assistance to war victims, but it is not a medical organization.

- In support of the human right to health care, MSF speaks out publicly on behalf of the populations it helps. The ICRC usually chooses diplomatic advocacy to ensure the rights of victims or war are protected.

MSF and the ICRC often work in close collaboration to deal with situations in which human rights are violated and the Geneva Conventions are obviously not being respected. When MSF provides medical assistance in conflict zones alongside the ICRC, it is contributing to the application of IHL. This becomes particularly obvious when MSF provides neutral and impartial medical and surgical care to war-wounded civilians or combatants.

Researching the NGO Job Market

There are hundreds of NGOs that employ health professionals. It is important that you take the time to learn about the mandate and activities of these NGOs so that you can identify the one that is closest to your personal and professional aspirations. Identifying an NGO that is well suited to your profile will likely help to ensure that you have a positive experience.

Some examples of Canadian NGOs working in the medical field are: MÉDECINS DU MONDE, based in Montreal; the CENTRE FOR STUDIES AND INTERNATIONAL COOPERATION (CECI), based in Montreal; the CANADIAN RED CROSS SOCIETY, VSO CANADA, based in Ottawa; CANADIAN PHYSICIANS FOR AID AND RELIEF, based in Toronto; and many church groups. (For a list of 223 Canadian NGOs, see the Profiles section in Chapter 38, NGOs in Canada. For a list of 410 US NGOs, see the Profiles section in Chapter 39, NGOs in the US.) A careful review of these lists and the accompanying resources will introduce you to the wide variety of organizations involved in international development and other international health work.

THE SKILLS REQUIRED

Prior to selecting what type of work you want to do and where you want to work overseas, you should first determine your motivation and suitability. This requires research and self-reflection. The following is a general list of skills that will help you in your self-assessment, career path development and research of specific organizations. As mentioned at the outset of this chapter, the emphasis in this discussion is on NGO-related health careers that involve working in conflict or emergency situations. By completing a review of the qualities presented here, you will be better able to choose an overseas position that will suit both your personal and professional profiles.

Sense of Commitment

To succeed in finding work with an international humanitarian NGO you must have a strong sense of personal commitment and a willingness to work in an international health environment. You must be able to describe the skills that illustrate your motivation. You must be able to articulate the reasons why you prefer to work with a specific NGO rather than with another one.

You will first need to undertake broad research of the NGOs operating in your field. (See the Profiles section in Chapter 38, NGOs in Canada; Chapter 39, NGOs in the US; and Chapter 40, NGOs in Europe & the Rest of the World.) You can then study in detail the mandate and projects of each NGO that you plan to approach. By linking your motivation and willingness to do international health work to the motivation and mandate of the NGO to which you are applying, you will be well placed to start the recruitment process and to speak directly to employers.

Teamwork

Living and working in teams is at the heart of most international health work situations, especially in field work—the front lines of most emergency health situations. You must be able to demonstrate your problem-solving skills in intensive group situations. North American/domestic experience can be valuable. Examples of relevant activities that may prepare you for this type of work are shared accommodation, group travel, outdoors activities, training programs, group dynamics and staged exercises. International recruiters are especially interested if you can describe specifically what you have learned about yourself through these experiences. You will need to convey your ability to face conflict; to understand that an expatriate's behaviour can jeopardize a field project; to question authority; to explore options to deal with/solve situations; to relate to locally hired personnel; to manage transition; to deal with changes; to build respect and trust; and to demonstrate self-confidence and leadership. Teamwork, as it relates to your interpersonal skills, is a key asset and will help you land an international job if you are able to describe your experience effectively to the recruiter.

Ability to Cope with Stress

International health recruiters will question you on your ability to cope with and manage stress. Are you able to cope with volatile security situations and related stress? If so, how? You will be asked questions about

- your tactics—methods you have developed that enable you to face high-risk situations and unknown environments—do you have a personal survival kit?

- your knowledge of what you can do to help alleviate your own stress. Do you know what can cause you extreme stress? Do you know the limit of the stress you can handle?

- your ability to cope with stress and manage a heavy workload, prioritize, delegate, assess your own capacity and communicate on a timely basis.

- your capacity to help others cope with stress.

Healthcare recruiters want to hear about how in the past you remained effective in stressful situations. Self-knowledge is a good indicator to recruiters that you can cope with stress and thus contribute to the success of your overseas mission. (For a more detailed review of the challenges of coping with overseas life, see the chapters in Part One, Your International IQ.)

Readiness to Undertake High-Risk Situations

To accept a position with an international NGO, you must be willing to consider taking risks by accepting work in unstable or volatile situations. Among the precarious security situations often encountered in the field while working overseas with NGOs are epidemics, famine, natural disasters, internally displaced populations and refugees, unrest and wars.

You must also be willing to consider taking personal health risks by agreeing to work in tropical zones and also to work intensively, without breaks, for long hours. It is important that you take the time to determine if your physical and psychological health is fit to match demanding work contexts.

You also must be prepared to comply with the health and safety requirements of the organization you plan to join. This means undertaking extensive health preparation prior to departure and medical follow-up upon return. Security rules in the field may entail, among other things, curfews, no driving, precautionary evacuations, radio communications, fixed rest and relaxation periods and other strict guidelines established in accordance with given situations.

Qualities that will be required by NGOs to which you apply include your awareness of security principles; your attention to relationships with local authorities; your ability to negotiate; your diplomacy, tact and calmness; your ability to demonstrate judgment; and your awareness of your responsibility to communicate with peers.

Ethical Behaviour

International health recruiters are interested in a broad category of skills termed "ethical behaviour." The health field is somewhat unique in emphasizing these characteristics, and those applying for international health work should take note. The nature of health delivery in war zones and refugee camps during famines and natural disasters requires that you are sensitive to and you have a vocabulary to describe the following: your understanding of ethical behaviour within the health delivery context at hand; your sensitivity to populations in danger and an understanding of their vulnerability; your ability to manage ethical misbehaviour; your ability to understand the importance of perception; your awareness of your obligations when representing an NGO while in the field; and your awareness that you must behave in accordance with universally accepted ethical and legal standards as well your own national laws and customs, while also respecting local laws and customs. All of these qualities, while perhaps elusive to the uninitiated, are crucial in any NGO field situation.

Language Abilities

Your ability to speak one or more languages other than your mother tongue is a strong asset. English is used in most countries, but your working knowledge of French, Portuguese and Spanish will be a strong asset that will increase your chance of getting overseas placements.

General Job Skills for International Health

It is difficult to capture the broad range of hard and soft skills specifically required to perform health work. We have therefore resorted to listing a series of questions that will help you envision the general requirements. The list of questions below may help you to initiate reflection on your motivation and to assess your level of experience.

- Are you willing to work in unknown environments?
- Are you familiar with some of the key issues linked to international emergency/relief aid and development?
- Do you have the capacity to develop, implement and monitor new health programs/infrastructures?
- Are you willing to provide health care to patients who do not speak your mother tongue and who stand for life values different than yours?
- Are you willing to coach/train health workers who have different experience and education than yours?
- Are you interested in advocating on behalf of patients to whom you provide medical care?
- Do you see yourself working with limited medical equipment/resources?
- Are you ready to learn more about medical practice in non-familiar settings?
- Are you able to count on your leadership and problem-solving skills to manage unpredictable events and fast change?
- Do you have some familiarity with international human rights laws?

- Do you have a highly developed understanding of ethical behaviours, especially in situations where ethics are constantly threatened?
- Are you willing to receive a lowered income to have the opportunity to work overseas?

Specific Areas of Expertise for International Health Programs

- Critical care
- Epidemiology, vaccination campaigns, cold chain
- Primary care
- General surgery
- HIV/AIDS: treatment and prevention
- Infectious diseases—HIV/AIDS, TB, etc.
- Northern nursing (Alaska or Canadian North)
- Nutrition surveys
- Public health
- Reproductive health, sexually transmitted illnesses (STIs)
- Sexual violence, mental health
- Statistics, medical advocacy
- Tropical medicine
- Water and sanitation
- Women's health, mother/child care

A Note on Entry-Level Skills

The selection process of most NGOs is based on specific criteria that are established in accordance with the organization's needs. However, some NGOs are less demanding than others for first-timers and do not ask for extensive previous experience; emphasis is placed on the personal attributes of candidates rather than on their array of experiences. For example, candidates who are flexible and ready to leave on short notice for a long-term period may have a better chance to be quickly retained. Indeed, it is important for first-timers to be able to demonstrate strong motivation and relevant personal attributes. Entry-level positions may include various medical positions (e.g., medical doctors, surgeons, anaesthesiologists), other health professional positions (e.g., nurses, midwives, laboratory technologists, mental health specialists), and non-medical positions (e.g., administrators, logisticians).

GAINING INTERNATIONAL HEALTH EXPERIENCE

A Selection of Educational Programs in Health

At the end of this chapter, we have profiled over 20 courses to help you with your international health career. This is a non-exhaustive list of high-calibre educational programs to help you increase your understanding of the complexity of health services delivery abroad, the various contexts of health programs, and related responsibilities. Most courses are short, and many are summer programs that are located in Canada, the US and Europe. Approximately one-third of the courses listed are not specifically geared to health but provide management training in support of health projects.

Other Ways to Build International Experience

It is important not to underestimate attributes gained from non-formal education and non-formal work experiences. Consider, for example, enrolling in courses or participating in social activities that could be of assistance to your preparation for living and working overseas. Here is a list of examples that constitute potential assets for building an international health career:

Training and Related Learning Experience

- first aid course
- home healthcare delivery to elderly or handicapped persons
- IT (information technology) training
- languages courses
- mechanical and other trades training
- memberships in professional organizations
- NGO training courses for international work
- occupational health and safety training
- participation in job fairs, recruitment conferences and exhibits
- professional honours and awards you have received
- publication of articles you have written
- seminars you have taught

Cross-Cultural Work and Volunteer Experience

- with immigrants and refugees in Canada
- in medical outposts in Alaska or the Canadian North
- with marginalized groups—e.g., street people
- with Aboriginal populations in your home country
- participation in international exchange programs
- unusual, offbeat travel (in your home country and overseas)
- community volunteer work in your home country
- experience with the media/public relations
- advocacy experience, speaking out experiences

TARGETING YOUR JOB SEARCH

It is important that you be as selective as possible in narrowing your choice and targeting a specific job. Decide what you want to do, where and with whom. The following key points will help you in your selection process:

- Identify what your professional strengths are and in which areas you can best share your knowledge and expertise.
- Know what your personal assets and weaknesses are and that you possess a good level of maturity and problem-solving skills.
- Know in which context you are likely to be best able to cope, based on your findings about the character, ethics, mandate and principles of the placement:
  - hospitals
  - private firms

- NGOs involved in international development in health
  - NGOs involved in emergency medical/relief aid
  - multilateral organizations
- Consider which region of the world you can best picture yourself living and working in. This may be based, for example, on previous travel experience and relationships with people from different background than yours. Do not hesitate to investigate your taste for new environments and cultures. Identify the places where you would *not* like to live and work.
- Visit Web sites of organizations that you would potentially like to work with. Complete the on-line application processes. Identify placements that will give you possible opportunities for professional development.
- Define the parameters for your departure.
  - Establish your availability/readiness to go overseas.
  - Establish for how long you are prepared to go.
  - Identify the dates on which you are prepared to leave.
  - Check what kind of leave notice is required at your current place of work.
  - Determine your availability to attend pre-departure training.
- Remain aware that there are risks in choosing to live and work abroad.
  - You may decide never to return to your previous lifestyle.
  - You may lose friends on the road.
  - You may experience illnesses, injuries and/or trauma—and much more that you could never have previously imagined.
- Create an inventory of your international health career skills so that you can match your profile to employers' requirements. (For more details, see Chapter 23, Selling Your International Skills.)
  - List your experience in organizing, training and supervising.
  - List your technical skills: communications, computers, languages, hobbies.
  - List activities you engage in outside of your paid job or course of study, such as any professional organizations you belong to, articles you have published, seminars you have taught, honours you have received and community or volunteer work you have done.
  - List your international experiences: travels, conferences, studies; exposure to immigrants, refugees, aboriginals, foreign students and tourists.
  - List any non-formal educational activities you have attended.
  - List your personal qualities, such as being analytical, open, creative, born to lead and others.
  - List experience such as internships, volunteer leadership positions, etc.
  - List three words that describe you best, and be prepared to explain why.
- Here are a few practical steps to ensure that you can leave on short notice:
  - Prepare any required documentation such as driver's licence, education and other accreditation documents.
  - Ensure that your passport is valid.

- Visit your family doctor to start familiarizing yourself with your health preparation.
- Inform your relatives and friends of your plan.
- Establish a calendar of action to finalize personal arrangements—e.g., finance, insurance, apartment lease, list of necessary purchases, personal documents, power of attorney, storage of belongings.

PERSONAL CAREER STORIES

The following are 11 personal career stories that outline the many varied perspectives on working in international health. A common trait that runs through all these stories is the wisdom that the individuals have achieved as they have contemplated the meaning of their experiences abroad. You'll see that courage and strength of character is in no short supply. (For two longer career stories, see John McNern's article, "The Fight Against Tuberculosis in Yunnan-China" in Appendix 33a, and Vanessa van Schoor's article, "Volunteering on a Health Project in Dili, East Timor" in Appendix 33b, on the CD-ROM.)

- **Doctor underlines the importance of training.** *I felt it was my responsibility to use my skills and background to help others in need. It is with this determination in mind that I first applied to volunteer with MÉDECINS SANS FRONTIÈRES (MSF) after completing my family practice residency in 1992. Since that time I have done 16 MSF missions over the last 11 years, in a variety of wars, famines, epidemics and natural disasters. These incredible experiences have had a profound impact on my life.*

  The more experience I obtained overseas the more I felt it necessary to seek additional training, to supplement my medical studies and to help me better understand and carry out the work of MSF. I first obtained a diploma in tropical medicine, followed by an epidemiology course at the CDC, and then sought training in humanitarian law and peacekeeping at the University of Santa Anna in Italy, as well as participated in a number of MSF management training courses. It is important to be as prepared as possible when joining an MSF field project. Adaptability and cultural sensitivity are essential elements to be able to work with populations in danger. My training strengthened my confidence when evaluating a new disaster, and provided me with sensitivity to the complex issues arising in, and from, crisis situations.

  In Canada, it is important to get the word out, to advocate and educate the Canadian public and the government on what is happening right now around the world. Unfortunately, the vast majority of our global population does not enjoy the privileges we have; basic rights such as access to health care, clean water, food and the absence of violence are only a dream for many.

- **Canadian nurse understands international health work.** *Over 15 years ago I read an article about a Canadian doctor who was working overseas with an emergency medical organization called MÉDECINS SANS FRONTIÈRES (MSF). I remember my heart racing and thinking, as a surgical nurse, that this is something I could and would love to do. I imagined it to be like one of those nurses running to get the wounded from the helicopters on M*A*S*H! I was excited to think how I could just run off and volunteer in the neediest war zone and help with the* *wounded. How wrong I was. I soon found out that most overseas medical work in conflict zones is not surgical but instead public health based. Although I did end up working in two conflict zones (Bosnia and Sri Lanka), I saw the majority of work of nurses in these areas was primary health care—setting up health posts, vaccination campaigns, treating tuberculosis and HIV/AIDS, mother and child heath care, nutrition and feeding centres. When I returned to Canada, I became a personnel and recruitment officer for MSF and I was often asked how one gets the type of experience needed to work overseas. As a nursing student, you can look for clinical placements in areas of public or community health, mother and child health or tropical or infectious diseases. You can volunteer overseas during your summer vacation, either as a student nurse or with a youth or development organization. A graduate nurse can work in First Nations or northern communities (nursing stations) where you will gather excellent experience in public health. But above all get out and travel and learn about what is happening in the world.*

Working overseas for a humanitarian aid organization changed my life and opened the world to me. My mother always told me to "help those who fall through the cracks" and working overseas allowed me to do that—I loved it!

- **Doctor alternates between work in Canadian North and overseas.** *My goal was always to work overseas doing work that somehow "made a difference." I decided to enter medicine, and do family medicine specifically. What I didn't anticipate was that I would come to find and enjoy meaningful work in Canada working with under-serviced populations here at home. I now intersperse periods overseas with stints working in Canada, and find it is the perfect mix.*

On finishing my residency, I went to work with the Cree people based in Moose Factory, Ontario. It was classic rural medicine, coping with anything and everything that came through the door. I learned a great deal about working together in teams, about cross-cultural living and practicing without the crutches of medical technology. These turned out to be common themes with my international work, and I found that, in turn, my international work gave me added skills for my work at home.

Much as I liked the work in the North, I wanted to get overseas. I signed up with MÉDECINS SANS FRONTIÈRES (MSF), the largest medical humanitarian agency in the world. The mission of MSF, to do emergency work in areas that need help combined with a commitment to address systemic issues by bearing witness to injustices, appealed to me. Ten years ago I left on my first mission to the former Yugoslavia. My job was to ensure that the hospitals and clinics in the wartorn areas had what they needed to stay open and functioning, and to implement a surveillance system to monitor disease outbreaks. Since that first experience, I have worked in refugee camps and managed epidemics of meningitis, cholera and dysentery. I have organized mass vaccination campaigns and set up feeding centres. I have worked in tuberculosis programs and implemented maternal child health care. The variety has been incredible and wherever I have been, it has been with a team of people who care about providing medical assistance to those who need it most. It is this commitment that has kept me hooked and coming back for more.

- **Logistician knows about the skills required.** *International health work involves a varied skill set, and there is no single profile that fits perfectly. One must plan* *ahead, work with minimal resources, work with people in a tight group with little privacy, and often function in a foreign language and culture. To prepare for a career as a logistician with MÉDECINS SANS FRONTIÈRES, a wide variety of backgrounds might be a good foundation. For example, a mechanic with some human resource management skills, a tree planter with some accounting experience, a corporate supply manager who does some camping or hunting, or a civil engineer who has volunteered as a scout master would have valuable logistical skills.*

I came to MSF as a logistician after 11 years in the Canadian forest industry. As a tree planter I was exposed to remote camp environments, isolation, group living, lack of "civilized" luxury, and hard work. As a project manager for a tree planting company, I hired and managed crews, organized camp set-ups (including some boat-based and fly-in scenarios), managed supply and did the accounting and payroll.

High levels of maturity and self-confidence are essential. One must take initiative, balance the sometimes unreasonable or conflicting demands of medical staff, deal with shocking and sometimes dangerous situations, adjust to the cultural needs of national staff and population, and often put in gruelling working hours.

As a career, one will never make a fortune working with MSF. However, with good planning, it is possible to have acceptable finances. The key is to reduce expenses at home to a bare minimum, and avoid large vacation spending. Since MSF pays all expenses in the field, virtually the entire salary or stipend can be banked. In many cases this will exceed what one could save while working in Canada after rent and living expenses.

- **Nurse follows varied career path in health management.** *To work as a nurse in Africa was definitely on my agenda since adolescence, however ill defined that romantic notion was for me at the time. I wanted to work overseas, meet people and understand the world that I lived in. I studied nursing, and then after gaining two years of solid work experience on medical wards at the Ottawa General Hospital, I moved to Switzerland at the age of 23 to begin practicing overseas. While in Europe, I became aware of an institute in Belgium that specialized in tropical medicine. I enrolled there in the hopes of preparing for the challenges of an African setting. I still had no clear design of how, when and where exactly I would apply this new knowledge until MÉDECINS SANS FRONTIÈRES (MSF) came recruiting at the institute. That was 12 years ago.*

  My first mission with MSF was in 1994 when I was sent to work in a team that provided health care for Somali refugees that had fled into Kenya during the Somali civil war. The people that we served there, my MSF colleagues and the national staff that worked alongside us literally captivated me for the next 10 years. I've since worked in many countries providing humanitarian assistance in the form of nutritional programs, primary health care, refugee health, emergency mass vaccination campaigns, war surgery etc... After five years of steady fieldwork in countries all over the globe, I relocated back to North America, to New York City this time in 1999. There I enjoyed working as a medical human resources recruiter and placement officer for MSF. In 2001, I shifted my focus to work with the program department that follows the developments in our fields of action and raises relevant humanitarian affairs in forums such as the US public media, the

UNITED NATIONS and the US government. Today, back in Canada since 2003, I hold a similar position as the government relations officer for MSF Canada. In addition to advocacy work, I also negotiate the grant contracts between the CANADIAN INTERNATIONAL DEVELOPMENT AGENCY (CIDA) and the MSF field projects that request Canadian funding.

I haven't stopped nursing though. Having done research and worked on the issue of rape in the refugee setting, I was able to translate that experience into an on-call nursing position here in Ottawa responding to victims of rape and domestic violence. I also eventually plan to indulge another dream on this agenda of mine, which is to work as an outpost nurse in Canada's great North. At MSF, we always say that Canadian outpost nurses do very well on the humanitarian field due to the similarity in experiences. Now it's my turn to see if the reverse is true!

- **Head nurse understands HIV/AIDS projects**. *I moved to Zimbabwe in 1988 for a two-year stint, leaving behind my position as head nurse of an emergency department in a large Canadian teaching hospital. The move seemed like a natural event, as I knew from early adulthood I would find myself in Africa one day. I did not go with a formal job, or with specific objectives. Rather, my interests were in learning about the context and environment on a culturally diverse continent. Upon departure, I can't say I knew where I would invest my energies. However, within a few weeks, it became apparent that HIV/AIDS had emerged as an important health issue and an area in need of healthcare professionals. I met with leaders of a number of community-based HIV/AIDS initiatives to learn about their priorities and challenges. My knowledge and interest in health and social issues guided my entrance into the area. I was recruited by a Canadian NGO interested in supporting community-based HIV/AIDS initiatives and gradually became part of a dynamic network of professionals and community activists collaborating with government and other stakeholders on developing a broad HIV/AIDS strategy. Adapting to the new terrain called for sensitivity to local wisdom and investments. As trust and credibility developed with local professionals, so did a willingness to grant me space to work autonomously and provide leadership. I remained in Zimbabwe for four years and continued to work with many committed and talented players in this field. I returned to Canada eight years later having further experienced life in South Africa as it emerged from years of apartheid. In all, I learned very many things: of the importance of humility and honesty in new work relationships; of the tremendous wisdom and lessons one encounters as a participant and observer in new contexts; and of how willing people are to welcome new energy and investment from outsiders genuinely interested in participating in advancing important work.*

- **Missionary nurse attracted to Africa.** *I don't know how many elderly people I have spoken to who have said to me, "I always wanted to go to Africa and work— but I never did." It never ceases to amaze me just how many people have the intention to go and work in Africa, even the desire to—but rarely do they follow through. When I ask them why they didn't go—they come up with things like, "I got married," "I had kids," or "I couldn't afford it." My personal favourite was, "I am afraid of snakes."*

I am thankful to say I won't ever have that regret. The decision to go and work in Africa was not really my own. From as far back as I can remember Africa has fascinated me. As a kid, seeing any picture that I knew was from Africa drew me in immediately. As a young teenager, I sat with a friend and pronounced, "Someday I will work in Africa." Strangely enough—I don't recall that moment—but my friend reminds me of it often. For me, Africa is a calling. It is where I am meant to be. It is what I am meant to do.

My work in Africa is as a missionary. I sought out several Christian organizations before settling with AFRICA INLAND MISSION (AIM). It is so important to find an organization that suits you with your strengths and needs. AIM was personable and small enough to give me the individualized attention I wanted, and yet established enough to ensure security and safety in those parts of Africa that are less stable, and to ensure proper medical care if needed. The focus of AIM is mission work; my medical expertise is used to minister to people in a variety of settings. That is what I wanted.

It isn't a stretch to say there is something out there for everyone. Take the time to seek out several organizations and find the perfect match for you.

- **Doctor alternates between work in Canada and overseas.** A private practice in Woodstock, New Brunswick is a far cry from curing populations in Asia or Africa, but both are experiences valued by Dr. Joni Guptill. An MSF volunteer since 1991, Dr. Guptill has done everything from vaccinating Kurdish refugees in Turkey to delivering babies and palliative care in New Brunswick. Dr. Guptill says that the chaos of her overseas postings has made her appreciate the sedate nature of her domestic practice more. Some of those overseas experiences have included working with MSF in Turkey, Somalia and China.

  In 1991, while completing a diploma in tropical medicine and hygiene in England, Dr. Guptill was recruited by MSF and soon thrust into a "front-line" medical position. The mass migration of thousands of Kurds across the mountains of northern Iraq into Turkey and then trying to administer healthcare to them was *"organized mayhem,"* says Dr. Guptill. It was a distressing first mission for the doctor but it quickly opened her eyes to the kinds of work done in the field.

  "The mixture of doing general practice and overseas work for me is a fantastic combination. One is very overwhelming at times and the other is too quiet at times, so the balance keeps me interested in both areas. I am constantly thinking of the next project [with MSF] and how I can get coverage for my practice here in New Brunswick. It is difficult in the current medical climate to get coverage at the same time that an emergency project requires your services."

- **Nurse on short-term NGO assignment in Nepal.** *I had been working as a nurse for six years in a downtown hospital when I decided it was time to take a leave of absence and head overseas. Along with a close friend who is also a nurse, we found a small NGO on the Internet and then met with the Canadian staff here in Toronto. After discussing mutual goals and expectations we were delighted to have the opportunity to spend four months in rural Nepal. With Nepali-based staff in Kathmandu, we were able to connect with local people and learn a little more about the community we were heading too. These contacts were invaluable in several ways, including arranging for a week of Nepali language lessons. It was a great asset to arrive in the village knowing a few words and phrases. While we arrived in Nepal with certain ideas about what types of work we would be doing, several informal community needs assessment meetings helped guide us in working* *with local members. Having met with the volunteer healthcare providers, teachers and members of the local community group we were able to better assess the needs of the community and enlist the support of those we would be working with around the issues of maternal/child health.*

While we achieved the goals we set out for ourselves, the work environment in a developing country can be quite different than the one we are used to in the Western world. What we saw as priorities for the community were not always the same as what they perceived, depending on many factors including weather (monsoon season) or during the time of a national election. The setting in which we worked was not as formal or structured as that which we were used too. We needed to be flexible, patient and open to other less conventional teaching methods such as song, dance and street theatre to convey information and education.

- **Nurse works as midwife in Sierra Leone.** *I was a nurse in Quebec City when I left for a mission with MSF to Sierra Leone in 2003. The reasons for leaving—I wanted to travel and see new places, but I also liked the idea of working with MSF because I really felt I could help people. When I arrived, Sierra Leone had just entered a peaceful period after the elections. The UN presence made the country more stable, but after the end of the war there were no health services. It was desolating to arrive in a country that had nothing. Food was just starting to arrive through the UN food program, which was greatly needed due to the high level of malnutrition in the population. Sierra Leone had qualified health personnel, but had no resources or health system in place. Medically, it was also very hard to see mothers die. Mothers are the central pillars of the society; if they die everything crumbles.*

On my mission with MSF I worked as a midwife, even though I was not officially trained as one in Canada. But in Sierra Leone, I worked with midwives who taught me how this work was done. My work with MSF in the field gave me an opportunity to do many different things that I could not have done in Canada. Personally, I learned how to live with little miracles, to grow personally and professionally in an environment that has hardly anything. It's when you come back to Canada that you learn to appreciate the comfort and the accessibility of things.

- **Logistician combines motivation with career path.** *What makes a person decide to volunteer overseas? Each person has a unique reason, which can range from a desire to help others to discovering a new culture. For myself, a Vancouver native who loved to travel, the decision to volunteer with MSF was not so obvious.*

Before joining MSF in 1997, I travelled for two years around the world on a motorcycle. It was during these travels that I first heard of and encountered MSF volunteers. I remember when my friend and I travelled trough remote areas in Ethiopia, people would come up to us asking for medicines and all I could say to them was "Sorry, I can't help you." But after I met some MSF volunteers working in Ethiopia, I felt that they were doing something worthwhile that I could also see myself doing.

Six months later, I returned to Canada to settle down and find a job. After several unlucky weeks searching, I finally decided to enrol in a job finding strategy course. When one of my counsellors suggested I look into international work, I suddenly remembered the MSF volunteers I had met in Ethiopia several months earlier. Five weeks after my first call to the MSF Vancouver office, I was sent to my first emergency mission as a logistician in the Democratic Republic of Congo. For the next seven years, I worked as a logistician in the Amazon, Angola, Mozambique, Rwanda, Tanzania and did everything from evacuate MSF volunteers in the Congo and save flood victims in Mozambique to helping malnourished families in Angola.

What advice would I give to a new volunteer? Work may seem so overwhelming in the field at times that a volunteer might feel he or she is just a drop in the bucket. But the work a volunteer does, no matter how small, can have far-reaching consequences in the lives of the people we work for.

A LAST WORD

You have completed your self-assessment, consulted with recruitment professionals, and researched information about medical programs and contexts among selected employers that match your personal and professional choices. You have searched and found a job. You are now ready to embark on your health career abroad.

An experienced nurse in Africa summarizes what it takes to be a successful healthcare manager overseas. *"Flexibility, diplomacy, a sense of ethics, maturity, perspective, a sense of initiative and openness to experience differences are essential qualities to acquire for achieving successful international humanitarian work."*

In the short term, providing international humanitarian assistance involves resilience, endurance, and perseverance. In the long term however, the rewards of devoting oneself to health care overseas are to be savoured for a lifetime.

ABOUT THE AUTHOR

Annik Chalifour (LLL) with the collaboration of MÉDECINS SANS FRONTIÈRES–CANADA (MSF-CANADA).

At the time of writing, Annik Chalifour has been the human resources director of MÉDECINS SANS FRONTIÈRES–CANADA for eight years in Toronto. Annik has more than 20 years' experience with NGOs involved in humanitarian assistance, advocacy, development education and intercultural programs, including 12 years with the CANADIAN RED CROSS SOCIETY coordinating their overseas personnel program; 2 years of international recruitment with the INTERNATIONAL FEDERATION OF RED CROSS and RED CRESCENT societies and the INTERNATIONAL COMMITTEE OF THE RED CROSS in Geneva. She was exposed to field operations located in Brazil, Mexico, Nigeria, Pakistan and Russia. She has lived and worked in Senegal, Colombia and Switzerland. She has also been involved in the implementation of several training courses for humanitarian workers and volunteers in Canada and overseas. Annik is about to embark on a consulting career in international human resources development and management. She will also be teaching cross-cultural effectiveness as part of the international project management post-graduate certificate at the HUMBER INSTITUTE OF TECHNOLOGY AND ADVANCED LEARNING. Annik holds a law degree from Laval University and is trilingual in French, English and Spanish.

APPENDIX ON THE CD-ROM

33a. "The Fight Against Tuberculosis in Yunnan-China," by John McNern

33b. "Volunteering on a Health Project in Dili, East Timor," by Vanessa van Schoor

RESOURCES

HEALTH CAREERS

If you are a healthcare professional interested in getting an overseas job in health care, your chances are fairly good. The healthcare field is considered a growth area. The more specialized your profession, the better your chances are. However, if you are a recent university graduate, you will find the search more difficult. A key ingredient for all positions is previous international work or cross-cultural experience. See also the related Resources section, Health Overseas, in Chapter 3, Living Overseas.

AlertNet 💻

www.alertnet.org/thepeople/jobs/?via=lnav ◆ This site boasts an excellent database of jobs in the international humanitarian aid and relief field. Filter your search by country, salary, field of expertise or location, or simply browse all jobs by country. [ID:2595]

Beresford Blake Thomas 👫

Beresford Blake Thomas, Suite 206, 40 Sheppard Ave. W., Toronto, ON M2N 6K9, Canada, www.bbtltd.com, 416-644-1078, fax 416-222-0624 ◆ Beresford Blake Thomas is an International organization headquartered in London, with regional offices in Canada, Australia, New Zealand, the UK, the UAE and South Africa. Its global network of offices assists health care professionals from all specialties to find and settle into overseas placements. [ID:2475]

CANADEM 👫

www.canadem.ca; 𝓕𝓇 ◆ Canadem maintains a national roster of Canadians skilled in human rights, peace building, democratization, admin-logistics, security, reconstruction and other international field experience. One way it achieves this goal is by administering the Junior Professional Consultant Program, which is one of the best-run internship programs around. Each year approximately 30 young Canadians are deployed to a number of host organizations (OSCE, IOM, UNDP to name a few) in Africa, Eastern Europe and Central Asia. Pre-departure training is excellent, as is post-deployment support. [ID:2616]

Canadian Association of Schools of Nursing (CASN) 👫

Canadian Association of Schools of Nursing (CASN), Suite 15, 99 Fifth Ave., Ottawa, ON K1S 5K4, Canada, www.casn.org, 613-235-3150, fax 613-235-4476 ◆ CASN is the bilingual national voice for nursing and nursing research; it represents nursing programs in Canada. As a nursing teacher or member of CASN, you can register with one of their databases. Most directly related to international work and study is the "Canadian International Nurse Researcher Database," This is a voluntary database of nurse researchers in the academic and clinical setting, which provides a mechanism to identify nurse researchers and their areas of expertise, to network and to promote new projects. The site also boasts a good job board that is frequently updated and sometimes contains international positions. [ID:2328]

Canadian Nurses Association 👫

Canadian Nurses Association (CNA), 50 Driveway, Ottawa, ON K2P 1E2, Canada, www.cna-nurses.ca, 800-361-8404, fax 613-237-3520; 𝓕𝓇 ◆ Through its International Bureau office, the Canadian Nurses Association (CNA) has worked with nursing associations in over 28 countries in Africa, Asia and Latin America. The office undertakes professional development projects overseas aimed at improving the quality of health services by upgrading nurses' skills and ensuring accessibility to health care through strong policy development and lobby activities. The CNA Overseas Development Program sends Canadian nursing volunteers to work with partners abroad on a short-term consultancy basis. Check out their excellent Web site and find links to other NGOs sending health care professionals overseas. In addition, the Helen K. Mussallem Library at the CNA subscribes to a number of nursing journals/newsletters from other countries which may provide information about employment opportunities. [ID:2144]

Canadian Society for International Health (CSIH) 🏛

Canadian Society for International Health, 1 Nicholas Street, Suite 1105, Ottawa, ON K1N 7B7, Canada, www.csih.org, 613-241-5785, fax 613-241-3845, csih@fox.nstn.ca; *Fr* ◆ This is a great Web site with numerous resources relating to overseas health careers and travellers' health. The CSIH is a network that extends across Canada and around the world, linking individuals and organizations from all health sectors. The CSIH maintains the International Health Human Resources Registry, which is open to health and health-related professionals experienced in working in developing countries or with expertise that is applicable internationally. Add your name to the roster through the CSIH Web site and check out the overseas health job board. Or if you want to do an internship in international health, you can choose from Ethiopia, Malawi, Mali, Paraguay and Thailand, to name a few. New site features include a direct link to the Student University Network for International Health and great information on CSIH projects in Bolivia, Ukraine, Russia, Guyana and the Philippines. Find travellers' health information and a list of contact information for every travellers' health clinic in every major centre in Canada. Their publication "Synergy Online" will keep you connected to events around the network. A great hit for aspiring overseas health professionals. [ID:2258]

DegreeHunter 🖥

www.degreehunter.com ◆ Engineering jobs, nursing jobs, medical jobs, health care jobs, legal jobs, physician jobs, legal jobs and MBA jobs can be found at DegreeHunter. DegreeHunter is the career search service that helps graduate degree candidates and other certified professionals find employment with a new career opportunity by focusing on distinct professions, providing pre-screened positions and resumes, and enabling real-time and confidential communication between candidates and recruiters. [ID:2823]

Effective Communication in Multicultural Health Care Settings 📖

1994, Gary Krebs, Elizabeth Kunimoto, 160 pages ➤ Sage Publications, 6 Bonhill Street, London, EC2A 4PU, UK, www.sagepub.com, $31.95 US; Credit Cards; (44) (171) 374-0645, fax (44) (171) 374-8741, subscription@sagepub.co.uk ◆ Through innovative descriptions of relevant theory and research, the presentation of realistic case histories and the development of specific communication recommendations, this book lays the groundwork for effective navigation of health care systems. It provides insights into the complexities of multicultural relations in health care and demystifies the many cultural influences on health and health care to achieve its ultimate goal: to help people get the most they can out of health care and facilitate the promotion of public health. Excellent for those planning to work in an overseas healthcare environment. [ID:2202]

Expats Direct 🖥

www.expatsdirect.com ◆ This UK Web site stakes its claim as the best on-line employment service for working overseas and it delivers. Browse literally thousands of overseas jobs; however, if you want to apply to them, you have to join. Membership costs £55 per year. It might well be worth your money for access to engineering, health care, technicial and managerial positions everywhere from Milan to Malaysia. [ID:2645]

Global Health Directory 📖 🖥

2003 ➤ Global Health Council, Suite 600, 1701 K Street N.W., Washington, DC 20006-1503, USA, www.globalhealth.org, $50 US, free online; VISA, MC; 202-833-5900, fax 202-833-0075 ◆ For anyone interested in overseas health careers, this directory is a great starting point. It contains accurate and up-to-date information on hundreds of organizations worldwide working to improve global health. Includes contact information, mission statements, details on service focus, regions/countries served and target groups. Expanded indexes make the "Global Health Directory 2003-2004" a comprehensive, easy-to-use reference tool. Available on-line for free. [ID:2533]

Health Professionals Abroad 📖

2000, Tim Ryder, Ian Collier, 256 pages ➤ Vacation Work, 9 Park End Street, Oxford, OX1 1HJ, UK, www.vacationwork.co.uk, £11.95; Credit Cards; (44) (0) (1865) 24-1978, sales@vacationwork.co.uk ◆ A comprehensive and complete guide to finding work overseas in all areas of health care. Covers both the state and private sectors in the large number of countries which need additional qualified and experienced staff in a wide range of disciplines. Includes details of opportunities in 34 countries and provides useful contact information for your overseas health search. [ID:2542]

Health, Population and Reproductive Health Resources 🖥

www.jhpiego.jhu.edu/websites/index.htm ◆ Those interested in a career in international health should check out this page of links to organizations involved in public health. [ID:2227]

HealthCareersCanada 🖥

www.healthcareerscanada.com ◆ Becoming a member of HealthCareersCanada is free. Find information on international career events, thousands of on-line job ads, hundreds of employer profiles, employment information, as well as education and salary data. It also offers a "Personal Job Search Agent" and a "Resume Builder/Download" at no cost. Once you complete your profile and upload your resume (or complete the on-line credentials) you can start applying for jobs that match your job search criteria, automatically pre-register for career events, and more. [ID:2835]

Helen Ziegler and Associates ⚕

Helen Ziegler & Associates, Suite 2403, 180 Dundas Street W., Toronto, ON M5G 1Z8, Canada, www.hziegler.com, 416-977-6941, fax 416-977-6128, hza@medhunters.com ◆ This organization has successfully recruited over 4,700 healthcare professionals: doctors, nurses, pharmacists, technologists, therapists, and administrators for major hospitals in Saudi Arabia and the United Arab Emirates. [ID:2229]

Helping Health Workers Learn 📖

1995, David Werner, Bill Bower, Hesperian Foundation, 632 pages ➤ Masters & Scribes Bookshoppe, 9938 - 81 Ave., Edmonton, AB T6E 1W6, Canada, www.mastersandscribes.com, $20 US; Credit Cards; 800-378-3199, fax 780-439-6879 ◆ Provides a people-centred approach to health care and presents strategies for effective community involvement through participatory education. [ID:2201]

International Health Exchange (IHE) ⚕

www.ihe.org.uk/recruit.htm ◆ This UK organization supports initiatives to bring about sustained improvements to people's health in developing countries by placing appropriately experienced people with organizations requiring their skills. They have a great publication called "The Health Exchange" which offers first-hand coverage of the challenges and success of health practitioners in developing countries. Links to other training courses offered by IHE and other organizations can help you keep your skills up-to-date. IHE administers an international register of health workers to help match workers with jobs. The recruitment centre is fantastic, with a searchable database that will get you on the road to an amazing overseas public health career! [ID:2709]

International Hospital Recruitments ⚕

International Hospital Recruitments, Suite 2403, 2300 Yonge Street, Toronto, ON M4P 1E4, Canada, www.ihrcanada.com/toc.htm, 416-221-2761, fax 416-222-6220 ◆ International Hospital Recruitments was established in 1994 to recruit medical personnel from North America. They have an office in Toronto and can assist you in finding a locum or permanent position in the United Arab Emirates and Saudi Arabia. [ID:2710]

International Jobs Center 📖

www.internationaljobs.org, $46 US for 3 months or $149 US for one year ◆ By becoming a member, you get access to late-breaking job openings and will receive the "International Career Employment Weekly" newspaper in hard copy or by e-mail. Take advantage of a comprehensive database of international jobs for professionals, but includes development jobs and internships as well. Noteworthy on this site are the listings of international health care, commerce and IT jobs. [ID:2583]

International Society of Travel Medicine 📖 🖥

www.istm.org ◆ This Georgia-based Web site is directed at health professionals specializing in the area of international travellers' health, but is also an excellent resource for anyone interested in the latest information about overseas health. Not only can you search for travellers' health clinics all around the world, but you can access the latest breaking overseas health information on the newsletter "NewsShare." The ISTM's "Responsible Traveller" initiative can provide you with information on how to lessen your public health impact when visiting other countries. And, if you're really keen, you can order the "Journal of Traveller's Health" on-line or in print for about $125.00 US per year. A great source of information and links for staying healthy overseas. [ID:2649]

Médecins Sans Frontières / Doctors Without Borders (MSF) 👪

Médecins Sans Frontières / Doctors Without Borders (MSF), Suite 5B, 355 Adelaide Street, Toronto, ON M5V 1S2, Canada, www.msf.org, 416-586-9820, fax 416-586-9821, msfcan@passport.ca ◆ MSF is a global NGO that has become the world's leading international medical relief organization. It establishes missions in areas of the globe where there is no medical infrastructure or where the existing one is unable to withstand the pressure to which it is subjected. MSF lobbies for political policy reform with repect to international public health, both domestically and internationally. The organization has an excellent Web site with information on how to become one of thousands of volunteer medical professionals that MSF sends to over 70 countries worldwide. There's a special section for medical students interested in working overseas and a resources page with publications and links relating to international public health and peace through health. A great resource for researching overseas health profession opportunities. (For more information, see their ad in the sponsor section at the end of this guide.) [ID:2273]

MedHunters 🖥

MedHunters, Suite 2403, 180 Dundas Street W., Toronto, ON M5G 1Z8, Canada, www.medhunters.com, 800-664-0278, fax 416-977-6128, jobs@medhunters.com ◆ This is an excellent job board for positions in the healthcare field. Browse hundreds of high quality jobs and view informative postings providing all the co-ordinates you'll need in to start the application process rolling. By registering for free, you can access career-building resources and online assignments and tutorials designed to help you come out on top of the pile and get the health job of your dreams. Check it out. [ID:2294]

Project Concern International 👪

Project Concern International, 3550 Afton Road, San Diego, CA 92123, USA, www.projectconcern.org, 858-279-9690, fax 858-694-0294 ◆ For over 40 years, San Diego-based Project Concern has been reaching people with its health care programs in 12 countries on five continents. Project Concern also places experienced volunteer healthcare professionals in hospitals and community clinics in Asia, Africa and South America. Check out their job board and internship program. [ID:2232]

Public Health Jobs Worldwide 🖥

www.jobspublichealth.com, $129 US/year (26 issues) ◆ This is a biweekly newspaper packed with current public health job openings in the US and around the world. View select international openings on-line or become a subscriber and receive the Public Health Jobs Worldwide newspaper by mail or on-line, along with Web access to "late-breaking" job openings that are not open to the public. Subscribers also get e-mail notification of special job openings. A great way for health professions to keep their eyes on the overseas job market! [ID:2760]

Science Careers 💻
http://aaas.sciencecareers.org ◆ Science Careers is a US Web site that allows you to search the latest openings from hundreds of employers, post your resume and create job alert agents. Create an account for free and the system will store multiple resumes and cover letters that you can use to apply to jobs posted on Science Careers. It will also save the jobs you have responded to so you can easily track and manage your applications. The database has a huge number of postings from all around the world, making this one of the best sites around for searching for international careers in science. [ID:2643]

Trillium Human Resources Inc. 👪
Trillium Human Resources Inc., Suite 210, 150 Consumers Road, Toronto, ON M2J 1P9, Canada, www.trilliumhr.com, 877-722-8522, fax 416-497-8491 ◆ Trillium is a placement agency that assists registered nurses, doctors, physical/occupational therapists, and speech pathologists in professional positions throughout Canada, the US and the UK. Applicants must be eligible to be licensed in other countries. Trillium recruits recent graduates and experienced candidates. Applicants pay no fees. Trillium's Web site offers an on-line application and lots of career planning resources that will help you with all facets of the job search. [ID:2295]

Where There Is No Doctor: A Village Health Care Handbook: Revised Edition 📖
2003, David Werner, Carol Thuman, Jane Maxwell, Hesperian Foundation, 632 pages ➤ Masters & Scribes Bookshoppe, 9938 - 81 Ave., Edmonton, AB T6E 1W6, Canada, www.mastersandscribes.com, $20 US; Credit Cards; 800-378-3199, fax 780-439-6879 ◆ Translated into over 90 languages, this US publication is considered the most accessible and widely used community health care manual in the world. This revolutionary health care "bible" has saved millions of lives around the world by providing vital information on diagnosing and treating common medical problems and diseases, and giving special emphasis to prevention. Includes sections detailing effective examination techniques, home cures, correct usage of medicines and their precautions, nutrition, caring for children, ailments of older individuals and first aid. [ID:2048]

Profiles of Health Training Programs

Twenty courses are profiled below. This is a non-exhaustive list of high-calibre educational programs are designed to help you build an international health career. Twelve of these courses are coded as Health Training. The other eight are coded as Management Training in Support of Health Project. Most courses are short, and many are summer programs. All are located in Canada, Europe or the US.

University of Arizona
Department of Family and Community Medicine, P.O. Box 245052, College of Medicine, Tucson, AZ, 85724, USA; 520-626-7962, fax 520-626-6134, www.globalhealth.arizona.edu/IHIndex.html

HEALTH TRAINING: Summer Course in International Health—Clinical and Community Care ◆ The University of Arizona's course on International Health: Clinical and Community Care is a highly rated three- or four-week course, usually offered in July. It is a multi-specialty, case-based problem-solving course which prepares medical students and primary care residents for healthcare experiences in developing countries. The course is also open to other healthcare professionals with clinical experience or those from any medical or public health field. Enrolment for the course is limited to 24, which allows case-based teaching in three groups of eight students. [ID:7223]

Boston University

School of Public Health, 715 Albany Street, T-4 West, Boston, MA, 02118,
USA; 617-638-5234, fax 617-638-4476, ih@bu.edu, www.international-health.org

HEALTH TRAINING: Summer Certificate Program in International Health ◆ The Boston University School of Public Health offers an annual Summer Certificate Program in International Health. It is an intensive 12-week program, that provides a comprehensive overview of factors that influence health and issues in the planning and delivery of health services in resource-constrained environments. It addresses challenges faced by developing and transitional economy countries. Participants earn 33 per cent of the credits for a Master of Public Health (MPH) degree at Boston University. [ID:7213]

University of British Columbia

Centre for Intercultural Communication (CIC), University of British Columbia,
Continuing Studies, 800 Robson Street, Vancouver, BC, V6Z 3B7, Canada;
604-822-1436, fax 604-822-0388, cic@cstudies.ubc.ca, http://cic.cstudies.ubc.ca

MANAGEMENT TRAINING IN SUPPORT OF HEALTH INTERVENTION: Certificate in Intercultural Studies ◆ The University of British Columbia Centre for Intercultural Communication offers an innovative program for people from any sector wanting to communicate effectively across cultures and adapt successfully to cultural change. The Centre offers a variety of programs, including the Certificate in Intercultural Studies.The program allows individuals from various sectors to improve their confidence in international and multicultural settings. The course will benefit those in health care and community service, and individuals in other fields. [ID:7222]

Columbia University

Mailman School of Public Health, Suite 1030, 722 West 168th Street,
New York, NY, 10032, USA; 212-305-3927, fax 212-342-1830,
ph-admit@columbia.edu, www.mailman.hs.columbia.edu/popfam/teach/mph_migrate.html

MANAGEMENT TRAINING IN SUPPORT OF HEALTH INTERVENTION: Course in Public Health in Complex Emergencies (PHCE) ◆ Columbia University's Mailman School of Public Health (in partnership with World Education, Inc.), offers a Public Health in Complex Emergencies (PHCE) program, which is a two-week course that focuses on critical health issues faced by NGO/PVO personnel, working in complex emergencies. The goal of the course is to enhance the capacity of humanitarian assistance workers and their organizations to respond to health needs of refugees and internally displaced persons affected by these emergencies. Participants in the program will gain knowledge in the following sectors: context of emergencies, epidemiology, communicable disease, environmental health, nutrition, reproductive health, weapons, violence and trauma, protection and security, psychosocial issues and coordination. [ID:7214]

University of Geneva

Uni-Mail, ppAH - Secrétariat, 40 bd du Pont d'Arve, Geneva 4, CH-1211, Switzerland;
(41) (0) 22-379-89-32, fax (41) (0) 22-379-89-39, ppah@unige.ch, www.unige.ch/ppah

MANAGEMENT TRAINING IN SUPPORT OF HEALTH INTERVENTION: Master's in Humanitarian Action ◆ The University of Geneva's multi-faculty program in humanitarian action (ppAH), offers a post-graduate degree, intended for people possessing a university degree (or equivalent) who have already been active in humanitarian fieldwork. People without a university degree, but with solid professional skills, are also eligible for this program. The aim of this program is to analyze humanitarian action from a multi-disciplinary perspective and to analyze its complex nature. The program consists of four reflection axes: armed conflict, natural disaster and associated population displacement as well as major social problems encountered in industrialized society (abuse, detention, exclusion and precariousness, etc.). [ID:7220]

Gorgas Memorial Institute of Tropical and Preventive Medicine (Peru)
University of Alabama at Birmingham, BBRB 203, 1530 Third Ave. S., Birmingham, AL, 35294-2170,
USA; 205-934-1630, fax 205-934-5600, info@gorgas.org, http://info.dom.uab.edu/gorgas/index.html

HEALTH TRAINING: Course in Clinical Tropical Medicine ◆ The Gorgas Memorial Institute of
Tropical and Preventive Medicine sponsors the Gorgas Course in Clinical Tropical Medicine, in
collaboration with the University of Alabama at Birmingham (UAB), the John J. Sparkman Center
for International Public Health Education, the US Naval Medical Research Center Detachment,
Lima (NMRCD) and the McGill Centre for Tropical Diseases. Given in Peru and taught in English,
this two-month introduction course to tropical medicine includes a unique format, composed of
lectures, case conferences, diagnostic laboratory and daily bedside teaching at a 35-bed tropical
medicine unit. The course is targeted toward physicians and public health professionals. [ID:7216]

Humber College Institute of Technology and Advanced Learning
INTERNATIONAL PROJECT MANAGEMENT
POSTGRADUATE PROGRAM
Program Coordinator, Lakeshore Campus, 3199 Lake Shore Blvd. W., Humber College
Institute Of Technology and Advanced Learning, Toronto, ON, M8V 1K8, Canada;
416-675-6622 ext. 3032, fax 416-252-0689, enquiry@humber.ca, www.humber.ca

MANAGEMENT TRAINING IN SUPPORT OF HEALTH INTERVENTION: Postgraduate
Certificate in International Project Management ◆ This one-year, post-graduate certificate program
in International Project Management prepares university graduates to work in the field of
international development and emergency relief as project or program officers and managers within
Canadian, US and intergovernmental, non-governmental and private sector organizations. (For more
information, see their ad in the sponsor section at the end of this guide and a more detailed profile
in Chapter 15, International Studies in Canada.) [ID:7159]

International Committee of The Red Cross
19 avenue de la Paix, Geneva, CH 1202, Switzerland;
(41) (22) 734-6001, fax (41) (22) 733-2057, www.icrc.org

MANAGEMENT TRAINING IN SUPPORT OF HEALTH INTERVENTION: Courses in
International Humanitarian Law (IHL) ◆ International humanitarian law (IHL) is composed of the
four Geneva Conventions of 1949 and the two Additional Protocols of 1977. These international
treaties contain the most important rules limiting the barbarity of war. They protect people who do
not take part in the fighting (civilians, medics, aid workers) and those who can no longer fight
(wounded, sick and shipwrecked troops, prisoners of war). The Geneva Conventions apply in times
of international wars and the Additional Protocols in times of civil wars. More than 190
governments have adhered to the conventions, which is almost every country in the world. All states
that have ratified the Conventions and Protocols have the obligation to abide by IHL. The
International Committee of the Red Cross (ICRC), which is a non-governmental Swiss
organization, based in Geneva, is responsible for the application of IHL and will act as neutral
intermediary with parties to a conflict. Various training courses, such as Humanitarian Assistance
Training HELP 1 (Health Emergencies in Large Populations) and HELP 2 (Health, Ethics, Law and
Politics), are offered by the organization. For more information on this course and others, please
visit www.icrc.org/Web/eng/siteeng0.nsf/html/help_course?OpenDocument. (For more information,
see the Canadian Red Cross profile in Chapter 38, NGOs in Canada.) [ID:7221]

Keele University
Centre for Health Planning and Management, Darwin Bldg., Newcastle-under-Lyme, Staffordshire,
ST5 5BG, UK; (44) (0) 1782-583191, fax 44 (0) 1782-711737, www.keele.ac.uk/depts/hm/index.htm

HEALTH TRAINING: MBA Health, Population and Nutrition in Developing Countries ◆ Keele
University's MBA in Health, Population and Nutrition in Developing Countries program, is
intended for senior health professionals, managers and policy-makers working in the health sector

in developing countries or countries in transition. The program combines the study of key principles in health policy and delivery with the Centre for Health Planning and Management's staff. Previous students have come from virtually all continents, but particularly Africa, Asia, Eastern Europe and transitional countries. The program is designed for one year's full-time attendance, leading to the MBA (health, population and nutrition). This comprises five four-week courses interspersed with single weeks for preparatory personal study and completion of essay assignments. [ID:7224]

University of Leeds
Nuffield Institute for Health, 71-75 Clarendon Road, Leeds, LS2 9PL, UK;
(44) (0) 113-343-6942, fax (44) (0) 113-246-0899, www.nuffield.leeds.ac.uk/content/home/home.asp

HEALTH TRAINING: MA or post-graduate diploma in Public Health—Low- and Middle-Income Countries ◆ The University of Leeds' Nuffield Institute for Health, offers a number of post-graduate programs, including MA in health management, planning and policy or a post-graduate diploma in health management, planning and policy, MA in hospital management or a post-graduate diploma in hospital management, as well as an MA in public health (low- and middle-income countries) or a post-graduate diploma in public health (low- and middle-income countries). [ID:7225]

The Lester B. Pearson Canadian International Peacekeeping Training Centre
121 Tribal Street, Cornwallis Park, Clementsport, NS, B0S 1E0, Canada;
902-638-8611 ext. 0, fax 902-638-8888, registrar@peaceoperations.org, www.peaceoperations.org

MANAGEMENT TRAINING IN SUPPORT OF HEALTH INTERVENTION: Courses in Peacekeeping ◆ The mission of the Pearson Peacekeeping Centre is to support and enhance the Canadian contribution to international peace, security and stability. The Centre offers an extensive range of formal courses including survey courses, those delving into various technical aspects of peacekeeping. The expression "peacekeeping" should be thought of as an umbrella term that embraces a host of international interventions. Today's peacekeeping operations frequently encompass response to complex emergencies, humanitarian/medical action, support of human rights, disarming and demobilization initiatives, support of development and democratization programs, as well at the traditional military observation and belligerent separation tasks. For more info please contact registrar@peaceoperations.org. (For more information, see Chapter 10, Short-Term Programs Overseas, and Chapter 38, NGOs in Canada.) [ID:7218]

Liverpool School of Tropical Medicine
Pembroke Place, Liverpool, L3 5QA, UK; (0) (151) 708-9393,
fax (0) (151) 705-3370, imr@liverpool.ac.uk, www.liv.ac.uk/lstm

HEALTH TRAINING: Master of Tropical Medicine and Master of Tropical Paediatrics ◆ The Liverpool School of Tropical Medicine offers a number of master's programs including Master of Community Health, Master of Tropical Medicine and Master of Tropical Paediatrics. Each master's course runs approximately 11 months and comprises orientation, taught modules and a research project leading to the submission of a dissertation. All master's courses begin in September with the exception of the community health course, which currently begins in January. [ID:7226]

McGill University
Faculty of Medicine, Department of Epidemiology and Biostatistics,
Room [27], Purvis Hall, 1020 Pine Ave. W., Montreal, QC, H3A 1A2, Canada;
514-398-6258, fax 514-398-8851, summer.epid@mcgill.ca, www.mcgill.ca/epi-biostat

HEALTH TRAINING: Courses in Epidemiology and Biostatistics ◆ McGill University's, Faculty of Medicine, offers an annual summer session in epidemiology and biostatistics. The summer session, beginning in May and ending in late June, provides health professionals the opportunity to gain familiarity with the principles of epidemiology and biostatistics. Courses are offered over one, two and four weeks, in health in developing countries, infectious and parasitic disease epidemiology, evaluation of health services, economics of health policy, etc. Courses are intended for health professionals (e.g., physicians, nurses, respiratory therapists, psychologists, social scientists, etc.) or professionals in related fields (e.g., industrial hygienists, environmental specialists, urban planners, engineers). For more information, please visit www.mcgill.ca/summer/special/medicine. [ID:7215]

Queen Margaret University College
International Office, Clerwood Terrace, Corstorphine Campus,
Edinburgh, EH12 8TS, UK; (0) (131) 317-3760, fax (0) (131) 317-3256,
international@qmuc.ac.uk, www.qmuc.ac.uk/courses/PGCourse.cfm?c_id=91

HEALTH TRAINING: MSc in International Health ◆ Queen Margaret University College's MSc in International Health program, equips health professionals and related workers for a wide range of roles within the field of international health. It is a one year full-time program, which is intended for middle- to senior-level health professionals working or planning to work in developing or transitional countries. Most students are from health ministries and the NGO sector. Those studying full-time, will normally undertake four modules in semester one and three modules in semester two and complete a dissertation project or research proposal. [ID:7227]

RedR Canada (Registered Engineers for Disaster Relief Training)
Suite 102, 9 Gurdwara Road, Ottawa, ON, K2E 7X6, Canada;
613-232-9999, fax 613-226-5991, info@RedR.ca, www.redr.ca

MANAGEMENT TRAINING IN SUPPORT OF HEALTH INTERVENTION: Training in Humanitarian Aid Work ◆ Through its affiliate, the International Health Exchange, RedR Canada is a non-partisan NGO that recruits and trains people in various aspects of humanitarian aid work, and provides people expertise to those countries needing relief/medical assistance. RedR looks for both men and women with resourcefulness, understanding and compassion, an ability to work on their own with limited resources and the ability to cope in very challenging environments. RedR members must adapt quickly to new cultures and harsh conditions that create the need for relief. They must work independently within a system yet remain flexible within highly demanding work situations. (For more information, see their ad in the sponsor section at the end of this guide and their profile in Chapter 38, NGOs in Canada.) [ID:7219]

Royal Tropical Institute
Course Co-coordinator ICHD, KIT Health, P.O. Box 95001, Amsterdam,
1090 HA, Netherlands; (31) (02) 0568-8256, fax (31) (02) 0568-8677, www.kit.nl

HEALTH TRAINING: International Course in Health and Development (ICHD) ◆ The Royal Tropical Institute's International Course in Health and Development is a 12-month course leading to a master's degree in public health. The course is conducted in English for senior staff, policy-makers and researchers in the field of health care. The course aims to develop the capacity of senior health managers, to use an integrated, multi-disciplinary approach to address the health problems in their country. The program is divided into three trimesters and covers various topics, including introduction to public health, epidemiology, health planning and management, reproductive health (including HIV/AIDS), and nutrition and disease control. The third trimester is devoted to thesis writing and includes a visit to the World Health Organization in Geneva. [ID:7155]

Seneca College of Applied Arts and Technology
INTERNATIONAL HEALTH SERVICE PROGRAM (IHP)
1750 Finch Ave. E., Toronto, ON, M2J 2X5, Canada; 416-491-5050, www.senecac.on.ca/fulltime/IHP.html

HEALTH TRAINING: Ontario College Graduate Certificate in International Health ◆ The International Health Service Program (IHP) offers a multidisciplinary approach to health care and the development of the knowledge and skills required to work in areas of the world disadvantaged by underdeveloped or depleted healthcare resources. This post-graduate program focuses on the individual's role as a health teacher, primary care worker and trainer for village health workers. This program is unique in North America and traditionally has participants from around the world.

This program delivers about 90% of the curriculum content—primarily the theory components—via distance education. Students have the opportunity to benefit from the knowledge and experience of individuals in the field and to develop hands-on skills through a one-month mandatory residency. IHP students enrol in the distance component of courses as their time allows. The courses cover subjects such as emergency preparedness, environmental issues and applied nutrition in developing areas, and issues in women's and children's health care. There is a specific stream of courses for regulated health professionals and another stream of courses for students who have a post-secondary diploma and are interested in the healthcare field. Students complete their residency and course work within three years to receive their certificate. [ID:7217]

Swiss Tropical Institute (STI)
Socinstrasse 57, Postfach, Basel, CH-4002, Switzerland;
(061) (284) 81-11, fax (061) (271) 86-54, courses-sti@unibas.ch, www.sti.ch

HEALTH TRAINING: Various Courses such as Health Care and Management in Tropical Countries ◆ The Swiss Tropical Institute (STI), offers a number of courses for health professionals who want to prepare themselves for work in public health at the national or international level. Facilitators for the courses come from both within STI and from other institutions of higher education and from international organizations. The involvement of teachers from the South is promoted and former course participants are often invited to participate in the teaching. These courses are taught in English. Courses offered by the STI include: Health Care and Management in Tropical Countries (HCMTC), Rational Drug Management in International Health, Health District Management: Planning and Programme Design, Medical Practice with Limited Resources. They also offer a Master in International Health (joint European Program). [ID:7156]

Uppsala University
International Maternal and Child Health (IMCH), Uppsala University Hospital,
Entrance 11, Uppsala, SE-751 85, Sweden; (46) (0) 186-1159-97, fax (46) (0) 185-080-13,
IMCH.education@kbh.uu.se, www.kbh.uu.se/imch/education/master.html; www.kbh.uu.se/imch

HEALTH TRAINING: Master's Programme in International Health ◆ Uppsala University's Master's Programme in International Health includes a minimum of 40 points of work. Master's students carry out a 20-point degree project after taking two compulsory courses and one or more elective course. Compulsory courses include International Health (10 points) and International Health Research Methods I (5 points). Elective courses include International Health Research Methods II (5 points), Health Programme Management in an International Perspective (5 points), Public Health in Humanitarian Assistance (5 points), Women's and Children's Nutrition in Low-income Countries (5 points). Students finish a master's degree during one academic year by completing their courses during the autumn and their degree project during the spring. Applications can only be accepted from physicians, nurses with advanced training and nutritionists. [ID:7157]

York University
CENTRE FOR REFUGEE STUDIES
Centre for Refugee Studies, Room 322, York Lanes, 4700 Keele Street, Toronto, ON,
M3J 1P3, Canada; 416-736-5663, fax 416-736-5837, summer@yorku.ca, www.yorku.ca/crs

MANAGEMENT TRAINING IN SUPPORT OF HEALTH INTERVENTION: Summer Course on Refugee Issues ◆ York University's Centre for Refugee Studies offers a summer course on refugee issues. The course offers post-graduate training in refugee issues for up to 70 practitioners inside and outside government who work on some aspect of refugee protection or assistance. The course includes panel discussions, case studies, a simulation exercise and lectures from international experts. A York University/Centre for Refugee Studies Certificate is awarded upon successful completion of the eight-day program. One of the course sessions offered by the Centre includes the Evolution of Public Health Response in Complex Humanitarian Emergencies. (For more information, see their profile in Chapter 15, International Studies in Canada.) [ID:7158]

CHAPTER 34

Spousal Employment & Freelancing Abroad

This chapter is written for spouses or partners of overseas employees, or for those going abroad with enough financial security and enough spunk to try and make it on their own. "Freelancer," "consultant" and "independent business person" are all words for people who earn money working for themselves rather than for a company or organization.

Working independently abroad has a great upside. If you are interested in part-time work or want to travel as well as work, your time is your own. You can often avoid the need for a work permit or skirt labour laws that restrict job opportunities for foreigners. You can work out of your home and you get a wonderful sense of accomplishment when you find work for yourself.

Self-employment is often the ideal solution for the spouse of someone who has the "real" job abroad. That's partly because self-employment, at least to start, is unlikely to bring in enough money to support one, never mind two or more people. It can also be frustrating and lonely if you're not used to working alone. And it takes a lot of motivation. You have to sell yourself every day, not just until you land a job.

That said, this section will give tips on which skills are best suited to self-employment, what it takes to work for yourself overseas and how to go about finding contracts.

WHAT CAN YOU DO ABROAD?

Certain skills and professions lend themselves to self-employment overseas more easily than others. The following are samples of the wide variety of skills that have brought in paid work for people abroad:

- writing, researching, journalism, editing (most of the examples in this chapter are drawn from these highly portable freelance careers)
- public relations work

- teaching English and other languages
- teaching music, yoga, aerobics, art, flower arranging and other crafts
- translation
- selling or teaching your arts and crafts, such as stained glass, paintings, quilts
- selling personal services such as picture framing, catering, facials
- selling services aimed at expatriates, including investment advice, resume writing or tax planning
- buying artifacts to sell in Canada
- computer services and skills
- counselling and therapy

PERSONAL STORIES

Successful international freelancers have many common traits. The following personal stories demonstrate how they have prevailed over the natural shyness of marketing themselves. They also show how persistent, curious, entrepreneurial, flexible and adaptable a self-employed person must be.

- An experienced journalist who moved to The Hague with her husband found it took longer than she had expected to get started. But, after a year and a half she had a wide variety of work: writing articles for an English-language trade magazine; selling reports to BBC and CBC radio; selling stories to Canadian and British magazines and newspapers; and writing and editing for two international development agencies based in the Netherlands. Some of the work she might have disdained at home. "I don't think I would have considered writing for a trade publication in Canada. But you have to start somewhere and it often leads to something more interesting."

- Among the expat spouses she met in The Hague over a two-year period, more than a dozen of them made work for themselves. One was an ornithologist who taught birdwatching once a week, and in the afternoons did bookkeeping for an English-language editing company owned by a neighbour. Another signed up for a docent course at the local art museum, and later led English-speaking women's clubs to art museums around Holland. Yet another was an accomplished picture framer who took a course in restoring antiques and old furniture. She opened her own antique shop when she moved back to Calgary.

- An American friend with energy to spare shows how someone with the right attitude can do almost anything. On a previous posting in Taiwan, she had taught business English to local business people. Through one of her contacts, she met someone who wanted to buy heavy equipment in Europe. She ended up travelling to Europe and closing the deal on his behalf. This time, with her husband based in The Hague, she again taught business English but also studied Russian on the side. With her Russian tutor, a refugee doctor, she compiled a list of medical doctors and professors in the former Soviet Union, which they then sold to pharmaceutical firms in the US.

BEFORE YOU GET THERE

Before you leave home, update your resume—perhaps bring a few versions highlighting different skills. Also bring letters of recommendation, especially if you've worked for well-known companies or institutions, and take along samples of your work where possible.

If you belong to a professional association, check for the names of companies based in the country you're headed for that use people in your field.

If you think you might need some equipment to get started—for example a computer or a tape recorder—think seriously about buying it in Canada. For one thing, it's always more difficult to find where to buy the right tools in a foreign country. And, as one reporter said to another who was wondering whether to buy a broadcast quality tape recorder before moving to Europe, *"well, if you don't have it, you certainly won't do radio reporting."*

It's helpful to talk to people who have been where you are going and get names of possible contacts. But keep in mind that some people you meet may not have had a positive experience trying to set up work for themselves. They could be more discouraging than helpful. A Canadian journalist who had lived in The Hague told another writer headed for the same city not even to think of working as a writer, and that the Dutch language was so difficult she'd have to write down every phone number she was given because she'd never find them in the phone book. The advice proved to be totally wrong on both counts.

Self-employment may be one of the few kinds of "jobs" where you're better off waiting until you get overseas to really get cracking. Especially if you're going along as a "spouse of," you're best not to commit yourself to anything beforehand. You don't know where you'll be living, how much time it will take to set up your family and household, and the pressures that you will face on arrival.

GETTING STARTED AND GETTING MOTIVATED

Looking for work always demands motivation, and making a job for yourself overseas takes all that you've got.

Many people who move overseas with a working spouse go with the best intentions, and then face depression and inertia almost as soon as they touch ground. This is normal. To be pulled up from your roots, without a job or career to tag next to your name, can be a tremendous blow to your self-esteem. Sometimes you have to wait for the worst to pass before getting started in your job search.

In many countries, just going out to do the shopping takes a huge amount of energy and initiative. You're not alone if you feel this way, so make sure you pat yourself on the back when you accomplish what seem like minor feats: opening a bank account, buying food for dinner, taking the bus downtown.

But everyone is different. One writer who has lived in India and the Sudan as the wife of a development worker says, *"Inertia sets in after a few months in a developing country so it's better to make use of the get-up-and-go that you bring from Canada while you still have it."*

One way to help yourself acclimatize is to study the local language. Don't expect to be able to converse after three months of twice-a-week classes, but you should know enough to perform your daily tasks with more confidence. This will also boost your self-esteem.

It is especially important to act professionally. Set up an office for yourself in your new apartment or house, even if it's just a desk and telephone in the corner of your living room. Making cold calls is hard for everyone, but if you set yourself a certain amount of time each week, or a certain number of calls, you'll feel like you're getting somewhere.

WHERE TO MAKE CONTACTS?

The ability to make and develop contacts differentiates those who find freelance work from those who do not.

When her husband was posted to the Sudan, a freelance writer brought c.v.'s, work samples and letters of reference from editors. *"When I got there I just started knocking on doors."* She heard that the Canadian chargé d'affaires to Cairo would be coming through Khartoum and that he always stayed at the Hilton Hotel. She telephoned him and arranged to meet him for tea. The official confided that the CANADIAN INTERNATIONAL DEVELOPMENT AGENCY (CIDA) was about to update its briefing report on the Sudan. Instead of flying someone in from Ottawa, she got the contract.

For the less brave, taking a volunteer job or becoming active in a social club for new arrivals will give you the confidence you need to look for paid contracts. And, for artisans and other people with items to sell, meeting other expats is the easiest way to get started. You can't fake enthusiasm, motivation or an outgoing personality—but you can make the most of what you have.

Get out and meet people, as many as you can. The writer who quickly nabbed the CIDA contract in the Sudan also made a job for herself in India by talking to the right people. She says it's not enough to talk to one person in an organization who can hand out contracts—talk to as many as you can. *"That way, when they meet each other your name may come up. And, while one might not have wanted to rock the boat, working together they might find something for you."*

"Be systematic," advises another experienced freelancer. Be creative in thinking up possibilities and use your common sense to hunt down information. One contact often leads to another. The Canadian (or foreign) community abroad is tightly knit and contracts or jobs for English-speakers are often awarded to competent friends or acquaintances because it's quicker than advertising.

If you're based in a city large enough to have clubs and associations geared to foreigners, these may offer you the best opportunity to advertise your services by word of mouth or through their newsletters. English-language schools offering evening courses for adults frequently need instructors. Women's groups can be hotbeds for people selling services or courses and a good way to get your name known, even if you don't think of yourself as someone who would normally join such a group. The Canadian consulate or embassy may be a good source of information about English-language associations that might otherwise take you months to track down.

Canadian embassies usually have a list of Canadian companies operating in the country. The commercial attaché may be loath to hand it out if you just state that you're looking for work, but the lists are not secret. Often there will be a chamber of commerce devoted to trade between Canada and the country you're in and it may be more helpful.

Do not neglect to contact the foreign missions and firms from the United States, Britain and other Western countries. Your familiarity with Western culture and your specialized skills will impress employers and individuals seeking consulting services.

BE CLEAR IN YOUR JOB OBJECTIVE

One important point to remember in freelance work is to state clearly to potential employers that you are looking for contract work. Use phrases in your cover letter, or at the top of your resume, such as *seeking freelance assignments, short-term consultancy, contract work, editing and writing services, temporary secretarial help, consultant*, etc. If your level of availability is a factor, mention your restrictions. Example: *available three days per week, mornings, between August and September.*

Your first reaction to this advice may be to say that it is too limiting and could discourage employers from offering you a full-time job. To the contrary, most employers find that it is a lot easier and less threatening to hire consultants and short-term workers. If a full-time job appears, the employer could well take the initiative to offer you an alternative work contract. But all in all, your chances of landing short-term work or selling your services on an assignment basis are much improved when you clearly state this objective.

HOW MUCH CAN YOU EARN AS A SELF-EMPLOYED PROFESSIONAL?

Your income from self-employment will depend on a number of factors: where you are based, how valuable your skills are, how much time you devote to the job and a certain amount of luck.

A Canadian in southern Africa lost his job as a development worker while overseas. However, the cost of living was so reasonable that he was able to earn enough money on a freelance basis to be able to afford to keep his four-bedroom house with a swimming pool and two servants.

When finding contracts or freelance work is difficult, trade is often an exciting option, especially in developing countries. Two Canadian students learning Chinese in Beijing plan to finance their next year's schooling at a Canadian university by buying silk scarves and pyjamas for next to nothing in China to sell in Vancouver on their return. An art dealer from Washington, who moved to Dubai with her oil industry boyfriend, made a lucrative business buying Moghul miniature paintings which she later sold through US galleries.

A Canadian journalist who moved to Amsterdam got enough contracts writing business stories and profiles for trade publications, both Dutch and Canadian, that his income almost equalled his wife's salaried wage within a year. Two Canadian journalists based in Ottawa set up a syndicated feature service specializing in the banking industry. They travel all over the world and earn very good incomes. One of them, who has been a freelancer for 10 years, has written for more than 100 publications in that time, and in some years has travelled outside Canada for more than 250 days. *"The key is to invest time by staying in touch through e-mail or by long distance phone calls because the nature of news is that what everyone knows in one place is news somewhere else. You can sell anything Canadian in Hong Kong more easily than in Canada—and vice versa. If you travel around, you become an expert on Asia in Europe and on Europe in Asia."*

Some people, including many journalists, can earn enough through freelance work to support a family. But for many, if not most people who are self-employed abroad, the work is enough to pay for some travel or supplement an already generous salary earned by the working spouse.

The Canadian journalist based in The Hague says that her work rarely took more than half her time. *"And luckily we weren't dependent on my income."* On the other hand, some of the new experience she gained through writing a book for an international agency broadened her c.v. and gained her another contract with the WORLD BANK upon her return to Canada.

TAXES AND LABOUR LAWS

Many countries have strict rules prohibiting the hiring of foreigners for jobs that locals can do. But often they do allow foreigners to start their own businesses or work for themselves. It is in your interest to check the labour and tax laws before you get serious, preferably by seeing a lawyer who can do it for you anonymously. If you're still a Canadian resident for tax purposes, you'll be paying taxes to the Canadian government; if you're a non-resident of Canada, you may be liable for income taxes in your country of residence. Some countries have wealth taxes (a percentage of your worldwide income) and it is better to check into the tax rules beforehand to ensure that it makes financial sense for you to work. In many countries, like Canada, a very low income won't be taxable, and you may not have to file.

A LAST WORD

One last word to those who are contemplating giving up a rewarding professional job in Canada for the exotic unknown of living abroad to accompany your working spouse. When you first arrive, the experience of being unable to define yourself through your job or profession may be ego-deflating and depressing. But once you have overcome that hurdle through gainful self-employment as a freelancer or (if no work is forthcoming) learning to define yourself differently, then you probably won't feel that fear so strongly again. Chances are you will be stronger and more optimistic. Freelancing can be a very liberating experience.

RESOURCES

FREELANCING ABROAD

There are limited resources available in this area of interest. This short list of books does not do justice to all the professional freelancing opportunities and strategies available abroad, but it's a start.

Adult Education Resources 💻

www.teleeducation.nb.ca ◆ Distance education is sometimes a faceless risk. Enter New Brunswick's excellent on-line learning support Web site. Access information on distance learning such as on-line courses available, admissions and transferral of credits. Check out listings of accrediting agencies and unaccredited institutions to avoid fly-by-night diploma mills. The "Learner Resources" section contains job postings and information on starting a business. [ID:2348]

All Freelance 💻

www.allfreelancework.com ◆ This US Web site is designed to assist freelance consultants in finding work. You can enter your consultant information, distribute your resume, create a career profile, access message boards and search projects matching your expertise. The site's database contains contract projects for which you can apply on-line. The site is well designed and easy to use with an excellent page of links to numerous freelance job sites. [ID:2620]

Career Flex 💻

www.careerflex.com ◆ A general directory of job finding resources on the Net. Specially focused directories on starting a business, working as a consultant, nursing and education. [ID:2426]

The Consulting Skills Manual 📖

Annual ➤ Sequus International, 381 Churchill Drive, Winnipeg, MB R3L 1W1, Canada, www.sequus.org, $100 CDN; Credit Cards; 204-992-2410, fax 204-478-5390, btrump@infobahn.mb.ca ◆ Winnipeg's Sequus International produces this workshop manual. It is widely used even by organizations that have not participated directly in Sequus's workshops. Part One deals with all of the details of the consulting process that are common to all consultants. The second part consists of a custom-tailored toolkit relating to each step in a six-part consulting process that forms the structure for the workshop. A great starting point for clarifying the opaque waters of international consulting. [ID:2535]

Contracted Work 💻

www.contractedwork.com ◆ This US-based Internet freelance market allows you to bid on contracts awarded in all sectors of the private marketplace: find the job that matches your skills, crunch your numbers and then post a bid. The lowest bid at the close of bidding wins the job. Browsing is free, but bidding costs. Bid from abroad and supplement your income while travelling! [ID:2621]

Culture Shock! A Wife's Guide 📖

2002, Robin Pascoe, 212 pages ➤ Graphic Arts Center Publishing Company, 3019 NW Yeon, Portland, OR 97210, USA, www.gacpc.com, $13.95 US; 503-226-2402, fax 503-223-1410 ◆ Written by a Canadian, the book is easy to read, and provides useful advice for the wife going overseas for the first time, especially if her husband is with Foreign Affairs or an international agency. Chapters on maids, entertaining and home leave may be off-putting, but after you've lived in Pascoe's shoes, they may seem pertinent. Has a useful chapter on getting a job or freelancing overseas. [ID:2085]

FreelanceWriting.com 💻

www.freelancewriting.com ◆ This US Web site is geared toward the freelance writer. Hundreds of job postings advertised with information on how to respond and apply. Get your writing career going from a beach in Thailand! No fees to apply. [ID:2622]

Starting and Running a B&B in France 📖

2003, Christine Hall, 192 pages ➤ How To Books Ltd., 3 Newtec Place, Magdalen Road, Oxford, OX4 1RE, UK, www.howtobooks.co.uk, £9.34; Credit Cards; (44) (1752) 202-301, fax (44) (1865) 202-331 ◆ As the title suggests, this British narrative shares the experiences of the author, who set up and ran a B&B in France. Humorous and genuine, this book is a good resource for someone wanting to set up an international small business in the tourism industry. [ID:2509]

The Translator's Handbook 📖

2002, 500 pages ➤ Schreiber Publishing, P.O. Box 4193, Rockville, MD 20849, USA, www.schreiberpublishing.com, $35.95 US; VISA, MC; 800-822-3213, fax 301-424-2336 ◆ This US book is a resource for translators and for anyone who is interested in joining the field. The fourth edition includes nearly 500 pages of essential information covering topics such career options, how to freelance, translator education (in the US) and translation techniques. [ID:2781]

Work Your Way Around The World 📖
2003, Susan Griffith, 576 pages ➤ Globe Pequot Press, P.O. Box 480, 246 Goose Lane, Guilford,
CT 06437, USA, www.globepequot.com, $19.95 US; VISA, MC; 888-249-7586, fax 800-820-2329
◆ Includes details on pre-trip preparation, red tape, visas and tax, getting a job before you go and
how to make speculative and opportunistic applications. Find information on how to travel around
the world for free, very cheaply or even get paid for your voyage. Read descriptions of different
types and areas of work including tourism, agriculture, teaching English, childcare, business and
industry, volunteering and many more. Vivid first-hand accounts from working travellers give a
flavour of what the work is actually like. [ID:2046]

PART FIVE
International Career Directories

CHAPTER 35

Private Sector Firms in Canada

The private sector is easily the largest employer in the international arena. It is also a sector where prospects for continued job growth are excellent. This chapter profiles over 251 Canadian firms with international activities, providing up-to-date contact information and appraisals of size, areas of expertise and preferred backgrounds. If a firm has an important or outstanding job page on their Web site, this is also mentioned.

Along with the Canadian government's endorsement of a wide array of bilateral, regional and multilateral trade agreements, widespread liberalization of international trade and investment continues to grow (with some opposition to these agreements by people who claim a variety of adverse effects). An increasing number of corporations have developed or expanded their international operations through export, partnering or other forms of strategic alliance over the last 10 years. Many Canadian firms have been at the forefront of this increasing global trend.

Several of the firms profiled in this chapter have worked and continue to work with government agencies, such as the CANADIAN INTERNATIONAL DEVELOPMENT AGENCY (CIDA) and INTERNATIONAL TRADE CANADA (ITCAN), as well as international organizations, such as the UNITED NATIONS, the WORLD BANK and the ASIAN DEVELOPMENT BANK.

In contrast to government agencies and international organizations, which are primarily involved in defining problems and funding projects, private firms are typically the implementing agents at the local level. For practical, hands-on individuals interested in the day-to-day operational aspects of international work, the private sector can provide a challenging and varied overseas career.

TYPES OF FIRMS PROFILED

The firms profiled in this chapter range from small consulting operations to large multinational corporations with several thousand staff. Companies are classified according to the size of their international operations: SMALL firms have international budgets of less than $500,000 per year; MID-SIZED firms, between $500,000 and $2 million per year; and LARGE firms, over $2 million per year.

A concerted effort has been made to accurately reflect those industries in which Canadian firms are globally competitive, such as mining, telecommunications, software, engineering and construction, food processing, communications, agriculture, forestry, petrochemicals, financial services, environmental services, and transportation. In addition, a significant number of consulting firms are profiled. Consulting companies are typically recipients of contracts tendered by CIDA and some of the larger UN agencies and international organizations.

QUALIFICATIONS

Private sector employers typically recruit candidates with very high skill levels, and look for a unique combination of technical business acumen and international know-how. You will be assessed on the basis of education, language skills, overseas experience and previous work experience. There are, of course, important exceptions noted in the profiles below.

Most firms require a master's or professional undergraduate degree with functional expertise. A generalist is often perceived to be less useful than someone with a professional designation or specialty in international finance, strategic planning, marketing or a specific sector. Typically, most of the larger firms profiled in this chapter state the specific education, experience and personal attributes they look for in an applicant. Many of the larger firms also offer internships, student opportunities (i.e., co-op placements, summer opportunities) and new graduate opportunities, to allow recent graduates to gain valuable and practical hands-on experience.

Competence in languages other than English and French is an asset. While specifications vary depending on the location of a firm's overseas contracts, Spanish currently seems in highest demand. Alongside foreign language proficiency, area expertise is actively recruited.

Less tangible skills are also evaluated: previous overseas experience, effective cross-cultural communication, adaptability and openness to change, and sensitivity to and respect for overseas cultures. An executive from a large consulting firm put it this way:

"We are interested if, on top of your education and technical expertise, you consider yourself an adaptable individual who is open to learning and new situations, and tolerant of ambiguity..."

HOW TO BEGIN

Overseas vacancies in the private sector are often advertised. Interested applicants can often search through international job postings on the Web sites of larger firms. Many firms now have specific careers pages on their Web sites, where they post employment opportunities, provide a breakdown of the benefits they offer their employees and often offer personal profiles of employees for interested applicants to view. They will also disclose whether they participate in campus career fairs and if they offer student, co-op, internship or new graduate opportunities. If a firm does not post employment opportunities, it will often provide an e-mail address to which interested applicants can send their resumes, or will have an electronic application system where applicants can complete an on-line profile and directly submit their information to the firm. Many firms maintain an active data bank for resumes, so don't be discouraged if prospective employers tell you that your application has been placed on file. Larger firms often provide resume and interview tips, as well, which can be very useful when applying to them and other firms. (For more information on preparing an effective international resume, see Chapter 24, International Resumes.)

Some companies are understandably reluctant to send new recruits overseas immediately. Many companies prefer to fill their international positions from within. Depending on your profession, then, you should be prepared to spend some time with a firm in Canada in order to position yourself for an eventual overseas posting. This is commonly the case in, for example, the banking industry. The up-side is that, once you've made that leap, the overseas opportunities can be extensive. Some firms actively encourage employees to groom themselves for work abroad and even offer foreign internships to nurture their staff's global vision.

Note that many firms with international operations prefer to work with local businesses and allow overseas partners to make all hiring decisions there, rather than in Canada. Sometimes you'll have to contact the local partners of Canadian firms, or even actually be in their country. As a rule, Canadian companies that never hire for foreign positions within Canada are not included in these profiles; an exception is made when the Canadian head office can help you learn about such contracts.

A LAST WORD

Prior to applying or making direct contact with an organization, it is very important to do some preliminary research on the organization you are interested in. Make sure you thoroughly understand a company's organizational objectives and international activities. Not only does this make it easier to determine which firms are compatible with your objectives, but it also shows the firm that you are a serious applicant. Call and ask for copies of annual reports and corporate brochures; keep abreast of relevant issues by reviewing business magazines and newsletters; read company and industry Web sites and newsgroups on the Internet, and make telephone inquiries.

Profiles of Private Firms

The following section profiles 251 Canada-based employers with significant overseas activities. As much as possible, we've tried to let companies speak for themselves. With only a few exceptions (generally professional organizations with Canadian partners), all of the companies listed meet the criteria of majority Canadian ownership.

It should be noted that, whenever possible, each firm's profile has been carefully written to describe its careers page, found on the firm's Web site. This description may include information regarding career opportunities that are posted, directions on how to apply for positions, whether the firm offers internships, student, co-op or new graduate opportunities, and any other useful information for job seekers.

Some general geographical patterns can be seen in the firms profiled in this chapter. Generally, mining and forestry firms tend to be located in Western Canada, as do petrochemical and energy firms. Engineering firms tend to be located all throughout Canada, as well as consulting firms. Telecommunications, high technology and financial services firms tend to be concentrated in central Canada. Law firms are not profiled in this chapter. (For more information on law careers, see Chapter 31, International Law Careers.)

Note that some subsidiaries are listed in addition to their parent company if they have their own separate hiring process. Visit the Web site of any company you intend to contact to find the most current contact information and learn more about the company's current operations and job opportunities.

AchieveGlobal

Suite 1300, 150 York Street, Toronto, ON, M5H 3S5, Canada; 416-214-2022,
fax 416-214-2023, contactus@achieveglobal.ca, www.achieveglobal.ca

LARGE MANAGEMENT CONSULTING FIRM: Consulting, Customer Services, Leadership Assessment, Management Consulting, Management Training, Organization Development

AchieveGlobal is the world leader in helping organizations translate business strategies into business results by developing the skills and performance of their people. The company's learning-based solutions focus on skills training and consulting services in sales performance, customer service, leadership and teamwork. It offers programs and services in more than 40 languages and dialects and its core competencies include sales performance, customer service, leadership and teamwork, consulting, customization and certification. The company has offices in South America, North America, Europe, Australia, Asia, the Middle East and Africa, and has completed projects in these regions.

AchieveGlobal employs approximately 35 people. An Employment page with opportunities may be found on the company's Web site. A resume database and employee biographies are also available to interested applicants. [ID:6812]

ACR Systems Inc.

Bldg. 210, 12960 - 84th Ave., Surrey, BC, V3W 1K7, Canada;
604-591-1128, fax 604-591-2252, enquiry@acrsystems.com, www.acrsystems.com

LARGE HIGH TECHNOLOGY FIRM: Advanced Technology, Engineering, Marketing, Technical Assistance

ACR Systems Inc. is one of the world's leaders in the design and manufacturing of compact self-powered data loggers. The company's precision electronic instruments (and related software) are used in a variety of industries to measure and record a broad range of parameters, including temperature, relative humidity, electric current, pressure, process signals, pulse frequency, power quality and more. It currently has more than 130 distribution points in over 40 countries and maintains an office in the United States. ACR Systems has served customers in Africa, South America, Europe, the Middle East, Asia, Australia and North America. The company employs approximately 30 engineers, technicians, production and marketing professionals. [ID:6766]

Acres International Limited (AIL)

1235 North Service Road W., Oakville, ON, L6M 2W2, Canada;
905-469-3400, fax 905-469-3404, hroakville@acres.com, www.acres.com

LARGE ENGINEERING FIRM: Consulting, Economics, Energy Resources, Engineering, Environment, Project Management, Technical Assistance, Telecommunications, Water Resources

Acres International Limited (AIL) provides consulting engineering services for all phases of the project cycle, from preliminary studies through engineering design, construction supervision and start-up operations. The company is active in power generation and transmission, ports and airports, irrigation and water resources development, industrial, environmental and waste management projects. The firm also has expertise in resource development planning, environmental management and institutional strengthening. AIL has provided services for over 123 countries worldwide. Activities are concentrated in developing countries including Asia, anglophone Africa, the Middle East and Latin America.

AIL has an overall staff of about 750 with 50 working abroad and 200 in Canada with international responsibilities. Applicants with professional engineer status (civil, mechanical, electrical), as well as economists and environmental scientists will be considered. Previous experience on engineering projects in developing countries is an asset. The company's Web site includes a careers page, which lists specific openings with the firm including overseas positions. The firm also maintains a data bank for resumes. [ID:6540]

Acumen Engineered Solutions International Inc. (AESI)

Suite 204, 310 Main Street E., Milton, ON, L9T 1P4, Canada;
905-875-2075, fax 905-875-2062, aesi@aesi-inc.com, www.aesi-inc.com

LARGE ENGINEERING CONSULTING FIRM: Business Development, Consulting, Energy Resources, Engineering, Information Technologies, Management Consulting, Project Management, Systems Engineering, Technical Assistance, Training and Technology Transfer

Acumen Engineered Solutions International Inc. (AESI) is an engineering and management consulting firm, specializing in business and operating processes and systems for electric utilities, industry, and government. AESI employs approximately 10 people. The firm's professional staff and associates offer a full range of services from strategic planning and feasibility analysis through project management, systems architecture, business process re-engineering, systems implementation, start-up and training. It has served both domestic and international clients including utilities, government agencies, resource companies, and manufacturers and suppliers through four distinct areas and services: power systems operations and planning, distribution utility services, power system facilities, and information and communications technologies. AESI maintains an office in the United States and has provided its services to clients in North America, South America, Europe and Asia. [ID:6803]

ADGA Group Consultants Inc.

Suite 600, 116 Albert Street, Ottawa, ON, K1P 5G3, Canada;
613-237-3022, fax 613-237-3024, adga@adga.ca, www.adga.ca 💻 *Fr*

LARGE ENGINEERING CONSULTING FIRM: Administration (General), Computer Systems, Engineering, Information Technologies, Media/Communications, Project Management

ADGA Group Consultants Inc. is a privately owned Canadian company offering systems engineering management consulting and technical services. The company provides services to diverse clients, which include government and private sector industries such as defence, aerospace, health, utilities and transportation. ADGA has offices in the US and Europe, and has completed thousands of projects on behalf of industry and government in the United States, Europe, the Middle East and Africa.

The company employs approximately 550 engineers and specialists. A careers page with current opportunities can be found on ADGA's Web site. ADGA seeks those with administrative, communications, engineering, planning, installation and information technology backgrounds. Interested candidates may submit their resumes to careers@adga.ca. [ID:6773]

ADI Group Inc.

Suite 300, 1133 Regent Street, Fredericton, NB, E3B 3Z2, Canada;
506-452-9000, fax 506-451-7451, adigroup@adi.ca, www.adi.ca

LARGE ENGINEERING FIRM: Construction, Consulting, Engineering, Environment, Project Management, Technical Assistance, Water Resources

The ADI Group Inc. is an employee-owned multidisciplinary group of companies organized into separate operations for each technology or service. The companies provide engineering, consulting, project management, architecture and construction services worldwide. Overseas operations are focused on the environmental sector, with projects ranging from environmental management to the engineering of water supply and treatment systems, to complete wastewater treatment systems on a turnkey basis.

ADI employs over 200 highly skilled professionals and has operations in over 30 countries worldwide. Offices are located throughout Eastern Canada, and there are US offices in New Hampshire and Maine. ADI holds numerous international patents and continues to expand the number of international projects. Prospective applicants should have a degree in environmental science or engineering coupled with experience in consulting or construction. Fluency in another language, Spanish in particular, is an asset. ADI participates in research and development, co-op placement, mentoring, EIT and funds three university scholarships in engineering. Contract positions are also considered. Interested applicants can contact the company through e-mail, fax, mail or phone. Unsolicited resumes are logged for future reference.

While the ADI Web site offers no specific advice to job seekers, it does list job opportunities within the firm's various offices across Canada. The site also offers an on-line newsletter profiling ADI's current projects and activities, which may be useful to interested applicants. [ID:6536]

Aecon Group Inc.

3660 Midland Ave., Toronto, ON, M1V 4V3, Canada;
416-754-8735, fax 416-754-1988, aecon@aecon.com, www.aecon.com ⬛ *Fr*

LARGE CONSTRUCTION FIRM: Construction

Aecon Group Inc. is Canada's largest publicly traded construction and infrastructure development company. The company provides design, building, operating, financing, procurement and development services to both the public and private sectors. Aecon builds condominiums, casinos, hotels, offices, power plants, factories, bridges and dams, and also lays power lines across ice and desert, mountains and cities. Some projects have included the St. Lawrence Seaway, the Trans-Canada Highway, the Ontario Legislature at Queen's Park, the SkyDome and the CN Tower. Aecon conducts international activities in places such as China, India, Israel, Korea and Poland. Aecon lists current job opportunities on the careers page found on their Web site. [ID:6526]

Aerosystems International Inc.

3538, rue Ashby, Saint-Laurent, QC, H4R 2C1, Canada; 514-336-9426,
fax 514-336-4383, info@aerosystems-international.com, www.aerosystems-international.com

LARGE HIGH TECHNOLOGY FIRM: Aerospace Technology, Air Transportation, Manufacturing, Research and Development, Software Development, Telecommunications

Aerosystems International Inc. designs and manufactures electronically based ground-support equipment and related systems, as well as automated remote monitoring systems for the radio spectrum, serving both the aerospace and telecommunications industries. The company has provided solutions to clients in Australia, Africa, Europe, South America, North America and Asia.

Aerosystems International employs 15 people. A careers page can be found on the company's Web site. The company asks that interested candidates e-mail their resumes to hr@aerosystems-international.com. Currently, Aerosystems is looking for software programmers, electronic technicians and electronic service personnel. [ID:6767]

AGF Management Ltd.

31st Floor, Toronto Dominion Bank Tower, 66 Wellington Street W.,
Toronto, ON, M5K 1E9, Canada; 416-367-1900, Tiger@agf.com, www.agf.com 💻*Fr*

LARGE INVESTMENT MANAGEMENT FIRM: Business/Banking/Trade, Investment Banking, Personal Taxation/Financial Planning, Trade and Investment

AGF Management Ltd. is one of Canada's premier investment management companies with offices across Canada and subsidiaries around the world. The company serves more than one million investors with offerings across the wealth continuum and assets totalling approximately $31 billion. AGF's products and services include a diversified family of over 50 mutual funds, the AGF Harmony tailored investment program, AGF Private Investment Management and AGD Trust GICs, loans and mortgages. The company has international operations in London, England, Dublin, Ireland, Singapore, Tokyo, Japan and Beijing.

A careers page with employment opportunities may be found on the company's Web site. Interested applicants may apply on-line by completing AGF's on-line application form. [ID:6813]

Agnew Consulting Group Limited (ACGL) Management Consultants

4 Eaglewing Court, West Hill, ON, M1E 4M1, Canada;
416-286-7265, fax 416-286-6511, info@acgl.com, www.acgl.com

MID-SIZED MANAGEMENT CONSULTING FIRM: Consulting, Human Resources, Management, Management Consulting, Management Information Systems, Management Training

Agnew Consulting Group Limited (ACGL) Management Consultants have over 20 years of experience providing strategic planning, process re-engineering, systems improvement and business advice to senior management across Canada and internationally. It is a Canadian-owned company of independent management consultants who have advised the leaders of many of Canada's largest organizations in both the public and private sectors. Clients are typically medium to large enterprises. The management levels served by the company include boards, executive management, functional (line of business) management and information systems management. Other services include directional planning, strategic planning, operational reviews, business re-engineering, systems selection, change management and human resources issues. ACGL's staff and associates have completed assignments all across Canada and have international consulting experience in the United States, the Caribbean, South America, Europe and Southeast Asia. The company also has offices in Toronto, Ottawa, Montreal, Halifax, Windsor, Edmonton and in the United Kingdom. [ID:6796]

Agriteam Canada Consulting Ltd.

Suite 200, 14707 Bannister Road S.E., Calgary, AB, T2X 1Z2, Canada;
403-253-5298, fax 403-253-5140, calgary@agriteam.ca, www.agriteam.ca

LARGE GENERAL CONSULTING FIRM: Adult Training, Agriculture, Business Development, Community Development, Consulting, Development Assistance, Development Education, Economics, Environment, Gender and Development, Human Resources, Human Rights, Law and Good Governance, Medical Health, Micro-enterprises, Project Management, Technical Assistance, Water Resources

Agriteam Canada Consulting Ltd. Is a Canadian consulting company specializing in international development. The company provides a full range of services to governments, businesses and financial institutions throughout the developing world. Agriteam is involved in all phases of the project cycle including project preparation, appraisal, implementation, monitoring and evaluation. Agriteam works in a wide range of sectors including education, health and population, agriculture and rural development, governance and environmental protection. Agriteam has implemented over 150 development projects in more than 30 countries throughout Asia, Africa, South and Central America, the Caribbean, Eastern Europe, and the former Soviet Union. The company is currently the executing agency for a portfolio of projects worth approximately $120 million. Clients of the company include the Canadian International Development Agency, the Asian Development Bank, the World Bank, the Inter-American Development Bank and the agencies of the United Nations as well as governments, private sector companies and non-governmental organizations.

Agriteam has an overseas staff of 15 and a Canadian-based corporate staff of 40. Its head office is in Calgary, with a satellite office in Gatineau and field offices in China, Ghana, Malawi, Pakistan, Peru, the Philippines, South Africa and Tanzania. It recruits candidates with graduate degrees related to agriculture, development, education, governance, human resources development, health and water resources. Previous overseas experience is required. Canadian citizenship is an asset, as is multiple language capability. Their Web site offers no information regarding employment. However, Agriteam does maintain a data bank for resumes. [ID:6611]

Agrium Inc.

13131 Lake Fraser Drive S.E., Calgary, AB, T2J 7E8, Canada;
403-225-7000, fax 403-225-7609, webmaster@agrium.com, www.agrium.com

LARGE AGRICULTURAL FIRM: Accounting, Agriculture, Computer Systems, Engineering, Environment, Project Management

Agrium Inc. is a leading global producer and marketer of agricultural nutrients and industrial products, and a major retail supplier of agricultural products and services in North America and Argentina. The company produces and markets three primary groups of nutrients: nitrogen, phosphate and potash as well as micronutrients; it is the largest producer of nitrogen in North America. Agrium has $2.5 billion US in revenues and employs over 5,000 employees throughout Canada, the United States, South America and Australia. It has production facilities in Canada, the United States and Argentina, as well as 14 wholesale operations in North America and South America. Agrium's products are sold to Australia, Chile, China, South Korea, Mexico, the Philippines, Thailand and Vietnam. Its wholesale operations in Argentina are conducted through its 50 per cent share in the Profertil S.A. joint venture with Repsol YPF, a large international oil and gas company based in Spain. Agrium operates 18 farm centres in Argentina, supplemented by two satellite outlets. The goal in establishing retail farm centres in Argentina was to introduce bulk blending and application equipment to the agricultural industry. These efforts have had a significant impact on the modernization of agriculture in Argentina.

Agrium has approximately 20 employees with extensive international responsibilities employed in their head office in Calgary, Canada. Key senior positions in foreign locations are filled by expatriates from either the Canadian or American operations. For other positions, typically Agrium hires employees locally for opportunities in Argentina. Agrium currently has five staff working on international assignments, but has had upwards of 30 expatriates in past years. Prospective applicants should have a related degree, combined with relevant industry experience. Preference is given to candidates with international experience and fluency in Spanish.

A careers page with employment opportunities may be found on the company's Web site. Agrium participates in campus recruiting and offers several programs to help new graduates gain experience. The company also offers a co-op program for hands-on experience. The company also offers an engineer-in-training program (EIT) to combine the technical training achieved at university with on-the-job training. Co-op students are recruited throughout the year, whereas EIT recruiting is done in the fall with the number of positions varying. Agrium suggests that interested candidates visit their school's co-op education centre or career services to find out when the company will be visiting and to review opportunities. Applicants may apply on-line. [ID:6827]

Agrodev Canada Inc.

Suite 100, 150 Isabella Street, Ottawa, ON, K1S 1V7,
Canada; 613-234-3300, fax 613-234-6601, www.agrodev.ca

MID-SIZED AGRICULTURAL CONSULTING FIRM: Agriculture, Business Development, Community Development, Consulting, Development Assistance, Economics, Environment, Fisheries, Forestry, Gender and Development, Project Management, Rural Development, Technical Assistance, Water Resources

Agrodev Canada is an international development consulting firm that has completed more than 300 projects in over 75 countries worldwide. The firm focuses on sustainable development and management of natural and human resources, and provides professional services in social development, institutional development and training, natural resources management, environmental management and fisheries, and aquaculture development. Clients include the World Bank, the Asian Development Bank, the Inter-American Bank, the Canadian International Development Agency, governments and private companies. The firm has undertaken projects in Brunei, Cambodia, Vietnam, Palestine, Pakistan, Bangladesh, Jordan, Nepal and Ghana. Agrodev has offices in Ottawa, Edmonton, Vancouver, Islamabad and Amman.

The firm has a staff of 25 with international responsibilities who work abroad or in Canada. Agrodev Canada is looking for candidates with the following qualifications: master's degree or doctorate in a related field, a minimum of five to 10 years of professional experience in a related field and overseas experience on international development projects, preferably working with international development agencies or banks. The firm maintains a data bank for resumes and suggests that those interested in applying submit their resumes to the office manager. [ID:6612]

Aiolos Engineering Corp.
100 - 2150 Islington Ave., Etobicoke, ON, M9P 3V4, Canada;
416-674-3017, fax 416-674-7055, marketing@aiolos.com, www.aiolos.com

LARGE ENGINEERING FIRM: Construction, Engineering, Project Management

Aiolos Engineering is a world leader in the design and construction of wind tunnels and related test facilities. The firm provides a complete array of services for the realization of aerospace and automotive test facilities including turnkey construction, project engineering and management, maintenance and feasibility studies for project-planning purposes. Typical facilities include aerodynamic and aeroacoustic wind tunnels, climatic wind tunnels and acoustic chambers. The firm's client list includes a wide range of automotive, aerospace, railroad, wind engineering and other companies such as Boeing, NASA, Porsche, Ford, Daimler Chrysler and the University of Western Ontario. Aiolos has offices in Canada, Luxembourg, South Korea and the United Kingdom. The firm has also completed projects in Korea, Italy, Malaysia, the United States, Canada, Germany, Austria and Spain.

Aiolos employs approximately 60 people. A careers page can be found on the firm's Web site. Typically, the firm hires additional staff in the areas of engineering and project management when needed. Aiolos asks that those with expertise in the areas of automotive or aerospace testing, test facility planning, acoustics, aerodynamics, vehicle emissions, industrial refrigeration systems or ProEngineer to submit their names and contact information to the database. [ID:6759]

Alcan Inc.
P.O. Box 6090, Montreal, QC, H3C 3A7, Canada; 514-848-8000, fax 514-848-8115, www.alcan.com ▱*Fr*

LARGE METALS FIRM: Aerospace Technology, Business Development, Computer Systems, Energy Resources, Engineering, Environment, Exchange Programs, Human Rights, Media/Communications, Medical Health, Project Management, Telecommunications

Alcan provides aluminum and packaging solutions worldwide. The company currently leads the competition in raw materials, primary metals and fabricated products, which include products and systems for the automotive and mass transportation markets, aerospace, aluminum sheet for beverage cans, as well as flexible and specialty packaging for aerospace and the food, pharmaceutical and personal care industries. Alcan operates in countries spanning four continents, making it one of the most internationally recognized metals firms in the world. Through subsidiaries and related companies around the world, Alcan's activities include bauxite mining, alumina refining, smelting, manufacturing, power generation, sales, recycling and recently aerospace technology. Alcan is also in the process of developing engineered products in the areas of casting, extrusions, forging and composites.

The company employs approximately 88,000 people in 63 countries. A careers page can be found on Alcan's Web site and promises an on-line resume submission form in the future. [ID:6613]

The Alder Group

Suite 200, 1306 Wellington Street, Ottawa, ON, K1Y 3B2, Canada;
613-241-8755, fax 613-241-8847, admin@aldergroup.com, www.aldergroup.com 🖳𝓕𝓻

MID-SIZED GENERAL CONSULTING FIRM: Advocacy, Consulting, Media/Communications, Medical Health, Project Management, Social Policy, Training and Education

The Alder Group is a bilingual Canadian consulting firm devoted to health promotion and social policy development. The company uses a comprehensive approach and offers a full range of services in the areas of communications, group facilitation, policy and program development, event management, consensus building, writing and editing, strategic planning, translation, Web development and training. The Alder Group has expertise in a number of program areas including healthy child development and aging, tobacco cessation, the Healthy Cities/Communities movement, public health and health communications, among others. The company involves itself in projects that support health, innovation and progressive social change. The Alder Group has project experience in Africa, Australia, the Middle East, Russia, South America, Mexico, the United States and Europe and has worked extensively with the World Health Organization. The Alder Group employs approximately 15 people. The Alder Group is not currently offering employment opportunities, but is available for consultation. [ID:6811]

ALS Canada Ltd.

212 Brooksbank Ave., North Vancouver, BC, V7J 2C1,
Canada; 604-984-0221, fax 604-984-0218, www.als.com.au

MID-SIZED BIOTECHNOLOGY FIRM: Administration (General), Advanced Technology, Chemicals, Environment, Laboratory Services, Mineral Handling, Mineral Resources, Mining

ALS Canada is the corporate head office for the ALS group of laboratories for North and South America, as well as a major minerals analytical laboratory and a major environmental analytical laboratory. ALS is a diversified international laboratory group which first established its operations in Queensland, Australia in 1975. The group has grown to 23 labs in countries throughout Australia, North America, South America and Asia. The company is now one of the largest analytical laboratories in the world. ALS provides a broad range of sophisticated state-of-the-art services to four main market segments: mining and mineral exploration, environmental monitoring, equipment maintenance through used lubricant analysis, and commodity analysis and certification. The group operates labs that specialize in analyzing geological materials such as soil and sediment samples, rock and drill cuttings and core samples. Worldwide clients include major mining and mineral exploration companies. ALS Chemex operates in 15 countries in various divisions with offices in Australia, Singapore, Hong Kong, Malaysia, Chile, Peru, Argentina, the United States and Mexico.

ALS Chemex has a staff of approximately 850 people. A careers link can be found on the company's Web site with current job postings. ALS asks that interested candidates tell them how they believe they can help the company fulfill its mission of being the premier supplier of analytical chemistry services to the mining and exploration industry. [ID:6532]

Alta Exports International Ltd. (AEI)

Suite 135, Edgeridge Terrace N.W., Calgary, AB, T3A 6C3, Canada;
403-547-4389, fax 403-547-5893, info@altaexports.com, www.altaexports.com

LARGE AGRICULTURAL FIRM: Agriculture, Development Assistance, Livestock Genetics, Marketing, Project Management, Training and Technology Transfer

Alta Exports International Ltd. (AEI) was established on January 1, 2000 by members of the Alta Genetics International Marketing team. The company markets livestock, embryos, genetic technologies and semen in specific export markets and is also involved in exporting forage seeds and farm equipment. AEI operates as Alta Genetics' exclusive representative in China and sources genetic products and livestock for a number of smaller markets. It is active in a number of technology transfer projects, providing expertise in embryo production and management, semen production, livestock management and production (beef and dairy), and has carried out a number of small ruminant (sheep and goats) management and embryo projects. The principals of AEI have been involved in contracts and commissioning of genetic products to over 50 countries worldwide. AEI's network of purebred livestock suppliers extends across Canada, the United States and to many countries which produce high quality breeding stock in cattle, goats, sheep, swine and specialty livestock. The company also performs project management and development services. AEI has an international office in China and has completed projects in China, Mexico, Russia, South America, Australia and Africa. [ID:6690]

AMEC Earth & Environmental

221-18th Street S.E., Calgary, AB, T2E 6J5, Canada;
403-248-4331, fax 403-248-2188, www.amec.com/earthandenvironmental

---

LARGE ENVIRONMENTAL FIRM: Consulting, Engineering, Environment, Water Resources

AMEC Earth & Environmental (a division of AMEC plc), is a full-service earth and environmental consulting firm providing multidisciplinary solutions covering all aspects of environmental services, geotechnical engineering, materials testing and water resource services. With more than 2,200 scientists, geologists, engineers, biologists, environmental planners and other specialists, AMEC offers an impressive depth and breadth of capabilities. The company has more than 90 offices internationally, including offices in Canada, the United States, the United Kingdom, Germany, Russia and China. Projects have been completed in more than 40 countries, ranging from urban environmental improvement and waste management to water optimization and flood control.

AMEC's Web site provides a comprehensive Careers page offering detailed information on current employment opportunities, internships, scholarships, training programs and graduate recruitment. Interested applicants can view current global opportunities on the Web site, searching by keyword, region or job category. [ID:6527]

AMEC plc

Americas Division, Suite 300, 36 Toronto Street, Toronto, ON, M5C 2C5, Canada;
416-644-3621, fax 416-644-3629, AMECToronto@amec.com, www.amec.com

---

LARGE ENGINEERING FIRM: Engineering

AMEC plc is an international engineering services company that provides design, project delivery and support for oil and gas, transport and infrastructure to industrial clients worldwide. The company has three major "home markets" including the United Kingdom, continental Europe and the Americas, with offices located throughout Canada, the United States, the United Kingdom, Germany, Switzerland, Russia, China, Hong Kong, Malaysia, Singapore and Australia. AMEC serves local clients as well as government departments and sector leaders. Clients include Shell, BP, ExxonMobil, Transco, the United Kingdom and French railways, General Electric, Dupont and GlaxoSmithKline.

The company employs 45,000 people across 40 countries worldwide. Interested applicants can view current global opportunities on AMEC's Web site, searching by keyword, region or job category. The majority of graduates recruited have an engineering background, but the company does recruit a small number of graduates from a variety of other disciplines for opportunities based in the United Kingdom. Internship and sponsorship opportunities are also posted on AMEC's Web site. For those beginning their careers, AMEC also offers structured training and development programs under the professional guidance of senior members. AMEC's Web site provides a comprehensive careers page with detailed information on current employment opportunities, internships, scholarships, training programs and graduate recruitment. [ID:6525]

Anadarko Canada Corporation

425 - 1st Street S.W., Calgary, AB, T2P 4V4, Canada; 403-231-0111,
fax 403-231-0187, HRCanada@anadarko.com, www.anadarko.com

LARGE ENERGY RESOURCES FIRM: Accounting, Engineering, Exploration and Development, Information
Technologies, Oil and Gas Exploration

Anadarko Canada Corporation, based in Calgary, is one of the world's largest independent oil
and gas exploration and production companies. It is a wholly owned subsidiary of Anadarko
Petroleum Corporation, based in Houston, Texas. Anadarko's operations extend to Canada, the
United States, Algeria, Venezuela and Qatar—the company is executing strategic exploration
programs in several other countries.

The company employs approximately 3,400 people worldwide, from engineers and
geoscientists to accountants and field personnel. Anadarko offers university and college graduates
the opportunity to build experience in the areas of accounting, engineering, exploration and
information technology services. Qualifications for these positions include top quartile average
academic performance, exceptional interpersonal and communication skills, leadership abilities and
a desire to experience practical application of theoretical studies. The company suggests that
interested candidates send their resume in MS Word format by e-mail to the human resources link
found on their Web site. [ID:6522]

APA Petroleum Engineering Inc.

Suite 1400, 800 - 5th Ave. S.W., Calgary, AB, T2P 3T6, Canada;
403-265-7226, fax 403-269-3175, pet-eng@apa-inc.com, www.apa-inc.com

LARGE PETROLEUM CONSULTING FIRM: Consulting, Energy Resources, Engineering, Project
Management

APA Petroleum Engineering Inc. is a petroleum engineering consulting firm specializing in
reservoir and production engineering studies. The firm has international experience in Europe,
Africa, South America, Australia, Asia, the Caribbean and North America. It has offices in
Calgary, Houston, Dallas, Halifax, St. John's, and provides practical solutions to complex problems
in more than 35 countries.

APA Petroleum Engineering employs approximately 35 people. An employment page may be
found on the firm's Web site. The firm is always interested in hearing from interested and qualified
people. Interested candidates may submit their resumes to pet-eng@apa-inc.com. [ID:6691]

Apotex Inc.

150 Signet Drive, Weston, ON, M9L 1T9, Canada; 416-749-9300, fax 416-401-3835, www.apotex.com

LARGE PHARMACEUTICAL FIRM: Medical Health

Apotex Inc. is the largest Canadian-owned diversified pharmaceutical company, having
exports to 115 countries around the world and international offices in a variety of regions including
Africa, the Middle East, Eastern Europe, Asia and the South Pacific. The company produces more
than 230 generic pharmaceuticals and it researches, develops, manufactures and distributes fine
chemicals, non-prescription and private label medicines, and disposable plastics for medical use.

Apotex currently has over 5,300 employees and over the past three years has hired over 1,000
new people in production, engineering, operations, quality assurance and research. Of their total
employee base, there are over 2,000 scientific staff, including more than 90 PhDs. The company
hires students directly from many science-related programs such as chemistry, laboratory
technology, pharmaceutical technology, as well as programs such as engineering and business
administration. Co-op and internship programs are a major component of Apotex's recruitment
strategy. Hiring sources for the company include internal job postings, newspapers, journals,
personnel agencies, college and university placement centres and career fairs. Employees are
offered the opportunity to upgrade their skills and knowledge on the job and/or after hours. Many of
their training programs are offered at their $3 million training centre in Toronto using instructor-led
and computer-based methods. Current Canadian job opportunities are posted on their Web site.
[ID:6590]

Applied International Marketing (AIM)

4657 Cove Cliff Road, North Vancouver, BC, V7G 1H7, Canada;
604-929-0940, fax 604-924-0767, info@aimtrade.com, www.aimtrade.com 💻 *Sp*

MID-SIZED GENERAL CONSULTING FIRM: Business Development, Business/Banking/Trade, Consulting,
Marketing, Tourism

Applied International Marketing (AIM) provides consulting services for companies
developing new markets in the western hemisphere. The company's areas of expertise include
international sales and marketing, export market development, cluster marketing, marketing to
Hispanics, strategic market planning, trade promotion, education and training, and tourism
development. Services provided by AIM include export diagnostics, global marketing strategy,
market-entry strategies, in-country sales support and implementation of international distribution
networks and strategic partnerships. Industry expertise includes prepared foods, agricultural
products, leather products, software, cut flowers, real estate, education and training, economic
development and export promotion. Their clients include government agencies, consulting
companies and small- to medium-sized enterprises developing international markets.

AIM's network of experienced associate consultants have mostly post-graduate degrees in
business, are multilingual, have local expertise and contact networks in the US, Canada, Mexico,
Central America, South America and the Caribbean. AIM hires senior and junior consultants on a
project-by-project basis. The company is not currently offering internships or employment opportunities. [ID:6814]

Artifex Media Group

Suite 402, 426 Sainte Helene Street, Montreal, QC, H2Y 2K7, Canada;
514-284-3023, fax 514-284-3043, imagine@artifexgroup.com, www.artifexgroup.com 💻 *Fr*

MID-SIZED COMMUNICATIONS FIRM: Business Development, Consulting, Information Technologies,
Marketing, Media/Communications

Artifex Media Group is a well-established media company specializing in multimedia and
branding services. Services provided by the company include advertising development and
applications, corporate identity development and applications, package design, Web applications,
and image and media consultation. The company has worked with clients across North and South
America (i.e., Colombia, Ecuador, Haiti, Peru and Venezuela), creating inventive and effective
advertising and promotional material for a variety of marketing purposes.

Artifex employs six people. A careers page with employment opportunities may be found on
their Web site. They continually seek new people to join the company. Interested applicants can
send their resumes to careers@artifexgroup.com. Artifex is currently interested in expanding its
business development department and is looking for those with this experience. [ID:6804]

Associated Mining Consultants Ltd. (AMCL)

Suite 415, 708 - 11th Ave. S.W., Calgary, AB, T2R 0E4, Canada;
403-264-9496, fax 403-263-7641, info@amcl.ca, www.amcl.ca, www.ae.ca

---

LARGE MINING CONSULTING FIRM: Consulting, Engineering

Associated Mining Consultants Ltd. (AMCL) provides comprehensive consulting and
engineering support to the minerals, energy, environmental and engineering sectors. AMCL is a
member of the IMC Group of Companies (www.imcgroup.co.uk), a major international consulting
technical services organization and is jointly owned by the Associated Engineering Group, a broad-
based, employee-owned engineering group with offices across Canada. AMCL's experience and
expertise covers precious metals, base metals, industrial minerals, precious stones, coal and oil
sands. The company offers support throughout the project life cycle, from resource evaluation for
investment decisions through project development and operation to site rehabilitation. In addition to
projects throughout Canada and the United States, AMCL has conducted large-scale geophysical
surveys in international locations including Nigeria, Guyana, Peru, Brazil, Venezuela, Cuba,
Guatemala, Indonesia, the Philippines, Papua New Guinea, New Caledonia and Australia. [ID:6712]

Aur Resources Inc.

Suite 2501, 1 Adelaide Street E., Toronto, ON, M5C 2V9, Canada;
416-362-2614, fax 416-367-0427, info@aurresources.com, www.aurresources.com

LARGE MINING FIRM: Exploration and Development, Metals, Mineral Handling, Mineral Resources, Mining

Aur Resources Inc. is a Canadian-based, international mining company active in the acquisition, exploration, development and mining of mineral properties. The company has three mining operations and derives approximately 95 per cent of its revenue from the production and sale of copper. It has activities in Canada, Central America, South America, and plans to expand its activities beyond the Americas in 2004 and focus on copper as well as gold deposits. The company has offices in Canada and Chile.

An employment page can be found on the company's Web site, which suggests that those interested in submitting an application for a position in North and Central America e-mail a resume to careers@aurresources.com. Those interested in submitting applications to one of Aur Resources' locations in Chile should e-mail their resume to careers@aurresources.cl. [ID:6826]

Aventis Pasteur Ltd.

Human Resources Dept., 1755 Steeles Ave. W., Toronto, ON, M2R 3T4, Canada;
416-667-2701, fax 416-667-2252, recruiting.canada@aventis.com, www.aventispasteur.ca 🖥️ *Fr*

LARGE BIOTECHNOLOGY FIRM: Advanced Technology, Manufacturing, Marketing, Medical Health, Research and Development

Aventis Pasteur Ltd. (owned by Aventis S.A), is Canada's largest vaccine company which develops and produces vaccines on an industrial scale. The company researches, develops, manufactures, markets and ships from one location in Toronto. The Canadian office manufactures and distributes more than 30 vaccines and immunotherapeutic products for protection against 17 diseases and common illnesses. The company's presence can be felt in over 150 countries worldwide including Canada, the United States and Mexico, as well as in 19 countries throughout Western Europe, Latin America, Eastern Europe, the Middle East, China and Japan.

Aventis Pasteur employs over 8,500 employees worldwide and 1,000 of those employees are found in Canada. Interested applicants can conduct specific job category searches, view all job postings and may apply on the company's Web site. (For more information, see their ad in the sponsor section at the end of this guide.) [ID:6647]

Aventis Pharma Inc.

2150 St-Elzear Blvd. W., Laval, QC, H7L 4A8, Canada;
514-331-9220, cainternet@aventis.com, www.aventis-pharma.ca 🖥️ *Fr*

LARGE BIOTECHNOLOGY FIRM: Advanced Technology, Manufacturing, Marketing, Medical Health, Pharmaceuticals, Research and Development

Aventis Pharma Inc. is the Canadian pharmaceutical arm of Aventis S.A. (who was formed with the merger in December 1999 of Hoechst AG and Rhone-Poulenc S.A.). The company's presence can be felt in over 150 countries worldwide including Canada, the United States and Mexico, as well as in 19 countries throughout Western Europe, Latin America, Eastern Europe, the Middle East, China and Japan.

Of the 8,500 people employed by Aventis Pasteur worldwide, 900 of those employees belong to Aventis Pharma. In December 2002, Aventis was named as Canada's 11th best employer in a survey conducted by "The Globe and Mail." Aventis Pharma maintains a resume database and regularly posts employment opportunities on the careers page of their Web site. [ID:6523]

Ballard Power Systems Inc.

4343 North Fraser Way, Burnaby, BC, V5J 5J9, Canada; 604-454-0900, fax 604-412-4700, www.ballard.com

SMALL ENGINEERING FIRM: Accounting, Administration (General), Business Development, Computer Systems, Engineering, Environment, Project Management, Research and Development, Science and Technology, Technical Assistance

Ballard Power Systems Inc. is recognized as the world leader in developing, manufacturing and marketing zero-emission proton exchange membrane (PEM) fuel cells for transportation and power generation applications. Ballard is also commercializing electric drives for fuel cell and other electric vehicles, power conversion products, and is a Tier 1 automotive supplier of friction materials for power train components. Counting six of the top ten automotive companies as customers, Ballard is also partnered with two of them (Ford and DaimlerChrysler) to develop the next generation of efficient and clean fuel cell engines for the world's vehicles such as transit buses and automobiles. In the rapidly changing world of power generation, Ballard is also working with companies like EBARA Corporation and MGE UPS Systems Inc. to lead the way in providing reliable, high-quality, revolutionary power generation solutions to customers. Ballard has sites in Canada, Germany and the United States, as well as an affiliate company in Japan.

Ballard's Web site has a good careers section that lists the major responsibilities and requirements for open positions and provides instructions on how to apply (international experience is not typically required). Ballard also maintains an on-line resume database and offers employment opportunities in all functional business areas. [ID:6698]

Barrick Gold Corp.

Suite 3700, P.O. Box 212, BCE Place, Canada Trust Tower, Toronto, ON, M5J 2S1, Canada; 416-861-9911, fax 416-307-3502, hr@barrick.com, www.barrick.com

LARGE MINING FIRM: Exploration and Development, Metals, Mining

Barrick Gold Corp. is a large international gold company with operating mines and development projects in Chile, Peru, Australia, Argentina and Tanzania, as well as in the US and Canada. The company has four major development projects currently underway and is actively exploring over 95 projects in nine countries.

In addition to its mining and exploration staff, the company employs full-time staff in each country of operation and at each operating site to oversee and implement its environmental and occupational health and safety policies and programs.

Barrick's Web site does have a careers page, but it does not list specific job opportunities. The company suggests e-mailing, faxing or mailing in a cover letter and resume. Interested applicants can read about the company's current and ongoing projects on the Web site. [ID:6614]

BDO Dunwoody LLP

P.O. Box 32, 33rd Floor, Royal Bank Plaza, 200 Bay Street, Toronto, ON, M5J 2J8, Canada; 416-865-0111, fax 416-367-3912, info@bdo.ca, www.bdo.ca ▯ℱr

LARGE FINANCIAL SERVICES FIRM: Accounting, Computer Systems, Consulting, Human Resources, Project Management

BDO Dunwoody LLP, Chartered Accountants and Advisors, is a Canadian partnership specializing in accounting, assurance, taxation, financing, personal financial planning and business advice. The firm has approximately 95 offices throughout Canada with partner offices in 99 countries through BDO International. BDO International is a worldwide network of public accounting firms, called BDO Member Firms and serving international clients. Each BDO member firm is an independent legal entity in its own country. BDO International has a staff of over 15,000 worldwide.

BDO Dunwoody LLP has a staff of approximately 1,600 in its Canadian offices. Prospective applicants should have an accounting designation and related work experience. BDO maintains a data bank for resumes and suggests that interested candidates contact a recruiter in a local office. Employment opportunities are regularly posted on the company's Web site and applicants can search by job title or location. BDO's Web site also provides direct access to information on the firm's international offices and activities. [ID:6592]

Bema Gold Corp.

P.O. Box 49113, Suite 3113, Three Bentall Centre, 595 Burrard Street, Vancouver, BC,
V7X 1G4, Canada; 604-681-8371, fax 604-681-6209, info@bemagold.com, www.bema.com

LARGE MINING FIRM: Exploration and Development, Gold and Metals Production, Mining

Bema Gold Corp. is an intermediate gold producer with operating mines and development projects in Russia, South Africa, Chile and Canada. The company has recently more than doubled its projected production for 2003 and plans to further increase its projected production by reopening the Refugio Mine in 2004.

Bema Gold employs approximately 45 people in Canada and more than 4,000 overseas. The bulk of Bema's overseas employees are locally hired. Canadian applicants should have a background in geology or mine-related engineering. Interested candidates may contact human resources at jobs@bemagold.com. Visitors to Bema's Web site can view slide shows and presentations of the company's projects, activities and objectives. However, no career-related information is provided on-line. [ID:6636]

Bennett Environmental Inc.

Suite 208, 1540 Cornwall Road, Oakville, ON, L6J 7W5, Canada;
905-339-1540, fax 905-339-0016, info@bennettenv.com, www.bennettenv.com 💻 *Fr*

LARGE ENVIRONMENTAL CONSULTING FIRM: Construction, Engineering, Environment, Waste Water Management

Bennett Environmental Inc. has been in the environmental business for over 25 years. The firm owns and operates the RSI high-temperature thermal treatment facility, for soil contaminated with PCBs, PAH and all other chlorinated and non-chlorinated hydrocarbons in St. Ambroise, Quebec. Bennett also owns and operates the MRR treatment facility in Cornwall, Ontario for PCBs and mercaptan, and owns the licence for the Eli Ecologic Process for the destruction of PCBs which is currently undergoing development. Bennett also provides complete remediation project management, specializing in large and small projects. Currently, exporting efforts are focused on the US although there has been some activity in Asia and Eastern Europe.

The company currently has 10 salaried staff with international responsibilities. Prospective applicants should have a sales and customer service background. Knowledge of hazardous waste treatment and disposal would be an asset. Useful educational backgrounds include environmental science, commerce, political science and engineering. Bennett Environmental's Web site has no career-related information. [ID:6637]

Bing Thom Architects

1430 Burrard Street, Vancouver, BC, V6Z 2A3, Canada; 604-682-1881,
fax 604-688-1343, office@btagroup.com, www.bingthomarchitects.com

MID-SIZED ARCHITECTURE AND PLANNING FIRM: Architecture and Planning, Community Development, Project Management, Urban Development

Bing Thom Architects has experience working with cultural institutions, corporations, universities, governments, developers and communities around the world. Services provided by the firm include architecture, interior design, urban design, landscape design, facilities programming and development feasibility analysis. The firm is recognized throughout Canada and internationally, and has experience in Asia, Europe and throughout North America.

Bing Thom Architects has a team of 45 who come from 13 different countries and speak 14 different languages. Most of the staff possess at least one other area of expertise on top of architecture. Interested candidates may send their resumes to careers@bingthomarchitects.com. [ID:6817]

Biomira Inc.

Human Resources, Edmonton Research Park, 2011 - 94th Street, Edmonton, AB,
T6N 1H1, Canada; 780-450-3761, fax 780-450-4772, www.biomira.com

SMALL BIOTECHNOLOGY FIRM: Accounting, Administration (General), Advanced Technology, Business
Development, Chemicals, Computer Systems, Engineering, Human Resources, Marketing,
Media/Communications, Medical Health, Pharmaceuticals, Project Management, Research and Development

Biomira Inc. is a biotech company applying its leading technology in immunotherapy and
organic chemistry for the development of cancer therapeutics. The company's commitment to the
development of products for the treatment of cancer is currently focused on synthetic therapeutic
vaccines and innovative strategies for immunotherapeutic treatment of cancer. Biomira has
subsidiary operations in the United States and Europe.

Biomira has a staff of 109. Prospective applicants should have a solid educational background
in pharmacology, immunology, toxicology, chemistry, biochemistry, microbiology or in a related
discipline. Biomira hires in the following fields: research and development, clinical operations,
regulatory affairs, business development/marketing/sales, operations, administration and support.
Previous professional international experience is an asset. Biomira maintains a data bank for
resumes. Those interested in the firm may send their resumes and cover letters to the firm's mailing
or e-mail address indicating the position sought. The firm considers applications for internships
throughout the year, with the majority of positions opening in the summer. Biomira maintains a
Web site that contains general information on the firm, copies of its annual reports, and some job-
related information. [ID:6638]

Biothermica Technologies Inc.

426 Sherbrooke E., Montreal, QC, H2L 1J6, Canada; 514-488-3881,
fax 514-488-3125, biotherm@biothermica.com, www.biothermica.com ⌨*Fr*

LARGE ENVIRONMENTAL CONSULTING FIRM: Consulting, Energy Resources, Engineering,
Environment, Technical Assistance

Biothermica Technologies Inc. is a technology company involved in the development, design
engineering and construction of turnkey projects related to thermal treatment of gases and waste.
The company's engineers, scientists and technicians are involved in the research and development
of tangible solutions to the various problems associated with air pollution and the production of
energy from waste. Biothermica's services focus on four areas: thermal oxidation of air pollutants in
process fumes, particle control from high-temperature gases, energy-oriented biomass valorization
and solid waste, and landfill gas management and valorization. Biomass energy conversion is one
of its main research activities. Outside Canada, the firm has done projects in France, El Salvador,
Barbados, Romania, Egypt, Tunisia, Morocco, Chile and French Guyana. Seasonal internship
positions are offered to students in Quebec. [ID:6707]

Bissett Resource Consultants Ltd.

250 - 839 - 5th Ave., Calgary, AB, T2P 3C8, Canada;
403-294-1888, fax 403-263-0073, mail@bissettres.com, www.bissettres.com

LARGE PETROLEUM CONSULTING FIRM: Construction, Drilling Services, Engineering, Oilfield Services,
Petrochemicals, Project Management

Bissett Resource Consultants Ltd. is an established Canadian petroleum engineering company
based in Calgary, Alberta. It is actively engaged in engineering, project management and field
supervision in the areas of construction, drilling and completion operations, workovers, production
operations and facilities. The company employs approximately 75 people and offers a variety of
consulting services throughout Canada and has successfully completed projects in the United
States, Europe, Africa and Asia. [ID:6774]

BMO Financial Group (BMO)

First Canadian Place, 100 King Street W., Toronto, ON, M5X 1A3, Canada;
416-867-5050, fax 416-867-4168, feedback@bmo.com, www.bmo.com 💻 *Fr*

LARGE FINANCIAL SERVICES FIRM: Administration (General), Economics

BMO Financial Group (BMO) is one of the largest financial services providers in North America, offering a broad range of retail banking, wealth management and investment banking products and solutions. BMO serves clients across Canada and the United States through its Canadian retail arm, BMO Bank of Montreal; Chicago-based Harris Bank, a major US mid-west financial services organization; The Harris Wealth Management Group; BMO Nesbitt Burns, one of Canada's leading full-service investment firms; and Harris Nesbitt, which provides investment banking services across the US. The bank is also represented in other global locations such as Barbados, Brazil, China, Ireland, Hong Kong, Mexico, Singapore, Taiwan and the United Kingdom.

Currently, the bank employs more than 33,000 people. The bank also offers several student and new graduate recruitment programs, which are all posted with application instructions on the bank's Web site. Recruiting is done year round (depending on the program) across the country and the bank participates in campus career fairs and has a student career library on its Web site. Employment opportunities are also posted on the Web site, as is a resume database. There is also an informative careers page, including tips for students and graduates looking for work, suggestions for interviews and hints for resume writing and networking. [ID:6705]

Bombardier Inc.

800 René Lévesque Blvd. W., Montreal, QC, H3B 1Y8, Canada;
514-861-9481, fax 514-861-7053, www.bombardier.com 💻 *Fr*

LARGE TRANSPORTATION MANUFACTURING FIRM: Accounting, Administration (General), Aerospace Technology, Business Development, Engineering, Human Resources, Media/Communications, Project Management

Bombardier Inc., based in Canada, is a world-leading manufacturer of innovative transportation solutions, from regional aircraft and business jets to rail transportation equipment. Bombardier Aerospace is a world leader in the design and manufacture of innovative aviation products and services for the business, regional and amphibious aircraft markets. This legacy of innovation consolidates more than 250 years of aviation history and has produced an unparalleled 14 new aircraft programs in the past 14 years. Bombardier Aerospace has full design and production facilities in three countries. Bombardier Transportation is the global leader in the rail equipment manufacturing and servicing industry. Bombardier Transportation has production facilities on five continents serving a diversified customer base around the world. Bombardier Capital is the financial services arm of the global transportation equipment manufacturer Bombardier Inc. With 30 years' experience in the financial services industry, Bombardier Capital provides lending, leasing and asset management services.

The company employs 65,000 people. Interested applicants can search for opportunities by job type, location and branch within the company. Resumes may be directly submitted to the Web site. Bombardier's careers page has a section specifically for students and recent graduates. This section offers various jobs for undergraduates, graduates and post-graduates in technical or business-related fields. Internships are available through the career centres of the universities that the company visits. The company's Web site lists these various universities and the dates of their upcoming visits. The careers page includes resume and interview tips, as well as personal experience stories. [ID:6639]

Bovar International Ltd.

P.O. Box 6620, Stn. D, Calgary, AB, T2P 3R3, Canada;
403-235-8300, fax 403-248-3306, jobs@orbus.ca, www.orbus.ca

LARGE ENVIRONMENTAL FIRM: Business Development, Consulting, Environment, Waste Water
Management

BOVAR International Ltd. (a division of Orbus Pharma Inc. as of May 2003, after a merger
with Orbus Life), is a fully integrated environmental and waste management operation, having its
core business in the treatment and disposal of hazardous and other regulated wastes, the sale of gas
monitoring and process control equipment, and environmental consulting and services. Bovar's joint
venture in Malaysia operates several facilities that install, operate and maintain a network of air and
water quality monitoring stations throughout Malaysia for the Malaysian Department of
Environment. Interested applicants are asked to e-mail the company for employment opportunities
at jobs@orbus.ca. [ID:6640]

Brascan Corporation

P.O. Box 762, Suite 300, BCE Place, 181 Bay Street, Toronto, ON,
M5J 2T3, Canada; 416-363-9491, fax 416-363-2856, www.brascancorp.com

LARGE INVESTMENT MANAGEMENT FIRM: Banking and Financial Services, Business Development,
Energy Resources, Forestry, Metals, Mining, Power Generation/Transmission/Distribution, Real Estate, Trade
and Investment

Brascan Corp. is an asset management company focused on the real estate and power
generation sectors. The company owns 55 premier office properties and 42 power generating
plants, primarily hydroelectric operations located in the northeastern parts of North America. It also
has an increasing portfolio of financial and other assets under management focused on alternative
investments, such as bridge and mezzanine financing and restructuring capital, and direct
investments in real estate, energy and resource assets. Brascan also provides a host of management
and advisory services, primarily in the real estate sector, to corporate and individual clients and is
recognized as a leading developer of master planned residential communities in both Canada and
the United States. The company has real estate operations across Canada, the United States and
South America, and has three hydroelectric power generation projects in development in Brazil.
Brascan employs 20,000 professionals. Interested applicants may submit their resume directly
to a specific business sector on the company's Web site. [ID:6549]

Breakwater Resources Ltd.

Suite 950, 95 Wellington Street W., Toronto, ON, M5J 2N7, Canada;
416-363-4798, fax 416-363-1315, investorinfo@breakwater.ca, www.breakwater.ca

LARGE MINING FIRM: Accounting, Administration (General), Engineering, Exploration and Development,
Metals, Mining

Breakwater Resources Ltd. is engaged in the acquisition, exploration, development and
mining of base and precious metal properties in North Africa and North, Central and South
America. In addition to its Canadian mines in Quebec, the Bouchard-Hébert Mine and the Langlois
Mine, which are both underground zinc/copper/gold/silver mines, the company owns and operates
El Mochito Mine, an underground zinc/lead/silver mine in Honduras; El Toqui Mine, a zinc/gold
mine in Chile and the Bougrine Mine, a zinc/lead mine in Tunisia. The company also has a
marketing office in Bridgetown, Barbados.
Although this expanding firm has a large number of overseas employees (three-quarters of its
approximately 2000 staff), the majority are locally hired. Candidates for overseas positions should
be seasoned professionals, generally mining or metallurgical engineers and geologists. The
company maintains a data bank for resumes. Interested applicants can view employment
opportunities on the company's Web site. [ID:6609]

Bregman + Hamann Architects (B+H)

Suite 300, 481 University Ave., Toronto, ON, M5G 2H4, Canada;
416-596-2299, fax 416-586-0599, email@bharchitects.com, www.bharchitects.com

LARGE ARCHITECTURE AND PLANNING FIRM: Architecture and Planning

Bregman + Hamann Architects (B+H) is a large architectural firm renowned for design, technical and project management excellence—it celebrated its 50th anniversary in 2003. It has designed award-winning buildings and collaborates with top international architects. The ability to work in diverse sectors at a range of scales is a hallmark of B+H's work with commercial, mixed-use, institutional, renewal, planning, hospitality, retail, health care, residential and transportation projects. Based in Toronto, the firm also has a full-service office in Shanghai, which has been very successful in the Chinese market.

B+H employs approximately 135 people. A careers page may be found on the firm's Web site. The firm continually seeks new people to join their team. Interested candidates may send their resumes to resume@bharchitects.com. [ID:6816]

Breton, Banville & Associates s.e.n.c. (BBA)

375 Sir-Wilfrid-Laurier Blvd., Mont-Sainte-Hilaire, QC, J3H 6C3,
Canada; 514-464-2111, fax 514-464-0901, bba@bba.ca, www.bba.ca 💻 Fr

MID-SIZED ENGINEERING FIRM: Consulting, Engineering, Technical Assistance

Breton, Banville & Associates (BBA) provides electrical engineering services in power systems, electro-technology, control and automation, and instrumentation. Their services include electrical and mechanical engineering, power generation, power studies, automation, advanced control, industrial computing, testing and commissioning, commercial and institutional engineering, project management and construction. The company serves the mining and metallurgy, chemical and petrochemical, aluminum plants, and pulp and paper sectors. BBA has worked on electrical energy projects in Cameroon, Colombia, Ivory Coast, Ghana, Guinea, Jamaica, Haiti, Mali, Peru, Senegal and Tunisia.

The company has more than 200 employees. Many employees have extensive international experience. The firm is always looking for engineers and senior technicians who specialize in electricity power systems.

BBA collaborates with a number of universities in the areas of recruitment, teaching and thesis direction, and offers both internship and training programs. The language of work is mainly French and a good knowledge of the language is required.

Breton, Banville & Associates maintains a data bank for resumes. The firm recommends forwarding a French version of your resume to the e-mail address specified on the Web site, as there are no specific career opportunities posted on the site. [ID:6641]

C.A.C. International

Suite 302, 3575 Saint-Laurent Blvd., Montreal, QC, H2X 2T7, Canada;
514-848-9993, fax 514-982-6182, info@cacinternational.com, www.cacinternational.com 💻 Fr

MID-SIZED GENERAL CONSULTING FIRM: Consulting, Development Assistance, Economic Development, Education, Human Resources, Institution Building, Law, Management, Media/Communications, Training and Education

C.A.C. International is a consulting firm with over 25 years of experience working in international development. The firm has been active on behalf of various multilateral, bilateral and non-governmental organizations, ministries and public/parapublic bodies, as well as private companies. C.A.C. International has developed a solid reputation among international aid agencies, including the Canadian International Development Agency (CIDA), the World Bank (WB), the United Nations Development Programme (UNDP), the United Nations Children's Fund (UNICEF), the International Labour Organization (ILO), the United Nations Population Fund (UNFPA) and the African Development Bank (AfDB), as well as diverse non-governmental organizations in Canada and around the world. The firm has carried out over 500 mandates in over 40 countries in North America, Africa, Latin America, the Caribbean, Asia, Central Europe and Eastern Europe.

C.A.C. International employs approximately 12 people in Canada who specialize in the fields of management, training, communications, law, basic education, good governance and evaluation. [ID:6830]

CAE Inc.

Suite 3060, Royal Bank Plaza, 200 Bay Street, Toronto, ON, M5J 2J1,
Canada; 416-865-0070, fax 416-865-0337, info@cae.com, www.cae.com ⌨ *Fr*

LARGE HIGH TECHNOLOGY FIRM: Advanced Technology, Air Transportation, Computer Systems, Information Technologies, Training and Technology Transfer

CAE Inc. is a world leader in providing advanced simulation and controls equipment and integrated training solutions for customers in the civil aviation, military and marine markets. The company exports 90 per cent of its products, which are sold throughout the world for the military, commercial airlines, business aircraft operators, aircraft manufacturers, naval warships, cruise lines, large passenger ferries and specialized cargo vessels. CAE is the world's leader in the design and production of civil flight simulators and associated visual systems. CAE is now the world's second largest training centre in strategic locations around the world. CAE is also a major provider of training and advanced simulation equipment for military markets, having supplied military training simulators to the defence forces of more than 30 nations. The company has developed the broadest rotary wing expertise of any simulator manufacturer, operates a major training base for submarines in the United Kingdom and has established a leading position in Europe in the supply of army command team and land-based training systems. It is also a world leader in the provision of marine automation systems for both naval and commercial shipping and has been selected to supply advanced automation technology for more than 100 ships in 16 navies and for more than 450 commercial ships worldwide. CAE has manufacturing operations and training facilities in 18 countries on five continents: North America, South America, Europe, Australia and Asia.

The company employs approximately 5,500 employees in Canada, the United States and around the world. A careers page with employment opportunities may be found on the company's Web site. Interested applicants may search by international location, level of experience and job category. During the last few years, CAE has hired 100 new graduates each year and has participated in career fairs which are also posted on the company's Web site. Interested applicants may submit their resume to the company's resume database. CAE's Web site also provides a very helpful careers section which offers resume tips and career FAQs. [ID:6768]

Caisse de dépôt et placement du Québec (CDP Capital)

1000, place Jean-Paul-Riopelle, Montreal, QC, H2Z 2B3, Canada;
514-842-3261, fax 514-847-2170, info@lacaisse.com, www.cdpcapital.com ⌨ *Fr*

LARGE FINANCIAL SERVICES FIRM: Accounting, Banking and Financial Services, Business/Banking/Trade, Human Resources, Personal Taxation/Financial Planning, Real Estate, Retirement/Estate Planning Overseas, Trade and Investment

Caisse de dépôt et placement du Québec (CDP Capital) is a financial institution that manages funds for public and private pension and insurance funds. The company offers private investment funds and real estate management services to external institutional investors. CDP Capital's areas of expertise include real estate, absolute return, business financing analysis and optimization, equities and fixed income. It has activities in Africa, Asia, Australia, Europe, South America and the United States.

A careers page can be found on CDP Capital's Web site. Interested applicants may submit their resume to the company. Currently, CDP Capital is seeking those with doctorate or post-graduate degrees in multiple disciplines, as well as those with human resources and financial management specializations. [ID:6821]

Calian Technology Ltd.

Calian Centre, 2 Beaverbrook Road, Kanata, ON, K2K 1L1, Canada;
613-599-8600, fax 613-599-8650, info@calian.com, www.calian.com

LARGE HIGH TECHNOLOGY FIRM: Administration (General), Engineering, Information Technologies, Project Management, Science and Technology, Technical Assistance, Training and Technology Transfer

Calian Technology Ltd. Is a full-service firm comprising two main divisions business and technology services, and systems engineering. The Business and Technology Services Division augments customer workforces with flexible short- and long-term placements of individuals and teams, provides access to critical recruiting capabilities and delivers outsourcing services for a variety of technical functions. The Systems Engineering Division plans, designs and implements solutions for many of the world's space agencies and leading communications satellite manufacturers and operators. Calian has grown rapidly and now services organizations in Canada, the United Sates, Europe and Asia. The company employs approximately 2,200 people.

A career resources page, along with employment opportunities, may be found on Calian's Web site. Interested applicants may submit a resume to the company's resume database. The career resources page includes resume and cover letter suggestions, interview and follow-up tips, and job hunting and networking hints. [ID:6769]

Cambior Inc.

C.P. 9999, 1075 - 3rd Ave. E., Val-d'Or, QC, J9P 6M1, Canada;
819-825-0211, fax 819-825-0342, info@cambior.com, www.cambior.com ⌨ *Fr*

LARGE MINING FIRM: Exploration and Development, Gold and Metals Production, Mining, Project Management

Cambior Inc. is a major diversified gold producer with operations, development projects and exploration activities in the Americas. The company's revenues are generated predominantly from the sale of gold with the remaining portion from the sale of ferroniobium, a strengthening additive used in the steel alloy industry. Cambior is also the third largest producer of niobium in the world with operating activities in Canada, the United States, Peru, Guyana and Suriname. It has also been active in Mexico and Chile. The company's existing projects are aimed at increasing gold reserves while maintaining a moderate diversification in base metals, primarily copper and zinc.

At the end of 2003, the company employed 2,500 individuals. Cambior states that it is looking for qualified personnel for its teams throughout the Americas and has employment opportunities in the following areas: engineering, geology, metallurgy, the environment, computer and administrative support. Interested candidates should have excellent English language skills with proven professional competence through progressively responsible supervisory experience, preferably in the mining industry. Experience working abroad is a definite asset. Cambior also maintains a resume database where interested candidates can post their resumes. [ID:6693]

Cameco Corp.

Human Resources Dept., 2121-11th Street W., Saskatoon, SK, S7M 1J3, Canada;
306-956-6200, fax 306-956-6539, employment@cameco.com, www.cameco.com

LARGE MINING FIRM: Accounting, Administration (General), Business Development, Community Development, Computer Systems, Energy Resources, Engineering, Environment, Exploration and Development, Human Resources, Media/Communications, Mining

The Cameco Corp., with its head office in Saskatoon, is the world's largest producer of combined uranium and conversion services. The company's competitive position is based upon its controlling ownership of the world's largest high-grade reserves and low-cost operations. Cameco's uranium products are used to generate clean electricity in nuclear power plants around the world, including in Ontario, where the company has a partnership to produce and generate nuclear electricity. The company also mines gold and explores for uranium in North America, Australia and Asia. Cameco also hires a wide range of staff beyond mining specialists. [ID:6694]

Canac International Inc.

3950 Hickmore Street, St. Laurent, QC, H4T 1K2,
Canada; 514-399-5741, info@canac.com, www.canac.com 🖳 𝓕𝓻

LARGE TRANSPORTATION CONSULTING FIRM: Consulting, Engineering, Logistics, Transportation

Canac International Inc. is the single-source provider of knowledge-based products and services for the rail industry. The company's solutions are used by freight and passenger railroads, investors and governments, and industries operating their own railroads throughout the United States, Canada, Mexico and elsewhere internationally. Since 1971, Canac has completed 700 major railway projects in 60 countries.

The number of staff working abroad fluctuates according to the number and importance of contracts. Recruiters look for candidates with degrees or equivalent expertise in transportation, engineering, management, information systems, telecommunications and related disciplines. Applicants with overseas experience are preferred. Canac International Inc. maintains a data bank for resumes. [ID:6642]

Canadian African Trade Centre Inc. (CATCI)

78 Erickson Drive, Whitby, ON, L1N 8Z2, Canada; 416-913-8281, fax 905-666-8830, catci@connection.com

---

SMALL GENERAL CONSULTING FIRM: Business Development, Business/Banking/Trade, Consulting, Development Assistance, International Law/International Agreements, Logistics, Management, Micro-enterprises, Trade and Investment

Canadian African Trade Centre Inc. (CATCI) is a wholly owned private international trade development company that is equipped with professional expertise and extensive linkage in Canada, the United States and key African countries. It has developed a special mandate to bridge the continents of North America and Africa and to make the necessary ties to increase trade and investment between Canadian and African-based small- and medium-sized enterprises. Since May 15, 1995, CATCI has been involved in: international trade, international trade consulting, trade regulations, export/import procedures, logistics and distribution, trade finance and negotiations, as well as financial and investment services. The company has experience working with countries such as Ghana, Nigeria Botswana, Côte d'Ivoire, Ethiopia, Guinea, Kenya, Sierra Leone and South Africa. CATCI employs approximately 10 people. The company's management team and staff consist of professionals from Canada, the United States and continental Africa. [ID:6801]

Canadian Fishery Consultants Ltd. (CFCL)

P.O. Box 606, 1489 Hollis Street, Halifax, NS, B3J 2R7, Canada;
902-422-4698, fax 902-422-8147, cfcl@canfish.com, www.canfish.com

---

MID-SIZED AGRICULTURAL CONSULTING FIRM: Business Development, Computer Systems, Construction, Consulting, Development Assistance, Economics, Engineering, Environment, Fisheries, Gender and Development, Project Management, Technical Assistance

Canadian Fishery Consultants Ltd. (CFCL) is an international consulting firm offering a variety of services to the fishery and marine sectors in Canada and around the world. The services provided by the firm include culturing, harvesting, processing and the marketing of fish species. CFCL's projects range from financial and technical feasibility studies to design, evaluation and retrofitting of fish processing facilities and increasing commercial use of fish landings by catching and processing wastes. The firm's work outside of Canada has taken it to Africa, the Caribbean, Central/South America, the Pacific and Southeast Asia overseeing the entire project cycle in the development of sustainable fisheries, aquaculture and marine transportation industries.

CFCL has eight staff members working out of Halifax. Recruitment of additional professionals is on a project-by-project basis for short-term assignments. CFCL recruits specialists in all aspects of the fishing and aquaculture industries. Specialists in the warm water species have been needed in the past. Expertise in fishing, fishing gear, fishing vessel design and construction, economics, biology, engineering, maintenance, environmental assessment and marketing are occasionally needed. Internships are considered during any season for individuals interested in fisheries and aquaculture. CFCL maintains a data bank for resumes.

Those who visit their Web site can view PowerPoint shows of past projects and activities, as well as read project summaries by client, location, date and project description. [ID:6643]

Canadian Higher Education Group (CHEG)

Penthouse Floor, 150 Isabella Street, Ottawa, ON, K1S 1V7, Canada;
613-237-2220, fax 613-237-7347, cheg@cheg.ca, www.cheg.org

MID-SIZED GENERAL CONSULTING FIRM: Administration (General), Computer Systems, Consulting, Development Assistance, Development Education, Education, Human Resources, Institution Building, International Education, Policy Development, Project Management

Canadian Higher Education Group (CHEG) is a unique combination of the private sector and the educational sector. This permanent partnership combines the marketing, management and business strengths of Hickling Corporation with the educational, training, management, research and business resources of four universities. CHEG's mission is to provide the best higher education services to international clients and its unique partnership has made it successful in the international development marketplace. CHEG is in partnership with the following universities: University of Guelph, McMaster University, University of Waterloo and the University of Western Ontario. The group is active in a broad range of educational projects at the basic, secondary and post-secondary levels. CHEG's expertise and that of its international roster of educational experts, is made available to countries that are engaged in strengthening and reforming their educational systems. The group is currently engaged in the following sectors: sector/system planning and policy development, decentralization, finance and investment, education and management, teacher and faculty development, computer application, university reform, curriculum and materials development, system efficiency, quality, access and equity, institutional strengthening and capacity building, labour market assessments, study tours and distance education. Clients of the group include international financial institutions, regional development banks, national governments and the Government of Canada. CHEG has project experience in Indonesia, Maldives, the Philippines, Papua New Guinea, Laos, Uzbekistan and Vietnam.

A careers page can be found on the group's Web site. Currently, CHEG is seeking highly qualified and experienced individuals with professional and consulting backgrounds in the following areas: education reform, strategic planning and policy development, education management, capacity building and institution strengthening, education finance and investment, decentralization of education systems, curriculum design, Education Management Information Systems (EMIS), monitoring and evaluation, and materials development. Consultants must have a minimum of five years experience in international education assignments. Consultants with doctorate degrees are also preferred. Interested and qualified individuals should forward a detailed electronic curriculum vitae showing all related consulting experience to hickling@hickling.ca. CHEG's Web site allows visitors to read through past projects of the group and learn more about their activities. [ID:6589]

Canadian Imperial Bank of Commerce (CIBC)

Human Resources Division, Commerce Court, Toronto, ON,
M5L 1A2, Canada; 416-980-2211, fax 416-784-6799, www.cibc.com 💻 *Fr*

LARGE FINANCIAL SERVICES FIRM: Banking and Financial Services

Canadian Imperial Bank of Commerce (CIBC), one of the largest banks in North America, is a highly diversified, full-service financial institution operating on a global basis. The financial institution provides a full range of products and services to over nine million customers across Canada and private banking centres around the world. CIBC is made up of three strategic business units: CIBC Retail Markets, CIBC Wealth Management and CIBC World Markets with branches and offices across Canada, the United States, the United Kingdom and Asia.

The institution employs more than 37,000 people worldwide. CIBC regularly posts job opportunities on its Web site and interested applicants can search by country, province/state, city and job category. Recruiters consider candidates from a wide variety of backgrounds depending on the position sought. The bank maintains a data bank for resumes. Co-op, summer and graduate work placements, as well as intake programs are also offered by the institution.

CIBC maintains a Web site that offers a number of on-line banking services and provides information on the bank's global activities. The careers page of the Web site also provides interested applicants with helpful job search resources. [ID:6644]

Canadian Natural Resources Ltd.

Suite 2500, 855 - 2nd Street S.W., Calgary, AB, T2P 4J8, Canada;
403-517-6700, fax 403-517-7350, employment@cnrl.com, www.cnrl.com

LARGE PETROCHEMICALS FIRM: Energy Resources, Oil and Gas Exploration, Petrochemicals, Research and Development

Canadian Natural Resources Ltd. is a senior independent oil and natural gas exploration, development and production company based in Calgary, Alberta. The company's operations are focused in Western Canada, the North Sea, offshore West Africa, and has offices located in Angola, Côte d'Ivoire and Scotland.

Canadian Natural Resources employs 1,700 employees. The company posts employment opportunities on its Web site and maintains a resume database. It asks those interested in international positions to please contact international offices posted on the site. Co-op, internship and student opportunities, as well as development programs are available. The company works closely with campus career placement offices and has various new grad positions. Canadian Natural Resources is currently scouting for people in the areas of engineering, accounting/finance, petroleum geology and suggests that those interested contact their local campus career placement office to check for current postings. [ID:6577]

Canadian Ocean Resource Associates Inc. (CORA)

Suite 901, TD Place, 140 Water Street, St. John's, NL, A1C 6H6,
Canada; 709-753-1015, fax 709-576-6777, info@cora.ca, www.cora.ca

MID-SIZED ENVIRONMENTAL CONSULTING FIRM: Accounting, Administration (General), Aerospace Technology, Architecture and Planning, Business Development, Business/Banking/Trade, Community Development, Computer Systems, Construction, Consulting, Development Assistance, Economics, Energy Resources, Engineering, Environment, Exchange Programs, Fisheries, Forestry, Gender and Development, Human Resources, Logistics, Media/Communications, Micro-enterprises, Project Management, Technical Assistance, Tourism, Volunteer

Canadian Ocean Resource Associates (CORA) Inc. is a consulting company based in Newfoundland that offers a variety of services including business planning and public/private sector partnerships, accessing governmental support programs, joint venture negotiation, technology transfer, small cap mergers and acquisitions, financial and operational due diligence, making company line departments profit centres, tax and financial planning for small companies and information technology consulting. Since 1993, CORA has managed $45 million in development projects in the public and private sectors. It has completed projects for clients in 35 countries throughout the world across a broad range of industries. The company also has an office in England.

The firm employs six full-time staff in Canada and an additional two overseas. Applicants should have a university degree and experience in private sector development issues. CORA maintains a data bank for resumes. [ID:6568]

CANARAIL Consultants Inc.

Suite 1050, 1140 Maisonneuve Blvd. W., Montreal, QC, H3A 1M8, Canada;
514-985-0930, fax 514-985-0929, inbox@canarail.com, www.canarail.com ❑ *Fr* ❑ *Sp*

LARGE TRANSPORTATION CONSULTING FIRM: Consulting, Economics, Engineering, Project Management, Railways, Technical Assistance, Transportation

CANARAIL Consultants Inc. is a consulting firm specializing in railway transportation. The firm combines the resources of engineers, managers and technicians. The group of consultants with the firm include economists, mechanical engineers and technical specialists, civil engineers and technical specialists, telecommunication engineers and technical specialists, railway operations specialists, procurement specialists, management consultants and information systems specialists. CANARAIL's primary focus is railway and urban transportation and has carried out numerous transportation projects in North America, Asia, Africa, Australia, Europe and Latin America.

Current CANARAIL staff includes both full-time employees in Canada and overseas. In addition, contractual employees are hired according to various project needs for short- or long-term contracts. Interested applicants can search for employment opportunities on the firm's Web site. CANARAIL continually searches for qualified professionals with solid experience in transportation, railway technical activities, engineers, transport planners, financial analysts, economists and telecommunications experts. The firm seeks consultants who are adaptable to change, have good listening skills and are sensitive to other cultures. CANARAIL maintains a resume data bank of potential consultants. Those who visit CANARAIL's Web site can read about past international projects to better understand the firm's activities. [ID:6648]

Canarc Resource Corp.

Suite 800, 850 West Hastings Street, Vancouver, BC, V6C 1E1,
Canada; 604-685-9700, fax 604-685-9744, www.canarc.net

SMALL MINING FIRM: Exploration and Development, Mining

Canarc Resource Corp. is a Canadian-based international gold exploration and mining company active in North, South and Central America. Canarc's overall focus is exploration and developing properties in the Americas. [ID:6610]

CanEd International Inc.

Suite 300, 4500 - 16th Ave. N.W., Calgary, AB, T3B 0M6, Canada;
403-266-1169, fax 403-261-3955, info@canedinternational.com, www.canedinternational.com

SMALL AGRICULTURAL FIRM: Agriculture, Business Development, Information Technologies, Marketing, Technical Assistance

CanEd International Inc. is a Canadian company that develops and distributes agricultural information systems to agricultural producers and agribusiness firms. The company's areas of expertise are in primary agriculture, agri-food processing and marketing, agricultural biotechnology and international agribusiness. CanEd's projects involve training, institutional strengthening and capacity building, and services are offered through domestic and international marketing studies, marketing plans, feasibility studies, business plans and technical assessments. The company has completed projects in the former Soviet Union, Central America, Egypt, Namibia, Zambia, Ukraine (for the Canadian International Development Agency, CIDA), El Salvador and Belize.

A careers page may be found on the company's Web site. The company asks that those interested in working as a project specialist to e-mail a copy of their resume in a Word document to CanEd International and they will review it for consideration. [ID:6761]

Canning & Pitt Associates Inc.

P.O. Box 21461, St. John's, NL, A1A 5G6, Canada;
709-738-0133, fax 709-753-4471, canpitt@nlnet.nf.ca, www.canpitt.ca

MID-SIZED ENVIRONMENTAL CONSULTING FIRM: Consulting, Economic Development, Economics, Environment, Fisheries, Geophysics, Media/Communications, Project Management

Canning & Pitt Associates Inc. is an economic and environmental assessment consulting firm particularly for the marine environment and fisheries, with extensive experience in communications, socio-economic impact analysis, impact mitigation and strategic planning. The company has experience in project management, land use planning, public consultation, conference planning and facilitation surveys. It also specializes in assisting geophysical surveys (seismic exploration) in environmental assessment, fisheries liaison and logistical support during surveys. The company has worked on projects for governments, private sector clients and industry groups throughout Atlantic Canada and the Arctic, in Scotland, Russia and elsewhere. [ID:6781]

Canora Asia Inc.

Suite 1500, 630 René Lévesque Blvd. W., Montreal, QC, H3B 1S6, Canada;
514-393-9110, fax 514-393-1511, canora@attglobal.net, www.canora-asia.com

LARGE ENVIRONMENTAL CONSULTING FIRM: Engineering, Environment, Waste Water Management

Canora Asia Inc. is a Canadian corporation which provides engineering and management services in the environment sector. The company is owned by a select group of highly qualified engineering and consulting companies from across Canada, as shareholders make up the Canora Group. While Canora is a Canadian company, its business is conducted entirely in Asia. Services are delivered in each country by utilizing the professional and financial resources within the Canora group of companies specific to project need. These resources are combined with local firms and individuals in each country that share Canora's project interests. As the company's profile grows in each country, Canora creates permanent establishments either through project or joint venture relationships in each Asian country. The company has provided services in over 20 countries including China, Vietnam, Laos, Indonesia, Thailand, Brunei and the Philippines. Clients of Canora have included the Asian Development Bank, the World Bank and the Canadian International Development Bank (CIDA). It has an office in Jakarta, Indonesia and is currently involved in several large projects in that country, including the JIEP Waste Water Treatment Project in Jakarta.

Canora has over 2,000 employees in its member companies. The company draws on their diverse backgrounds in the service, manufacturing and construction sectors. It helps its members identify opportunities and reduce the risks and costs of doing business in Asia. [ID:6681]

Canoro Resources Ltd.

Suite 2810, 715 - 5th Ave. S.W., Calgary, AB, T2P 2X6, Canada;
403-543-5747, fax 403-543-5740, mail@canoro.com, www.canoro.com

MID-SIZED ENERGY RESOURCES FIRM: Exploration and Development, Oil and Gas Exploration

Canoro Resources Ltd. is a Canadian international energy company, specializing in exploration, development and production of oil and gas. The company focuses on lower-risk international development projects, combined with upside growth potential through the exploration of its large land holdings. It currently operates two properties in Assam State in northeast India. Canoro is also represented in Russia by a wholly owned subsidiary known as Legasi Petroleum International, with development activities in Russia. [ID:6790]

CBCL Limited

P.O. Box 606, 1489 Hollis Street, Halifax, NS, B3J 2R7, Canada;
902-421-7241, fax 902-423-3938, info@cbcl.ca, www.cbcl.ca

MID-SIZED ENVIRONMENTAL CONSULTING FIRM: Construction, Engineering, Environment, Project Management, Science and Technology, Training and Technology Transfer

CBCL Limited is a multi-discipline engineering company providing a wide range of project management, design and construction management services for their clients. The firm provides all of the multi-discipline expertise required to see an assignment through from concept to completion, including liaison with regulatory agencies, planning, scheduling, cost estimating and budgeting, detailed design, procurement, contract administration, construction inspection, operational training and documentation. The firm has completed projects in Bermuda.

CBCL has a staff of approximately 200 people, including professional engineers, environmental scientists, technologists, technicians and support staff. An employment page can be found on the firm's Web site. [ID:6559]

C-CORE
Captain Robert A. Bartlett Bldg., Morrissey Road, St. John's, NL, A1B 3X5,
Canada; 709-737-8354, fax 709-737-4706, info@c-core.ca, www.c-core.ca

LARGE NATURAL RESOURCES FIRM: Advanced Technology, Engineering, Fisheries, Forestry, Geomatics, Geophysics, Information Technologies, Mining, Pulp and Paper

C-CORE is a global research and development corporation providing innovative engineering solutions to clients in the natural resource sectors. The company develops and applies advanced technologies to address production and market issues faced by natural resource sectors such as oil and gas, pipeline, mining, pulp and paper, forestry, fisheries and aquaculture. Collaboration with partners, clients and research institutions achieves exceptional results and contributes to economic growth in these industries. Although Canada is a major focus, the company also continues to increase its operations in the United States, Europe, Asia and offshore Russia. C-CORE's clients include large national and multinational corporations, small- and medium-size enterprises (SMEs), as well as government agencies.

C-CORE employs more than 50 research engineers. A careers page with employment opportunities may be found when posted. The careers page also lists C-CORE's current recruitment focus that interested applicants may view. [ID:6831]

Cedara Software Corp.
Human Resources, 6509 Airport Road, Mississauga, ON, L4V 1S7, Canada;
905-672-2100, fax 905-672-2307, info@cedara.com, www.cedara.com

LARGE MEDICAL IMAGING SOFTWARE FIRM: Accounting, Administration (General), Advanced Technology, Computer Systems, Engineering, Human Resources, Information Technologies, Management Training, Manufacturing, Marketing, Medical Health, Software Development, Technical Assistance

Cedara Software Corp. is a leading independent provider of medical technologies for many of the world's leading medical device and healthcare information technology companies. Cedara software is deployed in thousands of hospitals and clinics worldwide. Cedara's advanced medical imaging technologies are used in all aspects of clinical workflow, including the operator consoles of numerous medical imaging devices; Picture Archiving and Communications Systems (PACS); sophisticated clinical applications that further analyze and manipulate images; and even the use of imaging in minimally invasive surgery. Cedara is unique in that it has expertise and technologies that span all the major digital imaging modalities including magnetic resonance imaging (MRI), computed tomography (CT), digital X-ray, ultrasound, mammography, cardiology, nuclear medicine, angiography, positron emission tomography (PET) and fluoroscopy.

Cedara has over 250 employees and looks for individuals in the areas of sales, marketing, software development, information technology, administration, finance, clinical, human resources and technical support. Interested applicants can search through employment opportunities posted on Cedara's Web site and submit their resume on-line. [ID:6633]

Celestica Inc.
1150 Eglington Ave. E., Toronto, ON, M3C 1H7, Canada;
416-448-5800, fax 416-448-5895, contactus@celestica.com, www.celestica.com

LARGE HIGH TECHNOLOGY FIRM: Accounting, Advanced Technology, Business Development, Computer Systems, Engineering, Human Resources, Information Technologies, Marketing

Celestica Inc. is a world leader in the delivery of innovative electronics manufacturing services (EMS). Celestica operates a highly sophisticated global manufacturing network with operations in Asia, Europe and the Americas, providing a broad range of integrated services and solutions to leading OEMs (original equipment manufacturers). A recognized leader in quality, technology and supply chain management, Celestica provides competitive advantage to its customers by improving time-to-market, scalability and manufacturing efficiency. The company provides integrated services and solutions for OEMs operating in the aerospace and defence, automotive, communications, computing, consumer and industrial sectors. Services provided by the company include design, new product introduction, commodity management, engineering/lab services, order management, printed circuit board assembly, system assembly, enclosure assembly, logistics and after-market services. Celestica delivers comprehensive product solutions including power, memory, graphics, plastics, servers and workstations to customers seeking cost-effective, scalable ways to deliver their product to market. Celestica has operations in the United States, Canada, Mexico, Puerto Rico, Brazil, the United Kingdom, France, Ireland, Italy, Spain, the Czech Republic, China, Indonesia, Singapore, Taiwan, Thailand, Japan and Malaysia.

Celestica employs 43,000 people around the world. A careers page may be found on the company's Web site. Interested candidates may search by region and job category. The company typically recruits in the areas of business services, finance, human resources, information technology, operations, supply chain management, engineering, marketing, business development and sales. Student and new graduate opportunities are also available. Common positions include electrical engineering, mechanical engineering, procurement/component engineering, programmer analysts, marketing specialists, material planners and supply buyers, financial analysts and accountants, as well as technicians and technologists. Celestica's internship program lasts from 12 to 16 months, beginning in May and ending the following September. Application instructions may be found on the company's Web site. [ID:6779]

CFC International Inc. (CFCI)
Suite 800, 300 Léo Pariseau Street, Montreal, QC, H2X 4B3, Canada;
514-286-8212, fax 514-286-1500, sac@groupecfc.qc.ca, www.groupecfc.com ⌨ Fr

LARGE MANAGEMENT CONSULTING FIRM: Development Education, Human Resources, Project Management, Technical Assistance

CFC International Inc. (CFCI) is a consulting firm that provides human resource management consulting. The firm assists client organizations to improve their performance and competitiveness by transforming their culture, developing their management, optimizing their procedures and upgrading their human resources. The firm carries out strategic planning, organization, operation and appraisal of international projects, and offers the services of organizational alignment, organizational transformation and development, performance management and development of personal competencies. CFCI is a subsidiary of Group CFC, a leading Canadian firm in human resource management.

The firm has approximately 60 Canadian-based employees, some of whom have international responsibilities. Recruiters look for senior consultants with technical skills and expertise in management and human resources. Past international experience is required for international assignments. CFC International Inc. maintains a data bank for resumes. [ID:6645]

CIMA+
Suite 600, 3400 boul. du Souvenir, Laval, QC, H7V 3Z2, Canada;
450-688-4970, fax 450-682-1013, info@cima.ca, www.cima.ca ⌨ Fr

MID-SIZED ENGINEERING FIRM: Engineering, Project Management

CIMA+ is a multidisciplinary group active in engineering, advanced technologies and project management. The firm specializes in the following fields: energy, transport, telecommunications, civil engineering, effluent water treatment and building. These missions abroad are usually carried out in partnership with local organizations and/or engineering firms. CIMA+ has specialists located in Africa, Central America, China, Cuba and Argentina.

Currently, the company employs more than 650 people distributed among several major Quebec regions and overseas. Interested candidates can apply to jobs within Canada or internationally via e-mail. [ID:6710]

Cinram International Inc.

2255 Markham Road, Scarborough, ON, M1B 2W3, Canada;
416-298-8190, fax 416-298-0612, human.resources@cinram.com, www.cinram.com

LARGE HIGH TECHNOLOGY FIRM: Accounting, Administration (General), Business Development,
Computer Systems, Engineering, Human Resources, Logistics, Project Management

Cinram International Inc. is the world's largest independent provider of pre-recorded multimedia products and logistics services. With facilities in North America and Europe, Cinram manufactures and distributes pre-recorded DVDs, VHS video cassettes, audio CDs, audio cassettes and CD-ROMs for motion picture studios, music labels, publishers and computer software companies around the world. The company's shares are listed on the Toronto Stock Exchange (as CRW) and are included on the S&P/ TSX Composite Index. Cinram's head office is located in Scarborough, Ontario. The Canadian facilities provide manufacturing for DVD, CD, VHS and audio cassettes. The company's 20 major facilities worldwide include locations in the United States, France, Germany and the United Kingdom. In Latin America, the company owns 50 per cent of Cinram Latino-Americana, S.A. de C.V., a custom manufacturer of CD, DVD and VHS, located in Mexico City, Mexico.

Cinram has over 9,400 employees worldwide and posts employment opportunities on its Web site. Interested applicants can select employment opportunities by country. [ID:6709]

CODE Inc.

Suite 120, 2255 St. Laurent Blvd., Ottawa, ON, K1G 4K3, Canada;
613-260-3457, fax 613-260-3458, information@codeinc.com, www.codeinc.com

MID-SIZED GENERAL CONSULTING FIRM: Development Education, Election Monitoring

CODE Inc. delivers election and registration supplies worldwide. The company provides customized materials and professional services to support secure voting and successful registration events anywhere in the world. It has experience working with countries in Africa, Central America, Europe, Asia, Australia, the Caribbean, South America, North America and the Middle East. CODE Inc. employs eight people. CODE Inc. was founded in 1987 as the profit-making arm of CODE, a Canadian NGO based in Ottawa. [ID:6556]

Cognos Inc.

P.O. Box 9707, Stn. T, 3755 Riverside Drive, Ottawa, ON, K1G 4K9,
Canada; 613-738-1440, fax 613-738-0002, jobs@cognos.com, www.cognos.com

LARGE HIGH TECHNOLOGY FIRM: Computer Systems, Consulting, Engineering, Technical Assistance

Cognos, an international corporation, is one of the world's leading suppliers of business intelligence software. Cognos develops software that allows companies to improve and direct corporate performance by enabling all of the key steps in the management cycle, from planning and budgeting to reporting and analysis. The company serves the automotive, banking and insurance, energy and natural resources, government, health care, manufacturing and pharmaceutical sectors. Cognos serves over 22,000 customers in over 135 countries worldwide.

With more than 32 offices in 12 countries, Cognos employs more than 3,000 people worldwide in Australia, Belgium, France, Germany, Hong Kong, Italy, Japan, the Netherlands, Singapore, Sweden, the United Kingdom and the United States. Its US division is mainly a sales and marketing organization, requiring people with experience in sales, marketing, support and administration. The growing UK division typically requires software and marketing specialists as well as account managers and support staff. For college and university students, Cognos offers co-op placements and a scholarship program. Interested students may apply through notices posted in student co-op offices or contact the student recruiter on the company's Web site.

The company's Web site provides detailed information on job opportunities in the US and Canada, as well as instructions for employment in the UK. The site allows interested applicants to search for jobs by region, country and job category. [ID:6606]

Coles Associates Ltd.

P.O. Box 197, 197 Malpeque Road, Charlottetown, PE, C1A 7L3, Canada;
902-368-2300, fax 902-566-3768, hcoles@caltech.ca, www.colesassociates.com

MID-SIZED ENGINEERING CONSULTING FIRM: Architecture and Planning, Consulting, Engineering, Information Technologies, Transportation

Coles Associates Ltd. provides professional services to a diverse clientele in the United States, Canada and South America in the disciplines of architecture and engineering; specifically, structural, mechanical, civil, electrical and transportation engineering. The company's services portfolio embraces the disciplines of architecture, engineering, investigative engineering and information technologies. Coles Associates employs approximately 30 people. A careers page with regular job postings can be found on the company's Web site. [ID:6805]

Cominco Engineering Services Ltd. (CESL)

Suite 600, 200 Burrard Street, Vancouver, BC, V6C 3L9, Canada;
604-267-3050, fax 604-844-2681, info@cesl.com, www.cesl.com 💻*Sp*

MID-SIZED ENGINEERING FIRM: Engineering

Cominco Engineering Services Ltd. (CESL), a subsidiary of Teck Cominco Metals Ltd., has developed a hydrometallurgical process for the refining of copper and/or nickel from sulphide concentrates. This process is considered to be environmentally superior to smelting, as it does not produce sulphur dioxide gas and has no significant effluents. CESL is currently engaged in campaigns of process development and engineering studies in support of major US and South American mineral processing projects. The company's demonstration plant in Richmond, BC, closely replicates the equipment and operating conditions to be found in a commercial scale plant and provides necessary engineering design data. The smaller pilot plant in Vancouver facilitates the establishment of process parameters and flow sheet development.

CESL asks interested candidates to send a cover letter and resume to the company by regular mail or e-mail. The company also posts employment opportunities on its Web site. [ID:6561]

Comprehensive Care International (CCI)

Suite 301, 173 Dufferin Street, Toronto, ON, M6K 3H7,
Canada; 416-531-5950, fax 416-531-0427, www.ccihealth.com

MID-SIZED GENERAL CONSULTING FIRM: Consulting, Medical Diagnostics, Medical Health, Project Management, Training and Technology Transfer

Comprehensive Care International (CCI) is a project management firm specializing in comprehensive health care solutions. The firm serves hospitals in a variety of jurisdictions, both domestic and international, and in each case they strive to recognize the unique requirements of each community. CCI offers an array of services including population needs assessment and clinical programming, as well as staff education and training to create effective and efficient programs. They also create facilities designed to house these programs in an optimal manner. Their facility services include site selection, functional programming, interior and space design, tendering/procurement of all furniture and hospital equipment, or a complete turnkey service. An important emphasis of CCI is that they compliment the skills available in the client's hospital, adding expertise only as required. They apply global best practices to local needs. Their people are leading medical educators and practitioners, medical business consultants, designers of clinical medical programs and facilities, and hands-on project managers. In-depth knowledge of future directions in each medical field guides every solution, giving it the flexibility to accommodate growth or change. CCI has obtained recognition as a leader in its field. To date, CCI has completed projects in Brazil, Costa Rica, Argentina, Nicaragua, Trinidad and Tobago, and Canada.

An employment page with opportunities may be found on the company's Web site at www.ccihealth.com. Those interested are asked to contact or submit their resumes to careers@ccihealth.com. [ID:6802]

Conestoga-Rovers & Associates

651 Colby Drive, Waterloo, ON, N2V 1C2, Canada; 519-884-0510,
fax 519-884-0525, info@craworld.com, www.craworld.com ▢*Fr*▢*Sp*

LARGE ENGINEERING CONSULTING FIRM: Construction, Consulting, Energy Resources, Engineering, Environment, Project Management, Waste Water Management, Water Resources

Conestoga-Rovers & Associates (CRA) is an engineering, environmental consulting, construction and information technology services firm. The firm provides services in English, French, Spanish, Portuguese and several other languages. It specializes in environmental site assessment and remediation, water supply and wastewater treatment, and air quality and solid waste management, including energy recovery from landfill gas. CRA is involved in projects on a worldwide basis and has extensive experience working for both international agencies (e.g., the World Bank) as well as private industry. Recent projects have been completed in Argentina, Brazil, India, Germany, the Czech Republic, Italy, Jamaica and Africa. The firm also has over 50 offices across North America with additional offices in Brazil and the United Kingdom.

CRA employs over 1,700 people throughout its offices. A careers page can be found on the firm's Web site with employment opportunities. [ID:6762]

Consulting Resource Group International Inc. (CRG)

P.O. Box 418 Main, Abbotsford, BC, V2S 5Z5, Canada;
604-852-0566, fax 604-850-3003, info@crgleader.com, www.crgleader.com

---

MID-SIZED GENERAL CONSULTING FIRM: Business Development, Community Development, Consulting, Human Resources, Leadership Assessment, Organization Development, Personal Development, Publishing

Consulting Resource Group International Inc. (CRG) creates and publishes personality tests, educational tools and learning systems that enable individuals and organizations to realize their potential, access their true purpose and passion, and increase their productivity. The firm has helped more than one million people in fifty thousand organizations worldwide through learning assessments and solutions, facilitators and a global network of licensed associates who serve as consultants, coaches, trainers, counsellors and more. CRG has completed overseas contracts in nine countries around the world including the US, Japan, Australia, New Zealand, Sweden, the Netherlands, Hungary, and the UK, and has served both public and private sector clients. Past clients of CRG include AT&T, the Boeing Company, Chrysler Canada, IBM Canada Ltd., Microsoft Corporation, the RCMP and the Worker's Compensation Board.

Prospective applicants should be professional independent leaders in a defined region in one or more of the fields of consulting, training development, sales, marketing, personnel, education, career planning, and counselling; have a network of other professional contacts or intend to develop such a network; and have the required sales, marketing and financial capabilities to develop and support at least 10 associates. CRG's Web site provides information on distance learning. [ID:6649]

Corel Corporation

1600 Carling Ave., Ottawa, ON, K1Z 8R7, Canada; 613-728-8200, www.corel.com

---

LARGE HIGH TECHNOLOGY FIRM: Advanced Technology, Human Resources, Media/Communications, Quality Assurance, Research and Development, Software Development

The Corel Corporation is an internationally recognized developer and marketer of productivity applications, graphics and multimedia software. With the introduction of CorelDRAW® in 1989, Corel helped to define computer-generated graphics. Since that time, the company has built a global reputation for excellence in software innovation and design, earning it the trust and loyalty of millions of users worldwide. With CorelDRAW Graphics Suite and WordPerfect® Office, Corel continues to provide customers with two of the world's most recognized software titles. The company's headquarters is in Ottawa and has regional offices in the United States, Europe and Australia. Corel works with an established network of international partners to serve its customers around the globe.

Suitable candidates for software development positions hold bachelor's degrees in science, computer science, or computer engineering, or master's degrees or doctorates in science . Sales and marketing, product management, technical writing and quality assurance staff generally hold degrees in relevant disciplines and tend to be innovators in their field or seasoned high-tech professionals. Corel lists numerous employment opportunities on its Web site. Candidates can search for employment opportunities by category, country and city. The company also maintains a resume database. For more information, please visit www.corel.com/careers. [ID:6682]

Cott Corporation

Human Resources, Suite 340, 207 Queen's Quay W., Toronto, ON,
M5J 1A7, Canada; 416-203-3898, fax 416-203-8171, www.cott.com

LARGE FOOD PROCESSING FIRM: Manufacturing

Cott is the world's leading supplier of retailer brand carbonated soft drinks with beverage manufacturing facilities in Canada, the United States, the United Kingdom and Mexico, as well as a concentrate production plant and R&D centre in Columbus, Georgia. It produces and distributes a wide variety of retailer brand beverages for grocery, mass merchandise, drugstore and convenience store chains, as well as wholesalers in over 20 countries. It has primary subsidiaries in the US, UK and Australia and has additional production facilities in Norway. It plans further expansion in the US. The company operates seven bottling facilities in Canada.

Cott employs approximately 700 people across Canada. The company asks interested applicants to visit its Web site to submit some personal information (i.e., name, phone, e-mail address, area of interest, years of experience, preferred area of location, etc.), and also to directly submit a cover letter and resume to its resume database. Cott employs co-op students in Canada. Jobs with an overseas component are management positions. [ID:6708]

Cowater International Inc.

Suite 400, 411 Roosevelt Ave., Ottawa, ON, K2A 3X9, Canada;
613-722-6434, fax 613-722-5893, general@cowater.com, www.cowater.com

LARGE MANAGEMENT CONSULTING FIRM: Accounting, Adult Training, Banking and Financial Services, Community Development, Consulting, Development Assistance, Development Education, Economics, Engineering, Environment, Gender and Development, Human Resources, Institution Building, Law and Good Governance, Micro-enterprises, Policy Development, Project Management, Technical Assistance, Training and Technology Transfer, Water Supply, Waste Water Management

Cowater International Inc. is a multidisciplinary consulting company that carries out international development in four core areas: 1) water supply, sanitation and environment, 2) financial management, audit and accounting, 3) social development and 4) municipal services and enterprise development. The firm's mission is to provide high-quality consulting services which support social and economic development of self-reliance and sustainability through participatory development. Cowater is involved in all stages of the project cycle, from design and planning through implementation, to monitoring and evaluation, as well as policy development studies, sector reviews and training activities. Cowater has worked with 31 countries on four continents.

The firm has more than 25 overseas professional staff and 15 Canadian-based professional staff. Individuals are often hired for short-term contracts. Most candidates are required to have a master's degree and substantial experience. The firm prefers individuals with several years of international experience, as well as several years of experience in one or more of Cowater's core areas: project management, change management, institutional strengthening, training, capacity building, monitoring and evaluation, results-based management, human resources management, group facilitation and governance. Candidates should have a minimum of 10 years overseas experience in development and the ability to speak English, French, Spanish or Portuguese. The firm asks that applicants follow the resume format and application procedures indicated on its Web site. Cowater maintains a database of consultants for short- and long-term assignments. Cowater International occasionally accepts interns if the needs of the company can be matched with an applicant. [ID:6650]

CPCS Transcom Ltd.

72 Chamberlain Ave., Ottawa, ON, K1S 1V9, Canada;
613-237-2500, fax 613-237-4494, ottawa@cpcstrans.com, www.cpcstrans.com

LARGE TRANSPORTATION SERVICES FIRM: Consulting, Development Assistance, Economics, Engineering, Gender and Development, Marine

CPCS Transcom Ltd. specializes in international transportation commercialization and privatization projects. The company combines staff, resources and experience in the management and commercialization of infrastructure organizations, particularly roads, railways, ports and inter-modal terminal facilities for projects around the world. It has assisted the World Bank, the Canadian International Development Agency (CIDA), the African, Asian, Caribbean and Inter-American Development Banks, as well as the International Civil Aviation Organization and the United Nations Development Programme (UNDP). CPCS has completed over 700 projects in more than 60 countries, working on every continent. Clients include national governments, public transit authorities, private and state-owned transportation organizations and mining companies. It has offices in China, Barbados, Thailand, India and the US. CPCS Transcom employs approximately 40 people. A careers page with employment opportunities can be found on their Web site. [ID:6780]

CRC SOGEMA Inc.

Suite 454, East Tower, Complex St. Charles, 1111 St-Charles Street W., Longueuil, QC, J4K 5G4, Canada; 514-651-2800, fax 514-651-1681, www.crcsogema.com ☐*Fr*☐*Sp*

LARGE MANAGEMENT CONSULTING FIRM: Administration (General), Banking and Financial Services, Community Development, Computer Systems, Consulting, Environment, Human Resources, Project Management

CRC SOGEMA Inc. is a Canadian management consulting firm which works closely with developing countries in the fields of management, training and systemization. In addition, thanks to its subsidiary, CRC SIMA, its fields of expertise have extended to the management of geographic information, natural resources and the environment. The firm offers services in French, English and Spanish to institutions, companies, organizations and agencies in the public, parapublic and private sectors. CRC SOGEMA has carried out more than 250 projects throughout the world, including Africa, the Middle East, Latin America, the Caribbean and Eastern Europe.

The firm has more than 100 permanent consultants and employees working abroad and 60 managers and administrative staff in Canada with international responsibilities. CRC SOGEMA frequently looks for specialists who are willing to carry out short-term (less than six months) or long-term (six months and more) mandates in developing countries and who have experience in activity sectors, as specified on the Web site. Currently, the firm has projects underway in Africa, the Middle East, Central America, Eastern Europe and the Caribbean. Although there are specific requirements for each position to be filled, the firm gives priority to candidates with the following qualifications: undergraduate- or master's-level university education in a suitable branch of studies; between five and ten years of experience in the relevant sector of expertise; preferably, working experience in developing countries; an ability to work in a team; strong interpersonal and communication skills, as well as writing and speaking skills (according to assignment region); a strong degree of autonomy and ability to adapt to new environments and other cultures. The firm also recommends that applicants include some specific information when submitting resumes, which is outlined on the Web site. CRC SOGEMA Inc. maintains a database for resumes. [ID:6651]

Creo Inc.

3700 Gilmore Way, Burnaby, BC, V5G 4M1, Canada;
604-451-2700, fax 604-437-9891, marketing@creo.com, www.creo.com

LARGE HIGH TECHNOLOGY FIRM: Administration (General), Advanced Technology, Computer Systems, Customer Services, Manufacturing, Marketing

Creo Inc. is a global company with key strengths in imaging and software technology. It is a leading provider of prepress systems and assists more than 25,000 customers worldwide to adopt digital production methods which reduces costs, increases print quality and allows them to serve their customers more efficiently. The company's product lines include software and hardware computer-to-plate imaging systems for digital photography, scanning and proofing, as well as printing plates and proofing media. Creo has 50 offices worldwide, including product and manufacturing centres in Vancouver, West Virginia (United States), Herzlia (Israel), Pietermaritzburg (South Africa), as well as sales, support and distribution centres located throughout the world. The company also has regional offices in the United States, Japan, Hong Kong, Australia and Belgium. Creo has served customers in Africa, Australia, the Middle East, South America, Europe, North America and Asia.

The company employs 4,300 people around the world. A careers page can be found on Creo's Web site. Interested candidates may select regions for career opportunities (e.g., Canada, the United States and Latin America, Europe, Israel, Asia Pacific and Japan). Typical positions within the company span the product cycle, including manufacturing, product development, customer support, sales, marketing and general administration. Creo asks applicants to send their resume to resume_canada@creo.com. Co-op opportunities are listed within each region as well. [ID:6770]

Crown Energy Technologies
3001 Shepard Place S.E., Calgary, AB, T2C 4P1, Canada;
403-215-5300, fax 403-215-5303, sales@crown-energy.com, www.crown-energy.com

LARGE PETROLEUM INDUSTRY FIRM: Customer Services, Drilling Services, Oilfield Services, Technical Assistance

Crown Energy Technologies is a leading manufacturer of new oil field equipment, performs quality rig repair and retrofits, and offers a parts supply service. The company has activities in most major oil-producing locations in North America and has sales locations around the globe, including the United States, Russia, China and India. It specializes in custom-built simulation, drilling and workover equipment. Crown Energy's client list includes petroleum industry service companies and government organizations in all oil-producing regions of the world, including Canada, the United States, China, Indonesia, Russia, Kazakhstan, India, Iran, Romania, Argentina, Venezuela, as well as others.

Crown Energy Technology employs 450 people. A careers page with employment opportunities may be found on the company's Web site. Interested candidates may also submit their resumes to the company's resume database. [ID:6819]

Cumming Cockburn Limited
Suite 200, 9133 Leslie Street, Richmond Hill, ON, L4B 4N1, Canada;
905-763-2322, fax 905-763-9983, engineering@cclconsultants.com, www.cclconsultants.com

MID-SIZED ENGINEERING CONSULTING FIRM: Construction, Energy Resources, Engineering, Environment, Project Management, Water Resources

Cumming Cockburn Ltd. offers a wide range of professional engineering consulting services in such fields as municipal engineering, transportation engineering, land development, community planning, water resources, environmental studies, renewable energy, bridges, marine structures and coastal engineering, and drinking water protection. Typical projects include small hydro projects in Zimbabwe; the Philippines and Costa Rica; a bridge in Kenya; an aircraft maintenance complex in Antigua; a cruise ship berth in Dominica; feeder roads and jetties in St. Vincent; storage reservoir rehabilitation in Trinidad; a storm water management master plan in Barbados and a marina in Florida.

The firm has five staff working abroad and 130 staff in Canada. It has two offices in Florida that can be emailed to ccl@icanect.net. The company recruits professional personnel with language skills, flexibility and personality. The firm also maintains a data bank for resumes. Job listings are regularly posted on its Web site. [ID:6652]

CYME International Inc.

Suite 104, 1485 Roberval, St. Bruno, QC, J3V 3P8, Canada;
450-461-3655, fax 450-461-0966, info@cyme.com, www.cyme.com ▭*Fr*▭*Sp*

LARGE HIGH TECHNOLOGY FIRM: Computer Systems, Energy Resources, Engineering, Information Technologies, Training and Technology Transfer

CYME International Inc. is a respected worldwide supplier of high-quality, PC-based power engineering software designed for an international market. The company's software has been selected by a large number of electric utilities, industrial organizations, consultants, and research or teaching institutions as their standard for power engineering simulation purposes. More than 5,000 copies of the programs are being used in 105 countries around the world. The company has organized training sessions in North America, Europe, South America, Asia, Africa, the Middle East and Australia.

CYME has a staff of 40 engineers and computer specialists, with three holding PhDs in electrical engineering. A careers page with employment opportunities may be found on the company's Web site. CYME is currently seeking electrical engineers. Desirable additional qualifications include writing and speaking abilities in languages other than English. [ID:6776]

DALSA Corporation

605 McMurray Road, Waterloo, ON, N2V 2E9, Canada;
519-886-6000, fax 519-886-8023, Sales.Americas@dalsa.com, www.dalsa.com

---

LARGE HIGH TECHNOLOGY FIRM: Advanced Technology, Engineering, Manufacturing, Marketing, Quality Assurance, Research and Development, Science and Technology, Technical Assistance

The DALSA Corporation is an international high-performance semiconductor and electronics company that designs, develops, manufactures and markets digital imaging products and solutions, in addition to providing semiconductor products and services. DALSA's core competencies are in specialized integrated circuit and electronics technology and highly engineered semiconductor wafer processing. Products and services include image sensor components; electronic digital cameras, and semiconductor wafer foundry services for use in MEMS, high-voltage semi-conductors, image sensors and mixed-signal CMOS chips. DALSA is a public company listed on the Toronto Stock Exchange under the symbol DSA. Based in Waterloo, Ontario, the company has operations in Bromont, Quebec; Colorado Springs, Colorodo; Tucson, Arizona; Eindhoven, the Netherlands; Munich, Germany and Tokyo, Japan.

DALSA employs approximately 750 people. A careers page with employment opportunities may be found on the company's Web site. [ID:6829]

DataMirror Corporation

Suite 1100, 3100 Steeles Ave. E., Markham, ON, L3R 8T3, Canada;
905-415-0310, fax 905-415-0340, info@datamirror.com, www.datamirror.com

---

LARGE HIGH TECHNOLOGY FIRM: Administration (General), Computer Systems, Human Resources, Information Technologies, Technical Assistance

DataMirror Corporation is a leading provider of live on-demand data integration and protection solutions, and gives companies the power to manage, monitor and protect their corporate data in real time. The company's solutions help customers from around the world easily and cost effectively capture, transform and flow data throughout the enterprise. Approximately 1,800 companies have used DataMirror solutions, including FedEx Ground, GMAC, Tiffany & Co., Union Pacific Railroad, the French Navy, as well as many others. It has offices around the world including the United Kingdom, France, Germany, Hong Kong, the United States and Belgium.

DataMirror employs 305 people around the world. A careers page with Canadian, American, international and new graduate job postings may be found on the company's Web site. DataMirror recruits students from various universities and colleges to participate in cooperative teams and internship opportunities at the company. The company suggests that interested applicants visit their Web site for information on specific internships and co-op placements or contact the human resources department by e-mail at hr@datamirror.com. [ID:6800]

Delcan International Corporation

133 Wynford Drive, Toronto, ON, M3C 1K1, Canada;
416-441-4111, fax 416-441-4131, info@delcan.com, www.delcan.com

LARGE ENGINEERING FIRM: Architecture and Planning, Business Development, Construction, Consulting, Engineering, Environment, Global Communications, Information Technologies, Manufacturing, Project Management, Systems Engineering, Technical Assistance, Transportation, Waster Water Management, Water Supply

Delcan International is an international company engaged in three main fields: the management of major projects; information technology services and systems integration; and civil engineering and architecture. The organization is majority owned and managed by its employees. Delcan engages in program and project management, consulting, contracting, design-build, privatization and equity investments in projects. Delcan operates in the areas of transportation systems, information technology, information technology services, communications, highways, municipal roads and transit, water supply and sewage treatment, manufacturing facilities, as well as commercial and residential developments. Delcan has undertaken projects in Europe, Africa, Asia, Latin America and the Caribbean. Their offices are located in most major cities across Canada and in the US, Mexico, Ethiopia, Hong Kong, Malawi, Taiwan, Venezuela, Barbados, El Salvador, Israel, Greece and Turkey.

Delcan has 70 overseas staff and 20 Canadian staff who have international responsibilities. Candidates require a bachelor's degree in engineering, economics or management, and at least five years of experience in their area of expertise. International work experience is an asset and in some cases is absolutely necessary. Knowledge of Spanish or another language is an asset, especially the local language in the area of work. Demonstrated ability to adapt to local conditions and work with local people is also an asset. Delcan International posts employment opportunities on its Web site and maintains a data bank for resumes. [ID:6653]

Deloitte & Touche

P.O. Box 8, Suite 1200, 2 Queen Street E., Toronto, ON, M5C 3G7,
Canada; 416-874-3874, fax 416-874-3888, www.deloitte.ca ▢ℱ𝓇

LARGE FINANCIAL SERVICES FIRM: Accounting, Banking and Financial Services,
Business/Banking/Trade, Consulting

Deloitte & Touche is Canada's leading professional services firm, which provides audit, tax, financial advisory services and consulting through 47 locations across Canada and in over 140 countries worldwide. Deloitte & Touche LLP operates in Quebec as Samson Belair/Deloitte & Touche s.e.n.c.r.l. "Deloitte" refers to Deloitte & Touche LLP and affiliated entities. The firm is the only professional services firm to be named in "The Globe and Mail's Report on Business Magazine's" annual ranking as top employer for two consecutive years. Deloitte & Touche has professionals working in Africa, Asia, Europe, Latin America, the Middle East and North America.

The firm offers employment opportunities to experienced professionals, students and new graduates. Those interested in the firm may read through various postings and can apply on-line using the firm's application profile creator, which takes 15 to 30 minutes to complete. [ID:6585]

The Delphi Group

428 Gilmour Street, Ottawa, ON, K2P 0R8, Canada;
613-562-2005, fax 613-562-2008, www.delphi.ca ▢ℱ𝓇▢𝒮𝓅

MID-SIZED ENVIRONMENTAL CONSULTING FIRM: Development Assistance, Energy Resources, Environment, Policy Development, Project Management

The Delphi Group is a leading strategic consultancy to business leaders and policy-makers for the environment and clean energy sectors. The company assists private companies, governments and organizations with creative solutions to manage risk and the process of complex change and move toward a more competitive and sustainable future. It is engaged in policy and project implementation, the development and financing of technological initiatives and the promotion of international development objectives. Their project experience spans most regions of the world and virtually every sub-sector of the environment and clean energy markets. It has completed over 400 projects and has experience in Argentina, China, Egypt, Mexico, the Americas and India. [ID:6763]

Dessau-Soprin International Inc.

Suite 600, 1060, rue University, Montreal, QC, H3B 4V4, Canada; 514-281-1033, fax 450-875-9193, montreal@dessausoprin.com, www.dessausoprin.com ☐ *Fr* ☐ *Sp*

LARGE ENGINEERING FIRM: Administration (General), Business Development, Construction, Consulting, Development Assistance, Economics, Engineering, Environment, Fisheries, Gender and Development, Power Generation/Transmission/Distribution, Project Management, Quality Assurance, Technical Assistance, Urban Development, Waste Water Management, Water Supply

Dessau-Soprin International Inc. is a Canadian engineering company that is active in both national and international markets. The company has positioned itself in the industrial sector in the areas of process and services. Dessau-Soprin carries out projects in the fields of rural electrification, road rehabilitation, access to telecommunications, water supply and economic development, and has been active in the international market since the early 1970s in more than 30 countries around the world. For example, the company has worked in Peru, Venezuela, the Dominican Republic, China, the Caribbean, Burkina Faso, Thailand, Senegal, Niger, Algeria and Morocco. The company also has offices in the US (Florida), Peru and the Dominican Republic, and provides services in French, English, Spanish and Chinese.

Dessau-Soprin has a staff of 1,260 professional engineers, scientists and specialists in various sectors such as energy, transportation, environment, municipal engineering, urban planning, building engineering, telecommunications, as well as construction, administration and project management. For the most part, the company hires engineers with past overseas experience. Other qualifications include specific expertise in areas such as environmental planning, urban planning, economics, computers/systems and a good knowledge of French, English and Spanish. The company posts career opportunities on its Web site and maintains a data bank for resumes. [ID:6654]

Development Partnerships (The Devpar Group)

158 Armour Court, Cobourg, ON, K9A 4S6, Canada; 905-373-7214, fax 905-377-8986, clientservices@devpar.com, www.devpar.com

MID-SIZED GENERAL CONSULTING FIRM: Banking and Financial Services, Business Development, Community Development, Consulting, Development Assistance, Economics, Institution Building, Media/Communications, Micro-enterprises, Policy Development, Project Management, Technical Assistance

Development Partnerships (The Devpar Group) is an association of consulting firms working together to provide technical assistance in the conduct of projects in developing countries. The Devpar Group's focus is on development and improving the general welfare of people living in emerging, transitional and developing countries. The Devpar Group currently consists of three member firms representing Canada, the United Kingdom and the United States. It includes networked consulting firms and non-governmental organizations (NGOs) with which member firms work in partnership on projects. It also includes a number of local firms in developing countries that work closely with member firms to provide required inputs. The Devpar Group's areas of specialization include financial and capital market reform, public sector reform and governance, private sector development, regulatory and communications development, and program and project support services. Major clients include the World Bank, the Asian Development Bank, the United Nations Development Programme (UNDP), European Commission, the Canadian International Development Agency (CIDA), Swedish International Development and Cooperation Agency, among others. The Devpar Group has completed projects for countries in the Caribbean, Africa, Asia and Europe, and employs approximately 10 people. [ID:6806]

Diamond and Schmitt Architects Incorporated

Suite 600, 2 Berkeley Street, Toronto, ON, M5A 2W3, Canada;
416-862-8800, fax 416-862-5508, info@dsai.ca, www.dsai.ca

LARGE ARCHITECTURE AND PLANNING FIRM: Architecture and Planning, Urban Development

Diamond and Schmitt Architects Incorporated is an architectural firm whose services include architecture, urban planning, building conservation and interior design. The firm has received national and international design recognition with over 90 design awards. It has completed projects in Canada, Cuba, the Czech Republic, England, France, Israel, Malaysia, China, the US and the West Indies. The firm is comprised of 14 principals and includes 86 registered architects/university graduates, two urban planners and a support staff of 18, for a total of 120 employees. [ID:6833]

DiamondWorks Ltd.

4th Floor, 1311 Howe Street, Vancouver, BC, V6Z 2P3, Canada;
604-691-1793, fax 604-691-1794, info@diamondworks.com, www.diamondworks.com

LARGE MINING FIRM: Adult Training, Community Development, Energy Resources, Exploration and Development, Gold and Metals Production, Logistics, Project Management, Sustainable Development

DiamondWorks Ltd., the successor to Carson Gold, is a Canadian-based mining and mineral exploration and development group. The company is also active in the oil, gas and other supply industries in Africa. DiamondWorks' business is focused in three principal areas operating in an African context: mining and mineral projects, energy supply and logistics. The main countries that the company is focused on include Sierra Leone, Angola, Central African Republic, Zambia, Malawi, Kenya, Zimbabwe, Guinea and the Democratic Republic of Congo. DiamondWorks also has offices in Canada, the United Kingdom and South Africa. [ID:6704]

Dillon Consulting Limited

800 - 235 Yorkland Blvd., Toronto, ON, M2J 4Y8, Canada; 416-229-4646, fax 416-226-1707, www.dillon.ca

LARGE GENERAL CONSULTING FIRM: Architecture and Planning, Community Development, Development Assistance, Energy Resources, Engineering, Environment, Geophysics, Management Information Systems, Medical Health, Project Management, Sustainable Development, Transportation, Waste Water Management, Water Resources

Dillon Consulting Limited is a Canadian, employee-owned professional consultancy which provides service to government and the private sector in four major areas of business: infrastructure, environment, facilities planning and design, and community planning and development. Dillon has provided service in 40 countries in the Americas, Asia, Africa, Europe and the Caribbean. The firm is ethnically diverse and the combined staff of the company is fluent in 30 languages. In Canada, Dillon provides service in French and English. Typical international projects have a focus on roads and bridges, water, waste management, energy, environmental management, community planning, and development and institutional strengthening.

Dillon has 500 staff members with skills in over 30 distinct disciplines including professional engineers, architects, planners, economists, hydrologists, and physical and social scientists. Most employment opportunities offer the flexibility of working at one or several locations within a region. Candidates should have an accredited degree and technical experience in environmental engineering, planning, infrastructure or transportation; prior experience working overseas; cross-cultural sensitivity and good communication skills. Foreign language capability is an asset. Dillon has an employment opportunities page and maintains a data bank for resumes. [ID:6666]

Dipix Technologies Inc.

1051 Baxter Road, Ottawa, ON, K2C 3P2, Canada;
613-596-4942, fax 613-596-4914, info@dipix.com, www.dipix.com

LARGE HIGH TECHNOLOGY FIRM: Computer Systems, Customer Services, Engineering, Technical
Assistance, Training and Technology Transfer

Dipix Technologies Inc. is the leader in the design of high-speed, three-dimensional and two-dimensional inspection systems for on-line inspection of discrete processed food products. The company's machine-vision inspection systems are uniquely engineered to integrate leading-edge optical and electronic hardware, sophisticated industrial software and mechanical handling. The systems detect quality problems and trends before they are visible to human inspectors, giving plant operators the essential information to improve plant yield and quality of product delivered to their customers. The company provides full services to customers, including planning, equipment, commissioning, training and support. Dipix has successfully installed its systems with many of the world's leading bakers such as Nabisco, Keebler, Kellogg's and McDonald's, as well as many others. The company has completed projects for Algeria, Belgium, China, Denmark, Finland, France, Germany, Iceland, Iran, Israel, Japan, South Korea, Luxembourg, the Netherlands, Norway, Sweden, Taiwan, the United Kingdom and the United States. It also has distributors in the United Kingdom and Australia.

The company has approximately 42 employees. A careers page with employment opportunities can be found on Dipix's Web site. Interested candidates may also e-mail their resumes to careers@dipix.com. [ID:6771]

DPRA Canada

Suite 300, 7501 Keele Street, Concord, ON, L4K 1Y2, Canada;
905-660-1060, fax 905-660-7812, ier@dpra.com, www.dpra.com

LARGE ENVIRONMENTAL CONSULTING FIRM: Consulting, Environment, Information Technologies,
Institution Building, Management, Organization Development, Policy Development, Project Management,
Research, Social Policy, Systems Engineering, Technical Assistance, Training and Education, Waste Water
Management

DPRA Canada is an environmental consulting firm whose staff have training and consulting services experience in such diverse areas as environmental planning and assessment, socio-economic impact assessment, organizational analysis and management studies, strategic planning, public consulting services, program evaluation and planning for the needs of special populations, including Aboriginals and older adults. The firm's services have been retained by governments, Crown corporations, private organizations and community groups. Clients of the firm have included the United Nations Development Programme (UNDP), the World Bank, Canadian National Railway, International Minerals and Chemicals and De Beers Canada Mining. During the last two decades, DPRA has been active in international projects spanning the continents of North America, South America and Asia. Its fields of international activity have included policy development, institutional strengthening, capacity building, strategic planning, environmental/natural resource management, management of hazardous and solid wastes, public consultation, and workshop facilitation and training on a wide variety of social and environmental topics. The company has become a specialist in the design, development and implementation of international environmental projects and has extensive knowledge about the procurement of funding and technical collaboration for projects in developing countries. DPRA has wide-ranging international project experience in Nepal, Mexico, the United States, India, Bangladesh, Russia, Guyana, Jamaica, Indonesia and the Philippines.

DPRA employs approximately 25 people. A careers page with employment opportunities can be found on the company's Web site. Positions that DPRA frequently recruits for include research assistants, policy analysts, programmers, programmer/analysts and systems analysts. Individuals hired for these jobs help the company to provide analytical, technical and management services to support a wide range of clients in the public and private sectors. [ID:6820]

Duerden & Keane Consultants Inc.

26 Forest Road, Dartmouth, NS, B3A 2M3, Canada;
902-435-7562, fax 902-484-7639, www.duerdenandkeane.com

SMALL ENVIRONMENTAL CONSULTING FIRM: Consulting, Education, Engineering, Environment, Project Management, Science and Technology, Training and Technology Transfer

Duerden and Keane Consultants Inc. is an environmental management consulting company which has been providing consulting, training, and hazardous waste management services across Canada and around the world since 1994. The company specializes in environmental management systems, site assessments, training and education, environmental emergency and hazardous waste management. It has undertaken projects throughout the world, including China, Russia, the Caribbean, Bermuda and India. Duerden and Keane has a multidisciplinary staff including those with backgrounds in engineering, chemistry and biology. [ID:6777]

E.T. Jackson & Associates Ltd.

Suite 100, 858 Bank Street, Ottawa, ON, K1S 3W3, Canada;
613-230-5221, fax 613-230-0639, etjackson@etjackson.com, www.etjackson.com 💻 𝐹𝑟

MID-SIZED MANAGEMENT CONSULTING FIRM: Accounting, Administration (General), Adult Training, Advocacy, Agriculture, Business Development, Business/Banking/Trade, Community Development, Consulting, Development Assistance, Economics, Exchange Programs, Fundraising, Gender and Development, Human Resources, Human Rights, Humanitarian Relief, Micro-enterprises, Project Management, Technical Assistance, Volunteer

E.T. Jackson & Associates Ltd. is a management consulting firm, specializing in project management, evaluation and planning, public policy, education, governance and corporate social responsibility, as well as human resource development. The firm's activities range from stand-alone grassroots projects to sector-wide reform programs and works to help deliver efficient services, build institutional capacity and to improve policy. E.T. Jackson's goal is to work with governments, non-governmental organizations, educational and research institutions, and the private sector to reduce poverty and enhance the quality of life among marginalized populations. The firm has planned, operated, implemented, monitored and evaluated more than $2.5 billion worth of development interventions throughout Asia, Africa, the Americas and Eastern Europe, and operates offices in Bangladesh, Ghana and Vietnam.

E.T. Jackson employs 15 professionals. Interested candidates should have experience and skills in the firm's core lines of business: microfinance, local governance, social development, performance review and gender equality. The firm also offers a young professionals program which seeks to place young development professionals, especially recent graduates in field interventions in developing countries, to contribute to project implementation and to learn new skills and knowledge. Experience in South and Southeast Asia, West and southern Africa, Latin America, the Caribbean, and Central and Eastern Europe is desirable. E.T. Jackson & Associates maintains a data bank for resumes and a Web site that contains information about the company's activities. [ID:6656]

Eaton International Consulting Inc. (EIC)

Box 21148, 665 8th Street S.W., Calgary, AB, T2P 4H5,
Canada; 403-244-9015, info@eatonintl.com, www.eatonintl.com

SMALL GENERAL CONSULTING FIRM: Consulting, Education, Intercultural Briefings, Language Training, Marketing, Media/Communications, Training and Education

Eaton International Consulting Inc. (EIC) provides high-level expertise in educational consulting, language program marketing and cross-cultural education and training. The company also offers communications services. It serves both local and international clients and has worked with educational institutions, as well as corporate and non-profit clients. EIC employs a strong network of approximately 10 professionals in its day-to-day operations. [ID:6799]

EBA Engineering Consultants Ltd.

14940 - 123 Ave., Edmonton, AB, T5V 1B4, Canada;
780-451-2121, fax 780-454-5688, info@eba.ca, www.eba.ca

LARGE ENGINEERING CONSULTING FIRM: Administration (General), Agriculture, Air Transportation, Consulting, Engineering, Environment, Forestry, Geomatics, Mining, Project Management, Science and Technology, Transportation

EBA Engineering Consultants Ltd. provides a broad range of engineering and scientific consulting services nationally and internationally. Clients are served from 15 offices in Western and Northern Canada and the company's specializations include agricultural services, airport services, arctic engineering, design-build services, environmental services, First Nations services, forestry services, geotechnical engineering, GIS services, infrastructure services, materials engineering, mining services and transportation services. The company primarily serves the natural resources, urban development, transportation and environmental sectors. It has completed projects in Norway, the United States, Russia, Sweden, the United Kingdom, Denmark, Finland, Iceland and Japan.

EBA Engineering Consultants employs approximately 450 engineers, technologists and support staff. A careers page with employment opportunities may be found on the company's Web site. [ID:6818]

Econoler International

Office 200, 160 St-Paul Street, Quebec, QC, G1K 3W1, Canada;
418-692-2592, fax 418-692-4899, info@econolerint.com, www.econolerint.com 💻 *Fr* 💻 *Sp*

MID-SIZED ENERGY RESOURCES FIRM: Administration (General), Energy Resources, Engineering, Environment

Econoler International is a Canadian company specializing in energy efficiency, renewable energy, clean energy production, energy service companies (ESCO) and Kyoto mechanisms. It is one of the first energy service companies in the world. The company has implemented over 3,000 projects in more than 40 countries and its expertise is now internationally recognized. Econoler has completed projects in North America, South America, Europe, Africa, the Middle East and Asia. A subsidiary office for the company can be found in Tunisia, as well as project offices in India and Croatia and a representative office in Washington, DC. A careers page with postings by sector, including engineering, development and administration, can be found on their Web site. [ID:6631]

Econolynx International Ltd.

7 Briggs Ave., Ottawa, ON, K2E 6W2, Canada; 613-723-8698, fax 613-723-2641, www.econolynx.com

SMALL GENERAL CONSULTING FIRM: Accounting, Agriculture, Business Development, Consulting, Economics, Environment, Fisheries, Forestry, Gender and Development, Human Resources, Human Rights, Project Management, Telecommunications, Trade and Investment, Water Resources

Econolynx International is a Canadian company specializing in economic development, international trade, agri-industry research, program management and management systems. The company has over two decades of experience in the analysis of issues concerning international marketing, industrial development, regional planning, economic development, transportation and related problems. Recent assignments and studies include business opportunities in Poland, case studies of seven agricultural subsectors in eight Latin American countries, worldwide fisheries and marketing studies of Western Europe, Eastern Europe, the United States, South America, Japan, Australia and Southeast Asia.

Econolynx has a staff of eight. Fact-finding missions are sent abroad to support analysis and local consultants are hired on a subcontract basis as needs arise. Applicants should have development experience and/or a degree in economics. Language skills are an asset. Econolynx maintains a data bank for resumes. [ID:6533]

Econotec Inc. Consultants

5185 St-Laurent Blvd., Montreal, QC, H2T 1R9, Canada; 514-274-0106, fax 514-272-4480

MID-SIZED GENERAL CONSULTING FIRM: Consulting, Economics, Energy Resources, Gender and Development

Econotec Inc. Consultants is a mid-sized consulting firm specializing in development planning and economics, program and project monitoring and evaluation and institutional development. Sectors of experience include macroeconomic policy, energy, industrial development, state-owned enterprises and agriculture. [ID:6534]

EllisDon Corporation

Suite 800, 89 Queensway Ave. W., Mississauga, ON, L5B 2V2,
Canada; 905-896-8900, fax 905-896-8911, www.ellisdon.com

LARGE CONSTRUCTION FIRM: Construction, Project Management

The EllisDon Corporation is a leading, employee-owned, international construction company with over 530 full-time employees, completing more than $1 billion in industrial, commercial, institutional, civil and multi-unit residential construction annually. EllisDon also has the distinction of being Canada's most experienced builder of hospitals and related healthcare facilities with approximately $4 billion worth completed in recent years. EllisDon has successfully undertaken projects in Canada, the United States, Europe, the Middle East, Central America, the Caribbean, Malaysia and the former Soviet Union. The company is also working on projects in Greece for the 2004 Olympics. EllisDon's international work encompasses multiple market sectors. Their work in the Caribbean and Mexico has mainly been in the hotel and resort sector, however, EllisDon's expertise in healthcare facilities, sports facilities and office buildings has also been in demand. They provide project management, construction management, general contracting services and a variety of consulting services to international markets. Typically, EllisDon's international clients are seeking the high level of management expertise, the experience, the professionalism and the resources that EllisDon can bring to their projects.

EllisDon has a relationship with a few adult learning centres such as the Dufferin Peel Board Of Education's Adult Learning Centre. They take on co-op students who are looking for Canadian experience in order to gain a career in the Canadian construction industry. These placements can be up to 3 months long. In some cases, the student can be hired for full-time once the co-op term is complete. The human resources department has created a database where all potential resumes are stored and filed. This database contains both Canadian experience potentials as well as some with overseas experience. All of their career opportunities are posted on the EllisDon Web site and applicants can apply directly to a job posting or send their resume to the HR department. All of the hiring for EllisDon is done through the HR department. For the past three years, EllisDon has been named by "The Globe and Mail's Report on Business" as one of the 50 Best Employers in Canada, ranking an impressive sixth for 2004, as well as fourth for Best Senior Leadership, second for Best Career Opportunities and fifth for Best Workplace Resources. "The National Post" also named EllisDon for the second year in a row, one of the 50 Best Managed Companies in Canada. [ID:6597]

Enbridge Inc.

Suite 3000, Fifth Avenue Place, 425 - 1st Street S.W., Calgary, AB, T2P 3L8, Canada;
403-231-3900, fax 403-231-3920, webmaster@enbridge.com, www.enbridge.com

LARGE ENERGY RESOURCES FIRM: Energy Resources, Oil and Gas Distribution, Training and Technology Transfer

Enbridge Inc. (formerly known as IPL Energy) is a leading, publicly traded energy transportation and distribution company active in North America and internationally. The company operates in Canada and the United States and has the world's longest crude oil and liquids pipeline system. The company also has international opportunities and a growing involvement in the natural gas transmission and midstream businesses. Enbridge owns and operates Canada's largest natural gas distribution company and provides gas distribution services in the provinces of Ontario, Quebec and New Brunswick, as well as New York. Internationally, Enbridge has investments in the OCENSA crude oil pipeline in Colombia (24.7 per cent), which it operates, and in Compania Logistica de Hidrocarburos CLH (25 per cent), Spain's largest refined products transportation and storage business. Enbridge also offers a broad spectrum of proprietary pipeline operation technologies, including customized pipeline operator training, SCADA computer systems, operator qualification and technical support services. Over the past 30 years, Enbridge has completed over 500 consulting projects in over 30 countries around the world. In 2003, Enbridge's international business segment accounted for $72.3 million of the company's total $667.2 million in earnings.

Enbridge employs 4,000 people primarily in Canada, the United States and South America. The company posts job opportunities on its Web site and also has a student and recruitment process page, which provides tips and suggestions for success. Enbridge's campus recruiting strategy involves participation at career fairs, information sessions and other events. [ID:6701]

Ernst & Young
P.O. Box 251, Ernst & Young Tower, Toronto Dominion Centre, 222 Bay Street,
Toronto, ON, M5K 1J7, Canada; 416-864-1234, fax 416-864-1174, www.ey.com/ca ▭ *Fr*

LARGE MANAGEMENT CONSULTING FIRM: Accounting, Administration (General), Business Development, Business/Banking/Trade, Consulting, Logistics, Project Management, Technical Assistance

Ernst & Young LLP, a global leader in professional services, is committed to restoring the public's trust in professional services firms and in the quality of financial reporting. Its 103,000 people in more than 140 countries around the globe pursue the highest levels of integrity, quality and professionalism in providing clients with solutions based on financial, transactional and risk-management knowledge in Ernst & Young's core services of audit, tax and transaction advisory services. Ernst & Young refers to all the members of the global Ernst & Young organization.

Ernst & Young's culture is rooted in the belief that the firm succeeds when its people succeed. Ernst & Young hires both seasoned professionals and recent graduates and offers internships and co-op work terms. The firm has been named one of Canada's Top 100 Employers and has been listed as one of the 50 Best Employers in Canada. The company's Web site (for Canada, visit www.ey.com/ca, with links to international Ernst & Young offices) offers comprehensive information on both the firm and the work it does for clients. It also provides detailed information on what the company looks for when hiring (a background in accounting and business management is commonly required), the type of opportunities available, current job listings and the advantages enjoyed by people who work for Ernst & Young. Further information about Ernst & Young and its approach to a variety of business issues can be found at www.ey.com/perspectives. [ID:6595]

ESSA Technologies Ltd.
International Office, Suite 300, 1765 - 8th Ave. W., Vancouver, BC, V6J 5C6,
Canada; 604-733-2996, fax 604-733-4657, info@essa.com, www.essa.com

MID-SIZED ENVIRONMENTAL CONSULTING FIRM: Adult Training, Community Development, Computer Systems, Consulting, Development Education, Energy Resources, Environment, Fisheries, Forestry, Gender and Development, Project Management, Technical Assistance, Water Resources

ESSA Technologies Ltd. is an innovative Canadian company specializing in environmental consulting and decision support, and provides environmental consulting services and software solutions to industrial clients from around the world. The company's areas of expertise include fisheries and aquatic resource management, forestry and terrestrial resource management, environmental assessment, planning and management, as well as international development. The company has completed more than 1,300 projects in 33 countries worldwide and has three offices in Canada, as well as staff in Hanoi, Vietnam.

ESSA's professional staff of about 20 all have degrees in natural sciences, education, computing, engineering or social sciences. The company does post job opportunities on its Web site, as well as providing a broad range of information about the company. [ID:6598]

Eurasian Minerals Inc.

9th Floor, 570 Granville Street, Vancouver, BC, V6C 3P1, Canada;
604-689-1428, fax 604-682-3941, info@eurasianminerals.com, www.eurasianminerals.com

MID-SIZED METALS FIRM: Exploration and Development, Gold and Metals Production, Metals, Mining

Eurasian Minerals Inc. is a precious and base metals exploration company with locations in some of the world's most promising but under-explored frontier regions. The company is aggressively adding high-quality properties to its portfolios in Serbia and Turkey, located in the Tethyan metallogenic belt. In addition, the company has selected the Tien Shan metallogenic belt of Central Asia as highly prospective for the discovery of large, world class gold deposits. It has established a new office in the Kyrgyz Republic. [ID:6788]

EVS Consultants

195 Pemberton Ave., North Vancouver, BC, V7P 2R4, Canada;
604-986-4331, fax 604-662-8548, info@evsenvironment.com, www.evsenvironment.com

MID-SIZED ENVIRONMENTAL CONSULTING FIRM: Consulting, Environment, Fisheries, Forestry, Petrochemicals, Project Management, Technical Assistance, Water Resources

EVS Consultants provides clients with solutions to environmental problems, which often include developing technical criteria documents, strategic environmental planning, risk assessments, monitoring programs, environmental training, technology transfer and environmental toxicology. Services provided by the firm include consulting and advisory services, data collection, development, analysis and management, technical guidance documents and publications support. EVS has corporate offices in North Vancouver and Seattle, Washington, with project offices in Bangkok, Thailand and Jakarta, Indonesia, although their staff works on projects throughout North America, Australia, South America and Asia, addressing a wide range of environmental issues.

The firm has a staff of approximately 50, of which two work overseas and an additional 11 work in Canada and have primarily international responsibilities. Prospective applicants should have an MSc or PhD with practical multidisciplinary or specific experience in the environmental industry (particularly consulting). The firm also looks for candidates with technical backgrounds along with proven business development and project management skills. EVS does post employment opportunities on its Web site and maintains a data bank for resumes. [ID:6657]

Experco International

Suite 600, 150 Marchand Street, Drummondville, QC, J2C 4N1, Canada;
819-478-8191, fax 819-478-2994, expdrv@experco.com, www.experco.ca ⬜𝐹𝑟⬜𝑆𝑝

MID-SIZED ENGINEERING FIRM: Agriculture, Computer Systems, Construction, Consulting, Energy Resources, Engineering, Environment, Rural Development, Technical Assistance, Telecommunications, Transportation, Waste Water Management, Water Resources

Experco International, a subsidiary of Groupe HBA experts-conseils senc, has worked on international projects since 1972 and is known worldwide. The firm works in the fields of agriculture, rural development, transportation, environment, energy (electricity, gas), computerization and geomatic data processing, building and telecommunications, water supply and waste water treatment. International projects have been carried out in Africa (Mali, Rwanda, Burkina Faso, Senegal), Asia (Vietnam), Latin America (Colombia, Nicaragua, Honduras) and Eastern Europe (Romania). The firm currently employees over 300 people. Experco maintains a Web site that provides general information on the company and its range of activities. [ID:6600]

Fairmont Hotels & Resorts

P.O. Box 40, Toronto Dominion Centre, 100 Wellington Street W., Toronto, ON, M5K 1B7, Canada; 416-874-2600, fax 416-874-2601, pathfinder@fairmont.com, www.fairmont.com ⬜𝐹𝑟

LARGE CUSTOMER SERVICES FIRM: Administration (General), Customer Services, Management

Fairmont Hotels and Resorts (acquired by Canadian Pacific Hotels & Resorts in October, 1999) is a collection of world-class resorts and city centre hotels which enjoy unrivalled prominence in the communities in which they are located. Operating 43 properties throughout six countries, Fairmont is committed to providing guests with exceptional service in distinctive surroundings. Included in the hotel chain are such storied hotels as The Fairmont San Francisco, The Fairmont Banff Springs, Fairmont Le Chateau Frontenac and The Plaza. The company is headquartered in Toronto and is the largest hotel management company in North America. The hotel chain has locations throughout the United States, Canada, Bermuda, Barbados, Mexico and the United Arab Emirates.

An employment page with current employment opportunities posted for Canada, the United States, Mexico, Bermuda and Barbados can be found on the company's Web site. Fairmont is always seeking hospitality students and these students are invited to view the company's Student Work Experience Program Web site (SWEP) at www.fairmont.com/swep for more information. This program provides the opportunity to apply classroom learning and fine-tune skills in the day-to-day operations of the hotel chain. Every summer, hundreds of students are invited to participate in the program from May/June until the end of September. Various positions are available. Fairmont also offers a culinary apprenticeship program and employment for graduating students. Application instructions for SWEP are available on Fairmont's Web site. [ID:6562]

Falconbridge Ltd.
Suite 200, BCE Place, 181 Bay Street, Toronto, ON, M5J 2T3,
Canada; 416-982-7161, fax 416-982-7423, www.falconbridge.com

LARGE MINING FIRM: Computer Systems, Engineering, Human Resources, Marketing, Metals, Mining

Falconbridge is a leading producer of nickel, copper, cobalt and platinum group metals and is also one of the world's largest recyclers and processors of metal-bearing materials. The firm is the western world's second largest producer of primary nickel products and a significant producer of cobalt and copper. Falconbridge has operations in Canada, the Caribbean, South America, Africa, Australia, Asia, New Caledonia and Europe.

Founded in 1928, Falconbridge now employs 6,400 people in 13 countries. Employees work in engineering, geology, research, technology, finance, marketing, information systems and environmental roles. The company offers opportunities and specialized programs for recent graduates, including its innovative mining, metallurgical, electrical, mechanical and civil engineering development programs, and professional skills upgrading programs for designations and language training. Opportunities are available for engineering, as well as for professionals with science backgrounds in geology, process control, math or computer science. Those with backgrounds in finance, human resources, marketing or other key business areas are preferred. Falconbridge also posts job opportunities on its Web site and maintains a resume data bank. [ID:6601]

FEDNAV Group
Suite 3500, 1000 de la Gauchetiere ouest, Montreal, QC, H3B 4W5,
Canada; 514-878-6500, fax 514-878-6642, info@fednav.com, www.fednav.com 🖳 *Fr*

LARGE TRANSPORTATION SERVICES FIRM: Engineering, Law, Marine, Marine Engineering, Systems Engineering, Transportation

The FEDNAV Group has established itself as a leader in the international shipping business by combining innovative and practical solutions with technical and commercial experience. The company is Canada's largest ocean-going, dry-bulk, ship-owning and chartering group. Its primary activities are in the transportation of bulk and breakbulk cargoes on a worldwide basis. It is also engaged in the servicing of vessels and the handling of cargo through its terminals and by its agencies. The company's freight arm, Fednav International Ltd.'s fleet of about 70 owned and chartered ocean-going vessels, performs over 500 voyages and transports more than 12 million tons of cargo annually. The company operates a dedicated projects and business development unit that works closely with industrial partners in developing innovative and efficient solutions for the transportation of major bulk movements on a project basis. The FEDNAV Group has offices in

London, Tokyo, Antwerp, Hamburg, Brisbane, Rio de Janeiro and Singapore, as well as a number of local offices in Canada and the United States.

A careers page with employment opportunities can be found on the company's Web site. The company's projects and business development teams consist of maritime experts with engineering, design, legal, financial and operations backgrounds. [ID:6825]

Finning International Inc.
Suite 1000, 666 Burrard Street, Vancouver, BC, V6C 2X8,
Canada; 604-691-6444, fax 604-691-6440, www.finning.com

LARGE CONSTRUCTION FIRM: Construction, Customer Services, Information Technologies, Manufacturing, Merchandising

Finning International Inc. is a Canadian-based international corporation which sells, rents, finances and provides customer services for Caterpillar and complementary equipment. Finning's operations are located in Western Canada, the United Kingdom and South America (Argentina, Bolivia, Chile and Uruguay). Finning is one of the largest dealers in the world for products manufactured by Caterpillar Inc.

Finning employs more than 11,000 employees worldwide, including over 2,700 in Canada. The Finning Web site at www.finning.com provides a link to the company's Web sites for its Canadian and international operations. Typical positions include various levels of mechanics, field service technicians, sales and marketing representatives, and various finance and related head office functions. [ID:6695]

Fishery Products International (FPI)
P.O. Box 550, 70 O'Leary Ave., St. John's, NL, A1C 5L1, Canada;
709-570-0000, fax 709-570-0479, fpi@fpil.com, www.fpil.com

LARGE FOOD PROCESSING FIRM: Fisheries, Marketing

Fishery Products International (FPI) is an integrated seafood company engaged in harvesting, processing, global sourcing and marketing quality seafood products. Through their two business units, the Marketing and Value Added Group, and the Primary Group, they market value added and primary seafood to foodservice, retail and industrial customers throughout North America and internationally. The company has offices in England, Germany and China, and its activities extend from South America to the Far East, to the Arctic Circle, with suppliers in over 30 countries. FPI employs 3,400 people around the world and provides a careers page on its Web site with regular job postings. [ID:6703]

FORCE/Robak Associates Ltd.
115 Waggoners Lane, Fredericton, NB, E3B 2L4, Canada;
506-458-9676, fax 506-452-2141, ewr@fra.nb.ca, www.fra.nb.ca

SMALL FORESTRY CONSULTING FIRM: Consulting, Environment, Forestry, Information Technologies, Land Stewardship, Technical Assistance

FORCE/Robak Associates Ltd. is primarily engaged in the design, development, marketing and servicing of decision support technologies for the forestry and land management sectors. It has provided design, development and consultation services for everything from small information systems to large organization-wide forest management and business decision support systems. It has experience in Spain, India, Thailand and Canada, and employs two full-time people. [ID:6775]

Four Seasons Hotels Inc.
Human Resources, 1165 Leslie Street, Don Mills, ON, M3C 2K8, Canada; 416-449-1750,
fax 416-441-4341, jobs.corporateofficetoronto@fourseasons.com, www.fourseasons.com

LARGE CUSTOMER SERVICES FIRM: Administration (General), Customer Services, Marketing, Tourism

Four Seasons Hotels Inc. is the world's leading operator of luxury hotels and resorts. The company currently manages 61 properties in 29 countries primarily under the Four Seasons and

Regent brands, as well as offering a growing network of branded vacation ownership properties and residences. Four Seasons has hotels in North America, South America, the Middle East, Asia and Australia.

The company has approximately 21,000 employees. It is suggested that interested candidates visit the company's Web site to consult the human resources contacts list for each of their properties around the world, and to contact them directly regarding available positions, the application process and to answer any other questions. Currently, there are several opportunities for hospitality graduates, experienced managers and administration and service staff. [ID:6700]

Gardner Pinfold Consulting Economists Ltd.
1331 Brenton Street, Halifax, NS, B3J 2K5, Canada; 902-421-1720,
fax 902-422-5343, tpinfold@gardnerpinfold.ca, www.gardnerpinfold.ca

SMALL GENERAL CONSULTING FIRM: Consulting, Economics, Environment, Industrial Services, Management Consulting, Project Management

Gardner Pinfold Consulting is an independent, Halifax-based company. The general objective of the firm is to provide comprehensive professional services covering all aspects of economic consultancy. The firm specializes in assignments related to the economics of natural resources and industrial development and in the field of regional economics. Recent assignments have included cost-benefit analysis, program evaluation, economic impact assessment, forecasting, simulation modelling and advisory services in regulatory and judicial proceedings. Gardner is recognized as one of Canada's leading firms in terms of its analytical capabilities and experience related to the economics of natural resource development and management. It provides services to clients across Canada and internationally. The firm has offices in both Halifax and in Sechelt, BC, and employs approximately eight people. [ID:6835]

GCL Group Consulting
Suite 240, 3100 Cote-Vertu Blvd., Montreal, QC, H4R 2J8, Canada;
514-733-3000, fax 514-733-3439, gclgroup@gclgroup.com, www.gclgroup.com 💻 *Fr*

MID-SIZED MANAGEMENT CONSULTING FIRM: Computer Systems, Consulting, Customer Services, Human Resources, Management, Management Consulting, Management Information Systems, Management Training

The GCL Group is one of the leading management consulting firms in Canada and one of the largest in North America. The company is breaking new ground with the development of new computer products suited to customer needs. Services provided by the company include supply chain management, customer service, production planning, procurement, inventory control, warehousing, transportation, reverse logistics, cost management, information management and resource management. It has served many industry sectors, as well as clients in Mexico, the United Kingdom, Belgium, France, Singapore, China, Peru, the Caribbean, Argentina and Brazil.

The GCL Group employs approximately 10 people. A careers page with employment opportunities may be found on the company's Web site. [ID:6797]

Geac Computer Corporation Ltd.
Suite 300, 11 Allstate Parkway, Markham, ON, L3R 9T8, Canada;
905-475-0525, fax 905-475-3847, info@geac.com, www.geac.com

LARGE HIGH TECHNOLOGY FIRM: Computer Systems, Customer Services, Information Technologies, Manufacturing, Marketing, Project Management, Research and Development, Software Development

Geac Computer Corporation Ltd. is a global enterprise software company for business performance management, providing customers worldwide with the core financial and operational solutions and services to improve their business performance in real time. The company's solutions include cross-industry transaction processing applications for financial administration, and human resource functions and enterprise resource planning (ERP) applications for manufacturing, distribution and supply chain management. Geac also provides industry-specific applications to real estate, restaurant, property management and construction marketplaces, as well as a wide range of applications for libraries, local government administration and public safety agencies. Approximately 18,000 organizations around the world have employed the company's software and solutions. Geac has 55 locations worldwide, including Canada, the United States, Brazil, Europe, Asia and Australia.

Geac employs 2,400 people internationally. Interested applicants can search for employment opportunities on the company's Web site and apply on-line. [ID:6696]

Gender Equality Incorporated

P.O. Box 33, 422 Parliament Street, Toronto, ON, M5A 4N8, Canada;
416-928-0098, fax 416-928-2749, info@genderequality.ca, www.genderequality.ca

MID-SIZED GENERAL CONSULTING FIRM: Adult Training, Advocacy, Agriculture, Development Assistance, Education, Gender and Development, Human Resources, Institution Building, Intercultural Briefings, Medical Health, Photo Mapping, Policy Dialogue, Project Management, Social Justice and Development, Social Policy, Telecommunications, Training and Education, Transportation, Water Resources

Gender Equality Incorporated provides services to promote equality and success across gender and cultures. Services provided by the company include gender and social analysis, project submission, institutional analysis, gender and cross-cultural trainings, gender strategies and gender mainstreaming projects. The company specializes in planning and policy development, gender and social issues, international development, adult education and cross-cultural training. It has experience in working with the Canadian International Development Agency (CIDA) and numerous other organizations. Gender Equality has completed projects in Afghanistan, Brazil, Canada, Egypt, Jordan, Malawi, Peru, Thailand and the Philippines.

Gender Equality employs approximately 30 people. Team members have broad-ranging experience in gender and development work. Several languages are spoken by team members, including Portuguese, German, French, Afrikaans, Bengali, Dutch, Italian and Japanese, as well as other languages. [ID:6807]

General Woods and Veneers Consultants International Ltd.

1220 Marie Victorin Blvd., Longueuil, QC, J4G 2H9, Canada;
450-671-4957, fax 450-674-3494, gwvc@gwv.com, www.gwv.com ⌨Fr

LARGE FORESTRY CONSULTING FIRM: Consulting, Forestry, Manufacturing, Technical Assistance

General Woods and Veneers Consultants International Ltd. Is a worldwide organization designed to provide the most complete line of veneer, lumber and log products to an international marketplace. The company is involved in the following principal operations: manufacturing of veneers, distribution and sales, and the drying of lumber. Countries around the world have used the company and its offices can be found in Canada, the United States, China, the Czech Republic, Germany, Hungary, Japan, Myanmar, the Philippines, Russia, Switzerland and Vietnam.

General Woods and Veneers Consultants employs 250 people. Candidates should have an engineering degree in forestry with expertise in forest development programs, wood processing, wood product marketing, silviculture and reforestation. Consultants should have overseas experience. The firm maintains a data bank for resumes. [ID:6602]

Genivar

4th Floor, 5858 Côte-des-Neiges Road, Montreal, QC, H3S 1Z1,
Canada; 514-340-0046, fax 514-340-1337, www.genivar.com ⌨Fr⌨Sp

LARGE ENGINEERING CONSULTING FIRM: Aerial Surveys, Banking and Financial Services, Business Development, Construction, Engineering, Medical Health, Project Management

Genivar is a leader in global solutions for engineering-construction. It has experience in studies, engineering and aerial imagery, project and construction management, construction and strategic consulting. It also offers services in the development and financing of projects. Genivar carries out projects according to a variety of formulas including design construction, turnkey packages, engineering, procurement, construction, management, public-private partnerships, rental operation and built-own-operate-transfer. It has completed projects in El Salvador, Mexico,

Trinidad and Tobago, as well as in Haiti. The company has 20 offices across Quebec and Ontario. Genivar employs approximately 850 people. A careers page with employment opportunities may be found on the company's Web site. [ID:6557]

Geophysics GPR International Inc.

2545 DeLorimier Street, Longueuil, QC, J4K 3P7, Canada;
450-679-2400, fax 514-521-4128, gprmtl@videotron.ca, www.geophysicsgpr.com

MID-SIZED EARTH SCIENCES FIRM: Construction, Consulting, Energy Resources, Engineering, Geophysics, Oil and Gas Exploration, Water Resources

Geophysics GPR International Inc. is a company at the leading edge of technology with 30 years of experience. The company offers a complete range of specialized services in geophysics to consultants, general contractors, governments and their agencies, oil and gas exploration companies and to the mining industry worldwide. Geophysics GPR combines geophysics and geology and applies them to civil engineering. Branches of the company can be found in Zimbabwe with associate branches located in Peru, Morocco, Burkina Faso, Côte d'Ivoire and Ghana. The company has also completed several projects in India, Ghana, Malawi, the United States, Indonesia, Brazil, Tunisia, Madagascar, Guatemala, Panama, Bolivia, Nepal, Thailand, Guinea, Costa Rica, Sudan and Senegal.

Geophysics GPR has 30 employees. Candidates should have educational qualifications and work experience in geology or geophysics and international experience. Career opportunities as well as a resume data bank can be found on the company's Web site. The Web site provides a wide range of useful information on the geophysical services they provide and the techniques they use, as well as business opportunities and business links. [ID:6603]

Geostar Metals Inc.

1255 West Pender Street, Vancouver, BC, V6E 2V1, Canada;
604-669-4899, fax 604-685-2345, info@geostarmetals.com, www.geostarmetals.com

LARGE MINING FIRM: Advanced Technology, Exploration and Development, Mineral Resources

Geostar Metals Inc. (formerly Stellar Metals Inc.) is a junior resource company focused on the application of leading edge extraction technology developed to process nickel laterite. The intent is to apply such advanced technology to several laterite properties on which substantial exploration has already established the presence of a suitable resource. The objective of combining new technology with an appropriate laterite deposit is to direct Geostar toward becoming an integrated, low-cost nickel producer. The company is in the process of assembling properties with known deposits in the Philippines, where it has already developed extensive exploration experience. [ID:6635]

Glencairn Gold Corp.

Suite 500, 6 Adelaide Street E., Toronto, ON, M5C 1H6, Canada;
416-860-0919, fax 416-367-0182, info@glencairngold.com, www.glencairngold.com

LARGE MINING FIRM: Exploration and Development, Mineral Resources

Glencairn Gold Corp. is a gold producer with one operating gold mine, a second project under construction (expected to double the company's current gold output), and a third property at the prefeasibility stage, as well as an excellent portfolio of exploration targets. Glencairn's Limon Mine in Nicaragua is scheduled to produce 53,000 ounces of gold in 2004 and 60,000 ounces in 2005. The company's fully permitted Bellavista gold project in Costa Rica is expected to begin operating at a rate of 60,000 ounces per year by the end of 2004. The Vogel deposit in Timmins, Ontario, with a 261,100 ounces measured and indicated resource and a further 379,800 ounces inferred resource, is at the prefeasibility stage. The company's focus is on developing advanced gold projects in the Americas.

Glencairn employs approximately 500 people, mostly where their operations are located. The company generally employs a number of tradespeople and general office staff, as well as experienced miners. [ID:6521]

Golder Associates Ltd.

2390 Argentia Road, Mississauga, ON, L5N 5Z7, Canada;
905-567-4444, fax 905-567-6561, golder_hr@golder.com, www.golder.com ⌨Fr

LARGE ENGINEERING CONSULTING FIRM: Consulting, Energy Resources, Engineering, Environment, Fisheries, Forestry, Petrochemicals, Project Management, Water Resources

Golder Associates Ltd. is a premier global group of consulting companies specializing in ground engineering and environmental science. The firm has completed assignments in over 140 countries in the agricultural, forestry, finance, insurance, real estate, legal, land development, manufacturing, mining, oil and gas, power, transportation, waste management and water resource sectors. Golder has over 80 offices in 22 countries throughout Africa, Asia, Australia, Canada, South America and the United States.

Currently, Golder Associates has 3,000 employees worldwide. The company has approximately 800 staff in Canada. All professionals may be called on for international projects. Three-quarters of the staff have an advanced degree in engineering or science. Preferred candidates have a relevant post-graduate degree, in addition to five to 10 years experience in geotechnical engineering, hydrogeology or a related scientific field. Golder Associates occasionally considers applications for internships. Except for senior-level appointments, overseas experience is not essential. The company posts employment opportunities by region on its Web site and maintains a data bank for resumes. [ID:6604]

Graybridge International Consulting Inc.

76 Hôtel-de-Ville Street, Gatineau, QC, J8X 2E2, Canada; 819-776-2262,
fax 819-776-6491, success@graybridge.ca, www.graybridgemalkam.com ⌨Fr

MID-SIZED INTERCULTURAL CONSULTING: Adult Training, Consulting, Intercultural Briefings, Management Consulting, Project Management

Graybridge International Consulting Inc. provides professional consulting services in a wide range of areas linked to international training and overseas management. The company specializes in design, delivery and coordination of cross-cultural and overseas effectiveness training, organizational development training, professional skills development training and international/domestic event coordination. Graybridge provides consulting services to most of the principal Canadian government departments representing Canada overseas. In addition, the company provides an extensive range of services to an assortment of private sector firms and educational institutions, operating both in Canada and abroad. It has also worked with a number of development assistance projects sponsored by the Canadian International Development Agency (CIDA). The company has worked on the CIDA Women in Development Advisory Program throughout Indonesia and has provided support to the Government Ministry for Women in Indonesia.

A careers page with job postings for both overseas assignments and opportunities within Canada can be found on Graybridge's Web site. The company is always looking for Canadians who have recently worked or lived overseas, as well as country nationals who are willing to share their experiences and up-to-date knowledge about political, social, business and day-to-day realities of a specific country. Graybridge's Web site provides links to very helpful resources to those interested in working abroad. (In June 2004, Graybridge was about to merge with Malkam Consultants Ltd. See the Malkam Consultants profile in this chapter.) [ID:6596]

Groupe Conseil UDA Inc. (UDA)

International Division, 426 Chemin des Patriotes, Saint-Charles-sur-Richelieu, QC,
J0H 2G0, Canada; 450-584-2207, fax 450-584-2523, uda@udainc.com, www.udainc.com ⌨Fr

SMALL FORESTRY CONSULTING FIRM: Agriculture, Consulting, Development Assistance, Engineering, Environment, Forestry, Law, Management, Project Management, Research and Development, Sustainable Development, Urban Development, Water Resources

Groupe Conseil UDA Inc. (UDA) is committed to the challenge of contributing to the fields of agronomy and agricultural engineering, in particular, in their application to agriculture, forestry and agro-forestry environment, and maintaining its reputation in these fields. The firm has a broad range of interests including earth, water, forestry, agriculture, environment, consulting, management, design, supervision, research and development, forestry and agricultural production, small-scale and large-scale industries, as well as all levels of government. UDA's activities include management of resources and agricultural works, environmental management of agricultural and peri-urban lands, as well as biomass management, treatment and recycling. The firm has been working with several Canadian and international development agencies as well as private and public organizations to assist with evaluating resources and projects by providing training and extension services in biomass management, and treatment to soil and water conservation engineering. The firm has worked in the following countries: Russia, Hungary, Ukraine, Pakistan, Uruguay, Haiti, Nigeria, Egypt, Morocco, Costa Rica, Sudan, Algeria, Peru, Rwanda, Germany, Belgium, France, Holland and Switzerland for agencies such as the Canadian International Development Agency (CIDA), Foreign Affairs Canada (FAC) and International Trade Canada (ITCan).

UDA has 25 employees. The firm's team is made up of engineers, agronomists, biologists, forest engineers, environmental specialists, agricultural and forestry technicians. When needed, the firm also looks to other specialists for assistance, such as sociologists, geographers, urban planners, hydrogeologists and lawyers. Most of UDA's professionals have experience in the farming or forestry industries. [ID:6545]

Groupe RSW Inc.
Suite 2600, 800 René Lévesque Blvd. W., Montreal, QC, H3B 1Z1, Canada;
514-878-2621, fax 514-397-0085, rsw@rswinc.com, www.rswinc.com ▢ *Fr* ▢ *Sp*

MID-SIZED ENGINEERING CONSULTING FIRM: Construction, Consulting, Energy Resources, Engineering, Environment, Mining, Project Management, Training and Education, Transportation, Urban Development, Water Resources

Groupe RSW is a firm of consulting engineers specializing in design, engineering, construction, environment, project management and training, applied to the energy, industrial, urban infrastructure, building, environment, transportation and mining sectors. The firm's professionals cover the fields of engineering (civil, geo-technical, mechanical, electrical and environmental), computer science, training and management. Fields of activity include energy, industrial, buildings, environment, mining, transportation and urban infrastructure. Groupe RSW has completed assignments in more than 40 countries and has current operations in Africa (Algeria, Senegal, Egypt, Nigeria), Central America (Mexico, Costa Rica, Guatemala) and Asia (India, Iran, Pakistan).

Groupe RSW employs 300 people. Candidates must have either an engineering degree, a technical or administrative certificate, as well as expertise in energy transmission systems and automation. The firm also looks for overseas experience, good health and an interest in working abroad. Employment opportunities can be found on the firm's Web site, as well as a data bank for resumes. [ID:6670]

Hatch
Sheridan Science & Technology Park, 2800 Speakman Drive,
Mississauga, ON, L5K 2R7, Canada; 905-855-7600, fax 905-855-8270, www.hatch.ca

LARGE ENGINEERING FIRM: Construction, Consulting, Energy Resources, Engineering, Environment, Information Technologies, Management, Metals, Mineral Handling, Project Management, Transportation

Hatch supplies expertise, studies and project implementation in construction management, business and process consulting, energy, engineering, environment, project management, transportation, metallurgy, mineral processing and information technology. The firm has offices in Africa, Australia, Canada, Europe, South America, Southeast Asia and the United States.

Hatch has more than 4,400 salaried staff members. The firm asks that those who plan on becoming an engineer (civil, mechanical, structural, chemical, electrical, metallurgical, mining or environmental), an MBA graduate or computer technologist to please contact them. They are also interested in students involved in university co-op programs. Employment opportunities can also be found on the firm's careers page on their Web site. [ID:6539]

Hatfield Consultants Ltd.
201 - 1571 Ave., West Vancouver, BC, V7V 1A6, Canada;
604-926-3261, fax 604-926-5389, hcl@hatfieldgroup.com, www.hatfieldgroup.com

MID-SIZED GENERAL CONSULTING FIRM: Environment, Fisheries, Geomatics, Institution Building, Training and Education

The Hatfield Consultants Ltd. provides a wide array of consulting services ranging from full-scale, multi-faceted environmental impact assessments (EIAs) and monitoring of industrial operations, to fisheries evaluation and management, aquaculture site assessment facility design and operation, GIS/remote sensing applications, land use/land cover mapping and planning, institutional strengthening, human resources development and capacity building. Since 1974, it has provided high-quality services to over 1,000 private and public sector organizations. Services are provided to clients in the pulp and paper, forestry, oil and gas, petrochemical, mining and linear development industries, as well as governments, international financial institutions (e.g., Asian Development Bank, World Bank) and development agencies (Canadian International Development Agency). Hatfield has served clients in Asia and South America and has offices in Indonesia, Thailand, Chile and Canada.

Hatfield employs 60 people worldwide. A careers page with employment opportunities can be found on the company's Web site. Interested applicants may submit their resumes to: hcl@hatfieldgroup.com. [ID:6785]

Hauts-Monts Inc.
3645, boul. Saint-Anne, Beauport, QC, G1E 3L1, Canada; 418-667-1913,
fax 418-667-4606, hauts-monts@hauts-monts.com, www.groupealta.com 💻 Fr

LARGE EARTH SCIENCES FIRM: Advanced Technology, Aerospace Technology, Agriculture, Computer Systems, Consulting, Engineering, Environment, Forestry, Logistics, Photo Mapping, Project Management, Technical Assistance, Urban Development

Hauts-Monts Inc. specializes in aerial photography and applied geomatics. The company has completed projects such as orthophoto and photogrammetric ground control in Zimbabwe, a geodetic network in Paraguay, aerial coverage and analytic aerial triangulation of more than 170,000 square kilometres in GPS kinematics mode, as well as aerial photography in Barbados, Mali, Côte d'Ivoire and in many other countries. The company has also filled cartography orders from Gabon, Burkina Faso, Saudi Arabia and Brazil.

Hauts-Monts employs 95 professionals who are specialists in aerial photography and applied geomatics. Candidates should have a bachelor's or master's degree related to natural resources, computer sciences or environmental sciences in areas such as forestry, soil, water and air. They should also possess some background in the use of remote sensing, GIS, digital mapping and other advanced computer techniques. The company maintains a data bank for resumes. [ID:6569]

HGC Engineering Ltd. (Howe Gastmeier Chapnik Limited)
Suite 203, Plaza One, 2000 Argentia Road, Mississauga, ON, L5N 1P7, Canada;
905-826-4044, fax 905-826-4940, info@hgcengineering.com, www.hgcengineering.com

MID-SIZED ENGINEERING CONSULTING FIRM: Engineering, Environment

HGC Engineering Ltd. (Howe Gastmeier Chapnik Limited) is a consulting engineering firm specializing in environmental and industrial noise control, vibration and architectural acoustics. The firm's experience spans the spectrum of all types of industrial facilities, transportation noise, acoustics for building and sensitive spaces, acoustical assessments for land development, vibration isolation of entire buildings and acoustical design assistance for product development. It provides services to many industries, architects and engineers across North America, Europe and the Caribbean.

HGC Engineering employs approximately 15 people. The firm's Web site has a careers page and the firm is always looking for those with engineering degrees and experience in acoustics or vibration, excellent communications skills and the ability to meet deadlines. [ID:6786]

Hickling International
Penthouse Floor, 150 Isabella Street, Ottawa, ON, K1S 1V7, Canada;
613-237-2220, fax 613-237-7347, hickling@hickling.ca, www.hicklinginternational.ca

MID-SIZED MANAGEMENT CONSULTING FIRM: Business Development, Consulting, Development Assistance, Development Education, Gender and Development, Human Resources, Information Technologies, Institution Building, Medical Health, Micro-enterprises, Teaching, Trade and Investment

Hickling International is one of Canada's major management consulting companies, offering professional consulting services to the public and private sectors in Canada and around the world. The company provides service and expertise in the following service areas: education and training, health, information and communications technologies, labour markets, gender equity, micro credit, community development as well as monitoring and evaluation. International projects have taken the firm around the world, including Barbados, China, Russia, Croatia, Thailand, Indonesia, Vietnam, New Guinea, the Philippines, Jamaica, Malaysia, the Caribbean, Bangladesh, Uganda and South Africa.

Hickling International has about 60 to 65 employees including those regularly working overseas on short- and long-term assignments. Consultants for the firm must have a minimum of five years of successful experience in international assignments. Those interested are asked to please forward their resume to hickling@hickling.ca. Work experience in developing countries is a prerequisite. Knowledge of multilateral donors is an asset. The firm maintains a database for resumes. [ID:6550]

HN Telecom Inc.
1160 Douglas Road, Burnaby, BC, V5C 4Z6, Canada; 604-294-3401,
fax 604-299-6712, contact@hntelecom.com, www.hntelecom.com

MID-SIZED TELECOMMUNICATIONS FIRM: Computer Systems, Consulting, Engineering, Project Management, Telecommunications

HN Telecom Inc. is a consulting engineering firm specializing in the field of telecommunications. The firm provides planning, engineering and project management services for telecom transmission networks, broadband wireless access networks, network management systems and broadcast facilities. Clients of the firm include the United States, Iran, Nigeria, Saudi Arabia, Cameroon and the United Nations Development Programme.

Candidates should have a degree in electrical or electronics engineering and at least 10 years of experience in telecommunications. HN Telecom's Web site offers information on the company's mandate and services and provides several useful links to other telecommunication firms. [ID:6551]

HSBC Bank Canada
Suite 300, 885 West Georgia Street, Vancouver, BC, V6C 3E9,
Canada; 604-685-1000, fax 604-641-1849, info@hsbc.ca, www.hsbc.ca 🖥 *Fr*

LARGE FINANCIAL SERVICES FIRM: Banking and Financial Services, Business Development, Business/Banking/Trade

HSBC Bank Canada (formerly Hong Kong Bank of Canada) is a subsidiary of HSBC Holdings plc and is Canada's seventh largest bank. The bank offers a full range of commercial financial services including deposit services, treasury, cash management, electronic banking, asset management, term and operating credits, import and export financing, equipment leasing and investment capital financing. The bank also offers a full range of personal financial services, including deposit services, personal lending including mortgages, private banking, mutual funds, Internet and telephone banking, full-service investing and self-directed investing and trust services. The HSBC Group has more than 9,500 offices in 79 countries and territories.

HSBC has 6,000 employees in its 160 offices across Canada. The bank offers various training and development programs for its employees, as well as a careers page on its Web site that posts employment opportunities. For overseas positions, see also the careers section of the Web site for the HSBC Group: www.hsbcgroup.com. It provides a sample of international executive vacancies and graduate career opportunities. The annual recruitment campaign is also posted there. Although many openings do not require experience in banking, graduate career candidates should have a background in investment and international banking.

HSBC's Web site has an interesting "Canadians Abroad" page, which discusses support and network groups for Canadians working or travelling abroad, as well as tips and other links on topics such as contemplating a career move, managing your finances across borders and accessing your money while working abroad. [ID:6552]

HSI Health Services International Inc.
Suite 200, 638 - 11th Ave. S.W., Calgary, AB, T2R 0E2,
Canada; 403-410-3807, fax 403-410-3854, www.h-s-i.org

MID-SIZED GENERAL CONSULTING FIRM: Consulting, Development Assistance, Medical Health, Project Management, Trade and Investment

HSI Health Services International Inc. is an innovative, networked, globally experienced international health company specializing in health care. The company's main focus is healthcare development, investment, management and specialized consulting services for projects that have an investment mechanism. The company, in affiliation with associated companies, has completed projects in Canada, Mexico, China, Southeast Asia, Thailand, the Philippines and Malaysia. HSI has project offices in Canada, Hong Kong, Mexico and Beijing and has a permanent and contract staff of 30 professionals in all of its offices. [ID:6688]

Hummingbird Ltd.
1 Sparks Ave., North York, ON, M2H 2W1, Canada; 416-496-2200,
fax 416-496-2207, hr@hummingbird.com, www.hummingbird.com

LARGE HIGH TECHNOLOGY FIRM: Advanced Technology, Computer Systems, Information Technologies, Manufacturing, Marketing, Media/Communications, Project Management, Research and Development, Software Development

Hummingbird Ltd. (formerly Hummingbird Communications Ltd.) is a global enterprise software company whose revolutionary Hummingbird Enterprise, an integrated information and knowledge management suite, manages the entire life cycle of information and knowledge assets. Hummingbird Enterprise creates 360-degree views of enterprise content with a portfolio of products that are both modular and interoperable. The company has offices in Australia, the Netherlands, Belgium, Canada, France, Germany, Italy, Japan, Korea, Singapore, Sweden, Switzerland, the United Kingdom and the United States.

Interested applicants can search through job opportunities on the Web site and submit a resume to the company's on-line database. Hummingbird Ltd. generally seeks candidates with degrees in software engineering, systems engineering and analysis, and programming. The company's Web site is very helpful for job seekers. The site provides interview tips, a resume builder, tools and quizzes, interview FAQs, as well as links to associations, user groups and additional information on resume writing. [ID:6697]

Husky Energy Inc.
P.O. Box 6525, Stn. D, 707 - 8th Ave. S.W., Calgary, AB, T2P 3G7, Canada;
403-298-6111, fax 403-298-7464, webmaster@huskyenergy.ca, www.huskyenergy.ca

LARGE PETROCHEMICALS FIRM: Energy Resources, Oil and Gas Distribution, Petrochemicals

Husky Energy Inc. is an integrated energy and energy-related company that ranks among Canada's largest petroleum companies in terms of production and the value of its asset base. Upstream activities are currently focused in Western Canada, offshore Eastern Canada as well as in China. Husky Oil International Corporation is a large firm, specializing in the exploration and production of oil and natural gas. The firm has international operations in China and Indonesia and anticipates an increase in overseas assignments with new contracts.

Husky Energy Inc. employs approximately 2,900 people. Husky Oil International currently has 20 overseas staff and 36 Canadian-based staff who work on international projects. Husky Oil International recruits geologists, geophysicists, petroleum engineers and oil field operation personnel with five to 10 years experience. Interested candidates can view current employment opportunities on the Web site. Husky Energy uses an on-line recruiting system and offers recruitment programs for co-op/intern and summer students in all of their business areas. These programs are available year-round in the engineering, geology and accounting disciplines. The work terms can range in length from four to 16 months and locations vary. The majority of co-op/intern students are located in Calgary or Lloydminster. Another location is St. John's, Newfoundland and Labrador. Positions are posted at selected university and colleges and the company's Web site in January, May and September, while interviews are conducted in October, February and June. The summer student positions are designed for students who are interested in gaining experience in the oil and natural gas industry and who will be returning to school on a full-time basis in the fall. The positions are available for a wide variety of disciplines, in both the office and field environments, and are posted on the company's Web site in the fall and early winter for the upcoming summer. Husky also offers new graduate positions which are available year-round, however, the majority are hired in May and June. These positions are posted on the company's Web site and encompass the same disciplines as the company's student and co-op/intern positions. Husky Energy also typically recruits geologists, geophysicists, petroleum engineers and oil field operations personnel with five to 10 years' experience. Most positions are filled in-house and the company maintains a data bank for resumes. The Web site features a detailed careers section which lists openings in a wide variety of professions, mainly based in Canada. [ID:6553]

Hydro-Québec International (HQI)
20th Floor, 75 René Lévesque Blvd. W., Montreal, QC, H2L 1A4,
Canada; 514-289-4020, fax 514-289-4084, www.hydroquebec.com/hqi/en/ 💻 𝐹𝑟

LARGE ENGINEERING FIRM: Energy Resources, Engineering, Human Resources, Power Generation/Transmission/Distribution, Project Management, Research and Development

Hydro-Québec International (HQI) is a consulting engineering corporation that specializes in planning, design, construction and management of electrical power systems. Hydro-Québec's divisions, Hydro-Québec Production and Hydro-Québec TransEnergie, are responsible for international projects in their sphere of competence from planning to implementation. All projects are conducted under the Hydro-Québec International banner. The company operates 32,000 kilometres of line, serving 3.5 million customers in Quebec and currently has generation projects in Panama, Brazil, Poland, Ukraine, Iran, Cameroon and Vietnam. HQI also has transmission projects underway in the United States, Peru, Chile and Australia as well as generation projects in Panama.

HQI uses the services of engineers, accountants, economists, and MBAs specializing in hydroelectric projects, high voltage transmission, financial planning and administration. The firm generally employs people from Hydro-Québec. HQI maintains a data bank for internal resumes only. A careers page with employment opportunities can be found on the company's Web site, however, it can only be read in French. HQI's Web site also provides a variety of information on the firm's activities and services. [ID:6678]

Hydrosult Inc.
Bureau 400/410, 3333 Cavendish Blvd., Montreal, QC, H4B 2M5, Canada;
514-484-9973, fax 514-484-5298, hydrosult@hydrosult.com, www.hydrosult.com 💻 𝐹𝑟

LARGE GENERAL CONSULTING FIRM: Consulting, Engineering, Environment, Human Resources, Information Technologies, Institution Building, Project Management, Rural Development, Water Resources

Hydrosult Inc. is a large consulting firm specializing in engineering, planning and management of water resources and the environment, including related socio-economic and socio-cultural studies. It provides integrated services in agriculture, forestry, and hydrology in projects addressing integrated rural development. A typical past overseas contract involved the policy, planning and administration of water institutions in Indonesia. The company has also worked in China, Yemen, Africa, the Middle East, Bolivia, Niger, Haiti and Burkina Faso and has offices in France, Switzerland, Jordan and Indonesia. The company has a careers page on its Web site with employment opportunities posted. [ID:6535]

IMAX Corp.
2525 Speakman Drive, Mississauga, ON, L5K 1B1, Canada; 905-403-6500, fax 905-403-6450, www.imax.com

LARGE HIGH TECHNOLOGY FIRM: Camera and Projector Design, Film Distribution, Film Production and Post Productions, Manufacturing, Media/Communications, Project Management, Research and Development

IMAX Corporation is one of the world's leading entertainment technology companies with particular emphasis on film and digital imaging technologies including 3-D, post-production and digital projection. IMAX is a fully integrated, out-of-home entertainment enterprise with activities ranging from design, leasing, marketing, maintenance and operation of IMAX theatre systems to film development, productions, post-production and distribution of large-format films. IMAX also designs and manufactures cameras, projectors and consistently commits significant funding to ongoing research and development. The company has more than 220 affiliated theatres in 30 countries with the majority located in North America. The IMAX Corporation has offices in New York, Los Angeles, Europe, Singapore, Japan and three subsidiaries in the United States.

IMAX has a careers page on its Web site and regularly posts job opportunities for Canada, the United States and abroad. The company also maintains a resume database. [ID:6578]

IMP Group International Inc.
Suite 400, 2651 Joseph Howe Drive, Halifax, NS, B3L 4T1, Canada;
902-453-2400, fax 902-453-6931, webmaster@impgroup.com, www.impgroup.com

LARGE ENGINEERING FIRM: Accounting, Administration (General), Aerospace Technology, Air Transportation, Business Development, Human Resources, Project Management

IMP Group International Inc. is a privately owned diversified company headquartered in Halifax, Nova Scotia. The company is divided between three core operating divisions (Aerospace, Aviation and Commercial), and has a corporate investment portfolio. The IMP Group pursues a growth-oriented international strategy across Canada, the United States and Russia. IMP's corporate portfolio includes CanJet Airlines, the Moscow Aerostar Hotel in Russia, the Holiday Inn Select Halifax Centre in Nova Scotia, and the Oak Island Resort and Spa, also located in Nova Scotia.

The company has offices in Cyprus, Russia and Canada, and currently employs almost 3,000 people. Prospective applicants must have international work experience in the hospitality industry, but knowledge of Russian or Slavic languages is not required. IMP Group Inc. maintains a data bank for resumes. Their Web site provides basic information on the company's activities as well as job opportunities. [ID:6554]

Inco Ltd.
Suite 1500, 145 King Street W., Toronto, ON, M5H 4B7, Canada;
416-361-7511, fax 416-361-7781, inco@inco.com, www.inco.com

LARGE MINING FIRM: Marketing, Metals, Mineral Handling, Mining

Inco Limited is one of the world's premier mining and metals companies and the world's second largest producer of nickel. The company is also an important producer of copper, cobalt, precious metals and a major producer of value-added specialty nickel products. Inco's strength is built on a base of strong and profitable production from their global operations, the broadest range of value-added products in the industry and a worldwide marketing network that extends to over 40 countries. With two of the world's best nickel ore-bodies under development at Voisey's Bay in Newfoundland and Labrador, and at Goro in New Caledonia, they are expanding their production by 40 per cent. Processing operations are located in Canada and Indonesia, as well, along with the United States, Barbados, England, Germany, Thailand, Hong Kong, Taiwan, China and Japan.

Inco employs over 10,000 people around the world. The company's Web site has a careers section which includes job postings. Inco hires personnel for all aspects of geological exploration, mining and metals production, as well as for marketing and financial positions. Overseas staff is often, but not exclusively, hired locally. There is also a link for career information for students and graduates, entry-level positions, a university recruiting schedule, and information on Inco internships and co-ops. There are four-month and 16-month co-ops available, and the Ontario division offers maintenance/trade co-ops with Cambrian College of Sudbury. The firm maintains an attractive Web site that contains a wide variety of information on mining and on the company's activities. [ID:6555]

Intelcan Technosystems Inc.
69 Auriga Drive, Ottawa, ON, K2E 7Z2, Canada;
613-228-1150, fax 613-228-1149, info@intelcan.com, www.intelcan.com

MID-SIZED HIGH TECHNOLOGY FIRM: Advanced Technology, Aerospace Technology, Air Transportation, Computer Systems, Engineering, Media/Communications, Systems Engineering, Technical Assistance, Training and Technology Transfer

Intelcan Technosystems Inc. is Canada's premier total aviation systems integrator. Intelcan specializes in military and civil aviation systems and airport infrastructures. The company is involved in the sale and implementation overseas of multidisciplinary projects in telecommunications, power, civil aviation, transportation and machinery. Intelcan's activities include feasibility studies, technical assistance, equipment procurement and supply, system integration, on-site and in-factory training and ongoing operational maintenance. Offices for the company can be found in Europe, the Caribbean and in Canada. Intelcan has worked in Cuba, Bulgaria, Jamaica, Romania, Liberia, Zimbabwe, Guinea, Benin, Mali, Burkina Faso, Cameroon, Peru, Morocco, Iran, Congo, Africa and Nigeria.

Candidates should have an educational background in electrical engineering or computer science, or experience as a telecommunications technician. Overseas experience and language skills are assets. Intelcan considers applications for internships, particularly in the fields of engineering and computer science. The company has a careers page on its Web site and maintains a data bank for resumes. [ID:6658]

Intercan Development Company Ltd.
Suite 900, 275 Slater Street, Ottawa, ON, K1P 5H9, Canada;
613-238-6827, fax 613-236-3754, www.intercandevelop.com

MID-SIZED BUSINESS AND MANAGEMENT COMPANY: Adult Training, Business Development, Computer Systems, Consulting, Development Assistance, Economics, Engineering, Environment, Fisheries, Human Resources, Marketing, Media/Communications, Medical Health, Micro-enterprises, Project Management, Technical Assistance, Telecommunications, Tourism, Training and Technology Transfer, Water Resources

Intercan Development Company Ltd. is a mid-sized firm specializing in technology transfer, international business development, management consulting, international trade and commerce, feasibility studies, project management and professional services. The Canadian company is geared toward identifying potential market opportunities, developing market approaches, penetrating these markets, and catalyzing industry/technology transfer to enable successful opportunities in new ventures. The firm has a network of associates located in Europe, the Middle East, North Africa, the Mediterranean region, the Americas and southern Africa. [ID:6660]

Intercultural Systems / Systèmes interculturels (ISSI) Inc.
296 Sackville Street, Toronto, ON, M5A 3G2, Canada; 416-925-0479,
fax 416-925-9650, feedback@workingoverseas.com, www.workingoverseas.com

SMALL GENERAL CONSULTING FIRM: Project Management, Publishing

Intercultural Systems / Systèmes interculturels (ISSI) Inc. is the publisher of "The BIG Guide to Living and Working Overseas" (formerly "The Canadian Guide to Working and Living

Overseas"). The firm's activities revolve around publishing the print and Web editions of the guide. The author, Jean-Marc Hachey, conducts seminars and workshops on international careers across Canada. Clients include most Canadian universities, the Canadian International Development Agency (CIDA), Foreign Affairs Canada (FAC), the Centre for Intercultural Learning (CIL) and many non-governmental organizations (NGOs). ISSI Inc. has two other divisions. ISSI Consulting is a contact database design and consulting firm. WholePie Project Management (www.WholePie.com) offers project management training and consulting services to the public and private sectors in both French and English.

ISSI hires entry-level research staff for periodic research work and for six-month terms to update "The BIG Guide to Living and Working Overseas" once every three to four years. Research staff generally have a master's degree and overseas experience, whether it be work, volunteer or study. They possess solid writing skills, research and organizational abilities and are proficient in using computers and the Internet. Bilingualism is an asset. ISSI maintains a data bank for resumes.

Visit the ISSI Web site to access the Web edition of "The BIG Guide to Living and Working Overseas," as well as career tips such as "The BIG Guide's Top 100 Job Boards." [ID:6661]

Intermap Technologies Corp.
Human Resources, Suite 1000, 736 - 8th Ave. S.W., Calgary, AB, T2P 1H4,
Canada; 403-266-0900, fax 403-265-0499, info@intermap.ca, www.intermap.ca

LARGE INFORMATION SYSTEMS FIRM: Consulting, Geomatics, Photo Mapping, Project Management, Science and Technology, Software Development

Intermap Technologies Corp. produces highly accurate, low-cost digital elevation models (DEMs), including digital surface models (DSMs) and digital terrain models (DTMs), as well as cartographic products vital to producing accurate base maps, which drive a proliferation of GIS, GPS and 3-D visualization applications. The company works with both governments and private industry worldwide and collects data with its airborne STAR-3 inferometric synthetic aperture radar (IFSAR). The system allows the company to map large areas accurately, quickly and in overcast or dark conditions. Intermap Technologies has completed surveys and mapping projects in more than 85 countries, including Britain, Puerto Rico, Jamaica, Indonesia, Solomon Islands and the United States, and has offices in Germany and the United States.

The company employs 120 people and has a careers page on its Web site with employment opportunities posted. Interested applicants can apply on-line. Currently, Intermap is seeking those with experience in photogrammetry, mapping and editing. [ID:6659]

International Road Dynamics Inc. (IRD)
702 - 43rd Street E., Saskatoon, SK, S7K 3T9, Canada;
306-653-6600, fax 306-242-5599, info@irdinc.com, www.irdinc.com

LARGE TRANSPORTATION MANUFACTURING FIRM: Accounting, Administration (General), Advanced Technology, Business Development, Computer Systems, Engineering, Human Resources, Project Management, Systems Engineering, Technical Assistance

International Road Dynamics Inc. (IRD) is a multi-discipline technology company with expertise in integrating complementary ITS technologies into systems designed to solve unique and challenging transportation problems. IRD is a one source company which can offer multi-systems solutions by integrating a number of different technologies to the desired functionality. The company's multi-systems solutions include automated truck weigh stations, traffic data collection systems, automated toll systems, traffic safety and advisory systems, driver and fleet management systems, as well as customer service and support. IRD has international activities that have spanned five continents.

IRD has a staff of 150 and the majority of positions are based in Saskatoon; however, the company has engineering support based throughout Canada, the United States, South America and the Asia-Pacific region. Employment opportunities are posted on the company's Web site. Currently, there are employment opportunities in design and manufacturing, sales, installation, and service and support of systems and interfaces. [ID:6632]

John Roper & Associates

4660 Brentlawn Drive, Burnaby, BC, V5C 3V2, Canada; 604-299-9643,
fax 604-299-9643, roper@canadian-forests.com, www.canadian-forests.com

MID-SIZED FORESTRY CONSULTING FIRM: Development Assistance, Forestry, Policy Development,
Project Management

John Roper & Associates has more than 30 years experience working on international
development assistance programs in the forestry sector in Latin America and Africa. The company's
focus is to work for the conservation of tropical forests while at the same time meeting the
aspirations and needs of local people. It is engaged in project planning, management, monitoring
and strategic analysis, natural resource management and community forestry. Clients of the
company have included the Canadian International Development Agency (CIDA), the United
Nations Development Programme (UNDP) and the World Food Programme. John Roper &
Associates has international experience in Latin America, the Caribbean, Africa and Asia. A
careers page with employment opportunities can be found on the company's Web site listing various
organizations in the forestry industry. [ID:6558]

Kinross Gold Corp.

52nd Floor, Scotia Plaza, 40 King Street W., Toronto, ON, M5H 3Y2, Canada;
416-365-5123, fax 416-363-6622, info@kinross.com, www.kinross.com

LARGE MINING FIRM: Exploration and Development, Gold and Metals Production, Mining

Kinross Gold Corp. is the seventh largest primary gold producer in the world, producing
approximately 1.7 million ounces of gold equivalent annually. Approximately 50 per cent of
Kinross' production is based in the United States and over two-thirds in North America. This
largely North American presence provides Kinross with a stable base for its global portfolio of
mines. It has operations in North America (Canada and the United States), South America (Brazil
and Chile), Africa (Zimbabwe) and Asia (eastern Russia), as well as exploration and development
projects underway in North America, South America and Asia.

As of 2004, Kinross has 4,300 employees worldwide. An employment page with current
employment opportunities can be found on the company's Web site. [ID:6605]

Kleinfeldt Consultants Ltd.

Suite 102, 2400 Meadowpine Blvd., Mississauga, ON, M5N 6S2,
Canada; 905-542-1600, fax 905-542-2729, info@kcl.ca, www.kcl.ca

SMALL ENGINEERING FIRM: Engineering, Environment, Project Management

Kleinfeldt Consultants Limited provides consulting engineering services to government
agencies, building owners, property managers and land developers. The firm's qualified staff and
ample resources allow it to undertake a wide variety of assignments in the following disciplines:
building science, forensic services, environmental engineering, project management, structural
engineering, mechanical/electrical engineering, municipal engineering, building code and standards
development. Kleinfeldt has had more than 40 years of experience on domestic and international
projects. The majority of KCL's work is in Canada, although it has staff focused purely on Latin
America. The firm's consultants work overseas in the United Kingdom, Mexico and the Caribbean.
[ID:6662]

Klohn-Crippen Consultants Ltd.

5th Floor, 2955 Virtual Way, Vancouver, BC, V5M 4X6, Canada;
604-669-3800, fax 604-669-3835, admin@klohn.com, www.klohn.com

LARGE ENGINEERING FIRM: Energy Resources, Engineering, Environment, Mining, Project Management,
Transportation, Water Resources

Klohn-Crippen Consultants Ltd. is a leading integrated service provider in engineering,
management and environmental solutions. The firm has its origins in geotechnical and water
resources engineering and has evolved into one of Canada's pre-eminent consulting firms, offering

engineering, environmental and project management services across Canada and worldwide. It provides leading edge geotechnical, environmental, mining, power, transportation and water resources engineering solutions. Klohn-Crippen has a total of 48 office locations around the world, including Canada, the United States, Peru and Australia, and has completed projects in North America, South America, the Caribbean, Africa, Europe, Asia and the Middle East.

The firm employs 350 people. An employment board can be found on the firm's Web site with job postings. Klohn-Crippen asks that interested candidates forward their resumes to the human resources manager, unless a posting states otherwise. Candidates should have a minimum of two years' overseas experience and a transportation and water resource background. The ability to speak other languages is an advantage, but not essential. Candidates should be able to adapt to a cross-cultural setting and have a flexible attitude. The firm maintains a data bank for resumes. [ID:6663]

KOM International

Suite 2300, 300 Leo Pariseau, Montreal, QC, H2X 4B3,
Canada; 514-849-4000, fax 514-849-8888, www.komintl.com 🖳*Fr*🖳*Sp*

LARGE MANAGEMENT CONSULTING FIRM: Management Consulting, Management Information Systems

KOM International is a global leader in supply chain consulting services with over 40 years experience and 3,600 projects successfully completed. The company provides innovative and proven supply chain consulting services that enable companies around the world to manage their logistics activities more effectively. It has worked across a wide spectrum of industry sectors to deliver world class customer service levels at the lowest possible operating cost. KOM International's core competencies include supply chain strategy, distribution centre design and layout, improving existing distribution operations, supply chain technology solution selection and implementation, inventory management and warehouse and transportation management consulting. The company has served clients in Canada, the United States, Latin America, Europe and Asia. It also has international offices in Mexico, Venezuela, Colombia, Brazil and Chile.

A careers page with employment opportunities may be found on KOM International's Web site. Interested applicants may also submit their resume to the company's database. [ID:6795]

Komex

Suite 100, 4500 - 16th Ave. N.W., Calgary, AB, T3B 0M6, Canada;
403-247-0200, fax 403-247-4811, info@calgary.komex.com, www.komex.com

LARGE ENVIRONMENTAL CONSULTING FIRM: Engineering, Environment, Geophysics, Project Management, Sanitation, Waste Water Management

Komex is an international, full-service environmental consulting and engineering company. The company provides leading-edge technology and solutions to industries and governments worldwide. Its clients range from small private companies to multinational corporations, governments and international development agencies. Komex has offices on five continents (North America, South America, Africa, Europe and Asia), as well as four international operating centres. Each centre is responsible for operations within its international territories. Services provided by the company include brownfields, chlorinated solvents, contaminated site management and compliance and remediation, due diligence, environmental assessments and planning, engineering and project management, geophysics, MTBE, perchlorate, waste water treatment and solid waste management, as well as water management. Past clients of the company have included the Canadian International Development Agency (CIDA), the Asian Development Bank, the United Nations Development Programme (UNDP), the World Bank, the European Union, Canada, the United States, Kenya, Saudi Arabia, Ecuador, Yemen, Peru, Costa Rica, Bolivia, Brazil and Chile.

Komex employs approximately 180 people in Canada and roughly 350 people worldwide. A high percentage of their professional staff have a master's or a PhD. A careers page with employment opportunities may be found on the company's Web site, or resumes may be submitted to info@komex.com. [ID:6834]

KPMG LLP

P.O. Box 31, Stn. Commerce Court, Toronto, ON, M5L 1B6,
Canada; 416-777-8500, fax 416-777-8818, www.kpmg.ca ⌨ℱr

LARGE FINANCIAL SERVICES FIRM: Accounting

KPMG LLP is the Canadian member firm of KPMG International, the global network of professional services firms, whose aim is to turn understanding of information, industries and business trends into value. With 4,500 people in Canada and nearly 100,000 people worldwide, KPMG provides audit and risk advisory, tax, and financial advisory services from more than 750 cities in 150 countries.

KPMG views international assignments as an excellent development tool for their high-performing and high-potential people. The firm's Global Mobility Program is intended to provide career development opportunities for KPMG people who have an excellent track record. At any time, approximately 150 KPMG professionals from around the world are participating in long or short-term international assignments under Global Mobility. The firm has worked to develop fair and equitable global policies and tools to facilitate these assignments. For international transfers, KPMG seeks experienced individuals with strong technical skills in the firm's core disciplines of audit, tax and advisory services. Those considered will have a high degree of personal effectiveness, leadership skills and a commitment to knowledge sharing and client service. In Canada, KPMG recruits several hundred university students annually for student and co-op positions, typically leading to a CA designation. Applicants for these positions generally have a business or commerce degree. KPMG maintains a database of international opportunities available, which is accessible only by firm members. The firm's careers Web site at www.kpmg.ca/careers includes an e-recruitment system that accepts applicants' resumes. [ID:6664]

Kruger Inc.

3285, chemin Bedford, Montreal, QC, H3S 1G5, Canada;
514-737-1131, fax 514-343-3124, webadmin@kruger.com, www.kruger.com ⌨ℱr

---

LARGE FORESTRY FIRM: Forestry, Manufacturing, Marketing, Pulp and Paper

Kruger Inc. is a Canadian, privately owned company in the pulp and paper industry. The company meets the needs of its local and international customers and offers an array of products from virgin and recycled fibres, including newsprint, coated and supercalendered paper, linerboard, recovered paper, packaging, lumber, wood panels and tissue. The Kruger name is recognized both in Canadian and international markets, and the company conducts international activities in North America, Venezuela, Colombia and the United Kingdom. The company also has offices in Canada, the United States and England.

Kruger employs approximately 10,500 employees around the world. A careers page with employment opportunities may be found on the company's Web site. Kruger places a large emphasis on training and career development, as employees are encouraged to take courses and attend seminars at universities and technical schools. A tuition refund program has also been established. [ID:6824]

Lane Environment Ltd.

1663 Oxford Street, Halifax, NS, B3H 3Z5, Canada; 902-423-8197, fax 902-429-8089, lane@cs.dal.ca

---

SMALL ENVIRONMENTAL CONSULTING FIRM: Consulting, Development Assistance, Development Education, Environment, Sustainable Development, Water Resources

Lane Environment Ltd. is a consulting firm specializing in environmental and water resource management and sustainable development planning. It has pioneered methodologies in cumulative effects assessment, environmental impact assessments, ecological risk analysis and sustainability evaluation criteria. Overseas projects have included an innovative biotechnology project for water pollution abatement in Egypt, expert advice for the Bangladesh Flood Action Plan and special consultant services for environmental management and sustainability planning in Cuba. [ID:6665]

M.T. Ellis & Associates Ltd.

678 Southmore Drive W., Ottawa, ON, K1V 7A1, Canada;
613-523-5113, fax 613-523-8507, mtellis.consultant@sympatico.ca

MID-SIZED HUMAN RESOURCES FIRM: Adult Training, Human Resources, Management, Management Training, Organization Development, Project Management

M.T. Ellis & Associates Ltd. is a human resource and organizational development consulting organization that provides private and public institutional and organizational reforms, restructuring, capacity building, development and management services to a number of sectors: energy, environment, government, transportation, water supply, and sanitation. The firm operates in Africa, Asia, North America, Europe and the Middle East and currently employs four salaried staff overseas; an additional five stationed in Canada, the United States and Sri Lanka have international responsibilities. Short-term contractual assignments account for an additional three person-years per calendar year.

Prospective applicants should have as a minimum: a bachelor's degree, seven years of overseas working experience in developing countries and educational and/or training experience in one or more sectors of the firm's portfolio. Analytical, organizational and language (Spanish and Eastern European) skills are key assets, as are the abilities to work as a member of a team and communicate effectively. The company maintains a data bank of resumes. [ID:6667]

MacDonald, Dettwiler and Associates Ltd.

13800 Commerce Parkway, Richmond, BC, V6V 2J3, Canada;
604-278-3411, fax 604-273-9830, jobs@mda.ca, www.mda.ca

LARGE HIGH TECHNOLOGY FIRM: Computer Systems, Engineering, Information Technologies, Software Development, Systems Engineering

MacDonald, Dettwiler and Associates Ltd. is an information company that provides customers around the world with essential information used for decision-making in the workplace. It is active in data collection, information extraction and information distribution. The company's information products group delivers land information products and services in two categories: legal and asset information and geographical information. MacDonald, Dettwiler and Associates provides legal and asset information in the United States, the United Kingdom and Canada. The company's products provide access to current and accurate information on millions of properties, as well as providing essential information products to professionals such as lawyers, lenders and appraisers in the property transaction market. The company's growing range of information of geographic information products are used for a number of applications, including infrastructure planning and management, crop planning and monitoring, flood prevention and disaster response. Through a network of offices, subsidiaries and partnerships, MacDonald, Dettwiller and Associates services customers in North America, Europe and around the world. It has completed projects for clients in Algeria, Australia, Brazil, China, Indonesia, Iran, Japan, South Korea, Poland, Saudi Arabia, Taiwan, the United Kingdom and the United States. The company has business locations in the United States, Canada and the United Kingdom.

MacDonald, Dettwiler and Associates employs over 2,200 people. A careers page can be found on the company's Web site with employment opportunities. The company offers campus opportunities, including co-ops, internships as well as opportunities for new graduates. MacDonald, Dettwiler and Associates supports student placement programs in conjunction with local universities and colleges. Opportunities are given to students in electrical engineering, computer science, engineering physics, mathematics and computer science, to provide them with first-hand exposure to real-world projects. Each semester, the company posts its co-op openings with various campus recruiting offices across Canada. It is suggested that those interested in various programs contact their local co-op office. The company posts its co-op opportunities at school co-op offices every February, June and October. Interested candidates can submit their application packages (which should include a resume, a cover letter and latest transcripts) through their school coordinator. The company also maintains a resume database. [ID:6668]

Malkam Consultants Ltd.

Suite 5, 1309 Carling Ave., Ottawa, ON, K1Z 7L3, Canada; 613-761-7440,
fax 613-761-7481, manager@malkam.com, www.graybridgemalkam.com

---

MID-SIZED INTERCULTURAL CONSULTING: Adult Training, Consulting, Human Resources, Intercultural Briefings, Language Training, Teaching, Training and Education

Malkam Consultants Ltd. promotes linguistic and cultural diversity to build bridges that further employee understanding, communications and interactivity. The company builds upon the diversity of the client's employees, creating a valuable resource. Malkam's Cross-Cultural Training Program specializes in English as a second language and French as a second language, and offers courses in German, Mandarin, Portuguese, Spanish and other languages as requested. Malkam offers pre-employment programs that provide effective job search and workplace communication skills. Malkam also offers Resources and Information for Seeking Employment (RISE) and Language Assessment for Learning programs. Programs are available in cultural awareness, diversity, international preparedness and mentoring for success. The company delivers quality results, including information gathering, analysis, "best practices" and recommendations, comprehensive reporting and ongoing consultation, based on research findings.

A careers page can be found on Malkam's Web site along with employment opportunities. Those interested in cross-cultural training must have extensive experience in the design and delivery of training programs to private and public sector organizations. Bilingualism (French and English) is an asset. There is occasional need for culture-specific briefers in the following areas: Syria, Kuwait, Rwanda, Egypt, Jordan, Lebanon, Cyprus, Iraq, Cambodia, Korea, India, Pakistan, Zaire, Sierra Leone, East Timor, the western Sahara and the Democratic Republic of Congo. Facilitators must be native to the region that they are briefing, have lived in the area within the last seven years, have experience in delivering cultural briefings, and be fluent in English and the language of the region. Malkam is also looking for people for language training programs and pre-employment preparation. (In June 2004, Malkam was about to merge with Graybridge International Consulting Inc. See the Graybridge profile in this chapter.) [ID:6615]

Maple Leaf Foods International

Suite 2000, 3080 Yonge Street, Toronto, ON, M4N 3N1, Canada;
416-480-8900, fax 416-480-8950, info@mlfi.com, www.mlfi.com ⌨*Fr*⌨*Sp*

LARGE AGRICULTURAL FIRM: Accounting, Administration (General), Agriculture, Computer Systems, Economics, Engineering, Food and Agricultural Products Marketing, Human Resources, Logistics

Maple Leaf Foods International is one of the world's largest traders and niche marketers of food and agricultural products. The company strives to develop new and innovative products to meet the food requirements of a changing world. It has a global network of partners, producers, processors and retailers who work with the company to bring products to the market. Maple Leaf is a major exporter and marketer of wholesome meat products and is a source for some of the highest quality seafood products in the world. Maple Leaf is also a leader in marketing food products internationally. The company has offices in Japan, Hong Kong, Korea, Canada, the United Kingdom and Germany.

Maple Leaf Food International employs 100 people. A careers page can be found on the company's Web site and career opportunities are available across the globe. Currently, the company is looking for multilingual individuals possessing knowledge of international markets. Interested applicants may submit a resume to Maple Leaf's database. [ID:6699]

Maracon & Associates International Inc.

Suite 315, 4999 St. Catherine Street W., Montreal, QC, H3Z 1T3,
Canada; 514-487-9868, fax 514-487-9276, www.maracon.ca

SMALL INTERCULTURAL CONSULTING: Consulting, Intercultural Briefings, Management Consulting, Management Training

Maracon & Associates International Inc. is a management training and development firm, which specializes in negotiations and conflict resolution training and coaching worldwide. They also offer programs and consulting services in interpersonal and cross-cultural communication, team-building, train-the-trainer, presentation skills and facilitation skills. The firm collaborates with corporations in pharmaceuticals, telecommunications, finance and aerospace as well as with NGOs, governments and training institutions to assist them in adjusting management approaches to develop more open, productive teams and respond to cultural diversity. Maracon has 10 associates based in Europe, Africa, Latin America, Canada and the US who offer consulting and training in English, French, Spanish and German. [ID:6524]

Marshall Macklin Monaghan Ltd.

International Division, 80 Commerce Valley Drive E., Thornhill, ON, L3T 7N4, Canada; 905-882-1100, fax 905-882-0055, mmm@mmm.ca, www.mmm.ca

MID-SIZED ENGINEERING CONSULTING FIRM: Accounting, Administration (General), Architecture and Planning, Business Development, Community Development, Computer Systems, Consulting, Economics, Engineering, Environment, Geomatics, Photo Mapping, Project Management, Technical Assistance, Tourism, Waste Water Management, Water Resources

Marshall Macklin Monaghan Limited is a multidisciplinary professional services firm active in project development and management, civil and building engineering, as well as planning and geomatics. The firm specializes in the structuring and delivery of large-scale infrastructure projects through alternative means, such as public/private partnerships, design/build, etc. Services offered by the firm include project implementation, community planning and infrastructure, transportation, environment, building/structures and geomatics. Other services offered by the firm include water resource management and tourism development. In recent years, the firm has become increasingly involved in privately financed airport developments in Canada and 11 other countries. The firm is active internationally in airport development, environmental projects and geomatics. It has completed projects in Algeria, Barbados, Belize, Bermuda, Brazil, China, Colombia, Cuba, Egypt, Iran, Japan, Mexico, Oman, Puerto Rico, Russia, Saudi Arabia, Trinidad and Tobago and the United States. The firm has offices in Ontario, Alberta and in the United States.

Marshall Macklin Monaghan employs 450 people. A careers page can be found on the firm's Web site with current employment opportunities. It has representatives in Hungary, Turkey, Barbados, Ecuador, Honduras, Trinidad, Uruguay and the Middle East. Prospective applicants should have relevant educational backgrounds and experience in the fields of civil, mechanical, electrical and structural engineering, urban design or landscape architecture. The firm maintains a data bank for resumes. Marshall Macklin Monaghan provides a comprehensive Web site that documents domestic and international experience—it also lists corporate services and information. [ID:6616]

Martec Recycling Corporation

Suite 650, 1050 West Pender, Vancouver, BC, V6E 3S7, Canada; 604-687-7088, fax 604-687-7016, info@martec.ca, www.martec.ca

LARGE ENVIRONMENTAL FIRM: Administration (General), Business Development, Engineering, Environment, Manufacturing, Marketing

Martec Recycling Corporation specializes in asphalt recycling technology, and has developed the world's most technologically advanced, hot-in-place asphalt recycling train, the AR2000 Super Recycler. Martec is jointly owned by the Artec International Recycling Corporation of Canada, Marubeni Benelux S.A. of Belgium, the Marubeni Corporation of Japan, and the Green ARM Co. Ltd. of Japan. Martec's technology offers potential savings of up to 35 per cent in cost and 50 per cent in time over conventional resurfacing methods. The company has responded to the growing demand for economical and environment-friendly road rehabilitation technology, and offers their international customers several options for using Martec technology, from sales to leasing and joint ventures. Martec has completed many major projects worldwide and is currently expanding into Asia and Europe. Martec's team is made up of engineering, marketing, sales and administration people from many different countries. [ID:6591]

Masonite International Corp.

1600 Britannia Road E., Mississauga, ON, L4W 1J2, Canada;
905-670-6500, fax 905-670-6520, www.masonite.com

LARGE MANUFACTURING FIRM: Building Supplies, Manufacturing, Marketing, Merchandising

Masonite International Corp. offers a diverse line of interior and exterior doors to meet any design or budget. The company continues to be the brand that builders, remodellers and homeowners rely on in their quest to create homes of distinction. It has one of the largest private research and development facilities in the door industry. Masonite owns hundreds of international patents, trademarks and applications. The company has offices in Tampa, Florida; operates more than 70 facilities spanning North America, South America, Europe, Asia and Africa; and employs 12,000 people worldwide. The company also sells its products to a wide variety of customers in over 50 countries. [ID:6686]

McCain Foods Limited

107 Main Street, Florenceville, NB, E7L 1B2, Canada; 506-392-5541, fax 506-392-6062, www.mccain.com

LARGE FOOD PROCESSING FIRM: Accounting, Agriculture, Business Development, Engineering, Food and Agricultural Products Marketing, Human Resources, Information Technologies, Marketing, Research and Development, Systems Engineering

McCain Foods Limited is the world's largest producer of french fries, as well as a large producer of juices and drinks, desserts, vegetables, pizzas, oven-ready entrees, appetizers and more. The company has 55 production facilities on six continents, as well as 30 potato processing plants around the world. The company also has marketing and sales professionals representing McCain in more than 100 countries around the world. It is a world leader in new product innovation and development to please retail and food service customers alike. Countries of operation include Canada, the United Kingdom, the United States, the Netherlands, Belgium, France, Poland, Australia, New Zealand, Argentina, Mexico and South Africa. McCain also exports to more than 100 countries.

McCain employs approximately 18,000 people. A careers page with global career opportunities can be found on the company's Web site. Possible positions with the company include production, sales, marketing, engineering, finance, corporate development, agronomy, information systems, human resources and MQP continuous improvement. [ID:6778]

MDS Inc.

100 International Blvd., Toronto, ON, M9W 6J6, Canada;
416-675-6777, fax 416-675-0688, info@mdsintl.com, www.mdsintl.com ▢*Fr*

LARGE BIOTECHNOLOGY FIRM: Laboratory Automation Systems, Laboratory Services, Medical Diagnostics, Medical Health, Pharmaceuticals

MDS Inc. is an international health and life sciences company that provides enabling products and services for the development of drugs and the maintenance of disease. It is a leading provider of drug discovery and development solutions, highly sensitive analytical instruments, medical isotopes, gamma sterilization technology and is Canada's leader in diagnostic services and distribution of medical products. MDS operates in three segments: life sciences, health and proteomics. The company's operations are broadly international with a strong and growing presence in the advanced healthcare markets of North America, South America, Europe, Africa and Asia Pacific. Over 60 per cent of sales are in and to markets outside of Canada and MDS is the global market leader in a number of important niches in the health, pharmaceutical and biotechnology markets it serves. The company has employees in 24 countries around the world, including Argentina, Chile, South Africa, China, Hong Kong, Japan, Singapore, Taiwan and across Europe, from France and the United Kingdom, to Germany and Hungary.

MDS employs over 10,000 people around the world. A careers page can be found on the company's Web site with job postings. Interested applicants can complete an on-line application form on the Web site. Every employee at MDS has a personal development plan to develop skills and goals. The company offers a catalogue of courses offering sessions tailored to a variety of skills and knowledge. Other employee programs are offered through awards and opportunities to purchase shares in MDS at a discount from the market price. Interested candidates can read personal profiles of MDS employees on the company's Web site. [ID:6685]

MDSI Mobile Data Solutions Inc.
10271 Shellbridge Way, Richmond, BC, V6X 2W8, Canada;
604-207-0000, fax 604-207-0000, info@mdsi.bc.ca, www.mdsi-advantex.com

MID-SIZED HIGH TECHNOLOGY FIRM: Advanced Technology, Computer Systems, Telecommunications

MDSI Mobile Data Solutions Inc. is the largest provider of mobile workforce management solutions for the service industry worldwide. It services over 100 major blue-chip customers and has wirelessly enabled more than 80,000 mobile users around the world. The company's flagship product, Advantex, is a wireless application that schedules, assigns and wirelessly dispatches work orders to technicians in the utility, telecommunications, broadband and field service industries. The company serves customers in Africa, Europe, North America, Asia and Australia. MDSI has operations and support offices in the United States, Canada, Europe and Australia.

MDSI employs approximately 300 people. A careers page with employment opportunities may be found on the company's Web site. Interested applicants may send their resumes to jobs@mdsi.ca. The company encourages professional development and offers an in-house training program and tuition reimbursement for career-related courses. The company also offers a scholarship program. More information can be found on MDSI's Web site. [ID:6787]

Mega Engineering Ltd.
International Division, 625 - 4th Ave. S.W., Calgary, AB,
T2P 0K2, Canada; 403-263-0894, fax 403-263-6628, www.megaeng.ca

MID-SIZED PETROLEUM CONSULTING FIRM: Engineering, Management, Oilfield Services

Mega Engineering Ltd. provides engineering and management services for oil and gas drilling and production operations. The firm's main area of expertise is in planning, designing, and on-site engineering and geological supervision of oil and gas well drilling and completion operations throughout Western Canada and internationally. It has been responsible for drilling, well site geology and well completion operations on a considerable number of wells, ranging in depth from 10,000 to 16,000 feet in the geologically disturbed area of the Rocky Mountain foothills. Internationally, the firm has been engaged to provide similar services in diverse areas of the world petroleum industry, including the Middle East, the former Soviet Union, Northern Africa, Europe, South America and Asia since 1970.

Mega Engineering employs 15 people. Candidates should have a BSc in engineering, extensive experience in oil and gas operations and be open to working under unusual conditions in foreign cultures. Mega Engineering maintains a data bank for resumes. [ID:6617]

Met-Chem Canada Inc. (Met-Chem)
3rd Floor, 555 René Lévesque Blvd., Montreal, QC, H2Z 1B1, Canada;
514-288-5211, fax 514-288-7937, info@met-chem.com, www.met-chem.com ⌨ℱr

LARGE ENGINEERING CONSULTING FIRM: Accounting, Administration (General), Business Development, Computer Systems, Construction, Engineering, Environment, Human Resources, Logistics, Management Training, Project Management, Technical Assistance

Met-Chem Canada Inc. (Met-Chem) is an internationally renowned consulting engineering company, providing services in the mining, metallurgical and mineral processing sectors. The firm offers various services, including conceptual design, market research, feasibility studies, process design, basic and detailed engineering design, production management and field supervision, environmental management, start-up and commissioning, issuing certificates of acceptance, client personnel training, production improvement and optimization, maintenance warehouse organization and production management and technical assistance. Met-Chem has provided technical services in over 33 countries worldwide, touching all continents, including such countries as Argentina, China, Costa Rica, Guyana, India, Slovakia and the United States.

The firm employs 100 people including engineers, technicians and project management personnel. A careers page can be found on Met-Chem's Web site. Interested applicants should e-mail or mail their resumes to the human resources department, which can be found on the firm's Web site. The firm also offers co-op placements for students majoring in various engineering disciplines. Met-Chem also maintains a very good Web site that provides general information on the firm's activities and lists past and ongoing projects by country. [ID:6618]

Minefinders Corporation Ltd.

Suite 2288, 1177 West Hastings Street, Vancouver, BC, V6E 2K3, Canada;
604-687-6263, fax 604-687-6267, info@minefinders.com, www.minefinders.com

LARGE MINING FIRM: Exploration and Development, Gold and Metals Production, Mining

Minefinders Corporation Ltd. is a highly successful precious metals exploration company with advanced projects in Mexico and the United States. The company currently controls over 3.5 million ounces of gold resource and 160 million ounces of silver resource (in Mexico), and is actively seeking new discoveries. Offices for the company can be found in Vancouver, Nevada and Durango, Mexico. Minefinders' professional geologists, local specialists and technicians have been working continuously on MFL properties in Mexico and the US for seven years. Currently, there are several discoveries and projects underway in Mexico. When it requires additional staff or consultants, Minefinders seeks geologists, engineers and technically competent professionals. [ID:6538]

Mitel Networks

P.O. Box 13089, 350 Legget Drive, Kanata, ON, K2K 2W7,
Canada; 613-592-2122, fax 613-592-4784, www.mitel.com

LARGE TELECOMMUNICATIONS FIRM: Engineering, Marketing, Telecommunications

Mitel Networks is a market leader for voice, video and data convergence over broadband networks, with a focus on the user experience. The company delivers advanced communications solutions that are easily customized for individual business needs. Through intuitive desktop appliances and applications, businesses are provided with innovative ways to manage information and resources. Mitel has a total of 71 offices and manufacturing facilities worldwide, including the United Kingdom, Hong Kong, Dubai and the United States (Florida and Virginia).

Mitel employs approximately 2,000 people. The company's Web site has a careers page complete with job postings for Canada, Europe and the United States. Interested applicants can apply on the Web site. Mitel offers co-op opportunities to students at the world headquarters in Ottawa. New graduate programs are available for those finishing their degrees or recently graduated. Internship programs are available with Mitel. The company suggests that those interested in the internships please visit their local career services centre regarding these opportunities. Summer student opportunities for high school, college and university students to gain experience in customer service, finance, IT and marketing are also available with Mitel. Several universities partner with the company. [ID:6619]

National Bank of Canada/Banque Nationale du Canada

International Division, 5th Floor, 600 de la Gauchetière Street W., Montreal, QC,
H3B 4L3, Canada; 514-394-6400, fax 514-394-8276, telnat@bnc.ca, www.nbc.ca ☐𝐹𝑟

MID-SIZED FINANCIAL SERVICES FIRM: Accounting, Administration (General), Banking and Financial Services, Business Development, Business/Banking/Trade, Commerce, Customer Services, Investment Banking, Personal Taxation/Financial Planning, Services for International Businesses

The National Bank of Canada is the sixth largest chartered bank in Canada with assets in excess of $75 billion. The Canadian network of the bank boasts 546 branches, including 454 in Quebec. The bank is also increasingly active on the international scene with offices on all four corners of the globe. It has representative offices in England, Cuba and France (international commerce centres), and international centres in Hong Kong, Cuba, England, Bahamas, the United States and France. The bank is an integrated group that provides comprehensive financial services to consumers, small and medium-sized enterprises and large corporations in its core market, while offering specialized services to its clients elsewhere in the world. The bank offers a full array of banking services including retail, corporate and investment banking, and is involved in securities brokerage, insurance, wealth management, mutual fund and retirement plan management.

The National Bank of Canada, together with its subsidiaries, employs close to 17,000 people. A careers page can be found on the bank's Web site with job opportunities posted, as well as an on-line recruitment centre where interested candidates can apply. The bank offers various training programs and personalized training plans to employees. Each year, the bank ensures it is represented at some of Canada's largest universities. It regularly seeks graduates in the following fields: finance, accounting and administration, sales and service to individuals and businesses. The bank suggests that those interested in receiving more information should contact their university's employment office to find out the various recruitment activities the bank will be participating in. An internship program is also available with the bank to help students gain practical work experience related to their studies. [ID:6529]

ND LEA Consultants Ltd.
Suite 600, 1455 West Georgia Street, Vancouver, BC, V6G 2T3, Canada;
604-685-9381, fax 604-685-1728, international@ndlea.com, www.ndlea.com

MID-SIZED ENVIRONMENTAL CONSULTING FIRM: Computer Systems, Construction, Consulting, Engineering, Environment, Human Resources, Institution Building, Project Management, Railways, Roads, Technical Assistance, Transportation

ND LEA Consultants Ltd. is an employee-owned consulting engineering firm specializing in transportation infrastructure. Services are provided by the firm through two operating companies: ND LEA Consultants Ltd. in Vancouver and Williams Lake, British Columbia, and ND LEA Engineers and Planners Inc. in Winnipeg, Manitoba. The Vancouver office serves the British Columbia market and is the base for international projects. The firm's primary focus is transportation infrastructure for which planning, design, construction supervision and project management are provided for highways, bridges, transit infrastructure, parkades, railway infrastructure, airport airside and landside infrastructure, municipal roads and land development. Services are also provided relating to asset management, institutional strengthening and environmental assessments. The firm has offices in Indonesia, Sri Lanka, Nepal, Trinidad and Tobago, Guyana, the Philippines and Cambodia. It has also completed several projects in Asia, the Caribbean, South America, Central America and Africa.

ND LEA has approximately 150 employees. A careers page can be found on the firm's Web site with employment opportunities. Employment opportunities include road and highway technologists, highway engineers, transportation planners and environmental planners. Applicants are requested to submit an electronic resume to international@NDLEA.com, indicating the position sought by the applicant. All engineers interested in overseas work in the transportation sector are invited to submit their resume to ND LEA for consideration in new projects. New staff are chosen from the firm's database to fit upcoming projects. [ID:6528]

Nexen Inc.
801 - 7th Ave. S.W., Calgary, AB, T2P 3P7, Canada; 403-699-4000, www.nexeninc.com

MID-SIZED ENERGY RESOURCES FIRM: Chemicals, Energy Resources, Engineering, Exploration and Development, Geophysics, Oil and Gas Exploration

Nexen Inc. is an independent global energy and chemicals company, listed on the Toronto and New York stock exchanges. Nexen is expanding its exploration operations into the Gulf of Mexico, Yemen, West Africa and to the Athabasca oil sands of Alberta. The company's activities include full-cycle oil and gas exploration, development, production and marketing of crude oil and natural gas, as well as the manufacturing and marketing of sodium chlorate and chlor-alkali products.p

The company employs more than 2,800 people worldwide. Nexen offers a Graduate Development Program, a Summer Student Employment Program, as well as co-operative and internship work terms that allow students to gain practical experience. Further information regarding these programs and campus visits may be found on the company's Web site. Nexen also posts employment opportunities on its Web site. Nexen's Web site, especially its career and student programs section, is very detailed. The Web site also provides useful interview tips. [ID:6711]

NORAM Engineering & Constructors Ltd.
Suite 400, 200 Granville Street, Vancouver, BC, V6C 1S4, Canada;
604-681-2030, fax 604-683-9164, questions@noram-eng.com, www.noram-eng.com

MID-SIZED ENGINEERING FIRM: Advanced Technology, Chemicals, Engineering, Environment, Project Management, Waste Water Management

NORAM Engineering and Constructors Ltd. is a Canadian technology and engineering company specializing in the commercialization of new chemical processes. The company offers leading edge technologies to the chemical, pulp and paper, minerals processing and electrochemical industries. It has also become a supplier to the municipal and industrial waste water treatment market. The company has experience in waste water treatment, sulphuric acid, acid recovery and concentration, nitration, electrochemical, pulp and paper, and bleaching chemicals technologies. NORAM has completed projects on five continents involving the complete engineering and equipment supply for chemical and waste water treatment plants, the supply of proprietary equipment, engineering studies, and joint development projects.

The company employs 35 people. The staff is made up of engineers, designers and project management personnel. [ID:6560]

Noranda Inc.
Suite 200, BCE Place, 181 Bay Street, Toronto, ON, M5J 2T3, Canada;
416-982-7111, fax 416-982-7423, request@noranda.com, www.noranda.com ▢*Fr*

LARGE NATURAL RESOURCES FIRM: Accounting, Administration (General), Computer Systems, Engineering, Environment, Gold and Metals Production, Human Resources, Metals, Mineral Resources, Mining, Project Management

Noranda Inc. is a leading international mining and metals company with operations and offices in nine countries. It is one of the world's largest producers of zinc and nickel and is also a significant producer of copper, primary and fabricated aluminum, lead, silver, gold, sulpheric acid and cobalt. In addition, Noranda is a major recycler of secondary copper, nickel and precious metals. It has operations in Canada, the United States, Mexico, Peru, Chile, Brazil, Ireland, Norway, Switzerland, the Ivory Coast, New Caledonia and Australia.

Noranda employs 15,000 people in its worldwide operations and offices worldwide. An employment page with job postings can be found on the company's Web site. The company is a host organization for Career Edge, a Canadian private sector initiative which enhances youth employability by providing valuable, career-related experience through internships within successful Canadian organizations. [ID:6579]

Norenco Associated Ltd.
671 Kenwood Road W., Vancouver, BC, V7S 1S7, Canada; 604-925-0570, fax 604-925-0571

SMALL ENGINEERING CONSULTING FIRM: Engineering Management

Norenco Associated Ltd. offers professional services for civil engineering and transportation projects. Areas of expertise include feasibility studies, project planning, engineering management, project management, quality assurance and computer technology. Training and technology transfer are main components of the firm's international projects. Norenco provides consulting services for a wide range of projects in Canada and also in Africa, Asia and Latin America. [ID:6620]

Nortel Networks Corp.

Suite 100, 8200 Dixie Road, Brampton, ON, L6T 5P6, Canada;
905-863-0000, fax 905-863-8505, www.nortelnetworks.com

LARGE TELECOMMUNICATIONS FIRM: Administration (General), Engineering, Marketing, Research and Development, Telecommunications

Nortel Networks Corp. is an industry leader and innovator focused on transforming how the world communicates and exchanges information. The company is supplying its service provider and enterprise customers with communications technology and infrastructure to enable value-added IP data, voice and multimedia services spanning wireless, wireline, enterprise and optical networks. The company does business in more than 150 countries around the world and has offices in South America, Europe, Asia, Australia, North America, Africa and the Middle East.

Nortel Networks employs approximately 35,500 people. A careers page can be found on the company's Web site and candidates can search through employment opportunities and submit resumes to the company's resume database. The company also offers student and new graduate programs in locations around the world. Nortel Networks seeks applicants in technical disciplines such as computer science, systems and electrical engineering, as well as a limited number of opportunities in business, finance and marketing. [ID:6621]

Northern Orion Resources Inc.

Suite 250, 1075 West Georgia Street, Vancouver, BC, V6E 3C9, Canada;
604-689-9663, fax 604-434-1487, info@northernorion.com, www.northernorion.com

LARGE MINING FIRM: Environment, Exploration and Development, Gold and Metals Production, Metals, Mining, Sustainable Development

Northern Orion Resources Inc. is a low-cost copper and gold producer with a 12.5 per cent interest in the Bajo de la Alumbrera mine in northwestern Argentina. Alumbrera gives Northern Orion an estimated annual cash flow of $45 million US. The company is also developing its wholly owned Agua Rica (34 kilometres away from Alumbrera) copper/gold deposit which contains more than 10 million ounces of gold and 18 billion pounds of copper. It also conducts environmental assessments in the prefeasibility and feasibility studies at its advanced stage projects. [ID:6683]

Northwest Hydraulic Consultants Ltd. (NHC)

Manager, International Operations, 30 Gostick Place, North Vancouver, BC, V7M 3G2, Canada; 604-980-6011, fax 604-980-9264, jobs@nhcweb.com, www.nhcweb.com

LARGE WATER RESOURCES FIRM: Consulting, Development Assistance, Engineering, Environment, Project Management, Technical Assistance, Water Resources

Northwest Hydraulic Consultants (NHC) specializes in protecting, managing and developing water resources. The company's primary service areas are in river engineering, hydrology, hydraulic analysis and design, physical hydraulic modelling, sedimentation engineering and water resource development and management, as well as project management. NHC has been providing solutions to challenging water resource problems since 1972, from river crossings of the Trans Alaska Oil Pipeline in the Arctic, to large-scale riverbank stabilization works for the Jamuna and Meghna Rivers in Bangladesh. Clients of the company include organizations such as the United States Army Corps of Engineers, the Asian Development Bank and the Bangladesh Water Development Board, as well as other private engineering firms who rely on NHC's specialist services.

NHC employs approximately 100 people in offices in Western Canada and the United States, and on international project assignments primarily in Southeast Asia. The company also operates hydraulic modelling laboratories at its Vancouver and Edmonton locations in support of both its domestic and international work. The company has approximately 15 staff with international responsibilities based in Canada. NHC is particularly interested in hearing from those with backgrounds in complex project management and/or high-level hydrotechnical engineering or science. Resumes may be sent to jobs@nhcweb.com. [ID:6622]

Ophthalmic Technologies Inc.

Unit 16, 37 Kodiak Crescent, Toronto, ON, M3J 3E5, Canada;
416-631-9123, fax 416-631-6932, info@oti-canada.com, www.oti-canada.com

MID-SIZED MEDICAL IMAGING SOFTWARE FIRM: Advanced Technology, Information Technologies, Medical Diagnostics, Medical Health

Ophthalmic Technologies Inc. provides technologically advanced, easy-to-use equipment for ophthalmology. The company offers innovative systems with advanced imaging capabilities and provides tools that meet the needs of ophthalmologists and surgeons worldwide. In 2001, a subsidiary office opened in New Jersey to help the US market and an office was recently added in the UK at the University of Kent. Ophthalmic Technologies has a growing distribution network currently extending to over 40 countries around the world, touching Australia, South America, Asia, Europe, Africa and the Middle East. The company employs approximately 17 people. [ID:6798]

P.A. Services Conseils Inc.

Suite 800, 1 Westmount Square, Montreal, QC, H3Z 2P9, Canada; 514-932-8050,
fax 514-932-8960, info@paservicesconseils.com, www.paservicesconseils.com 💻 *Fr*

LARGE MANAGEMENT CONSULTING FIRM: Accounting, Administration (General), Adult Training, Agriculture, Banking and Financial Services, Business Development, Computer Systems, Consulting, Development Assistance, Development Education, Economic Development, Economics, Education, Gender and Development, Human Resources, Management Training, Micro-enterprises, Project Management, Technical Assistance

P.A. Services Conseils Inc. (also known as P.A. Consulting Services Inc.) specializes in the transfer of innovative and appropriate technology, to the public and private sectors at the national and international level to developing countries and to countries in transitional economies. The firm's team of specialists come from various disciplines with a great deal of experience in management, consulting and development. P.A. Services' professionals assist clients in strategic planning, organizational development, financial and human resources management, information system management, marketing, accounting, banking, as well as education and training. The firm's professionals can assume the creation and implementation of state-of-the-art administration and financial systems, allowing better utilization of resources and the enhancement of organizational and structural efficiency. Current projects of the firm include Zambia, Jamaica (in management and economics), United Arab Emirates (in education and training) and in Kuwait and Algeria (in computer science). The firm has also completed projects in Hungary, Croatia, Vietnam, the Democratic Republic of Congo, Morocco, Niger, Romania, Tunisia, Sierra Leone, Tanzania, Kuwait, Benin, Haiti, Indonesia and Senegal. P.A. Services has one international office in Romania.

The firm maintains a database of consultants that would like to conduct mandates abroad. Interested candidates should have a master's degree or PhD combined with 10 years' pertinent experience. [ID:6623]

Pacific Business Intelligence Ltd.

8916 Salish Place, Sidney, BC, V8L 4A5, Canada; 250-889-1414, fax 250-656-9183, www.pacificintel.com

SMALL GENERAL CONSULTING FIRM: Business/Banking/Trade, Economics, Marketing, Project Management, Research

Pacific Business Intelligence Ltd. provides professional consulting services in the core areas of international marketing, strategic planning, international trade and research and export development. It has also undertaken economic feasibility studies, industry and sector analysis, industrial development projects and has managed a wide variety of research programs. The company has undertaken consulting assignments for governments, multinational corporations, small- and medium-sized businesses, international agencies, research organizations and academic training institutions. Pacific Business Intelligence Ltd. has worked in Vietnam, Singapore, the Philippines, Malaysia, Taiwan, Thailand, Brunei, Australia, Indonesia, the United Kingdom, the United States and Canada. [ID:6784]

PendoPharm Inc.

8580, ave. de l'Esplanade, Montreal, QC, H2P 2R9, Canada;
514-384-6516, fax 514-384-9941, www.pendopharm.com

LARGE PHARMACEUTICAL FIRM: Manufacturing, Marketing, Medical Health, Pharmaceuticals, Research and Development

PendoPharm Inc. (formerly PanGeo Pharma Canada Inc.) is a specialty pharmaceutical company with core competencies in pharmaceutical manufacturing and marketing. The company manufactures and supplies a range of specialty pharmaceutical products and services to Canadian and international markets. It has worked with the Canadian International Development Agency (CIDA) and the World Bank for projects in Africa and the Caribbean. It has also completed contracts in Uganda, Tanzania, Kenya, Mali, Niger, Mozambique, Zambia, Jamaica, Trinidad and Cuba.

PendoPharm employs approximately 100 people working in three facilities. A careers page can be found on the company's Web site. It is suggested that interested applicants send their resumes to jobs@pendopharm.com. [ID:6793]

Petro-Canada

P.O. Box 2844, Calgary, AB, T2P 3E3, Canada; 403-296-8000,
fax 403-296-3030, investor@petro-canada.ca, www.petro-canada.ca 💻 *Fr*

LARGE PETROCHEMICALS FIRM: Accounting, Administration (General), Commerce, Computer Systems, Energy Resources, Engineering, Environment, Marketing, Oil and Gas Exploration, Petrochemicals, Research and Development

Petro-Canada is one of the largest integrated oil and gas companies in Canada and a significant international player. It has a strong reputation for ethical conduct, environmental responsibility and good corporate citizenship. Petro-Canada is building a world-class future on a solid and uniquely Canadian foundation. Petro-Canada is strategically focused on five core businesses: 1) North American Gas, which focuses on the exploration and production of natural gas in Western Canada, the marketing of natural gas in North America and the pursuit of high-potential exploration in other regions of North America including the Mackenzie Delta/Corridor, offshore Nova Scotia, and Alaska; 2) East Coast Oil, which focuses on the exploration, development, production and marketing of oil off Newfoundland; 3) Oil Sands, with the development and production of bitumen and synthetic crude oil in northeastern Alberta and conversion of the Edmonton refinery to process oil sands feedstock; 4) International, which focuses on the exploration, development, production and marketing of oil and natural gas focused in northwest Europe (production from the UK and Netherlands sectors of the North Sea, and exploration in Denmark), North Africa/Near East (production and exploration in Syria, Libya, Algeria and Tunisia) and northern Latin America (interest in a gas development offshore Trinidad and exploration in Venezuela). The company also has an office in London, England, from where it runs its international operations; 5) Refining and Sales & Marketing, which focuses on the conversion of crude oil into refined petroleum products, including gasoline, diesel, asphalt and high-quality lubricants and a network of over 1,600 retail and wholesale outlets in Canada. The company operates three refineries and a state-of-the-art lubricants facility in Canada.

Petro-Canada employs 4,500 people. Of those employees, 270 are employed in the International business. A careers page with employment opportunities can be found on the company's Web site. Petro-Canada offers a co-op/internship program. This program runs across their businesses and opportunities are available throughout the year. The company requires students from disciplines such as engineering, commerce, marketing, computer science, accounting, earth sciences and many more fields. The opportunities are posted through post-secondary institutions and the company asks that those interested check with their campus career centres. Petro-Canada also offers a new graduate program which provides an opportunity for new graduates to build their capabilities in an environment that supports learning, growth and performance. Those interested are also asked to check with their campus career centres for details. Petro-Canada also participates in campus career fairs. [ID:6608]

PGF Consultants Inc.

Suite 202, 291 Dalhousie Street, Ottawa, ON, K1N 7E5, Canada;
613-241-2251, fax 613-241-2252, inform@pgf.ca, www.pgf.ca 💻 *Fr*

MID-SIZED MANAGEMENT CONSULTING FIRM: Consulting, Development Assistance, Leadership
Assessment, Management Consulting, Organization Development, Social Policy, Social Science Research,
Training and Education

PGF Consultants Inc. provides management consulting services in organizational
development, training and social policy research. The company is made up of three divisions:
Organizational Development and Learning, Public Policy Research and Development, and
International. The International sector has developed working teams in learning, research and
international development. The combined experience of the company's team, which includes
consulting staff and associates, encompasses language skills in English, French, Spanish, Arabic,
German, Hebrew and Yiddish. PGF Consultants have assisted progressive governments,
corporations and not-for-profit groups with their customized leadership and organizational
development services. The company has also built a solid public policy research group that
provides expert advice and analysis to senior government and private sector officials. It has
undertaken some 400 projects in 30 countries, from Romania to Morocco, and has developed
several partnerships in Africa and the Middle East. It also has experience working with the
Canadian International Development Agency (CIDA) on million-dollar projects.

PGF Consultants has a full-time staff of 15 and a network of more than 40 associates from
across Canada. A careers page with employment postings may be found on the company's Web site.
Interested applicants may forward their resumes to info@pgf.ca. [ID:6808]

Phair-Sutherland Consulting Inc.

Suite 101, 475 Central Ave., London, ON, N6B 2G2, Canada; 519-472-2029, www.phair-sutherland.com 💻 *Sp*

MID-SIZED MANAGEMENT CONSULTING FIRM: Business Development, Consulting, Management
Consulting, Management Training, Marketing, Media/Communications, Telecommunications

Phair-Sutherland Consulting Inc. provides high-quality consulting services to the
telecommunications and high technology communities. The company consults on a broad range of
strategic marketing issues in projects lasting from three days to three years. It works with the
boards and executive teams of both multinationals and start-ups, assisting them in the definition of
strategic direction. Since 1986, the company has worked with 15 joint venture partnerships and
alliances and has particular expertise in assisting partners to improve their market performance. The
company works for equipment suppliers, applications and services suppliers, service providers and
carriers, as well as industry associations in the areas of wireless, broadband access, optical and
satellite networks. Phair-Sutherland provides various consulting services, including strategic
business and market planning, funding issues, marketing, communications planning, improving
market performance and training. The company has sold and delivered strategic marketing and
business solutions to a wide range of telecommunications companies in North America, South
America and Europe. Phair-Sutherland hires established consultants when required. [ID:6575]

Pharmascience Inc.

Suite 100, 6111, ave. Royalmount, Montreal, QC, H4P 2T4, Canada;
514-340-9800, fax 514-342-7764, service@pharmascience.com, www.pharmascience.com

LARGE PHARMACEUTICAL FIRM: Accounting, Administration (General), Manufacturing, Marketing,
Medical Health, Pharmaceuticals, Quality Assurance, Research and Development

Pharmascience Inc. is one of Canada's fastest growing pharmaceutical companies. The
company researches, develops, manufactures and markets generic and innovative products for both
prescription and over-the-counter sale. It produces more than 330 quality brandname and generic
products which are sold in over 30 countries around the world. Pharmascience has a global
presence as it holds distribution agreements in over 30 countries. It currently has partnership
agreements with companies in the United States, Europe, Asia and South America.

Pharmascience employs close to 1,000 people. A careers page with employment opportunities may be found on the company's Web site. The company offers a training and development program, as well as a rewards program. Positions are available in research and development, clinical research, quality control/quality assurance, regulatory affairs, sales and marketing, accounting and finance, as well as operations. [ID:6794]

Piteau Associates Engineering Ltd.

Suite 215, 260 West Esplanade, North Vancouver, BC, V7M 3G7, Canada;
604-986-8551, fax 604-985-7286, info@piteau.com, www.piteau.com

MID-SIZED GENERAL CONSULTING FIRM: Construction, Consulting, Engineering, Environment, Hydrographic Surveys, Project Management, Roads, Transportation, Waste Water Management, Water Resources

Piteau Associates Engineering Ltd. is an employee-owned company which offers a comprehensive range of services for resource development and management, transportation, construction, waste management and remediation. Services offered by the firm include groundwater resource management, contaminated site assessments, containment and remediation of contaminated soil and groundwater, mine design, construction and operation, mine waste management, waste management (from secure storage and containment of municipal and industrial wastes, to treatment and subsurface disposal of municipal waste water), resource development and management, transportation projects (including arterial highways, secondary roads, resource roads, railways, pipelines and transmission lines), civil and municipal construction. Piteau has provided services to projects in over 250 locations from Alaska to Tasmania and from Chile to China. The firm has opened a subsidiary office in Lima, Peru, to serve new and existing clients in Latin America. The firm also has a network of associates in offices in Argentina, Brazil, Chile, Colombia and Ecuador.

Piteau has 12 full-time staffers with extensive international responsibilities who are employed in Canada. They do not have overseas staff. Their engineering staff in Canada totals about 15. The company's team is made up of engineers, geoscientists and environmental specialists. Currently, some employees travel overseas for brief projects but there are no overseas postings. Only experienced engineers are sent on overseas projects. [ID:6570]

Placer Dome Inc.

P.O. Box 49330, Bentall Station, Vancouver, BC, V7X 1P1, Canada;
604-682-7082, fax 604-682-7092, goldpanner@placerdome.com, www.placerdome.com

LARGE MINING FIRM: Accounting, Administration (General), Computer Systems, Construction, Engineering, Exploration and Development, Human Resources, Metals, Mining, Project Management

Placer Dome Inc. is the world's sixth largest gold mining company pursuing quality assets around the world. The company's core gold business is strengthened by the contributions of the company's copper and silver assets. Placer Dome has interests in 18 mines in seven countries around the world. In 2004, the company expects to produce roughly 3.6 million ounces of gold and 400 million pounds of copper. Placer Dome has offices and operations in South Africa, Tanzania, Australia, Canada, Chile, the United States and Papua New Guinea.

The company maintains a careers page on its Web site containing contact information for each mine site and regional office. Interested applicants may contact one of the company's mine sites or offices directly. Alternatively, applicants may also send resumes to resumes@placerdome.com. [ID:6571]

PLAN:NET Ltd.

Suite 201, 1225a Kensington Road N.W., Calgary, AB, T2N 3P8, Canada;
403-270-0217, fax 403-270-8672, plannet@plannet.ca, www.plannet.ca

MID-SIZED MANAGEMENT CONSULTING FIRM: Community Development, Consulting, Development Assistance, Development Education, Environment, Gender and Development, Medical Health, Micro-enterprises, Organization Development, Policy Development, Project Management, Social Justice and Development, Technical Assistance, Training and Education, Urban Development

PLAN:NET Ltd. is an integrated planning and management corporation that provides comprehensive consulting and project management services to governments, non-governmental organizations, institutions and private clients. The firm's extensive and diverse roster of professionals has contributed their expertise to contracts in a wide range of service areas, including program/project management, monitoring and evaluation; results-based management and outcome measurement; gender and development, urban and rural planning; public and community health, environmental planning and management, community organization, participatory rapid assessment; social impact assessment and socio-economic policy analysis; organizational capacity building, training and education. PLAN:NET has worked with such multilateral institutions as the World Bank, the United Nations Development Programme, UN HABITAT, as well as IDRC, CIDA, FAC, ITCan and several other Canadian government departments, learning institutions, non-governmental organizations and public institutions, and the private sector. International assignments have included institutional evaluations in Sri Lanka, project design and monitoring in Africa, inputs evaluation in India, mid-term reviews of India, Sri Lanka, Bangladesh, Nepal and Pakistan. PLAN:NET has also had experience working with countries in Africa, the Middle East, Eastern Europe, the Caribbean, Latin America and North America.

The firm has approximately 30 professionals who have a wide range of national and international experience. No personnel are permanently stationed overseas. PLAN:NET staff are typically sent abroad on short-term assignments. PLAN:NET maintains a Web site that offers information on its programs and services. [ID:6655]

Policy Research International Inc. (PRI)

Suite 14, 6 Beechwood Ave., Ottawa, ON, K1L 8B4, Canada; 613-746-2554,
fax 613-744-4899, staff@pri.on.ca, www.pri.on.ca, www.policyresearch.ca

MID-SIZED GENERAL CONSULTING FIRM: Business Development, Development Education, Economics, Education, Energy Resources, Environment, Medical Health, Policy Development, Project Management, Science and Technology, Social Policy, Training and Technology Transfer

Policy Research International Inc. (PRI) is a Canadian-owned company based in Ottawa. The company specializes in the activities of research, strategy, policy and program design, evaluation and implementation of projects in the thematic areas of economics, education, energy, environment, health, social policy and technology transfer. It has worked on these issues and problems in Canada and internationally for 14 years. Clients of the company have included the governments of Canada, Australia and New Zealand; the Canadian International Development Agency (CIDA); the International Development Research Centre (IDRC); the World Bank; several agencies of the United Nations including the United Nations Environment Programme, as well as a number of non-governmental organizations and private firms. The firm undertakes between five and 15 contracts each year. These assignments usually require access to a broad knowledge base, experience and judgement, as well as the ability to integrate multidisciplinary skills and appropriate experience. PRI works with a small core group of staff, between four to six, and associates in Canada, Africa, Asia, Latin America and Europe, selecting team members based on the needs of individual projects. More information is available on the Web site.

PRI maintains a database of potential consultants. It believes it is important to share the outputs of its policy work widely, and to allow younger and highly motivated persons with less experience in issues of international development and policy to work with senior staff in the ongoing research and dissemination tasks. PRI has partnered with several universities in working with graduate research projects and has undertaken to host interns supported under the Canadian Youth Employment Strategy. [ID:6572]

Pratt & Whitney Canada (P&WC)
1000 Marie-Victorin Blvd., Longueuil, QC, J4G 1A1, Canada;
450-677-9411, fax 450-647-3620, human.resources@pwc.ca, www.pwc.ca ⬛ *Fr*

LARGE TRANSPORTATION MANUFACTURING FIRM: Aerospace Technology, Air Transportation, Customer Services, Engineering, Technical Assistance, Transportation

Pratt & Whitney Canada (P&WC), based in Longueuil, Quebec, is a world leader in aviation engines powering business, general aviation and regional aircraft and helicopters. The company also offers advanced engines for industrial applications. P&WC's operations and service network span the globe. It is a subsidiary of United Technologies Corporation (NYSE:UTX), a high-technology company based in Hartford, Connecticut.

P&WC's operations include production facilities in Canada, Poland and China; service centres in Canada, the United States, Brazil, South Africa, Australia, the United Kingdom, Germany and Singapore as well as engineering facilities in Russia. P&WC's engines are used in over 190 countries around the world.

Pratt & Whitney Canada employs more than 6,000 people in Canada and close to 2,500 people internationally. A careers page with employment opportunities for new graduates and those with specializations in engineering, product integrity, as well as others may be found on the company's Web site. Interested applicants may apply by completing the company's on-line application form or send their resumes to human.resources@pwc.ca. New graduates may send their resumes to newgrads@pwc.ca. [ID:6822]

Precision Drilling Corp.
Suite 4200, 150 - 6th Ave. S.W., Calgary, AB, T2P 3Y7, Canada;
403-716-4500, fax 403-716-4867, info@precisiondrilling.com, www.precisiondrilling.com

LARGE ENERGY RESOURCES FIRM: Drilling Services, Industrial Services, Oilfield Services, Research and Development

Precision Drilling Corp. is a global oil field services company, providing a broad range of drilling, production and evaluation services with a focus on fulfilling customer needs through fit-for-purpose technologies for the maturing oil fields of the 21st century. The company has offices in Calgary and Houston, Texas and research facilities in the United States and Europe, as well as people conducting operations in more than 30 countries. Regional operations' headquarters and service centres are located in Houston, Texas, Caracas (Venezuela), Jakarta (Indonesia), Abu Dhabi (United Arab Emirates) and Hanover (Germany). Staff in these locations support clients' drilling operations in Canada, the United States, Mexico, Latin America, Europe, the Middle East and the Asia Pacific.

Precision employs more than 10,000 people. A careers page complete with job postings can be found on the company's Web site. Interested applicants can fax or e-mail applications to the appropriate contact found on the Web site. [ID:6702]

Project Services International (PSI)
P.O. Box 1139, Stn.B, Ottawa, ON, K1P 5R2, Canada;
613-244-1049, fax 613-244-8315, mail@psi-spi.com, www.psi-spi.com

MID-SIZED GENERAL CONSULTING FIRM: Business Development, Community Development, Consulting, Development Education, Economic Development, Environment, Gender and Development, Human Resources, Institution Building, Law, Law and Good Governance, Logistics, Management Consulting, Micro-enterprises, Policy Development, Project Management, Research, Social Justice and Development, Social Policy

Project Services International (PSI) is a Canadian consulting firm specializing in international development consulting by attracting and building a core of experienced development professionals and networks with other small firms. The sole focus of the firm is international development and business. PSI's professionals each have over 15 years experience in international development, working and living in countries in Asia, Africa, the Caribbean, Europe and the Americas. The firm has international expertise in project identification, design, implementation, management and performance review, and specializes in the law and development, small and medium enterprise development, and financing and entrepreneurship development. PSI has international experience in institutional, capacity, social capital and human resources development, debt and equity financing, social economic and market research, business development, gender equality, participatory development, governance, enabling environments and policy development. Clients of the firm include the Canadian International Development Agency (CIDA), the United Nations Development Programme, the Asian Development Bank, Health Canada, the International Labour Organization, CARE International and the Aga Khan Foundation Canada.

Prospective applicants should have education and experience in economics, business, sciences or engineering. PSI maintains a data bank for resumes. [ID:6547]

Psion Teklogix
2100 Meadowvale Blvd., Mississauga, ON, L5N 7J9, Canada;
905-813-9900, ptinfo@psion.com, www.psionteklogix.com

LARGE HIGH TECHNOLOGY FIRM: Advanced Technology, Computer Systems, Engineering, Research and Development, Technical Assistance

Psion Teklogix is a global provider of solutions for mobile computing wireless data collection and integrated warehousing solutions. The company provides customers with fully integrated mobile computing solutions that include rugged hardware, secure wireless networks, robust software, professional services and exceptional support programs. Psion Teklogix serves various markets, including airports, automotive, cold chain, field service, government, ports/container yards, transportation, warehousing and distribution, as well as other markets. It has installed wireless systems in more than 60 countries around the world. The company has 35 sales and support offices in 16 countries, as well as customers in over 70 countries around the world who they service either directly or through their network of valued business partners which include independent distributors in North America, Europe, the Middle East, the Asia/Pacific rim, Australia, South America and Latin America. It also has additional offices in the United States, Europe and Asia.

Psion Teklogix employs approximately 600 people. A careers page with both international and national employment opportunities may be found on the company's Web site. [ID:6791]

Rally Energy Corp.
Suite 2000, 715 Fifth Ave. S.W., Calgary, AB, T2P 2X6, Canada;
403-538-0000, fax 403-538-3705, rally@rallyenergy.com, www.rallyenergy.com

LARGE PETROLEUM EXPLORATION FIRM: Oil and Gas Exploration, Oilfield Services, Petrochemicals

Rally Energy Corp. is an oil and gas exploration, development and production company. The company's international strategy is to enhance value in areas where discovered reserves already exist by applying Canadian development techniques and technology to the production of reserves. It is active in Egypt, Canada and Pakistan. [ID:6692]

RANA International Inc.
1 Russell Street W., Smiths Falls, ON, K7A 1N8, Canada;
613-284-0776, fax 613-283-6992, rana@ranaprocess.com, www.ranaprocess.com

MID-SIZED MANAGEMENT CONSULTING FIRM: Adult Training, Business Development, Consulting, Development Assistance, Development Education, Management, Project Management

RANA International Inc. is a Canadian company with roots in process consultation, facilitation, training and research development. It has international affiliations offering integrated organizational and management development services in Canada and abroad. The company has experience as process consultants and organizational development experts in government, industry and the non-governmental sectors. RANA has helped clients in the United States, Europe, South

America, the Caribbean, Australia and Africa. The company employs 20 consultants and also has an office in the United Kingdom. [ID:6809]

Resource Futures International (RFI)

Suite 103, 858 Bank Street, Ottawa, ON, K1S 3W3, Canada;
613-253-4343, fax 613-235-9916, info@rfigroup.com, www.rfigroup.com

MID-SIZED ENVIRONMENTAL CONSULTING FIRM: Consulting, Environment, Institution Building, Media/Communications, Policy Development, Project Management, Technical Assistance, Water Resources

Resource Futures International (RFI) is a Canadian company specializing in the provision of environmental policy analysis, management, assessment, institutional strengthening and communications strategies. The firm provides advanced and proven solutions to the sustainable development challenges encountered by communities, companies and governments. Currently, RFI has projects underway in China, India and Central America, but has completed hundreds of assignments for national and international agencies, governments, businesses and non-governmental organizations in the following countries: Bangladesh, Brazil, Cambodia, Costa Rica, China, Egypt, India, Indonesia, Laos, Malaysia, Mexico, Nepal, Pakistan, the Philippines, Thailand and the United States. Furthermore, the company has had experience with the Asian Development Bank, the United Nations Environment Programme, the United Nations Development Programme and the International Institute for Sustainable Development, to name a few.

RFI has five employees in Ottawa with international responsibilities and one consultant based in an associate office in Phnom Penh, Cambodia. RFI's staff includes experts working in specialized fields such as climate change, management strategies for chemicals and hazardous wastes, biodiversity, development and implementation of multilateral environmental agreements, environmental impact assessment and large project management. Prospective applicants should have relevant educational background in environmental policy or capacity development and some prior work experience. RFI maintains a data bank for resumes. [ID:6669]

RIM (Research In Motion)

295 Phillip Street, Waterloo, ON, N2L 3W8, Canada; 519-888-7465,
fax 519-888-7884, recruitment@rim.com, www.rim.com, www.blackberry.com

LARGE HIGH TECHNOLOGY FIRM: Advanced Technology, Engineering, Information Technologies, Marketing

RIM (Research In Motion) is a leading designer, manufacturer and marketer of innovative wireless solutions for the worldwide mobile communications market. The company provides platforms and solutions such as BlackBerry® for seamless access to time-sensitive information, including e-mail, phone, SMS messaging, Internet and Intranet-based applications. RIM technology also enables a broad array of third-party developers and manufacturers to enhance their products and services with wireless connectivity to data. The company operates offices in North America, Europe and Asia Pacific.

RIM's employee base has grown significantly since 1998, growing from approximately 200 to well over 2,000 people by 2004. This number continues to grow as RIM continues to expand further into the global wireless market. A careers page with employment opportunities may be found on the company's Web site. RIM participates in career fairs and overseas and student (co-op and intern) job opportunities are also posted on the careers page. [ID:6772]

RMC Resources Management Consultants Ltd.

Suite 100, 55 Ormskirk Ave., Toronto, ON, M6S 4V6, Canada;
416-762-8166, fax 416-762-1963, info@rmc-canada.com, www.rmc-canada.com

MID-SIZED MANAGEMENT CONSULTING FIRM: Computer Systems, Consulting, Human Resources, Medical Health, Project Management, Technical Assistance

RMC Resources Management Consultants Ltd. provides specialized high-quality expertise to the public and private sectors with particular emphasis on health, social services, education and justice. In addition to its active domestic practice, the firm has gained significant recognition for its work in the restructuring of healthcare systems. The firm has conducted successful projects in more than 40 countries, engaging hundreds of local and international specialists and professionals. Some of the services provided by the firm include health, social services and education, facility planning, equipment planning and commissioning, corporate planning and organizational development, management of information systems and human resources development. RMC has completed international projects in Albania, Armenia, Bahamas, Botswana, Canada, Dominica, Estonia, Georgia, Guyana, Hungary, Indonesia, Lithuania, Malaysia, Poland, Slovenia, Trinidad and Tobago, Turkey, Uganda, Ukraine and the United States.

The firm has a staff of 20 employees. The ideal international consultant possesses relevant post-graduate education, extensive experience in both consulting and management positions, speaks fluently in two or more languages, including English, and is culturally aware and sensitive. Preferred languages are English, Spanish, Polish, Ukrainian and Russian. RMC maintains a data bank for resumes. [ID:6576]

Roche Ltée., Groupe-Conseil/Roche Ltd. Consulting Group

3075 Chemin des Quatre-Bourgeois, Sainte-Foy, QC, G1W 4Y4,
Canada; 418-654-9600, fax 418-654-9699, srh@roche.ca, www.roche.ca 🖥 *Fr*

LARGE GENERAL CONSULTING FIRM: Architecture and Planning, Community Development, Construction, Consulting, Development Assistance, Energy Resources, Engineering, Environment, Forestry, Geomatics, Mining, Project Management, Technical Assistance, Transportation, Urban Development, Water Resources

Roche Ltd. Consulting Group/Roche Ltée., Groupe-Conseil is an integrated multidisciplinary design/build/operate company. It is also one of the largest engineering-construction companies in Canada. The company specializes in projects for industrial, commercial, government agency, municipal and institutional clients in the transportation, urban infrastructure, industry, real estate and environmental sectors. Roche has carried out thousands of projects in Quebec, throughout the rest of Canada and in over 50 other countries worldwide (including Honduras, Colombia, Bolivia, Peru, Egypt, Morocco, Mauritania, Guinea, Senegal, Côte d'Ivoire, Benin, India, Thailand, Vietnam, Indonesia, China, Nepal, Russia, Ukraine, Kazakhstan, Poland, Serbia and Montenegro, to name a few). These projects have generated annual revenues of approximately $90 million CDN.

Roche has a staff of approximately 850 in the following fields: industry, environment, transportation, forest/wood processing, energy, building, water, urban development and financial planning, as well as intellectual property. A careers page can be found on the company's Web site with opportunities posted. The site will also be available in English shortly. Interested candidates can also read more about Roche's past projects. [ID:6706]

Roger Billings & Associates

Suite 1122, 160 Bloor Street E., Toronto, ON, M4W 1B9, Canada;
416-927-0772, fax 800-692-5091, rogerbillings@msn.com, www.rogerbillings.com

MID-SIZED MANAGEMENT CONSULTING FIRM: Consulting, Human Resources, Leadership Assessment, Management, Management Consulting, Management Training, Marketing

Roger Billings & Associates offers key services in executive coaching and management and leadership development programs, as well as seminars. Clients of the company include Bell Canada, Ernst & Young, Codetel—Dominican Republic, Alcon Laboratorios do Brasil, British Airways, Kraft Canada, CIBC, Sony, Four Seasons Hotels and American Express, to name a few. The company has particular experience in Belgium, Brazil, the United Kingdom and the US. [ID:6689]

Royal Bank of Canada (RBC)

P.O. Box 1, Royal Bank Plaza, Toronto, ON, M5J 2J5, Canada;
416-974-5151, recruitmentservices@rbc.com, www.rbc.com ▢ *Fr*

LARGE FINANCIAL SERVICES FIRM: Administration (General), Adult Training, Banking and Financial Services, Business Development, Computer Systems, Customer Services, Human Resources, Information Technologies, Insurance, Investment Banking, Project Management, Retirement/Estate Planning Overseas, Services for International Businesses

The Royal Bank of Canada (RBC) is Canada's leader in financial services. The bank has five major lines of business: personal and commercial banking (RBC Banking), wealth management (RBC Investments), insurance (RBC Insurance), corporate and investment banking (RBC Capital Markets) and securities custody and transaction processing (RBC Global Services). RBC is one of North America's premier diversified financial services firms and Canada's largest company, as measured by assets and market capitalization. The bank serves more than 12 million personal, business and public sector clients worldwide from offices in more than 30 countries, including Canada, the United States, the Caribbean and the Bahamas.

RBC employs 60,000 employees and receives as many as 13,000 resumes every month. The bank has a careers section on its Web site with regular job postings and an on-line application system. There is also an "International Career Opportunities" link complete with employment opportunities in IT and sales. RBC offers a learning program which enables employees to advance their training, as well as offering student employment, internships and co-ops during both the summer and throughout the year. RBC also offers various new graduate programs and career opportunities, as well as programs for MBA graduates. The bank has a campus recruitment campaign where it visits a number of Canadian and American post-secondary institutions. Recruiters also participate in many recruitment events such as on-campus career fairs and on-line events. The bank's Web site is very good and provides helpful resume and interview tips. [ID:6671]

Sandwell International Inc.

Park Place, 666 Burrard Street, Vancouver, BC, V6Z 2X8, Canada;
604-684-0055, fax 604-684-7533, info@sandwell.com, www.sandwell.com

LARGE ENGINEERING CONSULTING FIRM: Bulk Materials Handling, Construction, Consulting, Energy Resources, Engineering, Mineral Handling, Project Management, Pulp and Paper, Railways

Sandwell International Inc. is a diversified engineering company operating internationally in the bulk handling, marine, energy and industrial sectors. The firm provides project management, design and detail engineering, procurement, contract management, construction management, start-up and operational assistance, as well as training. The firm also undertakes planning and feasibility studies, market studies, technical audits and reviews, as well as construction progress reviews. Sandwell has completed some 25,000 projects in Russia, China, Asia, South and Central America, Africa, India and Vietnam. The firm has ongoing operations in both Canada and the United States, as well as in Indonesia and Russia.

Sandwell employs approximately 800 people. A careers page can be found on the firm's Web site, complete with job postings and an on-line resume database. Employment opportunities with the firm include engineers, project and construction, managers, economists, planners, designers, technicians and support staff. Career development is fostered through Sandwell's College, an in-house, ongoing training program whose curriculum is designed to assist the firm's people in building their skills. [ID:6586]

SaskTel International

2121 Saskatchewan Drive, Regina, SK, S4P 3Y2, Canada; 306-777-4509,
fax 306-359-7475, sasktel.international@sasktel.sk.ca, www.sasktel-international.com

LARGE TELECOMMUNICATIONS FIRM: Administration (General), Advanced Technology, Computer
Systems, Construction, Consulting, Engineering, Marketing, Project Management, Software Development,
Technical Assistance, Telecommunications

SaskTel International has been providing marketing technology and software solutions
expertise to clients around the world since 1986. The company helps its clients around the world
develop, improve and expand their telecommunications systems. The company's leadership in the
application and provision of advanced technology—including fibre optics, microwave radio cellular
and trunked mobile radio, wireless and traditional access networks, advanced interactive and
Internet services—has been proven in many international markets. The company's main office is
home to its marketing division, software development and support groups and administration area.
In addition to its core staff members based in Regina, Saskatchewan, SaskTel International has a
regional office in Dar es Salaam, Tanzania. The company has installed a telecommunications
system in the English Chunnel, deployed fibre optics in the South China Sea, has provided over 550
telecentres in the rural Philippines and provides a communications network throughout Tanzania.
During the last 15 years, the company has worked in more than 30 countries (six continents in total)
on more than 60 projects. The company has also worked for the private sector and for governments
and international financial institutions. SaskTel International's projects have taken the company to
Western Europe (France, Belgium, Holland, Germany, Italy, Switzerland and the United Kingdom),
as well as the Ukraine, Poland, India, Malaysia, Argentina, Brazil, Chile, the Bahamas, Jamaica,
Puerto Rico, Honduras, Mexico, Canada and the United States.

SaskTel International employs 3,900 people. Some of its employees are posted in the
company's regional office in Dar es Salaam, Tanzania, along with a number of employees posted
overseas on assignments for clients or pursuing business opportunities. Prospective applicants
should have a background in engineering and high technology. Some marketing experience is also
desirable. SaskTel International maintains a data bank for resumes. [ID:6679]

Scotiabank

Scotia Plaza, 44 King Street W., Toronto, ON, M5H 1H1, Canada;
416-866-6161, fax 416-866-3750, email@scotiabank.ca, www.scotiabank.ca 💾 *Fr*

LARGE FINANCIAL SERVICES FIRM: Accounting, Administration (General)

Scotiabank is a major Canadian chartered bank with operations in some 50 countries around
the world, offering a broad range of retail, commercial, corporate, investment and international
banking services. Scotiabank's International Banking division provides worldwide retail,
commercial, and trade finance services, through branches, agencies, representative offices,
subsidiaries and affiliates. Scotiabank is the leading provider of financial services in the Caribbean
and has the broadest network of any Canadian bank. It is active in the Latin American market
through subsidiaries in Mexico and Central America, and has affiliates in Chile, Peru and
Venezuela.

Scotiabank employs over 48,000 people worldwide. Interested candidates can search through
current employment opportunities on the bank's Web site and may submit a resume to the bank's
database. Scotiabank also participates in campus events and posts where they will be visiting on
their Web site. Employees of the bank are also given the opportunity to increase their learning and
development needs through Scotiabank's Learning Management System where they are offered on-
the-job coaching and training programs. More than $51 million was spent on training at Scotiabank
in 2003, roughly $1,800 per employee. The bank's Web site has a very good careers page with a
useful tools and resources section. [ID:6684]

SEA Systems Limited
P.O. Box 1508, Stn. C, 22 Pearl Place, St. John's, NL, A1C 5N8,
Canada; 709-368-8832, fax 709-368-8734, www.seasystems.nf.ca

LARGE ENGINEERING FIRM: Advanced Technology, Engineering

SEA Systems Limited, a member of the Rutter Group of Companies, is a vendor-independent controls and automation systems integrator, electrical and instrumentation engineering company servicing the industrial, marine, oil and gas, utility and municipal sectors worldwide. SEA Systems provides services for control and safety systems integration such as design and engineering, project management, control systems integration, contract engineering, start-up and commissioning, panel design and fabrication, field service/calibration and contract manufacturing.

SEA Systems employs 170 highly skilled and experienced professionals throughout its operations in Canada, the United States, Brazil, Singapore and Korea. Its overseas functions are focused primarily in the oil and gas industry. Individuals possessing a degree in electrical engineering or a diploma as an electrical/instrumentation technician should forward their resumes to careers@seasystems.nf.ca. [ID:6782]

Seaforth Engineering Group Inc.
Suite 302, Inc. 780 Windmill Road, Dartmouth, NS, B3B 1T3, Canada;
902-468-3579, fax 902-468-6885, info@seaforthengineering.ca, www.seaforthengineering.com

MID-SIZED ENGINEERING FIRM: Energy Resources, Engineering, Environment, Geomatics, Geophysics, Marine Engineering, Project Management, Quality Assurance

Seaforth Engineering Group Inc. provides a full range of marine engineering and renewable energy technology solutions to its clients. Seaforth's primary focus is the provision of precise navigation and positioning, ocean-mapping services and innovative energy solutions for stakeholders operating in the marine environment and renewable energy sectors worldwide. Seaforth experience includes bottom and sub-bottom mapping, deep-ocean engineering, geophysical and geotechnical data acquisition, Health, Safety and Environmental Systems (HSE) consultation, interpretation and quality control services, project planning, management and report production, seismic vessel/drilling platform positioning and quality control services. The company has provided services to clients in North and South America, India, Africa, the Middle East and numerous other global locations.

Seaforth's team is made up of highly trained and dedicated professionals that include: geologists, geophysicists, hydrographers, land surveyors, project managers, electronic technologists and GIS (geographic information systems) and CAD (computer aided design) technicians. A careers page may be found on the company's Web site. Interested applicants may mail their resumes to the company or complete an on-line application form. [ID:6836]

Semex Alliance
130 Stone Road W., Guelph, ON, N1G 3Z2, Canada;
519-821-5060, fax 519-821-7225, info@semex.com, www.semex.com ▢Fr▢Sp

LARGE AGRICULTURAL CONSULTING FIRM: Agriculture, Business Development, Development Assistance, Livestock Genetics, Project Management, Technical Assistance

Semex Alliance develops and markets high-quality genetic technologies, products and services to benefit livestock producers around the world. The company owns and samples 350 bulls globally per year and offers a complete line of dairy and beef genetics, live cattle and embryos. Semex Alliance has a distribution network in over 70 countries around the world. Distributors can be found throughout North America, South America, Central America, the Caribbean, Europe, Asia, Australia, the Middle East and Africa.

Semex Alliance employs 35 people who have international responsibilities. A careers page with employment opportunities can be found on the company's Web site. Recruits should have academic training in animal health, breeding and management, hands-on farm experience and at least five years' work experience. Their extensive Web site provides a wide variety of information about the company's activities and the general state of livestock genetics. The Web site also provides information on training and a number of industry-related links. [ID:6587]

SENES Consultants Limited
Unit 12, 121 Granton Drive, Richmond Hill, ON, L4B 3N4, Canada;
905-764-9380, fax 905-764-9386, info@senes.ca, www.senes.ca

LARGE ENVIRONMENTAL CONSULTING FIRM: Consulting, Energy Resources, Engineering, Environment, Mining, Science and Technology, Technical Assistance, Waste Water Management, Water Resources

SENES Consultants Limited provides leading-edge environmental services on a broad spectrum of projects including environmental management systems, planning and strategies, due diligence, compliance and environmental monitoring, ecological and human health risk, radioactivity, air and aquatic assessment, solid waste management, site assessment, mining and mineral processing and public consultation. The company's affiliated firm, Decommissioning Consulting Services (DCS), provides expertise in technical disciplines related to site contamination. During its 24 years in business, SENES has participated in more than 4,000 projects in over 50 countries. Clients have included regulatory agencies, private sector companies, industrial associations and public organizations. The company also has extensive experience working with international aid and governmental agencies, including the Canadian International Development Agency (CIDA), the World Health Organization, the World Bank and the European Development Bank. SENES has offices in Canada (Toronto, Ottawa and Vancouver), Chile, the United States and India.

In total, the SENES group of companies employs a highly technical staff of 130 engineers, scientists, planners, technical specialists and support personnel. The technical backgrounds of the professional staff include various engineering disciplines, physical and natural sciences, mathematics, statistics, computer science, as well as geography and planning. Staff are from around the world and collectively speak more than 20 languages. An employment page can be found on the company's Web site with employment opportunities posted. [ID:6765]

SGA Energy Ltd.
Suite 302, 1376 Bank Street, Ottawa, ON, K1H 7Y3, Canada;
613-730-7421, fax 613-260-8082, www.sgaenergy.com

MID-SIZED GENERAL CONSULTING FIRM: Consulting, Development Assistance, Economics, Energy Resources, Engineering, Environment, Policy Development, Project Management, Social Science Research

SGA Energy Ltd. is a multidisciplinary, Canadian consulting firm of engineers, economists and environmental specialists in operation since 1988. The company is dedicated to bringing professional engineering and socio-economic services to key issues around sustainable energy use, energy production and the environmental impacts of energy. It has consulting experience in two major areas: energy services and climate change services. It also has experience in all aspects of planning and project preparation, supply/demand surveys, data management, forecasting, economic/financial analysis, sourcing, financing and policy development, for all sectors. SGA Energy has worked in both the rural and urban sectors of developing countries as well as in Canada. Clients of the company have included private industry, energy utilities, national, provincial and municipal governments in 12 countries, including Mexico, China, the Philippines, Jamaica, Kenya, India, Iran, Vietnam, Sierra Leone, Nepal, Sri Lanka and Bangladesh, as well as multilateral and bilateral development agencies, such as the World Bank, the United Nations Development Programme (UNDP), the Canadian International Development Agency (CIDA) and the Asian Development Bank. [ID:6810]

ShawCor Ltd.

25 Bethridge Road, Toronto, ON, M9W 1M7, Canada; 416-743-7111, fax 416-743-7199, www.shawcor.com

LARGE ENERGY RESOURCES FIRM: Administration (General), Energy Resources, Engineering, Human Resources, Information Technologies, Marketing, Oilfield Services, Project Management, Research and Development, Technical Assistance

ShawCor Ltd. (formerly Shaw Industries Ltd.) is a global energy services company specializing in products and services for the pipeline, exploration and production, and petrochemical and industrial segments of the oil and gas industry. The company operates through seven wholly owned business units: Bredero Shaw, Shaw Pipeline Services, Canusa-CPS, OMSCO, Guardian, DSG-Canusa and ShawFlex. It has operations in North America, Mexico, Africa, Europe, the Middle East, Asia and Australia.

ShawCor employs more than 5,000 people in over 20 countries around the world. A careers page with employment opportunities can be found on the company's Web site. Current opportunities are listed when they exist in administration, engineering/research and development/QA, finance and human resources, general manufacturing, manager/warehouse, information technology, operations, purchasing and materials, sales and marketing, skilled trades/inspectors, students and new graduates. [ID:6588]

Silver Standard Resources Inc.

Suite 1180, 999 West Hastings Street, Vancouver, BC, V6C 2W2,
Canada; 604-689-3846, fax 604-689-3847, www.silver-standard.com

LARGE MINING FIRM: Exploration and Development, Metals, Metals Distribution, Mining

Silver Standard Resources Inc. is a well-financed silver resource company with over $60 million in cash, excluding marketable securities. The company is focused on the development of silver deposits internationally. Its objective since 1994 has been to acquire significant in-ground silver resources and to develop these projects into silver-producing mines. On December 31, 2002, Silver Standard had interests in projects on three continents: Australia, South America (Argentina and Chile) and North America (the United States, Mexico and Canada). [ID:6607]

SNC-Lavalin International Inc.

455 René Lévesque Blvd. W., Montreal, QC, H2Z 1Z3, Canada;
514-393-1000, fax 514-866-0795, info@snclavalin.com, www.snclavalin.com ▢*Fr*

LARGE ENGINEERING FIRM: Agriculture, Business Development, Construction, Consulting, Development Assistance, Energy Resources, Engineering, Environment, Petrochemicals, Project Management, Technical Assistance, Telecommunications, Water Resources

SNC-Lavalin International Inc. provides engineering, procurement, construction, project management and project financing services to a variety of industry sectors, including agri-food, aluminum, biopharmaceuticals, chemicals, petroleum, environment, facilities and operations management, infrastructure, mass transit, mining and metallurgy, and power. The company has offices across Canada and in 30 other countries around the world and has worked in some 100 countries worldwide.

SNC-Lavalin employs approximately 6,000 people and regularly posts career opportunities on its Web site. It also offers to engineering students an award internship program, which is a paid four-month internship and a $2,000 scholarship. The internship program runs from May to August and allows students to combine theory with practice. Application instructions and forms are on the company's Web site and is available to students from schools across Canada. [ID:6674]

Sodexen Inc.

2519 Chomedey Blvd., Laval, QC, H7T 2R2, Canada;
450-973-7754, fax 450-973-7758, marketing@sodexen.com, www.sodexen.com ⬛*Fr*⬛*Sp*

MID-SIZED ENVIRONMENTAL FIRM: Chemicals, Engineering, Environment, Information Technologies, Project Management, Public Health, Quality Assurance, Science and Technology, Urban Development

Sodexen Inc. provides complete environmental diagnostic and protection services to a broad range of industrial, institutional and governmental clients. The company's professionals work on multidisciplinary teams covering all areas of environmental expertise, including: chemistry, biology, hygiene and public health, engineering, geology, urban planning, biotechnology, quality control, financing and economic analysis, project development, feasibility and pre-engineering studies, economic modelization and negotiation phases. Sodexen is internationally recognized by its urban environmental management expertise, notably in Southeast Asia. The company's international activities focus on waste-to-energy facilities in Vietnam. It has completed projects in the United States, Japan, Morocco, Vietnam, and other countries.

Sodexen employs approximately 30 people. A careers page may be found on the company's Web site. Interested candidates are asked to please forward their resumes (preferably in French) to the appropriate department. The company constantly recruits qualified individuals. [ID:6687]

SOFEG inc.

Bureau 101, 7, rue de la Commune ouest, Montreal, QC, H2Y 2C5,
Canada; 514-849-5927, fax 514-849-9250, info@sofeg.com, www.sofeg.com

LARGE GENERAL CONSULTING FIRM: Consulting, Development Assistance, Management, Social Policy, Technical Assistance

SOFEG inc., Société de formation et de gestion, est active sur le marché international depuis 1986. SOFEG offre des services de gestion de projets et de consultation dans les pays en développement et en transition principalement en Afrique du Nord, de l'Ouest et du Centre. Elle possède une expertise particulière dans les secteurs de l'éducation, de la formation, de l'appui aux PME et au secteur privé. SOFEG offre également des services de développement de solutions technologiques pour l'intégration des TiC (technologies de l'information et de la communication) en éducation et en appui au développement économique, appui institutionnel et gestion de projets. Depuis les dix dernières années, SOFEG a livré pour plus de cinquante millions de dollars canadiens de biens et de services dans le cadre de projets financés par l'ACDI, la Banque mondiale ou la Banque africaine de développement. Elle compte à son emploi une dizaine de salariés réguliers ainsi que plusieurs consultants spécialisés dans ses domaines d'intervention. [ID:7295]

SR Telecom Inc.

8150 Trans-Canada Highway, Montreal, QC, H4S 1M5, Canada;
514-335-1210, fax 514-334-7783, info@srtelecom.com, www.srtelecom.com ⬛*Fr*⬛*Sp*

LARGE TELECOMMUNICATIONS FIRM: Accounting, Administration (General), Advanced Technology, Business Development, Engineering, Logistics, Project Management, Technical Assistance, Telecommunications

SR Telecom Inc. is a world leader and innovator in fixed wireless access technology which links end-users to networks using wireless transmissions. The company's solutions include equipment, network planning, project management, installation and maintenance services. It offers one of the industry's broadest portfolios of fixed wireless products designed to enable carriers and service providers to rapidly deploy high-quality voice, high-speed data and broadband applications. Their products are used in over 130 countries and are among the most advanced and reliable available today. SR Telecom has installations and offices in all five continents. The company has a staff of 965 worldwide. A careers page with employment opportunities can be found on the company's Web site. Interested applicants can search opportunities by location and field type. [ID:6675]

Stantec Inc.

10160 - 112th Street, Edmonton, AB, T5K 2L6, Canada;
780-917-7000, fax 780-917-7330, hr@stantec.com, www.stantec.com

LARGE ENGINEERING FIRM: Aerial Surveys, Architecture and Planning, Consulting, Energy Resources, Engineering, Environment, Geomatics, Project Management, Transportation, Urban Development

Stantec Inc. provides comprehensive professional services in planning, engineering, architecture, interior design, landscape architecture, surveying and geomatics, environmental sciences, project management and project economics. Through both integrated and discipline-specific consulting and project delivery, Stantec works with clients in the public and private sectors in Central and Western Canada, as well as throughout the United States and selected international markets. Stantec's total infrastructure solutions are targeted toward five market segments: buildings, environmental, industrial, transportation and urban land. The firm delivers a comprehensive list of solutions to its international clientele, from prefeasibility and feasibility studies to design, procurement, construction supervision, commissioning, maintenance, operation and project management services. It has carried out projects funded by major international funding institutions, including the Caribbean Development Bank, Inter-American Development Bank and the Asian Development Bank. The firm's professionals have completed projects in more than 80 countries, from Australia to Zambia, for public and private sector clients. The global services offered by the firm assist clients with a full range of consulting services, focusing on the building, environmental, industrial, transportation, management systems and power sectors. The firm has offices in Canada, the United States, the Bahamas, Barbados, South Korea, Trinidad and Tobago, and Malawi.

The company employs 4,000 people operating out of 40 countries in North America and the Caribbean. A careers page with employment opportunities can be found on the firm's Web site. An international careers page can also be found on the Web site with regular job postings. Interested applicants are asked to please forward their resumes to the firm's human resources department: hr@stantec.com. Stantec also offers development and advancement opportunities. [ID:6676]

STAS - Unigec

1846 Outarde Street, Chicoutimi, QC, G7K 1H1, Canada;
418-696-0074, fax 418-696-1951, rh@stas-unigec.com, www.stas-unigec.com ▢Fr

LARGE ENGINEERING FIRM: Advanced Technology, Computer Systems, Construction, Consulting, Customer Services, Economics, Energy Resources, Engineering, Environment, Marketing, Research and Development, Science and Technology, Technical Assistance, Writing

STAS-Unigec (formerly Unigec Experts-Conseils) is a young, dynamic and entrepreneurial company specializing in the commercialization of new, technologically advanced equipment originating in research and development laboratories. The company serves the aluminum, mines, and pulp and paper sectors. The company is also a recognized leader in its innovative abilities to develop and fabricate sophisticated equipment used in various industry sectors to improve quality, reduce pollution and lower costs, using the latest in programmable automation systems. Services provided by STAS-Unigec include research and development and manufacturing and marketing for aluminum smelters. The company is completely devoted to the aluminum field and its activities are divided between two parts: design and marketing. The equipment offered by STAS-Unigec includes dross coolers, filters, degassing equipment, rotary injectors, crucible cleaning machines, automatic bale dewiring machines, automatic guidance systems for underground mines, and more.

The firm has about 10 overseas employees and 50 Canadian employees with international responsibilities. A careers page can be found on the company's Web site with employment opportunities. Candidates should have a bachelor's degree in science, have experience in the construction or engineering field and preferably speak both English and French. The firm maintains a data bank for resumes. [ID:6543]

Sterlite Gold Ltd.

Box 25, 199 Bay Street, Toronto, ON, M5L 1A9, Canada; 416-863-2753,
fax 416-863-2653, information@sterlitegold.com, www.sterlitegold.com

LARGE MINING FIRM: Exploration and Development, Metals, Mineral Resources, Mining

Sterlite Gold Ltd. is a Canadian company whose strategy is to find, develop and operate gold mines in Asia and the former Soviet Union. The company's strategic focus shifted to Asia in 1995. Current initiatives of Sterlite are located in Armenia, Myanmar and the Yukon Territory in Canada. [ID:6634]

Suncurrent Industries Inc.

P.O. Box 6044, Stn. A, Calgary, AB, T2H 2L3, Canada;
403-264-2880, fax 403-264-2881, www.suncurrent.ab.ca ▢*Sp*

MID-SIZED ENGINEERING CONSULTING FIRM: Advanced Technology, Construction, Energy Resources, Engineering, Environment, Project Management

Suncurrent Industries Inc. is a privately held Canadian corporation offering services and products in the construction and renewable energy industries and consulting services in the fields of management, transfer and marketing of new technologies. The company specializes in sustainable development through commercial real estate development. The company is also involved in renewable energy projects in Canada and the Caribbean and has experience in both Cuba and Jamaica. Suncurrent Industries employs approximately six people. A careers page with employment opportunities can be found on the company's Web site. [ID:6764]

Syndel International Inc.

9211 Shaughnessy Street, Vancouver, BC, V6P 6R5, Canada;
604-321-7131, fax 604-321-3900, info@syndel.com, www.syndel.com

MID-SIZED PHARMACEUTICAL FIRM: Agriculture, Consulting, Environment, Food Security, Marketing, Medical Health, Project Management, Science and Technology

Syndel International Inc. is a world leader in aquatic animal reproduction. It is a privately held Canadian company that has developed and marketed high-quality aquaculture chemicals and pharmaceutical products (Ovaprim and Ovaplant) worldwide for more than 20 years. The company's products are currently available in more than 40 countries through an established network of agents and distributors. The company's challenge is to provide health product leadership to meet a growing consumer demand for farmed seafood and to address increasing government responsibility for safety and quality. Syndel is also active in educating farmers, purchasing agents and government officials in disease prevention and detection, and in the safe, efficient use of its products. It has agents and/or distributors in North America (Canada), Asia (Malaysia, Indonesia and Singapore, India, Pakistan, Hong Kong, Taiwan), Australia, South America (Colombia, Chile), Europe (Ireland, the United Kingdom) and Africa (Nigeria, Benin).

The company employs eight people with primary international responsibilities. Candidates should possess a combination of appropriate education (minimum BSc), technical expertise, overseas experience, as well as language and intercultural skills. Syndel maintains a data bank for resumes. [ID:6580]

Sypher:Mueller International Inc.

International Division, Suite 500, 220 Laurier Ave. W., Ottawa, ON, K1P 5Z9,
Canada; 613-236-4318, fax 613-236-4850, mail@sypher.aero, www.sypher.aero

MID-SIZED TRANSPORTATION CONSULTING FIRM: Air Transportation, Architecture and Planning, Consulting, Economics, Engineering, Management, Management Consulting, Project Management, Transportation

Sypher:Mueller International Inc. provides consulting services to enhance its clients success through improvements to their management, operations, facilities and profitability. The firm offers its clients a diversified, one-stop source of expertise in all areas of aviation. Its primary objective is to assist clients through the provision of innovative professional services in airport planning and development, airport design and construction program management, airport management and business planning, air service development and marketing, civil aviation planning and airport security. Clients of the firm include the aviation and corporate real estate sectors. The firm has offices in the United States, Canada, and the Caribbean and operates throughout the world. It has undertaken projects in over 54 countries in North America, South America, Europe, Africa, the Middle East, Australia and Asia.

Sypher:Mueller employs four people overseas and 15 in Canada. Employees have extensive training and experience in program management, engineering, architecture, finance, economics, business management, statistics, operations research, civil aviation management and safety analysis. A careers page with employment opportunities may be found on the firm's Web site. [ID:6581]

Talisman Energy Inc.

Suite 3400, 888 - 3 Street S.W., Calgary, AB, T2P 5C5, Canada;
403-237-1234, fax 403-237-1902, tlm@talisman-energy.com, www.talisman-energy.com

LARGE ENERGY RESOURCES FIRM: Oil and Gas Distribution, Petrochemicals

Talisman Energy Inc. is a large, internationally diversified oil and gas producer, a major North American natural gas supplier and over the last decade has successfully expanded into a number of international areas. The company operates in North America (Canada and the United States), the North Sea, Southeast Asia (Indonesia, Malaysia and Vietnam), the Caribbean (Trinidad and Tobago) and Latin America (Colombia), as well as in Africa (Algeria) and the Middle East (Qatar). Talisman's subsidiaries also conduct business in Trinidad and Tobago, Colombia and Qatar. The company's international offices are located in Scotland, Indonesia and Malaysia.

A careers page with Canadian and overseas job postings can be found on their Web site. There are many opportunities for movement between operating groups, cross-functionally and internationally. Technical training and personal development are encouraged and educational assistance is available as employees broaden their skills and work toward their career objectives. [ID:6583]

TD Bank Financial Group

TD Tower, Toronto, ON, M5K 1A2, Canada; 416-982-8222, fax 416-944-6955, recruit@td.com, www.td.com

LARGE FINANCIAL SERVICES FIRM: Administration (General), Banking and Financial Services, Business Development, Business/Banking/Trade, Commerce, Customer Services, Human Resources, Insurance, Investment Banking, Retirement/Estate Planning Overseas, Services for International Businesses

TD Bank Financial Group (TDBFG), headquartered in Toronto and with offices around the world, offers a full range of financial products and services through TD Canada Trust, TD Commercial Banking, TD Asset Management, TD Waterhouse and TD Securities. The Toronto Dominion Bank and its subsidiaries are collectively known as TD Bank Financial Group (TDBFG)—they offer a full range of financial products and services to approximately 13 million customers worldwide through three key business lines: personal and commercial banking (including TD Canada Trust), wealth management (including the global operations of TD Waterhouse) and wholesale banking (including TD Securities). TDBFG had more than $274 billion CDN in assets as of October 31, 2003, and ranks as one of the top on-line financial services providers in the world, with more than 4.5 million on-line customers. TD Securities works with clients around the world, focusing selectively and strategically on markets from offices in key financial centres.

TDBFG employs 51,000 people in offices around the world. The bank's Web site suggests that those interested in employment with the bank should visit their career services centre for TDBFG job opportunities offered through campus recruitment. Interested applicants may also e-mail, fax or mail resumes to the bank, but are asked to follow the hiring manager's application instructions when applying to a specific job. Internships are also available with the bank, which attempt to match the student's interests to roles and responsibilities, as well as to improve the student's skills and increase their marketability. TDBFG is also in partnership with Career Edge, a national not-for-profit corporation that offers a youth internship program for new graduates in partnership with organizations such as TDBFG, enhancing new graduates employability. The bank recruits from a number of post-secondary institutions by participating in campus career fairs. The dates of these visits are posted on the bank's Web site. The bank also offers a Personal Performance Development Program, which allows employees to set their own performance and development objectives each year, and to establish a clear link between individual and business performance and the employee's total cash compensation. TDBFG's Web site provides helpful tools and resources including resume and interview tips, a useful FAQs page, as well as providing profiles of employees in specific job roles. [ID:6541]

Teck Cominco Ltd.
Suite 600, 200 Burrard Street, Vancouver, BC, V6C 3L9, Canada;
604-687-1117, fax 604-687-6100, info@teckcominco.com, www.teckcominco.com

---

LARGE MINING FIRM: Gold and Metals Production, Mining

Teck Cominco Ltd. and its subsidiary companies are a diversified mining, smelting and refining group headquartered in Vancouver, BC. The company mines zinc, lead, copper, gold, metallurgical coal, as well as producing a number of by-product metals and chemicals through its two zinc refining facilities in Canada and Peru. Teck Cominco holds interests in 12 producing mines in Canada, the United States and Peru and has offices located in nine countries.

The company has a career page on its Web site with current job postings. Teck Cominco is actively recruiting candidates under 35, especially graduates in geology and metallurgical, chemical, and mechanical engineering. It offers university scholarships at all levels. After gaining experience in Canada, employees can go overseas. [ID:6646]

TECSULT
85 Ste-Catherine Street W., Montreal, QC, H2X 3P4, Canada;
514-287-8500, fax 514-287-8643, ressources@tecsult.com, www.tecsult.com 💻 *Fr*

LARGE ENGINEERING CONSULTING FIRM: Accounting, Administration (General), Construction, Consulting, Economics, Energy Resources, Engineering, Environment, Forestry, Geomatics, Human Resources, Information Technologies, Project Management, Water Resources

TECSULT is one of the most important engineering firms in Canada and is a leader in many fields of activities such as engineering, resource management, environment, forestry, geomatics, information systems, human resource development, as well as other areas. The firm has offices in Quebec, Ontario and Nova Scotia, as well as 25 countries around the world. TECSULT has carried out assignments in North America, Central America, South America, Africa, Asia and Europe. The firm's international offices are located throughout North America, South America, the Middle East, Africa and Asia. A career page with employment opportunities can be found on the firm's Web site. Interested applicants can forward their resumes to ressources@tecsult.com. [ID:6584]

Teleglobe International Holdings
1000 de la Gauchetière Street W., Montreal, QC, H3B 4X5, Canada;
514-868-7272, fax 514-868-7234, jobs@teleglobe.com, www.teleglobe.com 💻 *Fr*

LARGE TELECOMMUNICATIONS FIRM: Accounting, Administration (General), Advanced Technology, Business Development, Engineering, Global Communications, Human Resources, Information Technologies, Telecommunications

Teleglobe International Holdings is a leading carrier of international voice, wireless roaming and data/IP services, which enables telecommunications, Internet and mobile service providers around the world to offer the most advanced and reliable global services to their customers at competitive prices. The company owns and operates one of the world's most extensive networks, providing reach to over 240 countries and territories with advanced data capabilities. The company also has 272 direct and bilateral relations, as well as ownership in over 100 sub-sea and terrestrial cable systems directly connecting over 90 countries to North America. It is also one of the largest providers of satellite capacity connecting the Internet. Teleglobe has over 1,000 wholesale customers and a network that carries close to 7.5 billion international minutes. Offices for the company can be found in the United States, the United Kingdom, Hong Kong, Spain and Germany.

Teleglobe's Web site has a careers page with job postings listed, however, interested applicants may also send a resume to the human resources link provided on the Web site. It regularly has openings in countries around the globe, typically involving sales or management work, or occasionally having technical positions in areas such as software engineering or network planning. [ID:6530]

Telesat
1601 Telesat Court, Gloucester, ON, K1B 5P4, Canada;
613-748-0123, fax 613-748-8712, info@telesat.ca, www.telesat.ca 💻 *Fr*

MID-SIZED TELECOMMUNICATIONS FIRM: Advanced Technology, Business Development, Consulting, Engineering, Technical Assistance

Telesat is one of the early pioneers in satellite communications and systems management. The company operates a fleet of satellites for the provision of broadcast distribution and telecommunications services and is a highly respected consultant and partner in satellite ventures around the world. Telesat has offices in Canada, the United States and Brazil.

The company has approximately 500 employees. A careers page can be found on the company's Web site with current employment opportunities. Typical positions include satellite engineers, field technicians and software developers, among others. Telesat also offers opportunities to students. Interested candidates may submit their resumes to the company's database. [ID:6593]

TELUS Corp.
3777 Kingsway, Burnaby, BC, V5H 3Z7, Canada;
604-432-2151, fax 604-432-9681, hr@telus.com, www.telus.com

MID-SIZED TELECOMMUNICATIONS FIRM: Telecommunications

Telus Corp. is the largest telecommunications company in Western Canada and the second largest in the country with more than $7 billion of annual revenue, 4.9 million network access lines and 3.4 million wireless subscribers. The company provides subscribers with a full range of telecommunications products and services including voice and wireless solutions across Canada, utilizing next-generation, Internet-based technologies. It has served the United Kingdom, the United States, Brazil, Iran, Japan and Mexico.

Telus employs more than 25,000 Canadians. A careers page with employment opportunities can be found on the company's Web site. There is some overseas work available, primarily establishing telecommunication systems in developing countries. Prospective applicants should have relevant educational background and work experience in the telecommunications sector. Telus maintains a data bank for resumes. [ID:6594]

Tembec
Bureau 1050, 800 René-Levésque Blvd. W., Montreal, QC, H3B 1X9, Canada;
514-871-0137, fax 514-397-0896, corporate.human.resources@tembec.com, www.tembec.com 💻 *Fr*

LARGE FORESTRY FIRM: Forestry, Manufacturing, Pulp and Paper, Reforestation, Sustainable Development

Tembec is a leading integrated forest products company well established in North America and France. With sales of approximately $4 billion and some 11,000 employees, it operates over 50 market pulp, paper and wood product manufacturing units and produces chemicals from by-products of its pulping process. Tembec markets its products worldwide and has sales offices in Canada, the United States, the United Kingdom, Switzerland, China, Korea, Japan and Chile. It also manages 40 million acres of forest land in accordance with sustainable development principles and has committed to obtaining Forest Stewardship Council (FSC) certification for all forests under its care by the end of 2005. Tembec's common shares are listed on the Toronto Stock Exchange under the symbol TBC.

A careers page can be found on the company's Web site. Interested applicants may send their resumes to the human resources department at corporate.human.resources@tembec.com. Additional information on Tembec is available on its Web site at www.tembec.com. [ID:6823]

Teshmont Consultants LP

1190 Waverley Street, Winnipeg, MB, R3T 0P4, Canada;
204-284-8100, fax 204-475-4601, teshmont@teshmont.com, www.teshmont.com

MID-SIZED ENGINEERING CONSULTING FIRM: Construction, Energy Resources, Engineering, Power Generation/Transmission/Distribution, Project Management, Technical Assistance, Training and Technology Transfer

Teshmont Consultants LP is a world leader in high voltage power transmission engineering. Teshmont is a leader in the engineering of EHV AC and HVDC transmission systems and has provided services to projects that represent more than 50 per cent of the world's installed capacity of HVDC power transmission. It has carried out comprehensive economic and technical feasibility studies for many of the major HVDC and EHV AC transmission systems around the world. Teshmont specializes in system studies, specification and design of HVDC converter stations, SVC and FACTS devices, EHV AC terminal stations, DC ground and sea electrodes, communications systems, electrical and structural design of EHV transmission lines and in construction supervision and commissioning of complete transmission systems. Teshmont has provided services for many DC projects in North America, Asia and around the world. Services offered by Teshmont include transmission system studies, system integration studies, engineering services, project management, equipment expediting and inspection, on-site construction supervision and commission, as well as training. Teshmont has participated in projects in Brazil, Bosnia and Herzegovina, Norway, Poland, Ireland, Egypt, Jordan, China, Thailand, India, Korea, Japan, Pakistan, Malaysia, Peru, the United Kingdom, Venezuela, Australia and New Zealand.

Teshmont Consultants LP has 45 employees. A careers page can be found on the company's Web site. Currently, Teshmont is looking for electrical engineers, eligible for registration in Manitoba with good oral and written communication skills in English, as well as more than three years experience in electrical utility engineering. A willingness to travel within Canada and overseas is also important. Teshmont is also looking for electrical technologists with the same qualifications. Interested applicants are asked to please submit their resumes to employment@teshmont.com. [ID:6680]

TransGlobe Energy Corporation

Suite 2900, 330 - 5th Ave. S.W., Calgary, AB, T2P 0L4, Canada;
403-264-9888, fax 403-264-9898, contact@trans-globe.com, www.trans-globe.com

MID-SIZED PETROLEUM EXPLORATION FIRM: Accounting, Energy Resources, Engineering, Geophysics

The TransGlobe Energy Corporation employs a multi-disciplined team of 10 professionals in Canada to manage international and domestic exploration and development operations. The company currently has two producing properties in the Republic of Yemen and three in Alberta with an additional two projects under development. TransGlobe Energy is focused on growth in the Middle East/North African oil exploration industry. There are no permanent overseas employees and the current Calgary staff has very experienced global knowledge. [ID:6828]

Triathlon Ltd.

MacDonald Dettwiler Bldg., 13800 Commerce Parkway, Richmond, BC, V6V 2J3,
Canada; 604-233-5000, fax 604-233-5043, hr@triathloninc.com, www.triathloninc.com

LARGE EARTH SCIENCES FIRM: Advanced Technology, Aerial Surveys, Consulting, Engineering, Hydrographic Surveys, Information Technologies, Photo Mapping, Project Management

Triathlon Ltd. (formerly Terra Surveys Ltd., now owned by MacDonald, Dettwiler and Associates Ltd.) provides customers with essential information for decision-making from the real estate industry to local governments. The company develops information systems for armed forces and police forces and is one of the world's largest and most productive photogrammetric service organizations. It is a full-service geomatics firm, providing traditional photogrammetric topographic, planimetric and cadastral mapping, in addition to digital orthophoto production, Geographic Information Systems (GIS), field surveying and consulting engineering services. Triathlon specializes in city and county GIS basemapping and updating services, as well as agriculture, forestry, pipeline, electric transmission line and transportation mapping. The company has completed projects in the United States, Canada, Ghana, Guyana, United Arab Emirates, Argentina and Puerto Rico.

There are three employees currently working overseas and 50 employees in Canada working on international projects, primarily in the Middle East and Asia Pacific. A careers page can be found on Triathlon's Web site with current job postings. The company asks that all resumes be forwarded to the human resources department by mail, fax, or e-mail (hr@triathlon.com). It is an asset, but not essential for candidates to have international work experience or experience in a remote area of Canada. Applicants must have experience in a specific field to qualify for international positions. Particular project language skills may be important. Triathlon maintains a data bank for resumes. [ID:6548]

Trudell Medical International (TMI)

725 Third Street, London, ON, N5V 5G4, Canada; 519-455-7060,
fax 519-455-6329, tmi@trudellmed.com, www.trudellmed.com

LARGE PHARMACEUTICAL FIRM: Medical Health, Pharmaceuticals

Trudell Medical International (TMI) is a member of the Trudell Medical Group of companies. It is a leader in the development and manufacture of aerosol drug delivery devices and asthma management products. It is also a supplier to many of the major pharmaceutical companies involved in respiratory medicine. The company's strength lies in product development around core capabilities in mechanical, electronic and software engineering design, complemented by a state-of-the-art aerosol research laboratory and the experience gained by marketing products in over 90 countries worldwide. A careers page with employment opportunities can be found on the company's Web site. [ID:6792]

TTA Technology Training Associates Ltd.

Suite 702, 555 Seymour Street, Vancouver, BC, V6B 3H6, Canada;
604-412-7706, fax 604-688-7037, tta@techtraining.org, www.techtraining.org 💻*Sp*

MID-SIZED TRANSPORTATION CONSULTING FIRM: Adult Training, Consulting, Economics, Human Resources, Project Management, Technical Assistance, Transportation

TTA Technology Training Associates Ltd. offers clients corporate and industry training and consulting services, and also provides customized, flexible and relevant training for professional growth and career success. The firm has strong connections with local, national and international businesses, industry partnerships and project management. TTA's strength is in developing human resources in organizations, seeking continuous growth and customized training programs, to support the transportation, environment, energy, infrastructure development and construction sectors. Services provided by the firm include planning, design and delivery. The firm has been working for the International Financial Institute (IFI) on major projects in regions like the Asia Pacific, South Africa and South America. TTA has partnerships with the World Bank, the Asian Development Bank and various government agencies. It has also successfully implemented international projects in Asia, Africa and the Caribbean.

The firm employs eight people. It seeks candidates with experience and a relevant educational background in transportation and/or training. TTA maintains a data bank for resumes. [ID:6582]

UMA Group Ltd.

Suite 1700, 1066 West Hastings Street, Vancouver, BC, V6E 3X2, Canada;
604-689-3431, fax 604-685-1035, careers@umagroup.com, www.umagroup.com

LARGE ENGINEERING CONSULTING FIRM: Architecture and Planning, Community Development, Construction, Consulting, Development Assistance, Engineering, Environment, Forestry, Geomatics, Project Management, Roads, Sanitation, Transportation, Waste Water Management, Water Resources

UMA Group Ltd. provides consulting, engineering and project management services to the community infrastructure, earth and water, transport and industrial market sectors. The firm's specialties include building municipal water and sewer systems, as well as roadways and bridges. In addition to studies, conceptual and detailed planning, surveying, cost estimating and design development, UMA brings extensive experience in public consultation. The firm's experience and abilities address a broad spectrum that includes civil, structural, mechanical, electrical and instrumentation design. UMA has also developed niche skills in Arctic engineering, hydrocarbon recovery, engineered wood products, irrigation, underground services, renovations and intermodal facilities. Offices for the firm can be found throughout Canada and Mexico.

UMA employs 1,000 people, two-thirds of whom are professional engineers and technologists. A careers page can be found on the firm's Web site with job postings. Interested applicants can search by category and location. UMA offers a career development program comprised of assessment and review sessions done throughout the year, providing employees the opportunity to assess their contributions and achievements. [ID:6542]

Universalia Management Group Ltd.

Suite 310, 5252 de Maisonneuve Street W., Montreal, QC, H4A 3S5, Canada;
514-485-3565, fax 514-485-3210, universalia@universalia.com, www.universalia.com ▢*Fr*▢*Sp*

MID-SIZED MANAGEMENT CONSULTING FIRM: Adult Training, Consulting, Development Assistance, Development Education, Human Resources, Management, Management Consulting, Management Training, Organization Development, Research

Universalia Management Group Ltd. is a management consulting firm based in Montreal and Ottawa, and has developed extensive expertise in planning and executing performance improvements and management changes in organizations throughout Canada and 90 other countries. Universalia can assist organizations in areas such as assessment, change management, strategic planning, results-based management and program evaluation. The firm brings together individuals with a wide spectrum of backgrounds and experiences in fields such as program evaluation and monitoring, education, human resources management, strategic planning and project management, among others. Since 1980, Universalia has been working in the area of international development and has served an increasingly broad and diverse range of international agencies (e.g., the African Development Bank, the Canadian International Development Agency, the World Bank and the United Nations Development Programme), government departments of various levels (i.e. Foreign Affairs Canada and International Trade Canada), private sector companies and Aboriginal organizations. Universalia has project experience on all continents except Antarctica and has international offices in Kosovo and Moscow.

The firm has a staff of 40 people and operates in three languages, as well as capability in 13 other languages. Universalia's Web site has a careers page with job opportunities posted on it. Candidates must be university educated and have experience in education, administration and international development. Interested applicants are asked to submit their resume to the firm's database. Those interested in learning more about the firm can visit the Web site and click onto each continent to learn more about past projects completed by Universalia. [ID:6544]

Vaughan International

P.O. Box 2045, Stn. M, Suite 1100, 1505 Barrington Street, Halifax, NS,
B3J 2Z1, Canada; 902-425-3980, fax 902-423-7593, www.mgnet.ca

---

LARGE ENGINEERING CONSULTING FIRM: Consulting, Engineering, Environment, Project Management, Pulp and Paper, Waste Water Management, Water Resources

Vaughan International is part of the MacDonnell Group, a Canadian team of companies and professionals committed to world-class engineering and management consulting solutions with locations and clients across Canada and other key centres throughout the world. Vaughan provides services for industrial and manufacturing facilities, heavy civil projects, and building and municipal engineering projects. Services provided to clients include feasibility studies, reports, cash flow assessments, designs, facilities audits, specifications, construction inspection and full project management services. The company has also expanded its activities to include mechanical, pulp and paper mill projects, power plant projects, management facilities, wharfs, buildings, bridges, water and sewer services, shipyards, large structural projects and environmental services. Vaughan

International is a part of a three-party consortium with the Canadian International Development Agency (CIDA) and has completed projects in Jamaica. Through its subsidiary, Novaport, Vaughan played an important role in contributing to a multi-faceted study of solid waste management in the Organization of Eastern Caribbean States (OECS) and has completed projects in El Salvador and Costa Rica (Vaughan Engineering).

Vaughan employs over 100 professionals and technical staff, including engineers, scientists, planners, CG specialists, GIS specialists and management consultants. The company's Web site has a careers page with current job postings. Vaughan suggests mailing or e-mailing a resume to the appropriate contact for each job posting. [ID:6537]

Wardrop Engineering Inc.

International Division, 6th Floor, 6725 Airport Road, Mississauga, ON, L4V 1V2, Canada; 905-673-3788, fax 905-673-8007, toronto@wardrop.com, www.wardrop.com

LARGE GENERAL CONSULTING FIRM: Aerospace Technology, Agriculture, Business Development, Community Development, Computer Systems, Consulting, Development Assistance, Development Education, Engineering, Environment, Forestry, Industrial Services, Information Technologies, Logistics, Management Consulting, Mining, Power Generation/Transmission/Distribution, Project Management, Technical Assistance, Water Resources

Wardrop Engineering Inc. is an international consulting firm providing engineering, environmental, information technology and business solutions to both private industry and public sector organizations throughout the world. The firm has made contributions as far away as the International Space Station and has responded to some of the world's most complex challenges, including the Chernobyl and World Trade Center disasters. The firm serves the forest product, healthcare, infrastructure (including transportation and water and waste), manufacturing, mining, oil and gas, nuclear and power sectors. Wardrop has seven offices across Canada (Calgary, Mississauga, Saskatoon, Sudbury, Thunder Bay, Toronto and Winnipeg); one office in the United States (Minneapolis, Minnesota); and three international offices (Uganda, Ghana, and Nigeria). Wardrop has completed projects in Algeria, Brazil, Canada, Ghana, India, Japan, Kenya, Togo, Vietnam, the United States and many more.

Wardrop currently has a staff of approximately 400 and has been named a Top 100 Employer for a 4th consecutive year. The firm has also been the recipient of numerous business achievement awards, including the most recent Award of Excellence and Best in Show Keystone Award from the Consulting Engineers of Manitoba. Wardrop's international projects provide interested staff with a unique opportunity to travel to other countries to work in diverse cultures. A careers page with employment opportunities can be found on the company's Web site. Interested applicants can submit a resume to the firm's resume database. [ID:6546]

Water & Earth Sciences Associates Ltd. (WESA)

P.O. Box 430, 3108 Carp Road, Ottawa, ON, K0A 1L0, Canada; 613-839-3053, fax 613-839-5376, wesacarp@wesa.ca, www.wesa.ca ▣ Fr ▣ Sp

LARGE EARTH SCIENCES FIRM: Administration (General), Banking and Financial Services, Business Development, Engineering, Environment, Medical Health, Project Management, Science and Technology, Waste Water Management, Water Resources, Water Supply

Water & Earth Sciences Associates Ltd. (WESA) is a leading environmental sciences and engineering consulting group, providing professional services to business, industry, government and other sectors. Services provided by the company include all aspects of environmental sciences, environmental management and environmental engineering. It has completed thousands of assignments and has established relationships with leading engineering firms in the United States, Central and South America, the Pacific Rim, Europe and Africa and routinely provides project management and technical expertise to these markets. WESA has worked in over 25 countries around the world in the fields of water supply developments, waste management, waste water treatment, industrial audits, environmental business planning and industrial health and safety. The company works daily in English, French and Spanish, and has subsidiary companies in Britain and

El Salvador. WESA is currently active in nine countries including: Jamaica, Trinidad, India, Kenya, Belize, Honduras, Mexico, Guatemala, El Salvador, the United States and Canada.

WESA employs approximately 80 highly qualified scientists, engineers, industrial hygienists, environmental auditors, project managers, financial specialists and support personnel. An employment page with opportunities may be found on the company's Web site. [ID:6815]

Whyte Reynolds International Inc.

703 - 14th Street, Calgary, AB, T2N 2A4, Canada; 403-283-6690,
fax 403-283-0286, whytereynolds@telusplanet.net, www.whytereynolds.com

MID-SIZED MANAGEMENT CONSULTING FIRM: Business Development, Economic Development, Human Resources, Management Consulting, Management Training, Marketing

Whyte Reynolds International Inc. is a Canadian management consulting company which has been in operation since 1982. The company serves business, industry and governments worldwide with specific expertise in doing business in Southeast Asia, Eastern Europe and Latin America. It specializes in international strategic alliances, feasibility studies and business plans, entrepreneurship and small and medium enterprise (SME) development, training and human resource development, economic development strategies, market analysis and marketing strategies. Whyte Reynolds employs approximately 25 people and has completed projects in North America, Southeast Asia, Europe and Latin America. [ID:6760]

Yamana Gold Inc.

Suite 1902, 150 York Street, Toronto, ON, M5H 3S5, Canada;
416-815-0220, investor@yamana.com, www.yamana.com

LARGE METALS FIRM: Exploration and Development, Gold and Metals Production, Metals, Mining

Yamana Gold Inc. is a Canadian gold producer with significant gold production, gold and copper development stage properties, exploration properties and land positions in all major mineral areas in Brazil. The company also holds gold exploration properties in Argentina, subject to earn-in. The company also plans to build on this base by targeting other gold consolidation opportunities in Brazil and throughout Latin America. [ID:6789]

Zeidler Partnership Architects

315 Queen Street W., Toronto, ON, M5V 2X2, Canada; 416-596-8300,
fax 416-596-1408, mail@zeidlerpartnership.com, www.zeidlerpartnership.com

LARGE ARCHITECTURE AND PLANNING FIRM: Architecture and Planning, Computer Systems, Project Management, Urban Development

Zeidler Partnership Architects' projects cover virtually the entire range of architectural, urban and interior design. The company's projects vary from large mixed-use complexes, hospitals and performing arts centres, to small residences and offices. Its major body of work is located in Canada and the United States and has also developed a significant international presence in Europe and Asia, as well as having offices in China, Germany, Canada, the United States and the United Kingdom.

The company has a staff of approximately 140 professionals and support staff members. The staff's specialties also include interior design, signage, life-cycle costing, master planning, feasibility studies, urban planning, project management, systems development and programming. [ID:6783]

CHAPTER 36

Private Sector Firms in the US

Of the estimated 4.1 million Americans living overseas, many work for private firms. Opportunities to work with American firms abroad are increasing, and while employees used to have to work their way up the corporate ladder to be considered for international positions, it is now becoming more common for culturally aware and language-able individuals to be able to apply to a company directly for an overseas position. This chapter profiles over 306 American firms that have international activities, providing contact information, a description their areas of expertise and notes on applying for jobs.

Many firms profiled in this chapter have active contracts with government agencies, such as the UNITED STATES AGENCY FOR INTERNATIONAL DEVELOPMENT (USAID), and international organizations like the UNITED NATIONS. Many of the companies profiled not only are involved in international work, but also have international offices and are effectively multinational corporations with headquarters in the United States. The international work of these companies varies from the laborious field work of civil engineers to the desk work of financial investors. We have generally stayed away from listing multinationals that send only long-term career-track employees overseas, and have concentrated on listing firms that regularly rotate staff overseas as part of their core business. This chapter profiles 306 US Private sector firms.

TYPES OF FIRMS PROFILED

The firms profiled in this chapter range from small consulting operations with a handful of employees to large multinational corporations, some exceeding 100,000 staff worldwide. Companies are loosely classified according to the number of employees and annual revenues. Small companies include those with fewer than 200 employees and less than $10 million US in annual revenues; Mid-Sized companies are those with 200 to 1,000 employees and $10 million to $1 billion US in annual revenues; companies with over 1,000 employees and over $1 billion US in revenues are classified as Large. In many instances, where the number of employees and revenues did not align with the pre-set categories, the level of international activities was used to indicate size.

Most industries have at least some companies operating internationally. International work is common in industries such as business and management, communications, engineering, investment, transportation and law. American consulting companies involved in environmental, engineering and development consulting are often recipients of contracts tendered by USAID, some UN agencies and international organizations.

THE AMERICAN PRIVATE SECTOR AND CANADIANS

Few differences exist between the Canadian and American private international job sectors except in terms of size. If there is a perception that American companies offer more international opportunities than their Canadian counterparts, it is mainly attributable to the sheer size and number of American private sector organizations: they employ a vastly larger number of people, their profits are higher, and they thus have the ability to spread their girth and operate with more offices in more locations around the world. The US government plays an important role in feeding private sector work overseas.

Increased visa restrictions and the economic uncertainty since September 11, 2001 has made it more difficult for Canadians to work in the US although the North American Free Trade Agreement (NAFTA) does allow for the free movement of many designated professionals. In terms of international work with US-based firms, talented professionals are always in demand, and companies are quick to acquire work visas for exceptional candidates. Very few US companies mention citizenship or visa requirements for their overseas positions. American companies can offer exceptional international opportunities for Canadians if they have superior talents, international experience and/or language training. Be sure to browse through this list of companies; it may send you in a direction that you've never considered.

WEB SITES AND OTHER RESOURCES

American private sector Web sites are generally informative and very visually appealing. Details found on company Web sites commonly include a company overview, investor and product or service information, the latest press releases and employment information.

The majority of companies profiled in this chapter have excellent on-line employment sites where you can browse through information about company culture and employee benefits, and read employee profiles. In addition, you will often find pages designed to provide specific recruitment information to college graduates and experienced professionals.

Most multinationals and many large companies allow you to search job openings by country or geographical location, which makes an international job search quick and easy. Companies that do not allow you to search by location often indicate that inquiries for international positions can be found on individual branch office Web sites, or they specify that the applicant must contact the geographic location directly to learn about specific international opportunities.

The majority of companies now allow you to apply for positions immediately on-line, or provide you with an e-mail address to which you can send your resume. You will also find it helpful that many Web sites host consultant or resume databases that enable you to submit your application once and be considered for current and future openings. Some companies no longer accept paper resumes sent by mail, so be sure to read the application instructions on the Web site before mailing a resume. There is a multitude of different jobs available; and even if you don't like the idea of working in the private sector, take a look—you might be surprised at what is available.

A LAST WORD

For more information about qualifications, how to enter the private sector and resources, see the chapter introduction for Chapter 35, Private Sector Firms in Canada, and all of Part Three: The International Job Search, as well as Chapter 30, Careers in International Development; Chapter 32, Engineering Careers Abroad; Chapter 33, Health Careers Abroad; Chapter 34, Spousal Employment & Freelancing Abroad; and Chapter 21, Resources for the International Job Search.

Profiles of Private Firms

Profiles of the organizations' international activities, as well as complete contact information for each of the US private sector firms indexed here, are available on the companion CD-ROM. (See Appendix 36a, "Profiles for Chapter 36: Private Sector Firms in the US.")

The following list provides an overview of 306 American private sector companies. The companies listed are headquartered in the United States and have significant international activities. In most cases, the company descriptions have been quoted directly from the firm's Web site. To help you with your job search, we have also provided comments about on-line employment pages found on these sites.

Both US NGOs and private sector organizations are highly concentrated in the American North East, but you'll find many spread across the rest of the US too. 161 US private sector organizations listed in THE BIG GUIDE are based in the North East - primarily in Washington D.C., New York City, Boston, and surrounding areas. Of the remaining international companies, 49 are based in Arlington, VA, Atlanta, GA and the rest of the South East; 32 are located around Chicago and other cities in the Mid West; 46 can be found in the West, especially in the areas surrounding Los Angeles and San Francisco; and finally, 15 major private sector companies are spread throughout the South West, with a high concentration in Texas.

Other general geographical patterns appear in the firms profiled in this chapter. Generally, civil engineering, energy and petrochemical companies tend to be headquartered in Texas. Other engineering firms and consulting firms are dispersed throughout the country. Technology firms tend to be concentrated along the western seaboard, but can also be found dispersed throughout the eastern seaboard as well. Law firms, communication companies, and financial and management companies are also located across the country but often have headquarters or a major base of operation in New York City, Washington, DC, Boston or Chicago. Note that American law firms are profiled in Chapter 31, International Law Careers.

We have listed some subsidiaries in addition to their parent company listing if they have their own on-line employment pages. Private sector job availability is subject to market, economic and political forces, so make sure to visit companies' Web sites to find current information about operations and job opportunities.

Index to Private Sector Firms in the US

Use this index to quickly scan for field types (written in uppercase) and organization Web site addresses. Check out the CD-ROM for descriptions of the organizations' international activities and for complete contact information. (See Appendix 36a, "Profiles for Chapter 36: Private Sector Firms in the US.")

A.T. Kearney Inc.
MANAGEMENT CONSULTING FIRM
www.atkearney.com [ID:6328]

ABB Lummus Global
PETROCHEMICALS FIRM
www.abb.com/lummus [ID:5787]

Abt Associates, Inc.
GENERAL CONSULTING FIRM
www.abtassociates.com [ID:5934]

Accenture
MANAGEMENT CONSULTING FIRM
www.accenture.com [ID:6330]

ADE Corporation
HIGH TECHNOLOGY FIRM
www.ade.com [ID:6454]

Adobe Systems Inc.
HIGH TECHNOLOGY FIRM
www.adobe.com [ID:6264]

Advanced Engineering Associates
International (AEAI)
ENVIRONMENTAL CONSULTING FIRM
www.aeaiinc.com [ID:6377]

Advanced Systems Development, Inc. (ASD)
INFORMATION SERVICES FIRM
www.asd-inc.com [ID:5935]

Advanstar Communications Inc.
COMMUNICATIONS FIRM
www.advanstar.com [ID:5895]

AECOM Technology Corporation
GENERAL CONSULTING FIRM
www.aecom.com [ID:6431]

Agilent Technologies
GENERAL CONSULTING FIRM
www.agilent.com [ID:6447]

Aguirre International Inc.
GENERAL CONSULTING FIRM
www.aguirreinternational.com [ID:6383]

American Express Company
FINANCIAL SERVICES FIRM
www.americanexpress.com [ID:6492]

American Information Technologies
GENERAL CONSULTING FIRM
www.aitusa.com [ID:6384]

American International Group, Inc. (AIG)
FINANCIAL SERVICES FIRM
www.aigcorporate.com [ID:5872]

AMEX International, Inc.
GENERAL CONSULTING FIRM
www.amexdc.com [ID:5937]

AMR Corporation
TRANSPORTATION SERVICES FIRM
www.amrcorp.com [ID:6471]

AMS
BUSINESS AND MANAGEMENT COMPANY
www.ams.com [ID:6422]

Aon Corporation
MANAGEMENT CONSULTING FIRM
www.aon.com [ID:6430]

APL Limited
TRANSPORTATION SERVICES FIRM
www.apl.com [ID:6400]

Apollo Ship Chandlers, Inc.
TRANSPORTATION SERVICES FIRM
www.apolloships.com [ID:6006]

ARCADIS
GENERAL CONSULTING FIRM
www.arcadis-us.com [ID:6449]

ARD, Inc.
GENERAL CONSULTING FIRM
www.ardinc.com [ID:5938]

Arkel International, Inc.
CONSTRUCTION FIRM
www.arkel.com [ID:5939]

Arthur D. Little
MANAGEMENT CONSULTING FIRM
www.adl.com [ID:5982]

ASET International
COMMUNICATIONS FIRM
www.asetquality.com [ID:6503]

Associated Press (AP)
COMMUNICATIONS FIRM
www.ap.org [ID:6349]

Astec Industries, Inc.
TRANSPORTATION MANUFACTURING FIRM
www.astecindustries.com [ID:6448]

ATI Transport International, LLC (ATI)
TRANSPORTATION SERVICES FIRM
www.ati-sky.com [ID:5721]

Atlantic Management Center, Inc. (AMCI)
BUSINESS AND MANAGEMENT COMPANY
www.amciweb.com [ID:6386]

Aurora Associates International, Inc.
GENERAL CONSULTING FIRM
www.aurorainternational.com [ID:6388]

Automation Research Systems, Ltd. (ARS)
INFORMATION SERVICES FIRM
www.arslimited.com [ID:5940]

Bain & Company, Inc.
MANAGEMENT CONSULTING FIRM
www.bain.com [ID:5983]

Baker Hughes Incorporated
PETROLEUM INDUSTRY FIRM
www.bakerhughes.com [ID:6428]

BAX Global Inc.
TRANSPORTATION SERVICES FIRM
www.baxglobal.com [ID:6478]

BBDO Worldwide
COMMUNICATIONS FIRM
www.bbdo.com [ID:6371]

BearingPoint, Inc.
MANAGEMENT CONSULTING FIRM
www.bearingpoint.com [ID:6332]

Bechtel
ENGINEERING FIRM
www.bechtel.com [ID:5941]

Berlitz International, Inc.
COMMUNICATIONS FIRM
www.berlitz.com [ID:6004]

Bernard Hodes Group
COMMUNICATIONS FIRM
www.hodes.com [ID:6457]

BJ Services Company
PETROLEUM INDUSTRY FIRM
www.bjservices.com [ID:6267]

Black and Veatch Corporation
ENGINEERING CONSULTING FIRM
www.bv.com [ID:5943]

Bloomberg
COMMUNICATIONS FIRM
www.bloomberg.com [ID:6354]

The Boeing Company
TRANSPORTATION MANUFACTURING FIRM
www.boeing.com [ID:5873]

Bonhams & Butterfields
CUSTOMER SERVICES FIRM
www.butterfields.com [ID:6499]

Booz Allen Hamilton
GENERAL CONSULTING FIRM
www.boozallen.com [ID:5944]

The Boston Consulting Group (BCG)
GENERAL CONSULTING FIRM
www.bcg.com [ID:5981]

The Brink's Company
TRANSPORTATION SERVICES FIRM
www.brinkscompany.com [ID:6477]

Brodeur Worldwide
COMMUNICATIONS FIRM
www.brodeur.com [ID:6510]

Buchart Horn, Inc and Basco Associates
GENERAL CONSULTING FIRM
www.bh-ba.com [ID:5970]

The Bureau of National Affairs, Inc.
COMMUNICATIONS FIRM
www.bnai.com [ID:6382]

Burns and Roe Enterprises (BR)
ENGINEERING FIRM
www.roe.com [ID:5971]

CACI International Inc
INFORMATION SERVICES FIRM
www.caci.com [ID:5972]

Caesars Entertainment, Inc.
BUSINESS AND MANAGEMENT COMPANY
www.caesars.com [ID:6494]

CalRecovery Inc
ENVIRONMENTAL CONSULTING FIRM
www.calrecovery.com [ID:6389]

Camp Dresser and McKee, Inc. (CDM)
GENERAL CONSULTING FIRM
www.cdm.com [ID:5973]

Cap Gemini Ernst & Young
MANAGEMENT CONSULTING FIRM
www.capgemini.com [ID:6331]

Carana Corporation
GENERAL CONSULTING FIRM
www.carana.com [ID:6391]

Cargill Industrial Oils & Lubricants
BUSINESS AND MANAGEMENT COMPANY
www.cargill.com [ID:6423]

Carlson Companies
CUSTOMER SERVICES FIRM
www.carlson.com [ID:6497]

The Carlyle Group
BUSINESS AND MANAGEMENT COMPANY
www.thecarlylegroup.com [ID:6460]

Carnival Cruise Lines
TRANSPORTATION SERVICES FIRM
www.carnival.com [ID:6007]

Carter and Burgess, Inc.
GENERAL CONSULTING FIRM
www.c-b.com [ID:5974]

Casals & Associates, Inc.
BUSINESS AND MANAGEMENT COMPANY
www.casals.com [ID:6393]

CB Richard Ellis Group, Inc.
BUSINESS AND MANAGEMENT COMPANY
www.cbre.com [ID:6488]

CB&I
ENGINEERING FIRM
www.chicagobridge.com [ID:5878]

CDM
GENERAL CONSULTING FIRM
www.cdm.com [ID:6390]

Celebrity Cruises
TRANSPORTATION SERVICES FIRM
www.celebrity.com [ID:6008]

Cendant Corporation
BUSINESS AND MANAGEMENT COMPANY
www.cendant.com [ID:6495]

Checchi and Company Consulting, Inc.
GENERAL CONSULTING FIRM
www.checchiconsulting.com [ID:5879]

Chemonics
GENERAL CONSULTING FIRM
www.chemonics.com [ID:5880]

ChevronTexaco Corporation
ENERGY RESOURCES FIRM
www.chevrontexaco.com [ID:5874]

Christie Digital
HIGH TECHNOLOGY FIRM
www.christiedigital.com [ID:5778]

Citigroup
INVESTMENT MANAGEMENT FIRM
www.citigroup.com [ID:6343]

Clapp & Mayne (C&M)
MANAGEMENT CONSULTING FIRM
www.cmusa.com [ID:5912]

Clark & Weinstock
MANAGEMENT CONSULTING FIRM
www.clarkandweinstock.com [ID:5716]

Clark Consulting International, Inc (CCI)
COMMUNICATIONS FIRM
www.ccimarketing.com [ID:5915]

Clear Channel
COMMUNICATIONS FIRM
www.clearchannel.com/ [ID:5774]

C-Level Solutions, LLC (C-LS)
COMMUNICATIONS FIRM
www.c-levelsolutions.com [ID:6380]

CMS Energy
ENERGY RESOURCES FIRM
www.cmsenergy.com [ID:5913]

Coca-Cola Enterprises Inc.
FOOD PROCESSING FIRM
www.cokecce.com [ID:6459]

Commodity Components
International (CCI), Inc.
HIGH TECHNOLOGY FIRM
www.cci-inc.com [ID:5911]

The Communities Group
GENERAL CONSULTING FIRM
www.thecommunitiesgroup.com [ID:5914]

Computer Assisted Development, Inc. (CADI)
HIGH TECHNOLOGY FIRM
www.cadi-usa.com [ID:5916]

ConAgra Foods Inc.
FOOD PROCESSING FIRM
www.conagrafoods.com [ID:6441]

ConocoPhillips Company
ENERGY RESOURCES FIRM
www.conocophillips.com [ID:6268]

Constellation Brands, Inc.
FOOD PROCESSING FIRM
www.cbrands.com [ID:6436]

Continental Airlines, Inc.
TRANSPORTATION SERVICES FIRM
www.continental.com [ID:6470]

Creative Artists Agency, Inc. (CAA)
MANAGEMENT CONSULTING FIRM
www.caa.com [ID:5772]

Creative Associates International Inc (CAII)
COMMUNITY ASSISTANCE FIRM
www.caii.net [ID:5882]

Crowley Maritime Corporation
TRANSPORTATION SERVICES FIRM
www.crowley.com [ID:6484]

Cummins Inc.
ENERGY CONSULTING FIRM
www.cummins.com [ID:6480]

Cushman & Wakefield, Inc.
BUSINESS AND MANAGEMENT COMPANY
www.cushmanwakefield.com [ID:6489]

The D&B Corporation
BUSINESS AND MANAGEMENT COMPANY
www.dnb.com [ID:6504]

Darlington Incorporated
COMMUNICATIONS FIRM
www.darlington.com [ID:5918]

Datex, Inc
GENERAL CONSULTING FIRM
www.datexinc.com [ID:5919]

DDB Worldwide Communications Group, Inc.
COMMUNICATIONS FIRM
www.ddb.com [ID:5713]

Deloitte
GENERAL CONSULTING FIRM
www.deloitte.com [ID:5984]

Delta Air Lines, Inc.
TRANSPORTATION SERVICES FIRM
www.delta.com [ID:6472]

Delta Scientific Corporation
ENGINEERING FIRM
www.deltascientific.com [ID:6394]

Development Alternatives, Inc (DAI)
GENERAL CONSULTING FIRM
www.dai.com [ID:5752]

Development Associates, Inc
GENERAL CONSULTING FIRM
www.devassoc1.com [ID:5712]

**Development Dimensions
International, Inc. (DDI)**
HUMAN RESOURCES FIRM
www.ddiworld.com [ID:5724]

DevTech Systems, Inc
GENERAL CONSULTING FIRM
www.devtechsys.com [ID:6395]

DF Young
TRANSPORTATION SERVICES FIRM
www.dfyoung.com [ID:5917]

DFI International
GENERAL CONSULTING FIRM
www.dfi-intl.com [ID:6381]

Digicon Corporation
HIGH TECHNOLOGY FIRM
www.digicon.com [ID:6396]

DMJM & Harris, Inc.
ENGINEERING FIRM
www.dmjmharris.com [ID:5729]

Dorst MediaWorks
COMMUNICATIONS FIRM
www.dorstmediaworks.com [ID:6379]

Dow Jones & Company
COMMUNICATIONS FIRM
www.dowjones.com [ID:6355]

Doyle New York
CUSTOMER SERVICES FIRM
www.doylenewyork.com [ID:6500]

DPK Consulting
GENERAL CONSULTING FIRM
www.dpkconsulting.com [ID:6378]

DPRA, Inc
ENVIRONMENTAL CONSULTING FIRM
www.dpra.com [ID:5730]

E. & J. Gallo Winery
FOOD PROCESSING FIRM
www.gallo.com [ID:6437]

Earth Satellite Corporation (EarthSat)
GENERAL CONSULTING FIRM
www.earthsat.com [ID:5731]

Earth Tech
ENGINEERING FIRM
www.earthtech.com [ID:6265]

Edelman
COMMUNICATIONS FIRM
www.edelman.com [ID:6375]

Electroteck Concepts
HIGH TECHNOLOGY FIRM
www.electrotek.com [ID:6397]

Ernst & Young
GENERAL CONSULTING FIRM
www.ey.com [ID:5985]

ExxonMobil Corporation
ENERGY RESOURCES FIRM
www.exxonmobil.com/corporate/ [ID:6196]

FedEx Corporation
TRANSPORTATION SERVICES FIRM
www.fedex.com [ID:6476]

Financial Markets International, Inc. (FMI)
FINANCIAL SERVICES FIRM
www.fmi-inc.net [ID:6398]

Fiserv, Inc.
HIGH TECHNOLOGY FIRM
www.fiserv.com [ID:6445]

Fitch Ratings
INVESTMENT MANAGEMENT FIRM
www.fitchibca.com [ID:6341]

**Fleishman Hillard International
Communications**
COMMUNICATIONS FIRM
www.fleishman.com [ID:6353]

Fluor Corporation
ENGINEERING FIRM
www.fluor.com [ID:5733]

Ford Models, Inc.
MANAGEMENT CONSULTING FIRM
www.fordmodels.com [ID:5775]

Foreign Policy
COMMUNICATIONS FIRM
www.foreignpolicy.com [ID:6357]

Foster Wheeler Inc.
ENGINEERING FIRM
www.fwc.com [ID:5734]

Fox Entertainment Group, Inc.
COMMUNICATIONS FIRM
www.newscorp.com/feg/index.html [ID:6366]

Futures Group
GENERAL CONSULTING FIRM
www.futuresgroup.com [ID:5735]

The Gallup Organization
GENERAL CONSULTING FIRM
www.gallup.com [ID:6427]

Gannett Fleming Inc.
ENGINEERING CONSULTING FIRM
www.gannettfleming.com [ID:5736]

Gavin Anderson & Company
COMMUNICATIONS FIRM
www.gavinanderson.com [ID:6399]

GCI Group
COMMUNICATIONS FIRM
www.gcigroup.com [ID:6511]

General Electric Company (GE)
HIGH TECHNOLOGY FIRM
www.ge.com [ID:6318]

The GEO Group, Inc.
GENERAL CONSULTING FIRM
www.thegeogroupinc.com [ID:6485]

Gilead
PHARMACEUTICAL FIRM
www.gilead.com [ID:6408]

Glamis Gold Ltd.
MINING FIRM
www.glamis.com [ID:6263]

Global Container Lines Limited (GCL)
TRANSPORTATION SERVICES FIRM
www.gogcl.com [ID:6401]

Global-Change Associates (GCA)
ENERGY CONSULTING FIRM
www.global-change.com [ID:6385]

Goldin-Rudahl Systems, Inc. (GRS)
HIGH TECHNOLOGY FIRM
www.goldin-rudahl.com [ID:6424]

Goldman Sachs Group, Inc.
INVESTMENT MANAGEMENT FIRM
www.gs.com [ID:6334]

GTSI Corp.
GENERAL CONSULTING FIRM
www.gtsi.com [ID:6402]

Halliburton
PETROLEUM INDUSTRY FIRM
www.halliburton.com [ID:6316]

Hay Group, Inc
GENERAL CONSULTING FIRM
www.haygroup.com [ID:5986]

Hazen and Sawyer
ENGINEERING CONSULTING FIRM
www.hazenandsawyer.com [ID:6404]

Heery International, Inc.
CONSTRUCTION FIRM
www.heery.com [ID:5737]

Hellmuth, Obata & Kassabaum, Inc (HOK)
ENVIRONMENTAL CONSULTING FIRM
www.hok.com [ID:5738]

Hershey Foods Corporation
FOOD PROCESSING FIRM
www.hersheys.com [ID:6515]

Hewitt Associates, Inc.
HUMAN RESOURCES FIRM
www.hewitt.com [ID:6351]

Hewlett-Packard Company (HP)
HIGH TECHNOLOGY FIRM
www.hp.com [ID:6516]

Hill & Knowlton Inc.
COMMUNICATIONS FIRM
www.hillandknowlton.com [ID:6509]

Hill International, Inc.
CONSTRUCTION FIRM
www.hillintl.com [ID:6452]

Hyatt Corporation
CUSTOMER SERVICES FIRM
www.hyatt.com [ID:6493]

ICON International, Inc.
FINANCIAL SERVICES FIRM
www.icon-intl.com [ID:5717]

IMG
MANAGEMENT CONSULTING FIRM
www.imgworld.com [ID:5773]

Input/Outpub, Inc. (I/O)
HIGH TECHNOLOGY FIRM
www.i-o.com [ID:5898]

Intelex, Ltd.
INFORMATION SERVICES FIRM
www.intelexltd.com [ID:6505]

Intelsat Global Service Corporation
HIGH TECHNOLOGY FIRM
www.intelsat.com [ID:6266]

Inter-Con Security Systems, Inc.
GENERAL CONSULTING FIRM
www.icsecurity.com [ID:6487]

International Business and Technical Consultants Inc. (IBTCI)
BUSINESS AND MANAGEMENT COMPANY
www.ibtci.com [ID:6406]

International Business Machines Corporation (IBM)
HIGH TECHNOLOGY FIRM
www.ibm.com [ID:6319]

International Creative Management, Inc. (ICM)
MANAGEMENT CONSULTING FIRM
www.icmtalent.com [ID:5723]

International Data Group (IDG)
COMMUNICATIONS FIRM
www.idg.com [ID:5777]

International Finance Corporation (IFC)
FINANCIAL SERVICES FIRM
www.ifc.org [ID:6407]

International Resources Group (IRG)
GENERAL CONSULTING FIRM
www.irgltd.com [ID:5739]

International Science and Technology Institute (ISTI)
GENERAL CONSULTING FIRM
www.istiinc.com [ID:6033]

InterPro Solutions Ltd
GENERAL CONSULTING FIRM
www.interpro-solutions.com [ID:6506]

Investor Risk Management Incorporated
GENERAL CONSULTING FIRM
www.invrm.com [ID:6456]

J. Walter Thompson Company
COMMUNICATIONS FIRM
www.jwtworld.com [ID:6370]

John Snow, Inc.
GENERAL CONSULTING FIRM
www.jsi.com [ID:5955]

John T. Boyd Company
MINING CONSULTING FIRM
www.jtboyd.com [ID:5945]

Johnson & Johnson
PHARMACEUTICAL FIRM
www.jnj.com [ID:6320]

Jones Lang LaSalle Incorporated
FINANCIAL SERVICES FIRM
www.joneslanglasalle.com [ID:6490]

JP Morgan Chase & Co.
FINANCIAL SERVICES FIRM
www.jpmorganchase.com [ID:6335]

Ketchum
COMMUNICATIONS FIRM
www.ketchum.com [ID:5714]

KPMG
MANAGEMENT CONSULTING FIRM
www.kpmg.com [ID:5993]

Kroll Inc.
GENERAL CONSULTING FIRM
www.krollworldwide.com [ID:6486]

L.T. Associates, Inc
GENERAL CONSULTING FIRM
www.ltassociates.com [ID:5901]

Labat-Anderson Inc.
GENERAL CONSULTING FIRM
www.labat.com [ID:5956]

Land O'Lakes
AGRICULTURAL FIRM
www.international.landolakes.com [ID:5902]

Lehman Brothers
INVESTMENT MANAGEMENT FIRM
www.lehman.com [ID:6338]

Logical Technical Services (LTS) Corporation
INFORMATION SERVICES FIRM
www.ltscorporation.com [ID:5957]

The Louis Berger Group, Inc.
ENGINEERING FIRM
www.louisberger.com [ID:5942]

LTG Associates, Inc.
GENERAL CONSULTING FIRM
www.ltgassociates.com [ID:6464]

Macfadden & Associates, Inc. (MAI)
BUSINESS AND MANAGEMENT COMPANY
www.macf.com [ID:6465]

Macro International Inc.
MANAGEMENT CONSULTING FIRM
www.macroint.com [ID:6466]

Management Sciences for Development, Inc. (MSD)
GENERAL CONSULTING FIRM
www.msdglobal.com [ID:6467]

Management Sciences for Health (MSH)
GENERAL CONSULTING FIRM
www.msh.org [ID:6468]

Management Systems International (MSI)
MANAGEMENT CONSULTING FIRM
www.msiworldwide.com [ID:6469]

ManTech International Corporation
HIGH TECHNOLOGY FIRM
www.mantech.com [ID:6416]

Marriott International, Inc.
CUSTOMER SERVICES FIRM
www.mariott.com [ID:6496]

Marsh & McLennan Companies, Inc.
BUSINESS AND MANAGEMENT COMPANY
www.marshmac.com [ID:6342]

Mathtech, Inc.
GENERAL CONSULTING FIRM
www.mathtechinc.com [ID:5958]

The McGraw-Hill Companies, Inc.
INFORMATION SERVICES FIRM
www.mcgraw-hill.com [ID:6444]

McKinsey & Company
MANAGEMENT CONSULTING FIRM
www.mckinsey.com [ID:5994]

Merck & Co.
PHARMACEUTICAL FIRM
www.merck.com [ID:6321]

Merrill Lynch
INVESTMENT MANAGEMENT FIRM
www.ml.com [ID:6337]

Metcalf & Eddy International
ENVIRONMENTAL CONSULTING FIRM
www.m-e.com [ID:5959]

Microsoft Corporation
HIGH TECHNOLOGY FIRM
www.microsoft.com [ID:6322]

Millennium Engineering and Integration Company (MEI)
ENGINEERING FIRM
www.meicompany.com [ID:6420]

MMM Design Group
ENGINEERING FIRM
www.mmmdesigngroup.com [ID:5960]

Monitor Group
MANAGEMENT CONSULTING FIRM
www.monitor.com [ID:6329]

Montgomery Watson Harza (MWH)
GENERAL CONSULTING FIRM
www.mwhglobal.com [ID:5961]

Moody's Corporation
INVESTMENT MANAGEMENT FIRM
www.moodys.com [ID:6340]

Morgan Stanley
INVESTMENT MANAGEMENT FIRM
www.morganstanley.com [ID:6336]

Morrison-Maierle, Inc.
ENGINEERING FIRM
www.m-m.net [ID:5962]

MWH
GENERAL CONSULTING FIRM
www.mwhglobal.com [ID:6403]

Nathan Associates
GENERAL CONSULTING FIRM
www.nathaninc.com [ID:5963]

National Fuel
ENERGY RESOURCES FIRM
www.natfuel.com [ID:6433]

National Geographic Society
COMMUNICATIONS FIRM
www.nationalgeographic.com [ID:6442]

National Public Radio (NPR)
COMMUNICATIONS FIRM
www.npr.com [ID:6368]

Navigant Consulting, Inc.
GENERAL CONSULTING FIRM
www.navigantconsulting.com [ID:5964]

NBC Universal
COMMUNICATIONS FIRM
www.nbc.com [ID:6367]

NCR Corporation
HIGH TECHNOLOGY FIRM
www.ncr.com [ID:6479]

New York Times
COMMUNICATIONS FIRM
www.nytco.com [ID:6358]

Newmont Mining Corporation
MINING FIRM
www.newmont.com [ID:6491]

Newsweek
COMMUNICATIONS FIRM
www.newsweek.com [ID:6360]

The Nielsen-Wurster Group Inc.
GENERAL CONSULTING FIRM
www.nielsen-wurster.com [ID:6451]

Northwest Airlines Corporation
TRANSPORTATION SERVICES FIRM
www.nwa.com [ID:6474]

Ogilvy & Mather Worldwide
COMMUNICATIONS FIRM
www.ogilvy.com [ID:6372]

OMI Corporation
TRANSPORTATION SERVICES FIRM
www.omicorp.com [ID:6435]

Omnicom Group Inc.
COMMUNICATIONS FIRM
www.omnicomgroup.com [ID:6462]

Oracle
HIGH TECHNOLOGY FIRM
www.oracle.com [ID:6512]

Overseas Strategic Consulting, Ltd. (OSC)
COMMUNICATIONS FIRM
www.oscltd.com [ID:6481]

PADCO, Inc.
GENERAL CONSULTING FIRM
www.padcoinc.com [ID:5965]

PAREXEL International Corporation
PHARMACEUTICAL FIRM
www.parexel.com [ID:5897]

Parsons
ENGINEERING FIRM
www.parsons.com [ID:5732]

Parsons Brinckerhoff (PB)
ENGINEERING FIRM
www.pbworld.com [ID:6483]

Pearson Education, Inc
COMMUNICATIONS FIRM
www.pearsoned.com [ID:6446]

PeopleSoft Inc.
HIGH TECHNOLOGY FIRM
www.peoplesoft.com [ID:6514]

The Pepsi Bottling Group, Inc. (PBG)
FOOD PROCESSING FIRM
www.pbg.com [ID:6461]

Petroleum Helicopters, Inc. (PHI)
TRANSPORTATION SERVICES FIRM
www.phihelico.com [ID:5722]

Pfizer Inc.
PHARMACEUTICAL FIRM
www.pfizer.com [ID:6323]

Philip Morris Companies Inc.
AGRICULTURAL FIRM
www.philipmorris.com [ID:6324]

**Planning and Learning
Technologies, Inc. (Pal-Tech)**
HIGH TECHNOLOGY FIRM
www.pal-tech.com [ID:6482]

Porter Novelli International
COMMUNICATIONS FIRM
www.porternovelli.com [ID:5715]

The Pragma Corporation
GENERAL CONSULTING FIRM
www.pragmacorp.com [ID:5758]

PricewaterhouseCoopers
MANAGEMENT CONSULTING FIRM
www.pwcglobal.com [ID:5995]

Princess Cruises
TRANSPORTATION SERVICES FIRM
www.princess.com [ID:6010]

Process Consulting Services, Inc.
ENGINEERING FIRM
www.revamps.com [ID:6409]

Procter & Gamble (P&G)
FOOD PROCESSING FIRM
www.pg.com [ID:6325]

Provant, Inc
GENERAL CONSULTING FIRM
www.provant.com [ID:5725]

Quest Diagnostics Incorporated
BIOTECHNOLOGY FIRM
www.questdiagnostics.com [ID:5896]

Radisson Seven Seas Cruises
TRANSPORTATION SERVICES FIRM
www.rssc.com [ID:6011]

Rainier Overseas Movers Inc.
TRANSPORTATION SERVICES FIRM
www.rainieros.com [ID:6439]

Rand McNally & Company
COMMUNICATIONS FIRM
www.randmcnally.com [ID:6443]

Raytheon Company
ENGINEERING FIRM
www.raytheon.com [ID:5887]

The Rendon Group, Inc. (TRG)
COMMUNICATIONS FIRM
www.rendon.com [ID:6410]

The Robert Mondavi Corporation
FOOD PROCESSING FIRM
www.robertmondavi.com [ID:6458]

RONCO Consulting Corporation
GENERAL CONSULTING FIRM
www.roncoconsulting.com [ID:6411]

Ruder Finn
COMMUNICATIONS FIRM
www.ruderfinn.com [ID:6376]

Ryder Scott Company Petroleum Consultants
PETROLEUM CONSULTING FIRM
www.ryderscott.com [ID:6455]

Saatchi & Saatchi
COMMUNICATIONS FIRM
www.saatchi.com [ID:6373]

SBC Communications Inc.
TELECOMMUNICATIONS FIRM
www.sbc.com [ID:6326]

Schlumberger Limited
ENERGY CONSULTING FIRM
www.slb.com [ID:6429]

Science Applications International Corporation (SAIC)
ENGINEERING FIRM
www.saic.com [ID:6434]

Sheladia Associates, Inc
GENERAL CONSULTING FIRM
www.sheladia.com [ID:5883]

Sibley International
MANAGEMENT CONSULTING FIRM
www.sibleyinternational.com [ID:6412]

Sigma One Corporation
AGRICULTURAL CONSULTING FIRM
www.sigmaone.com [ID:6413]

SIRVA
CUSTOMER SERVICES FIRM
www.sirva.com [ID:6438]

Smith Brandon International
INFORMATION SERVICES FIRM
www.smithbrandon.com [ID:6507]

Social Impact
MANAGEMENT CONSULTING FIRM
www.socialimpact.com [ID:6415]

SoftInWay Inc.
ENGINEERING FIRM
www.softinway.com [ID:6453]

Sotheby's
CUSTOMER SERVICES FIRM
www.sothebys.com [ID:6501]

Standard & Poor's
INVESTMENT MANAGEMENT FIRM
www2.standardandpoors.com [ID:6339]

Stanley Consultants Inc
ENGINEERING CONSULTING FIRM
www.stanleygroup.com [ID:6450]

Starboard Cruise Services, Inc.
TRANSPORTATION SERVICES FIRM
www.starboardcruise.com [ID:6009]

Starbucks Corporation
FOOD PROCESSING FIRM
www.starbucks.com [ID:5771]

Starwood Hotels & Resorts Worldwide, Inc.
CUSTOMER SERVICES FIRM
www.starwood.com [ID:6498]

Stickle Enterprises
TRANSPORTATION SERVICES FIRM
www.stickle.com [ID:6387]

STV Group, Inc.
GENERAL CONSULTING FIRM
www.stvinc.com [ID:5976]

Sun Microsystems, Inc.
HIGH TECHNOLOGY FIRM
www.sun.com [ID:6425]

Sybase
HIGH TECHNOLOGY FIRM
www.sybase.com [ID:6513]

Taking Off
EXCHANGE GROUP
www.els.com [ID:6005]

TAMS Consultants, Inc (TAMS)
ENGINEERING FIRM
www.tamsconsultants.com [ID:5977]

TechTrans International, Inc.
GENERAL CONSULTING FIRM
www.tti-corp.com [ID:6508]

Telos Corporation
HIGH TECHNOLOGY FIRM
www.telos.com [ID:6417]

Tempest Environmental Systems
WATER RESOURCES FIRM
www.aquapura.com [ID:6418]

Tetra Tech, Inc
ENGINEERING CONSULTING FIRM
www.tetratech.com [ID:6419]

Time Inc.
COMMUNICATIONS FIRM
www.aoltimewarner.com [ID:6361]

Time Warner Inc.
COMMUNICATIONS FIRM
www.aoltimewarner.com [ID:6362]

Towers Perrin
HUMAN RESOURCES FIRM
www.towers.com [ID:6350]

Transport International Pool Inc. (TIP)
TRANSPORTATION SERVICES FIRM
www.tiptrailers.com [ID:5720]

Tri Star Engineering, Inc.
ENGINEERING FIRM
www.star3.com [ID:6421]

Tribune Company
COMMUNICATIONS FIRM
www.latimes.com [ID:6359]

UAL Corporation
TRANSPORTATION SERVICES FIRM
www.united.com [ID:6473]

United Parcel Service, Inc. (UPS)
TRANSPORTATION SERVICES FIRM
www.ups.com [ID:6475]

United Press International (UPI)
COMMUNICATIONS FIRM
www.upi.com [ID:6356]

Unitrans International Corporation
TRANSPORTATION SERVICES FIRM
www.unitrans-us.com [ID:6440]

University Research Co., LLC (URC)
GENERAL CONSULTING FIRM
www.urc-chs.com [ID:5978]

URS Corporation
ENGINEERING FIRM
www.urscorp.com [ID:6432]

US News and World Report, L.P.
COMMUNICATIONS FIRM
www.usnews.com [ID:6364]

VERITAS DGC Inc.
PETROLEUM CONSULTING FIRM
www.veritasdgc.com [ID:5899]

Viacom Inc.
COMMUNICATIONS FIRM
www.viacom.com [ID:6365]

Wal-Mart Stores, Inc.
CUSTOMER SERVICES FIRM
www.walmartstores.com [ID:6327]

The Walt Disney Company
COMMUNICATIONS FIRM
www.disney.go.com [ID:5718]

Washington Consulting Group, Inc. (WCG)
GENERAL CONSULTING FIRM
www.washcg.com [ID:5979]

Washington Group International
ENGINEERING FIRM
www.wgint.com [ID:5884]

The Washington Post Company
COMMUNICATIONS FIRM
www.washingtonpost.com [ID:6363]

Watson Wyatt & Company Holdings
GENERAL CONSULTING FIRM
www.watsonwyatt.com [ID:6352]

Wilbur Smith Associates (WSA)
GENERAL CONSULTING FIRM
www.wilbursmith.com [ID:5885]

Wilhelmina Models
BUSINESS AND MANAGEMENT COMPANY
www.wilhelmina.com [ID:5776]

Wimberly Allison Tong & Goo (WATG)
ARCHITECTURE AND PLANNING FIRM
www.watg.com [ID:5980]

Xerox Corporation
HIGH TECHNOLOGY FIRM
www.xerox.com [ID:6426]

CHAPTER 37
Canadian Government

The federal government employs over 150,000 Canadians working in diverse fields in over 1,000 locations throughout Canada and the rest of the world. Among these are development specialists working in sub-Saharan Africa, diplomats filling Canada's seats in the many intergovernmental organizations in Geneva, trade officials on all four corners of the globe and immigration authorities processing a steady stream of applicants. You will find opportunities for international government employment in many fields, but your chances of working in the international sphere are greatest in the areas of development, diplomacy and trade promotion. Keep in mind also that many international jobs with the federal government are actually based in Canada and these are primarily in Ottawa.

If you are a recent graduate, it is an ideal time to start a career in the public service. Over the next few years a large number of baby boomers will be retiring. As a young professional, your chances of climbing the management ladder have never been better! Numerous management positions will be opening up and you can expect promotions early in your career.

Most of the federal government's recruitment is handled by the PUBLIC SERVICE COMMISSION OF CANADA (PSC), although some departments and agencies do their own recruitment, including a few with international mandates like EXPORT DEVELOPMENT CANADA (EDC) and the INTERNATIONAL DEVELOPMENT RESEARCH CENTRE (IDRC). These organizations, along with 68 other provincial, territorial and federal departments, agencies and Crown corporations, are profiled in this chapter.

While the majority of international opportunities are with the federal government, provincial governments also have some ongoing international activities, especially in the fields of tourism, trade and investment promotion. Even large municipalities sometimes have international positions related to specific projects and activities, such as international conferences or the upcoming 2010 Olympic Winter Games in Vancouver. Application procedures and opportunities will be different for each jurisdiction, so make sure that you take the time to investigate each independently. This chapter profiles 61 government profiles.

HOW THIS CHAPTER IS ORGANIZED

The first section of this chapter will introduce you to the PUBLIC SERVICE COMMISSION OF CANADA (PSC), the various programs it offers and advice on how to identify and apply for vacancies through the PSC's e-recruitment system. This is then followed by profiles of the government's four largest international employers. The first profile covers two departments: FOREIGN AFFAIRS CANADA (FAC) and INTERNATIONAL TRADE CANADA (ITCAN). The second profile is of the CANADIAN INTERNATIONAL DEVELOPMENT AGENCY (CIDA) and the third is of the CANADIAN ARMED FORCES.

The last section of this chapter profiles in alphabetical order the 68 remaining federal, provincial and territorial government departments, agencies and Crown corporations.

RESOURCES

CANADIAN GOVERNMENT

For more government resources, see the other Resources sections in this chapter—Foreign Affairs Canada and Canadian International Development Agency.

Asia Pacific Review 📖
Annual, 72 pages ➤ Asia Pacific Foundation of Canada, Suite 666, 999 Canada Place, Vancouver, BC V6C 3E1, Canada, www.asiapacific.ca, $34.95 CDN; VISA, MC; 604-684-5986, fax 604-681-1370; Fr ◆ This annual survey examines Canada's relationship with Asia and the impact on business of major developments during the year. The report includes a Canada-Asia report card which examines in depth nine key areas of the Canada-Asia relationship, assigning letter grades to each performance indicator. The Review is also available in French. [ID:2393]

Asian Outlook 📖 🖥
Quarterly, variable ➤ Asia Pacific Foundation of Canada, Suite 666, 999 Canada Place, Vancouver, BC V6C 3E1, Canada, www.asiapacific.ca, Free; VISA, MC; 604-684-5986, fax 604-681-1370 ◆ Offers a concise survey of the latest political and economic trends in 14 Asia Pacific economies of interest to Canadian business. Includes a succinct listing of developments to watch for in the months ahead, including a tabulation of major economic indicators. [ID:2395]

Canada Business Service Centres 🖥
www.cbsc.org; Fr ◆ Designed to serve Canadian business people, the CBSC Internet site contains searchable collections of information on federal and provincial government services, programs and regulations. The site also allows the user to contact Business Information Officers by e-mail. This is an excellent site for those interested in government. [ID:2245]

Canada Post Corporation ♙
www.canadapost.ca; Fr ◆ Canada Post's Web site allows easy and convenient access to Canadian postal codes, parcel rates, delivery confirmation and postal outlet locations. [ID:2331]

Canadian Passport Office ♙
www.ppt.gc.ca ◆ This site is dedicated especially to topics about passports. Includes details on obtaining passports on-line, travel tips and advisories, and what to do if you lose your passport. Your best source for passport information. [ID:2354]

Canadian Representatives Abroad 💻

Foreign Affairs Canada (FAC), www.dfait-maeci.gc.ca/world/embassies/cra-en.asp, Free on-line; *Fr* ◆ This is a bilingual directory of Government of Canada diplomatic and consular missions overseas, as well as a resource for finding Canada-based staff at those missions. You can search the directory, choose a region on the map below or access a list by city, country or surname. Finally, access a list of Canadian Missions to international organizations. This is an excellent tool to use if you want to learn about the size of a mission abroad. For embassies, note that many can be found just by entering the name of a city or country within www.***.gc.ca (e.g., www.losangeles.gc.ca, www.london.gc.ca, and www.india.gc.ca). Good luck in your search! [ID:2027]

Export Development Corporation 🏛

www.edc.ca; *Fr* ◆ The Export Development Corporation assists Canadians wishing to do business with foreign countries. Services include risk assessment, export insurance, credit profiles of foreign customers, market trends analysis, export readiness tools and financial management assistance. A fabulous service for the international entrepreneur. [ID:2285]

ExportSource.ca 💻

www.ExportSource.ca; *Fr* ◆ ExportSource.ca is a service for Canadians in international export development. Publications include a guide to locating opportunities for bidding on international contracts, searching for bidding partners, and developing and evaluating bid proposals. The Web site has links to on-line databases of business opportunities in Canada and internationally. [ID:2829]

Government Electronic Directory Services 💻

http://direct.srv.gc.ca/cgi-bin/direct500/TE?FN=index.htm ◆ The Government Electronic Directory Services (GEDS) provides an integrated directory of all federal public servants. This is an invaluable service that provides the public with access to public servant's names, titles, telephone and facsimile numbers, departmental names, office locations and position titles within the governmental structure. In all the site includes information on over 170,000 public servants. This site is obviously great for gaining the contact information of government officials. Perhaps more importantly, however, this service is probably the easiest way to see the bureaucratic structure of federal departments. [ID:2234]

Government of Canada Primary Internet Site 💻

http://canada.gc.ca/main_e.html; *Fr* ◆ The government at your fingertips. This site provides access to all federal departments and programs, as well as links to provincial governments and several international organizations. [ID:2284]

Government of Canada Telephone Directory: National Capital Region 📖

2003, Supply and Services Canada, 3,192 pages ➤ Renouf Publishing Co. Ltd., Unit 1, 5369 Canotek Road, Ottawa, ON K1J 9J3, Canada, www.renoufbooks.com, $39.95 CDN; Credit Cards; 888-767-6766, fax 613-745-7660; *Fr* ◆ For those within the federal government and for those that deal frequently with the federal government, the regional telephone directory provides quick and easy access to the right people in the Canadian government. This directory offers a complete listing of federal government contacts and services available by region. [ID:2071]

MERX 💻 🏛

www.merx.com, $24.95 CND per month; *Fr* ◆ A national electronic tendering service that advertises government goods and services contracts. MERX is like the classifieds for contracts with most federal government departments, some provincial and territorial ministries, and some municipalities. At this site you'll find contracts to work with CIDA, FAC, ITCan, the World Bank and on other international projects. Essential for any businesses working in international development and a great way for university students starting out to see exactly the type of projects that Canadians work on throughout the world. [ID:2313]

Department of National Defence Canada 🏛

www.dnd.ca; *Fr* ◆ From information on the latest UN peacekeeping operations to recruiting guidelines, this is the gateway to Canada's military. It also provides a statement of defence policy and information on financial management assistance. [ID:2268]

Public Service Commission of Canada 🏛

http://jobs.gc.ca/menu/alljobs_e.htm; *Fr* ◆ This is the main recruitment site for careers in the Canadian civil service. Search jobs by field or geographic location. You can also access resources such as resume builders, alerts and advanced search tools from this page. Don't miss the extensive list of links to other government organization job sites, such as the National Film Board and National Research Council. [ID:2592]

Le Québec International 📖

Annual, Denis Turcotte, 150 pages ➤ Les Éditions Québec dans le monde, C.P. 8503, Ste-Foy, QC G1V 4N5, Canada, www.quebecmonde.com, $49.95 CDN; VISA; 418-659-5540, fax 418-659-4143 ◆ Cet annuaire recense plus de 1000 intervenants internationaux québécois et partenaires étrangers. On y retrouve différents organismes publics, associations et organisations internationales, exportateurs, établissements, ambassades et consulats, organismes non gouvernementaux, bureaux de coopération et centres d'études. [ID:2563]

Western Economic Diversification Canada 🖥

www.wd.gc.ca ◆ A department of the Government of Canada, Western Economic Diversification Canada (WD) works to strengthen western Canada's economy and advance the interests of the West in national economic policy. This is a great Web site with information on entrepreneurship, exporting and e-business. Through the "Business Service Network" database, you can find the office nearest you. [ID:2346]

Youth Link 🖥

Human Resources and Skills Development Canada, www.youth.gc.ca, Free on-line; *Fr* ◆ Not to be confused with the Canadian government's Web site, YouthPath, Youth Link is publication that includes more than 250 programs, services and resources for young people between the ages of 15 and 30. It is also a valuable resource for career counsellors, parents, educators, employers and community groups. From the YouthPath index, navigate to "Publications" and search for Youth Link. [ID:2703]

The Public Service Commission (PSC)

West Tower, L'Esplanade Laurier, 300 Laurier Street W,
Ottawa, Ontario, K1A 0M7; www.psc-cfp.gc.ca, info-com@psc-cfp.gc.ca [ID:7204]

The PUBLIC SERVICE COMMISSION OF CANADA (PSC) is the independent agency responsible for recruiting new employees and filling vacancies in 75 of the federal government's departments and agencies. The PSC's mandate is to ensure that federal government employees are highly competent, non-partisan and representative of Canada's diverse population. Its appointments are based on merit, reflecting the PSC's values of fairness, equity of access and transparency. Through its employment equity program, the federal government actively recruits people with disabilities, members of visible minority groups, Aboriginal peoples and women in non-traditional occupations.

In the eyes of one employee, the federal government is a great employer that allows her to enjoy both a fulfilling professional and personal life:

"The Canadian government is in many ways an ideal employer; you have a sense of helping others and promoting values, both in Canada and abroad. The federal government is a leader in Canada, offering great benefits like flex-time, fully paid maternity leave, ability to work from home, training and development opportunities, generous vacation allowances and pension packages. While some may find working in a large bureaucracy frustrating, there is a strong sense of public service amongst my colleagues, and we know that the Canadian government is a fair and equitable employer."

If you're interested in working for the public service—whether you are in high school, university or a senior executive—the http://jobs.gc.ca page is the central portal for your job search. The following sections explain the various opportunities that are open to Canadians at all levels of professional careers. The first section explains how you can search and apply for temporary, permanent and executive positions with the federal government. The following two sections are devoted respectively to recent graduates and students. The final section explores some lesser-known and backdoor strategies to finding your way into the public service.

JOBS OPEN TO THE PUBLIC

Permanent and Temporary Positions

The "Jobs Open to the Public" page allows you to search for temporary or permanent positions according to the region you live in. However, if you're interested in an internationally focused career, you're best to focus your job search on the national capital region.

After selecting a region to search for jobs, you'll be presented with a list of available job opportunities. Clicking on a job title will bring you to a job description. The first sentence of each job description indicates whether it is a term position—usually lasting anywhere from three to twelve months—or a permanent position. Remember that getting your foot in the door is the most important thing, so you should be prepared to accept any opportunity that gets you into a department that interests you. Don't wait and hold out for a permanent position.

Once you find a job that you're interested in applying for, select the "Apply On-Line" link at the bottom of each job description. You'll then automatically be brought to one of the PSC's two e-recruitment systems, the "Public Service Resourcing System" or the "Resume Builder System." Very occasionally, an applicant is directed to apply using a department's internal recruitment system. Both of the e-recruitment systems are relatively easy to use and you should have little difficulty creating your on-line profile. You should also be aware that the PSRS is presently being test-piloted and is used for all of the PSC's Post-Secondary Recruitment Programs. It is expected that this system will eventually be used for all of the PSC's recruitment.

Both of the PSC's e-recruitment systems allow you to save your on-line profile, making it easy to apply for new positions. Make sure, though, that you tailor your on-line profile for every new position you apply to according to the "Statement of Quali-fications" that is found at the bottom of each job description. The Statement of Qualifications contains detailed information about each available job and is extremely important! Print it off and use it to complete your on-line profile. Also refer to it if you are required to complete a questionnaire that will ask you to provide examples of your professional experience.

The PSRS and the Resume Builder System also have some features that will assist you in your job search. The PSRS includes a "Match Profile to Job" function that generates a list of available jobs according to the qualifications and preferences that you indicate in your on-line profile. This allows you to identify some opportunities that you might not notice otherwise. Make sure that you regularly log in to your account to see if there are any new jobs that match your profile.

After completing your on-line profile on the Resume Builder System you can register on the job alert function to regularly receive e-mails that match your job search criteria and ensure you don't miss out on any opportunities.

Finally, make sure that you visit the Jobs Open to the Public page often, as some jobs are open for as little as 48 hours! The fact that some jobs are advertised for such a short time should alert you to the fact that some jobs, especially temporary positions, are more vacant than others. Indeed, many positions are unofficially reserved for incumbents. So don't get discouraged if you don't get an interview for a position you were perfect for. Getting your foot in the door of the public service is hard to do and there are many other avenues besides the PSC Web site that are explored later in this chapter.

Executive Positions

The "Executive Programs" interface can be accessed through the http://jobs.gc.ca page. It provides information for senior executives with extensive experience that are interested in becoming public service executives. Be aware that this site contains limited information and is only of value to seasoned professionals. If you possess international experience and you fall into this category, you should directly contact a department that you are interested in working for.

UNIVERSITY GRADUATES

Tens of thousands of public service employees are set to retire over the next five years. Most of these positions will be filled by new graduates through one of the Canadian government's programs for university graduates. The main graduate programs that are accessible through the PSC Web site are described below. If you're interested in a specific department you should visit its Web site or contact it to determine its policies on graduate recruitment.

Post-Secondary Recruitment

The federal government conducts most of its recruitment for recent or expectant graduates through the PSC's Post-Secondary Recruitment (PSR) program, an annual competition held each year in the fall. Other entry-level positions are posted throughout the year on the Jobs Open to the Public page of the PSC's Web site.

Specific recruitment campaigns, including those for foreign officer positions with FAC and ITCAN and development officer positions with CIDA are called *Tested Opportunities*. As the name suggests, you must complete certain tests to participate in these campaigns. Since these recruitment programs take place in the fall, you should check the PSC Web site in the summer. Make sure you complete your on-line profile and pre-register for these tests! (For more specific information about FAC, ITCAN and CIDA recruitment campaigns, see the following sections in this chapter.)

Management Trainee Programs

If you have a master's degree you might want to take a look at the four-year Management Trainee Program (MTP) that develops highly qualified individuals for key positions of responsibility in the federal government. The Accelerated Economist Training Program (AETP) is an option for those with master's degrees in economics, public administration or a related discipline. This two-year program gives participants the opportunity to work alongside Canada's top decision-makers on a number of social, economic and international policy agendas. FAC, ITCAN and CIDA all participate in these programs, although FAC and ITCAN rarely take on people through the MTP.

STUDENT EMPLOYMENT

You'll quickly realize that a lack of experience is the single greatest obstacle to finding your first job. Participating in one of the federal government's student employment programs will provide you with this much-sought-after experience and allow you to make valuable contacts. No matter what your career plans, don't pass up the opportunity to work for the government as a summer student, a co-op placement, an intern, a temporary employee, or by working through a temp agency or a firm with a federal government service contract.

Federal Student Work Experience Program

The Federal Student Work Experience Program (FSWEP) offers full-time high school, CEGEP, college, technical institute and university students the opportunity to apply for student jobs with the federal government. There are only a few overseas assignments available under FSWEP. (For example, see the VETERANS AFFAIRS CANADA'S Student Guide Program in France, in the Profiles section of Chapter 10, Short-Term Programs Overseas.) If you are lucky however, you may be placed with a federal government department or agency involved in international activities and based in Canada. While the FSWEP offers excellent opportunities, it is nonetheless a lottery system and not a surefire way of gaining international-related work experience. You can increase your chances by emphasizing your international credentials, but realistically you'll have to use parallel strategies if you want summer work with the government. The most useful thing you can do is simply to contact the hiring manager in a section of a department you are interested in spending the summer with. Have your international skills "elevator pitch" ready and be prepared with an international resume. (See Chapter 23, Selling Your International Skills and Chapter 24, International Resumes.)

Post-Secondary Co-operative Education and Internship Program

The federal public service is Canada's single largest employer of students in co-op programs. On average, students from over 100 institutions across Canada carry out more than 7,000 work terms with the government each year.

To be eligible for a co-op placement you must be a post-secondary student enrolled in a cooperative education or internship program where work experience is a mandatory requirement for graduation. By selecting "approved programs," you'll enter a search engine where you can search the various internship programs that are offered by Canadian colleges and universities. Co-op placements are paid and usually last for four months. Co-op students may be re-employed into an FSWEP position following their initial co-op placement or internship. Your chances for targeting an international position (most likely based in Canada) are much better under this program than they are under FSWEP.

For those with entrepreneurial instincts, there may even be informal internship possibilities where you approach a civil servant with a research project on an international subject. There are also pseudo-internships like the unpaid ones offered by The NORMAN PATERSON SCHOOL OF INTERNATIONAL AFFAIRS at CARLETON UNIVERSITY for its students.

Bridging Mechanisms for Students

Bridging mechanisms are a little known way that you can be appointed into the public service right after completing your studies without going through a competitive process. There are two bridging mechanisms that are open to students, but you must first be employed in an FSWEP position or co-op program.

The first bridging mechanism allows students to apply for jobs that are only open to members of the public service. The second bridging mechanism allows students to be directly appointed into a position without competition. Students are only eligible for non-competitive bridging if they complete their post-secondary education in the 18-month period preceding the date of the without-competition appointment.

The managers responsible for hiring in the international branches of several departments indicated that they extensively rely upon bridging mechanisms to fill their vacancies.

GETTING IN THE BACK DOOR

Opportunities for government sector employment, especially permanent positions in the federal public service, are limited. If you want to work for the federal government, you'll probably have to find a way to get in through the back door. Getting that first assignment is the toughest, so you have to be prepared to work hard and take risks to secure that elusive first job. Working as a student and taking advantage of one of the bridging mechanisms is probably your best bet. And it never hurts to directly contact the managers in the division you are interested in working for. Here are some more suggestions that might help you get your foot in the door:

- **Move to the National Capital Region:** It won't take you long to realize that virtually every internationally focused job with the Canadian government is based in Ottawa or Gatineau. Being there is the only way that you'll be able to accept temporary assignments, to network and to immerse yourself in Ottawa's distinct political culture.

- **Learn or improve your french:** Most federal positions require bilingualism. And while the government does provide language training, managers are interested in hiring people who come on board with the necessary skills and don't require further training that will take them away from their jobs.

- **Apply for a security clearance:** Many federal positions require an enhanced reliability or secret security clearance that you can only apply to if sponsored by an employer. A way to get one without already having a job is to contact an employment agency and indicate that you are interested in temporary government work. If you have a suitable background the employment agency will sponsor you for a security clearance. The basic enhanced reliability clearance takes about six weeks to process and is valid for five years. A secret clearance can take up to four months to process and is valid for ten years.

- **Work as an administrative assistant:** If you are bilingual and possess a security clearance you should have no problem finding a temporary job as an administrative assistant. This is a great way to gain experience while familiarizing yourself with the inner workings of government. These positions—along with numerous other government contracts—are often recruited through employment agencies. Contact the agencies directly or look for advertisements in the *Ottawa Citizen*, at Careerclick.com or on HRDS's job bank.

- **Contact a department directly:** If you are a young professional with an international background, you should contact a department's international division directly. Make sure you have done your research and have a resume prepared so that you it can be sent immediately after hanging up the phone.

- **Volunteer on a political campaign:** This is the best way to network and potentially get a job as a political staffer on Parliament Hill. Many political staffers eventually find their way into the federal government or join the ranks of Ottawa's ubiquitous consultants. Those who work for three years on a cabinet minister's staff can apply to be entered on the ministers' staffs priority inventory. Those with a ministers' staffs priority are entitled to be appointed without competition to any position in the public service that they are qualified for.

- **Network, network, network:** The reality is that many people working for Canada's government found their jobs because they knew someone. So get out there, meet people, and let them know that you're looking for work. Start by going to Darcy McGee's Irish Pub on a Friday evening where you'll enjoy a pint while bearing witness to some intense networking; or join an ultimate Frisbee team, a peculiar obsession for some federal government employees.

Foreign Affairs Canada (FAC) and International Trade Canada (ITCAN)

Lester B. Pearson Bldg. 125 Sussex Drive, Ottawa, Ontario, K1A 0G2; 613-944-4000
Fax: 613-996-9709 www.fac-aec.gc.ca, www.itcan-cican.gc.ca, enqserv@dfait-maeci.gc.ca [ID:7205]

As of early 2004, the DEPARTMENT OF FOREIGN AFFAIRS AND INTERNATIONAL TRADE (DFAIT) ceased to exist as a federal department. Its services, programs and activities are now the responsibility of two separate federal departments: FOREIGN AFFAIRS CANADA (FAC) and INTERNATIONAL TRADE CANADA (ITCAN).

FAC is responsible for promoting peace, prosperity and Canadian values around the world. It is responsible for Canada's diplomatic relationships with foreign governments and international organizations and ensures that Canadians abroad continue to receive the necessary consular services. FAC will administer the foreign service of Canada.

ITCAN is the new centralized department that will provide integrated federal trade support and investment promotion. It offers Canadian businesses and entrepreneurs a variety of services that will help them succeed in an increasingly competitive international marketplace. The new department incorporates INVESTMENT PARTNERSHIPS CANADA from INDUSTRY CANADA, which is a central component of Canada's foreign investment strategy, designed to attract foreign direct investment in Canada, particularly from multinational enterprises. ITCAN will also negotiate and administer Canada's trade and investment agreements.

At the time of publication, the departmental restructuring was still in progress. Despite the restructuring, the two departments will be jointly administered and headquartered in the Lester B. Pearson Building. As a result, current employees will not be greatly affected by the changes and the recruitment process will likely remain the same. More detailed information will be posted on the departments' new Web sites that are currently being developed.

WORKING FOR THE FOREIGN SERVICE

A career in the Canadian foreign service is a way of life. Typically, it involves extensive overseas travel, stimulating assignments and diverse international experiences. FAC and ITCAN seek highly qualified, creative people with strong analytical and communication skills to fill a variety of international positions. Employees keep the Canadian government apprised of the international situation and represent Canada's diplomatic, trade and human interests abroad.

As a member of the foreign service, you can expect to spend roughly one-half of your career working and living outside of Canada. The remainder of your time will be spent in Ottawa, or, if you are a trade commissioner, at one of the international trade centres located across Canada. This ongoing job rotation can be very difficult for you and your family, who must be comfortable dealing with frequent and dramatic change. If you can meet this challenge, FAC and ITCAN offer interesting and meaningful international careers.

Canadian Missions Abroad

Canada has diplomatic and consular missions in 270 locations in approximately 180 foreign countries. These missions are staffed by a variety of Canadian public servants from a number of federal departments and locally engaged staff. The focus of individual missions varies from country to country, but all are responsible for representing and enhancing Canada's political, economic and cultural relations in the international sphere. Most of the missions are accredited to specific countries, although there are also a number of multilateral missions that serve Canada's interests at international bodies such as the UNITED NATIONS and the NORTH ATLANTIC TREATY ORGANIZATION (NATO). The work on multilateral missions is mostly political in nature, concerned with working with other countries to ensure that Canada's values are incorporated into international law and ensuring that Canada's voice is heard. (For a detailed list of our diplomatic and consular missions abroad, see Canadian Representatives Abroad in the Foreign Affairs Canada Resources following this profile.)

Canada's bilateral missions offer a wide range of services to Canadians travelling, working, studying or living abroad. Every year, over two million Canadians who run into difficulty while abroad receive Canadian consular services. An ever increasingly important component of Canadian representation abroad is to help Canadian businesses promote and sell their goods and services in foreign markets and attract foreign investment into Canada. Missions abroad also work toward the economic, technical, educational and social advancement of developing countries. Finally, for Canadians abroad these missions can be an oasis of familiar territory in unfamiliar places, where you can simply relax and read a week-old copy of *The Globe and Mail*.

Canadian Diplomatic Terminology

All Canadians who work and live abroad should be familiar with the terminology used to describe Canadian representations abroad—an important aspect of your international IQ.

- *Mission* is the generic term for a Canadian government office abroad. A mission may be a large operation with as many as 100 Canadians and other locally engaged staff, or a 1-person satellite office.

- A mission in a foreign capital is called an *embassy*, unless the other country is a member of the Commonwealth in which case it is called a *high commission*.

- Where there is an office in a city other than the capital of a country, for example New York in the United States or Osaka in Japan, it is called a *consulate*. If it is relatively large, delivers several programs or has satellite offices, it is called a *consulate general*.

- A *liaison office* functions for a special purpose, such as coordination of Canadian military operations.

- A Canadian government *trade* (or *aid*) *office* has a single assigned function and is usually a satellite of a larger mission.

- A *permanent mission* is the Canadian representation at the UNITED NATIONS or one of its agencies, or other multilateral bodies.

FAC AND ITCAN STAFF

Together FAC and ITCAN have more than 8,500 employees working in Canada and throughout the world. More than half of these are Canadian and locally engaged staff that provide administrative assistance and are a source of invaluable institutional knowledge to rotational staff. Support staff positions are advertised on the individual Web sites of Canadian missions throughout the world and on the PSC Web site.

Officers in the Canadian Foreign Service commit to work on a rotation basis in Ottawa and at Canadian missions abroad. Spending half of your career abroad sounds great at first, but frequently moving between cultures and continents is emotionally and socially very difficult. Indeed, you must be adaptable and willing to deal with the challenges and difficulties that come with having a constantly changing working and living environment. On the flip side, many foreign service officers and their families greatly enjoy change and the experience of new cultures. They revel in all that this exciting and interesting lifestyle has to offer.

Rotational staff belong to one of the following occupational groups: executive (EX), foreign service (FS), administrative services (AS), administrative support (CR and ST-SCY), computer systems administration (CS) and electronics (EL) groups. Foreign service (FS) is by far the largest rotational occupational group.

FS officers with FAC promote Canada's interests bilaterally and in multilateral forums, assess the political climate of countries, meet with international counterparts, participate in the fair running of elections and project Canadian values abroad. They must be very adaptable and possess excellent analytical and communication skills.

ITCAN Trade Commissioners promote Canada's economic interests in the global marketplace by encouraging foreign investment into Canada and by assisting the Canadian business community to penetrate and succeed in foreign markets. As the contact point for Canadian businesses abroad, trade commissioners must be outgoing, service oriented and capable of networking in a diversity of cultures and business climates.

FS immigration officers are recruited through the same process as other FS, but work for CITIZENSHIP AND IMMIGRATION CANADA (CIC), a separate federal department. Roughly 70 per cent of CIC's immigration officers are assigned to visa offices overseas and have the difficult task of selecting candidates to become permanent residents of Canada and making decisions on the visa applications of visitors, students and temporary workers. Immigration officers must possess excellent judgment and be able to delicately balance humanitarian impulses with security concerns. (For more information on CIC, see the Profiles section at the end of this chapter.)

Management and consular affairs officers (MCO) at Canadian diplomatic missions overseas manage FAC and ITCAN's business lines—those being assistance to Canadians abroad, passport services, corporate services and services to other government departments.

Other rotational staff such as CS/EL, AS and CRs provide the necessary support to ensure the smooth operation of programs abroad.

FAC and ITCAN also employ a large number of non-rotational staff from different occupational groups. These employees are recruited through the PSC. The key difference between non-rotational and rotational staff is the former are not recruited from the viewpoint of their availability to work abroad. However, a non-rotational employee may be given an opportunity to work abroad once or twice during his or her career.

Rotational Life

Rotational personnel are posted abroad for period of two to four years. After each posting they either return to Ottawa or are assigned to another foreign post. Frequently moving into and out of different cultural milieus is very demanding (but also addictively enticing for many). Rotational staff and their families must be versatile, adaptable and prepared to face new challenges constantly.

As a new recruit, you may face stiff competition from your peers over popular assignments. You may want to be posted to Washington or London, where you will find many top diplomats, lots of high-level political activity, a firmly entrenched hierarchy and greater opportunities for spousal employment. Or, like most new recruits, you may prefer the option of working in a smaller mission where you will take on greater responsibilities and be involved in a wider variety of activities than you would at a larger, more specialized post.

While in Ottawa, FS officers take up responsibilities as desk officers for particular countries or groups of countries, or in one of the functional branches dealing with trade, economic policy, cultural liaison, management or corporate services. MCOs manage resources for these branches, conduct mission audits and provide domestic support for overseas emergency situations. FS immigration officers work at CIC in various branches. They may provide operational support to their colleagues in offices overseas, monitor aspects of the CIC's program overseas, analyze or develop strategies for dealing with financial or administrative issues or develop CIC programs and policies.

Salary and benefits are comparable to those of other Canadian government employees. However, once assigned to a post you will also receive a premium for serving abroad, a cost of living or hardship allowance where applicable and payment of some leave travel costs.

Life overseas does have its drawbacks. A life travelling throughout the world might seem glamorous, but it can be very difficult on families that must continually adjust to new locations and unfamiliar cultures. Spouses often postpone career opportunities, accept limited local employment or do not work at all, while children must frequently say goodbye to friends and find their way in new schools. FAC and ITCAN make efforts to ease the strain on families by providing counsellors and subsidizing education costs for children who generally attend international schools. Single people face other challenges, such as loneliness and a perceived lack of a social support network. Yet, despite these difficulties, many people consider that working in the foreign service is extremely rewarding, interesting and exciting.

An excellent source of information on life in the foreign service is the Professional Association of Foreign Service Officers (PAFSO). In their publication,

Bout de Papier, members recount overseas experiences, discuss issues of importance to FS, and provide invaluable insights into FS officers' work and lifestyles. (For information on this publication, see the Foreign Affairs Canada Resources at the end of this profile.)

FAC AND ITCAN RECRUITMENT

For the time being, FAC and ITCAN will continue to recruit for the foreign service through the same four-part process that includes the following steps: application, examination, screening phase and selection phase.

The Application Process

Every fall, over 6,000 applicants compete for about 75 to 100 positions as FS officers and MCOs through the PSC's Post-secondary Recruitment Campaign. Applicants are required to be Canadian citizens and meet the educational requirements stated in the recruitment campaign. The MCO competition is a separate career choice usually open to business administration and management graduates. Otherwise the screening process is identical.

You apply to participate in the campaign by completing your PSRS on-line profile as explained in the PSC section. You will also have to pre-register to write the required tests, which are only written once a year, on the third Saturday in the month of October, so don't miss the registration deadline! You can also arrange to write the test overseas by contacting the PSC.

The Foreign Service Exam

If you are a Canadian interested in a career in international affairs you have probably heard about the Foreign Service Exam. Since 1928, it has been the sole route to obtaining an entry-level position with the foreign service. The present test used by FAC and ITCAN, however, bears little resemblance to the traditional Foreign Service Exam that tested an individual's knowledge of world affairs. Today FAC and ITCAN use a situational judgment test along with two other standardized tests administered by the PSC. These tests are held in succession on the same date, and take between fifty-five minutes and two and a half hours each to write. The exams are written on university campuses and government offices throughout Canada, or at Canadian diplomatic missions abroad. (For a personal perspective on completing the Foreign Service Exam, see "Writing the Foreign Service Exam", by E. Thomas, in Appendix 37a on the CD-ROM.)

These tests serve to eliminate the bottom 80 percentile from consideration for FS positions; great news if you excel at standardized tests, but not the most encouraging news if they are not your forte.

The first exam is the Graduate Recruitment Test (GRT) that measures your ability to use reasoning to solve problems. It contains four question types: similarities, arithmetic problems, figure analogies and number series. The GRT consists of 55 multiple-choice questions that you have 90 minutes to complete.

The second exam is the Written Communication Proficiency Test that assesses your ability to communicate in writing. You will be asked to read 13 short passages and answer questions such as identifying errors in grammar, determining the best word to insert in a blank, choosing the best title for a passage, ordering sentences or choosing the best summary of a text. You have 1 hour and 40 minutes to read all of the texts and answer 50 questions.

The third and final exam is the Situational Judgement Test. The test consists of a series of scenarios, followed by a series of actions that you could take in that situation. You are asked to select what you think are the most and least effective actions. There are 73 actions to be rated over 70 minutes. When answering these questions you should keep in mind that you are writing a test that is designed to test your judgment as a bureaucrat, not an individual!

To get past this stage of the campaign, you will have to place in the top 15 to 20 per cent. The PSC informs candidates of their test results on its Web site and forwards the names and applications of top performers to FAC, ITCAN and CIC.

The Selection Phase

Applications received from the PSC are reviewed and a few hundred candidates are invited to participate in interviews and a group simulation exercise. The interviews are generally held in February. They take place across Canada and in selected Canadian missions abroad. Candidates assume responsibility for any travel or personal costs they incur as a result of attending the interview.

On the morning of the specified day, candidates have a 45-minute personal interview with a 4-person interview team. The interviewers will ask a range of questions to assess how you handle yourself in different situations and roles. Some of the characteristics they are looking for are the ability to analyze and evaluate situations, oral communication skill, and the ability to plan, organize and control projects. The nature of the work also dictates that successful candidates have strong interpersonal skills, display leadership and teamwork ability, exercise good judgment, have personal integrity and are creative, flexible and adaptable.

In the afternoon candidates participate in a group simulation exercise administered by the interviewers. Each candidate is given a topic and asked to present the proposal to the group, which must then arrive at a consensus on the merits of the different project proposals. The purpose of the exercise is to strike a balance between promoting a project and facilitating a group decision. Candidates are thereby expected to demonstrate those abilities and characteristics required of a foreign service officer representing Canada abroad, while being closely observed by members of the interview team.

The Human Resources Branch evaluates all information from the application, examination, interview and references, and retains approximately one-quarter of those interviewed as final candidates. The candidate's score from the interview report is used in establishing the list of final candidates. Other aspects of a candidate's background, such as a demonstrated interest and experience in foreign cultures or "fluency" in a particular discipline, may emerge in the interview process.

If you are a final candidate and decide to accept the stream for which you have been chosen, you will be asked to provide detailed personal background information to finalize your security clearance. If you pass this last hurdle, you become a successful FS officer ready to join FAC, ITCAN or CIC.

THE FOREIGN SERVICE DEVELOPMENT PROGRAM

If you are one of the few to make it through the selection process and are headed for the FS or MCO streams, you'll probably begin your career in language training. You'll have 12 months to become proficient in both official languages, during which time you will be paid 80 per cent of your FS starting salary.

If, at the end of the Foreign Service Development Program, you have successfully met all performance measures you will graduate from the program to the next level.

THE MCO PROGRAM

As a Management and Consular Affairs Officers (MCO) recruit you will undertake training similar to, but separate from, FS officers. First international assignments last between two to four years, after which MCOs may be cross-posted or return to Ottawa. The MCO probation period is only one year.

From this point on, promotions for FS and MCOs are achieved through competition or promotion exercises and are based on relative merit. You should also be aware that the federal government's employment equity program dictates that efforts be made to encourage the promotion of people with disabilities, members of visible minority groups, Aboriginal peoples and women.

CONTRACT EMPLOYMENT WITH FAC AND ITCAN

Various divisions within FAC and ITCAN hire short-term employees or contractors to work on special projects or to fill staff positions on a temporary basis. You will have to keep your eyes open to find these opportunities. Many are posted on the PSC's Web site, while others appear on HRDS's job bank or in Ottawa area newspapers. Some divisions rely on employment agencies to do their recruitment, while other positions are only "advertised" by word of mouth.

An officer with FAC points out that she often encounters people who want to do contract work with FAC, but fail to realize that it is a large department that covers a multitude of very different regional and policy areas. She recommends that you search FAC and ITCAN's Web sites and find sections or policy issues that interest you and then contact people in that section. They will be able to offer you some suggestions about their work and let you know if they anticipate having future hiring or research needs. Another contract employee gives this advice:

"If you are a graduate student, plan to do some research at FAC or ITCAN. This is an excellent way to make contacts. While you might not speak directly to those with the authority to hire, others you do meet may be helpful."

STUDENT OPPORTUNITIES

Every year, FAC and ITCAN hire summer students through the Federal Student Work Experience Program (FSWEP). Getting a summer job through FSWEP is akin to winning the lottery and something you can't plan for. A more secure avenue for a student to gain invaluable professional experience is to participate in one of the federal government's co-operative programs, which are open to students enrolled in cooperative programs at universities or colleges. Every year, FAC and ITCAN take on about 60 to 75 students through this program. Most are second- or third-year political science or economics students who work on projects similar to those of an entry-level FS officer.

The departments also offer a number of enticing fellowship opportunities for students. The Norman Robertson Fellowship is awarded to a scholar in an advanced stage of doctoral research in economics, political economy or political science to work with the Trade and Economic Analysis Division. The Cadieux-Léger Fellowship is a foreign policy research position in the Policy Planning Division awarded to a candidate who has completed his or her doctorate or master's degree on a topic of relevance to Canada's foreign policy. Every year, FAC and ITCAN also fund five to seven Human Security Fellowships that are administered by the CANADIAN CONSORTIUM ON HUMAN SECURITY. (For more information on this group, see Chapter 38, NGOs in Canada. For more information on the Human Security Fellowships, see Chapter 14, Awards & Grants.)

Some countries and international organizations offer Canadian scholars additional opportunities that would be of interest to students interested in studying abroad. (For more information visit the "Education" section found in the "Culture Education and Youth" page on the FAC Web site.)

FAC AND ITCAN INTERNSHIPS

If you are interested in an international career, then you simply cannot pass up the opportunity to participate in Young Professionals International (YPI). The Canadian government should be lauded for putting in place this excellent initiative that provides young Canadian graduates who are having trouble finding employment in the international field with their first overseas paid work assignment. The field experience you'll gain is a invaluable asset that will substantially bolster your future career prospects. Some placements also offer the prospect of being hired back by an organization.

YPI is delivered in partnership with the private sector, intergovernmental and non-governmental organizations and are broadly grouped under the three pillars of Canada's foreign policy: prosperity, security and identity. Projects in the prosperity category often take place with private sector firms and focus on promoting the expansion of international trade, commerce and investment. Those in the security category address issues such as the promotion of international peace and security, human security, war-affected children, human rights and democratic development. Projects in the identity category promote Canadian culture and values. (For more information about the program, visit the "Youth" section of FAC's Web site or see the section "Canadian International Government Internships" in Chapter 17, Internships Abroad.) Don't miss this excellent career enhancing opportunity. It is almost a must for launching your international career!

A LAST WORD ON FAC AND ITCAN

FOREIGN AFFAIRS CANADA (FAC) and INTERNATIONAL TRADE CANADA (ITCAN) offer exciting and challenging opportunities for experienced professionals, as well as students wanting to build career experience. Rotational staff can expect a lifetime of travel, with postings in such diverse places as Kabul and Osaka. For students, a summer or semester working at the Lester B. Pearson Building will provide you with valuable experience within the federal government, allow you to establish important contacts and help increase your international IQ.

APPENDIX ON THE CD-ROM

37a. "Writing the Foreign Service Exam," by E. Thomas

RESOURCES

FOREIGN AFFAIRS CANADA

This list includes resources for FOREIGN AFFAIRS CANADA (FAC) and INTERNATIONAL TRADE CANADA (ITCAN).

Bout de papier 📖
Quarterly ➤ Professional Association of Foreign Service Officers, Suite 412, 47 Clarence Street, Ottawa, ON K1N 9K1, Canada, www.pafso.com, $16 CDN for 1 year or $30 CDN for 2 years; Cheque or Money Order; 613-241-1391, fax 613-241-5911; *Fr* ◆ A must-read for all those interested in Canadian diplomacy and foreign service. Each issue features guest columnists, tales and photos from far and wide, special interviews, book reviews, and media coverage of Canadian diplomacy. Delves into major policy issues and provides first-hand accounts of life in diplomatic postings abroad. [ID:2082]

Canada Corps 👥
www.CanadaCorps.gc.ca; *Fr* ◆ At the time of printing, the Canadian government made a commitment to create Canada Corps under Foreign Affairs Canada (FAC). Canada Corps will enhance linkages among existing Canadian efforts and explore new partnerships with other levels of government and the private sector. The initiative will harness the energy and experience of Canadian experts, volunteers and young professionals to deliver international assistance in the areas of governance and institution building. Keep an eye on their Web site for exciting developments about this new initiative. [ID:2839]

Canada World View 📖
Quarterly ➤ Enquiries Service, Foreign Affairs Canada (FAC), 125 Sussex Drive, Ottawa, ON K1A 0G2, Canada, www.fac-aec.gc.ca, Free; 800-267-8376, fax 613-996-9709; *Fr* ◆ Provides an overview of Canada's perspective on foreign policy issues and highlights the Government of Canada's international initiatives and contributions. A good primer. [ID:2485]

CanadExport 📖
Biweekly ➤ Enquiries Service, Foreign Affairs Canada (FAC), 125 Sussex Drive, Ottawa, ON K1A 0G2, Canada, www.fac-aec.gc.ca, Free; 800-267-8376, fax 613-996-9709; *Fr* ◆ Foreign Affairs' primary publication for keeping the Canadian business community and exporters informed about key trade matters. A biweekly newsletter, it provides timely information on business opportunities, trade fairs and other related matters. [ID:2119]

Canadian Foreign Service Institute (CFSI) 👥
Canadian Foreign Service Institute (CFSI), Lester B. Pearson Bldg. A4-235, 125 Sussex Drive, Ottawa, ON K1A 0G2, Canada, www.dfait-maeci.gc.ca/cfsi-icse, 613-944-0011, fax 613-996-4381; *Fr* ◆ The Canadian Foreign Service Institute (CFSI) is the part of Foreign Affairs Canada (FAC) that is responsible for providing the learning tools designed to foster more effective international relations. The CFSI provides training to FAC employees, as well as offering a series of courses to other Canadians that allow them to acquire practical knowledge and skills for living and working on assignments abroad. If you are a professional or youth planning to go overseas, consult the course calendar to see which courses you might benefit from attending. [ID:2699]

Canadian Representatives Abroad 💻

Foreign Affairs Canada (FAC), www.dfait-maeci.gc.ca/world/embassies/cra-en.asp, Free on-line; *Fr* ◆ This is a bilingual directory of Government of Canada diplomatic and consular missions overseas, as well as a resource for finding Canada-based staff at those missions. You can search the directory, choose a region on the map below or access a list by city, country or surname. Finally, access a list of Canadian Missions to international organizations. This is an excellent tool to use if you want to learn about the size of a mission abroad. For embassies, note that many can be found just by entering the name of a city or country within www.***.gc.ca (e.g., www.losangeles.gc.ca, www.london.gc.ca, and www.india.gc.ca). Good luck in your search! [ID:2027]

The Canadian Trade Commissioner Service ⛪

International Trade Canada (ITCAN), www.infoexport.gc.ca; *Fr* ◆ On this Government of Canada Web site, you can find trade commissioner offices in Canada and abroad. Navigate by country or industry sector to the region you're interested in and find the latest trade information on market prospects, key local contacts, local company information, visitor information and market intelligence. The best feature of the Web site is the virtual trade commissioner. Register on-line at no cost and receive a personalized Web page containing market information and business leads that match your international business interests. [ID:2249]

Consular Affairs: Information and Assistance for Canadians Abroad ⛪

www.voyage.gc.ca, fax (800) 575-2500; *Fr* ◆ The Canadian government produces this great Web site, featuring essential travel, including country and regional reports, travel updates, maps, pre-departure information, and emergency contacts. Check out the weekly travel bulletin on safety "hot spots" for the most current information. [ID:2756]

Diplomat & International Canada 📖

Bimonthly, Jennifer Campbell, 48 pages ➤ Ganlin Media Inc.Teachers' Overseas Recruiting Fair, P.O. Box 1173, Stn. B, Ottawa, ON K1P 5R2, Canada, www.diplomatcanada.com, $4.95 CDN per issue; Cheque or Money Order; 613-789-6890, fax 613-789-9313 ◆ This magazine is Canada's only news journal for the diplomatic and international community and boasts a circulation of 11,000. [ID:2069]

Export Services for Small- and Medium-Sized Enterprises 📖

2001 ➤ Enquiries Service, Foreign Affairs Canada (FAC), 125 Sussex Drive, Ottawa, ON K1A 0G2, Canada, www.fac-aec.gc.ca, 800-267-8376, fax 613-996-9709; *Fr* ◆ This pamphlet explains the activities of the export services for the Small and Medium-Sized Enterprises Division (TSME) of the Canadian Trade Commissioner Service. [ID:2484]

Exporting from Canada: A Practical Guide to Finding
and Developing Export Markets for Your Product or Service 📖

2002, Gerhard Kautz, 192 pages ➤ Self-Counsel Press, 1481 Charlotte Road, North Vancouver, BC V7J 1H1, Canada, www.self-counsel.com, $21.95 CDN; VISA, MC; 800-663-3007, fax 604-986-3947, sales@self-counsel.com ◆ This book provides Canadian exporters and would-be exporters with easy-to-follow information and advice on the strategies and issues involved in doing business outside the country. Includes reference guides, Internet sites, business contacts and practical pointers on visiting foreign countries. [ID:2125]

Foreign Affairs Canada (FAC) ⛪

www.fac-aec.gc.ca; *Fr* ◆ FAC's Web site provides information on international trade and the countries and regions that make up the international system within which Canada exists. Authoritative fact sheets, population data and highlights of special issues complement the usual political and economic information available. A good source of trustworthy information. [ID:2267]

Foreign Representatives in Canada 💻

Foreign Affairs Canada (FAC), www.dfait-maeci.gc.ca/protocol, Free on-line; *Fr* ◆ Foreign Affairs Canada's Office of Protocol updates this bilingual monthly publication and complementary search tool every 24 hours. It allows you to find accurate information on foreign missions and international organizations accredited to Canada. It also has a function that allows members of the diplomatic community, governmental agencies, businesses and Canadians alike to access the names and titles of foreign representatives with diplomatic, consular or official status in Canada. Many sources can be easily downloaded and printed, including a PDF version of the publication: "Diplomatic, Consular and Other Representatives in Canada." From the Diplomatic Gateway to Canada index, click on "Foreign Representatives in Canada." Easy-to-use and recommended. [ID:2026]

Foreign Service 📖
1993, John Kneale, 240 pages ➤ Captus Press Inc., Units 14 & 15, 1600 Steeles Ave. W., Concord, ON L4K 4M2, Canada, www.captus.com, $14.95 CDN; VISA; 416-736-5537, fax 416-736-5793 ◆ A candid, insightful and personal account of a career as a Foreign Service Officer in Algeria, Iran, Ecuador, Mexico and New York. This penetrating narrative brings exotic cultures to life and exposes the difficulties of representing Canada's interests abroad when faced with unfamiliar foreign politics and, frequently, domestic political indifference. Kneale's wry humour and eye for the incongruous makes this thoughtful critique of Canada's management of its foreign missions a fascinating read. [ID:2096]

ITCan Directory 👬
www.itcan-cican.gc.ca/menu-en.asp, Free on-line; 𝐹𝑟 ◆ This handy directory allows you to find any of member of International Trade Canada (ITCan's) staff quickly and easily. From the ITCan home page, click on "What We Do" and then navigate to "Directory of Departmental Employees." Search employees by name and position. You can also search the directory by building, organization and trade mission abroad. [ID:2334]

Professional Association of Foreign Service Officers (PAFSO) 👬
Professional Association of Foreign Service Officers, Suite 412, 47 Clarence Street, Ottawa, ON K1N 9K1, Canada, www.pafso.com, Cheque or Money Order; 613-241-1391, fax 613-241-5911 ◆ The Professional Association of Foreign Service Officers (PAFSO) is both the bargaining agent and the professional association for Canadian foreign service officers. Visit its Web site to see the latest news about the working conditions of foreign service officers, including information about expected employment trends. [ID:2700]

A Rich Broth: Memoirs of a Canadian Diplomat 📖
1993, David Chalmer Reese, 231 pages ➤ McGill-Queen's University Press, 3430 McTavish Street, Montreal, QC H3A 1X9, Canada, www.mqup.mcgill.ca, $19.95 CDN; VISA, MC; 514-398-3750, fax 514-398-4333 ◆ A witty autobiography containing a mix of insight and humour based on a 38-year career in the Canadian foreign service. [ID:2095]

Strategis 💻
http://strategis.ic.gc.ca, Free on-line; 𝐹𝑟 ◆ Strategis is Canada's business and consumer Web site, through which Industry Canada innovatively disseminates business information intended to improve conditions for investment and promote economic growth among Canada's businesses. The site is a comprehensive collection of company directories, business information by sector, economic analysis and statistics, as well as information on financing, licences and consumer information. Entrepreneurs: bookmark this site!

Strategis also features a number of informative guides on subjects like starting a business, financing, exporting, e-commerce and researching markets. Of particular interest to international entrepreneurs is the Guide to Exporting, which is accessible by clicking "Exporting" from the menu of Strategis Guides on the home page.

Here you'll find eight excellent resources including "Trade Data Online," through which you can access information and statistics on new markets and existing competition for your products; "Trade Team Canada Sectors," which provides information about services and activities for the trade promotion of Canada's key industries; "International Trade Centres," regional bodies that provide export counselling services and market entry support; "Trade Shows," highlighting opportunities to showcase products abroad; "Export Your Services," which is a fabulous tool that walks you through the stages of exporting your product; "Services 2000," which contains information on the national and international trade agreements; and "Building Abroad," which is especially for the construction industry abroad. There's also a link to "ExportSource," which is included as a separate resource write-up. [ID:2317]

Working Abroad: Unravelling the Maze 📖
2003, 32 pages ➤ Enquiries Service, Foreign Affairs Canada (FAC), 125 Sussex Drive, Ottawa, ON K1A 0G2, Canada, www.fac-aec.gc.ca, 800-267-8376, fax 613-996-9709; 𝐹𝑟 ◆ Preparation and careful planning go a long way to ensuring a safe and successful international work experience. The goal of "Working Abroad: Unravelling the Maze" is to provide the overseas job hunter with practical information to maximize the chances of a successful venture and advice on what to do if things don't work out as planned. [ID:2490]

WWW Virtual Library: International Affairs Resources 🖥
www.etown.edu/vl ◆ This excellent Web site is a section of the WWW Virtual Library system and presents over 2,600 annotated links to a wide range of international affairs, international development, international studies and international relations Web sites. Browse for resources organized by media sources, organizations, regions and countries, and topics. An excellent source of information on international affairs. Also, if your career interest is in international affairs or international development, you can canvass organizations using this list. A great resource. [ID:2761]

Canadian International Development Agency (CIDA)

5th Floor, Place du Centre, 200 Promenade du Portage, Hull, Québec K1A 0G4
(800) 230-6349, (819) 997-5006; Fax: (819) 953-6088 www.acdi-cida.gc.ca, info@acdi-cida.gc.ca [ID:7206]

In the 1960s, Prime Minister Lester B. Pearson announced that developed states should contribute at least 0.7 per cent of their annual GDP to international development efforts. Since then, international development has been close to the hearts of many Canadians; none closer, than the committed staff of the Cᴀɴᴀᴅɪᴀɴ Iɴᴛᴇʀɴᴀᴛɪᴏɴᴀʟ Dᴇᴠᴇʟᴏᴘᴍᴇɴᴛ Aɢᴇɴᴄʏ (CIDA), the federal agency that is responsible for distributing almost 80 per cent of Canada's development assistance. The remainder is dispersed by Fᴏʀᴇɪɢɴ Aꜰꜰᴀɪʀꜱ Cᴀɴᴀᴅᴀ (FAC), the Dᴇᴘᴀʀᴛᴍᴇɴᴛ ᴏꜰ Fɪɴᴀɴᴄᴇ, the Iɴᴛᴇʀɴᴀᴛɪᴏɴᴀʟ Dᴇᴠᴇʟᴏᴘᴍᴇɴᴛ Rᴇꜱᴇᴀʀᴄʜ Cᴇɴᴛʀᴇ (IDRC) and the Iɴᴛᴇʀɴᴀᴛɪᴏɴᴀʟ Cᴇɴᴛʀᴇ ꜰᴏʀ Hᴜᴍᴀɴ Rɪɢʜᴛꜱ ᴀɴᴅ Dᴇᴍᴏᴄʀᴀᴛɪᴄ Dᴇᴠᴇʟᴏᴘᴍᴇɴᴛ, otherwise known as Rɪɢʜᴛꜱ ᴀɴᴅ Dᴇᴍᴏᴄʀᴀᴄʏ.

Throughout the 1990s the work of CIDA was hampered by significant cuts to the International Assistance Envelope (IAE), which contains the budgetary allocations by the federal government to international assistance. In the first years of this century, it fell to an embarrassing low of 0.22 per cent of GDP, far below the standard that Canadians expect. In the last budget of the Chrétien era, the federal government announced an immediate 8 per cent increase in the IAE and committed to doubling it by 2010. Unfortunately, if the 2004 budget is any indication, the Liberal government's commitment to double its contributions to IAE will not be kept.

Even if this commitment is not met, international development should continue to receive increases in funding, a necessity given that governments are beginning to recognize that the world is interconnected and the only way to protect citizens from threats like terrorism or communicable diseases is to ensure that people throughout the world are provided with the means to live dignified, prosperous lives.

The recognition that the world's inequalities must be addressed should increase the number of jobs open to Canadians working in international development. You'll also be buoyed by the news that almost 40 per cent of CIDA's workforce is eligible for retirement within the next 5 years. In short, a combination of demographics and the "dark side" of globalization dictates that CIDA should be doing a lot of hiring over the next decade.

If you want to work in international development you should also keep in mind that CIDA is far from the only organization that offers careers in international development. Hundreds of Canadian NGOs are active in the field fighting AIDS; international organizations are developing strategies to reduce poverty in communities around the world; and US private consulting firms are playing an ever increasingly large role in their country's international development efforts. (For a broad overview of international development, see Chapter 30, Careers in International Development.)

WHAT DOES CIDA DO?

CIDA oversees the delivery of Canada's ODA program in developing countries with a view toward reducing poverty and contributing to a more secure, equitable and prosperous world. To understand fully CIDA's role in international development, it is helpful to think of a hierarchy at the top of which CIDA sits.

Being at the top of the hierarchy means that CIDA is responsible for setting Canada's international development priorities and agenda. Once the priorities have been set, CIDA collaborates with partners to determine the type of projects that can best meet the identified international development priority areas. Finally, CIDA filters its financial resources down the hierarchy to the organizations that will deliver most of Canada's aid through international development projects.

CIDA recently identified the importance of social development and is accordingly increasing its funding in four priority areas: health and nutrition, HIV/AIDS, basic education and child protection, with gender equality as an integral part of all of these priority areas. It also identified nine priority countries that will receive significant new aid resources.

CIDA, however, engages in very little hands-on development work. It instead provides the guidance and the resources to organizations that fall in the middle of Canada's international development hierarchy. The organizations that fall into this unofficial middle hierarchy manage and implement CIDA-sponsored projects that include an assortment of Canadian individuals, NGOs, private companies and even a few international organizations. These entities apply for CIDA funding and bid on contracts to deliver Canada's aid around the world.

Here it is important to appreciate fully that international development is a very large industry that is becoming increasingly professionalized. Your typical international development worker is now highly educated and brings an extensive array of skills and experience to the field. More than a few young starry-eyed Canadians are surprised to learn the degree to which international development is a business that is designed to benefit both people around the world and those at home.

Every year, hundreds of NGOs receive grants from CIDA, and over 2,000 businesses and more than 50 universities and colleges receive aid-related contracts. CIDA itself highlights that 70 cents of every ODA dollar find their way back into the Canadian economy, and that the jobs of more than 33,000 Canadians are sustained through its programs.

At the bottom of the international development hierarchy are local partners, active at the grassroots level. This includes local organizations, communities, governments or private sector firms. CIDA, or the Canadian organizations it funds, work closely with these local organizations and communities to ensure that Canada's development aid is delivered effectively and to the most deserving communities.

You should also be aware that since 1995, CIDA has been responsible for administering most of Canada's Official Assistance (OA) program in countries in transition in Central and Eastern Europe, where the focus is on supporting democratic development and promoting economic liberalization. The economies of many of these countries are too advanced to receive ODA, although a few do qualify for development assistance. If your interest is in working in this branch of CIDA, you should focus on developing skills related to international economics rather than those typically associated with international development.

WHAT IS IT LIKE TO WORK AT CIDA?

Individuals are interested in working at CIDA for a variety of reasons. Many are motivated by a personal commitment to international development. Others view a stint at CIDA as a stepping stone in a career with the public service. Still others value the satisfaction and prestige associated with managing the "big money" that tends to go with CIDA programming work. What is clear is that CIDA, owing to the diversity of its programs and the agencies and institutions with which it interacts, offers its employees an extremely wide and varied field of opportunity. Furthermore, CIDA offers the excitement of international work and travel without the personal and family upheaval that accompanies long-term overseas postings.

It is important to understand that CIDA's 1,700 employees are first and foremost public servants who oversee Canada's delivery of ODA. Situated at the top of the hierarchy, CIDA's staffers are responsible for managing and directing Canada's delivery of aid. They review the grants submitted by NGOs, travel to developing countries to consult with local partners, manage projects and write reports assessing the overall progress of development issues. The work is quite technical in nature and insiders advise that your individual success within CIDA often depends on your acceptance of the bureaucratic process and your ability to make the system work for you.

A small number of CIDA's staff—roughly 100 individuals—are posted overseas. Usually the postings are for two or three years with an option for an additional year. Based in Canadian missions and program support units, they administer programs, consult with partner organizations and identify situations where CIDA could contribute to the sustainable development efforts of the over 100 countries it operates in. These individuals are CIDA's eyes and ears on the ground and they play the important role of ensuring that there is no disconnect between CIDA's staff in Ottawa and what is happening in the field. Employees assigned overseas normally have five years' experience with CIDA in program planning and project management, and possess a broad knowledge of bilateral, multilateral and partnership policies and procedures. There are few, if any, entry-level overseas positions.

TERM OR PERMANENT WORK WITH CIDA

CIDA is quite unique as a government agency because it not only has permanent and term staff, but also hires cooperants and works closely with consultants and a variety of Canadian organizations. The following sections review the various paths to finding work at CIDA.

Like other federal institutions, CIDA's core staff are either permanent or term staff that are recruited through the PUBLIC SERVICE COMMISSION (PSC). Most of CIDA's positions are filled through internal PSC competitions, although occasionally you will find jobs open to the public advertised on the PSC Web site. (For information on how to apply to these jobs, consult the PSC section found at the start of this chapter.)

CIDA has a long-standing policy of hiring staff with international development experience. This ensures that CIDA staffers are familiar with the types of challenges that development workers face in the field and allows them to anticipate problems and manage projects effectively. If your long-term goal is to work with CIDA, you should attempt to acquire as much international development experience as possible.

When filling vacancies, CIDA also looks for individuals with relevant educational backgrounds, language skills, leadership abilities and cross-cultural sensitivity. CIDA has also adopted results-based management (RBM) as its central tool in its management philosophy and practice. Being trained in RBM techniques is not only an advantage to potential applicants, but, some would say, an increasing necessity for individuals who want to work with CIDA.

Post-Secondary Recruitment

In the mid-1990s CIDA realized that it would have to be more aggressive in its recruitment efforts and instituted a post-secondary recruitment program similar to that used by the former DFAIT.

CIDA now recruits about 20 development officers (DOs) a year through its Post-Secondary Recruitment Campaign. Applicants must possess at least a master's degree in a related field and most successful applicants have some overseas international development experience.

Successful applicants enter the five-year-long Career Management Program for new DOs. The CMP combines structured work environments and classroom training in order to provide new recruits with the necessary skills and experience to become effective DOs in CIDA's program and policy branches. Participants are expected to become proficient in a wide variety of functions in a minimum of one geographic program branch (the Americas, Asia, Africa and the Middle East, and Central and Eastern Europe), as well as one of the non-geographic branches (policy, multilateral programs, performance review, communications, legal services and Canadian partnership). An effort is made to give each participant a short assignment overseas or sometimes with CIDA's partner organizations.

Cooperants

CIDA currently has about 80 cooperants working overseas. Cooperants are individuals with extensive professional experience who are hired on a contract basis to work on specific CIDA projects. The contracts are usually for two-year periods and the cooperant is considered to be a self-employed worker. Cooperants receive a fee based on the amount they would be paid for similar work in Canada. CIDA also pays certain benefits, such as an overseas allowance, pension contributions, housing and school benefits.

If you are interested in becoming a cooperant you will first have to register your personal details in a database that is maintained and managed by the CORPORATE CONTRACTING OPERATIONS AND TECHNICAL ASSISTANCE SECTION. To register, you must have at least three years of relevant experience in your professional area of expertise. Currently, the main sectors in which professional and technical expertise are required are good governance, education, health, agriculture, forestry, financial management, project management, international development and the environment.

If you meet the above requirements, you can register simply by sending in your resume. CIDA prefers that you send in a chronological resume, as opposed to a functional resume. You will be contacted annually to see if you want to continue to be considered for cooperant positions. Keep in mind that cooperants are professionals with significant experience.

Contracting with CIDA

If you are going to work in the field of international development, it helps if you are familiar with the contracting opportunities offered by CIDA. Contracts for the delivery of both goods and services are awarded to Canadian individuals, not-for-profit organizations and companies that have established their expertise and ability to complete projects.

Most of CIDA's projects originate from the three bilateral branches (Africa and the Middle East, Asia, and the Americas). These branches are responsible for planning and delivering Canada's bilateral assistance, which is typically delivered by Canadian individuals or organizations. CIDA also has an Unsolicited Proposal Mechanism that allows organizations to submit original, unsolicited proposals related to development issues.

If you're just starting, out or are still in university, you should take the time to become familiar with the types of contracts that CIDA offers. CIDA's "Projects at the Planning Stage" section of their Web site is a great resource that allows you to take a look at the projects that CIDA is planning to implement around the world. Looking at these contracts will help you understand the types of skills, training and experience you'll have to hone if you want to work in international development. *CIDA's Contracts and Agreements* is a publication that serves as an excellent starting point for an international job search. (For more information on this, see the CIDA Resource section following this profile.) Review the lists of individuals and firms that have CIDA contracts and approach them in your job search.

Consulting with CIDA

CIDA often makes use of consultants who provide services across a spectrum of technical, professional, scientific and managerial fields. The length of the consulting assignments can vary greatly, anywhere from three weeks to one year, and can be based in Canada or overseas. The main consulting areas include human resource development, education and training, environment, health and nutrition, institutional development, agriculture, energy and population. The types of projects that a consultant might work on include preparing country program reviews; developing corporate, strategic and operational planning; conducting project management; overseeing structural adjustment programs and working to improve the delivery of gender programs.

CIDA's mandate includes coordinating Canada's emergency response to humanitarian crises or natural disasters. To fulfill these tasks, CIDA often needs to hire consultants on the quick and will often do so through informal channels. Because of this, it is very important for consultants to network and let relevant managers know of their continued availability. Consultants can also bid on contracts, usually for the delivery of services.

Another source of employment for both junior and senior professionals is CONSULTING AND AUDIT CANADA (CAC). The INTERNATIONAL SERVICES DIRECTORATE (ISD) of CAC provides management consulting and audit services to international development projects funded by CIDA and FAC. In 2003–2004, ISD carried out over 500 service delivery assignments.

ISD maintains a permanent pool of over 1,200 private sector consultants who have passed a screening process. New consultants are added regularly and the list includes junior consultants. Candidates should have a bachelor's degree and preferably a master's or doctorate in any field related to development as well as consulting experience in international development. (For more information, see CONSULTANT AND AUDIT CANADA in the Profiles section of this chapter.)

STUDENT OPPORTUNITIES WITH CIDA

CIDA is very committed to including young Canadians in its international development work. It hires full-time students for summer or part-time work through the PSC's Federal Student Work Experience Program (FSWEP), and also takes on students through the Post-Secondary Co-operative Education and Internship Program. These students make valuable contacts and sometimes receive short-term contracts at headquarters or in the regions. (For more information on these programs, see the PSC section at the start of this chapter.)

CIDA's International Youth Internship Program

If you are serious about working in the field of international development, the best way you can jump-start your career is by participating in CIDA's International Youth Internship Program (IYIP).

Since its inception in 1997, about 3,500 young professionals have gained valuable international experience and exposure through CIDA's IYIP. The IYIP is very similar to the FAC and ITCAN Young Professionals International initiative, with the key difference being that CIDA's partners work in the field of international development. The internships are roughly divided according to the following 10 sectors: civil society, communications, education, environment, finance and marketing, health, industry, natural resources, social services and water/sanitation.

The length of the internships last anywhere from 6 to 12 months, and all include at least a 5-month placement overseas. Applicants must be under 30 and unemployed or underemployed, working in a job that is not directly linked to their academic training.

CIDA now offers roughly 400 internships every year. The list of internships is posted on CIDA's Web site and is very user-friendly. You can search internships by country, by the internship's title, by sector, by status, by Canadian organization or by country/overseas host organization.

When applying for internships, also make sure to visit the Canadian organization's home page for detailed information. If you have student loans, make sure to check how much money you'll actually receive from the organization. CIDA provides $15,000 for each internship with an understanding that the Canadian organization will take no more than 20 per cent for administration costs, but how much you receive varies greatly by organization. Generally larger organizations seem to be a bit better in simply taking off a fair amount that covers their administrative costs, but some NGOs require you to incur costs to participate in the program.

CIDA's International Youth Internship Program is a tremendous opportunity for young Canadians; for this, the Canadian government should be lauded for its support. We cannot overstate the importance of gaining field experience, so make sure you participate in this excellent program.

A LAST WORD ON CIDA

Working in the field of international development is extremely challenging. Often you must work in difficult conditions, put your own safety in jeopardy and deal with issues that are often overwhelming in their depth of despair. At the same time, devoting yourself to improving the lives of people throughout the world can be tremendously rewarding. CIDA allows experienced professionals the opportunity to continue contributing to international development efforts while settling down to build their lives in Canada. CIDA offers young Canadians the chance to participate in internships that can serve as springboards to careers in international development.

RESOURCES

CANADIAN INTERNATIONAL DEVELOPMENT AGENCY

For related resources consult Chapter 30, Careers in International Development and Chapter 38, NGOs in Canada.

Aid As a Peacemaker: Canadian Development Assistance and Third World Conflict 📖
1994, Robert Miller, 224 pages ➤ McGill-Queen's University Press, 3430 McTavish Street, Montreal, QC H3A 1X9, Canada, www.mqup.mcgill.ca, $19.95 CDN; VISA, MC; 514-398-3750, fax 514-398-4333 ◆ Does development by its nature produce conflict? Are there times when Canada should take sides in Third World conflict? Are there ways that Canadian aid can be used to promote peace? Experts in Third World development pursue answers to these questions. Still interesting as a primer on Canadian aid and the nexus between development and conflict. [ID:2163]

Association of Consulting Engineers of Canada (ACEC) ⚏
Association of Consulting Engineers of Canada (ACEC), Suite 616, 130 Albert Street, Ottawa, ON K1P 5G4, Canada, www.acec.ca, 613-236-0569, fax 613-236-6193, info@acec.ca ◆ ACEC has a task force on Canadian International Development Agency (CIDA) contracting. This task force

publishes reports that will be of interest to all professional engineers interested in independent consulting work. The Web site provides links to national and international engineering associations and the 1,400+ member firms can be searched by international characteristics. [ID:2797]

Canadian International Development Agency (CIDA) ⅲ

www.acdi-cida.gc.ca; *Fr* ◆ This bilingual Canadian government Web site provides a thorough overview of Canada's international development activities. Here you will find detailed information on CIDAs official policies, publications and programs. There are informative sections profiling regions and countries of the world where CIDA is active, youth internships, and all aspects of the CIDA project cycle, including how businesses can access development assistance grants. International job seekers looking to work in overseas development will benefit from the information and useful links to other development agencies and development organizations. [ID:2233]

CIDA Public Inquiries ⅲ

Canadian International Development Agency (CIDA), Public Inquiries, 200 Promenade du Portage, Gatineau, QC K1A 0G4, Canada, www.acdi-cida.gc.ca, 800-230-6349, fax 819-953-6088, info@acdi-cida.gc.ca ◆ Call (800) 230 6349 and helpful staff endeavour to answer any and all questions relating to CIDA's overseas development assistance program. A good place to start when searching for contacts elsewhere in the organization. [ID:2309]

CIDA Publications 📖

Canadian International Development Agency (CIDA), Communications Branch, 200 Promenade du Portage, Gatineau, QC K1A 0G4, Canada, www.acdi-cida.gc.ca, Free; 819-997-5006, fax 819-953-6088; *Fr* ◆ CIDA publishes a wide array of documents in the form of policies, strategies and research papers. Topics covered include sustainable development, health, globalization, opportunities in international development, and gender equity, to name a few. CIDA operates a library that is open to the public, but for job seekers not living in the Ottawa region, these documents can be accessed on-line by following the link to "Resources" and then "Publications" from the home page.These documents are available free of charge and are excellent resources for those interested in Canada's role in overseas development assistance. [ID:2308]

CIDA Development Information Program ⅲ

Canadian International Development Agency (CIDA), Communications Branch, 200 Promenade du Portage, Gatineau, QC K1A 0G4, Canada, www.acdi-cida.gc.ca, 819-997-5006, fax 819-953-6088; *Fr* ◆ Established by CIDA to encourage public understanding of international development issues, this program financially supports the development of mass media and education initiatives aimed at increasing awareness and understanding of international development and cooperation issues among Canadians. The DIP has three components: a mass-media initiative, which funds the production of media features targeting the Canadian public; a global classroom initiative, which supports the development and delivery of school-based global education activities and a journalism and development initiative, which provides support to Canadian journalists interested in gaining more professional experience in the international development field. Access the DIP Web site by following the link from CIDA's home page. [ID:2311]

CIDA International Development Photo Library (IDPL) ⅲ

Canadian International Development Agency (CIDA), Communications Branch, 200 Promenade du Portage, Gatineau, QC K1A 0G4, Canada, www.acdi-cida.gc.ca, 819-997-5006, fax 819-953-6088; *Fr* ◆ IDPL is a resource of over 80,000 slides depicting life in the South, international development and Canada's role in it. Staff will provide photo editing/research services to the public for a nominal fee. Those in the Ottawa area can schedule a time to view these photos in the photo library. Requests take five to 10 working days to complete. Call 613-953-6530 for more information. [ID:2312]

CIDA's Contracts and Agreements 📖

Quarterly, 100 pages ➤ Canadian International Development Agency (CIDA), Communications Branch, 200 Promenade du Portage, Gatineau, QC K1A 0G4, Canada, www.acdi-cida.gc.ca, Free; 819-997-5006, fax 819-953-6088; *Fr* ◆ This publication seeks to help individuals, small- and medium-sized businesses (SME), and other organizations to identify potential opportunities for subcontracting to organizations responsible for implementing programs and projects funded by the Canadian International Development Agency (CIDA). The information about current major CIDA projects, recipient countries and Canadian organizations involved in international development is an excellent starting point for an international job search. [ID:2383]

Cross-Cultural Effectiveness: A Study of Canadian Technical Advisors Overseas 📖

2001, Daniel Kealey, 70 pages ➤ Foreign Affairs Canada (FAC) - Centre for Intercultural Learning, 125 Sussex Drive, Ottawa, ON K1A 0G2, Canada, www.dfait-maeci.gc.ca/cfsi-icse/cil-cai/menu-en.asp, $18.95 CDN; 800-267-8376; Fr ◆ This study's findings challenge commonly held beliefs about what it takes to be effective in living and working in a new culture. Defines the interpersonal skills and pre-departure attitudes which are predictive of overseas success and links these to the practical issues of selection and training. A must read for anyone interested in an international and intercultural job experience. [ID:2031]

Development Business 📖 💻

Weekly ➤ United Nations Publications, Sales and Marketing Section, Room DC2-853, Department I004, New York, NY 10017, USA, www.un.org/Pubs/sales.htm, $550 US/year; Credit Cards; 800-253-9646, fax 212-963-3489 ◆ This United Nations Department of Public Information publication is available only by subscription and is the single best way that suppliers and consultants can find the information needed to successfully win contracts generated from projects financed by development banks governments and the United Nations. Graphically and organizationally excellent, this site includes an on-line Business Directory with links to the Web sites of companies involved in international business, which can be used for job searches and to locate potential business partners. A great resource [ID:2083]

Virtual Library on International Development 💻

http://w3.acdi-cida.gc.ca/virtual.nsf ◆ The Virtual Library is published by CIDA and contains an excellent collection of links to international development-related sites and documents on the Internet. Organized by topic, country, region and organization, the site allows for easy and comprehensive searches. A great way to search for overseas jobs in your area of interest. [ID:2224]

Your Guide to Working with CIDA 💻 👬

Canadian International Development Agency (CIDA), Communications Branch, 200 Promenade du Portage, Gatineau, QC K1A 0G4, Canada, www.acdi-cida.gc.ca, Free on-line; 819-997-5006, fax 819-953-6088; Fr ◆ This guide is intended mainly for Canadian firms, individual consultants, and voluntary organizations and institutions that are not currently involved with CIDA and would like to know how to bid on service contracts, how the unsolicited proposal mechanism works, how the Industrial Co-operation Program operates, what sectors are currently a priority for CIDA and how to access opportunities from multilateral organizations. The guide is accessible by navigating to "Publications" and then clicking on "Your Guide to Working with CIDA" under the "Business and Employment" heading. [ID:2314]

Your Guide to Working With CIDA - The Contracting Process 💻

Canadian International Development Agency (CIDA), Communications Branch, 200 Promenade du Portage, Gatineau, QC K1A 0G4, Canada, www.acdi-cida.gc.ca, Free on-line; 819-997-5006, fax 819-953-6088 ◆ This guide is accessible through the Your Guide to Working with CIDA site by clicking on "The Contracting Process." It is an indispensable guide that provides an overview of CIDA's contracting processes. It includes an introduction into how to find contracting opportunities with CIDA, goes over the various types of contracts that are available and explains what type of individuals or organizations can bid on the different categories of contracts. It includes information and links for further information on CIDA's bilateral unsolicited proposal mechanism, Projects at the Planning Stage (Pipeline), how the MERX-Electronic Tendering Service works and a great deal more information on contracting with CIDA. [ID:2698]

Department of National Defence (DND) and the Canadian Forces

Major-General George R. Pearkes Building, 101 Colonel By Drive, Ottawa, Ontario, K1A 0K2
(613) 995-2534; Fax: (613) 995-2610; www.forces.gc.ca, information@forces.gc.ca [ID:7207]

When considering an international career many young professionals forget about the Canadian organization that makes the single-greatest Canadian contribution to brining peace to the world: CANADA'S ARMED FORCES. Whether they are delivering humanitarian relief or establishing and consolidating peace in the Balkans and other war-torn areas, the members of the Canadian Forces make a remarkable contribution to the security and well-being of Canadians and greatly improve the fate of thousands of people throughout the world.

Moreover, when you decide to leave the military your skills and experience will be in demand by NGOs outside of Canada and IGOs. Many of these international groups are on the lookout for former military personnel who bring with them excellent training and have an insider's knowledge of military culture which is especially important in Peace Support Operations.

Canada's defence portfolio includes several separate but interconnected organizations and agencies in which CANADIAN FORCES (CF) members and civilian employees work side by side to achieve common objectives.

The national defence "family" comprises more than 100,000 Canadians, including members of the Regular and Reserve Forces, the Canadian Rangers, and civilian employees of defence. The Canadian Forces is made up of members of the navy, army and air force and has the important mandate of defending Canada, its interests and values, while contributing to international peace and security. In particular, the three main roles of the Canadian Forces are

- to protect Canada;
- to defend North America in cooperation with the United States of America;
- to contribute to peace and international security.

Canada's sailors, soldiers and air personnel represent every province and territory, as well as the cultural, linguistic and regional diversities found within Canada. There are more than 100 different professions, occupations and trades available in the CF—ranging from doctors, lawyers and engineers, to technicians, mechanics and chefs.

A UNIQUE INTERNATIONAL CAREER

Since 1947, more than 100,000 Canadian Force members have taken part in peacekeeping and peace enforcement missions in hot spots all over the world. These missions have been conducted under the auspices of the UNITED NATIONS (UN) and the NORTH ATLANTIC TREATY ORGANIZATION (NATO), and within coalitions of like-minded countries.

Assignments as part of peace support operations are traditionally the largest contribution of CF personnel on the international stage. Most recently, Canada's contributions to Afghanistan, Bosnia, the Persian Gulf and Haiti have combined to see more than 3,500 sailors, soldiers and air force personnel deployed at any one time.

Other opportunities for international employment while serving in uniform include service with inter-country units, such as NATO headquarters in Brussels or NORAD headquarters in Colorado; exchange postings to foreign units, military schools and academic institutions as students or faculty; and employment in military attaché and embassy staff positions. Multi-year postings to these types of locations are normally considered "accompanied" positions, meaning immediate families are posted with uniformed personnel.

Due to safety concerns on peace support operations, CF members will be deployed without their families for the duration of their tour of duty—normally about six months in length. To ensure military personnel can focus on their very important deployment jobs, the CF provides services and support to spouses and dependents through Military Family Resource Centres.

REGULAR FORCE FULL-TIME CAREERS

With more than 100 different occupations and professions, the Canadian Forces is both combat capable and self-sustaining. Each year the CF hires roughly 5,000 new people in Regular Force (or full-time) positions.

Opportunities are available for people joining the workforce out of secondary school, community college and university. There are also positions available that see successful applicants subsidized to complete studies in technical disciplines at community colleges, or to attain an undergraduate degree at university. Most applicants in this plan will attend the ROYAL MILITARY COLLEGE OF CANADA in Kingston, Ontario, but many attend other Canadian institutions as well. Medical and dental students also have the opportunity to be subsidized for their studies.

Currently, the Canadian Forces are looking for qualified health services professionals, technicians, engineers and others. In many of these areas, qualified applicants may be eligible for signing bonuses of $10,000 to $20,000 for technicians, $25,000 for dentists, $40,000 for engineers, and $225,000 for practicing family physicians.

Specific benefits include full medical and dental coverage, 20 days of paid vacation per year (25 days after 5 years of service), competitive salaries, second-language training, full fitness facilities, and opportunities for continuing education and subsidized post-graduate education. There are also resources and facilities available to support the spouses and dependents of serving members.

RESERVE FORCE PART-TIME CAREERS

Approximately 5,000 Reserve Force (part-time) positions are available annually. Reserve personnel can normally expect to work one evening a week and one weekend each month while serving with a reserve unit. There are also opportunities to participate in extended summer training and full-time work without the requirement to move locations. Reserve personnel also have the opportunity to participate in international deployments alongside Regular Force members.

RECRUITING PROCESS

All applicants to the Canadian Forces follow the same process regardless of whether they're seeking full- or part-time employment. Applicants will complete aptitude and fitness tests, a medical screening, a background check, and an interview. Upon completion of these steps, applicants will be selected in competition with others for available positions in a desired occupation.

Basic training at the Canadian Forces Leadership and Recruit School in St-Jean, Quebec, will follow enrolment. Officers, leaders or managers, will complete a 14-week basic training, while non-commissioned members will complete a 10-week course.

A LAST WORD ON THE CANADIAN FORCES

For more information about opportunities with the Canadian Forces, contact your local recruiting office at 1-800-856-8488, or on-line at www.recruiting.forces.gc.ca.

Profiles of Government Organizations in Canada

There are 61 profiles included in this chapter. They cover a range of international opportunities in the government sector. Fourteen profiles deal with federal government departments and agencies, 13 with international activities carried out by provincial governments, and 13 with Crown corporations. There are also 7 profiles dealing with government-funded institutes and research councils with international activities. Ontario has 34 of the 61 profiles, Quebec has 11, and other provinces and territories have one or two each. In terms of Canadian government international activities, this list is extensive but not exhaustive.

Agriculture and Agri-Food Canada
Room 1009, Market and Industry Services Branch, Sir John Carling Bldg., 930 Carling Ave.,
Ottawa, ON, K1A 0C5, Canada; 613-759-1000, fax 613-759-7499, agr@agr.gc.ca, www.agr.gc.ca ⌨*Fr*

LARGE, FEDERAL GOVERNMENT: Administration (General), Agriculture

Agriculture and Agri-Food Canada (AAFC) provides information, research and technology, and policies and programs to help ensure that Canada is a world leader in producing safe, high-quality food for Canadian and international markets in an environmentally responsible way using innovative methods.

Federal, provincial, and territorial Ministers of Agriculture have pledged to meet today's challenges in the agriculture and agri-food sector by jointly developing and signing on to the comprehensive Agricultural Policy Framework (APF). The APF's international component is designed to maximize international opportunities arising from progress on the domestic front. It is composed of four elements: gaining recognition and building markets, improving market access, overcoming technical barriers, and enhancing international development.

More than 100 AAFC employees have international responsibilities. Most work in either the International Markets Bureau or the International Trade Policy Directorate. A few specialists work abroad in priority markets including Japan, South Korea, Singapore, Taiwan, Dubai and Mexico.

AAFC has some very interesting options for those interested in an international career. Economists analyze foreign markets and macroeconomic trends, trade negotiators present Canada's position before multilateral organizations like the World Trade Organization, and other officials market Canada's agricultural products abroad. AAFC maintains a Web site that provides information about vacancies and recruitment initiatives. [ID:7152]

Alberta Economic Development

6th Floor, Commerce Place, 10155 - 102 Street, Edmonton, AB, T5J 4L6, Canada;
780-415-1319, fax 780-422-1759, hr.aed@gov.ab.ca, www.alberta-canada.com

LARGE, PROVINCIAL GOVERNMENT: Business Development

Alberta Economic Development provides strategic information and planning input for Alberta's economy. The Department facilitates a coordinated approach to address Alberta's economic challenges in collaboration with other government ministries. The Department works to support a provincial government strategy called Securing Tomorrow's Prosperity that endorses a more diversified and competitive Alberta.

Alberta Economic Development has approximately 200 staff in Edmonton, Calgary and in 10 regional offices to serve the economic needs of Alberta communities. The Department also operates international business offices in Hong Kong, Japan, South Korea, Taiwan, the UK, Mexico, and Germany; and two offices in China to facilitate access to international markets, create business networks, and generate a positive business climate.

Candidates interested in working at Alberta Economic Development should have a degree in commerce, business or economics and some relevant business experience in international marketing, policy, or industry-specific or regional economic development. Successful applicants will have demonstrated abilities and skills in more than one language, written and oral communication, team work, time management, and project management experience. Jobs are posted on the Government of Alberta's job board. [ID:7153]

Alberta's Wild Rose Foundation (WRF)

International Development Program, Room 907, Standard Life Centre,
10405 Jasper Ave., Edmonton, AB, T5J 4R7, Canada; 780-422-2315,
fax 780-427-4155, comdev.communications@gov.ab.ca, www.cd.gov.ab.ca/wrf

SMALL, PROVINCIAL AGENCY: Business Development, Development Assistance, Development Education, Gender and Development, Human Resources, Human Rights

The Wild Rose Foundation, a foundation funded by Alberta government lotteries, serves to enhance and encourage Alberta's humanitarian presence in international development through the International Development Granting Program. This initiative provides financial assistance to improve the health, social and economic conditions in eligible developing countries. Assistance is provided in cooperation with registered and recognized NGOs, and promotes a spirit of volunteerism and respect for the culture, environment, dignity and independence of the beneficiaries.

The Wild Rose Foundation very occasionally has employment and contract opportunities, which are posted on the Ministry of Community Development's Web site. [ID:7167]

Atomic Energy of Canada Limited (AECL)

2251 Speakman Drive, Mississauga, ON, L5K 1B2,
Canada; 905-823-9060, fax 905-823-8006, www.aecl.ca 💻 Fr

LARGE, FEDERAL CROWN CORPORATION: Energy Resources, Engineering, Power Generation/Transmission/Distribution, Project Management

Atomic Energy of Canada Limited (AECL) is a nuclear technology and engineering company that designs and develops the CANDU nuclear power reactor, as well as other advanced energy products and services. There are 34 CANDU reactors completed or under construction worldwide and the AECL has international offices in Buenos Aires, Beijing, Seoul, Bucharest and Maryland.

The AECL has 3,600 staff working in Canada and overseas. There are many international openings for engineers and scientists. Information about these and other opportunities can be found on the AECL Web site's Career Opportunity page. This site also contains information for student opportunities and a resume database for future openings. [ID:7154]

Bank of Canada
234 Wellington Street, Ottawa, ON, K1A 0G9, Canada; 613-782-8111,
fax 613-782-7713, paffairs@bankofcanada.ca, www.bankofcanada.ca 💻 𝓕𝓻

MID-SIZED, FEDERAL CROWN CORPORATION: Economics, Investment Banking, Trade and Investment

The Bank of Canada's international activities are conducted primarily through its International Department. The International Department has four divisions that provide analysis of current and prospective developments in foreign countries, liaise with international financial institutions, and undertake advanced research on currency markets, international capital markets and economic trends.

The Bank of Canada employs about 1,200 people, some of whom have international responsibilities. A staff of 42 works in the International Department, located at the Bank's head office in Ottawa.

The Bank's Web site has superb career information and houses a resume databank, co-op and internship opportunities, and information about university recruitment. Employees of the Bank enjoy a beautiful working environment, a fitness centre and a number of flex-options. [ID:7181]

British Columbia Ministry of Forests
Economics and Trade Branch, 2nd Floor, 1520 Blanshard Street, Victoria, BC,
V8W 3C8, Canada; 250-356-9804, fax 250-387-5050, www.for.gov.bc.ca

SMALL, PROVINCIAL GOVERNMENT: Economics, Forestry

The British Columbia Ministry of Forests manages the province's trade in forestry products, with an annual value of $15 billion. Work centres on trade issues such as tariffs, log export restraints and regulatory policies.

The ministry currently has 10 salaried staff in Canada with international responsibilities. It also works closely with overseas agents and ITCan.

Vacancies are posted on the British Colombia government's Web site. Prospective applicants should have a post-graduate degree in business, trade policy or economics, and/or comparable field experience. Those with experience in forest-related issues are preferred. [ID:7175]

British Columbia Ministry of Small Business and Economic Development
8th Floor, 1810 Blanshard Street, Victoria, BC, V8W 9N3,
Canada; 250-952-0610, fax 250-952-0600, www.gov.bc.ca/sbed

LARGE, PROVINCIAL GOVERNMENT: Business Development, Project Management

The British Columbia Ministry of Small Business and Economic Development works to establish a competitive investment climate by removing barriers to business, making it easier and faster to do business in British Columbia. The Ministry assists investors and exporters in a number of ways including informing investment and export proponents of potential joint ventures, identifying key private sector projects, providing information on government policies, establishing contacts between clients and developing industry sector trade opportunities.

The staff of 157 are action-oriented, highly-focused professionals with extensive experience at senior levels in both the private and public sectors. Their expertise includes international business development, international government relations, project development and management, commercial and investment banking, and trade and public policy. [ID:7176]

Business New Brunswick

Centennial Bldg., 670 King Street, Fredericton, NB, E3B 1G1, Canada;
506-444-5228, fax 506-453-5428, www@gnb.ca, www.gnb.ca/bnb-enb ⬛ 𝐹𝑟

LARGE, PROVINCIAL GOVERNMENT: Business Development, Information Technologies

Business New Brunswick works closely with the business community, other government departments and the academic sector to stimulate positive growth in the province's economy. A particular focus is placed on building the province's strength in natural resources and capitalizing on new technology-based opportunities.

The Department has about 180 employees with some international responsibilities. Most work in the Investment and Exports Division or the Trade Policy Branch. Most employees are bilingual and the Department seeks individuals with backgrounds in international commerce, marketing and practical business experience. Vacancies are posted on the government's Web site. [ID:7193]

Canada Mortgage and Housing Corporation (CMHC)

International Relations Division, 700 Montreal Road, Ottawa, ON, K1A 0P7, Canada;
613-748-2461, fax 613-748-2302, international@cmhc.ca, international@cmhc.ca ⬛ 𝐹𝑟

MID-SIZED, FEDERAL CROWN CORPORATION: Trade and Investment

CMHC is a Crown Corporation whose international activities are conducted by CMHC International. The Corporation has staff at both the National Office in Ottawa as well as at its five regional offices in Halifax, Montreal, Toronto, Calgary and Vancouver.

CMHC International represents Canada on housing and urban environment issues in various international forums, such as the OECD and the UN Commission on Human Settlements (UN-HABITAT).

On the industry side, CMHC International supports and promotes the export of Canadian housing products and expertise by identifying market opportunities and providing practical information and advice to the housing industry. It is an invaluable source of information and intelligence on foreign markets for Canadian exporters. CMHC International is also increasingly becoming recognized as a global provider of housing and housing finance solutions, with a growing list of clients around the world.

Candidates applying to CMHC International should be multilingual and have backgrounds in one or several of the following: housing policy and programs, housing finance, urban and regional planning, and Canadian social policy.

CMHC maintains an excellent Web site that provides information to prospective employees and has specific information for new graduates and students seeking employment or co-op placements. [ID:7177]

Canada Post International Limited (CPIL)

International Business Division, Suite C0115, 2701 Riverside Drive, Ottawa, ON, K1A 0B1,
Canada; 613-734-9800, fax 613-734-4698, cpi@canadapost.ca, www.canadapost.ca ⬛ 𝐹𝑟 ⬛ 𝑆𝑝

LARGE, FEDERAL CROWN CORPORATION: Consulting, Technical Assistance

Canada Post International Limited (CPIL) is a subsidiary of Canada Post that provides postal consulting services on a commercial basis. Since 1990 it has carried out more than 160 projects in over 60 countries, and has been successful in transferring Canadian-based technology and management expertise as well as that of its teaming partners to all corners of the world. Through its work, CPIL has developed a reputation for its proven Postal Technologies, Postal Transformation, e-Commerce capabilities and Consulting Services. CPIL employs and recruits through Canada Post's Career Web site. Assignments are staffed primarily from internal Canada Post subject matter specialists. [ID:7179]

Canada Revenue Agency (CRA)

International Relations Coordination Office, Albion Tower, 25 Nicholas Street,
Ottawa, ON, K1A 0L5, Canada; 613-957-9775, fax 613-941-6618, www.cra-arc.gc.ca ▭*Fr*

MID-SIZED, FEDERAL GOVERNMENT: Accounting, Policy Development, Trade and Investment

The Canada Revenue Agency (CRA) is mandated to collect revenues; administer tax laws both for the federal government and on behalf of some provinces and territories; administer trade policies and legislation; provide border services; and make certain social and economic payments to individuals and corporations.

The CRA has primary responsibility for administering certain laws pertaining to revenue collection such as the Income Tax Act and the Customs Act. As well, it helps administer several other pieces of legislation while working in close cooperation with other federal government departments, and provincial and territorial governments. This spirit of cooperation extends to the customs and revenue agencies of other countries, thereby providing jobs and stimulating economic growth by facilitating trade and investment. Its administration of international customs and tax agreements benefits legitimate international commerce.

The CRA's international activities are managed by its International Relations Coordination Office in Ottawa. The department also has representatives at the Canadian embassies in Brussels (European Union) and Tokyo. Applications for employment must be made through the Public Service Commission. CRA maintains a Web site that provides information on its mandate and activities, and presents a number of on-line publications. [ID:7197]

Canadian Border Service Agency (CBSA)

Customs Information Services, 15th Floor, Sir Richard Scott Bldg., 191 Laurier Ave. W.,
Ottawa, ON, K1A 0L5, Canada; 800-461-9999, comments_cbsa@rc.gc.ca, www.cbsa.gc.ca ▭*Fr*

LARGE, FEDERAL AGENCY: Immigration Services, Media/Communications, Trade and Investment

The Canada Border Services Agency (CBSA) created in 2003, brings together all the major players involved in facilitating legitimate cross-border traffic and supporting economic development while stopping people and goods that pose a potential risk from entering Canada. It integrates several key functions previously spread among three organizations: the Customs program from the Canada Customs and Revenue Agency; the Intelligence, Interdiction and Enforcement program from Citizenship and Immigration Canada; and the Import Inspection at Ports of Entry program from the Canadian Food Inspection Agency. The CBSA manages Canada's borders by administering and enforcing about 75 domestic laws that govern trade and travel, as well as international agreements and conventions.

The CBSA operates at about 1,370 service points across Canada and nearly 40 locations abroad. It employs 10,000 public servants who serve some 170,000 commercial importers and more than 98 million travellers each year. More information is available on the CBSA Web site. [ID:7147]

Canadian Broadcasting Corporation (CBC) / Radio Canada

International Relations, P.O. Box 3220, Stn. C, Ottawa, ON, K1Y 1E4,
Canada; 613-724-5710, fax 613-724-5699, www.cbc.radio-canada.ca ▭*Fr*

MID-SIZED, FEDERAL CROWN CORPORATION: Accounting, Administration (General), Business
Development, Computer Systems, Consulting, Engineering, Human Resources, Media/Communications,
Project Management, Telecommunications

The Canadian Broadcasting Corporation (CBC)/Radio-Canada provides radio, television and Internet broadcasts in both English and French. It has foreign offices in London, Paris, Washington and at the UN headquarters in New York, as well as foreign correspondents in major cities throughout the world.

The CBC is also active internationally, marketing its original programming to foreign broadcasters at international program festivals and competitions. The International Relations section is responsible for international program and staff exchanges, festivals and competitions, as well as for international training and arranging agendas for foreign visitors.

In 2004 the CBC was featured as one of Canada's Top 100 Employers. As Canada's national public broadcaster, CBC/Radio-Canada offers Canadians a wide range of media services that reflect and celebrate our country's diverse heritage, cultures and stories. It uses an e-recruitment system and on-line job board on its Web site. Alternately, submit a general application to CBC/Radio-Canada, at HRRecruit_admin@cbc.ca, telling CBC/ Radio-Canada about your interests and qualifications so that you can be notified when opportunities that match your background are available. If you're interested in becoming a foreign correspondent you might you need at least 10 years of broadcasting experience. [ID:7150]

Canadian Commercial Corporation (CCC)

Overseas Division, 1100 - 50 O'Connor Street, Ottawa, ON, K1A 0S6,
Canada; 613-996-0034, fax 613-995-2121, info@ccc.ca, www.ccc.ca 💻 Fr

MID-SIZED, FEDERAL CROWN CORPORATION: Business Development, Investment Banking, Trade and Investment

The Canadian Commercial Corporation (CCC) assists in the development of trade, which it does by signing and managing over $1 billiion in export contracts, and by providing related services to Canadian exporters and foreign buyers in over 30 countries each year. CCC helps to provide access to foreign government procurement markets and sales with private sector buyers, and assists Canadian companies with project promotion, contract structuring and negotiation, and contract management.

As prime contractor, CCC provides privileged access to the US public sector aerospace and defence market. CCC supports Canadian companies wishing to sell to civilian agencies and to state and local governments in the US, and helps Canadian exporters identify business leads for sales to governments in the US and other markets by matching thousands of global business opportunities to Canadian companies and their products and services.

CCC has about 90 employees, including lawyers, contract specialists, engineers, risk analysts and project administrators. Vacancies are posted on its Web site and the CCC accepts resumes at any time from individuals with a university degree in economics or business, and experience working in the international marketplace. [ID:7182]

Canadian Commission for UNESCO

P.O. Box 1047, 7th Floor, 350 Albert Street, Ottawa, ON, K1P 5V8, Canada;
613-566-4414, fax 613-566-4390, unesco.comcdn@canadacouncil.ca, www.unesco.ca 💻 Fr

SMALL, INSTITUTE/RESEARCH COUNCIL: Culture, Development Education, Human Rights

The Canadian Commission for UNESCO operates under the aegis of the Canada Council for the Arts. It acts as a forum for governments and civil society, and encourages the participation of Canadian organizations and committed individuals in UNESCO's mandated areas of education, the natural and social sciences, culture and communication.

The Commission has 11 very active employees that educate Canadians about human rights, promote the status of the arts and foster cross-cultural understanding. Employment and internship opportunities are advertised on the Web site of the Canada Council for the Arts. [ID:7183]

Canadian Heritage

International and Intergovernmental Affairs Sector, 13-G-27, 13th Floor, 25 Eddy Street,
Gatineau, QC, K1A 0M5, Canada; 819-997-1288, fax 819-997-2553, www.pch.gc.ca 💻 Fr

MID-SIZED, FEDERAL GOVERNMENT: Advocacy, Business Development, Culture, International Business

The International and Intergovernmental Affairs Sector at Canadian Heritage includes several branches that advance Canadian culture, cultural trade and sport internationally. The International Affairs Branch builds international support for Canadian domestic cultural policy objectives with various stakeholders including other countries and multilateral organizations such as UNESCO and La Francophonie. The Trade and Investment Branch provides expertise and policy advice on cultural trade and investment issues such as trade negotiations and disputes, and provides support to

Canadian arts as well as small and medium-sized cultural enterprises for international business development and export preparedness.

Canadian Heritage has approximately 80 staff with international responsibilities. New staff are usually former FSWEP participants or co-op students who are hired through the merit-based bridging mechanisms discussed in the PSC section of its Web site. To be considered for student employment you should have a background in international relations or a related discipline and have proficiency in both official languages. Heritage's Web site provides extensive information about its international programs and policies. [ID:7184]

Canadian Institutes of Health Research (CIHR)
9th Floor, 410 Laurier Ave. W., Ottawa, ON, K1A 0W9, Canada;
613-941-2672, fax 613-954-1800, info@cihr-irsc.gc.ca, www.cihr-irsc.gc.ca 💻 *Fr*

SMALL, INSTITUTE/RESEARCH COUNCIL: Exchange Programs, Medical Health, Public Health, Research

As Canada's premier health research organization, CIHR supports research and training in four pillars of health research: biomedical science, clinical science, health services and systems research, as well as social, cultural and environmental determinants of population health. Each of CIHR's 13 multi-disciplinary "virtual" institutes is dedicated to a specific area of health research. Every institute supports and links researchers in universities, hospitals and research centres across Canada.

CIHR encourages international collaborations through its core operating grants, CIHR Group and Clinical Trials programs as well as its University-Industry and R&D partnered programs. It also promotes the establishment of collaboration through international exchange and research programs. The exchange programs are open to Canadian and permanent resident researchers who desire to establish potential collaboration with researchers abroad. [ID:7189]

Canadian International Development Agency (CIDA)
Communications Branch, 5th Floor, Place du Centre, 200 Promenade du Portage,
Gatineau, QC, K1A 0G4, Canada; 819-997-5006, fax 819-953-6088, http://w3.acdi-cida.gc.ca 💻 *Fr*

LARGE, FEDERAL GOVERNMENT: Agriculture, Community Development, Consulting, Development Assistance, Development Education, Economics, Environment, Exchange Programs, Fisheries, Forestry, Gender and Development, Human Rights, Humanitarian Relief, Intercultural Briefings, Media/Communications, Medical Health, Micro-enterprises, Technical Assistance, Telecommunications, Volunteer, Water Resources

See the detailed profile at the beginning of this chapter. (For information on their international internships see the Canadian Government International Internships profile in Chapter 17, Internships Abroad.) [ID:7206]

Canadian International Grains Institute (CIGI)
Suite 1000, 303 Main Street, Winnipeg, MB, R3C 3G7, Canada;
204-983-5344, fax 204-983-2642, cigi@cigi, www.cigi.ca

MID-SIZED, INSTITUTE/RESEARCH COUNCIL: Agriculture, Marketing, Training and Education

The Canadian International Grains Institute (CIGI) is a non-profit market development organization promoting Canada's field crop industries in international and domestic markets through educational programming and technical activities. CIGI offers programs on the handling, marketing and commercial applications for food and feed end uses of Canadian grains, oilseeds, pulses and special crops. CIGI's 30 staff members work with the Canadian agriculture industry to build and maintain relationships with domestic and international customers of Canadian field crops. Through its international programs, CIGI brings together representatives from as many as 20 countries at a time. Vacancies are posted on CIGI's Web site. [ID:7185]

Canadian International Trade Tribunal (CITT)
15th Floor, 333 Laurier Ave. W., Ottawa, ON, K1A 0G7, Canada;
613-993-3595, fax 613-998-1322, secretary@citt-tcce.gc.ca, www.citt.gc.ca ⌨Fr

SMALL, FEDERAL GOVERNMENT: Economics, Law

The Canadian International Trade Tribunal (CITT) is the main quasi-judicial institution in Canada's trade remedy system. It conducts inquiries into whether dumped or subsidized imports have caused, or are threatening to cause, material injury to a domestic industry, conducts safeguard inquiries and provides advice on economic, trade and tariff issues.

The Tribunal is composed of up to nine full-time members who are appointed by the Governor in Council for a term of up to five years. Members of the Tribunal have extensive government experience, usually relating to international trade. [ID:7186]

Canadian Security Intelligence Service (CSIS)
Headquarters, P.O. Box 9732, Stn. T, Ottawa, ON,
K1G 4G4, Canada; 613-993-9620, www.csis-scrs.gc.ca ⌨Fr

LARGE, FEDERAL GOVERNMENT: Intelligence and Security

The Canadian Security Intelligence Service (CSIS) investigates, analyzes and reports to the government on threats to the security of Canada. It has liaison officers posted abroad who are involved in the exchange of security intelligence by liaising with various police, security and intelligence organizations, and assisting Citizenship and Immigration Canada in screening prospective immigrants and travellers. CSIS has offices in most major cities across Canada and overseas, of which only London, Paris and Washington have, for personnel security reasons, been publicly acknowledged. CSIS has an estimated workforce of some 2,330 people. The number of overseas personnel is not available.

The range of CSIS activities means that its employees must possess a variety of academic backgrounds and abilities. Reference the CSIS Web site for detailed information about vacancies and the selection process for Intelligence Officers (IOs). IOs must be a Canadian citizen with a university degree, possess a valid driver's license and agree to relocate anywhere in Canada, depending on the requirements of the Service. The Service is looking for motivated people who possess strong interpersonal skills and an ability to take the initiative, who are empathetic and sensitive to the cultural mores of a changing Canadian society, and who are adaptable and embrace new experiences with confidence. Applicants should be aware that they will undergo a very stringent background check. [ID:7187]

Canadian Space Agency (CSA)
John H. Chapman Space Centre, 6767 route d'Aeroport, Saint-Hubert, QC, J3Y 8Y9,
Canada; 450-926-4800, fax 450-926-4352, info@space.gc.ca, www.space.gc.ca ⌨Fr

LARGE, FEDERAL AGENCY: Aerospace Technology, Forestry

The Canadian Space Agency promotes the peaceful use and development of space to meet Canada's social and economic needs and to develop an internationally recognized and technically capable space industry. In addition to delivering its own programs, the CSA is responsible for coordinating all federal and civil space-related policies and programs pertaining to science and technology research, industrial development, and international cooperation.

The CSA maintains close international partnerships and has ties to various space agencies, most notably NASA and the European Space Agency. It has a staff of about 579 employees and 80 students. It has international offices in Washington, Paris and Houston. The CSA's Web site includes a careers page that provides information about jobs, student opportunities and explains that those interested in becoming astronauts, perhaps the most international of all jobs, will have to wait for the CSA's next recruitment campaign. (The last one was in 1992.) [ID:7162]

Canadian Transportation Agency

15 Eddy Street, Gatineau, QC, K1A 0N9, Canada; 819-997-0344,
fax 819-953-8353, cta.comment@cta-otc.gc.ca, www.cta-otc.gc.ca ▪*Fr*

MID-SIZED, FEDERAL AGENCY: Air Transportation, Marine, Railways, Transportation

The Canadian Transportation Agency is responsible for administering the licensing system for Canadian and foreign air carriers with domestic and international operations relevant to Canada. It also administers and participates in negotiating international air agreements, including the regulation of international air tariffs. Currently, there are about 40 salaried staff in Canada with international responsibilities.

The Agency maintains a Web site that describes its mandate and activities; it also provides information on transportation regulations, agency decisions and orders, and transportation of travellers with disabilities. [ID:7191]

Citizenship and Immigration Canada (CIC)

International Region, 16th Floor, Jean Edmonds Tower S., 365 Laurier Ave. W.,
Ottawa, ON, K1A 1L1, Canada; 613-996-8436, fax 613-996-8048, www.cic.gc.ca ▪*Fr*

LARGE, FEDERAL GOVERNMENT: Immigration Services, Medical Health, Social Policy

At the Department of Citizenship and Immigration Canada (CIC), Foreign Service Immigration Officers provide policy and procedural advice on international immigration trends and developments. They deliver Canada's immigration program overseas, including screening and processing applications from prospective immigrants and refugees, students, temporary workers and visitors.

There are currently 300 Foreign Service Immigration Officers, assisted by some 1,100 local employees at 89 Canadian missions abroad. Foreign Service Immigration Officers are recruited through a post-secondary recruitment program jointly administered by the Department of Citizenship and Immigration Canada and the departments of Foreign Affairs Canada (FAC) and International Trade Canada (ITCan). This recruitment is usually held in the fall of each year. (For more infromation, see the FAC profile in this chapter.)

CIC is also responsible for the Medical Immigration Program overseas. The Medical Officers decide on the medical admissibility of potential immigrants, long-term visitors, students and temporary workers, and they manage a large network of designated local doctors who conduct the immigration medical examinations. They also take part in the delivery of the Public Service Health Program, which ensures access to adequate health care for Canadian diplomatic staff and their families posted in Canadian missions abroad.

The Foreign Service Immigration Officer and Medical Officers are rotational employees. They are assigned to periods of duty of from two to four years in Canada at a time and the same at a Canadian post abroad.

If you are interested in these rotational jobs at Citizenship and Immigration Canada, you should consult the Public Service Commission's job Web site under the "Post-Secondary Recruitment Program (PSR)" or "Jobs Open to the Public." [ID:7163]

Communications Security Establishment

Sir Leonard Tilley Bldg., 719 Heron Road, Ottawa, ON, K1G 3Z4,
Canada; 613-991-7600, webmaster@cse-cst.gc.ca, www.cse-cst.gc.ca ▪*Fr*

SMALL, FEDERAL GOVERNMENT: Computer Systems, Intelligence and Security

The Communications Security Establishment (CSE) is Canada's national cryptologic agency. CSE acquires and provides foreign signals intelligence, protects the government's electronic infrastructure, computer systems and networks, and provides assistance to federal police and security agencies in the performance of their lawful duties. CSE actively recruits people who are interested in challenging positions involving mathematics, engineering, computer science, physics, foreign languages and intelligence analysis. Vacancies and information for co-op students is posted on its Web site, as is information about the Paul Sargent Memorial Scholarship for Foreign

Language Studies. This scholarship is open to post-graduate students that have at least an intermediate level of competence in an Asian, Middle Eastern, North African or Eastern European language. Those awarded scholarships are also given a summer job and employment for two years after the completion of their studies. Applicants should be aware that the entire selection process for positions with the CSE may take more than one year to complete. For more information please visit the CSE Web site. [ID:7178]

Consulting and Audit Canada (CAC)
International Services Directorate, 112 Kent Street, Ottawa, ON,
K1A 0S5, Canada; 613-996-1577, fax 613-995-9203, www.cac.gc.ca 💻 ℱr

LARGE, FEDERAL GOVERNMENT: Accounting, Administration (General), Adult Training, Community Development, Consulting, Development Assistance, Development Education, Economics, Environment, Exchange Programs, Gender and Development, Human Resources, Human Rights, Humanitarian Relief, Intercultural Briefings, Logisitics, Project Management, Technical Assistance, Telecommunications, Tourism, Water Resources

Canadian public service standards are recognized for their excellence worldwide. As a Canadian government agency, CAC has earned a solid reputation in the international community for providing high quality consulting and audit services in more than 40 countries. CAC's client roster includes United Nations agencies, the Canadian International Development Agency (CIDA), the Foreign Affairs Canada/International Trade Canada (FAC/ITCan) and the World Bank. Their assignments in the international arena are as varied as their clients. They include: planning to complete public service reform, establishing public sector consulting services, enhancing government audit capacity and evaluating a wide variety of development projects.

ISD maintains a pool of private sector consultants, with new candidates added regularly through a competitive screening process. Candidates should have a bachelor's degree and preferably a master's or PhD in any field related to development activities, as well as consulting experience in international development. You can register on-line at www.cac.gc.ca. [ID:7164]

Department of Human Resources and Skills Development (HRSD)
Place du Portage, Phase IV, 140 Promenade du Portage,
Gatineau, QC, K1A 0J9, Canada; www.hrsdc.gc.ca 💻 ℱr

SMALL, FEDERAL GOVERNMENT: Human Resources

The Department of Human Resources and Skills Development (HRSD) is responsible for providing Canadians with the tools they need to thrive and prosper in the workplace and community. It works with a wide range of countries, partners and international organizations to further this goal within the context of globalization, most notably through its involvement with the International Labour Organization (ILO).

The five members of the International Affairs Branch coordinate HRSD's international activities and provide strategic advice to the department. There are about 16 individuals within the Strategic Policy and International Labour Affairs Branch that have international responsibilities, including managing Canada's participation in the ILO, coordinating Canada's involvement in the North American Agreement on Labour Cooperation and addressing international labour issues.

Staff with international responsibilities have diverse educational backgrounds ranging from international relations, labour law, human rights and economics. Most also have significant professional experience dealing with foreign delegations, conducting policy or economic analysis and possess a sound knowledge of the federal government.

HRSD participates in the Federal Student Work Experience Program and posts vacancies for permanent and term position on the PSC Web site. [ID:7180]

Elections Canada
257 Slater Street, Ottawa, ON, K1A 0M6, Canada; 613-993-2975, www.elections.ca ⌨*Fr*

LARGE, FEDERAL GOVERNMENT: Election Monitoring, Institution Building, Technical Assistance

Elections Canada plays an active role on the world scene, offering its experience to new democracies and international organizations dedicated to the promotion of democratic electoral processes. Since 1990, it has been involved in more than 355 international democratic missions in 100 countries, advising on constitutional and election law provisions, conducting pre-election evaluations, providing professional support and technical assistance, and conducting bilateral exchanges of information and knowledge.

Election Canada's international missions range in length from 10 days to 6 months and are carried out by individuals selected from the CANADEM Roster of International Election Experts. Prospective election observers often receive no salary, must deploy rapidly, and have prior regional and election-related experience. (For more information on CANADEM see Chapter 38, NGOs in Canada.) [ID:7165]

Environment Canada (EC)
351 St. Joseph Blvd., Gatineau, QC, K1A 0H3, Canada;
819-997-2800, enviroinfo@ec.gc.ca, www.ec.gc.ca ⌨*Fr*

LARGE, FEDERAL GOVERNMENT: Economics, Environment, Policy Dialogue

Environment Canada (EC) contributes to the Canadian government's international environmental agenda by advancing and sharing science and know-how, as well as through negotiations and policy dialogue in international forums.

The International Relations Directorate (IRD) plays the central policy and coordination role for Environment Canada's international activities. It provides strategic advice on international relations, develops the strategic framework within which the department's international activities are managed, participates in the negotiation and implementation of international agreements, and provides policy and operational support to the Minister, Deputy Minister and senior management on international activities. The directorate's responsibilities also include managing the department's bilateral and regional relations (e.g. North American Agreement on Environmental Cooperation) as well as participation in international organizations such as the International Joint Commission (IJC), the Organization for Economic Cooperation and Development (OECD), the United Nations Environment Program(UNEP) and the G8.

Many of EC's 5,000 staff have some international responsibilities.

EC has a number of excellent opportunities for students, including the Science Horizons Youth Internship Program, which offers young scientists and post-secondary graduates hands-on experience working on environmental projects under the mentorship and coaching of experienced scientists and program managers. This is a separate program from the International Environment Youth Corps, which fosters long-term employability for Canadian youth in the environment industry sector while at the same time strengthening the capacity of this sector to expand Canadian exports and trade. Other student opportunities at EC include Co-op/Internship Programs that allow full-time post-secondary students to alternate academic semesters with career-related placements and the Federal Student Work Experience Program (FSWEP), whereby students can be recruited for temporary jobs. Upon graduation, EC may use student bridging mechanisms to facilitate the hiring of recently employed students into the public service. EC's Web site includes an excellent careers page that has an abundance of information for job seekers. [ID:7166]

Export Development Canada (EDC)

151 O'Connor Street, Ottawa, ON, K1A 1K3, Canada;
613-598-2500, fax 613-237-2690, export@edc4.edc.ca, www.edc.ca 🖳*Fr*

LARGE, FEDERAL CROWN CORPORATION: Accounting, Administration (General), Business
Development, Economics, Engineering, Human Resources, Media/Communications, Trade and Investment

Export Development Canada (EDC) is a financially self-sufficient crown corporation devoted exclusively to providing trade finance services to support Canadian exporters and investors in some 200 markets, 130 of which are in developing markets. EDC offers a range of financial services including credit insurance, bonding and guarantees, political risk insurance, direct loans to buyers and lines of credit in other countries to facilitate access to Canadian markets. EDC operates on commercial principles, charging fees and premiums for its products and interest on its loans.

EDC employs approximately 1,000 people who work in 12 offices across Canada, as well as a small number of representatives in China, Brazil, Mexico and Poland. EDC employees indicate that working in the fast-paced global marketplace is one of the most rewarding aspects of their jobs. They especially enjoy the experience of supporting smaller Canadian companies, which make up nearly 90 per cent of EDC's clients, that are trying to gain a foothold in foreign markets.

EDC's professional staff have backgrounds in commerce, business administration, finance, economics, law or marketing. When recruiting, EDC also looks for candidates who have strong analytical, organizational, written and oral communication skills, as well as interpersonal skills. Knowledge of both official languages is also strongly valued.

EDC staff can choose to work in a variety of areas in the Ottawa head office or in regional offices. Business development managers, financial service managers on EDC's business teams and regional managers in the International Markets division provide financial and risk management advice to exporters and deal with other lending institutions, development banks and foreign governments. These positions require frequent travel abroad. Other areas of employment include economics, political and risk assessment, project financing and equity groups, treasury operations, corporate finance and government relations, public affairs and communications, marketing, legal services, information services, administration and human resources.

The EDC has implemented an excellent Education & Youth Employment strategy through which it recruits the best and brightest business and economics students. At the heart of its efforts is a million dollar scholarship fund that annually provides 25 undergraduate students with a $3,000 scholarship and two $5,000 scholarships for MBA students. Winners are also offered a four-month work term within the year they receive the scholarship, which pushes the total award for undergraduate students to $14,000. Check out the student section on EDC's Web site for information about these and other student opportunities.

Vacancies for EDC jobs, including student opportunities, are posted on its Web site. Applicants must use EDC's e-recruitment system to apply for positions. Overall, the EDC Web site is very well done and contains a wealth of information to potential applicants, including numerous tips about resumes and interview skills. [ID:7188]

Department of Finance Canada

19th Floor, East Tower, 140 O'Connor Street, Ottawa, ON,
K1A 0G5, Canada; 613-992-1573, fax 613-992-0938, www.fin.gc.ca 🖳*Fr*

LARGE, FEDERAL GOVERNMENT: Economics, Investment Banking, Policy Dialogue

The Department of Finance is responsible for providing analysis and advice on the economic and financial affairs of Canada. It is concerned with all aspects of the performance of the Canadian economy, following the development of external factors that bear on domestic economic performance, and examining the economic actions taken by other levels of government.

Several branches at the Department have international responsibilities, although the three divisions within the International Trade and Finance Branch do most of the international work. The International Finance and Development Division takes the lead on most aspects of Canada's international financial relations, focusing on the financing of Canadian exports and development assistance. The International Policy and Institutions Division manages Canada's relations with international financial institutions (IFI), such as the Bretton Woods institutions and regional development banks, and leads Canadian participation in a range of international groupings such as the G7 and G20 finance ministers and central bank governors' processes. The International Trade Policy Division contributes to the development and management of Canada's international trade and investment policies and is responsible for most aspects of Canadian import policy. Finance has a relatively small staff that includes 350 policy analysts and economists. It also has a number of overseas positions in G7 countries, with some IFIs and in other intergovernmental organizations. They recruit for economists and analysts, doctoral researchers and tax legislation officers, through PSC post-secondary recruitment programs. [ID:7168]

Department of Fisheries and Oceans (DFO)

International Affairs Directorate, 13th Floor, 200 Kent Street, Ottawa, ON, K1A 0E6, Canada; 613-993-1873, fax 613-993-5995, info@dfo-mpo.gc.ca, www.dfo-mpo.gc.ca 🖳 *Fr*

SMALL, FEDERAL GOVERNMENT: Fisheries, International Law/International Agreements, Policy Development, Trade and Investment

The Department of Fisheries and Oceans International Affairs Directorate conducts international fisheries relations and negotiates international fisheries agreements of a bilateral and multilateral nature, for the conservation and the sustainable management of fisheries and ocean resources. The directorate administers and coordinates the implementation of these agreements, formulates and represents Canadian fisheries positions and participates in bilateral and multilateral fisheries commissions as well as United Nations (UN) bodies such as the UN General Assembly, UNICPOLOS and the FAO .

The directorate currently has 14 staff, including one director general, two directors, and various officers and support staff. The backgrounds of the staff vary, but most have degrees in the social sciences, commerce or law. There are occasional opportunities for consulting in specialized areas of research. [ID:7169]

Department of Foreign Affairs and International Trade (DFAIT)

Lester B. Pearson Bldg., 125 Sussex Drive, Ottawa, ON, K1A 0G2, Canada; 613-996-3386, fax 613-995-1405, www.dfait-maeci.gc.ca 🖳 *Fr*

LARGE, FEDERAL GOVERNMENT: Agriculture, Business Development, Consulting, Culture, Development Assistance, Economics, Exchange Programs, Human Rights, Intercultural Briefings, Media/Communications, Peace and Security, Policy Development, Trade and Investment

As of 2004 the Department of Foreign Affairs and International Trade no longer exists as a federal department. All of its services, programs and activates are now offered by two separate departments: Foreign Affairs Canada (FAC) and International Trade Canada (ITCan). These departments are profiled together at the beginning of this chapter. [ID:7205]

Health Canada

International Affairs Directorate (IAD), 3rd Floor, Jeanne Mance Bldg., Tunney's Pasture, Postal Locator 1903A, Ottawa, ON, K1A 0K9, Canada; 613-957-2991, fax 613-952-7417, iad-dai@hc-sc.gc.ca, www.hwc.ca 🖳 *Fr*

MID-SIZED, FEDERAL GOVERNMENT: International Law/International Agreements, Medical Health, Public Health

Health Canada's International Affairs Directorate (IAD) advances the Government of Canada's perspective on health issues and coordinates the sharing of knowledge and technical expertise with other countries seeking to build their healthcare capacity. The IAD manages the international aspects of the department's strategies on major health issues such as HIV/AIDS, global health security and tobacco control, and represents Canada in meetings at key international health organizations where it promotes health issues based on Canada's health values and principles. It also builds relationships with other countries in the health field to improve the exchange of information on health policy and practices, facilitates technical capacity building, and looks for opportunities to promote the use of Canadian healthcare products and expertise.

The IAD has about 24 staff and is occasionally in a position to recommend Canadian technical experts to international organizations and agencies, such as the World Health Organization (WHO) or Pan-American Health Organization (PAHO). The IAD's staff have backgrounds in Canadian health policy, medicine, international affairs and trade, HIV/AIDS, gender health, economics, environmental health, health of Indigenous Peoples and a broad knowledge of international health policy. [ID:7170]

Industry Canada
International Trade and Investment Policy Branch, 5th Floor, 235 Queen Street E., Ottawa, ON, K1A 0H5, Canada; 613-947-7466, fax 613-954-6436, www.ic.gc.ca 💻 *Fr*

LARGE, FEDERAL GOVERNMENT: Business Development, Environment

Industry Canada works with Canadians throughout the economy to foster a competitive, knowledge-based Canadian economy. Its efforts are increasingly focused on increasing Canada's share of global trade and encouraging foreign investment. Program areas include developing industry and technology capability, fostering scientific research, setting telecommunications policy, promoting tourism and small business development, and setting rules and services that support the effective operation of the marketplace.

Industry Canada has almost 6,000 full-time employees working in Ottawa and in 15 regional offices across Canada. The further integration of the global economy dictates that many of its employees' functions include international aspects. The work of many of their employees covers international issues. They work on issues such as the impact of trade negotiations on industry sectors, macroeconomic analysis, trade promotion and providing information about markets to Canadian businesses. Internationally-focused staff generally have backgrounds in international marketing, trade policy, international relations and technology issues. Industry Canada's Web site includes a Careers page that provides information for prospective employees and about several internship programs open to students and young professionals. [ID:7171]

International Development Research Centre (IDRC)
250 Albert Street, Ottawa, ON, K1G 3H9, Canada; 613-236-6163, info@idrc.ca, www.idrc.ca 💻 *Fr* 💻 *Sp*

LARGE, INSTITUTE/RESEARCH COUNCIL: Accounting, Administration (General), Agriculture, Business Development, Community Development, Computer Systems, Development Assistance, Development Education, Economics, Environment, Fisheries, Forestry, Fundraising, Gender and Development, Human Resources, Media/Communications, Micro-enterprises, Water Resources

Canada's International Development Research Centre (IDRC) is a public corporation, created by the Parliament of Canada in 1970. The Centre helps developing countries use science and knowledge to find practical, long-term solutions to the social, economic and environmental problems they face. In particular, it strives to optimize the creation, adaptation and ownership of the knowledge that the people of developing countries judge to be of the greatest relevance to their own prosperity, security and equity.

IDRC is dedicated to fostering a work environment that encourages creativity and innovation, rewards competence and team work, and is managed in a fair and equitable manner. Its success depends on highly effective and imaginative staff working well together. The IDRC head office is in Ottawa and there are regional offices in Kenya, Senegal, Egypt, Uruguay, Singapore and New Delhi. Regional offices are staffed with people hired locally and from Canada.

As of 2004, the IDRC has 300 employees working in Ottawa and 52 working in regional offices. The IDRC actively recruits graduates from a variety of academic disciplines ranging from the arts, commerce and law to science, engineering and accounting. The qualities the Centre looks for in its staff include being a team player, leadership, good communication skills, creativity and previous experience in developing countries. These are all listed as desirable non-academic qualifications. Graduates would occupy positions such as program officer, project officer, research officer, helpdesk analyst, financial analyst, systems analyst/manager, administrative assistant, administration officer and research information specialist, etc.

The Centre provides new employees with coverage under its benefits plan. Tuition subsidies are also available for employees interested in furthering their education. New employees receive four weeks of paid vacation allowance after their first year. The average starting salary falls within the range of $45,001-$50,000 CDN.

The best method for initial contact for those seeking employment is through the Centre's Web site. Job postings as well as announcements regarding IDRC's summer employment program can also be found on the Web site. The IDRC hires co-op and summer students. Awards and internship programs are also available at IDRC. [ID:7173]

Island Investment Development Inc.

2nd Floor, 94 Euston Street, Charlottetown, PE, C1A 1W4, Canada;
902-894-0351, www.gov.pe.ca/development/iidi-info/index.php3

SMALL, PROVINCIAL CROWN CORPORATION: Banking and Financial Services, Trade and Investment

Island Investment Development Inc. (IIDI) is a crown corporation established to administer the Island Funds and the Prince Edward Island Century 2000 Fund through the federal government's Immigrant Investor Program. The program's objective is to encourage and facilitate the immigration of experienced business persons from abroad who will make a positive contribution to the province's economy by applying their risk capital and business acumen to Canadian business ventures that create jobs for Canadians. IIDI presently has four staff and advertises for open positons on the PEI's government Web site. [ID:7208]

Department of Justice Canada

External Liaison Unit, Room 209, 239 Wellington Street, Ottawa, ON,
K1A 0H8, Canada; 613-952-8346, fax 613-941-4165, http://canada.justice.gc.ca 💻 *Fr*

MID-SIZED, FEDERAL GOVERNMENT: Development Assistance, Development Education, Gender and Development, Human Rights, International Law/International Agreements, Technical Assistance

The Department of Justice is responsible for the legal affairs of the federal government, and for ensuring that fair federal acts and regulations responsive to Canadian needs are effectively administered. It also serves as legal advisor to the Governor General, represents the Crown in litigation, and provides legal counsel to federal departments and agencies.

The department represents Canada at legal meetings in several international forums, including the United Nations Commission on International Trade Law (UNCITRAL), the Hague Conference on Private International Law, the International Institute for the Unification of Private Law (Unidroit), the International Civil Aviation Organization (ICAO), the Organization of American States (OAS), and the Council of Europe.

The department is involved in legal technical assistance with a number of countries including the Czech Republic, Slovakia, Ukraine, Haiti and South Africa. Currently, two Justice officials are posted abroad and the Department contributes to the salary of another federal official posted at the Canadian Embassy to the European Union in Brussels. The Department also runs the Visiting Professional Interchange Program, which facilitates placement of qualified staff in unique law-related employment situations both within and outside of Canada.

There are some opportunities for students including articling positions with the Department of Justice. For details on these, the Visiting Interchange Program and general recruitment, visit their Web site. (See the multi page profile of the Department of Justice at the beginning of Chapter 31, International Law Careers.) [ID:7174]

Manitoba Trade and Investment Corporation (MTI)

1100 - 259 Portage Ave., Winnipeg, MB, R3B 3P4, Canada; 204-945-2466,
fax 204-957-1793, mbtrade@itt.gov.mb.ca, www.gov.mb.ca/itm/trade 💻 *Fr* 💻 *Sp*

MID-SIZED, PROVINCIAL AGENCY: Business Development

Manitoba Trade and Investment Corporation (MTI) is an agency of Manitoba Industry, Trade and Mines. Its mission is to help build the Manitoba economy through industrial development, export and investment marketing opportunities. The Corporation coordinates its activities with agencies and organizations of other governments, in Canada and abroad.

Manitoba Trade currently has 37 staff members based in Canada and seven agents overseas. Applicants should have a business background. Desired qualifications and experience for candidates include a degree in business and/or international trade, overseas business experience, cross-cultural skills, and language capabilities. Vacancies are posted on the Manitoba government's Web site. [ID:7151]

Department of National Defence (DND)

Recruiting, Canadian Forces Recruiting Services Headquarters,
P.O. Box 1000 Stn. Main, Bldg. 0-110, Canadian Forces Base Borden,
Borden, ON, L0M 1C0, Canada; , fax 613-992-2272, www.recruiting.dnd.ca ☐ Fr

LARGE, FEDERAL GOVERNMENT: Defence and Peacekeeping, Peace and Security

The Canadian Forces have four main areas of international activity: peacekeeping and contingency operations for collective security agencies such as the UN; service in inter-country units, such as at NATO Headquarters in Brussels or NORAD Headquarters in Colorado; exchange postings to foreign units, military schools and academic institutions as students or faculty; and employment in military attaché and embassy staff positions.

Members of the Canadian Forces are not hired specifically for overseas employment. Depending on requirements and your military occupation, you may have several opportunities to serve overseas. Currently, there are approximately 30 officer military occupations and 110 non-commissioned member occupations. Most of these can serve overseas in their trade area or in a general service capacity. There are also approximately 60,000 regular force personnel, of which 2,900 are based overseas. Service in the Primary Reserves is the closest the Canadian Forces has to an internship program. There is extensive information about recruitment on the Department of National Defence's Web site. (This department has a more extensive profile earlier in this chapter.) [ID:7207]

National Film Board of Canada (NFB)

International Program, 3155 Cote de Liesse Road, Montreal, QC, H4N 2N4,
Canada; 514-283-9461, fax 514-282-2573, international@nfb.ca, www.nfb.ca ☐ Fr

MID-SIZED, FEDERAL CROWN CORPORATION: Culture, Marketing

The Distribution Branch of the National Film Board of Canada promotes, markets and sells NFB French and English productions around the world. They are also shown in over 250 international film festivals each year. With two international offices located in Paris and New York, along with a Montreal-based marketing manager for the Asia Pacific region and an agent based in Los Angeles responsible for Latin America, the Distribution Branch assures that National Film Board productions are seen around the globe. In all, NFB has about 45 staff working in its distribution team. Vacancies are posted on the NFB's Web site. [ID:7190]

Natural Resources Canada (NRCan)

580 Booth Street, Ottawa, ON, K1A 0E4, Canada; 613-995-0947,
fax 613-995-5576, ihelpdes@nrcan.gc.ca, www.nrcan.gc.ca ☐ Fr

MID-SIZED, FEDERAL GOVERNMENT: Energy Resources, Environment, Mineral Resources

Natural Resources Canada (NRCan) plays a pivotal role in helping shape the important contributions of the natural resources sector to the Canadian economy, society and environment. The nature of NRCan's work dictates that all of its sectors—earth sciences, energy, forests, and minerals and metals—have international responsibilities. Internally, each of these four sectors has its own international division, which, together with a central coordinating group, collectively ensures that Canada meets its international commitments related to natural resources and that global markets remain open for Canadian products, services and technology.

NRCan's staff with international responsibilities work in the international arena to promote Canada's objectives of encouraging economic and market reform, advocating environmental stewardship and energy efficiency, promoting Canadian industry access to foreign markets and technical cooperation. Most have backgrounds in policy development, economics, international relations, law, environmental studies or related fields.

NRCan has an excellent careers page on its Web site, where extensive information about employment and other opportunities can be found, including the Policy Analyst Recruitment and Development Program that is used to recruit about 15 to 20 students a year. NRCan also participates in numerous career fairs. [ID:7192]

New Brunswick Department of Intergovernmental and International Relations

Cooperation Division, P.O. Box 6000, 670 King Street, Fredericton, NB, E3B 5H1, Canada; 506-444-5418, fax 506-453-2995, NBInter@gov.nb.ca, www.gnb.ca/0056/index-e.asp 💻 *Fr*

MID-SIZED, PROVINCIAL GOVERNMENT: Business Development, Policy Dialogue, Trade and Investment

The Department of Intergovernmental and International Relations is responsible for implementing the province's first-ever international strategy, Prospering in the Global Community: New Brunswick's International Strategy. The strategy will ensure coordination across all provincial departments and identify priorities for engaging partners and stakeholders involved in international activities. Specific parts of the world are also designated for higher levels of attention, including the United States, the United Kingdom and China. The province's membership in La Francophonie is also acknowledged as an important gateway to pursue New Brunswick's immigration, investment and trade, and cultural interests. It also commits the province to engaging specific member countries in a strategic fashion.

The Department has about 25 staff members. Most have backgrounds in international relations or international business and all are fully bilingual. Vacancies are posted on the provincial government's Web site. [ID:7203]

Newfoundland and Labrador Department of Innovation, Trade and Rural Development

P.O. Box 8700, Confederation Bldg., St. John's, NL, A1B 4J6, Canada; 709-729-7000, fax 709-729-7244, ITRDinfo@gov.nl.ca, www.NLbusiness.ca

MID-SIZED, PROVINCIAL GOVERNMENT: Business Development

The Newfoundland and Labrador Department of Innovation, Trade and Rural Development promotes the province's diversification and growth. A major component of this agenda is forging links between Newfoundland and Labrador and the international community. Its work includes assisting Newfoundland and Labrador businesses to develop an export plan for entry into new markets, find new export business partners and research new national and international market opportunities. It also specializes in attracting new investment, new companies and new industries to the province.

About 20 staff members have international responsibilities. Most have backgrounds in commerce or economics and provide business and marketing advice to local companies looking for export opportunities. Vacancies are posted on the province's Public Service Commission Web site. [ID:7194]

Newfoundland and Labrador Department of Tourism, Culture and Recreation

Tourism Development Division, P.O. Box 8700, St. John's, NL, A1B 4J6, Canada; 709-729-2831, fax 709-729-0057, info@tourism.gov.nf.ca, www.gov.nf.ca/tourism 💻 *Fr*

SMALL, PROVINCIAL GOVERNMENT: Media/Communications, Tourism

The Newfoundland Department of Tourism, Culture and Recreation's Tourism Development Division works in cooperation with Canadian embassies and the Atlantic Canada Tourism Partners in the area of trade development.

Prospective applicants should have knowledge of French and German, and an education in travel or commerce. Paid summer internships relating to visitor services and public relations are typically available. The department maintains a data bank for resumes. [ID:7195]

Northwest Territories Department of Resources, Wildlife and Economic Development

P.O. Box 1320, 6th Floor, Scotia Centre, Yellowknife, NT,
X1A 2L9, Canada; 867-873-7115, www.gov.nt.ca/RWED

MID-SIZED, PROVINCIAL GOVERNMENT: Business Development, Trade and Investment

The Northwest Territories, Department of Resources, Wildlife and Economic Development promotes economic self-sufficiency and growth through the sustainable development of natural resources and enhances the creation of new opportunities in the traditional and wage economies.

The Department has a staff of almost 300 and posts vacancies on its Web site related to environment, parks and tourism, economic development, wildlife and fisheries, policy, legislation and communications, and human resources. [ID:7209]

Nova Scotia Business Inc. (NSBI)

P.O. Box 2374, Suite 520, 1800 Argyle Street, Halifax, NS, B3J 3E4, Canada;
902-424-6650, fax 902-424-5739, nsbi@gov.ns.ca, www.novascotiabusiness.com

MID-SIZED, PROVINCIAL CROWN CORPORATION: Business Development, Trade and Investment

Nova Scotia Business Inc. (NSBI) is a business-focused, private sector-led organization charged with bringing fresh ideas and new energy to the work of helping companies grow and, in turn, expanding economic choices for all Nova Scotians. NSBI focuses on attracting new businesses to the province, helping established companies expand, identifying global business opportunities, assisting new exporters to find markets for their goods and services, and providing financial products and services that help Nova Scotian companies expand. Nova Scotia Business Inc. has 65 employees. Most have backgrounds in commerce, business, marketing, finance and international relations. Vacancies are posted on its Web site [ID:7149]

Ontario Ministry of Economic Development and Trade

8th Floor, Hearst Block, 900 Bay Street, Toronto, ON, M7A 2E1, Canada;
416-325-6666, fax 416-325-6688, info@edt.gov.on.ca, www.ontariocanada.com ▫ℱr

MID-SIZED, PROVINCIAL GOVERNMENT: Business Development, Trade and Investment

The mandate of the Ontario Ministry of Economic Development and Trade is to promote economic growth within the province of Ontario. Faced with an increasingly competitive global marketplace, the Ministry aims to accomplish this by creating a culture of innovation, promoting investment and expanding exports to world markets.

The Ministry includes several offices that promote Ontario's economic interests throughout the world. The Office of International Relations and Protocol (OIRP) provides the government with policy advice concerning Ontario's international interests and activities. It works to advance Ontario's position with International Trade Canada (ITCan), foreign countries and jurisdictions and with international organizations. The OIRP serves as the Ontario government's point of contact with over 100 diplomatic and consular representatives in the province and provides guidance on international protocol practices. Its Protocol section advises on and manages the organization of royal and official visits, trade delegations and government conferences.

The OIRP's staff have backgrounds in fields such as international relations, economics, commerce and marketing. Vacancies are posted on the Government of Ontario Web site. [ID:7212]

Privy Council Office (PCO)

Room 1000, 85 Sparks Street, Ottawa, ON, K1A 0A3, Canada;
613-957-5153, fax 613-995-0101, info@pco-bcp.gc.ca, www.pco-bcp.gc.ca ▫ℱr

MID-SIZED, FEDERAL GOVERNMENT: Policy Development

The Privy Council Office (PCO) is both the Cabinet secretariat and the prime minister's source of public service advice across the entire spectrum of policy questions and operational issues facing the government. PCO provides the prime minister with advice on the most pressing national security, foreign and defence policy issues. It also provides support to the PM when he meets with leaders and representatives of other countries and international organizations.

Most of PCO's staff are senior public servants with significant experience. About 20 staff have international responsibilities and work on Canada's most important and sensitive international files. Typically they have a master's degree with extensive research, policy and international experience. Positions are usually filled from within the public service, but occasionally jobs are advertised on the PSC Web site, particularly for regional experts. [ID:7148]

Public Safety and Emergency Preparedness Canada (PSEPC)
340 Laurier Ave. W., Ottawa, ON, K1A 0P8, Canada; 613-991-3283,
fax 613-990-9077, communications@psepc-sppcc.gc.ca, www.psepc-sppcc.gc.ca 💻*Fr*

MID-SIZED, FEDERAL GOVERNMENT: Computer Systems, Telecommunications

Public Safety and Emergency Preparedness Canada (PSEPC) is a new federal department responsible for protecting Canadians and maintaining a safe, peaceful society. It brings together the core functions of national security, emergency preparedness, crisis management, corrections, policing, crime prevention and border services.

PSEPC's International Relations Division works closely with foreign governments (particularly the United States) and multinational organizations, such as the OECD and NATO, to protect critical infrastructure from physical or cyberthreats. These international partnerships allow for the exchange of best practices and early detection of potential threats. [ID:7146]

Public Service Commission
21st Floor, West Tower, L'Esplanade Laurier, 300 Laurier Ave. W., Ottawa, ON,
K1A 0M7, Canada; 613-996-8436, fax 613-954-7541, www.psc-cfp.gc.ca/jobs.htm 💻*Fr*

LARGE, FEDERAL GOVERNMENT:

See the detailed profile at the beginning of this chapter. [ID:7204]

Québec: Ministère des Relations internationales (MRI)
525, boul. René-Lévesque est, Édifice Hector-Fabre, Quebec, QC, G1R 5R9, Canada;
418-649-2300, fax 418-649-2656, communications@mri.gouv.qc.ca, www.mri.gouv.qc.ca 💻*Sp* 💻*En*

LARGE, PROVINCIAL GOVERNMENT: Administration (General), Commerce, Culture, Economics, Law, Management, Science and Technology, Tourism

Le ministère des Relations internationales dirige l'action internationale du gouvernement de manière à promouvoir et défendre les intérêts et les valeurs du Québec Il contribue ainsi, par sa mission, à la prospérité, à l'affirmation de l'identité et à la sécurité de la société québécoise ainsi qu'à son rayonnement sur le plan international.

Actif à l'étranger depuis le XIXe siècle, le gouvernement du Québec s'est donné depuis 1967 un ministère spécialisé dans les rapports avec l'étranger, en particulier dans les relations avec les gouvernements et les organisations internationales.

Pour accomplir sa mission, le ministère conseille le gouvernement, planifie, organise et dirige son action à l'étranger ainsi que celle de ses ministères et organismes, et coordonne leurs activités au Québec en matière de relations internationales. À cet égard, il peut convenir, avec chacun des ministres concernés, de modalités de collaboration.

Le ministère assure les communications officielles du gouvernement avec les gouvernements étrangers et les organisations internationales; il dirige la représentation du Québec à l'étranger. Il veille aux négociations internationales et au respect de la compétence constitutionnelle du Québec dans les engagements internationaux. Le rapport annuel contient les données sur les réalisations du ministère, sur les programmes et sur les ressources humaines, matérielles et financières dont il dispose pour réaliser son mandat.

Les Ressources Humaines

L'effectif du ministère s'établit à plus de 652 employés à temps complet. 374 personnes travaillent au siège du Ministère, soit 357 à Québec et 17 à Montréal. 278 personnes travaillent outre-mer, dont 70 fonctionnaires et 208 employés recrutés localement où sont situées les représentations du Québec à l'étranger (ces employés sont soit des Canadiens résidant à l'étranger, soit des citoyens du pays visé).

Le ministère poursuit ses démarches pour renouveler son personnel en ayant recours à des listes de déclarations d'aptitudes issues de concours de recrutement universitaire et collégial. Toute personne intéressée peut faire parvenir sa candidature et son curriculum vitae à la direction des ressources humaines du ministère des Relations internationales. La direction les informera alors des possibles concours de recrutement ouverts aux candidats qui ne font pas déjà partie de la fonction publique québécoise.

Le Réseau

Les bureaux du gouvernement à l'étranger assurent des fonctions de représentation et renseignent le gouvernement sur le sens des développements économiques, politiques ou sociaux susceptibles d'avoir des incidences sur le Québec. Ils constituent une base d'intervention pour la prospection de ressources (immigration, investissements, etc.) et la promotion du Québec comme terre d'accueil et en tant que partenaire gouvernemental. Dans les pays où le Québec détient des ententes de coopération avec le gouvernement, la représentation contribue à en faciliter l'application. Le représentant du Québec est le porte-parole officiel et l'interlocuteur des autorités publiques dans le pays d'accueil, et veille à la transmission des communications envoyées par les autorités québécoises.

C'est également le rôle des représentations d'offrir l'infrastructure, la coordination et l'accompagnement nécessaires aux autorités québécoises, ainsi qu'aux responsables et aux experts de l'Administration gouvernementale, en mission à l'étranger. Ces établissements constituent aussi une source de références et de soutien pour les particuliers et les entreprises qui souhaitent faire affaire sur le territoire couvert.

Les fonctions et le statut administratif des différentes représentations varient selon les villes ou les pays. Selon leurs attributions, elles peuvent traiter notamment les questions économiques et commerciales, l'immigration, les affaires culturelles, l'éducation, le tourisme, les relations institutionnelles et la coopération intergouvernementale, en plus d'assurer de façon générale la promotion du Québec. La charge de délégué général comporte la capacité de représenter le Québec dans tous les secteurs d'activités qui sont de compétence constitutionnelle du Québec.

Les délégations générales et les délégations sont dirigées par un représentant (délégué général, délégué). D'autres bureaux du Québec sont dirigés par des fonctionnaires affectés par le ministre des Relations internationales.

Le gouvernement du Québec possède 28 représentations à l'étranger, soit 6 délégations générales (la plus complète des représentations du Québec à l'étranger), 4 délégations, 9 bureaux, 6 antennes et 3 agents d'affaires. Le Québec dispose de délégations générales à Bruxelles, Londres, Mexico, New York, Paris, Tokyo. Les quatre délégations se trouvent à Boston, Buenos Aires, Chicago, Los Angeles. Les bureaux, antennes et agents d'affaires se trouvent dans les plus grandes régions du monde.

Les Stages Jeunesse

Différents stages sont offerts dans un autre pays ou dans une organisation internationale. Pour plus d'informations, consulter le site Internet du ministère. Deux types de programmes de stages sont proposés : Québec sans frontière est un programme de stages pour les personnes qui s'intéressent à la coopération internationale. Chaque année, plus de 400 jeunes âgés de 18 à 35 ans participent à ce programme et vivent une expérience de solidarité internationale en Afrique francophone, en Amérique latine ou au Québec, au sein d'un organisme de coopération internationale. Des jeunes des pays du Sud (actifs au sein d'organismes partenaires) peuvent également participer en venant effectuer un stage au Québec.

Le programme des Stages dans les organisations internationales s'adresse aux universitaires de 2e et 3e cycles qui désirent vivre une expérience d'initiation au marché du travail international. Une cinquantaine de stages par année sont organisés à la suite des engagements du gouvernement pris après la tenue du Sommet du Québec et de la jeunesse en février 2000. Voici quelques-unes des organisations associées au ministère des Relations internationales : Organisation des Nations Unies pour l'éducation, la science et la culture (UNESCO), Organisation mondiale de la santé, Organisation de coopération et de développement économiques (OCDE), Organisation universitaire interaméricaine (OUI). [ID:7334]

Radio Canada International - Canadian Broadcasting Corporation (RCI-CBC)

International Programming, 1400 boul. René-Lévesque est, Montreal, QC,
H2L 2M2, Canada; 514-597-7500, fax 514-284-9550, info@rcinet.ca, www.rcinet.ca ▢*Fr*▢*Sp*

LARGE, FEDERAL CROWN CORPORATION: Information Technologies, Telecommunications

Radio Canada International (RCI) is the external short-wave radio service of the CBC that transmits radio programming abroad. It provides international audiences with programs reflecting Canadian life and culture, national interests and policies, and a spectrum of Canadian viewpoints on national and international affairs. The service broadcasts news, information and entertainment programs from the English and French domestic networks. Programs are in English, French, Russian, Ukrainian, Spanish, Mandarin and Arabic.

Broadcasts are aimed at audiences in Europe, Asia, Latin America, the Caribbean, the Middle East, Africa and the US. RCI has approximately 120 staff members, all of whom are based in Canada, with the majority working in programming.

Minimum requirements for journalists and announcer-producers include a university degree, five years of relevant experience, fluency in English and French, as well as the appropriate third language for those working in foreign-language sections, and knowledge of Canadian and international affairs. Opportunities arise from time to time for freelance journalists, analysts, and commentators. Freelancers are commissioned in Canada.

RCI has a very interesting Web site that offers real-time audio news in several languages as well as a wealth of information on the organization's activities. [ID:7196]

Rights and Democracy (The International Centre for Human Rights and Democratic Development)

1100 suite, 1001 boul. de Maisonneuve est, Montreal, QC, H2L 4P9, Canada;
514-283-6073, fax 514-283-3792, ichrdd@ichrdd.ca, www.ichrdd.ca ▢*Fr*▢*Sp*

MID-SIZED, INSTITUTE/RESEARCH COUNCIL: Advocacy, Gender and Development, Human Rights

Rights and Democracy is a non-profit, non-partisan, charitable organization that was created by, but operates at arm's length from, Canada's government. Through its programs, Rights and Democracy supports universal values of human rights and promotes democratic ideals throughout the world. Its partnerships with various stakeholders uniquely place it to act as an intermediary between civil society organizations and governments in Canada and abroad. Rights and Democracy's global programs focus on four themes: democratic development, women's human rights, globalization and human rights, and the rights of Indigenous Peoples.

Rights and Democracy has 29 staff members and posts vacancies and internship opportunities on its Web site. Applicants should have a university degree in a relevant field, knowledge of human rights issues and international human rights protection mechanisms and organizations. Knowledge of and experience with non-governmental organizations, computer literacy and, in some cases, languages other than English and French are also required. [ID:7172]

Royal Canadian Mounted Police (RCMP)

RCMP Headquarters - Public Information Branch, Room 316, 1200 Vanier Parkway,
Ottawa, ON, K1A 0R2, Canada; 613-993-7267, fax 613-993-5894, www.rcmp-grc.gc.ca ▢*Fr*

MID-SIZED, FEDERAL AGENCY: Intelligence and Security

The Royal Canadian Mounted Police (RCMP) maintains a network of 36 Liaison Officers in 20 locations around the world. RCMP members serve as points of contact for law enforcement matters, working from various Canadian missions (embassies, high commissions, and consulates general). The liaison officers also assist foreign police services in the exchange of investigative or police-related information pertaining to Canada. Each liaison officer is responsible for pursuing Canadian law enforcement interests in numerous countries of accreditation.

Liaison officers are regular members or peace officers of the RCMP, and are selected for foreign assignment based on their specific policing experience and ability to work effectively in a complex international environment. Experience in the following areas are considered prerequisites for service in the International Operations Branch: drugs and organized crime, financial crime, border integrity, international policing, national security and major case investigations. The ability to communicate effectively in both of Canada's offical languages, as well as those used in the areas of foreign coverage are a definite asset. The RCMP's Web site offers information on the force and provides recruiting information for interested parties. [ID:7198]

Saskatchewan Institute of Applied Science and Technology (SIAST)
International Services Division, P.O. Box 556, Albert South Centre, Regina, SK, S4P 3A3, Canada; 306-787-0113, fax 306-787-4840, international@siast.sk.ca, www.siast.sk.ca

LARGE, INSTITUTE/RESEARCH COUNCIL: Technical Assistance

The Saskatchewan Institute of Applied Science and Technology (SIAST) is a leader in superior education, focused on students and lifelong learning—a catalyst for advancing the social and economic prosperity of Saskatchewan. SIAST employs more than 1,500 staff.

In Canada, the International Services Division of SIAST promotes development awareness within the broader institution. Over the past 15 years, International Services has delivered technical and vocational education and training services in over 33 countries, providing international working opportunities for faculty, staff, students and graduates. Currently, SIAST has projects in Africa, the Caribbean, South Asia, Southeast Asia and China.

The Institute works closely with the Association of Canadian Community Colleges and the Canadian International Development Agency on its international projects. Consultants and interns are hired on a project-by-project basis. Vacancies are advertised on SIAST's Web site and applicants can apply to positions through SIAST's e-recruitment system. It also maintains a resume databank for international consultants. Applicants must have cross-cultural sensitivity and flexibility, along with strong academic and professional credentials in their particular fields. Currently, there are six staff in Canada with international responsibilities. [ID:7199]

Saskatchewan Trade and Export Partnership (STEP)
P.O. Box 1787, 320 - 1801 Hamilton Street, Regina, SK, S4P 3C6, Canada; 306-787-9210, fax 306-787-6666, inquire@sasktrade.sk.ca, www.sasktrade.sk.ca 💻*Sp*

MID-SIZED, PROVINCIAL CROWN CORPORATION: Business Development, Trade and Investment

Saskatchewan Trade and Export Partnership (STEP) is a non-profit, membership driven, industry-government partnership that promotes the growth of Saskatchewan's export industry. STEP assists provincial businesses to realize global marketing opportunities through specially tailored services and programs. STEP pursues growth in existing foreign markets and opens doors to new ones. Members include both businesses that are experienced and those that are new to international trade. STEP's team of over 30 professionals have international business experience and knowledge. Vacancies are posted on its very informative Web site. [ID:7210]

Social Sciences and Humanities Research Council of Canada (SSHRC)
P.O. Box 1610, Constitution Square, 350 Albert Street, Ottawa, ON, K1P 6G4, Canada; 613-992-0691, fax 613-992-1787, z-info@sshrc.ca, www.sshrc.ca 💻*Fr*

LARGE, INSTITUTE/RESEARCH COUNCIL: Research, Social Science Research

The Social Sciences and Humanities Research Council (SSHRC) is a federal agency that promotes and supports university-based research and training in the social sciences and humanities. SSHRC-funded research fuels innovative thinking about real-life issues including economy, education, health care, the environment, immigration, globalization, language, ethics, peace, security, human rights, law, poverty, mass communication, politics, literature, addiction, pop culture, sexuality, religion, Aboriginal rights, the past and our future.

The SSHRC has 150 employees, all based in Ottawa. It offers several programs for researchers interested in exploring issues concerning globalization and international relations. Post-graduate students should visit the SSHRC Web site to learn about awards available to master's and doctoral students who are citizens or permanent residents of Canada. The Web site also includes a careers section where vacancies are posted. Generally SSHRC recruits for individuals with at least an honours bachelor degree in the humanities or social sciences and knowledge of the university research environment. They must also be familiar with the work of other granting agencies active at the national or international level. The Council also recruits, from time to time, specialists in information technology, Web design, electronic services delivery, public policy, statistics, accounting, graphic design and journalism. [ID:7200]

Statistics Canada (SC)

International Relations Division, 25th Floor, R.H. Coats Bldg., Tunney's Pasture, Ottawa, ON, K1A 0T6, Canada; 613-951-8917, fax 613-951-1231, infostats@statcan.ca, www.statcan.ca 🖵 *Fr*

MID-SIZED, FEDERAL GOVERNMENT: Accounting, Economics, Social Science Research, Statistics

Statistics Canada's International Relations Division supports and advises the agency's senior management on matters of international relations and participates in a wide range of international statistical activities with the objective of improving the Canadian statistical system through bilateral and multilateral consultation. The nine members of the division are also responsible for overseeing the delivery of technical assistance in its fields of competence to governmental entities in foreign countries and to international organizations on a cost-recovery basis.

Statistic Canada's Web site includes an employment section that details the post-secondary recruitment campaigns that target economists and mathematical statisticians. [ID:7201]

Telefilm Canada (TFC)

Suite 700, 360 St. Jacques Street, Montreal, QC, H2Y 4A9, Canada; 514-283-6363, fax 514-283-8212, www.telefilm.gc.ca 🖵 *Fr*

SMALL, FEDERAL CROWN CORPORATION: Culture, Marketing, Media/Communications

Telefilm Canada is a federal cultural agency dedicated to the development and promotion of the Canadian film, television, new media and music industries. With the objective of building larger audiences for Canadian cultural products, the corporation acts as a partner to the private sector through investments in diverse productions with wide appeal.

Telefilm Canada's International Operations ensures that the Canadian industry is a competitive player on the global scene. It oversees a number of activities, ranging from certifying official co-productions to coordinating Canada's presence at international festivals and markets.

Employment opportunities and information about working with Telefilm Canada are posted on its Web site. [ID:7202]

Yukon Department of Economic Development

P.O. Box 2703, Whitehorse, YK, Y1A 2C6, Canada; 867-393-7014, fax 867-393-6944, ecdev@gov.yk.ca, www.economicdevelopment.gov.yk.ca

MID-SIZED, PROVINCIAL GOVERNMENT: Business Development, Trade and Investment

The Yukon Department of Economic Development provides trade and investment services and promotes new development opportunities in all of Yukon's economic sectors including information technology, service industries, natural resources, construction, film production, energy innovation, tourism, infrastructure and telecommunications. It is particularly active working with other agencies in the natural resource sector and facilitating new business opportunities with Yukon's First Nations and the private sector. The Department of Economic Development also provides a wide range of statistical forecasts, reviews and reports related to the Yukon economy.

The Department employs approximately 30 people. All recruitment is coordinated through the Public Service Commission. Job postings are listed on the home page of the Yukon government (www.employment.gov.yk.ca). [ID:7211]

CHAPTER 38

NGOs in Canada

Thousands of groups based in the North operate worldwide on a non-profit basis in the public interest. These groups are known as "non-governmental organizations" or NGOs. In the field of international development, they are usually volunteer agencies, working in partnership with like-minded groups in developing countries for social justice, human rights, HIV/AIDS prevention, environmental initiatives and the eradication of poverty. Unions, religious institutions, professional associations, cooperatives, and research departments of universities and colleges also operate as NGOs. This chapter profiles 223 Canadian NGOs—the most extensive list anywhere.

Canada is known throughout the world as having one of the most extensive government-supported NGO sectors, and non-government grassroots organizations now operate in Europe, USA and Australia. Working for Canadian or foreign NGOs is possible, especially if you have language skills or other special skills that may be in short supply. (For more information and profiles on non-Canadian NGOs, see Chapter 39, NGOs in the US; and Chapter 40, NGOs in Europe & the Rest of the World.)

A BRIEF HISTORY OF NGOs

Long before any official Canadian government involvement in foreign aid programs, Canadian volunteer agencies were at work in developing countries. While missionary groups were active before the turn of the century, the first Canadian government aid program, the Colombo Plan, wasn't launched until the post–World War II era of the early 1950s.

In 1968 the federal CANADIAN INTERNATIONAL DEVELOPMENT AGENCY (CIDA) was established. Within CIDA, a non-governmental organizations (NGO) division was set up, with a mandate to promote Canadian participation in development activities, provide government assistance to nations through non-governmental channels, and tap the expertise and resources of non-governmental sectors for development purposes.

In the 1990s, CIDA's NGO division encouraged and facilitated the participation of Canadians in international development by co-financing projects and programs of autonomous Canadian NGOs that are compatible with Canadian foreign and development policies. It also supported the efforts of people in the South, particularly the least privileged, to meet their basic human needs and to improve their quality of life through sustainable development, a development process that supports the use of local resources.

NGOs have traditionally been regarded as an effective alternative to government aid programs, mainly because they are exempt from some of the constraints involved in government-to-government (bilateral) aid. NGOs are generally better able to work at the grassroots level and are flexible in the type of work they engage in. Most recently, work is being done in partnership with Southern-based NGOs or local people's movements. It is also common to find a range of small to large NGOs with well-defined socio-political agendas that consider issues such as HIV/AIDS, gender, micro-enterprise, and democracy and good governance. Given the current unstable political climate, collapse of urban infrastructures and environmental ecosystems, terrorism, and increase of refugees from war-torn countries, many NGOs have reverted back to providing primary health, education and small-income-generating activities.

WHO FUNDS NGOs?

The NGO community has grown, with increasing public support and government funding. NGOs receive much of their funding through government channels. It now administers some 20 per cent of Canada's official development assistance (ODA) to developing countries. However, the strength of NGOs depends greatly on financial donations from individuals and private businesses. Not only do these donations contribute substantially to the programming capacity of NGOs, but they also indicate to government that the Canadian public values the goals and activities of NGOs. We strongly recommend that you become a regular donor or volunteer with an NGO. Making a regular contribution to a large organization such as CARE CANADA, CUSO or OXFAM, or a smaller group like WATERCAN or INTER PARES, will go a long way! Your support is needed.

CIDA's contribution to NGOs has remained fairly constant since the late 1980s. In 1996–1997 CIDA supported approximately 250 NGOs through various thematic and regional programs. CIDA's NGO division respects the independence, integrity and personality of NGOs, and seldom provides more than a part of the funds necessary for a project or program. Generally, CIDA supplements funds raised by the NGOs through a matching grant system. Project/program planning, implementation and management, and liaison with countries in the South are the responsibility of the NGO.

THE WORK OF NGOs OVERSEAS

NGOs have historically been linked in the public mind with emergency aid. Less attention has been given to the principal work of NGOs: long-term development and advocacy on behalf of Southern NGOs and people's movements. NGOs strive to head off famine and environmental disintegration by promoting health, education, food self-sufficiency and other basic needs. They have become effective innovators in the field of development and have demonstrated an edge over government in effectiveness due to their closeness to the people and their community-based approach.

The current wisdom among NGOs is to respond to requests for assistance from like-minded groups in the South rather than to initiate projects. Community-based, or so-called grassroots activities, refer to projects that are initiated indigenously, and embraced and directed by the people themselves. More and more, NGOs are listening to what people in the developing countries have to say about their own development. They act increasingly as advocates on behalf of their developing country partners, often placing on their agendas broad causes such as disarmament, social justice, HIV/AIDS drug rights, gender equality issues and genetic patenting of plant species,. As such, they have come to be known as global goodwill ambassadors.

NGO workers typically receive the lowest salaries in the international field, although these days many development workers have adopted the formal attire and customs of the business world. While NGOs remain committed to working on the front line of development, you may be hard pressed to find the sandals and backpacks of the past.

APPLYING FOR A JOB

Given the limited resources available to most NGOs, it is important for them to be as efficient and effective as possible in their activities. For this reason, most people who are employed in NGOs are highly-skilled, motivated individuals. Finding a job within the NGO community is very challenging, but certainly not impossible. The following tips will assist you in your job search strategy.

If you are a graduate in international studies, be conservative in your expectations of finding work in the areas of development policy or planning economic models. The work of development is 80 per cent administration, no matter where you work, and no matter what sector of international development you work in. Most overseas NGO employees must be able to write a project work plan, formulate budgets, understand basic accounting systems, fundraise and create personnel policies.

Consider the other special skills required for grassroots development: advocacy, community relations, facilitation, community-building and negotiating skills, organizing, organizing, and more organizing. It helps to be a proficient writer and public speaker. It is also beneficial to be fluent in two languages and be willing to learn others throughout your career.

Be strategic, creative and proactive when approaching NGOs. You can obtain information on job opportunities among member organizations of coordinating bodies such as the CANADIAN COUNCIL FOR INTERNATIONAL CO-OPERATION (CCIC) or its provincial councils in British Columbia, Saskatchewan, Manitoba, Ontario and the Atlantic region. Other provincial councils are the DEVELOPMENT EDUCATION CO-ORDINATING COUNCIL OF ALBERTA (DECCA), and ASSOCIATION QUÉBÉCOISE DES ORGANISMES DE COOPÉRATION INTERNATIONALE (AQOCI). Other leads can be found on Web sites such as www.charityvillage.com, www.careerswithoutborders, www.dev-zone.org, www.canadem.ca, and www.devnetjobs.org. (For more information, see the NGO Job Boards Resources in Chapter 30, Careers in International Development.)

JOBS OVERSEAS

Many development groups are shifting away from overseas program support toward fundraising and advocacy work on behalf of an increasing number of partner NGOs based in developing countries. Even for jobs in Canada, many of the NGOs listed here demand previous experience overseas. Consider first supporting yourself through volunteering or internships overseas. (See Chapter 10, Short-Term Programs Overseas and Chapter 17, Internships Abroad.)

Many opportunities abroad still remain, but stringent hiring requirements reflect the increasing tendency of developing countries to train and hire indigenous development workers. Six major Canadian NGOs send skilled volunteers or cooperants to developing countries; they are VSO, CCI, CUSO, WUSC, CECI and OxFAM-QUÉBEC. (For a detailed description of each organization, see the Profiles section at the end of this chapter.) Note that while the working language of these organizations is either English or French, all six organizations work in both French- and English-speaking developing countries. The average volunteer is approximately 37 years old and has accumulated technical or professional experience in Canada. Assignments usually last for two years. NGOs work in a variety of fields; for example, VSO Canada works in international development and recruits volunteers from more than 80 occupations including health professionals, teachers, business advisors, IT specialists, social and community workers, and technical and natural resource professionals. (For more information on VSO Canada, see their ad in the sponsor section at the end of this guide. Also, see their profile at the end of this chapter.)

NGO staff tend to integrate more with the local population than employees of the UN, CIDA or industry, a compensatory consequence of their lower salaries and general commitment to grassroots development. Take time to get to know your hosts and absorb the popular culture—in itself a rewarding experience! Learn their needs and aim for mutual confidence and co-operation. Bring a sense of humour, patience and tolerance. Before you go, ask yourself: Are you aware of your personal needs and limitations while under stress? Do you open up easily to others? Are you naturally relaxed, positive and non-judgmental? Can you sustain this positive outlook in hot, sticky climates while barraged by unfamiliar sights, sounds, smells and customs?

VOLUNTEERING IN CANADA

A sure-fire way of finding work is to demonstrate volunteer leadership in almost any international or cross-cultural organization. Some people get hired by NGOs after doing extensive volunteer work with them. Get active with local committees of the CANADIAN CATHOLIC ORGANIZATION FOR DEVELOPMENT AND PEACE, CANADIAN CROSSROADS INTERNATIONAL, UNICEF, etc. Confirm your commitment to yourself—don't do it just to pad your resume. Most NGO workers have a long history of volunteering in the international community.

Investigate local activities such as benefits and awareness-raising events. Volunteer to billet visitors to Canada from developing countries. (See Chapter 11,

Hosting Programs.) Join or initiate NGO advocacy campaigns if you want to directly influence economic and social progress. Get involved in NGO community outreach programs that form the foundation of public support. NGOs have pioneered many new approaches—including global education, Canada–South twinning programs between communities, and organizational partnerships and networks. (For an excellent example of an organizational partnership twinning program, see CANADIAN CROSSROADS INTERNATIONAL (CCI) in the Profiles section at the end of this chapter.)

WORDS OF ADVICE

NGOs have some key suggestions regarding the appropriate attitude and experience for those contemplating working in the challenging field of overseas grassroots development. Much of the advice given by NGOs is related to the attitude an individual must possess to adapt well to a new culture. The first step is to ask yourself why you want a career working in developing countries—then learn as much as you can about the part of the world that interests you. It is important to go with an open mind. No amount of professional training will prepare you for the different life you will live. Be willing to adjust to whatever the circumstances require, and don't expect others to adjust to you. The old cliché, "When in Rome, do as the Romans do," certainly rings true for Canadians working overseas. Living and working in the ways of your host country expands your understanding and lets you grow by leaps and bounds.

Other advice given by NGOs is linked to the underlying philosophy and goal of their activities. Most NGOs work towards a more just and equitable global community, and place importance on human dignity and self-determination of the communities in which they work. So, as a Canadian working overseas, you must direct your first efforts to learning from the poor and the marginalized. Never assume that more sophisticated technology will improve the lifestyles of those you seek to help. Let indigenous people teach you their ways and inform you of their own needs—do not teach them your way and attribute needs to them that are not their own. In other words, don't bring a superior Western attitude, but be willing to learn and share ideas and expertise. Development work is a process by which local people increase control over the decisions that affect their lives. Active involvement and full participation of the local people—men and women—is crucial to the success of any development activity.

Working on a project overseas requires a great deal of flexibility. Don't expect to have all the necessary tools, equipment and materials that would be readily available in your home country. Instead, you must adapt easily to the environment and to the help that is available there. Set realistic goals and expectations of what can be accomplished during your one- or two-year posting. It is virtually impossible to make radical changes in the short term. Be certain of your commitment before taking on a position. The scope of responsibilities involved, and the limited financial and other resources of most international development NGOs mean that they cannot afford drop-outs.

And most importantly, have a sense of humour! You most probably will need it.

A LAST WORD

Ask most staff members of an NGO how to establish a career in international development, and you will learn first that competition in this field is fierce; however, there are a variety of ways that individuals can beat the competition and gain valuable experience.

First, to start a career in international development it is often necessary to have work experience in a developing country. This prerequisite is often attainable only through a volunteer experience that requires a sacrifice in terms of financial compensation. However, the other rewards more than make up for this short-term sacrifice.

If you are unable to go overseas as a volunteer, one way to gain international development exposure is to get involved in development-related activities in Canada, even as a volunteer. The activity can be focused on international or domestic development issues. Be knowledgable and skilful in your particular area of endeavour. It is also important to demonstrate your ability and interest in broadening your horizons, both personally and professionally. Increasingly, agencies are looking for people who already have some understanding of development issues or development-related experience prior to their placements overseas.

In terms of formal academic qualifications, it is valuable to have a university degree that has a practical application overseas, such as administration, nursing, medicine, teaching or engineering. Many academic programs offer an optional or sometimes mandatory field experience component as part of their "hands-on" approach to education. If after gaining practical experience overseas you feel like you still want to work in the area of international development, NGO management, or political studies, pursue a master's degree in this or a related field. You almost certainly have to complete an internship to start off your career.

As NGOs continue to expand, change their focus and diversify their interests, less traditional fields are just as critical to overseas projects. Professionals with backgrounds in law, business, information technology, public relations and media are needed to contribute to specific NGO requests.

RESOURCES

CANADIAN NGOS

All of these NGO resources are related to Canada.

Aid As a Peacemaker: Canadian Development Assistance and Third World Conflict 📖
1994, Robert Miller, 224 pages ➤ McGill-Queen's University Press, 3430 McTavish Street, Montreal, QC H3A 1X9, Canada, www.mqup.mcgill.ca, $19.95 CDN; VISA, MC; 514-398-3750, fax 514-398-4333 ◆ Does development by its nature produce conflict? Are there times when Canada should take sides in Third World conflict? Are there ways that Canadian aid can be used to promote peace? Experts in Third World development pursue answers to these questions. Still apropos and interesting as a priimer on Canadian aid and the nexus between development and conflict. [ID:2163]

Association of Universities and Colleges of Canada ♦♦♦
www.aucc.ca ◆ AUCC and its 93 member universities have carried out more than 2,000 international development projects in the past 30 years. The focus is on international opportunities that enhance other countries' resources and lead to improvements in their living standards. AUCC

also administers more than 150 scholarship, fellowship and internship programs on behalf of governments, foundations and private sector companies. Each year more than 3,500 scholarships are delivered to young people interested in pursuing higher education. The site is well-designed; searching for scholarships or university programs is a breeze. [ID:2148]

Au Courrant 💻
Semi-annual ➤ Canadian Council for International Cooperation (CCIC), Suite 300, 1 Nicholas Street, Ottawa, ON K1N 7B7, Canada, www.ccic.ca, Free on-line; VISA; 613-241-7007, fax 613-241-5302 ◆ This bilingual newsletter is a source of news, analysis and opinion on official development aid, foreign policy, domestic and international economic policy. Available online on CCIC's Web site. [ID:2029]

Bridges of Hope? Canadian Voluntary Agencies and the Third World 📖
1988, Tim Brodhead, 173 pages ➤ North-South Institute, Suite 200, 55 Murray Street, Ottawa, ON K1N 5M3, Canada, www.nsi-ins.ca, $14 CDN; Credit Cards; 613-241-3535, fax 613-241-7435 ◆ An excellent Canadian book summarizing a two-year study of Canadian NGOs. Assesses NGO effectiveness, strengths and weaknesses and provides recommendations. A great primer on the efficacy of the NGO system of overseas development. [ID:2062]

Canada's Council to End Global Poverty 💻
www.ccic.ca ◆ This Canadian Web site is an excellent resource for searching jobs in international development and educating yourself on global poverty issues. There's a good job board that is frequently updated and worth checking periodically. The site offers an outstanding resources page containing an extensive collection of PDF documents on gender, ethics, peace building, trade and poverty, and Canadian foreign policy, to name just a few. Start networking with over 100 NGO member organizations all over Canada and find the development job you want! [ID:2630]

Canadian Development Report 2003 📖
Annual, North-South Institute, 112 pages ➤ Renouf Publishing Co. Ltd., Unit 1, 5369 Canotek Road, Ottawa, ON K1J 9J3, Canada, www.renoufbooks.com, $30 CDN; Credit Cards; 888-767-6766, fax 613-745-7660 ◆ This report looks at multilateral trade arrangements from the perspectives of both the North and the South. Highlights development issues such as those regarding market access and the WTO Intellectual Property Agreement. Includes up-to-date statistics and analyses related to social and economic indicators of developing countries along with statistics regarding the Canadian government's trade-related involvement with developing countries. A valuable reference tool for students and international job seekers with interests in development and trade. [ID:2260]

Canadian International Development Agency (CIDA) 👪
www.acdi-cida.gc.ca; Fr ◆ This bilingual Canadian government Web site provides a thorough overview of Canada's international development activities. Here you will find detailed information on CIDAs official policies, publications and programs. There are informative sections profiling regions and countries of the world where CIDA is active, youth internships, and all aspects of the CIDA project cycle, including how businesses can access development assistance grants. International job seekers looking to work in overseas development will benefit from the information and useful links to other development agencies and development organizations. [ID:2233]

Care Canada 👪
www.care.ca; Fr ◆ This site gives detailed job information not only about positions with Care Canada, but also about overseas work in general. In its "Job Centre" sub-directory, you will find information on the employment sectors Care is involved in, important characteristics for overseas work, current job openings, internship programs and overseas volunteer opportunities. You can submit your resume into a database and instantly be considered for upcoming job openings with this internationally respected organization. [ID:2223]

Careers Without Borders ▣

Careers Without Borders, Suite 100, 9 Gurdwara Road, Ottawa, ON K2E 7X6, Canada, www.careerswithoutborders.com, 800-965-1830 ◆ This Ottawa site bills itself as the first central recruitment site devoted to assisting both development professionals seeking international jobs and development organizations seeking new recruits. It allows you to create your on-line profile and resume, after which the database is scanned regularly, matching development professionals to international jobs. You can also browse "Current Openings" and apply to as many as you like. Apply on-line and receive an automatic confirmation every time. A great new site with lots of features and advice that promises soon to be a fixture on international ID job seekers' favourites lists. (For more information, see their ad in the sponsor section at the end of this guide.) [ID:2762]

The Communication Initiative ▣

www.comminit.com/vacancies.html ◆ This Canadian Web site is the main initiative of the Communications Initiative's (CI's) mandate to foster dialogue and debate on development issues. The job board is updated daily with interesting and challenging positions in the field of development that are not readily found elsewhere. Lots of postings for program managers, public health officials and technical support officers. If it's capacity-building development work you're after, look no further. [ID:2659]

Focus ▣

Quarterly ➤ Canadian Executive Service Organization (CESO), Suite 700, 700 Bay Street, Toronto, ON M5G 1Z6, Canada, www.ceso-saco.com, Free on-line; 416-961-2376, fax 416-961-1096 ◆ This newsletter features articles about the organization's worldwide activities. CESO is a non-governmental voluntary agency that sends Canadians with professional, technical and managerial skills to be volunteer consultants to business organizations in Canadian aboriginal communities and in developing countries. [ID:2030]

In Common Directory ▣

BC Council for International Cooperation (BCCIC) www.bccic.org, Free on-line; ◆ An alphabetical directory of Canadian organizations working toward the common purpose of achieving a more equitable world through involvement in overseas projects, global education and raising public awareness in BC. A fabulous departure point for your research on overseas work with NGOs! Also has a small job board. [ID:2561]

Ngoma: The Talking Drum ▢

Quarterly ➤ CODE, 321 Chapel Street, Ottawa, ON K1N 7Z2, Canada, www.codecan.org, VISA; 613-232-3569, fax 613-232-7435, codehq@codecan.com ◆ Ngoma is the official newsletter of the CODE and is distributed to supporters in Canada and abroad to keep them informed of CODE's literacy-building programs. [ID:2481]

Sustainable Times Webzine ▣

CUSO, Suite 500, 2255 Carling Ave., Ottawa, ON K2B 1A6, Canada, www.cuso.org, 613-829-7445, fax 613-829-7996 ◆ This Web zine explores practical alternatives to the ways business is done. Featuring original articles from Canada and the Third World, the Sustainable Times Web zine is for those seeking down-to-earth answers to our most pressing problems. [ID:2483]

Who's Who in International Development ▢

2003, 316 pages ➤ Canadian Council for International Cooperation (CCIC), Suite 300, 1 Nicholas Street, Ottawa, ON K1N 7B7, Canada, www.ccic.ca, $40 CDN or $25 CDN for CCIC members; VISA; 613-241-7007, fax 613-241-5302; ℱ ◆ This book profiles over 100 Canadian NGOs, providing information on the overseas activities, regions of interests, publications, finances and affliations of each. Includes addresses and personnel, as well as geographical and sector/program bibliographies. [ID:2238]

Profiles of Canadian NGOs

The following is the most extensive list of Canadian NGOs available anywhere. All of them work in international development. There are 223 Canadian NGOs listed in this chapter. NGO profiles are categorized by 20 field types (written in upper case below the address) which are too numerous to mention here.

The greatest concentration of NGO head offices is in Ottawa, with clusters in Montreal and Toronto, which reflects the organizations' continuing dependence on federal government funding. Western Canada has a thin but solid spread of NGOs. A very few NGOs are based in the Maritimes. But even a very remote community can harbour a branch or committee. 63 of the NGOs have their headquarters in Ottawa, with 64 in Toronto, 23 in Montreal, 9 in Quebec City, 10 in Winnipeg and 15 in Vancouver and Victoria. Provincially, the number of NGOs is as follows: Alberta, 8; British Columbia, 20; Manitoba, 11; New Brunswick, 2; Nova Scotia, 2; Ontario, 140; Quebec, 37; Saskatchewan, 2. Many NGOs have regional offices or have local volunteer committees even in the smallest communities.

Action Canada For Population Development (ADPD)

Suite 300, 260 Dalhousie Street, Ottawa, ON, K1N 7E4, Canada;
613-562-0880, fax 613-562-9502, info@acpd.ca, www.acpd.ca 🖥 Fr

MID-SIZED COORDINATING BODY: Advocacy

Action Canada for Population Development (ACPD) is a non-partisan organization that mobilizes public support for international population and development issues. ACPD focuses on the inter-relationships between population growth and structure, the environment, over-consumption, poverty, sexual and reproductive health and rights, gender equity and equality, human rights, migration, economics and other development issues. Through dialogue, education, advocacy and coalition building, ACPD is the only Canadian NGO that promotes the full implementation of the Programme of Action generated at the 1994 International Conference on Population and Development (ICPD). ACPD works with non-governmental organizations throughout the world that share its goals and principles to promote public policy discussion on population and development issues. ACPD has 10 staff members in Canada. [ID:6906]

Adventist Development and Relief Agency Canada (ADRA CANADA)

1148 King Street E., Oshawa, ON, L1H 1H8, Canada; 905-433-8004, fax 905-723-1903, www.adra.ca

MID-SIZED RELIEF AND DEVELOPMENT AGENCY: Adult Training, Agriculture, Community Development, Development Assistance, Gender and Development, Humanitarian Relief, Medical Health, Project Management, Water Resources

The Adventist Development and Relief Agency Canada (ADRA Canada) is the development and relief agency sponsored by the Seventh-day Adventist Church. The ADRA network operates worldwide in over 100 countries while ADRA Canada is currently working in about 40 of these countries. The international projects are mainly concentrated in Africa, Inter-America, South Asia and East Asia. Its relief and development programs include disaster relief, health, agriculture, water and sanitation, education, community and institutional development, and women in development. Through the provision of financial, material and technical resources, ADRA will support, rehabilitate and enhance the quality of life and well-being of underprivileged peoples without reference to their ethnic, political or religious associations. ADRA encourages self-reliance and determination, with particular emphasis upon the needs of the very poor. ADRA also has a national program focusing on community assistance programs in Canada. For the latest information visit their Web site.

ADRA Canada has over a dozen staff in Canada. At present it no longer recruits volunteers. Senior staff have spent some time working overseas and have several years experience in international development. Most senior staff hold university degrees. ADRA does not currently maintain a data bank for resumes. [ID:7007]

Africa Community Technical Service (ACTS)
P.O. Box 1515, Comox, BC, V9N 8A2, Canada;
250-339-1212, fax 250-339-1300, info@acts.ca, www.acts.ca

MID-SIZED COMMUNITY DEVELOPMENT GROUP: Agriculture, Development Assistance, Religious, Technical Assistance, Training and Education, Water Resources

Africa Community Technical Service (ACTS) is a Christian technical mission currently at work in Uganda, East Africa. Volunteers assist rural communities in achieving their development goals in cooperation with the local church. Current development priorities include rural water supply, agroforestry, ecotourism for income generation, and skills transfer. There are 3 staff members in Canada and 15 located overseas depending on the season. Longer-term volunteer postings require Christian commitment and the active support of one's church congregation. ACTS overseas personnel should be prepared and adaptable to meet the challenges of cross-cultural life and work, and possess excellent communication skills. ACTS also offers six-month internships for recent graduates in the social or environmental sciences and engineering, through CIDA's youth internship program. Contact ACTS directly for more information on how you might help. Volunteer postings are listed on their Web site. [ID:6868]

Africa Inland Mission International Canada (AIM)
1641 Victoria Park Ave., Scarborough, ON, M1R 1P8, Canada;
416-751-6077, fax 416-751-3467, general.can@aimint.net, www.aimcanada.org

LARGE EVANGELICAL GROUP: Accounting, Administration (General), Adult Training, Agriculture, Community Development, Consulting, Development Assistance, Medical Health, Project Management, Religious, Teaching

Africa Inland Mission Canada (AIM) is an inter-denominational foreign mission organization. AIM's primary goal is to establish and develop maturing churches through the evangelization of people and the effective preparation of church leaders.

AIM has missions in over 15 Central and East African countries including Chad, Sudan and Mozambique, as well as on Indian Ocean islands such as the Seychelles. AIM supports over 700 active missionaries, and the types of ministries include medicine, evangelism, public health, church-planting, bible school, avionics, agriculture, water development, veterinary medicine, community development and missionary children's education. Missions are also established in three urban centres in the US, including prison ministries and evangelism in local black churches.

AIM examines an applicant's Christian character, academic achievements, emotional stability and ability to work with others. Successful applicants complete a thorough application and orientation procedure, then seek funds for their travel and monthly expenses. AIM offers some internship positions in various African countries for periods ranging from two months to two years. AIM posts job openings on their Web site. [ID:7008]

African Canadian Continuing Education Society (ACCES)
2441 Christopherson Road, Surrey, BC, V4A 3L2, Canada;
604-538-7267, fax 604-538-7267, acces@acceskenya.org, www.acceskenya.org

MID-SIZED DEVELOPMENT ASSISTANCE GROUP: Education

The mission of the African Canadian Continuing Education Society (ACCES) is to help young Africans obtain the skills and education needed to benefit themselves and their society. ACCES has three particular projects: a long-term training program, a primary education program and an HIV/AIDS awareness program. The long-term training program provides educational opportunities for bright and needy post-secondary students. Four hundred and fifty students have completed the program and another 400 students are now enrolled in training institutions. The primary education project is for children who have never gone to school due to poverty. About 860 of these children are now being taught by Kenyan teachers in their own communities. ACCES is also committed to an HIV/AIDS awareness education program by which hundreds of teachers and other members of the community are taught how to prevent the spread of the disease.

ACCES has 15 volunteer staff members in Canada and at present has people in place to accomplish the major tasks of running the society—bookkeeping, publications and secretarial work. As time goes on, other volunteers may be needed to do this work. Currently volunteers are needed for fundraising. [ID:6902]

African Centres for Peace Education and Training (ACPET)

Canadian Centres for Teaching Peace, P.O. Box 70, Okotoks, AB, T1S 1A4,
Canada; 403-938-5335, fax 403-938-4117, www.peace.ca/africa.htm

SMALL DEVELOPMENT EDUCATION GROUP: Adult Training, Advocacy, Conflict Prevention, Consulting, Development Education, Gender and Development, Literacy, Media/Communications, Research and Development, Teaching

The objective of African Centres for Peace Education and Training (ACPET) is to deepen the pedagogical skills of African peace educators and trainers in active non-violence. Special emphasis is placed on peaceful settlement of disputes and knowledge of conflict prevention for community leaders and grassroots peace activists. Activities include training non-violent conflict resolution activists to serve the entire African network; maintaining effective communication links with similar bodies both within and outside Africa; and building a formidable African Peace Team for deployment to crisis-torn environments.

ACPET has two staff in Canada and 20 overseas. Volunteer positions are available, check their Web site to see how you can use your skills to help. [ID:6907]

African Medical and Research Foundation (AMREF)

Suite 407, 489 College Street, Toronto, ON, M6G IA5, Canada;
416-961-6981, fax 416-961-6984, amref@web.ca, www.amref.org

MID-SIZED COMMUNITY HEALTH GROUP: Administration (General), Adult Training, Community Development, Development Assistance, Development Education, Environment, Fundraising, Humanitarian Relief, Medical Health

The African Medical and Research Foundation (AMREF) is an independent non-profit, non-governmental organization whose mission is to improve the health of disadvantaged people in Africa as a means for them to escape poverty and improve the quality of their lives. AMREF has defined the following priority areas for intervention: HIV/AIDS, tuberculosis, malaria, safe water and environmental sanitation, family health, clinical outreach, disaster management and emergency response, health training and development of health learning materials. Wherever possible AMREF takes a holistic approach and implements its activities within the context of community-based health care. AMREF Canada runs a variety of innovative projects that emphasize appropriate, low-cost health care for people in rural areas.

AMREF maintains three staff to provide fundraising and support for programs administered from its headquarters in Nairobi, Kenya. It maintains 600 paid staff overseas, but does not recruit staff in Canada for overseas work. All such applications are processed by the Nairobi office. AMREF also does not recruit volunteers for overseas placement, but volunteers are always welcome in the Toronto office. For staff in Canada, knowledge of health care in East Africa, fundraising skills, and development education skills are required. [ID:7009]

AFS Interculture Canada (AFS)

1425 Rene-Levesque W. Blvd., Montreal, QC, H3G 1T7, Canada;
514-288-3282, fax 514-843-9119, info-canada@afs.org, www.afscanada.org 🖳 *Fr*

LARGE EXCHANGE GROUP: Administration (General), Community Development, Development Assistance, Development Education, Environment, Exchange Programs, Gender and Development, Human Rights, Humanitarian Relief, Intercultural Briefings, Medical Health, Teaching, Volunteer

AFS Interculture Canada (AFS) is a volunteer-driven, non-profit organization. An educational movement, AFS promotes global education and intercultural understanding through quality exchange programs for youth and adults. AFS Interculture Canada is a member of AFS Intercultural Programs, the largest exchange network in the world. This international network comprises 52 member countries and more than 100,000 volunteers and 500 employees around the world. The AFS experience promotes the core values of the organization: dignity, respect for differences, harmony, sensitivity and tolerance, and also enables its participants to act as responsible, global citizens working for peace and understanding in a diverse world. The national office is managed by a team of professionals who work together with volunteers to coordinate support activities for program participants.

The length of AFS student exchange programs are one year or a semester for young Canadians between 15 and 18. Adults between 18 and 29 can choose from international community service, dialogue or internship programs. Visit the AFS Web site for job postings. (For more information on AFS, see Chapter 10, Short-Term Programs Overseas and Chapter 11, Hosting Programs.) [ID:7010]

Aga Khan Foundation Canada (AKFC)

Suite 1220, 360 Albert Street, Ottawa, ON, K1R 7X7, Canada;
613-237-2532, fax 613-567-2532, info@akfc.ca, www.akfc.org 🖳 *Fr*

LARGE DEVELOPMENT ASSISTANCE GROUP: Most Job Categories

Aga Khan Foundation Canada (AKFC) is a non-profit international development agency that supports economic and social development projects designed to benefit poor communities in East Africa and South and Central Asia. The foundation aims to enhance the quality of education, improve healthcare and increase rural incomes. It is also concerned with gender equity, preserving the environment, promoting small enterprise development and strengthening non-governmental organizations.

Programs are enhanced by AKFC's links to the worldwide Aga Khan Development Network. Local expertise in developing countries ensures initiatives are designed and implemented to respond to the needs of local communities while investing in long-term self-sufficiency. Many of AKFC's programs are undertaken in partnership with the Canadian International Development Agency (CIDA), including the Youth and Young Professionals Program, which sends recent Canadians graduates and young professionals overseas to learn first-hand about development.

AKFC has 22 personnel in Canada and overseas programs are staffed through partners of the Aga Khan Development Network—usually they are locals. AKFC places non-staff members overseas through internships and through a relatively small program called CADEX, which sends Canadian development professionals to work on specific projects with local partners. (For more information on AKFC, see Chapter 10, Short-Term Programs Overseas.) [ID:7029]

L'Aide médicale internationale à l'enfance (L'AMIE)

1001 route de l'Église, Bureau 207, Sainte-Foy, QC, G1V 3V7, Canada;
418-653-2409, fax 418-653-3262, amie.quebec@globetrotter.net, www.amie.ca 🖳 *Sp* 🖳 *En*

SMALL COMMUNITY HEALTH GROUP: Humanitarian Relief, International Education, Literacy, Volunteer

L'Aide médicale internationale à l'enfance est une organisation de coopération internationale qui oeuvre pour le mieux-être des enfants défavorisés à travers le monde. L'AMIE soutient différents projets de développement en Amérique latine, en Afrique et dans les Caraïbes et établit un partenariat avec les communautés locales des pays afin de les aider à développer leur autonomie. L'AMIE est également responsable d'un programme de parrainage. Elle réalise des stages de coopération qui visent à soutenir l'exercice des droits fondamentaux des enfants en assurant leur protection, leur accès à l'éducation et leur épanouissement. [ID:7240]

Alberta Council for Global Cooperation (ACGC)

Main P.O. Box 11535, Edmonton, AB, T5J 3K7, Canada;
780-469-6088, fax 780-469-6099, acgc@web.ca, www.web.net/acgc

SMALL COORDINATING BODY: Community Development

The Alberta Council for Global Cooperation (ACGC) is a coalition of over 40 international development, social justice and environmental non-governmental organizations (NGOs) working both internationally and in Alberta. It is committed to advocating harmonious relations among nations and to promoting equitable community development within nations that is people-centred, democratic, just, sustainable, inclusive and respectful of indigenous cultures. Members of ACGC pursue this goal through supporting public engagement programs and participatory development projects throughout the world.

ACGC has one staff person. ACGC sits on the board of the Canadian Council for International Cooperation, which gives members direct access to research and analysis, national forums, databases and other information. It also collaborates with six other provincial councils and various provincial, national and international networks, and provides members with a direct communication link to CIDA. [ID:6908]

Alternatives

Bureau 300, 3720, ave. du Parc, Montreal, QC, H2X 2J1, Canada;
514-982-6606, fax 514-982-6122, alternatives@alternatives.ca, www.alternatives.ca 💻Fr

LARGE COMMUNITY DEVELOPMENT GROUP: Development Assistance, Environment, Gender and Development, Human Rights, Policy Dialogue

Alternatives provides training and financial assistance to hundreds of popular organizations in such areas as policy formulation and research, planning, education, gender equity, environmental protection, service delivery, conflict resolution, mobilization, communication and evaluation. Alternatives also helps set up networks, coalitions and South-South and North-South encounters in order to foster direct exchanges and the development of common solutions and actions. Alternatives works with community groups in Canada, Africa, Asia, the Middle East, South America and Eastern Europe.

Alternatives has 30 staff in Canada and three overseas. Every year Alternatives sends young people from all over Canada overseas to work with partners and gain valuable field experience. Electronic Communication Internships in international development are offered. For three months, Montreal participants work with organizations interested in creating their own Web sites, while learning technical, linguistic and various other skills needed for the project. Participants then go overseas for another three months to work with grassroots organizations creating Web sites, helping define electronic communication needs, and training future administrators. To be notified when new internships are available, send an email to stages@alternatives.ca. For more information check their Web site. [ID:7028]

Amnistie internationale (section canadienne francophone)

6250, boul. Monk, Montreal, QC, H4E 3H7, Canada; 514-766-9766,
fax 514-766-2088, info@amnistie.qc.ca, www.amnistie.qc.ca 💻En

MID-SIZED ADVOCACY GROUP: Administration (General), Advocacy, Human Rights, Media/Communications, Project Management

Amnistie internationale est un mouvement mondial, indépendant et impartial, formé de bénévoles qui interviennent directement pour la défense des droits de la personne, partout où ils ne sont pas respectés. Elle base son action sur une recherche rigoureuse des faits et appuie ses interventions sur le droit international, conformément à son mandat. Amnistie ne dépend d'aucune subvention gouvernementale.

La section canadienne francophone est l'une des quelque 55 sections nationales du mouvement et elle compte environ 20 000 membres et sympathisants. Quatre fois l'an, la section publie son périodique AGIR dont le mandat est d'informer la population sur l'évolution des droits de la personne dans le monde ainsi que sur les activités d'Amnistie. Le site internet d'Amnistie internationale, section canadienne francophone, informe de la situation des droits de la personne dans le monde et propose des actions concrètes.

La section francophone canadienne d'Amnistie internationale n'est pas à la recherche de personnel. Toutefois, les candidats peuvent faire parvenir leur C.V. au secrétariat national. L'organisme accueille à l'occasion des stagiaires (non rémunérés), qui détiennent une formation en politique internationale, en communications, en informatique et en bureautique. [ID:7241]

Asia Pacific Foundation of Canada (APFC)

Suite 666, 999 Canada Place, Vancouver, BC, V6C 3E1, Canada;
604-684-5986, fax 604-681-1370, info@asiapacific.ca, www.asiapacific.ca 💻 *Fr*

SMALL ADVOCACY GROUP: Business Development, Intercultural Briefings, Media/Communications, Micro-enterprises

The Asia Pacific Foundation of Canada (APFC) is an independent, non-profit research think tank that examines Canada's relationship with the Asia Pacific region. Its mandate is to provide guidance on Asia Pacific topics for business and governments, and to enhance links among policy, business and research communities in areas relating to Canada's ties with Asia Pacific.

APFC has 26 staff and senior management based in their Vancouver office. It is also the hub of the Canada Asia Pacific Research Network, a national network built around 500 academic experts and other regional specialists from across Canada involved in Asia Pacific research. Junior research analysts are hired in May and September of each year to assist with the research and analysis program of the foundation, which covers policy and business issues related to Canada-Asia economic relations, development cooperation, people-to-people linkages, and institutional, political and security relations. Qualifications include a soon-to-be completed MA/MSc or PhD in the social sciences, preferably with emphasis on the Asia Pacific; ability in business or policy issues related to the Asia Pacific; living/working experience in Asia; and Asian language ability.

The Web site contains analysis, statistics, information and Internet links detailing trade and investment; development cooperation, people-to-people relations; political, security and industrial relations; and economic, political, social and institutional relations with the Asia Pacific. (For more information on APFC, see Chapter 14, Awards & Grants.) [ID:7030]

Association of Canadian Community Colleges (ACCC)

International Services Bureau, Suite 200, 1223 Michael Street N., Ottawa, ON,
K1J 7T2, Canada; 613-746-2222, fax 613-746-6721, postmaster@accc.ca, www.accc.ca 💻 *Fr*

LARGE COORDINATING BODY: Accounting, Administration (General), Adult Training, Agriculture, Architecture and Planning, Business Development, Computer Systems, Consulting, Development Assistance, Development Education, Energy Resources, Environment, Gender and Development, Human Resources, Media/Communications, Micro-enterprises, Project Management, Teaching, Technical Assistance, Telecommunications, Water Resources

The Association of Canadian Community Colleges (ACCC) is a national voluntary membership organization created to represent colleges and institutes to government, business and industry in Canada and overseas. ACCC organizes conferences and workshops for college staff, students and board members to facilitate networking and participation in national and international activities such as sector studies, awards programs and linkages. As a membership association, ACCC has access to 30,000 college instructors and administrators, the capability to identify college/institute strengths and areas of optimum contribution to human resource development, as well the target groups they are best able to serve and the best models of project implementation.

ACCC's international experience includes over 300 projects in 70 countries. Community college instructors and professionals are hired for international contract work based on their business, industry and trade experience. The secretariat operates with 64 full-time staff. Field offices are located in 9 countries around the world. ACCC maintains a data bank for resumes. Visit the ACCC Web site for consulting and teaching job postings. [ID:7031]

Association of Universities and Colleges of Canada (AUCC)
International Relations, Suite 600, 350 Albert Street, Ottawa, ON, K1R 1B1, Canada; 613-563-1236, fax 613-563-9745, info@aucc.ca, www.aucc.ca 💻 Fr

MID-SIZED COORDINATING BODY: Accounting, Administration (General), Adult Training, Advocacy, Aerospace Technology, Agriculture, Architecture and Planning, Business Development, Community Development, Computer Systems, Construction, Consulting, Development Assistance, Development Education, Economics, Energy Resources, Engineering, Environment, Exchange Programs, Fisheries, Forestry, Gender and Development, Human Resources, Human Rights, Humanitarian Relief, Intercultural Briefings, Logistics, Media/Communications, Medical Health, Micro-enterprises, Project Management, Teaching, Technical Assistance, Telecommunications, Water Resources

The Association of Universities and Colleges of Canada (AUCC) represents 93 public and private non-profit universities and university degree-level colleges in Canada and abroad. Its mandate is to facilitate the development of public policy on higher education and to encourage cooperation among universities, governments, industry, communities and institutions in other countries. AUCC and member universities have carried out more than 2,000 international development projects in the past 30 years. The focus has been on international opportunities that enhance other countries' resources and lead to improvements in their living standards.

AUCC has approximately 20 staff based in Canada involved in international relations. The organization represents Canadian universities at international meetings and meetings with foreign government officials, education leaders, development organizations and members of the diplomatic community. AUCC offers information about Canada's university system; promotes scientific, scholarly and technical exchanges between Canadian universities and international universities; and administers programs linking Canadian and foreign universities.

AUCC maintains databases on Canadian university involvement in international development projects and on international exchange agreements between Canadian and foreign universities for students and faculty and for the purpose of research collaboration. It organizes workshops and international conferences, publishes newsletters, and reports on the increasingly important role of Canadian universities in international affairs.

AUCC also administers a large number of graduate and undergraduate scholarships and exchange programs offered by Canadian and foreign governments, Canadian corporations and other agencies.

Qualifications for work with AUCC include a master's degree in international relations, and 5 to 10 years' experience in international development or international affairs. Proficiency in French and English is also an asset. Visit the AUCC Web site for information on university development, exchange programs and job openings at member universities. (For more information on AUCC, see Chapter 14, Awards & Grants and Chapter 10, Short-Term Programs Overseas.) [ID:7033]

Association québécoise des organismes de coopération internationale (AQOCI)
1001, rue Sherbrooke est, Bureau 540, Montreal, QC, H2L 1L3, Canada; 514-871-1086, fax 514-871-9866, aqoci@aqoci.qc.ca, www.aqoci.qc.ca

MID-SIZED COORDINATING BODY: Development Assistance, Development Education, Environment, Exchange Programs, Policy Dialogue

L'AQOCI, une association sans but lucratif, regroupe 52 organismes de coopération et d'éducation à la solidarité internationale qui oeuvrent au Québec. La mission de l'AQOCI consiste à promouvoir et à soutenir le travail de ses membres et leurs initiatives en faveur de la solidarité internationale. Son engagement dans la société québécoise témoigne d'un intérêt concret pour la création de ponts entre les communautés du Nord et du Sud : activités de sensibilisation et de mobilisation du public, publications d'analyses de fond et prises de position face à la politique extérieure canadienne et aux événements nationaux et internationaux. Ses membres travaillent sur tous les continents. Ces organismes envoient des volontaires et stagiaires à l'étranger et administrent des fonds publics d'aide au développement. [ID:7242]

Atlantic Council for International Cooperation (ACIC)

125 South Knowlesville Road, Knowlesville, NB, E7L 1B1, Canada;
506-375-4795, fax 506-375-9013, info@acic-caci.org, www.acic-caci.org ▯*Fr*

LARGE COORDINATING BODY: Training and Education

The Atlantic Council for International Cooperation (ACIC) is a coalition of organizations, institutions and branches working in the Atlantic region that are committed to achieving global sustainability in a peaceful and healthy environment, with social justice, human dignity and participation for all. ACIC supports its members in international cooperation and education through collective leadership, networking, information, training and coordination, and represents their interests when dealing with government and others. The council sponsors events such as conferences, seminars, lectures and professional development workshops. Part of ACIC's strategic plan includes engaging Atlantic Canadians in tourism and international cooperation issues, as well as promoting solidarity with those involved in people's movements in the South and in the North. As part of a CIDA-funded consortium of Canadian and Nigerian organizations, ACIC has developed a partnership with the Non-Governmental Organization Coalition for the Environment (NGOCE), a coalition-based out of Calabar, Nigeria.

There are three personnel working for ACIC and 25 volunteers/interns across Canada working in various capacities, including the Board of Directors. There are also intern placements in Canada and overseas in a variety of countries. Job postings can be found on their Web site. Qualifications and experience depend on the position. [ID:6893]

Bellanet

IDRC, P.O. Box 8500, c/o IDRC, Ottawa, ON, K1G 3H9, Canada;
613-236-6163, fax 613-238-7230, info@bellanet.org, www.bellanet.org ▯*Fr*

MID-SIZED DEVELOPMENT EDUCATION GROUP: Advocacy, Computer Systems

Bellanet's IDRC division supports collaboration in the development community by sharing its expertise in information and communication technologies as well as its skills in facilitating organizational learning and the sharing of knowledge. It delivers its program through three main program lines: on-line communities, knowledge sharing and open development. In addition, three important crosscutting areas are woven into all aspects of Bellanet's work: gender equality, capacity development, and monitoring and evaluation.

Bellanet has 17 full-time staff; 14 are based in Canada and three are posted as overseas locally-engaged staff. It offers short-term work in the Ottawa office (summer and occasionally in the course of the year). Bellanet looks for people with relevant educational background and work experience, as well as fluency in languages. Recruitment and hiring processes are handled by the human resources department of IDRC for summer and occasional positions. Applications are considered according to the interests of the applicant and the needs of the various units and programs. Applicants can make explicit their interest to work with Bellanet. Following this process, each unit, including Bellanet, receives a selection of requests and the hiring process follows. IDRC and Bellanet post the openings for summer positions early in January. Applications should be directed to the address listed above or by e-mail to competitions@idrc.ca. [ID:6909]

Brace Centre for Water Resources Management

Macdonald Campus, McGill University, 21-111 Lakeshore Road, Ste-Anne-de-Bellevue, QC,
H9X 3V9, Canada; 514-398-7833, fax 514-398-7767, brace@macdonald.mcgill.ca, www.mcgill.ca/brace

MID-SIZED INTERNATIONAL RESEARCH GROUP: Adult Training, Consulting, Development Education, Energy Resources, Engineering, Environment, Water Resources

The Brace Centre for Water Resources Management, located at McGill University, integrates staff from several of the university's faculties to engage in research and development, studies, teaching and specialized short-term training in water resources management in Canada and internationally. It specializes in developing methods for desalination of sea or brackish water used by local populations.

There are 19 university staff working at the Centre, as well as associates of non-university related experts. The Centre organizes short-term training sessions for visitors from developing countries and provides assistance to similar groups in areas such as Central Asia, the Middle East, India, Pakistan, the Caribbean, Central America and Africa. Applicants should be bilingual, possess an engineering or technical degree and be interested in the development of arid and rural zones. The Centre maintains a data bank for resumes and posts job openings on their Web site. [ID:7034]

British Columbia Council for International Co-operation (BCCIC)
P.O. Box 21651, 1424 Commercial Drive, Vancouver, BC, V5L 5G3, Canada;
604-899-4475, fax 604-899-4436, info@bccic.org, www.bccic.org

MID-SIZED COORDINATING BODY: Accounting, Administration (General), Advocacy, Development Education, Volunteer

The British Columbia Council for International Co-operation (BCCIC) is a coalition of 40 international development organizations across the province of British Columbia. BCCIC's role is to provide key coordination and policy and advocacy support to the member agencies, and to work in partnership with government agencies to ensure that global development issues are addressed. It provides a forum for action on global development at the provincial level and brings a B.C. perspective to national policy discussions through its participation in committees, working groups and coalitions.

Although primarily volunteer and membership driven, there is one BCCIC staff in Canada backed by a dynamic board of directors. The membership includes various non-governmental organizations involved in education, health, social and rural development, faith-based organizations, development education centres and the regional office of the Canadian International Development Agency (CIDA). BCCIC supports the work of member agencies, shares information and communication about global issues, organizes professional development and skills training for members, coordinates and represents members' interests to governments and establishes support for international development in communities not currently part of established networks.

Job and volunteer openings at member organizations are posted on the BCCIC Web site. Visit the "Links" section of the Web site to find helpful connections to national and international development organizations. [ID:7035]

Canada World Youth (CWY)
3rd Floor, 2330 Notre Dame Street W., Montreal, QC, H3J 1N4, Canada;
514-931-3526, fax 514-939-2621, cwy-jcm@cwy-jcm.org, www.cwy-jcm.org 💻 𝓕𝓻

LARGE EXCHANGE GROUP: Community Development, Development Education, Exchange Programs, Fundraising, Intercultural Briefings, Project Management, Volunteer

Canada World Youth (CWY) is a national, non-profit organization that promotes international cooperation and understanding through international exchanges and educational programs for youth. Young adults focus on volunteer work and community development in a cross-cultural setting.

CWY offers many different programs involving thousands of young adults. The Core Program is for youth between the ages of 17 to 20. It involves six- to seven-month exchanges, where participants spend half their time living and working as volunteers in a host community in Canada, and the other half in Africa, Asia, Latin America or the Caribbean. The Central and Eastern Europe Programs follow a similar structure and are adapted to the realities of these regions. The NetCorps Canada International Program allows those aged 19 to 24 to work on volunteer projects related to information and communication technology in Brazil, Ecuador, Guatemala, Jamaica, Russia and Poland/Ukraine. The Customized Programs meet the needs of specific clientele or partners or are designed around a specific theme. They respect the underlying philosophy of CWY's educational programming while customizing the structure, components and form to fit the specific project. The Overseas Internship Programs are offered exclusively overseas and provide the opportunity to gain work experience in fields such as information and communication technology, health, community intervention and popular education. Lastly, the Academic and Community Partnerships are international educational programs designed by representatives from high schools, colleges, universities or youth groups with the assistance and guidance of CWY staff.

CWY has around 50 permanent staff at the head office in Montreal, as well as regional and satellite offices. CWY hires project supervisors to implement program objectives by working with young people in host communities and supervising its exchanges. Qualifications for these positions include a college or university degree, bilingualism, and experience in a developing country or in a cross-cultural context. Experience in budget planning, project coordination and supervision are assets. (For more on CWY, see Chapter 10, Short-Term Programs Overseas.) [ID:7039]

CANADEM
Suite 1102, 1 Nicholas Street, Ottawa, ON, K1N 7B7, Canada;
613-789-3328, fax 613-789-6125, canadem@canadem.ca, www.canadem.ca 💻 *Fr*

MID-SIZED COORDINATING BODY: Community Development, Gender and Development, Housing/Human Settlements, Human Rights, Law and Good Governance, Peace and Security

CANADEM is a human resources and consulting non-profit agency. Delivering Canadian expertise internationally, its purpose is to bolster peace, order, and good governance efforts worldwide.

CANADEM employs 10 staff in Canada. The core of CANADEM's personnel is a roster of almost 5,000 screened Canadians with skills in human rights, peace-building, rule of law, governance, democratization, elections, policing, security, admin-logistics, and reconstruction. Funded by Foreign Affairs Canada (FAC), this national roster enables international agencies, governments and other non-profit organizations to connect with Canadian specialists at no charge. Drawing on this pool of Canadian talent, CANADEM also delivers security sector reform programs through its operational arm CANPOL (www.canpol.ca). Most positions require work experience in the area of expertise, a university degree, previous international experience, experience working for the requesting agency or another similar agency, good language skills including English and possibly a second language, solid interpersonal skills, and culture and gender sensitivity. CANADEM also has many useful resources that provide members with information on relevant job, internship, and volunteer opportunities abroad. [ID:7117]

Canadian Auto Workers' Social Justice Fund (CAW-SJF)
205 Placer Court, Toronto, ON, M2H 3H9, Canada; 416-497-4110,
fax 416-495-6559, cawint@caw.ca, www.caw.ca/whatwedo/socialjusticefund 💻 *Fr*

MID-SIZED DEVELOPMENT ASSISTANCE GROUP: Development Education, Gender and Development, Human Rights, Refugee Services, Trade Unions

The Canadian Auto Workers' Social Justice Fund (CAW-SJF) is working to strengthen trade unions and improve labour conditions in Canada, South Africa, the Middle East, Asia and Central America. Its overseas development projects are developed in conjunction with other NGOs and focus on refugees and displaced persons, trade union support, human rights, civics and gender issues. CAW-SJF currently has two staff in Canada and numerous project partners overseas. Only North-South exchanges of CAW and project partner members are facilitated. More information is available in the Social Justice Fund section of the CAW Web site. [ID:7040]

Canadian Bar Association (CBA)
CBA Young Professionals International Program, Suite 500, 865 Carling Ave.,
Ottawa, ON, K1S 5S8, Canada; 613-237-2925, fax 613-237-8860, info@cba.org, www.cba.org 💻 *Fr*

LARGE COORDINATING BODY: Children's Rights, Human Rights, Law and Good Governance, People's Organizations

The Canadian Bar Association (CBA) is a professional organization that provides educational and networking opportunities for lawyers. The CBA represents more than 37,000 lawyers, judges, notaries, law teachers and law students from across Canada. It is committed to enhancing the professional and commercial interests of a diverse membership and to protecting the independence of the judiciary and the Bar.

CBA has over 100 staff, 10 of whom work in the International Development division. The International Development Committee (IDC) was established as a special committee of the CBA whose mission is to enhance the rule of law in democratizing countries through systematic change. IDC programs are developed in response to membership interest and the perceived need for the project, and in consideration of available funding, membership expertise and the administrative capacity of the CBA. CBA is involved in South Africa, Bangladesh and China.

The CBA also administers a Young Professionals International Internship Program, which is funded by Foreign Affairs Canada (FAC) and International Trade Canada (ITCan). Through this program, young lawyers are placed in eight-month internships (they are overseas for between six and seven of the eight months) to work with human rights legal organizations on issues such as women's rights, labour rights, constitutional rights, children's rights and indigenous people's rights, in Southern and Central Africa and Latin America. In order to apply, write a letter of application describing your interest and attach your resume. [ID:6882]

Canadian Bureau for International Education (CBIE)

Suite 1100, 220 Laurier Ave. W., Ottawa, ON, K1P 5Z9, Canada;
613-237-4820, fax 613-237-1073, info@cbie.ca, www.cbie.ca 💻 *Fr*

LARGE COORDINATING BODY: Advocacy, Community Development, Development Assistance, Development Education, Exchange Programs, Human Resources, Intercultural Briefings, Media/Communications, Membership Relations, Project Management, Technical Assistance

The Canadian Bureau for International Education (CBIE) is an umbrella organization comprised of 200 colleges, universities, schools, school boards, educational organizations and businesses across Canada. It offers a wide variety of services and publications to members, international students and the Canadian public. Internationally, CBIE engages in cooperative projects in capacity building, institutional strengthening and human resource development. CBIE works in partnership with educational institutions, community-based organizations and governments in Africa, the Middle East, Asia, the Americas, the former Soviet Union and Central and Eastern Europe.

CBIE employs 30 staff in Canada. It manages projects, counsels students, researches, writes, edits and manages publications, promotes programs and services, as well as develops new programs. Occasionally, CBIE employs consultants for research projects or special training. For staff positions, CBIE prefers candidates with developing country experience and graduate degrees in relevant fields. Bilingualism (English-French) is either required or considered an asset for virtually all positions. Other languages are an asset, as is work experience in an educational institution.

CBIE also offers youth internships programs with placements ranging from accounting and banking to the mining and energy sectors. CBIE also gives out International Learning Grants, and facilitates the J. Armand Bombardier Internationalist Fellowship and Lucent Global Science Scholars Program. CBIE has a specialized Web site for Canadians interested in study/work abroad and for international students who wish to study in Canada: www.destineducation.ca. (For more information on CBIE, see Chapter 14, Awards & Grants.) [ID:7041]

Canadian Centre for International Studies and Cooperation (CECI)

Recruitment Director, 3185 Rachel Street E., Montreal, QC, H1W 1A3,
Canada; 514-875-9911, fax 514-875-6469, info@ceci.ca, www.ceci.ca 💻 *Fr* 💻 *Sp*

LARGE DEVELOPMENT ASSISTANCE GROUP: Administration (General), Adult Training, Agriculture, Business Development, Community Development, Computer Systems, Consulting, Development Assistance, Development Education, Economics, Engineering, Environment, Exchange Programs, Fisheries, Forestry, Fundraising, Gender and Development, Human Resources, Human Rights, Humanitarian Relief, Intercultural Briefings, Literacy, Media/Communications, Medical Health, Micro-enterprises, Project Management, Technical Assistance, Volunteer, Water Resources

The Canadian Centre for International Studies and Cooperation (CECI) is a non-profit organization whose mission is to fight poverty and exclusion and to promote sustainable development. It seeks to involve Canadians in international development notably as volunteer cooperants, preparing them to be effective development agents overseas and in Canada. It provides support and capacity-building services to developing country partners and communities. It also takes part in the ongoing exchange of ideas on international cooperation and educates the Canadian public towards building equitable relations with developing countries. CECI meets these objectives mainly through its decentralized offices; a CIDA-funded volunteers program carried out in partnership with WUSC-Ottawa; a small youth internship program; development projects funded by various agencies and/or CECI fundraising implemented in collaboration with local partners; and humanitarian initiatives carried out in a similar way. Volunteers for CECI provide professional input, ideally acting as a bridge between a local and a similar Canadian organization. Volunteer assignments are from six months to two years. For youth interns they are six months or less.

CECI currently has 60 staff based in Canada, 100 volunteers and youth interns overseas, as well as some 500 local staff, most of whom are tied to specific projects. For volunteers and youth interns, desired education and work experience in Canada varies. Depending on the country, they work in French, English or Spanish. CECI maintains a data bank for resumes, and posts job openings and applications on their Web site. [ID:7056]

Canadian Centre on Disability Studies (CCDS)
50 The Promenade, Winnipeg, MB, R3B 1H9, Canada; 204-287-8411,
fax 204-284-5343, ccds@disabilitystudies.ca, www.disabilitystudies.ca

LARGE RESEARCH INSTITUTE: Education, Research

The Canadian Centre on Disability Studies (CCDS) is a consumer-directed, university-affiliated centre dedicated to research, education and information dissemination on disability issues. Through their activities, CCDS promotes full and equal participation of people with disabilities in all aspects of society. This is accomplished on a local, national and international level in partnership with the disability community, the corporate sector, the academic world and governments. CCDS has 11 staff members in Canada.

The CCDS International Program (IP) is a response to the global demand for new knowledge and best practices in the area of disability studies and disability issues. The overall purpose of the IP of CCDS continues to be the promotion of disability studies as an academic discipline internationally, with a focus on curriculum development, education, research, policy development and dissemination of knowledge on disability issues. The active model of partnership developed through the CCDS' first international project—Winnipeg-Stavropol (Russia) Development Project—continues to be a model for social change and is the foundation for the IP and CCDS as a whole.

CCDS also offers internships through CIDA's Youth International Internship Program (IYIP). The IYIP is an employment program for young Canadian professionals, offering post-secondary graduates the opportunity to gain valuable international development work experience. The program's focus is in the area of disability studies and related issues, and initiates a worldwide research and knowledge-based network. Currently, the project has five six-month placements in Russia, Ukraine, Thailand and Mexico. For more details, please see their Web site. [ID:6869]

Canadian Centre on Minority Affairs Inc.
Suite 400, 1200 Eglinton Ave., North York, ON, M3C 1H9, Canada;
416-441-3249, fax 416-441-2068, info@ccmacanada.org, www.ccmacanada.org

MID-SIZED DEVELOPMENT ASSISTANCE GROUP: Development Assistance, Education, Exchange Programs, Policy Dialogue, Youth and Development

The Canadian Centre on Minority Affairs Inc. (CCMA) is an organization dedicated to promoting and encouraging the full participation of Black and Caribbean Canadians into the mainstream of Canadian society through the development and sustainability of a broad range of social development projects and institutional collaboration in both Canada and the Commonwealth Caribbean. Current project emphases include information technology, health promotion, social development and youth initiatives. CCMA has four staff members. Volunteers are welcome to get involved by contacting CCMA directly. [ID:7115]

Canadian Coalition for the Rights of Children (CCRC)

Suite 201, 383 Parkdale, Ottawa, ON, K1Y 4R4, Canada;
info@rightsofchildren.ca, www.rightsofchildren.ca 📖 *Fr*

SMALL ADVOCACY GROUP: Human Rights

The Canadian Coalition for the Rights of Children (CCRC) monitors and promotes Canada's implementation of the United Nations Convention on the Rights of the Child and related international children's rights instruments, as well as commitments including Canada's National Action Plan from the UN Special Session on Children. CCRC undertakes a variety of activities primarily in Canada but also abroad. The Coalition carries out its mandate by monitoring the implementation of the Convention in Canada in respect of Canadian domestic and international policies, programs and legislation; establishing national, provincial, regional, local and international links with organizations concerned with the well-being of children; fostering the education and awareness in Canada of the rights of children, especially among young Canadians; acting as an informal information network in Canada for materials related to the Convention; and urging the federal government to ensure Canadian representation to the United Nations Committee on the Rights of the Child. The work of the Coalition is based on volunteer contributions, and paid employment opportunities fluctuate over time. [ID:7116]

Canadian Consortium on Human Security (CCHS)

Liu Institute for the Study of Global Issues, University of British Columbia,
6476 N.W. Marine Drive, Vancouver, BC, V6T 1Z2, Canada; 604-822-1877,
fax 604-822-6966, cchs.hq@ubc.ca, www.humansecurity.info 📖 *Fr*

SMALL COORDINATING BODY: Research and Development

The Canadian Consortium on Human Security (CCHS) is an academic-based network promoting policy-relevant research on human security, funded by Foreign Affairs Canada and International Trade Canada. CCHS's core mission is to facilitate the analysis and the exchange of research relating to human security in Canada and internationally. Human security is a people-centered approach to foreign policy that recognizes that lasting stability cannot be achieved until people are protected from violent threats to their rights, safety or lives.

CCHS is involved in the following activities: publishing the quarterly "Human Security Bulletin", which presents policy-relevant human security research currently being pursued in Canada and internationally; running the annual Human Security Fellowship Programme, which helps foster innovative research and policy development on a range of human security issues; providing funding for human security-related conferences, seminars and workshops; and maintaining a mailing list of people interested in human security research. CCHS is also developing the Human Security Gateway, a fully-searchable research and information database devoted to human security issues, including a bibliographic database, teaching resources, a directory of human security-oriented institutions and a roster of human security experts. CCHS has one full-time staff member and five part-time workers in Vancouver, Toronto and Halifax. [ID:6910]

Canadian Co-operative Association (CCA)

Suite 400, 275 Bank Street, Ottawa, ON, K2P 2L6, Canada; 613-238-6711,
fax 613-567-0658, info@CoopsCanada.coop, www.coopcca.com

LARGE DEVELOPMENT ASSISTANCE GROUP: Accounting, Administration (General), Agriculture,
Business Development, Community Development, Development Assistance, Development Education,
Exchange Programs, Fundraising, Logistics, Micro-enterprises, Project Management, Technical Assistance,
Volunteer

The Canadian Co-operative Association (CCA) is the international development arm of cooperatives and credit unions in English-speaking Canada. It is a non-profit national umbrella organization owned by its members, who come from many sectors of the economy, including finance, insurance, agri-food and supply, wholesale and retail, housing, health and the service sector. CCA works with partner cooperatives throughout South America, Africa, Asia and Eastern Europe on behalf of co-operatives in Canada, aiming ultimately to reduce poverty.

There are 36 staff members based in Canada. CCA seeks cultrually-sensitive, flexible university graduates with direct experience overseas or with a cooperative/credit union.

CCA programs activities include the following: 1) Technical Co-operants: Managed by CCA Ottawa, this is an electronic database matching Canadian candidates with their partner's requirements. Working as technical cooperants, these candidates share their skills and experience on assignments ranging from short-term training to long-term management. 2) Women's Mentoring: This program provides professional development training and exposure programs, involving women from Africa, Asia and the Americas. 3) Study Tours: Development education study tours are offered, combining tourism with co-op education. 4) Co-op Connections: This gives an opportunity for people in Canadian cooperatives or credit unions to develop a unique relationship with a similar organization in the developing world. 5) Youth Experiences International (YEI): This program engages young Canadian graduates who want a chance to participate in six-month internships with its co-op partners. If interested, complete an on-line application and reference form and send an electronic copy of your resume to interns@coopscanada.coop. For more information, contact the CCA Ottawa office or the regional development education coordinator in your region to arrange for an information workshop. CCA maintains a data bank for resumes. [ID:7043]

Canadian Council for International Co-operation (CCIC)
Suite 300, 1 Nicholas Street, Ottawa, ON, K1N 7B7, Canada;
613-241-7007, fax 613-241-5302, info@ccic.ca, www.ccic.ca ▢ *Fr*

LARGE COORDINATING BODY: Advocacy, Economics, Environment, Gender and Development, Human Rights, Media/Communications

The Canadian Council for International Co-operation (CCIC) advocates for Canadian policies and programs that will reduce global poverty and promote sustainable human development. It also seeks to strengthen the role of the voluntary sector in development cooperation. CCIC is a coalition of Canadian organizations that seek to change the course of human development in ways that favour social and economic equity, democratic participation, environmental integrity and respect for human rights. The council conducts research, disseminates information and creates learning opportunities for its members. CCIC coordinates their collective efforts to shape new models for world development, press for national and international policies that serve the global public interest, and strive to build a social movement for global citizenship in Canada.

CCIC has 20 staff members in Ottawa. It also consists of more than 100 Canadian non-profit organizations working in Canada and overseas, which include religious and secular development groups, professional associations and labour unions. They work with NGOs, cooperatives and citizens' groups in the South in order to enable people in Africa, Asia and Latin America to meet basic needs for food, shelter, education, health and sanitation. Many conduct research and campaign with their Southern partners for fair trade, global security, children's rights, biodiversity or forgiveness of multilateral debt. Some members work exclusively in Canada, designing education materials for use in classrooms and resource centres. Others use their overseas program experience as a springboard for public awareness campaigning in Canada. [ID:7011]

Canadian Council of Churches (CCC)
159 Roxborough Drive, Toronto, ON, M4W 1X7, Canada;
416-972-9494, fax 416-927-0405, admin@ccc-cce.ca, www.ccc-cce.ca ▢ *Fr*

SMALL COORDINATING BODY: Human Rights, Religious, Social Justice and Development

In Canada, the Canadian Council of Churches (CCC) provides churches with an agency for consultation and common planning and actions. It encourages ecumenical understanding and action throughout Canada. CCC relates to the World Council of Churches and to other agencies serving the worldwide ecumenical movement. Work includes gathering and sharing information and theological-ethical reflection related to peace and justice, human rights, health care and biotechnology in Canada and around the world. The CCC occasionally sponsors exchange programs or exposure tours. It employs six staff in Canada. For job openings, see their Web site. [ID:7012]

Canadian Crossroads International (CCI)

Ontario Regional Office, 317 Adelaide Street W., Toronto, ON, M5V 1P9,
Canada; 416-967-1611, fax 416-967-9078, ontario@cciorg.ca, www.cciorg.ca 💻 Fr

LARGE EXCHANGE GROUP: Agriculture, Community Development, Development Education, Education,
Environment, Exchange Programs, Gender and Development, Human Rights, Intercultural Briefings, Volunteer

Canadian Crossroads International (CCI) is an international development agency working in
partnership with local organizations in 15 countries. The key sectors CCI works in are:
health/HIV/AIDS; education and literacy; human rights, good governance and democratization;
agriculture; community, economic and rural development; and environment and natural resources
management. CCI brings NGOs in developing countries and Canadian non-profit organizations
working on similar issues into long-term partnerships. Their shared mission is to ensure sustainable
development in developing countries by increasing the capacity of CCI's developing partners to
meet the needs of their communities. Partners define their needs and what projects can best support
them. The job of the volunteers on placement, either in Canada or in developing countries, is to
facilitate the sharing of knowledge and skills between partner organizations and communities that
will increase the capacity of partners beyond CCI's involvement. Volunteers are recruited
throughout the year. See CCI's Web site for volunteer job postings.

CCI has 31 staff in Canada and hundreds of volunteers in Canada and overseas who assist in
the delivery of its program. CCI has four regional offices in Halifax, Montreal, Toronto and
Vancouver and does not have offices overseas. Postings for staff positions can be found on their
Web site. (For more information on CCI, see Chapter 10, Short-term Programs Overseas and
Chapter 11, Hosting Programs.) [ID:7013]

Canadian Education Centre Network (CEC Network)

Suite 578, 999 Canada Place, Vancouver, BC, V6C 3E1, Canada;
604-408-0588 ext. 3322, fax 604-641-1238, info@cecnetwork.ca, www.cecnetwork.ca 💻 Fr

LARGE COORDINATING BODY: Exchange Programs, Intercultural Briefings, Lifestyle/Cultural Orientation,
Tourism, Training and Education, Volunteer, Youth and Development

The Canadian Education Centre Network (CEC Network) markets and promotes Canada as a
study destination for international students. It also promotes Canada's expertise in training and
skills upgrading by sourcing and managing international education projects, and placing Canadian
teachers worldwide.

The CEC Network has about 100 staff in Canada and overseas. It does not have volunteers. It
offers a number of opportunities for Canadians interested in working, studying or travelling abroad.

Six-month internships may be available at selected overseas Canadian Education Centres
(CECs) in Asia, Australia, Latin America and Europe. Interns assist CEC staff with a variety of
tasks related to the promotion of Canada as a study destination. Applicants must be post-secondary
graduates between the ages of 18 and 30, with an interest in international affairs and/or
international marketing. For more information about internship opportunities, including
requirements and deadlines, please visit www.cecnetwork.ca.

The CEC Network also operates Canadian Cultural and Language Institutes in selected
countries, offering overseas students an introduction to Canada and a chance to learn English or
French as a second language through courses taught by Canadian teachers. As well, the CEC
Network works with foreign governments around the world to provide technical assistance in
education and to deliver ESL programs and teacher training programs at primary, secondary and
college levels. It also works with private schools across Latin America, Asia and the Middle East to
identify and select teachers for ESL and other disciplines. For information on teaching abroad,
please contact teacher.recruitment@cecnetwork.ca or visit www.trainingcanada.ca.

The CEC Network's Go Abroad Fair gives young Canadians a chance to meet exhibitors from
cultural and education organizations, study abroad programs, universities, travel agencies, and work
and volunteer abroad programs. For Go Abroad Fair dates and information, please visit
www.goabroadfair.ca. (For more information about the Go Abroad Fair, see their ad in the sponsor
section at the end of this guide.) [ID:6867]

Canadian Environmental Network (CEN)
National Director, Suite 300, 945 Wellington Street, Ottawa, ON, K1Y 2X5,
Canada; 613-728-9810, fax 613-728-2963, info@cen-rce.org, www.cen-rce.org 💻 *Fr*

MID-SIZED COORDINATING BODY: Environment

The Canadian Environmental Network (CEN) facilitates networking between environmental organizations and others who share its mandate to protect the earth and promote ecologically sound ways of life. CEN works directly with concerned citizens and organizations striving to protect, preserve and restore the environment, and to affect how society thinks about environmental issues. The Network provides coordination, communication, research and networking services to more than 800 Canadian environmental groups affiliated through one of CEN's 11 regional networks. CEN has seven staff based at the national office in Ottawa and does not provide overseas placements. [ID:7014]

Canadian Executive Service Organization (CESO)
Suite 700, P.O. Box 328, 700 Bay Street, Toronto, ON, M5G 1Z6, Canada;
416-961-2376, fax 416-961-1096, toronto@ceso-saco.com, www.ceso-saco.com 💻 *Fr* 💻 *Sp*

LARGE VOLUNTEER GROUP: Most Job Categories

The Canadian Executive Service Organization (CESO) is a non-profit, volunteer-sending organization that transfers social and economic development expertise to Canadian Aboriginal Peoples, non-Aboriginal Canadians, developing nations and emerging market economies. CESO international services' mission is to transfer Canadian expertise to businesses and organizations in countries in Africa, Asia, the Caribbean, Central and South America, as well as Central and Eastern Europe, in order to help them achieve their goals of economic and technical self-sufficiency.

CESO maintains approximately 70 salaried staff across Canada, and recruits hundreds of volunteer advisers (VA) every year to work in Canada and overseas. Most VAs are retired or semi-retired and have the time and the willingness to share their expertise without pay. The average age of a volunteer is 62 years. CESO posts employment opportunities on their Web site and individuals wishing to volunteer should forward their resume to CESO's Roster Manager. [ID:7057]

Canadian Federation of Agriculture (CFA)
Suite 1101, 75 Albert Street, Ottawa, ON, K1P 5E7,
Canada; 613-236-3633, info@cfafca.ca, www.cfa-fca.ca 💻 *Fr*

MID-SIZED COORDINATING BODY: Advocacy, Agriculture, Policy Development

The Canadian Federation of Agriculture (CFA) was formed in 1935 to answer the need for a unified voice to speak on behalf of Canadian farmers. It continues today as a farmer-funded national umbrella organization representing provincial general farm organizations and national commodity groups. Through its members, CFA represents over 200,000 Canadian farm families from coast to coast. The CFA's mission is to promote the interests of Canadian agriculture and agri-food producers, including farm families, through leadership at the national level and to ensure the continued development of a viable and vibrant agriculture and agri-food industry in Canada.

CFA employs eight full-time staff and several contractors in Ottawa to fill a variety of policy, project management and communications roles. Ottawa staff openings are advertised through CFA's own networks of members, and posted on Canadian employment sites such as www.charityvillage.com.

Each year CFA also offers five to 10 international internship placements in the Young Professionals International Program (YPI), sponsored by Foreign Affairs Canada and International Trade Canada. These placements are open to Canadian citizens or permanent residents of Canada under 30 years of age and are typically with international organizations such as the International Federation of Agricultural Producers (IFAP) based in Paris, or the UN Food and Agriculture Organization (FAO) based in Rome; national agriculture organizations outside Canada, such as the US National Farmers Union based in Washington, DC; or other local organizations and research institutes abroad. Information on YPI can be found on CFA's Web site. [ID:6883]

Canadian Feed the Children Inc. (CFTC)

174 Bartley Drive, Toronto, ON, M4A 1E1, Canada; 416-757-1220,
fax 416-757-3318, cftc@canadianfeedthechildren.ca, www.canadianfeedthechildren.ca

LARGE RELIEF AND DEVELOPMENT AGENCY: Accounting, Administration (General), Computer
Systems, Fundraising, Humanitarian Relief, Project Management, Volunteer

Canadian Feed the Children Inc. (CFTC) is an independent registered charity whose goal is to
alleviate the impact of poverty on children. With financial support from individual, community and
corporate donors, CFTC works with local partners in Bolivia, Canada, Ethiopia, Ghana, Haiti,
Sierra Leone and Uganda to develop community-based programs in the areas of food security, clean
water access, health and hygiene, sustainable agriculture and education. CFTC currently employs a
staff of 19 who work out of its Toronto office as well as three paid indigenous field representatives
who live and work in Bolivia, Haiti and Uganda. [ID:7015]

Canadian Food for the Hungry International (CFHI)

Personnel Director, Suite 201, 2580 Cedar Park Place, Abbotsford, BC,
V2T 3S5, Canada; 800-667-0605, fax 604-853-4332, info@cfh.ca, www.cfh.ca

LARGE RELIEF AND DEVELOPMENT AGENCY: Community Development, Development Assistance,
Development Education, Environment, Fundraising, Gender and Development, Human Rights, Humanitarian
Relief, Medical Health, Micro-enterprises, Project Management, Religious, Teaching, Technical Assistance,
Volunteer, Water Resources

Canadian Food for the Hungry International (CFHI) is a Christian charitable organization
dedicated to sustainable development and emergency response worldwide. Their purpose is to send
appropriate people, ideas and resources to areas of need, to influence society as advocates for the
poor, and empower the Christian community with a biblical view of poverty and injustice. CFHI's
long-range development programs in 20 developing countries focus on agricultural training,
community development, microenterprise, child survival, reforestation, wells/irrigation, primary
health care, education and literacy, and emergency relief. All programs emphasize the
organization's Christian motivation.

CFHI has 11 staff based in Canada and five overseas employees who work with over 1,000
staff members of their partner agency, Food for the Hungry International. Applicants should have a
biblically-based Christian worldview and possess education or work experience in food production,
land reclamation, agro-forestry, primary health care, relief and development, or health-related
fields. Business or management experience is useful, but not necessary. CFHI maintains a data bank
for resumes. Visit their Web site for job openings. [ID:7016]

Canadian Foodgrains Bank Association Inc. (CFGB)

P.O. Box 767, Suite 400, 280 Smith Street, Winnipeg, MB, R3C 2L4, Canada;
204-944-1993, fax 204-943-2597, cfgb@foodgrainsbank.ca, www.foodgrainsbank.ca

MID-SIZED RELIEF AND DEVELOPMENT AGENCY: Accounting, Consulting, Development Assistance,
Humanitarian Relief, Project Management, Relief and Development

Canadian Foodgrains Bank Association Inc. (CFGB) is a Christian organization that provides
development assistance. Working as a cooperative of 13 Canadian church organizations, it is the
largest private food aid provider in the world. Canadian Foodgrains Bank member agencies carry
out food and food security programming in developing countries by working with partner
organizations that are directly involved with local communities. It also works closely with various
government organizations, including CIDA and the World Food Program. It evolved with food
justice policy and education issues both in Canada and internationally.

CFGB has 24 staff members working in Canada and two working in Ethiopia. Generally staff
have backgrounds in development aid and famine relief. Vacancies are posted on their Web site.
[ID:7017]

Canadian Foundation for the Americas (FOCAL)

Suite 720, 1 Nicholas Street, Ottawa, ON, K1N 7B7, Canada;
613-562-0005, fax 613-562-2525, focal@focal.ca, www.focal.ca ⬛ *Fr*

MID-SIZED INTERNATIONAL RESEARCH GROUP: Development Education, Economics, Social Science Research

The Canadian Foundation for the Americas (FOCAL) is an independent, non-governmental organization dedicated to deepening and strengthening Canada's relations with countries in Latin America and the Caribbean through policy discussion and analysis. FOCAL's mission is to develop a greater understanding of important hemispheric issues and to help build a stronger community of the Americas.

FOCAL's Internship Program provides an opportunity for college and university graduates to receive international experience that could propel them to a career overseas. A long-term commitment to working with the poor and marginalized, demonstrated by the completion of appropriate studies as well as a past record of community and/or volunteer work is important for acceptance to this program. Participants receive a taxable stipend to cover the cost of living expenses for six months, and travel in Canada and abroad. Preference will be given to applicants with a degree in international development, international relations, politics, economics, international law, public policy or public health. Candidates must have demonstrated interest in Latin America through course selection and travel, as well as possess a high degree of fluency in Spanish.

FOCAL offers placements at different Inter-American organizations in Washington, DC and in non-governmental organizations throughout the hemisphere. These placements are six-month projects that begin in June and end in December. Job openings are posted on FOCAL's Web site every year, between the months of March and April. [ID:7044]

Canadian Friends of Burma (CFOB)

Suite 206, 145 Spruce Street, Ottawa, ON, K1R 6P1, Canada;
613-237-8056, fax 613-563-0017, cfob@cfob.org, www.cfob.org

SMALL ADVOCACY GROUP: Advocacy, Fundraising, Human Rights, Humanitarian Relief, Media/Communications, Refugee Services

Canadian Friends of Burma (CFOB) supports the Burma pro-democracy movement in the struggle for peace, democracy, human rights and equality in Burma. It raises Canadian awareness about the political, human rights and socio-economic situation in Burma.

CFOB has one staff member in Canada. Occasionally it offers short-term contracts or internships in the areas of public advocacy and human rights. It also welcomes volunteers who can assist with campaigns and public awareness initiatives. [ID:7129]

Canadian Harambee Education Society (CHES)

446 Kelly Street, New Westminster, BC, V3L 3T9, Canada; 604-521-3416,
fax 604-521-3416, canadianharambee@shaw.ca, www.canadianharambee.ca

MID-SIZED DEVELOPMENT EDUCATION GROUP: Education, Gender and Development, Volunteer

The Canadian Harambee Education Society (CHES) is dedicated to educating young African girls. CHES provides scholarships for poor, bright high school girls in Kenya and Tanzania. CHES also supports special projects, such as the provision of books for libraries and the building of a science lab, dormitories and a computer building. CHES sends volunteers from the ranks of retired teachers and other professionals to act as agents, helping to administer the scholarship program and other projects.

CHES employs one office assistant and has many volunteers in Canada. CHES sends agents overseas on six-month terms, with four agents volunteering at one time. For more information on CHES and how to become an agent overseas, please visit their Web site. [ID:6903]

Canadian Human Rights Foundation (CHRF)

Executive Director, Suite 407, 1425 René-Lévesque Blvd. W., Montreal, QC,
H3G 1T7, Canada; 514-954-0382, fax 514-954-0659, chrf@chrf.ca, www.chrf.ca ▭ *Fr*

MID-SIZED ADVOCACY GROUP: Human Rights, International Education

The Canadian Human Rights Foundation (CHRF) delivers human rights education training in Canada, Africa, Eastern Europe, Asia and Central Asia. Thematic regional training programs include the protection and promotion of the rights of female child domestic workers, migrant workers and minorities; the teaching of trainers; capacity-building for national human rights institutions; and human rights monitoring and advocacy.

The CHRF has 18 employees in Canada and branch offices in Jakarta, Indonesia and Almaty, Kazakhstan. The CHRF maintains a data bank for resumes and considers internship positions from those who have funding. [ID:6999]

Canadian Institute of Cultural Affairs (ICA Canada)

655 Queen Street E., Toronto, ON, M4M 1G4, Canada;
416-691-2316, fax 416-691-2491, ica@icacan.ca, www.icacan.ca

SMALL ORGANIZATIONAL TRAINING GROUP: Business Development, Community Development

The Canadian Institute of Cultural Affairs (ICA Canada) is a non-profit training and research organization. It exists to develop the capacity of people to contribute to positive social change through research, publishing, education and social change projects. ICA Canada has the Youth as Facilitative Leadership Program (YFL), where candidates receive intensive training in order to give them the skills to become leaders, and teach other youth the techniques of facilitative leadership. They also sponsor the Youth in Trades project, which is being developed to encourage youth to access vocational training. Full details of ICA Canada's activities can be found on their Web site.

There are four staff working in Canada, which is member of an international network of 32 sister organizations worldwide. Several international ICA organizations accept volunteers on a six- or 12-month basis. All requests should be directed to the specific country office. For more, information visit ICA's international Web site: www.icaworld.org. [ID:7045]

Canadian Institute of Planners (CIP)

Suite 801, 116 Albert Street, Ottawa, ON, K1P 5G3, Canada;
613-237-7526, fax 613-237-7045, general@cip-icu.ca, www.cip-icu.ca ▭ *Fr*

MID-SIZED COORDINATING BODY: Community Development, Human Resources, Technical Assistance, Training and Education, Urban Development

The Canadian Institute of Planners (CIP) is the national organization of professional planners in Canada. CIP and seven provincial-level affiliate organizations based across Canada provide membership services to 5,800 professional planners in Canada and overseas.

CIP is active in several international initiatives that rely on volunteers and internships. WorldLink, the International Internship Program for Planners, provides entry-level professional work experience to recent graduates interested in gaining their first paid overseas work experience in the planning field. Working in partnership with other Canadian private and non-profit organizations managing international planning projects, the WorldLink program has successfully placed over 65 recent graduates in internship positions in 20 developing countries and economies in transition.

CIP has been active in the Caribbean since 1988 through its relationship with the Commonwealth Association of Planners. CIP is working with the Government of Trinidad and Tobago and the city of Port of Spain to design a participatory governance framework to enable the coordinated delivery of priority social development projects and services through a local area planning process in East Port of Spain. CIP is also collaborating with China's Ministry of Land and Resources to establish a land-use planning professional system for China, including the development of a professional institute, the standardization and improvement of planning education, and the reform of China's framework for land planning.

CIP is run by four full-time staff in Canada. There are no full-time staff overseas. Responsibilities for international project management are shared amongst staff. CIP is seeking individuals with experience in a broad range of areas related to urban and regional planning. Preference is given to individuals with membership in CIP. CIP offers approximately six overseas internship placements annually for recent graduates of planning and planning-related university programs. Employment, volunteer and internship opportunities are posted on their Web site and circulated electronically. [ID:6870]

Canadian Jesuits International (CJI)

1325 Bay Street, Toronto, ON, M5R 2C4, Canada;
416-962-4500, fax 416-962-4501, cji@jesuits.ca, www.jesuits.ca

MID-SIZED COMMUNITY DEVELOPMENT GROUP: Adult Training, Advocacy, Agriculture, Community Development, Development Assistance, Development Education, Environment, Gender and Development, Humanitarian Relief, Medical Health, Religious, Volunteer

Canadian Jesuits International (CJI) is committed to the service of faith and the promotion of justice among poor and marginalized groups in the global community. CJI currently works with Jesuit and other partners in India, Nepal, Africa, Jamaica and Eastern Europe, supporting efforts by the local community in the following areas: education, agriculture, cooperatives, humanitarian assistance and pastoral work. CJI fosters a holistic approach to human development and honours the transformative power of respect for elders, women and children. CJI promotes dialogue and understanding among world religions and ethnic groups and supports educational advocacy.

CJI has two staff in Canada and approximately 30 Canadian Jesuits overseas. Those interested in volunteer work overseas are usually directed to Jesuit Volunteer International, P.O. Box 25478, Washington, DC, 20007, USA; (202) 944-1594, www.jesuitvolunteers.org. [ID:7046]

Canadian Labour Congress (CLC)

International Department, 2841 Riverside Drive, Ottawa, ON, K1V 8X7, Canada;
613-521-3400, fax 613-521-4655, communications@clc-ctc.ca, www.clc-ctc.ca 🖥*Fr*

LARGE COORDINATING BODY: Adult Training, Advocacy, Community Development, Computer Systems, Development Assistance, Development Education, Exchange Programs, Gender and Development, Human Rights, Humanitarian Relief, Project Management, Technical Assistance

The Canadian Labour Congress (CLC) strives to build international trade union solidarity through technical, material, humanitarian and financial assistance overseas, and through projects sponsored by Third World union organizations. CLC staff assist project partners in the field where CLC international development projects take place. CLC international staff manages projects in Africa, the Americas, the Caribbean, Central and Eastern Europe, Asia and the Middle East.

CLC has 117 staff in Canada. Their hiring process entails circulating the postings internally first, and then, depending on the position, externally to labour councils, federations of labour, universities, affiliates, various civil society organizations and special interest groups. Most professional positions involve performing trade union related work in various fields—for example, workers' rights, globalization and free trade-related issues, workplace literacy, workplace training, research on the labour movement, women's studies, anti-racism and human rights issues. Organizers, trainers, campaigners and professionals experienced in policy development, international development, research, etc. are needed. [ID:7047]

Canadian Lawyers for International Human Rights (CLAIHR)

Human Rights Research and Education Centre, University of Ottawa, 57 Louis Pasteur Street, Ottawa, ON, K1N 6N5, Canada; 613-562-5800 ext. 3353, fax 613-562-5125, contact@claihr.org, www.claihr.org 🖥*Fr*

SMALL HUMAN RIGHTS ORGANIZATION: Advocacy, Education, Human Rights, Law

Canadian Lawyers for International Human Rights (CLAIHR) is a non-profit organization established to promote human rights globally through legal education, advocacy and law reform. CLAIHR analyses laws, institutions and practices affecting human rights; contributes to developing and strengthening laws and institutions that protect human rights; promotes awareness of human rights issues within the legal community; and supports lawyers, legal organizations and others dedicated to achieving human rights. It focuses on the situations of indigenous people, workers and women, particularly in Africa, Asia and Latin America.

CLAIHR assists the Canadian Bar Association in the selection of applicants for six-month Youth Employment Strategy internships for young lawyers. Interns work with human rights legal organizations in developing countries on issues such as women's rights, labour rights, constitutional rights, children's rights and indigenous people's rights. The program is designed to provide foreign partner organizations abroad with interns who have the legal expertise and give young lawyers international experience to help them obtain employment in international human rights legal work. Applicants should be recently graduated lawyers or students-at-law under 30, Canadian citizens or permanent residents, who are unemployed or under-employed, and who have not had previous career-related, paid employment overseas. Most partner organizations are in Africa and Latin America. Placements in Latin America are Spanish-speaking and Portuguese-speaking. CLAIHR is interested in developing new placements, in particular those that are French-speaking. Interns are required to raise $1,000 as their contribution to the $15,000 cost of the placement. [ID:7075]

Canadian Lutheran World Relief (CLWR)
1080 Kingsbury Ave., Winnipeg, MB, R2P 1W5, Canada;
204-694-5602, fax 204-694-5460, clwr@clwr.mb.ca, www.clwr.org

LARGE RELIEF AND DEVELOPMENT AGENCY: Administration (General), Agriculture, Community Development, Consulting, Development Assistance, Development Education, Environment, Gender and Development, Human Resources, Humanitarian Relief, Medical Health, Project Management, Technical Assistance, Water Resources

Canadian Lutheran World Relief (CLWR) is the service delivery arm for development programming and overseas relief for the Evangelical Lutheran Church in Canada and Lutheran Church-Canada. CLWR facilitates and supports development programs in Africa, Asia, Latin America and the Middle East. Efforts are focused in the areas of development assistance, peace building, development education and advocacy, refugees and immigration, and emergency relief and material aid.

There are five staff working in Canada and two staff overseas. Any job openings are posted on their Web site. Applications can be sent to the CLWR office in Winnipeg. Positions normally require an international development education background and/or experience; familiarity with CIDA policies; and management and communication skills. The ability to speak Spanish, Portuguese or French is also an asset. There are no internship programs offered. [ID:7048]

Canadian Manufacturers & Exporters (CME)
Suite 1500, 1 Nicholas Street, Ottawa, ON, K1N 7B7, Canada;
613-238-8888, fax 613-563-9218, national@cme-mec.ca, www.cme-mec.ca 💻 Fr

LARGE TRADE ORGANIZATION: Advanced Technology, Advocacy, Business Development, Manufacturing, Trade and Investment, Training and Education

Canadian Manufacturers & Exporters (CME) represents the interests of Canadian business, keeping members on the competitive edge of world-class manufacturing and trade. Its mission is to continually improve the competitiveness of Canadian industry and to expand export business through effective advocacy to government at all levels; timely, relevant information, programs and support of superior quality and value; opportunities for networking, learning and professional growth; and promoting the development and implementation of advanced technology. CME has an international network of similar organizations that it works with around the world.

CME has 70 staff across Canada. Professional staff postings are advertised through the CME Web site. Resumes are kept on file until positions are available. Internships are offered under the CIDA Youth Employment Strategy. For more details contact CME directly. [ID:6871]

Canadian Museums Association (CMA)

Suite 400, 280 Metcalfe Street, Ottawa, ON, K2P 1R7,
Canada; 613-567-0099, fax 613-233-5438, www.museums.ca 💻 *Fr*

LARGE COORDINATING BODY: Science and Technology, Training and Education, Youth and Development

The Canadian Museums Association (CMA) is the national organization for the advancement of the Canadian museum community. It unites, represents and serves museums and museum workers across Canada. Members are non-profit museums, art galleries, science centres, aquaria, archives, sports halls of fame, artist-run centres, zoos and historic sites across Canada. All are dedicated to preserving and presenting our cultural heritage to the public.

CMA has 13 staff working in Ottawa, and it has approximately 1,500 individual members and 500 institutional members. It administers three Youth Employment Programs funded by the Government of Canada, in museums across Canada and abroad. Young Professionals International (YPI) gives young adults under 30 their first paid, career-related international work experience through six-month overseas placements. Young Canada Works in Heritage Organizations provides summer jobs for high school, college and university students who are 30 and under. Young Canada Works at Building Careers in Heritage (YCW-BCH) supports a small number of internships for underemployed and unemployed graduates under 30. These experiences last from four to 12 consecutive months (four months for internships in Canada and six months for international internships). All applications for youth opportunities are posted on their Web site. Also, the careers section of CMA's Web site is a free job posting service, created jointly by the Canadian Museums Association and the Canadian Heritage Information Network. It lists job postings for administrative, interpretive and technical jobs associated with museum work across Canada. [ID:6885]

Canadian Network for International Surgery (CNIS)

Suite 205, 1037 W. Broadway, Vancouver, BC, V6H 1E3, Canada;
604-739-4708, fax 604-739-4788, office@cnis.ca, www.cnis.ca

SMALL MEDICAL ASSISTANCE GROUP: Medical Health

The Canadian Network for International Surgery (CNIS) is a non-profit organization that promotes the delivery of essential surgical care to the underprivileged. CNIS is a nation-wide membership of physicians, surgeons, and other concerned citizens who share a commitment to improving the health of people in low-income countries. It wants to empower low-income countries to create an environment where the risk of injuries is minimal and all people receive adequate surgical care. Three people staff the Vancouver office. Requests for medical-related and support staff volunteers to work in Canada and Africa are listed on their Web site. [ID:6904]

Canadian Nurses Association (CNA)

50 Driveway, Ottawa, ON, K2P 1E2, Canada; 613-237-2133,
fax 613-237-3520, info@cna-aiic.ca, www.cna-aiic.ca 💻 *Fr*

LARGE COORDINATING BODY: Public Health, Training and Education

The Canadian Nurses Association (CNA) is a federation of 11 provincial and territorial nursing associations representing more than 120,000 registered nurses. CNA employs 58 staff in Ottawa, including nine in its Department of International Policy and Development (IPD) either in the capacity of Nurse Consultant or Administrative/Financial Support. IPD is partially supported financially by the Government of Canada through the Canadian International Development Agency (CIDA) on two international health partnership programs. These programs enable the exchange of expertise and best practices to support leadership development in nursing, public and regulatory policy, primary health care, and HIV/AIDS, with over 20 national nursing associations in Eastern Europe, sub-Saharan Africa, Asia and Latin America. CNA's international projects are advanced with support of Canadian nurses on technical and/or monitoring missions.

CNA works mostly through its member provincial associations to identify nurse consultants with relevant skills and expertise to volunteer in its IHP. An honorarium is offered to the volunteers, and all travel, accommodation and per diem expenses are paid by CNA. To volunteer, you must be a registered nurse (RN) and a CNA member. Candidates should be baccalaureate prepared (or equivalent), and possess proven, relevant knowledge and expertise, as well as language skills, where indicated. Interested candidates may contact their provincial professional association or submit a resume to CNA for consideration. [ID:6892]

Canadian Organization for Development through Education (CODE)

Development Department, 321 Chapel Street, Ottawa, ON, K1N 7Z2, Canada;
613-232-3569, fax 613-232-7435, codehq@codecan.com, www.codecan.org 🖳 *Fr*

LARGE DEVELOPMENT ASSISTANCE GROUP: Development Education, Fundraising, Media/Communications, Project Management

The Canadian Organization for Development (CODE) is a Canadian charitable organization that has been promoting education and literacy in the developing world for more than 40 years. CODE builds the bridge of literacy by developing partnerships that provide resources for learning, promote awareness and understanding, and encourage self-reliance. Overseas, CODE works with 13 partner organizations in nine countries: eight in Africa and one in the Caribbean. CODE's target group is primary school-aged children. The organization is committed to supporting communities where children have inadequate access to literacy resources and skilled teachers. CODE also carries out development education programs in Canada to raise awareness of the need to support literacy and education in the developing world. It has received many awards including a Canada Post Flight for Freedom Literacy Award and a UNESCO International Prize for Literacy.

CODE has 17 employees all based in Canada. Generally, a candidate must have a relevant degree and/or equivalent educational qualifications; an understanding of international development plus a minimum of two years' experience working in a developing country; excellent project/program management, administrative and organizing skills; and good interpersonal skills. CODE does not have an overseas volunteer program. CODE maintains a database of resumes for hiring. [ID:7049]

Canadian Peace Alliance (CPA)

P.O. Box 13, 427 Bloor Street W., Toronto, ON, M5S 1X7, Canada;
416-588-5555, fax 416-588-5556, cpa@web.ca, www.acp-cpa.ca 🖳 *Fr*

SMALL COORDINATING BODY: Advocacy, Conflict Prevention, Education

The Canadian Peace Alliance (CPA) is the largest umbrella peace organization in Canada. Its member groups act as a broad coalition in order to provide a strong, coordinated voice for peace issues at the national level. Common goals among member groups include redirecting funds from military spending to human needs; working toward global nuclear disarmament; making Canada a consistent leader for world peace; strengthening world institutions for the peaceful resolution of conflict; and protecting the rights of all people to work for social and economic justice. These goals are attained through public education and political lobbying. The Canadian Peace Alliance is staffed by two co-coordinators. They do not send staff overseas. [ID:6905]

Canadian Physicians for Aid and Relief (CPAR)

1425 Bloor Street W., Toronto, ON, M6P 3L6, Canada;
416-369-0865, fax 416-369-0294, info@cpar.ca, www.cpar.ca

LARGE RELIEF AND DEVELOPMENT AGENCY: Accounting, Administration (General), Computer Systems, Construction, Development Assistance, Development Education, Engineering, Environment, Forestry, Gender and Development, Humanitarian Relief, Medical Health, Water Resources

Canadian Physicians for Aid and Relief (CPAR) is a non-profit, non-sectarian organization supporting vulnerable, low-income people in the developing world to achieve good health by helping individuals, communities and grassroots organizations to become increasingly self-reliant. CPAR also works locally to inform Canadians about the global effort for health and development. CPAR is currently in Ethiopia, Tanzania, Malawi and Uganda. CPAR minimizes expatriate involvement and maximizes local involvement to ensure that local people are adequately trained to sustain the program once expatriates withdraw.

There are 10 Canadian staff and approximately 200 local staff overseas. The Canadian office is responsible for support and administration, fundraising, development education and public relations. Successful applicants will have hands-on experience or skills in agroforestry, health, engineering, management or administration. Experience living and working in the developing world is an asset. CPAR looks for innovative, self-directed, and resourceful people willing to commit to a minimum of two years overseas. All expatriate staff, excluding senior management positions, are expected to undertake voluntary work for CPAR in Canada following a position overseas. CPAR maintains a data bank for resumes. [ID:7050]

Canadian Public Health Association (CPHA)

International Programs, Suite 400, 1565 Carling Ave., Ottawa, ON, K1Z 8R1, Canada; 613-725-3769, fax 613-725-9826, info@cpha.ca, www.cpha.ca ⊒*Fr*

LARGE COMMUNITY HEALTH GROUP: Advocacy, Community Development, Development Education, Gender and Development, Medical Health, Project Management

The Canadian Public Health Association (CPHA) is a national, independent, non-profit, voluntary association representing public health in Canada with links to the international public health community. CPHA's members believe in universal and equitable access to the basic conditions that are necessary to achieve health for all Canadians. CPHA's mission is to constitute a special national resource that advocates for the improvement and maintenance of personal and community health according to the public health principles of disease prevention, health promotion and protection, and healthy public policy. CPHA's membership is composed of health professionals from over 25 health disciplines and is active in conducting and supporting health and social programs both nationally and internationally. CPHA stresses its partnership role by working with federal and provincial government departments and international agencies, non-governmental organizations and the private sector in conducting research and health services programs.

CPHA employs a total of 60 employees; 19 of whom are with the Global Health Programs (one is overseas). Through its Global Health Programs, and with the support of CIDA, CPHA cooperates with public health and similar organizations in Africa, the Caribbean, Latin America, and Central and Eastern Europe. CPHA manages several international projects including the Family and Reproductive Health Project (Malawi and Zambia), the Aboriginal and Rural Women's Health Project (Argentina), the Strengthening of Essential Public Health Functions Project (Balkans), the Caribbean HIV/AIDS Project and the Southern African AIDS Trust. Through the Canadian International Immunization Initiative (CIII), CPHA recruits Canadian technical experts to assist the World Health Organization (WHO), the United Nation's Children's Fund (UNICEF) and local Ministries of Health to strengthen childhood immunization. In addition, CPHA occasionally seeks other public health experts for volunteer short-term assignments overseas, particularly for the Strengthening of Public Health Associations Program. CPHA maintains a data bank for resumes. [ID:7051]

Canadian Red Cross Society (CRCS)

Suite 300, 170 Metcalfe Street, Ottawa, ON, K2P 2P2, Canada; 613-740-1900, fax 613-740-1911, feedback@redcross.ca, www.redcross.ca ⊒*Fr*

LARGE RELIEF AND DEVELOPMENT AGENCY: Accounting, Administration (General), Advocacy, Agriculture, Community Development, Development Assistance, Development Education, Humanitarian Relief, Logistics, Media/Communications, Medical Health, Technical Assistance, Volunteer, Water Resources

The Canadian Red Cross Society (CRCS) is a non-profit, humanitarian organization and a branch of the International Red Cross and Red Crescent Movement. The mission of CRCS is to help people deal with situations that threaten their survival and safety, their security and well-being, and their human dignity. Canadian operations include international relief and development assistance, a domestic tracing and family reunion service, and educational and international humanitarian law dissemination activities.

There are 6,644 Canadian Red Cross staff across the country, both full- and part-time. CRCS sends approximately 120 professional relief workers on overseas missions yearly. These people are recruited and trained for overseas assignments with the International Committee of the Red Cross (ICRC) and the International Federation of Red Cross and Red Crescent Societies in its international relief operations. Assignments, organized in response to natural disasters and conflict, are six to 12 months in length. Overseas positions include working with displaced persons and unaccompanied children, working in places of detention, or in finance and administration, telecommunications, water and sanitation, medical/health, disaster preparedness, relief administration, and information dissemination. Individuals recruited for these assignments have five years work experience in their fields.

People are recruited both from within the CRCS and on a contract basis. Applicants are recruited through regional and zonal offices and must first participate in the Basic Training Course for Overseas Personnel. The CRCS also manages a large domestic emergency response program and encourages potential international staff to become actively involved as volunteers at the local level. Applicants should contact their regional office. General information about employment opportunities is available on the CRCS Web site. For those interested in disaster relief, the "International" section on the Web site has an excellent source of up-to-date information on relief activities. [ID:7052]

Canadian Rotary Committee for International Development (CRCID)
1579 Hyde Park Road, London, ON, N6H 5L4, Canada;
519-473-2100, fax 519-471-8982, www.crcid.org

MID-SIZED COMMUNITY DEVELOPMENT GROUP: Agriculture, Business Development, Community Development, Development Education, Gender and Development, Human Resources, Medical Health, Micro-enterprises, Teaching, Technical Assistance, Volunteer, Water Resources

The mission of the Canadian Rotary Committee for International Development (CRCID) is to champion the principles of sustainable development among Rotarians throughout Canada, while assisting Canadian Rotary Clubs and Districts to obtain matching funds from CIDA for overseas development assistance. CRCID supports community development through project development, assessment, funding and management. It also monitors and evaluates existing projects, and has a development education program.

Program areas include water and sanitation, agriculture and forestry, community/social development, primary education, primary health care, and microenterprise. The individual projects are planned and implemented by volunteer Rotarians in Canada and in the eligible developing countries with the financial assistance and international development expertise of CRCID personnel. Rotary volunteers are selected to monitor and evaluate the projects once they are completed.

CRCID has three professional staff and 23 volunteer regional members in Canada with international development expertise. Limited opportunities exist for Canadians seeking employment. The Rotary International Web site has many volunteer opportunities; check it out at www.rotary.org/programs/volunteers. [ID:7053]

Canadian Teachers' Federation (CTF)
International Programs, 2490 Don Reid Drive, Ottawa, ON, K1H 1E1,
Canada; 613-232-1505, fax 613-232-1886, info@ctf-fce.ca, www.ctf-fce.ca ☐ Fr

LARGE ORGANIZATIONAL TRAINING GROUP: Development Assistance, Teaching, Volunteer

The Canadian Teachers' Federation (CTF) is a national bilingual umbrella organization of 14 provincial and territorial teacher associations with a membership of approximately 240,000 teachers across Canada. CTF's major areas of interest include defending public education; promoting the teaching profession; providing support to member organizations and teachers across Canada; addressing societal issues that affect the health and well-being of children and youth in Canada and abroad; and providing assistance and support to teacher colleagues in developing countries.

Project Overseas is a joint endeavour by the CTF and its members to work with fellow teachers in developing countries to provide in-service training. Project Overseas has now assisted teacher organizations in over 50 countries of Africa, Asia and the Caribbean. As many as 50 volunteers are sent to approximately 12 countries for between three and six weeks in the summer. Additional Canadian teachers volunteer their time and talents for Inter-Action, which links resource persons to teacher organization projects that extend the reach of quality public education in their countries. Types of assistance range from teacher and leadership training to organizational skills development and secretariat support. Requirements for direct participation include five years of Canadian teaching experience. Teachers must apply through their provincial or territorial teacher organizations or, in Ontario, through their OTF affiliates. Complete applications and further details are on the CTF Web site. (For more information on CTF, see Chapter 10, Short-Term Programs Overseas.) [ID:7054]

CARE Canada
Suite 200, 9 Gurdwara Road, Ottawa, ON, K2E 7X6, Canada;
613-228-5600, fax 613-226-5777, info@care.ca, www.care.ca ☐ *Fr* ☐ *Sp*

LARGE DEVELOPMENT ASSISTANCE GROUP: Accounting, Administration (General), Agriculture, Business Development, Community Development, Computer Systems, Construction, Consulting, Engineering, Environment, Fisheries, Forestry, Fundraising, Gender and Development, Human Resources, Human Rights, Humanitarian Relief, Logistics, Media/Communications, Medical Health, Micro-enterprises, Project Management, Water Resources

CARE Canada implements development projects throughout the world in water supply and sanitation, agroforestry and natural resources, income generation, emergency assistance and small economic activities. Its major programs are agriculture, forestry, public health, water supply, construction, emergency response and project management. CARE Canada facilitates lasting change by strengthening capacity for self-help, influencing policy decisions at all levels, providing economic opportunity, addressing discrimination in all its forms and delivering relief in emergencies.

CARE Canada has approximately 60 Canadian staff working in Canada and another 60 Canadian staff overseas. CARE Canada recruits staff to work within projects, to manage projects, to administer and manage field office functions and to provide technical advice. Contract length is variable and dependent on project activity, duration and funding. Interested candidates must have a university degree or college diploma and at least two to three years of relevant work experience working with a development or emergency program overseas. To apply for current or future openings, interested applicants should register on-line via the CARE Canada Web site or through www.careerswithoutborders.com.

CARE Canada also offers a limited number of internships each year. Some are funded through CIDA's International Youth Internship Program, which is a federally-funded program aiming to give recent graduates their first international work experience in development programming. Internship opportunities are posted on the CARE Canada and/or CIDA Web sites as they become available. [ID:7055]

Carrefour de solidarité internationale (CSI)
165, rue Moore, Sherbrooke, QC, J1H 1B8, Canada; 819-566-8595,
fax 819-566-8076, info@csisher.com, www.csisher.com

SMALL DEVELOPMENT ASSISTANCE GROUP: Adult Training, Agriculture, Community Development, Development Assistance, Development Education, Environment, Exchange Programs, Gender and Development, Human Resources, Human Rights, Logistics, Media/Communications, Project Management, Teaching, Technical Assistance, Volunteer, Water Resources

Le Carrefour solidarité internationale (CSI) est une ONG régionale qui, dans sa programmation régulière, développe des liens de partenariat avec des organismes au Mali, en République Dominicaine, à Haïti, au Nicaragua, et au Pérou. Sa programmation intégrée comprend trois volets: soutien de projet de développement, stages d'échange et communications sociales. CSI organise également, en Estrie, des activités de sensibilisation aux enjeux internationaux.

Carrefour solidarité international dispose d'un personnel de 7 employés au Canada. Le CSI évalue les demandes de stages dans les domaines de l'organisation communautaire, la santé, l'agriculture et le développement durable. [ID:7261]

Carrefour tiers-monde (CTM)

365, boul. Charest est, Quebec, QC, G1K 3H3, Canada; 418-647-5853,
fax 418-647-5856, info@carrefour-tiers-monde.org, www.carrefour-tiers-monde.org

SMALL DEVELOPMENT EDUCATION GROUP: Adult Training, Community Development, Development Assistance, Development Education, Exchange Programs, Gender and Development, Human Rights, Media/Communications

Carrefour tiers-monde est une organisation non gouvernementale vouée à l'éducation du public de la région de Québec à la solidarité internationale. Trois employés travaillent à temps complet et deux sont contractuels. Les objectifs de l'organisme sont de sensibiliser la population à la réalité des peuples des pays en voie de développement, d'offrir des possibilités de formation sur les différents aspects du développement, de servir de lieu de rencontre et d'offrir des ressources aux groupes et aux individus qui s'intéressent aux questions de développement international. Par ailleurs, elle organise aussi, par exemple, des conférences publiques, des sessions de formation et des campagnes d'actions de solidarité internationale. Elle possède son propre centre de documentation. CTM produit des outils pédagogiques en lien avec l'éducation au développement et à la solidarité internationale. [ID:7319]

CAUSE Canada (CC)

Overseas Program Director, P.O. Box 8100, Canmore, AB, T1W 2T8, Canada;
403-678-3332, fax 403-678-8869, info@cause.ca, www.cause.ca

MID-SIZED DEVELOPMENT ASSISTANCE GROUP: Agriculture, Community Development, Construction, Development Education, Environment, Forestry, Fundraising, Gender and Development, Humanitarian Relief, Medical Health, Micro-enterprises, Water Resources

CAUSE Canada (CC) is an international relief and development agency committed to supporting sustainable development projects in geographical regions underrepresented by the international aid community. Assistance is focused in West Africa and Central America, especially Guatemala, Honduras, Sierra Leone and Ivory Coast. Development priorities include primary health care, water and sanitation, reforestation, gender-specific development, microenterprise projects, post-conflict reintegration and rehabilitation (peacebuilding). CC is committed to the challenge of assisting their developing partners in the establishment and strengthening of their own non-governmental organization communities.

CAUSE Canada employs six staff in Canada and 13 overseas. CC seeks individuals with university degrees in business management, health-related disciplines and accounting. Previous overseas experience and fluency in Spanish or French is a must. Individuals must also be able to work in a team environment with flexibility and initiative. CC maintains a data bank for resumes and offers six-month internships with stipends. Volunteer positions are also available depending on the candidate and country needs (very small honorariums are given and accommodation is normally covered). Current areas of focus for internships are health, agriculture, accounting, business development and gender equality promotion. [ID:7125]

Centre de coopération internationale en santé et développement

2180, chemin Ste-Foy, C.P. 2208, terminus Québec, Quebec, QC, G1K 7P4,
Canada; 418-656-5525, fax 418-656-2627, ccisd@ccisd.org, www.ccisd.org ▭*Sp* ▭*En*

LARGE DEVELOPMENT ASSISTANCE GROUP: Community Development, Development Assistance, Development Education, Human Rights, Medical Health, Project Management

Le Centre de coopération internationale en santé et développement (CCISD) est une organisation sans but lucratif qui se spécialise dans la conception et la gestion de projets en matière de santé sur la scène internationale. Le mandat du CCISD est de contribuer à l'amélioration de la santé des populations les plus démunies par le renforcement des ressources du secteur de la santé et des groupes communautaires qui travaillent en collaboration avec celles-ci.

Établi au Québec depuis 1987, le CCISD compte sur les services professionnels et l'expertise de plus de 175 personnes qui travaillent au siège social et à l'étranger pour la réalisation de projets en Afrique, en Amérique latine et en Asie.

Le CCISD appuie de nombreuses causes, telles que la lutte contre le sida et les maladies transmissibles sexuellement, la veille épidémiologique et les nouvelles technologies de l'information, la santé des femmes, les soins de santé de base, l'intervention en faveur de la petite enfance, la problématique des rapports entre les sexes dans un contexte de développement international, le renforcement des moyens des communautés dans le secteur de la santé et enfin, le soutien aux établissements et aux organismes qui se consacrent à la santé des populations. [ID:7238]

Centre de solidarité internationale du Saguenay-Lac-Saint-Jean
C.P. 278, Bureau 206, 425 Sacré-Cœur ouest, Alma, QC, G8B 5V8, Canada;
418-668-5211, fax 418-668-5638, centreso@centreso.saglac.org, www.centreso.saglac.org

SMALL VOLUNTEER GROUP: Administration (General), Development Assistance, Development Education, Media/Communications, Project Management, Technical Assistance, Volunteer

Le Centre de solidarité internationale du Saguenay-Lac-Saint-Jean (CSI), travaille à mettre en œuvre des actions de solidarité internationale avec la population du Saguenay-Lac-Saint-Jean dans une perspective de développement durable et dans le but de bâtir un monde juste et équitable. Ses programmes de coopération permettent à des communautés de pays du Sud (particulièrement l'Équateur et le Burkina Faso) d'acquérir les moyens techniques, matériels et humains pour prendre en charge leur propre développement. Le CSI réalise un travail d'ouverture sur le monde, notamment auprès des jeunes. Parmi ses volets d'actions, soulignons des stages outre-mer, des activités de sensibilisation et financement, la mise sur pied de projets de développement outre-mer et l'engagement bénévole à la solidarité internationale. [ID:7320]

Centre for Social Justice
Suite 303, 489 College Street, Toronto, ON, M6G 1A5, Canada;
416-927-0777, fax 416-927-7771, justice@socialjustice.org, www.socialjustice.org

MID-SIZED ADVOCACY GROUP: Education, Human Rights, Research, Social Justice and Development

The Centre for Social Justice conducts research and promotes education and advocacy. It is committed to working for change in partnership with various social movements and recognizes that effective change requires the active participation of all sectors of our community. Although the Centre is based in Ontario, its work increasingly takes place across Canada and in the international arena. The programmatic content of the Centre's work may change from year to year, but there is an ongoing interest in working strategically to narrow the gap between rich and poor, challenging the corporate domination of Canadian politics, and pressing for policy changes that promote economic and social justice.

The Centre for Social Justice has four staff members and seven interns working as researchers, adult educators and organizers. All have degrees in the social sciences. When positions become available they are advertised on www.charityvillage.com. [ID:6923]

Change for Children Association (CFCA)
Suite 221, 9624 - 108th Ave., Edmonton, AB, T5H 1A4, Canada; 780-448-1505,
fax 780-448-1507, cfca@changeforchildren.org, www.changeforchildren.org

MID-SIZED COMMUNITY DEVELOPMENT GROUP: Community Development, Development Assistance, Development Education, Project Management

Change for Children Association (CFCA) primarily undertakes grassroots projects in Latin America and the Caribbean. Indigenous cooperants determine project sectors, priorities and costs. They also administer and implement projects. In Canada, CFCA has an extensive development education program that educates Canadians on such issues as social justice, international cooperation and the root causes of poverty.

CFCA has two staff in Edmonton: one in charge of project management and financial administration of the organization and another responsible for the development education program. CFCA also has numerous volunteers in Canada and hundreds of indigenous volunteers overseas. Canadians wishing to visit CFCA's overseas projects must do so at their own expense and initiative.

CFCA participates in CIDA's International Youth Internship Program, with one or two interns per year. The program offers young Canadian post-secondary graduates the opportunity to gain valuable international development work experience. Internships are 10 months in duration: four months are spent working in the Edmonton office and six months are spent working overseas with one of CFCA's partner organizations. Opportunities are posted on their Web site.

For employment in Canada, CFCA requires a strong commitment to the ideals of development assistance and social justice. Depending on the position, applicants should have strong administrative skills or a meaningful background in international development, combined with an ability to articulate the concepts of development and social justice. CFCA maintains a data bank for resumes. [ID:7058]

CHF
Deputy Director, 323 Chapel Street, Ottawa, ON, K1N 7Z2, Canada;
613-237-0180, fax 613-237-5969, info@partners.ca, www.chf-partners.ca

LARGE DEVELOPMENT ASSISTANCE GROUP: Accounting, Administration (General), Adult Training, Advocacy, Agriculture, Community Development, Development Assistance, Development Education, Fundraising, Gender and Development, Human Rights, Micro-enterprises, Project Management, Technical Assistance

CHF is a non-profit organization dedicated to enabling poor rural communities in developing countries to attain sustainable livelihoods. Forty years ago CHF was involved in community development in India. Today, in partnership with NGOs in developing countries, CHF helps to bring food, water, energy, and most importantly, self-reliance to people in over 40 countries in Africa, Asia and the Americas.

CHF currently employs 20 staff in Canada and four overseas. It seeks individuals who have technical and management expertise, leadership skills and the ability to relate to the social and cultural milieu of the countries where CHF implements programs. [ID:7004]

Christian Blind Mission International - Canada (CBMI)
P.O. Box 800, Stouffville, ON, L4A 7Z9, Canada;
905-640-6464, fax 905-640-4332, cbmi@cbmi-can.org, www.cbmicanada.org

LARGE SPECIAL NEEDS GROUP: Administration (General), Adult Training, Blindness Rehabilitation, Community Development, Humanitarian Relief, Logistics, Medical Health, Project Management, Teaching, Technical Assistance

Christian Blind Mission International (CBMI) is a leading agency working towards the prevention and cure of blindness and towards enabling people with disabilities in developing countries. Christian Blind Mission International - Canada makes Canadians aware of the needs of blind and otherwise disabled people in developing countries. With more than 50 ongoing projects in 30 countries, CBMI-Canada provides funds and personnel to help partners meet the tremendous needs of the projects. Working together with national churches, other mission organizations, and national self-help groups, CBMI-Canada seeks to bring physical help and spiritual hope to people with disabilities in developing nations.

CBMI assigns over 100 expatriates of various nationalities to overseas posts and also employs over 10,000 skilled nationals. Seconded co-workers are most commonly ophthalmologists and orthopaedic surgeons, teachers of the blind and deaf, vocational trainers and CBR (community-based rehabilitation) experts. Most of the assignments are in Africa, but there are also some opportunities in Asia and Latin America.

CBMI requires workers who can take a hands-on approach and have the ability to motivate and lead others, as well as deal with frustrations and difficult situations. CBMI especially needs creative, innovative people who are able to work with patience and determination for the sake of others. English language skills are required, while French and/or Spanish is useful. Applicants should have a university or equivalent degree and at least two to three years of professional experience, and should be prepared to accept a two- to four-year contract. Applicants should also be willing to work in a Christian environment. In addition to salary, CBMI provides overseas co-workers with a benefits package and cost of living allowance. [ID:7059]

Christian Children's Fund of Canada (CCFC)
1027 McNicoll Ave., Toronto, ON, M1W 3X2, Canada; 416-495-1174,
fax 416-495-9395, sponsors@ccfcanada.ca, www.ccfcanada.ca

LARGE DEVELOPMENT ASSISTANCE GROUP: Adult Training, Agriculture, Business Development, Community Development, Development Assistance, Development Education, Environment, Exchange Programs, Fundraising, Gender and Development, Human Rights, Humanitarian Relief, Micro-enterprises, Project Management, Teaching, Volunteer, Water Resources

Christian Children's Fund of Canada (CCFC) is an international development organization that provides financial and technical assistance to children and community development projects. CCFC works in 11 countries, affecting the lives of over 250,000 children and families each year. Programs begin by trying to meet the basic needs of children: adequate food, water, housing, clothing, education and health care. Additional programs provide basic development services such as potable water, irrigation, housing projects and sanitation. In selected projects, CCFC cooperates with the community in developing programs for income generation, food production, education and institutional strengthening to achieve self-sufficiency.

CCFC has approximately 45 staff in Canada. All overseas work is done in partnership with indigenous church or community agencies in an effort to strengthen organizations and encourage participation in programs that affect local lives. CCFC seeks workers with skills in education, health care, agriculture, sanitation, engineering related to irrigation and water projects, small business management and basic construction. Multilingualism, strong planning and administrative skills are also assets. Candidates must be self-directed, work well under very limited supervision and be able to find solutions to the inevitable problems that occur in a development project. Applicants must commit to an egalitarian relationship with partners in developing countries. CCFC considers internship applications on an individual basis. [ID:7060]

Christian Reformed World Relief Committee of Canada (CRWRC)
P.O. Box 5070, Stn. LCD 1, 3475 Mainway, Burlington, ON, L7R 3Y8,
Canada; 905-336-2920, fax 905-336-8344, crwrc@crcna.ca, www.crwrc.org

LARGE DEVELOPMENT ASSISTANCE GROUP: Adult Training, Agriculture, Business Development, Community Development, Development Education, Fisheries, Micro-enterprises, Project Management, Religious, Teaching, Water Resources

The Christian Reformed World Relief Committee of Canada (CRWRC) is a relief, development and educational ministry supported by the Christian Reformed Church in North America. In North America and 30 countries around the world, CRWRC works with people and communities struggling with poverty to create permanent and positive change. CRWRC works in partnership with local Christian agencies, strengthening their organizational capacities, and helping them carry out programs of integrated community development and relief in times of disaster. In community development, CRWRC works to improve leadership skills, food production, income, health education, literacy and spiritual growth. Its programs promote justice, gender equity and environmental integrity. In relief, CRWRC responds to urgent needs in human and natural disasters around the world. It works in partnership with Christian agencies, including the Canadian Foodgrains Bank and the Foods Resource Bank, to provide food, shelter, seed and tools. It also provides reconstruction services through trained volunteers. In justice education, CRWRC helps people in North America and around the world to develop and act from a Christian perspective on issues of poverty, hunger and justice.

CRWRC has 12 staff in Canada and 76 working overseas. CRWRC hires a variety of skilled, development-minded Christians. All have training or comparable experience in agriculture, health, social work, literacy, management or community development. Job postings are available on their Web site. CRWRC maintains a data bank for resumes. [ID:7061]

Christian Veterinary Missions of Canada (CVM)
P.O. Box 31059, Guelph, ON, N1H 8K1, Canada; 905-304-6146, www.cvmcanada.org

SMALL DEVELOPMENT ASSISTANCE GROUP: Education

Christian Veterinary Missions of Canada (CVM) is a fellowship of veterinarians, veterinary students and others interested in the opportunity to minister through their profession to the needs of veterinarians, people and their animals worldwide. The organization is committed to empowering veterinarians, technicians and veterinary students to Christian ministry through the veterinary profession. Currently CVMC is involved in two long-term projects overseas in Mongolia and Sierra Leone.

CVM has two staff in Canada and is an active partner in the CVM US short-term and long-term ministry programs. Through these programs, veterinarians, technicians and veterinary students have the opportunity to work overseas in the developing world for anywhere from one week to six months, usually at the site of a current CVM US long-term project. Also, long-term assignments are available for veterinarians who want to use their skills on a full-time basis in the developing world. The length of term varies from two to three years, with the possibility of extending beyond that time. For more details on these overseas programs, please contact CVMC directly. [ID:6917]

CLUB 2/3
Bureau 510, 1259 rue Berri, Montreal, QC, H2L 4C7, Canada;
514-382-7922, fax 514-382-3474, club@2tiers.org, www.2tiers.org

MID-SIZED DEVELOPMENT EDUCATION GROUP: Administration (General), Agriculture, Community Development, Development Education, Education, Environment, Global Communications, Media/Communications, Medical Health, Micro-enterprises, Project Management, Youth and Development

Le CLUB 2/3 est un organisme d'éducation et de coopération internationale fondé en 1970 par un groupe d'étudiants et d'intervenants en milieu scolaire. Il a pour mission de sensibiliser les jeunes d'ici et d'ailleurs à l'interdépendance des peuples, de les amener à vivre en citoyens du monde respectueux de la diversité culturelle par le biais des valeurs de justice, d'équité et de solidarité. Le CLUB 2/3 réalise avec les jeunes et leur communauté des programmes de coopération qui répondent à leurs besoins réciproques et qui s'inscrivent dans une perspective de développement durable. Le CLUB 2/3 soutient des organismes jeunesse au Bénin, au Brésil, au Burkina Faso, en Haïti, au Népal, au Paraguay, au Pérou et au Togo et mène un programme de sensibilisation dans 200 écoles secondaires du Québec. Le CLUB 2/3 offre des stages d'initiation à la coopération internationale (70 jours en groupe de 6 à 10) pour les jeunes âgés de 18 à 30 ans et des stages pour jeunes professionnels (stages individuels de six mois) dans l'un ou l'autre des pays où se concentrent les activités de l'organisation. [ID:7243]

Coady International Institute
St. Francis Xavier University, P.O. Box 5000, Antigonish, NS, B2G 2W5, Canada;
902-867-3960, fax 902-867-3907, coady@stfx.ca, www.stfx.ca/institutes/coady

LARGE ORGANIZATIONAL TRAINING GROUP: Adult Training, Advocacy, Community Development, Development Education, Environment, Gender and Development, Human Rights, Media/Communications, Micro-enterprises, Project Management

The Coady International Institute, at St. Francis Xavier University, is world-renowned as a centre of excellence in community-based development education, innovation and action. The institute focuses on strengthening and building the capacity of people, their communities and societies to foster the growth of a more just, inclusive, participatory and sustainable society. It promotes this by providing training, consultancies, participatory evaluation and technical assistance to organizations working with disadvantaged communities in developing countries. Areas of expertise include asset-based community development, adult education, microfinance, advocacy and networking, peacebuilding and conflict transformation, community-based resource management and gender development. The training is offered each year in Antigonish, Nova Scotia, and in developing countries at the request of groups and institutions. The institute also engages in public education about development, mainly in Atlantic Canada. The institute is committed to working with partner organizations worldwide to help them strengthen their ability to educate and train local development workers, hence developing a global shared-learning network of development leaders and organizations. The Coady International Institute is also collaborating with global partners to initiate a new distance learning program that will increase access to educational programs.

The institute has 10 full-time teaching staff. It looks for candidates at the MA and PhD levels with expertise in adult education, community development, cooperatives and credit unions, program planning, implementation and evaluation. International experience in people-based development is preferred. The Coady International Institute keeps resumes on file for two years. The institute also offers the International Youth Internship Program, a six-month overseas work internship aimed at engaging young Canadians and providing them with experiences and education that will encourage their participation as global citizens. Qualifications, duration and honorariums vary and depend upon the program offering funding. For openings and new internship opportunities, potential applicants should check their Web site. [ID:7062]

CoDevelopment Canada (CoDev)

Programme Director, Suite 101, 2747 East Hastings Street, Vancouver, BC, V5V 1T9, Canada; 604-708-1496, fax 604-708-1497, codev@codev.org, www.codev.org

MID-SIZED DEVELOPMENT EDUCATION GROUP: Advocacy, Community Development, Development Assistance, Development Education, Environment, Fundraising, Gender and Development, Human Rights, Intercultural Briefings, Teaching

CoDevelopment Canada (CoDev) works to form partnerships between groups in BC and in Latin America in order to build alliances for social change. It has partnerships with more than 16 unions and groups in BC and with 23 community groups, women's organizations and unions in Latin America and Cuba. CoDev seeks to strengthen civil society groups, particularly those representing historically disadvantaged sectors of the population such as women, workers, indigenous people and poor communities. Gender equity, women's empowerment and labour rights are central themes in the work that CoDev supports. Poverty eradication through education, community development and income generating activities is another. The 30 projects currently underway include a broad range of activities such as leadership training, human and labour rights education, institutional strengthening, basic health education, income generation projects and cultural exchanges between students.

CoDev has four staff based in Canada. CoDev welcomes volunteers for general office support, to billet partners from Latin America, to translate documents, to do outreach at events and conferences and to help with fundraising. [ID:7000]

Collaboration santé internationale (CSI)

1001, chemin de la Canardière, Quebec, QC, G1J 5G5, Canada; 418-522-6065, fax 418-522-5530, csi@csiquebec.org, www.csiquebec.org

MID-SIZED MEDICAL ASSISTANCE GROUP: Development Education, Medical Health, Volunteer

Santé internationale est une organisation non gouvernementale, sans but lucratif, qui a pour mission de venir en aide aux populations des pays en voie de développement dans leurs efforts de prise en charge de leur propre développement en matière de santé. CSI appuie les missionnaires canadiens et leurs associés qui oeuvrent en développement durable dans les secteurs de la santé et de l'éducation en les approvisionnant en appareils, accessoires, équipements, mobilier, médicaments et en s'associant à leurs projets. Collaboration Santé internationale est présente dans 95 pays. [ID:7244]

Comité régional d'éducation pour le développement international de Lanaudière (CREDIL)

200, de Salaberry, Joliette, QC, J6E 4G1, Canada; 450-756-0011,
fax 450-759-8749, credil@videotron.ca, www.credil.qc.ca

SMALL ADVOCACY GROUP: Administration (General), Development Education, Gender and Development, Technical Assistance

Le Comité régional d'éducation pour le développement international de Lanaudière (CREDIL) a pour objectifs l'éducation au développement international dans la région de Lanaudière, la solidarité avec des organisations populaires, et l'initiation et le support d'engagements concrets en appui aux efforts de justice dans le monde. Pour ce faire, il entretient des liens directs avec l'Afrique australe et sahélienne, le Moyen-Orient et l'Amérique latine et organise chaque année des stages de coopération internationale en Amérique du Sud et en Afrique d'une durée de 70 jours, pour les gens âgés de 18 à 30 ans. Le CREDIL accueille également les nouveaux arrivants et réfugiés humanitaires dans Lanaudière. [ID:7321]

Commonwealth Games Canada

Suite 216, 720 Belfast Street, Ottawa, ON, K1G 0Z5, Canada; 613-244-6868, fax 613-244-6826, cslc@commonwealthgames.ca, www.commonwealthgames.ca, www.jeuxcommonwealth.ca 🖳*Fr*

LARGE COORDINATING BODY: Development Education

Commonwealth Games Canada's mission is to strengthen sport within Canada and throughout the Commonwealth through participation in the Commonwealth Games and by using sport as a development tool. Commonwealth Games Canada programs operate in Africa and the Caribbean. The programs have a strong emphasis on enhancing the opportunities available for women, youth at risk, people with a disability and social development.

Commonwealth Games Canada annually employs 15 local staff and 10 to 25 interns to work in their international programs. Commonwealth Games Canada maintains an active database for application packages. Their Web site lists information on job postings, programs and application procedures, and has information on past participants and their placements. Every four years mission staff are hired to support the team that travels to the Commonwealth Games. (For more information on their internships, see Chapter 10, Short-Term Programs Overseas.) [ID:6872]

Compassion Canada

International Division, 985 Adelaide Street S., London, ON, N6A 4A3, Canada;
800-563-5437, fax 519-686-1107, info@compassion.ca, www.compassion.ca

LARGE RELIEF AND DEVELOPMENT AGENCY: Adult Training, Community Development, Development Education, Fundraising, Humanitarian Relief, Media/Communications, Micro-enterprises, Religious, Teaching, Water Resources

Compassion Canada exists as an advocate for children. The organization seeks to help children with their spiritual, economic, social and physical well-being, enabling them to become responsible and fulfilled Christian adults. Working in Africa, Asia, Latin and South America, Compassion provides one-on-one child sponsorship and also facilitates community development focused on providing clean drinking water, health care, microfinance, agriculture and literacy programs. Compassion has 30 Canadian staff and only employs nationals in field countries. Student internships are offered and are posted with other job listings on their Web site. [ID:7063]

Conseil d'Affaires et de Culture Québec-Bulgarie

771, des Calcédoines, Charlesbourg, QC, G2L 2N8, Canada;
418-623-8474, fax 418-623-5012, quebec@bulgarie.net, www.bulgarie.net 🖳*En*

SMALL EXCHANGE GROUP: Business Development, Trade and Investment

Le Conseil d'Affaires et de Culture Québec - Bulgarie (CACQB) est un organisme sans but lucratif qui œuvre depuis 1996 dans le développement et la promotion des échanges commerciaux et culturels entre le Canada et la Bulgarie. Le Conseil organise des missions commerciales canadiennes en Bulgarie et accueille des missions bulgares au Québec. Il assure la rédaction de deux portails Internet sur les échanges entre le Canada et la Bulgarie - le Business Portail Canada Bulgarie www.bulgarie.net et le Business Portail Canada - www.Canada-business.net. Le CACQB offre également des services de traduction et d'organisation de sessions d'information et de soutien à l'intégration économique des immigrants. L'équipe de CACQB compte une quinzaine d'employés et bénévoles spécialisés en commerce international, en communication et en informatique, selon les projets en cours. Les membres participent à divers programmes de stages rémunérés et non rémunérés. [ID:7337]

Cooperation Canada Mozambique (COCAMO)

323 Chapel Street, Ottawa, ON, K1N 7Z2, Canada; 613-233-4033, fax 613-233-7266, cocamo@magma.ca, www.cocamo.com 💻*Fr*

SMALL COORDINATING BODY: Administration (General), Agriculture, Civil Society, Community Development, Development Education, Logistics, Medical Health

Cooperation Canada Mozambique (COCAMO) is a coalition of non-governmental and church-based development organizations and unions. COCAMO engages the public on Mozambican and African development and social justice issues and also supports Mozambican civil society organizations to be effective and responsive to the marginalized in northern Mozambique. The coalition provides technical assistance and emergency aid as well as supports local NGOS working in education, water, agriculture, small industries, health and development education in Mozambique and Canada. During the last four years, COCAMO has administered an integrated mine action program with governmental departments, international and local NGOs and community groups. COCAMO employs three staff in Canada and Mozambique. [ID:7064]

Crossroads Christian Communications, Inc.

Missions, 1295 North Service Road, Burlington, ON, L7R 4M2, Canada; 905-335-7100, fax 905-332-6655, crossroads@crossroads.ca, www.crossroads.ca 💻*Fr*

LARGE RELIGIOUS GROUP: Children's Rights, Community Development, Education, Film Production and Post Productions, Humanitarian Relief, Medical Health, Micro-enterprises, Nutrition

Crossroads Christian Communications, Inc. strives to provide relief and assistance to people affected by disaster, famine, poverty and war, and to facilitate sustainable development programs in their countries. Program needs are presented through the national television broadcast flagship program, 100 Huntley Street, and other select media, allowing the mission's conscience and response of the viewers to direct their relief and development efforts. Crossroads partners with established indigenous organizations, churches and non-governmental organizations already working in the developing countries.

The organization's Emergency Response & Development Fund has responded to death, destruction and psychological trauma caused by natural disaster, war and poverty in the developing countries of the world. Emergency response activities include food and medical aid, earthquake and flood relief, and the rebuilding of homes. It also services a short-term need in developing countries by shipping quality donated goods in containers. Long-term investments involve five priority areas of social development: health and nutrition, basic education, HIV/AIDS, child protection and microeconomic development.

Crossroads looks for recent university or college graduates to fill eight-month CIDA Youth Internship positions on established overseas projects. Volunteers are also needed to receive, pack and ship containers and to assist with fixing computers, sewing and tailoring, bicycle repair, and the pick-up and delivery of donated items. Volunteers usually give two to four hours per week according to ability and need. If you wish to be involved in some way at the Crossroads Global Activity Centre, send an e-mail to missionswarehouse@crossroads.ca. [ID:6873]

CUSO

Suite 500, 2255 Carling Ave., Ottawa, ON, K2B 1A6, Canada;
613-829-7445, fax 613-829-7996, cuso.secretariat@cuso.ca, www.cuso.org ☐ *Fr*

LARGE VOLUNTEER GROUP: Administration (General), Adult Training, Advocacy, Agriculture, Business Development, Community Development, Development Assistance, Development Education, Environment, Fisheries, Forestry, Fundraising, Gender and Development, Human Rights, Intercultural Briefings, Micro-enterprises, Project Management, Technical Assistance, Volunteer, Water Resources

CUSO supports alliances for global social justice with people striving for freedom, self-determination, gender and racial equality, and cultural survival. The CUSO program concentrates on four areas: livelihoods, environment, rights and HIV/AIDS. There are three main activities within the program: recruitment of skilled Canadians to work on two-year postings in developing countries; funding of locally-controlled, sustainable projects that are sensitive to the environment and to women's issues; and raising public awareness in Canada regarding international development issues and the causes of global economic imbalances. CUSO provides strategic, technical and professional support to its development partners in Asia, the Pacific, Africa, the Caribbean and Latin America.

CUSO employs about 70 staff in Ottawa and about 65 overseas. Most have experience in international development. CUSO also has approximately 230 volunteers (cooperants) overseas, working on two-year contracts. These include health workers, trades people, engineers, fisheries advisors, forestry specialists, agriculturalists, teachers and community development workers. All are experienced in their fields and have academic qualifications or trade papers. In some cases (forestry and fisheries, for example), many years of on-the-job experience is sufficient. Cooperants are generally paid a local wage adequate to cover overseas living costs and provided with a benefits package. To apply on-line for cooperant postings, visit the Overseas Volunteers section on their Web site or contact the local office in your region.

CUSO is also a member of NetCorps Canada International, a youth internship program that focuses on information and communications technology (ICT). Internships link youth between 19 and 30 years of age with partner organizations for four- to six-month ICT placements in developing countries. This program is separate from CUSO's mainstream volunteer-sending program. CUSO looks for dynamic, community-minded Canadians to participate in this program. For staff positions in Canada and overseas, apply to the human resources department in CUSO's Ottawa office. (For more information, see their ad in the sponsor section at the end of this guide.) [ID:7065]

Cybersolidaires

1264, rue Dorion, Montreal, QC, H2K 4A1, Canada;
514-525-8805, info@cybersolidaires.org, www.cybersolidaires.org

SMALL ADVOCACY GROUP: Administration (General), Computer Systems, Development Assistance, Gender and Development, Human Rights, Media/Communications

Cybersolidaires est un organisme sans but lucratif ayant pour mandat de renforcer la défense des droits de la personne, essentiellement les droits économiques, sociaux et culturels des femmes ainsi que leur droit à la communication. L'organisme fait également la promotion du féminisme en favorisant le réseautage au sein du mouvement des femmes francophones et en soutenant leur utilisation des technologies. Cybersolidaires tient aussi un site Internet qui diffuse de l'information sur les violences faites aux femmes, la montée de la droite, la prostitution, les droits des femmes, l'économie, les conjoints (es) de même sexe, les autochtones, ainsi que sur les luttes pour la démocratie et la paix, pour une mondialisation solidaire et pour que les femmes prennent leur place dans la société de l'information et de la communication. Cybersolidaires coordonne également des couvertures en direct d'événements, tant locaux qu'internationaux, et fait la promotion de campagnes, d'événements, de ressources et d'initiatives de solidarité. Des formations sur mesure et des services d'accompagnement à l'intégration des TiC sont également offerts. [ID:7161]

Defence for Children International - Canada (DCI-Canada)

25 Spadina Road, Toronto, ON, M5R 2S7, Canada;
dci-canada@sympatico.ca, www.defence-for-children.org

SMALL ADVOCACY GROUP: Children's Rights

Defence for Children International - Canada (DCI-Canada) is a non-profit charitable organization committed to upholding the rights of children and youth as outlined in the United Nations Convention on the Rights of the Child. DCI-Canada has both domestic and international projects. It is currently developing a project to support young people in conflict/post-conflict situations in Africa, funded through the Canadian International Development Agency's Canada Fund for Africa. DCI-Canada is part of a worldwide network with a secretariat based in Geneva, Switzerland. [ID:7145]

Developing Countries Farm Radio Network (DCFRN)

Suite 101, 416 Moore Ave., Toronto, ON, M4G 1C9, Canada;
416-971-6333, fax 416-971-5299, info@farmradio.org, www.farmradio.org ⬛*Fr*

MID-SIZED MEDIA DEVELOPMENT GROUP: Administration (General), Agriculture, Fundraising, Media/Communications, Volunteer

Developing Countries Farm Radio Network (DCFRN) is a Canadian-based, non-profit organization. It supports over 500 radio partners in Africa, Asia and Latin America to strengthen their radio programming for rural audiences. DCFRN researches and produces radio materials to help broadcasters fight poverty and food insecurity in their regions. Materials focus on simple, practical methods of farming, health and nutrition, and community development. Radio scripts and a partner newsletter with resources, training tips and content ideas for broadcasters are distributed quarterly. Script packages are published in English, French and Spanish. DCFRN has five full-time staff in Canada and none overseas. [ID:7066]

Development and Peace (CCODP)

Suite 420, 10 St. Mary Street, Toronto, ON, M4Y 1P9, Canada;
416-922-1592, fax 416-922-0957, ccodp@devp.org, www.devp.org ⬛*Fr* ⬛*Sp*

LARGE DEVELOPMENT ASSISTANCE GROUP: Accounting, Administration (General), Advocacy, Computer Systems, Development Education, Fundraising, Media/Communications, Project Management, Technical Assistance

Development and Peace (CCODP) helps people of all faiths through community development programs in Africa, Asia and Latin America. Launched in 1967 as Canada's official Catholic overseas development organization, it promotes awareness about the causes of poverty and underdevelopment through education and action programs in Canada and solidarity with people in developing countries. Development and Peace is Caritas Canada, a member of Caritas Internationalis, the Rome-based international Catholic emergency response network of international development and aid organizations.

CCODP has 79 staff responsible for programs in Canada and overseas. It does not have staff based overseas; rather, their program officers, who are based in Canada, work and visit regularly with partners in developing countries. The organization looks for people with experience in advocacy, pertinent work experience both in Canada and in developing countries, and sufficient knowledge of the Catholic Church and its commitments in the field of international development. Being bilingual, which includes both speaking and writing the languages required in certain developing countries, is required of all program officers. CCODP keeps suitable resumes on file for six months. Visit their Web site for job openings and internship positions. [ID:7042]

Développement international Desjardins (DID)

150, ave. des Commandeurs, Lévis, QC, G6V 6P8, Canada;
418-835-2400, fax 418-833-0742, info@did.qc.ca, www.did.qc.ca 💻*Sp* 💻*En*

LARGE DEVELOPMENT ASSISTANCE GROUP: Accounting, Administration (General), Business
Development, Computer Systems, Development Assistance, Micro-enterprises, Project Management, Technical
Assistance

Développement international Desjardins (DID) est une société canadienne spécialisée en
appui technique et en investissement dans le secteur de la finance communautaire dans les pays en
voie de développement et en émergence. DID appuie actuellement des organisations dans une
vingtaine de pays d'Afrique, d'Amérique latine, des Antilles, d'Asie et d'Europe centrale et de l'Est.

La mission de DID est de renforcer la capacité d'agir et d'entreprendre des populations moins
nanties des pays en voie de développement ou en transition en favorisant la maîtrise d'institutions
financières à propriété collective et à rayonnement communautaire.

En vue d'assurer la pérennité des institutions qu'elle appuie, DID intervient dans plusieurs
domaines. Son expertise est sollicitée pour mettre en place des institutions de base, les organiser en
réseau, introduire de nouveaux produits financiers, redresser des situations de crise, moderniser les
opérations, esquisser des stratégies de supervision, élaborer des lois sur les coopératives d'épargne
et de crédit, et former les différents acteurs de la scène financière locale. En tant que filiale du
Mouvement des caisses Desjardins, DID bénéficie du soutien et de l'expertise de cette institution
bancaire.

L'équipe de DID regroupe une centaine d'employés, dont près de la moitié travaillent à
l'étranger. DID recherche des candidats possédant un diplôme universitaire relié au domaine de la
finance, maîtrisant l'anglais ou l'espagnol, en plus du français, et ayant une solide expérience dans
le domaine bancaire. Les personnes intéressées à se joindre à l'équipe peuvent déposer leur
candidature à partir du site Internet du Mouvement Desjardins: www.desjardins.com, ou encore
consulter le site de DID: www.did.qc.ca [ID:7327]

Disabled Peoples International (DPI)

748 Broadway, Winnipeg, MB, R3G 0X3, Canada;
204-287-8010, fax 204-783-6270, info@dpi.org, www.dpi.org 💻*Fr* 💻*Sp*

MID-SIZED COORDINATING BODY: Administration (General), Adult Training, Advocacy, Development
Assistance, Fundraising, Gender and Development, Human Rights

Disabled Peoples International (DPI) is a network of national organizations or assemblies of
disabled people, established to promote human rights of disabled people through full participation,
equalization of opportunity, and development. Headquartered in Canada, DPI has National
Assemblies in 135 countries, operating regional offices in Africa, Asia/Pacific, Europe, Latin
America and the Caribbean, working in English, French and Spanish. A major goal of DPI is the
full participation of all disabled people in the mainstream of life, particularly those in developing
countries who form the vast majority of the world's 600 million disabled people. DPI works closely
with the UN to ensure that disabled people's needs are recognized and responded to by national and
international bodies. One of their central activities has been the organization of training seminars,
through which participants gain the leadership qualities and marketable skills they require to take a
more active role in their communities. DPI members have also initiated a variety of income-
generating projects, among them a textile factory in Botswana, a technical aids factory in
Nicaragua, and a network of agricultural cooperatives in Zimbabwe.

DPI has four staff in Canada. Canadian regional offices are in charge of their own hiring. DPI
occasionally offers internships of less than one year if sponsorships are available. [ID:7067]

Emmanuel International of Canada

P.O. Box 4050, Stouffville, ON, L4A 8B6, Canada;
905-640-2111, fax 905-640-2186, info@e-i.org, www.e-i.org

MID-SIZED EVANGELICAL GROUP: Accounting, Administration (General), Adult Training, Agriculture, Community Development, Forestry, Humanitarian Relief, Logistics, Medical Health, Micro-enterprises, Project Management, Religious, Water Resources

Emmanuel International of Canada is an inter-denominational, evangelical agency which assists local churches worldwide to meet the physical and spiritual needs of the poor. The agency seeks to give responsibility back to local church bodies by fostering partnerships between churches in Canada and churches in developing countries. Emmanuel International of Canada currently works in 10 different countries: Brazil, Ethiopia, Haiti, Indonesia, Malawi, Mozambique, the Philippines, Sudan, Tanzania and Uganda. Overseas staff work under the authority of a national church in projects on primary health, water, sanitation, agricultural assistance, reforestation, income generation, cottage industry, evangelism and discipleship.

Emmanuel International of Canada is the head office for Emmanuel Relief and Rehabilitation International, an international organization with five offices worldwide. The Canadian office currently has seven staff in Canada, and 12 staff and 10 volunteers serving overseas. Applicants must be over 18 and agree with Emmanuel's Statement of Faith. Emmanuel International of Canada accepts mature, ministering Christians, active in, and recommended by, their local church. International experience is also an asset, as is training/experience in specific project areas. It also offers recent university or college graduates one-year CIDA Youth Internship positions. Job postings are listed on their Web site and they maintain a data bank for resumes. [ID:7068]

Engineers Without Borders - Canada (EWB)

Suite 201, 188 Davenport Road, Toronto, ON, M5R 1J2, Canada;
416-481-3696, fax 416-222-0166, info@ewb.ca, www.ewb.ca ▣ *Fr*

MID-SIZED RELIEF AND DEVELOPMENT AGENCY: Agriculture, Community Development, Development Education, Energy Resources, Engineering, Water Resources

Engineers Without Borders - Canada (EWB) works in partnership with developing communities around the world to provide long-term sustainable solutions to issues that hinder development. Using engineering principles it helps communities access appropriate technologies in four major areas: water and sanitation, agriculture and food processing, information and computer technology, and sustainable energy development. EWB has sent over 70 young Canadians to work on 35 projects in 20 countries. Closer to home, 6,000 members across the country strive to make Canada the most development-friendly and sustainable country in the world.

EWB employs six full-time staff and has 21 chapters at universities across Canada. Overseas volunteers have all shown long-term commitment to development work. Many of the people placed overseas have volunteered with an EWB chapter at their university, or have some work experience in developing countries. EWB looks for a variety of skills but often requires people with water, sanitation or agricultural experience. Not all of the people sent overseas are engineers. When overseas positions are available they are posted on their Web site. (For more information, see their ad in the sponsor section at the end of this guide.) [ID:6874]

Environmental Youth Alliance

P.O. Box 34097, Stn. D, Vancouver, BC, V6J 4M1, Canada;
604-689-4463, fax 604-689-4242, info@eya.ca, www.eya.ca

SMALL ENVIRONMENTAL ACTION GROUP: Education, Environment, Volunteer, Youth and Development

Environmental Youth Alliance (EYA) is a non-profit charity dedicated to creating sustainable living alternatives. Work initiatives consist of building rooftop gardens, developing urban agriculture options, environmental building projects, alternative energy solutions and creating education strategies. Each year EYA sends youth to both developing and developed countries to gain job experience in their focus areas. At the time of publication, EYA will be sending youth to France, Germany and Kenya. Youth interns are selected from a wide range of backgrounds. Its hope is to educate Canadian youth in the importance of protecting our world's ecosystems while giving them work experience to increase employability. For more details visit EYA's Web site. [ID:6887]

Equip KIDS In Developing Societies International

63 Burrard Road, Toronto, ON, M9W 3T4, Canada;
416-695-9339, info@equipkids.org, www.equipkids.org 💻*Sp*

SMALL COMMUNITY DEVELOPMENT GROUP: Consulting, Development Assistance, Human Rights, Medical Health, Teaching, Technical Assistance, Volunteer

Equip KIDS In Developing Societies International is a development organization helping children with disabilities in developing countries. The organization works to promote and improve rehabilitation services, human rights and access to assistive technology in order to improve quality of life and productiveness at the individual, family and community levels. Current projects are located in Peru and Bolivia, with other projects planned throughout Latin America.

Equip KIDS has one permanent staff and several Canadian volunteers overseas. International positions are primarily volunteer positions in the areas of physiotherapy, occupational therapy, speech-language pathology, assistive technology, education and other disability-related fields. In the field, Equip KIDS also works with local volunteers and professionals. Candidates should be flexible, patient and have excellent interpersonal skills. Experience working with children with disabilities and/or in international education as well as knowledge of Spanish are definite assets. Equip KIDS maintains a data bank of resumes. For more information on projects and volunteer opportunities, visit their Web site. [ID:6911]

ETC Group

Suite 200, 478 River Ave., Winnipeg, MB, R3L 0C8, Canada;
204-453-5259, fax 204-284-7871, etc@etcgroup.org, www.etcgroup.org

---

MID-SIZED INTERNATIONAL RESEARCH GROUP: Advanced Technology, Engineering, Environment, Human Rights, Research, Sustainable Development

ETC Group, the Action Group on Erosion, Technology and Concentration, is dedicated to the conservation and sustainable advancement of cultural and ecological diversity and human rights. The organization supports socially responsible developments of technologies useful to the poor and marginalized and it addresses international governance issues and corporate power. ETC Group works in partnership with civil society organizations (CSOs) and social movements, especially in Africa, Asia and Latin America, for cooperative and sustainable self-reliance within disadvantaged societies, by providing information and analysis of socio-economic and technological trends and alternatives.

ETC Group has six full-time and two part-time staff and nine board members scattered over five continents. It works primarily at the global and regional (continental or sub-continental) levels. ETC Group does not undertake grassroots, community or national work. It supports partnerships with community, national or regional CSOs but does not make grants or funds available to other organizations. ETC Group does accept a limited number of interns and volunteers. Potential volunteers should be self-motivated and willing to help on any aspect of the organization's work — from cataloguing books and photocopying, to searching and deciphering patents, to editing. Contact ETC Group directly for further information. [ID:6912]

Evangelical Medical Aid Society (EMAS)

30 - 5155 Spectrum Way, Mississauga, ON, L4W 5A1, Canada;
905-625-4457, fax 905-625-1812, main@cmds-emas.ca, www.cmds-emas.ca

---

MID-SIZED EVANGELICAL GROUP: Adult Training, Medical Health

The Evangelical Medical Aid Society (EMAS) is a Christian, inter-denominational, charitable organization based in Canada and Hong Kong. EMAS coordinates and organizes professional teaching and service teams of Christian physicians, dentists and students who participate in joint ventures with host country partners. It currently has projects in Romania, the Ukraine, Ecuador, Cuba, Costa Rica, Haiti, Vietnam, India, the Philippines, Nigeria, Ghana and Angola.

There are four part-time staff members working across Canada and over 200 personnel working on overseas mission projects at various times throughout the year. Mission team participants require medical/dental degrees or other healthcare related training. EMAS maintains a data bank of resumes of professionals who would like to be notified about pending short-term mission needs. The opportunity section of their Web site contains national and overseas job postings. [ID:7069]

Falls Brook Centre (FBC)

125 South Knowlesville Road, Knowlesville, NB, E7L 1B1,
Canada; 506-375-8143, fax 506-375-4221, www.fallsbrookcentre.ca ▢*Fr* ▢*Sp*

MID-SIZED COMMUNITY DEVELOPMENT GROUP: Agriculture, Community Development, Energy Resources, Environment, Forestry, Training and Technology Transfer

Falls Brook Centre (FBC) is an environmental community development demonstration and training centre in rural New Brunswick. FBC works to demonstrate the practical application and implementation of sustainable development and resource stewardship. Appropriate technology applications of solar energy, wind energy, composting and recycling, as well as forest trails, certified organic gardens, an arboretum, herbarium and a forest museum attract visitors on a regular basis. With a solar- and wind- powered conference centre, FBC is able to host small meetings and provide accommodation and certified-organic catering for up to 25 people on-site. FBC has four main program areas: forest stewardship, sustainable agriculture, appropriate technology and community development.

Falls Brook Centre has 10 permanent staff at the centre who direct the four main program areas alongside programming in international youth internships, environmental education, climate change and non-timber forest products. FBC's youth internships give young Canadians international work experience to develop skills in international relations and sustainable development. Successful applicants will start and finish their work experience in rural New Brunswick at FBC. These positions require determined, self-starting individuals who are willing to work in a team, under difficult conditions and unpredictable circumstances. The successful applicant will be given a moderate financial stipend to cover living expenses and a unique opportunity to gain experience in an international environment. For specific details see their Web site. [ID:6855]

Federation of Canadian Municipalities (FCM)

International Centre for Municipal Development, 3rd Floor, 24 Clarence Street, Ottawa, ON,
K1N 5P3, Canada; 613-241-8484, fax 613-241-7117, international@fcm.ca, www.icmd-cidm.ca

LARGE COMMUNITY DEVELOPMENT GROUP: Accounting, Administration (General), Consulting, Development Assistance, Media/Communications, Project Management

The Federation of Canadian Municipalities (FCM) is a national organization representing the interests of local governments on policy and program matters within federal jurisdiction across Canada. Consistent with the overall mission of FCM, its International Program serves municipal governments internationally, fosters their economic opportunities and directs local energies in pursuit of sustainable development. Through the International Centre for Municipal Development, an extensive international program of municipal partnerships is administered that includes urban professional exchanges and training in local government through its partnerships, technical assistance, knowledge sharing and policy development. The International Office manages a large number of municipal partnerships in Africa and a major training program for municipal officials in China. It has expanded its focus to include municipal exchange programs and training activities in Latin America, Southeast Asia, the Caribbean and the Middle East.

FCM employs 21 staff in Canada, with no staff overseas. Generally, applicants require a university degree and work experience related to urban studies and international development. Second languages or other specialized skills and expertise are viewed as assets. FCM maintains a data bank for resumes and has a good resource section on their Web site. [ID:7070]

Fondation CRUDEM

2240, rue Fullum, Montreal, QC, H2K 3N9, Canada;
514-527-4082, fax 514-527-4082, crudem@sympatico.ca, www.crudem.ca

MID-SIZED DEVELOPMENT ASSISTANCE GROUP: Adult Training, Agriculture, Business Development, Construction, Development Assistance, Development Education, Environment, Gender and Development, International Education, Medical Health, Technical Assistance

La Fondation CRUDEM œuvre dans les secteurs de l'éducation et de la santé. Dans l'ensemble de sa programmation, la Fondation accorde une grande importance à la participation des femmes au développement et à la prise en charge de leur milieu. Bien que la Fondation ait œuvré dans près de 17 pays différents, elle concentre maintenant son appui à Haïti, au Mali et au Cameroun, où elle fonctionne sur une base de programmes triennaux.

Les bureaux permanents de la Fondation CRUDEM sont situés à Montréal où trois employés à temps plein assurent la coordination de l'ensemble des activités avec les membres et partenaires outre-mer. Sur le terrain, la Fondation CRUDEM bénéficie de trois représentants, au Mali, en Haïti et au Cameroun. La Fondation dispose également d'un bureau au Mali où l'on retrouve toute la documentation sur les programmes entrepris au pays. La Fondation n'engage aucun coopérant pour l'extérieur. [ID:7245]

Fondation Paul Gérin-Lajoie

Bureau 900, 465, rue St-Jean, Montreal, QC, H2Y 2R6, Canada;
514-288-3888, fax 514-288-4880, fpgl@fondationpgl.ca, www.fondationpgl.ca

LARGE RELIEF AND DEVELOPMENT AGENCY: Adult Training, Community Development, Computer Systems, Construction, Development Assistance, Project Management, Teaching, Technical Assistance

La Fondation Paul Gérin-Lajoie s'est donnée pour mission de contribuer à l'éducation de base des enfants et à l'alphabétisation des adultes dans les pays les plus démunis, de même qu'à la sensibilisation aux réalités internationales chez les enfants des écoles primaires au Canada. La Fondation tente d'offrir aux élèves des pays en voie de développement un milieu d'apprentissage adéquat en construisant et rénovant les salles de classe et autres infrastructures scolaires. Elle œuvre au Sénégal, au Mali, au Niger, au Bénin, au Burkina Faso, à Haïti et en Équateur.

La Fondation emploie une vingtaine de personnes au Canada et plus de 200 à l'étranger. Les candidats nationaux sont sélectionnés d'après leurs compétences et leur formation générale. Les candidats recherchés comme volontaires en coopération internationale sont des diplômés universitaires en éducation ou en sciences sociales avec une expérience en enseignement ou en animation pédagogique. Ces futurs coopérants doivent également maîtriser le français et faire preuve d'engagement social, d'esprit d'initiative et d'une capacité de travailler en équipe. Des stages en coopération sont disponibles strictement dans le domaine de l'éducation dans des projets outre-mer pour des volontaires canadiens. Les stages et postes sont tous affichés sur le site Internet de la Fondation Paul Gérin-Lajoie. [ID:7294]

Forum of Federations

Suite 700, 325 Dalhousie Street, Ottawa, ON, K1N 7G2, Canada;
613-244-3360, fax 613-244-3372, forum@forumfed.org, www.forumfed.org 🖵 Fr

MID-SIZED COORDINATING BODY: Civil Society, Conflict Prevention, Energy Resources, Environment, Human Rights, Law and Good Governance, Medical Health, Social Justice and Development

The Forum of Federations, an international network on federalism, seeks to strengthen democratic governance by promoting dialogue on and understanding of the values, practices, principles and possibilities of federalism.

The Forum of Federations employs 25 staff in Ottawa and offers six-month internships with its international liaison partners in federal countries around the world for young Canadian practitioners and landed immigrants in Canada. A session on federalism for young practitioners from all federal countries occurs in the summer. For qualifications and application details for the internship program and summer session, see the "Youth Programs" page under "Programs" on the Forum Web site. The Forum of Federations posts its current job openings on its Web site. [ID:6876]

Foster Parents Plan of Canada
Suite 1001, 95 St. Clair Ave. W., Toronto, ON, M4V 3B5, Canada;
416-920-1654, fax 416-920-9942, info@fosterparentsplan.ca, www.fosterparentsplan.ca

LARGE DEVELOPMENT ASSISTANCE GROUP: Adult Training, Agriculture, Business Development, Community Development, Consulting, Development Assistance, Development Education, Fundraising, Gender and Development, Medical Health, Micro-enterprises, Technical Assistance

Foster Parents Plan of Canada recruits Canadian sponsors and links them to an individual child in a developing country, providing information and reports about that specific child and his or her family. In addition, it facilitates the exchange of communications between sponsors and sponsored children. Foster Parents Plan of Canada fundraises within Canada to attract new sponsors and other donors, and is involved with development education and advocacy. The organization operates in 45 countries throughout Africa, Asia, South and Central America and the Caribbean.

The Canadian office, based in Toronto, has approximately 60 employees primarily focused on sponsor and donor relations, finance, fundraising and program management. There are volunteer opportunities within several departments. Visit the Volunteer Opportunities section of the Web site to view descriptions of all volunteer positions. Send inquiries about overseas employment directly to the Plan International address: Plan, International Headquarters, Chobham House, Christchurch Way, Woking, Surrey, GU21 6JG, UK. [ID:7001]

Foundation for International Training (FIT)
Suite 110, 7181 Woodbine Ave., Markham, ON, L3R 1A3, Canada;
905-305-8680, fax 905-305-8681, info@ffit.org, www.ffit.org

MID-SIZED ORGANIZATIONAL TRAINING GROUP: Economic Development, Environment

The Foundation for International Training (FIT) is a non-profit development services organization with a goal to further social and economic progress in developing countries by strengthening human capabilities. FIT's programs are designed to foster and increase the capacities of local institutions and to strengthen human resources for development. Areas of work include social and economic development, public sector strengthening and environmental management. Since its inception FIT has completed more than 500 projects in over 60 countries in Africa, Asia, the Caribbean, Central and Eastern Europe, Latin America and the Middle East, financed by the Canadian International Development Agency (CIDA), the World Bank, the Asian Development Bank and United Nations agencies, as well as the governments of developing countries themselves.

FIT has 15 staff members in Canada and five staff overseas. FIT offers CIDA-funded, eight-month internships for youth from 19 to 30, in a variety of areas such as women's and children's human rights, NGO institutional strengthening, HIV/AIDS prevention, agriculture and microenterprise development. Locations include: China, South Africa, Sri Lanka, India, Egypt and Jamaica. Contact FIT directly for more information. [ID:7130]

The Future Group (TFG)
P.O. Box 61284, RPO Brentwood, Calgary, AB, T2L 2K6, Canada;
info@thefuturegroup.org, www.thefuturegroup.org

SMALL RELIEF AND DEVELOPMENT AGENCY: Advocacy, Community Development, Development Education, Fundraising, Human Rights, Humanitarian Relief, Volunteer

The Future Group (TFG) is based on the principle that a new approach is required to address the challenges that the future holds. The group is driven towards building a freer and safer future by protecting individual freedom, promoting justice and advancing democracy in Southeast Asia.

In May-August 2001, 2002 and 2003, four Canadians went to Cambodia to help children victimized by sex slavery and trafficking. Through the course of 100 days, the team worked with local organizations in all parts of the country to implement often lifesaving projects. Highlights of the 10 projects include reaching 80,000 children at high risk living along Cambodia's trafficking corridors; developing small business training for recovering victims; supplying First Aid training and materials to people on the front lines of this overwhelming challenge; and deterring would-be child sex offenders through the launch of a new sex trafficking Web site called www.youwillbecaught.com. To date, more than 50 tips have been processed from the on-line portal.

The Future Group has more than two dozen volunteers across Canada. Positions within the organization include research, humanitarian aid, fundraising and communications. Interested individuals should have some knowledge of humanitarian issues in Southeast Asia, and experience in international work is an asset, but not necessary. While TFG is pleased to consider volunteer applications, they are not currently in a position to offer paid employment positions. [ID:7143]

Gems of Hope (GEMS)

Executive Director, Suite 304, 675 King Street W., Toronto, ON, M5V 1M9, Canada;
416-362-4367, fax 416-362-4170, gems@gemsofhope.org, www.gemsofhope.org

MID-SIZED COMMUNITY DEVELOPMENT GROUP: Accounting, Administration (General), Community Development, Development Assistance, Development Education, Fundraising, Gender and Development, Micro-enterprises, Project Management

Gems of Hope (GEMS) is a small Toronto-based charity with a global focus. It supports international development projects that empower women by providing microcredit (small scale loans), skills training and basic health services to marginalized women in developing nations. GEMS currently has projects in Bangladesh, Bolivia, Brazil, Peru and Vietnam. Gems of Hope has one full-time and two part-time staff in Canada and does not place people overseas, preferring to work with local partners in the countries involved. GEMS relies on volunteers to assist with general administration, fundraising and event planning. [ID:7077]

Global Development Group (GDG)

Suite 100, 9 Gurdwara Road, Ottawa, ON, K2E 7X6, Canada;
613-228-5646, fax 613-226-7288, info@globaldev.org, www.globaldev.org

MID-SIZED DEVELOPMENT EDUCATION GROUP: Human Resources, Information Technologies, Trade and Investment

Global Development Group (GDG) is an independent, non-profit organization providing human resource (HR), information technology (IT) and international trade solutions to development NGOs, non-profit organizations, government agencies, universities and private institutions. GDG was created by former professionals of the HR and IT divisions of CARE Canada in response to globalization over the previous decade and the growing need of development agencies to have equal and affordable access to state-of-the-art but customizable HR, IT and trade solutions.

Operating independently since 1995, GDG designs, implements and supports human resource development and expatriate service solutions, knowledge management and access to global trading environments on behalf of its clients in a strictly non-partisan manner. Its mission is to improve organizational effectiveness so that those it serves can help spread the benefits of globalization. Some of GDG's clients include CARE International, CIDA, Red Cross, Save the Children, Christian Children's Fund, Governments of Zambia and Mozambique, WUSC, Health Canada, University of Toronto and Cowater International. GDG also manages a Program Support Unit (PSU) in Kabul, Afghanistan, that provides finance, administration, logistics and programming services.

GDG has employees in Afghanistan, France, Belgium, Honduras and Canada. It also recruits, contracts, deploys and administers to another 35 countries on behalf of other agencies. The organization offers a highly competitive compensation package with superior benefits. Employees enjoy a dynamic and supportive work environment with numerous opportunities to expand their personal and professional horizons. GDG has also launched Careers Without Borders, the first full-feature central Web site devoted to international development employment. To register, view and apply for employment opportunities for GDG and many other agencies, visit www.careerswithoutborders.com. GDG also maintains a database of development professionals for possible employment, consultancies and internships. It also provides a limited number of paid and unpaid internships and volunteer opportunities. Interested individuals should register with www.careerswithoutborders.com. (For more information, see their ad in the sponsor section at the end of this guide.) [ID:6900]

Global Vision

Junior Team Canada, 13 Berthier Street, Cantley, QC, J8V 2V5, Canada;
819-827-2838, fax 819-827-2571, info@gvconnects.com, www.gvconnects.com

SMALL EXCHANGE GROUP: Business Development, Education

Global Vision is dedicated to providing youth, aged 16 to 25, with the skills, experience and knowledge necessary to become the business leaders of tomorrow. The program strives to produce a generation of young leaders knowledgeable in the field of international trade and development, and on Canada's key growth sectors and development strategies within the international marketplace. Global Vision is active in Chile, China, Europe, Japan, Korea, Singapore, Malaysia, Thailand, Mexico, Taiwan and the southern US.

Global Vision targets youth in a program called Junior Team Canada (JTC), which includes JTC Regional Centres, JTC International Trade Missions, and JTC Ambassador Programs. JTC Regional Centres take place in every province and bring together youth to work alongside local community and business leaders in order to learn more about their future careers in the global economy. The JTC International Trade Missions travel to foreign markets where team members meet with industry and government leaders to explore business opportunities on behalf of their partners and promote cross-cultural understanding. The JTC Ambassador Program provides youth with the opportunity to put their leadership skills into action while working on a project that will make a difference in their respective communities.

Global Vision has four employees in Canada. Staff have experience and knowledge of different socio-economic regions of the world, language skills and multi-tasking skills, as well as strong people skills. Global Vision maintains a data bank for resumes and on-line registration for the JTC program. [ID:7114]

Greenpeace Canada

Suite 605, 250 Dundas Street W., Toronto, ON, M5T 2Z5, Canada;
416-597-8408, fax 416-597-8402, members@yto.greenpeace.org, www.greenpeace.ca 🖳*Fr*

LARGE ENVIRONMENTAL ACTION GROUP: Accounting, Administration (General), Advocacy, Environment, Fundraising, Media/Communications

Greenpeace Canada campaigns throughout the world on today's most pressing environmental issues and is known for its non-violent but direct action. It has over 100,000 members in Canada and 2.5 million members worldwide. Greenpeace Canada is focusing campaign efforts on climate change, ancient forests, genetic engineering, nuclear, oceans and toxins.

Greenpeace Canada has between 40 and 50 staff in three offices across Canada. Greenpeace Canada advertises its vacancies in local and/or national newspapers, depending on the position, and also posts jobs on their Web site. For overseas jobs with Greenpeace International, which includes the Marine Service and Scientific Unit, visit the Greenpeace International Web site, www.greenpeace.org/jobs.shtml. Volunteers are encouraged to contact their local Greenpeace branch for job opportunities. (For more information on Greenpeace International, see Chapter 40, NGOs in Europe and the Rest of the World.) [ID:7128]

The Group of 78

Suite 206, 145 Spruce Street, Ottawa, ON, K1R 6P1, Canada;
613-230-0860, fax 613-563-0017, group78@web.net, www.hri.ca/partners/G78 🖳*Fr*

SMALL ADVOCACY GROUP: Accounting, Administration (General), Arms Control, Development Assistance, Editing, Fundraising, Gender and Development, Human Rights, Humanitarian Relief, Religious, Research, Translation, Writing

The Group of 78 is an informal association of Canadians who promote global priorities for peace and disarmament, equitable development for all, and a strong and revitalized United Nations system. The Group's work includes organizing conferences to address needed changes in foreign policy, lunching with invited speakers, and producing publications on conference findings and special issues. The Group of 78 has one paid staff member in Canada. [ID:7078]

Habitat for Humanity Canada Inc.
40 Albert Street, Waterloo, ON, N2L 3S2, Canada;
800-667-5137, fax 519-885-5225, habitat@habitat.ca, www.habitat.ca ▢*Fr*

LARGE VOLUNTEER GROUP: Accounting, Administration (General), Adult Training, Architecture and Planning, Business Development, Community Development, Computer Systems, Construction, Consulting, Engineering, Environment, Exchange Programs, Fundraising, Human Resources, Media/Communications, Project Management, Religious, Teaching, Water Resources

Habitat for Humanity Canada Inc. is a non-profit, faith-based organization that works in partnership with low-income families to help them become homeowners. Habitat for Humanity Canada Inc. has dedicated more than 700 homes from coast to coast since its inception. There are currently 61 affiliates in all 10 provinces helping to eliminate poverty housing.

There are approximately 20 staff members at the national office in Canada and thousands of volunteers around the world. The Canadian organization operates in conjunction with Habitat for Humanity International Inc. Internationally, Habitat for Humanity is active in over 92 countries. Habitat for Humanity is dependent on volunteers who can assist locally in their own communities or travel to another location to help build. Contact the Canadian affiliates directly by calling 1-800-667-5137, or contact Habitat for Humanity International's Global Village Program for a list of short-term projects worldwide. Volunteers can also work as international partners on long-term projects in development and construction. For international partners, a three-year commitment is required; volunteers work on a stipend basis and living costs are paid. They must have an attitude of service and of partnering with local people, and must have both education and work experience that relates to community development and home construction. [ID:7079]

Handicap International Canada
448, place Jacques-Cartier, Montreal, QC, H2Y 3B3, Canada; 514-908-2813,
fax 514-288-8090, info@handicap-international.ca, www.handicap-international.org

SMALL ADVOCACY GROUP: Adult Training, Agriculture, Development Assistance, Human Rights, Medical Health, Project Management, Teaching, Technical Assistance, Volunteer

Handicap International est une ONG de solidarité internationale. Elle a pour mission d'agir et de militer pour la restauration des capacités d'action des personnes en situation de handicap, et pour l'amélioration de leurs conditions de vie et de leur participation sociale. Au Canada, l'association emploie une personne à temps plein, soutenue par une équipe de bénévoles. La section canadienne a pour mission de partager et de mettre à profit l'expérience de l'association en mobilisant les ressources techniques, humaines, administratives et financières indispensables à la réalisation des programmes sur le terrain. L'association recrute des volontaires et des professionnels physiothérapeutes, médecins, psychologues, ergothérapeutes, organisateurs communautaires, etc., qui ont choisi de consacrer leur énergie et leurs compétences aux personnes handicapées. Cofondatrice de la Campagne internationale pour l'interdiction des mines antipersonnel, l'association est corécipiendaire du Prix Nobel de la Paix 1997. [ID:7292]

Help the Aged Canada (HTAC)
Unit 205, 1300 Carling Ave., Ottawa, ON, K1Z 7L2, Canada;
613-232-0727, fax 613-232-7625, info@helptheaged.ca, www.helptheaged.ca ▢*Fr*

MID-SIZED SPECIAL NEEDS GROUP: Administration (General), Fundraising, Project Management, Technical Assistance

Help the Aged Canada (HTAC) is the only non-denominational and international charity in Canada dedicated exclusively to assisting elderly people living in poverty. Programs focus on the areas of primary health care, food aid, emergency assistance, capacity-building, training and sponsorship in 11 countries.

HTAC has five staff in Canada, and overseas programs are coordinated through local charitable organizations such as the Oblate missionaries, the Salvation Army, the St. Vincent de Paul Society, and the Red Cross Society. Volunteers throughout Canada are needed to assist with the creation of Help the Aged Chapters and Groups. HTAC has a low staff turnover, but normally looks for individuals with past work experience in the country in which a specific grant program is offered. HTAC works in partnership with the Canadian International Development Agency (CIDA) to provide young professionals with an opportunity for employment in a developing country, providing them valuable practical experience that will assist them in the transition from the classroom to the work force. Position descriptions are carefully designed to meet the needs of the overseas partner and to provide a meaningful experience for the intern. The overseas portion of the internship lasts from five to eight months. All travel and living expenses are provided, including a small honorarium. For more information on application procedures, see their Web site. [ID:7080]

HOPE International Development Agency
Suite 214, 6th Street, New Westminster, BC, V3L 3A2, Canada; 604-525-5481,
fax 604-525-3471, hope@hope-international.com, www.hope-international.com

LARGE DEVELOPMENT ASSISTANCE GROUP: Accounting, Administration (General), Agriculture, Community Development, Construction, Consulting, Development Assistance, Development Education, Engineering, Environment, Forestry, Fundraising, Gender and Development, Human Resources, Humanitarian Relief, Medical Health, Micro-enterprises, Project Management, Teaching, Technical Assistance, Volunteer, Water Resources

HOPE International Development Agency offers an overseas development education program for Canadians interested in international development. The program is open to anyone aged 18 to 35 who demonstrates a willingness to serve and learn about other cultures and issues of poverty and development. On a part-time basis, a group of eight to 12 people spend three to five months learning HOPE's development education curriculum in Canada. Participants then spend six to eight weeks working in a developing country at the community level. The Understanding Needs in Other Nations (UNION) program takes place each summer in a variety of developing countries, most often including the Dominican Republic, Cambodia and South Africa. HOPE has 13 staff in Canada and five overseas personnel. (For more information on HOPE, see Chapter 10, Short-Term Programs Overseas.) [ID:7081]

Horizons of Friendship (Horizons)
P.O. Box 402, 50 Covert Street, Cobourg, ON, K9A 4L1, Canada;
905-372-5483, fax 905-372-7095, info@horizons.ca, www.horizons.ca ▭*Sp*

MID-SIZED DEVELOPMENT ASSISTANCE GROUP: Administration (General), Agriculture, Community Development, Gender and Development, Medical Health, Volunteer

Horizons of Friendship (Horizons) is an international development agency committed to addressing the root causes of poverty and injustice through the cooperation of people from the South and North. Horizons supports Central American and Mexican partner organizations that undertake local initiatives that further this goal. Horizons incorporates gender into its joint community development projects that support health, low-cost housing, agriculture, irrigation, training of women and indigenous communities. In Canada, Horizons raises awareness on global issues and works with Canadian organizations at the local and national levels to bring about positive and lasting change. Horizons of Friendship employs six staff and recruits volunteers to work in Canada. All available positions and their requirements are posted on their Web site. [ID:7082]

Human Concern International (HCI)
P.O. Box 3984, Stn. C, Ottawa, ON, K1Y 4P2, Canada; 613-742-5948,
fax 613-742-7733, info@humanconcern.org, www.humanconcern.org

MID-SIZED RELIEF AND DEVELOPMENT AGENCY: Agriculture, Community Development, Fundraising, Human Resources, Humanitarian Relief, Medical Health, Trades, Water Resources

Human Concern International (HCI) runs various programs in relief, development and restoration, rehabilitation and reconstruction aimed at fostering self-reliance and preserving human dignity. HCI initiates projects to help refugees and displaced people help themselves. It fully utilizes the local labour force in these projects.

HCI has five staff in Canada and 50 overseas. It is supported by numerous volunteers across Canada, as well as five volunteers overseas. HCI seeks volunteer workers with degrees from recognized universities and experience dealing with refugees, displaced people and disaster victims in developing countries. Applicants must also have extensive experience in international development work, mainly in the areas of health, agriculture and water resource projects. Sensitivity to, and full understanding of, local cultures and traditions is very important. HCI maintains a data bank for resumes. [ID:7083]

IN Network - Canada

Canadian Administrative Office, P.O. Box 1288, Aldergrove, BC, V4W 2V1, Canada;
604-702-9805, fax 604-702-9806, inc@inter-nationalneeds.org, www.inter-nationalneeds.com

MID-SIZED RELIGIOUS GROUP: Community Development

The IN Network connects Christian partners in the developed and developing world in evangelism, discipleship and community development. IN Network is convinced that the most effective way to reach the developing world religiously is through Christians in the developing countries. It has projects in more than 26 countries around the world.

IN Network has a small administrative staff. Those wishing to become involved with this organization should contact them directly. IN Network does not normally send people overseas, although on occasion, short-term mission trips take place. [ID:7072]

Infant Feeding Action Coalition Canada (INFACT)

6 Trinity Square, Toronto, ON, M5G 1B1, Canada; 416-595-9819,
fax 416-591-9355, info@infactcanada.ca, www.infactcanada.ca

SMALL SPECIAL NEEDS GROUP: Infant/Youth Health, Maternal and Infant Nutrition

Infant Feeding Action Coalition Canada (INFACT) participates in the International Baby Food Action Network (IBFAN) and supports breastfeeding promotion and protection projects in Nicaragua and Africa. It has four personnel working in Canada, and it works overseas through the global network structure of IBFAN.

Those interested in applying to INFACT should possess a health education background, have experience in primary health care and/or have worked internationally. INFACT maintains a data bank for resumes and sometimes considers internships. [ID:7084]

L'Institut de l'Énergie et de l'Environnement de la Francophonie (IEPF)

56, rue Saint-Pierre, 3e étage, Quebec, QC, G1K 4K1, Canada;
418-692-5727, fax 418-692-5644, iepf@iepf.org, www.iepf.org

SMALL ENVIRONMENTAL ACTION GROUP: Energy Resources, Environment, La Francophonie

L'Institut de l'Énergie et de l'Environnement de la Francophonie (IEPF), organe subsidiaire de l'Agence intergouvernementale de la francophonie, a pour mission de contribuer au renforcement des capacités nationales, sur les plans institutionnels et individuels, ainsi qu'au développement des partenariats dans le domaine de l'énergie et de l'environnement. Les activités de formation, information, actions de terrain et concertation de l'IEPF visent à promouvoir le développement durable. [ID:7272]

Institute for Media, Policy and Civil Society (IMPACS)

Suite 910, 207 West Hastings, Vancouver, BC, V6B 1H7, Canada;
604-682-1953, fax 604-682-4353, media@impacs.org, www.impacs.bc.ca 💻 Fr

LARGE MEDIA DEVELOPMENT GROUP: Media/Communications, Research and Development

The Institute for Media, Policy and Civil Society (IMPACS), is a Canadian charitable organization committed to the protection and expansion of democracy and to strengthening civil society. IMPACS believes that a strong democracy requires three key elements: an articulate and vocal civil society; an accountable and accessible media; and government policies that foster democratic development. IMPACS is currently working in the following areas: Afghanistan, Guyana, Sri Lanka and with a roving South Asia editor's forum.

IMPACS has a staff of 12 and another dozen around the globe, managing local projects in Canada. IMPACS' trainers roster currently has more than 130 members (mostly journalists) with extensive professional experience in radio, TV, print, Internet and related fields such as media and elections, media and law, media management, and strategic communications. The high level of expertise and skills of IMPACS trainers include international training, facilitation skills, language abilities and the flexibility to adapt to difficult situations. Trainers are required to learn and share IMPACS' approach to international media development, and it is essential they understand the current political and social context of their field placements. Being respectful of the people, possessing cultural sensitivity, and being ready to engage in the field are qualities that IMPACS values highly.

News about IMPACS' work is published in their free monthly electronic newsletter, eCatalyst. You can also check the news page of their Web site for program updates, new publications, breaking news and employment opportunities. [ID:7071]

Institute of Peace and Conflict Studies (IPACS)
Conrad Grebel University College, 140 Westmount Road N.,
Waterloo, ON, N2L 3G6, Canada; 519-885-0220 ext. 380, fax 519-885-0014,
ipacs2@uwaterloo.ca, www.grebel.uwaterloo.ca/academic/undergrad/pacs/ipacs.shtml

---

SMALL INTERNATIONAL RESEARCH GROUP: Adult Training, Advocacy, Development Education, Exchange Programs, Research, Teaching

The mandate of the Institute of Peace and Conflict Studies (IPACS), located within Conrad Grebel University College, is to undertake research and public education and provide support for peacemaking efforts at various levels. Housed in an academic institution, it bridges the gap between academic research and the more practical work of NGOs. Currently IPACS researchers give leadership in three areas: 1) Project Ploughshares works with churches and related organizations, as well as governments and non-governmental organizations to identify, develop and advance approaches that build peace and prevent war. 2) The World Order and Regional Conflict (WORC) Program-Horn of Africa, is jointly sponsored by Project Ploughshares and IPACS to monitor regional conflict and arms flow in the region. For more information, please see www.ploughshares.ca (For a full description, see Project Ploughshares, Chapter 38, NGOs in Canada). 3) Conflict Resolution Network Canada develops, promotes and extends the use of conflict resolution and restorative justice processes such as negotiation, mediation, consensus building and peacemaking circles. It serves as a network for organizations and individuals involved in these processes in Canada. For more information, please see www.crnetwork.ca.

The Certificate Program in Conflict Management offers workshops that combine skill and theory while empowering participants to respond in creative and positive ways to the conflict each may face in daily life. Workshops may be taken for interest only or to obtain a Certificate in Conflict Management. Additional IPACS activities include workshops, seminars, public lectures and publications on current issues related to human conflict and peace.

IPACS offers internships, many of which are overseas, for a period of four months. It also has an internship program that sends a dozen Peace and Conflict Studies students overseas. (For more information on the internship program, see Chapter 13, Study Abroad.) [ID:7085]

Inter Pares
221 Laurier Ave. E., Ottawa, ON, KlN 6P1, Canada;
613-563-4801, fax 613-594-4704, info@interpares.ca, www.interpares.ca ▣ *Fr*

MID-SIZED COMMUNITY DEVELOPMENT GROUP: Community Development

Inter Pares is a social justice organization working to build understanding about the causes and effects of poverty and injustice, and the need for social change. Inter Pares builds relationships with existing developing country groups by offering support to their locally determined, community-based programs, their efforts to challenge the structural obstacles to self-determination and their alternative development approaches. Inter Pares learns from and attempts to enlighten Canadians about efforts by developing country groups, particularly through global justice advocacy at national and international levels. It currently works in Africa, Asia and Latin America.

Inter Pares is not a volunteer-sending agency; nor do they have offices overseas. They work primarily with local organizations. Inter Pares currently has 16 staff based in Canada. Inter Pares also links Canadian social and economic justice issues and social action at home with social change in developing countries. Inter Pares has a small staff with low turnover. If actively recruiting Canadian staff, they post positions on their Web site. [ID:7086]

Interagency Coalition on AIDS and Development (ICAD)

Suite 726, 1 Nicholas Street, Ottawa, ON, K1N 7B7, Canada;
613-233-7440, fax 613-233-8361, info@icad-cisd.com, www.icad-cisd.com 💻 Fr

SMALL ADVOCACY GROUP: Development Education, Medical Health

The Interagency Coalition on AIDS and Development (ICAD) develops and promotes positions on HIV/AIDS issues. It advocates for appropriate responses to these issues among major stakeholders such as the Canadian government, NGOs, multilateral agencies, the Canadian public and the media. An important component of ICAD's work is researching the capacities, activities and attitudes of Canadian NGOs regarding AIDS prevention, support and care in developing countries. ICAD informs NGOs of the impact of AIDS in developing countries through its organization of workshops and conferences, the production of a bilingual newsletter and maintenance of a comprehensive resource centre.

ICAD has five employees in Canada. CIDA internships offer post-secondary graduates the opportunity to gain valuable international development work experience. ICAD's strategy is to link organizations in Canada with similar organizations abroad. Consequently, each intern will be attached to a Canadian host agency for two months—one month before and one month after the overseas placement. Each of the Canadian host agencies is responsible for recruitment and selection. Please contact the relevant agency for more information; details are listed on the Youth Connection section of ICAD's Web site.

ICAD also has an on-line Information Exchange where any kind of request or offer of assistance related to HIV/AIDS can be posted. ICAD's Web site also has a Job Board, listing a variety of employment opportunities within their network. [ID:7087]

Intercultural Institute of Montréal (IIM)

4917 St-Urbain Street, Montreal, QC, H2T 2W1, Canada;
514-288-7229, fax 514-844-6800, info@iim.qc.ca, www.iim.qc.ca 💻 Fr

MID-SIZED INTERNATIONAL RESEARCH GROUP: Advocacy, Community Development, Consulting, Culture, Development Education, Environment, Human Rights, Intercultural Briefings, Religious

The Intercultural Institute of Montréal (IIM) is a non-profit research and social action organization, dedicated to promoting an ever-deepening understanding of cultural pluralism, intercultural relations and social change. Its scope is at once local, national, and international. It engages in research action on pluralism and interculturalism; advocacy of people's rights to cultural identity with a special focus on Aboriginal and First Nations; and cultural studies on and advocacy of the knowledge systems of peoples, cultures and communities in the following areas: health and healing, education, agriculture and food, economy and sustenance, environment and ecology, politics and social movements, and spirituality. The institute gives intercultural teaching and training workshops and produces and provides intercultural resource materials. In addition, they offer intercultural referral and consulting services.

IIM employs nine staff in Canada, and there are possibilities for internship and volunteer work. Those interested in a permanent position or an internship should apply directly to the Executive Director. Job postings are posted mainly through their network and in the community and regular newspapers. [ID:7088]

International Association for Transformation (IAT)

P.O. Box 30090, Saanich Centre, Victoria, BC, V8X 5E1, Canada;
250-744-3240, fax 250-744-3241, iat@iatcan.org, www.iatcan.org

SMALL DEVELOPMENT ASSISTANCE GROUP: Agriculture, Development Education, Education, Gender and Development, Medical Health, Reforestation, Self-Help Projects, Youth and Development

The International Association for Transformation (IAT) raises the awareness of humanity concerning global conditions. IAT's efforts are centered on community-based, small-scale, self-help programs in the Philippines. Specific programs include multicultural youth development and leadership training; environmental protection and restoration; and tropical agriculture and organic farming. As well, IAT is currently developing a new initiative—an Eco-village and Global Youth Training and Development Centre in Costa Rica.

In Canada IAT also promotes awareness through development education programs. IAT's all-volunteer support staff works in Canada and has 11 Filipino staff overseas. Dedicated volunteers with skills in business administration, fundraising, event and volunteer coordination are needed in Canada. In the Philippines and Costa Rica, volunteers with experience in agroforestry and conservation, permaculture, organic agriculture, small-scale enterprise, community economic development and construction trade skills are welcome. Opportunities are available for volunteers and co-op students to participate in the Philippines and Costa Rica programs. [ID:7089]

International Christian Aid Canada (ICA Canada)

P.O. Box 5090, 1005 Skyview Drive, Burlington, ON, L7R 4G5, Canada;
905-331-7799, fax 905-331-7699, icac@sympatico.ca, www.acdi-cida.gc.ca

LARGE RELIEF AND DEVELOPMENT AGENCY: Administration (General), Humanitarian Relief, Medical Health, Micro-enterprises, Water Resources

International Christian Aid Canada (ICA Canada) conducts relief and development work in East Africa, Southeast Asia and Central America, contributing in the areas of water supply, agriculture, medicine, education and emergency relief.

There are approximately 99 salaried staff overseas, supported by four staff in Canada. ICA Canada no longer hires persons for overseas work. It uses local personnel and works through local NGOs in the countries where it operates. [ID:7090]

International Development and Relief Foundation (IDRF)

1063 McNicoll Ave., Scarborough, ON, M1W 3W6, Canada;
416-497-0818, fax 416-497-0686, office@idrf.ca, www.idrf.ca

MID-SIZED DEVELOPMENT ASSISTANCE GROUP: Agriculture, Community Development, Construction, Development Assistance, Development Education, Gender and Development, Human Resources, Humanitarian Relief, Medical Health

The International Development and Relief Foundation (IDRF), established in 1985, is a registered Canadian non-governmental organization. Since that time, IDRF has provided emergency relief support and development assistance through partners in various parts of the world to people who are coping with privations caused by poverty, wars or natural disasters. The mission of IDRF is based on the Islamic principles of human dignity, self-reliance and social justice. IDRF's main focus is development projects aimed at helping people, particularly women and children, overcome conditions of endemic poverty. The projects have a particular emphasis on primary level education; basic health care, sanitation and health education; access to clean water; agriculture; microcredit; and skills training. IDRF has implemented relief and development projects in 19 countries in Africa, Asia, Eastern Europe and the Middle East, often with financial support from the Canadian International Development Agency (CIDA). It has seven staff and no personnel overseas. [ID:7091]

International Federation of L'Arche

381 Rachel est, Montreal, QC, H2W 1E8, Canada; 514-844-1661,
fax 514-844-1960, office@larchecanada.org, www.larchecanada.org 💻 Fr

MID-SIZED SPECIAL NEEDS GROUP: Humanitarian Relief, Volunteer

International Federation of L'Arche is an international federation of faith-based communities creating homes and day programs with people who have developmental disabilities. There are over 100 L'Arche communities in 30 countries. L'Arche operates in India, Haiti, Honduras, Australia, Dominican Republic, Mexico, Brazil and throughout Africa and Europe.

L'Arche Canada is the national organization linking the 26 L'Arche communities across the country. Only volunteers are sent overseas. The most important requirement for volunteers is the desire to share daily life with people with a mental challenge. Applicants must be mature, responsible, and have worked at least 12 months with L'Arche Canada before going overseas. [ID:7032]

International Institute for Sustainable Development (IISD)

6th Floor, 161 Portage Ave. E., Winnipeg, MB, R3B 0Y4, Canada;
204-958-7750, fax 204-958-7710, info@iisd.ca, www.iisd.org

SMALL ENVIRONMENTAL ACTION GROUP: Accounting, Administration (General), Agriculture, Business Development, Community Development, Development Assistance, Development Education, Economics, Energy Resources, Environment, Fisheries, Forestry, Fundraising, Media/Communications

The International Institute for Sustainable Development (IISD) contributes to sustainable development by advancing policy recommendations on international trade and investment, economic policy, climate change, measurement and indicators, and natural resources management. By using Internet communications, it reports on international negotiations and broker knowledge gained through collaborative projects with global partners, resulting in more rigorous research, capacity-building in developing countries and better dialogue between the North and South. IISD's vision is better living for all—its mission is to champion innovation, enabling societies to live sustainably.

IISD has 43 employees in Canada and seven overseas. In addition, 30 to 35 interns have been placed with partnership organizations overseas on six-month term placements. Employees have knowledge of sustainable development, policies and considerable international experience. IISD maintains a data bank for resumes. Job postings can be found on IISD's Web site. [ID:6997]

International Society of Bangladesh (ISB)

2e étage #17, 419 St-Roch, (Métro Parc), Montreal, QC, H3N 1K2,
Canada; 514-271-9499, fax 514-271-2162, isb1989@hotmail.com 💻 Fr

SMALL INTERNATIONAL RESEARCH GROUP: Development Education, Research, Volunteer

The International Society of Bangladesh (ISB) is a voluntary research organization whose mission is to identify medium- to long-term social and economic problems in Bangladesh/South Asia, and to provide an international forum on possible solutions to these problems. ISB sponsors and supports national and international study, research and seminars that promote public awareness of these issues. ISB also works with youth, making them aware of social problems and how they can assist with the integration of South Asian immigrants in Canada.

ISB has five staff in Canada, as well as more than 20 volunteers in Canada and two overseas. Applicants can find out about volunteer postings through local newspapers, Parc Extension Quertier en Santé (PEQS) community postings and bulletins, and at the Centre des femmes du Bangladesh. [ID:7092]

Jamaican Self Help (JSH)

Unit 9, 129½ Hunter Street W., Peterborough, ON, K9H 2K7, Canada;
705-743-1671, fax 705-743-4020, jsh@ptbo.igs.net, www.jshcanada.org

MID-SIZED COMMUNITY DEVELOPMENT GROUP: Development Assistance, Development Education

Jamaican Self-Help (JSH) is working in partnership with sister organizations in Jamaica to help improve the living circumstances of Jamaican people by fostering self-sustaining programs such as literacy, skills training, community development, health care and sanitation, and institutional strengthening. JSH currently assists six projects with funding and networking support. This alliance of Canadians and Jamaicans is contributing to the capacities of marginalized women, men and children to work towards self-reliance. JSH has two part-time staff and over 100 volunteers in Canada. [ID:7093]

Jeunesse du monde (JDM)

920, rue Richelieu, Quebec, QC, G1R 1L2, Canada; 418-694-1222,
fax 418-694-1227, jeune@jeunessedumonde.qc.ca, www.jeunessedumonde.qc.ca

MID-SIZED DEVELOPMENT EDUCATION GROUP: Development Assistance, Development Education, Environment, Human Rights, Youth and Development

Jeunesse du monde (JDM) est une organisation sans but lucratif dont le mandat est l'éducation et la formation des jeunes de 13 à 25 ans à la solidarité internationale, au développement et à l'entraide communautaire. Pour ce faire, elle intervient dans les milieux scolaires canadiens, dans les milieux religieux et culturels, et ceci, en Afrique, en Asie et en Amérique latine. L'organisation emploie une douzaine de personnes au Canada et sept à l'étranger. Le site Internet de JDM donne plusieurs informations sur les pays où les stages sont effectués. [ID:7246]

Journalists for Human Rights (JHR)

8 Gibson Ave., Toronto, ON, M5R 1T5, Canada; 416-413-0240, info@jhr.ca, www.jhr.ca ▣ *Fr*

MID-SIZED MEDIA DEVELOPMENT GROUP: Human Rights, Media/Communications

Journalists for Human Rights (JHR) is a charitable organization dedicated to informing Africans about their rights through local African media. By concentrating on increasing the quality and quantity of human rights reporting in selected African countries, JHR empowers Africans to protect their own, and others, rights. This work improves human security, democracy and economic development.

JHR has offices in Toronto and Accra, Ghana. JHR has two permanent staff members and six full-time volunteers. The majority of JHR's overseas work is done by full-time volunteers and experts on short-term contracts. JHR is currently expanding its overseas operations, and many new positions will become available over the next year. The majority of positions available at JHR are for journalists and human rights experts. Please refer to the JHR Web site for updated working and volunteering opportunities. [ID:6856]

KAIROS: Canadian Ecumenical Justice Initiatives

129 St. Clair Ave. W., Toronto, ON, M4V 1N5, Canada; 416-463-5312,
fax 416-463-5569, info@kairoscanada.org, www.kairoscanada.org ▣ *Fr*

MID-SIZED DEVELOPMENT EDUCATION GROUP: Development Education, International Education, Religious

KAIROS: Canadian Ecumenical Justice Initiatives, is an inter-church coalition and network of community-based ecumenical groups that work for global justice. Areas of study include Aboriginal rights, Canadian social development (including refugees, health and anti-poverty), ecological and economic justice, and international human rights. There are 25 staff members in Canada, and KAIROS does not send staff overseas. Volunteer assistance is welcome. For listings on employment opportunities, visit their Web site. [ID:7127]

LifeCycles Project Society

527 Michigan Street, Victoria, BC, V8V 1S1, Canada; 250-383-5800,
fax 250-386-3449, international@lifecyclesproject.ca, www.lifecyclesproject.ca

MID-SIZED COMMUNITY DEVELOPMENT GROUP: Agriculture, Development Education, Exchange
Programs, Fundraising, Micro-enterprises

LifeCycles Project Society is a non-profit, community-based organization dedicated to
cultivating awareness of and initiating action around food, health and urban sustainability in the
Greater Victoria community. This predominantly youth-driven organization is geared toward
education and building community connections through hands-on projects that work toward
creating better local and global food security. LifeCycles works with international partners to grow
food, teach farmers organic techniques and engage the public in ways to make the food system local
and sustainable.

Most of LifeCycles' international work is based in Latin America and the Caribbean; projects
range from green mapping, community gardening, environmental education, urban agriculture and
waste management systems. For example, LifeCycles has an ongoing partnership project in Havana,
Cuba, focusing on urban agriculture and food security.

There are six full-time LifeCycle personnel based in Canada. In addition, LifeCycles offers
contract or short-term positions on a regular basis (approximately 15 contracts per year) in the
following program areas: school gardening, classroom education, resource development and
community economic development. LifeCycles posts any available opportunities on their Web site
and through listservs and accept resumes to put on file.

Internationally, LifeCycles offers internship positions through the Building Bridge program.
This program places interns with international partners working on active projects for six to seven
months. Interns conduct job-specific training in Victoria and are provided support and debriefing
upon their return home. Spanish fluency, community development experience and agricultural
knowledge are necessary. Positions are posted on their Web site in early June with a start date for
mid-July. Positions are subject to funding and eligibility criteria. [ID:6877]

London Cross Cultural Learner Centre (LCCLC)

505 Dundas Street, London, ON, N5W 1W4, Canada;
519-432-1133, fax 519-660-6168, cclc@lcclc.org, www.lcclc.org

MID-SIZED COMMUNITY DEVELOPMENT GROUP: Media/Communications

London Cross Cultural Learner Centre (LCCLC) reaches out to the London and area
community to increase awareness of global issues and to provide opportunities for involvement.
Through their Library and Resource Centre, community groups can access extensive information on
multiculturalism, diversity, various international and global issues, as well as information on issues
and challenges faced by newcomers (ESL and employment resources). LCCLC provides events and
workshops to the general public throughout the year. Their Speakers Bureau highlights a vast array
of local expertise that specialize in different topics, such as environmental awareness, race
relations, cultural sensitivity and appreciation of diversity. The Centre also offers programs for
students at every level, from elementary to post-secondary. LCCLC publishes a monthly quarterly
and also maintains up-to-date contact information for various ethno-cultural groups and faith
groups in London. Fact sheets and bibliographies are produced occasionally.

LCCLC has 30 permanent staff. Volunteers are welcome in every area of LCCLC
programming. LCCLC works in partnership with other social service agencies, cultural groups, and
the government and private sectors to reduce discrimination and increase understanding about the
benefits of diversity and to ensure that London is able to respond adequately to the needs of its
changing community. [ID:6954]

Manitoba Council for International Co-operation (MCIC)

Suite 302, 280 Smith Street, Winnipeg, MB, R3C 1K2, Canada;
204-987-6420, fax 204-956-0031, mcic@web.ca, www.mcic.ca

MID-SIZED COORDINATING BODY: Administration (General), Advocacy, Community Development,
Development Assistance, Development Education, Fundraising, Humanitarian Relief

The Manitoba Council for International Co-operation (MCIC) is a coalition of organizations
involved in international development that are committed to respect, empowerment and self-
determination for all peoples; development that protects the world's environment; and global
understanding, cooperation and social justice. It coordinates information and resources among its
members and promotes public awareness of development issues in Manitoba by holding workshops,
sponsoring speakers and distributing literature. It also administers the Manitoba Government
Matching Grant Program.

MCIC employs four permanent staff in Canada. It seeks team players with good interpersonal,
oral, writing and word processing skills, as well as experience in international development. While
MCIC does not arrange overseas employment, it does act as an information resource for those
interested in becoming involved in any of its member agencies that operate throughout the
developing world. [ID:7094]

MAP-Canada

5722, rue St-André, Montreal, QC, H2S 2K1, Canada;
514-843-7875, fax 514-843-3061, info@mapcan.org, www.mapcan.org 🖥 *Fr*

MID-SIZED MEDICAL ASSISTANCE GROUP: Medical Health

MAP-Canada provides medical assistance and funding to health centres and community
development projects in Lebanon, Jordan and Palestine. Through its office in Jerusalem, MAP-
Canada works closely with its local partners, which identify projects defined by the local
population in the areas of health, education, gender and development, the environment, agriculture
and fisheries. It also provides technical assistance and humanitarian assistance and relief where
necessary. In Canada, MAP-Canada publishes a quarterly newsletter and regularly sponsors
lectures, film and video screenings, theatrical performances and other cultural events.

MAP-Canada's staff consists of two full-time employees and several volunteers in Canada.
Work is primarily in the areas of fundraising, documentation, lobbying and public relations. Staff
are usually university-educated, with some experience in project development and management.
MAP-Canada also hires experts on a contract basis. It encourages groups and individuals, including
health professionals, to offer their time and experience to MAP-Canada's activities. Several trips
are organized to the Palestinian territories. Montreal-area volunteers are welcome to participate in
fundraising activities and public awareness activities that are organized by MAP Canada's head
office in Montreal. [ID:7095]

Maquila Solidarity Network (MSN)

606 Shaw Street, Toronto, ON, M6G 3L6, Canada; 416-532-8584,
fax 416-532-7688, info@maquilasolidarity.org, www.maquilasolidarity.org 🖥 *Fr* 🖥 *Sp*

MID-SIZED ADVOCACY GROUP: Advocacy, Social Justice and Development

The Maquila Solidarity Network (MSN) is a Canadian network promoting solidarity with
groups in Mexico, Central America and Asia that defend the rights of maquiladora and export
processing zone workers. It believes that groups in the North and developing countries must work
together to win employment with dignity, fair wages and working conditions, and healthy
workplaces and communities. MSN has coordinated several campaigns pressuring Canadian and
US retailers to take responsibility for the conditions under which their apparel products are made.

MSN does not send volunteers overseas or provide internships. Volunteers are encouraged to
become involved in MSN's work in Canada through their solidarity campaigns and by using the
educational resources in their local communities. For more information, please visit their Web site.
[ID:6857]

Marine Institute (MI)

Memorial University of Newfoundland, P.O. Box 4920, St. John's, NL,
A1C 5R3, Canada; 800-563-5799, miintl@mi.mun.ca, www.mi.mun.ca

LARGE RESEARCH INSTITUTE: Education, Environment, Fisheries, Marine, Research and Development, Water Resources

The Marine Institute of Memorial University of Newfoundland is North America's most comprehensive institute dedicated to education, training and industrial support in oceans industries. MI International (MI), the international arm of MI, is a six-person unit dedicated to the design, development and management of international project activity. To date, MI International has secured more than 70 funded projects in over 35 countries, from Argentina to Zanzibar. With more than 20 years' international experience and more than 90 MI personnel who have overseas experience, MI International has helped make the Marine Institute one of Canada's leading colleges in the international arena. This experience is backed by an articulated Internationalization Strategy with the following key components: international development projects; internationalization of programs and curriculum; contract training and consultancies; international mobility for students and graduates; international student recruitment and services; and international professional development for MI faculty and staff. MI has 270 faculty and staff, including six full-time positions at MI International.

MI International's Global Graduate Placement Program (GGPP) is a Government of Canada funded program designed to provide post-secondary Canadian graduates with global experience, thereby assisting them in making the transition from school to work. Overseas positions are typically four to seven months in duration and focus on broad themes including fisheries resource management, aquaculture, coastal zone management and marine environmental technology. To find out more about MI International, visit their Web site at http://www.mi.mun.ca/mi_international. [ID:6875]

Marquis Project

Executive Director, 707 Rosser Ave., Brandon, MB, R7A 0K8, Canada;
204-727-5675, fax 204-727-5683, marquisp@mts.net, www.marquisproject.com

SMALL DEVELOPMENT ASSISTANCE GROUP: Accounting, Administration (General), Adult Training, Agriculture, Arms Control, Community Development, Computer Systems, Consulting, Development Assistance, Development Education, Environment, Exchange Programs, Forestry, Fundraising, Gender and Development, Human Resources, Human Rights, Intercultural Briefings, Media/Communications, Medical Health, Micro-enterprises, Project Management, Tourism, Water Resources

The Marquis Project is a non-profit, charitable organization which aims to educate Canadians on international development issues. It is active in partnerships with NGOs in Central America and East Africa. The Marquis Project supports HIV/AIDS education, fair trade in East Africa, the emancipation of women and children, and concentrates on environmental concerns, including organic production and reforestation. The Marquis Project is also involved in community development and multicultural work in Brandon and south-western Manitoba. In addition, the group is active in development education with schools and youth and operates a Worldly Goods craft shop as part of its educational and fundraising work.

The Marquis Project has four staff based in Canada. The project currently has interns and welcomes other inquiries and proposals. [ID:7002]

MATCH International Centre

15 Croissant Grenfell Crescent, Nepean, ON, K2G 0G3, Canada; 613-238-1312,
fax 613-238-6867, info@matchinternational.org, www.matchinternational.org ▣*Fr* ▣*Sp*

MID-SIZED COMMUNITY DEVELOPMENT GROUP: Accounting, Administration (General), Gender and Development

MATCH International Centre supports women through overseas partnership initiative funding in Africa, Asia, the Caribbean and Latin America. It also raises awareness on development issues through public education in Canada. MATCH and its sister organizations in developing areas are committed to a feminist vision of sustainable development—the eradication of all forms of injustice, in particular the exploitation and marginalization of women. Current priority areas include violence against women, words of women and critical concerns of women.

MATCH employs seven staff in Canada. It does not send people overseas and has no overseas offices. Candidates must have educational and work experience relevant to MATCH's job positions. Candidates must also be active in the women's movement. [ID:7096]

Médecins du Monde Canada (MDM Canada)
338 Sherbrooke Street E., Montreal, QC, H2X 1E6, Canada; 514-281-8998, fax 514-281-3011, info@medecinsdumonde.ca, www.medecinsdumonde.ca 💻 Fr

MID-SIZED MEDICAL ASSISTANCE GROUP: Humanitarian Relief, Medical Health

Médecins du Monde (MDM) is a non-governmental organization providing medical and humanitarian assistance to the world's most vulnerable populations in times of crisis, war, natural disaster and involuntary displacement. Médecins du Monde was created in France in 1980 by a group of physicians. Today, it has twelve autonomous and operational national delegations (Argentina, Belgium, Canada, Cyprus, France, Greece, Italy, Portugal, Spain, Sweden, Switzerland and the United States), as well as six representative offices. Médecins du Monde carries out missions involving over 2,500 medical and other professionals in 57 countries throughout the world.

Based in Quebec, Médecins du Monde Canada (MDM Canada) has been incorporated since 1996 as a non-profit organization by the Inspector General of Financial Institutions of the Government of Quebec. It is also registered with Revenue Canada. MDM Canada is managed by a board of directors of 15 members, 75 per cent of whom are from the medical community. Its projects are financed by private donations and sponsors such as the Canadian International Development Agency (CIDA) and the Secrétariat à l'aide internationale du Gouvernement du Québec (SAI). MDM Canada has current projects in Afghanistan, Haiti, Iraq , Malawi, Nicaragua, Palestine, Romania, Vietnam and Montreal, and has plans for others in Burkina Faso and Zimbabwe. In addition, MDM Canada has participated in emergency humanitarian missions in the following countries: Venezuela, Mozambique, Kosovo, Iran and Salvador.

Médecins du Monde Canada recruits doctors, nurses, psychologists, social workers, logisticians, administrators and coordinators for their projects overseas. These volunteers are under contract to Medecins du Monde Canada for various durations, generally from six months to one year, depending on the project. Emergency project volunteers stay for shorter periods. [ID:7139]

Médecins Sans Frontières/Doctors Without Borders (MSF)
Recruitment Manager, Suite 402, 720 Spadina Ave., Toronto, ON, M5S 2T9, Canada; 416-964-0619, fax 416-963-8707, msfcentral@msf.ca, www.msf.ca 💻 Fr

LARGE MEDICAL ASSISTANCE GROUP: Advocacy, Construction, Engineering, Fundraising, Humanitarian Relief, Logistics, Medical Health, Volunteer, Water Resources

Médecins Sans Frontières/Doctors Without Borders (MSF) is an international humanitarian medical relief organization that works with populations affected by war, political instability, epidemics and natural disasters. It provides medical care regardless of race, religion or political affiliation. MSF Canada focuses on the recruitment of field personnel, fundraising and advocacy. Project contexts and responsibilities vary from refugee or displaced persons camps to nutrition programs, drug distribution, training programs and projects such as HIV/AIDS, tuberculosis, malaria, sleeping sickness and more. Worldwide, MSF operates projects in over 75 countries, with about 2,500 expatriate volunteers departing each year.

MSF has 23 staff in their national office in Toronto. The majority of volunteers on mission abroad are given a contract for a specific time period—usually six to 12 months. Volunteers receive a monthly indemnity to help cover their fixed costs at home and to help them re-integrate after a mission. They also receive an allowance for personal expenses, and the cost of living, accommodation and transportation in the project country are covered.

MSF utilizes a variety of health professionals, but is in greatest need of medical doctors with experience in one or more of the following areas: public health, obstetrics and gynecology, paediatrics, anaesthesiology, infectious diseases, HIV/AIDS/STDs, tuberculosis, family practice, emergency medicine and general surgery. Paramedical personnel such as nurses, midwives, lab technologists and nutritionists are also needed. MSF also recruits non-medical personnel such as technical and general logisticians, financial controllers, project coordinators and heads of mission/country managers. Generally, country managers must have prior MSF experience, but persons with strong experience in management of development or relief work should apply.

Previous work or travel experience in Africa, Asia, Central and South America, or in remote areas such as the Canadian North is an advantage. This experience indicates direct interaction with local populations for a substantial amount of time—several months at least. The ability to train others, act independently and organize are prerequisites. Language skills (French, Portuguese, Spanish, Russian or Arabic as well as English) are also a strong asset. Preference will be given to candidates who are bilingual (English and French). Those interested can find profiles of various professions, general requirements and an on-line application form at www.msf.ca/overseas. (For more information, see their ad in the sponsor section at the end of this guide.) [ID:6976]

Mennonite Brethren Mission and Service International (MBMS)
Suite 2, 169 Riverton Ave., Winnipeg, MB, R2L 2E5, Canada; 204-669-6575 ext. 258,
fax 204-654-1865, winnipeg@mbmsinternational.org, www.mbmission.org

MID-SIZED EVANGELICAL GROUP: Community Development, Religious

Mennonite Brethren Mission and Service International (MBMS) sends missionaries to communities all over the world, including Latin America, Asia, Africa and Europe, primarily to engage in church planting and community development activities. MBMS International currently works in 60 countries. MBMS International has 15 permanent Canadian staff, many of whom coordinate international services. For job postings and missionary and service-related opportunities, visit their Web site at www.mbmsinternational.org. [ID:6977]

Mennonite Central Committee, Canada (MCC Canada)
Personnel Services, 134 Plaza Drive, Winnipeg, MB, R3T 5K9, Canada;
204-261-6381, fax 204-269-9875, canada@mennonitecc.ca, www.mcc.org

LARGE RELIEF AND DEVELOPMENT AGENCY: Adult Training, Agriculture, Community Development, Development Assistance, Development Education, Environment, Exchange Programs, Humanitarian Relief, Religious, Teaching, Technical Assistance, Volunteer

The Mennonite Central Committee (MCC) is the relief and development agency of the Mennonite and Brethren in Christ Churches in Canada. MCC works in Africa, Europe, the Middle East, Asia and Latin America in the areas of development, emergency relief, social concerns, peace and justice. MCC is involved in a broad range of projects in agriculture, education, economic and technical development, health and social services.

MCC has over 800 personnel, of which about 450 are scattered coast-to-coast across Canada (100 in Winnipeg) and the US; 350 staff are based overseas on three-year assignments in over 50 countries. MCC covers living expenses, travel costs and provides a subsistence allowance. MCC overseas assignments generally require a university or college degree, or equivalent experience. Candidates must be active members of a Christian church and show commitment to a lifestyle of non-violence and peacemaking. For postings of specialized and urgent openings, as well as information about serving with MCC, visit the "Service Tree" section of their Web site. [ID:6978]

Mennonite Economic Development Associates (MEDA)
Suite 302, 280 Smith Street, Winnipeg, MB, R3C 1K2, Canada;
204-956-6430, fax 204-942-4001, meda@meda.org, www.meda.org

LARGE DEVELOPMENT ASSISTANCE GROUP: Adult Training, Agriculture, Economics, Human
Resources, Micro-enterprises, Project Management, Technical Assistance

The Mennonite Economic Development Associates (MEDA) is an association of Christians in business and the professions who share their faith, abilities and resources to address human needs through economic development. MEDA brings hope, opportunity and economic well-being to low-income people around the world, through a business-oriented approach to development. Areas of expertise include microfinance, business development services, investment and trade. MEDA has operations in Bolivia, Haiti, Nicaragua, Mozambique, Peru and Tanzania and provides consulting and other services in over 20 countries.

Worldwide staff include 36 in North America, seven expatriate staff living overseas, and 89 local nationals. Candidates must have overseas experience, appropriate language ability, related university degrees, management experience and an understanding and support of MEDA's faith and values. MEDA is currently operating internships for Canadian university graduates through CIDA's International Youth Internship Program. For job postings, visit their Web site. [ID:6979]

MiningWatch Canada (MWC)
Suite 508, City Centre Bldg., 880 Wellington Street, Ottawa, ON, K1R 6K7, Canada;
613-569-3439, fax 613-569-5138, canada@miningwatch.ca, www.miningwatch.ca 💻 *Fr* 💻 *Sp*

SMALL ADVOCACY GROUP: Mining

MiningWatch Canada (MWC) is a pan-Canadian initiative supported by environmental, social justice, Aboriginal and labour organizations from across the country. MWC has extensive networks of partner organizations working on the social, economic and environmental impacts of mining activities in many parts of the world. It addresses the urgent need for a coordinated public interest response to the threats to public health, water and air quality, fish and wildlife habitat and community interests posed by irresponsible mineral policies and practices in Canada and around the world. MWC has four staff members. Internships are available depending on funding. MWCs Web site is a valuable resource for people looking for policy or project-specific information. [ID:6914]

Mission Aviation Fellowship of Canada (MAF Canada)
264 Woodlawn Road W., Guelph, ON, N1H 1B6, Canada;
519-821-3914, fax 519-823-1650, info@mafc.org, www.mafc.org

LARGE RELIEF AND DEVELOPMENT AGENCY: Accounting, Administration (General), Adult Training,
Air Transportation, Community Development, Computer Systems, Construction, Development Assistance,
Development Education, Humanitarian Relief, Media/Communications, Religious, Teaching, Technical
Assistance, Telecommunications

Mission Aviation Fellowship of Canada (MAF Canada) is part of a worldwide aviation association supporting Christian outreach and humanitarian assistance in over 30 developing countries. MAF Canada serves the logistics, transportation and communication needs of close to 400 different overseas agencies by providing air support for hospitals, schools, water projects, agricultural improvement projects, medical clinics and church outreach. Much of MAF Canada's work is medical, and has helped save thousands of lives. Most flying is to remote and inhospitable parts of the world, using tiny, primitive airstrips with minimal or no navigational or radio aids.

Internationally, MAF employs roughly 450 families overseas who serve as pilots, aircraft engineers, teachers and other aviation-related specialists—servicing and flying a fleet of over 145 aircraft. MAF Canada currently has 30 workers overseas and employs 12 in Canada. MAF seeks workers who have a Christian commitment. It looks for qualified pilots, mechanics, avionics technicians, IT and logistics professionals, and grade-school teachers to serve the needs of their programs overseas. To apply on-line, visit their Web site. [ID:6980]

National Council on Canada-Arab Relations (NCCAR)
Suite 301, 63 Sparks Street, Ottawa, ON, K1P 5A6, Canada;
613-238-3795, fax 613-235-9135, nccar@nccar.ca, www.nccar.ca

SMALL COORDINATING BODY: Advocacy, Education

The National Council on Canada-Arab Relations (NCCAR) works with governments, the private sector and community organizations to promote and assist programs that increase Canadian awareness and knowledge of the Arab world, and to encourage the expansion of commercial, scientific, educational and cultural links between Canadian and Arab institutions.

NCCAR has three staff in Canada. It coordinates eight to ten placements in the government's Young Professionals International Program (YPI). All eight placements are located in the Arab region of the world and have a six-month overseas work experience component. NCCAR YPI placements are exciting, excellent learning opportunities and effective in career development. The Parliamentary Internship Program is available to young Canadians of Arab origin who are currently enrolled in a Canadian post-secondary educational institution. It provides interns with exposure to the Canadian political process and serves as an eye-opener to the challenges and opportunities that members of the Canadian Arab community face in the Canadian political arena. NCCAR has many events and activities within which volunteers can participate. Specific application procedures for intern programs and volunteer opportunities are listed on their Web site. [ID:6888]

Near East Cultural and Educational Foundation of Canada (NECEF)
106 Duplex Ave., Toronto, ON, M5P 2A7, Canada; 416-483-6467,
fax 416-483-5732, info@acdi-cida.gc.ca, www.acdi-cida.gc.ca ☐*Fr*

SMALL HUMAN RIGHTS ORGANIZATION: Education, Human Rights, Research, Social Justice and Development

The Near East Cultural and Educational Foundation of Canada (NECEF) focuses on promoting respect for human rights and democratic development, as well as building community mental health capacities to cope with the consequences of war and systematic oppression in the Near East. Activities are geared towards a general understand of history, culture and the contemporary situation, centred in the countries of Iraq, Israel, Lebanon and Palestine. It assists educational research, training, humanitarian and development projects. In addition, it produces a newsletter and organizes speaking tours for partner organizations.

NECEF has no full-time staff, but have 12 volunteers in Canada who work as support staff. NECEF welcomes volunteers who are interested in writing resource materials for the classroom, or have fundraising talents. NECEF does not send volunteers overseas directly, but will help individuals facilitate communication links with partners in the Near East. If you are interested in volunteering, please contact NECEF directly. [ID:6915]

The North-South Institute (NSI)
Suite 200, 55 Murray Street, Ottawa, ON, K1N 5M3, Canada;
613-241-3535, fax 613-241-7435, nsi@nsi-ins.ca, www.nsi-ins.ca ☐*Fr*

LARGE RESEARCH INSTITUTE: Accounting, Civil Society, Conflict Prevention, Corporate Ethics, Economics, Gender and Development, Human Rights, Media/Communications, Micro-enterprises, Project Management, Resource Centre Management, States and Markets, Statistics

The North-South Institute (NSI) is dedicated to eradicating global poverty and enhancing social justice through research that promotes international cooperation, democratic governance and conflict prevention. It is Canada's first independent, non-governmental and non-partisan research institute focused on international development. The NSI provides research and analysis on foreign policy and international development issues for policy-makers, educators, business, the media and the general public. The institute's research results, publications and seminars help foster understanding, discussion and debate about the challenges facing Canadians and the citizens of the developing world.

The NSI employs 20 staff in Canada. Research staff have graduate degrees or work experience in international finance, trade, states and markets, civil society, conflict prevention or gender and development areas. Researchers do hire interns. The NSI maintains a data bank for resumes and job openings are posted on their Web site. [ID:6981]

One Sky - The Canadian Institute for Sustainable Living

P.O. Box 3352, Smithers, BC, V0J 2N0, Canada;
250-877-6030, fax 250-877-6040, info@onesky.ca, www.onesky.ca

MID-SIZED COMMUNITY DEVELOPMENT GROUP: Advocacy, Agriculture, Business Development, Community Development, Energy Resources, Exchange Programs, Forestry, Fundraising, Gender and Development, Human Rights, Media/Communications, Micro-enterprises, Project Management, Technical Assistance

One Sky - The Canadian Institute for Sustainable Living's mission is to promote sustainable living globally. It promotes a global approach to living sustainably because it recognizes the interdependence of bioregions in a globalized world. By working internationally in very difficult social and environmental locations, One Sky hopes to both positively support local struggles and radicalize Canadian perspectives regarding our planet's well-being. One Sky has been concentrating on making the links between human security and the environment a development niche. It seeks out existing effective change agents that are exemplifying sustainable living, and supports them both morally and financially. One Sky draws from effective lessons learned around the world and tries to promote these solutions in Canada. The key to this work is capacity-building, both individually and with similarly focused organizations, through networking and mentorship programs. Its current international projects are in Sierra Leone and Nigeria.

One Sky has four full-time personnel in Canada and five staff overseas. It seeks multilingual overseas staff with the ability to be adaptable, flexible and resourceful; with a degree or diploma in a relevant field; and with direct or related work experience. One Sky is engaged in CIDA's Youth Internship Program and sends young Canadians who are 19 to 30 overseas. For more details, visit their Web site. [ID:6878]

Ontario Council for International Cooperation (OCIC)

Suite 506, 10 Mary Street, Toronto, ON, M4Y 1P9, Canada;
416-972-6303, fax 416-972-6996, info@ocic.on.ca, www.ocic.on.ca

SMALL COORDINATING BODY: Administration (General), Advocacy, Development Education, Education, Environment, Fundraising, Media/Communications, Volunteer

The Ontario Council for International Cooperation (OCIC) is an umbrella group of 55 Ontario NGOs who work in international development and global education. OCIC assists its members through information exchanges on members' activities; skills development workshops for members; and networking with special interest groups and communities in Ontario.

OCIC has one full-time staff member. OCIC is not directly involved in overseas or local placements, but does share overseas and volunteer placement information from their membership groups and other international development organizations. [ID:7097]

Operation Eyesight Universal

4 Parkdale Crescent N.W., Calgary, AB, T2N 3T8, Canada; 403-283-6323,
fax 403-270-1899, info@operationeyesight.ca, www.operationeyesight.ca ☐Fr

LARGE MEDICAL ASSISTANCE GROUP: Accounting, Administration (General), Community Development, Consulting, Development Education, Fundraising, Gender and Development, Media/Communications, Medical Health, Project Management, Volunteer

Operation Eyesight Universal is the original Canadian response to global blindness. Operation Eyesight is a charitable organization with offices in Vancouver, Calgary, Toronto and Montreal. Their work has touched millions of people through sight restoration and blindness prevention activities throughout India and other parts of South Asia, as well as parts of Africa and Latin America. All overseas work is performed by indigenous medical teams that receive resources, equipment and training. Future efforts will focus on equipping these partner programs to build sustainable, comprehensive eye care programs in their communities.

Twenty Canadian staff are employed in areas of fund development, pubic relations, volunteer management and accounting. Overseas (indigenous) staff represent the areas of opthalmology, hospital administration, program monitoring and a wide range of medical support functions associated with eye health. There are no overseas opportunities for Canadian nationals at the time of publication. [ID:7098]

Operation Rainbow Canada (ORC)

P.O. Box 64008, 528B Clarke Road, Coquitlam, BC, V7J 7V6, Canada; 888-956-3399, fax 604-530-1588, info@operationrainbowcanada.com, www.operationrainbowcanada.com

SMALL MEDICAL ASSISTANCE GROUP: Medical Health, Volunteer

Operation Rainbow Canada (ORC) is a private, non-profit volunteer medical services organization providing reconstructive surgery and related health care to poor children and young adults in developing countries. ORC also provides education and training to physicians and other healthcare professionals in the host countries to achieve long-term self-sufficiency.

ORC has no paid staff in Canada and relies strictly on volunteer assistance. It organizes volunteer medical missions to developing countries each year, which may include 15 to 20 members. The missions are non-denominational medical and humanitarian exchange trips. Each mission provides a chance for working professionals to exchange ideas and to learn about each other's cultures while providing free humanitarian medical services to needy children.

The teams include surgeons, anesthesiologists, nurses and non-medical staff, all volunteering their time and skills. CVs and evidence of language skills are requested from all applicants. The experience is both rewarding and challenging and lasts one to two weeks. In addition to reviewing medical skills, participants are encouraged to prepare for the physical adjustments of the trip as well as the emotional impact of working in a challenging environment. Residents in plastic surgery and pediatric anesthesiology are also encouraged to apply for opportunities to join their international missions. For an on-line volunteer application and specific details, see their Web site. [ID:7074]

OPIRG-Carleton

326 Unicentre, Carleton University, 1125 Colonel By Drive, Ottawa, ON, K1S 5B6, Canada; 613-520-2757, fax 613-520-3989, opirg@carleton.ca, www.opirg-carleton.org

SMALL ADVOCACY GROUP: Environment, Human Rights, Social Justice and Development

OPIRG-Carleton (Ontario Public Interest Research Group at Carleton University) works on a variety of human rights, social justice and environment issues. Its resource centre has extensive sections on international issues, food, human rights and peace. Working groups, which are the hub of the Centre's educational programming, are organized by theme: Southeast Asia, Multilateral Agreement on Investment, and the impacts of Dams and Reservoir. For more information and links to other PIRGs across Canada, visit their Web site. [ID:7073]

Opportunity International Canada (OIC)

Suite 502, 50 Gervais Drive, Toronto, ON, M3C 1Z3, Canada; 416-444-2448, fax 416-444-8166, info@opportunitycanada.ca, www.opportunitycanada.ca

SMALL DEVELOPMENT ASSISTANCE GROUP: Micro-enterprises

Opportunity International Canada (OIC) is a Christian microenterprise development organization providing the poor with small loans and training so they can work their way out of poverty with dignity. Programs are located in Latin Africa, Latin America and Eastern Europe. OIC has established a team of experts continually researching and developing initiatives aimed at holistically bettering the lives of clients. OIC has six staff members in Canada. Postings are advertised as they become available in areas such as fundraising, programming, communications and office management. [ID:6879]

OXFAM-Canada
Suite 400, 880 Wellington Street, Ottawa, ON, K1R 6K7, Canada;
613-237-5236, fax 613-237-0524, enquire@oxfam.ca, www.oxfam.ca

LARGE RELIEF AND DEVELOPMENT AGENCY: Accounting, Administration (General), Advocacy, Community Development, Development Education, Fundraising, Gender and Development, Human Resources, Humanitarian Relief, Media/Communications, Project Management

OXFAM-Canada supports grassroots, community-based development activities of popular organizations in Southern Africa, the Horn of Africa, the Caribbean, Central America, the Andean region of South America and Canada. Its programs focus on institutional capacity-building, promoting environmentally sustainable development and issues of gender and development. Its contacts with community-based organizations also provide an effective mechanism for responding to emergency needs in times of war and natural disaster. In Canada the organization supports groups involved in community development and undertakes fundraising, development education and advocacy work in support of its domestic and overseas programs.

OXFAM-Canada has 45 staff in Canada and two overseas positions filled on a permanent basis. It is not involved in the short- or medium-term placement of staff or volunteers overseas; however, it does promote exchanges between community development groups overseas and in Canada, providing opportunities for Canadian volunteers to participate in activities such as election monitoring. Candidates must have extensive knowledge and experience in the region of concentration, proven program development and administrative skills, the ability to direct one's own work with minimal supervision, and demonstrated commitment (through paid or volunteer work) to international development issues. It works in cooperation with nine other organizations that share the OXFAM name around the world. Each works independently and administers its own employment program, maintaining large overseas staffs. OXFAM-Canada maintains a data bank for resumes and has limited internships when funding is available. [ID:7099]

OXFAM-Québec
Bureau 200, 2330, rue Notre-Dame ouest, Montreal, QC, H3J 2Y2, Canada;
514-937-1614, fax 514-937-9452, info@oxfam.qc.ca, www.oxfam.qc.ca

LARGE VOLUNTEER GROUP: Community Development, Environment, Gender and Development, Human Rights, Humanitarian Relief, Micro-enterprises, Social Justice and Development, Sustainable Development

OXFAM-Québec, membre de la grande famille OXFAM INTERNATIONAL, est une organisation non gouvernementale, non partisane et non religieuse de coopération et de solidarité internationale. La mission d'OXFAM-Québec est d'appuyer les populations défavorisées des pays en voie de développement qui luttent pour leur survie, leur progrès, la justice sociale et le respect des droits de la personne. En outre, OXFAM-Québec a pour mandat de mobiliser la population du Québec et faciliter l'expression de sa solidarité pour un monde plus équitable.

Dans une perspective de développement durable, OXFAM-Québec oeuvre dans les domaines du renforcement institutionnel, des activités économiques des femmes, de la micro-entreprise et du microcrédit, de l'environnement (eau et reboisement), de l'autosuffisance et la sécurité alimentaires, de la santé, du développement communautaire et de la formation en développement. Dans une perspective d'action humanitaire, OXFAM-Québec intervient dans l'aide humanitaire d'urgence, la reconstruction et la réhabilitation.

OXFAM-Québec dispose d'un effectif de 35 employés au Canada et une centaine de coopérants-volontaires outre-mer. Pour son programme de coopération volontaire et pour satisfaire les besoins exprimés par ses partenaires, OXFAM-Québec requiert les services de personnes ayant une formation universitaire, une expérience pertinente, de la flexibilité et une bonne capacité d'analyse et d'adaptation. [ID:7258]

Pacific Peoples' Partnership (PPP)

Suite 407, 620 View Street, Victoria, BC, V8W 1J6, Canada; 250-381-4131,
fax 250-388-5258, general@pacificpeoplespartnership.org, www.pacificpeoplespartnership.org

SMALL ADVOCACY GROUP: Advocacy, Development Education, Environment, Gender and Development,
Intercultural Briefings, Project Management

Pacific Peoples' Partnership (PPP) is dedicated to promoting the aspirations of people of the
Pacific Islands for peace, cultural integrity, social justice, human dignity and environmental
sustainability. Aside from providing support to community-based organizations in the South
Pacific, PPP offers a range of effective community development and education programs in
Canada. Over the past five years, through their Indigenous Peoples Abroad Programme (IPAP),
PPP has sent close to 50 young First Nations leaders for six-month work placements in indigenous,
non-profit organizations in the South Pacific, offering them their first overseas career-related work
experience, and an intense introduction to global environmental, political, economic and social
issues. PPP also has a rich history of innovative programming in high schools, universities and
friendship centres, and has produced countless conferences, cross-cultural tours and educational
materials for a variety of audiences across the country.

Other than within the context of IPAP, PPP does not recruit and place staff overseas; nor does
it usually hire given its small and stable staff. PPP does provide orientation briefings and resources
for people who will be working and living in the Pacific Islands for a fee. [ID:6984]

The Parliamentary Centre

Suite 802, 255 Albert Street, Ottawa, ON, K1P 6A9, Canada;
613-237-0143, fax 613-235-8237, parlcent@parl.gc.ca, www.parlcent.ca 💻 Fr

LARGE COORDINATING BODY: Development Assistance, Development Education, Law and Good
Governance, Project Management, Research and Development, Training and Education

The Parliamentary Centre is an independent, non-profit organization whose mission is to
strengthen legislatures in Canada and around the world. It is not part of the Parliament of Canada,
though it works closely with the Parliament through Canadian programs and the involvement of
Canadian members of Parliament in overseas work. The Parliamentary Centre services include
assisting legislatures through assessment missions, capacity-development and confidence-building
programs, research and publications, and workshops and courses specializing in anti-corruption,
poverty reduction and e-parliament.

The Parliamentary Centre employs about 30 staff and associates who have expertise in a
variety of areas including parliamentary committee, research and information systems, the budget
process, and parliamentary organization and administration. Job postings are listed under the
"Career Opportunities" section of their Web site. [ID:6918]

Partnership Africa Canada (PAC)

323 Chapel Street, Ottawa, ON, K1N 7Z2, Canada;
613-237-6768, fax 613-237-6530, info@pacweb.org, www.pacweb.org 💻 Fr

MID-SIZED DEVELOPMENT ASSISTANCE GROUP: Advocacy, Policy Dialogue, Research

Partnership Africa Canada (PAC) is a coalition of Canadian and sub-Saharan African NGOs
working together on issues of human rights, human security and sustainable development. In
collaboration with its members and other organizations, PAC undertakes research and policy
dialogue initiatives on issues affecting Africa. PAC has four staff in Canada that work in
collaboration with a team of researchers. [ID:7102]

PATH Canada

Executive Director, Suite 1105, 1 Nicolas Street, Ottawa, ON, K1N 7B7, Canada;
613-241-3927, fax 613-241-7988, admin@pathcanada.org, www.pathcanada.org 💻 *Fr*

MID-SIZED COMMUNITY HEALTH GROUP: Community Development, Consulting, Medical Health,
Technical Assistance, Volunteer

PATH Canada is a non-profit NGO whose goal is to improve health in developing countries,
particularly the health of women and children. PATH Canada has four main sectors of activity:
food and nutrition, malaria control, tobacco control and reproductive health. It works with local
partners to design and implement projects that bridge the gap between user and provider of primary
health services. PATH Canada has worked in over 30 countries in Africa, Asia, Latin America, the
Caribbean and Canada, with project sites in Bangladesh, Vietnam and India.

PATH has three staff members in Ottawa and 10 overseas staff. It maintains a roster of
consultants available in Ottawa and internationally for short- and medium-term assignments in the
areas of nutrition, malaria control, reproductive health and tobacco control. These assignments
require expertise and experience in a wide range of technical disciplines (for example: food
fortification, micronutrient supplementation, insecticide-treated bed nets, malaria drug therapy,
maternal health care, respiratory diseases, HIV/AIDS/STD and toxicology). The ability to speak
multiple languages, and work experience in various countries with various members of the health
sector (NGOs, Ministries of Health, UN, etc.) is valued. The assignments usually require travel, and
the consultant should have Internet access. [ID:7005]

Peace Brigades International - Canada (PBI)

Suite 201, 427 Bloor Street W., Toronto, ON, M5S 1X7, Canada;
416-324-9737, fax 416-324-9757, pbican@web.ca, www.peacebrigades.org 💻 *Fr*

SMALL HUMAN RIGHTS ORGANIZATION: Human Rights

Peace Brigades International (PBI) is a unique grassroots organization exploring and
implementing non-violent approaches to peacebuilding. PBI maintains international
observer/protective accompaniment teams in conflict areas at the request of local human rights
defenders and organizations, creating a breathing space in which they can continue working for
peace and social justice. Currently, PBI works in Colombia, Mexico (Chiapas—through a joint
project with SIPAZ), Indonesia, and has recently re-opened its Guatemala project. PBI's work is
supported by a global network of organizations and individuals and by 18 PBI country groups.

PBI Canada has two staff in Toronto. Volunteers conduct protective accompaniment,
facilitate workshops on peace education and disseminate first-hand reports to the international
community. Candidates should be 25 or older and have the following: understanding of and
commitment to non-violence, experience working overseas, in human rights and/or with NGOs,
appropriate language skills, discretion and diplomacy, flexibility, ability to work well under stress
and within a team setting, and cross-cultural sensitivity. Volunteers must also be able to commit to
one year of service. PBI provides comprehensive training, a monthly living stipend and
incomparable field experience. For more information and application forms, visit their Web site or
contact the PBI Canada office. [ID:6866]

Peacefund Canada (PFC)

Suite 206, 145 Spruce Street, Ottawa, ON, K1R 6P1, Canada;
613-230-0860, fax 613-563-0017, pfcan@web.net, www.web.net/~pfcan

SMALL DEVELOPMENT EDUCATION GROUP: Administration (General), Advocacy, Development
Education, Fundraising, Human Rights, Media/Communications, Project Management, Volunteer

Peacefund Canada (PFC) is an independent fundraising and granting organization with three
key objectives: to help individuals and groups in Canada and around the world work for a just and
sustainable peace through adult education; to initiate and fund projects that increase public support
for disarmament, equitable development and reduction of global tensions; and to use and support
existing networks engaged in peace education. PFC gives priority to educational activities that seek

to inform, educate and mobilize public opinion about peace, equitable development and global security.

PFC has three staff based in Ottawa and does not sponsor overseas volunteers. Staff generally have experience in conflict resolution, adult education, non-violence training, international politics or development, or human rights. Peacefund Canada welcomes the time and skills of volunteers in the Ottawa area. [ID:7103]

Pearson Peacekeeping Centre (PPC)

P.O. Box 100, Clementsport, NS, B0S 1E0, Canada; 902-638-8611 ext. 0,
fax 902-638-8888, info@peaceoperations.org, www.peaceoperations.org ⌨ Fr

LARGE INTERNATIONAL RESEARCH GROUP: Adult Training, Peace and Security

The Pearson Peacekeeping Centre (PPC) is a gathering point for education, training and research on all aspects of peace operations. Its main activity is training—providing practical knowledge and skills to individuals and organizations involved in peace operations worldwide. Courses are delivered at PPC's two campuses in Cornwallis and Montreal, and in other major cities across Canada and Africa. PPC also hosts round tables, conferences and seminars on emerging peace operations issues. It engages in research on emerging issues that shape the future of peace operations. Findings support the development of learning services, as well as public and policy discussion. Capacity-building initiatives are designed to enhance the ability of other education and training institutions to develop and deliver their programs. PPC supports missions in the field through delivery of education and training services to peace operation missions on-site.

PPC employs approximately 100 staff. It hires external faculty who are subject-matter experts in peace operations-related issues, professional staff and support staff. A minimum of several years of field experience in some aspect of a peace operation and relevant academic and professional credentials are necessary. The working language is primarily English in Cornwallis and French in Montreal, but knowledge of French, English and/or Spanish is also desirable for both campuses. To apply for a job, send your resume to employment@peaceoperations.org. PPC also has an internship program for young professionals who are interested in a career in peace operations or international relations. For more information, e-mail internships@peaceoperations.org. (For more information on PPC internships, see Chapter 10, Short-Term Programs Overseas.) [ID:6891]

Planned Parenthood Federation of Canada (PPFC)

Suite 430, 1 Nicholas Street, Ottawa, ON, K1N 7B7, Canada; 613-241-4474, admin@ppfc.ca, www.ppfc.ca

MID-SIZED COMMUNITY HEALTH GROUP: Public Health

The Planned Parenthood Federation of Canada (PPFC) is the only non-governmental organization in Canada that provides services, information and counselling exclusively on sexual and reproductive health. For almost 40 years, PPFC has worked nationally and internationally to ensure that people have access to universal, reliable information and services in order to make informed decisions related to their sexual and reproductive health. Twenty-two independent Planned Parenthood affiliates in 68 communities across Canada provide clinical services, education and counselling to over 310,000 Canadians every year; 90 per cent of these clients are under 30 years of age, the vast majority of whom are women. As a member of the International Planned Parenthood Federation, PPFC actively supports projects to improve the sexual and reproductive health of women, men and youth in developing countries. Internationally, PPFC works in Brazil, Colombia, El Salvador, Jamaica and Pakistan. PPFC projects work in partnership with local governments and non-governmental institutions.

PPFC has a staff of 12 employees and 5 volunteers working in conjunction with the executive director. To volunteer with PPFC, look up the office near you on their Web site. [ID:6880]

Plenty Canada

Cooperant Department, RR 3, Lanark, ON, K0G 1K0, Canada;
613-278-2215, fax 613-278-2416, info@plentycanada.com, www.plentycanada.com

MID-SIZED DEVELOPMENT ASSISTANCE GROUP: Administration (General), Agriculture, Development
Assistance, Medical Health, Social Justice and Development, Sustainable Development

Plenty Canada promotes self-sufficiency and human dignity in developing countries. It
responds to locally identified needs for technically oriented programs that support sustainable
development. It works among indigenous peoples in Guatemala and Nicaragua and with The Six
Nations of the Grand River in Brantford, Ontario. Other projects are located in El Salvador, Cuba,
Sri Lanka, India, South Africa, Botswana and Lesotho.

Plenty Canada has four employees in Canada, and overseas positions are filled by its local
partners. It hires persons with civil engineering or agricultural degrees and looks for workers with
administrative experience and a background in international studies or rural planning and
development. Plenty Canada maintains a data bank for resumes. [ID:7104]

Potash & Phosphate Institute of Canada (PPIC)

Suite 704, CN Tower, Midtown Plaza, Saskatoon, SK, S7K 1J5, Canada;
306-652-3535, fax 306-664-8941, ppic@ppi-ppic.org, www.ppi-ppic.org

MID-SIZED DEVELOPMENT ASSISTANCE GROUP: Agriculture

The Potash & Phosphate Institute of Canada (PPIC) administers an active international
agronomic research and education program that emphasizes the importance of balanced fertilization
in sustainable crop production systems. PPIC's Saskatoon headquarters links programs throughout
Asia, Latin America and South America and operates offices in Brazil, Canada, China, Ecuador,
India, Singapore and the US. The institute also maintains relations with consultancies located in
Bangladesh, Pakistan, Mexico and Australia/New Zealand.

PPIC has 10 professional employees overseas and four Canadian-based employees with
international responsibilities. Candidates must possess post-graduate training, preferably a PhD in
agronomy, soil fertility or plant nutrition. Demonstrated interest in international agriculture
development and related experience is a prerequisite for employment. [ID:6988]

Presbyterian Church in Canada (PCC)/
Presbyterian World Service & Development (PWS&D)

International Ministries, 50 Wynford Drive, Toronto, ON, M3C 1J7, Canada;
416-441-1111, fax 416-441-2825, pwsd@presbyterian.ca, www.presbyterian.ca/pwsd

LARGE COMMUNITY DEVELOPMENT GROUP: Accounting, Administration (General), Advocacy,
Agriculture, Community Development, Engineering, Human Resources, Human Rights, Humanitarian Relief,
Medical Health, Project Management, Religious, Teaching, Water Resources

The Presbyterian Church in Canada (PCC) sends people overseas through International
Ministries. International Ministries staff may work with overseas partners on relief and
development programs funded by Presbyterian World Service & Development (PWS&D).
International positions have included medical doctors, project managers and teachers. There are
various levels of appointment, including regular appointments (five years) and volunteers (up to
three years). International Ministries staff may also include ministers and lay leaders working
alongside churches in ministry positions. There are currently 36 mission personnel including
spouses in 18 countries. Staff are recruited through a variety of channels.

Presbyterian World Service & Development (PWS&D) is the relief and development agency
of The Presbyterian Church in Canada. PWS&D raises funds to support relief and development
work separate from the funds that support the national church office of The Presbyterian Church in
Canada. PWS&D is a member of the Canadian Foodgrains Bank and Action by Churches Together,
a Geneva-based alliance through which PWS&D supports emergency relief and long-term
development programs in basic education, skills training, primary health care, water, small-scale

enterprise and income generation. Development projects and emergency relief programs may be located anywhere in the world, including Canada.

PWS&D employs five full-time staff in Canada: a director, two program coordinators, a resource and communications coordinator, and a coordinator of administration, finance and refugees. PWS&D does not send people overseas. PWS&D often employs students to work as interns alongside the staff in the summer. [ID:6919]

Primate's World Relief and Development Fund (PWRDF)
600 Jarvis Street, Toronto, ON, M4Y 2J6, Canada;
416-924-9192, fax 416-924-3483, pwrdf@pwrdf.org, www.pwrdf.org

SMALL DEVELOPMENT ASSISTANCE GROUP: Education

The Primate's World Relief and Development Fund (PWRDF) is a Christian organization, committed to a vision of international development and global justice that is founded on theological reflection and a faith-based analysis. PWRDF supports projects in 20 countries implemented by local people working for local development partners. The PWRDF's Youth Initiative Network is made up of youth and youth leaders from across the Anglican Church of Canada. The growing network seeks to connect young people from different countries and to deepen engagement through global education and action, in the struggle for justice in Canada and around the world. PWRDF does not send Canadians overseas; nor do they provide placements with local partners. [ID:6920]

Probe International
225 Brunswick Ave., Toronto, ON, M5S 2M6, Canada; 416-964-9223,
fax 416-964-8239, probeinternational@nextcity.com, www.probeinternational.org

SMALL ADVOCACY GROUP: Administration (General), Advocacy, Energy Resources, Environment, Water Resources

Probe International is an independent environmental advocacy organization concerned with the environmental effects of Canada's aid and trade activities in developing countries. Probe International helped create a worldwide information network of citizens' groups to expose environmental wrongdoing in developing countries. Special emphasis is now given to the impact of hydro-electric dams, mining projects, forced resettlement and the projects and policies of financing agencies. Probe International has four staff in Canada. They have volunteers in the office who usually work as administrative assistants. [ID:7105]

Project Ploughshares
57 Erb Street W., Waterloo, ON, N2L 6C2, Canada; 519-888-6541,
fax 519-888-0018, plough@ploughshares.ca, www.ploughshares.ca

MID-SIZED COMMUNITY DEVELOPMENT GROUP: Community Development, Conflict Prevention

Project Ploughshares is an ecumenical agency of the Canadian Council of Churches, established to implement the churches' imperative to seek peace and pursue justice in Canada and abroad. Its mandate is to work with churches and related organizations, as well as governments and non-governmental organizations to identify, develop and advance approaches that build peace and prevent war, and promote the peaceful resolution of political conflict. The focus of Project Ploughshares' research and policy development program is in four broad thematic areas: eliminating weapons of mass destruction; reducing the use of military force to resolve political conflict; controlling the weapons trade; and building the conditions for sustainable peace. Programs are often undertaken in collaboration with overseas partners.

In the national office, Project Ploughshares has 10 regular staff and two contract staff, plus an intern. It offers approximately 10 internship positions, lasting six months, in Canada and abroad. The internship program provides an opportunity for Canadian youth (under 30) to work with non-governmental organizations that are engaged in activities related to international peace building and security. Participants are typically graduates of post-secondary programs such as peace and conflict studies, political science, history, international studies and communications, and will have an interest in pursuing full-time career opportunities in emerging areas of international peace and security. There is funding to cover travel and living expenses for the placements. Also included is a small monthly stipend plus the cost associated with any visas, medical insurance or vaccinations that may be required.

Project Ploughshares is affiliated with the Institute of Peace and Conflict Studies (IPACS), Conrad Grebel University College, University of Waterloo. (For more information on IPACS see Chapter 38, NGOs in Canada.) [ID:6921]

Pueblito Canada
Suite 418, 720 Spadina Ave., Toronto, ON, M5S 2T9, Canada;
416-963-8846, fax 416-963-8853, pueblito@pueblito.org, www.pueblito.org

MID-SIZED COMMUNITY DEVELOPMENT GROUP: Childcare, Community Development, Gender and Development, International Education, Volunteer

Pueblito Canada's mission is to work with families and communities to support the growth of healthy and happy children in Latin America. Pueblito works in partnership with local NGOs to provide capacity-building and financial assistance to develop culturally appropriate, innovative early childhood development programs that benefit children directly. Projects are exclusively in the Spanish- and Portuguese-speaking countries of the Americas and Caribbean—in Brazil, Mexico and the Dominican Republic. Pueblito Canada is also committed to increasing awareness in Canada about the causes and effects of child abandonment and poverty in Latin America.

There are six staff positions in the Toronto office and numerous volunteer positions available in Canada. Pueblito Canada welcomes volunteers in high school co-op programs and university internship placements to carry out awareness programs and assist in fundraising. Contact Pueblito directly for more details. [ID:7106]

RedR Canada (Registered Engineers for Disaster Relief Training)
Suite 102, 9 Gurdwara Road, Ottawa, ON, K2E 7X6, Canada;
613-232-9999, fax 613-226-5991, info@RedR.ca, www.redr.ca ☐*Fr*

SMALL RELIEF AND DEVELOPMENT AGENCY: Architecture and Planning, Engineering, Engineering Management, Global Communications, Housing/Human Settlements, Technical Assistance, Transportation, Urban Development, Waste Water Management, Water Supply

RedR Canada (Registered Engineers for Disaster Relief) is part of RedR International—an organization that relieves suffering by selecting, training and providing competent and efficient personnel to humanitarian aid agencies worldwide. RedR members provide technical assistance vital to refugee camps and affected communities, such as rebuilding roads and bridges; re-establishing fresh water supplies; managing waste; restoring communications; coping with emergencies; and managing financial, material and human resources. RedR looks for both men and women who are resourceful, understanding and compassionate, able to work on their own with limited resources, and able to cope in very challenging environments. RedR members must adapt quickly to new cultures and harsh conditions that create the requirement for relief. They must work independently within a system yet remain flexible within highly demanding work situations.

RedR Canada is growing fast, with 45 members and members-in-training as of June 2004; eight members are currently on assignment overseas. Most assignments are geared towards engineers and technicians with a wide range of skills and experience. Nearly 800 assignments have been undertaken by RedR members through 90 different relief agencies in over 50 countries. Contact RedR if you have the requisite skills and want to become directly involved. (For more information, see their ad in the sponsor section at the end of this guide.) [ID:6913]

RESULTS Canada
President, Suite 104, 153 Chapel Street, Ottawa, ON, T2S 2Z2, Canada;
613-562-9240, fax 613-241-4170, alec@results-resultats.ca, www.results-resultats.ca ☐*Fr*

LARGE ADVOCACY GROUP: Community Development, Human Rights, People's Organizations

RESULTS Canada (Responsibility for Ending Starvation Using Legislation, Trimtabbing and Support) is a non-partisan and non-denominational grassroots network of citizens working to create the political will to end hunger and poverty in Canada and around the world. It is active in seven provinces and its focus is on universal access to basic human needs and access to microcredit as a dignified route out of poverty. RESULTS has sister organizations in the US, the UK, Germany, Japan, Australia and Mexico with whom it lobbies the international financial institutions.

RESULTS has three staff members in their Canadian offices. There are no internship programs in place, but from time to time there are individuals who assist staff in the office. [ID:7003]

Right to Play International (RTP)

19th Floor, 65 Queen Street W., Toronto, ON, M5H 2M5, Canada;
416-498-1922, fax 416-498-1942, info@righttoplay.com, www.righttoplay.com

---

LARGE ADVOCACY GROUP: Advocacy, Children's Rights, Infant/Youth Health, Project Management, Training and Education, Volunteer, Youth and Development

Right to Play International (RTP) is committed to improving the lives of the most disadvantaged children and their communities through sport for development. RTP develops and delivers its SportWorks and Sport Health programs in Africa, Asia, Eastern Europe and the Middle East in collaboration with implementing partners such as the United Nations High Commissioner for Refugees (UNHCR), United Nations Children's Fund (UNICEF) and local community organizations.

International volunteers, who commit to 12- to 24-month contracts, require skills that include the following: project implementation and management with overseas experience preferred; a high degree of professionalism; written and verbal communication skills that can be used effectively in a cross-cultural environment; and training, with emphasis on training low-literacy adult and youth populations using non-traditional methods. In addition, RTP volunteers must be comfortable representing themselves and RTP to high level officials, international agencies, community organizations, teachers and children; be at ease in working with various sectors of the population in the host community; have an ability to be flexible and respond to project needs; and, in some locations, be willing to live with minimal communication services and basic living conditions. Volunteers have a variety of work and educational experience and typically come from one of the following backgrounds: children and development of children's activities; HIV/AIDS awareness and health promotion; teacher trainers and coaches; communications, working with all forms of media; community development and capacity-building; curriculum development; people with disabilities; and sport and physical activity. Additional requirements are fluency in written and spoken English, with French, Portuguese, Spanish, Swahili, Amharic, Armenian or Thai a requirement or an asset in some locations. Computer literacy is required.

RTP employs 36 staff in Toronto. Volunteer applications may be sent at any time; however, RTP schedules two training dates per annum, both of which have application deadlines. For more details on volunteer and work opportunities, visit their Web site. [ID:6922]

Rooftops Canada

Suite 207, 2 Berkeley Street, Toronto, ON, M5A 4J5, Canada;
416-366-1445, fax 416-366-3876, info@rooftops.ca, www.rooftops.ca ▢ Fr

---

MID-SIZED DEVELOPMENT ASSISTANCE GROUP: Development Education, Housing/Human Settlements, Project Management, Technical Assistance

Rooftops Canada is the international development program of cooperative and social housing organizations in Canada working with partner organizations to improve housing conditions, build sustainable communities and develop a shared vision of equitable global development. Its focus is on disadvantaged communities in Africa, Asia, Latin America, the Caribbean and Eastern Europe.

Rooftops Canada has five staff in Canada and it sends approximately 12 short- and long-term technical assistants overseas each year. Technical assistants require extensive experience in cooperative and/or social housing, including financing, land and housing development, administration and training. Working languages are English, French and Portuguese. Rooftops Canada also has the Young Professional Internship Program. Each year, approximately seven interns participate in six-month placements with overseas partners. Interns engage in legal research on housing and land rights, architectural design of housing cooperatives, development of HIV/AIDS training modules, community microfinance projects, and special needs housing policies. For a monthly e-bulletin providing up-to-date information on Rooftops Canada's overseas projects and partners, recruitment notices and volunteer opportunities, visit the "What's New" section of their Web site. [ID:7107]

SalvAide

Suite 411, 219 Argyle Ave., Ottawa, ON, K2P 2H4, Canada;
613-233-6215, fax 613-233-7375, salvaide@web.net, www.salvaide.ca 🖳*Sp*

MID-SIZED COMMUNITY DEVELOPMENT GROUP: Administration (General), Advocacy, Community Development, Development Education, Exchange Programs, Fundraising, Human Rights, Project Management

SalvAide supports economic development and organizational strengthening programs in rural communities in El Salvador. In Canada, SalvAide engages in policy, information and educational work to inform decision-makers and the Canadian people about issues affecting development in El Salvador.

SalvAide has one full-time and two part-time staff in Canada and one full-time staff member overseas. SalvAide's personnel have a variety of professional qualifications and a demonstrated commitment to build social and economic justice and democracy with the people of El Salvador. Interns work in rural El Salvador for five to six months in two main areas: youth and gender. To work in El Salvador, the ability to communicate in Spanish is essential. [ID:7108]

Salvation Army Overseas Development Department

2 Overlea Blvd., Toronto, ON, M4H 1P4, Canada; 416-425-2111,
Public_Relations@can.salvationarmy.org, www.salvationarmy.ca

LARGE DEVELOPMENT ASSISTANCE GROUP: Administration (General), Adult Training, Agriculture, Community Development, Construction, Consulting, Development Assistance, Development Education, Environment, Exchange Programs, Fundraising, Gender and Development, Human Resources, Humanitarian Relief, Media/Communications, Medical Health, Project Management, Religious, Teaching, Technical Assistance, Volunteer, Water Resources

The Salvation Army carries out evangelical and humanitarian work in 109 countries and 145 languages. Both in Canada and overseas, it provides healthcare services; housing for single mothers and the elderly; food, shelter and clothing for disadvantaged groups; counselling and rehabilitation centres; day care; and education services.

The Toronto office is part of an international network of overseas partners. It currently has four staff based in Canada. Several volunteers work overseas but come under the jurisdiction of their respective territories. Employees should possess some understanding of the international aspect of the Salvation Army. Overseas experience in developing countries is a definite advantage. The current staff have experience in public relations, fundraising, government relations, and community development as well as administrative, technical, and tour experience in 30 countries. [ID:7109]

Samaritan's Purse - Canada (SPC)

P.O. Box 20100, Calgary Place, Calgary, AB, T2P 4J2, Canada;
403-250-6565, fax 403-250-6567, canada@samaritan.org, www.samaritanspurse.ca

LARGE RELIEF AND DEVELOPMENT AGENCY: Accounting, Administration (General), Adult Training, Agriculture, Business Development, Community Development, Humanitarian Relief, Micro-enterprises, Project Management, Teaching

Samaritan's Purse - Canada (SPC) is an international Christian relief and development organization that is currently working in more than 100 countries around the world such as Mexico, Nicaragua, Brazil, Cambodia, India, Afghanistan, Ethiopia and Sudan. SPC seeks to help those who are suffering from the effects of war, famine, disease, extreme poverty or natural disaster. SPC projects benefit all people regardless of race, gender, religion or political persuasion. It focuses on improving the situation of the world's vulnerable, and all projects are a reflection of this. SPC relief initiatives include water, emergency food supplies, medical and shelter. Development projects include clean water programs, community health development, microenterprise, construction and rebuilding projects, education and a variety of children's programs.

SPC has 45 permanent staff in the Canadian office and approximately 25 staff in the field. SPC works closely with an international network of overseas partners to develop, implement and maintain development projects, but also employs Canadians to assist and oversee these processes. In addition, SPC, in partnership with the Canadian International Development Association (CIDA), offers an internship program through their water project, to post-secondary graduates. SPC maintains a data bank for resumes. [ID:6881]

Saskatchewan Council for International Co-operation (SCIC)

2138 McIntyre Street, Regina, SK, S4P 2R7, Canada;
306-757-4669, fax 306-757-3226, scic@web.net, www.earthbeat.sk.ca

SMALL COORDINATING BODY: Development Education, Housing/Human Settlements, Humanitarian Relief

The Saskatchewan Council for International Co-operation (SCIC) is comprised of a coalition of over 30 Saskatchewan-based international development NGOs. SCIC supports its members' international programs and communicates with governments on concerns between Saskatchewan, Canada and developing countries. The council administers both the Saskatchewan government's Matching Grants in International Aid Programs and its Emergency Aid Program for emergency relief projects. It also manages a Small Projects Fund for short-term development education projects and promotes public education on international issues.

Six staff members and approximately 200 volunteers work for SCIC. The council manages the Global Connections database, which matches Saskatchewan residents with international expertise to local businesses and institutions seeking such expertise. SCIC's Youth Committee plans local education and skills-building activities for young people (14 to 29) interested in international development, and the Youthbeat Web page collects information about youth opportunities locally, nationally and internationally. To join, send an e-mail to the SCIC Youth Committee at scicyouth@earthbeat.sk.ca. [ID:7110]

Save A Family Plan (SAFP)

Executive Director, P.O. Box 3622, London, ON, N6A 4L4, Canada;
519-672-1115, fax 519-672-6379, safpinfo@safp.org, www.safp.org

LARGE DEVELOPMENT ASSISTANCE GROUP: Agriculture, Community Development, Environment, Gender and Development, Housing/Human Settlements, Medical Health, People's Organizations, Public Health, Sanitation, Technical Assistance, Training and Education, Water Resources

Save A Family Plan (SAFP), which is based at St. Peter's Seminary in London, Ontario, is involved in partnering with the poor for a just world. Since 1965, SAFP has been implementing sustainable family and community development programs in India and is presently working in five states (Andhra Pradesh, Gujarat, Karnataka, Kerala and Tamil Nadu) with 41 Diocesan Social Service Societies, 26 Homes of Healing, approximately 10,550 Sanghams (grassroots community-based organizations), and over 15,000 poor families. Programs are developed through participatory needs assessments with the partnering families and include the following initiatives: housing, water, sanitation, health and hygiene, income generation, environment, natural resource management and conservation practices (including drinking water systems/waterwells and rainwater, harvesting, watersheds, organic farming, waste management, pollution control, renewable energy/biogas and solar energy), gender, capacity-building, disaster management and rehabilitation, and microcredit.

SAFP Canada employs six full-time staff who are supported by approximately 70 volunteers. Volunteer regional representatives are located throughout Canada and the United States. At the SAFP India level, 12 full-time staff are employed and are supported by thousands of community level volunteers. The SAFP Canada office can make arrangements for North American supporters to visit the SAFP India operations and projects in India. It also welcomes anyone who is interested in volunteering both in the offices in Canada and in India. For further details or contact information, visit the SAFP Web site. [ID:7111]

Save the Children Canada

Suite 300, 4141 Yonge Street, Toronto, ON, M2P 2A8, Canada; 416-221-5501, fax 416-221-8214, sccan@savethechildren.ca, www.savethechildren.ca 💻*Fr* 💻*Sp*

LARGE DEVELOPMENT ASSISTANCE GROUP: Accounting, Administration (General), Advocacy, Community Development, Development Assistance, Fundraising, Human Rights, Humanitarian Relief, Project Management, Volunteer

Save the Children is a leading child-rights organization, working for over 85 years to improve the quality of children's lives through the realization of their rights. Save the Children Canada is a member of the International Save the Children Alliance. With Save the Children member organizations in 29 countries and operating programs in over 100 countries, the alliance is the world's largest global movement for children. Through community development and advocacy initiatives in partnership with local communities in Canada and overseas, Save the Children Canada assists, enables and empowers communities to improve the quality of life for children. It works primarily in the areas of education, HIV/AIDS, exploitation and abuse, and armed conflict and disaster.

There are 25 staff working in Canada, and Canadian volunteer, internship and co-op placements are offered. For more information, visit their Web site or e-mail them at volunteering@savethechildren.ca. [ID:7112]

Scarboro Foreign Mission Society (SFMS)

Lay Mission Office, 2685 Kingston Road, Scarborough, ON, M1M 1M4, Canada; 416-261-7135, fax 416-261-0820, info@scarboromissions.ca, www.scarboromissions.ca

SMALL COMMUNITY DEVELOPMENT GROUP: Administration (General), Adult Training, Community Development, Development Education, Engineering, Human Rights, Medical Health, Religious, Teaching, Technical Assistance, Volunteer, Water Resources

Scarboro Foreign Mission Society (SFMS) is a Roman Catholic missionary organization founded in 1918 to train and send missionary priests to China. Scarboro Missions has evolved to include lay missionaries and serve the Catholic Church, not only in China but in other parts of Asia, South America, the Caribbean, Africa and Canada. The Lay Mission Office coordinates the training and placing of lay missioners who serve for three years in overseas settings. Applicants must be between 23 and 65 years of age, Canadian citizens and Catholic. The skills of lay missioners are matched to the needs of the receiving community and include teaching, health care, pastoral work, community building, maintenance work and social work.

Currently SFMS has 49 priests and 28 lay people serving. Current placement countries include China, Malawi, Thailand, Ecuador, Brazil and Guyana; however, placement possibilities do change over time. Applicants must be motivated by faith and a desire to serve and to learn, and have post-secondary education and/or applicable work experience. Lay missioners have their basic expenses covered and receive a small stipend. [ID:7113]

Serving in Mission Canada (SIM)

10 Huntingdale Blvd., Scarborough, ON, M1W 2S5, Canada; 416-497-2424, fax 416-497-2444, info@sim.ca, www.sim.ca 💻*Fr*

LARGE EVANGELICAL GROUP: Agriculture, Community Development, Environment, Forestry, Humanitarian Relief, Medical Health, Religious, Water Resources

Serving in Mission Canada (SIM) is a national office of SIM International, a privately supported, independent mission agency involved in activities overseas such as church ministries, education, translation, health, relief, development, and HIV/AIDS awareness and prevention. SIM International is currently active in 17 countries in Africa, eight countries in Asia, and six countries in South America. SIM works in direct partnership with national churches and community groups. Community development activities include community health care, literacy, skills training, agriculture, crop research, reforestation, environmental conservation, water development and natural disaster relief.

SIM Canada has 15 staff members and over 170 active members. Actual qualifications will vary with the requirements set by the host country. SIM looks for individuals with good interpersonal skills who are able to spend time developing genuine relationships with local people. [ID:6991]

Seva Canada Society

Suite 100, 2000 West 12th Ave., Vancouver, BC, V6J 2G2, Canada;
604-713-6622, fax 604-733-4292, admin@seva.ca, www.seva.ca

MID-SIZED DEVELOPMENT ASSISTANCE GROUP: Administration (General), Business Development, Computer Systems, Consulting, Development Assistance, Development Education, Fundraising, Human Resources, Media/Communications, Medical Health, Micro-enterprises, Project Management, Teaching, Technical Assistance

Seva Canada Society supports development programs in national and international communities. Seva's principal activities abroad focus on the prevention and reversal of blindness in Nepal, Tibet, India and Tanzania. Seva's emphasis is on building self-sustaining programs with committed local partners.

Seva has 3.5 Canadian staff and none overseas. Seva Canada Society is known for promoting volunteerism and strengthening the volunteer sector. Volunteers are given jobs that match their skills—in office administration, working at special events, or in the fundraising and research sectors. Seva Canada Society accepts requests from overseas partners regarding their volunteer needs. These requests from overseas partners are very rare. [ID:7126]

Sierra Club of Canada (SCC)

Suite 412, 1 Nicholas Street, Ottawa, ON, K1N 7B7, Canada;
613-241-4611, fax 613-241-2292, info@sierraclub.ca, www.sierraclub.ca 💻*Fr*

LARGE ENVIRONMENTAL ACTION GROUP: Development Education, Environment, Forestry, Fundraising, Human Resources, Media/Communications

The Sierra Club of Canada (SCC) is spread across Canada through various chapters and working groups, working on public policy and environmental awareness. SCC has developed major national campaigns within four program areas: health and environment, protecting biodiversity, atmosphere and energy, and transition to a sustainable economy. SCC's action alerts provide important information about government action (and inaction) on the environment.

There are 15 staff in the Ottawa office and overseas. Volunteers are welcome to apply to the national office and specific chapters across Canada for opportunities matching their skills. From time to time interns are brought in to work on specific projects. Career opportunities are posted on their Web site. [ID:7119]

Sir Edmund Hillary Foundation

222 Jarvis Street, Toronto, ON, M58 2B8, Canada; 416-941-3315,
fax 416-941-2321, zoconno@sears.ca, www.thesiredmundhillaryfoundation.ca

SMALL MEDICAL ASSISTANCE GROUP: Conservation, Education, Medical Health

The Sir Edmund Hillary Foundation, established in 1979, funds the construction of schools, bridges, water pipelines and the reconstruction of three monasteries. Literary programs have also been established. The foundation is also involved in a reforestation program in the Sagarmatha National Park and recruits medical doctors for volunteer work in hospitals in Nepal. Partners in developing countries make final decisions on medical candidates based on qualifications and needs. Medical professionals who are interested should inquire directly at the Sir Edmund Hillary Foundation. [ID:6992]

Smiles Foundation

Suite 301, 2727 Steeles Ave. W., Toronto, ON, M3J 3G9, Canada;
416-663-0445, fax 416-663-1973, info@smilesfoundation.org, www.smilesfoundation.org

MID-SIZED MEDICAL ASSISTANCE GROUP: Education, Medical Health

Smiles Foundation is dedicated to giving the children of the developing world the opportunity for a healthier existence. The foundation's primary goal is to offer curative dental treatments and preventive health education to children and adults through its permanent and mobile dental clinics in the Dominican Republic. Community development projects and computer education programs for youth are newly developed areas of work. Smiles Foundation's long-term vision is to expand and amplify its community development agenda. Short-term and long-term programs give volunteers the opportunity to come face to face with global issues and to become part of productive solutions in the Dominican Republic in targeted health care, education and social development.

Smiles Foundation is currently working with volunteers only; there are no staff members. Candidates must be enrolled or have obtained some form of post-secondary education, be 21 years of age or older in good health and have a basic knowledge of Spanish. In Canada, Smiles Foundation is always in search of volunteers in the areas of public relations, office work and fundraising. If you are interested in volunteering in the Toronto office, please contact the Smiles Foundation directly. [ID:6854]

The Social Justice Committee

Suite 320, 1857, boul. de Maisonneuve ouest, Montreal, QC, H3H 1J9,
Canada; 514-933-6797, fax 514-933-9517, sjc@web.ca, www.s-j-c.net ☐ℱr

SMALL ADVOCACY GROUP: Economics, Human Rights, Social Justice and Development

The Social Justice Committee seeks to analyze the underlying structural and global causes of poverty, human rights violations and other social injustices. Its program focuses on global economic justice, especially cancelling Third World debt and human rights abuse, especially in Central America and Mexico. Popular education tools and national and international advocacy campaigns are used to inform people worldwide of how Western lifestyles, governments and institutions have an impact upon the lives of people living in developing countries.

The Social Justice Committee has five staff in Canada. It welcomes enthusiastic volunteers or interns to work on either a sub-committee or general office administration. The sub-committees meet in the evenings and organize public events. The office needs people with communication and graphic skills. As there is a lot of work done with Latin America and Canadian government and associations, language skills in Spanish, French or English are very useful. Basic office skills are also necessary for daily tasks. [ID:6916]

Société Mer et Monde

340, rue St-Augustin, Montreal, QC, H4C 2N8, Canada;
514-495-8583, fax 514-937-7652, info@monde.ca, www.monde.ca

MID-SIZED DEVELOPMENT ASSISTANCE GROUP: Adult Training, Community Development, Development Assistance, Environment, Gender and Development, Human Rights, Medical Health, Micro-enterprises

La Société Mer et Monde a comme objectif principal d'appuyer le travail des ONG qui œuvrent auprès des personnes appauvries des pays en développement et au Canada. Mer et Monde privilégie les occasions de contacts, d'échanges et de partenariat entre les gens du Sud et du Nord. La société collabore avec les organisations qui s'impliquent dans diverses activités de coopération au Honduras ou au Sénégal en santé, éducation, intervention sociale et environnement. Mer et Monde offre des stages pour adultes d'une durée de 6 à 12 semaines et propose quelques semaines de découverte aux jeunes de 15 à 19 ans. Mer et Monde emploie quatre personnes à Montréal pour les programmes de stage, en plus d'une équipe de formation de quatre personnes. À l'étranger, Mer et Monde emploie deux personnes à temps plein au Sénégal, et deux au Honduras; un personnel occasionnel s'ajoute selon les besoins. [ID:7274]

SOCODEVI (Société de coopération pour le développement international)

1245, chemin Ste-Foy, Bureau 2300, Quebec, QC, G1S 4P2, Canada;
418-683-7225, fax 418-683-5229, info@socodevi.org, www.socodevi.org ⌨*Sp* ⌨*En*

MID-SIZED DEVELOPMENT ASSISTANCE GROUP: Accounting, Administration (General), Agriculture, Business Development, Consulting, Development Assistance, Development Education, Forestry, Gender and Development, Insurance, Media/Communications, Micro-enterprises, Project Management, Technical Assistance

Formée d'institutions coopératives et mutualistes, SOCODEVI a pour mission de contribuer à l'avancement de pays en voie de développement par la promotion et le renforcement de la formule coopérative ou de toute formule apparentée en favorisant l'engagement de ses institutions membres dans ses programmes.

SOCODEVI intervient particulièrement dans les secteurs de l'agroalimentaire, les assurances et services financiers, la foresterie, la production industrielle, les services funéraires et autres. Elle détient des mandats en Bolivie, au Pérou, au Nicaragua, au Honduras, au Guatemala, au Togo, en République démocratique du Congo (RDC) et au Viêtnam.

Pour assurer la maîtrise d'œuvre de ses projets, SOCODEVI compte sur une équipe de professionnels qualifiés dont une vingtaine à son siège social et une quinzaine outre-mer. De plus, les institutions membres mobilisent des experts-conseils qui fournissent des appuis d'appoint spécialisés dans des secteurs précis.

Les candidats recherchés par SOCODEVI doivent posséder une formation et une expérience de travail reliées au domaine de l'emploi. Ils doivent avoir acquis une certaine connaissance du monde coopératif et des pays en voie de développement et démontrer un niveau de compétence confirmée en gestion de projets. SOCODEVI utilise, entre autres, un répertoire de candidatures pour combler les postes disponibles, et recrute occasionnellement des stagiaires. [ID:7328]

SOPAR

1 chemin des Érables, Gatineau, QC, J8V 1C1, Canada;
819-243-3616, fax 819-243-6280, sopar@sopar.ca, www.sopar.ca ⌨*Fr*

MID-SIZED DEVELOPMENT ASSISTANCE GROUP: Humanitarian Relief, Micro-enterprises

SOPAR (Society for Partnership) is a non-profit organization working towards reducing poverty in developing countries and promoting solidarity and cooperation in Canada. In particular it aims to: reduce poverty in developing countries by supporting local initiatives that strengthen the capacities of local populations to enhance their autonomy and improve their quality of life; and inform Canadians about international cooperation and encourage them to actively engage in the development of their world. Key program areas are: women and development; watershed management and access to safe drinking water; and education, training and capacity building in India.

SOPAR has three staff in Canada and one staff overseas. SOPAR greatly depends on the enthusiasm of volunteers to carry out various roles including: being a member of their board of directors or one of their three committees; giving presentations on international cooperation in schools, churches and amongst community organizations; assisting with events and administrative duties; and offering specific skills that will enhance the overall performance and success of the organization. If you are interested in volunteering your time with SOPAR please contact them directly. [ID:6982]

SOS Children's Villages Canada

National Director, Suite 200, 244 Rideau Street, Ottawa, ON, K1N 5Y3, Canada;
800-767-5111, fax 613-232-6764, info@soschildrensvillages.ca, www.soschildrensvillages.ca ⌨*Fr*

LARGE SPECIAL NEEDS GROUP: Children's Rights, Fundraising, Orphaned Children

SOS Children's Villages Canada operates in 131 countries around the world. It provides permanent family homes and a supportive community to over 50,000 children who might otherwise have been forgotten—innocent victims of family breakdowns, extreme poverty, wars or natural disasters. SOS Children's Villages also operates hundreds of training centres and schools, medical clinics, family counselling centres and other community-based programs to the benefit of an additional 400,000 children and their families each year. SOS Children's Villages Canada employs only six staff, relying heavily on the kindness of volunteers to meet its mandate to help give children at risk a brighter future filled with hope and opportunity. [ID:7003]

South Asia Partnership Canada (SAP)

Suite 200, 1 Nicholas Street, Ottawa, ON, K1N 7B7, Canada;
613-241-1333, fax 613-241-1129, sap@sapcanada.org, www.sapcanada.org

LARGE COORDINATING BODY: Advocacy, Development Assistance, Gender and Development, Human Rights, Intercultural Briefings, Media/Communications, Policy Dialogue

South Asia Partnership Canada (SAP) is a coalition of 27 Canadian organizations that support the long-term human development of socially and economically disadvantaged people in South Asia. Canadian constituents include South Asian-Canadian organizations; non-governmental organizations (NGOs); activists; social justice and solidarity groups, networks and alliances; women's groups; journalists; student organizations, academic organizations and research institutes; and consulting firms, business associations and businesses.

SAP Canada currently manages the South Asian Regional People and Policy, and Building Community programs. SAP Canada works through counterpart SAP organizations in Bangladesh, India, Nepal, Pakistan and Sri Lanka, which identify, select and monitor projects partnered with Canadian development organizations covering a wide spectrum of community development and policy activities.

The Asian SAP organizations employ local program staff. SAP Canada employs seven people in Canada, and occasionally hires consultants for specific projects. For these staff and contractual positions, candidates should possess a blend of formal training and relevant experience. SAP maintains a file for resumes. For job openings and volunteer information for SAP Canada, as well as its members, visit the "Jobs" and "Get Involved" sections on their Web site. [ID:6983]

Steelworkers Humanity Fund

8th Floor, 234 Eglinton Ave. E., Toronto, ON, M4P 1K7, Canada;
416-487-1571, fax 416-487-5548, uswa@uswa.ca, www.uswa.ca 💻 *Fr*

MID-SIZED DEVELOPMENT ASSISTANCE GROUP: Advocacy, Food Security, Labour, Medical Health

The Steelworkers Humanity Fund raises aid and supports community development in developing countries and in Canada. It lends financial support to development initiatives, primarily in the areas of food security, primary health care, potable water, income generation and social communications. In Canada, it carries out development education activities through week-long labour courses and mini courses related to its areas of focus. Steelworkers Humanity Fund has three staff based in Canada. [ID:6985]

The Stephen Lewis Foundation

Robertson Bldg., 215 Spadina Ave., Toronto, ON, M5T 2C7, Canada; 416-533-9292,
fax 416-850-4910, info@stephenlewisfoundation.org, www.stephenlewisfoundation.org

SMALL DEVELOPMENT ASSISTANCE GROUP: HIV/AIDS, Humanitarian Relief, Medical Health

The Stephen Lewis Foundation's purpose is threefold: to provide care at the community level to women who are dying so that their last weeks, days and hours are free from pain, humiliation and indignity; to assist orphans and other AIDS-affected children, in every possible way, from the payment of school fees to the provision of food; and to support associations of people living with HIV/AIDS so that the courageous men and women who have openly declared their status can educate themselves and share information with the broader community on prevention, treatment, care and the elimination of stigma.

The Foundation funds, or plans to fund, grassroots projects in Kenya, Tanzania, Zambia, Malawi, Zimbabwe, Lesotho, Namibia, Botswana, Mozambique, Rwanda, Uganda, South Africa and Swaziland. The Foundation currently operates with a small dedicated team, and does not have the mandate or capacity to send or refer people to work/volunteer overseas. (For more information, see their ad in the sponsor section at the end of this guide.) [ID:7341]

Street Kids International

Suite 201, 38 Camden Street, Toronto, ON, M5V 1V1, Canada;
416-504-8994, fax 416-504-8977, ski@streetkids.org, www.streetkids.org

MID-SIZED SPECIAL NEEDS GROUP: Administration (General), Adult Training, Children's Rights, Development Education, Fundraising, Media/Communications, Micro-enterprises, Project Management, Technical Assistance

Street Kids International is a Canadian-based international non-profit organization that is consistently recognized and honoured globally for its cutting-edge practices and approaches to working with marginalized youth around the world. Its mandate is to give street-involved youth in Canada and around the world the options, skills and opportunities to make better lives for themselves. Street Kids International operates primarily as a capacity builder in partnership with a broad array of agencies serving the children and youth that live and work on city streets in developing, transitional and industrialized countries.

Street Kids International has eight staff based in Canada, and recruits interns for work overseas. Specific language and education requirements vary according to position. Street Kids International looks for candidates with overseas experience and a demonstrated participatory (youth-centred) approach. They also seek candidates with strong written and oral communications skills (fluency in English and other languages), and energetic, positive, efficient self-starters who collaborate well with others. Street Kids maintains a data bank for resumes. Internship applications are considered on an individual basis. Look for job openings and volunteer positions on their Web site [ID:6998]

SUCO

Bureau 210, 1453, rue Beaubien est, Montreal, QC, H2G 3C6, Canada;
514-272-3019, fax 514-272-3097, montreal@suco.org, www.suco.org

LARGE DEVELOPMENT ASSISTANCE GROUP: Environment, Gender and Development, Sustainable Development

SUCO est un organisme de coopération internationale qui a pour mission l'appui au développement durable des communautés et l'éducation à la solidarité internationale. La mission de solidarité de SUCO repose sur l'envoi de coopérants volontaires qui, en collaboration avec les organisations et les communautés, participent à l'identification des besoins et à la mise en œuvre des projets. La programmation de SUCO contribue au renforcement de la démocratie participative et du pouvoir local pour contrer les principales formes d'exclusions (sociale, politique, économique et culturelle). SUCO appuie les collectivités afin qu'elles soient les maîtres d'œuvre de leur développement, condition essentielle au développement durable. SUCO développe des projets en partenariat avec des organismes non gouvernementaux en Amérique latine (Nicaragua et Pérou) ainsi qu'en Afrique (Mali) et dans les Caraïbes (Haïti). Les actions de SUCO s'organisent autour de trois axes majeurs: la place des femmes dans le développement; la protection de l'environnement dans une perspective de développement durable; et la sensibilisation du public à la solidarité internationale. Le siège social de SUCO est situé à Montréal et l'équipe est composée d'une dizaine de personnes. [ID:7228]

TakingITGlobal (TIG)

Suite 505, 19 Duncan Street, Toronto, ON, M5H 3H1, Canada;
416-977-9363, info@takingitglobal.org, www.takingitglobal.org ⌨Fr⌨Sp

LARGE COORDINATING BODY: Volunteer, Youth and Development

TakingITGlobal (TIG) is an innovative international youth-led organization based in Toronto. TakingITGlobal.org is a global on-line community, providing youth with inspiration to make a difference and the opportunities to take action, and is also a source of information on issues, as well as a bridge to get involved locally, nationally and globally. Membership is free of charge and allows you to interact with various aspects of the Web site, to contribute ideas, experiences and actions.

TIG has approximately 25 paid staff within its Toronto headquarters. It also offers a variety of summer, volunteer and term co-op placements. TIG offers international internships that are designed to provide participants with a unique and powerful career-related work experience, giving young people opportunities to be agents of change. [ID:6924]

Ten Thousand Villages
65B Heritage Drive, New Hamburg, ON, N3A 2J3, Canada; 519-662-1879,
fax 519-662-3755, inquiry.ca@TenThousandVillages.com, www.tenthousandvillages.com

LARGE DEVELOPMENT ASSISTANCE GROUP: Business Development, Community Development, Development Assistance

Ten Thousand Villages provides vital, fair income to Third World people by marketing their handicrafts and telling their stories in North America. Ten Thousand Villages works with artisans who would otherwise be unemployed or underemployed, providing sustainable income through fair trade. This income helps pay for food, education, health care and housing. The organization is a non-profit program of Mennonite Central Committee (MCC), the relief and development agency of Mennonite and Brethren in Christ churches in North America. Thousands of volunteers in Canada and the United States work with Ten Thousand Villages in their home communities. Their Web site provides ample information about the products they sell and the communities they support. Volunteer opportunities are available within stores and warehouses across North America. Job opportunities at the Canadian and US headquarters are also listed on their Web site. [ID:7144]

Terre des Hommes Canada Inc. (TDH Canada)
Bureau 5, 2520, rue Lionel-Groulx, Montreal, QC, H3J 1J8,
Canada; 514-937-3325, fax 514-933-7125, www.tdh.ca ▤ *Fr*

SMALL SPECIAL NEEDS GROUP: Orphaned Children

The primary work of Terre des Hommes Canada Inc. (TDH Canada) is in Vietnam, where it has established relationships with several provinces. TDH pour les Enfants provides parents with guidance through the process of file preparation, and completes for the prospective parents all the procedures required in Vietnam for the adoption of a child, from presentation of the parent dossier to final immigration procedures. Representatives accompany adoptive parents through the final steps which require the parent's presence in Vietnam. TDHE also maintains small adoption programs in Honduras, Moldova, Slovakia, and soon, in Russia. Contact staff directly for more information on these programs.

TDHE has five staff in Canada. A number of their volunteers participate in its fund-raising efforts for projects in developing countries. Interested persons can contact TDH directly. [ID:6986]

The United Church of Canada (UCC)
3250 Bloor Street W., Toronto, ON, M4X 2Y4, Canada; 416-231-5931,
fax 416-231-3103, gmp@united-church.ca, www.united-church.ca ▤ *Fr*

LARGE DEVELOPMENT ASSISTANCE GROUP: Accounting, Administration (General), Adult Training, Advocacy, Community Development, Construction, Development Assistance, Development Education, Environment, Gender and Development, Human Rights, Medical Health, Micro-enterprises, Project Management, Teaching, Technical Assistance, Volunteer

The United Church of Canada (UCC) is the largest Protestant denomination in Canada. It is a national church, with congregations, community services and offices across the country from coast to coast. The UCC sends personnel overseas in response to specific requests by overseas partners in Africa, the Caribbean, Latin America, East and South Asia, the Pacific Islands and the Middle East.

The UCC currently has approximately 30 personnel serving overseas in both stipendiary and volunteer capacities. Appointments are normally for three years, though shorter-term appointments ranging from three months to two years are also made. Eligible candidates for overseas service have training and experience relevant to the articulated needs of the overseas partners. The UCC requires a Christian commitment from its overseas personnel, including active involvement in the work of the Christian community. Previous cross-cultural experience is an asset, as is previous work with marginalized people. Current positions for which candidates are being sought is posted on their Web site and is also available from the Global Mission Personnel office of the UCC. [ID:6987]

United Nations Association in Canada (UNA-Canada)
Suite 300, 309 Cooper Street, Ottawa, ON, K2P 0G5, Canada;
613-232-5751, fax 613-563-2455, info@unac.org, www.unac.org 💻𝐹𝑟

MID-SIZED ADVOCACY GROUP: Business Development, Defence and Peacekeeping, Environment, Human Rights, Sustainable Development

The United Nations Associations in Canada (UNA-Canada) is a registered charity, founded in 1946, with a mandate to educate and engage Canadians in support for and understanding of the United Nations and its issues that have a global impact.

With a professional, national secretariat in Ottawa (currently a staff of about 12), UNA-Canada derives much of its strength and community outreach from its network of 14 volunteer-based branches. Working with the private and public sector, academia, community leaders, like-minded NGOs, as well as multilateral organizations, UNA-Canada provides a place for Canadians to offer their made-in-Canada solutions to challenges confronting the global commons and to develop skills in living together in peace and prosperity. Key programs target Canadian youth, human rights, sustainable development, environment, peacebuilding and corporate social responsibility.

Employees must have an interest in international affairs, and applicants with related degrees or past experience are welcome. Degree of expertise required depends on the position. Bilingualism is an asset, and often obligatory, and computer knowledge is required. UNA Canada maintains a data bank for resumés and it is also one of several implementing agencies for the Canadian government's Youth International Internship Program. [ID:6969]

USC Canada
Suite 705, 56 Sparks Street, Ottawa, ON, K1P 5B1, Canada;
613-234-6827, fax 613-234-6827, info@usc-canada.org, www.usc-canada.org 💻𝐹𝑟

LARGE DEVELOPMENT ASSISTANCE GROUP: Adult Training, Agriculture, Business Development, Community Development, Development Education, Environment, Gender and Development, Micro-enterprises

USC Canada (also known as the Unitarian Service Committee of Canada) works to help the poor of developing countries meet basic needs and improve their standard of living, as well as to promote human development and self-reliance. USC also provides emergency relief to areas of extreme need in countries where it has programs. It supports projects in Mali, Ethiopia, Lesotho, South Africa, Nepal, Bangladesh and Indonesia. The organization works in a variety of fields including education, health, income earning and employment creation, agriculture, rehabilitation, community development and reforestation. Overseas partner offices are managed and run by local professionals in those countries.

USC Canada employs approximately 25 people in its Canadian offices. Positions range from administrative support to education professionals to professionals in international development and programming to academics. The USC operates a national volunteer program in Canada, and has provincial offices in Ontario and British Columbia that focus on volunteers and development education. [ID:6970]

Voluntary Service Overseas Canada (VSO Canada)
Suite 806, 151 Slater Street, Ottawa, ON, K1P 5H3, Canada;
613-234-1364, fax 613-234-1444, inquiry@vsocan.org, www.vsocan.org 💻𝐹𝑟

MID-SIZED VOLUNTEER GROUP: Agriculture, Business Development, Community Development, Computer Systems, Development Education, Energy Resources, Engineering, Environment, Fisheries, Forestry, Intercultural Briefings, Media/Communications, Medical Health, Teaching, Trades, Volunteer, Water Resources

Volunteer Service Overseas Canada (VSO Canada) is a partner of VSO, an international development agency headquartered in London, UK, that promotes volunteering to fight global poverty and disadvantage. With 1,500 volunteers working in more than 30 developing countries, VSO is the world's largest independent volunteer-sending agency.

VSO Canada recruits volunteers who are living in Canada and the US. VSO Canada has 19 staff based in Ottawa and approximately 120 North American volunteers currently working overseas. This covers only a small percentage of VSO's international staff, which includes 39 field offices and over 1,800 volunteers from North America and Europe.

VSO Canada recruits volunteers from more than 80 occupations, including health professionals, teachers, business advisors, IT specialists, social and community workers, and technical and natural resource professionals. Placements through VSO's Volunteer Sending Program are usually for two years. VSO also sends Canadian IT professionals on six-month internships through NetCorps Canada International. Shorter-term secondment opportunities are available for business and management specialists through the VSO Business Partnership program. VSO provides a thorough and comprehensive package of training and support to volunteers, including coverage of expenses relating to pre-departure training, airfare, health insurance, immunizations, overseas accommodation and a living allowance.

Most VSO placements require that volunteers and interns have relevant qualifications and experience in the field in which they will be working (one year of post-qualification experience for NetCorps, usually two or more years for the Volunteer Sending Program). Application information can be obtained by visiting VSO's Web site, or by contacting the VSO Canada office. (For more information, see their ad in the sponsor section at the end of this guide.) [ID:6971]

Volunteers in Mission (VIM), Anglican Church of Canada
The Anglican Church of Canada, 80 Hayden Street, Toronto, ON, M4Y 3G2, Canada;
416-924-9192, fax 416-969-9797, vim@national.anglican.ca, www.anglican.ca/vim

SMALL EVANGELICAL GROUP: Administration (General), Community Development, Forestry, Fundraising, Medical Health, Religious, Water Resources

The Volunteers in Mission Program (VIM) of the Anglican Church of Canada provides opportunities for qualified Canadians to serve overseas or in Canada, usually for two years, in response to specific requests.

Ten to fifteen volunteers are overseas at any given time. Volunteers generally fill requests for teachers at the primary, secondary and post-secondary levels, teachers of English as a Second Language, physicians, other health personnel, agriculturalists, pastors, theological educators and translators. Volunteers are required to raise the funds necessary to cover the costs of such expenses as return airfare, medical insurance and a modest living allowance, while host organizations provide housing. Requests come from the regions of Africa, Asia and the Pacific, Latin America and the Caribbean. For more details, visit their Web site. [ID:6972]

Volunteers International Christian Service (VICS)
Suite 3, 843 Youville Drive W., Edmonton, AB, T6L 6X8, Canada;
780-485-5505, fax 780-485-5510, vics1@telusplanet.net, www.volunteerinternational.ca

LARGE VOLUNTEER GROUP: Community Development, Development Assistance, Medical Health, Teaching, Technical Assistance, Volunteer

Volunteer International Christian Service (VICS) is a lay volunteer program providing professional and technical personnel the opportunity to assist and work alongside the peoples of developing countries around the world. Men and women of all ages, single and married, share professional and technical skills to aid in the struggle to conquer disease, ignorance and social injustice.

Developing countries in areas such as Africa, Asia, South America and the South Pacific approach VICS requesting professional trained and licensed technically-skilled individuals. In response to these specific requests, VICS seeks volunteers with qualifications suited to these overseas assignments: medical personnel, licensed trades people, construction supervisors, qualified teachers and graduates with degrees in English, math and sciences. Volunteers must be between the ages of 21 and 65 and be in excellent health. In addition, it is recommended that VICS volunteers have some job experience in their fields. VICS recruits "witnesses"; not those who see themselves as preachers or experts. Volunteers commit to a minimum term of two years overseas. There is also an orientation session prior to going abroad. VICS pays for volunteers' airfare, accommodation and health/accident insurance. VICS also provides a cost of living allowance to volunteers.

There is one staff person in Edmonton as well as regional representatives across the country and 20-25 volunteers overseas at one time. Please contact VICS for more information. [ID:6842]

War Child Canada

Suite 204, 401 Richmond Street W., Toronto, ON, M5V 3A8, Canada;
416-971-7474, fax 416-971-7946, info@warchild.ca, www.warchild.ca

MID-SIZED DEVELOPMENT ASSISTANCE GROUP: Advocacy, Children's Rights, Development Education

War Child Canada is dedicated to providing urgently needed humanitarian assistance to war-affected children around the world. Working closely with the music industry, War Child Canada helps generate awareness, support and advocacy for children's rights everywhere. International projects reach more than 10 regions of the world, helping thousands of children and youth who have lived through war. Thousands of young people across North America have become involved in their campaigns, taking the initiative and organizing projects in their schools and communities, and hundreds more are creating a network of youth working for peace around the world.

War Child Canada is headed by two medical doctors and 10 local staff, and includes varying numbers of summer interns and volunteers in Canada. A large proportion of War Child Canada's employees started as volunteers or interns, so becoming familiar with the office is a very good way of getting yourself known in the organization. War Child Canada has a small database of interested people to whom they send out upcoming job vacancies. You can receive this information by signing up for their e-newsletter on their Web site. War Child Canada partners with local organizations abroad and does not send volunteers overseas. [ID:6901]

WaterCan

321 Chapel Street, Ottawa, ON, K1N 7Z2, Canada; 613-230-5182 ext. 224,
fax 613-230-0712, info@watercan.com, www.watercan.com

MID-SIZED DEVELOPMENT ASSISTANCE GROUP: Development Education, Fundraising, Water Supply

WaterCan supports integrated water supply, sanitation and hygiene promotion projects that assist rural communities and the urban poor in Africa. As an organization focused solely on the water and sanitation sector, WaterCan has developed specialized expertise in working with local partner organizations, identifying and organizing capacity-building opportunities for these partners, and supporting knowledge networks that facilitate collaboration among local and international stakeholders. In Canada, WaterCan carries out a variety of development education activities to raise awareness of the health and development benefits of clean water in the developing world.

WaterCan has five staff in Ottawa that manage the organization's international, development education and fundraising programs. WaterCan does not have an overseas volunteer program; however, enquires regarding volunteer opportunities in Canada are welcome. [ID:6973]

World Accord (WA)

1C-185 Frobisher Drive, Waterloo, ON, N2V 2E6, Canada; 519-747-2215,
fax 519-747-2644, waccord@worldaccord.org, www.worldaccord.org

MID-SIZED DEVELOPMENT ASSISTANCE GROUP: Development Assistance

World Accord (WA) works in partnership with local indigenous community organizations and NGOs in Asia and Latin America on a range of development activities, with local institutional capacity-building central to all its activities. WA supports micro-enterprise and cooperative development, environmental agriculture, agroforestry, rice production, milling, storage and marketing, women's rights, health and education. It works primarily in the Philippines, Nepal, Sri Lanka, India, Honduras and Guatemala.

WA has four staff based in Canada. Staff generally have experience in international development and are dedicated to eliminating world poverty and inequality. Development education is a critical part of the work done in Canada. Other skills such as accounting, office administration, communications and desktop publishing are also required for positions. [ID:6989]

World Federalist Movement - Canada (WFM-C)

Suite 207, 145 Spruce Street, Ottawa, ON, K1R 6P1, Canada;
613-232-0647, fax 613-563-0017, wfcnat@web.net, www.worldfederalistscanada.org

SMALL ADVOCACY GROUP: Administration (General), Advocacy, Editing, Fundraising, Volunteer, Writing

World Federalist Movement - Canada (WFM-C) is a national organization that promotes global awareness and political support for world institutions of law and governance. There are five branches across Canada. WFM-C is one of 22 national members of the World Federalist Movement (WFM), an accredited NGO at the United Nations.

Two staff, an executive director and an administrator, are based in Ottawa. In general, all staff have university degrees in political science or the social sciences and an extensive history of participation in volunteer organizations. Bilingualism is an asset. [ID:6990]

World Literacy of Canada (WLC)

Studio 236, 401 Richmond Street W., Toronto, ON, M5V 3A8, Canada;
416-977-0008, fax 416-977-1112, info@worldlit.ca, www.worldlit.ca

SMALL DEVELOPMENT ASSISTANCE GROUP: Adult Training, Community Development, Development Education, Gender and Development, Literacy, Social Justice and Development, Teaching

World Literacy of Canada (WLC) promotes international development and social justice in South Asia through the funding of community-based programs that emphasize adult literacy and non-formal education. WLC supports literacy programs that integrate health, housing, vocational training, and credit and savings programs in a holistic approach to community development. Particular attention is given to the needs of disadvantaged women. In Canada, WLC promotes public awareness and understanding of literacy and international development issues through their own projects and in cooperation with other Canadian agencies.

For their overseas projects, WLC stands by its commitment to employ local people who have the necessary expertise to work on their own projects. WLC currently employs five full-time staff in Canada and 16 in India. Local languages, cultural knowledge, and gender equity are fundamental to considerations for staffing overseas. Although staff turnover is minimal, WLC maintains a data bank for resumes. [ID:6993]

World Relief Canada (WRC)

Communications Director, Suite 310, 600 Alden Road, Markham, ON, L3R 0E7, Canada; 905-415-8181, fax 905-415-0287, worldrelief@wrcanada.org, www.wrcanada.org

MID-SIZED RELIEF AND DEVELOPMENT AGENCY: Development Assistance

World Relief Canada (WRC) is a Christian relief and development agency that partners with the evangelical church in Canada and overseas to respond to the basic needs of the world's most oppressed, poor and suffering people. WRC has 12 staff members, works exclusively through its overseas partners and does not send personnel overseas. [ID:6994]

World University Service of Canada (WUSC)

1404 Scott Street, Ottawa, ON, K1Y 4M8, Canada;
613-798-7477, fax 613-798-0990, wusc@wusc.ca, www.wusc.ca ▢*Fr*

LARGE VOLUNTEER GROUP: Adult Training, Business Development, Community Development, Computer Systems, Development Assistance, Development Education, Economics, Environment, Exchange Programs, Forestry, Gender and Development, Human Resources, Logistics, Media/Communications, Micro-enterprises, Project Management, Teaching, Technical Assistance, Telecommunications, Volunteer

Across Canada, World University Service of Canada (WUSC) implements development education programs through its network of members and local committees on college and university campuses. The organization supports approximately 30 refugee students each year and up to 100 international trainees under WUSC-administered scholarship and training programs. It works with and actively encourages linkages between academic institutions in Canada and those overseas.

WUSC works with indigenous NGOs, government and sector partners in its program countries. WUSC also implements bilateral development projects in Africa, Latin America, the Middle East and Southeast Asia. Its overseas programming targets the following sectors: small enterprise (private sector) development, education and training, agriculture and rural development, HIV/AIDs, community development and institutional strengthening. For updates on projects, programs and related opportunities, refer to their Web site.

In 2004, WUSC began working with the Canadian Centre for International Studies and Cooperation (CECI) to administer a joint volunteer program. At the same time, CECI joined WUSC as the Canadian cooperating agency for the United Nations Volunteers Programme (UNV), handling the recruitment process for Canadians and permanent residents on behalf of UNV headquarters in Bonn, Germany. UNV offers mid-career professionals the opportunity to volunteer overseas in humanitarian efforts. Thousands of people from more than 100 countries volunteer as specialists and field workers. For more information, consult the UNV Web site at www.unv.org.

WUSC has approximately 60 staff at its secretariat office in Ottawa. It has field offices in six countries abroad. Through its volunteer and public engagement programs, the organization fields approximately 100 volunteers and students overseas each year. WUSC recruits Canadian volunteers and technical experts for capacity-building programs and projects in selected African, Asian and South American countries. (For more information on WUSC, see Chapter 10, Short-Term Programs Overseas.) [ID:6995]

World Youth Centre (WYC)

147 Portland Street, Toronto, ON, M5V 2N4, Canada; 416-927-1992,
fax 416-960-3940, info@worldyouthcentre.com, www.worldyouthcentre.com

SMALL COORDINATING BODY: Education, Social Justice and Development, Youth and Development

World Youth Centre (WYC) is a new organization that exists to recognize, galvanize and enable the global, youth-driven, social change movement. Based in Toronto, WYC brings together young people from Canada and around the world to develop their enterprising ideas for social change in their communities and significantly influence public thought and action on issues that matter most to them.

Upon completion of the centre in 2007, the international headquarters for youth-driven efforts of social change will provide a curriculum in social entrepreneurship and sustainable development; a cultural centre for sharing and understanding through the arts; a spiritual centre for sharing belief systems, social justice issues and self-growth; a park, recreation and activity centre for learning through sport, fitness and activity; a resource centre of youth-serving and youth-driven programs and organizations, internationally; classrooms and conference/seminar/workshop rooms; and regular programming that highlights the exceptional work being done by youth around the world in the area of systemic/social change. [ID:6897]

YMCA Canada

International Office, 6th Floor, 42 Charles Street E., Toronto, ON, M4Y 1T4,
Canada; 416-967-9622, fax 416-967-9618, services@ymca.ca, www.ymca.ca ☐ Fr

LARGE DEVELOPMENT ASSISTANCE GROUP: Administration (General), Development Assistance,
Development Education, Project Management

The YMCA in Canada is dedicated to the growth of all persons in spirit, mind and body, and to a sense of responsibility for each other and the global community. There are 18 Canadian YMCAs and YMCA-YWCAs partnered with YMCAs in other countries worldwide. Overseas projects are generally implemented by indigenous YMCA staff and volunteers, and support a wide variety of sectors: education, health, agriculture, community development, leadership training, and refugees and rehabilitation.

There are two International Program staff in the YMCA Canada office and about 15 staff involved in the International Program across the country. A very limited number of opportunities exist to go overseas as part of a Partnership Exchange. Selection and orientation of individuals for overseas opportunities is done by local associations.

Mano Sin Fronteras (Hand-to-Hand without Borders) is an annual four-week Youth Exchange Program between the United States, Mexico and Canada. Selection and orientation of individuals for overseas opportunities is done by local associations. Candidates should have previous volunteer involvement with the YMCA, YMCA-YWCA or other community services, and commit themselves to sharing their experience with YMCA staff, volunteers and the community upon their return. For more information, visit the YMCA Canada Web site. [ID:6996]

Youth Challenge International (YCI)
Suite 305, 20 Maud Street, Toronto, ON, M5V 2M5, Canada;
416-504-3370, fax 416-504-3376, generalinfo@yci.org, www.yci.org ▢*Fr*

MID-SIZED SPECIAL NEEDS GROUP: Business Development, Community Development, Development Assistance, Development Education, Gender and Development, Human Resources, Medical Health

Youth Challenge International (YCI) promotes global youth development and believes youth-driven solutions are a critical component of their work. YCI aspires to a world where youth can reach their full potential and are valued for their contributions; where youth are full and welcomed participants; and where youth have access to education, meaningful employment and freedom from HIV/AIDS. To achieve these aims, YCI works within an international network and a global constituency for youth in Canada.

YCI employs five full-time and two part-time personnel. Overseas staff numbers vary from 10 to 30, depending on the time of year. International youth volunteers aged 18 to 30 play a key role in the planning and implementation of development projects and the achievement of long-term, sustainable outcomes. Since 1989, YCI has successfully involved over 2,000 Canadian youth volunteers in international development programs in Central America, South America, Africa and the South Pacific. Programs include HIV/AIDS peer education in Guyana, youth skills summits in Tanzania and young rural women's income generation training in Costa Rica. (For more on YCI's short-term programs, see Chapter 10, Short-Term Programs Overseas.) [ID:7021]

YWCA of Canada
Canadian Headquarters, Suite 422, 75 Sherbourne Street, Toronto, ON, M5A 2P9,
Canada; 416-962-8881, fax 416-962-8084, national@ywcacanada.ca, www.ywcacanada.ca ▢*Fr*

SMALL COMMUNITY DEVELOPMENT GROUP: Development Assistance, Development Education

YWCA of Canada is the oldest and largest women's service organization in Canada. It is a member of the World YWCA that unites 25 million women and girls in over 100 countries. YWCA Canada is headquartered in Toronto and works actively for the improved status of women and responsible social and economic change. Thirty-eight YWCAs and YMCA-YWCAs operate across the country, meeting the needs of more than one million women and their families annually. The YWCA is a turning point for women, offering them safety and economic security. It is the largest national provider of shelter and non-profit housing, and the second largest provider of employment and childcare services.

Check with specific local Association's for a complete listing of their employment courses such as employment training, pre-employment courses, life skills, entrepreneurship, career skills development, job search and non-traditional training. Although YWCA Canada does not place volunteers overseas, you can contact local Associations in Canada, the World YWCA or individual national YWCA overseas as they may be able to provide some assistance to interested individuals seeking volunteer work overseas. Contact information for YWCA in Canada or the World can be found at www.ywca.ca. [ID:7020]

CHAPTER 39

NGOs in
the US

There are an estimated 4.1 million Americans living overseas, and the number is growing fast. American expats working with NGOs can literally be found on every continent, providing assistance in even the most remote corners of the earth. Around the world, NGOs from the US are known for their size, wealth, innovation and reach. American NGOs dominate and lead NGO activity throughout the world, and no other country has as large an NGO presence as the US. American NGOs working overseas tend to have fairly narrow specializations. Often they focus on only one or two causes and develop numerous programs that support their cause in a range of geographic areas. This chapter profiles 410 US NGOs.

USAID AND NGOs

The United States history of government involvement in foreign assistance dates back to after World War II. The Marshall Plan, an American program designed to help stabilize post-war Europe, initiated a series of programs that led to the Foreign Assistance Act and the creation of The United States Agency for International Development (USAID) in 1961. (For more information about NGOs in general and applying for jobs with NGOs, see Chapter 38, NGOs in Canada.)

Annually, USAID is allotted less than 0.5 per cent of the US federal budget. The Agency supports programs of economic growth, agriculture, trade, global health, democracy, conflict prevention and humanitarian assistance in Sub-Saharan Africa, Asia and the Near East, Latin America and the Caribbean, Europe and Eurasia. USAID provides funding and contracts to over 3,500 American companies and over 300 American NGOs, many of which are profiled in this chapter. (For more information on USAID contracts to American private firms, see Chapter 36, Private Sector Firms in the US.)

THE US NGO JOB MARKET FOR CANADIANS

Differences between Canadian and American NGOs tend to be slight, and most information provided applies to both Canadian and American organizations. There are hundreds of different types of NGO occupations overseas. (For more information on job types, see Chapter 30, Careers in International Development Jobs.)

American NGOs receive less funding from government than their Canadian counterparts, so most US NGOs must seek additional funding from charitable foundations, private citizens and corporations. Despite the smaller amount of funding from the US government, currently the largest difference between Canadian and American NGOs is the increased availability of funds and contracts from the US federal government for national or international security. Because of September 11, 2001, there is a massive reallocation of resources toward international security by all types of US agencies operating abroad. Although most funding for these projects lands in the hands of American private industry, some NGOs have also benefited. As well, protection for those living overseas has increased as a result of the renewed interest in international security.

American NGOs range in size from small, family-run groups to large multinational organizations. A significant number of US NGOs have over 500 staff, including large overseas contingents. Because of visa restrictions, Canadians are generally not employed in US headquarters; however, Canadians can obtain overseas positions with US NGOs. Overseas positions are generally advertised and managed through the Web sites of NGOs' American headquarters. American NGOs offer good opportunities for Canadians to work overseas, and Canadians with French language skills and international experience make for highly desirable overseas employees. Canadians are also eligible for many consulting contracts with American NGOs, and currency rates allow Canadians to offer organizations the added enticement of lower consulting fees than American consultants. Alternatively, Canadians can take advantage of overseas volunteer opportunities with American organizations, and can often find direct employment with US NGOs while travelling or living overseas. All of this means that American NGOs should not be overlooked by Canadians. US NGOs offer some excellent opportunities for Canadians to build their careers and gain international work.

US NGO WEB SITES

American NGO Web sites have dramatically improved over the last few years. Most Web sites are visually attractive and laden with information. Details found on NGO Web sites commonly include information about who they are, what they do, where they work, employment, contact information, pictures, related broadcast news reports and newsletters. Also, due to the practice among American NGOs of eliciting funding from private citizens, it is not uncommon to find on-line donation forms on the same Web page that provides employment information.

Employment pages on NGO Web sites are now found on all but the smallest sites. Job pages often contain information about the culture of the organization, and sometimes offer testimonials from staff or volunteers. The number of jobs listed on a Web site varies from one to one hundred depending on the size of the organization, funding situation and job availability. Job descriptions are usually detailed and highly specific. Most Web sites also offer information about internships—formal or informal, paid or unpaid.

Many NGO Web sites also provide a listing of organizations that they work with or endorse. Where these lists are available, you will find them particularly helpful for finding similar jobs in similar organizations. You might also find it helpful that many Web sites allow you to apply to positions on-line, and some even maintain consultant or resume databases that enable you to be considered for current and future openings. Even if you are not interested in working for an American NGO, it is still worth your while to check out a few Web sites to see the types of jobs available and to familiarize yourself with the terminology in the field.

A LAST WORD

For related information, see Chapter 38, NGOs in Canada, and Chapter 40, NGOs in Europe & the Rest of the World.

RESOURCES

US NGOS

These are a few resources on NGOs in the US. Many more US NGOs can be found on the Internet and in the numerous American books listed in International Job Search Books Resources in Chapter 21, Resources for the International Job Search.

Foreign Policy Association 🖳
Foreign Policy Association, www.fpa.org ◆ International job postings categorized by development assistance, education, environment, humanitarian relief, health and population, research, youth and other. Also a great listing of internships and volunteer opportunities. Highly recommended. [ID:2579]

ForeignAID.com 🖳
www.foreignaid.com ◆ The ForeignAID.com International Funding Directory is a database of over 700 foundations and donors in the U.S., Europe, and worldwide that give over $1 Billion every year in grants and scholarships to individuals and projects. Subscription price is $499 US per year. [ID:2844]

Internet Public Library: Associations on the Net 🖳
www.ipl.org/ref/AON ◆ A comprehensive US guide to Web sites of prominent organizations and associations, listed by sector. An excellent resource for background research for your job search. [ID:2412]

Jobs and Careers with Nonprofit Organizations 📖
1999, Caryl Krannich, Ronald Krannich, 259 pages ➤ Impact Publications, Suite N, 9104 North Manassas Drive, Manassas Park, VA 20111-5211, USA, www.impactpublications.com, $17.95 US; Credit Cards; 703-361-7300, fax 703-335-9486 ◆ This US book provides information on over 300 US and international non-governmental organizations. Each organization is summarized in terms of purpose, activities, budget and number of employees. The book also includes Web sites. Rich with insights, tips, sample resumes and letters, contact information and recommended resources, this book is essential reading for anyone interested in exploring a job and career opportunities with non-governmental organizations. [ID:2183]

Peace Corps 👭
www.peacecorps.gov ◆ The United States Peace Corps is one of the world's most successful and respected development organizations. Peace Corps sends volunteers overseas to work in

development-related, 27-month projects. The organization also hires overseas and domestic program administrators, so be sure to check out those opportunities! [ID:2625]

Policy Library 🖳
www.policylibrary.com ◆ Policy Library Web site is a social, economic and foreign policy resource—updated daily with the latest jobs, research and events. An annual membership costs $70 CDN and allows access to hundreds of jobs, internships and scholarships from all around the world. A good resource for policy buffs. [ID:2644]

SIL International 🖳
www.sil.org/sildc/ThinkTanks_DC.htm ◆ This US Web site provides a comprehensive list of hyperlinks to US research and policy-development think tanks. Recommended as a great starting point for anyone looking for employment in this sector. [ID:2664]

USAID ⅲ
www.usaid.gov/careers ◆ This is the recruitment Web site of the US Government's overseas development assistance agency. USAID is the largest funding agency in the world, with job postings listed for US citizens interested in working in development. [ID:2668]

World Press Review List of Think Tanks and NGOs 🖳
www.worldpress.org/library/ngo.htm ◆ This Web site provides links to numerous international think tanks. An indispensable site for people interested in policy research or related fields. [ID:2663]

Profiles of US NGOs

Profiles of the organizations' international activities, as well as complete contact information for each of the US NGOs indexed here are available on the companion CD-ROM. (See Appendix 39a, "Profiles for Chapter 39: NGOs in the US" on the CD-ROM.)

Of the thousands of American NGOs in existence, 410 are listed in this chapter. NGO profiles are categorized by 20 field types (written in upper case below the field type) which are numerous to mention here.

The geographic distribution of US NGOs is very similar to that of the American private sector international firms. The Northeast is home to 213 NGOs primarily located in Washington, D.C., New York City, Boston, Baltimore, and surrounding areas. The Southeast is the base for 67 NGOs, mainly concentrated around Arlington, VA; Atlanta, GA and throughout Florida. Of the remaining NGOs listed in this guide, 42 are located in the Midwest region surrounding Chicago and Minneapolis; 74 are located in the West, surrounding Los Angeles, San Francisco, and Seattle; and 12 are located in the Southwest – a small scattering throughout the state of Texas.

Index to US NGOs

Use this index to quickly scan for field types (written in uppercase) and organization Web site addresses. Check out the CD-ROM for descriptions of the organizations' international activities and for complete contact information. (See Appendix 39a, "Profiles for Chapter 39: NGOs in the US" on the CD-ROM.)

A Self-Help Assistance Program (ASAP)
DEVELOPMENT ASSISTANCE GROUP
www.asapafrica.org [ID:6045]

Academy for Educational Development (AED)
ADVOCACY GROUP
www.aed.org [ID:5815]

ACCION International
COMMUNITY DEVELOPMENT GROUP
www.accion.org [ID:5816]

ACDI/VOCA
RELIEF AND DEVELOPMENT AGENCY
www.acdivoca.org [ID:5824]

Action Against Hunger
RELIEF AND DEVELOPMENT AGENCY
www.aah-usa.org [ID:6046]

Action for Enterprise (AFE)
DEVELOPMENT ASSISTANCE GROUP
www.actionforenterprise.org [ID:6047]

The Adoption Exchange, Inc.
SPECIAL NEEDS GROUP
www.adoptex.org [ID:6048]

**Adventist Development and Relief
Agency International (ADRA)**
RELIEF AND DEVELOPMENT AGENCY
www.adra.org [ID:5822]

The Africa-America Institute (AAI)
ADVOCACY GROUP
www.aaionline.org [ID:5759]

**African Community Resource
Center, Inc. (ACRC)**
ADVOCACY GROUP
www.africancommunitycenter.org [ID:5760]

**The African Methodist Episcopal
Church Service & Development
Agency, Inc. (AME-SADA)**
RELIEF AND DEVELOPMENT AGENCY
www.amecnet.org/sada/sada.htm [ID:5761]

African Wildlife Foundation (AWF)
ENVIRONMENTAL ACTION GROUP
www.awf.org [ID:5762]

Africare, Inc.
DEVELOPMENT ASSISTANCE GROUP
www.africare.org [ID:5823]

Aid to Artisans, Inc.
DEVELOPMENT ASSISTANCE GROUP
www.aidtoartisans.org [ID:6049]

**International Association for
Students in Economics and Business
Management (AIESEC)**
EXCHANGE GROUP
www.aiesec.org [ID:6001]

Air Serv International
RELIEF AND DEVELOPMENT AGENCY
www.airserv.org [ID:5825]

Amazon Conservation Team (ACT)
COMMUNITY DEVELOPMENT GROUP
www.amazonteam.org [ID:6050]

Amazon-Africa Aid Organization
COMMUNITY DEVELOPMENT GROUP
www.amazonafrica.org [ID:6051]

**America-Mideast Educational &
Training Services (AMIDEAST)**
COMMUNITY DEVELOPMENT GROUP
www.amideast.org [ID:6053]

**American College of
Nurse-Midwives (ACNM)**
MEDICAL ASSISTANCE GROUP
www.midwife.org [ID:6054]

American Council on Education (ACE)
ADVOCACY GROUP
www.acenet.edu [ID:6055]

**American Enterprise Institute for
Public Policy Research (AEI)**
RESEARCH INSTITUTE
www.aei.org [ID:5969]

American Friends Service Committee (AFSC)
RELIEF AND DEVELOPMENT AGENCY
www.afsc.org [ID:5827]

American Geophysical Union (AGU)
DEVELOPMENT ASSISTANCE GROUP
www.agu.org [ID:6056]

American Himalayan Foundation
FOUNDATION
www.himalayan-foundation.org [ID:6057]

American Institute for Research (AIR)
RESEARCH INSTITUTE
www.air.org [ID:5936]

American Jewish Committee (AJC)
ADVOCACY GROUP
www.ajc.org [ID:5803]

**The American Jewish Joint
Distribution Committee, Inc. (JDC)**
COMMUNITY DEVELOPMENT GROUP
www.jdc.org [ID:6058]

American Jewish World Service (AJWS)
RELIEF AND DEVELOPMENT AGENCY
www.ajws.org [ID:6023]

**American Latvian Association
in the United States, Inc. (ALA)**
COMMUNITY DEVELOPMENT GROUP
www.alausa.org [ID:6059]

American Leprosy Missions (ALM)
MEDICAL ASSISTANCE GROUP
www.leprosy.org [ID:6060]

American Medical Resources Foundation, Inc.
MEDICAL ASSISTANCE GROUP
www.amrf.com [ID:6061]

American Near East Refugee Aid (ANERA)
RELIEF AND DEVELOPMENT AGENCY
www.anera.org [ID:6062]

American Red Cross
RELIEF AND DEVELOPMENT AGENCY
www.redcross.org [ID:5804]

American Red Magen
 David for Israel (ARMDI)
MEDICAL ASSISTANCE GROUP
www.armdi.org [ID:6063]

American Refugee Committee (ARC)
COMMUNITY DEVELOPMENT GROUP
www.archq.org [ID:5831]

American Soybean Association (ASA)
COORDINATING BODY
www.soygrowers.com [ID:6064]

American-Nicaraguan Foundation, Inc. (ANF)
FOUNDATION
www.aidnicaragua.org [ID:6065]

AmeriCares Foundation, Inc.
RELIEF AND DEVELOPMENT AGENCY
www.americares.org [ID:5805]

America's Development
 Foundation, Inc. (ADF)
COMMUNITY DEVELOPMENT GROUP
www.adfusa.org [ID:6052]

Ananda Marga Universal
 Relief Team, Inc. (AMURT)
RELIEF AND DEVELOPMENT AGENCY
www.amurt.net [ID:6066]

Armenia Fund U.S.A., Inc.
DEVELOPMENT ASSISTANCE GROUP
www.armeniafundusa.org [ID:6067]

Armenian Assembly of America, Inc.
ADVOCACY GROUP
www.aaainc.org [ID:6068]

Armenian Eyecare Project (AECP)
MEDICAL ASSISTANCE GROUP
www.eyecareproject.com [ID:6069]

Armenian Relief Society, Inc. (ARS)
RELIEF AND DEVELOPMENT AGENCY
www.ars1910.org [ID:6070]

Armenian Technology Group, Inc. (ATG)
DEVELOPMENT ASSISTANCE GROUP
www.atgusa.org [ID:6071]

Ashoka
DEVELOPMENT ASSISTANCE GROUP
www.ashoka.org [ID:5806]

The Asia Foundation
FOUNDATION
www.asiafoundation.org [ID:6072]

Aspen Institute
RESEARCH INSTITUTE
www.aspeninstitute.org [ID:5832]

Assist International
RELIEF AND DEVELOPMENT AGENCY
www.assistinternational.org [ID:6073]

Association for International
 Practical Training (AIPT)
EXCHANGE GROUP
www.aipt.org [ID:5996]

Atlantic States Legal Foundation, Inc.
ENVIRONMENTAL ACTION GROUP
www.aslf.org [ID:6074]

Bay Area International Development
 Organizations (BAIDO)
COORDINATING BODY
www.baido.org [ID:6022]

Benetech
HUMAN RIGHTS ORGANIZATION
www.benetech.org [ID:6024]

Benevolent Healthcare Foundation
RELIEF AND DEVELOPMENT AGENCY
www.projectcure.org [ID:6075]

Bethany Christian Services International, Inc.
SPECIAL NEEDS GROUP
www.bethany.org [ID:6076]

Better Africa Foundation
COMMUNITY DEVELOPMENT GROUP
www.betterafrica.org [ID:6025]

Bill & Melinda Gates Foundation
FOUNDATION
www.gatesfoundation.org [ID:6043]

Blessings International
MEDICAL ASSISTANCE GROUP
www.blessing.org [ID:6078]

BoardSource
DEVELOPMENT ASSISTANCE GROUP
www.boardsource.org [ID:6079]

Books For Africa, Inc. (BFA)
DEVELOPMENT EDUCATION GROUP
www.booksforafrica.org [ID:6080]

The Brackett Foundation
FOUNDATION
http://brackett.colgate.edu [ID:6081]

Bread for the World
ADVOCACY GROUP
www.bread.org [ID:5807]

The Brookings Institution
RESEARCH INSTITUTE
www.brook.edu [ID:5989]

Brother's Brother Foundation (BBF)
DEVELOPMENT ASSISTANCE GROUP
www.brothersbrother.org [ID:6082]

C.I.S. Development Foundation, Inc. (CISDF)
DEVELOPMENT ASSISTANCE GROUP
www.cisdf.com [ID:6083]

CARE USA
INTERNATIONAL NGO
www.care.org [ID:5843]

Carelift International
MEDICAL ASSISTANCE GROUP
www.carelift.org [ID:6084]

Caribbean Conservation Corporation
& Sea Turtle Survival League (CCC/STSL)
ENVIRONMENTAL ACTION GROUP
www.cccturtle.org [ID:6085]

Caribbean/Latin American Action (CCAA)
ADVOCACY GROUP
www.claa.org [ID:6086]

Carley Corporation
DEVELOPMENT EDUCATION GROUP
www.carleycorp.com [ID:6392]

Carmen Pampa Fund
DEVELOPMENT EDUCATION GROUP
www.carmenpampafund.org [ID:6087]

Carnegie Endowment for
International Peace (CEIP)
RESEARCH INSTITUTE
www.ceip.org [ID:5833]

The Carter Center, Inc.
HUMAN RIGHTS ORGANIZATION
www.cartercenter.org [ID:6014]

Catholic Medical Mission
Board, Inc. (CMMB)
MEDICAL ASSISTANCE GROUP
www.cmmb.org [ID:6088]

Catholic Near East Welfare
Association (CNEWA)
EVANGELICAL GROUP
www.cnewa.org [ID:6089]

Catholic Relief Services (CRS)
RELIEF AND DEVELOPMENT AGENCY
www.catholicrelief.org [ID:5808]

Cato Institute
RESEARCH INSTITUTE
www.cato.org [ID:5991]

Center for Citizen Initiatives (CCI)
ADVOCACY GROUP
www.ccisf.org [ID:6090]

Center for Communications,
Health and the Environment (CECHE)
ADVOCACY GROUP
www.ceche.org [ID:6091]

Center for International Rehabilitation (CIR)
SPECIAL NEEDS GROUP
www.cirnetwork.org [ID:6092]

The Center for Justice
and Accountability (CJA)
HUMAN RIGHTS ORGANIZATION
www.cja.org [ID:6026]

Center for Strategic and
International Studies (CSIS)
RESEARCH INSTITUTE
www.csis.org [ID:5992]

Center for Victims of Torture (CVT)
COMMUNITY DEVELOPMENT GROUP
www.cvt.org [ID:6093]

The Centre for Development and
Population Activities (CEDPA)
ADVOCACY GROUP
www.cedpa.org [ID:5809]

Chapin Living Waters Foundation
FOUNDATION
www.chapinlivingwaters.org [ID:6094]

CHF International
COMMUNITY DEVELOPMENT GROUP
www.chfhq.org [ID:5828]

Child Family Health International (CFHI)
MEDICAL ASSISTANCE GROUP
www.cfhi.org [ID:6027]

Child Health Foundation
FOUNDATION
www.childhealthfoundation.org [ID:6095]

Child Welfare League of
America, Inc. (CWLA)
ADVOCACY GROUP
www.cwla.org [ID:6096]

ChildHope Foundation
ADVOCACY GROUP
www.childhopeusa.com [ID:6097]

Childreach/Plan USA
DEVELOPMENT ASSISTANCE GROUP
www.planusa.org [ID:5810]

Children International
DEVELOPMENT ASSISTANCE GROUP
www.children.org [ID:6098]

Children of Chernobyl
Relief Fund, Inc. (CCRF)
MEDICAL ASSISTANCE GROUP
www.childrenofchornobyl.org [ID:6099]

The Children of War (TCOW)
DEVELOPMENT ASSISTANCE GROUP
www.thechildrenofwar.org [ID:6100]

Children's Christian Storehouse, Inc. (CCS)
DEVELOPMENT ASSISTANCE GROUP
www.geocities.com/ccstorehouse [ID:6101]

Children's Emergency
Relief International (CERI)
RELIEF AND DEVELOPMENT AGENCY
www.bcfs.net/ceri.htm [ID:6102]

Children's HeartLink
MEDICAL ASSISTANCE GROUP
www.childrensheartlink.org [ID:6103]

Children's Home Society
of Minnesota (CHSM)
COORDINATING BODY
www.chsm.com [ID:6104]

Children's Hunger Relief Fund, Inc. (CHRF)
RELIEF AND DEVELOPMENT AGENCY
www.chrf.org [ID:6105]

Children's Network International
RELIEF AND DEVELOPMENT AGENCY
www.childrensnetworkinternational.org
[ID:6106]

China Foundation, Inc.
FOUNDATION
www.chinafoundation1.org [ID:6107]

Christian Blind Mission International (CBMI)
SPECIAL NEEDS GROUP
www.cbmi-usa.org [ID:6108]

Christian Children's Fund (CCF)
RELIEF AND DEVELOPMENT AGENCY
www.christianchildrensfund.org [ID:5811]

Christian Medical & Dental Associations
EVANGELICAL GROUP
www.cmdahome.org [ID:6109]

Christian Mission Aid (CMA)
RELIEF AND DEVELOPMENT AGENCY
www.cmaid.org [ID:6110]

Christian Reformed World
Relief Committee (CRWRC)
RELIEF AND DEVELOPMENT AGENCY
www.crwrc.org [ID:6111]

Christian World Adoption (CWA)
COORDINATING BODY
www.cwa.org [ID:6112]

Church World Service (CWS)
RELIEF AND DEVELOPMENT AGENCY
www.churchworldservice.org [ID:5812]

CitiHope International, Inc.
RELIEF AND DEVELOPMENT AGENCY
www.citihope.org [ID:6113]

Citizens Development Corps, Inc. (CDC)
DEVELOPMENT ASSISTANCE GROUP
www.cdc.org [ID:6114]

The Citizens Network for
Foreign Affairs (CNFA)
DEVELOPMENT ASSISTANCE GROUP
www.cnfa.com [ID:6115]

Colorado China Council (CCC)
EXCHANGE GROUP
www.asiacouncil.org [ID:6013]

Committee to Protect Journalists (CPJ)
ADVOCACY GROUP
www.cpj.org [ID:5829]

Compassion International
RELIEF AND DEVELOPMENT AGENCY
www.compassion.com [ID:5813]

Compatible Technology International (CTI)
DEVELOPMENT ASSISTANCE GROUP
www.compatibletechnology.org [ID:6116]

Concern Worldwide US, Inc.
RELIEF AND DEVELOPMENT AGENCY
www.concernusa.org [ID:6117]

Conservation International (CI)
ENVIRONMENTAL ACTION GROUP
www.conservation.org [ID:5881]

Constituency for Africa
ADVOCACY GROUP
[ID:6118]

Convoy of Hope (COH)
RELIEF AND DEVELOPMENT AGENCY
www.convoyofhope.org [ID:6119]

Cooperative Housing Foundation (CHF)
DEVELOPMENT ASSISTANCE GROUP
www.chfhq.org [ID:6120]

Coptic Orphans Support Association
DEVELOPMENT ASSISTANCE GROUP
www.copticorphans.org [ID:6121]

The Corporate Council on Africa (CCA)
ADVOCACY GROUP
www.africacncl.org [ID:6122]

Council for International
Exchange of Scholars (CIES)
COORDINATING BODY
www.cies.org [ID:5726]

Council of the Americas
COORDINATING BODY
www.americas-society.org [ID:5727]

Council on Foreign Relations
RESEARCH INSTITUTE
www.cfr.org [ID:5728]

Council on International
Educational Exchange (CIEE)
EXCHANGE GROUP
www.ciee.org [ID:5745]

Counterpart International, Inc.
DEVELOPMENT ASSISTANCE GROUP
www.counterpart.org [ID:6123]

Covenant House
DEVELOPMENT ASSISTANCE GROUP
www.covenanthouse.org [ID:6124]

The Crafts Center at CHF International
DEVELOPMENT ASSISTANCE GROUP
www.craftscenter.org [ID:6125]

The Creative Connections Project
EXCHANGE GROUP
www.ccproject.org [ID:6019]

Creative Learning, Inc.
COMMUNITY DEVELOPMENT GROUP
www.creativelearning.org [ID:6126]

Cross International
RELIEF AND DEVELOPMENT AGENCY
www.crossinternational.org [ID:5864]

CrossLink International, Ltd.
RELIEF AND DEVELOPMENT AGENCY
www.crosslinkinternational.net [ID:5865]

Cuban American National
Council, Inc. (CNC)
COMMUNITY DEVELOPMENT GROUP
www.cnc.org [ID:5866]

Curamericas
MEDICAL ASSISTANCE GROUP
www.curamericas.org [ID:5867]

CURE International, Inc.
SPECIAL NEEDS GROUP
www.cureinternational.org [ID:5868]

Deep Roots Incorporated
DEVELOPMENT EDUCATION GROUP
www.deeproots.org [ID:6020]

The Dian Fossey Gorilla Fund
International (DFGFI)
ENVIRONMENTAL ACTION GROUP
www.gorillafund.org [ID:5870]

Direct Relief International
RELIEF AND DEVELOPMENT AGENCY
www.directrelief.org [ID:5814]

Disability Rights Education
and Defense Fund (DREDF)
SPECIAL NEEDS GROUP
www.dredf.org [ID:5886]

Doctors of the World, Inc.
RELIEF AND DEVELOPMENT AGENCY
www.doctorsoftheworld.org [ID:5753]

Ducks Unlimited
ENVIRONMENTAL ACTION GROUP
www.ducks.org [ID:5754]

E&Co
ENVIRONMENTAL ACTION GROUP
www.energyhouse.com [ID:5755]

Earth Day Network (EDN)
ENVIRONMENTAL ACTION GROUP
www.earthday.net [ID:5756]

Earth Island Institute, Inc.
ENVIRONMENTAL ACTION GROUP
www.earthisland.org [ID:5757]

EARTH University Foundation, Inc.
FOUNDATION
www.earth-usa.org [ID:6127]

Earthwatch Institute
RESEARCH INSTITUTE
www.earthwatch.org [ID:5746]

EastWest Institute (EWI)
ADVOCACY GROUP
www.ewi.info [ID:6128]

EcoLogic Development Fund
ENVIRONMENTAL ACTION GROUP
www.ecologic.org [ID:6129]

Education Development Center, Inc. (EDC)
DEVELOPMENT EDUCATION GROUP
main.edc.org [ID:5818]

Educational and Research Foundation
for the American Academy of Facial and
Reconstructive Plastic Surgery (AAFPRS
Foundation)
MEDICAL ASSISTANCE GROUP
www.aafprs.org [ID:6130]

Elizabeth Glaser Pediatric AIDS Foundation
FOUNDATION
www.pedaids.org [ID:6131]

Enersol Associates, Inc.
COMMUNITY DEVELOPMENT GROUP
www.enersol.org [ID:6132]

Engender Health, Inc.
COMMUNITY HEALTH GROUP
www.engenderhealth.org [ID:6133]

Enterprise Development International
DEVELOPMENT ASSISTANCE GROUP
www.endpoverty.org [ID:6134]

Enterpriseworks Worldwide, Inc. (EWW)
DEVELOPMENT ASSISTANCE GROUP
www.enterpriseworks.org [ID:6135]

Environmental Defense Fund (EDF)
INTERNATIONAL NGO
www.environmentaldefense.org [ID:5841]

Eritrean Development Foundation (EDF)
RELIEF AND DEVELOPMENT AGENCY
www.edfonline.org [ID:6136]

Esperanca, Inc.
MEDICAL ASSISTANCE GROUP
www.esperanca.org [ID:5819]

Ethiopian Community Development
Council, Inc. (ECDC)
COMMUNITY DEVELOPMENT GROUP
www.ecdcinternational.org [ID:6137]

The Fabretto Children's Foundation, Inc
FOUNDATION
www.fabretto.org [ID:6138]

Family Care International (FCI)
ADVOCACY GROUP
www.familycareintl.org [ID:6139]

Family Health International (FHI)
INTERNATIONAL NGO
www.fhi.org [ID:5842]

Federation of Jain Associations in North
America
ADVOCACY GROUP
www.jaina.org [ID:6140]

Feed the Children, Inc.
RELIEF AND DEVELOPMENT AGENCY
www.feedthechildren.org [ID:6141]

The Field Museum of Natural History
RESEARCH INSTITUTE
www.fieldmuseum.org [ID:6142]

Financial Services Volunteer
Corps, Inc. (FSVC)
DEVELOPMENT ASSISTANCE GROUP
www.fsvc.org [ID:6143]

First Voice International
MEDIA DEVELOPMENT GROUP
www.firstvoiceint.org [ID:6315]

Floresta USA, Inc.
ENVIRONMENTAL ACTION GROUP
www.floresta.org [ID:6144]

Florida Association of Voluntary Agencies
for Caribbean Action, Inc. (FAVACA)
COMMUNITY DEVELOPMENT GROUP
www.favaca.org [ID:6145]

Food for the Hungry, Inc.
RELIEF AND DEVELOPMENT AGENCY
www.fh.org [ID:5820]

Food For The Poor, Inc. (FFP)
RELIEF AND DEVELOPMENT AGENCY
www.foodforthepoor.org [ID:6146]

Ford Foundation
FOUNDATION
www.fordfound.org [ID:6036]

Foreign Policy Association (FPA)
RESEARCH INSTITUTE
www.fpa.org [ID:5747]

The Foundation for a Civil Society, Ltd.
FOUNDATION
www.fcsny.org [ID:6147]

Foundation for Democracy in Africa (FDA)
FOUNDATION
www.democracy-africa.org [ID:6148]

Foundation for Global Community
FOUNDATION
www.fgconline.org [ID:6149]

**Foundation for International
Community Assistance, Inc. (FINCA)**
DEVELOPMENT ASSISTANCE GROUP
www.villagebanking.org [ID:6150]

**Foundation for Russian/American
Economic Cooperation (FRAEC)**
FOUNDATION
www.fraec.org [ID:6151]

**Foundation for Sustainable Development
(FSD)**
COMMUNITY DEVELOPMENT GROUP
www.fsdinternational.org [ID:6029]

**Foundation for Understanding
and Enhancement (FUNEN)**
FOUNDATION
www.funen.org [ID:6152]

**Foundation of Compassionate
American Samaritans (FOCAS)**
EVANGELICAL GROUP
www.focas-us.org [ID:6153]

Freedom From Hunger
DEVELOPMENT ASSISTANCE GROUP
www.freefromhunger.org [ID:5821]

Freedom House
HUMAN RIGHTS ORGANIZATION
www.freedomhouse.org [ID:5830]

Friends of the Americas
RELIEF AND DEVELOPMENT AGENCY
www.friendsoftheamericas.org [ID:6154]

Friends of the Orphans (FOTO)
DEVELOPMENT ASSISTANCE GROUP
www.helptheorphans.org [ID:6155]

Fund for Armenian Relief, Inc. (FAR)
RELIEF AND DEVELOPMENT AGENCY
www.farusa.org [ID:6156]

**The Fund for International
Nonprofit Development (FIND)**
ORGANIZATIONAL TRAINING GROUP
www.find-usa.org [ID:6028]

**The German Marshall Fund
of the United States (GMF)**
RESEARCH INSTITUTE
www.gmfus.org [ID:6157]

Gifts in Kind International
COORDINATING BODY
www.giftsinkind.org [ID:6158]

Global Assistance, Inc.
MEDICAL ASSISTANCE GROUP
www.globalassistance.org [ID:6159]

**Global Environment &
Technology Foundation (GETF)**
FOUNDATION
www.getf.org [ID:6160]

Global Health Action, Inc. (GHA)
DEVELOPMENT ASSISTANCE GROUP
www.globalhealthaction.org [ID:6161]

Global Health Council
ADVOCACY GROUP
www.globalhealth.org [ID:5856]

Global Health Ministries (GHM)
MEDICAL ASSISTANCE GROUP
www.ghm.org [ID:6162]

Global Impact, Inc.
ENVIRONMENTAL ACTION GROUP
www.globalimpact.org [ID:6163]

Global Links
MEDICAL ASSISTANCE GROUP
www.globallinks.org [ID:6164]

**Global Operations & Development/
Giving Children Hope (GO&D)**
MEDICAL ASSISTANCE GROUP
www.godaid.com [ID:6165]

Global Peace Initiative
RELIEF AND DEVELOPMENT AGENCY
www.globalpeacenow.com [ID:6166]

Global Volunteers
VOLUNTEER GROUP
www.globalvolunteers.org [ID:6839]

Goodwill Industries International, Inc
DEVELOPMENT ASSISTANCE GROUP
www.goodwill.org [ID:5794]

Grameen Foundation USA (GF-USA)
FOUNDATION
www.gfusa.org [ID:6168]

The Grant Foundation
MEDICAL ASSISTANCE GROUP
www.hashaiti.org [ID:6169]

**Grupo de Apoyo a La
Democracia, Inc. (GAD)**
ADVOCACY GROUP
www.gadcuba.org [ID:6170]

Habitat for Humanity International, Inc.
DEVELOPMENT ASSISTANCE GROUP
www.habitat.org [ID:5795]

**Hadassah, The Women's Zionist
Organization of America, Inc.**
COMMUNITY DEVELOPMENT GROUP
www.hadassah.org [ID:6171]

The Haitian Health Foundation
MEDICAL ASSISTANCE GROUP
www.haitianhealthfoundation.org [ID:6172]

Half the Sky Foundation
DEVELOPMENT ASSISTANCE GROUP
www.halfthesky.org [ID:6173]

The Halo Trust (USA), Inc
RELIEF AND DEVELOPMENT AGENCY
www.halousa.org [ID:6174]

Healing Hands International, Inc (HHI)
RELIEF AND DEVELOPMENT AGENCY
www.hhi-aid.org [ID:6175]

Healing the Children Northeast, Inc.
MEDICAL ASSISTANCE GROUP
www.htcne.org [ID:6176]

Health Alliance International (HAI)
MEDICAL ASSISTANCE GROUP
www.depts.washington.edu/haiuw [ID:6177]

Health for Humanity (HH)
MEDICAL ASSISTANCE GROUP
www.healthforhumanity.org [ID:6178]

Health Volunteers Overseas, Inc. (HVO)
MEDICAL ASSISTANCE GROUP
www.hvousa.org [ID:6179]

Heart to Heart International, Inc.
RELIEF AND DEVELOPMENT AGENCY
www.hearttoheart.org [ID:6180]

Heifer International, Inc.
DEVELOPMENT ASSISTANCE GROUP
www.heifer.org [ID:5796]

Helen Keller Worldwide (HKW)
COMMUNITY HEALTH GROUP
www.hki.org [ID:5797]

Help the Afghan Children (HTAC)
DEVELOPMENT ASSISTANCE GROUP
www.helptheafghanchildren.org [ID:6181]

The Heritage Foundation
RESEARCH INSTITUTE
www.heritage.org [ID:5748]

Hermandad, Inc.
COMMUNITY DEVELOPMENT GROUP
www.hermandad.org [ID:6182]

The Hesperian Foundation
FOUNDATION
www.hesperian.org [ID:6030]

**Holt International Children's
Services, Inc. (HI)**
COMMUNITY DEVELOPMENT GROUP
www.holtinternational.org [ID:6184]

**Hoover Institution on War,
Revolution and Peace**
RESEARCH INSTITUTE
www-hoover.stanford.edu [ID:5749]

Hope Haven, Inc.
SPECIAL NEEDS GROUP
www.hopehaven.org [ID:6183]

Hope International
DEVELOPMENT ASSISTANCE GROUP
www.givehope.org [ID:6185]

HOPE Worldwide, Ltd.
DEVELOPMENT ASSISTANCE GROUP
www.hopeww.org [ID:6186]

Hudson Institute
RESEARCH INSTITUTE
www.hudson.org [ID:6037]

Human Rights Watch (HRW)
HUMAN RIGHTS ORGANIZATION
www.hrw.org [ID:5750]

The Hunger Project
DEVELOPMENT ASSISTANCE GROUP
www.thp.org [ID:5798]

Imani House, Inc. (IHI)
COMMUNITY DEVELOPMENT GROUP
www.imanihouse.org [ID:6187]

Impact Teams International
RELIEF AND DEVELOPMENT AGENCY
www.impactkids.org [ID:6189]

Independent Institute
RESEARCH INSTITUTE
www.independent.org [ID:5834]

Innovative Resources Management Inc. (IRM)
ENVIRONMENTAL ACTION GROUP
www.irmgt.com [ID:6405]

**Institute for Democracy in
Eastern Europe (IDEE)**
ADVOCACY GROUP
www.idee.org [ID:6190]

Institute for Policy Studies (IPS)
RESEARCH INSTITUTE
www.ips-dc.org [ID:5835]

**Institute for Social & Economic
Development (ISED)**
RESEARCH INSTITUTE
www.ised.org [ID:6191]

Institute for Sustainable Communities (ISC)
RESEARCH INSTITUTE
www.iscvt.org [ID:5854]

**The Institute for Transportation
and Development Policy (ITDP)**
RESEARCH INSTITUTE
www.itdp.org [ID:6192]

Institute of Cultural Affairs (ICA)
COMMUNITY DEVELOPMENT GROUP
www.ica-usa.org [ID:6193]

Institute of International Economics
RESEARCH INSTITUTE
www.iie.com [ID:5851]

Institute of International Education (IIE)
COORDINATING BODY
www.iie.org [ID:5799]

Inter-American Development Bank (IADB)
COMMUNITY DEVELOPMENT GROUP
www.iadb.org [ID:6038]

InterExchange
EXCHANGE GROUP
www.interexchange.org [ID:5800]

Interlocken International
EXCHANGE GROUP
www.interlocken.org [ID:6002]

International Agricultural
  Exchange Association (IAEA)
  EXCHANGE GROUP
  members.ozemail.com.au/~iaea/ [ID:6003]
International Aid (IA)
  RELIEF AND DEVELOPMENT AGENCY
  www.gospelcom.net/ia/ [ID:5801]
International Campaign to
  Ban Landmines (ICBL)
  INTERNATIONAL NGO
  www.vvaf.org [ID:5838]
International Center for
  Journalists, Inc. (ICFJ)
  MEDIA DEVELOPMENT GROUP
  www.icfj.org [ID:6223]
International Center for
  Research on Women (ICRW)
  ADVOCACY GROUP
  www.icrw.org [ID:5802]
International Children's Heart Foundation
  MEDICAL ASSISTANCE GROUP
  www.babyheart.org [ID:5871]
International Development and
  Educational Associates (IDEAS)
  RELIEF AND DEVELOPMENT AGENCY
  www.ideasworld.org [ID:5869]
International Development Enterprises (IDE)
  COMMUNITY DEVELOPMENT GROUP
  www.ideorg.org [ID:5857]
International Executive Service Corps (IESC)
  DEVELOPMENT ASSISTANCE GROUP
  www.iesc.org [ID:5875]
International Executive Service Corps (IESC)
  DEVELOPMENT ASSISTANCE GROUP
  www.iesc.org [ID:5859]
International Development Exchange (IDEX)
  COMMUNITY DEVELOPMENT GROUP
  www.idex.org [ID:6031]
International Eye Foundation (IEF)
  MEDICAL ASSISTANCE GROUP
  www.iefusa.org [ID:5860]
International Food Policy
  Research Institute (IFPRI)
  RESEARCH INSTITUTE
  www.ifpri.org [ID:5740]
International Foundation for
  Education and Self-Help (IFESH)
  DEVELOPMENT ASSISTANCE GROUP
  www.ifesh.org [ID:5876]
International Foundation
  for Election Systems (IFES)
  RESEARCH INSTITUTE
  www.ifes.org [ID:5853]
International Foundation for Hope
  DEVELOPMENT ASSISTANCE GROUP
  www.ifhope.org [ID:5920]

International Health Organization (IHO)
  MEDICAL ASSISTANCE GROUP
  www.ihousa.org [ID:6077]
International Institute for
  Energy Conservation (IIEC)
  ENVIRONMENTAL ACTION GROUP
  www.iiec.org [ID:5921]
International Justice Mission (IJM)
  HUMAN RIGHTS ORGANIZATION
  www.ijm.org [ID:5990]
International Medical Corps (IMC)
  MEDICAL ASSISTANCE GROUP
  www.imc-la.com [ID:5850]
International Medical Equipment
  Collaborative of America (IMEC)
  MEDICAL ASSISTANCE GROUP
  www.imecamerica.org [ID:5922]
International Medical Services
  for Health (INMED)
  MEDICAL ASSISTANCE GROUP
  www.inmed.org [ID:5923]
International Orthodox Christian
  Charities, Inc. (IOCC)
  RELIEF AND DEVELOPMENT AGENCY
  www.iocc.org [ID:5924]
International Relief and Development (IRD)
  RELIEF AND DEVELOPMENT AGENCY
  www.ird-dc.org [ID:6194]
International Relief Teams
  RELIEF AND DEVELOPMENT AGENCY
  www.irteams.org [ID:6195]
International Rescue Committee (IRC)
  INTERNATIONAL NGO
  www.intrescom.org [ID:5844]
International Schools Services (ISS)
  EXCHANGE GROUP
  www.iss.edu [ID:5741]
International Service Center
  DEVELOPMENT ASSISTANCE GROUP
  www.isc1976.com [ID:5903]
International Social Service,
  American Branch (ISI)
  DEVELOPMENT ASSISTANCE GROUP
  www.iss-usa.org [ID:5904]
International Tuberculosis
  Foundation, Inc. (ITF)
  MEDICAL ASSISTANCE GROUP
  www.itfweb.org [ID:5905]
International Youth Foundation (IYF)
  DEVELOPMENT ASSISTANCE GROUP
  www.iyfnet.org [ID:5907]
Interns for Peace, Inc. (IFP)
  ORGANIZATIONAL TRAINING GROUP
  www.internsforpeace.org [ID:5908]
Internships International
  EXCHANGE GROUP
  www.rtpnet.org/~intintl [ID:5997]

Ipas, Inc.
ADVOCACY GROUP
www.ipas.org [ID:5909]

Jesuit Volunteers International
DEVELOPMENT ASSISTANCE GROUP
www.jesuitvolunteercorps.org [ID:6041]

Joint Center for Political and Economic Studies, Inc.
ADVOCACY GROUP
http://jointcenter.org [ID:5910]

Jubilee House Community, Inc (JHC)
COMMUNITY DEVELOPMENT GROUP
www.jhc-cdca.org [ID:6198]

Junior Achievement International
ORGANIZATIONAL TRAINING GROUP
www.jaintl.org [ID:6199]

Katalysis Partnership, Inc.
DEVELOPMENT ASSISTANCE GROUP
www.katalysis.org [ID:6200]

Kettering Foundation
RESEARCH INSTITUTE
www.kettering.org [ID:6345]

Kids Around the World, Inc.
DEVELOPMENT ASSISTANCE GROUP
www.kidsaroundtheworld.com [ID:6201]

Kurdish Human Rights Watch, Inc. (KHRW)
DEVELOPMENT ASSISTANCE GROUP
www.khrw.com [ID:6202]

LakeNet
ENVIRONMENTAL ACTION GROUP
www.worldlakes.org [ID:6203]

Landmine Survivors Network (LSN)
SPECIAL NEEDS GROUP
www.landminesurvivors.org [ID:6204]

LASPAU - Academic and Professional Programs for the Americas
COORDINATING BODY
www.laspau.harvard.edu [ID:5861]

Life for Relief & Development
RELIEF AND DEVELOPMENT AGENCY
www.lifeusa.org [ID:6205]

Lions Clubs International
COMMUNITY DEVELOPMENT GROUP
www.lionsclubs.org [ID:6015]

Living Water International (LWI)
EVANGELICAL GROUP
www.living-water.org [ID:6211]

Lutheran World Relief
RELIEF AND DEVELOPMENT AGENCY
www.lwr.org [ID:5925]

Lutheran Immigration and Refugee Service (LIRS)
ADVOCACY GROUP
www.lirs.org [ID:5863]

The Maasai Heritage Preservation Foundation, Inc.
FOUNDATION
www.maasai-heritage.org [ID:6212]

Mano a Mano Medical Resources
COMMUNITY HEALTH GROUP
www.manoamano.org [ID:6213]

MAP International
RELIEF AND DEVELOPMENT AGENCY
www.map.org [ID:5926]

Maternal Life International, Inc. (MLI)
MEDICAL ASSISTANCE GROUP
www.maternallifeintl.com [ID:6210]

Matthew 25: Ministries, Inc.
RELIEF AND DEVELOPMENT AGENCY
www.m25m.org [ID:6232]

Médecins Sans Frontières/ Doctors Without Borders (MSF)
RELIEF AND DEVELOPMENT AGENCY
www.doctorswithoutborders.org [ID:5817]

Medical Care Development, Inc (MCD)
COMMUNITY DEVELOPMENT GROUP
www.mcd.org [ID:6221]

MediSend International
MEDICAL ASSISTANCE GROUP
www.medisend.org [ID:6222]

Mennonite Central Committee (MCC)
RELIEF AND DEVELOPMENT AGENCY
www.mcc.org [ID:5927]

Mercy Corps
RELIEF AND DEVELOPMENT AGENCY
www.mercycorps.org [ID:5852]

Mercy Ships
MEDICAL ASSISTANCE GROUP
www.mercyships.org [ID:6231]

Meridian International Center
EXCHANGE GROUP
www.meridian.org [ID:5742]

Mission Without Borders International
DEVELOPMENT ASSISTANCE GROUP
www.mwbi.org [ID:6214]

Mobility International USA (MIUSA)
SPECIAL NEEDS GROUP
www.miusa.org [ID:6021]

NAFSA: Association of International Educators
EXCHANGE GROUP
www.nafsa.org [ID:5743]

National Wildlife Federation (NWF)
ENVIRONMENTAL ACTION GROUP
www.nwf.org [ID:5788]

The Nature Conservancy
ENVIRONMENTAL ACTION GROUP
www.nature.org [ID:6237]

Nazarene Compassionate Ministries, Inc. (NHCM)
MEDICAL ASSISTANCE GROUP
www.ncmi.org [ID:6197]

Near East Foundation (NEF)
FOUNDATION
www.neareast.org [ID:5744]

OIC International
COMMUNITY DEVELOPMENT GROUP
www.oicinternational.org [ID:5789]

Open Society Institute
FOUNDATION
www.soros.org [ID:5836]

Operation Smile, Inc.
MEDICAL ASSISTANCE GROUP
www.operationsmile.org [ID:6239]

Operation USA, Inc
COMMUNITY DEVELOPMENT GROUP
www.opusa.org [ID:6519]

Opportunities Industrialization Centers International, Inc (OICI)
DEVELOPMENT ASSISTANCE GROUP
www.oicinternational.org [ID:5858]

Opportunity International
COMMUNITY DEVELOPMENT GROUP
www.opportunity.org [ID:5791]

ORBIS International
MEDICAL ASSISTANCE GROUP
www.orbis.org [ID:6016]

Oxfam America
RELIEF AND DEVELOPMENT AGENCY
www.oxfamamerica.org [ID:5792]

PACT (Private Agencies Collaborating Together)
COORDINATING BODY
www.pactworld.org [ID:5793]

Partners for Democratic Change (Partners)
DEVELOPMENT ASSISTANCE GROUP
www.partnersglobal.org [ID:6241]

Partners for Development (PFD)
DEVELOPMENT ASSISTANCE GROUP
www.pfd.org [ID:6249]

Partners of the Americas
EXCHANGE GROUP
www.partners.net [ID:5928]

Pathfinder International
MEDICAL ASSISTANCE GROUP
www.pathfind.org [ID:5929]

Peace Corps
DEVELOPMENT ASSISTANCE GROUP
www.peacecorps.gov [ID:6032]

Peacebuilding and Development Institute
RESEARCH INSTITUTE
www.american.edu/sis/peace/summer
[ID:6520]

Pearl S. Buck International, Inc. (PSBI)
DEVELOPMENT ASSISTANCE GROUP
www.pearl-s-buck.org [ID:6250]

The Peregrine Fund
ENVIRONMENTAL ACTION GROUP
www.peregrinefund.org [ID:6276]

Physicians for Human Rights (PHR)
HUMAN RIGHTS ORGANIZATION
www.phrusa.org [ID:5931]

Planned Parenthood Federation of America, Inc. (PPFA)
ADVOCACY GROUP
www.plannedparenthood.org [ID:5932]

Population Action International (PAI)
ADVOCACY GROUP
www.populationaction.org [ID:5933]

Population Council
RESEARCH INSTITUTE
www.popcouncil.org [ID:5839]

Population Reference Bureau (PRB)
RESEARCH INSTITUTE
www.prb.org [ID:5888]

Population Services International (PSI)
MEDICAL ASSISTANCE GROUP
www.psi.org [ID:5889]

Program for Appropriate Technology in Health (PATH)
COMMUNITY HEALTH GROUP
www.path.org [ID:5890]

Project Concern International
COMMUNITY HEALTH GROUP
www.projectconcern.org [ID:5946]

Project HOPE
MEDICAL ASSISTANCE GROUP
www.projhope.org [ID:5930]

ProLiteracy Worldwide
COMMUNITY DEVELOPMENT GROUP
www.proliteracy.org [ID:5862]

RAND Corporation
RESEARCH INSTITUTE
www.rand.org [ID:5779]

Rare Center for Tropical Conservation
ENVIRONMENTAL ACTION GROUP
www.rarecenter.org [ID:6018]

Refugees International (RI)
ADVOCACY GROUP
www.refugeesinternational.org [ID:5948]

Relief International (RI)
RELIEF AND DEVELOPMENT AGENCY
www.ri.org [ID:5826]

Research Triangle Institute (RTI)
RESEARCH INSTITUTE
www.rti.org [ID:5947]

Results Educational Fund
ADVOCACY GROUP
www.results.org [ID:6034]

Results Educational Fund (RFF)
RESEARCH INSTITUTE
www.rff.org [ID:6040]

The Rockefeller Foundation
FOUNDATION
www.rockfound.org [ID:6042]

The Rodale Institute
RESEARCH INSTITUTE
www.rodaleinstitute.org [ID:5780]

Royal Caribbean International
EXCHANGE GROUP
www.aupairsaccord.com [ID:6012]

Rural Development Institute (RDI)
ADVOCACY GROUP
www.rdiland.org [ID:6039]

Samaritan's Purse
RELIEF AND DEVELOPMENT AGENCY
www.samaritanspurse.org [ID:6293]

Save the Children, USA
RELIEF AND DEVELOPMENT AGENCY
www.savethechildren.org [ID:5949]

SCI International Voluntary Service
EXCHANGE GROUP
www.sci-ivs.org [ID:5998]

Search for Common Ground (SFCG)
DEVELOPMENT ASSISTANCE GROUP
www.sfcg.org [ID:5845]

Self-Help International
DEVELOPMENT ASSISTANCE GROUP
www.selfhelpinternational.org [ID:6517]

Sierra Club
ENVIRONMENTAL ACTION GROUP
www.sierraclub.org [ID:5840]

Smithsonian Institution
RESEARCH INSTITUTE
www.si.edu [ID:6414]

Social Science Research Council (SSRC)
RESEARCH INSTITUTE
www.ssrc.org [ID:5846]

Special Olympics
SPECIAL NEEDS GROUP
www.specialolympics.org [ID:5950]

SRI International
RESEARCH INSTITUTE
www.sri.com [ID:5975]

Sustainable Sciences Institute (SSI)
MEDICAL ASSISTANCE GROUP
www.ssilink.org [ID:6035]

TechnoServe, Inc.
COMMUNITY DEVELOPMENT GROUP
www.technoserve.org [ID:5951]

Trees for Life, Inc.
DEVELOPMENT ASSISTANCE GROUP
www.treesforlife.org [ID:6518]

Trees for the Future
DEVELOPMENT ASSISTANCE GROUP
www.treesftf.org [ID:6240]

Unitarian Universalist
Service Committee (UUSC)
HUMAN RIGHTS ORGANIZATION
www.uusc.org [ID:5953]

United Nations Association of the
United States of America (UNA-USA)
ADVOCACY GROUP
www.unausa.org [ID:5847]

United States Fund for UNICEF
RELIEF AND DEVELOPMENT AGENCY
www.unicefusa.org [ID:5952]

United States Olympic Committee (USOC)
COORDINATING BODY
www.olympic-usa.org [ID:5782]

Urban Institute
RESEARCH INSTITUTE
www.urban.org [ID:5783]

Urgent Action Fund (UAF)
COMMUNITY DEVELOPMENT GROUP
www.urgentactionfund.org [ID:6238]

The US-China Business Council (USCBC)
RESEARCH INSTITUTE
www.uschina.org [ID:5781]

The Vaccine Fund
MEDICAL ASSISTANCE GROUP
www.vaccinefund.org [ID:5768]

Vellore Christian Medical
College Board (USA), Inc.
MEDICAL ASSISTANCE GROUP
www.vellorecmc.org [ID:5769]

Viet-Nam Assistance for
the Handicapped (VNAH)
SPECIAL NEEDS GROUP
www.vnah-hev.org [ID:5770]

Vietnam Veterans Memorial Fund
ADVOCACY GROUP
www.vvmf.org [ID:6296]

Visions in Action
DEVELOPMENT ASSISTANCE GROUP
www.visionsinaction.org [ID:6297]

The Voice of the Martyrs
ORGANIZATIONAL TRAINING GROUP
www.persecution.com [ID:6298]

Volunteer Missionary
Movement (VMM-USA)
RELIEF AND DEVELOPMENT AGENCY
www.vmmusa.org [ID:6299]

Volunteers for Inter-American
Development Assistance (VIDA)
RELIEF AND DEVELOPMENT AGENCY
www.vidausa.org [ID:6300]

Volunteers for Peace
EXCHANGE GROUP
www.vfp.org [ID:5999]

Volunteers in Technical Assistance (VITA)
DEVELOPMENT ASSISTANCE GROUP
www.vita.org [ID:5954]

Volunteers of America, Inc.
COMMUNITY DEVELOPMENT GROUP
www.volunteersofamerica.org [ID:6301]

W.K. Kellogg Foundation
FOUNDATION
www.wkkf.org [ID:6317]

Water For People (WFP)
COMMUNITY DEVELOPMENT GROUP
www.waterforpeople.org [ID:6302]

Water Missions International
RELIEF AND DEVELOPMENT AGENCY
www.watermissions.org [ID:6017]

The WILD Foundation
ENVIRONMENTAL ACTION GROUP
www.wild.org [ID:5906]

WildAid, Inc.
ENVIRONMENTAL ACTION GROUP
www.wildaid.org [ID:6303]

**Winrock International Institute for
Agricultural Development**
DEVELOPMENT ASSISTANCE GROUP
www.winrock.org [ID:6304]

Women for Women
DEVELOPMENT ASSISTANCE GROUP
www.womenforwomen.org [ID:6305]

**Woodrow Wilson International
Center for Scholars**
RESEARCH INSTITUTE
http://wwics.si.edu [ID:5848]

**World Association for Children
and Parents (WACAP)**
COORDINATING BODY
www.wacap.org [ID:6306]

World Concern
RELIEF AND DEVELOPMENT AGENCY
www.worldconcern.org [ID:5891]

World Conference of Religions for Peace
ADVOCACY GROUP
www.religionsforpeace.org [ID:6307]

**World Council of Credit
Unions, Inc. (WOCCU)**
COORDINATING BODY
www.woccu.org [ID:5892]

World Education
DEVELOPMENT ASSISTANCE GROUP
www.worlded.org [ID:5893]

World Emergency Relief (WER)
RELIEF AND DEVELOPMENT AGENCY
www.worldemergency.org [ID:6308]

World Environment Center (WEC)
ENVIRONMENTAL ACTION GROUP
www.wec.org [ID:6309]

World Help
EVANGELICAL GROUP
www.worldhelp.net [ID:6310]

World Hope International
RELIEF AND DEVELOPMENT AGENCY
www.worldhope.net [ID:6311]

World Institute on Disability (WID)
SPECIAL NEEDS GROUP
www.wid.org [ID:6312]

World Learning
RESEARCH INSTITUTE
www.worldlearning.org [ID:5784]

World Neighbors
COMMUNITY DEVELOPMENT GROUP
www.wn.org [ID:5785]

World Rehabilitation Fund, Inc. (WRF)
SPECIAL NEEDS GROUP
www.worldrehabfund.org [ID:6313]

**World Relief Corporation of
National Association of Evangelicals**
EVANGELICAL GROUP
www.wr.org [ID:5894]

World Resources Institute (WRI)
RESEARCH INSTITUTE
www.wri.org [ID:5849]

World Vision International
INTERNATIONAL NGO
www.wvi.org [ID:5837]

World Wildlife Fund, Inc. (WWF)
ENVIRONMENTAL ACTION GROUP
www.worldwildlife.org [ID:6314]

Worldwatch Institute
RESEARCH INSTITUTE
www.worldwatch.org [ID:5968]

CHAPTER 40

NGOs in Europe & the Rest of the World

Over the past few decades non-governmental organizations have proliferated throughout the world. They can now be found in virtually every country of the world, often picking up the slack for governments that are unable to deliver basic services to their people. Others work from centres of power where they undertake research that is designed to shape public policy.

This chapter offers a glimpse of the types of NGOs operating in Europe and throughout the rest of the world. It includes 60 profiles of some of the world's largest and most respected organizations in Europe, as well as a few smaller organizations doing important work in Africa and Asia.

European NGOs

There are thousands of NGOs operating throughout Europe, including some of the world's largest and most respected NGOs. Most are concentrated in England, France, Switzerland and Northern Europe, although there are numerous smaller NGOs operating throughout the continent, including in the transitional countries of Eastern Europe.

Many North Americans are drawn to European NGOs because of their innovativeness and thoroughly developed policies. In many respects these NGOs are reflective of the European populace, which generally tends to have a much greater understanding of world issues. Moreover, many European NGOs receive broader bases of revenue and are therefore not as reliant upon government funding. This allows them to remain committed to long-term projects, unlike so many North American NGOs that react to government "cause célèbres" and tend to work in global hot spots that are in the news.

WORKING WITH EUROPEAN NGOs

The variety and excellence of the work being done by European NGOs attracts a high number of applicants for all vacancies. Getting one of these coveted jobs is no easy task, especially for North Americans, who often have difficulty getting the necessary legal authorization to work in Europe. Most NGOs go so far as to tell all non-EU citizens not to bother applying for positions based in Europe unless they already have a legal right to work in the home country. In short, unless you have dual citizenship, your chances of simply applying for a job with a European NGO and having success, are slim.

That being said, thousands of North Americans currently work for European NGOs and there are still ways to obtain work in Europe—it'll just take more work and commitment than simply writing a great cover letter and resume.

There are essentially three avenues to finding a job with a European NGO: volunteer or intern in Europe, join a European short-term program overseas, or work for a European NGO overseas.

First, in Europe it is common for recent graduates to spend several months volunteering or interning with an NGO to gain professional experience. This path is equally open to North Americans, and if you prove yourself, an employer might be tempted to complete the necessary paperwork to retain your services. Like any other job, it is relevant, practical work experience that employers look for. Finding a volunteer position or an internship with an NGO that specifically meets your career building needs requires work. If you are bold, well organized, and take initiative, you will succeed. Consider taking a six-month European backpacking vacation, but start the first three months with a volunteer posting. Make use of government sponsored student work visas to build professional experience while in Europe—rather than working as a bar maid in Paris, for example. (For information on government sponsored student work visas, see for example the SWAP profiles in the Profiles section of Chapter 10, Short-Term Programs Overseas.)

Second, join a European short-term program overseas. Like the many programs based in Canada or the US, North Americans are often eligible to apply for the volunteer programs run by European NGOs. These experiences will put you into the loop and can serve as a stepping stone to permanent jobs abroad with European NGOs. At the least, you will gain valuable cross-cultural experience, more so than if you joined a North American program. Your international resume will have greater punch for years to come when you list your participation in a European short-term program overseas. (To find information on European programs, see the Resources section in Chapter 10, Short-Term Programs Overseas.)

Third—and most important—European NGOs are free to hire whomever they want for overseas positions. Increasingly these positions are being filled by locally engaged staff, but there are still numerous overseas vacancies. Most, however, tend to be more senior positions that require management experience or specific technical skills. But there are a limited number of entry-level positions, particularly for those who are willing to live in difficult conditions and who possess language skills. For instance, many European NGOs actively recruit bilingual Canadians with French and English language skills to work on their overseas development projects in Africa. Bilingual Spanish-speaking Americans are also recruited by European NGOs to work in Latin America. If you have a professional designation, such as engineering or nursing, this may be your in. Regardless of the angle, search the European NGO job boards—these are revolutionizing the application process and opening up the job world to all, regardless of citizenship. (For more sources of information, see the NGO Job Boards Resources in Chapter 30, Careers in International Development.)

JOBS IN ASIA, AFRICA AND THE MIDDLE EAST

Profiles of 10 NGOs based in countries throughout Africa, the Middle East and Asia are included in this chapter. These are meant to provide you with a sampling of the type of NGOs that are active around the world.

Permanent positions with these NGOs are generally reserved for individuals from the home country, although it is not uncommon to find a North American or European working for an Asian or African NGO. While there are few permanent positions, these NGOs do offer numerous opportunities for students and young professionals to gain overseas professional experience through internships or volunteering.

Working for a local or grassroots NGO is a great way to gain professional overseas experience and develop your cross-cultural skills. The drawback is that few of these organizations will be able to offer you any remuneration, although funding is out there. Try contacting your government, school or the NGO itself to find out about possible funding sources. Search especially for North American NGOs that have had past partnership agreements with NGOs in the South. A North American NGO can often provide you with an introduction to a partner in the developing world.

A LAST WORD

One successful strategy used by many North Americans is to parlay an overseas posting into a job with a non–North American NGO. Whether you are backpacking abroad, interning abroad, or on your first professional assignment, you should consider knocking on the doors of NGO offices wherever you are. It is much easier for a European NGO to hire a North American when you are already working or travelling abroad. Start by requesting a short consulting contract, and build from there. Remember, be bold and daring in your job search because these are the same characteristics that will make you succeed in your international work. Go forth and become a citizen of the world by working for an NGO based outside of your home country. The world needs more global citizens such as you!

RESOURCES

NGOS IN EUROPE & THE REST OF THE WORLD

The resources below are presented with a view to assisting you in broader, more extensive searches.

Centre d'Information sur le Volontariat International 🖥

www.civiweb.com/default.asp?action=offres; *Fr* ◆ Centre d'Information sur le Volontariat International : site français avec des offres de volontariat à travers le monde et conseils pour devenir volontaire. [ID:2676]

The Directory of Work & Study in Developing Countries 📖
1997, Robert Miller, 256 pages ➤ Vacation Work, 9 Park End Street, Oxford, OX1 1HJ, UK, www.vacationwork.co.uk, £9.99; Credit Cards; (44)(0)(1865) 24-1978, sales@vacationwork.co.uk
◆ For those who wish to experience life in a developing country as more than a tourist. Thousands of short- and long- term opportunities for work and study with over 400 organizations in Africa, the Middle East, Asia, the Far East, the Pacific, Latin America and the Caribbean, including health care, engineering, disaster relief, agriculture, business, teaching, archaeology, economics, oil, irrigation, etc. [ID:2047]

German Development Service 👫
www.ded.de ◆ The German Development Service (DED) is one of the leading European development services for personnel cooperation. It was founded in 1963; since then, more than 13,000 development workers have committed themselves to improving the living conditions of people in Africa, Asia and Latin America. Almost 1,000 development workers are currently working in 40 countries. Search DED development job postings all over the world. [ID:2476]

NGLS Handbook 🖥
Biennial ➤ United Nations Non-Governmental Liaison Service (UN/NGLS), Room FF 346, United Nations, New York, NY 10017, USA, www.un.org/partners/civil_society/ngo/ngo-ngls.htm, Free on-line; 212-963-3125, fax 212-963-8712 ◆ Find in-depth profiles of UN agencies, programs, and funds working for economic and social development. In addition to information on each agency and its work program, the Handbook also describes how they cooperate with NGOs. [ID:2335]

World Press Review List of Think Tanks and NGOs 🖥
www.worldpress.org/library/ngo.htm ◆ This Web site provides links to numerous international think tanks. An indispensable site for people interested in policy research or related fields. [ID:2663]

Yearbook of International Organizations 2003/2004 📖
Annual, Union of International Associations (Geneva) ➤ Thomson K. G. Saur Verlag, Ortlerstrasse 8, Munich, 81373, Germany, www.saur.de, €1,498; (49) (0) 769-02-239, fax (49) (0) 89-769-02-250; Available in large libraries ◆ The most up-to-date and comprehensive reference work on international non-profit organizations. Profiles 25,979 of the most important organizations active in the world today, including 2,552 intergovernmental (IGOs) and 23,427 international non-governmental organizations (NGOs). An excellent job hunting resource. [ID:2056]

Profiles of NGOs in Europe & the Rest of the World

Profiles of the NGO's international activities, as well as complete contact information for each are available on the companion CD-ROM. (See Appendix 40a, "Profiles for Chapter 40: NGOs in Europe & the Rest of the World" on the CD-ROM.)

There are a total of 60 profiles listed in this chapter. These NGOs have been chosen because they are large and important within their own country and because they provide a representative sample of the thousands of NGOs based outside of North America. If you are to be an "international person" you should learn about what other international organizations exist in your field, and you should consider working for them as part of a long-term career building strategy.

Index to NGOs in Europe & the Rest of the World

Use this index to quickly scan for field types (written in uppercase) and organization Web site addresses. Check out the CD-ROM for descriptions of the organizations' international activities and for complete contact information. (See Appendix 40a, "Profiles for Chapter 40: NGOs in Europe & the Rest of the World" on the CD-ROM.)

International Center
ORGANIZATIONAL TRAINING GROUP
www.internationalcenter.cl [ID:5751]

International Chamber of Commerce (ICC)
ADVOCACY GROUP
www.iccwbo.org [ID:5594]

**International Committee
of the Red Cross (ICRC)**
HUMAN RIGHTS ORGANIZATION
www.icrc.org [ID:5569]

International Crisis Group (ICG)
ADVOCACY GROUP
www.crisisweb.org [ID:5555]

**International Federation of Red Cross
and Red Crescent Societies**
RELIEF AND DEVELOPMENT AGENCY
www.ifrc.org [ID:5611]

**International Institute for
Applied Systems Analysis (IIASA)**
RESEARCH INSTITUTE
www.iiasa.ac.at [ID:5566]

International Peace Research Institute (PRIO)
RESEARCH INSTITUTE
www.prio.no [ID:5550]

**International Planned
Parenthood Federation (IPPF)**
COMMUNITY HEALTH GROUP
www.ippf.org [ID:5613]

International Service
RELIEF AND DEVELOPMENT AGENCY
www.internationalservice.org.uk [ID:5576]

**International Social Security
Association (ISSA)**
COORDINATING BODY
www.issa.int [ID:5614]

IUCN -The World Conservation Union
COORDINATING BODY
www.iucn.org [ID:5573]

Kiel Institute for World Economics
RESEARCH INSTITUTE
www.uni-kiel.de/ifw/homeeng.htm [ID:5552]

Médecins du Monde
MEDICAL ASSISTANCE GROUP
www.medecinsdumonde.org [ID:7336]

Merlin
COMMUNITY HEALTH GROUP
www.merlin.org.uk [ID:5553]

Mine Action (MAG)
RELIEF AND DEVELOPMENT AGENCY
www.magclearsmines.org [ID:5542]

Norwegian Refugee Council (NRC)
RELIEF AND DEVELOPMENT AGENCY
www.nrc.no [ID:5556]

Overseas Development Institute (ODI)
RESEARCH INSTITUTE
www.odi.org.uk [ID:5534]

**Pacific Economic Cooperation Council
(PECC)**
COORDINATING BODY
www.pecc.org [ID:5533]

Peace Brigades International (PBI)
HUMAN RIGHTS ORGANIZATION
www.peacebrigades.org [ID:5567]

Plan
COMMUNITY HEALTH GROUP
www.plan-international.org [ID:5572]

SNV Netherlands Development Organisation
RELIEF AND DEVELOPMENT AGENCY
www.snvworld.org [ID:5620]

SOLIDARITÉS
RELIEF AND DEVELOPMENT AGENCY
www.solidarites.org [ID:7270]

**Stockholm International
Peace Research Institute (SIPRI)**
RESEARCH INSTITUTE
www.sipri.se [ID:5616]

Tearfund
RELIGIOUS GROUP
www.tearfund.org [ID:5624]

Terre des Hommes (TDH)
RELIEF AND DEVELOPMENT AGENCY
www.tdh.ch [ID:5543]

Third World Network - Africa
RESEARCH INSTITUTE
http://twnafrica.org [ID:5493]

Transparency International (TI)
ADVOCACY GROUP
www.transparency.org [ID:5617]

War Child Netherlands
DEVELOPMENT ASSISTANCE GROUP
www.warchild.nl [ID:5535]

WOMANKIND Worldwide
DEVELOPMENT ASSISTANCE GROUP
www.womankind.org.uk [ID:5621]

**Women in Security, Conflict Management
and Peace (WISCOMP)**
RESEARCH INSTITUTE
www.furhhdl.org [ID:5529]

World Economic Forum
ADVOCACY GROUP
www.weforum.org [ID:5570]

World Wide Fund for Nature (WWF)
ENVIRONMENTAL ACTION GROUP
www.panda.org [ID:5565]

ZOA-Refugee Care
RELIGIOUS GROUP
www.zoaweb.org [ID:5536]

CHAPTER 41

United Nations & Other IGOs

Following the Second World War, the states of the world came together and decided that international peace, security and prosperity could only be maintained by creating a truly international society that would be governed by states acting through institutions that are now commonly referred to as intergovernmental organizations (IGOs).

The United Nations would rest at the centre of the international system and was given the mandates of preventing international conflict, promoting human rights, ensuring respect for the international rule of law, supporting the peaceful settlement of disputes, and promoting social and economic progress.

Specialized agencies of the UN and other autonomous IGOs were subsequently created to oversee particular areas of responsibility. The Bretton Woods institutions were created to coordinate the international economic system, the WORLD HEALTH ORGANIZATION (WHO) would promote international cooperation aimed at improving the health of the world's people, and the INTERNATIONAL LABOUR ORGANIZATION (ILO) would continue the work it began in 1919 of improving international labour standards. The family of IGOs continues to grow, and in 2002 the international community welcomed the long-overdue creation of the INTERNATIONAL CRIMINAL COURT (ICC).

Below this first layer of IGOs are numerous regional governmental organizations that likewise have mandates covering an array of fields like security, economics, health and human rights. The NORTH ATLANTIC TREATY ORGANIZATION (NATO) provides security to Europe, the AFRICAN DEVELOPMENT BANK GROUP promotes economic liberalization throughout Africa, while the PAN AMERICAN HEALTH ORGANIZATION (PAHO) deals with international public health issues in the Americas.

As this sampling indicates, IGOs are usually specialized and focused on specific issues. The individuals whom these organizations seek to work for them are likewise highly specialized professionals who are committed to working in the public interest. Landing one of these highly sought-after jobs, however, is anything but easy. This chapter will provide you with some of the advice you'll need if you want to work for an IGO. It also includes profiles for 78 IGOs.

WORKING FOR AN IGO

Intergovernmental organizations (IGOs) are the largest international employers. The UN and its affiliated programs alone employ slightly over 50,000 full-time staff, not including thousands of short-term contractors. Nor does this statistic include the WORLD BANK or the CONSULTATIVE GROUP ON INTERNATIONAL AGRICULTURAL RESEARCH (CGIAR), each of which employs over 10,000 employees. There are at least 100,000 full-time positions with IGOs, covering every imaginable field and sector. One of these is waiting for you! Now all you have to do is find it—something that might take some patience and perseverance.

If you're a specialist you probably already know the IGOs that operate in your area of specialization. Certainly explore these IGOs to identify appropriate entry points, but don't make the mistake of limiting your job search to a few organizations. Take the time to explore all the opportunities that are out there. Engineers might be surprised to learn that organizations working in refugee camps desperately need their skills, and it might not occur to economists that the CGIAR offers them some very interesting and unique research opportunities. Looking around is especially important for those in professions like information technology, human resources and law, which are required by all IGOs.

Don't limit yourself or rush your job search. Take an appropriate amount of time to carefully research the various organizations that exist and the potential they have for you as employees. Even if you aren't yet ready to apply for a job, you should visit the career pages of IGOs. As a student, this will help you understand the type of training that will assist you to get a job.

The following section will provide you with an idea of the categories of employment that exist for seasoned professionals and those seeking entry-level positions.

Professional Categories

Most IGOs follow the UN's system of categorizing professional staff into two categories: the professional, or "P", levels (P-1 through P-5) and the director, or "D", levels (D-1 and D-2). P-1 is the entry-level category, although these positions are hardly ever advertised and seem, for the most part, to have become redundant due to the large number of internship positions with IGOs and the various associate or junior professional positions that are out there. The most junior positions that vacancies are posted for now seem to be at the P-2 level, although even these are rare.

The scarcity of entry-level jobs tells you that IGOs don't train. They're looking for seasoned professionals that already possess experience and bring transferable skills with them. It is this factor—experience—that separates the various professional categories from each other. At least two years direct experience is required at the P-2 level and at least 20 years experience at the D-2 level. Most advertised positions are at the P-3 or P-4 levels, which require anywhere from five to 12 years of related professional experience.

Along with experience, almost all IGO positions require an advanced degree and knowledge of English and French, or one of the other working languages of the UN. If you're considering a master's degree, try to stay away from a general international relations degree. Instead try to specialize and develop an expertise in an area where your skills will be in demand, such as economics, environmental studies or law. Cross-cultural skills are also prized, and it is good to be able to demonstrate experience working in a cross-cultural or multicultural environment. When applying for jobs, you should also remember that IGOs, especially the UN, are hierarchical organizations that are rather formal. Always be very professional. (For one insider's account of what you'll need to get a job with an IGO, see "Careers in Public International Law" by Ken Roberts, in Appendix 31b on the CD-ROM.)

Salaries and Benefits

The base salary of international civil servants working in the UN common system is based on the Noblemaire principle, which holds that employees should receive a level of remuneration equal to those in countries where, for comparable qualifications, the salaries are the highest. In practice this means that UN salaries are determined by ensuring that the salaries of UN staff in the New York headquarters are equivalent to those paid to US civil servants in Washington, after factoring in cost-of-living differences. A 15 to 20 per cent margin is then added to offset the disadvantages of expatriation.

In addition to this base salary, staff are accorded a post adjustment supplement. This ensures that the purchasing power of all professional staff is equal, regardless of their duty station. Occasionally, staff also receive a daily living allowance and a recruitment allowance. UN salaries are not tax free, as all professional staff are responsible for paying an internal staff assessment that is comparable to a national income tax. That being said, the staff assessment is hardly excessive, running on average at about 25 per cent.

The vast majority of IGOs follow the salary structure of the UN, with the exception of the international development banks, which have a looser (and much higher) salary structure that is reviewed each year and is increasingly based on comparable salaries in the private sector. Unlike the UN, these salaries are completely tax free.

Along with competitive salaries, staff of IGOs enjoy excellent benefits. Chief among these are the six weeks of vacation that you'll receive right off the bat. Then there are numerous other benefits such as educational grants for children, rental subsidies and spousal support. Salaries with the UN start at $42,944 US and top out at $186,144 US.

The Drawbacks

The idea of living abroad and travelling throughout the world can seem very attractive at first, but after several years it can begin to take a toll on individuals. Being away from family and friends is also difficult. Then there are the difficulties of relationships. (See Robin Pascoe's article, "Moving Your Marriage" in Appendix 3b on the CD-ROM.)

Working for an IGO can also be extremely frustrating for people who go in with high-minded ideals and a commitment to improve the world. It's not that such ideals are misplaced, but that most IGOs are huge bureaucracies that are often cumbersome or inefficient. You'll also quickly discover that not everyone working for IGOs shares a commitment to effect positive change. Too many are there to get a paycheque. Most people who end up leaving IGOs do so out of the frustration of working within a large bureaucracy.

ENTRY-LEVEL POSITIONS

There are virtually no professional entry-level positions with the UN. You're expected to be able to step into a position already possessing the necessary skills, training, education and experience. The same applies for most IGOs, although some do have entry-level positions or traineeship programs. Increasingly the way to get your foot in the door of the UN system and IGOs is by completing an internship. Indeed, an internship is one of the only ways to get invaluable direct professional experience with an IGO. The following section explains the four ways to get your foot in the door: Junior Professional Officer (JPO) programs, paid internships, unpaid internships and the United Nations Volunteers program (UNV). (For profiles on approximately 35 UN and other IGO internship programs, see the Profiles section in Chapter 17, Internships Abroad.)

Associate or Junior Professional Officer Positions

Many IGOs offer a limited number of associate or junior professional officer (JPO) positions or similar trainee positions. These entry-level training contracts generally last for one to three years. These positions are reserved explicitly for young professionals who are at an early stage in their career. These positions offer excellent opportunities to gain professional experience, including much-prized field experience.

These positions are available to the nationals of states that pay for them. For Canadians these positions are limited whereas the United States and many governments throughout Europe fund much larger numbers of JPOs. As of 2004 Canada funds 17 JPOs. (See the Junior Professional Officer Program (JPO) in the Profiles section in Chapter 17, Internships Abroad.)

Unpaid Internships

All UN bodies and most IGOs have internship programs that are open to students and recent graduates. The intent of these programs is to provide an introduction to international work, and they are the most secure avenue through which to gain professional work experience with an IGO.

The overriding drawback of these internships is that they are usually completely unpaid. Some IGOs do offer a limited stipend, but for most you'll have to cover all of your living expenses and a flight overseas. This is especially difficult given that the living expenses in cities like Geneva, New York and London are among the highest in the world. Canadians should budget for at least $1,500 a month, if they're willing to live modestly! An alternative is to try to arrange to be placed in a regional or field office. The flight might set you back quite a bit more, but the reduced living expenses and the opportunity to live in a truly unique culture is a decision that in the long-term will pay dividends.

Another drawback with internships is that you are sometimes not eligible to be hired back with a UN agency for a six-month period following the completion of your internship. Similar moratoriums of varying durations exist with some, but not all, IGOs. On the reverse side of this equation, there are backdoor strategies that may be available to the talented intern who has the support of his or her intern manager.

Given today's ever-rising tuitions, it is difficult to contemplate an unpaid internship that is overseas and usually in a very expensive city. At the same time, if you're serious about a career with an IGO, this is exactly the type of bold decision that could separate you in the minds of future employers.

Paid Internships

While the UN does not itself offer remuneration for interns, some IGOs do. Most of these paid internships are with the international financial institutions (IFIs), which don't seem to suffer the same budgetary restraints as other IGOs. For example, the IMF offers about 35 to 40 summer internships that pay about $4,500 US a month over the summer.

If you're not interested in finance or economics, your best chance for receiving a paid internship is with the Canadian government's international internship program. The bulk of these internships are with smaller organizations, so make sure you identify, very early in the calendar year, the Canadian organizations that offer internships with IGOs, as most of these internships begin early in the summer. Keep your eye on the Web sites of Canadian organizations like the UNITED NATIONS ASSOCIATION IN CANADA, the ATLANTIC COUNCIL OF CANADA and CANADEM which all offer excellent internships with IGOs. (For more information about the Canadian Government International Internship Programs, see Chapter 17, Internships Abroad.)

United Nations Volunteers Program (UNV)

The United Nations Volunteers (UNV) program supports human development globally by promoting volunteerism and mobilizing volunteers. It is administered by the United Nations Development Programme (UNDP). Every year 5,500 UN volunteers from more than 150 different nationalities actively support the programs of the United Nations itself and almost all UN funds, programs and specialized agencies. Job vacancies for postings all over the world are listed on-line. Currently, applicants must be at least 25 years of age, have a minimum of five years' work experience, and possess a good working knowledge of at least one of these languages: Arabic, English, French, Portuguese, Russian or Spanish. Assignments usually last 24 months; however, assignments of six to 12 months are increasingly common. (For more information on UNV, see the Profiles section in Chapter 10, Short-Term Programs Overseas.)

Finding and Applying for Jobs

Most IGOs maintain excellent Web sites that provide career information to prospective applicants, including listings of all current vacancies. The UN, however, is not counted among these organizations. The UN's career page does provide detailed information about how to apply for jobs through its e-recruitment system and does clearly list all vacancies. Other than that, though, the information on the UN site is rather sparse.

The most important piece of information that is lacking at the UN site is that there are many other UN jobs advertised on other sites. If you are interested in a particular UN agency, make sure you visit its Web site to see whether it lists jobs separately from the main UN employment site. Two major sites you should include in your job search are the UNITED NATIONS PEACEKEEPING OPERATIONS site, which lists jobs for civilians interested in working with peace support operations, and RELIEFWEB's vacancy page. This site, found at www.reliefweb.int and maintained by the UN OFFICE FOR THE COORDINATION OF HUMANITARIAN AFFAIRS (OCHA), is an indispensable source of information for anyone interested in working for the UN. Also make sure to include www.eurobrussels.com in your search for jobs with IGOs, particularly those based in Europe. (For more detailed information on these and other sites, see the UN & Other IGOs Resources at the end of this chapter.)

Applying for jobs has been greatly facilitated by the increasing use of e-recruitment systems by IGOs, including the UN. These on-line resumes take time to fill out, but once you've completed them, they are relatively easy to update and it is very easy to apply for new positions. When completing your on-line profile, remember to include as many keywords from the job description that you're applying to as possible.

You'll still have to send in paper applications for some UN positions. Often you'll be asked either to submit an international resume (which includes information like age, sex and marital status) or to complete a UN P.11 form, which is essentially the equivalent of the on-line form used in the UN's e-recruitment system. If you have to complete a P.11, make sure you save it on your computer as it takes some time to complete.

If you don't have significant experience, your chances of getting a job are greatest if you'll accept a hardship post or one in a conflict zone. In the end it might not be your six years of university and three languages that get you the job—it could be your willingness to sleep in a tent! Be aware also that many IGOs maintain quota systems for employees, based on the level of financial contribution by a country. Both Canada and the US are large contributors to most IGOs and therefore our nationalities are well represented.

A LAST WORD

Finding a job with an IGO takes persistence. While the odds are challenging, our experience shows that many young professionals do succeed—but they do so through the backdoor. Consider working in hardship locals. When there, look at trading up, by networking for other jobs within the same organization or, more productively, by looking for work with other IGOs working in the same place. Consider also working for the thousands of contractors who are employed by IGOs. There are many consulting opportunities, and entry-level professionals are well positioned for employment with these firms. Research the "procurement" pages of UN and other IGO Web sites to research firms with service contracts. Good luck with your search!

RESOURCES

UN & OTHER IGOS

The list of books below is presented with a view to assisting you in embarking on an international career with the United Nations or related agencies.

Asian Development Bank Business Opportunities 💻 🏛
Monthly ➤ Central Operations Services Office, Asian Development Bank, P.O. Box 789, Manila Central Post Office, 0980 Manila, Philippines, www.adb.org, $30 US/year; (632) 632-4444, fax (632) 636-2444 ◆ The ADB is based in Manila and funds development projects and programs in the Asian and Pacific regions. The goal is to generate opportunities for the business communities of member countries. The Business Opportunities page of the site is found by navigating from the index to "Opportunities" and then to "Business Opportunities." It provides information on the requirements for goods, work and services of projects under consideration by ADB. [ID:2286]

Basic Facts About the United Nations 📖
2000, United Nations Publications, 364 pages ➤ Information Office, United Nations Association in Canada, Suite 900, 130 Slater Street, Ottawa, ON K1P 6E2, Canada, www.unac.org, $12.50 US; VISA, MC; 613-232-5751, fax 613-563-2455 ◆ This updated edition reflects the wide range of concerns and multitude of ways in which the United Nations touches the lives of people everywhere. It chronicles the work of the organization in such areas as peace, development, human rights, refugees, disarmament and international legal order. In describing the work of the UN System, this publication provides a blueprint of our concerns, problems and determined efforts to find solutions. Essential reading for the overseas job seeker. [ID:2077]

CANADEM-International Trends and Opportunities 🏛
www.canadem.ca; *Fr* ◆ CANADEM is a national level roster of civilians with a broad range of skills including human rights, peacebuilding, democratization, admin-logistics, security and reconstruction. It serves primarily as a rapid reaction source of skilled Canadians for the UN, OSCE, other international organizations, NGOs and the Canadian government. CANADEM's Web page, "International Trends and Opportunities," provides a synopsis for international job hunters by monitoring all major UN field missions including the UN Department of Peacekeeping. For more information, see the specific mission updates on this excellent site. [ID:2837]

Careers in International Affairs 📖
2003, Maria Pinto Carland, Lisa A. Gihring, Georgetown University Graduate School of Foreign Affairs, 371 pages ➤ Scholarly Books, www.sbookscan.com, $39.53 US ◆ This US book is one of the best resources available for information on careers in international affairs. Provides a basic understanding of the different international career fields and what each offers, insights into the skills and requirements employers find necessary for success, heightened awareness of career options and broad guidelines for helping you make important career decisions. The book is painstakingly researched in conjunction with one of the oldest foreign affairs institutions in the US. Structurally, it starts with a well-written overview of the international affairs job market, followed by chapters on interview and Internet job hunting skills. Finally, you'll have a head start with hundreds of organizational profiles at your fingertips. An invaluable resource. Highly recommended! [ID:2043]

Development Business 📖 💻
Weekly ➤ United Nations Publications, Sales and Marketing Section, Room DC2-853, Department I004, New York, NY 10017, USA, www.un.org/Pubs/sales.htm, $550 US/year; Credit Cards; 800-253-9646, fax 212-963-3489 ◆ This United Nations Department of Public Information publication is available only by subscription and is the single best way that suppliers and consultants can find the information needed to successfully win contracts generated from projects financed by development banks, governments and the United Nations. Graphically and organizationally excellent, this site includes an on-line Business Directory with links to the Web sites of companies

involved in international business, which can be used for job searches and to locate potential business partners. A great resource [ID:2083]

Encyclopedia of Associations: International Organizations 📖
2004, Linda Irvin, three volumes ➤ Thomson Gale, 835 Penobscot Bldg., 645 Griswold Street, Detroit, MI 48226-4094, USA, www.gale.com, $765 US; Credit Cards; 800-877-4253 ext. 1330, fax 800-414-5043; Available in large libraries ◆ This classic three-volume reference covers multinational and national membership organizations from Afghanistan to Zimbabwe, including US-based organizations with a binational or multinational membership. Entries provide the names of directors, executive officers or other personal contacts; telephone, fax, telex, electronic mail, Web sites and bulletin boards. Also presents the group's history, governance, staff, membership, budget and affiliations. Entries are arranged in general subject chapters allowing users to browse in sections that interest them. Three indexes—geographic, executive and keyword—help speed research. An invaluable resource for your international job search! [ID:2042]

Euro Brussels 💻
www.eurobrussels.com/index.php ◆ Find your perfect job in Brussels, EU institutions or international organizations. Euro Brussels bills itself as the number one site in the business of European affairs and international relations, and it delivers. With 200,000 hits per month and literally hundreds of postings for some of the more obscure international jobs, searchable by category: international organizations, NGOs and political consultancies, EU institutions, law firms, academic and private think tanks, internships and industry associations. Many positions are high level, but there are some entry-level positions. Subscribe to their excellent newsletter. [ID:2607]

European Bank for Reconstruction and Development (EBRD) 👪
European Bank for Reconstruction and Development (EBRD), One Exchange Square, London, EC2A 2JN, UK, www.ebrd.com, (44) (20) 7338-6000, fax (44) (20) 7338-6100 ◆ EBRD provides funding for development projects in Europe and Asia. It provides a list of current and proposed projects and links to press releases and related stories. [ID:2827]

IDB Project and Procurement Information 💻
Inter-American Development Bank, 1300 New York Ave. N.W., Washington, DC 20577, USA, www.iadb.org, Free on-line; 202-623-1000, fax 202-623-3096 ◆ This is the main source of Inter-American Development Bank funded project procurement information. Navigate to the "Projects" section of the IADB home page and click on "Procurement." You'll find yourself at the "Project and Procurement Information" Web page table of contents. "Project Pipeline" is a database of projects under consideration for financing, which are tracked from initial identification until they receive official approval. "Approved Projects" provides the same information for those projects officially approved. Both provide continuously updated information on anticipated consulting and business opportunities. You'll also find procurement notices, contract award information, policies, procedures and standard form procurement documents, all intended to help you in your bid for a consultancy or supply contract. [ID:2287]

IFInet 💻
www.infoexport.gc.ca/ifinet/menu-e.htm, Free on-line ◆ The International Financing Information Network offers information designed to help Canadian companies prosper in the booming international development business market. IFInet can help you find out how to supply your goods and services to development and humanitarian projects; where to find project financing and guarantees for your investments in developing and transition economies; how other companies are thriving in this market, and who in the Trade Commissioner Service can best support your efforts. From the World Bank to the United Nations, from health sector reform to wastewater treatment, IFInet helps Canadian international entrepreneurs prosper in international development. [ID:2316]

Image and Reality: Questions and Answers About the United Nations 📖
2003, 56 pages ➤ United Nations Publications, Sales and Marketing Section, Room DC2-853, Department I004, New York, NY 10017, USA, www.un.org/Pubs/sales.htm, $5 US; Credit Cards;

800-253-9646, fax 212-963-3489 ◆ This book provides simple answers to some of the most frequently asked questions about the UN, including, how are peacekeeping operations organized? What is the organization doing to promote human rights? How is the UN addressing environmental problems? How is the budget determined? Is the organization overstaffed? What reforms are being undertaken to improve its work? This book helps the reader to understand and appreciate the work of this world body. [ID:2516]

Information on Applying for Employment with the United Nations 💻

www.un.org/Depts/OHRM/brochure.htm ◆ This is the general information site for the United Nations regarding recruitment. Information about applying for jobs in each of the organization's recruitment areas: administration, economics, electronic data processing, finance, language and related work, legal, library, public information, social development and statistics. A good start for learning about the UN recruitment system. [ID:2587]

Inter-Parliamentary Union 💻

www.ipu.org/strct-e/otherjobs.htm ◆ An excellent collection of links to the employment opportunity pages of other international organizations. [ID:2586]

Department of National Defence Canada ♛

www.dnd.ca; Fr ◆ From information on the latest UN peacekeeping operations to recruiting guidelines, this is the gateway to Canada's military. It also provides a statement of defence policy and information on financial management assistance. [ID:2268]

NGLS Handbook 💻

Biennial ➤ United Nations Non-Governmental Liaison Service (UN/NGLS), Room FF 346, United Nations, New York, NY 10017, USA, www.un.org/partners/civil_society/ngo/ngo-ngls.htm, Free on-line; 212-963-3125, fax 212-963-8712 ◆ Find in-depth profiles of UN agencies, programs, and funds working for economic and social development. In addition to information on each agency and its work program, the Handbook also describes how they cooperate with NGOs. [ID:2335]

Permanent Missions to the United Nations 📖

2003, 348 pages ➤ United Nations Publications, Sales and Marketing Section, Room DC2-853, Department I004, New York, NY 10017, USA, www.un.org/Pubs/sales.htm, $30 US; Credit Cards; 800-253-9646, fax 212-963-3489 ◆ Information on the United Nations' permanent missions worldwide. An excellent resource for starting your international job search, since missions have been known to hire independently of Human Resources in Geneva. Check it out. [ID:2517]

Renouf Catalogue 💻 ♛

Renouf Publishing Co. Ltd., Unit 1, 5369 Canotek Road, Ottawa, ON K1J 9J3, Canada, www.renoufbooks.com, Credit Cards; 888-767-6766, fax 613-745-7660 ◆ This Web site is produced by the North American specialty distributor Renouf, which features the publications of international and governmental organizations such as the United Nations and governments of Canada, US and the EU. The list of titles is extensive, featuring many of interest to the overseas job seeker looking to expand his or her international IQ. Highly recommended. Renouf also has a distribution office in the US: 812 Proctor Avenue, Ogdensburg, NY 13669-2205, USA, 888-551-7470 fax 888 568-8546. [ID:2180]

UNDP Jobs 💻

www.undp.org/jobs ◆ This job site offers a wide range of international opportunities at various levels, at the headquarters in New York, as well as in the field in locations such as Addis Ababa, Bangkok, Beirut, Bratislava, Dakar, Kathmandu, Nairobi, Oslo and Panama City. Jobs are in the organization's six key areas of operation: democratic governance, poverty reduction, energy and environment, crisis prevention and recovery, HIV/AIDS and management. Often updated with easy-to-access job postings. You can even apply on-line. Highly recommend site by a well-respected organization. [ID:2585]

United Nations Chronicle 📖

Quarterly, 78 pages ➤ United Nations Publications, Sales and Marketing Section, Room DC2-853, Department I004, New York, NY 10017, USA, www.un.org/Pubs/sales.htm, $8 US; Credit Cards; 800-253-9646, fax 212-963-3489; *Fr* ◆ A must read for every aspiring overseas worker, the "United Nations Chronicle" is a quarterly, easy-to-read report on the work of the United Nations and its agencies. Every issue covers a wide range of United Nations-related activities: from fighting the drug war to combatting racial discrimination, from relief and development to nuclear disarmament, terrorism and the worldwide environmental crisis. Written in English and available in French, Spanish and Arabic, the "United Nations Chronicle" includes a review of current Security Council and General Assembly sessions as well as information on future United Nations conferences and publications. [ID:2518]

United Nations Handbook 📖

Annual, Ministry of External Relations & Trade ➤ New Zealand High Commission, Suite 727, 99 Bank Street, Ottawa, ON K1P 6G3, Canada, $20 US; Money Order; 613-238-5991, fax 613-238-5707, www.mfat.govt.nz ◆ Comprehensive and up-to-date, the handbook lists all of the organizations in the United Nations family, including their aims, committee structure and legal basis. Also highlights subsidiary organizationss established under the UN Charter. Does not cover non-governmental organizations and intergovernmental organizations. An excellent resource. [ID:2061]

United Nations International Civil Service Commission 🖥

http://icsc.un.org ◆ Probably the best links page on the Net for fingertip access to job vacancies at all the UN agencies and the main international IGOs. [ID:2590]

United Nations Jobs 🖥

https://jobs.un.org/release1/Vacancy/Vacancy.asp ◆ This is the main UN vacancy page. Also contains information on the application process, remuneration and frequently asked questions. Postings are frequently updated and easily accessible. You can apply on-line. [ID:2589]

United Nations Jobs in Peacekeeping Operations 🖥

www.un.org/Depts/dpko/field/vacancy.htm ◆ This Web site lists the current job openings in UN Peacekeeping Operations. [ID:2591]

United Nations Publications Catalogue 🖥 👭

Annual ➤ United Nations Publications, Sales and Marketing Section, Room DC2-853, Department I004, New York, NY 10017, USA, www.un.org/Pubs/sales.htm, Free on-line; Credit Cards; 800-253-9646, fax 212-963-3489 ◆ This UN Web catalogue is a compendium of the all the United Nations' publications. Also available on CD-ROM. [ID:2790]

United Nations System 🖥

www.un.org ◆ This is the home page for the United Nations. It's full of information on the organization's make-up and policies, as well as links to daily briefings, media, maps and documents, publications and events. The kids' site, "CyberSchoolBus," is a great resource for teaching children about the value of the UN. For job vacancies, click on the link to "UN Employment." If you want your information immediately, you can receive the UN Webcast streamed 24 hours. A fabulous site to this fascinating human endeavour into international governance. [ID:2274]

United Nations Volunteers (UNV) 🖥

www.unv.org ◆ This program offers mid-career professionals the opportunity to volunteer overseas in a humanitarian effort. Every year some 5,000 UN Volunteers from more than 150 different nationalities take part in the programs of the United Nations itself as well as UN funds, programs and specialized agencies. This informative and user-friendly site has all the information you need to become a UN Volunteer and gain international experience. [ID:2153]

US Department of State International Vacancy Announcements 💻
www.state.gov/p/io/rls/iva/2004/29546.htm ◆ This site is updated every two weeks and contains an
extensive list of job openings at the United Nations and other international organizations. [ID:2588]

The World Bank Group ♔
World Bank, www.worldbank.org ◆ This flashy Web site is the information portal for the World
Bank Group, complete with organizational information, country information, statistics, employment
opportunities and more. [ID:2275]

**World Concerns and the United Nations: Model Teaching
Units for Primary, Secondary and Teacher Education** 📖
192 pages ➤ United Nations Publications, Sales and Marketing Section, Room DC2-853,
Department I004, New York, NY 10017, USA, www.un.org/Pubs/sales.htm, $19.95 US; Credit
Cards; 800-253-9646, fax 212-963-3489 ◆ Provides model teaching units for primary and secondary teachers directly applicable to the classroom. In addition to dealing with the aims and activities
of the United Nations and its system, the 26 model units in the collection follow a young person's
development, progressing through the interests characteristic of each age. The units are particularly
sensitive to youth's deep concern for justice, the environment, equal opportunities and full
participation in the life of society. The book also includes reading lists and illustrations. An
excellent resource for introducing your children to a new life as a UN overseas worker. [ID:2519]

World Trade Organization 💻
www.wto.org ◆ This is the WTO's official Web site. You'll find information on the organization and
its constituent members, as well as trade policy and statistics, legal documents and research reports.
There's also a job site and internship vacancies page. [ID:2288]

Yahoo's Search Directory of International Organizations 💻
www.yahoo.com/Government/International_Organizations ◆ Here you'll find hyperlinks to 667
international organizations around the world. [ID:2276]

Yearbook of International Organizations 2003/2004 📖
Annual, Union of International Associations (Geneva) ➤ Thomson K. G. Saur Verlag, Ortlerstrasse
8, Munich, 81373, Germany, www.saur.de, €1,498; (49) (0) 769-02-239, fax (49) (0) 89-769-02-
250; Available in large libraries ◆ The most up-to-date and comprehensive reference work on
international non-profit organizations. Profiles 25,979 of the most important organizations active in
the world today, including 2,552 intergovernmental (IGOs) and 23,427 international non-
governmental organizations (NGOs). An excellent job hunting resource. [ID:2056]

Profiles of UN & Other IGOs

The following 78 profiles have been put together to give you a good grounding in the
UN system along with other intergovernmental organizations (IGOs).

African Development Bank Group (ADBG)
Personnel Office, Rue Joseph Anoma, 01 BP 1387, Abidjan 01, Côte d'Ivoire;
(225) 20-20-44-44, fax (225) 20-20-49-59, afdb@afdb.org, www.afdb.org 💻 *Fr*

REGIONAL DEVELOPMENT BANK ◆ The African Development Bank Group (ADBG) is a
regional multilateral development bank supported by 77 nations from Africa, North and South
America, Europe and Asia. It consists of three institutions: the African Development Bank (ADB),
the African Development Fund (ADF) and the Nigeria Trust Fund (NTF).
　　　　The ADB promotes the economic development and social progress of its Regional Member
Countries (RMC) through loans, equity investments and technical assistance. The ADF provides

development finance on concessional terms to low-income RMCs that are unable to borrow on the non-concessional terms of the ADB, and the NTF assists the development efforts of poorer member countries.

Most of the staff work for the ADB. Canadians are eligible for employment with the ADB and can find vacancy information on its Web site. Applicants should possess an advanced degree, experience working in developing countries and be proficient in English and French. The ADB is actively recruiting qualified applicants in a number of specialized fields, including agronomy experts, engineers, financial analysts and information technology experts. [ID:5597]

Asian Development Bank (ADB)
P.O. Box 789, 6 ADB Ave., Mandaluyong, 0401 Metro Manila, 0980 Manila,
Philippines; (63) (2) 632-4444, fax (63) (2) 636-2444, information@adb.org, www.adb.org

REGIONAL DEVELOPMENT BANK ◆ The Asian Development Bank (ADB) is a regional development finance institution that engages in mostly public sector lending for development purposes in its developing member countries. The ADB focuses its efforts on poverty reduction by emphasizing sustainable economic growth, social development and good governance.

The ADB has over 2,000 employees from nearly 50 countries. Vacancies are posted on its Web site and applicants must generally have a very good academic background, including a post-graduate degree, and be willing to work with other nationalities and different cultures. The ADB provides facilities for qualified consultants to register the details of their capabilities and expertise.

The ADB's Young Professionals Program (YPP) is a three-year fixed-term appointment that lays the foundation for a career with the ADB. Canadians are also eligible for the ADB's summer internship program, although nominations must be directed through registered academic institutions. For a list of Canadian institutions that are registered, and other career information, consult the ADB Web site. [ID:5598]

Caribbean Development Bank (CDB)
P.O. Box 408, Wildey, St. Michael, Barbados; 246-431-1600,
fax 246-426-7269, info@caribank.org, www.caribank.org

REGIONAL DEVELOPMENT BANK ◆ The Caribbean Development Bank (CDB) contributes to the harmonious economic growth and development of the member countries in the Caribbean and promotes economic cooperation and integration among them, having special and urgent regard to the needs of the less developed members of the region.

It has 200 staff members from 11 countries, including 99 professionals in fields such as environmental sciences, law, macroeconomics and project management. The CDB looks for mature individuals who understand development and possess sound interpersonal and communication skills. It also maintains an on-line register of consultants. [ID:5540]

Committee on the Peaceful Uses of Outer Space (COPUOS)
Office for Outer Space Affairs, Vienna International Centre, P.O. Box 500,
A - 1400 Vienna, Austria; (43) (1) 26060-4950, fax (43) (1) 26060-5830,
oosa@unvienna.org, www.oosa.unvienna.org/COPUOS/copuos.html

GENERAL ASSEMBLY ◆ The Committee on the Peaceful Uses of Outer Space (COPUOS) is a permanent body that reviews the scope of international cooperation in peaceful uses of outer space, devises programs in this field to be undertaken under United Nations auspices, encourages continued research and the dissemination of information on outer space matters, and studies legal problems arising from the exploration of outer space.

The Committee and its two standing subcommittees, the Scientific and Technical Subcommittee, and the Legal Subcommittee, meet annually to consider and make recommendations regarding reports and questions submitted by the General Assembly, and issues raised by the Member States. Jobs with the COPUOS are listed on the general UN job page. [ID:5670]

Commonwealth Secretariat

Marlborough House, Pall Mall, London, SW1Y 5HX, UK; (44) (0) 20-7747-6500,
fax (44) (0) 20-7930-0827, info@commonwealth.int, www.thecommonwealth.org

MULTILATERAL INSTITUTION ◆ The Commonwealth Secretariat is the main intergovernmental agency of the Commonwealth. It facilitates the advancement of democracy, human rights, and sustainable economic and social development within its 53 member countries and beyond. The Secretariat currently has 400 staff from over 30 countries and is responsible for the recruitment of staff for the numerous Commonwealth Centre Youth Programmes and development experts for activities in developing Commonwealth countries. The Secretariat also maintains a database of suitably experienced and qualified professionals. The Commonwealth has yet to move to an e-recruitment system, so visit its recruitment site for information on how to apply. [ID:5607]

Consultative Group on International Agricultural Research (CGIAR)

1818 H Street N.W., Washington, DC, 20433, USA; 202-473-8951,
fax 202-473-8110, cgiar@cgiar.org, www.cgiar.org ▣ Fr ▣ Sp

SCIENTIFIC RESEARCH NETWORK ◆ The Consultative Group on International Agricultural Research (CGIAR) is a strategic alliance of countries, international and regional organizations, and private foundations supporting 15 international agricultural research centres that work with national agricultural research systems, the private sector and civil society. The alliance mobilizes agricultural science to reduce poverty, foster human well-being, promote agricultural growth and protect the environment. Research is geared toward producing higher-yielding food crops and more productive livestock, fish and trees, improving farming systems that are environmentally benign and enhancing scientific capacities in developing countries. The 15 centres are located throughout the world and together have over 8,500 scientists and scientific staff conducting cutting-edge research in more than 100 countries. Over a thousand of CGIAR's scientists are recruited internationally from over 50 countries. Typically these researchers have advanced degrees in biological sciences (including livestock and fishery science), agricultural research or economics. The centres also employ a large number of professionals with policy and development backgrounds. Each research centre recruits international staff through independent recruitment processes. Visit each of their Web sites for a list of vacancies, as well as information about numerous fellowship opportunities. Links to the recruitment Web site of each of the centres can be accessed by visiting the "Employment Opportunities" page of the CGIAR Web site. [ID:5599]

Economic and Social Commission for Western Asia (ESCWA)

P.O. Box 11-8575, Riad el-Solh Square, Beirut, Lebanon; (961) (1) 981-301,
fax (961) (1) 981-510, webmaster-escwa@un.org, www.escwa.org.lb

ECOSOC COMMISSION ◆ The Economic and Social Commission for Western Asia (ESCWA) assists in the economic and social development of that region and strives to strengthen economic relations among member countries and other parts of the world. Principal areas of work include development planning, agriculture, natural resources, human settlements, transportation, communications and tourism, social development and population, statistics, technical cooperation, and the environment. The majority of activities under the regular program of work are regional in dimension. There are, however, a limited number of activities that are country-specific but have regional implications.

While ESCWA's Web site provides little information regarding general qualifications for employment with the Commission, it does list professional and general vacancies, as well as details about ESCWA's internship program. (For ESCWA internship information, see Chapter 17, Internships Abroad). [ID:5683]

Economic Commission for Africa (ECA)

Personnel Section, P.O. Box 3001, Africa Hall, Addis Ababa, Ethiopia;
(251) (1) 51-72-00, fax (251) (1) 51-44-16, ecainfo@uneca.org, www.uneca.org ▢*Fr*

ECOSOC COMMISSION ◆ The Economic Commission for Africa (ECA), the regional arm of the UN in Africa, is mandated to support the economic and social development of its 53 member states, foster regional integration and promote international cooperation for Africa's development. To these ends, ECA engages in policy analysis and advocacy, technical assistance, communication and knowledge sharing, and support for sub-regional activity.

The ECA has headquarters in Addis Ababa, Ethiopia, and employs a staff of more than 200 professionals. ECA has five sub-regional offices (SROs) located in Niger, Morocco, Zambia, Rwanda and Cameroon. The SROs have a total staff of approximately 50 professionals. ECA commonly recruits individuals with backgrounds as economists, MBAs, social scientists, administrators, and a number of other specialties to work in areas such as research, policy formulation, information dissemination, advocacy, and administration.

Professional level vacancies are listed on the ECA's Web site; general services positions are open to internal candidates only. Past vacancies are archived on the job page, providing useful information and descriptions for interested job seekers. [ID:5684]

European Bank for Reconstruction and Development (EBRD)

One Exchange Square, London, EC2A 2JN, UK; (44) (20) 7338-6000,
fax (44) (20) 7338-6100, generalenquiries@ebrd.com, www.ebrd.com ▢*Fr*

REGIONAL DEVELOPMENT BANK ◆ The European Bank for Reconstruction and Development (EBRD) assists countries in Central and Eastern Europe, and the Commonwealth of Independent States (CIS) that are committed to democratic principles to make the transition to a market-based economy. The largest investor in the region, the EBRD provides project financing for banks, industries and businesses, both new ventures and investments in existing companies. It also works with publicly owned companies, to support privatization, restructure state-owned firms and improve municipal services.

The EBRD's 1,200 staff members work in a challenging and culturally diverse environment. 400 of the staff work in the 27 countries where EBRD is active. The EBDR offers a wide range of opportunities for contractors, jobseekers, debt investors, asset managers, co-financiers, consultants and NGOs. Recruiters look for outstanding educational qualifications and several years of relevant experience and are especially interested in individuals with financial backgrounds who have Russian language skills or experience working in Eastern Europe and Central Asia.

Job vacancies are posted on EBRD's Web site; the Bank has ongoing vacancies for bankers, legal counsel and people with financial management experience. It also has an excellent entry-level analyst program. [ID:5709]

European Space Agency (ESA)

8 - 10 rue Mario Nikis, 75738, Paris CEDEX 15, France;
(33) (1) 53-69-76-54, fax (33) 1-53-69-75-60, mailcom@esa.int, www.esa.int ▢*Fr*▢*Sp*

MULTILATERAL INSTITUTION ◆ The European Space Agency (ESA) was established exclusively to promote peaceful purposes and cooperation among European states in their pursuit of space research, technology and space applications. Its mission is to shape the development of Europe's space capability and ensure that investment in space continues to deliver benefits to the citizens of Europe. The ESA is composed of European states, although Canada does participate in some projects under cooperation agreements. Just under 2,000 people work for the ESA, which posts vacancies on its Web site. [ID:5574]

Food and Agriculture Organization (FAO)
Viale delle Terme di Caracalla, 00100 Rome, Italy; (39) (06) 57051,
fax (39) (06) 5705-3152, FAO-HQ@fao.org, www.fao.org ▣ Fr ▣ Sp

SPECIALIZED AGENCY ◆ The Food and Agriculture Organization's (FAO) mandate is to improve agricultural productivity, to raise levels of nutrition and standards of living, and to better the condition of rural populations. The FAO offers development assistance to developing countries on a range of technical assistance projects, provides information to stakeholders, advises governments and provides a neutral forum where all nations can meet to discuss and formulate policy on major food and agriculture issues.

The FAO has 1,500 professional staff and 2,200 general service staff working in its headquarters, regional offices and 78 country offices. The FAO posts its vacancies on its Web site and maintains a number of consultant databases for short-term opportunities. Consult its Web site for information about the FAO's Associate Professional Officer (APO) Program, which Canadians apply to through the Canadian International Development Agency (CIDA). [ID:5557]

Inter-American Development Bank (IADB)
1300 New York Ave. N.W., Washington, DC, 20577, USA;
202-623-1000, fax 202-623-3096, pic@iadb.org, www.iadb.org ▣ Fr ▣ Sp

REGIONAL DEVELOPMENT BANK ◆ The Inter-American Development Bank (IADB) Group is made up of the Inter-American Development Bank (IDB), the Inter-American Investment Corporation (IIC) and the Multilateral Investment Fund (MIF). The IADB supports economic and social development, and regional integration in Latin America and the Caribbean by lending to public institutions and funding private projects in infrastructure and capital markets development. The IIC finances small- and medium-scale private companies, and the MIF is an autonomous fund managed by the IADB that supports private sector development, mainly in the microenterprise sector. Collectively these institutions work to achieve poverty reduction, social equity and environmentally sustainable growth.

The IADB has about 1,500 staff in its Washington headquarters and another 550 working in country offices in Latin America, Europe and Japan. The staff includes professionals in economics, finance, social areas, infrastructure and the environment, as well as in policy and institutional management.

The IADB uses an e-recruitment system and posts vacancies on its Web site. It offers a number of excellent entry-level positions including a two-year Junior Professionals Program. It also offers both summer and winter employment programs for undergraduate students and an internship program for graduate students. If you are an Aboriginal person you are also eligible for the IADB's unique Diversity Internship Program for Indigenous Peoples. [ID:5559]

International Atomic Energy Agency (IAEA)
P.O. Box 100, Wagramer Strasse 5, A - 1400 Vienna, Austria;
(43) (1) 2600-0, fax (43) (1) 2600-7, Official.Mail@iaea.org, www.iaea.org

RELATED UN AGENCY ◆ The International Atomic Energy Agency (IAEA) is the world's centre of cooperation in the nuclear field. The IAEA works with its Member States and multiple partners worldwide to promote safe, secure and peaceful nuclear technologies.

The IAEA's 2,229 professional and support staff conducts research on atomic energy for peaceful purposes, facilitates the exchange of technical and scientific information, and establishes global safety standards. The IAEA hosts an internship and has a diversity of professional opportunities, but is of particular interest to scientists, engineers and those from related disciplines. Vacancies are posted on its Web site, which provides excellent information about working with the IAEA. (For IAEA internship information, see Chapter 17, Internships Abroad). [ID:5698]

International Bank for Reconstruction and Development (IBRD)

Personnel Office, 1818 H Street N.W., Washington, DC, 20433,
USA; 202-477-1234, fax 202-477-6391, www.worldbank.org 🖥 *Fr* 🖥 *Sp*

WORLD BANK GROUP ◆ The International Bank for Reconstruction and Development (IBRD)
(also known as the World Bank) lends funds to carry out projects or to finance economic and
institutional reform programs in less-developed member countries. The bank is also attempting to
increase the proportion of funding allocated to directly assist the poorest people in these countries.
IBRD is one of three member organizations comprising the World Bank Group. (For World Bank
internship information, see Chapter 17, Internships Abroad.) [ID:5677]

International Centre for Settlement of Investment Disputes (ICSID)

1818 H Street N.W., Washington, DC, 20433, USA;
202-458-1534, fax 202-522-2615, www.worldbank.org/icsid

WORLD BANK GROUP ◆ The International Centre for Settlement of Investment Disputes
(ICSID) is one of five organizations that constitute the World Bank Group. ICSID was designed to
facilitate the settlement of investment disputes between governments and foreign investors. ICSID
is the designated dispute settlement forum of choice in most bilateral investment treaties (BITs). In
addition to its dispute settlement activities, ICSID carries out advisory and research activities
relevant to its objectives and has a number of publications. The Centre also collaborates with other
World Bank Group units in meeting requests by governments for advice on investment and
arbitration law. Its Web site is an essential resource for anyone interested in BITs or doing research
on international investment laws. Vacancies are also posted on the World Bank's Web site. [ID:7346]

International Civil Aviation Organization (ICAO)

999 University Street, Montreal, QC, H3C 5H7, Canada;
514-954-8219, fax 514-954-6077, icaohq@icao.org, www.icao.int 🖥 *Fr* 🖥 *Sp*

MULTILATERAL INSTITUTION ◆ The International Civil Aviation Organization (ICAO)
develops the principles and techniques of international air navigation, and fosters the planning and
development of international air transport with a view to ensuring the safe and orderly growth of
international civil aviation throughout the world. The ICAO headquarters are in Montreal and it has
seven regional offices. Vacancies are posted on its Web site. [ID:5560]

International Computing Centre (ICC)

Palais des Nations, 1211 Geneva 10, Switzerland; (41) (0) 22-929-1444, callcentre@unicc.org, www.unicc.org

MULTILATERAL INSTITUTION ◆ The International Computing Centre (ICC) is an inter-
organizational facility that provides a variety of services to governmental entities,
intergovernmental and non-governmental organizations, as well as other not-for-profit institutions.
Its 200 staff provide services including Internet hosting, managed storage and IT consultancy. The
ICC offers an internship program for students specializing in information technology or other
relevant disciplines. Vacancies are advertised on its Web site. [ID:5575]

International Court of Justice (ICJ)

Peace Palace, 2517 KJ, The Hague, Netherlands; (31) (70) 302-2323,
fax (31) (70) 364-9928, information@icj-cij.org, www.icj-cij.org 🖥 *Fr*

INTERNATIONAL COURT OF JUSTICE ◆ The International Court of Justice (ICJ) is the
principal judicial organ of the United Nations. The court has a dual role: to settle in accordance
with international law the legal disputes submitted to it by states, and to provide advisory opinions
on legal questions referred to the ICJ by duly authorized international organs and agencies.

　　Both professional and general services vacancies with the ICJ are posted on the ICJ Web site.
Graduates from Yale, McGill, New York University, the University of Michigan and Strasbourg
University are all eligible for the ICJ's clerkship program. [ID:7351]

International Criminal Court (ICC)
Maanweg, 174, 2516 AB, The Hague, Netherlands;
(31) (70) 515-8515, fax (31) (70) 515-8555, pio@icc-cpi.int, www.icc-cpi.int ⬛*Fr*

MULTILATERAL INSTITUTION ◆ The International Criminal Court (ICC) is an independent international organization that was established by the Rome Statute of the International Criminal Court on July 17, 1998. The ICC is the first permanent treaty-based international criminal court established to promote the rule of law and ensure that the gravest international crimes do not go unpunished. Even though the Statute entered into force on July 1, 2002, it will take some time before the Court begins prosecuting cases.

The seat of the Court is The Hague. As a new organization, the ICC seeks creative, professional and highly-motivated individuals who are proficient in one of the working languages of the Court, which are English and French. The ICC seeks to fill posts by nationals of a State Party to the Statute of Rome, or of a state which has signed or acceded to the Statute and is engaged in the ratification process, but nationals from non-state parties may also be considered. Canadians are already well represented at the Court and there are still many opportunities for experienced professionals. The Court offers excellent clerkship and internship opportunities. It has an excellent Web site that contains detailed information about the various opportunities that the Court offers. Applications are maintained on an active roster for a period of one year. [ID:7344]

International Criminal Police Organization (OIPC - INTERPOL)
200, quai Charles de Gaulle, 69006 Lyon, France; (33) 7244-7000,
fax (33) 7244-7163, cp@interpol.int, www.interpol.int ⬛*Fr*⬛*Sp*

MULTILATERAL INSTITUTION ◆ The International Criminal Police Organization (INTERPOL) is the world's largest international police organization. Founded in 1923, it promotes global police cooperation by helping officers from different police forces, countries, languages and cultures to work together to solve crime. Crucial to this work is its state-of-the-art electronic police communications system, called I-24/7. The Interpol general secretariat in Lyon employs approximately 265 international civil servants who work alongside about 135 seconded police officers. Overall, at any one time, between 50 and 60 different nationalities are represented. Interpol has four official languages: English, French, Spanish and Arabic. Candidates should have relevant professional experience and knowledge of at least two, preferably three, of these languages, including an excellent command of either English or French. [ID:5608]

International Development Association (IDA)
Recruitment Division Personnel, 1818 H Street N.W., Washington, DC, 20433, USA;
202-473-1000, fax 202-477-6391, opportunities@worldbank.org, www.worldbank.org/ida

WORLD BANK GROUP ◆ The International Development Association (IDA), part of the World Bank Group, promotes economic development by providing finance to the world's poorest countries on much more concessionary terms than those of conventional loans. Responding to recent changes in the international development environment, IDA works closely with borrowers and other development partners to develop sustainable, country-based strategies that help developing countries participate in the global economy, and promote equity and inclusive growth for their poorest citizens. All IDA vacancies are posted on the World Bank Group Web site. [ID:5710]

International Energy Agency (IEA)
9, rue de la Fédération, 75739 Paris CEDEX 15, France;
(33) (1) 40-57-65-00, fax (33) (1) 40-57-65-59, info@iea.org, www.iea.org

MULTILATERAL INSTITUTION ◆ The International Energy Agency (IEA) is an autonomous agency associated with the Organization for Economic Co-operation and Development (OECD). The IEA brings its 26 member states together to ensure and increase energy security by promoting a diversification of energy suppliers and more efficient uses of energy resources. Nationals of OECD member states, including Canada, are eligible for IEA vacancies that are posted on its recruitment page. [ID:5609]

International Finance Corporation (IFC)

2121 Pennsylvania Ave., N.W., Washington, DC, 20433, USA;
202-473-1000, fax 202-477-6391, webmaster@ifc.org, www.ifc.org ☐ *Fr* ☐ *Sp*

WORLD BANK GROUP ◆ The International Finance Corporation (IFC) is the largest multilateral source of loan and equity financing for private sector projects in the developing world. It promotes sustainable private sector development by financing private sector projects and helping private companies find financing for projects in developing countries.

Slightly more than half of the IFC's 2004 staff work in Washington, with the others stationed in one of the IFC's 85 field offices in 67 countries. Recent graduates can apply for the two-year Investment Analyst Program. If you have an MBA or an equivalent graduate degree and experience in international corporate finance you are eligible to join the IFC's global transaction team (GTT), the starting point for entry-level investment officers (IO's). The IFC also offers an excellent summer internship program for graduate students in finance with an interest in international development. The IFC's careers Web page is excellent and provides an abundance of information about these and other opportunities. [ID:5561]

International Fund for Agricultural Development (IFAD)

Via del Serafico 107, 00142 Rome, Italy; (39) (6) 54591, fax (39) (6) 504-3463, ifad@ifad.org, www.ifad.org

UN SPECIALIZED AGENCY ◆ The International Fund for Agricultural Development (IFAD) is a specialized agency of the United Nations dedicated to eradicating poverty and hunger in developing countries. Through grants and low-interest loans the IFAD finances projects that enable rural poor people to overcome poverty themselves. Since it began operations in 1978, IFAD has invested $8.5 billion US in loans and grants in 653 rural development projects and programs in 115 countries and territories throughout the world.

IFAD employs 134 professionals and 182 general service staff from 45 nations. It also engages the services of consultants, conference personnel and other temporary staff. Vacancies are posted on IFAD's Web site, as is information about its Associate Professional Programme for young professionals and its internship program. (For IFAD internship information, see Chapter 17, Internships Abroad.) [ID:5703]

International Labour Organization (ILO)

4 route des Morillons, 1211 Geneva 22, Switzerland;
(41) (22) 799-6111, fax (41) (22) 798-8685, ilo@ilo.org, www.ilo.org ☐ *Fr* ☐ *Sp*

MULTILATERAL INSTITUTION ◆ The International Labour Organization (ILO) promotes opportunities for women and men to obtain decent and productive work in conditions of freedom, equity, security and human dignity by formulating international policies, creating international labour standards and designing programs that enhance international technical cooperation. The ILO has a unique tripartite structure, with workers and employers participating as equal partners with governments in the work of its governing organs.

The ILO employs 1,900 officials at its Geneva headquarters and in 40 field offices and multidisciplinary teams around the world, as well as 600 experts undertaking missions in all regions of the world. The International Training Centre in Turin, Italy, the ILO's training arm, employs 60 training and subject matter specialists.

An e-recruitment system is used to recruit professionals with several years of experience, an advanced university degree and knowledge of two of the ILO's three working languages. Canada does not participate in the ILO's Associate Expert Program, although Canadians are eligible for internships. Recruitment for short-term employment or consultancy opportunities is decentralized to the individual departments, which candidates should contact directly to find out about opportunities. Not surprisingly, ILO staff members enjoy excellent benefits. [ID:5562]

International Maritime Organization (IMO)

4 Albert Embankment, London, SE1 7SR, UK;
(44) (0) 20-7735-7611, fax (44) (20) 7587-3210, info@imo.org, www.imo.org

SPECIALIZED AGENCY ◆ The International Maritime Organization (IMO) is responsible for designing measures to improve the safety and security of international shipping and preventing marine pollution from ships. It is also involved in legal matters, including liability and compensation issues and the facilitation of international maritime traffic. The IMO has nearly 300 permanent staff members and posts information about vacancies and internship opportunities on its Web site. [ID:5563]

International Monetary Fund (IMF)

Recruitment Division, 700 - 19th Street N.W., Washington, DC, 20431, USA;
202-623-7300, fax 202-623-6278, publicaffairs@imf.org, www.imf.org ▢*Fr*▢*Sp*

SPECIALIZED AGENCY ◆ The International Monetary Fund (IMF) promotes international monetary cooperation, facilitates the expansion and balanced growth of international trade, promotes exchange rate stability and assists in the establishment of a multilateral system of payments and the elimination of foreign exchange restrictions. The IMF also provides temporary financial assistance to help countries improve balance of payment difficulties.

The IMF employs about 2,633 staff members from over 133 countries. The bulk of these are economists, although the IMF also employs an assortment of other professionals. The IMF offers excellent benefits, and competition for openings is fierce. Every year it receives about 20,000 applications and hires about 200 staff worldwide. The IMF uses an e-recruitment system and posts vacancies for experienced economists and other professionals on its Web site.

The IMF offers a number of excellent entry-level positions, but again these are highly competitive and applicants must have an exemplary academic record. Every summer it offers internships to about 35 to 40 graduate students to carry out a research project under the supervision of an experienced economist. The two-year Economist Program is the gate of entry into the IMF for recently graduated economists with at least a master's degree. The two-year Research Assistant Program provides recent BA graduates with an opportunity to gain useful work experience before pursuing further studies or moving on to other employment opportunities. The IMF's Web site is an excellent resource and provides detailed information about each of these programs. [ID:5564]

International Organization for Migration (IOM)

C.P. 71, 17 route des Morillons, CH - 1211 Geneva 19, Switzerland;
(41) (22) 717-9111, fax (41) (22) 798-6150, info@iom.int, www.iom.int ▢*Fr*▢*Sp*

MULTILATERAL INSTITUTION ◆ The International Organization for Migration (IOM) works with migrants and governments to provide humane responses to refugees, displaced persons and other persons in need of international migration assistance. The IOM encourages social and economic development through migration, advances understanding of migration issues and upholds the human dignity and well-being of migrants. The IOM has 19 regional field offices and a global network of over 150 country missions.

The IOM has 150 staff working in its head office. Vacancies are posted on its Web site and are either one-year fixed-term contracts or special short-term contracts. Applicants must be willing to work in the field, and have an advanced degree and three years of professional experience in their field of expertise. [ID:5612]

International Seabed Authority (ISA)

14-20 Port Royal Street, Kingston, Jamaica; (876) 922-9105,
fax (876) 922-0195, webmaster@isa.org.jm, www.isa.org.jm ▢*Fr*▢*Sp*

MULTILATERAL INSTITUTION ◆ The International Seabed Authority is an autonomous international organization established under the 1982 United Nations Convention on the Law of the Sea (UNCLOS) and the 1994 Agreement relating to the Implementation of Part XI of UNCLOS. The Authority is the organization through which all states party to the Convention organize and control activities within national jurisdictions, with particular focus on resource administration. The ISA Web site contains detailed information on the organs of the Authority and lists all vacancies as they arise. [ID:5602]

International Telecommunication Union (ITU)

Palais des Nations, CH - 1211 Geneva 20, Switzerland;
(41) (22) 730-5111, fax (41) (22) 733-7256, itumail@itu.int, www.itu.int 💻*Fr*💻*Sp*

MULTILATERAL INSTITUTION ♦ The International Telecommunication Union (ITU), the United Nations agency for telecommunications, promotes international cooperation among its government and private sector members. The activities of the three sectors of the ITU, Radiocommunication (ITU-R), Telecommunication Standardization (ITU-T) and Telecommunication Development (ITU-D), cover all aspects of telecommunication, from setting standards that facilitate seamless interworking of equipment and systems on a global basis to adopting operational procedures for the vast and growing array of wireless services and designing programs to improve telecommunication infrastructure in the developing world.

The ITU has 765 staff members from 82 countries working in its headquarters and 11 field offices throughout the world. The ITU recruits professionals with specializations in radio and satellite communications, switching, network, transmission, mobile communications, administrative restructuring and regulatory policy. [ID:5600]

International Trade Centre (ITC)

54-56 rue de Montbrillant, CH 1211, Geneva, Switzerland; (41) (22) 730-0111,
fax (41) (22) 730-0803, itcreg@intracen.org, www.intracen.org 💻*Fr*💻*Sp*

SPECIALIZED AGENCY ♦ The International Trade Centre (ITC) is the technical cooperation agency of the United Nations Conference on Trade and Development (UNCTAD) and the World Trade Organization (WTO) that works with developing countries to set up effective national trade promotion programs for expanding their exports and improving their import operations. In particular the ITC works very closely with these countries' private sectors.

ITC has its headquarters in Geneva where it employs a handful of Canadian professional and support staff, and offers an internship program. ITC maintains a consultant roster, occasionally bringing on consultants for short-term contracts.

All vacancies including consultancies and temporary secretarial posts are listed on the ITC's Web site on their "About ITC" page. (For ITC internship information, see Chapter 17, Internships Abroad.) [ID:7348]

International Tribunal for the Law of the Sea (ITLOS)

Am Internationalen Seegerichtshof 1, 22609 Hamburg, Germany;
(49) (40) 35607-0, fax (49) (40) 35607-245, itlos@itlos.org, www.itlos.org 💻*Fr*

MULTILATERAL INSTITUTION ♦ The International Tribunal for the Law of the Sea (ITLOS) is an independent judicial body established to adjudicate disputes arising out of the interpretation and application of the UN Convention on the Law of the Sea. The Tribunal is composed of 21 independent members, elected from among persons enjoying the highest reputation for fairness and integrity and of recognized competence in the field of the law of the sea. Pursuant to the provisions of its statute, the Tribunal has formed the following Chambers: the Chamber of Summary Procedure, the Chamber for Fisheries Disputes and the Chamber for Marine Environment Disputes.

Both professional- and general service-level vacancies are posted on the ITLOS Web site; applicants are required to complete a United Nations Personal History Form. ITLOS also hosts an internship program. (For ITLOS internship information, see Chapter 17, Internships Abroad.) [ID:7345]

Inter-Parliamentary Union (IPU)
C.P. 330, 5 chemin du Pommier, CH - 1218 Le Grand-Saconnex, Geneva, Switzerland;
(41) (22) 919-4150, fax (41) (22) 919-4160, postbox@mail.ipu.org, www.ipu.org 💻 *Fr*

MULTILATERAL INSTITUTION ◆ The Inter-Parliamentary Union (IPU) is the international organization of parliaments of sovereign states, established in 1889. Located in Geneva, Switzerland, the IPU is the focal point for worldwide parliamentary dialogue and works for peace and cooperation among peoples and for the firm establishment of representative democracy. The IPU works in close cooperation with the United Nations, regional inter-parliamentary organizations, and international intergovernmental and non-governmental organizations that are motivated by the same ideals.

The IPU posts all current vacancies on its Web site, along with detailed application instructions. The IPU maintains a consultant roster of suitably qualified and experienced experts who are generally parliamentarians and parliamentary staff (serving or retired). Successful candidates will have a university degree (or equivalent) in political science or social science/public administration/governance, at least five years of experience working in a parliamentary setting (as an MP or parliamentary staff), previous parliament-related consultancy work, and proficiency in the IPU's working languages: English, French, Spanish. [ID:5603]

Joint United Nations Programme on HIV/AIDS (UNAIDS)
20 Ave. Appia, CH - 1211, Geneva 27, Switzerland;
(41) (22) 791-3666, fax (41) (22) 791-4187, unaids@unaids.org, www.unaids.org

RELATED UN PROGRAM ◆ The Joint United Nations Programme on HIV/AIDS (UNAIDS) is the main body advocating for global action on HIV/AIDS. It leads and supports an international response aimed at preventing transmission of HIV, providing care and support for those infected and affected by the disease, reducing the vulnerability of individuals and communities to HIV/AIDS, and alleviating the socio-economic and human impact of the epidemic. UNAIDS monitors and evaluates global efforts, mobilizes resources and promotes civil society engagement.

UNAIDS Web site has a useful Human Resources section, with information for interested applicants, as well as postings for professional fixed-term posts (normally two years) and short-term openings (between six months and one year). Vacancies in the general services category are also advertised on the Web site, but are usually filled locally. All applications for employment to UNAIDS must be made via the World Health Organization's e-recruitment system. UNAIDS also runs an internship program. (For UNAIDS internship information, see Chapter 17, Internships Abroad.) [ID:5695]

Multilateral Investment Guarantee Agency (MIGA)
Suite 1200, 1800 G Street, N.W., Washington, DC, 20433,
USA; 202-473-6163, fax 202-522-2630, www.miga.org

WORLD BANK GROUP ◆ The Multilateral Investment Guarantee Agency (MIGA) facilitates foreign direct investment into emerging economies by offering political risk insurance to investors and lenders, and by helping developing countries attract and retain private investment. It promotes investment by offering investors guarantees against the risks of currency transfer, expropriation and other political risks. It also provides technical assistance to host governments to enhance their ability to attract foreign direct investment.

MIGA's staff works in the Guarantees, Investment Marketing Services, and Legal and Claims departments, as well as the Policy and Evaluation Unit. Vacancies are posted on its Web site where you can also access detailed information about the general requirements for employment in each of MIGA's operational departments. [ID:5604]

North Atlantic Treaty Organization (NATO)
Blvd. Leopold III, B - 1110 Brussels, Belgium; (32) (2) 728-4111,
fax (32) (2) 728-4579, natodoc@hq.nato.int, www.nato.int ⬛ *Fr* ⬛ *Sp*

REGIONAL SECURITY ORGANIZATION ◆ The North Atlantic Treaty Organisation (NATO) is a collective security organization comprising most of the world's large, developed and wealthy democracies. Its fundamental role is to safeguard the freedom and security of its member countries by political and military means. During the last 15 years, NATO has also played an increasingly important role in crisis management and peacekeeping.

There are 3,150 full-time staff at NATO Headquarters in Brussels, the political headquarters of the alliance and the permanent home of the North Atlantic Council. Of these, 1,400 are members of national delegations and national military representatives to NATO, while there are 1,300 civilian members of the international staff and 350 members of the international military staff.

The working languages of NATO are French and English, and only nationals of member countries can apply for openings. Vacancies are posted on NATO's Web site, as is information about several fellowships. NATO does not offer internships, although if you are a young graduate you can contact Canada's national delegation at the headquarters to set up an internship. [ID:5588]

Office of the United Nations High Commissioner for Human Rights (OHCHR)
8-14 ave. de la Paix, 1211 Geneva 10, Switzerland; (41) (22) 917-9000,
fax (41) (22) 917-9024, personnel@unhchr.ch, www.unhchr.ch ⬛ *Fr* ⬛ *Sp*

UN SPECIALIZED AGENCY ◆ The Office of the United Nations High Commissioner for Human Rights (OHCHR) has the principal responsibility for United Nations human rights activities. The OHCHR is committed to working with other parts of the United Nations to integrate human rights standards throughout the work of the organization. OHCHR engages in dialogue with governments on human rights issues with a view to enhancing national capacities in the field of human rights and towards improved respect for human rights; it provides advisory services and technical assistance when requested, and encourages governments to pursue the development of effective national institutions and procedures for the protection of human rights.

The OHCHR has its headquarters in Geneva, and has regional offices across Africa, the Middle East, the Asia Pacific region, Europe, Central Asia and the Caucasus, as well as in Latin America and the Caribbean.

OHCHR's Web site lists current vacancies and provides information regarding field operations, as well as internship and fellowship opportunities. (For OHCHR internship information, see Chapter 17, Internships Abroad.) [ID:5691]

Organisation for Economic Co-operation and Development (OECD)
2 rue Andre Pascal, F-75775 Paris CEDEX 16, France; (33) (1) 4524-8200,
fax (33) (1) 4524-8500, webmaster@oecd.org, www.oecd.org ⬛ *Fr*

MULTILATERAL INSTITUTION ◆ The Organisation for Economic Co-operation and Development (OECD) is a group of 30 like-minded industrialized countries committed to a market economy and pluralistic democracy. It collaborates with a large number of emerging and developing economies, as well as with business, labour and civil society.

There are 2,300 staff at the OECD secretariat in Paris, including 700 economists, lawyers, scientists and other professional staff that provide research and analysis to the OECD's 12 substantive directorates. The majority of job vacancies are for the positions of economist, policy analyst, senior economist, senior policy analyst, or principal administrator. Note that recruitment of young professionals is extremely limited.

Successful candidates generally have a strong background in economics, international exposure, three to seven years of relevant professional experience, an advanced university degree in a relevant field, and excellent knowledge of English or French with a working knowledge of the other language. Knowledge of other member country languages or of major non-member country languages is an advantage.

The OECD occasionally accepts graduate students as unpaid trainees whose area of study is directly related to the OECD's work program. You can find information about the highly competitive Young Professionals Program on the OECD's Web site. Competition for traineeships is very strong, especially during the summer months. [ID:5589]

Organisation for the Prohibition of Chemical Weapons (OPCW)

Johan de Wittlaan 32, 2517 JR ■ The Hague, Netherlands,
(31) (70) 416-3300, inquiries@opcw.org, www.opcw.org ▢*Fr*▢*Sp*

MULTILATERAL INSTITUTION ◆ The Organisation for the Prohibition of Chemical Weapons (OPCW) implements the provisions of the Chemical Weapons Convention in order to achieve a world both free of chemical weapons and in which cooperation in chemistry for peaceful purposes for all is fostered. The OPCW has a staff of about 500 with diverse backgrounds. It is particularly interested in professionals with backgrounds in chemistry, related sciences and engineering. Vacancies are posted on its Web site. [ID:5546]

Organisation internationale de la Francophonie (OIF)

Secrétariat général, 28, rue de Bourgogne, 75007, Paris, France;
(33) (0) 1-44-11-12-50, fax (33) (0) 1-44-11-12-76, oif@francophonie.org, www.francophonie.org

MULTILATERAL INSTITUTION ◆ L'Organisation internationale de la Francophonie (OIF) est une institution fondée sur le partage d'une langue et de valeurs communes. Elle compte à ce jour 51 États et gouvernements membres (dont le Québec et le Nouveau-Brunswick) et 5 États observateurs. L'OIF conduit des actions dans les domaines de la politique internationale et de la coopération multilatérale. Environ 600 personnes travaillent pour l'organisation de par le monde. Le siège est situé à Paris et l'OIF dispose de nombreuses représentations dans différentes métropoles : New York, Genève, Bruxelles, Addis-Abeda, Lomé, Libreville, Hanoi, Québec et Bordeaux.

Le recrutement du personnel de l'Agence intergouvernementale de la Francophonie, qui est l'opérateur principal de l'OIF, se fait par la voie d'avis de vacance de postes, consultables sur le site Internet de l'agence: www.agence.francophonie.org. Les offres d'emplois des autres opérateurs directs de l'OIF se retrouvent sur leurs sites Internet respectifs (voir la liste sur le site de l'OIF). [ID:7268]

Organization for Security and Co-operation in Europe (OSCE)

Kärntner Ring 5-7, 4th Floor, 1010, Vienna, Austria; (43) (1) 514-36-0,
fax (43) (1) 514-36-96, employment@osce.org, www.osce.org

REGIONAL SECURITY ORGANIZATION ◆ The Organization for Security and Co-operation in Europe (OSCE) is the largest regional security organization in the world with 55 participating states from Europe, Central Asia and North America. It is active in early warning, conflict prevention, crisis management and post-conflict rehabilitation. The OSCE deals with a wide range of security-related issues including arms control, preventive diplomacy, confidence- and security-building measures, human rights, democratization, election monitoring, and economic and environmental security.

The OSCE has 370 staff in its institutions and about 1,000 international and 2,000 locally-engaged staff working in its 18 missions and in field operations in Southeastern Europe, the Caucasus, Eastern Europe and Central Asia. The OSCE is a non-career organization that frequently rotates seconded and contracted staff. The international staffing of field operations is based on secondments that are usually for a period of six months, with a possibility of extension.

Vacancies for both seconded and contracted positions are posted on the OSCE's Web site. To apply for contracted positions you must complete an on-line application form and send it directly to the secretariat. Canadians that are interested in seconded positions must register with CANADEM, through which you also register to be considered for short- and long-term assignments as OSCE election monitors. The OSCE also maintains a resume database for various experts that are considered for inclusion in Rapid Expert Assistance and Co-operation Teams (REACT). [ID:5568]

Organization of American States (OAS)

17th Street & Constitution Ave. N.W., Washington, DC, 20006, USA;
202-458-3000, fax 202-458-3967, info@oas.org, www.oas.org ⌨ *Fr* ⌨ *Sp*

MULTILATERAL INSTITUTION ◆ The Organization of American States (OAS) is a regional organization comprising 35 member states that serves as the primary political forum for multilateral dialogue and actions in the Americas. Its programs throughout the region focus on strengthening democracy, advancing human rights, promoting peace and security, expanding trade and developing strategies to deal with the complex problems caused by poverty, drugs and corruption.

The OAS has 674 staff members at its Washington headquarters and in regional offices in member countries. Of these, only 17 are Canadian, so if you are fluent in Spanish you should definitely look at the OAS vacancies posted on its Web site. You can also find information on its Web site about the several hundred fellowships for graduate studies offered by the OAS. [ID:5590]

Pan American Health Organization (PAHO)

525 - 23rd Street N.W., Washington, DC, 20037, USA;
202-974-3000, fax 202-974-3663, webmaster@paho.org, www.paho.org ⌨ *Sp*

MULTILATERAL INSTITUTION ◆ The Pan American Health Organization (PAHO) is the World Health Organization's Regional Office for the Americas. Its mission is to improve the health and living standards of the region's people. Working out of the Washington headquarters, 27 country offices and nine scientific centres, PAHO scientists and technical experts work with the countries of Latin America and the Caribbean to strengthen national and local health systems.

The PAHO has almost 900 staff members and is always looking for healthcare professionals with Spanish language skills. Vacancies are posted on the PAHO Web site and must be applied for through an e-recruitment system. [ID:5571]

Preparatory Commission for the Comprehensive Nuclear-Test-Ban Treaty Organization

P.O. Box 1200, Vienna International Centre, A - 1400 Vienna, Austria;
(43) (1) 26030-6200, fax (43) (1) 26030-5823, info@ctbto.org, www.ctbto.org

RELATED UN PROGRAM ◆ The Preparatory Commission for the Comprehensive Nuclear-Test-Ban Treaty Organization (CTBTO Preparatory Commission) is an international organization established by the States Signatories to the Treaty on 19 November 1996. It carries out the necessary preparations for the effective implementation of the Treaty, and prepares for the first session of the Conference of the States Parties to the Treaty. The Commission's main task is the establishment of the 337 facility International Monitoring System and the International Data Centre, and the development of operational manuals, including on-site inspections.

Located in Vienna, Austria, the Commission recruits individuals with expertise in areas such as seismology, geophysics, computer science, accounting, finance, human resource management or law, and is a non-career employer. Professional-level staff are internationally recruited, while General Services Staff are locally recruited, with the exception of a few positions requiring highly specialized technical or scientific qualifications, for which the Commission recruits internationally. The Commission encourages qualified individuals to submit their resumes for ongoing consultancies, and has an ongoing internship program. (For CTBTO Preparatory Commission internship information, see Chapter 17, Internships Abroad.) [ID:5692]

United Nations Children's Fund (UNICEF)

Development Section, Division of Personnel (H-5F), UNICEF House, 3 United Nations Plaza, New York, NY, 10017, USA; 212-326-7000, fax 212-888-7465, netmaster@unicef.org, www.unicef.org ⌨ *Fr* ⌨ *Sp*

RELATED UN PROGRAM ◆ The United Nations Children's Fund (UNICEF) is mandated to advocate for the protection of children's rights, to help meet their basic needs and to help them reach their full potential. UNICEF works to ensure special protection for the most disadvantaged children: victims of war, disasters, extreme poverty, all forms of violence and exploitation, and those with disabilities.

With six headquarter offices in New York, Geneva, Denmark, Italy, Belgium and Japan, as well as seven regional offices and 126 country offices, UNICEF employs more than 7,000 people in 158 countries. UNICEF recruits specialists in areas such as child protection, public health, nutrition, education, HIV/AIDS, water and sanitation, administration, accounting, information systems, logistics, communication, fundraising, marketing and management. Successful applicants generally have a master's degree or equivalent experience, relevant professional work experience, including some in a developing country, and proficiency in English and one other UN working language.

UNICEF's Web site has a great job page, listing all vacancies, short-term opportunities, internships, as well as information about the Young Professional and Junior Professional programs. (For UNICEF internship information, see Chapter 17, Internships Abroad.) [ID:5688]

United Nations Commission on International Trade Law (UNCITRAL)
P.O. Box 500, Vienna International Centre, Wagramerstrasse 5, A - 1400 Vienna, Austria;
(43) (1) 26060-4061, fax (43) (1) 26060-5813, uncitral@uncitral.org, www.uncitral.org ⬜ *Fr* ⬜ *Sp*

GENERAL ASSEMBLY ◆ The United Nations Commission on International Trade Law (UNCITRAL) is the core legal body within the United Nations system in the field of international trade law, with the mandate to further the progressive harmonization and unification of international trade law. For employment as an entry level (P-3) legal officer, successful applicants will have an advanced university degree in law with particular emphasis on commercial, economic and comparative private law, as well as six years of professional experience in international trade law and a sound background in the experience of a particular legal system. An advanced degree (PhD or equivalent) may be substituted for two years of professional experience. The UNCITRAL secretariat also hosts an internship program for young lawyers.

UNCITRAL's Web site has no job page, but offers some employment-related information on the FAQs page. Vacancies are posted on the UN job page. (For UNCITRAL internship information, see Chapter 17, Internships Abroad.) [ID:7347]

United Nations Conference on Trade and Development (UNCTAD)
Palais des Nations, 8 - 14 ave. de la Paix, 1211 Geneva 10, Switzerland;
(41) (22) 917-1234, fax (41) (22) 917-0043, info@unctad.org, www.unctad.org ⬜ *Fr* ⬜ *Sp*

RELATED UN PROGRAM ◆ The United Nations Conference on Trade and Development (UNCTAD) has a few principal functions: it promotes international trade, particularly between countries at different levels of development, formulates and implements principles and policies on international trade and related problems of development, facilitates the coordination of activities of other institutions within the UN system in the field of trade, initiates actions for the negotiation and adoption of multilateral legal instruments in the field, and acts as a centre for the harmonization of trade and related development policies of governments and regional economic groups.

UNCTAD employs approximately 400 people. Vacancies in technical cooperation are listed on the UNCTAD Web site, while those for professional posts are available on the UN job page. UNCTAD's job page offers advice for job seekers at all levels interested in working with UNCTAD and other UN agencies. [ID:7350]

United Nations Department of Peacekeeping Forces (DPKO)
Field Administrator, Logistics Division, UN Headquarters, New York, NY,
10017, USA; 212-963-8079, fax 212-963-9222, www.un.org/Depts/dpko ⬜ *Fr* ⬜ *Sp*

SECURITY COUNCIL ◆ The United Nations Department of Peacekeeping Operations (DPKO) is dedicated to assisting the Member States and the Secretary-General in their efforts to maintain international peace and security. The Department plans, prepares, manages and directs UN peacekeeping operations, and works to integrate the efforts of the UN with those of governmental and non-governmental organizations.

Peacekeeping operations often consist of several components, including a military component, which may or may not be armed, and various civilian components encompassing a broad range of disciplines. At the time of publication, the DPKO was involved in 13 peacekeeping operations: Golan Heights, Lebanon, the Middle East, Cyprus, Georgia, Kosovo, East Timor, India/Pakistan, Côte d'Ivoire, Liberia, the Democratic Republic of Congo, Ethiopia and Eritrea, Sierra Leone and the Western Sahara. There are currently around 235 Canadians involved in these missions in various capacities.

Personnel are recruited according to needs that arise in each field mission; an extensive list of occupational groups for which personnel are often recruited is included on the DPKO Web site. The DPKO job page lists field vacancies, provides links to related UN job pages, and outlines the key soft skills necessary for success in DPKO field missions. [ID:5704]

United Nations Development Fund for Women (UNIFEM)
15th Floor, 304 East 45th Street, New York, NY, 10017, USA;
212-906-6400, fax 212-906-6705, unifem@undp.org, www.unifem.undp.org

UN PROGRAM AND FUND ◆ United Nations Development Fund for Women (UNIFEM) provides financial and technical assistance to innovative programs and strategies that promote women's human rights, political participation and economic security. Within the UN system, UNIFEM promotes gender equality and links women's issues and concerns to national, regional and global agendas by fostering collaboration and providing technical expertise on gender mainstreaming and women's empowerment strategies.

In addition to its headquarters in New York, UNIFEM has 13 field offices and works in over 100 countries. UNIFEM employs five sub-regional gender advisors, two gender and HIV/AIDS advisors, and has a growing network of affiliated gender advisors and specialists in Africa, the Arab States, the Asia Pacific, Central and Eastern Europe and the Commonwealth of Independent States, Latin America and the Caribbean. UNIFEM relies heavily on volunteers and hosts an internship program for outstanding graduate students. UNIFEM's Web site lists all vacancies, and offers some information on their internship program. (For more information on UNIFEM internships, see Chapter 17, Internships Abroad.) [ID:5690]

United Nations Development Programme (UNDP)
Division of Personnel, 1 United Nations Plaza, New York, NY, 10017, USA;
212-906-5558, fax 212-906-5364, hq@undp.org, www.undp.org ▢*Fr*▢*Sp*

RELATED UN PROGRAM ◆ The United Nations Development Programme (UNDP), the coordinating body for the UN's global development network, assists developing countries by accelerating their economic and social development and by providing systematic and sustained assistance geared to the development objectives of the concerned states. The UNDP's substantive focus is helping countries build and share solutions to the challenges of such issues as democratic governance, poverty reduction, crisis prevention and recovery, energy and environment, and HIV/AIDS. UNDP also engages in extensive advocacy work.

With over 7,000 staff working in 166 countries through 136 country offices in developing regions, the UNDP is headquartered in New York City, and has administrative and coordinating offices in Geneva, Brussels, Denmark, Tokyo and a liaison office in Washington, DC. UNDP employs approximately 90 Canadian professional and support staff. The UNDP job page lists all vacancies, and offers advice for expert practitioners and consultants. The UNDP also hosts an internship program. (For UNDP internship information, see Chapter 17, Internships Abroad.) [ID:5673]

United Nations Economic and Social
Commission for Asia and the Pacific (ESCAP)

Office 1508A, United Nations Bldg., Rajadamnern Ave., Bangkok, 10200, Thailand;
(66) (2) 288-1234-1, fax (66) (2) 282-1000, escap-registry@un.org, www.unescap.org

ECOSOC COMMISSION ◆ The Economic and Social Commission for Asia and the Pacific (ESCAP) is the regional arm of the United Nations Secretariat for the Asia Pacific region. ESCAP coordinates and supports the development of that region with a view to raising the standard of living and the level of economic activity. To this end, the Commission promotes regional and sub-regional cooperation and integration, acts as an executing agency for relevant operational projects, provides substantive and secretariat services and documentation, carries out studies, research and other activities within the terms of reference of the Commission, and provides advisory services to governments at their request.

ESCAP is located in Bangkok, Thailand, and employs a staff of over 200 professionals, 380 general service staff plus a number of consultants. All professional and general services vacancies are posted on the ESCAP Jobs page. The ESCAP Web site also offers a useful "Quick Links" section, with links to job pages for a number of other UN Agencies. ESCAP hosts an internship program for graduate students. (For ESCAP internship information, see Chapter 17, Internships Abroad.) [ID:5682]

United Nations Economic Commission for Europe (ECE)

Secretariat Recruitment Section, Palais des Nations, CH - 1211 Geneva 10, Switzerland;
(41) (22) 917-1234, fax (41) (22) 917-0505, info.ece@unece.org, www.unece.org

ECOSOC COMMISSION ◆ The United Nations Economic Commission for Europe (ECE) is one of five regional commissions of the United Nations. ECE works to generate and improve economic relations among its member states, as well as with other countries, and to strengthen intergovernmental cooperation and coordination, particularly in the areas of environment, transport, statistics, trade facilitation and economic analysis. The Commission's experts provide technical assistance to the countries of Southeast Europe and the Commonwealth of Independent States (CIS). This assistance takes the form of advisory services, training seminars and workshops where countries in transition can share their experiences and receive support from other countries in the region.

ECE job opportunities are listed on the UN Job page. Occasionally, the Commission will also post internship opportunities on its Web site. (For ECE internship information, see Chapter 17, Internships Abroad.) [ID:5696]

United Nations Economic Commission for
Latin America and the Caribbean (ECLAC)

Casilla de Correo 179-D, Vitacura, Santiago, Chile;
(56) (2) 210-2000, fax (56) (2) 208-0252, www.eclac.org 💻*Sp*

ECOSOC COMMISSION ◆ The UN Economic Commission for Latin America and the Caribbean (ECLAC) is one of five regional commissions of the United Nations. ECLAC promotes the economic and social development of member countries and seeks to maintain and expand economic relations among member countries and with other countries of the world. ECLAC also provides governments and other regional intergovernmental organizations with timely statistical information. Major themes include economic development, social development and humanitarian affairs, international trade, transnational corporations, food and agriculture, science and technology, population, human settlements, natural resources, energy, environment, transport and statistics.

ECLAC provides no specific job-related information on their Web site. Professional level employment opportunities with ECLAC are published on the UN job page. Information on local positions at ECLAC headquarters can be found on ECLAC's Web site under "About ECLAC." ECLAC has an internship program for graduate students from the Latin American and Caribbean region. (For ECLAC internship information, see Chapter 17, Internships Abroad.) [ID:5685]

United Nations Educational, Scientific and Cultural Organization (UNESCO)
Office of Public Information, 7 place de Fontenoy, 75352 Paris 07 - SP, France;
(33) (1) 4568-1000, fax (33) (1) 4567-1690, bpiweb@unesco.org, www.unesco.org 💻 *Fr* 💻 *Sp*

SPECIALIZED AGENCY ◆ The United Nations Educational, Scientific and Cultural Organization (UNESCO) works to contribute to peace and security by promoting collaboration among nations in the areas of education, science, and culture. Through their work, UNESCO aims to further universal respect for justice, the rule of law, and the fundamental human rights and freedoms affirmed by the global community.

UNESCO employs approximately 30 Canadian professional and support staff. Posts in UNESCO are mainly filled by people in occupations linked to the organization's main activities: culture, education, science and communication. There are also opportunities for employment in fields such as administration, finance, human resources and information technology. Junior program and administrative posts (generally for people under 30) require a university degree, two to three years of related professional experience, as well as functional French and English. Mid- and high-level posts require an MA and several years of relevant experience in responsible positions.

UNESCO's job page is comprehensive and informative. UNESCO's job page lists all vacant professional posts as well as specialized and general support staff vacancies. The site also provides information on applying for the Young Professionals Programme, the Associate Expert Programme, and the organization's internship program. (For UNESCO internship information, see Chapter 17, Internships Abroad.) [ID:5672]

United Nations Environment Programme (UNEP)
Recruitment Unit, P.O. Box 30552, United Nations Ave., Gigiri, Nairobi, Kenya;
(254) (2) 621-234, fax (254) (2) 624-489, unepinfo@unep.org, www.unep.org 💻 *Fr*

RELATED UN PROGRAM ◆ The United Nations Environment Programme (UNEP) is comprised of three entities: a Governing Council, a Secretariat, and a supplementary Environment Fund. UNEP's chief functions are to promote international cooperation in the environmental field, to recommend policies to this end, and to provide leadership and general guidance regarding the direction and coordination of environmental programs implemented by the UN system, member-states and individuals. The Environment Fund finances such programs as regional and global environmental monitoring, assessment and data-collecting systems; environmental research; informational exchange, and the dissemination of research information to develop forms of economic growth compatible with sound environmental management.

UNEP's Web site lists international employment and internship opportunities, provides links to general UN Job pages, and offers detailed directions regarding the application process. (For UNEP internship information, see Chapter 17, Internships Abroad.) [ID:5671]

United Nations Framework Climate Change Convention (UNFCCC)
P.O. Box 260124, D-53153 Bonn, Germany; (49) (228) 815-1000,
fax (49) (228) 815-1999, secretariat@unfccc.int, http://unfccc.int 💻 *Fr* 💻 *Sp*

RELATED UN PROGRAM ◆ The United Nations Framework Climate Change Convention (UNFCCC) secretariat supports cooperative action by states to combat climate change and its impacts on humanity and ecosystems. Guided by the parties to the Convention, the UNFCC secretariat provides organizational support and technical expertise to negotiations and institutions while facilitating the flow of authoritative information on the implementation of the Convention.

Located in Bonn, the working language of the UNFCC is English; therefore fluency in both written and spoken English is essential for employment with the organization. All current vacancies are listed on the UNFCCC job page under the "Secretariat" tab of their Web site, as is information regarding UNFCCC's internship program. (For UNFCCC internship information, see Chapter 17, Internships Abroad.) [ID:7349]

United Nations High Commissioner for Refugees (UNHCR)

Career Development and Recruitment Section, C.P. 2500, CH - 1211, Geneva, 2, Depot,
Switzerland; (41) (22) 739-8111, fax (41) (22) 731-9546, webmaster@unhcr.ch, www.unhcr.ch

RELATED UN PROGRAM ◆ The mandate of the United Nations High Commissioner for
Refugees (UNHCR) is to provide international protection and material assistance to refugees, and
to search for permanent solutions to their ongoing plight. In seeking such solutions, UNHCR
attempts to help those refugees wishing to go home in reintegrating into their home communities.
When this is deemed unfeasible, UNHCR works to help refugees in countries of asylum or, failing
that, to resettle them in other countries.

UNHCR now has over 5,000 staff working in more than 120 countries. Employment-related
information, including current vacancies and information about their Junior Professional Officer
Programme is available on the UNHCR Web site in the "Administration" section. In addition, the
UNHCR solicits resumes several times a year that match certain professional profiles to store in an
"International Professional Roster." Even when not actively accepting resumes, UNHCR provides
"standard post profiles" to inform interested candidates of positions for which they may begin
recruiting. [ID:5669]

United Nations Human Settlements Programme (UN-HABITAT)

P.O. Box 30030, UN Office at Nairobi, Nairobi, Kenya; (254) (20) 623-120,
fax (254) (20) 623-477, infohabitat@unhabitat.org, www.unhabitat.org

ECOSOC COMMISSION ◆ The United Nations Human Settlements Programme (UN-HABITAT)
is mandated to promote socially and environmentally sustainable towns and cities with the goal of
providing adequate shelter for all. The agency focuses on a range of issues and special projects it
helps to implement, including a joint UN-HABITAT/World Bank slum upgrading initiative called
the Cities Alliance, and a number of major projects in post-war societies such as Afghanistan,
Kosovo, Somalia, Iraq, Rwanda and the Democratic Republic of Congo.

With its headquarters in Nairobi, Kenya, UN-HABITAT has over 200 international and local
staff working on 154 technical programmes and projects in 61 countries around the world. The
agency has regional offices in Fukuoka, Japan, Rio de Janeiro, Brazil, and Nairobi.

UN-HABITAT's Web site lists current vacancies and provides information regarding
applying for their internship program. (For UN-HABITAT internship information, see Chapter 17,
Internships Abroad.) [ID:5679]

United Nations Industrial Development Organization (UNIDO)

P.O. Box 300, Vienna International Centre, A - 1400 Vienna, Austria;
(43) (1) 260-260, fax (43) (1) 26926-9, unido@unido.org, www.unido.org ▣Fr

SPECIALIZED AGENCY ◆ The United Nations Industrial Development Organization (UNIDO) is
dedicated to promoting sustainable industrial development in countries with developing and
transitional economies. UNIDO mobilizes knowledge, skills, information and technology to
promote productive employment, a competitive economy and a sound environment.

UNIDO's activities are concentrated in strengthening industrial capacities, and in cleaner and
sustainable industrial development. The organization's activities are focused geographically on
least-developed countries, in particular in Africa; sectorally on agro-based industries; and
thematically on small- and medium-sized enterprises (SMEs).

Current vacancies are posted in the "About UNIDO" section of their Web site. The Web site
also provides information regarding jobs at various levels including field project experts and
consultants, associate experts and junior professional officers, general services and internships. (For
UNIDO internship information, see Chapter 17, Internships Abroad.) [ID:5678]

United Nations Institute for Disarmament Research (UNIDIR)
Palais des Nations, CH - 1211 Geneva 10, Switzerland; (41) (22) 917-3186,
fax (41) (22) 917-0176, unidir@unog.ch, www.unidir.org 🖳 *Fr*

OTHER UN BODY ◆ The United Nations Institute for Disarmament Research (UNIDIR), an intergovernmental organization within the United Nations, undertakes independent research on disarmament and security-related issues. The organization provides the international community with data on problems relating to disarmament, development, and all forms of security (regional, national, global), with a view to facilitating progress through negotiations toward greater security as well as economic and social development for all peoples.

At UNIDIR researchers are recruited to work at the Institute on a specific project or outside experts are commissioned to undertake the work. UNIDIR accepts visiting fellows supported by their national governments, philanthropic foundations or sponsored through the institute's fellowship program. Employment and fellowship opportunities are listed on UNIDIR's Web site. UNIDIR also offers a limited number of unpaid internships. (For UNIDIR internship information, see Chapter 17, Internships Abroad.) [ID:5668]

United Nations Institute for Training and Research (UNITAR)
Palais des Nations, 8 - 14 ave. de la Paix, CH - 1211 Geneva 10, Switzerland;
(41) (22) 917-1234, fax (41) (22) 917-8047, info@unitar.org, www.unitar.org 🖳 *Fr*

OTHER UN BODY ◆ The United Nations Institute for Training and Research (UNITAR) is an autonomous body within the UN that provides training to assist countries in social and economic development and international cooperation; performs related applied research; and partners with other UN agencies, governments and non-governmental organizations to develop and implement training and capacity-building programs to meet the needs of member states.

To this end, UNITAR prepares distance learning training packages, workbooks, as well as software and video training packs, and undertakes research to facilitate improvement and innovation in training methods. Currently, UNITAR organizes some 120 different programs, fellowships, seminars and workshops every year, benefiting in excess of 5,500 participants over five continents. UNITAR's Web site offers no job-related information. Job openings for UNITAR are listed on the UN Job page. [ID:5707]

United Nations International Research and Training
Institute for the Advancement of Women (INSTRAW)
César Nicolás Penson 102-A, Santo Domingo, Dominican Republic;
(809) 685-2111, fax (809) 685-2117, comments@un-instraw.org, www.un-instraw.org 🖳 *Fr* 🖳 *Sp*

OTHER UN BODY ◆ The United Nations International Research and Training Institute for the Advancement of Women's (INSTRAW) objective is to stimulate and assist, through research, training, and the collection and dissemination of information, the advancement of women and their integration in the development process, both as participants and beneficiaries.

INSTRAW employs a small team of professional, technical and support staff (generally less than 50), and maintains a roster of consultants. Consultants often work in INSTRAW's head office, while some work on a short-term basis on specific research and training projects. Other opportunities with INSTRAW exist through INSTRAW's internship program, as well as through the UN's Volunteer Programme and Associate Expert Programme.

All professional level vacancies are listed on INSTRAW's Web site. General services posts are not listed, but are filled locally. (For INSTRAW internship information, see Chapter 17, Internships Abroad.) [ID:5694]

United Nations Interregional Crime and Justice Research Institute (UNICRI)
Viale Maestri del Lavoro, 10, 10127 Turin, Italy;
(39) (11) 653-7111, fax (39) (11) 631-3368, unicri@unicrit.it, www.unicri.it

OTHER UN BODY ◆ United Nations Interregional Crime and Justice Research Institute's (UNICRI) objective is to contribute, through research, training, field activities and the collection, exchange and dissemination of information, to the formulation of improved policies in the field of crime prevention and control. Due regard is paid to the integration of such policies within broader policies for socio-economic change and development, and the protection of human rights.

UNICRI's small staff of 22 are recruited through the UN Secretariat. The UNICRI Web site provides information about the Institute's internship program. (For UNICRI internship information, see Chapter 17, Internships Abroad.) [ID:5687]

United Nations Office for Project Services (UNOPS)
Information Section, 4th Floor, 405 Lexington Ave., New York, NY, 10174, USA;
212-457-4000, fax 212-457-4001, unops.newyork@unops.org, www.unops.org

RELATED UN PROGRAM ◆ The United Nations Office for Project Services (UNOPS) provides specialized services to ensure the successful implementation of projects undertaken by United Nations Member States. UNOPS services include program and project management, loan administration and project supervision, procurement of goods and services, recruiting and advisory services.

Professional and general service vacancies are posted on UNOPS Web site. UNOPS maintains a consultant registry of recognized specialists or authorities in specific fields who are interested in working with UNOPS. Generally, consultants have at least one university degree and considerable professional experience in their area of expertise. However, significant professional experience (including military experience) may compensate for a lack of formal education. UNOPS does offer internships, but instructs interested applicants to contact the organization directly for more information. [ID:5700]

United Nations Office on Drugs and Crime (UNODC)
P.O. Box 500, Vienna International Centre, A - 1400 Vienna, Austria;
(43) (1) 26060-0, fax (43) (1) 26060-5866, unodc@unodc.org, www.unodc.org

RELATED UN PROGRAM ◆ The United Nations Office on Drugs and Crime (UNODC) is mandated to assist UN Member States in their struggle against illicit drugs, crime and terrorism. To this end, the UNODC performs three key functions: it provides research and analytical work to increase knowledge and understanding of drug and crime issues and expand the evidence-base for policy and operational decisions; it performs normative work to assist states in the ratification and implementation of the international treaties, and the development of domestic legislation on drugs, crime and terrorism; and it coordinates field–based technical cooperation projects to enhance the capacity of member states.

UNODC employs over 500 people at its Vienna headquarters, New York liaison office and 21 field offices around the world. Professional level job postings with UNODC are available on the UN Job page, while project-level vacancies are posted on UNODC's Web site. [ID:5708]

United Nations Population Fund (UNFPA)
Personnel Office, 17th Floor, 220 East 42nd Street, New York, NY, 10017,
USA; 212-297-5000, fax 212-297-4908, hq@unfpa.org, www.unfpa.org ▭*Fr*▭*Sp*

RELATED UN PROGRAM ◆ The United Nations Population Fund (UNFPA), is the world's largest international source of funding for population and reproductive health programs. UNFPA works with governments and NGOs in over 140 countries at their request to improve reproductive health care and to promote sustainable development. UNFPA supports programs that help people plan their families and avoid unwanted pregnancies, undergo pregnancy and childbirth safely, avoid sexually transmitted diseases (STDs), and combat violence against women. The fund also provides data on population and its effects on human rights, quality of life, economic development, and the environment.

All UNFPA vacancies and application directions are posted on the organization's Web site. For professional postings, UNFPA seeks candidates with an advanced degree in a study pertinent to the Fund's program (e.g. demography, public health, population studies, etc.) and experience in a developing country, preferably with a development organization similar to UNFPA. Fluency in English is required; speaking and reading ability in one other United Nations language, preferably French or Spanish, is desirable. UNFPA also participates in the UN Junior Professional Programme, and has an internship program. (For UNFPA internship information, see Chapter 17, Internships Abroad.) [ID:5702]

United Nations Relief and Works Agency for Palestine Refugees in the Near East (UNRWA)

P.O. Box 140157, HQ Gaza, Amman 11814, Jordan; (972) (8) 677-7333,
fax (972) (8) 677-7555, unrwapio@unrwa.org, www.unrwa.org ▱*Sp*

OTHER UN BODY ◆ The UN Relief and Works Agency for Palestine Refugees in the Near East (UNRWA) carries out relief and works programs for Palestinian refugees in collaboration with local governments. UNRWA's three principal areas of activity are education, health services, and relief and social services. UNRWA provides essential services to eligible Palestinian refugees residing in its five fields of operations: Jordan, Lebanon, the Syrian Arab Republic, the West Bank and Gaza Strip.

The Agency's Headquarters is divided between Gaza and Amman and houses 453 staff. The Agency also has a field office in each of its fields of operation, and employs a total of over 24,300 staff, the majority of whom are Palestine refugees. The largest single group of staff employed with UNRWA are teachers, followed by health services, relief and social services staff, and administrative and support staff. There are normally only about six international staff in a field office.

Vacancies are posted on the UNRWA Web site and are usually advertised in the international press. Priority consideration is given to applications from registered Palestine refugees, though the United Nations New York funds 109 international posts. For professional-level posts, successful applicants will frequently have an advanced degree and several years of relevant work experience. Senior posts require solid managerial experience in an organization. At the time of publishing, UNRWA was not hosting interns due to security issues in the area. [ID:5680]

United Nations Research Institute for Social Development (UNRISD)

Palais des Nations, 1211 Geneva 10, Switzerland; (41) (22) 917-3020,
fax (41) (22) 917-0650, info@unrisd.org, www.unrisd.org ▱*Fr*▱*Sp*

RELATED UN PROGRAM ◆ The United Nations Research Institute for Social Development (UNRISD) is an autonomous UN agency that undertakes multidisciplinary research on the social dimensions of contemporary problems affecting development. UNRISD research is guided by two core values: that every human being has a right to a decent livelihood and that all people should be allowed to participate on equal terms in decisions that affect their lives. UNRISD is the only United Nations organization that engages exclusively in research on social development.

UNRISD looks for candidates with a post-graduate university degree, work experience with an intergovernmental or non-governmental organization in the development field, cultural literacy, and research interests in social development and social justice, poverty eradication, democratization, human rights, gender equity and environmental sustainability. Successful candidates will also have an excellent working knowledge of English, French or Spanish.

UNRISD's Web site posts vacancies for the Institute under the "Help and FAQs" pages of the site, but offers no other professional employment-related information. In lieu of an internship program, UNRISD has a Graduate Student Programme. (For UNRISD internship information, see Chapter 17, Internships Abroad.) [ID:5681]

United Nations System Staff College (UNSSC)
Viale Maestri del Lavoro, 10, 10127 Turin, Italy; (39) (11) 653-5911, fax (39) (11) 653-5902, www.unscc.org

UN SPECIALIZED AGENCY ◆ The United Nations System Staff College (UNSSC) is the United Nations institution for system-wide knowledge management, learning and training, and plays a pivotal role in organization change and reform, and in the development of a common culture within the system. The Staff College is intended to be the UN system's pre-eminent learning arm. It is charged with building capacity to enable the organizations of the United Nations system to fulfill their mandates, particularly system-wide mandates, more effectively.

The UNSSC hosts an internship program and recruits for positions requiring a broad range of skills. The College's Web site has a great Job page that lists all current professional and general services vacancies, as well as vacancies in the Associate Collaborator category, which are appointed for a fixed period on the basis of expertise and experience to become either resident scholars, associates or senior associates, as appropriate. (For UNSSC internship information see Chapter 17, Internships Abroad.) [ID:5697]

United Nations University (UNU)
53-70, Jingumae 5-chome, Shibuya-ku, Tokyo 150, Japan;
(81) (3) 3499-2811, fax (81) (3) 3499-2828, mbox@hq.unu.edu, www.unu.edu ▣ Fr ▣ Sp

OTHER UN BODY ◆ The United Nations University (UNU) is a system of decentralized academic institutions integrated into the world university community. UNU is devoted to action-oriented research on the global problems of human survival, development, and welfare, and to post-graduate training of young scholars and research workers. Current program activities are focused on four areas: peace and governance, development, environment, and science and technology.

Most professional UNU staff are internationally recruited; advertisements are posted on the UNU Web site as well as in specialized, international journals focused on the targeted academic discipline. Professional staff are often recruited from universities, research institutions and international organizations, or on secondment for fixed terms. A wide variety of nationalities and cultures are represented. All general service staff are locally recruited and recruitment advertisements placed in the local press. (For UNU internship information, see Chapter 17, Internships Abroad.) [ID:5667]

Universal Postal Union (UPU)
International Bureau, P.O. Box 13, 3000 Berne 15, Switzerland;
(41) (31) 350-3111, fax (41) (31) 350-3110, info@upu.int, www.upu.int ▣ Fr

SPECIALIZED AGENCY ◆ The Universal Postal Union (UPU) sets the rules for international mail exchanges and provides technical assistance, training and consultant services aimed at improving the quality of international postal services and helping implement new systems in developing countries. Virtually all professional staff working at the UPU's International Bureau are recruited from the postal administrations of member countries.

Vacancies for positions in general services are commonly advertised and filled from within Switzerland. The UPU occasionally requires specific technical or specialist expertise for projects, or expands its search for qualified candidates. Recruitment takes place through UPU's Web site as well as through vacancy announcements in the international or national press. [ID:5705]

World Bank Group
www.worldbank.org

WORLD BANK GROUP ◆ The World Bank Group is a specialized agency of the UN that is composed of five closely associated institutions that specialize in different aspects of development but use their comparative advantages to work collaboratively toward reducing global poverty. The term World Bank refers specifically to two of the institutions: the International Bank for Reconstruction and Development (IBRD) and the International Development Association (IDA). For information about the World Bank see the profile description above. The World Bank Group's other three institutions are the International Finance Corporation (IFC), the Multilateral Investment Guarantee Agency (MIGA) and the International Centre for Settlement of Investment Disputes (ICSID). (For more information, see the IFC and MIGA profiles in this chapter and the ICSID profile in Chapter 31, International Law Careers.) [ID:5545]

The World Bank
1818 H Street N.W., Washington, DC, 20433, USA; 202-473-1000,
fax 202-477-6391, opportunities@worldbank.org, www.worldbank.org ☐ *Fr* ☐ *Sp*

WORLD BANK GROUP ◆ The International Bank for Reconstruction and Development (IBRD) aims to reduce poverty in middle-income and credit-worthy poorer countries by promoting sustainable development through loans, guarantees and advisory services. The International Development Association (IDA) helps the world's poorest countries reduce poverty by providing credits, which are loans at zero interest with a 10-year grace period and maturities of 35 to 40 years. Together, the IBRD and the IDA form the World Bank.

The World Bank employs 10,000 development professionals from 160 countries. About 7,000 work in the Bank's Washington office, with 3,000 working in 109 country offices. The Bank's staff works with governments in developing countries around the world, assists people in all areas of development, from policy and strategic advice to the identification, preparation, appraisal and supervision of development projects. Development professionals come from a variety of backgrounds, and the Bank has a Web feature that provides sample skills requirements for various professionals including economists, environmental specialists and education specialists.

The World Bank's Web site is superb and contains a wealth of information about careers with the Bank. The site also contains information about Bank sponsored scholarships and fellowships, and a Staff Profiles page that explains the career paths of some of the Bank's professional staff. (For World Bank internship information see Chapter 17, Internships Abroad.) [ID:5706]

World Food Programme (WFP)
Via C.G.Viola 68, Parco dei Medici, Roma 00148, Italy;
(39) (06) 65131, fax (39) (06) 6513 2840, wfpinfo@wfp.org, www.wfp.org

MULTILATERAL INSTITUTION ◆ The World Food Programme (WFP) is the United Nations frontline agency mandated to combat global hunger, which afflicts one out of every seven people on earth. The WFP fights hunger in least-developed and low-income countries where victims of natural disasters, refugees, internally-displaced persons and the hungry poor face severe food shortages. The front line in the fight against global hunger stretches from sub-Saharan Africa and the Middle East to Latin America and the Asia Pacific.

The WFP has 621 staff working in its Rome headquarters and another 2,063 staff working in the field. When a vacancy occurs, WFP managers look for suitable candidates on its e-recruitment system's database. If you are interested in working for the WFP make sure you complete an on-line personal profile. WFP managers also use the database to select interns. If you are interested in joining the WFP as a Junior Professional Officer you should contact the Canadian International Development Agency (CIDA). The WFP recruits committed university graduates with a knowledge of two of its official working languages. [ID:5592]

World Health Organization (WHO)
Avenue Appia 20, 1211 Geneva 27, Switzerland;
(41) (22) 791-2111, fax (41) (22) 791-31116, inf@who.int, www.who.int ☐ *Fr* ☐ *Sp*

SPECIALIZED AGENCY ◆ The World Health Organization (WHO) is the United Nations' specialized agency for health. It works toward the attainment of the highest possible level of health for all of the world's people. Health is defined in the WHO's Constitution as a state of complete physical, mental and social well-being and not merely the absence of disease or infirmity. The WHO has 3,700 staff working at its headquarters, six regional offices and in the field. It generally seeks applications from health-related professionals, such as medical officers, epidemiologists, health economists and other public health specialists who have a post-graduate degree and experience working in public health or international development.

The WHO uses an e-recruitment system and has an excellent Web site where its many vacancies are posted. The WHO also has an Associate Professional Officers program, but Canadians are not eligible as Canada does not participate in the program. [ID:5595]

World Meteorological Organization (WMO)
7 bis ave. de la Paix, C.P. 2300, 1211 Geneva 2, Switzerland;
(41) (22) 730-8111, fax (41) (22) 730-8181, ipa@wmo.int, www.wmo.ch ☐ *Fr* ☐ *Sp*

MULTILATERAL INSTITUTION ◆ The World Meteorological Organization (WMO) is the international community's authoritative scientific voice on the state and behaviour of the Earth's atmosphere and climate. The WMO coordinates global scientific activity to allow increasingly prompt and accurate weather information and other services for public, private and commercial use, including international airline and shipping industries. The WMO employs 246 full-time staff and posts vacancies on its human resources management division Web page. It also has information about the hundreds of fellowships offered by the WMO in the fields of meteorology and operational hydrology and related sciences. [ID:5596]

World Tourism Organization (WTO)
Capitán Haya 42, E-28020 Madrid, Spain; (34) (1) 567-8100,
fax (34) (1) 571-3733, omt@world-tourism.org, www.world-tourism.org ☐ *Fr* ☐ *Sp*

SPECIALIZED AGENCY ◆ The World Tourism Organization (WTO) acts as an umbrella organization for world tourism. It promotes and develops tourism with a view to contributing to economic development, international understanding, peace, prosperity and universal respect for, and observance of, fundamental human rights and freedoms for all peoples. The WTO has about 90 full-time staff working in its Madrid headquarters. If you are interested in being considered for vacancies you must complete a personal history form and return it to the personnel section. [ID:5491]

World Trade Organization (WTO)
154 rue de Lausanne, Centre William Rappard, 1211 Geneva 21, Switzerland;
(41) (22) 739-5111, fax (41) (22) 731-4206, enquiries@wto.org, www.wto.org ☐ *Fr* ☐ *Sp*

SPECIALIZED AGENCY ◆ The World Trade Organization (WTO) secretariat administers multilateral trade agreements that reduce barriers to trade, expand international trade and promote economic development. Trade in goods, services, intellectual property and investment, trade and environment questions, and trade in agricultural goods are some of the issues the WTO secretariat deals with. It also administers a dispute settlement mechanism for trade conflicts.

The 550 staff carry out a variety of duties including the preparation of reports, economic and legal research, and work with the delegations of member states. The WTO recruits applicants with graduate degrees in economics, international relations or trade law who have at least five years of relevant experience. WTO is particularly interested in individuals with strong drafting and language skills. It offers a small internship program for post-graduate university students wishing to gain practical experience and a deeper knowledge of the multilateral trading system. [ID:5558]

INDEXES

Resources
by Subject

THE BIG GUIDE publishes 830 resources under the 62 subject areas listed below. Some of these subject areas are repeated for ease of reference.

Resources
by Title

There are 830 resources indexed below. Many have multiple page references because they fall in more than one resource subject area. A resource is either a Web site 🖳, book 📖, or organization ⛨ providing international job hunting services.

Cities in Canada & the US with International Contacts

There are two indexes in this section: an index to Canadian cities appearing in print, and an index to US cities appearing on the CD-ROM. Both offer a quick way to find out about international activities in your part of North America.

Cities in Canada

This is a list of 120 Canadian cities appearing in the print edition and sorted alphabetically by city. The province or territory is listed after each city.

Montreal, QC: 157, 158, 160, 164, 173, 176, 178, 182, 183, 194, 221, 232, 233, 238, 240, 248, 618, 649, 680, 701, 705, 709, 710, 712, 713, 717, 719, 721, 730, 735, 738, 740, 741, 744, 748, 753, 754, 756, 759, 760, 764, 765, 766, 777, 778, 782, 783, 786, 847, 852, 854, 866, 867, 869, 871, 873, 881, 893, 897, 903, 907, 911, 913, 916, 918, 924, 936, 939, 940, 984

Mont-Sainte-Hilaire, QC: 712

Nepean, ON: 917

New Hamburg, ON: 940

New Westminster, BC: 173, 880, 908

North Vancouver, BC: 702, 705, 737, 763, 767, 819

North York, ON: 747, 874

Oakville, ON: 697, 708

Okotoks, AB: 865

Oshawa, ON: 863

Ottawa, ON: 157, 158, 160, 161, 162, 163, 164, 165, 166, 167, 168, 169, 170, 171, 174, 179, 188, 193, 195, 229, 230, 231, 232, 233, 234, 235, 236, 237, 238, 239, 240, 241, 243, 244, 245, 246, 248, 249, 251, 252, 618, 621, 622, 625, 629, 630, 631, 681, 697, 700, 702, 716, 722, 724, 725, 726, 729, 732, 733, 734, 746, 750, 755, 756, 766, 768, 769, 771, 776, 780, 787, 832, 834, 835, 836, 837, 838, 839, 840, 841, 842, 843, 844, 845, 846, 847, 849, 850, 852, 853, 854, 862, 863, 866, 868, 869, 870, 872, 873, 875, 876, 878, 880, 881, 882, 883, 884, 885, 886, 887, 888, 891, 895, 896, 897, 902, 903, 905, 906, 907, 908, 910, 911, 920, 921, 923, 924, 925, 926, 927, 930, 932, 935, 937, 938, 941, 943, 944, 978

Peterborough, ON: 914

Pointe-Claire, QC: 166

Quebec City, QC: 734

Quebec, QC: 159, 181, 850, 889, 894, 909, 914, 937

Regina, SK: 181, 774, 853, 933

Richmond Hill, ON: 727, 776

Richmond, BC: 723, 755, 759, 784

Russell, MB: 180

Saint-Charles-sur-Richelieu, QC: 743

Sainte-Foy, QC: 772, 866

Saint-Hubert, QC: 839

Saint-Laurent, QC: 698

Saskatoon, SK: 714, 751, 928

Scarborough, ON: 722, 864, 912, 934

Sherbrooke, QC: 164, 888

Sidney, BC: 764

Smithers, BC: 922

Smiths Falls, ON: 770

St. Bruno, QC: 728

St. John's, NL: 180, 717, 718, 720, 739, 775, 848, 917

St. Laurent, QC: 715

Ste-Anne-de-Bellevue, QC: 870

Stouffville, ON: 891, 900

Surrey, BC: 696, 864

Sydney, NS: 284, 287

Thornhill, ON: 757

Toronto, ON: 161, 168, 172, 174, 183, 184, 189, 190, 194, 222, 246, 247, 250, 619, 620, 624, 629, 677, 679, 681, 682, 696, 698, 699, 703, 706, 707, 710, 711, 712, 713, 716, 720, 723, 725, 729, 731, 736, 737, 738, 741, 742, 749, 750, 752, 754, 756, 758, 762, 764, 771, 772, 773, 774, 777, 780, 781, 788, 849, 865, 872, 876, 877, 878, 879, 881, 882, 885, 890, 892, 898, 900, 901, 904, 905, 906, 909, 914, 916, 918, 921, 922, 923, 926, 928, 929, 930, 931, 932, 934, 935, 936, 938, 939, 940, 942, 943, 944, 945, 946

Val-d'Or, QC: 714

Vancouver, BC: 159, 160, 235, 247, 248, 617, 678, 708, 718, 723, 731, 736, 737, 739, 742, 746, 752, 757, 760, 761, 762, 763, 767, 773, 777, 780, 782, 785, 868, 871, 875, 877, 884, 894, 900, 909, 935

Victoria, BC: 834, 912, 915, 925

Waterloo, ON: 222, 724, 728, 771, 907, 910, 929, 943

West Hill, ON: 699

West Vancouver, BC: 745

Weston, ON: 704

Whitby, ON: 306, 715

Whitehorse, YK: 854

Winnipeg, MB: 172, 177, 195, 222, 248, 689, 784, 838, 846, 874, 879, 883, 899, 901, 913, 916, 919, 920

Yellowknife, NT: 849

Cities in the US on the CD-ROM

This is a list of 263 US cities sorted by state and city with US NGOs or US Private Sector firms. Figures in (brackets) indicate the number of NGOs operating in the city and the figure without brackets indicate the number of US private firms. These cities are published on the CD-ROM and are easily searchable.

AR-Bentonville: (1)

AR-Little Rock: 1, (1)

AR-Morrilton: 1,

AZ-Phoenix: 2,

AZ-Scottsdale: 1

AZ-Tempe: 1

CA-Aliso Viejo: (1)

CA-Berkeley: 3

CA-Beverly Hills: (2)

CA-Burbank: (1)

CA-Burlingame: (1)

CA-Camarillo: 1

CA-Carlsbad: 1

CA-Concord: 1, (1)

CA-Cypress: (1)

CA-Davis: 1

CA-Dublin: (1)

CA-Emeryville: 1

CA-Foster City: (1)

CA-Fresno: 1

CA-Inglewood: (1)

CA-Irvine: (1)

CA-Long Beach: (1)

CA-Los Angeles: 4, (2)

CA-Menlo Park: 1
CA-Modesto: (1)
CA-Monrovia: 1
CA-Newport Beach: 1
CA-Oakland: 3, (2)
CA-Oakville: (1)
CA-Ojai: 1
CA-Palo Alto: 2, (2)
CA-Pasadena: (3)
CA-Petaluma: 1
CA-Placentia: 1
CA-Pleasanton: (1)
CA-Redwood Shores: (1)
CA-San Diego: 3, (1)
CA-San Francisco: 14, 4
CA-San Jose: (1)
CA-San Ramon: (1)
CA-Santa Barbara: 1
CA-Santa Clara: (1)
CA-Santa Clarita: (1)
CA-Santa Monica: 2
CA-Santa Rosa: 1
CA-Scotts Valley: 1
CA-Stanford: 1
CA-Stockton: 1
CA-Turlock: (1)
CA-Valencia: (1)
C-O, Boulder: 2
CO-Aurora: 1
CO-Broomfield: (2)
CO-Centennial: 1
CO-Colorado Springs: 3
CO-Denver: 1, (1)
CO-Fort Collins: (1)
CO-Highlands Ranch: (1)
CO-Lakewood: 1
CO-Littleton: 1
CT-Fairfield: (1)
CT-Greenwich: (1)
CT-Hartford: 1
CT-New Canaan: 1
CT-New Milford: 1
CT-Norwalk: 1
CT-Norwich: 1
CT-Stamford: (4)
CT-Westport: 1
DC-Washington: 90, (32)
FL-Boca Raton: 1, (1)
FL-Coral Gables: 1
FL-Deerfield Beach: 1
FL-Fort Lauderdale: (1)
FL-Gainesville: 1
FL-Miami: 2, (4)
FL-Orlando: 1
FL-Tallahassee: 1
G-A, Roswell: 1
GA-Americus: 1
GA-Atlanta: 6, (5)
GA-Brunswick: 1

GA-Peachtree City: 1
HI-Honolulu: (1)
IA-Cedar Rapids: (1)
IA-Coralville: 1
IA-Rock Valley: 1
IA-Waverly: 1
ID-Boise: 1, (1)
IL-Champaign: (1)
IL-Chicago: 4, (9)
IL-Dundee: (1)
IL-Elk Grove Township: (1)
IL-Evanston: 1
IL-Lincolnshire: (1)
IL-Oak Brook: 2
IL-Rockford: 1
IL-Skokie: (1)
IL-Westmont: (1)
IL-Wilmette: 1
IN-Bedford: (1)
IN-Columbus: (1)
IN-Elkhart: 1
IN-Indianapolis: 1
IO-Muscatine: (1)
KS-Manhattan: (1)
KS-Olathe: 2
KS-Overland Park: (1)
KS-Wichita: 1
LA-Baton Rouge: 1, 1
LA-Lafayette: (1)
M-A, Westwood: (1)
MA-Amherst: (1)
MA-Boston: 5, (9)
MA-Brockton: 1
MA-Burlington: (1)
MA-Cambridge: 3, (4)
MA-Maynard: 1
MA-Newton: 1
MA-North Chelmsford: 1
MA-Peabody: (1)
MA-Wakefield: (1)
MA-Waltham: (2)
MA-Watertown: 2, (1)
M-D, Kensington: 1
MD-Annapolis: 1
MD-Baltimore: 7
MD-Bethesda: (5)
MD-Calverton: (1)
MD-Columbia: 2
MD-Potomac: 1
MD-Rockville: 3, (4)
MD-Silver Spring: 5, (1)
ME-Augusta: 1
ME-Portland: 1
MI-Ann Arbor: 1
MI-Battle Creek: 1
MI-Grand Rapids: 2
MI-Grandville: 1
MI-Jackson: (1)
MI-Southfield: 1

MI-Spring Lake: 1
M-N, Eagan: (1)
MN-Arden Hills: (1)
MN-Mendota Heights: 1
MN-Minneapolis: 5, (2)
MN-St. Paul: 4
M-O, Kansas City: 1
MO-Springfield: 1
MO-St. Louis: 1, (2)
MT-Butte: 1
MT-Great Falls: 1
MT-Helena: (1)
NC-Boone: 1
NC-Chapel Hill: 1
NC-Durham: 1, (1)
NC-Raleigh: 2
NC-Research Triangle Park: 1, (1)
NE-Omaha: (1)
NH-Hillsborough: 1
NH-Portsmouth: 1
NJ-Bloomfield: 1, (1)
NJ-Clinton: (1)
NJ-East Brunswick: 1
NJ-East Orange: (1)
NJ-Jersey City: (1)
NJ-Little Silver: 1
NJ-Marlton: (1)
NJ-New Brunswick: (1)
NJ-Oradell: (1)
NJ-Princeton: 1, (2)
NJ-Short Hills: 1, (1)
NJ-Teterboro: (1)
NJ-Upper Saddle River: (1)
NJ-Whitehouse Station: (1)
NJ-Woodcliff Lake: (1)
NV-Las Vegas: (1)
NV-Reno: 1
NY-Andes: 1
NY-Armonk: (1)
NY-Brooklyn: 1
NY-Fairport: (1)
NY-Garden City: (1)
NY-Getzville: 1
NY-Hamilton: 1
NY-Long Beach: 1
NY-New York: 48, (60)
NY-Saratoga Springs: 1
NY-Somers: (1)
NY-Syracuse: 2
NY-Watertown: 1
NY-White Plains: (1)
NY-Williamsville: (1)
OH-Cincinnati: 1, (1)
OH-Cleveland: (1)
OH-Dayton: 1, (1)
OH-Loveland: 1
O-K, Oklahoma City: 2
OK-Bartlesville: 1
OK-Tulsa: 1

OR-Eugene: 2
OR-Lake Oswego: 1
OR-Portland: 1
PA-)Bridgeville: (1)
PA-Akron: 1
PA-Bala Cynwyd: 1
PA-Canonsburg: (1)
PA-Devon: (1)
PA-Douglassville: (1)
PA-Harrisburg: 2, (1)
PA-Hershey: (1)
PA-Kutztown: 1
PA-Lancaster: 1
PA-Perkasie: 1
PA-Philadelphia: 3, (2)
PA-Pittsburgh: 3
PA-Wayne: 1
PA-York: (1)
RI-Warwick: 1
SC-Charleston: 2
SC-Columbia: (1)
SC-Greenville: 2
SC-Rock Hill: 1

SC-Wando: (1)
TN-Bristol: 1
TN-Chattanooga: (1)
TN-Memphis: 2, (1)
TN-Nashville: 1
TX-Dallas: 1
TX-Fort Worth: (2)
TX-Garden Valley: 1
TX-Houlton: (1)
TX-Houston: 1, (8)
TX-Irving: (1)
TX-San Antonio: 1, (1)
TX-Stafford: (1)
TX-The Woodlands: (1)
VA-Alexandria: 4, (2)
VA-Arlington: 9, (11)
VA-Ashburn: (1)
VA-Burke: 1
VA-Chantilly: (1)
VA-Crozet: 1
VA-Fairfax: 2, (2)
VA-Fall Church: (1)
VA-Falls Church: 1, (2)

VA-Forest: 1
VA-McLean: 1, (3)
VA-Merrifield: 1
VA-Millwood: 1
VA-Norfolk: 1, (1)
VA-Oakton: (1)
VA-Reston: 1, (1)
VA-Richmond: 1, (1)
VA-Springfield: 1
VA-Sterling: 2
VA-Vienna: 2, (1)
VA-Warrenton: 1
VT-Belmont: 1
VT-Burlington: (1)
VT-Montpelier Montpelier: 1
WA-Freeland: 1
WA-Newcastle: (1)
WA-Redmond: (1)
WA-Seattle: 8, (1)
WI-Brookfield: (1)
WI-Greendale: 1
WI-Madison: 1
WV-Grafton: 1

Countries & Regions of the World

This index offers you a quick way to find any mention of a country or region of the world listed anywhere in the print edition of this book. (Countries and regions published on the CD-ROM are easily searchable and are therefore not listed here.)

Countries are usually sorted by continent, with a few exceptions based on various considerations: *Africa, Americas* (excluding the Caribbean), *Asia and Oceania, Caribbean* (including Bermuda), *Europe and Eurasia* (includes Turkey) and the *Middle East*.

Sub-regions are indexed at the top of each regional section, followed by an alphabetical listing of country names. All countries in the world have been indexed (if they appear in the book), but some non-standard regions may not be indexed. No attempt has been made to cross-reference sub-regions to specific countries. French country names (if different from the English name) are shown in brackets if they appear in the book and are denoted by parentheses.

Côte d'Ivoire: 715, 717, 742, 745, 772, 979

Democratic Republic of Congo (République démocratique du Congo): 621, 659, 672, 731, 756, 764, 937, 997

Egypt: 452, 519, 521, 522, 524, 544, 709, 718, 730, 741, 744, 754, 756, 757, 770, 771, 772, 784, 845, 904

Eritrea: 994

Ethiopia: 67, 543, 671, 674, 715, 729, 879, 885, 900, 932, 941, 982, 994

Gabon: 745

Gambia: 85, 414, 524

Ghana: 56, 79, 80, 83, 161, 165, 184, 210, 220, 221, 243, 387, 401, 414, 441, 442, 443, 456, 522, 524, 641, 700, 701, 712, 715, 733, 742, 785, 787, 879, 901, 914

Guinea: 543, 705, 712, 715, 716, 731, 742, 746, 750, 767, 772

Kenya: 62, 116, 161, 190, 314, 315, 425, 452, 524, 579, 659, 668, 715, 727, 731, 753, 765, 776, 787, 788, 845, 865, 880, 900, 938, 996, 997

Lesotho: 928, 938, 941

Liberia: 78, 659, 750, 994

Libya: 522, 765

Madagascar: 336, 742

Malawi: 67, 116, 524, 674, 700, 729, 731, 741, 742, 779, 885, 886, 900, 918, 934, 938

Mali: 67, 124, 161, 164, 674, 712, 737, 745, 750, 765, 888, 903, 939, 941

Maroc: 523

Mauritania: 772

Morocco: 111, 522, 524, 709, 730, 742, 744, 750, 764, 766, 772, 778, 982

Mozambique: 92, 125, 659, 672, 765, 864, 896, 900, 905, 918, 920, 938

Namibia: 188, 190, 554, 718, 938

Niger: 161, 730, 749, 764, 765, 903, 982

Nigeria: 80, 87, 92, 117, 163, 441, 457, 478, 522, 659, 672, 705, 715, 744, 746, 750, 780, 787, 870, 901, 922, 979

Rwanda: 24, 587, 590, 611, 621, 623, 657, 659, 672, 737, 744, 756, 938, 982, 997

Senegal (Sénégal): 123, 161, 183, 672, 712, 730, 737, 742, 744, 764, 772, 845, 903, 936

Seychelles: 864

Sierra Leone: 79, 80, 84, 587, 590, 597, 601, 623, 671, 715, 731, 756, 764, 776, 879, 889, 893, 922, 994

Somalia: 654, 659, 670, 997

South Africa: 28, 126, 176, 183, 184, 186, 380, 522, 523, 524, 610, 621, 669, 673, 700, 708, 715, 727, 731, 746, 758, 767, 769, 785, 846, 872, 873, 904, 908, 928, 938, 941

Sudan: 449, 450, 451, 522, 654, 659, 685, 686, 742, 744, 864, 900, 932

Swaziland: 161, 557, 938

Tanzania: 115, 117, 165, 186, 190, 449, 450, 452, 641, 672, 700, 707, 764, 765, 767, 774, 880, 885, 900, 920, 935, 938, 946

Togo: 92, 161, 210, 300, 441, 787, 893, 937

Tunisia: 522, 524, 709, 711, 712, 734, 742, 764, 765

Uganda: 186, 243, 524, 746, 765, 772, 787, 864, 879, 885, 900, 938

Western Sahara: 994

Zambia: 447, 542, 641, 718, 731, 764, 765, 779, 886, 905, 938, 982

Zimbabwe: 50, 52, 58, 77, 83, 129, 161, 287, 355, 457, 522, 659, 669, 727, 731, 742, 745, 750, 752, 899, 918, 938, 976

Americas- Regions

Americas: 157, 158, 213, 217, 226, 258, 284, 496, 500, 558, 561, 614, 623, 632, 703, 706, 714, 718, 720, 728, 730, 731, 733, 742, 750, 770, 824, 825, 873, 876, 880, 882, 891, 930, 954, 956, 959, 960, 969, 992

Central America (Amérique Centrale): 327, 403, 421, 500, 558, 560, 583, 699, 705, 706, 718, 721, 722, 726, 735, 744, 761, 771, 773, 774, 775, 782, 871, 872, 889, 904, 908, 912, 916, 917, 924, 936, 946

Latin America (Amérique latine): 37, 39, 41, 43, 92, 94, 150, 160, 166, 174, 177, 179, 202, 214, 225, 245, 252, 253, 262, 263, 264, 266, 267, 268, 273, 276, 291, 314, 323, 345, 358, 400, 402, 403, 460, 475, 477, 479, 481, 483, 485, 496, 497, 498, 499, 500, 501, 502, 503, 504, 515, 516, 555, 574, 581, 582, 583, 613, 619, 622, 623, 624, 629, 631, 632, 673, 697, 706, 713, 718, 722, 726, 727, 729, 733, 734, 737, 752, 753, 757, 762, 765, 767, 768, 769, 770, 774, 781, 788, 847, 851, 852, 866, 871, 873, 876, 877, 880, 883, 884, 886, 890, 891, 894, 895, 897, 898, 899, 901, 902, 904, 911, 914, 915, 917, 919, 922, 923, 926, 928, 930, 931, 936, 939, 940, 942, 943, 945, 947, 953, 965, 966, 983, 990, 992, 994, 995, 1002

North America (Amérique du Nord): 19, 21, 23, 24, 26, 27, 28, 29, 31, 32, 38, 40, 43, 44, 49, 51, 56, 57, 58, 60, 61, 63, 65, 66, 67, 79, 83, 84, 86, 87, 91, 100, 103, 105, 113, 129, 130, 152, 158, 164, 166, 171, 175, 177, 189, 191, 203, 207, 209, 241, 242, 253, 268, 298, 300, 301, 302, 321, 322, 325, 327, 329, 332, 341, 344, 345, 351, 360, 363, 372, 379, 380, 381, 426, 428, 441, 468, 475, 478, 485, 492, 493, 499, 506, 507, 509, 520, 526, 527, 528, 530, 536, 537, 555, 559, 560, 563, 565, 589, 596, 597, 605, 633, 634, 635, 636, 637, 638, 639, 640, 641, 644, 646, 651, 655, 660, 668, 675, 681, 696, 697, 698, 700, 702, 704, 708, 710, 711, 713, 714, 715, 716, 718, 722, 724, 727, 728, 729, 732, 734, 735, 737, 738, 739, 740, 745, 749, 752, 753, 754, 755, 758, 759, 763, 765, 766, 768, 770, 771, 773, 775, 777, 779, 780, 781, 782, 783, 784, 788, 790, 830, 841, 842, 892, 917, 920, 933, 940, 942, 943, 955, 963, 964, 965, 966, 977, 991

South America: 88, 188, 189, 190, 327, 378, 496, 501, 503, 523, 558, 676, 696, 697, 698, 699, 700, 702, 703, 704, 705, 706, 711, 713, 715, 722, 723, 727, 728, 732, 734, 736, 737, 738, 739, 740, 743, 744, 745, 751, 752, 753, 758, 759, 761, 763, 764, 766, 770, 771, 775, 777, 780, 781, 782, 785, 787, 867, 875, 878, 895, 919, 924, 928, 934, 942, 945, 946, 979

Americas- Countries

Argentina (Argentine): 237, 403, 496, 500, 501, 504, 700, 702, 707, 721, 723, 724, 727, 730, 739, 740, 758, 759, 763, 767, 774, 777, 785, 788, 886, 917, 918

Belize: 74, 339, 718, 757, 788

Bolivia (Bolivie): 67, 161, 172, 190, 500, 504, 579, 674, 739, 742, 749, 753, 772, 879, 901, 905, 920, 937

Brazil (Brésil): 158, 165, 176, 221, 237, 402, 448, 496, 500, 501, 502, 563, 672, 705, 710, 711, 721, 723, 724, 740, 741, 742, 745, 748, 752, 753, 755, 757, 762, 767, 769, 771, 772, 774, 775, 783, 784, 787, 788, 843, 871, 893, 900, 905, 913, 927, 928, 930, 932, 934, 997

Chile: 92, 188, 243, 314, 496, 500, 501, 504, 555, 700, 702, 706, 707, 708, 709, 711, 714, 739, 745, 748, 752, 753, 758, 762, 767, 774, 776, 777, 780, 783, 906, 995

Costa Rica: 74, 77, 88, 153, 158, 165, 175, 187, 188, 189, 221, 288, 452, 496, 500, 504, 555, 723, 727, 742, 744, 753, 759, 771, 787, 901, 912, 946

Colombia: 121, 243, 500, 501, 659, 672, 705, 712, 736, 737, 753, 754, 757, 767, 772, 780, 781, 834, 926, 927

Ecuador (Équateur): 96, 120, 187, 188, 190, 500, 504, 705, 753, 757, 767, 820, 871, 980, 901, 903, 928, 934

El Salvador: 500, 583, 709, 718, 729, 741, 787, 788, 927, 928, 932

Guatemala: 161, 165, 187, 500, 504, 705, 742, 744, 788, 871, 889, 926, 928, 937, 943

Guyana: 67, 189, 278, 456, 674, 705, 709, 714, 732, 759, 761, 772, 785, 910, 934, 946

Honduras: 158, 177, 183, 500, 711, 737, 757, 772, 774, 788, 889, 905, 913, 936, 937, 940, 943

Mexico: 20, 28, 33, 43, 94, 158, 176, 177, 186, 187, 202, 243, 263, 354, 358, 464, 475, 481, 493, 496, 497, 498, 499, 500, 501, 502, 503, 504, 505, 555, 558, 646, 672, 700, 702, 703, 705, 706, 710, 714, 715, 721, 722, 725, 729, 730, 732, 735, 738, 740, 741, 744, 747, 752, 753, 757, 758, 760, 761, 762, 769, 771, 774, 776, 777, 783, 786, 788, 820, 832, 833, 843, 851, 874, 906, 913, 916, 926, 928, 930, 931, 932, 936, 946

Nicaragua: 158, 164, 500, 723, 737, 742, 888, 899, 909, 918, 920, 928, 932, 937, 939

Panama: 158, 505, 742, 748, 977

Paraguay: 67, 158, 500, 674, 745, 893

Peru (Pérou): 87, 164, 165, 172, 187, 190, 258, 403, 500, 505, 555, 679, 700, 702, 705, 707, 712, 714, 730,

740, 741, 742, 744, 748, 750, 753, 762, 767, 772, 774, 782, 784, 888, 893, 901, 905, 920, 937, 939

Suriname: 161, 714

Uruguay: 448, 500, 739, 744, 757, 845

USA: 158, 159, 165, 166, 171, 172, 174, 178, 180, 181, 184, 186, 187, 188, 189, 194, 196, 231, 241, 242, 247, 252, 309, 310, 312, 313, 315, 317, 018, 485 - 496, 616, 620, 020, 628, 629, 631, 632, 677, 678, 679, 690, 696, 697, 699, 700-707, 709, 710, 711, 713, 714, 715, 716, 720-725, 727, 728, 730, 732, 734-739, 741-744, 746, 747, 748, 749, 751, 752, 753, 754, 755, 757-764, 766, 767, 769, 770-779, 781, 782, 783, 785, 787, 788, 789, 791, 848, 850, 882, 918, 933, 940, 946, 978, 979, 981, 983, 984, 985, 986, 987, 989, 992, 993, 994, 999, 1002

Venezuela: 201, 210, 444, 445, 448, 496, 500, 502, 505, 555, 704, 705, 727, 729, 730, 753, 754, 765, 769, 774, 784, 918

Asia and Oceania - Regions

Asia (Asie): 29, 37, 42, 51, 78, 79, 113, 122, 150, 157, 160, 163, 164, 174, 189, 190, 213, 214, 217, 220, 221, 226, 245, 252, 258, 266, 269, 273, 274, 278, 313, 323, 327, 333, 336, 355, 358, 363, 369, 370, 372, 373, 376, 378, 379, 402, 429, 452, 475, 477, 479, 481, 485, 508, 515, 519, 523, 524, 525, 527, 528, 529, 530, 532, 555, 558, 560, 561, 574, 581, 582, 583, 610, 617, 619, 621, 622, 623, 624, 629, 631, 632, 636, 647, 650, 670, 673, 676, 680, 688, 696, 697, 698, 699, 702, 704, 708, 709, 713, 714, 716, 718, 719, 720, 722, 727, 728, 729, 730, 731, 732, 733, 734, 737, 738, 740, 741, 743, 744, 745, 751, 752, 753, 755, 757, 758, 759, 761, 762, 763, 764, 766, 768, 769, 770, 771, 773, 775, 777, 780, 781, 782, 784, 785, 788, 802, 824, 825, 847, 852, 867, 868, 871, 872, 873, 875, 876, 877, 878, 881, 882, 883, 884, 888, 890, 891, 895, 897, 898, 899, 901, 904, 911, 912, 914, 916, 917, 919, 926, 928, 931, 934, 938, 942, 943, 947, 952, 963, 965, 966, 976, 979, 990, 994, 995, 1002

Asia Pacific: 29, 358, 369, 370, 475, 477, 479, 481, 524, 525, 527, 529, 530, 532, 561, 610, 617, 621, 624, 727, 758, 769, 771, 785, 802, 847, 868, 990, 994, 995, 1002

Central Asia: 279, 304, 514, 607, 625, 626, 629, 673, 737, 866, 871, 881, 982, 990, 991

East Asia: 43, 202, 262, 264, 266, 268, 273, 276, 863

(Moyen-Orient): 895

Oceania (Océanie): 217

Pacific Islands: 925, 940

Pacific Rim: 267, 345, 623, 787

South Asia: 118, 273, 416, 429, 525, 533, 561, 625, 853, 863, 910, 913, 922, 938, 940, 944

Southeast Asia: 41, 42, 83, 119, 221, 373, 378, 379, 414, 425, 447, 461, 471, 483, 524, 526, 530, 531, 560, 639, 699, 715, 733, 734, 744, 747, 763, 778, 781, 788, 853, 902, 904, 905, 912, 923, 945

Western Asia: 308, 981

Asia and Oceania - Countries

Australia (Australie): 31, 74, 152, 158, 162, 166, 170, 173, 174, 176, 177, 179, 180, 184, 189, 216, 228, 230, 240, 242, 278, 280, 284, 285, 287, 359, 363, 368, 376, 482, 525, 527, 528, 530, 531, 532, 562, 577, 647, 648, 655, 673, 696, 698, 700, 702, 703, 704, 705, 707, 713, 714, 718, 722, 724, 725, 727, 728, 732, 734, 737, 738, 740, 741, 743, 744, 747, 748, 753, 755, 758, 759, 762, 763, 764, 767, 768, 769, 770, 771, 775, 777, 779, 780, 781, 784, 855, 877, 913, 928, 931

Bangladesh: 100, 299, 336, 414, 579, 621, 701, 732, 733, 746, 754, 763, 768, 771, 776, 873, 905, 913, 926, 928, 938, 941

Bhutan: 328, 545

Burma (Myanmar): 741, 780, 880

Cambodia: 621, 623, 701, 756, 761, 771, 904, 908, 932

China: 31, 32, 36, 41, 42, 95, 96, 117, 119, 120, 124, 165, 188, 206, 221, 237, 239, 282, 372, 430, 477, 482, 483, 492, 502, 516, 524, 525, 526, 529, 530, 531, 532, 554, 555, 562, 563, 621, 646, 666, 670, 673, 687, 698, 700, 702, 703, 706, 710, 719, 721, 726, 727, 730, 731, 732, 733, 739, 740, 741, 746, 747, 749, 755, 757, 758, 759, 767, 769, 771, 772, 773, 774, 776, 783, 784, 788, 833, 843, 848, 853, 873, 881, 902, 904, 906, 928, 934, 954, 961, 967

Fiji: 221, 243

Hong Kong: 24, 39, 42, 206, 282, 336, 345, 372, 379, 475, 501, 502, 524, 525, 526, 527, 530, 531, 532, 555, 604, 629, 631, 641, 687, 702, 703, 710, 722, 727, 728, 729, 746, 747, 749, 756, 758, 760, 780, 782, 833, 901

India: 24, 31, 52, 92, 106, 111, 114, 161, 165, 182, 190, 243, 252, 278, 286, 379, 414, 477, 482, 485, 496, 520, 525, 531, 532, 685, 686, 698, 719, 724, 726, 727, 730, 732, 733, 734, 739, 742, 744, 756, 759, 768, 771, 772, 773, 774, 775, 776, 780, 784, 787, 788, 871, 882, 891, 901, 904, 913, 922, 926, 928, 932, 933, 935, 937, 938, 943, 944, 994

Indonesia: 85, 89, 92, 206, 385, 447, 448, 451, 525, 526, 544, 555, 606, 611, 659, 705, 716, 719, 721, 727, 732, 737, 742, 743, 745, 746, 748, 749, 751, 755, 761, 764, 769, 771, 772, 773, 780, 781, 881, 900, 926, 941

Japan: 31, 32, 34, 38, 39, 40, 94, 107, 132, 158, 169, 173, 178, 184, 237, 239, 243, 246, 247, 249, 262, 278, 279, 280, 281, 286, 288, 294, 317, 345, 373, 403, 477, 482, 524, 525, 526, 527, 530, 531, 532, 543, 546, 554, 555, 558, 559, 561, 562, 577, 699, 706, 707, 721, 722, 724, 727, 728, 732, 734, 741, 747, 749, 755, 756, 757, 758, 778, 783, 784, 787, 811, 832, 833, 906, 931, 983, 993, 997, 1001

Korea, North: 659

Korea, South: 454, 524, 525, 526, 527, 700, 701, 732, 755, 779, 832, 833

Laos: 221, 716, 719, 771

Malaysia: 42, 82, 83, 86, 88, 92, 243, 280, 283, 373, 377, 379, 448, 501, 524, 525, 530, 531, 532, 648, 674, 701, 702, 703, 711, 721, 731, 735, 746, 747, 764, 771, 772, 774, 780, 781, 784, 906

Maldives: 716

Marshall Islands: 188

Mongolia: 893

Myanmar (see Burma)

Nepal (Népal): 187, 421, 444, 446, 448, 646, 654, 659, 670, 701, 732, 742, 761, 768, 771, 772, 776, 882, 893, 935, 938, 941, 943

New Zealand: 74, 158, 162, 173, 183, 184, 240, 243, 278, 287, 525, 527, 531, 532, 562, 573, 577, 673, 724, 758, 768, 784, 928, 978

Pakistan: 111, 115, 287, 455, 520, 532, 533, 659, 672, 700, 701, 744, 756, 768, 770, 771, 780, 784, 871, 927, 928, 938, 994

Philippines: 28, 67, 80, 286, 370, 379, 425, 447, 448, 525, 529, 531, 532, 547, 674, 700, 705, 716, 719, 727, 732, 741, 742, 746, 747, 761, 764, 771, 774, 776, 900, 901, 912, 943, 975, 980

Singapore: 42, 206, 220, 221, 279, 373, 379, 448, 480, 490, 501, 524, 525, 526, 530, 531, 532, 548, 629, 699, 702, 703, 710, 721, 722, 739, 740, 747, 749, 758, 764, 769, 775, 780, 832, 845, 906, 928

Solomon Islands: 86, 751

Sri Lanka: 243, 667, 755, 761, 768, 776, 904, 910, 928, 938, 943

Taiwan: 229, 249, 301, 501, 525, 526, 528, 531, 555, 558, 562, 564, 684, 710, 721, 729, 732, 749, 755, 758, 764, 780, 832, 833, 906

Thailand: 31, 62, 67, 158, 165, 187, 190, 206, 221, 313, 379, 382, 448, 452, 477, 482, 524, 525, 526, 531, 532, 543, 555, 621, 645, 674, 689, 700, 719, 721, 726, 730, 737, 739, 741, 742, 745, 746, 747, 749, 764, 771, 772, 784, 874, 906, 934, 995

Tonga: 221

Vanuatu: 189

Western Samoa: 532

Caribbean - Regions

Caribbean (Caraibes): 43, 92, 150, 160, 163, 174, 202, 206, 214, 226, 232, 264, 268, 276, 278, 314, 403, 485, 496, 504, 558, 583, 619, 622, 699, 704, 705, 713, 715, 722, 726, 729, 730, 731, 733, 735, 738, 740, 745, 746, 750, 752, 753, 761, 765, 768, 770, 771, 773, 774, 775, 779, 780, 781, 785, 787, 852, 853, 871, 874, 878, 880, 881, 882, 885, 886, 888, 890, 895, 897, 899, 902, 904, 915, 917, 924, 926, 930, 931, 934, 940, 942, 947, 953, 955, 960, 966, 980, 983, 990, 992, 994, 995

West Indies: 731

Antilles: 899

Caribbean - Countries

Bahamas: 504, 655, 760, 772, 773, 774, 779

Barbados: 709, 710, 711, 726, 727, 729, 738, 745, 746, 749, 757, 779, 980

Europe and Eurasia - Regions

Europe and Eurasia - Countries

Russia: 31, 39, 128, 165, 175, 208, 220, 279, 281, 306,
     482, 496, 508, 513, 514, 516, 517, 518, 519, 563,
     625, 629, 646, 672, 674, 702, 703, 708, 718, 719,
     720, 727, 732, 733, 734, 741, 744, 746, 749, 752,
     757, 769, 772, 773, 871, 874, 940
Serbia and Montenegro: 772
Slovakia: 505, 519, 759, 846, 940
Slovenia: 505, 519, 772
Spain (Espagne): 31, 35, 76, 94, 96, , 152, 158, 160, 162,
     175, 177, 221, 243, 280, 281, 360, 378, 397, 403,
     482, 505, 511, 512, 513, 555, 558, 563, 700, 701,
     721, 736, 739, 782, 881, 918, 1003
Sweden (Suède): 166, 170, 232, 233, 238, 281, 288, 505,
     513, 682, 722, 724, 732, 734, 747, 918
Switzerland (Suisse): 39, 76, 162, 166, 171, 175, 176,
     243, 281, 284, 286, 311, 314, 316, 317, 318, 505,
     513, 518, 626, 628, 632, 654, 655, 668, 672, 678,
     679, 682, 703, 741, 744, 747, 749, 762, 774, 783,
     898, 918, 963, 984, 986, 987, 988, 989, 990, 993,
     995, 997, 998, 1000, 1001, 1002, 1003
Turkey: 39, 285, 505, 511, 513, 518, 519, 543, 549, 555,
     670, 729, 737, 757, 772
UK: 32, 40, 74, 75, 76, 92, 97, 150, 151, 152, 153, 154,
     156, 158, 160, 161, 162, 165, 173, 179, 180, 193,
     204, 205, 208, 213, 214, 215, 216, 218, 219, 226,
     227, 228, 229, 231, 232, 235, 243, 248, 250, 258,
     278, 279, 281, 282, 283, 284, 286, 287, 288, 358,
     359, 360, 363, 364, 366, 367, 368, 376, 377, 378,
     379, 478, 483, 493, 494, 504, 505, 506, 509, 510,
     511, 512, 513, 521, 523, 531, 558, 561, 562, 573,
     574, 575, 576, 578, 582, 585, 613, 619, 624, 625,
     630, 631, 632, 648, 650, 655, 673, 674, 675, 677,
     679, 680, 681, 689, 699, 701, 703, 710, 713, 716,
     721, 722, 724, 725, 728, 730, 731, 732, 734, 739,
     740, 747, 752, 754, 755, 756, 758, 760, 764, 765,
     769, 771, 772, 774, 780, 782, 783, 784, 788, 833,
     848, 904, 931, 941, 966, 976, 981, 982, 987
Ukraine: 67, 266, 505, 517, 519, 674, 718, 744, 748, 772,
     774, 846, 871, 874, 901
Uzbekistan: 81, 716
Vatican City: 138

Middle East - Regions

Middle East: 20, 38, 41, 52, 104, 137, 150, 213, 214, 217,
     226, 230, 245, 252, 262, 268, 278, 327, 358, 376,
     379, 397, 425, 475, 481, 483, 485, 519, 520, 521,
     522, 524, 558, 560, 561, 583, 624, 632, 639, 696,
     697, 702, 704, 706, 722, 726, 727, 728, 729, 734,
     735, 740, 749, 750, 753, 755, 757, 759, 763, 764,
     766, 768, 769, 770, 775, 777, 781, 782, 784, 785,
     824, 825, 841, 852, 867, 871, 872, 873, 877, 882,
     883, 902, 904, 912, 919, 931, 940, 945, 965, 966,
     990, 994, 1002

Middle East - Countries

Bahrain: 519, 520
Iran: 519, 543, 589, 659, 727, 732, 744, 746, 748, 750,
     755, 757, 776, 783, 820, 918
Iraq: 519, 590, 659, 670, 756, 918, 921, 997
Israel: 153, 247, 283, 519, 520, 521, 522, 620, 698, 727,
     729, 731, 732, 921, 952
Jordan: 519, 521, 701, 741, 749, 756, 784, 916, 1000
Kuwait: 519, 521, 756, 764
Lebanon: 308, 477, 519, 756, 916, 921, 981, 994, 1000
Oman: 519, 757
Qatar: 519, 520, 704, 781
Saudi Arabia: 100, 104, 519, 520, 521, 654, 655, 675,
     745, 746, 753, 755, 757
Syria: 519, 756, 765
United Arab Emirates: 519, 655, 675, 738, 764, 769, 785
West Bank and Gaza Strip: 1000
Yemen: 519, 520, 659, 749, 753, 761, 784

Job Categories

Job categories are listed just before the symbol ◆ and help to indicate the variety of job opportunities available with that organization. There are three indexes in this section: The first is for chapters in the print edition: Chapter 35, Private Sector firms in Canada; Chapter 37, Canadian Governement; Chapter 38, NGOs in Canada. The second and third indexes are for job categories on the CD-ROM: Appendix 36a, Private Sector Firms in the US; and Apendix 39a, NGOs in the US.

Readers should note that that not all organizations have been assigned job categories (example, chapters related to gaining experience or those on academic study). However, they also offer a variety of job opportunities. The surest way to find job opportunities is to scan the contents of profiles in all chapters.

Accounting: 700, 704, 707, 709, 710, 711, 713, 714, 717, 720, 722, 725, 729, 733, 734, 736, 749, 751, 754, 756, 757, 758, 759, 760, 762, 764, 765, 766, 767, 774, 778, 782, 784, 836, 841, 843, 845, 854, 864, 868, 869, 871, 875, 879, 885, 886, 888, 891, 898, 899, 900, 902, 905, 906, 907, 908, 913, 917, 920, 921, 922, 924, 928, 932, 934, 937, 940

Administration (General): 697, 702, 707, 709, 710, 711, 714, 716, 717, 720, 722, 726, 728, 730, 733, 734, 736, 737, 739, 749, 751, 756, 757, 759, 760, 762, 763, 764, 765, 766, 767, 773, 774, 777, 778, 781, 782, 787, 832, 836, 841, 843, 845, 850, 864, 865, 866, 867, 868, 869, 871, 873, 875, 879, 883, 885, 886, 888, 890, 891, 893, 895, 896, 897, 898, 899, 900, 902, 905, 906, 907, 908, 912, 913, 916, 917, 920, 922, 924, 926, 928, 929, 932, 934, 935, 937, 939, 940, 942, 944, 945

Adult Training: 699, 725, 731, 733, 736, 741, 743, 750, 755, 756, 764, 770, 773, 785, 786, 841, 863, 864, 865, 868, 869, 870, 873, 882, 888, 889, 891, 892, 893, 895, 897, 899, 900, 901, 903, 904, 907, 910, 917, 919, 920, 927, 932, 934, 936, 939, 940, 941, 944

Advanced Technology: 696, 702, 706, 709, 713, 720, 724, 726, 728, 742, 745, 747, 750, 751, 759, 762, 764, 770, 771, 774, 775, 778, 779, 780, 782, 783, 784, 883, 901

Advocacy: 702, 733, 741, 837, 852, 863, 865, 867, 869, 870, 871, 873, 876, 878, 880, 882, 883, 885, 886, 891, 893, 894, 897, 898, 899, 904, 906, 910, 911, 916, 918, 921, 922, 924, 925, 926, 928, 929, 931, 932, 934, 938, 940, 943, 944

Aerial Surveys: 741, 779, 784

Aerospace Technology: 698, 701, 710, 717, 745, 749, 750, 769, 787, 839, 869

Agriculture: 699, 700, 702, 718, 733, 734, 737, 741, 743, 745, 756, 758, 764, 775, 777, 780, 787, 832, 838, 844, 845, 863, 864, 868, 869, 873, 875, 877, 878, 882, 883, 886, 887, 888, 889, 891, 892, 893, 896, 897, 898, 900, 902, 903, 904, 907, 908, 912, 913, 915, 917, 919, 920, 922, 928, 932, 933, 934, 937, 941, 983

Air Transportation: 698, 713, 734, 749, 750, 769, 780, 840, 920

Architecture and Planning: 708, 712, 717, 723, 729, 731, 757, 772, 779, 780, 785, 788, 868, 869, 907, 930

Arms Control: 906, 917

Arts: 837

Banking and Financial Services: 711, 713, 716, 725, 726, 729, 730, 741, 746, 760, 764, 773, 781, 787, 846

Blindness Rehabilitation: 891

Building Supplies: 758

Bulk Materials Handling: 773

Business Development: 697, 699, 700, 701, 705, 707, 709, 710, 711, 714, 715, 717, 718, 720, 722, 724, 729, 730, 733, 734, 736, 741, 746, 749, 750, 751, 757, 758, 759, 760, 764, 766, 768, 769, 770, 773, 775, 777, 778, 781, 782, 783, 787, 788, 833, 834, 835, 836, 837, 843, 844, 845, 846, 848, 849, 853, 854, 868, 869, 873, 875, 881, 883, 887, 888, 892, 895, 897, 899, 903, 904, 906, 907, 913, 922, 932, 935, 937, 940, 941, 944, 946

Business/Banking/Trade: 699, 705, 713, 715, 717, 729, 733, 736, 746, 760, 764, 781

Camera and Projector Design: 749

Chemicals: 702, 709, 732, 761, 762, 778

Childcare: 930

Civil Society: 896, 903, 909, 921, 956

Commerce: 716, 754, 755, 757, 760, 765, 781, 784, 833, 835, 850, 968

Commonwealth: 811, 874, 881, 895, 981, 982, 994, 995

Community Development: 699, 700, 708, 714, 717, 724, 725, 726, 730, 731, 733, 736, 757, 768, 769, 772, 785, 787, 833, 838, 841, 845, 863, 864, 865, 866, 867, 869, 871, 872, 873, 875, 877, 879, 881, 882, 883, 886, 887, 888, 889, 890, 891, 892, 893, 894, 895, 896, 897, 900, 902, 903, 904, 905, 907, 908, 909, 910, 911, 912, 913, 916, 917, 919, 920, 922, 924, 926, 928, 929, 930, 932, 933, 934, 936, 940, 941, 942, 944, 946, 955

Computer Systems: 697, 700, 701, 707, 709, 713, 714, 715, 716, 717, 720, 722, 726, 728, 732, 736, 737, 738, 740, 745, 746, 747, 750, 751, 755, 756, 757, 759, 761, 762, 764, 765, 767, 770, 771, 773, 774, 779, 787, 788, 836, 840, 845, 850, 868, 869, 870, 873, 879, 882, 885, 888, 897, 898, 899, 903, 907, 917, 920, 935, 941, 944

Conflict Prevention: 865, 885, 903, 921, 929

Conservation: 935, 951, 953, 954, 958, 960, 968

Construction: 698, 701, 708, 709, 715, 717, 719, 724, 727, 729, 730, 735, 737, 739, 741, 742, 744, 759, 761, 767, 772, 773, 774, 777, 779, 780, 782, 784, 785, 869, 885, 888, 889, 903, 907, 908, 912, 918, 920, 932, 940

Consulting: 696, 697, 698, 699, 700, 702, 703, 704, 705, 707, 709, 711, 712, 715, 716, 717, 718, 722, 723, 724, 725, 726, 729, 730, 731, 732, 733, 734, 735, 736, 737, 739, 740, 741, 742, 743, 744, 745, 746, 747, 748, 750, 751, 754, 756, 757, 761, 763, 764, 766, 767, 768, 769, 770, 771, 772, 773, 774, 776, 777, 778, 779, 780, 782, 783, 784, 785, 786, 787, 793, 794, 795, 798, 799, 800, 825, 826, 827, 835, 836, 838, 841, 844, 864, 865, 868, 869, 870, 873, 879, 883, 888, 901, 902, 904, 907, 908, 911, 917, 922, 926, 932, 935, 937

Corporate Ethics: 921

Culture: 817, 837, 844, 847, 848, 850, 854, 895, 911

Customer Services: 696, 726, 727, 732, 737, 739, 740, 760, 769, 773, 779, 781

Defence and Peacekeeping: 847, 941

Development Assistance: 699, 700, 702, 712, 715, 716, 717, 725, 726, 729, 730, 731, 733, 741, 743, 746, 747, 750, 752, 754, 763, 764, 766, 768, 770, 772, 775, 776, 777, 778, 785, 786, 787, 827, 833, 838, 841, 844, 845, 846, 860, 863, 864, 865, 866, 867, 868, 869, 873, 874, 875, 879, 882, 883, 885, 886, 887, 888, 889, 890, 891, 892, 894, 897, 899, 901, 902, 903, 904, 905, 906, 907, 908, 912, 913, 914, 916, 917, 919, 920, 925, 928, 932, 934, 935, 936, 937, 938, 940, 942, 943, 944, 945, 946, 961

Development Education: 699, 716, 721, 722, 725, 736, 746, 754, 764, 768, 769, 770, 786, 787, 833, 837, 838, 841, 845, 846, 857, 865, 866, 868, 869, 870, 871, 872, 873, 875, 877, 879, 880, 882, 883, 885, 886, 887, 888, 889, 890, 891, 892, 893, 894, 895, 896, 897, 898, 900, 903, 904, 905, 908, 910, 911, 912, 913, 914, 915, 916, 917, 919, 920, 922, 924, 925, 926, 931, 932, 933, 934, 935, 937, 939, 940, 941, 943, 944, 945, 946

Drilling Services: 709, 727, 769

Economic Development: 712, 718, 764, 769, 788, 833, 834, 849, 854, 904, 920

Economics: 697, 699, 700, 710, 715, 717, 718, 725, 726, 730, 733, 734, 735, 740, 750, 756, 757, 764, 768, 776, 779, 780, 782, 785, 834, 838, 839, 841, 842, 843, 844, 845, 850, 854, 869, 873, 876, 880, 913, 920, 921, 936, 944, 951, 957, 968

Editing: 906, 944

Education: 712, 716, 733, 735, 741, 764, 768, 798, 807, 817, 826, 843, 864, 865, 874, 877, 880, 882, 885, 890, 893, 896, 900, 906, 912, 917, 921, 922, 929, 935, 936, 945, 951, 955, 958, 962, 979

Election Monitoring: 722, 842

Energy Resources: 697, 701, 704, 709, 711, 714, 717, 724, 727, 728, 729, 731, 734, 735, 736, 737, 742, 743, 744, 747, 748, 752, 761, 765, 768, 772, 773, 775, 776, 777, 779, 780, 782, 784, 833, 847, 868, 869, 870, 900, 902, 903, 909, 913, 922, 929, 941

Engineering: 696, 697, 698, 700, 701, 703, 704, 705, 707, 708, 709, 710, 711, 712, 714, 715, 717, 719, 720, 721, 722, 723, 724, 725, 726, 727, 728, 729, 730, 731, 732, 733, 734, 737, 738, 741, 742, 743, 744, 745, 746, 748, 750, 751, 752, 753, 755, 756, 757, 758, 759, 760, 761, 762, 763, 765, 767, 769, 770, 771, 772, 773, 774, 775, 776, 777, 778, 779, 780, 782, 783, 784, 785, 786, 787, 791, 792, 797, 799, 833, 836, 843, 869, 870, 873, 885, 888, 900, 901, 907, 908, 918, 928, 930, 934, 941

Engineering Management: 762, 930

Environment: 697, 698, 699, 700, 701, 702, 703, 707, 708, 709, 711, 714, 715, 717, 718, 719, 724, 725, 726, 727, 729, 730, 731, 732, 733, 734, 736, 737, 739, 740, 743, 744, 745, 748, 750, 752, 753, 754, 757, 759, 761, 762, 763, 765, 767, 768, 769, 771, 772, 775, 776, 777, 778, 779, 780, 782, 785, 786, 787, 838, 841, 842, 845, 847, 865, 866, 867, 868, 869, 870, 873, 876, 877, 878, 879, 882, 883, 885, 888, 889, 892, 893, 894, 897, 900, 901, 902, 903, 904, 906, 907, 908, 909, 911, 913, 914, 917, 919, 922, 923, 924, 925, 929, 932, 933, 934, 935, 936, 939, 940, 941, 944, 953, 956, 962, 967, 988, 996

Exchange Programs: 701, 717, 733, 838, 841, 844, 866, 869, 871, 873, 874, 875, 877, 882, 888, 889, 892, 907, 910, 915, 917, 919, 922, 932, 944

Exploration and Development: 704, 706, 707, 708, 711, 714, 718, 719, 731, 737, 742, 752, 760, 761, 763, 767, 777, 780, 788

Film Distribution: 749

Film Production and Post Productions: 749, 896

Fisheries: 700, 715, 717, 718, 720, 730, 734, 736, 737, 739, 743, 745, 750, 838, 844, 845, 869, 873, 888, 892, 897, 913, 917, 941, 988

Food and Agricultural Products Marketing: 756, 758

Food Security: 780, 938

Forestry: 700, 711, 717, 720, 734, 736, 737, 739, 741, 743, 745, 752, 754, 772, 782, 783, 785, 787, 834, 838, 839, 845, 869, 873, 885, 888, 889, 897, 900, 902, 908, 913, 917, 922, 934, 935, 937, 941, 942, 944

Fundraising: 733, 845, 865, 871, 873, 875, 879, 880, 885, 888, 889, 891, 892, 894, 895, 897, 898, 899, 904, 905, 906, 907, 908, 913, 915, 916, 917, 918, 922, 924, 926, 932, 934, 935, 937, 939, 942, 943, 944

Gender and Development: 699, 700, 715, 717, 725, 726, 730, 733, 734, 735, 736, 741, 746, 764, 768, 769, 833, 838, 841, 845, 846, 852, 863, 865, 866, 867, 868, 869, 872, 873, 876, 877, 879, 880, 882, 883, 885, 886, 887, 888, 889, 891, 892, 893, 894, 895, 897, 899, 903, 904, 905, 906, 908, 912, 917, 921, 922, 924, 925, 930, 932, 933, 936, 937, 938, 939, 940, 941, 944, 946

General: 703, 741, 795, 830, 844, 846, 887, 918, 978, 980, 992, 993, 998

Geomatics: 720, 734, 745, 751, 757, 772, 775, 779, 782, 785

Geophysics: 718, 720, 731, 742, 753, 761, 775, 784

Global Communications: 729, 782, 893, 930

Gold and Metals Production: 708, 714, 731, 737, 752, 760, 762, 763, 782, 788

HIV/AIDS: 822, 844, 845, 855, 856, 857, 864, 865, 877, 884, 886, 896, 897, 904, 911, 917, 918, 919, 926, 931, 932, 934, 938, 946, 977, 989, 993, 994

Housing/Human Settlements: 872, 930, 931, 933

Human Resources: 699, 706, 707, 709, 710, 712, 713, 714, 716, 717, 720, 721, 722, 724, 725, 726, 728, 733, 734, 738, 739, 740, 741, 746, 748, 749, 750, 751, 755, 756, 758, 759, 761, 762, 764, 767, 769, 771, 772, 773, 777, 781, 782, 785, 786, 788, 804, 815, 833, 836, 841, 843, 845, 868, 869, 873, 881, 883, 887, 888, 905, 907, 908, 912, 917, 920, 924, 928, 932, 935, 944, 946, 977, 989

Human Rights: 699, 701, 733, 734, 821, 833, 837, 838, 841, 844, 846, 852, 866, 867, 869, 872, 873, 875, 876, 877, 879, 880, 881, 882, 888, 889, 890, 891, 892, 893, 894, 897, 899, 901, 903, 904, 906, 907, 911, 914, 917, 921, 922, 923, 924, 926, 928, 930, 932, 934, 936, 938, 940, 941, 957, 959, 960, 967, 990

Humanitarian Relief: 733, 838, 841, 863, 865, 866, 869, 873, 879, 880, 882, 883, 885, 886, 888, 889, 891, 892, 895, 896, 900, 904, 906, 908, 912, 913, 916, 918, 919, 920, 924, 928, 932, 933, 934, 937, 938

Hydrographic Surveys: 767, 784

Immigration Services: 836, 840

Industrial Services: 740, 769, 787

Infant/Youth Health: 909, 931

Information Technologies: 697, 704, 705, 713, 714, 718, 720, 723, 728, 729, 732, 739, 740, 744, 746, 747, 748, 755, 758, 764, 771, 773, 777, 778, 782, 784, 787, 792, 835, 852, 905

Institution Building: 712, 716, 725, 730, 732, 741, 745, 746, 748, 761, 769, 771, 842

Insurance: 773, 781, 937

Intelligence and Security: 839, 840, 852

Intercultural Briefings: 733, 741, 743, 756, 838, 841, 844, 866, 868, 869, 871, 873, 877, 894, 897, 911, 917, 925, 938, 941

International Affairs: 808, 821, 837, 841, 844, 975

International Business: 796, 835, 837

International Development: 699, 701, 712, 718, 719, 726, 730, 741, 743, 744, 745, 751, 752, 753, 765, 766, 768, 770, 776, 786, 787, 789, 791, 801, 802, 821, 822, 827, 828, 829, 833, 838, 841, 845, 853, 855, 858, 861, 862, 866, 871, 873, 884, 887, 898, 904, 908, 912, 918, 933, 947, 948, 952, 958, 965, 983, 985, 1001, 1002

International Education: 716, 866, 873, 881, 903, 914, 930, 957

International Law/International Agreements: 715, 844, 846

Investment Banking: 699, 760, 773, 781, 834, 837, 843

La Francophonie: 837, 848, 909

Laboratory Automation Systems: 758

Laboratory Services: 702, 758

Labour: 712, 770, 841, 882, 938, 969, 986

Land Stewardship: 739

Language Training: 733, 756

Law: 699, 712, 725, 738, 743, 769, 792, 839, 846, 850, 872, 882, 903, 925, 971, 987, 988, 993, 1002

Law and Good Governance: 699, 725, 769, 872, 903, 925

Leadership Assessment: 696, 724, 766, 772

Lifestyle/Cultural Orientation: 877

Literacy: 865, 866, 873, 885, 944

Livestock Genetics: 702, 775

Logistics: 715, 717, 722, 731, 736, 745, 756, 759, 769, 778, 787, 869, 875, 886, 888, 891, 896, 900, 918, 944, 993

Management: 696, 697, 699, 710, 712, 715, 716, 720, 729, 731, 732, 737, 740, 743, 744, 753, 755, 756, 759, 764, 766, 769, 770, 771, 772, 774, 778, 780, 781, 786, 787, 788, 793, 796, 797, 807, 812, 816, 824, 850, 870, 910, 951, 957, 968

Management Consulting: 696, 697, 699, 740, 743, 753, 756, 766, 769, 772, 780, 786, 787, 788

Management Information Systems: 699, 716, 731, 740, 753

Management Training: 696, 699, 720, 740, 755, 756, 759, 764, 766, 772, 786, 788

Manufacturing: 698, 706, 720, 725, 726, 728, 729, 739, 740, 741, 747, 749, 754, 757, 758, 765, 766, 783, 883

Marine: 726, 738, 775, 840, 875, 906, 917, 988

Marine Engineering: 738, 775

Marketing: 696, 702, 705, 706, 709, 718, 720, 726, 728, 733, 738, 739, 740, 747, 749, 750, 754, 757, 758, 760, 763, 764, 765, 766, 771, 772, 774, 777, 779, 780, 788, 829, 838, 847, 854, 975, 976, 977, 978, 979, 989

Maternal and Infant Nutrition: 909

Media/Communications: 697, 701, 702, 705, 709, 710, 712, 714, 717, 718, 724, 730, 733, 747, 749, 750, 766, 771, 836, 838, 843, 844, 845, 848, 854, 865, 867, 868, 869, 873, 876, 880, 885, 886, 888, 889, 890, 893, 895, 897, 898, 902, 906, 907, 909, 913, 914, 915, 917, 920, 921, 922, 924, 926, 932, 935, 937, 938, 939, 941, 944

Medical Diagnostics: 723, 758, 764

Medical Health: 699, 701, 702, 704, 706, 709, 720, 723, 731, 741, 746, 747, 750, 758, 764, 765, 766, 768, 771, 780, 785, 787, 838, 840, 844, 863, 864, 865, 866, 869, 873, 879, 882, 883, 884, 885, 886, 887, 888, 889, 891, 893, 894, 896, 900, 901, 903, 904, 907, 908, 911, 912, 916, 917, 918, 922, 923, 926, 928, 932, 933, 934, 935, 936, 938, 940, 941, 942, 946

Membership Relations: 873

Merchandising: 739, 758

Metals: 706, 707, 711, 723, 737, 738, 742, 744, 749, 762, 763, 767, 777, 780, 788

Metals Distribution: 777

Micro-enterprises: 699, 715, 717, 725, 730, 733, 746, 750, 764, 768, 769, 838, 845, 868, 869, 873, 875, 879, 887, 888, 889, 891, 892, 893, 895, 896, 897, 899, 900, 904, 905, 908, 912, 915, 917, 920, 921, 922, 923, 924, 932, 935, 936, 937, 939, 940, 941, 944

Mineral Handling: 702, 706, 744, 749, 773

Mineral Resources: 702, 706, 742, 762, 780, 847

Mining: 702, 705, 706, 707, 708, 711, 714, 718, 720, 732, 734, 737, 738, 744, 749, 752, 760, 762, 763, 767, 772, 776, 777, 780, 782, 787, 788, 798, 920

Most Job Categories: 866, 878

Nutrition: 896

Oil and Gas Distribution: 735, 747, 781

Oil and Gas Exploration: 704, 717, 719, 742, 761, 765, 770

Oilfield Services: 709, 727, 759, 769, 770, 777

Organization Development: 696, 724, 732, 755, 766, 768, 786

Orphaned Children: 937, 940

Peace and Security: 844, 847, 872, 927

Personal Development: 724

Personal Taxation/Financial Planning: 699, 713, 760

Petrochemicals: 709, 717, 737, 743, 747, 765, 770, 777, 781

Pharmaceuticals: 706, 709, 758, 765, 766, 785

Photo Mapping: 741, 745, 751, 757, 784

Policy Development: 716, 725, 729, 730, 732, 752, 768, 769, 771, 776, 836, 844, 849, 878

Policy Dialogue: 741, 842, 843, 848, 867, 869, 874, 925, 938

Power Generation/Transmission/Distribution: 711, 730, 748, 784, 787, 833

Project Management: 697, 698, 699, 700, 701, 702, 704, 707, 708, 709, 710, 714, 715, 716, 717, 718, 719, 721, 722, 723, 724, 725, 726, 727, 729, 730, 731, 732, 733, 734, 735, 736, 737, 740, 741, 743, 744, 745, 746, 747, 748, 749, 750, 751, 752, 753, 755, 757, 759, 761, 762, 763, 764, 767, 768, 769, 770, 771, 772, 773, 774, 775, 776, 777, 778, 779, 780, 782, 784, 785, 786, 787, 788, 833, 834, 836, 841, 863, 864, 867, 868, 869, 871, 873, 875, 879, 882, 883, 885, 886, 888, 889, 890, 891, 892, 893, 897, 898, 899, 900, 902, 903, 905, 907, 908, 917, 920, 921, 922, 924, 925, 926, 928, 931, 932, 934, 935, 937, 939, 940, 944, 945

Public Health: 778, 838, 844, 884, 886, 927, 933

Publishing: 724, 750, 803, 861, 977

Pulp and Paper: 720, 754, 773, 783, 786

Quality Assurance: 724, 728, 730, 766, 775, 778

Railways: 717, 761, 773, 840

Real Estate: 711, 713

Reforestation: 783, 912

Refugee Services: 872, 880

Relief and Development: 879, 929, 958

Religious: 864, 876, 879, 882, 892, 895, 900, 906, 907, 911, 914, 919, 920, 928, 932, 934, 942

Research: 698, 706, 707, 709, 717, 724, 728, 732, 740, 743, 747, 748, 749, 751, 758, 763, 764, 765, 766, 768, 769, 770, 771, 777, 779, 786, 793, 800, 801, 804, 821, 838, 845, 853, 865, 868, 874, 875, 882, 890, 901, 906, 909, 910, 913, 917, 921, 923, 925, 951, 955, 958, 960, 967, 968, 970, 974, 981, 987, 998, 999, 1000

Research and Development: 698, 706, 707, 709, 717, 724, 728, 740, 743, 747, 748, 749, 758, 763, 765, 766, 769, 770, 777, 779, 865, 875, 909, 917, 925

Resource Centre Management: 921

Retirement/Estate Planning Overseas: 713, 773, 781

Roads: 761, 767, 785

Rural Development: 700, 737, 748, 848, 961

Sanitation: 753, 785, 933

Science and Technology: 707, 714, 719, 728, 733, 734, 751, 768, 776, 778, 779, 780, 787, 850, 853, 884

Self-Help Projects: 912

Services for International Businesses: 760, 773, 781

Social Justice and Development: 741, 768, 769, 876, 890, 903, 916, 921, 923, 924, 928, 936, 944, 945

Social Policy: 702, 732, 741, 766, 768, 769, 778, 840

Social Science Research: 766, 776, 853, 854, 880, 961

Software Development: 698, 720, 724, 740, 747, 751, 755, 774

States and Markets: 921

Statistics: 854, 921

Sustainable Development: 731, 743, 754, 763, 771, 783, 901, 913, 924, 928, 939, 941, 956

Systems Engineering: 697, 714, 729, 732, 738, 750, 751, 755, 758

Teaching: 746, 756, 864, 865, 866, 868, 869, 879, 887, 888, 891, 892, 894, 895, 901, 903, 907, 908, 910, 919, 920, 928, 932, 934, 935, 940, 941, 942, 944, 979

Technical Assistance: 696, 697, 698, 699, 700, 707, 709, 712, 714, 715, 717, 718, 720, 721, 722, 725, 727, 728, 729, 730, 732, 733, 736, 737, 739, 741, 745, 750, 751, 757, 759, 761, 763, 764, 768, 769, 770, 771, 772, 774, 775, 776, 777, 778, 779, 783, 784, 785, 787, 825, 835, 838, 841, 842, 846, 853, 864, 868, 869, 873, 875, 879, 881, 882, 883, 886, 887, 888, 890, 891, 895, 897, 898, 899, 901, 903, 904, 907, 908, 919, 920, 922, 926, 930, 931, 932, 933, 934, 935, 937, 939, 940, 942, 944, 961

Telecommunications: 697, 698, 701, 734, 737, 741, 746, 750, 759, 760, 763, 766, 774, 777, 778, 782, 783, 836, 838, 841, 850, 852, 868, 869, 920, 944, 988

Tourism: 705, 717, 739, 750, 757, 841, 848, 850, 877, 917, 1003

Trade and Investment: 699, 711, 713, 715, 734, 746, 747, 834, 835, 836, 837, 843, 844, 845, 846, 848, 849, 853, 854, 883, 895, 905

Trade Unions: 872

Trades: 881, 908, 941

Training and Education: 702, 712, 732, 733, 741, 744, 745, 756, 766, 768, 838, 864, 870, 877, 881, 883, 991, 023, 931, 933

Training and Technology Transfer: 697, 702, 713, 714, 719, 723, 725, 728, 732, 733, 735, 750, 768, 784, 902

Translation: 906

Transportation: 710, 715, 717, 723, 729, 731, 734, 737, 738, 741, 744, 752, 761, 767, 769, 772, 779, 780, 785, 840, 930, 957

Urban Development: 708, 730, 731, 743, 744, 745, 768, 772, 778, 779, 788, 881, 930

Volunteer: 717, 733, 809, 838, 858, 864, 865, 866, 871, 873, 874, 875, 877, 879, 880, 882, 886, 887, 888, 889, 890, 892, 894, 897, 898, 900, 901, 904, 907, 908, 913, 914, 918, 919, 922, 923, 926, 930, 931, 932, 933, 934, 939, 940, 941, 943, 944, 955, 961, 001, 070, 998

Waste Water Management: 708, 711, 719, 724, 725, 730, 731, 732, 737, 753, 757, 762, 767, 776, 785, 786, 787, 930

Water Resources: 697, 698, 699, 700, 703, 724, 727, 731, 734, 736, 737, 741, 742, 743, 744, 748, 750, 752, 754, 757, 763, 767, 771, 772, 776, 777, 782, 785, 786, 787, 838, 841, 845, 863, 864, 868, 869, 870, 873, 879, 883, 885, 886, 887, 888, 889, 892, 895, 897, 900, 907, 908, 912, 917, 918, 928, 929, 932, 933, 934, 941, 942

Water Supply: 725, 729, 730, 787, 930, 943

Writing: 779, 814, 818, 906, 944

Youth and Development: 874, 877, 884, 893, 900, 912, 914, 931, 939, 945

Job Categories of US Organizations on the CD-ROM

Below are two Job Category indexes for Appendix 36a, "Profiles for Chapter 36: Private Sector Firms in the US" and Appendix 39a, "Profiles for Chapter 39: NGOs in the US." Since these files are electronically searchable on the CD-ROM, what is shown is the number of hits for each Job Category.

INDEX TO APPENDIX 36a: Private Sector Firms in the US

Accounting, 56
Administration (General), 59
Adult Training, 3
Advanced Technology, 14
Advocacy, 3
Aerospace Technology, 1
Agriculture, 9
Air Transportation, 11
Architecture and Planning, 11
Arts, 2
Banking and Financial Services, 42
Business Development, 48
Chemicals, 4
Civil Society, 1
Commerce, 1
Community, 1
Computer Systems, 23
Conservation, 2
Construction, 26
Consulting, 36
Culture, 1
Customer Services, 38
Economic Development, 4
Economics, 14

Editing, 14
Education, 10
Energy Resources, 11
Engineering, 71
Engineering Management, 1
Environment, 38
Exchange Programs, 1
Exploration and Development, 3
Film Production and Post
    Productions, 1
Food and Agricultural Products
    Marketing, 3
Forestry, 1
Gender and Development, 2
Geophysics, 6
Global Communications, 12
Housing/Human Settlements, 1
Human Resources, 47
Human Rights, 1
Humanitarian Relief, 1
Industrial Services, 4
Information Technologies, 82
Institution Building, 8
Insurance, 3

Intelligence and Security, 3
Laboratory Services, 1
Language Training, 2
Law, 43
Law and Good Governance, 5
Logistics, 16
Management, 67
Management Consulting, 18
Management Information Systems, 3
Management Training, 1
Manufacturing, 23
Marine, 2
Marine Engineering, 1
Marketing, 67
Maternal and Infant Nutrition, 2
Media/Communications, 56
Medical Health, 5
Merchandising, 2
Metals, 1
Mineral Resources, 1
Mining, 4
Most Job Categories, 5
Oil and Gas Distribution, 1
Oil and Gas Exploration, 4

Oilfield Services, 3
Organization Development, 3
Petrochemicals, 4
Pharmaceuticals, 5
Policy Development, 3
Procurement Management, 4
Project Management, 38
Public Health, 3
Publishing, 8
Quality Assurance, 16
Real Estate, 7

Relief and Development, 2
Research, 34
Research and Development, 8
Science and Technology, 10
Social Justice and Development, 3
Social Policy, 1
Software Development, 16
Systems Engineering, 7
Teaching, 1
Technical Assistance, 21
Telecommunications, 7

Tourism, 10
Trade and Investment, 10
Training and Education, 13
Training and Technology Transfer, 6
Translation, 2
Transportation, 22
Urban Development, 2
Waste Water Management, 2
Water Resources, 8
Water Supply, 1
Writing, 13

INDEX TO APPENDIX 39a: NGOs in the US

Administration (General), 5
Adult Training, 30
Advanced Technology, 1
Advocacy, 40
Agriculture, 39
Air Transportation, 1
Arts, 2
Arts and Sciences, 2
Banking and Financial Services, 7
Business Development, 33
Childcare, 12
Civil Society, 9
Community Development, 45
Conflict Prevention, 3
Conservation, 18
Construction, 1
Consulting, 7
Culture, 9
Development Assistance, 20
Development Education, 4
Economic Development, 19
Economics, 13
Education, 115
Energy Resources, 6
Engineering, 4
Environment, 51
Exchange Programs, 21
Food Security, 20
Fundraising, 6
Gender and Development, 1

Geophysics, 1
Housing/Human Settlements, 2
Human Resources, 1
Human Rights, 13
Humanitarian Relief, 51
Immigration Services, 1
Infant/Youth Health, 16
Information Technologies, 5
Institution Building, 3
Intelligence and Security, 1
Intercultural Briefings, 4
International Affairs, 1
International Education, 2
International Law/International
     Agreements, 2
Journalism, 2
Language Training, 1
Law, 8
Law and Good Governance, 3
Literacy, 3
Marketing, 3
Maternal and Infant Nutrition, 11
Media/Communications, 5
Medical Health, 63
Micro-enterprises, 31
Most Job Categories, 2
Nutrition, 3
Organization Development, 1
Peace and Security, 1
Pharmaceuticals, 3

Policy Development, 37
Policy Dialogue, 8
Project Management, 1
Public Health, 23
Publishing, 3
Refugee Services, 13
Relief and Development, 2
Religious, 22
Research, 49
Research and Development, 10
Rural Development, 3
Sanitation, 5
Self-Help Projects, 1
Social Justice and Development, 12
Social Policy, 3
Social Science Research, 1
Statistics, 1
Sustainable Development, 5
Teaching, 5
Technical Assistance, 17
Tourism, 1
Trade and Investment, 1
Training and Education, 39
Translation, 1
Transportation, 3
Urban Development, 1
Volunteer, 8
Water Resources, 9
Youth and Development, 12

Organizations

The index below is sorted alphabetically by organization name. THE BIG GUIDE contains 2,215 organizations listed under 17 seperate categories in 16 chapters. There are three sets of profiles: *Part Two, Acquiring International Experience* has seven chapters with profiles; *Part Four, The Professions* has two chapters with profiles; and *Part Five: International Career Directories* has seven chapters with profiles. Four chapters are indexed within their chapter and the profiles are on the CD-ROM. The CD-ROM also has a searchable index with hotlinks to all the organizations indexed below.

Organizations by Chapter

Index to Organizations

INDEX TO SPONSORS

The following organizations want to inform you about their services and products. Please take a moment to browse through these pages – you might find just what you are looking for!

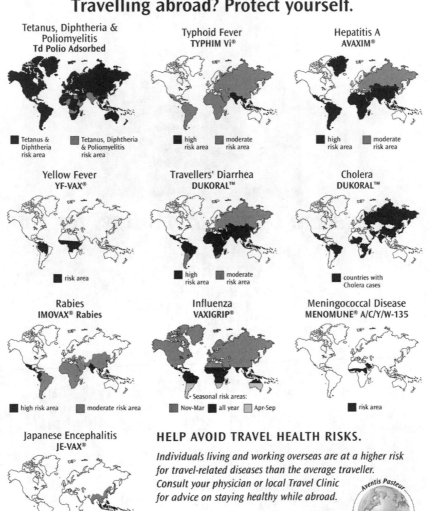

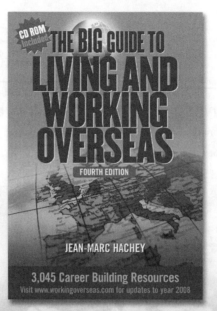

International
Career Seminars

by Jean-Marc Hachey
Author of The BIG Guide to Living and Working Overseas

*Jean-Marc Hachey is a leading authority on international
careers, a writer, consultant and engaging public speaker.
He has shared his international employment strategies with
thousands of university students and professionals of all ages.*

About the Seminars

Mr. Hachey's seminars are exciting, dynamic and encouraging for all
those thinking about launching an international career. In these seminars,
participants will learn about:

- personal and professional skills to succeed overseas
- establishing long-term career strategies
- acquiring relevant experience to land overseas placements
- developing cross-cultural communication skills
- creating an international resume
- clinching international interviews
- conducting an international job search

✓ Most Popular Seminars:

- Launching Your International Career (2 hour presentation)
- The International Job Search is Different (1 day seminar)

Key Note Speaker - Canada & USA

✓ University Career Fairs   ✓ International Symposiums
✓ HR Conferences   ✓ Professional Development Days

 Contact us at 416-925-0479 or seminars@workingoverseas.com

For more information, see the "About Us" section at
www.workingoverseas.com

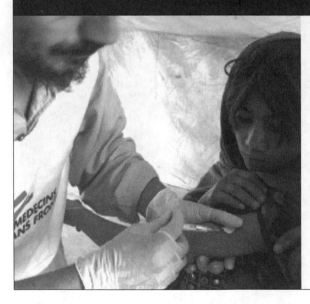

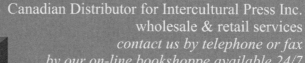

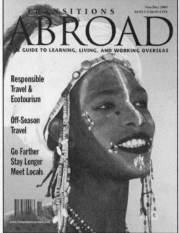

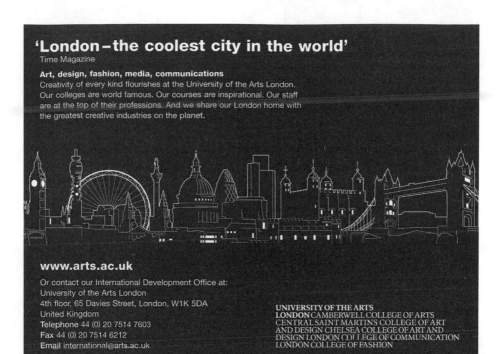

INDEX TO SPONSORS

The following organizations want to inform you about their services and products. Please take a moment to browse through these pages – you might find just what you are looking for!

About the Author

Jean-Marc Hachey is a leading authority on international careers. A writer, consultant and engaging public speaker, he has shared his international employment strategies with thousands. Hachey speaks from experience: he has worked overseas for the United Nations High Commissioner for Refugees, World University Service of Canada, Canadian Crossroads International, and the German Volunteer Service. Fluent in French and English, Hachey has a BBA from the University of New Brunswick and an MA in Political Science from l'Université Laval in Québec City.

Since 1990, he has been mentoring students, recent graduates and others interested in pursuing opportunities abroad. Hachey has also consulted on international job skills to the Canadian International Development Agency, Foreign Affairs Canada and numerous NGOs and universities. Most recently, Hachey has been active in conducting seminars for 24 universities across the continent as well as for international internship programs. Hachey's popular seminars and workshops crackle with tips, true stories and humour, and continue to help launch many international careers.

Why did the Author Write a Book on International Careers?

"During the start of my international career, I was often approached by friends for advice on finding overseas jobs. With no idea of where to start and unaware of the extent of international opportunities, most international job searchers were discouraged. Few understood the international IQ skills employers look for. Hence, I knew there was the need for a "road map" on international careers."

How this Book
Was Researched

The process of updating the Fourth Edition of THE BIG GUIDE TO LIVING AND WORKING OVERSEAS was particularly exciting because Internet technologies have greatly impacted the research process (90 percent of our research was accessed through the Web), the work place environment (60 percent of our staff worked from home), the business model for publishing (we are the first in our field to launch a Web edition), and most fundamentally—the international job hunting process (job boards and e-mail have greatly changed the playing field for the international job seeker).

There were three major phases in the production of THE BIG GUIDE. PHASE I, from October 15th 2003 to January 15th 2004, involved reviewing our procedures manuals, management systems and databases. PHASE II, from January 15th to June 1st 2004, was for research and writing. Over 5,000 organizations and resources were studied, 12 how-to chapters were completely re-written or created from scratch, and 29 chapters were up-dated. Also during this phase, we designed the business model for our new Web edition, launched a new Web site and re-branded our publication with a new name (the former title was *The Canadian Guide to Working and Living Overseas*). PHASE III, from June 1st to August 30th 2004, was the copy editing and layout phase for both the print and Web editions.

The First Edition of THE BIG GUIDE required five years to complete, the Second Edition required nine months, the Third Edition 10 months, and this Fourth Edition, also 10 months. Twenty-eight staff worked together to produce the book. There were 10 researchers, three writers, three designers, one Web manager, one computer programmer, one hardware installer, one marketing manager, one translator, three copy editors, three layout persons, and one organized author happily and steadily plying his craft.

The project started in mid-October 2003 in an office rented in Cabbagetown in downtown Toronto—600 square feet in a renovated historical building with a large bank of south-facing windows overlooking a treed lane (yes, we loved this space).

Computer hardware prices have declined dramatically since the last edition, and memory has increased exponentially. We can now manage the entire book in one single file (the last edition required three files). Generating an index is now done in a matter of minutes, while during the last edition we would launch the index feature and leave the computer running for the whole evening. Seven Dell computers were purchased and networked for this project. PC configuration included 2.4 GHz processing speed, 512 MB of RAM, 40 GB hard drives, and the latest new technologies—CD Read-Write drives, flat screen monitors, and our most treasured StarWars-like gizmo—a 525MD USB Flash Drive for fast backups. Software for the print edition included *Microsoft Word, Outlook, Excel* and *Access 2002*; *Adobe Acrobat 6.0*; *MYOB Accounting*; virus protection and zip software. Our high speed Internet connection was provided by ROGERS cable. The software used to create the initial design of our site *www.workingoverseas.com* was *Photoshop 7*. The coding and building of the non-database components of our Web site was completed using *Dreamweaver MX*. We also made ample use of *www.Xdrive.com* to store and transfer large files to staff working outside the office and were constrained by size limitations in e-mail attachments.

The office ran on a flotilla of project management principals—but one mantra dominated all—*"plan before you execute"*. ISSI staff were coached and sometimes cajoled into managing with itemized running to-do-list, master to-do-list, strict file-naming procedures, one-page project plans, Gantt charts and indispensable audit tables. There was basically no task completed without an accompanying control tool.

One of our most important tasks was to update and maintain the 250 page *ISSI Procedures Manual*. This "office bible" was indispensable for managing the 18 database types in the organization database and the 61 resource types in the bibliography database, ensuring consistency, facilitating staff training, helping us structure work plans and record decisions. Our very efficient Access database systems, developed six years ago for our previous edition, remained basically unchanged except for a new module to e-mail organizations. Our databases allowed staff to track research leads, e-mail and print organization profiles, and generate status reports to measure progress and data integrity. The survey process for updating an organization's profile followed a 24-step flowchart, from initial contact to final printing. The process for updating the resources followed a 12-step flowchart.

The Internet played a major role in shaping how we managed our human resources. Recruitment was made much easier with the use of Internet job boards. We had over 700 job applicants, and hired highly qualified staff (almost everyone had a Masters degree) often within an astonishing one week turnaround time from posting the job to making the offer. Eleven researchers were assigned roles by chapter; others were assigned to bibliography research, marketing, writing/editing, Web design and layout. Communication was done almost solely by e-mail (faxing was the dominant communication method in our previous edition). It should be noted that an old-fashioned initial phone call was still made to establish a personal relationship with almost every organization profiled in the book. Many freelancers were hired, all worked remotely in the areas of computer programming, copy editing, translation, Web design and database, cover design, and hardware installation. Over half the staff worked from their home offices (we in fact never personally met two of our staff, and saw three others only once). This occasioned a re-thinking of many management functions, the merits of e-mailing over a phone call, assessing staff training and creating a common office culture. The Internet has indeed added much new value to this project. It especially facilitated easy communications. For example, without the Internet, we could not have so easily assembled the 27 articles in the Appendix written by Emerging Writers Contest winners and expert guest contributors. The Internet changed our business model. We have strong hopes for the Web edition of THE BIG GUIDE. While we have had a Web site since 1994, we believe that this is the correct time to introduce subscription fee-based publishing—allowing us to deliver our services to a wider audience at a reduced cost. All in all, the Internet has made this project very exciting. We live in very interesting times!

While we have simplified the layout of this new edition (to conform to the requirements for the Web edition), we still required more than 100 styles in *Microsoft Word*. To increase efficiency and not go beyond our maximum page count (1,104 pages) we reduced the font size in the "how-to" sections of the book to 10 point, and the profile and resource font size was set at 8.5 point. The font used for the body of the text is *Century Old Style* and the headings use *Verdana*. The final version was formatted with *Microsoft Word 2002* and printed on a *Brother Laser Printer* (model HL-1870N network ready, 1,200dpi). The book cover was designed on a *Power Mac G4* computer using *Quark Xpress 5.0*, *Adobe Illustrator 10.0* and *Adobe Photoshop 7.0*. The actual printing of the book took three weeks.

The final result for THE BIG GUIDE means the print edition contains 1,104 pages and the CD-ROM 518 pages. The grand total of pages is 1,622. The guide is divided into 41 chapters with 750 headings (chapter names, headings and sub-headings). The accompanying CD-ROM has files containing organization profiles, 27 articles, and three major indexes. There are 3,045 records: (830 resources and 2,215 organizations). And for trivia buffs, THE BIG GUIDE contains 763,859 words (41 percent more than in the Third Edition).

For information on the publisher, INTERCULTURAL SYSTEMS / SYSTÈMES INTERCULTURELS (ISSI), see Chapter 35, Private Sector Firms in Canada.

—BON VOYAGE—

CONTENTS AT A GLANCE

THE BIG GUIDE TO LIVING AND WORKING OVERSEAS (Fourth Edition)